THE OXFORD HANDBOOK OF

INTERNATIONAL
ENVIRONMENTAL LAW

THE OXFORD HANDBOOK OF

INTERNATIONAL ENVIRONMENTAL LAW

Edited by

DANIEL BODANSKY

JUTTA BRUNNÉE

AND

ELLEN HEY

OXFORD
UNIVERSITY PRESS

OXFORD

UNIVERSITY PRESS

Great Clarendon Street, Oxford OX2 6DP

Oxford University Press is a department of the University of Oxford.
It furthers the University's objective of excellence in research, scholarship,
and education by publishing worldwide in

Oxford New York

Auckland Cape Town Dar es Salaam Hong Kong Karachi
Kuala Lumpur Madrid Melbourne Mexico City Nairobi
New Delhi Shanghai Taipei Toronto

With offices in

Argentina Austria Brazil Chile Czech Republic France Greece
Guatemala Hungary Italy Japan Poland Portugal Singapore
South Korea Switzerland Thailand Turkey Ukraine Vietnam

Oxford is a registered trade mark of Oxford University Press
in the UK and in certain other countries

Published in the United States
by Oxford University Press Inc., New York

British Library Cataloguing in Publication Data
Data available

Library of Congress Cataloging in Publication Data
Data available

Typeset by Newgen Imaging Systems (P) Ltd., Chennai, India
Printed in Great Britain
on acid-free paper by
Ashford Colour Press Ltd., Gosport, Hampshire

ISBN 978–0–19–926970–9 (Hbk.)
ISBN 978–0–19–955215–3 (Pbk.)

1 3 5 7 9 10 8 6 4 2

Preface

As the length of this volume attests, international environmental law has become a substantial field during its relatively brief history. The *Handbook* aims to take stock of the field as a whole, exploring its core assumptions and concepts, basic analytical tools, and key challenges. Although it focuses on international environmental *law*, it examines international environmental law from a broader policy and theoretical perspective, drawing on insights from other disciplines such as political science, economics, and philosophy. In doing so, it aims to strike a balance between practice and theory. Each chapter is a free-standing essay that examines an issue that is central to current scholarly debates or policy development. At the same time, the *Handbook* is structured as a whole to provide readers with both a 'bigger picture' of international environmental law and a more in-depth understanding of its preoccupations. In our view, this approach is particularly important at a time in the development of international environmental law when the emergence of increasingly specialized subfields obscures unifying themes and cross-cutting challenges.

Editing a volume with more than 40 authors might seem a daunting task, but, in this case, it has been a pleasure, thanks to the exceptional group of scholars and practitioners who agreed to contribute to the *Handbook*. We could not have asked for a more talented, knowledgeable, and reliable group of colleagues, who always remained good humoured through what often must have seemed like an interminable editorial process. For us, it has been a privilege to work with them.

A book of this nature, however, would never see the light of day without the contributions of those who work 'behind the scenes' and whose names do not appear in the list of contributors. We are particularly grateful to Stacy Belden, the copy-editor for the *Handbook*, for working with us on the manuscript and dealing with the authors' and our own varied understandings of the English language. We also thank our student assistants for taking on a variety of tasks related to the *Handbook*: Paul Simpelaar and Gijs van der Velden at Erasmus University Rotterdam; Jennifer Edwards, Amy Hsiao, and Briant Mildenhall at the University of Georgia; and James Hunter at the University of Toronto. Last but certainly not least, we thank John Louth, at Oxford University Press, for entrusting us with this project and for his good humour and patience, even when confronted with the inevitable unmet deadline or two.

Daniel Bodansky, Jutta Brunnée, and Ellen Hey
July 2006

CONTENTS

....

PART II ANALYTICAL TOOLS
AND PERSPECTIVES

PART III BASIC ISSUE AREAS

PART IV NORMATIVE DEVELOPMENT

PART V KEY CONCEPTS

PART VI ACTORS AND INSTITUTIONS

PART VII   IMPLEMENTATION
AND ENFORCEMENT

Table of Cases

NOTES ON THE CONTRIBUTORS

Steinar Andresen is Senior Research Fellow at the Fridtjof Nansen Institute, Norway. He was Research Director from 1992–7 and a Professor of Political Science at the University of Oslo, Norway from 2002–6. He has published extensively on international regimes related to the environment or natural resources.

Scott Barrett is Professor of Environmental Economics and International Political Economy and Director of the International Policy Program at the School of Advanced International Studies at Johns Hopkins University, United States.

Russel Lawrence Barsh studied anthropology and law at Harvard University, United States. Besides teaching, he has participated in UN studies and negotiations on indigenous peoples from 1981–2001 as representative of an indigenous non-governmental organization and adviser to UN agencies. He runs an ecological research laboratory in the San Juan Islands near Seattle, Washington.

Ulrich Beyerlin, Dr. iur., is Professor in the Law Faculty at Heidelberg University, and at the Max Planck Institute for Comparative Public Law and International Law in Heidelberg, Germany.

Daniel Bodansky is Professor of Law and holds the Emily and Ernest Woodruff Chair in International Law at the University of Georgia School of Law, United States. He served as the US Department of State's Climate Change Coordinator from 1999–2001 and is on the Editorial Board of the *American Journal of International Law*.

Laurence Boisson de Chazournes is Professor and Director of the Department of Public International Law and International Organization in the Faculty of Law at the University of Geneva, Switzerland. She is also Visiting Professor at the Graduate Institute of International Studies in Geneva. She acts as expert and counsel for various states and international organizations.

Alan Boyle is Professor of Public International Law at the University of Edinburgh School of Law, United Kingdom, and a practising barrister at Essex Court Chambers in London. He has acted as counsel in the Chile/EC *Swordfish* case, the *MOX Plant* arbitration, and the *Pulp Mills* case.

Jutta Brunnée is Professor of Law and holds the Metcalf Chair in Environmental Law in the Faculty of Law at the University of Toronto, Canada. She was Co-Editor-in-Chief of the *Yearbook of International Environmental Law* and serves on the Editorial Board of the *American Journal of International Law*.

Kyle W. Danish is a member of the law firm of Van Ness Feldman, PC, in Washington DC. He is also on the Adjunct Faculty of the Washington College of Law at the American University, United States.

John S. Dryzek is Professor in the Research School of Social Sciences at the Australian National University, Australia. His recent books include *The Politics of the Earth* (2nd edition) and *Deliberative Global Politics: Discourse and Democracy in a Divided World*.

Jeffrey L. Dunoff is Charles Klein Professor of Law and Government and Director of the Institute for International Law and Public Policy at the James E. Beasley School of Law at Temple University, United States. He writes in the areas of public international law, and interdisciplinary approaches to international law.

Pierre-Marie Dupuy is Professor of Public International Law at Paris Panthéon-Assas University, France, and the European University Institute, Italy. He has been counsel in many cases before the International Court of Justice and adviser to the Organisation for Economic Co-operation and Development, the UN Environment Programme, and several other international organizations.

Jonas Ebbesson is Professor of Environmental Law and Director of the Stockholm Environmental Law and Policy Centre at Stockholm University, Sweden.

Malgosia Fitzmaurice holds a Chair of Public International Law in the Department of Law, Queen Mary College, at the University of London, United Kingdom. Her main interests include international environmental law, the law of treaties, international water law, and indigenous peoples. In 2001, she delivered the Hague Academy of International Law lectures.

David Freestone is Deputy General Counsel, Advisory Services in the Legal Vice Presidency of the World Bank. Formerly Professor of International Law at the University of Hull, United Kingdom, he is Editor-in-Chief of the *International Journal of Marine and Coastal Law*.

Thomas Gehring is Professor of International Relations in the Faculty of Social and Economic Sciences at the Otto Friedrich University in Bamberg, Germany. His main research topics focus on the operation and development of international economic and environmental institutions as well as the European Union.

Peter Haas is Professor of Political Science at the University of Massachusetts Amherst, United States. He has published on international relations theory, constructivism, international environmental politics, global governance, and the interplay of science and international institutions at the international level.

Günther Handl is Eberhard Deutsch Professor of Public International Law at Tulane University Law School, United States. He is the founder and former Editor-in-Chief of the *Yearbook of International Environmental Law* and a recipient of the Prix Elisabeth Haub for 'exceptional achievements in the field of international environmental law.'

Lisa D. Hawke was a Law Fellow at the Center for International Environmental Law from 2005–6. Currently, she works for a large energy company. She is admitted to practice law in Massachusetts and New York and lives in New York City.

Ellen Hey is Professor and Head of the Department of Public International Law at Erasmus University Rotterdam, The Netherlands. She was Co-Editor-in-Chief of the *Yearbook of International Environmental Law* and is a member of the editorial board of the *Netherlands Yearbook of International Law*.

Benedict Kingsbury is Murry and Ida Becker Professor of Law and Director of the Institute for International Law and Justice at the New York University School of Law, United States.

Jan Klabbers is Professor of International Organizations Law at the University of Helsinki, Finland, and Director of the Academy of Finland Centre of Excellence in Global Governance Research.

Ludwig Krämer teaches European Environmental Law in Brugge and Gent, Belgium, and is Honorary/Visiting Professor in Bremen, Germany; Copenhagen, Denmark; and London, United Kingdom. From 1972–2004, he worked in the environmental department of the European Commission.

Daniel Barstow Magraw is President of the Center for International Environmental Law in Washington DC, United States. He was a US government official for ten years, during which time he participated in negotiating environmental, trade and other international instruments.

Thilo Marauhn is Professor of Public Law, European Law, and International Law at the Justus Liebig University in Giessen, Germany, and is a permanent Visiting Professor of Constitutional Theory at the University of Lucerne, Switzerland.

John G. Merrills is Edward Bramley Professor of Law at the University of Sheffield, United Kingdom. A former Dean of the Faculty of Law, he is the author of *International Dispute Settlement* and several other books, as well as numerous articles.

Karin Mickelson is Associate Professor at the Faculty of Law, University of British Columbia, Canada. Her main research area has been the South-North dimension of international law, with a focus on international environmental law.

Ronald B. Mitchell is Professor of Political Science at the University of Oregon, United States. He has published extensively on international environmental issues, particularly on the effects and effectiveness of international environmental agreements.

Jason Morrison is Director of the Economic Globalization and the Environment Program of the Pacific Institute, United States, and Chair of the ISO/TC 207 NGO Task Group.

Steven R. Ratner is Professor of Law at the University of Michigan Law School, United States. His current research interests include international humanitarian law, corporate responsibility, and issues of moral philosophy and international law. He is a member of the Board of Editors of the *American Journal of International Law*.

Rosemary Rayfuse is Associate Professor and the Director of International Law Programs in the Faculty of Law at the University of New South Wales, Australia. Her research interests include law of the sea and international fisheries law, with particular reference to issues of sustainability, compliance and enforcement and polar governance.

Catherine Redgwell is Professor of International Law in the Faculty of Laws at University College London, United Kingdom. She has published extensively on international law, with particular focus in her teaching and research on international environmental law, international energy law, and treaty law. She is General Editor of the *International and Comparative Law Quarterly*.

Naomi Roht-Arriaza is Professor of Law in the Hastings College of the Law at the University of California, United States. She is the author of several articles on private standards and an Associate Editor of the *Yearbook of International Environmental Law*.

Cesare P.R. Romano is Associate Professor at Loyola Law School Los Angeles, United States, and Assistant Director of the Project on International Courts and Tribunals (PICT).

Ian H. Rowlands is Associate Professor in Environment and Resource Studies at the University of Waterloo, Canada. He is also Associate Dean of Research for the Faculty of Environmental Studies at the University of Waterloo.

Salman M.A. Salman is Lead Counsel with the Environmentally and Socially Sustainable Development and International Law Group of the Legal Vice Presidency of the World Bank, Bank Adviser on water law, and the Editor of the *Law, Justice, and Development Series* of the Legal Vice Presidency.

Peter H. Sand is a lecturer in international environmental law at the University of Munich, Germany, and a former Legal Adviser/Environmental Affairs Officer for several international organizations and institutions (the Food and Agriculture Organization of the UN (FAO), the World Conservation Union, the UN Environment Programme, the UN Economic Commission for Europe, the UN Conference on Environment and Development, and the World Bank).

Dinah Shelton is Patricia Roberts Harris Research Professor of Law at the George Washington University Law School, United States, a member of the Board of Editors of the *American Journal of International Law*, and author of numerous publications on international law, international environmental law, and human rights.

Jon Birger Skjærseth is Senior Research Fellow at the Fridtjof Nansen Institute, Norway. He has published extensively on international environmental cooperation, national environmental policy, and corporate environmental strategies.

Peter J. Spiro is Charles R. Weiner Professor of Law in the James E. Beasley School of Law at Temple University, United States. He has written widely on the role of non-state actors in international law-making.

Richard B. Stewart is Professor and Director of the Center for Environmental and Land Use Law at New York University School of Law, United States. He writes on administrative and environmental law and co-directs the New York University Project on Global Administrative Law.

Christopher D. Stone is J. Thomas McCarthy Trustee Professor of Law at the University of Southern California, United States.

Dan Tarlock is Distinguished Professor of Law at the Chicago-Kent College of Law, United States and Honorary Distinguished Professor in the International Water Law Institute at the University of Dundee, Scotland.

Stephen J. Toope is President of the University of British Columbia, Canada. He was President of the Pierre Elliott Trudeau Foundation between 2002 and 2006 and, previously, Dean of the Faculty of Law at McGill University. He also served as Chair of the United Nations Working Group on Disappearances and is a former President of the Canadian Council on International Law.

Geir Ulfstein is Professor of Law and Director of the Norwegian Centre for Human Rights at the University of Oslo, Norway. He has written extensively on the law of the sea, the law on the use of force, and international environmental law. He was Co-Editor-in-Chief of the *Yearbook of International Environmental Law* and is Co-Editor of *Implementing the Climate Regime: International Compliance*.

Jørgen Wettestad is Senior Research Fellow at the Fridtjof Nansen Institute, Norway. He has published extensively on questions related to the effectiveness and design of international environmental institutions, with particular emphasis on European air and climate change politics.

Jonathan B. Wiener is Perkins Professor of Law and of Environmental Policy at Duke University, United States and a University Fellow of Resources for the Future. He earned degrees in economics and in law at Harvard University, United States. He has written extensively on precaution, risk-risk tradeoffs, and climate change policy. He thanks the Engene T. Bost, Jr. Research Professorship of the Charles A. Cannon Charitable Trust No 3 at Duke Law School for support.

David A. Wirth is Professor of Law and Director of International Programs at Boston College Law School, United States. He earned degrees in chemistry from Princeton and Harvard Universities and in law from Yale University, United States. He is a member of the US Council on Foreign Relations and has published extensively on international environmental law and policy.

Abbreviations

....

AAU	assigned amount unit
AIA	advanced informed agreement
AOSIS	Alliance of Small Island States
ASEAN	Association of Southeast Asian Nations
ATS	Antarctic Treaty System
BAN	Basel Action Network
BAT	best available technique/technology
BATNEEC	best available technology not entailing excessive costs
BEP	best environmental practices
BINGO	business and industry non-governmental organization
BNFL	British Nuclear Fuels Ltd
BSE	Bovine Spongiform Encephalopathy
CalPERS	California Public Employees' Retirement System
CASCO	(ISO) Committee on Conformity Assessment
CBD	Convention on Biological Diversity
CBDR	common but differentiated responsibilities
CCAMLR	Commission for the Conservation of Antarctic Marine Living Resources
CCSBT	Commission for the Conservation of Southern Bluefin Tuna
CDM	Clean Development Mechanism
CEC	(NAAEC) Commission for Environmental Cooperation
CEM	continuous emissions monitoring
CEN	Comité Européen de Normalisation/European Committee for Standardization
CENELEC	European Committee for Electrotechnical Standardization
CER	certified emission reduction
CERES	Coalition for Environmentally Responsible Economies
CFC	chlorofluorocarbon
CIEL	Center for International Environmental Law
CITES	Convention on International Trade in Endangered Species
CMS	Convention on the Conservation of Migratory Species of Wild Animals
COP/MOP	Conference of the Parties/Meeting of the Parties

DAWN	Development Alternatives with Women for a New Era
DOE	designated operational entity
DSU	(WTO) Understanding on Rules and Procedures Governing the Settlement of Disputes
EATS	emissions and allowance tracking system
EB	executive board
EBRD	European Bank for Reconstruction and Development
EC	European Community
ECG	(OECD) Working Party on Export Credits and Credit Guarantees
ECJ	Court of Justice of the European Communities
ECOSOC	(UN) Economic and Social Council
ECtHR	European Court of Human Rights
EEZ	exclusive economic zone
EIA	environmental impact assessment
EICC	Electronic Industry Code of Conduct
EMAS	(EU) Eco-Management and Audit Scheme
EMEP	Co-operative Programme for Monitoring and Evaluation of the Long-range Transmission of Air Pollutants in Europe
EMS	environmental management system
EPA	(US) Environmental Protection Agency
ERU	emission reduction unit
ETS	emissions trading system
EU	European Union
EURATOM	European Atomic Energy Community
FEI	Fédération Economique Internationale
FMD	foot and mouth disease
FSC	Forest Stewardship Council
GAD	gender and development
GATT	General Agreement on Tariffs and Trade
GDP	gross domestic product
GEF	Global Environment Facility
GESAMP	Joint Group of Experts on the Scientific Aspects of Marine Pollution
GHG	greenhouse gas
GLP	good laboratory practice
GMO	genetically modified organism
GPA	Global Programme of Action for the Protection of the Marine Environment from Land-Based Activities
GRI	Global Reporting Initiative
IAEA	International Atomic Energy Agency
IAF	International Accreditation Forum

IAS	invasive alien species
IBRD	International Bank for Reconstruction and Development (World Bank)
ICAO	UN International Civil Aviation Organization
ICCAT	International Commission for the Conservation of Atlantic Tunas
ICCPR	International Covenant on Civil and Political Rights
ICJ	International Court of Justice
ICRW	International Convention for the Regulation of Whaling
IDA	International Development Association
IEC	International Electrotechnical Commission
IEL	international environmental law
IFAD	International Fund for Agricultural Development
IFC	International Finance Corporation
IFCS	(WHO) Intergovernmental Forum on Chemical Safety
IFI	international financial institution
IGO	intergovernmental organisation
IL	international law
ILA	International Law Association
ILC	International Law Commission
ILO	International Labour Organization
IMCO	International Maritime Consultative Organisation (now the IMO)
IMF	International Monetary Fund
IMO	International Maritime Organization
INC	intergovernmental negotiating committee
IO	international organization
IOMC	Inter-Organization Programme for the Sound Management of Chemicals
IPCC	Intergovernmental Panel on Climate Change
IPOA	international plan of action
IPR	intellectual property rights
IR	international relations
ISA	International Seabed Authority
ISEAL	International Social and Environmental Accrediting and Labelling Alliance
ISO	International Organization for Standardization
ITL	international transactions log
ITLOS	International Tribunal for the Law of the Sea
ITPGRFA	International Treaty on Plant Genetic Resources for Food and Agriculture
IUCN	World Conservation Union (formerly International Union for the Conservation of Nature)

IUU	illegal, unregulated and unreported
IWC	International Whaling Commission
JI	joint implementation
LBS	land-based sources and activities of marine pollution
LMO	living modified organism
LOSC	(UN) Convention on the Law of the Sea
LOT	load-on-top system (oil pollution)
LRTAP	Long-Range Transboundary Air Pollution (Convention)
MDG	Millennium Development Goal
MEA	multilateral environmental agreement
MEPC	(IMO) Maritime Environment Protection Committee
MFMP	Multilateral Fund for the Implementation of the Montreal Protocol
MSC	Marine Stewardship Council
MSY	maximum sustainable yield
NAAEC	North American Agreement on Environmental Cooperation
NAFO	Northwest Atlantic Fisheries Organization
NAFTA	North American Free Trade Agreement
NAO	(US) National Audit Office
NASCO	North Atlantic Salmon Conservation Organization
NEPAD	New Partnership for Africa's Development
NGO	non-governmental organization
NIEO	New International Economic Order
NOW	(US) National Organization for Women
NPM	new public management
NTTAA	(US) National Technology Transfer and Advancement Act
OAS	Organization of American States
ODA	official development assistance
ODS	ozone-depleting substance
OECD	Organisation for Economic Cooperation and Development
OHCHR	Office of the United Nations High Commissioner for Human Rights
OIE	World Organisation for Animal Health (formerly Organisation International Epizootique)
OP/BP	operational policy / bank policy
OSHA	(US) Occupational Safety and Health Administration
OSPAR	Convention for Protection of the Marine Environment of the North-East Atlantic
P&I	protection and indemnity club
PCB	polychlorinated biphenyl
PCF	Prototype Carbon Fund
PD	prisoner's dilemma
PEFC	Program for the Endorsement of Forest Certification Schemes

PGCT	(Code of Conduct for) Plant Germoplasm Collecting and Transfer
PIC	prior informed consent
POP	persistent organic pollutant
PP	precautionary principle
PPM	process and production method
PRAM	(OSPAR) Programs and Measures Committee
RAINS	(LRTAP) Regional Acidification Information and Simulation
REACH	(EU Framework for) Registration, Evaluation and Authorization of Chemicals
RIA	regulatory impact analysis
RMU	removal unit
RTB	race to the bottom
SADC	Southern African Development Community
SAICM	Strategic Approach to International Chemicals Management
SAP	structural adjustment programme
SBT	southern bluefin tuna
SDR	special drawing right
SEAFO	South-East Atlantic Fisheries Organisation
SEP	supplemental environmental project
SRI	socially responsible investment
TEAP	(Montreal Protocol) Technology and Economic Assessment Panel
TNC	transnational corporation
TRAFFIC	Trade Records Analysis of Flora and Fauna in Commerce
TRIPS	Trade-Related Aspects of Intellectual Property Rights
TWAIL	third world approaches to international law
UN	United Nations
UNCC	United Nations Compensation Commission
UNCED	United Nations Conference on Environment and Development (Rio Conference)
UNCERD	United Nations Committee on the Elimination of Racial Discrimination
UNCHE	United Nations Conference on the Human Environment (Stockholm Conference)
UNCHR	United Nations Commission on Human Rights
UNCSD	United Nations Commission on Sustainable Development
UNDP	United Nations Development Programme
UNECE	United Nations Economic Commission for Europe
UNEP	United Nations Environment Programme
UNESCO	United Nations Educational, Scientific and Cultural Organization
UNFAO	United Nations Food and Agriculture Organization
UNFCCC	United Nations Framework Convention on Climate Change
UNGA	United Nations General Assembly

UNHCR	United Nations High Commissioner for Refugees
UNIDO	United Nations Industrial Development Organization
UNITAR	United Nations Institute for Training and Research
USAID	United States Agency for International Development
USSR	Union of Soviet Socialist Republics
VOC	volatile organic compound
WAD	Women and Development
WBCSD	World Business Council for Sustainable Development
WCAR	World Conference against Racism
WCD	World Commission on Dams
WCED	World Commission on Environment and Development (Brundtland Commission)
WCN	World Charter for Nature
WCS	World Conservation Strategy
WEDO	Women's Environment & Development Organization
WEO	World Environmental Organization
WESD	Women, Environment and Sustainable Development
WHO	World Health Organization
WID	Women in Development
WIPO	World Intellectual Property Organization
WRI	World Resources Institute
WSF	World Social Forum
WSSD	World Summit on Sustainable Development (Johannesberg Conference)
WTO	World Trade Organization
WWF	Worldwide Fund for Nature (formerly World Wildlife Fund)

CHAPTER 1

INTERNATIONAL ENVIRONMENTAL LAW
MAPPING THE FIELD

DANIEL BODANSKY

JUTTA BRUNNÉE

ELLEN HEY

INTERNATIONAL environmental law is still a relatively new field (see Chapter 2 'Evolution of International Environmental Law'). For example, the UN Charter of 1945 does not list environmental protection among the purposes and principles that it aims to promote, and it was only in the 1970s that a UN body specifically devoted to environmental matters, the United Nations Environment Programme (UNEP), was established. Of course, legal issues that, today, we would describe as environmental issues are not entirely new,[1] nor are legal arrangements that, today, we would describe as environmental agreements or institutions.[2] However, the underlying issues were not usually conceived of as 'environmental'. Instead, they were seen as *resource* issues, primarily relating to the conservation of wildlife for human uses.

This anthropocentric outlook not only has a long lineage,[3] but also came to carry a historical burden that still encumbers contemporary efforts to address global environmental problems (see Chapter 12 'Critical Approaches'). International environmental law continues to struggle with the complaint that it reflects the concerns of developed countries more than those of developing countries and that it merely rearticulates some of the patterns of colonial exploitation in environmental terms. Just as colonial empires tended to treat their 'outlying possessions' as providers of resources—places where it was 'convenient to carry on the production of sugar, coffee and a few other tropical commodities'[4]—some of the earliest conservation treaties, although concerned with the preservation of flora and fauna in Africa, excluded native populations from these reserves and glossed over the fact that threats to the protected areas and resources actually stemmed from white hunters and colonial exploitation rather than from indigenous uses.[5] It is not difficult to see the debates over colonialism being replayed in the ongoing debates over whether developing countries, for example, should preserve biological resources of global concern or should reduce their greenhouse gas emissions and, if so, how much financial support developed countries should provide for such efforts (see Chapter 26 'Sustainable Development', Chapter 27 'Equity', and Chapter 41 'Technical and Financial Assistance').

---

[1] See, e.g., *Bering Fur Seals Arbitration Assistance* (1898) 1 Moore's International Arbitration Awards 755, reprinted in 1 I.E.L. Rep. 43, 67 (1999).

[2] See, e.g., the 1909 Treaty between the United States and Great Britain Respecting Boundary Waters between the United States and Canada, which also established the International Joint Commission to deal with transboundary water issues.

[3] As Clive Ponting shows in his book, *A Green History of the World: The Environment and the Collapse of Great Civilizations* (New York: Penguin Books, 1991), such resource (or 'environmental') issues have actually existed for most of human history.

[4] John Stuart Mill, *Principles of Political Economy* (1848), quoted in K. Mickelson, 'South, North, International Environmental Law, and International Environmental Lawyers' (2000) 11 Y.B. Int'l Envt'l L. 52 at 56.

[5] *Ibid.* at 58–60 (referring to the 1900 Convention for the Preservation of Wild Animals, Birds, and Fish in Africa and the 1933 Convention on the Preservation of Flora and Fauna in Their Natural State). See also A. Anghie, 'Colonialism, Environmental Damage, and the Nauru Case' (1993) 34 Harv. Int'l L.J. 445 (on the efforts by a former dependent territory to get redress for the impact of colonial resource exploitation).

In the evolution of what, today, we refer to as international environmental law, attention initially focused on visible, immediate environmental issues, which tended to be local or regional in character, primarily in Europe or North America. Most early international efforts concerned transboundary resource use or pollution—the hunting of migratory birds, for example, the shared use of river basins, or the fumes emitted by the Trail Smelter in Canada, which drifted south across the border, causing damage to crops in the United States (see Chapter 2 'Evolution of International Environmental Law'). The international legal responses to these problems were generally ad hoc and episodic, involving the application of traditional principles of customary international law grounded in state sovereignty, and related to territorial integrity and state responsibility.[6] Overuse of resources on the high seas was also an early concern, leading to the development of international regimes to conserve fish and fur seals for future harvesting.

International environmental law began to emerge in a significant way, however, only in the late 1960s and 1970s, as part of a growing concern about environmental problems in many developed countries and their growing awareness of the international and global nature of many environmental issues.[7] During this period, states negotiated conventions on the protection of the marine environment from oil pollution, trade in endangered species, dumping of hazardous wastes at sea, wetlands, and world heritage sites, in some cases with significant involvement by international organizations and non-governmental organizations (NGOs). The United Nations convened the Stockholm Conference on the Human Environment in 1972, which was the first in a series of UN mega-conferences including the 1992 Rio Conference on Environment and Development and the 2002 Johannesburg World Summit on Sustainable Development. Stockholm, in turn, resulted in the UN General Assembly (UNGA) establishing the first multilateral environmental institution, UNEP, headquartered in Nairobi.

Since then, despite ebbs and flows in international concern about the environment, there has been a remarkable growth, overall, in the number and range of international instruments and institutions addressing environmental problems.[8] Indeed, such is the growth of the discipline that, by now, the study of international environmental law has become virtually an industry. It is taught in law schools around the world and is the subject of major treatises and teaching texts,[9] several specialty law

---

[6] T. Kuokkanen, *International Law and the Environment: Variations on a Theme* (The Hague: Kluwer Law International, 2002).

[7] See, e.g., R. Carson, *Silent Spring* (Boston: Houghton Mifflin, 1962); and D.L. Meadows et al., *The Limits to Growth: A Report to the Club of Rome* (New York: Universe Books, 1972).

[8] A periodically updated compilation of international environmental law documents has grown to more than 20 volumes and counting. B. Rüster and B. Simma, *International Protection of the Environment: Treaties and Related Documents* (Dobbs Ferry, NY: Oceana, 1975–82, second series, 1990–present).

[9] See the list of general reading at the end of this chapter.

journals,[10] and a burgeoning number of monographs dealing with an array of increasingly specialized topics within international environmental law.

As far as specialization is concerned, international environmental law has come a long way from its origins in the application of broad principles derived from state sovereignty to environmental issues. Not only has the number of specialized environmental instruments and institutions grown to the point where some commentators have warned of treaty congestion,[11] but sub-specialties have also developed within many of these regimes. Thus, worries over the 'fragmentation of international law' no longer concern merely the impact of the emergence of fields such as international environmental law, human rights law, or international economic law and the attendant proliferation of international courts and tribunals.[12] Concerns have also come to be voiced with respect to the fragmentation of international environmental law itself.[13] Indeed, an expert on the law of marine environmental protection might find it difficult to navigate an air pollution agreement. Similarly, an expert on the rules governing carbon sinks may have trouble communicating with an expert on international emissions trading, notwithstanding the fact that both issues fall under the Kyoto Protocol on climate change.

Whether the phenomenon of increasing specialization within international environmental law is cause for concern is bound to be a matter for debate. But, along with the exponential growth of the field, it is one of the reasons why the present *Handbook* endeavours to step back and take stock of this growing field as a whole, and to discern its overarching features. It includes chapters surveying the main issue areas—air, water, biological resources, and hazardous materials (see Part III: 'Basic Issue Areas'). However, its primary purpose is not to describe in depth the substantive rules of international environmental law—several treatises have already performed this task admirably.[14] Instead, it seeks to analyse the field in more conceptual terms, focusing on issues of structure and process rather than on issues of content. Important topics include:

- *Legal design*—At what level should environmental governance be exercised: global, regional, or national (see Chapter 5 'Levels of Environmental Governance')? What are the principal issues in choosing among regulatory instruments (see Chapter 8

---

[10] See, e.g., the *Colorado Journal of International Environmental Law and Policy*, the *Georgetown International Environmental Law Review*, the *Review of European Community and International Environmental Law*, and the *Yearbook of International Environmental Law*.

[11] E. Brown Weiss, 'International Environmental Law: Contemporary Issues and the Emergence of a New World Order' (1993) 81 Geo. L.J. 675.

[12] See G. Hafner, 'Risk Ensuing from the Fragmentation of International Law', in International Law Commission, *Report of the Working Group on Long-Term Programme of Work*, UN Doc. ILC (LII)/WG/LT/L./Add.1 (2000).

[13] See, e.g., S. Andresen, 'Global Environmental Governance: UN Fragmentation and Coordination', in O. Stokke and O.B. Thommessen, eds., *Yearbook of International Co-operation on Environment and Development 2001/2002* (London: Earthscan, 2001) 19.

[14] See list of general reading at the end of this chapter.

'Instrument Choice')? To what extent is the distinction between formal and informal norms important (see Chapter 6 'Formality and Informality')? What impact do paradigms and discourse, and science and technology have on legal design (see Chapter 3 'Paradigms and Discourses' and Chapter 9 'Science and Technology')? How might we understand the present design of global environmental governance (see Chapter 4 'Global Environmental Governance as Administration')? How does international environmental law relate to other areas of international law (see Chapter 7 'Relationship between International Environmental Law and Other Branches of International Law')?

- *Analytical tools*—How can other disciplines, such as international relations, economics, ethics, and critical perspectives help us to better understand international environmental issues and the role that law can play in addressing them (see Part II: 'Analytical Tools and Perspectives')?
- *Normative development*—How do international environmental law norms emerge and develop? What is the role of policies, principles, and rules (see Chapter 18 'Different Types of Norms in International Environmental Law'); custom (see Chapter 19 'Formation of Customary International Law and General Principles'); treaty mechanisms (see Chapter 20 'Treaty Making and Treaty Evolution'); or private and quasi-private standard-setting processes (see Chapter 21 'Private and Quasi-Private Standard Setting')?
- *Key concepts*—What is the deeper conceptual structure of international environmental law? What are the key concepts underlying the more specific rules, doctrines, and processes (see Part V: 'Key Concepts')?
- *Actors and institutions*—Who are the principal actors in the international environmental process? What roles do they play in its formation, implementation, and enforcement (see Part VI: 'Actors and Institutions')?
- *Implementation and enforcement*—To what extent is international environmental law effective and how is compliance best promoted (see Chapter 39 'Compliance Theory')? How is it implemented and enforced (see Part VII: 'Implementation and Enforcement')?

Although some may continue to contend, as Ian Brownlie once did,[15] that international environmental law is nothing more than the application of international law to environmental problems, the picture that emerges overall is a different one. It suggests that international environmental law has, to a significant degree, become a distinct field—distinct not simply in the sense of addressing a discrete set of problems through a discrete set of substantive rules, but also in the stronger sense of having its own characteristic structure and process, and its own set of conceptual tools and methodologies. To be sure, international environmental law remains rooted in international law and draws upon much of its repertoire, such as the rules

---

[15] I. Brownlie, 'Editor's Preface,' in B.D. Smith, *State Responsibility and the Marine Environment: The Rules of Decision* (Oxford: Clarendon Press, 1988).

governing customary law, the law of treaties, the law of state responsibility, and juris-dictional rules. Such rules, moreover, also are relevant in determining the rela-tionship between international environmental law and other substantive areas of international law, such as human rights law or international economic law (see Chapter 7 'Relationship between International Environmental Law and Other Branches of International Law'). However, as this *Handbook* demonstrates, inter-national environmental law now comes complete with its own distinctive cast of characters, legislative and administrative processes, and concepts.

1 Some Distinctive Features of International Environmental Problems

In understanding the special characteristics of international environmental law, it is useful, at the outset, to consider several features of international environmental problems that serve to distinguish them from other international problems.

International environmental problems are caused primarily by private conduct. International law primarily addresses questions of governmental conduct: claiming territory, using force against other states, suppressing human rights, exercising juris-diction, and so forth. Some environmental problems are also the product of govern-mental conduct—for example, the blowing up of Kuwaiti oil wells by Iraq during the first Gulf War. Yet most pollution and natural resource depletion result from private activities. Consider climate change, for example. Emissions of carbon dioxide and other 'greenhouse gases' result from generating and consuming electricity, driving cars, manufacturing products, growing food, and cutting trees—activities that qual-ify as private rather than governmental. The same is true of other international envir-onmental problems as well: threats to African elephants come from the consumers who wish to purchase ivory products and from the poachers who satisfy that demand by killing elephants; oil pollution results from the combined actions (or inactions) of oil producers, shipbuilders, shippers, and, ultimately, individuals who consume oil for transportation and other purposes; deforestation results from demand by local populations for fuel wood and for agricultural land, and by local and more distant populations for timber. Virtually all human activity involves, to one degree or another, the consumption of resources or the generation of wastes and, thus, con-tributes to environmental problems.

The challenge for international environmental law is to develop effective ways of regulating these private activities. Traditionally, international law has governed the conduct of states, not individuals. Thus, in order to control private activities, it must either do so at one step removed, by requiring states to regulate or otherwise influence the behaviour of the relevant non-state actors within their borders, or it must find ways to engage private actors more directly (see Chapter 31 'Changing Role of the State').

International environmental problems have a physical and technological basis. Most problems addressed by international law are predominantly political in nature: war, human rights abuses, trade protectionism. These are failures of human behaviour, which international law seeks to address through the development of rules, institutions, and other modalities of international governance. Environmental issues, of course, also have political dimensions. But they have an additional dimension as well, which is not generally shared by other international problems: they involve impacts, often technology driven, on extremely complicated physical processes, which can be understood only with the aid of science (see Chapter 9 'Science and Technology'). The ozone problem, for example, results from the incidental release of synthetic compounds such as chlorofluorocarbons (CFCs), which migrate to the upper atmosphere and catalytically react with ozone, thereby breaking down the ozone layer. The problem was created by technology, diagnosed through Nobel Prize-winning science, and, ultimately, addressed through the development of new technologies.

International environmental problems involve significant scientific uncertainties. Although international environmental disputes are often attributable to differences in interests and values among states, they are complicated by uncertainties concerning the facts. Many modern environmental problems have effects that are widely dispersed and long term, with long latency periods. Given the complexity of the physical, economic, and social processes involved, we often do not know for sure how serious a problem is, what its causes are, how expensive it will be to address, whether it is even a problem at all, and, if it is, whether it is still possible to address. Is the buildup of greenhouse gases in the atmosphere causing global warming, and, if so, how much warming will occur and with what effects? Do genetically modified organisms pose a danger to other species and to human health? Are human fertility rates declining, and, if so, to what extent is this decline attributable to persistent organic pollutants? On these and many other questions, scientists cannot provide conclusive answers. Some argue, for example, that we do not know enough about climate change to justify potentially costly preventive policies; others predict dangerous levels of warming and argue that, if we delay action in order to get better scientific information, it will become too late to act. No matter what choice we make, it may have serious consequences. Decisions must be made in the face of uncertainty (see Chapter 25 'Precaution').

International environmental problems are extremely dynamic. Environmental problems present a moving target. In part, this fact results from changes in scientific knowledge. When the Montreal Protocol on Substances That Deplete the Ozone Layer (Montreal Protocol) was adopted in 1987, the Antarctic ozone hole had just been discovered and its significance was not fully understood. By 1990, it had become clear that the Montreal Protocol's requirement to reduce the production and con-sumption of ozone-depleting substances by 50 per cent was inadequate and that stronger control measures were needed. In response, the parties adopted the London Amendments, which provided for the complete phase-out of the principal ozone-depleting substances. Since then, the ozone regime has continued to evolve as our scientific understanding of the problem has developed. Moreover, not only does scientific understanding develop, environmental problems themselves change as human behaviour and technology change. For example, economies grow, consuming more resources and producing more wastes; new chemicals are created, sometimes replacing more harmful substances but sometimes creating new risks; a fish stock becomes depleted, so fishermen move on to other fisheries and begin to overfish them. International environmental law is a Heraclitian world, in which there are few constants except change itself.

International environmental problems are interconnected and need to be addressed holistically. It is by now almost a cliché that everything is interconnected and that addressing one problem may contribute to another. In the early twentieth century, for example, factories built taller smokestacks in order to disperse pollutants more widely and thereby reduce local air pollution. But this 'solution' merely converted air pollution from a local to a regional concern. Similar kinds of interconnections char-acterize a wide variety of environmental issues. Some of the leading replacements for ozone-depleting substances are greenhouse gases, which therefore contribute to global warming. The protection of one species may allow it to multiply, with adverse effects for other species. The limitations on nuclear energy may result in greater use of fossil fuels and higher emissions of carbon dioxide. Environmental problems do not come packaged as discrete units that can be treated in isolation, without regard to their wider repercussions. Instead, they need to be addressed on a more holistic basis (see Chapter 24 'Ecosystems').

With respect to many environmental issues, states and people around the world are interdependent as well. For example, the Earth has only one ozone layer and one climate system, so that no state can immunize itself against harmful effects or address ozone depletion and climate change without cooperating with other states. Likewise, states benefit from preventive steps taken by other states. Relationships of inter-dependence, and the need for cooperation, similarly exist with respect to regional and transboundary environmental concerns.

2 TRADITIONAL STATE-CENTRIC APPROACH

As traditionally conceived, international law sought to regulate the interactions of states by defining their respective rights and obligations. Despite its tremendous development, international environmental law remains rooted in this inter-state system and, to a significant degree, can still be understood as an effort to reconcile the differing and often competing concerns of states.

Within this state-centric paradigm, environmental problems become legally relevant when activities within one state inflict significant harm within the territory of another. Under classical principles of international law, the concept of state sovereignty gives rise to two potentially contradictory notions: the principle of territorial integrity recognizes the right of states to be free of interference from others, and the principle of territorial sovereignty recognizes the freedom of states to do as they like within their own territory. International environmental law aims to strike a balance between territorial integrity and territorial sovereignty, since neither can be absolute in the environmental context. This goal is reflected in the obligation not to cause significant transboundary harm, which represents a 'cornerstone' of international environmental law (see Chapter 22 'Transboundary Impacts'). The need to balance the competing sovereign interests involved is even more clearly reflected in the principle of 'equitable utilization', which is set forth in the UN Convention on the Law of Non-Navigational Uses of International Watercourses (Watercourses Convention) (see Chapter 15 'Oceans and Freshwater Resources'), and reflected in the International Law Commission's 2001 Draft Articles on the Prevention of Transboundary Harm from Hazardous Activities, which calls for solutions based on 'an equitable balance of interests'.[16]

From an economic perspective, the no-harm rule can be understood as an effort to 'internalize' significant transboundary externalities. Externalities are the costs of an activity that are not borne by the actor but that fall on others. For example, one country emits sulphur dioxide that causes acid rain to fall on its neighbour downwind or it discharges pollution into a river, causing damage to lower riparians. To the extent that a country is able to 'externalize' the costs of polluting, it has no economic incentive to stop. The no-harm rule is meant to address this problem, by prohibiting one state from imposing significant environmental costs on another.

Although the no-harm principle has, by now, achieved canonical status, in practice, it is not consistently applied to resolve specific environmental disputes by courts or tribunals. Despite considerable efforts to codify the rules of state responsibility for transboundary pollution (see Chapter 44 'International Responsibility and Liability'), the *Trail Smelter* case, which arose between the United States and Canada in the 1920s,[17] remains the only case where a state has been found legally responsible for failure to prevent transboundary pollution. Even the massive transboundary pollution caused by the Chernobyl and Sandoz accidents did not lead to legal claims by the victim states.

Instead, transboundary impacts have been addressed, if at all, in a more pragmatic way, through negotiations among the states concerned to reach a mutually satisfactory

---

[16] This terminology apparently was not intended to qualify the polluting state's duty to avoid significant transboundary harm (see Chapter 22 'Transboundary Impacts').

[17] *Trail Smelter Case (United States v. Canada)*, Award, 1941, 3 U.N.R.I.A.A. 1905.

outcome—and, in some cases, to establish institutional arrangements that can manage the externalities on an ongoing basis. Examples include the International Joint Commission, which has been operating for close to a century under the 1909 US–Canada Boundary Waters Treaty, and the Long-Range Transboundary Air Pollution (LRTAP) regime in Europe. To some degree, the no-harm rule and the equitable utilization principle form part of the legal context in which these solutions are negotiated and implemented.

However, neither the principles of international environmental law nor the existence of transboundary institutions guarantee the expeditious resolution of transboundary pollution problems. There is some irony in the fact that the Trail Smelter itself is again the subject of disagreement between Canada and the United States and that the no-harm rule, which the first *Trail Smelter* case so famously helped crystallize, has not played a significant role in the resolution of the current dispute. Nor has the International Joint Commission been able to resolve the matter, notwithstanding the fact that the issue is one of transboundary water pollution, and that the commission is a well-established institution. Indeed, the inter-state level and international environmental law have been by-passed through efforts by governmental and nongovernmental actors within the United States to apply US law to the Smelter's activities and its alleged transboundary impacts.[18] In short, the inter-state paradigm is under strain even in the 'classical' transboundary context in which the basic, sovereignty-derived rules of international environmental law originated.

3 New Types of Environmental Concerns in International Law

The traditional state-centric approach conceptualizes international environmental problems in terms of the mutual rights and responsibilities of polluting and victim states. Yet international environmental law has evolved considerably from its state-centric roots, and now encompasses a much wider set of concerns.

3.1 Common Concerns

To begin with, many international environmental issues reflect not the interests of individual states, but rather the common concerns of the international community (see Chapter 23 'Common Areas, Common Heritage, and Common Concern').

---

[18] See, e.g., A.L. Parrish, '*Trail Smelter* Déjà Vu: Extraterritoriality, International Environmental Law, and the Search for Solutions to Canadian-U.S. Transboundary Water Pollution Disputes' (2005) 85 B.U. L. Rev. 363.

Along with transboundary impacts, environmental impacts that affect areas beyond national jurisdiction—such as the high seas and, arguably, Antarctica—were among the first topics of international environmental regulation.[19] These impacts are obviously of common concern, not only because the harms fall on all of the users of the commons, rather than on only a single state, but also because protection of the commons requires collective action. The same is true, of course, for the relatively more recent concerns over the degradation of globally shared resources, such as the ozone layer or the climate system. In all of these cases, since no single state can comprehensively regulate access or use, states must agree on mutual restraints in order to prevent a tragedy of the commons.

Today, the range of environmental problems that are considered 'common concerns' has grown significantly, and encompasses as well the protection of resources that, while found within a particular country, are considered to provide global benefits, for example, world heritage sites and biological diversity. Although these resources—unlike, say, high seas resources or the climate system—could potentially be protected by the territorial sovereign, it may lack the incentive to do so on its own, especially to the extent that the benefits of the resources go to the international community. And it remains unclear to what extent individual states owe obligations to protect such resources *erga omnes*—that is, under customary international law and to the international community as a whole.

When environmental impacts affect a commons area or common interests, collective action is thus required for a number of reasons. Legally speaking, individual states lack rights that they could effectively invoke to demand protection of a commons or of resources located within other states. Practically speaking, states' interdependence in terms of both contributions and solutions demands cooperation in addressing collective environmental concerns. The response by international environmental law, therefore, has tended to consist of efforts to build multilateral, treaty-based regimes. The enduring challenge, not surprisingly, is to bring sufficient numbers of key states to participate in a given regime and then to ensure the compliance of participating states with their commitments.

Typically, solutions to collective action problems depend on a feature generally absent at the international level—that is, governmental institutions. Viewed from this perspective, the task of international environmental institutions is to provide governance without government—that is, to influence state conduct in order to produce collective benefits. The use of international environmental law to provide global collective benefits raises two important questions. First, how can international institutions be designed in order to accomplish this objective? Specifically, how can states be motivated to join an international environmental regime and then to comply with the standards it sets? And, second, how should the burden of producing collective benefits, such as restoring the ozone layer, preserving biological diversity, or mitigating climate change, be shared among the international community?

---

[19] See *Bering Fur Seals Arbitration*, note 1 above.

The first question has been the subject of lively scholarly debates, in which international lawyers have increasingly engaged with the insights of other disciplines, notably international relations and economics, to gain new insights into institution building. Thus, recent economics and rationalist international relations literature has focused upon such design variables as the nature and stringency of a regime's commitments (soft versus hard, general versus precise, shallow versus deep), its rules regarding membership and voting, and its compliance system (see Chapter 10 'International Relations Theory' and Chapter 11 'Economic Theory of International Environmental Law').[20] According to this literature, to the extent that mutual restraint produces a net benefit, it should be possible, in theory, to design an international environmental regime to distribute this gain so as to leave every state better off—in other words, it should be possible to find a solution that provides a Pareto benefit. But, even if this were in practice possible, it might not be enough to induce states to cooperate. In cooperative games such as the prisoner's dilemma, both sides benefit from cooperation, but, nonetheless, each party has an incentive to defect. The same is true of environmental problems. When the gain from environmental cooperation is what economists refer to as a public good—protection of the ozone layer, mitigation of climate change, and so forth—states share in that gain whether or not they participate in producing it. As a result, effective environmental regimes require design elements that reward participation and penalize free riding (see Chapter 11 'Economic Theory of International Environmental Law').

By contrast, constructivist international relations theory suggests that an exclusive focus on states' interests and their strategic pursuit of these interests may be unduly narrow. In particular, it neglects the question of where states' interests come from in the first place and, thus, the important possibility that they are at least in part shaped through states' interactions. These interactions, in turn, are framed by international norms.[21] Actors' conduct, one line of reasoning goes, is shaped not only by a logic of consequences (the rational pursuit of material interests), but also by a logic of appropriateness, leading actors to assess their conduct in light of applicable norms and attendant expectations of other actors.[22] For global regime building, the important lesson is that shared normative understandings must be gradually cultivated and deepened, and that regimes must be designed so as to maximize the opportunities for normative interaction, and pressures on states to justify their conduct in

---

[20] See, e.g., B. Koremenos, C. Lipson, and D. Snidal, eds., 'The Rational Design of International Institutions' (2005) 55 Int'l Org. 761. To the extent that states behave rationally to pursue their interest in mutual cooperation, this literature not only helps us understand how institutions should be designed but also helps to explain how international institutions are in fact designed.

[21] J.G. Ruggie, 'What Makes the World Hang Together? Neo-Utilitarianism and the Social Constructivist Challenge' (1998) 52 Int'l Org. 855.

[22] See J.G. March and J.P. Olsen, 'The Institutional Dynamics of International Political Orders,' in P.J. Katzenstein et al., eds., *Exploration and Contestation in the Study of World Politics* (Cambridge, MA: MIT Press, 1998) 309.

light of applicable standards.[23] Many international environmental regimes follow this design logic through a progressive deepening of initial framework treaties (see Chapter 20 'Treaty Making and Treaty Evolution'), and ongoing law-making and justificatory processes, including compliance procedures (see Chapter 43 'Compliance Procedures'). Of course, precisely this 'transformational' regime-building strategy has been criticized by the rationalist strands of international relations theory, on the ground that it is unlikely to succeed where a regime requires states to make costly policy changes.[24]

The second question, regarding burden sharing, raises the issue of intra-generational equity, which has taken on a strong North-South dimension (see Chapter 12 'Critical Approaches' and Chapter 27 'Equity'). A variety of equity principles have been suggested to allocate burdens, including historical responsibility and ability to pay. The principle of common but differentiated responsibilities has emerged as the most commonly invoked burden-sharing concept, but it does not specify exactly how responsibilities should be differentiated. Some formulations of the principle, such as Article 3 of the UN Framework Convention on Climate Change (UNFCCC), include the phrase 'and respective capabilities', suggesting that capacity to pay is relevant along with historical responsibility. Similarly, Principle 7 of the Rio Declaration on Environment and Development highlights both 'the different contributions to global environmental degradation' and 'technologies and financial resources' as bases for differentiation.

The invocation of these equitable principles also leaves unanswered the questions what it is that developed countries are to pay for and how much they are to pay. While the latter issue is one that can be resolved only through negotiation, the former question has been answered, at least to some extent, through the emergence of the notion of incremental costs. It demands that developed countries pay for the costs of measures taken in developing countries that benefit the international community as a whole, instead of only the state in which a measure is taken. The notion of incremental costs, however, remains controversial for at least two reasons. First, it is often difficult to distinguish which costs of measures produce global, as opposed to local, benefits. Second, and more fundamentally, the opinions of developing and developed states differ greatly as to the appropriateness of applying the principle of common but differentiated responsibilities only to measures benefiting the international community. Thus, it seems fair to say that while the international community has progressed in identifying issues that are of common concern, considerably less progress has been made in developing a shared conceptualization of how to deal with these issues in the North-South context.

[23] See A. Chayes and A. Handler Chayes, *The New Sovereignty: Compliance with International Regulatory Agreements* (Cambridge, MA: Harvard University Press, 1995).

[24] G.W. Downs et al., 'The Transformational Model of International Regime Design: Triumph of Hope or Experience?' (2000) 38 Colum. J. Transnat'l L. 465.

3.2 Future Generations

Issues such as biodiversity, climate change, and, more generally, sustainable development expand the ambit of environmental concern along an additional dimension: into the future. Although some types of environmental damage are transitory, the consequences of many environmental problems are long term and, in some cases, irreversible. When a species becomes extinct, for example, the loss is permanent. Similarly, current emissions of greenhouse gases will have effects far into the future, due to the inertia of the climate system. In both cases, our actions now impose environmental impacts not only on other countries but also on future generations.

The principles of sustainable development (see Chapter 26 'Sustainable Development'), inter-generational equity (see Chapter 27 'Equity'), and precaution (see Chapter 25 'Precaution') all reflect this concern about the future—sustainable development and inter-generational equity most directly, precaution through its particular focus on irreversible damage. According to the most widely quoted definition of sustainable development, 'sustainable development is development that meets the needs of the present without compromising the ability of future generations to meet their own needs.'[25] The problem with definitions such as these—and there are now literally hundreds of them—is to determine what they mean in practice. Although it is easy to agree that we should be concerned not merely with our own welfare but also with that of future generations, it is far less clear how we need to act in order to give that principle effect. In practice, these inter-temporal principles tend to be most relevant in shaping international environmental discourse and framing treaty-based regimes, which can then flesh out what precautionary actions are to be taken, or define sustainable resource use or emissions levels in a given context.

From an economic perspective, harm to future generations represents a type of externality, which, if it is to be dealt with, must be internalized by putting appropriate values on future damages and factoring those costs into present-day decision-making. Such cost internalization is, in economic terms, the function of the international regimes addressing such issues as climate change and biodiversity. But, of course, economics cannot answer the many hard distributional questions that are raised by inter-temporal environmental concerns.

A central debate concerning the principles of sustainable development and inter-generational equity is whether they imply the need to conserve any particular resources—what might be considered 'global heirlooms' (see Chapter 13 'Ethics and International Environmental Law'). If, as mainstream economics assumes, natural resources are infinitely substitutable, including by human and technological resources, then there is no need to protect any particular resources for the benefit of future generations. The emerging field of ecological economics, however, challenges

---

[25] World Commission on Environment and Development, *Our Common Future* (Oxford: Oxford University Press, 1987) at 43.

this assumption of infinite substitutability. According to ecological economics, some natural resources are non-substitutable, and need to be protected for the sake of future generations—for example, resources that are critical to life support, such as the climate system and the stratospheric ozone layer, as well as unique resources, such as world heritage sites. Yet this perspective raises further questions: Should we preserve such resources without regard to cost? Do they, in essence, have infinite value? Will the resources that we consider critical today be those that future generations consider critical? How are we to make those choices on behalf of future generations when they are not here to tell us what they want? No matter which choices we make, we will be taking decisions that affect future generations—this is the philosophical and moral conundrum that we face. The principles of sustainable development and inter-generational equity squarely raise these difficult questions, but do not answer them.

3.3 From Anthropocentrism to Environmental Protection as an End in Itself?

In general, international environmental law has an anthropocentric bias. It focuses on protecting the environment, not for its own sake, but because of its value to humans—its importance for human health, economics, recreation, and so forth. The very first international agreement to be negotiated, in 1900, addressed the protection of African wildlife for the benefit of European hunters, and most subsequent agreements continue to have a utilitarian focus. The landmark Stockholm Conference was entitled, significantly, the Stockholm Conference on the Human Environment. And the principle of sustainable development, which today serves as the organizing principle for international environmental law, focuses on the needs of humans, as did the Rio Conference and the Johannesburg Summit.

The human interest in environmental protection has also found, more recently, direct expression through human rights law. While a specific right to a clean environment has not emerged in international law, there is ample evidence that established human rights, such as the rights to life, health, property, or privacy, can be interpreted to encompass environmental concerns (see Chapter 28 'Environmental Rights'). In addition, procedural rights, such as rights of participation in environmental decision-making and of access to justice, have become entrenched through treaty law (see Chapter 29 'Public Participation').

Yet, increasingly, international environmental law has displayed a more ecocentric approach, despite the philosophical challenges that such an approach poses (see Chapter 13 'Ethics and International Environmental Law'). The ten-year follow-up to the Stockholm Declaration on the Human Environment was entitled the World Charter for Nature and declared that 'every form of life is unique, warranting respect regardless of its worth to man.'[26] Similarly, the 1992 Convention on Biological Diversity speaks of the 'intrinsic value' of biological diversity (although it defines biological resources in terms of resources with 'actual or potential use or value to humans'). The evolution from a utilitarian to a more environmentally oriented ethic can be seen in the international whaling regime, which started as an effort to conserve whales in order to make possible the orderly development of the whaling industry, but which has become, in essence, a preservationist regime, prohibiting commercial whaling of all species, whether or not they are endangered (see Chapter 16 'Biological Resources'). A number of international environmental agreements have also recognized the intrinsic value of ecosystems (see Chapter 24 'Ecosystems'). The 1991 Protocol on Environmental Protection to the Antarctic Treaty is an example in the global commons context. At the regional level, the first joint Ministerial Meeting of the Baltic Marine Environment Protection Commission, and the Commission for the Protection of the Marine Environment of the North East Atlantic, in 2003, agreed to adopt an ecosystem approach to the management of human activities.[27] In this approach, human activities are treated as a component of ecosystems, and are to be managed in accordance with the capacity of ecosystems. In the transboundary context, Article 20 of the Watercourses Convention provides that states 'shall individually and, where appropriate, jointly protect and preserve ecosystems of international watercourses' (see Chapter 15 'Oceans and Freshwater Resources'). Significantly, in an agreement that is otherwise concerned with a traditional balancing of states' respective sovereign rights, this provision envisages ecosystem protection duties that are independent from significant impacts on neighbouring states.

4 ACTORS AND INSTITUTIONS

Contemporary international environmental law not only encompasses a much wider range of concerns, but it also involves an increasingly complex array of actors. States, international institutions, individuals, NGOs, business, and technical experts— these categories only begin to capture the rich variety of actors. NGOs can have many different characteristics. For example, they can be international or domestic, large membership organizations or small think tanks, advocacy or programmatic organizations. Business can be green or brown, domestic or multinational. International institutions include traditional international organizations, as well as treaty bodies and regional integration organizations.

---

[26] UN General Assembly Resolution 37/7 (1982).
[27] *Record of the First Joint Meeting of the Helsinki and OSPAR Commissions*, Bremen, 25–6 June 2003, Annex 5.

These various actors can be analysed along several interrelated dimensions (see Chapter 33 'Non-Governmental Organizations and Civil Society'). First, we can study the types and degree of influence they exercise at different junctures in the policy cycle: agenda setting, normative development, implementation, and enforcement. For example, NGOs can help define an issue, promote it on the policy agenda, exert pressure on national delegations during the negotiations, monitor state compliance, and, in some cases, even bring complaints regarding inadequate enforcement. International institutions such as UNEP traditionally have played a catalytic role in helping to set the environmental agenda, but, today, international institutions are increasingly a site of normative development.

Second, actors can be analysed in terms of the basis on which they exercise influence or power. The basis of scientists' influence is, of course, expertise, and, for this reason, they tend to be less influential in the process of normative development, which involves questions of value, and more influential at stages in the policy process that involve issues with objective answers (for example, are there adequate substitutes for halons in fire extinguishers?). Some NGOs also play an expert role, but others have a representative basis, deriving their influence from their membership. Businesses too can be a source of expertise but can also exert market and financial power.

Finally, actors can be analysed by focusing on the different causal pathways through which they exercise influence. For example, many NGOs and businesses still operate primarily through states (see Chapter 31 'Changing Role of the State'). They exercise influence by pushing their own state to support a policy internationally or to implement its international obligations. Increasingly, however, NGOs and the business sector participate more directly in international institutions. And, sometimes, NGOs also act directly in the national or international marketplace through the threat or use of consumer boycotts.

4.1 States

Despite the increasing importance of other actors in the international environmental process, states remain the dominant players in both the development and implementation of international environmental law (see Chapter 31 'Changing Role of the State'). Most of the substantive content of international environmental law— whether in the form of treaties or softer instruments such as codes of conduct or guidelines—has developed through a process of inter-state negotiation, even if other actors may play significant roles in that process. And implementation of these norms depends primarily on national action: enactment of international standards into domestic law, establishment of domestic permitting procedures, monitoring and reporting on regulated activities, punishment of violations, and judicial application (see Chapter 40 'National Implementation').

However, although states remain central, the nature of the state system is itself changing. The state is becoming more porous not only economically but also environmentally. As a result, it is increasingly difficult to draw a clear separation between international and domestic environmental policy. A problem such as climate change is not just a foreign relations problem. It has implications for virtually every aspect of domestic policy: energy, transportation, construction, and land use. And, as the most recent *Trail Smelter* case serves to illustrate, even more localized transboundary pollution problems implicate a variety of governmental, and non-governmental, actors and will not necessarily be resolved through traditional inter-state channels.

International environmental law also has eroded the principle of the sovereign equality of states by differentiating among states in terms of both their obligations and their rights and, thus, has acknowledged the reality that states are heterogeneous rather than homogeneous. This development is reflected not only in the 'principle of common but differentiated responsibilities', which differentiates among states according to their contributions to a given problem and their capacity for problem-solving, but also finds expression in the decision-making procedures of institutions such as the Global Environment Facility (GEF), and the Montreal Protocol and Kyoto Protocol compliance committees, which require double-majorities of developed and developing states (see Chapter 32 'International Institutions').

4.2 International Institutions

The development of international environmental law during the second half of the twentieth century and, in particular, after the Stockholm Conference in 1972 cannot be grasped without taking into consideration the role of international institutions (see Chapter 2 'Evolution of International Environmental Law'). These institutions are not a homogenous set of actors, and they perform a variety of functions in the development and implementation of international environmental law. International institutions, furthermore, interact through, and are linked to, each other by a variety of arrangements (see Chapter 32 'International Institutions').

Within this complex web of institutions, the United Nations, through, in particular, the UNGA, the Economic and Social Commission, and the Commission on Sustainable Development, plays a coordinating role. The UNGA, for example, convened the three major environmental summits—Stockholm, Rio, and Johannesburg—and established UNEP. These summits have played an important role in generating political consensus on the issues to be addressed in international law and policy.

International institutions, such as UNEP and various UN specialized agencies, perform a catalytic role in problem identification, and in the negotiation and further development of environmental regimes. They play a role in problem identification, in particular, by providing forums for coordinating scientific research (see Chapter 9 'Science and Technology'); they support the development and implementation of international environmental treaties by hosting the secretariats for negotiating conferences and for, so-called, multilateral environmental agreements (MEAs). MEAs, in turn, also have generated a large number of international institutions, including conferences of the parties, which are not international organizations, as traditionally understood, but have traits and perform roles that closely resemble those generally attributed to international organizations (see Chapter 38 'Treaty Bodies'). International financial institutions, such as the World Bank and the GEF, coordinate the transfer of financial and technological resources and thus play a role in the implementation of the principle of common but differentiated responsibilities (see Chapter 41 'Technical and Financial Assistance'). Monitoring and verification programmes and compliance procedures, furthermore, are coordinated through, in particular, institutions associated with MEAs (see Chapter 42 'Monitoring and Verification' and Chapter 43 'Compliance Procedures'). In addition, a number of courts and tribunals, at least in principle, have jurisdiction to consider environmental disputes (see Chapter 45 'International Dispute Settlement').

In the course of performing these functions, many international institutions both engage in normative development, and administer international environmental law (see Chapter 20 'Treaty Making and Treaty Evolution' and Chapter 32 'International Institutions'). These activities have contributed to the emergence of a distinctive type of law, now often referred to as global administrative law (see Chapter 4 'Global Environmental Governance as Administration').

4.3 Non-State Actors

Two distinctive features of international environmental problems have had particular implications for the non-state actors involved in the international environmental process. First, the fact that environmental problems have a physical basis means that science figures much more prominently in international environmental regimes than in other areas of international law (see Chapter 9 'Science and Technology'). Scientists often operate through expert networks that share a common knowledge base, and whose individual members exercise influence at both national and international levels of policy-making. The role of scientists is perhaps greatest in the agenda-setting process, although technical experts can also play a significant role in the process of elaborating and implementing international environmental regimes (see Chapter 34 'Epistemic Communities'). Many pressing environmental problems, such as climate change or ozone depletion, were not immediately apparent; they were recognized as problems only as a result of science. For example, when CFCs—the principal ozone-depleting substances—were first invented in the 1920s, they were considered completely benign—not flammable, explosive, or toxic. They became an international issue only decades later, in the 1970s, as a result of the Nobel-prize winning work of two atmospheric chemists who realized that, over time, CFCs would

migrate to the upper atmosphere and catalytically react with ozone, thereby destroying the stratospheric ozone layer. Similarly, in the 1980s, climate change became an
important political issue due to both significant advances in basic science and the
entrepreneurship of a small number of scientific knowledge brokers, who pushed the
issue through a series of international meetings and hearings at the national level.
Their efforts provided knowledge about the existence of the problem, raised public
awareness and concern, influenced national policy-makers, and helped begin an
international dialogue, initially at the non-governmental level but, as the issues
gained prominence, increasingly among governments as well.

   Second, because most environmental problems are caused primarily by conduct
that qualifies as private rather than governmental, the business community has
an unusually high stake in international environmental regimes (see Chapter 35
'Business'). Typically, although states are the direct addressees of international environmental obligations, private actors are the ultimate regulatory target. Some international environmental regimes actually define the applicable standards of private
conduct directly. For example, the International Convention for the Prevention of
Pollution from Ships (MARPOL Convention) establishes detailed construction and
design standards for oil tankers, which ship builders and vessel operators must follow—states act merely as transmission belts, applying the MARPOL Convention's
standards to their flag vessels. Other international environmental agreements require
states to adopt elaborate regulatory machinery to control private conduct, including
permitting schemes for waste disposal or for trade in endangered species, or prior
informed consent requirements for transport of hazardous materials. Still other
international environmental regimes, such as the Kyoto Protocol, simply require
states to bring about a particular result but leave it up to states to decide how to influence private conduct in order to achieve this result.

   Since private actors are the ultimate target of most international environmental
regulation, they are particularly active in the international standard-setting and
implementation processes. Businesses typically influence policy and rule-making
in order to further their own business interests—in the case of 'green' business, by
gaining a competitive advantage through the adoption of more stringent environmental measures; in the case of 'brown' business, by seeking to stall the adoption of
more stringent measures in order to continue doing business as usual. Sometimes
industries develop environmental standards on their own in order to enhance their
image, forestall governmental regulation, or influence the development of internationally uniform standards in anticipation of governmental regulation. These private and quasi-private standard-setting efforts are an increasingly significant feature
of international environmental law, and raise important issues of participation and
legitimacy (see Chapter 21 'Private and Quasi-Private Standard Setting').

   Finally, environmental NGOs play a significant role in virtually every aspect
of the international environmental process (see Chapter 33 'Non-Governmental
Organizations and Civil Society'). Depending on their membership, they may be

regarded either as 'giving the environment a voice' and thus acting in the common interest or as representing the particular interests of their membership in preserving a specific natural environment. International NGOs such as Greenpeace and the World Conservation Union are examples of the former; NGOs representing local populations or indigenous peoples are examples of the latter (see Chapter 36 'Indigenous Peoples'). Although typically, NGOs wield influence by attempting to influence states, in some cases, NGOs play a more direct role in international environmental regimes. For example, under the Montreal Protocol, they may provide information on state compliance to the Secretariat, while under the Convention on International Trade in Endangered Species of Wild Fauna and Flora (CITES), NGOs have quasi-official roles in monitoring and reporting processes. As mentioned, NGOs also act directly in the national or international marketplace by using or threatening consumer boycotts. Relevant examples are the campaigns against the consumption of ivory and seal fur.

5 Normative Development

The dynamic quality of international environmental issues has necessitated the development of more dynamic and flexible standard-setting processes. Treaties remain the basis of most international environmental regulation. But, in most international environmental regimes, they no longer reflect a static set of rules agreed to by states for an indefinite period of time. Instead, they establish iterative processes, which allow international environmental law to develop more rapidly in response to the emergence of new problems and new knowledge and understanding (see Chapter 20 'Treaty Making and Treaty Evolution'). Broad framework agreements, such as the LRTAP Convention or the UNFCCC, which establish the basic principles and institutions of their respective regimes, are elaborated by more precise regulatory protocols addressing particular pollutants or activities. Technical details are assigned to annexes that can be amended more easily, usually through tacit consent procedures. Vague treaty norms, such as the 'wise use' requirement for wetlands, set forth in the Convention on Wetlands of International Importance Especially as Waterfowl Habitat, are elaborated through decisions of treaty bodies. In essence, modern environmental treaties establish ongoing regulatory processes that exemplify what has been referred to more generally as global administrative law (see Chapter 4 'Global Environmental Governance as Administration').

The result is that, in most international environmental regimes, the treaty text itself represents just the tip of the normative iceberg. The majority of the norms develop through more flexible and dynamic processes, which result in formally non-legally binding decisions. This is the reason why, in order to understand international environmental regimes such as the regime on trade in endangered species, one needs to consult not merely the CITES agreement itself but also the CITES handbook—a thick book that compiles the various decisions by the CITES parties on the listing process, reporting, compliance, and so forth.

In this more flexible process of normative development, it is worth highlighting two related features, which not only aim to promote community interests in the environment but also raise concerns about the legitimacy of the international environmental process (see Chapter 30 'Legitimacy'). First, the need for collective action has eroded the requirement of state consent, which traditionally served to legitimize international law. Of course, ordinary consent-based methods still play a role in regime development. For example, when an agreement is amended or when an additional treaty, such as a protocol, is adopted, individual states are bound only when they consent to these instruments. But more and more regulatory detail is adopted through decisions of a treaty's Conference of the Parties, without subsequent formal consent by individual states. Under the climate change regime, for example, the bulk of the regulatory work has been accomplished through simple decisions of the plenary body.

Second, regime-based law-making processes provide an arena in which actors other than states, such as international organizations, NGOs, individuals, or business entities, can directly participate (see Chapter 29 'Public Participation' and Chapter 32 'International Institutions'). Although, in a formal sense, law-making remains firmly in the hands of states, actors other than states have opportunities to provide input into law-making processes and help shape their outcomes. To the extent that these other actors, although unelected, represent broader constituencies, their involvement in the international environmental process might be seen as reflecting a more inclusive approach to the environmental concerns of the wider international community.

These trends are reinforced by the extensive use of informal methods of environmental standard-setting—codes of conduct, guidelines, and their like (see Chapter 6 'Formality and Informality'). Although even soft standards are subject to tough and protracted negotiations, their non-binding character to some extent may facilitate reaching agreement upon collective action. In some cases, informal norms may be sufficient in themselves (the ISO 14000 standards are perhaps an example); in others, they serve as intermediary steps on the road towards a binding agreement;[28] in still others, they are adopted in the context of a binding agreement. In all of these cases, informal standard-setting processes allow speedier regime development, and adjustment, than processes that require ratification by individual states.

---

[28] For example, the prior informed consent procedures for hazardous substances, which were originally developed in the UNEP's Cairo and London guidelines, served as the basis for the Basel Convention on the Control of Transboundary Movements of Hazardous Wastes and Their Disposal and the Convention on the Prior Informed Consent Procedure for Certain Hazardous Chemicals and Pesticides in International Trade.

In this dynamic standard-setting process, one traditional source of international law that has diminished in importance is customary law (see Chapter 19 'Formation of Customary International Law and General Principles'). The decentralized, and uncoordinated, nature of the customary law-making process make it ill-suited for generating the kinds of detailed rules necessary to regulate the use of hazardous materials, the trade in endangered species, or the emissions of long-range pollutants. As a result, most of the action in international environmental law relates to treaty regimes rather than custom. The customary law process is able to generate only quite general principles, such as the duty to prevent transboundary harm. Apart from an occasional international or national case where norms of customary law might be invoked, these norms operate as broad principles that frame legal discourse and diplomacy—so their formal legal status is of only limited practical significance. They play a significant role in the broader process of persuasion and justification that characterizes international environmental law, rather than as rules that govern behaviour (see Chapter 18 'Different Types of Norms in International Environmental Law').

6 COMPLIANCE

International environmental law illustrates the limitations of the classical approach in international law to compliance. In traditional international legal theory, compliance focuses on such concepts as breach, state responsibility, invocation of responsibility by another state, dispute settlement, and, ultimately, remedies such as restitution and compensation (see Chapter 44 'International Responsibility and Liability'). However, as is well known, this general model is seldom applied in international law generally, and even less so in international environmental law. States rarely try to enforce international environmental law by invoking state responsibility, and few cases of non-compliance are ever addressed through traditional dispute settlement (see Chapter 45 'International Dispute Settlement'), perhaps because environmental disputes, due to their multilateral nature, are not satisfactorily addressed by dispute settlement procedures that typically have a bilateral and adversarial character.

The need to achieve the greatest possible degree of compliance by the widest possible range of parties has resulted in the emergence of tailor-made procedures that assess parties' compliance with their treaty commitments, and provide for a range of measures to facilitate or compel compliance (see Chapter 43 'Compliance Procedures'). In general, these compliance processes combine pragmatic and legal elements. The compliance bodies usually are comprised of government representatives rather than independent experts, in contrast to the human rights field. And their objective is not so much to determine state responsibility, and impose remedies, as to make the regime more effective in the future, by determining why a country is not complying and helping it to do better. Against this backdrop, their formal legal status seems to be of secondary importance. Significantly, although the non-legally binding nature of these compliance procedures helps make them acceptable to treaty parties, it does not appear to make them any less effective than binding measures might be.

7 CONCLUSION: IS INTERNATIONAL ENVIRONMENTAL LAW A DISTINCT FIELD?

Given the development of new types of concerns, new actors, and new standard-setting and compliance processes, it is no exaggeration to say that international environmental law has emerged as a distinct field. This distinctiveness is reflected in the very terminology of international environmental law, which speaks of 'commitments' rather than 'obligations', 'non-compliance' rather than 'breach', and 'consequences' rather than 'remedies' or 'sanctions'.[29] Is this distinctiveness cause for celebration or concern? Does it serve to undermine the fundamental unity and coherence of international law?

As international environmental regimes, institutions, and tribunals have proliferated, some have expressed concern about threats to the coherence of international law. But the emergence of new approaches to standard setting and compliance could be viewed, instead, as an entirely appropriate response to the distinctive characteristics of international environmental problems. These problems are not only political but also physical and involve a great deal of technical complexity. They result primarily from private, rather than governmental, conduct. They are highly uncertain and rapidly changing. All of these factors mean that, to address international environmental problems, we need complex regulatory regimes, which involve more flexible and dynamic standard-setting processes, and we need to take a pragmatic and forward-looking approach.

International environmental regimes have led to new types of normative development, blurring the distinction between legally binding and non-legally binding norms, public and private standard setting, and international and domestic law. Indeed, as these other distinctions have blurred, the distinction between legal scholarship and non-legal scholarship has itself blurred in international environmental law. There is tremendous interaction between scholars from different fields,

---

[29] M. Koskenniemi, 'Breach of Treaty or Non-Compliance? Reflections on the Enforcement of the Montreal Protocol' (1992) 3 Y.B. Int'l Envt'l L. 123.

which is why the *Handbook* includes a section examining other disciplinary perspectives, and why about a quarter of its authors do not have a legal background.

Are the new features of international environmental law unique to this field? Of course not. International environmental law, however, more than other areas of international law has adapted to significant societal changes, which are associated with the processes of globalization, and emphasize the relationships of inter-dependence across the globe. Perhaps most importantly, international environmental law has had to find ways of accommodating the distinct interests of a large variety of states and other actors, whose participation in international environmental regimes, albeit in different ways, is crucial if environmental problems are to be addressed with at least some measure of success. International environmental law has by no means addressed all the attendant challenges successfully, as critical contributions to this *Handbook* illustrate. So there may well be the potential for fertilization—in both directions—between international environmental law and other fields of international law. However, in thinking about such possibilities of cross-fertilization, it is important to identify first what is new and distinctive about international environmental law rather than to see it as simply a continuation of the past. The aim of this *Handbook* is to assist in this task.

RECOMMENDED READING

U. Beyerlin, *Umweltvölkerrecht* (Munich: C.H. Beck, 2000).

P.W. Birnie and A.E. Boyle, *International Law and the Environment*, 2nd edition (Oxford: Oxford University Press, 2002).

L. Boisson de Chazournes et al., *Protection internationale de l'environnement* (Paris: Editions Pedone, 2005).

D. Hunter, J. Salzman, and D. Zaelke, *International Environmental Law and Policy*, 2nd edition (New York: Foundation Press, 2002).

A.C. Kiss and J.-P. Beurier, *Droit International de L'Environnement* (Paris: Editions Pedone, 2000).

—— and D. Shelton, *International Environmental Law*, 4th edition (Ardsley, NY: Transnational Publishers, 2004).

V.P. Nanda and G.R. Pring, *International Environmental Law and Policy for the Twenty-First Century* (Ardsley, NY: Transnational Publishers, 2003).

P. Sands, *Principles of International Environmental Law*, 2nd edition (Cambridge: Cambridge University Press, 2003).

PART I

GENERAL
ISSUES

CHAPTER 2

THE EVOLUTION OF INTERNATIONAL ENVIRONMENTAL LAW

PETER H. SAND

FEW legal disciplines have evolved as rapidly as international environmental law, which is variously described as a 'special field', a 'new branch', or an emergent 'autonomous special area' of international law. Although some would contest, or at least qualify, this claim to autonomy—mainly on the grounds that there is presently no overall systemic coherence, let alone authoritative codification, of the diverse international norms applicable (see Chapter 7 'Relationship between International Environmental Law and Other Branches of International Law')—the debate is somewhat academic, given the sheer volume of materials now appearing under this subject heading.[1]

It is important to keep in mind, though, that the field is not—as usually conceived—confined to public international law but that it also encompasses transnational/private international law—that is, 'the entire corpus of international law, public and private, relevant to environmental issues or problems.'[2] Moreover, the continuous impact of domestic environmental law, public and private, on international law-making in this field as well as the related 'problem of scale'[3]—that is, the need to assess the transferability of empirical generalizations, causal inferences, and theoretical models from one level to another (see Chapter 5 'Levels of Environmental Governance') makes comparative information and analysis indispensable.[4]

Close interaction with national laws and policies has indeed been the major driving force for innovation in international environmental law—to the point where economists have noted with some perplexity the 'non-ergodic world' of environmental regimes,[5] which is subject not only to unforeseeable natural and technological changes (see Chapter 9 'Science and Technology'), but also teeming with regulatory approaches that are new, often divergent, and competing (see Chapter 8 'Instrument Choice').

Most descriptions of the historical evolution of international environmental law distinguish three or four major 'periods' or 'phases':

- the 'traditional era' until about 1970 (preceding the 1972 United Nations Stockholm Conference on the Human Environment), which is sometimes sub-divided into a pre-1945 and a post-1945 period;

---

[1] See, e.g., W.E. Burhenne and M. Jahnke, eds., *International Environmental Law: Multilateral Treaties* (Berlin: Erich Schmidt Verlag, 1974–2006), and W.E. Burhenne and M. Jahnke, eds., *International Environmental Soft Law: Collection of Relevant Instruments* (Dordrecht: Martinus Nijhoff, 1993–2006).

[2] P.W. Birnie and A.E. Boyle, *International Law and the Environment*, 2nd edition (Oxford: Oxford University Press, 2002) at 2.

[3] O.R. Young, *The Institutional Dimensions of Environmental Change: Fit, Interplay, and Scale* (Cambridge, MA: MIT Press, 2002) at 139.

[4] See, e.g., N.A. Robinson, ed., *Comparative Environmental Law and Regulation* (Dobbs Ferry, NY: Oceana, 1993–2006).

[5] D.C. North, 'Dealing with a Non-Ergodic World: Institutional Economics, Property Rights, and the Global Environment' (1999) 10 Duke Envt'l L. and Pol'y F. 1. According to the *Web Dictionary of Cybernetics and Systems* (*Principia Cybernetica*, 2005), the term 'non-ergodic'—from the field of statistical mathematics—refers to systems that are incomprehensible through observation, either for lack of repetition or for lack of stabilities.

- the 'modern era' from Stockholm to the 1992 United Nations Conference on Environment and Development (UNCED) in Rio de Janeiro; and
- the 'post-modern era' after Rio.

However, it has rightly been pointed out that the reality of international law is 'historically and synchronically discontinuous'[6]—that is, contemporary law reflects traditional, modern, and post-modern elements alike. Even though it may be possible to put dates on the first international formulation of some environmental legal approaches, the bulk of law developed during earlier periods continues to be relevant simultaneously with new concepts today. Nor did the absence of specific environmental terminology during the so-called traditional era preclude the development of pertinent transnational rules and legal regimes as far back as the eighteenth century.

The same caveat applies to the distinction frequently drawn between the period prior to the Second World War and the post-war period, which is said to be characterized by the transition from an 'international law of coexistence' to an 'international law of cooperation'. While it is true that the establishment of the UN, and of the post-war generation of global and regional organizations, laid the ground for new international law-making—especially for the global commons and for novel pollution risks—it is just as well to remember that certain cooperative arrangements and institutions in issue areas now labelled as 'environmental' had already existed long before. Even so, the three-layer (traditional–modern–post-modern) perspective helps to understand the historical context.

1 TRADITIONAL ERA

Natural resource management has been a subject of international law-making for well over two hundred years—starting with bilateral and regional regulatory agreements, and dispute settlement arrangements over the shared utilization of water, wildlife, and fisheries in transboundary areas (see Chapter 22 'Transboundary Impacts') and over the allocation and exploitation of 'fugitive' marine resources outside national jurisdiction.

What emerged during this period—especially under the label of 'vicinage' or 'good neighbourship law' (*bon voisinage, Nachbarschaftsrecht*)—were typical territorial regimes of reciprocity, either between contiguous states or for the users of geographical areas customarily designated as 'global commons'. Hence, many international law textbooks continue to address environmental problems primarily under the doctrinal headings of territorial sovereignty and 'internationally used spaces and

---

[6] M. Koskenniemi, 'Letter to the Editors of the Symposium on Methods in International Law' (1999) 93 A.J.I.L. 351 at 359.

resources'—on the premise that 'cold-eyed application of [traditional] legal analysis may be just as fruitful as the invention of a new vehicle such as "international environmental law".'[7] Among the most frequently cited examples of this classical approach are the arbitration awards in the *Pacific Fur Seal* case (*United States v. Great Britain*, 1893: living resources in the global commons); the *Trail Smelter* case (*United States v. Canada*, 1938–41: transboundary air pollution); and the *Lake Lanoux* case (*Spain v. France*, 1957: transboundary freshwaters). Simultaneously, if less well publicized, a number of similar transnational disputes were resolved by domestic court decisions on classical territorial grounds under the applicable rules of conflict of laws or 'international administrative law'.[8] Examples include the *Roya River* case (*France–Italy*: transboundary waters, Italian Supreme Court, 1939); the *Poro* case (*France–Germany*: transboundary air pollution, German Court of Appeals, 1957); and the *Salzburg Airport* case (*Germany–Austria*: transboundary aircraft noise, Austrian Supreme Administrative Court, 1969).[9]

At the same time, 'green' policies began to make their appearance in treaty regimes from the middle of the nineteenth century onwards,[10] echoing a transition in national laws from 'single-use-oriented' regimes (for example, for fisheries) to multiple use and 'resource-oriented' regulation (for example, for river basins). And, even though the legal history of economic development is often associated with the unbridled over-exploitation of resources such as of the forests in Europe and North America,[11] the history of conservation can also be traced back to enlightened legislative models such as Jean-Baptiste Colbert's 1669 *Ordonnance des eaux et forêts*,[12] which may in turn be seen as precursors of contemporary environmental law.

The initial policy motives for much of this law-making were utilitarian and self-serving—the avowed reason for Colbert's forest legislation was to secure long-term timber supplies for French naval construction. 'Anthropocentric' lines of reasoning were prominent in early multilateral 'environmental' treaties (see Chapter 13 'Ethics and International Environmental Law'), such as the 1900 London Convention Designed to Ensure the Conservation of Various Species of Wild Animals in Africa

---

[7] I. Brownlie, 'Editor's Preface,' in B.D. Smith, *State Responsibility and the Marine Environment: The Rules of Decision* (Oxford: Clarendon, 1987).

[8] One of the earliest scholarly surveys of this field was Karl Neumeyer's monumental treatise on *International Administrative Law* (*Internationales Verwaltungsrecht*), volume 2, part 2 (Munich: Schweitzer, 1922), chapter 8 on the transnational regulation of natural resources at 1.

[9] P.H. Sand, *Transnational Environmental Law: Lessons in Global Change* (The Hague: Kluwer Law International, 1999) at 87, 89, and 90.

[10] E.g., Article 22 (regulations 'to prevent destruction of the fishery' in the Bidassoa River) of the 1856 Bayonne Boundary Treaty between France and Spain, and further examples referenced in B. Rüster and B. Simma, eds., *International Protection of the Environment: Treaties and Selected Documents*, volume 9 (Dobbs Ferry, NY: Oceana, 1977) at 4319–792.

[11] See, e.g., J.W. Hurst, *Law and Economic Growth: The Legal History of the Lumber Industry in Wisconsin, 1836–1915* (Washington, DC: Belknap, 1964).

[12] A. Trout, *Jean-Baptiste Colbert* (Boston: Twayne, 1978) at 149. See also P.W. Bamford, *Forests and French Sea Power, 1660–1789* (Toronto: University of Toronto Press, 1956) at 21. It was Colbert who inspired the first scientific elaboration of the 'sustainability' concept by H.C. von Carlowitz, *Sylvicultura Oeconomica* (1713), 2nd edition (Leipzig: Braun, 1732) at 57–8.

That Are Useful to Man or Inoffensive and the 1902 Paris Convention to Protect Birds Useful to Agriculture. The 1931, 1937, and 1946 International Conventions for the Regulation of Whaling were also primarily aimed at resource management for commercial uses, and the 1929 and 1951 International Plant Protection Conventions—like their ancestor, the 1878 Phylloxera Convention—were solely concerned with cultivated, that is, agricultural, crops.

Yet the twentieth century also marks the entry of genuine conservation ethics on the treaty agenda, reflecting new concerns of the international community for common natural heritage and the prevention of global risks (see Chapter 23 'Common Areas, Common Heritage, Common Concern'): from President Theodore Roosevelt's first abortive attempt at convening an International Conservation Conference at The Hague in 1909, to the 1940 Washington Convention on Nature Protection and Wildlife Preservation in the Western Hemisphere; from the colonial powers' 1933 London Convention Relative to the Preservation of Fauna and Flora in Their Natural State, to the post-colonial 1968 Algiers African Convention on the Conservation of Nature and Natural Resources; and from the 1955 UN General Assembly Resolution Establishing the Scientific Committee on the Effects of Atomic Radiation (which was later attached to the UN Environment Programme (UNEP)), to the 1963 Nuclear Test Ban Treaty.

Although pre-war efforts to translate these concerns into new intergovernmental institutions failed at the time, the 'para-governmental' International Union for the Protection of Nature, which was established in 1948 (renamed in 1956 the International Union for Conservation of Nature and Natural Resources (IUCN) and later the World Conservation Union), became an influential source of subsequent treaty initiatives. In 1959, the International Maritime Consultative Organization (IMCO, now IMO) was designated to deal with global marine pollution risks under the 1954 International Convention for the Prevention of Pollution of the Sea by Oil. Its ensuing treaty work and technical standard-setting in this field (see Chapter 18 'Different Types of Norms in International Environmental Law'), together with that of several other UN specialized agencies and bodies which during the post-war period assumed new environment-related functions (Food and Agriculture Organization (FAO), International Atomic Energy Agency (IAEA), International Labour Organization (ILO), UN Educational, Scientific and Cultural Organization (UNESCO), World Health Organization (WHO), and UN Economic Commission of Europe (ECE)), further contributed to the growing stock of international law and governance practice now available.

2 MODERN ERA

The beginning of 'modern' international environmental law is usually dated to 5 June 1972, the opening day of the first UN Conference on the Human Environment in Stockholm, which is now annually celebrated as World Environment Day. However, it really was the culmination of an intense preparatory process going back to Resolution 1346 (XLV) of the UN Economic and Social Council on 30 July 1968, endorsed by UN General Assembly Resolution 2398 (XXIII) on 6 December 1968. The Stockholm 'watershed' or 'paradigm shift' so initiated must be seen in the context of several concurrent discourses (see Chapter 3 'Paradigms and Discourses'):

- a global rise in environmental risks, highlighted by a series of eco-disasters starting with the 1967 *Torrey Canyon* case (oil pollution in the North Sea) and the 1971 *Minamata* cases (river pollution by organo-mercury in Japan);
- a growing public awareness of the 'world eco-crisis', alerted by media attention, and by seminal publications such as Rachel Carson's 1962 *Silent Spring*, Max Nicholson's 1969 *Environmental Revolution*, and the Club of Rome's 1972 *Limits to Growth*—readily espoused by the civic protest movements of the late 1960s and early 1970s; and
- innovative examples of national legislation enacted in response to the environmental challenge, including Japan's 1967 Kogai Act, Sweden's 1969 Miljöskyddslag, and the 1970 US National Environmental Policy Act.

In terms of international environmental law, the Stockholm process produced a new type of global institution (UNEP), with a de-centralized action plan assigning environmental responsibilities to a wide spectrum of existing institutions, and a plethora of new legal instruments ('hard' and 'soft') within a network of functional (risk-oriented) international regimes.

UNEP, which was established by UN General Assembly Resolutions 2997 and 3004 (XXVII) in 1972, with headquarters in Nairobi, continues to serve as the centrepiece of environmental activities within the UN family of organizations. Its budget, executive director, and Governing Council membership (58 states) are determined by the UN General Assembly, to which it reports through the Economic and Social Council. This legal status sets it apart from the semi-autonomous UN specialized agencies, among which it always had difficulty asserting a cross-sectoral coordinating function—not unlike national environmental agencies among their sectoral counterparts in traditional cabinet ministries. Yet, although UNEP originally did not even have a formal international legislative mandate (see Chapter 32 'International Institutions'), it has succeeded in initiating and negotiating no less than 48 multilateral environmental conventions and protocols since 1976—through diplomatic conferences convened under its auspices and, from 1982 onwards, in the context of a government-approved Programme for the Development and Periodic Review of Environmental Law (Montevideo Programme). At the same time, beginning with the 1972 Stockholm Declaration on the Human Environment, it has promoted extensive international norm-making through the development of 'soft law' (see Chapter 6 'Formality and Informality').

The new generation of legal instruments that were emerging no longer fitted the territorially defined 'Procrustean bed' into which environmental issues had been forced before. The spectrum of international environmental relations (see Chapter

10 'International Relations Theory') had expanded well beyond the stereotype of 'transboundary matters' on the one hand and 'governance of the commons' on the other, to match not only the growing environmental agenda of regional regimes but also the growing catalogue of environmental problems that had once seemed local, yet had turned out to be globally shared. Accordingly, the scope and focus of international law-making shifted towards 'functional' regulation, depending on the ecosystems affected or the specific environmental risks addressed, and largely irrespective of traditional territorial limitations.[13]

2.1 Treaty Developments

Compared to the traditional (pre-Stockholm) period, the number of multilateral environmental agreements more than doubled during the 20 years from Stockholm to Rio. The institutional structure for implementing this multitude of treaties was highly de-centralized—not to say chaotic—even for those negotiated and adopted under UNEP auspices. It essentially consisted of a network of quasi-autonomous 'conferences of the parties' (see Chapter 38 'Treaty Bodies'), some without permanent headquarters, though for the most part they were hosted by different existing international organizations and, hence, became a prime object of inter-agency rivalries and turf wars. There were also notable incremental changes, both in terms of treaty subjects and treaty design. Instead of the classical risks of natural resource scarcity and extinction (for example, treaties to preserve wildlife habitats or species and to prevent their over-exploitation by fishing, hunting, or commercial uses (see Chapter 16 'Biological Resources'), the new man-made risks of industrial pollution and resource degradation by hazardous substances or activities now moved into the focus of legal drafting (for example, international regulations for the carriage of dangerous goods or for the production and use of chemicals (see Chapter 17 'Hazardous Substances and Activities')—sometimes through near-instant law-making, as in the case of the 1986 IAEA conventions adopted in the wake of the Chernobyl nuclear power disaster. At the same time, the pattern of treaty design shifted (see Chapter 20 'Treaty Making and Treaty Evolution') from ad hoc single-issue diplomatic conventions towards 'dynamic' regulatory regimes open to future change by supplementary review and negotiation, with periodic adjustment of standards through technical annexes (and increasingly geared towards prevention rather than remediation of damage, as illustrated by the package of IMO marine pollution conventions adopted in response to the series of tanker accidents between 1967 and 1989). Best reflected in Maurice Strong's credo that 'the process is the policy', the idea of a 'framework

---

[13] In the view of sociologist Niklas Luhmann, globalization is characterized by a shift from territorial to functional boundaries; see N. Luhmann, *Das Recht der Gesellschaft* (Frankfurt: Suhrkamp, 1993) at 571, English translation (by K.A. Ziegert) *Law as a Social System* (Oxford: Oxford University Press, 2004) at 481.

convention' (supplemented by optional 'protocols') first emerged in 1974 from a Spanish draft proposal for what later became the UNEP-sponsored Convention for the Protection of the Mediterranean Sea against Pollution, which served as the design model for numerous subsequent environmental treaties.[14]

2.2 Developments in Dispute Settlement

Similar trends—that is, focus on anthropogenic risks and on preventive regulatory design—made their appearance in international/transnational environmental dispute settlement during this period (see Chapter 45 'International Dispute Settlement'), primarily in the field of transfrontier river pollution, as in the *Rhinesalt* cases adjudicated—as a matter of conflict of laws—by the European Court of Justice in 1976 and by Dutch and French national courts in 1983–90; and in the field of marine pollution, as in the *Montedison* cases decided by Italian and French courts in 1974–85, and the *Amoco Cadiz* judgment rendered by a US court in 1992. Significantly, the Rhine chloride waste problem was eventually resolved by a cost-sharing scheme negotiated among the riparian states in 1991, and the bulk of claims for ship-based oil pollution shifted away from liability suits to the quasi-insurance scheme set up—in response to the *Torrey Canyon* and *Amoco Cadiz* accidents—under the 1971 and 1992 International Oil Pollution Compensation Funds (see Chapter 44 'International Responsibility and Liability').

Even though most multilateral environmental agreements contain formal provisions for dispute settlement by recourse to international adjudication or arbitration, those clauses have remained notoriously unused. By contrast, environment-related disputes became frequent topics for quasi-judicial proceedings in the context of the General Agreement on Tariffs and Trade (GATT), starting with the *Tuna-Dolphin* cases (*Mexico v. United States*, 1991); and the environmental damage caused by the 1991 Gulf War generated an unprecedented volume of state responsibility claims that were settled by the UN Security Council's Compensation Commission (UNCC).[15]

2.3 Developments in National Law

Simultaneously, the Stockholm-to-Rio period witnessed the momentous 'horizontal diffusion' of innovative environmental laws and policies worldwide, with a dual effect on international law. On the one hand, through a voluntary process of social learning

---

[14] J.A. Yturriaga, 'Regional Conventions on the Protection of the Marine Environment' (1979) 162 Recueil des cours 319 at 339.

[15] P.H. Sand, 'Compensation for Environmental Damage from the 1991 Gulf War' (2005) 35 Envt'l Pol'y & L. 244.

and imitation sometimes referred to as *mimesis*,[16] 'legal formants' spreading across national and cultural boundaries produced a certain degree of convergence and harmonization that tended to facilitate consensus in treaty-making. A prime example is the 'environmental impact assessment' (EIA) technique, which originated in section 102(C) of the 1970 US National Environmental Policy Act and rapidly spread to more than 80 countries worldwide. Even though proposals for a global EIA treaty never materialized, the technique was incorporated into a 1985 Council Directive of the European Union (EEC Directive 85/337, amended in 1997 by EC Directive 97/11); into the 'soft' UNEP Goals and Principles of Environmental Impact Assessment in 1987; as well as into several of UNEP's regional seas conventions, and the 1991 UNECE Convention on Environmental Impact Assessment in a Transboundary Context. In addition, it became in 1989 a condition for World Bank loans, a practice that has since been followed by other multilateral development banks.

On the other hand, international environmental agreements also borrowed concepts and language from this partially harmonized core of domestic environmental law, across a wide spectrum of both 'command and control' and 'economic instruments' of regulation, thereby creating a distinct 'vertical transplant' effect.[17] In some instances, though, the elements that were transplanted from the national level have tended to act as 'legal irritants' which unleashed an evolutionary dynamic perturbing and potentially transforming the recipient (international) regimes[18]—illustrated, for example, by the 'precautionary principle' (see Chapter 25 'Precaution'), which prevailed in the 1987 Montreal Protocol on Substances That Deplete the Ozone Layer (Montreal Protocol) (see Chapter 14 'Atmosphere and Outer Space'), but which continued to prove controversial in subsequent biosafety (see Chapter 16 'Biological Resources') and chemical safety negotiations (see Chapter 17 'Hazardous Substances and Activities').

2.4 Development of International Environmental Law as a Discipline

By the end of the 1980s at the latest, international environmental law had 'emerged as a *distinct academic discipline*.'[19] Indeed, the 'greening' of international law, politics,

---

[16] A. Toynbee, *A Study of History: 12. Reconsiderations* (Oxford: Oxford University Press, 1961) at 343. See also W.C. Clark, J. Jäger, J. van Eijndhoven, and N.M. Dickson, eds., *Learning to Manage Global Environmental Risks* (Cambridge, MA: MIT Press, 2001).

[17] J.B. Wiener, 'Something Borrowed for Something Blue: Legal Transplants and the Evolution of Global Environmental Law' (2001) 27 Ecology L.Q. 1295.

[18] D. Nelken, 'Beyond the Metaphor of Legal Transplants? Consequences of Autopoietic Theory for the Study of Cross-Cultural Legal Adaptation,' in J. Přibaň and D. Nelken, eds., *Law's New Boundaries: The Consequences of Legal Autopoiesis* (Aldershot: Ashgate, 2001) 265.

[19] *Harvard Law Review* Editors, 'Developments in the Law: International Environmental Law' (1991) 104 Harv. L. Rev. 1484 at 1489.

and institutions had become something of a missionary goal and meta-narrative to an entire generation of committed environmental activists. Several worldwide professional networks of 'international environmental lawyers' had come into existence, amply qualified as a new 'epistemic community' (see Chapter 34 'Epistemic Communities') (if promptly suspected of 'overspecialization' by the international law establishment),[20] for example, the International Council of Environmental Law, the IUCN Commission on Environmental Law, and the Environmental Law Alliance Worldwide. They were active not only as expert participants in intergovernmental and non-governmental conferences and institutions, but also in the global dissemination of innovative environmental legislation, through numerous new programmes for technical drafting assistance and legal 'capacity building' in developing countries in particular (for example, by the FAO Development Law Service, the IUCN Environmental Law Centre, the UNEP Environmental Law Unit, and the World Bank Legal Department). Voluntary international standardization and certification schemes for environmental quality of products and services contributed to technical-legal harmonization in a number of sectors, including eco-labels for sustainably harvested products certified by the Forest Stewardship Council and the Marine Stewardship Council, and the ISO 14000 series by the International Organization for Standardization (see Chapter 21 'Private and Quasi-Private Standard Setting').

There now was a rush of international initiatives for the trans-sectoral codification of environmental law 'principles'. Following the World Charter for Nature, which was initiated by the IUCN and adopted as a 'soft' UN General Assembly Resolution (37/7) in 1982, and the Montreal Rules of International Law Applicable to Transfrontier Pollution, which were adopted in 1982 by the (non-governmental) International Law Association, the 1987 Brundtland Commission report recommended a set of legal principles on 'transboundary natural resources and environmental interferences.' The UN International Law Commission began to struggle with the topic of responsibility and liability for environmental harm (see Chapter 44 'International Responsibility and Liability'), and, in 1991, the Institut de Droit International embarked on its own formulation of rules applicable to the environment and to environmental damages (finalized at Strasbourg in 1997).

At the regional level also (see Chapter 5 'Levels of Environmental Governance'), environmental topics had begun to enter—and at times, to dominate—the normative agenda of the European Communities (see Chapter 37 'Regional Economic Integration Organizations'), the Organisation for Economic Cooperation and Development (OECD), the UN regional economic commissions, and several autonomous regional regimes including the Antarctic Treaty (with its 1991 Madrid

---

[20] See I. Brownlie, 'State Responsibility and International Pollution: A Practical Perspective,' in D.B. Magraw, ed., *International Law and Pollution* (Philadelphia: University of Pennsylvania Press, 1991) 120 at 122.

Protocol on Environmental Protection). In parallel to the global codification of marine environment rules in Part XII of the 1982 UN Convention on the Law of the Sea (see Chapter 15 'Ocean and Freshwater Resources'), the 1976 Convention for the Protection of the Mediterranean Sea against Pollution became the model for a series of UNEP-sponsored 'regional seas' programmes, which generated a total of 40 conventions and protocols for different marine and coastal regions of the world. One characteristic of this new type of regional treaties (which distinguishes them from earlier conventions for the North Sea and the Baltic Sea) was the prominent role of 'Southern' developing countries, which was also reflected in a thematic expansion from environmental to development issues.

The North-South discourse, which has been an integral part of international environmental governance ever since the 1971 Founex report (preparatory to Stockholm), may be said to have evolved from a pre-Stockholm era of contestation to active participation and engagement during the 'modern' era. In terms of international environmental law, the consequences were twofold, including, on the one hand, formal recognition of the need for built-in financial transfers in order to compensate for structural North-South handicaps in global environmental agreements[21] and, on the other hand, the emergence of new bipolar institutions, exemplified by the governance structure of the Montreal Protocol's Multilateral Fund since 1990 (the '7+7' formula) and the Global Environment Facility's 'double majority' balance, not unlike the ritual institutional parity formerly observed in East-West relations.[22] The major difference, however, is that the North-South categories are mutually exclusive and do not allow for a third, neutral, or 'non-aligned' position. While states may *de facto* 'graduate' from the status of developing countries or may in turn drop below the ominous World Bank threshold of *per capita* annual income,[23] there is no non-alignment option—poverty rarely is a matter of choice (see Chapter 12 'Critical Approaches').

3 POST-MODERN ERA

Inevitably perhaps, the proliferation of new multilateral environmental instruments and norms also raised new questions, as critical observers expressed alarm over 'treaty congestion' and a lack of synergy in international law-making and institution

---

[21] P.H. Sand, 'Carrots without Sticks? New Financial Mechanisms for Global Environmental Agreements' (1999) 3 Max Planck Y.B. UN L. 363.

[22] On the 'semicircles syndrome' introduced by UNCED PrepCom 4, see P.H. Sand, 'International Environmental Law after Rio' (1993) 4 Eur. J. Int'l L. 377 at 388.

[23] In the World Bank, when a borrowing member country reaches a certain level of *per capita* gross national income (originally, US $4,000 at 1989 value; currently, US $5,685), a review is made to phase out and ultimately end bank lending. The Global Environment Facility applies similar eligibility thresholds.

building. With the state of the world's environment continuing to deteriorate, and new mega-risks arising at the same time (for example, to the ozone layer and global climate), international environmental law as a grand narrative or 'mobilizing myth' suffered a severe loss of credibility—a symptom typical of post-modernity.[24] Hence, the focus of attention shifted to the 'effectiveness' of the existing international legal structure (see Chapter 39 'Compliance Theory'), its empirical verification, and procedural/institutional anchorage (see Chapter 42 'Monitoring and Verification' and Chapter 43 'Compliance Procedures'). Closer linkage with national implementation and compliance—the legislative, judicial, and administrative 'domestication' of international environmental law (see Chapter 40 'National Implementation')—proved to be a key factor, given the growing significance of 'role-splitting' (*dédoublement fonctionnel*) and 'two-level games' between international and national action in this field, as well as the ensuing need for more de-centralized rules and networks (see Chapter 31 'Changing Role of the State'), such as the International Network for Environmental Compliance and Enforcement.[25]

The 1992 Rio conference (UNCED) offered an opportunity for reflection and reform. While adding yet another layer of environmental treaties (UN Framework Convention on Climate Change, and the Convention on Biological Diversity) and soft law (Rio Declaration on Environment and Development, and Agenda 21), it also invigorated the trend towards diversification and pluralism at three distinct levels.

In the North-South context, the UNCED concept of 'common but differentiated responsibilities' (see Chapter 27 'Equity') acknowledged the breakdown of traditional egalitarian fictions and the emergence of a new legal polycentricity. More specifically, it confirmed the differential treatment of developing countries under most recent environmental agreements, on account of their special circumstances and needs—not only in economic terms but also possibly in terms of a wider multicultural 'universalization' of international law[26]—albeit at the price of asymmetry and fragmentation.

The inter-generational dimension of the 'sustainable development' concept—although traceable to earlier sources such as the 1987 Brundtland Commission report, the 1980 IUCN World Conservation Strategy, or even seventeenth-century forestry economics—formally recognized the need to balance equitable interests between generations (see Chapter 26 'Sustainable Development'). The constraints thus imposed on present resource users for the benefit of previously unrepresented people yet unborn have found their way into numerous Rio and post-Rio legal texts

---

[24] See J.F. Lyotard, *The Post-Modern Condition: A Report on Knowledge* (Minneapolis: University of Minnesota Press, 1984) at xxiv.

[25] D. Zaelke, D. Kaniaru, and E. Kružíková, eds., *Making Law Work: Environmental Compliance and Sustainable Development* (London: Cameron May, 2005). See also A. Nollkaemper, 'Compliance Control in International Environmental Law: Traversing the Limits of the National Legal Order' (2002) 13 Y.B. Int'l Envt'l L. 165.

[26] C. Weeramaantry, *Universalising International Law* (The Hague: Martinus Nijhoff, 2004).

(for example, Article IV of the revised 2003 African Convention on the Conservation of Nature and Natural Resources). It has also provided new directions for inter-national economics (see Chapter 11 'Economic Theory of International Environmental Law'), and even prompted doctrinal proposals to replace environmental law by a new kind of 'sustainable development law'.

Finally, the 'participatory revolution' at Rio (with more than 1,400 non-govern-mental organizations registered as observers and 8,000 at the parallel Global Forum) (see Chapter 29 'Public Participation') prepared the ground not only for subsequent reforms in UN accreditation rules (UN Economic and Social Council Resolution 1996/31), but also for the public-private partnerships eventually formalized at the 2002 Johannesburg World Summit on Sustainable Development. It served as a power-ful reminder of the legitimate claim of civil society to take part in international deci-sion-making (see Chapter 33 'Non-Governmental Organizations and Civil Society'), which has since been recognized in a number of new environment-related insti-tutions admitting non-state actors to legal or quasi-legal proceedings: the World Bank Inspection Panel established in 1993, the Commission on Environmental Cooperation established in 1994 under the North American Free Trade Agreement, and especially the 1998 UNECE Convention on Access to Information, Public Participation in Decision-Making and Access to Justice in Environmental Matters (Aarhus Convention). Non-governmental participants thus acceded to the Aarhus Compliance Committee established in 2002, both as complainants and as adjudi-cants. These developments mark a momentous change away from the traditional reciprocal rules of state responsibility for environmental harm, and towards a new type of collective accountability owed by all governments for their proper manage-ment of environmental resources vis-à-vis global civil society, present and future (see Chapter 30 'Legitimacy').

The three-dimensional shift towards pluralism initiated at the Rio conference may indeed be linked to a more fundamental paradigm shift in post-modern ecological theory (see Chapter 24 'Ecosystems'), from the old stereotype of a presumed 'balance of nature' (that is, a stable equilibrium to be preserved against change) towards a holistic/biocentric 'new ecology' based on dynamic non-equilibrium—open to nat-ural change but ready to control the risks of excessive anthropogenic interference and, hence, moving towards 'an environmental law that welcomes change and cares about consequences rather than categories.'[27] This approach has also been defined in terms of 'reflexive' environmental law as a self-organizing process (*autopoiesis*), albeit externally induced through a new generation of 'informational regulation', relying on enforced transparency of decision-making rather than on traditional 'command and control' or market-based instruments (see Chapter 8 'Instrument

---

[27] J.B. Wiener, 'Law and the New Ecology: Evolution, Categories, and Consequences' (1995) 22 Ecology L.Q. 325 at 334; see also A.D. Tarlock, 'The Nonequlibrium Paradigm in Ecology and the Partial Unraveling of Environmental Law' (1994) 27 Loy. L.A. L. Rev. 1121.

Choice'). Perhaps the most prominent example of this new approach is civil society's hard-won right of access to environmental risk information, be it government-held or industry-held (the 'right to know').

On the whole, international law for the environment has coped rather well with the challenges of global change. It seems a little too soon, therefore, to predict 'the end of environmental law'[28] or to surmise that it 'has gone rather quickly from maturation to an infirm old age' because of an alleged loss of vigour in responding to change.[29] On the contrary, there may now be a countervailing risk of the post-modern 'dynamic' construct of sustainable development reducing international law—and international environmental law in particular—to a mere technique for managing change in the guise of global governance. In the face of the uncertain promises of the 'governance mindset', it may well be time to strengthen some of the more resilient foundations of international environmental law (forcefully re-affirmed in the 2004 IUCN International Covenant on Environment and Development)[30] as part of a 'formalist' culture of the international legal process—'a culture of resistance to power, a social practice of accountability, openness and equality.'[31]

Recommended Reading

S. von Ciriacy-Wantrup, *Resource Conservation: Economics and Policies*, 3rd edition (Berkeley: University of California Division of Agricultural Sciences, 1968).

M. Holdgate, *The Green Web: A Union for World Conservation* (London: Earthscan, 1999).

A.C. Kiss and J.P. Beurier, *Droit international de l'environnement*, 3rd edition (Paris: Pedone, 2004).

T. Kuokkanen, *International Law and the Environment: Variations on a Theme* (The Hague: Kluwer Law International, 2002).

K. Mickelson, 'South, North, International Environmental Law and International Environmental Lawyers' (2000) 11 Y.B. Int'l Envt'l L. 52.

E.W. Orts, 'Autopoiesis and the Natural Environment,' in J. Přibaň and D. Nelken, eds., *Law's New Boundaries: The Consequences of Legal Autopoiesis* (Aldershot: Ashgate, 2001) 159.

[28] L. Farmer and G. Teubner, 'Ecological Self-Organization,' in G. Teubner, L. Farmer, and D. Murphy, eds., *Environmental Law and Ecological Responsibility: The Concept and Practice of Ecological Self-Organization* (Chichester: John Wiley and Sons, 1994) 3 at 3.

[29] D.M. Driesen, 'Thirty Years of International Environmental Law: A Retrospective and Plea for Reinvigoration' (2003) 30 Syracuse J. Int'l L. & Com. 353 at 353.

[30] Commission on Environmental Law of the World Conservation Union, *Draft International Covenant on Environment and Development*, IUCN Environmental Policy and Law Paper no. 31/Rev. 2, 3rd edition (Bonn: IUCN Environmental Law Centre, 2004).

[31] M. Koskenniemi, *The Gentle Civilizer of Nations: The Rise and Fall of International Law, 1870–1960* (Cambridge: Cambridge University Press, 2001) at 500.

C.P.R. Romano, *The Peaceful Settlement of International Environmental Disputes: A Pragmatic Approach* (The Hague: Kluwer Law International, 2000).

P.H. Sand, 'A Century of Green Lessons: The Contribution of Nature Conservation Regimes to Global Governance' (2001) 1 Int'l Envt'l Agreements: Politics, Law and Economics 33.

P. Sands, *Principles of International Environmental Law*, 2nd edition (Cambridge: Cambridge University Press, 2003), chapter 2 (history).

E. Brown Weiss, 'International Environmental Law: Contemporary Issues and the Emergence of a New World Order' (1993) 81 Georgetown L.J. 675.

CHAPTER 3

PARADIGMS AND DISCOURSES

JOHN S. DRYZEK

1 INTRODUCTION

BOTH paradigms and discourses are a type of inter-subjective understanding that condition individual action, and social outcomes, in the international system no less than elsewhere. They have no formal existence resembling that of organizations, constitutions, laws, and treaties. Yet they can be none the less effective in coordinating the behaviour of large numbers of actors, and this is especially true in a political system as de-centralized as the international one, where formal sources of order are weak. Even in the presence of laws and formal organizations, discourses in particular constitute the 'software' that is important in explaining how institutions work. Indeed, discourses are important aspects of institutions, conditioning the 'logic of appropriateness' that J.G. March and J.P. Olsen see as the hallmark of 'new institutionalism' in social science.[1] It is impossible to understand international environmental law without coming to grips with the informal understandings that condition its creation and operation.

2 BASIC CONCEPTS

The concept of paradigm has its origins in the philosophy of science, notably in the work of Thomas Kuhn.[2] The word is much overused, and the concept can be stretched in a direction that would cover pretty much any kind of frame of reference (the same might be said for discourse). In this chapter, I will stick to a Kuhnian meaning. Paradigms have their origins in academic disciplines, and are oriented in the first instance to generating explanations of aspects of the natural or social world. Paradigms structure the world and, in particular, its problems or aspects requiring explanation. They are cultivated by their adherents, and the acceptance of a paradigm may be the passport to academic respectability in a discipline. Beyond policing professional boundaries in this fashion, paradigms have no necessary orientation to social power (though they can be deployed by those whose power rests on other bases). When it comes to international environmental institutions and practices, relevant paradigms can come from both natural sciences and social sciences. From natural sciences might come paradigms in Darwinian biology or systems ecology. From social sciences might come paradigms in neoclassical microeconomics, ecological economics, or cultural theory.

---

[1] J.G. March and J.P. Olsen, *Rediscovering Institutions* (New York: Free Press, 1989).
[2] T. Kuhn, *The Structure of Scientific Revolutions* (Chicago: University of Chicago Press, 1962).

A discourse is by definition composed of shared concepts, categories, and ideas that enable actors to understand situations. Thus, any particular discourse will entail and include judgments, assumptions, capabilities, dispositions, and intentions, establishing the foundations for analysis, debates, agreements, and disagreements. Those who subscribe to a discourse will then be able to put together pieces of information into coherent accounts organized around storylines that can be shared in ways that are meaningful to fellow subscribers. Discourses establish meanings, identify agents in contrast to those who can only be the object of action, confirm relations between actors and other entities, set the boundaries for what is legitimate knowledge, and generate what is accepted as common sense.[3] Practices as well as words enter discourses, for social actions are always associated with the language that establishes their meaning. Power is internal to discourses as they constitute norms and perceptions, serving some interests while squashing others. While discourses are often thought of as a source of order, particular discourses can also be disruptive (think of the role of neo-conservatism and Islamic radicalism in disrupting the international system in recent years). An emphasis on the constitutive role of discourses is consistent with a constructivist position in international relations theory (though constructivists do not have to be discourse analysts).

With this characterization of discourses in mind, we are in a better position to see the difference between paradigms and discourses. Both paradigms and discourses are constitutive, but they constitute subjects in different ways. Scientists are educated within paradigms and, indeed, become scientists within the framework provided by paradigms. Individuals are generally socialized into discourses, rather than formally educated in them. In social life, discourses can come before subjects—that is, in large measure, individuals are the creations of the discourses in which they move. However, individuals can sometimes escape the terms of particular discourses. One aspect of modernization is the capacity of individuals to subject discourses to critical attention. Paradigms are normally a matter of conscious awareness on the part of those who deploy them, at least (for example) to the point where a biologist could say 'I am a Darwinian'. Discourses, in contrast, can be so ingrained that subjects are unaware of their presence (Michel Foucault and his followers write histories of discourses in this idiom). What an outsider can see as a discourse, an insider will often take for granted as the natural order of things. The dominant discourse relevant to environmental affairs before the 1960s—industrialism—had exactly this character, which long prevented the conceptualization of such a thing as 'the environment'. The kind of distinction I have drawn between paradigms and discourses is not always followed in the literature, especially by those who extend the idea of a 'paradigm' beyond scientific communities and into society at large.[4]

---

[3] J. Milliken, 'The Study of Discourse in International Relations: A Critique of Research and Methods' (1999) 5 Eur. J. Int'l Rel. 225.

[4] See, e.g., M. Colby, *Environmental Management in Development: The Evolution of Paradigms*, World Bank Discussion Paper no. 80 (New York: World Bank, 1990).

While policy analysis based on paradigms may feed into debates on the construction of international laws, treaties, and regimes, any given paradigm is rarely decisive in determining outcomes. When they are decisive, it is largely a matter of what Peter Haas calls an epistemic community mobilizing around a particular paradigm, and prioritizing the interpretations, problems, and broad solutions it has identified (see Chapter 34 'Epistemic Communities'). Neoclassical economics could claim to be exceptional here in terms of its more direct influence. However, any influence it exercises is never simple and direct. Rather, it occurs when economic analysis is taken up by a particular discourse. Discourses that have taken up microeconomics include ecological modernization and market liberalism (and its 'Washington consensus'), but these discourses deploy resources provided by the paradigm to a very different effect. In ecological modernization, microeconomics is used simply as a source of some policy ideas (such as green taxes). In market liberalism, it is seen as capable of yielding truths on which government should be based.

For all of these reasons, the focus of this chapter will be on discourses rather than paradigms; paradigms will be treated mainly in terms of how they are taken up by, and take effect through, particular discourses. Discourses have origins that can be both multiple and complex. Sometimes they are an outgrowth of an ingrained social order (for example, medieval discourses about sin and punishment). Sometimes skilled rhetoricians can bend established discourses in new directions. A discourse may prove functional for a dominant economic system (Marxists often saw the discourse of liberal democracy in this light as providing cover for the injustices of capitalism). There is no plausible general theory of the origins of discourses—which means that the best way to account for where they come from and how they change is to write their histories.

Industrialism constitutes the background against which environmental discourses develop, so let me now turn to a categorization and analysis of the major discourses of environmental concern, positioning them first of all in terms of the character of their departure from, and challenge to, industrialism.

3 MAPPING ENVIRONMENTAL DISCOURSES

The defining feature of industrialism is its dedication to growth in the amount of goods and services that society produces and in the human material well-being that results. Industrialism develops along with industrial society, which has witnessed diverse ideological currents, ranging from liberalism and fascism to conservatism, socialism, and Marxism. Yet from the perspective of environmentalism, these ideologies can actually seem very similar, however much this similarity might surprise, and be disputed by, their proponents. None was especially interested in the environment (setting aside some Nazi interest in Aryan nature). Even what we now recognize as environmental concerns were treated mainly as inputs to industrial processes or, at most, a matter of public health. Consider, for example, the US conservation movement of the early twentieth century in the United States, under the leadership of Gifford Pinchot. Pinchot and his movement wanted resources such as minerals, timber, and fish to be used carefully rather than in a profligate free-for-all—such that resources could better support industrial growth. Industrialism does not have to require that particular resources be infinite. Yet it must deny the existence of systemic limits to human economic activity, stemming, for example, from the finite character of the ecosystems in which society is embedded.

Industrialism was not vanquished by the rise of the environmentalism that began in the 1960s and persisted into the twenty-first century. When President George W. Bush announced US withdrawal from the Kyoto Protocol to the UN Framework Convention on Climate Change in 2001, he justified it mainly on the grounds that US economic interests were more important than global environmental protection, and that the protocol would impose an unacceptable burden on US industry. He did not even feel the need to make any hypocritical reference to his administration's concern about the climate change issue, highlighting instead alleged scientific uncertainty surrounding the issue. The international trade regime for its part has routinely ruled against environmental protection measures that affect international trade by interpreting them as simply 'restraints on trade'. This interpretation confirms the subordination of environmentalist to industrialist discourse under the General Agreement on Tariffs and Trade—though there are signs this situation is changing.

Environmental discourses can be positioned in terms of how they differ from the industrialism from which they depart—and which is the main protagonist of all of them, their engagement with industrialism generally being more pronounced than their engagement with each other. On one dimension, this departure can range from reformist to radical; on another, from prosaic to imaginative. Prosaic discourses accept as given the character of the game set by industrial society—environmental issues are conceptualized principally as difficulties run into by the industrial political economy. The response required does not involve social transformation, though it can be substantial and indeed radical in its character. For example, some environmentalists believe that economic growth must be curbed and perhaps even stopped but, at the same time, they want to manage this transition only by deploying instruments and institutions developed in industrialism, especially strong central administration guided by scientific expertise.

Imaginative departures from industrialism reconfigure the game, mainly by conceptualizing environmental issues as opportunities, not troubles. In particular, environmental values are not placed in opposition to economic values but in potential complementarity. The environment can then be welcomed into cultural, social, and economic systems, not just seen as generating difficulties for these systems from the outside. While imaginative, the desired social change can range from the incremental and reformist to the extensive and radical. The two dimensions—reformist to radical and prosaic to imaginative can be combined to give four cells, which are presented in Table 1.[5]

Environmental Problem Solving is prosaic and reformist, taking the political economy of industrial society pretty much as given but requiring some policy changes to deal with environmental issues. Three main types of change are available, stressing respectively citizens organized into politics, consumers and producers organized into markets, and experts organized into governmental administration. The result is three discourses of environmental problem solving: liberal pragmatism, economic rationalism, and administrative rationalism. There is room for dispute about the relative merits of these three discourses or their suitability for different purposes. Some want to curb pollution through administrative control, others by the application of economic incentives.

Survivalism is prosaic and radical, arriving with a splash in the early 1970s. Especially influential was the 1972 report to the Club of Rome, *The Limits to Growth*. Though no longer so dominant, the discourse of limits and survival still has many adherents. Survivalism charges that economic and population growth must at some point encounter limits given by the Earth's supply of natural resources and the ability of ecosystems to support agricultural and industrial activity and assimilate wastes. This discourse is radical in its rejection of economic growth, and in its desire to centralize political power in the hands of experts who would steer the global political economy in the required direction. Survivalism is prosaic for it sees a simple conflict between economy and environment, and conceptualizes solutions in terms set in industrialism, involving control by elites, administrators, and scientists.

Sustainability began in the 1970s, and was confirmed as the dominant discourse in global environmental politics with the publication of the Brundtland report in 1987.[6] Sustainable development features imaginative dissolution of the clash between environment and economy that underlines discourses of problem solving and limits alike. Growth and development become thought of in ways that undermine the limits discourse's predictions of overshoot and collapse—the whole idea of limits fades into the background (though it does not quite disappear). With the urgency of limits thus receding, sustainability discourse does not have to be radical (and with time its centre

---

[5] This categorization is explored at greater length in J.S. Dryzek, *The Politics of the Earth: Environmental Discourses*, 2nd edition (Oxford: Oxford University Press, 2005).

[6] World Commission on Environment and Development, *Our Common Future* (Oxford: Oxford University Press, 1987).

of gravity becomes less radical). Also in the 1980s, a discourse of ecological modernization appeared in northern Europe. Ecological modernization also believes economic growth and environmental conversation can be complementary. While originally concerned mainly with re-engineering developed economies, ecological modernization eventually spread to other parts of the world. So far its impact at the international level has been limited, and so I will not address it further (although A.P.J. Mol suggests that businesses and governments from developed countries pursuing ecological modernization at home may take the discourse into the global political economy).[7] While sustainable development and ecological modernization have many similarities, ecological modernization lacks the breadth of sustainable development that extends to social justice, the developing world, and global concerns. Their origins are different, with ecological modernization growing alongside some actual public policy and corporate practice in northern Europe.

Green Radicalism combines imagination and radicalism, rejecting both the fundamental structure of industrial society and how this society conceptualizes 'the environment'. Industrialism's conceptualizations are replaced by some very different ways of thinking about people, society, and humanity's position in the world. Green radical discourse has had many internal divisions: animal liberationists versus more holistic ecological thinkers, social ecologists versus deep ecologists, romantics versus rationalists, lifestyle advocates versus political activists, and (in Germany) *Fundis* favouring grassroots action in streets and neighbourhoods versus *Realos* committed to parliamentary action. Green radicals vary in their degree of ecocentrism as well as in the degree to which they might be willing to compromise ecological concerns for the sake of other values such as social justice. Yet all of these disputants have more similarities with each other than with either industrialism or the other three environmental discourses, especially when it comes to the need to move towards a different kind of society that has ecological concerns at its core.

I will now take a closer look at the discourses I have enumerated, with special reference to how they manifest themselves in international environmental affairs and to what effect they have upon the outcomes.

Table 1 Classifying Environmental Discourses

	Reformist	Radical
Prosaic	Problem solving	Survivalism
Imaginative	Sustainability	Green radicalism

---

[7] A.P.J. Mol, 'Ecological Modernization and the Global Economy' (2002) 2(2) Global Envt'l Pol. 92.

4 MAJOR ENVIRONMENTAL
DISCOURSES

4.1 Survivalism and Its Promethean Opposite

The heyday of the discourse of limits and survival was the 1970s, otherwise known as the doomsday decade.[8] An earlier contribution came in Paul Ehrlich's 1968 declaration that the Earth was about to be hit by a 'population bomb', which would be more devastating than nuclear weapons.[9] Other population biologists such as Garrett Hardin added their warnings to the debate—a case of a discourse (survivalism) making use of a scientific paradigm (population biology). The *Limits to Growth* forecasts received massive publicity, and the book sold over four million copies worldwide.[10] While the timetable was a little hazy depending on the assumptions input into the analysis, the book forecast that at some point by the middle of the twenty-first century the world was going to hit absolute ecological limits. Unless action could be taken to forestall matters, the consequence would be overshoot and collapse,[11] meaning economic crash and decimation of human numbers. The Organization of Petroleum Exporting Countries oil embargo of 1973 showed what resource shortages might look like (though the embargo was politically engineered, not in any sense a matter of natural scarcity). In the waning days of the Carter presidency in the United States, his administration's *Global 2000* report was published, anticipating a miserable world beset by scarcities 20 years hence. The action seen as necessary in all of these survivalist tracts was coordinated and global in order to steer global systems away from uncontrolled economic and population growth.

Survivalism's impact has been limited. Occasionally figures in high places have endorsed survivalism and this was especially true in the 1970s. Much later, in a speech in 2003, UK Environment Minister Michael Meacher compared the human race to a virus capable of destroying the Earth.[12] Occasionally, countries have followed population control policies that have been enforced in heavy-handed fashion, consistent with the idea of limits and survival—the best example being China. It is harder to discern the lasting impacts of the discourse on international regimes and institutions— hard but not impossible. D.H. Meadows, D.L. Meadows, and J. Randers, in their 1992

---

[8] For particularly gloomy prognostications, see R. Heilbroner, *An Inquiry into the Human Prospect* (New York: W.W. Norton, 1974); W. Ophuls, *Ecology and the Politics of Scarcity* (New York: W.H. Freeman and Company, 1977); and G. Hardin and J. Baden, *Managing The Commons* (San Francisco: W.H. Freeman and Company, 1977).

[9] P. Ehrlich, *The Population Bomb* (New York: Ballantine Books, 1968).

[10] D.H. Meadows et al., *The Limits to Growth* (New York: Universe Books, 1972).

[11] W.R. Catton, *Overshoot: The Ecological Basis of Revolutionary Change* (Urbana: University of Illinois Press, 1980).   [12] *The Guardian* (14 February 2003).

follow-up to *Limits to Growth*, themselves believe that the success of the 1987 Montreal Protocol on Substances That Deplete the Ozone Layer (Montreal Protocol) demonstrates that at the all-important global level we can indeed move 'back from beyond the limits'.[13] However, this claim is not especially plausible, given that cheap technological solutions have been at hand to deal with the ozone issue, while there is no suggestion in the Montreal Protocol that economic or population growth should be curbed or even redirected. According to Peter Haas, a united epistemic community of atmospheric scientists motivated global action, exactly as survivalist discourse would require. However, it should be noted that there are competing accounts of the dynamics of the ozone issue (one of which I will discuss later).[14] And survivalists should not draw too much comfort from the ozone issue, especially in light of the global failure to tackle the arguably much more important issue of climate change, despite consensus among atmospheric scientists on its reality.

More recently, the limits discourse has been revived and sometimes localized under the heading of 'environmental security', energized by the danger of states and others coming to blows over declining resources such as fresh water and land.[15] A 2003 study commissioned by the US Department of Defense anticipated massive security fallout from climate change accompanied by famine, drought, energy shortages, and coastal flooding, on a time scale of two decades.[16] This study met with no policy response from the United States government. This mixed record does not mean survivalism is wrong in its emphasis on global limits. If nothing else, by identifying some apocalyptic horizons, survivalism has confirmed that the environment is a vital issue and, perhaps, the most important issue that humanity will confront in the twenty-first century.

Survivalism's opposite is a Promethean discourse that simply denies the existence of ecological and resource limits, mostly on the grounds that no global scarcities have ever turned out to limit human economic activity because human ingenuity always finds a way around them ('Cornucopian' is sometimes used to describe this discourse, but it is a less appropriate title because it implies bounty without human effort). However, the implicit assumption that such a happy situation can be projected indefinitely into the future should not be accepted uncritically. In fact, no evidence is capable of finally adjudicating the dispute between Prometheans and survivalists, short of global shortages and ecological collapse someday vindicating survivalism. Prometheans adduce evidence from the past, concerning, for example, trends that show resources are becoming less scarce with time (because their prices

---

[13] D.H. Meadows, D.L. Meadows, and J. Randers, *Beyond the Limits: Confronting Global Collapse, Envisioning a Sustainable Future* (Post Mills: Chelsea Green, 1992) at 141–60.

[14] P.M. Haas, 'Banning Chlorofluorocarbons: Efforts to Protect Stratospheric Ozone' (1992) 46 Int'l Org. 187.

[15] T. Homer-Dixon, *Environment, Scarcity, and Violence* (Princeton: Princeton University Press, 1999).

[16] P. Schwartz and D. Randall, *An Abrupt Climate Change Scenario and Its Implications for National Security* (Emeryville: Global Business Network, 2003).

are falling) and that global indicators of well-being have been moving in positive directions. Survivalists can argue that even if trends currently look fine, global limits will eventually be hit. The two discourses really do offer contending interpretations of the world. Inasmuch as they both draw on scientific paradigms, survivalism utilizes population biology and ecology (many prominent survivalists have a background in biology), while Promethean discourse utilizes micro-economics (many Protheans have a background in economics). The economic connection provides the key mechanism for Protheans: if resources become scarce their price will rise, providing incentives to develop substitutes.

In some ways, Promethean discourse is an extension of the exuberance of industrialism. The difference is that while industrialism simply took economic growth for granted as the highest good, Protheans must articulate a defence of perpetual economic growth in light of the survivalist critique. In addition, the collective management of particular resources can be accommodated within industrialism but less easily in Promethean discourse, which is completely wedded to the market in a way that industrialism is not. Promethean discourse has been especially influential in the US presidencies of Ronald Reagan and George W. Bush. The Promethean economist, Julian Simon was influential in the Reagan administration.[17] Simon's counterpart as the leading Promethean publicist in the George W. Bush era was Bjørn Lomborg, who had ties to the government of Denmark rather than the United States, although Republican congressional candidates were pointed in Lomborg's direction in the 2004 US election campaign.[18]

When it comes to international environmental affairs, the opposition of both the Reagan and G.W. Bush presidencies to coordinated global environmental protection (with the important exception of the 1987 Montreal Protocol) can be attributed to their domination by Promethean and industrialist discourse. In the 1980s, the United States renounced international environmental governance, ending support and finance for international treaties or programmes concerning transboundary air pollution (especially acid rain), the trade of nuclear materials, population control, and the United Nations Environment Program.[19] The Reagan administration refused to ratify the United Nations Convention on the Law of the Sea, preferring a free-for-all when it came to ocean resources rather than global management, and it was sceptical concerning the 1989 Basel Convention on the Control of Transboundary Movements of Hazardous Wastes and Their Disposal. In the 2000s, US withdrawal from the Kyoto Protocol symbolized Promethean hostility to international environmental

[17] J. Simon, *The Ultimate Resource* (Princeton: Princeton University Press, 1981); and J. Simon and H. Kahn, eds., *The Resourceful Earth: A Response to Global 2000* (New York: Blackwell, 1984).

[18] B. Lomborg, *The Skeptical Environmentalist: Measuring the Real State of the World* (New York: Cambridge University Press, 2001).

[19] L. Caldwell, 'The World Environment: Reversing U.S. Policy Commitments,' in N.J. Vig and M.E. Kraft, eds., *Environmental Policy in the 1980s: Reagan's New Agenda* (Washington, DC: Congressional Quarterly Press, 1984) 319.

protection—though the United States did ratify the 2001 Stockholm Convention on Persistent Organic Pollutants and, by 2004, the George W. Bush administration had supported ratification of the United Nations Convention on the Law of the Sea (although it had yet to be secured from Senate at the time of writing).

4.2 Problem Solving Discourses

The three discourses of environmental problem solving are liberal pragmatism, economic rationalism, and administrative rationalism. All developed initially in the context of a liberal democratic state operating within a capitalist economy. Thus, all three require modification in translation to the international level because each assumes a sovereign state capable of organizing and implementing problem-solving activity in its territory. Of the three, administrative rationalism is particularly problematic in the absence of a sovereign state to organize the apex of any hierarchy of administrative authority (see Chapter 5 'Levels of Environmental Governance'). Hierarchical international organizations with some capacity to exercise binding authority are also in short supply. There is no World Environment Organization analogous to the World Trade Organization (WTO). Organizations such as the United Nations Environment Program have little in the way of the sort of implementation capacity that administrative rationalism requires. Transnational networks composed of administrators from different jurisdictions may exist, but they operate as networks, not as administrative hierarchies. Multilateral agreements such as the 1973/1978 International Convention for the Prevention of Pollution from Ships may rely on the mobilization of expertise in their implementation, but again the tight connection of expertise to administrative hierarchy is missing.

Democratic pragmatism fares somewhat better. Dealing in interactive problem solving, it can more easily escape its origins in the sovereign liberal democratic state. Even in their domestic affairs, such states increasingly yield to networked forms of social problem solving that involve interactions among government officials, interest organizations, corporations, labor unions, and political activists.[20] The term 'governance' is often used to describe such activity. Given that 'governance without government' is a staple of international politics,[21] interactive democratic pragmatism is potentially at home here too. For example, transnational forest product certification is carried out by a network of non-governmental organizations (NGOs), including the Worldwide Fund for Nature and the Rainforest Alliance.[22] J. Braithwaite and

[20] R.A.W. Rhodes, *Understanding Governance: Policy Networks, Reflexivity, and Accountability* (Buckingham: Open University Press, 1997).

[21] J.N. Rosenau and E.O. Czempiel, eds., *Governance without Government: Order and Change in World Politics* (Cambridge: Cambridge University Press, 1992).

[22] E.E. Meidinger, 'Forest Certification as a Global Civil Society Regulatory Institution,' in E.E. Meidinger, C. Elliott, and G. Oesten, eds., *Social and Political Dimensions of Forest Certification*

P. Drahos show how activists and NGOs, along with government officials, can create a global web of business regulation—including environmental regulation.[23] Such regulation is beyond the reach of administrative rationalism. The kind of dialogue created around Local Agenda 21—pursued around the world by local governments in the wake of the 1992 United Nations Conference on Environment and Development— is also consistent with a discourse of democratic pragmatism (see Chapter 33 'Non-Governmental Organizations and Civil Society').

Economic rationalism can be defined in terms of its fixation on the deployment of market mechanisms to achieve public ends (see Chapter 11 'Economic Theory of International Environmental Law'). Market-type instruments (tradeable permits to pollute or extract resources, green taxes, and so forth) were endorsed in passing in the Brundtland report, and have been advocated by the Organisation for Economic Cooperation and Development.[24] The stress on markets is consistent with the market liberal discourse that dominates international economic affairs. The 1987 Montreal Protocol provides for limited international trade in quotas for chloro-fluorocarbon emissions. The US delegation at Kyoto in 1997 pushed for international trade in quotas for emissions of greenhouse gases, although the United States has rarely implemented such schemes at home (with a few exceptions, notably for trade in permits for sulphur dioxide emissions across coal-burning utilities). Other developed countries are less keen on the idea (though the United Kingdom began exploring carbon dioxide emissions trading in 2002). Several countries (the four Nordic countries and the Netherlands) have implemented a carbon tax in order to reduce greenhouse emissions. In 2001, the United Kingdom introduced a climate change levy on fossil fuels used by industries and government bodies. These carbon taxes illustrate the degree to which a discourse (economic rationalism) can coordinate the behaviour of actors (states) in the absence of any formal authority (though the states I have mentioned have all signed the Kyoto Protocol). However, there are limits to the degree that economic rationalist instruments can be deployed in the absence of a central governmental body. This limit can be highlighted in the context of T.L. Anderson and D.R. Leal's suggestion that 'whales can also be "branded" by genetic prints and tracked by satellite' in order to create secure property rights in an international market for whales.[25] Conservationists could buy whales to save them, whalers could buy whales to kill them, and the market would determine the optimal balance. The problem is that no international authority stands ready to enforce the

---

(Remagen: Oberwinter, 2003) 265. Democratic pragmatism deals in multiple centres of power, not popular sovereignty, so any lack of accountability of NGOs to publics is not an issue.

[23] J. Braithwaite and P. Drahos, *Global Business Regulation* (Cambridge: Cambridge University Press, 2000) at 256–96.

[24] Organisation for Economic Cooperation and Development (OECD), *Economic Instruments for Environmental Protection* (Paris: OECD, 1989).

[25] T.L. Anderson and D.R. Leal, *Free Market Environmentalism* (San Francisco: Westview Press for the Pacific Research Institute for Public Policy, 1991) at 34.

property rights in question; certainly the International Whaling Commission (IWC) is not up to the task.

In short, discourses of environmental problem solving that have dominated environmental problem solving within liberal democratic states over the past three or four decades have had somewhat less impact in international environmental affairs. Yet the basic idea of problem solving still infuses many multilateral environmental agreements. Let me now turn to the discourse that has in many ways defined international environmental affairs since the mid-1980s.

4.3 Sustainability

Sustainable development's discursive domination of the global environmental stage was confirmed in 1987 by Brundtland and has persisted since then (see Chapter 26 'Sustainable Development'). The precise meaning of sustainable development remains a matter of some contention. Gro Harlem Brundtland herself famously characterized the matter: 'Humanity has the ability to make development sustainable—to ensure that it meets the needs of the present without compromising the ability of future generations to meet their own needs'.[26] Subsequently, definitions have proliferated and been contested. Yet in many ways this proliferation and contestation constitute the whole point—sustainable development is a discourse, not a concept, and still less a scientific concept. Within this discourse, the essence of sustainability is contested. For the World Business Council on Sustainable Development, 'development' is closely linked to economic growth. Environmentalists might try to build a respect for intrinsic values in nature into the 'sustainable' aspect of the discourse that is conspicuously missing in the Brundtland report. Third World advocates would stress the need for global redistribution and highlight the needs of the poor.

Just as contestation over what democracy means is central to the discourse of democracy, so contestation over what sustainable development means is central to the discourse of sustainability. However, the discourse has boundaries. These are defined by a rejection of four other discourses. The earlier discourse of limits and survival is rejected because, while global ecological limits can still lurk in the background, they are treated as capable of being dealt with.[27] Green radicalism is rejected because no wholesale change in the basic structure of the international political economy is deemed necessary. Market liberalism and Promethean discourses are rejected because markets alone are thought incapable of achieving sustainability. Instead, conscious, coordinated, collective action is required. More positively, sustainable development rests on the assumption that environmental

---

[26] World Commission on Environment and Development, see note 6 above at 8.

[27] O. Langhelle, 'Why Ecological Modernization and Sustainable Development Should Not be Conflated' (2000) 2 J. Envt'l Pol'y & Planning 303.

conservation and economic growth can be mutually reinforcing rather than conflicting values.

The United Nations Conference on Environment and Development in Rio in 1992 confirmed that sustainable development was now a discourse for North and South, rich and poor. However, the rich eventually forgot (or never really accepted) the global equity central to Brundtland.[28] The 2002 World Summit on Sustainable Development (WSSD) agreed to a 'plan of implementation' for the Rio Conference's Agenda 21. Despite its title, the 2002 plan was thin on concrete targets, actions, and responsibility for actions.[29] Sustainable development's status was unintentionally confirmed as that of a discourse, not a plan for action. The WSSD witnessed significant repositioning within the discourse. Rich states that once promoted environmental values now stressed development through economic globalization and, thus, bent sustainable development in the direction of industrialism. Third World governmental delegations showed new appreciation of their own environmental problems, rather than dismissing conservation as a luxury.[30] Corporations established the presumption of a major role for business in the production of solutions, which was very different from business's older image as a generator of environmental problems. Hundreds of business partnerships with NGOs and government were created at the summit. From a sceptical view, this was 'the privatization of sustainable development',[31] transforming the discourse into commercial projects.[32]

Sustainable development pervades the discourse of international institutions, though its impact on multilateral environmental agreements remains patchy. The World Bank's 2002 *World Development Report* had sustainable development at its centre, arguing that wealthy states should become still richer so as to create larger markets for the exports of the poor. The European Union inserted sustainable development into its constituent treaties and, at the WSSD, showed far greater enthusiasm for sustainability than the United States. The United States is actually unique in the degree to which sustainable development does not pervade environmental discourse, mainly because its environmental policy debates are stuck in a standoff between supporters and opponents of the regulatory systems established in the 1970s.[33]

If we were to look for sustainable development as an accomplished fact, where would we find it? The answer is surely: nowhere. According to a recent study of 142 countries carried out for the World Economic Forum, the top performer is

---

[28] J. Meadowcroft, 'Sustainable Development: A New(ish) Idea for a New Century?' (2000) 48 Pol. Stud. 370 at 379.

[29] I. von Frantzius, 'World Summit on Sustainable Development Johannesburg 2002: A Critical Assessment of the Outcomes' (2004) 13 Envt'l Pol. 467 at 470.

[30] P. Wapner, 'World Summit on Sustainable development: Toward a Post-Jo'burg Environmentalism' (2003) 3 (1) Global Envt'l Pol. 1 and 4–6.   [31] von Frantzius, see note 29 above at 469.

[32] Wapner, see note 30 above at 4.

[33] G.C. Bryner, 'The United States: Sorry-Not Our Problem,' in W.M. Lafferty and J. Meadowcroft, eds., *Implementing Sustainable Development: Strategies and Initiatives from High Consumption Societies* (Oxford: Oxford University Press, 2000) 273 at 277.

Finland.[34] However, if the developmental path taken by Finland were to be followed by all of the countries in the world, the result would surely be intolerable stress on the world's ecosystems. Moreover, though Finland comes out on top, there is no suggestion that its performance is currently adequate by any standard of sustainability. This drives home the point that sustainable development cannot be conceptualized as a path taken by wealthy countries such as Finland, which could be followed by others, but rather should be thought of as a discourse that requires fundamentally reconceptualizing the development process.

One such path would involve a 'de-centred' approach encouraging local experiments in the practice of sustainability.[35] Commitment to the discourse itself would be the main glue holding these various experiments together, absent any centralized governmental control. Such a de-centred approach can arguably be found in what H. Bruyninckx refers to as 'post Rio regimes' or 'sustainable development regimes' such as the Convention to Combat Desertification in Those Countries Experiencing Serious Drought and/or Desertification, which was negotiated in the wake of the 1992 Earth Summit.[36] Such regimes adopt aspects of the sustainability discourse highlighted in Agenda 21, notably in terms of stakeholder involvement, de-centralization, and local knowledge. There is no guarantee that such a de-centred approach will produce adequate global (or even local) sustainability performance, but given the ineluctable breadth of the sustainable development discourse it is hard to see what any better alternative might be.

4.4 Green Radicalism

Green radicalism can be defined in terms of its presumption that the liberal capitalist political economy cannot be sustained, and that intersecting concerns relating to social and environmental justice, conservation, and congenial human existence require fundamental structural transformation. The discourse is home to a wide variety of philosophical viewpoints, repertoires, and political movements. As befits a radical discourse, its origins lie in oppositional movements confronting governments, corporations, and other centres of power. However, there are times when aspects of green radicalism have been influential on these centres of power or have constituted countervailing power.

---

[34] World Economic Forum study, text available at <http://www.ciesin.org./indicators/ESI/rank.html> (5 November 2005).

[35] D. Torgerson, 'The Uncertain Quest for Sustainability: Public Discourse and the Politics of Environmentalism,' in F. Fischer and M. Black, eds., *Greening Environmental Policy: The Politics of a Sustainable Future* (New York: St. Martin's Press, 1995) 3.

[36] H. Bruyninckx, 'The Convention to Combat Desertification and the Role of Innovative Policy Making Discourses: The Case of Burkina Faso' (2004) 4(3) Global Envt'l Pol. 107 at 108.

In common with many other social movement discourses, some of the impact of green radicalism is found in cultural change—in lifestyles and consumer behaviour. P. Wapner suggests that when it comes to international environmental affairs, 'NGO cultural politics may be more politically significant than NGO policy efforts'[37] (though, of course, not all NGO activities are radical). While cultural change might seem remote from law and institutions, it can also be thought of as an alternative to the more conventional political and legal route. One way of inducing behavioural change is through law and another is through culture. People can choose to recycle, conserve energy, boycott forest products from old growth logging, and so forth without laws requiring them to do so.

Green radical discourse has sometimes succeeded in provoking international institutions to the point where it at least merits a response, for example, as one among a number of discourses present in the anti-corporate globalization movement in recent years. Initially derided as incoherent and contradictory, this movement has at least forced global institutions such as the International Monetary Fund, the World Bank, and the WTO to take seriously some concerns they would have preferred to ignore.[38] Just occasionally, green radicalism may undermine some of the pillars of the international order. For example, in 1995, the Shell Corporation proposed disposing of a redundant oil storage platform, the Brent Spar, in the deep waters of the north Atlantic. Protests across Europe organized by Greenpeace, along with the occupation of the platform, eventually forced Shell to another disposal option. The British government was prepared to use force to dislodge the occupiers and to stand firm in the face of protests, and was horrified by Shell's capitulation. For good reason—the Greenpeace action undermined notions of private property and national sovereignty, which the British government held dear and which are foundational to the contemporary international order. (There was an environmental case for deep water disposal, but this is irrelevant in explaining the British government's response.)

For the most part, green radical discourse is practised and cultivated in an oppositional public sphere.[39] The green public sphere is home to all kinds of creative and varied thinking, but only very occasionally is its influence felt in the dominant institutions of national and international society. Sometimes this influence comes in the form of affecting the terms of discourse, as in the anti-corporate globalization case, or in establishing 'environmental justice' as a principle that must be addressed, in international affairs no less than elsewhere. Sometimes influence comes with the threat of political instability that can accompany the discourse. At the national level, it was such a threat that led to the pioneering burst of environmental law

[37] P. Wapner, 'Horizontal Politics: Transnational Environmental Activism and Global Cultural Change' (2002) 2 Global Envt'l Pol. 37 at 51.

[38] J. Stiglitz, *Globalization and Its Discontents* (New York: W.W. Norton and Company, 2002) at 20.

[39] D. Torgerson, *The Promise of Green Politics: Environmentalism and the Public Sphere* (Durham: Duke University Press, 1999).

and policy in the United States around 1970. President Nixon was keen to draw the nascent environmental movement away from the radicalism of the counterculture and into the political mainstream—and he succeeded brilliantly.[40] The price his presidency had to pay was substantial in terms of laws such as the National Environmental Policy Act and institutions such as the federal Environmental Protection Agency.

5 RELATIVE IMPORTANCE OF DISCOURSES

International environmental affairs are, then, home to a constellation of discourses. Yet they are home to many other influences too. How important are discourses in conditioning outcomes compared to these other influences? This question can be hard to answer when discourses are entwined with these other influences. For example, the dominant discourse in the international political economy is market liberalism. States generally abide by its prescriptions of free trade and capital mobility because they fear punishment by disinvestment and capital flight if they are (say) over-zealous in the environmental regulation of business. However, in large measure, the punishment occurs because investors perceive such states as being inhospitable to business. And investors perceive this because they, too, are under sway of the discourse of market liberalism. So, is the ultimate influence here rooted in the material facts of international markets or in the facts of discourse? The answer is 'both'. Discourses can provide the 'software' that makes international regimes work, while more formal organizations and rules provide the 'hardware'.

How, then, are we to demonstrate the importance of discourse? One way is to examine the history of particular episodes and look for discourse shifts that are followed by changed outcomes. K.T. Litfin's study of 'ozone discourses' is exemplary.[41] Litfin argues that the 1987 Montreal Protocol was made possible by a widely accepted shift to a 'discourse of precautionary action' that interpreted existing and still inconclusive scientific evidence in a new way. The idea of an 'ozone hole' as a piece of rhetoric that dramatized changed seasonal variations in ozone levels in Antarctic regions was crucial. The fact that the discourse shift was followed by policy shift does not of itself prove that the discourse shift was crucial, and so Litfin has to consider and disprove alternative explanations (for example, one stressing the role of an epistemic community).

---

[40] J.S. Dryzek et al., *Green States and Social Movements: Environmentalism in the United States, United Kingdom, Germany, and Norway* (Oxford: Oxford University Press, 2003) at 59.

[41] K.T. Litfin, *Ozone Discourses: Science and Politics in Global Environmental Cooperation* (New York: Columbia University Press, 1994).

The ozone case reveals the conversion of important actors from one discourse to another in a short space of time. Yet discourses can also undergo a slow shift in their content with time—and the consequences of such gradual shifts ought to be traceable too. Consider, in this light, sustainable development. The discourse has its roots in the 1970s in challenges to conventional development models, pushed mainly by advocates for the poor and marginalized in the Third World, in opposition to transnational capitalism.[42] Brundtland in 1987 deradicalized the discourse somewhat by accepting the desirability of substantial global economic growth—while retaining a concern for global redistribution. With time, the discourse became still more business-friendly, culminating in the dominant role played by business at the 2002 WSSD. However, sustainable development and market liberalism can still be cast in opposition sometimes. At the WSSD, a number of national delegations argued that any agreements on trade reached at the summit should take place within the parameters provided by WTO rules—suggesting sustainable development be subordinated to market liberalism. With time, however, the increasingly business-friendly character of sustainable development means that rapprochement with market liberalism becomes easier. In terms of outcomes, what this rapprochement makes possible are measures such as the raft of partnerships involving business that were the main tangible outcome of the WSSD.

Gradual change can also be played out in contests between discourses. Consider, for example, the issue of commercial whaling. The IWC agreed upon a moratorium on commercial whaling beginning in 1986. The commission began with the idea of regulating whaling in the days when whales were seen as simply a natural resource. The moratorium was not agreed upon as a result of the objective consideration of the depletion of whale stocks and what could be done to restore them. By 1986, evidence of severely depleted whale numbers had existed for decades, but little had been done by the IWC in response. The moratorium was more the result of a discourse shift that involved a reconceptualization of whales as beautiful sentient creatures with intrinsic value. This conceptualization, with roots in green radicalism, took hold in a majority of national delegations to the IWC. Iceland, Norway, and Japan remained committed to an older industrialist treatment of whales as a source of useful products for human consumption (though they also had to add a 'culturalist' overlay to this commitment in order to make it more palatable internationally).

The whaling example illustrates long-running discourse contestation. Outcomes such as the persistence or abolition of the commercial whaling moratorium depend crucially on the relative weight of competing discourses. In the whaling case, unlike sustainable development and market liberalism, there has been no rapprochement across competing discourses.

[42] D. Carruthers, 'From Opposition to Orthodoxy: The Remaking of Sustainable Development' (2001) 18 J. Third World Stud. 93.

6 CONCLUSION

Discourses pervade international environmental affairs no less than other realms of social life. How important are they compared to other influences on collective outcomes? It is hard to generalize because discourses are bound up with regimes, other institutions, material forces, and non-linguistic practices. Indeed, such practices help constitute discourses, which are not just a matter of words. Often their influence is constitutive rather than causal—discourses constitute the subjective dispositions and capacities of the actors. To the degree that a discourse is pervasive in this constitutive sense, it may even go unnoticed as a set of background assumptions shared by all or most actors. The influence of discourses and, in particular, discourse change can be discerned only by writing histories of particular cases. However, in the end, there is one reason to expect discourses to be more consequential in the international system than in the internal affairs of states. Formal institutions are relatively weak in the international system, meaning that coordination (and disruption) across actors has to be supplied by informal mechanisms such as discourses.

RECOMMENDED READING

M. Colby, *Environmental Management in Development: The Evolution of Paradigms* (New York: World Bank, 1990).

É. Darier, ed., *Discourses of the Environment* (Oxford: Basil Blackwell, 1999).

J.S. Dryzek, *The Politics of the Earth: Environmental Discourses*, 2nd edition (Oxford: Oxford University Press, 2005).

M.A. Hajer, *The Politics of Environmental Discourse: Ecological Modernization and the Policy Process* (Oxford: Oxford University Press, 1995).

K.T. Litfin, *Ozone Discourses: Science and Politics in Global Environmental Cooperation* (New York: Columbia University Press, 1994).

D. Torgerson, *The Promise of Green Politics: Environmentalism and the Public Sphere* (Durham: Duke University Press, 1999).

CHAPTER 4

....

GLOBAL ENVIRONMENTAL GOVERNANCE AS ADMINISTRATION

IMPLICATIONS FOR INTERNATIONAL LAW

....

BENEDICT KINGSBURY

1 INTRODUCTION

THIS chapter argues for the analysis of global and transnational environmental governance as administration. This approach sheds light on some important but neglected themes in international environmental law scholarship. The chapter begins by outlining several basic administrative concepts that call for analysis under such an approach (section 2), then sets forth an analytical framework of five structures of administration in global governance (sections 3–6). The five structures include the following (these are archetypes—practice often combines them or blurs the divisions).[1] *Distributed administration* is performed largely by organs of national governments, acting pursuant to international agreements or other transnational regimes. *International administration* is performed by a formal intergovernmental body with a defined organization and competence, usually established by treaty. *Inter-governmental network administration* is performed by networks of national government officials that operate with less formal definition. *Hybrid administration* is performed by a joint institution, or a less formal coordination, involving public and private actors in a transnational context. It will be considered together with *private administration*, conducted by actors that are not governmental or intergovernmental.

It will be argued that governance of fundamental global and transnational environmental problems is being displaced from distributed administration, which has been the predominant model, towards direct administration by intergovernmental organizations or networks on the one side or towards hybrid or private administration on the other. Distributed administration is instead becoming part of the process of diffusion of national environmental law and policy approaches as well as a residuum for special inter-state situations. This change is having fundamental effects on international environmental law, but has not been sufficiently incorporated into scholarship in the field.

Due to space limitations, this chapter must focus largely on positive law and analytic issues. However, these issues are bound up with fundamental normative questions, which the administrative approach opens up for consideration.[2] Normative appraisal in administrative law is often conducted by reference to basic public law values, such as legality, proportionality, rationality, accuracy, effectiveness, efficiency, and respect for basic rights. Political theory inquiries into democracy and legitimacy in global governance may be given more applied purchase by distilling normative values and implicit trade-offs, embodied in such legal-administrative components as transparency, notification, participation, reason-giving, and review. Inflections in the

---

[1] B. Kingsbury, N. Krisch, and R.B. Stewart, 'The Emergence of Global Administrative Law' (2005) 68 L. & Contemp. Probs 15.

[2] Normative issues are addressed in several of the papers in B. Kingsbury, N. Krisch, R.B. Stewart, and J.B. Wiener, eds., 'Symposium: The Emergence of Global Administrative Law' (2005) 68 L. & Contemp.

design and operation of different administrative systems may have impacts on distributive outcomes, procedural fairness, and other elements of justice. These considerations feed back into the normative theory of institutional design under conditions of power asymmetry, uneven information flows and filtering, and pervasive uncertainties in each governance unit about which policies to choose and what their consequences will be amid continuous mutual jostling, adjustment, and re-clustering.

2 Administrative Law Concepts in Global Environmental Governance

Analysing global environmental governance as administration provides a framework for developing, from an administrative law standpoint, several key concepts that are at present treated rather differently in political science. Administrative law concepts that should be central to the international law understanding of global environmental governance include, among others, delegation, accountability, reasoned deliberation, professional expertise, local knowledge, dynamic effects, and the generality or specificity of norms. Space permits only cursory notations on these concepts to indicate areas of future politico-legal research.

2.1 Delegation

Delegation is the voluntary transfer of power from one actor or group of actors to another. Those delegating power may intend that the role of the delegate be to follow their wishes (a principal-agent structure)[3] or that the role of the delegate be to act in the best interests of the delegators or designated third parties (a trustee-beneficiary structure). The powers of the delegate may be tightly specified by detailed rules or loosely stated.[4] The creation of inter-state organizations is typically modelled as a delegation of powers by the member states. Delegations may also occur from one international organization to another, but, even if this form is used, the key actors in

Probs 1; and in N. Krisch and B. Kingsbury, eds., 'Symposium: Global Governance and Global Administrative Law in the International Legal Order' (2006) 17 Eur. J. Int'l L. 1.

[3] D. Hawkins, D. Lake, D. Nielson, and M.J. Tierney, 'Delegation under Anarchy: States, International Organizations, and Principal-Agent Theory,' in D.G. Hawkins et al., *Delegation and Agency in International Organizations* (Cambridge: Cambridge University Press, 2006) 3.

[4] R. Grant and R. Keohane, 'Accountability and Abuses of Power in World Politics' (2005) 99 Am. Pol. Sci. Rev. 1.

practice may be governments who have decided to re-delegate their powers. The multiplicity of actors, and the overlaps and discontinuities in controls exerted on these various actors, means that the dense interactions in any specific area of global regulatory governance may not be adequately modelled by a simple delegation theory. In world politics, many actors are primordial, often self-constituted, as might be the case of a non-governmental organization (NGO) that issues certificates that coffee is shade-grown without anyone else deliberately conferring on it the power to do so.

2.2 Accountability

Accountability can be understood functionally in terms of its components: account-ability of whom; to whom; for what; and by what means? Global environmental governance increasingly encompasses fledgling efforts to build accountability of its administrators to the actors (usually state governments) who empowered them or, in some cases, to those who are affected by them. The accountability may be for the consequences of general policies or (more robustly) of specific decisions affecting identifiable actors and concrete interests. The mechanisms of accountability are often political, including the threat of non-renewal of appointments or cuts in finances, or they are loosely 'reputational'. In some cases, formal review processes may have a more legal character, including quasi-judicial or judicial tribunals. Limiting the term 'accountability' to situations where one actor can impose a sanc-tion on another actor, in accordance with a reasoned decision based on previously defined standards, has the advantage of tying the concept more closely to legal modalities. Yet a broader approach has the advantage of reflecting the real politics of many transnational governance regimes. These accountability mechanisms may contribute to policy changes, very occasionally to annulment or amendment of deci-sions or to disciplinary measures and, episodically, to disguised or *ex gratia* compen-sation or compensatory measures. Very seldom do they result in formal legal liability.

Accountability is often linked to delegation because it provides a means for hold-ing the delegate to the terms of the delegation. Control of the delegate may be per-formed directly by the principal or beneficiary, or it may be triggered or exercised by third parties. The US Congress gave affected private parties rights to seek judicial review of action by executive branch agencies partly as a means to mobilize focused interests to the task of keeping the agencies aligned with policies that Congress had adopted by statute. Such *ex-post* mobilization of third parties to support the object-ives of those delegating power is less common in global environmental governance. It can occur where the possibility exists for third parties to trigger review processes, as with the right of persons claiming to be affected by a violation of the World Bank's own policies to file a request for investigation with the World Bank Inspection Panel; the possibility of such review can press members of the bank's staff (management) to comply with policies adopted by the bank's board (which itself is responsive to the member states who create, finance, and use the bank).

Potentially important structures of legal accountability operate where actions can be brought (or defences raised) in national administrative agencies or national courts relying on the terms of international environmental agreements and implementing statutes. Thus the Natural Resources Defense Council sought to have a US Federal Court review a rule adopted by the US Environmental Protection Agency, on the plausible ground that the rule did not comply with an administrative decision of the Meeting of the Parties to the Montreal Protocol concerning methyl bromide. But in August 2006 the court held that this COP decision was to be regarded as a political commitment and not as part of US law. A different, and more attenuated modality, involving a review of legal accountability, is exemplified by the North American Commission for Environmental Cooperation procedure for individuals and groups to submit arguments that a state is failing effectively to enforce its own environmental laws, potentially triggering a decision by the inter-governmental council to have the Secretariat prepare a factual record.

State responsibility provides the traditional international law system of accountability. Treating international law largely as an inter-state system requires ensuring allocation among states of the necessary powers to regulate conduct by all other actors as well as specification of the responsibility of states for their own actions or regulatory failures. Problems of evasion of responsibility through delegation are addressed by attributing to each state responsibility for the non-state actors it controls, for certain conduct in the territory that is not part of the state but in which it exercises control, for complicity in violations of international law by other states, and, conceivably, for unremedied acts of international organizations in which it is a leading power or simply a member. Whether such mechanisms are sufficient to structure accountability in contemporary global governance is doubtful. Yet proponents argue that the authority and clarity of international law in the traditional state responsibility system is preferable to the deformalized, purposive, and rather variable normativity embraced by the models of governance and accountability.

2.3 Deliberation and Reason-Giving

Governance mechanisms can be arrayed along a spectrum between essentially political and essentially legal modes of operation, based upon the degree of commitment to deliberation and reason-giving in their decision-making. A purely political mechanism, such as the casting of votes in a secret ballot, involves no obligation to give any reasons or to seek to persuade anyone else. Conversely, a judicial mechanism usually involves an obligation to state reasons and a considerable effort to make these reasons convincing to the parties and to the relevant audience. In between are modalities that are more political but have a deliberative, rather than arbitrary decisionist, mode of operation. In developing such an analysis, John Ferejohn has hypothesized that purely political mechanisms (such as electoral choices) that play a vital part in national democracies can seldom be routinized in global administration, where democratic legitimation of political decision-making is not achievable. As a substitute, actors with the power (individually or in coalition) routinely to impose political decisions must usually give reasons to overcome the legitimacy deficit that otherwise would generate contestation or non-cooperation from necessary parties.[5]

The demand to increase reason-giving and deliberation in global governance, as a substitute for unattainable democratic legitimacy, confronts two basic dilemmas that beset all institutional design in global environmental administration. The first is the dilemma of expertise and the second is the dilemma of local knowledge. The dilemma of expertise arises in relation both to effective rule-making and to the administration of rules. The continuous increase in regulatory complexity means that only experts can draft workable technical rules and amend them in response to practical experience and new knowledge. The real work of detailed rule-making must be done administratively (not by national legislatures and not by international treaties). A political body may formally approve the detailed rules, but it will probably not be able to deliberate in a reasoned way over most issues arising in them, and cannot deliberate too extensively without causing so much delay as to frustrate the effective administration of a workable regime. The technical complexity also means that no one other than experts can really review rules for compliance with substantive standards or can review the substance of complex administrative decisions taken under the rules.[6] Thus, a system of independent judicial or administrative review is unlikely to be effective on substantive issues, although it may be a control on the procedures used by experts in rule-making and administration. If this dilemma of expertise is inevitable, one of the problems to address is whether such rule-making powers, and rule-review powers, which involve problems of expertise, should themselves be established and limited by detailed rules or by more general standards (see discussion later in this chapter).

The dilemma of *local* knowledge arises from the tension between the advantages of uniformity, and centralization, of standard setting (market integration, reduced transaction costs, pooling of expertise, and so on), and the advantages of policy-making and administration being carried out by those with specific local knowledge and involvement. As James C. Scott argues, in denouncing the failures of high-modernist state planning in land collectivization, agriculture, and scientific forestry, '[t]he necessarily simple abstractions of large bureaucratic institutions . . . can never adequately represent the actual complexity of natural or social processes.'[7] Capitalist

---

    [5] J. Ferejohn, *Accountability in a Global Context*, unpublished manuscript, 2006 [on file with author]. Also valuable is ongoing work by M. Philp and R. B. Stewart.

    [6] M. Shapiro, ' "Deliberative," "Independent" Technocracy versus Democratic Politics: Will the Globe Echo the EU?' (2005) 68 L. & Contemp. Probs 341.

    [7] J.C. Scott, *Seeing Like a State: How Certain Schemes to Improve the Human Condition Have Failed* (Binghampton, NY: Vail-Ballou Press, 1998) at 262.

markets and state minimalism are the Hayekian solution to the problem of energiz-
ing local knowledge and responding rapidly to its changing experiences. Scott's
rejoinder addresses a subset of cases, relating particularly to large-scale infrastructure and industrial or agribusiness projects: '[L]arge-scale capitalism is just as much
an agency for homogenization, uniformity, grids, and heroic simplification as the
state is, with the difference being that, for capitalists, simplification must pay.'[8] Global
environmental governance increasingly seeks to utilize market mechanisms, local
consultations, and, in some cases, community initiation of activities. These can be
structured through locally driven experiments, the results of which are reported,
diffused, and framed as generalized benchmarks to help raise standards in local
governance elsewhere. However, such solutions are often flawed in practice. Global
environmental governance thus typically co-exists with forms of resistance and
counter-power as well as special interest rent-seeking and welfare-reducing local
chauvinisms.

2.4 Dynamic Effects

Comparative literature on administration in global environmental governance frequently addresses static design, for instance, in comparing the design of compliance
mechanisms or technical amendment procedures or financing mechanisms among
different multilateral environmental treaties. Yet a dynamic analysis is often essential.
Administration produces information (which may be asymmetrically distributed),
shapes behaviour of the administered, and may generate demand for altered rules or
different institutions. Administrators, the administered actors, and third parties
often operate in mutually responsive relations entailing some reflexivity. Thus, anticipated evolutionary effects should influence the initial choice of administrative
system, and actual evolutionary experience may affect its subsequent redesign. This
dynamic is intensified where an administrative system has direct current competitors
or might in the future be substituted by another. The certification of forest management and forest products is an illustrative case. The formation of the Forest
Stewardship Council (FSC), with its environmental NGO orientation and very
detailed performance standards, prompted the establishment of more forest-industry
oriented organizations such as the Sustainable Forestry Initiative in the United States
and the Program for the Endorsement of Forest Certification (PEFC) in Europe.
The PEFC was initially organized on national lines with considerable government
involvement, but, from 2003, it began to operate outside Europe and in looser ways.
The FSC had a global focus and a sectoral structure from the beginning, but it did not
admit governments and did not even admit government forestry companies until
2002. Although they initially differed in levels of transparency, both soon came to follow notice-and-comment processes in setting standards, and they both responded

---

[8] *Ibid.* at 8.

quickly to changes in expectations about consultation as well as to demands from large retailers, government procurement agencies, industry, consumers, regulators, and many other actors. Some of these actors are in turn affected or even shaped by the standard setters.[9]

2.5 General versus Specific Norms

Issues relating to the generality or specificity of legal norms are a recurrent, if elusive, theme in debates about administrability of international environmental regimes. The debate in US legal scholarship on standards versus rules has solidified some basic premises. Standards have the advantages of being less costly to devise, politically easier to agree on, flexible rather than ossifying as new information or new policy objectives emerge, and conducive to continued deliberation and dialogue each time their meaning must be determined in a concrete case. Rules have the advantages of being less costly to apply, providing more predictable outcomes, embodying precise solutions to collective action problems so as better to assure capture of gains from cooperation, and increasing the role of the rule-makers as against the courts or other reviewing bodies. Transposing these themes to inter-state environmental agreements, rationalist analysis suggests that states will prefer standards, except where substantial gains can really be captured by a rule-defined equilibrium solution to a collective action problem (as in the stratospheric ozone regime), or where an agreement confers substantial powers on a third party, which states prefer to hem in by rules (as with the detailed rules defining powers of the Executive Board under the clean development mechanism, which is discussed later).[10] The inter-state picture becomes more complicated when internal politics of states are factored in, as detailed rules in an international agreement might have the effect of empowering one government agency against others, or might be used by national courts when general standards would not, or might be used by a group currently in power to lock in policies it fears its successors will reverse. The standard model may also be departed from when a hegemonic state, or a first-mover, seeks to use international agreements to export its own detailed regulatory scheme, whether for idealistic or ideological reasons or to capture relative gains from convergence around its standard.

The rules versus standards analysis usually focuses on an orthodox principal-agent model of administration in international environmental governance, in which an inter-state body makes the rules and an administrative body 'implements' them.[11] Yet

    [9] E. Meidinger, 'The Administrative Law of Global Public-Private Regulation: The Case of Forestry' (2006) 17 Eur. J. Int'l L. 47.

    [10] D. Bodansky, 'Rules versus Standards in International Environmental Law' (2004) 98 Proc. Am. Soc. Int'l L. 275.

    [11] This is exemplified by the Instrument Establishing the Global Environment Facility, which provides that the Secretariat's first function is to 'implement effectively the decisions of the Assembly and the Council.'

the shift in administrative philosophy, from setting rules for administrators to defining goals for them to meet, changes the structures of discretion. Whether the goals are defined in contracts, in voluntary codes and performance standards, or in some international agreements, if the administrator is given only a very small number of measurable goals, discretion is largely limited to a choice of means. However, if the number of goals proliferates, the administrator makes substantive choices about which goals to pursue in which combination, given the inevitability of prioritization and the likelihood that the returns to the administrator of focusing on some goals vastly exceed those for other goals.

Choices between standards and rules are thus highly contextual. The Global Environmental Facility (GEF) illustrates this point. The GEF's Principles of Cooperation among the Implementing Agencies (UN Development Programme, UN Environment Programme, and the World Bank) are written very generally, and envisage the building of trust and long-term relations rather than elaborate rules of inter-agency demarcation. The Instrument Establishing the Global Environment Facility uses more precise rules about the organization of its constituencies and who gets what. Finally, very detailed World Bank rules are used to insulate the World Bank's trusteeship administration of the GEF Fund monies from risks of depredations by member states or staff, and from pressures by other organizations.

2.6 Overview

Consideration of the elements mentioned in this section—delegation in principal-agent and trustee models, accountability, dilemmas of expertise and local knowledge, deliberative reason-giving, the dynamic effects of administration, and the choice between standards and rules—points to some of the central politico-legal issues in design of global and transnational environmental governance regimes. International law scholarship has been rather slow to address these issues, although they are familiar from administrative law as well as political science. Innovative legal theorizing of the administration of global environmental governance has thus been influenced largely by debates on national regulatory reform.

A commitment to find substitutes for direct government administration of utilities and social services and for command-and-control regulation of business operations affecting the environment has been widely espoused since the 1980s. Many states have adopted measures aimed at involving civil society groups and businesses in environmental governance, including public-private eco-label schemes, public-private partnerships to craft national sustainable development strategies, and legislation on public access to environmental information.[12] On more fundamental issues, efforts to theorize substitute approaches have been contentious and unstable. The New Public

---

[12] P.-O. Busch, H. Jörgens, and K. Tews, 'The Global Diffusion of Regulatory Instruments: The Making of a New International Environmental Regime' (2005) 598 Annals Am. Acad. Pol. & Soc. Sci. 146.

Management (NPM) approach, which has been increasingly applied in many Organisation for Economic Co-operation and Development (OECD) and developing countries since the 1980s, separates the determination of overall strategy and goals (set by politicians and expert consultants) from the pursuit of these by professional managers or contractors, whose performance is measured by performance indicators and by surveys of customer satisfaction. This separation facilitates outsourcing and governance by contract, provided performance targets are measurable. Yet the NPM struggles with cross-cutting issues where a wide range of ecologic, social, and economic initiatives must be integrated. A reaction in some sectors (for example, education) has been to switch to interactive governance, with significant powers devolved to very local levels, but this has overwhelmed some local actors who lack expertise or capacity on aspects of complex issues, and runs into problems where local practices do not aggregate to a sound macro policy.[13] NPM-type approaches have been extended to transnational governance, with the European Union (EU) providing the most intricate body of practice, loosely characterized in Europe as 'new governance'. By comparison with traditional hierarchical public command-and-control governance, 'new governance' tends towards heterarchy, networks, wide participation (including by private governance actors), reflexively revisable standards rather than hard rules, voluntary agreements or contracts or mutual recognition rather than substantive central legislation, the use of environmental taxes and other market instruments, eco-labels, technology-based standards, benchmarks, guidelines, indicators, peer review, self-reporting and monitoring, naming/shaming rather than fines, conciliation/negotiation, and limited or no formal judicial control or justiciability.[14] These re-orientations in national regulatory approaches in different parts of the world, and the practical development of them in transborder contexts in the EU, have significantly affected the administration of international environmental governance. However, direct transposition from administration in national policy or the EU to administration in global regimes is perilous. There remains a pressing need for a theory of international law responsive to such administrative approaches but adapted to global politics and problems.

3 DISTRIBUTED ADMINISTRATION

The standard model of international environmental law is of rules set by agreement among states, usually in a formal treaty-based intergovernmental organization (IO) or an informal intergovernmental network, then implemented (administered) by

---

[13] C. Sabel, 'Beyond Principal-Agent Governance: Experimentalist Organizations, Learning and Accountability,' in E. Engelen and M. Sie Dhian Ho, eds., *De Staat van de Democratie: Democratie voorbij de Staat* (Amsterdam: Amsterdam University Press, 2004) 173.

[14] G. de Burca et al., *New Modes of Governance in Europe (NEWGOV), Taskforce on Legal Issues II, Working Agenda 2005-06*, 2005 [on file with author].

public authorities in each state (see Chapter 31 'Changing Role of the State'). The agreement is thus the first part of a solution to a collective action problem—if it is specific enough, it singles out one among several possible equilibria, makes it into a focal point, and so enables valuable coordination or assists the capture of gains from collaboration. The second part of the solution is the administration of the agreement by states. If the agreement is simply one of coordination, so that once it is made no state has an incentive to breach it, the state's administration can be expected to align its conduct with the agreement, unless the administering agency has different preferences or reflects different interests than the treaty-maker or unless there are capacity or cost problems inhibiting administration. If the agreement is one which the state's leaders have substantial reasons not to aim effectively to administer, as with Kyoto Protocol emissions reduction requirements (which many governments of rich countries found too costly to deliver on), insulating the administrators from the state's political leadership may be a useful strategy to increase the likelihood of the agreement being accurately implemented. This may be done by empowering independent agencies that are insulated much as national central banks are, or by building the agreement into a wider programme that is difficult to change (such as a general property rights or taxation system), or by making the agreement readily enforceable in the national courts.

The standard model of distributed administration in international environmental law is of administration by each state of an agreement it chooses to make, and no strong external principal for whom the state can realistically be described as an agent. The Aarhus Convention on Access to Information, Public Participation in Decision-making and Access to Justice in Environmental Matters, the Convention on Biological Diversity, and the Ramsar Convention on Wetlands of International Importance Especially as Waterfowl Habitat, are among the many examples. Even regimes such as the Basel Convention on the Control of Transboundary Movements of Hazardous Wastes and Their Disposal and the Antarctic Treaty system follow this pattern, although external actors may be able to trigger state action. There is a continuum from this pattern to another model of distributed administration, in which the national authorities can be regarded as the administering agents of norms prescribed by the IO or network even where the state itself did not participate in making the norm. This latter model may operate where the national officials respond primarily to an international body rather than to their own government, which may result from national officials participating in epistemic communities and the rewards of international recognition or from the provision of foreign consultants or administrators. This may happen in relatively innocuous ways, for example where state officials collect uncontroversial information required by an international agency, but the issues may involve much higher political stakes. The political leverage that enables an external agency to coopt state administrators may exist where the administering state is highly dependent on an external agency—for example, a state in great need of World Bank financing for ecotourism might decide to administer all of its forests along lines prescribed by the bank's internal forests policy. Leverage also exists where an international body's policies reflect the wishes of major states, and are strongly buttressed by their bilateral pressure on the target state, as occurs in some marine mammal conservation regimes (for example, US pressure on states to administer the regime defined by the Inter-American Tropical Tuna Commission). States that are anxious to join an external agency, such as the EU or the World Trade Organization (WTO), may also commit many of their administrative agencies to guidance from Brussels or from experts purporting to be authorities on the meaning of certain WTO rules.

Cases of this latter model of distributed administration, with the international agency as principal and the state as agent, blend into direct international administration. They tend to be imposed on poorer or weaker states or to be by-products of economic integration regimes (the EU above all). Georges Scelle's conception of *dédoublement fonctionnel*[15] of a national authority acting as the implementing agency of international society, advocated this model as a means of realizing international law without world government, but it meets normative resistance because it may conflict with the values of national democracy and national accountability, and with the associated expectation that national officials who have sworn an oath of office in the national system ought not to act lightly as the agent for someone else.

Distributed administration of a treaty on a non-environmental issue may also impose constraints on state administration of environmental policies. An example is the WTO Appellate Body's requirements that the United States, in administering its unilateral turtle-protecting legislation restricting shrimp imports, also administer the WTO General Agreement on Tariffs and Trade properly by providing potentially affected countries advance notice of the reasons for the proposed restrictions, an opportunity to be heard, a reasoned decision, and a review procedure.[16] The US turtle-protecting policy was set unilaterally, but, in certain circumstances, the same WTO logic could have applied had the United States been implementing an international environmental treaty.

Loose systems of distributed administration of internationally specified norms may be both one cause and one consequence of the puzzling phenomena of multiple states adopting similar regulatory policies at roughly the same time when not forced to do so. Parallel policy adoption may, in some cases, arise simply because the same problem begets the same regulatory response in each state without regard to what other states are doing, or, conversely, it may result from strong pressure from a powerful state or an IO or network, so that adoption is not a 'choice' at all. Where states make choices that take into consideration what other states have chosen, they may do so as adaptation to changed conditions created by the choices of other states or,

[15] G. Scelle, Le phénomène juridique du dédoublement fonctionnel,' in W. Schätzel and H.-J. Schlochauer, eds., *Rechtsfragen der internationalen Organisation: Festschrift für Hans Wehberg* (Frankfurt am Main: Klostermann, 1956) 324.

[16] *United States—Import Prohibition of Certain Shrimp and Shrimp Products*, Appellate Body Report, Doc. WT/DS58/AB/R (6 November 1998) at para. 180.

instead, by learning from what other states have done. Adaptation may produce divergence—if many countries have adopted a high environmental standard imposing economic costs, another state may adopt a lower standard to gain a competitive advantage or to benefit from premium prices for a now-scarce product. Learning may produce divergence too—if a policy has bad results in some countries, other similarly situated countries may adopt a different policy. Yet frequently, adaptation stimulates convergence to maintain parity with competitors, or to benefit from network externalities (including further improvements) where a growing number of states have adopted the same policy, or when a tipping point is reached that makes a particular policy choice now seem legitimate or at least immune from attack by others.[17] Likewise, learning often prompts convergence—states study a small subset of celebrated models, or borrow from countries that are prominent or that they are close to. It is often prudent to utilize an existing model rather than bear the costs and risk of developing a new one.[18]

4 International Administration

In most areas of international environmental governance, intergovernmental institutions do not act directly on non-state corporations or individuals. Generally, they rely on individual states to conduct that administration (under distributed administration models), but some special cases are beginning to appear in which global governance agencies seek themselves to construct and shape global markets—the example of the Kyoto Protocol's clean development mechanism (CDM) will be considered. Somewhat more frequently, intergovernmental institutions act as direct administrators vis-à-vis individual states, for example, by finding a state in non-compliance with an international standard and, hence, authorizing remedial measures or the limitation of a state's privileges under the regime or by issuing a certificate or a warning that alters the market conditions affecting that state (the example of the Office International des Epizooties (OIE) will be discussed later in this chapter).

The CDM under the Kyoto Protocol on climate change is unusual, but it is perhaps indicative of future patterns in that an inter-state environmental agreement confers substantial powers on an international institution to directly administer a regime affecting private market actors as well as state agencies. The CDM enables developed countries to receive credits towards their emission reduction obligations for projects undertaken, often by private entities, in developing countries, with the aims of both

---

[17] S. Barrett, *Environment and Statecraft: The Strategy of Environmental Treaty-Making* (Oxford: Oxford University Press, 2003).

[18] Z. Elkins and B. Simmons, 'On Waves, Clusters, and Diffusion: A Conceptual Framework' (2005) 598 Annals Am. Acad. Pol. & Soc. Sci. 33.

promoting development and enabling emissions reductions at a reduced cost. The CDM's ten-member Executive Board (EB) consists of representatives of states parties to the Kyoto Protocol, elected for two-year terms, and complemented by a further ten alternate members who are actively involved in its work. Its powers and responsibilities are defined in very detailed rules adopted by the inter-state Conference of the Parties/Meeting of the Parties (COP/MOP). However, some of these rules themselves are influenced by the EB's own practice and drafting, including the work of panels established by the EB, such as the CDM Small Scale Project Activities Panel. In these cases, the EB and the panels have an authorial role, with the COP/MOP exercising an editorial and approval role. The COP/MOP uses rules rather then general standards as a means to limit the EB's discretion, but the rules do not cover all issues, and considerable power is left to the EB in the administration of the CDM. The EB's power can be exercised by super-majority votes if consensus cannot be attained. This power is hemmed in at the operational project level by the system under which designated operational entities (DOEs) validate proposed CDM projects and verify and certify reductions in emissions. The final certification by the DOE results automatically in the issuance by the CDM registry administrator of the specified number of certified emission reductions (CERs), unless the EB exercises its power of review, which is limited to fraud, malfeasance, or incompetence of the DOE.[19] Thus, much of the power to create CERs, which are in effect an internationally constructed property right, rests with the DOEs, which are themselves market actors that are not created by intergovernmental action (albeit each DOE needs approval by the EB and the COP/MOP) and are contracted by the project parties in relation to each project. There exists therefore in this case a chain of delegations, from states parties to the COP/MOP, from the COP/MOP to the EB, and from the EB to the DOEs. The delegations to the EB and to the DOEs are framed by very detailed rules. Significant discretionary powers are conferred, but these are checked in various ways. The DOEs are likely to be subject to market disciplines and to reputational accountability constraints, provided they are repeat players and are unable to establish monopolies or to capture their own regulator. The EB faces little market pressure (except perhaps if rival emissions certification and trading systems become its competitors), and its individual members face only limited constraint through the system for EB elections (they serve two-year terms and can be re-elected once, but individual performance may well be outweighed by other political issues in re-election dynamics). The EB is constrained by rules about openness in its meetings, by limits on its finances and expertise, by limitations on its own powers in relation to particular projects, and by powers of review in the COP/MOP.

The logic leading to this pattern in international administration of market-oriented environmental governance is readily intelligible. The high stakes of climate

---

[19] For an overview, see F. Yamin and J. Depledge, *The International Climate Change Regime: A Guide to Rules, Institutions and Procedures* (Cambridge: Cambridge University Press, 2004).

change and the need for precision to define property rights and to establish a pre-dictable regime for market actors militate for detailed rules. Nevertheless, the result is a highly regulated and bureaucratic structure, whose coherence may suffer where competing political interests pull in different directions, for example, on whether to grant credits for projects that would have been undertaken anyway or on whether to grant credits for controversial tree plantations. The success of this regime may prove to depend in part on its inability to monopolize administration. More space may be needed for 'local' knowledge and practices—it can be difficult for an indigenous group to repackage an emissions-reducing practice, such as Aboriginal Australian traditional fire management, in the terms of the CDM system. National or regional regulation may be vital. International administration will certainly play a role even in the long term, in conjunction with partial substitutes that are likely to emerge for it. In the current transitional phase, it provides some opportunities for learning (build-ing private sector and public sector expertise on emissions reduction and trading), for redistribution (for example, encouraging the formation of DOEs in smaller developing countries receiving little foreign investment), and for dynamically build-ing a wider constituency for regulation.

International administration vis-à-vis member states is carried out by the World Organization for Animal Health (OIE), which was established in 1924. The OIE Scientific Commission for Animal Diseases, consisting of five members (all veterin-arians) elected by the inter-governmental plenary body (the International Committee), operates a register of countries (or parts of countries) that are free of foot and mouth disease (FMD). Member states seeking such status submit data in prescribed form to the Scientific Commission, which invites scientific comments from all member states and, if necessary, is assisted by an expert panel. Decisions are ultimately adopted by resolution of the International Committee. However, the commission itself has the authority to certify that a previously FMD-free country, subsequently affected by an FMD outbreak, should once again be classed as FMD-free. This model has been extended to other animal diseases, including a scheme for bovine spongiform encephalopathy. Such certifications are of considerable importance in international trade. They may have substantial consequences for entire national economies in agri-cultural societies. Despite the high stakes, this area of international administration has operated without great public controversy on the understanding that universal scientific criteria provide the right basis for decisions and are best implemented by technocratic experts. This regime is unusual in that it has not (yet) become highly proceduralized—in its documents, the technical but substantive criteria for disease-free status preponderate over detailed specification of the procedures of the relevant bodies, perhaps reflecting the dominance in the OIE of animal health scientists rather than lawyers. The commission's position is buttressed by its use of detailed scientific criteria administered by reputable scientists, by the political control exer-cised by member states through the International Committee, and perhaps also by the bureaucratic control exercised by the director general. However, if a major controversy were to arise, it would rapidly focus political attention on the adequacy of the commission's procedures and on the substantive propriety of such a commission having these powers.

The CDM and the OIE have in common the absence of a process to review actions of the EB or the Scientific Commission, other than through the intergovernmental plenary bodies. No formal mechanism exists for challenges by private actors, let alone for compensation to states or individuals if the administering agency acts wrongly. Accountability mechanisms are thus limited to political bodies protecting the collective interests of the states that delegated power. Yet contrasts between the CDM and OIE systems have also been highlighted. These suggest important research questions: under what conditions are broad delegations of power to international administrators politically possible in environmental governance, and when are such delegations reined in?[20] In what circumstances do different classes of states, and different interests within states, agree to rely on the vicissitudes of *ex post* control rather than insisting on strong *ex ante* control by detailing the rules? What are the results when such delegations are tightly circumscribed by substantive rules with more discretion as to procedures or by detailed procedures with less *ex-ante* agreement on substantive rules? If a separate review mechanism to protect private parties or individual states is established, the collectivity of states will likely also prefer to limit its discretion, using precise rules rather than vague standards.

Measures of administration against non-member states are difficult for most environmental IOs, unless the non-member wishes to cooperate. The 1995 Agreement for the Implementation of the Provisions of the United Nations Convention on the Law of the Sea Relating to the Conservation and Management of Straddling Fish Stocks and Highly Migratory Fish Stocks provides, in Article 17, that regional fisheries management organizations may take measures against vessels from non-member states and denies such states the power to authorize fishing for the relevant straddling or highly migratory stocks. Yet the difficulties of extended enforcement are illustrated by the intergovernmental Commission for the Conservation of Southern Bluefin Tuna (CCSBT). It has members, cooperating non-members, and a provision in its 2000 action plan for pressure by member states on third states whose vessels are undermining the SBT conservation regime, including through denial of access to the lucrative Japanese sashimi market. The trade measures provision is limited by the requirement that they be 'consistent with the members' international obligations.' In practice, such measures have not been seriously contemplated against any state, even though Indonesia, in particular, has resisted becoming a cooperating non-member and has had vessels catching hundreds of tonnes of SBT annually with little monitoring. The difficulties of real international administration of these fisheries have meant

---

[20] D.L. Nelson and M.J. Tierney, 'Delegation to International Organizations: Agency Theory and World Bank Environmental Reform' (2003) 57 Int'l Org. 241.

that the independent powers given to fisheries commissions such as the CCSBT have been very limited, except occasionally in relation to research and scientific determinations, and that they therefore operate more as cases of distributed administration. This continues to be a common pattern in international environmental law more generally.

5 NETWORK ADMINISTRATION

The informality of international networks of government officials means they have seldom been designed to exercise appreciable administrative powers. However, the advantages to government officials of creating administrative structures through networks rather than treaties are prompting various efforts to institutionalize such networks. In some cases, the network operates directly as an international administration, in others it uses techniques such as continuous information assessment, review, peer pressure, socialization, and participatory revision of objectives to exercise administrative power. This section deals with cases in these two categories, rather than cases in which networks set policies that are administered in discretionary fashion by national authorities (a model closer to distributed administration). A network can act quickly, adopting norms and establishing supervisory mechanisms without needing to seek approvals from national legislatures. Specialist government agencies rather than foreign ministries may lead the process, which can make convergence between negotiators easier, facilitate close articulation between policies adopted by the network and policies followed by the national agencies staffed by the same people, and reduce the diverting effects of linkages with other diplomatic issues.

The most dramatic examples of administration by networks occur in the areas of international security and financial markets regulation (for example, the Proliferation Security Initiative and the Financial Action Task Force). Some of these networks have no aspiration to universality—they are self-constituted coalitions of the willing or the like-minded and may aim to exert considerable pressure on non-participants. The administrative powers of environmental management networks are less intrusive but can be significant, as two OECD examples illustrate.[21]

The OECD Council has taken legally binding decisions establishing a system of mutual acceptance by member states of test data on chemicals (for toxicity, skin irritation, and so on) conducted in laboratories approved in any participating state, and the OECD has adopted over 100 guidelines covering various tests of chemicals as well

---

[21] J. Salzman, 'Decentralized Administrative Law in the Organization for Economic Cooperation and Development' (2005) 68 L. & Contemp. Probs 189.

as a set of Principles of Good Laboratory Practice (GLP Principles) to be followed by public and private laboratories engaged in such testing. Each of the guidelines is approved by the OECD's Environment Policy Committee after peer review and scientific validation involving some 7,000 experts. The GLP Principles are kept up to date by a working group, which has also established a system of 'mutual joint visits', under which teams from three other national authorities inspect each country's GLP compliance supervisory agency. Specialist environmental and animal welfare NGOs participate actively in the processes of establishing and reviewing guidelines and GLP Principles (although not in the mutual joint visit system), along with industry and labour groups that have an organized role in many OECD structures. States that are not members of the OECD may adhere to the GLPs, with the result that the system, although far from universal, is gradually expanding. This set of arrangements is avowedly technocratic and establishes highly specific standards, while proceeding in a much less definitive way on compliance issues, and carefully avoiding fundamental policy questions such as which chemicals to approve or what levels of risk should be accepted.

The OECD adopted in December 2003 (and subsequently updated) a Recommendation on Common Approaches on Environment and Officially Supported Export Credits, prompted by a combination of NGO lobbying and the US Export-Import Bank, which had adopted an environmental policy in 1995 and was concerned about being undercut by other states' export credit agencies that were not constrained by such a policy. The common approaches, which are now followed by all OECD members, do not set sharp or justiciable standards for evaluating the substance of decisions to finance particular projects, and they provide only limited specifications as to how to conduct environmental impact assessments or other reviews, but they do set forth process obligations to conduct these. They rely on monitoring and peer or public pressure and, to this end, establish general obligations of publication and of member state reporting on standard electronic forms to the OECD's Working Party on Export Credits and Credit Guarantees (ECG).

These OECD examples are typical of network governance in several respects. The controlling rules are readily updated and amended and, usually, do not involve national legislatures. The network is ultimately controlled mainly by governments, but it is not limited to government agencies, and often includes corporate and labour interests as well as highly specialized NGOs (including NGO coalitions) dedicated to that very forum and able also to coordinate among national NGOs. These networks often incorporate standards developed in other institutions by different processes, as with the references in the ECG recommendation to member states benchmarking certain projects against standards and guidelines of the World Bank Group or relevant regional development banks. Such cross-incorporation of standards can add considerable specificity to apparently more general norms, although it can also muddy the normative analysis where different norms compete.

6 HYBRID AND PRIVATE ADMINISTRATION

Legal differences between administration by entirely private entities, and hybrid administration that involves both private actors and state authority, are potentially important. Measures taken under state authority are subject to international trade and investment rules that do not necessarily apply to private conduct—for example, some scholars argue that WTO rules do not reach purely private eco-labelling schemes. Rules of the WTO plurilateral agreement on government procurement do not cover purchases by private actors unconnected to state activities. Governments and their agencies can incur liability under human rights treaties, and perhaps even responsibility for the acts of intergovernmental organizations, in ways that private entities do not. IOs, too, when involved in hybrid administration may attract public law obligations that do not apply to private actors. Conversely, administrative entities involving states and IOs may be able to claim immunities and formal recognition that private entities cannot. The legal uncertainties indicate that international law has struggled to keep up with hybrid public-private rule-making and decisions, which are proliferating in global governance, and in which public entities may seek to minimize their exposure while ensuring their leverage (see Chapter 21 'Private and Quasi-Private Standard Setting' and Chapter 33 'Non-Governmental Organizations and Civil Society').

In functional terms, separating hybrid from private administration is often artificial. Even in the case of forest standard-setting and certification, which is outwardly dominated by private bodies such as the FSC, the private structure works against a backdrop of state and inter-state policies and rules, ranging from support by national forestry regulators of private companies, to decisions of state-owned forestry companies, to government procurement policies (for example, in the United Kingdom) designed to force supplier standards upwards, to national laws protecting trademarks used by the FSC and its competitors, to global trade rules and national and international legal incorporation of International Organization for Standardization (ISO) standards. On this issue of administration, as in political economy generally, there is no sharp separation of states and markets or of public and private.

Hybrid and private bodies are often used by states, or by inter-state organizations, to perform administrative functions in a state-defined scheme of global governance. Private corporations provide routine laboratory testing, environmental impact assessments, ship safety certificates, and other such services as agents for state principals, in which the standard problems for states include preventing the agent firms from shirking, from pursuing private interests incompatible with those of the state agents, or from balancing different state principals off against each other.

Accountability may be established under national statutory or private law or under transnationalized contract and arbitration arrangements, although the agents may in practice be more constrained by the costs of losing business and reputation. Such hybrid or private bodies may provide concentrated expertise that states lack, and may be better able to mobilize local knowledge than state bureaucracies can. Although these situations of delegation involve important operational issues, more challenging conceptually are situations in which the hybrid or private bodies exercise norm-setting or decision powers without direct accountability to or through states.

With respect to norm-setting by hybrid or private bodies, the International Social and Environmental Accrediting and Labelling Alliance (ISEAL), which consists of eight non-state organizations including the FSC, has promulgated a code of practice for social and environmental standard setting. This code emphasizes transparency, participation, and reason-giving. Thus, it requires two rounds of public comments on proposed standards, and a public written response to each material issue raised in such comments. It requires that standard setting strive for consensus among a balance of interested parties, although the ISEAL defines consensus for this purpose as '[g]eneral agreement, characterized by the absence of sustained opposition to substantial issues by any important part of the concerned interests and by a process seeking to take into account the views of interested parties.' The more venerable standard-setting bodies, led by the ISO (established in 1947), have moved in similar directions. The ISO has itself promulgated a modern code of practice on standardization, and it seeks to reach into the predicates for its own processes by setting detailed requirements as to how ISO member bodies should consult different interests within their home country before coming to vote within the ISO. The ISO makes unusual use of a reason-giving requirement to reduce risks of hold-outs and capture as well as to discourage oppositional bloc voting. Member bodies are obliged to provide substantive reasons if they vote against the final adoption of a proposed standard in the ISO. States have also sought to indirectly regulate the ISO, through the interstate WTO, whose Agreement on Technical Barriers to Trade provides that states benefit from a rebuttable presumption of WTO compatibility where their technical restrictions on imports comply with 'international standards'. The WTO has issued a Code of Good Practice for the Preparation, Adoption and Application of Standards, which in effect sets guidance on the ways in which the ISO must operate if ISO standards are to operate as a safe harbour under WTO rules.

These codes of practice on norm-making do not generally prescribe levels of specificity (for example, rules versus standards). It may be expected that a body that controls the interpretation and application of its own standards, or whose leading members control the decisions on application, will prefer general standards, whereas a body that has difficulty controlling the decision-making administrators will prefer highly specific rules. The FSC's norms provide such a model, utilizing general global principles, but becoming increasingly specific in relation to individual issues and countries or forest regions. These rules tend to be performance based, aiming for outcomes that are objectively measurable. By contrast, rival organizations set up by the forestry industry and landowners frustrated by their lack of influence in the FSC, or (as in British Columbia in 2002) spurred to action when the FSC adopted regional standards that the industry found too stringent or costly, initially favoured less specific norms than the FSC.[22] Instead of performance standards, they preferred environmental management systems based on continuous improvement and other ISO 14000 techniques. Increasingly, the various systems have converged, with the FSC adjusting regulations to get greater industry support, and industry needing more credible standards for customers.

7 CONCLUSION

This chapter has highlighted the need to evaluate systematically the reasons for, and the consequences of, different choices of means for administration in different contexts of global environmental governance. Understanding exactly how those administrative structures work, and how they might be improved, requires more legal analysis of concepts used in political science and in national administrative law, such as delegation, accountability, anticipated dynamic effects, reason-giving, expertise, local knowledge, and specificity of norms. While the traditional model of distributed administration continues to be prevalent in global environmental governance, some displacement is occurring from this model along the continuum towards more centralized administration by international organizations or intergovernmental networks or towards hybrid or private administration. Distributed administration itself should increasingly be analysed not in the internationalist mode advocated by Georges Scelle but, instead, as a dimension of processes of national policy diffusion, in which international environmental agreements may generate governance but only modest centralized legal demands. This chapter has focused on positive rather than normative dimensions, but, in both dimensions, the analysis of global environmental governance as administration offers promising new pathways for research and practice in the field of international environmental law.

---

[22] See generally J. Kirton and M. Trebilcock, eds., *Hard Choices, Soft Law: Combining Trade, Environment, and Social Cohesion in Global Governance* (New York: Ashgate, 2004) at 65–94.

RECOMMENDED READING

L. Boisson de Chazournes, 'Qu'est-ce que la pratique en droit international?' in Société française pour le droit international, Colloque de Genève, *La pratique et le droit international* (Paris: Editions Pedone, 2004) 13.

D. Bodansky, 'The Legitimacy of International Environmental Governance: A Coming Challenge for International Environmental Law?' (1999) 93 A.J.I.L. 596.

J. Brunnée, 'COPing with Consent: Law Making under Multilateral Environmental Agreements' (2002) 15 Leiden J. Int'l L. 1.

B.S. Chimni, 'Co-Option and Resistance: Two Faces of Global Administrative Law' 37 N.Y.U. J. Int'l L. & Pol. 799.

C. Joerges, I.-J. Sand, and G. Teubner, eds., *Transnational Governance and Constitutionalism* (Oxford: Hart Publishing, 2004).

B. Kingsbury, N. Krisch, R.B. Stewart, and J.B. Wiener, eds., 'Symposium: The Emergence of Global Administrative Law' (2005) 68 L. & Contemp. Probs 1.

N. Krisch and B. Kingsbury, eds., 'Symposium: Global Governance and Global Administrative Law in the International Legal Order' (2006) 17 Eur. J. Int'l L. 1.

D. Lazer, 'Regulatory Capitalism as a Networked Order: The International System as an Informational Network' (2005) 598 Annals Am. Acad. Pol. & Soc. Sci. 52.

J.B. Wiener, 'On the Political Economy of Global Environmental Regulation' (1999) 87 Geo. L.J. 749.

O. Young, 'Environmental Governance: The Role of Institutions in Causing and Confronting Environmental Problems' (2003) 3 Int'l Envt'l Agreements: Pol., L. and Econ. 377.

CHAPTER 5

LEVELS OF ENVIRONMENTAL GOVERNANCE

JEFFREY L. DUNOFF

1 INTRODUCTION

WHO should make the decisions that determine the planet's ecological health? Which groups or institutions—local, national, regional, or global—are best placed, and have the greatest claim, to manage the earth's resources? Questions about how environmental decisions are made and who makes them—that is, questions of environmental governance—lie at the heart of environmental law and policy. This chapter focuses on one important aspect of governance, namely the allocation of authority over environmental issues among different levels of governance. The fundamental question is which political community should govern which environmental issues, and, more specifically, when should responsibility over particular environmental issues be vested at the local, national, regional, or global level?

A large body of scholarship attempts to identify and explain general principles to determine when more, or less, centralized environmental governance systems are most appropriate. The arguments have been developed in diverse literatures, including writings on federalism, de-centralization, European integration, globalization, and regional and multilateral regimes. It is not possible to do justice to these rich literatures in this chapter; instead I shall try to summarize and abstract the most recurrent and influential arguments that are found in this scholarship. To do so, this chapter proceeds as follows. The first section sets the stage by briefly reviewing the trends that are moving towards more centralized environmental governance and describes some of the factors explaining this trend. The next section examines, from a normative standpoint, several leading approaches to debates over the appropriate level of environmental governance. The third section identifies analytic inquiries that can advance current debates over environmental governance and the final section offers a brief conclusion.

2 TRENDS IN ENVIRONMENTAL GOVERNANCE

The past three decades have witnessed overwhelming trends leading towards the centralization of environmental authority at the national, regional, and international levels. During this time, many governments in both developed and developing states were creating national environmental ministries, and enacting complex national environmental regimes. Regional treaties and regimes also proliferated. While the European Union's (EU) complex environmental regime represents the most advanced regional system, notable regional efforts have also been undertaken in North America, southeast Asia, and elsewhere. In addition, scores of important multilateral environmental agreements (MEAs) have been negotiated since the 1972 Stockholm Conference on the Human Environment first placed environmental issues on the global agenda.

To be sure, the moves towards centralization have been uneven. In the United States, for example, a flurry of legislative activities in the 1970s that created a set of comprehensive national regulatory programs were followed by episodic efforts to extend and refine, and occasionally retract, federal regulatory authority. Similarly, on the international plane, efforts to create centralized governance have ebbed and flowed. An initial burst of activity, starting in the late 1960s and culminating in the 1972 Stockholm Conference was followed by a relatively quiet period during the late 1970s and early 1980s. Another burst of law-making activity in connection with the 1992 Conference on Environment and Development has been followed by a phase marked by less attention to norm creation, and a greater focus on implementation issues.

Efforts to explain and justify patterns of environmental governance are rendered difficult, in part, because many national, regional, and international efforts to centralize environmental governance have arisen in an ad hoc and fragmented manner. For example, centralized environmental regimes frequently arise in response to dramatic, high-profile environmental events such as the Bhopal disaster, the *Torrey Canyon* spill, the Seveso chemical plant explosion, the Basel warehouse fire, the *Exxon Valdez* spill, and other environmental catastrophes. More generally, various national and international mechanisms for environmental governance are created in response to the essentially random emergence of environmental issues onto the political agenda as well as the political pressures that various constituencies can bring to bear on different issues at different times.

Moreover, efforts to understand and explain the allocation of authority over environmental issues are further complicated by the fact that contemporary environmental governance addresses not a single problem, but instead, a complex set of issues including pollution control, natural resource management, and human health and safety. In addition, every instance of more centralized environmental governance reflects, in part, highly particularized and contextual factors. The creation of a regional environmental regime in Europe, for example, cannot be understood without reference to Europe's shared cultural heritage and historical experiences. Other regional regimes, such as the North American Agreement on Environmental Cooperation between Canada, Mexico, and the United States, cannot be explained by reference to similar factors and instead reflects power asymmetries and domestic political calculations. Similarly, multilateral efforts follow very different patterns. Some MEAs, such as the global agreement on persistent organic pollutants, build upon regional efforts, while others have no regional antecedents. Some multilateral efforts, such as those that address ozone depletion and biodiversity, represent dynamic and evolving regimes, while others, such as those that combat desertification, are virtually moribund. Finally, the motivations for some efforts to create more central-ized environmental governance have little to do with the environment. Most of the parties that negotiated the Convention on Long-Range Transboundary Air Pollution, for example, were much more interested in promoting East-West *détente* through cooperation on an issue area of little apparent importance than they were in eliminat-ing acid rain.

An ad hoc and fragmented system that relies upon historical accident, luck, and blunder to allocate environmental authority is unlikely to produce a sensible govern-ance system. In particular, it is likely to over-centralize governance authority in some cases and under-centralize it in others. Perhaps as a result, substantial scholarly and diplomatic energies have been devoted to developing more coherent, and principled, approaches to determining the appropriate level of environmental governance. The section that follows discusses the leading approaches to these debates.

3   NORMATIVE APPROACHES TO ENVIRONMENTAL GOVERNANCE

Despite the diversity of problems that have been presented, and the context-specific features that are critical to every effort to centralize governance, most scholarly efforts to address the levels of environmental governance issue cluster around a rela-tively small number of theories or approaches. For ease of exposition, I first outline the most influential arguments commonly offered in favour of less centralized envir-onmental governance. In the aggregate, these arguments constitute a background presumption against centralization. I then discuss the most important arguments offered in favour of more centralized environmental governance.

3.1 Presumption against Centralization

A variety of normative arguments are typically offered in support of less centralized forms of environmental governance. First, de-centralized authority structures permit regulation to better reflect geographical variations in preferences for collective goods such as environmental quality and localized knowledge about how best to produce those goods. In particular, as resource levels, background political and social con-ditions, policy priorities, risk tolerance, and assimilative capacity diverge across different parts of a state or the world, tailoring environmental standards to local cir-cumstances can increase aggregate social welfare. Second, non-centralized decision-making enables different jurisdictions to experiment with diverse policies and act as 'laboratories' for innovative regulatory approaches. De-centralization permits jurisdictions to try new policies and generate evidence about the effectiveness and administrative feasibility of alternative programmes. Other jurisdictions can then adopt, modify, or avoid these programmes. Third, not only do different jurisdictions experiment with different policy approaches, they also compete with one another for mobile firms. This inter-jurisdictional competition may encourage socially desirable levels of environmental protection in much the same way that competition among firms in private markets produces socially desirable levels of goods and services. Together with de-centralization and experimentation, competition among juris- dictions is thought to promote efficient and effective regulation. Finally, dispersal of regulatory authority is also said to promote 'self-determination' and political par- ticipation, since individuals can generally participate more easily and more meaning- fully in local governance processes. These normative arguments are said to have a special force in the environmental realm, as natural environmental conditions, pat- terns of resource use and economic development, and environmental values often vary widely across jurisdictions.

The factors supporting de-centralized environmental decision-making have both contributed to, and been reinforced by, background constitutional and legal norms in many political systems that favour the de-centralized exercise of regulatory author- ity. In many federal states, including Australia, Canada, Germany, Switzerland, and the United States, national constitutions provide that sub-national jurisdictions have authority over all matters not constitutionally delegated to the national government. In the EC, a similar presumption in favour of de-centralized authority finds expres- sion in the concept of 'subsidiarity' (see Chapter 37 'Regional Economic Integration Organizations'). The treaties creating the EC provide that under this principle, the Community shall act 'only if and in so far as the objectives of the proposed action cannot be sufficiently achieved by the Member States and can therefore, by reason of the scale or effects of the proposed action, be better achieved by the Community'. As a result of these and similar norms in other legal systems, many debates over the appropriate level of environmental governance take place against a strong back- ground presumption in favour of de-centralization.

3.2 Approaches that Favour Centralization

Scholars and advocates have developed a series of arguments designed to overcome the presumption against centralization, which I label the 'externality', 'game theory', 'regulatory competition', 'public choice', and 'polycentric governance' approaches. The general rhetorical structure of these arguments is to identify structural features of recurrent fact patterns that render de-centralized environmental governance insufficient and, therefore, by implication, more centralized governance desirable.

Many of the arguments in these approaches are informed by rational choice methodologies. Rational choice is an umbrella term that includes many approaches and theories. All assume that the actors engage in a purposive, means-end calculation to pursue their goals (see Chapter 10 'International Relations Theory' and Chapter 11 'Economic Theory of International Environmental Law'). As described later in this chapter, much of the rational choice-influenced literature attempts to 'match' the scope or level of regulatory authority with the scope or level of the underlying environmental problem. Hence, the focus is primarily on the 'vertical' dimensions of governance, and the central inquiry is whether environmental problems are best addressed through more centralized (say, international or national) or less centralized (say, national or provincial) governance mechanisms.

3.2.1 *Externalities*

The clearest justification for moving regulatory authority to a more centralized—that is, a hierarchically and vertically superior—level is found in the case of environmental 'externalities' or 'spillovers' that are generated in one jurisdiction but cause harm in another jurisdiction. The paradigmatic case involves pollution generated in jurisdiction A that travels downstream or downwind into jurisdiction B. Jurisdiction A may have little incentive to regulate the polluting activity as it enjoys the full benefits of the activity that causes the externality, and exports some or all of the resulting environmental harm. Jurisdiction B may have sufficient incentive to regulate, but lack the effective legal authority to regulate or enforce judgments against parties located in other jurisdictions. Environmental spillovers present a strong argument for moving environmental governance from a sub-national to a national level or from a national to a regional or an international level—the purpose of which is to attempt to match the scale of political governance to the physical scale of the externality.[1]

The presence of interjurisdictional externalities is the most commonly offered justification in both the academic literature and the political arena for vesting authority over environmental issues in a vertically superior body. Many federal environmental laws in the United States purport to address interstate externalities. Similarly, numerous regional and international efforts purport to address transboundary spillovers. A recent example is the Agreement on Transboundary Haze Pollution, which was entered into by the ten member states of the Association of Southeast Asian Nations (ASEAN) in response to the 1997–8 fires in Indonesia, which caused pollution and economic loss throughout the region. Moreover, concerns over spillovers have sometimes given rise to interesting bilateral or inter-regional governance structures involving commissions, task forces, or agencies. In the Upper Rhine Valley, for example, the Swiss cantons of Basel-Land and Basel-Stadt, the French department

---

[1] Similar arguments support more centralized governance in cases of shared resources, such as migratory birds, or where a resource, such as a river, forms a boundary between two jurisdictions.

Haut-Rhin, and the German district Basel-Stadt have developed a range of transnational structures that address a variety of environmental (and other) issues.

As a normative matter, the case of transboundary pollution presents a very strong argument for shifting regulatory authority to a more centralized level of governance. Surprisingly, however, despite broad general trends towards centralization in environmental governance—and the frequent invocation of transboundary harm to justify this trend—much transboundary pollution is still not the subject of centralized governance regimes. On the international plane, treaties, UN declarations, and other international instruments regularly proclaim states' responsibilities to ensure that activities within their jurisdiction or control do not cause damage to the environment of other states or to areas beyond the limits of national jurisdiction. However, despite the centrality of this principle (see Chapter 22 'Transboundary Impacts'), relatively little effective governance of transboundary pollution exists. For example, notwithstanding some notable exceptions,[2] most treaties that address transboundary pollution focus primarily upon information sharing and consultation rather than on the imposition of substantive limitations on transboundary pollution or creation of liability regimes for transboundary harm, for instance. In short, neither a comprehensive nor an effective transboundary pollution regime exists at the international level, and 'transboundary pollution seems much more the rule than the exception in interstate relations.'[3]

Similar patterns exist on the national level. In the United States, for example, major federal statutes such as the Clean Air Act and the Clean Water Act largely fail to address directly pollution between different states.[4] More specifically, neither statute's core provisions can be understood as an effort to control interstate pollution nor have the relatively small number of provisions directed at controlling interstate pollution been terribly effective.[5] Paradoxically, then, although we find much centralized environmental governance, it largely fails to address the circumstances that environmental governance theories identify as its strongest justification.

3.2.2 *Game Theoretic Approaches*

The literature on externalities introduced rational choice methodologies into environmental governance debates. The next key analytic move in the literature was to shift from an analysis of static environments, where actors simply respond to events,

---

[2] One important exception is the Convention on Long Range Transboundary Air Pollution, which is discussed in detail in Chapter 14 'Atmosphere and Outer Space' in this text.

[3] D. Bodansky, 'Customary (and Not So Customary) International Law' (1995) 3 Ind. J. Global Legal Stud. 105 at 110–11.

[4] This and the other generalizations in text necessarily paint with a very broad brush. As is generally true of generalizations, notable exceptions exist, including, in this instance, the US Clean Air Act's acid rain programme and ozone transport provisions.

[5] See, e.g., R.L. Revesz, 'Federalism and Interstate Environmental Externalities' (1996) 144 U. Pa. L. Rev. 2341.

to the study of strategic environments, where actors understand that the consequences of their actions depend, in part, on what other actors do. To do so, scholars employ 'game theory' and, in particular, an analysis of 'collective action' problems in order to generate a powerful set of counter-intuitive insights regarding how parties might predictably fail to act together to increase joint gains (see Chapter 11 'Economic Theory of International Environmental Law').

3.2.2.1 *Prisoner's Dilemma*

The Prisoner's Dilemma (PD) provides an important example of how individually rational behaviour can produce individually and collectively sub-optimal outcomes. In essence, this 'game' involves two prisoners accused of jointly committing a crime who have been arrested and are awaiting trial. The prisoners are separated and not permitted to communicate. The prosecutor presents each with the following terms: (1) if neither prisoner provides evidence to the prosecution, each will be convicted of a minor crime and spend a year in jail; (2) if one prisoner provides evidence and the other does not, the first prisoner will go free and his accomplice will receive a ten-year prison term; and (3) if both provide evidence, each will receive a five-year term. Given this incentive structure, each prisoner will quickly come to realize that, whether or not the other prisoner provides evidence, he is better off providing evidence (in game theoretic terms, 'defecting'). Yet this rational pursuit of individual self-interest will produce the sub-optimal result (from the prisoners' perspective) of both prisoners providing evidence and serving five-year terms.

The PD is thought to capture the complex and conflicting incentives that individuals and states often face. More specifically, these actors often face 'mixed motives', where each not only has an incentive to cooperate, but also incentives to defect or engage in opportunistic behaviour that negatively affects others. More importantly, the PD illustrates the frequent divergence between individual and collective rationality in situations marked by interdependence.[6] In these circumstances, shifting governance from the parties themselves to a more centralized level can provide a means for the enforcement of voluntary agreements between the parties through monitoring and compliance mechanisms.[7] More broadly, centralized governance structures in

---

[6] While the Prisoner's Dilemma (PD) is the game most commonly used in environmental governance debates, a variety of other games have also been invoked. See, e.g., S. Barrett, *Environment and Statecraft: Strategies of Environmental Treaty-Making* (Oxford: Oxford University Press, 2003). For current purposes, these variations among games change little in terms of the justifications for more centralized governance.

[7] Rational choice approaches suggest that several other potential solutions to the PD will not be effective. Permitting the prisoners to communicate is not effective because, absent binding commitments, there is no way to know whether promises to cooperate are simply intended to deceive others into cooperating while the promissor defects. Changing the game into a repeated (or 'iterated') game is often thought to sustain cooperation. However, this outcome is far from certain, particularly if the participants expect to play the game a finite number of times. If, for example, the players expected to play 20 times, it might seem advantageous for both players to forego short-term gains and cooperate. However, the

these circumstances can improve the quantity and quality of information available to the parties, provide a set of stable expectations, and minimize the transaction costs associated with monitoring behaviour and enforcement mechanisms. In these ways, greater centralization enables parties to restrain themselves (and others) from pursuing counter-productive actions, and enables actors to engage in cooperative behaviour that otherwise would not occur.

3.2.2.2 *Tragedy of the Commons*

The Tragedy of the Commons extends the structure and logic of the two-player PD to situations involving 'commons' resources and any number of actors. The 'tragedy' occurs when, as in the PD, individually rational decisions produce individually and collectively sub-optimal results. The paradigmatic example, popularized by Garret Hardin, involves herdsmen grazing cattle on an open pasture. Since each herdsman enjoys all of the benefits associated with adding an additional cow to the herd but internalizes only a fraction of the costs that the extra animal imposes upon the grazing lands, he has every incentive to increase the size of his herd. However, each herdsman faces the same incentive structure, hence, the tendency is to add too many cattle, eventually depleting the amount of grass available to the herd. The generalized idea is that when a resource is freely available to all, every actor has an incentive to maximize consumption of the resource, and no actor has an incentive to invest in the resource, even though the ultimate result may be the destruction of the resource itself. As Hardin explains:

> Therein is the tragedy. Each man is locked into a system that compels him to increase his [consumption] without limit—in a world that is limited. Ruin is the destination toward which all men rush, each pursuing his own best interest in a society that believes in the freedom of the commons. Freedom in a commons brings ruin to all.[8]

Hardin's arguments have served as the starting point for much subsequent analysis of commons problems. It, and the PD, are commonly thought to illustrate how self-interested actors left to their own devices will frequently generate individually and collectively sub-optimal outcomes. Yet there is also a second important message. While certain resource allocations seem likely to induce tragic outcomes, tragedy is not the inevitable result. Rather, a move to more centralized forms of governance can avert these tragic tendencies. A number of potential solutions have been described, including privatization, taxes, subsidies, regulation, unified management, and auctions.[9] In fact, virtually all of the solutions involve some vertically superior form of

dominant strategy in the last round of the game would still be to defect. Knowing this, each player assumes defection in the final round of the game and reasons that he or she will benefit from defection in the second-to-last round of the game. This process of 'backward induction' may eventually lead players to choose defection as a dominant strategy in each round of the game.

[8] G. Hardin, 'The Tragedy of the Commons' (1968) 162 Science 1243.

[9] Some solutions will not be appropriate for certain resources—for example, one cannot privatize the atmosphere—and solutions will be more difficult in some political contexts than others (that is, efforts

governance authority that imposes restraints on the use of the commons resource.[10] We can understand international agreements on the marine environment, Antarctica, outer space, and the atmosphere as efforts to create more centralized governance structures for commons areas and to avoid potentially devastating tragedies of the commons (see Chapter 23 'Common Areas, Common Heritage, and Common Concern').

3.2.3 *Regulatory Competition*

The arguments reviewed earlier in this chapter typically focus on the physical scale of the environmental problem. There is an alternative approach that applies similar logic but focuses on the scale of economic interactions among relevant actors. This alternative approach highlights the possibility of regulatory competition among jurisdictions, often characterized as a 'race to the bottom' (RTB).

RTB arguments most commonly appear in the context of economic liberalization or integration efforts, and the most common version of this argument rests on the claim that differences in environmental standards can distort economic competition. Specifically, firms operating in low-standard jurisdictions will, other things being equal, enjoy a competitive advantage over firms operating in jurisdictions with more rigorous environmental standards. As a result, firms in low standard jurisdictions will enjoy increased sales, market share, and profitability, with corresponding losses to firms in high-standard jurisdictions. High-standard jurisdictions thus confront the prospect of declining tax revenues, job loss, and, eventually, industrial relocation to low-standard jurisdictions.

Of course, high-standard jurisdictions facing these prospects will be tempted to lower environmental standards (or, at least, relax the enforcement of environmental norms) from the levels they would otherwise choose. However, if a high-standard jurisdiction relaxes its environmental standards, low-standard jurisdictions will then have an incentive to lower their standards even more to recapture economic advantage. These acts, in turn, may prompt additional reductions in standards. The resulting dynamic is characterized as a 'race to the bottom'.

One way to address the pressures prompting this 'race' is for high-standard jurisdictions to use tariffs, quotas, subsidies, and other trade policy instruments to eliminate the market advantage that products from low-standard jurisdictions would otherwise enjoy. However, these types of trade measures may violate economic integration and trade liberalization agreements (see Chapter 7 'Relationship between

---

to address international commons areas, such as the high seas, will in general be more difficult to address than national commons areas).

[10] Scholars have also identified informal structures that mimic more formal governance regimes. See, e.g., R.C. Ellickson, *Order without Law: How Neighbors Settle Disputes* (Cambridge, MA: Harvard University Press, 1991); and E. Ullman-Margalit, *Emergence of Norms* (Oxford: Clarendon Press, 1977).

International Environmental Law and Other Branches of International Law'). Moreover, the use of environmental subsidies or other trade measures may spark similar measures from other jurisdictions, thereby triggering yet another form of regulatory competition.

A more common response to the competitiveness concerns sparked by differential environmental standards is the harmonization of standards.[11] Harmonization can take different forms. Sometimes harmonized standards establish minimum environmental norms that lower-level jurisdictions are free to surpass, while, at other times, harmonized standards are intended to serve as ceilings.[12] Moreover, some harmonization schemes address product standards, while others address production processes or methods. However, in most instances, harmonized environmental standards are associated with the creation of a more centralized authority in national or supranational rules and bodies. Thus, federal states such as the United States and regional entities such as the European Community have employed a variety of harmonization strategies in response to competitiveness concerns. On the international front, harmonization often occurs through MEAs that set out standards for all parties to meet.

Centrally set harmonized standards need not be implemented in a uniform manner in all jurisdictions—for example, the US Clean Air Act permits states to use differentiated standards; the EU's 'new approach' to harmonization grants considerable flexibility to member states with respect to the means of implementation; and MEAs such as the Montreal Protocol on Substances That Deplete the Ozone Layer provide for differential timetables for developed and developing states.[13] Yet, whether or not differentiated standards are used, moves towards harmonization through the centralization of governance are designed to ensure that wide variations in levels of

---

For more on the use of formal and informal norms as governance tools, see Chapter 6 'Formality and Informality' in this text.

[11] The argument in the text describes why high-standard jurisdictions might seek harmonization. Low-standard jurisdictions who fear that high environmental standards can act as unjustified barriers to the free movement of goods might also seek harmonized standards. Moreover, private actors doing business across jurisdictions might also seek harmonized standards, to address concerns that different standards in different jurisdictions can fragment markets and frustrate economies of scale. Of course, agreement among different actors on harmonization as a strategy to address competitiveness concerns does not suggest that these actors would necessarily agree on how stringent or lax these standards should be.

[12] And sometimes centralized governance generates both floors and ceilings. In the EU, for example, minimum harmonization measures establish floors below which no member state may fall. Member states may enact stricter measures—so long as they are consistent with the EC Treaty, including provisions on the free movement of goods. Thus, the harmonization measure constitutes the floor, and the treaty the ceiling. A similar dynamic can be found in federal states such as the United States. Some federal environmental legislation permits states to enact more stringent standards, subject to the limitations imposed by the US constitution, particularly the commerce clause.

[13] MEAs also use other tools to address competitiveness concerns, including carefully designed entry into force clauses. The Kyoto Protocol, for example, came into force only after 55 parties ratified, representing at least 55 per cent of total carbon dioxide emissions for 1990 of industrialized state parties.

environmental regulation are reduced over time, thereby obviating the pressures thought to trigger regulatory competition.

RTB arguments are politically potent. Perhaps as a result, they have come under sharp challenge on both normative and positive grounds. As a normative matter, the RTB argument that competition among jurisdictions will produce sub-optimal levels of environmental regulation is countered by those who argue that competition among jurisdictions for mobile firms will produce socially desirable levels of environmental protection in much the same way that competition in private markets generates socially optimal levels of goods and services. A large and rich literature addresses whether competition among jurisdictions produces sub-optimal or socially beneficial outcomes.[14]

Critics also claim that there is little empirical support for the RTB. They point out that states within the United States with stronger environmental policies have generally not experienced slower rates of economic growth or development than low-standard states. Similarly, on the international plane, states with higher standards have generally not suffered economically. Finally, critics argue that, notwithstanding increased economic integration among states with widely divergent environmental regimes, there is little empirical evidence that firms relocate to other jurisdictions to take advantage of lower environmental regulations.[15]

Experience suggests that competitiveness arguments are sometimes successfully deployed to block the adoption of new environmental regulations. For example, an energy tax proposed by President Bill Clinton floundered in the face of concerns over competitive disadvantage, and similar carbon taxes proposed in Australia and the EU were rejected due largely to competitiveness concerns. On the other hand, there is some evidence that processes triggered by economic integration can sometimes lead to more concentration of environmental governance and higher standards. For example, one of the motivations for providing the European Community with competence over environmental matters was the fear by some high-standard states, notably Germany and the Netherlands, that they would suffer a competitive disadvantage vis-à-vis low-standard states. More recently, the political dynamic generated by negotiations to increase economic integration has often created the political space for high-standard jurisdictions to pressure low-standard jurisdictions to raise environmental standards. Changes in Mexico during the negotiations of the North

Similarly, the Montreal Protocol required that 11 countries, together accounting for at least two-thirds of the 1986 level of global consumption of controlled substances, ratify prior to entry into force.

[14] See, e.g., D.C. Esty and D. Geradin, eds., *Regulatory Competition and Economic Integration: Comparative Perspectives* (Oxford: Oxford University Press, 2001); J. Bhagwati and R.E. Hudec, eds., *Fair Trade and Harmonization: Prerequisites for Free Trade?* (Cambridge, MA: MIT Press, 1996).

[15] For a review of the empirical literature on firm relocation, see Organization for Economic Co-operation and Development, *Environmental Issues in Policy-Based Competition for Investment: A Literature Review*, Doc. ENV/EPOC/GSP(2001)11/Final (4 April 2002). For a discussion of the difficulties in conducting empirical research into the impact of environmental policy on firm relocation, see J. Clapp, 'Foreign Direct Investment in Hazardous Industries in Developing Countries: Rethinking the Debate' (1998) 7 Envt'l Pol'y 92.

American Free Trade Agreement and in Turkey as it attempts to advance its efforts to join the EU are examples of this phenomenon. In each case, higher-standard states used the leverage of enhanced market access to bring pressure on lower-standard states to strengthen environmental protections, in part to reassure domestic constituencies otherwise threatened by closer economic integration. Ironically, then, environmental advocates have in some cases skilfully used concerns over the lowering of environmental standards to generate pressures that actually strengthen environmental protections.

3.2.4 *Public Choice*

'Public choice' arguments are sometimes used to justify more centralized forms of environmental governance. Public choice approaches apply the tools of economic analysis to political processes, and treat the law-making process as a microeconomic system that produces laws in response to pressures of supply and demand. In the environmental context, public choice analysis begins with the observation that the costs of environmental regulation are generally more concentrated and tangible than the benefits. In particular, costs are often borne by well-organized and easy-to-identify firms and sectors. The countervailing interest in environmental quality is shared by individuals whose personal stake is small and who face formidable difficulties in organizing for collective action. As a result, interests opposing environmental regulation have greater incentive and ability to organize than do those favouring environmental quality and generally have more effective representation before administrative and legislative bodies.

The public choice argument for greater centralization in environmental governance rests upon the claim that '[t]he comparative disadvantage of environmental groups will often be reduced . . . if policy decisions are made at [more centralized] level[s].'[16] Environmental interests can exert more leverage by organizing into one or a few units at a centralized level, as opposed to multiple units in multiple jurisdictions. Even if industrialized interests enjoy similar scale economies for industrial interests, these are likely to be less significant, particularly if the industrial interests are already national in scope. Moreover, 'effective representation may be less a function of comparative resources than of attainment of a critical mass of skills, resources, and experience . . . [A more centralized] forum for decision may greatly lessen the barriers to environmental interests' achievement of organizational critical mass, sharply reducing the disparity in effective representation.'[17]

As a positive matter, it is surely the case that more centralized governance is sometimes more protective of environmental values than less centralized governance.

---

[16] An early and influential statement of this claim is found in R.B. Stewart, 'Pyramids of Sacrifice? Problems of Federalism in Mandating State Implementation of National Environmental Policy' (1977) 86 Yale L.J. 1196.   [17] *Ibid.* at 1214.

Casual empiricism suggests, however, that significant counter-examples exist, including examples where regulated firms advocate for uniform national standards to avoid stronger local standards[18] and examples where de-centralized jurisdictions are more aggressive than more centralized jurisdictions in addressing environmental problems.[19] Perhaps because of this mixed empirical record, the salience of public choice arguments seems to ebb and flow over time,[20] and the arguments are not, at present, prominent in the environmental governance literature.

3.2.5 *Polycentric Governance: Multi-Level and Multi-Regime Models of Environmental Governance*

One final dimension of the environmental governance literature deserves mention. A primarily descriptive component of environmental governance scholarship is less concerned with identifying *the* appropriate level of environmental governance than with describing and analysing the *multiple* sources and levels of governance for environmental problems. This scholarship thus emphasizes the *polycentric* nature of much contemporary environmental governance.[21]

Much of the polycentric governance scholarship has focused on the vertical dimension of 'multilevel governance', which is seen within the United States and the EU as well as internationally. This scholarship has explored, for example, the promise and problems associated with the United States's use of 'cooperative federalism', where federally set standards are implemented by state authorities as a model of environmental governance. Other times, this scholarship highlights the horizontal dimensions of polycentric governance, such as when several partially overlapping regimes govern a particular subject area with no agreed upon hierarchy among them. Examples of such 'regime complexes'[22] include forests, which are addressed by the Food and Agriculture Organization's (FAO) Committee on Forestry in Rome, the International Tropical Timber Organization in Yokohama, and the UN Forum on Forests in New York; and plant genetic resources, which are addressed in the International Convention for the Protection of New Varieties of Plants, the Convention on Biological Diversity, the Consultative Group on International

---

[18] E.D. Elliott, B.A. Ackerman, and J.C. Millian, 'Toward a Theory of Statutory Evolution: The Federalization of Environmental Law' (1985) 1 J.L. Econ. & Org. 313.

[19] An important example is in the area of climate change, where many US states have been more aggressive then the federal government in addressing climate change.

[20] Public choice arguments were prominent in environmental discourse in the United States in the 1970s and then again in the mid and late 1990s. Public choice arguments have been less prominent in the EU and the multilateral contexts.

[21] In a sense, the approaches surveyed earlier in this chapter implicitly assume polycentric governance as norms adopted at more centralized levels frequently need to be adopted and implemented by less centralized jurisdictions.

[22] This term is borrowed from K. Raustiala and D.G. Victor, 'The Regime Complex for Plant Genetic Resources' (2004) 56 Int'l Org. 277.

Agriculture Research, the World Trade Organization (WTO) Agreement on Trade-Related Aspects of Intellectual Property Rights, and the FAO.

Significantly, the polycentric governance scholarship reveals wide divergences in the levels of integration and coordination within different governance regimes. For example, in some areas of international environmental governance, regional efforts are closely and, in some cases, systematically linked to global conventions and agreements and are useful in supporting the implementation of global instruments. The regional seas conventions and the Global Programme of Action for the Protection of the Marine Environment from Land-based Activities illustrate this phenomenon. Similarly, the provisions in regional seas conventions on pollution from oil and other harmful substances and on dumping are operationally linked to the International Maritime Organization's marine pollution conventions in these areas, and the various independent regional treaties and memoranda of understanding negotiated under the auspices of the Convention on the Conservation of Migratory Species of Wild Animals are the primary mechanisms for achieving the goals of the parent convention. In these contexts, the regional and global treaties form a tightly woven 'global mosaic' for addressing environmental issues. Yet this sort of close integration among clusters of treaties addressing similar or related topics is more the exception than the rule. The regional fisheries conventions, for example, all address similar issues but lack the programmatic and institutional relationships that mark the regional seas conventions and action plans.

The polycentric governance scholarship raises important questions about the appropriate level of integration and coordination in both specific issue areas and the entirety of global environmental governance. The centrality of these questions is underscored by the diplomatic attention recently given to the policy gaps, incoherent decision-making structures, and lack of meaningful coordination resulting from the current fragmented, polycentric structure of global environmental governance. Moreover, international organizations and states increasingly emphasize that the sheer proliferation of institutions, issues, and agreements places serious stress on the system, ranging from the inability of parties to participate meaningfully in all of these activities given limited resources and capacities to the inability of a highly fragmented system to address issues in a comprehensive manner.

At least implicitly, then, one implication of polycentric governance scholarship is the need for more coherent and integrated approaches that can generate coordination and synergies among the various entities involved—in other words, for greater centralization. This type of centralization could take various forms, which range from sectoral clustering among activities of different governance systems, for example, with regard to the atmosphere or chemicals and wastes, to the upgrading of the UN Environment Programme (UNEP) or the UN Governing Council/Global Ministerial Environment Forum, to the creation of a new World Environment Organization (WEO). Indeed, renewed debate over the desirability of establishing a WEO[23] reflects, in part, a reaction to the lack of coherence and coordination highlighted in the polycentric governance scholarship (see Chapter 32 'International Institutions').

4 ADVANCING DEBATES OVER ENVIRONMENTAL GOVERNANCE

The 'externality', 'game theory', 'regulatory competition', 'public choice', and 'polycentric governance' approaches outlined earlier have framed much of the discourse over the appropriate level of environmental governance. However, in many respects, environmental governance debates have reached an impasse—many of the arguments for or against centralization have generated well-founded critiques or counterarguments. The section that follows outlines some analytic moves that can supplement conventional approaches, and shed additional light on debates over levels of environmental governance.

4.1 Comparative Institutional Analysis

Most of the approaches surveyed earlier in this chapter generally engage in single institution analysis. Thus, the analysis focuses on one level of environmental governance and identifies certain 'failures' associated with this level. For example, de-centralized governance 'fails' when sub-national jurisdictions generate pollution spillovers, engage in a race to the bottom, or confront a prisoner's dilemma. After identifying the failure at one level, conventional analysis concludes that the solution involves governance at a more centralized level. Hence, conventional analysis teaches, for example, that spillovers and regulatory competition among sub-national jurisdictions necessitates national level governance, and prisoner's dilemmas among countries justify the creation of regional or multilateral regimes.

However, this form of analysis is unconvincing unless it examines whether the alternative level of governance is subject to failures of its own, which may be as great as or greater than the failures of the original level of governance.[24] Thus, for example,

---

[23] For a sense of the debate, see generally F. Biermann and S. Bauer, eds., *A World Environmental Organization: Solution or Threat for Effective Environmental Governance?* (Aldershot: Ashgate, 2005); S. Charnovitz, 'A World Environmental Organization' (2002) 27 Colum. J. Envt'l L. 3232; and K. von Moltke, 'The Organization of the Impossible' (2001) 1 Glob. Envt'l Pol. 23.

[24] The leading work developing this argument is N.K. Komesar, *Imperfect Alternatives: Choosing Institutions in Law, Economics, and Public Policy* (Chicago: University of Chicago Press, 1994).

a national legislature or international body may be subject to capture by special interests, and generate a regulatory solution worse than the conditions produced by subnational or national jurisdictions. The call for comparative analysis is, of course, not new. In fact, environmental scholarship has generated important insights through comparative analysis of the efficacy of different regulatory tools (see Chapter 8 'Instrument Choice'). Yet most environmental scholarship to date has not made the analytic and conceptual shift from comparing the efficacy of various *regulatory mechanisms* to comparing the efficacy of various *levels of governance*.[25] Moreover, to the extent that scholars have engaged in comparative institutional analysis, they have tended to focus primarily upon comparisons among governance mechanisms located on the same horizontal plane. In other words, they compare the relative strengths of, say, domestic legislatures and courts to address an issue, or whether a proposed WEO would be more or less effective than an enhanced UNEP. But most environmental governance scholarship has not, to date, engaged in a comparative analysis of governance mechanisms on different vertical planes, such as a comparison of regional versus national governance.

The prevalent use of single institution analysis ignores the insight that all governance structures are subject to one or more 'failures'. For current purposes, the question is not whether one level of environmental governance will fail in a particular instance, but whether a proposed alternative level of governance can perform better. Environmental governance scholarship would benefit immensely from engaging in this comparative inquiry.

4.2 Explaining the Incidence, Stringency, and Evolution of Environmental Governance

The approaches outlined in the section above purport to identify the circumstances in which the greater centralization of environmental governance is most appropriate. However, the approaches say little about the incidence, stringency, or effectiveness of more centralized governance. Consider, again, the problem of transboundary externalities. As noted earlier, inter-jurisdictional spillovers present a very strong case for shifting regulatory authority to a more centralized level of governance, yet relatively little meaningful regulation of transboundary pollution actually exists. Similarly, some situations involving game theoretic collective action problems have given rise to more centralized regimes, while others have not.

The inability to predict the incidence of more centralized environmental governance is a serious limitation in conventional approaches to environmental governance. Again, however, it is possible to extend conventional approaches. Why, for

---

[25] For a notable exception, see D.C. Esty, 'Toward Optimal Environmental Governance' (1999) 74 N.Y.U. L. Rev. 1495.

example, should there be relatively little centralized governance of transboundary pollution on the international plane? We might supplement conventional accounts by noting that in many transboundary contexts, the costs and benefits of the polluting activity, and the regulation of that activity, are strongly asymmetrical between source and victim jurisdictions. This asymmetrical distribution of costs and benefits means that a source state has little incentive to agree to more centralized governance structures.[26] Unless some form of compensation is offered, the source state (or, in the multilateral context, unless the treaty imposes non-uniform obligations), it is difficult to see how more centralized regimes will arise—unless, of course, these more centralized structures impose little by way of meaningful substantive obligations. Thus, by incorporating distributional concerns, scholars can begin to generate richer theories about the incidence of more centralized environmental governance.[27]

The analysis can be extended to generate insights about the stringency of more centralized environmental regimes. For example, at least some, and perhaps most, transboundary pollution impacts the source state before it crosses into another jurisdiction. To the extent that a source jurisdiction suffers harm, it has an incentive to regulate the polluting activity to protect its constituents, with indirect benefits to the neighbouring jurisdiction.[28] These internal regulations can then serve as a basis for more centralized governance regimes. A good example is the 1991 United States–Canada agreement on acid rain, which was reached only after many years of contentious debate between the two states. This agreement commits both states to caps on sulphur and nitrogen oxide emissions. However, the agreement only obligates the United States to emissions reductions that had already been legislated in 1990 amendments to the US Clean Air Act. Canada likewise had already assumed, through domestic law, many of the emissions reductions contained in the bilateral agreement. Thus, in this agreement, the parties

[26] Alternatively stated, we might expect to see a higher incidence of centralized governance where inter-jurisdictional pollution runs in both directions than where it runs primarily in one direction.

[27] Similar observations about the gains to be achieved by factoring distributional considerations into the analysis are relevant to the standard form PD and Tragedy of the Commons analysis discussed earlier in this chapter. As a general matter, the explanatory and predictive powers of these game theoretic models depend on the 'payoff matrix'—the costs and benefits that actors receive from cooperation or defection. Yet these payoffs are virtually always endogenous to the models. In other words, they are simply assumed, and conventional game theoretic models shed no light on how net benefits from cooperation are distributed among various actors. Moreover—and even more unrealistically—game theoretic models frequently assume that the payoffs that actors enjoy from collaboration are symmetric (that is, by confessing, both prisoners receive five years in jail; if neither had confessed, they each would have served only one year). However, real world states are rarely similarly situated, national interests are typically asymmetrical, and disagreements over the distribution of the benefits of cooperation are central to real world environmental impasses. This suggests that fact patterns viewed as PDs or tragedies of the commons are frequently dominated by distributional issues. Standard renditions of the PD and tragedy of the commons, which take payoff structures as given and unalterable, obscure this dynamic driver of much environmental politics.

[28] For a fuller elaboration of this argument, see T. Merrill, 'Golden Rules for Transboundary Pollution' (1997) 46 Duke L.J. 931.

promised to do little beyond what they had already decided to do as a matter of domestic environmental governance.

These examples are intended to illustrate some of the ways that standard arguments about environmental governance are underdeveloped, and to suggest the sorts of analytic moves that can be used to extend the analysis. A progressive research agenda would build upon these suggestions, and extend standard approaches to explore the incidence, stringency, effectiveness, and evolution of more centralized systems of environmental governance.

4.3 Disaggregating Environmental Governance

Most of the approaches surveyed earlier in this chapter take the level of environmental governance as an all-or-nothing proposition. The arguments suggest that environmental governance should occur at this or that level of governance. Yet environmental governance encompasses a wide variety of tasks and activities. Disaggregating governance into its component parts can generate more nuanced approaches to debates over appropriate levels of governance. For example, contemporary environmental governance relies critically upon the collection and interpretation of scientific information, including problem identification, data collection, epidemiological and ecological analysis, harm valuation, quantitative risk assessments, and the like. As these and related tasks require significant amounts of technical expertise and exhibit significant scale economies, a strong argument for centralization exists. Moreover, centralization of scientific and technical tasks can change the underlying political dynamics of environmental governance debates. To the extent that political conflict over the need for more centralized regimes rests upon disagreement over empirical data or the causal mechanisms driving environmental change, as illustrated by the acid rain and ozone contexts, centralized scientific processes can generate credible information that enables relevant actors to better understand and pursue their interests.

On the other hand, other governance tasks, such as implementation and enforcement, often rely upon highly localized information. In practice, even in relatively highly centralized national systems, many governance functions are delegated to sub-national actors. For example, in the United States, the federal Environmental Protection Agency has delegated or authorized primary responsibility to states for implementing many day-to-day programmatic activities, such as issuing permits, conducting compliance programs, and monitoring environmental conditions. Similarly in the EU, such responsibilities rest with the member states.

Thus, disaggregating the various component elements of environmental governance can help advance debates over levels of governance. Some issues will turn on highly localized information and should in general be de-centralized, while others may benefit from significant economies of scale and should typically occur at more centralized levels.

4.4 The Elusive Quest for Optimality: The Limits of Environmental Governance Debates

The arguments outlined in this section are intended to suggest ways to enrich conventional debates over environmental governance. However, they are not intended to suggest that conventional approaches can answer all governance questions. Indeed, debates over levels of governance often implicate much deeper questions about the nature and purpose of environmental governance. Consider, one last time, the arguments for more centralized governance to address transboundary spillovers. While there is little disagreement that spillovers justify some centralization of regulatory authority, there is much controversy over what constitutes a relevant spillover. In particular, there is significant debate over whether 'psychic' or 'psychological' spillovers justify greater centralization of environmental governance. For example, if a large number of citizens in EU member states were appalled by bullfighting in Spain, but suffered no economic or physical harm as a result of this activity, would such psychological spillovers justify legislation at the EU level?

Proponents of recognizing the relevance of psychological spillovers argue that environmental resources have both 'use' and 'non-use' values, and that individuals may derive utility from the avoidance of environmental harm even if they are not physically or economically affected by that harm. More broadly, if public policy, including environmental policy, is intended to maximize collective preferences or social utility, then it should take this form of environmental preference 'seriously'.[29] Opponents counter that under this argument the local residents in target jurisdictions would unfairly bear the costs of satisfying the preferences of citizens of other jurisdictions. And even if, say, developed state citizens were willing to pay the economic costs of saving the African elephant or Brazil's rainforest, citizens in source states might legitimately object that their national environmental policies need not attempt to maximize the preferences of citizens from other states.[30]

We can understand the debate over psychic spillovers as an instantiation of the debate that the levels of governance debate attempt to resolve: the identification of the appropriate jurisdiction (and, hence, political community) to govern any particular resource. Whether, and when, an individual or political community has a

[29] W.P.J. Wils, 'Subsidiarity and EC Environmental Policy: Taking People's Concerns Seriously' (1994) 6 J. Envt'l L. 85 at 89.

[30] One concrete example of this sort of dynamic is found in the biodiversity context. Genetic resources were traditionally regarded as part of the 'common heritage of mankind.' However, developing states objected to early drafts of the Convention on Biological Diversity, which identified genetic resources as the 'common heritage of mankind.' The treaty itself rejects the 'common heritage' concept. Instead, preambular language in the treaty refers to genetic resources as the 'common concern' of mankind, and the treaty asserts sovereign rights over genetic resources. The recent International Treaty on Plant Genetic Resources for Food and Agriculture likewise abandons the 'common heritage of mankind' language in the context of plant genetic resources.

legitimate interest in an environmental resource or problem is a critical inquiry that bedevils national, regional, and global efforts at environmental governance. It recurs in contexts as diverse as US courts trying to determine whether a US citizen has 'standing' to file a lawsuit to protect elephants and species in Sri Lanka; European tribunals trying to determine whether the Dutch government can lawfully prosecute a local delicatessen owner for selling wild birds killed lawfully in the United Kingdom; and the WTO's Appellate Body trying to determine whether the United States has a legitimate interest in restricting the import of shrimp caught by Thai and Malaysian shrimpers in their local waters in ways that harm endangered migratory sea turtles.[31] As these disputes indicate, there can be little doubt that many individuals and jurisdictions treat environmental concerns as transcending individual or local interest, and as not being limited by physical and economic harms. Whether and when the law should recognize these concerns remains a critical and highly contested question.

The approaches to environmental governance surveyed earlier provide no satisfying formula or metric to resolve these sorts of questions. Rather, the question of whether the law respects these psychological preferences involves a complex cluster of historical, cultural, and political contingencies. The legal recognition of these preferences will reflect, in part, evolving conceptions of human and ecological interdependence as well as the various and shifting ways that individuals sort out the relative importance of their membership in multiple communities—many of which transcend political boundaries.

5 Conclusion

Despite the volume and sophistication of the levels of environmental governance literature, it would be a mistake to view any of the standard arguments in this literature as presenting an algorithm capable of determining with precision the appropriate level of environmental governance in any particular instance. Moreover, there is little reason to believe that what constitutes an 'optimal' environmental governance structure at one time will be optimal for all times. Circumstances change. As major sources of pollution and waste are addressed, new production and consumption patterns generate unexpected problems; novel technologies render one or another regulatory approach more effective; and governance structures that successfully addressed past problems may not be well-suited to new economic and social realities.

---

[31] See, e.g., *Lujan v. Defenders of Wildlife*, 504 U.S. 555, 112 S. Ct. 2130 (1992); Case C-169/89 *Criminal Proceedings against Gourmetterie Van den Burg*, [1990] E.C.R. I-2143; *United States–Import Prohibition on Certain Shrimp and Shrimp Products*, Appellate Body Report, Doc. WT/DS58/AB/R (6 November 1998).

Nonetheless, scholarship addressing environmental governance can deepen our understanding, and provide reasons to believe that one or another level of governance is more or less likely to be appropriate. More importantly, debates over governance properly focus our attention on the central issues underlying environmental law and policy. Choices among alternative levels of governance will often determine what environmental policy is pursued. Thus, decisions about governance can mark the difference between environmental improvement or harm and between success and failure in managing ecosystems and natural resources.

Recommended Reading

S. Barrett, *Environment and Statecraft: Strategies of Environmental Treaty-Making* (Oxford: Oxford University Press, 2003).

E.D. Elliott, B.A. Ackerman, and J.C. Millian, 'Toward a Theory of Statutory Evolution: The Federalization of Environmental Law' (1985) 1 J. L. Econ. & Org. 313.

D.C. Esty, 'Toward Optimal Environmental Governance' (1999) 74 N.Y.U. L. Rev. 1495.

—— and D. Geradin, eds., *Regulatory Competition and Economic Integration: Comparative Perspectives* (Oxford: Oxford University Press, 2001).

G. Hardin, *The Tragedy of the Commons* (1968) 162 Science 1243.

T. Merrill, 'Golden Rules for Transboundary Pollution' (1997) 46 Duke L.J. 931.

R.L. Revesz, 'Federalism and Interstate Environmental Externalities' (1996) 144 U. Pa. L. Rev. 2341.

——, P. Sands, and R.B. Stewart, eds., *Environmental Law, the Economy and Sustainable Development: The United States, the European Union and the International Community* (Cambridge: Cambridge University Press, 2000).

R.B. Stewart, 'Pyramids of Sacrifice? Problems of Federalism in Mandating State Implementation of National Environmental Policy' (1977) 86 Yale L.J. 1196.

D. Vogel, *Trading Up: Consumer and Environmental Regulation in a Global Economy* (Cambridge, MA: Harvard University Press, 1995).

CHAPTER 6

FORMALITY AND INFORMALITY

STEPHEN J. TOOPE

THIS chapter explores contested terrain in the no-man's land between international law and politics—the work of 'norms' in social, including legal, change. International environmental law has served as the crucible for much of the theoretical debate, and a central focus of this debate has been on the effectiveness of various types of formal and informal norms. The category of 'norm' is inclusive and general. A norm may be vague or specific—it may mean a widespread social practice, a social prescription, a legal principle articulated to shape the evolution of a regime, or a precise legal rule. The common core of the concept of 'norm' is that the desideratum contained in the norm is intended to influence human conduct. Note the word 'influence': norms do not necessarily determine human action.[1] They help to shape behaviour, but they rarely if ever dictate it. Since norms operate in many different ways, they relate to the concepts of formality and informality differentially as well. Norms can be formal rules of law, but they can also be informal social guides to proper conduct. More surprisingly, as we will see, norms can be informal and precise as well as informal and vague; formal and precise as well as formal and vague. The key point, as Friedrich Kratochwil has argued so persuasively, is that 'formality' is not an appropriate test for the existence or non-existence of law.[2]

In legal discourse, 'formal' has varied and sometimes conflicting meanings. The concept of the 'formal' may be related to the employment of specific forms. 'Form'

[1] See, e.g., F. Kratochwil, *Rules, Norms, and Decisions: On the Conditions of Practical and Legal Reasoning in International Relations and Domestic Affairs* (Cambridge: Cambridge University Press, 1989).　　　　　　　　　　　　　　　　　　　　　　[2] *Ibid.* at 200–1.

itself has various denotations. It is sometimes linked to process and procedure, as in discussions of writs of action in the common law. 'Form' is also used in counterpoint to substance, as in debates over whether it matters what legal instrument is employed to pursue a policy agenda, be it legislation, regulation, contract, interpretative statement, or negotiated implementing arrangements. 'Formal' law is also used as a term of art to mean law that is created using precise constitutional processes—here, the concept links to discussions of sources in international law and to positivist understandings of law generally. In a related usage, 'formal' is a term employed to describe law that is 'hard' and to distinguish it from norms that are not produced through specified sources or processes. In the international milieu, this use of 'formal' extends one step further to describe the distinction between law and non-law or between legal 'rule' and social 'norm'. Formal law is that which fits within the categories contained in Article 38 of the Statute of the International Court of Justice. Other possible norms, however influential, are 'informal' or 'soft'. 'Hard' law is commonly assumed to be more precise than 'soft' law and is often linked to processes of adjudication. In this combined substantive and institutional sense, it is said to be more 'formal' as well. Although all of these invocations of the concept of formality will find expression in this chapter, the principal focus will be upon the ways in which international environmental law undermines the common assumption that 'hard' law is inevitably more effective than 'soft' law.

It is difficult even to categorize certain rules as formal or informal. This measure, like law itself, seems to exist on a continuum. Even theorists who describe themselves as formalist do not agree on what the nomenclature means. Larry Alexander's version of formalism is based upon the assumption that adherence to a norm's prescription ('compliance' in the contemporary international law terminology) does not depend upon the congruence of the norm with its background reasons. In other words, a norm is formal when we refuse to look behind it at all—it might or might not serve the reasons for its enunciation, but we will still comply.[3] Another way of phrasing the same point is that the category of 'formal legal norm' may be conflated with the category of 'binding rule'. On this view, the binding quality of the rule is based in the formality of its production and not in any substantive justification. It is this pure formalism—this refusal of any need to justify the norm—that Alexander uses to distinguish law from other forms of normativity, such as morality. For Alexander a 'serious rule' will be determinate, a 'factual predicate or hypothesis and a prescription'.[4]

Determinateness can arise only in communities where a social fact of agreement on terms exists. Members of a given community do not need to be correct about the meaning of the terms incorporated in a rule—the meanings need only be consistent with each other. This version of formalism would appear to lack robust explanatory

---

[3] L. Alexander, ' "With Me, It's All er Nuthin": Formalism in Law and Morality' (1999) 66 Univ. Chi. L. Rev. 530 at 531.   [4] Ibid. at 541 and 544.

power in an international setting where the notion of community is so weak that one cannot presume deeply shared meanings that can give rise to determinate rules. The common complaint about international environmental law 'principles' such as sustainable development (see Chapter 26 'Sustainable Development') or precaution (see Chapter 25 'Precaution')—that they are often woolly, vague, or obtuse—is a manifestation of this situation. However, if we accept that such principles do have influence, this influence cannot be explained by Alexander's version of formal law.

Somewhat more promising is Ernest Weinrib's conception of formalism, which 'postulates that law is intelligible as an internally coherent phenomenon'.[5] In complete opposition to Alexander, Weinrib suggests that formalism is a theory of legal justification:

> As a theory of *justification*, formalism considers law to be not merely a collection of posited norms or an exercise of official power, but a social arrangement responsive to moral argument. As a theory of *legal* justification, formalism focuses on the phenomena most expressive of the juridical aspect of our social lives: on interactions between parties who regard their interests as separate, and on the role of courts in resolving the consequent controversies.[6]

When applied in the context of international law, this theoretical perspective rightly emphasizes that law cannot be explained in terms of hierarchies of rules (the positivist fallacy) nor in terms of various purely external measures of utility (the 'law and . . .' phenomenon). Law seeks to carve out a sphere of influence and action where the phenomenon of law is measured against its own internal aspirations. Lon Fuller's concept of the 'internal morality of law' is a closely related idea.[7]

Weinrib also joins Fuller in conceiving of law as relational. However, while Fuller's view of legal relations is largely, though not exclusively, *process* focused, Weinrib's formalism emphasizes the internal structure of the legal relationship. This structure, which is tripartite with opposing agents and a neutral decision-maker, supports free agency—a rational agency that can change the world. Building upon Hegelian and Kantian theories of natural right, Weinrib believes that law is created through practical reason, which is the 'unity of reason and practice'.[8]

Where Weinrib's formalism causes difficulties for international environmental law is in his emphasis upon the form of court adjudication as the archetype for all 'legal' relationships. It goes without saying that courts, and even other forms of third party adjudication, play a relatively minor role in international law generally and in environmental law in particular. If law's autonomy and influence depend upon courts, then international law will not be able to effectively shape other social structures to which law relates.

---

[5] E.J. Weinrib, 'Legal Formalism: On the Immanent Rationality of Law' (1988) 97 Yale L.J. 949 at 951.
[6] E.J. Weinrib, 'The Jurisprudence of Legal Formalism' (1993) 16 Harv. J. L. & Pub. Pol'y 583 at 583.
[7] L.L. Fuller, *The Morality of Law*, revised edition (New Haven: Yale University Press, 1969).
[8] Weinrib, see note 6 above at 590.

It is the desire to carve out a role for law distinct from the goals or imperatives of power politics that motivates contemporary international law formalists. Chief among them are two theorists who hold otherwise conflicting views. For Philip Allott, law arises in the interaction of *ideas* from philosophy, politics, sociology, or elsewhere and the concrete decisions and actions of juridical actors, generally termed *practice*. However, law becomes itself through specific juridical processes and legal relations that serve to found law's independent justification.[9] Allott's formalism is therefore of a very particular kind. It is limited to the claim that law is related to, but ultimately independent from, other social constructions. Although the aspiration to a more humane world—one imbued with 'public' values—links law and politics, their inter-subjective practices and modes of justification are fundamentally different. Allott is formalist, then, only in believing that there is a clear break between law and non-law. In all other ways, Allott is anti-formalist because he rejects the possibility of 'right' answers and specifically eschews legal positivism.

The complication in Allott's approach is that he reifies law, treating it as the great mystery that links all thought and all politics:

The extraordinary progress of the human species would not have been possible without law. We have created a vast world-law in which collective human effort is organized through law, a world of unlimited possibilities of complexity and sophistication.[10]

The reification is itself rooted in a striking assertion: that human social life is shaped by a 'common human experience, an international consciousness'.[11] This Hegelian construct runs counter to post-colonial conceptions of social pluralism and political and cultural diversity. If the autonomy of international law must be rooted in a hegemonic, universalist image, it is unlikely to attract the allegiance of wide swaths of world opinion. It is not wise to try to ground international environmental law, for example, primarily in shared environmental values. If, *pace* Allott, law is not completely autonomous from politics, as I will argue later in this chapter, then the discursive complexities of political argument must be considered. This perspective implies that persuading actors of the need for effective environmental law will require arguments that blend identity and interest and that pay due attention to imbalances of power. This is exactly what concepts such as common heritage (see Chapter 23 'Common Areas, Common Heritage, and Common Concern') or common but differentiated responsibilities (see Chapter 27 'Equity') seek to do.

The most thoroughgoing formalists in contemporary international legal theory are a surprising group—the so-called critical, or new stream, scholars. Of this group, Martti Koskenniemi is the most intriguing interlocutor. Finding no way to ground concrete legal decisions in inter-subjective practice because of the inability to choose rationally between dialectic principles or what he calls 'conceptual oppositions', such

---

[9] P. Allott, 'The True Function of Law in the International Community' (1997–8) 5 Ind. J. Global Legal Stud. 391.   [10] *Ibid.* at 394.

[11] P. Allott, *Eunomia: New Order for New World* (Oxford: Oxford University Press, 1990) at 293.

as rule/process and consent/justice,[12] Koskenniemi argues for a strongly formal answer to what constitutes law. The answer is 'validity':

[N]either studying law as an instrument for external purposes (power) nor examining its legitimacy pull provides any significant room for the concept of validity. And inasmuch as *that* concept gets thrown away, nothing is left of law but a servile instrument for power (of what works) to realize its objectives (of what should work).[13]

The central point is to reverse the instrumental position that law is the handmaiden of power or of extra-legal aims and to assert that law itself is the external measure against which power is to be evaluated. What is more, the emphasis upon validity recognizes and treasures the diversity of global societies. Koskenniemi quotes Terry Nardin in suggesting that it is only law understood in a non-instrumental way, as authoritative independently of particular purposes, that 'is compatible with the freedom of its subjects to be different'.[14] Note that the assertion is the exact inverse of Allott's claim that it is universal law, grounded in shared human consciousness, that establishes law's potential autonomy.

In what does 'validity' consist? Despite numerous forays on the subject, Koskenniemi has never explicitly articulated what he means by the concept. In the absence of a new reading of the idea, one is driven back to older conceptions. Here, it is instructive that the only reference Koskenniemi provides is to a discussion of Hans Kelsen.[15] Andreas Fischer-Lescano is more open about his theoretical allies. Supporting Koskenniemi's defence of formal validity, Fischer-Lescano roots it directly in Kelsen, explaining that the famous *grundnorm* is:

Kelsen's attempt to *positivize* the foundation of validity of law and free it from political will, natural law or religious and other transcendental points of view. Kelsen's legal pacifism and the pure legal theory were decidedly characterized by opposing a different model to the 'real political' legal instrumentalism in the tradition of Carl Schmitt. The basic intention of Kelsen was to show that it is the legal order that constitutes the political system; that law cannot be found in a legal vacuum and that it is not politics but rather the idea of the 'grundnorm' and its presupposed and hypothetical validity that the norms of international law derive their own validity. The basic problem of the international legal order as Kelsen saw it is the auto-interpretive or instrumental approach which nations applied when dealing with international law. This required that a world legal system be placed over and against it. 'No law without a court' wrote Kelsen and in another place he lamented, 'there exists no authority accepted generally and obligatorily as competent to settle international conflicts'.[16]

---

[12] M. Koskenniemi, *From Apology to Utopia: The Structure of International Legal Argument* (Helsinki: Finnish Lawyer's Publishing Company, 1989) at 40–1 and 449–50.

[13] M. Koskenniemi, 'Carl Schmitt, Hans Morgenthau, and the Image of Law in International Relations,' in M. Byers, ed., *The Role of Law in International Politics: Essays in International Relations and International Law* (Oxford: Oxford University Press, 2000) 17 at 33.

[14] T. Nardin, quoted in M. Koskenniemi, 'What Is International Law For?' in M. Evans, ed., *International Law*, 1st edition (Oxford: Oxford University Press, 2003) 89 at 102.

[15] Koskenniemi, see note 14 above at 107, n. 24.

[16] Andreas Fischer-Lescano, *Redefining Sovereignty via International Constitutional Moments?* in M. Bothe, M.E. O'Connell, and N. Ronzitti, eds., *Redefining Sovereignty: The Use of Force after the End of*

The difficulty is that one cannot simply separate out the plea for legal autonomy through validity from the rest of the Kelsenian superstructure. Unless a clear alternative reading is provided, to rely on Kelsen's view of validity is to accept the generation of all law through a formal hierarchy of norms rooted in the *grundnorm*. It is to say that law is nothing more than the emanation of the state. It is to deny the normative evolution of the last 50 years, which has seen the growing status of individuals as 'formal' subjects of law and of civil society organizations as informal but influential generators of legal norms. The extraordinary role played by non-governmental organizations in the lead-up to Rio and Johannesburg, for example, and their impact upon the elaboration of new environmental law principles finds no echo in Koskenniemi's concept of legal validity. With these developments in mind—and one should also recall similar patterns in international human rights law—recourse to Kelsenian validity seems a rearguard action indeed.

Attempts to resurrect formal validity are particularly troubling when one considers the evolution of international environmental law. Indeed, a fair reading would be that Kelsen's understanding of law would render nugatory most of what we currently conceive as the global law of the environment. Very little of it is linked to court adjudication, and implementation is largely dependent on what, from a positivist legal approach, are considered to be voluntary and negotiated compliance arrangements. Indeed, Koskennemmi is troubled by exactly this set of developments, arguing that the move from obligation to 'commitment', and from 'breach' to 'non-compliance', signal an undoing of international law (see Chapter 43 'Compliance Procedures').[17]

Is there any way to protect the autonomy of international law from instrumentalism, from service to purely external aspirations or raw power, without resorting to outdated concepts of state positivism? Both Allott and Koskenniemi gesture in this direction by eschewing rigid formalism. As noted earlier, Allott's formal preoccupations are designed only to insulate law, as a constellation of ideas and practices, from raw power. Even Koskenniemi, while stressing the central importance of validity, goes on to argue:

[L]aw unites an *instrumentalist* logic, one that looks for the realization of objectives through law, with a *formalist* logic, one that establishes standards of behaviour. Now it is obvious that neither logic is fully constraining.[18]

Another way of thinking about this tension between formalism and instrumentalism is to trace out their philosophical roots. Aristotle argued that all human action is to some purpose. Law should not be excluded. Hobbes stressed what we would now call a positivist, self-referential, and self-explaining quality in social systems, including

the Cold War—New Options, Lawful and Legitimate? (Ardsley, NY: Transnational Publishers, forthcoming) [footnotes omitted].

    [17] M. Koskenniemi, 'Breach of Treaty or Noncompliance? Reflections on the Enforcement of the Montreal Protocol' (1992) 3 Y.B. Int'l Envt'l L. 123 at 123–8.

    [18] Koskenniemi, see note 14 above at 104.

law. Drawing these strains of thinking together, which both Allott and Koskenniemi at least implicitly undertake, results in the *relative* autonomy of international law.

Relative autonomy means that there is no identity between law and power or between law and politics. Might does *not* make right, and law is not merely the infinitely malleable tool of political aspiration. At the same time, neither law and power nor law and politics are opposites. Law embodies both substantive and procedural values that provide it with relative independence from unmediated power and politics. Law 'is the work of its everyday participants, a continuous effort to construct and sustain a common institutional framework to meet the exigencies of social life in accordance with certain ideals'.[19] This understanding of law is connected to Habermasian discourse theory. However, Habermas's dependence upon a shared 'lifeworld' as a basis for communicative action causes immense problems for those international lawyers who doubt the existence of such a common lifeworld in international society.[20]

Lon Fuller explains that law is rooted in two different 'moralities'—one might also call them 'logics' if one wants to adopt a purely rationalist reading. The 'morality of aspiration' is closely allied to aesthetics or to Aristotelian 'virtue'.[21] It is the desire and struggle to make the most of one's life, to be the best (or most fully realized) that one can be, both as a person and as a society. The 'morality of duty', which is more commonly associated with law, is the base common denominator, providing the minimum standards of appropriate conduct that make life in society possible. The conjuncture of the two moralities reflects Fuller's understanding that both consensus and conflict are inevitably present in human interaction through law. Fuller argues, however, that because the building of a legal system is a purposive activity, it partakes of the morality of aspiration more than is commonly credited. Aspiration is often manifested first in informal norms. Fuller nonetheless recognizes that law's immediate aim is the imposition of duties upon actors within the system.[22] For Fuller, however, it is the aspirational morality that gives rise to tests of legality that apply to both individual rules and systems of rule-making: the generality of rules, promulgation, limiting cases of retroactivity, clarity, the avoidance of contradiction, not asking the impossible, constancy over time, and the congruence of official action with underlying rules.[23]

What does all this mean for the question of formality in international environmental law? To summarize the broad theoretical argument, if the existence of a

---

[19] K.I. Winston, 'Three Models for the Study of Law,' in W.J. Witteveen and W. van der Burg, eds., *Rediscovering Fuller: Essays on Implicit Law and Institutional Design* (Amsterdam: Amsterdam University Press, 1999) 51 at 63.

[20] J. Habermas, *Moral Consciousness and Communicative Action*, translated by C. Lenhardt and S.W. Nicholsen (Cambridge, MA: MIT Press, 1995).

[21] Aristotle, *The Nicomachean Ethics*, translated by J.A.K. Thomson and H. Tredennick (London: Penguin Books, 1976) I:vii at 76; II:vi at 100; and VI:ii at 205.   [22] Fuller, see note 7 above at 42–3.

[23] *Ibid.* at 46–91 and 155.

category called 'law' is dependent upon a collection of tests related primarily to the internal characteristics of rules, then the mere formal articulation of the rule provides little guidance as to its likely influence or effect. To understand the social phenomenon of law, it is not enough to measure validity, as a product of a formal hierarchy or sources or legislative competency. Nor is it useful to reify law because law cannot be transcendent—it always emerges from the mixing together of ideas and practices. Law is a special form of practical reasoning that requires testing in the muck of social interaction. Rules emerge on a continuum with two concurrent scales of measure: aspiration (ideas) and duty (practice).

Formal and informal approaches to shaping behaviour are therefore inextricably intertwined. Nowhere is this more apparent than in the range of issue areas brought together under international environmental law. Within international environmental law, formal and informal styles are expressed in three distinct ways. First, we see varied processes of law-making, ranging from the negotiation of formal treaties to the implicit amendment of treaty rules through subsequent practice or through frank political negotiation in conferences of the parties (see Chapter 20 'Treaty Making and Treaty Evolution' and Chapter 38 'Treaty Bodies'). For example, at the first Meeting of the Parties to the Kyoto Protocol to the UN Framework Convention on Climate Change (UNFCCC) in December 2005, the parties agreed to adopt the protocol's compliance procedure by simple decision. They postponed consideration of the formal amendment that would be required under the terms of the protocol to make any compliance consequences legally binding. This arrangement allowed the compliance procedure to operate even while disagreements over its proper legal form remained unresolved. Second, in the content of international environmental law norms, we often see nebulous standards or principles with ill-defined scope contained in formal instruments. For example, treaties may set out duties to notify or cooperate that are not clearly related to particular circumstances, or parties may simply be told to exercise precaution. Conversely, soft law instruments may contain rather precise obligations of what might be termed an 'administrative' nature (see Chapter 4 'Global Environmental Governance as Administration' and Chapter 32 'International Institutions'), designed to promote the implementation of the 'binding' nebulous standard or to provide guidance as to the scope of application of the principle. Third, within international environmental law, stipulated dispute settlement processes range from rarely used and highly formal processes of binding adjudication to the entirely negotiated settlement of controversies (see Chapter 45 'International Dispute Settlement').

There does not appear to be any predictable connection between formal and informal approaches across these three arenas. One can see imprecise norms in binding treaties with largely informal dispute resolution procedures, for example in the 1979 Convention on Long-Range Transboundary Air Pollution, which contains broad principles and a preference for negotiated dispute settlement. One also sees relatively precise norms in informal instruments or processes with an attempt at more formal dispute resolution. Within the Kyoto Protocol framework, for example, a decision of the Conference of the Parties setting out eligibility requirements for the use of the Kyoto mechanisms will be subject to Kyoto's non-compliance procedure. There are many variations lying between these two poles.

It is no accident that normative debates have often played themselves out most heatedly in the issue areas covered by international environmental law. The superficial explanation is that international environmental law is a relatively new field at the forefront of developments in international law concerning the broadening of participation in norm creation, the expansion of legitimate sources of normative inspiration, and the so-called de-centring of the state. International environmental law is at the heart of globalization debates because it is recognized that environmental problems often resist any temporal or spacial delimitation, and that they implicate states, individuals, and corporations. Transboundary effects of pollution are commonplace, as with acid rain (see Chapter 22 'Transboundary Impacts'). Some environmental risks project themselves far into unknown futures. Consider the transport and storage of hazardous waste, most notably of nuclear waste (see Chapter 17 'Hazardous Substances and Activities'). Other problems are global in scale, for example, climate change, and present all the difficulties inherent in the protection of common spaces, including free rider problems and classic prisoner's dilemmas (see Chapter 14 'Atmosphere and Outer Space'; Chapter 11 'Economic Theory of International Environmental Law'; and Chapter 23 'Common Areas, Common Heritage, and Common Concern'). Underlying these rather obvious points is a connecting theme that is conceptually more fruitful. International environmental law exists because of the need to address problems described years ago by Michael Polanyi in economics and philosophy, and Lon Fuller in law, as 'polycentric', and it is precisely such problems that challenge us most directly to articulate sophisticated theories of normative influence.

Polycentric problems are those with complex ramifications—they have no 'essence' but can be recast in many ways from many different perspectives. The range of people affected by the problem cannot easily be foreseen, and those who can participate in decision-making are not clear exactly what issues they should or can address.[24] Polycentricity is not amenable to precise definition. It is self-consciously metaphoric and suggestive, rather than directive. Nonetheless, Fuller's transposition of Polanyi's image into the realm of law is evocative and certainly speaks to a central problem with environmental concerns:

We may visualize this kind of [polycentric] situation by thinking of a spider web. A pull on one strand will distribute tensions after a complicated pattern throughout the web as a whole. Doubling the original pull will, in all likelihood, not simply double each of the resulting tensions but will rather create a different complicated pattern of tensions. This would

---

[24] R.A. Macdonald, 'Legislation and Governance,' in Witteveen and van der Burg, see note 19 above 279 at 279–99; and J.W.F. Allison, 'Legal Culture in Fuller's Analysis of Adjudication,' in Witteveen and van der Burg, see note 19 above 346 at 346–50.

certainly occur, for example, if the doubled pull caused one or more of the weaker strands to snap. This is a 'polycentric' situation because it is 'many centered'—each crossing of strands is a distinct centre for distributing tensions.[25]

This description fits to a tee the problems surrounding the negotiation and implementation of the Kyoto Protocol, but it also suits less obviously overwhelming matters such as the transboundary transport for disposal of solid wastes or the exploitation rights of upper riparians in shared watercourses. As Jeffrey Dunoff suggests in Chapter 5 of this *Handbook*, complex problems may require polycentric governance, blurring the lines between state-based and international regulation. The point here is that polycentric problems may also require access to a rich variety of normative strategies, both formal and informal, if exceedingly complex matters are to be addressed with any hope of efficacy.

Waiting for the negotiation of a binding treaty may not be possible when many-centred tensions are building—the web may snap before the final text is concluded. Similarly, it may be necessary for a principle to be invoked and promoted to convince actors to modify behaviour in the absence of a precise rule. This is the very essence of 'precaution', to take but one example. Finally, formal adjudication may not be successful in drawing into consideration the wide range of facts generated by a polycentric problem. Negotiation or consensus building may be preferred options. This seems to be the case when one is trying to address conflicts among upper and lower riparians. They almost never resort to formal adjudication even when it is provided for in bilateral or multilateral treaties. Indeed, the same is true for multilateral environmental agreements generally. With few exceptions, their dispute settlement clauses have remained unused. This is not to suggest that polycentric problems can be addressed only informally, merely that informal and formal acts and processes may need to be employed in a strategic amalgam.

Since the advent of the American Legal realists in the 1920s, there is no more damning criticism of legal analysis—at least in North America—than that it is 'formalistic'. The implicit charge against formalism is that it sacrifices an honest assessment of 'real' problems to mere categorization and definition. Of course, the tension between formal and substantive analysis in law is age-old. In the evolution of the common law tradition, equity emerged as a kind of 'shadow' law to balance against the formal manner in which common law cases could be brought: '[O]utside the writs, there was no common law, no way to state a case or get before a judge' (see Chapter 27 'Equity').[26] Similarly, in the civil law tradition, it took almost a thousand years for plaintiffs to be able to gain access to a judge without the equivalent of the Roman praetor formulating the specific issue that the judge was allowed to decide—finally breaking away from what was a close analogy to the common law writ. The fixation

---

[25] L.L. Fuller, 'The Forms and Limits of Adjudication' (1978) 92 Harv. L. Rev. 353 at 395.

[26] H.P. Glenn, *Legal Traditions of the World: Sustainable Diversity in Law* (Oxford: Oxford University Press, 2000) at 210 and 237.

of some international legal doctrine with sources of law, as represented by Article 38 of the Statute of the International Court of Justice, is emblematic of a different kind of 'formalistic' thrust to law. Here, the formalism relates to what counts, substantively, as law. Yet the impulse is the same—to create rigid definitional barriers around what can be described as law, be it procedurally or substantively. The policy-science analysis of the New Haven School, a direct spawn of the legal realists, epitomizes the contemporary anti-formalist challenge.

The great difficulty with the debate between upholders of the formal in the face of self-styled realists is the wide degree of division over what is meant by *formalism* in law. The various conceptions of the formal discussed at the outset of this chapter are often conflated. What is more, formalism is often simply employed as an accusing epithet in fundamental legal theoretic disputes. To add to the confusion, many particular rules can be cast as formal or informal, depending upon one's underlying theoretical commitments. Take, for example, the principle of common but differentiated responsibilities (see Chapter 26 'Sustainable Development' and Chapter 27 'Equity'), which began its explicit textual life, albeit in muted terms, in the Vienna Convention for the Protection of the Ozone Layer (Vienna Convention). The preamble of this convention includes reference to the need to consider 'the circumstances and particular requirements of developing countries'. Preambles are generally considered not to be binding on the parties, but they frequently express principles that inform both interpretation and further negotiation. So the idea of paying special attention to the needs and circumstances of the developing world was included in a formal legal text, but in a section that could be viewed as 'informal', in the sense of not being intended as binding. Yet, the concept would come to have formal legal implications in the light of further practice and further negotiation.

Later developments provide more conceptual challenges. The full-blown concept of 'common but differentiated responsibilities' is stated in Principle 7 of the Rio Declaration, an instrument that was not a binding treaty. One could suggest, therefore, that this principle could not be more than an 'informal' desideratum. Yet the principle was included in an explicit, negotiated text resulting from a major intergovernmental conference and, in this sense, was very 'formal'. Although the principle was not at this point imperative, it clearly had begun to take on a life of its own, shaping future negotiations. So for many legal theorists, at this point there was no 'formal' rule, but there was at the very least a set of expectations, shared by many states, that a norm was emerging. The Montreal Protocol on Substances That Deplete the Ozone Layer (Montreal Protocol) to the Vienna Convention then included a specific provision allowing developing countries a ten-year grace period before the obligations to reduce and eliminate the production of ozone-depleting substances would apply. This was, on most accounts, a legal rule. Does it represent a precise, binding, and, therefore, 'formal' instantiation of a wider informal principle of common but differentiated responsibilities or merely a highly specific, textually grounded rule? The answer will likely depend upon one's theory of obligation in international law, the role of consent in rule generation, the interplay of custom and treaty, and a theory of interpretation. At what point might an informal principle have transmuted into a formal rule?

Aside from the substantive question whether or not a formal legal rule exists, which we have just considered, the further question arises whether it matters greatly in a practical sense whether or not a norm is formal or informal, in the sense of 'binding' or not 'binding'. Relevant in this context are the various arguments stating that formal rules encompassed within treaties should not be evaluated solely in terms of 'compliance'. In international environmental law, it is commonly suggested that even when formal treaty rules are unlikely to generate changes of behaviour, the articulation of the rule can have a beneficial educative effect and can open up avenues for effective future advocacy. This argument is now advanced quite commonly in relation to the Kyoto Protocol and is linked to the recognition that this protocol, even if fully implemented, will not produce the needed reductions in greenhouse gas emissions. In other words, even if the substantive outcomes of the treaty are not likely to be adequate to the challenges we face on climate change, Kyoto is worth promoting for its secondary, educative effects that may make it possible for future negotiations on a more forceful regime to succeed.

Another example from the climate regime is equally telling. The principle of common but differentiated responsibilities appears in the operative text of the UNFCCC (Article 3 on 'principles'), where it is phrased in hortatory terms. The Kyoto Protocol embodies and makes operational the same principle. Yet this is precisely why certain states have refused to join Kyoto and why they continue to deny the existence or utility of the common but differentiated responsibilities 'principle'. However, the principle refuses to go away and has proven to be remarkably 'sticky' and hard to undermine. The only choice left is non-participation in the regime.

If these arguments have any merit, what does it mean to differentiate between a 'formal' legal norm, often called a 'rule' and an 'informal' norm? Usually, the difference is said to relate to one of two seemingly competing conceptualizations. For most international relations (IR) scholars, formality is likely to be treated explicitly as an element related to effectiveness—to the concrete social impact of the formal norm. For most international lawyers, the formality of a rule pertains primarily to its binding quality as 'law'. The implicit assumption for many lawyers is that binding law is effective. For some, this is simply an article of faith; for others 'binding' actually means 'effective.' For the majority of IR theorists and international lawyers, then, formalism is tied to evaluations of likely effectiveness.

Yet, the creation of explicit legal rules is no guarantee that the rules will be effective in shaping behaviour. An entire generation of freshwater treaties was structured around the premise that the regulation of competitive uses was the abiding need in this issue area. While these treaties contained explicit 'no significant harm' and 'equitable allocation' rules, these rules had little impact because of the dominant competitive use paradigm. As mentioned earlier, these treaties typically contained detailed formal adjudicative procedures that were never employed. The effect of the weak rules and the failure to employ the formal adjudicative procedures was that environmental protection concerns, although formally part of the legal regime, did not weigh heavily in competitive use calculations. Formal law and formal institutional structures could not produce noticeable effects. It did not matter how formal the rules were.[27]

If notionally binding rules are often not effective in practice, it is equally true that informal, non-binding norms may come to shape practice quite effectively. To continue with the freshwater example, the informal interactions promoted among the riparian states of the Nile Basin through the World Bank-sponsored Nile Basin Initiative seem to have generated new norms of cooperation in a previously and potentially highly conflictual setting.[28] In other broader contexts, the vague and contested concept of 'sustainable development' has had a profound influence in the interstices of legal rules, on their interpretation, and in negotiations for further normative evolution.[29] Moreover, informal processes of deliberation may prove to be more influential than formal adjudication. To pursue an example drawn from the ozone agreements, the Montreal Protocol provided for an informal Implementation Committee. The goal of the procedure is to facilitate compliance rather than define non-compliance. Reports suggest that the committee's discussions have been sufficient to induce compliance by most parties or, at least, to lead to agreement on future compliance (see Chapter 43 'Compliance Procedures').

It is time to put the most difficult matter before us—state consent. As was suggested earlier, the formalism based in Kelsenian validity is grounded in one central idea—that international law is the product of willing, the willing of artificial persons called sovereign states. On this reading of international law, rules can emerge only when states sense that rules are in their interest. A rule cannot exist unless the 'community' of states wills the rule into being. What is more, states that do not consent to the rule are not bound, either because they refuse to ratify a treaty or because they persistently object to the formation of a custom.

This structuring of the international rule of law has been creaking and groaning for some time. J.L. Brierly argued 40 years ago that 'in the practical administration of international law, states are continually treated as bound by principles which they cannot, except by the most strained construction of the facts, be said to have consented to'.[30] More recently, even scholars of a positivist bent have suggested that

---

[27] J. Brunnée and S.J. Toope, 'Environmental Security and Freshwater Resources: Ecosystem Regime Building' (1997) 91 A.J.I.L. 26.

[28] J. Brunnée and S.J. Toope, 'The Changing Nile Basin Regime: Does Law Matter?' (2002) 43 Harv. J. Int'l L. 105.

[29] V. Lowe, 'The Politics of Law-Making: Are the Method and Character of Norm Creation Changing?' in Byers, see note 13 above, 207.

[30] J.L. Brierly, *The Law of Nations: An Introduction to the International Law of Peace*, 6th edition (Oxford: Clarendon Press, 1963) at 52.

the edges of consent have been 'softening'.[31] Allott opines that the idea that states must consent to any abridgement of their 'liberty' is 'a cynical misappropriation of some part of the ethos of revolutionary democracy'.[32] The evolution of norms in international environmental law especially is no longer clearly dependent upon the express consent of states. We see this change most clearly in the growing role of principles such as precaution and sustainability in shaping concrete regimes and in the role of consensual mechanisms, such as conferences of the parties, in elaborating detailed rules.[33]

Does the 'softening' of consent mean that international lawyers no longer need to concern themselves with 'binding'—a special type of 'formal'—rules? Is the formal articulation of rules a dead letter? Perhaps surprisingly, the answer to both of these questions is a firm 'no'. International lawyers continue to worry about the reality of their discipline, and we search for the magical quality that will make law effective, binding actors to the substantive outcomes of the processes of law creation. That is why positivist normative hierarchies have proven to be so attractive. Law can still be distinguished from other forms of social normativity by the specific type of rationality apparent in the internal processes that make law possible—a rationality dependent upon reasoned argument—and by reference to past practice, contemporary social aspirations, and the deployment of analogy. When achieved, law's specific form of rationality tends to attract adherence. Law is then viewed as legitimate, possessing the capacity to generate moral commitment. The binding quality of law is an internal quality of the subjects (and creators) of the legal system—bindingness is self-bindingness.

If the binding quality of law remains important, even when de-linked from the pre-occupation with enforcement, then the concept of 'formal' law retains a prominent, though not exclusive, place in the shaping of behaviour in international society. Although consent has been softened, it has not been excluded as a test for formal law. Rather than revisiting the sterile 'sources of law' debate that has swirled around Article 38 of the Statute of the International Court of Justice, it is more useful to invert the question and to ask how we should treat 'informal' norms. In international environmental law, this question has tended to be framed in the context of 'soft law'. Although the term is often misleading, it remains current. The final section of this chapter will therefore tie together the theoretical insights traced out earlier in the light of 'soft law' discourse in international environmental law.

---

[31] B. Simma, 'From Bilateralism to Community Interest' (1994, VI) 250 Recueil des cours 217 at 225–7. See also S.J. Toope, 'Powerful but Unpersuasive? The Role of the United States in the Evolution of Customary International Law,' in M. Byers and G. Nolte, eds., *United States Hegemony and the Foundations of International Law* (Cambridge: Cambridge University Press, 2003) 287 at 302–16.

[32] P. Allott, 'The Concept of International Law,' in Byers, see note 13 above, 69 at 77.

[33] J. Brunnée, 'COPing with Consent: Lawmaking under Multilateral Environmental Agreements' (2001) 15 Leiden J. Int'l L. 1.

The term 'soft law' is employed in a number of different contexts in more or less precise ways. The most common meaning ascribed to the term is a non-binding written instrument setting out international principles (see Chapter 18 'Different Types of Norms in International Environmental Law'). This definition includes voluntary resolutions, declarations, sets of rules, and codes of conduct. Some of these instruments contain relatively precise statements of guiding principle or even excruciatingly detailed and technical rules very much like domestic 'regulations' under a statute, while others contain much more general concepts intended to shape practice. In other words, 'precision' is not a good way to distinguish between what is 'hard' and what is 'soft' law. Well-known examples of soft law instruments include the 1972 Stockholm Declaration on the Human Environment, the 1974 Organisation for Economic Co-operation and Development's Principles Concerning Transfrontier Pollution, the 1992 Rio Declaration on Environment and Development, the UN Environment Programme's (UNEP) 1995 Global Programme of Action for the Protection of the Marine Environment, and the International Organization for Standardization's standards. Such instruments are commonly drafted and approved by international organs and conferences, but they are not ratified by states.

Some authors suggest that soft law may be 'legal' or 'non-legal', but this distinction is confusing. Although 'international principles' may sometimes be expressed in what superficially appears to be a binding legal form, the principles do not thereby become directly binding upon states or other international actors. For example, a treaty, which is indisputably a formal legal instrument, may contain soft law principles—in this case, meaning imprecise norms not designed to condition specific conduct. Numerous treaties, such as the 1992 Convention on Biological Diversity and the 1994 Convention to Combat Desertification in Those Countries Experiencing Serious Drought and/or Desertification contain goals related to the imprecise concept of sustainable development. The form of normative expression, however, is not the only key to understanding the potential operation of soft law. Pierre-Marie Dupuy argues that to identify soft law one must go so far as to reject the formal criterion of obligation, and assess instead substantive criteria including the nature and specificity of behaviour required of states.[34] In other words, the 'softness' of law may relate either to the form of expression or to the content of a norm.

Soft law as content, rather than form, is based upon the premise that certain principles are important, and should ideally shape international law and policy even if they are not binding. A more expansive understanding of soft law would include even the articulation of principles by individual actors with some authority in a relevant international regime (for example, the executive director of UNEP, a member of a treaty monitoring body, or the leader of an influential non-governmental

---

[34] P.M. Dupuy, 'Soft Law and the International Law of the Environment' (1991) 12 Michigan J. Int'l L. 420 at 430.

organization).[35] Such articulations help to create shared expectations of particular state conduct.

To suggest that soft law is not binding, either because it is contained in non-binding forms or because it is stated in non-binding terms, is not to say that it is without influence. Indeed, it is increasingly common for international lawyers to speak of a progression along a continuum from soft to hard law, although this progression is by no means inevitable or invariably desirable. One way of conceptualizing this process is that soft law may come to play a role in 'interstitial lawmaking', where principles (or concepts) come to influence the interpretation of binding norms because the principles are useful or even necessary to practical decision-making.[36] Alternatively, more precise articulations may migrate through negotiation from informal instruments to formal and binding instruments of law. There can be no doubt that one of the reasons prompting the articulation of the concept of soft law was to assist in the progressive development of binding international law. In the words of Christine Chinkin:

While soft law may not be directly used to found a cause of action it has both a legitimising and a delegitimising direct effect: it is extremely difficult for a State that rejected some instrument of soft law to argue that behaviour in conformity with it by those who accepted it is illegitimate.[37]

This comment expresses one mode of operation of soft law perfectly. States are entirely free to hold themselves apart from a soft norm, as it is not binding. However, because it may possess the legitimacy of wide support, it is difficult for a state to claim that others are not free to voluntarily act according to the norm's terms. The conceptual difficulty is that when soft law sets forth a requirement, duty, or prohibition, as opposed to a permission or license, and when enough states choose to abide by this norm, it can be used to criticize inconsistent conduct by a state that initially rejected the norm, as has been done with the concept of common but differentiated responsibilities, discussed earlier. Ultimately, the new norm may crystallize into binding custom. Identifying the point on the continuum where the 'soft' norm becomes 'hard' is notoriously challenging. This is precisely why so much ink is spilled in trying to assess whether concepts such as precaution or sustainable development have become binding. Moreover, soft law statements and instruments may come to influence a treaty regime, both through the interpretation and application of treaty rules and in the further elaboration of treaty regimes. The latter is particularly likely when framework treaties are made more specific through protocols and decisions of conferences of the parties. Consent remains important, but its role is subtle and fluid. Soft law establishes shared understandings that may limit the practical ability to withhold consent.

[35] C.M. Chinkin, 'The Challenge of Soft-Law: Development and Change in International Law' (1989) 38 Int'l & Comp. L.Q. 850.

[36] Lowe, see note 29 above at 212–17. See also J. Ellis, *Soft Law as Topos: The Role of Principles of Soft International Law in the Development of International Environmental Law* (DCL dissertation, McGill University, Montreal, 2001).   [37] Chinkin, see note 35 above at 850–51.

Participants in the construction of international law, including states, non-governmental actors, and individuals, rely on non-binding principles to map out terrain that they wish to occupy and even conquer. The metaphor suggests that the process of normative evolution is oftentimes conflictual. Informal, non-binding norms can move the signposts without creating borders that need defending. Sometimes international actors will 'choose' to promote and negotiate informal soft norms, either by choosing a non-binding instrument or by articulating principles that are not intended to condition specific conduct. They may 'choose' in this way because this is what is politically possible. At other times, there is no active 'choice' involved—ideas emerge through the wonders of the human intellect and spirit, they are promoted, and the messy interactions of actors (practice) take them up. Over time, the informal blends into processes that can render norms formal, through the specifying in practice of heretofore vague principles or through the negotiation of binding texts. What René-Jean Dupuy called 'revolutionary custom' may be generated when states come to believe that a particular innovative practice is now required.[38]

Various actors may also promote the conclusion of binding instruments, employing previously informal norms in new contexts. Even here there is no inevitable straight line trajectory—informal norms can find their way into seemingly binding texts as preambular statements, and as aspirational statements within the operational sections of treaties. They remain informal in the sense that they are not meant to produce legal rights and duties for state parties. A striking example of the latter type of informal—but influential—norm is Article 3 of the UNFCCC, which enumerates key guiding 'principles' such as sustainable development, intergenerational equity, precaution, and common but differentiated responsibilities. In this and other cases, the norms serve as guidelines in the interpretation, application, and elaboration of the regime. What is more, the attempt to promote formal law may fail for various reasons, but this does not inevitably mean that the underlying informal norms cannot continue to influence behaviour. To continue with the climate change example, the principles underlying the UNFCCC and its Kyoto Protocol are likely to survive efforts to undermine the protocol's operation in practice.

It is nonetheless true that participants in the processes of international law-making oftentimes manifest a desire to promote formal, binding law. They may be seeking ways to protect important interests, to foster perceived core values, or simply to engender greater predictability in relationships. They look to binding law and, typically, to formal instruments such as treaties to encompass their intentions and hopes. If they ensure that the desired rules are created through inclusive processes and that the rules meet internal tests of legality including generality of rules, promulgation, limiting cases of retroactivity, clarity, avoidance of contradiction, not asking the impossible, constancy over time, and congruence of official action with the underlying rules, chances are that the rules will be perceived as legitimate and that the

[38] R.-J. Dupuy, 'Coutume Sage et Coutume Sauvage,' in S. Bastid et al., eds., *Mélanges Offerts a Charles Rousseau: La Communauté Internationale* (Paris: Editions Pedone, 1974) 75 at 83–4.

self-binding quality of law can be generated. In international environmental law, this process has taken place on numerous occasions, such as with the creation of modern water basin agreements or rules on the transportation of hazardous waste.

Formal and informal norms operate side by side. Each can be influential and each can fail to influence. Rarely can one simply choose to employ either a formal or an informal 'tool'. Indeed, this metaphor is quite simply wrong. Neither formal rules nor informal norms are mere tools for law is never purely instrumental. Law relates to our deepest hopes and fears. It is rooted in our collective aspirations for a better world and in our experiences of failure and success in seeking out that world. At the same time, law is itself an expression of the values that we trust to shape a better world. If purported law fails to manifest those values, it will not work as law because it will not command our adherence. Its illegitimacy will destroy our hopes and reinforce our fears. Since law is rooted in both the logics of aspiration and of duty, it will always be necessarily and appropriately both informal and formal.

RECOMMENDED READING

P. Allott, 'The Concept of International Law,' in M. Byers, ed., *The Role of Law in International Politics: Essays in International Relations and International Law* (Oxford: Oxford University Press, 2000) 69.

M. Barnett and M. Finnemore, *Rules for the World: International Organizations in Global Politics* (Ithaca, NY: Cornell University Press, 2004).

J. Brunnée and S.J. Toope, 'Persuasion and Enforcement: Explaining Compliance with International Law' (2002) 13 Finnish Y.B. Int'l L. 273.

——, 'International Law and Constructivism: Elements of an Interactional Theory of International Law' (2000) 39 Colum. J. Transnat'l. L. 19.

T. Gruchalla-Wesierski, 'A Framework for Understanding "Soft Law" ' (1984) 30 McGill L.J. 37.

H. Hillgenberg, 'A Fresh Look at Soft Law' (1999) 10 Eur. J. Int'l L. 499.

M. Koskenniemi, 'What Is International Law For?' in M. Evans, ed., *International Law*, 1st edition (Oxford: Oxford University Press, 2003) 89.

F. Kratochwil, *Rules, Norms and Decisions: On the Conditions of Practical and Legal Reasoning in International Relations and Domestic Affairs* (Cambridge: Cambridge University Press, 1989).

V. Lowe, 'The Politics of Law-Making: Are the Method and Character of Norm Creation Changing?' in M. Byers, ed., *The Role of Law in International Politics: Essays in International Relations and International Law* (Oxford: Oxford University Press, 2000) 207.

G.J. Postema, 'Implicit Law' (1994) 13 L. & Phil. 361.

S.J. Toope, 'Emerging Patterns of Governance and International Law,' in M. Byers, ed., *The Role of Law in International Politics: Essays in International Relations and International Law* (Oxford: Oxford University Press, 2000) 91.

CHAPTER 7

....

RELATIONSHIP BETWEEN INTERNATIONAL ENVIRONMENTAL LAW AND OTHER BRANCHES OF INTERNATIONAL LAW

....

ALAN BOYLE

1 INTRODUCTION

INTERNATIONAL law empowers, constrains, and compels governments in various ways and at various levels. For example, a country that enters into free trade agreements gains economic advantages it would not otherwise enjoy but, at the same time, its freedom to pursue other policies will be affected. It may no longer be permitted to protect domestic industries, thus increasing unemployment in some sectors of the economy, and making it more difficult to promote the economic and social welfare of some of its citizens. Other parts of its economy may develop more rapidly, putting pressure on land, natural resources, water supply, and air quality, leading to unsustainable development, environmental degradation, and poorer conditions of health. It may thus be harder to meet commitments undertaken in the International Covenant on Economic, Social and Cultural Rights or at the UN Conference on Environment and Development. Equally, those same commitments may restrict certain forms of economic development and limit the country's ability to benefit from free trade in natural resources. Ultimately, governments make policy choices about how to balance competing objectives of this kind on political, social, economic, or ethical grounds. These choices will be reflected in the agreements they sign or in the state practice that contributes to general international law. The relationship between these environmental concerns, international trade policy and human rights law is best negotiated by states acting through the United Nations, the World Trade Organization (WTO), and other international organizations. However, few governments can foresee in detail all of the consequences of the commitments they make. Even when they do foresee them, it is not always possible to secure the agreement of other governments on how to address whatever tensions may arise out of the interaction of the commitments into which they have entered. In this chapter, we consider how international law deals with such unforeseen or unresolved conflicts, specifically as they affect the environment.

Before turning to the main subject of this chapter, however, it is worth making some preliminary points about what is encompassed by the term 'international environmental law'. International environmental law is neither a separate nor a self-contained system or sub-system of law. Rather, it is simply part of international law as a whole. It is true that many 'environmental' treaties and other legal instruments have been negotiated over the past half-century and that the study of international environmental law is to a significant extent a study of these treaties and other instruments. Nevertheless, unlike WTO law, the law of the sea, or human rights law, international environmental law has never been systematically codified into a single treaty or group of treaties. There is neither a dedicated international environmental organization nor an international dispute settlement process with the ability to give it coherence.

Undoubtedly, there are specifically environmental norms that have attained the status of customary international law or have become accepted by states as general principles of law (Chapter 19 'Formation of Customary International Law and General Principles'). Environmental impact assessment, transboundary risk management, and the precautionary principle or approach spring immediately to mind in this context (see Chapter 22 'Transboundary Impacts' and Chapter 25 'Precaution'). However, as international litigation amply demonstrates, contemporary international environmental disputes will often require us to consider both this body of specifically environmental law, and the application of general international law to environmental problems.[1] In the real world, it is simply not possible to address many of the legal issues posed by international environmental problems without also considering the law of treaties, state responsibility, jurisdiction, the law of the sea, natural resources law, dispute settlement, private international law, human rights law, international criminal law, and international trade law, to name only the most obvious. All of these topics have environmental dimensions or affect the resolution of environmental problems and disputes.

It should also be noted that there is no magic in categorizations such as 'international environmental law', 'international trade law', 'international human rights law', 'the law of the sea', 'natural resources law', and so on. These are no more than convenient labels, which help us locate what we think we are talking about as lawyers. They are not stockades to be defended from impurity. Moreover, even within those discrete bodies of law, specifically environmental norms or applications can also be found. Part XII of the 1982 UN Convention on the Law of the Sea (LOSC) deals with 'protection and preservation of the marine environment' and is one of the most important environmental agreements currently in existence. The preamble to the 1994 Marrakech Agreement Establishing the World Trade Organization (WTO Agreement) refers to 'sustainable development', and to this extent it encompasses environmental concerns, as do the exceptions listed in Article XX of the General Agreement on Tariffs and Trade (GATT). Human rights law has an increasingly important environmental dimension, as we observe later in this chapter in *Hatton v. United Kingdom* and in the *Ogoniland* case. Much of contemporary international environmental law deals with the sustainable use of freshwater, fisheries, forests, biological diversity, or endangered species. This is simply natural resources law—or perhaps the law of sustainable development—from another perspective. Bearing all of this in mind, it is worth re-emphasizing that 'international environmental law' is nothing more, or less, than the application of international law to environmental problems and concerns.

What then matters is that the regulation of international environmental concerns, however categorized, generally entails the application of international law as a whole. The sometimes difficult question is how to do so in an integrated and

---

[1] See especially *Case Concerning the Gabčíkovo-Nagymaros Project (Hungary/Slovakia)*, Judgment of 25 September 1997, [1997] I.C.J. Rep. 92 [*Gabčíkovo-Nagymaros*].

coherent manner. Given the great variety of potentially relevant environmental and other treaties and rules and principles of general international law, how do we determine their precise interaction? In this chapter, we will consider this question in the context of some of the more contentious topics—notably WTO law and human rights law. Yet what follows is not uniquely about the intersection of environment, trade, and human rights. Much of it is equally relevant to the interaction of treaties on other subjects and to the integration of international law in general.

How courts resolve the potential for conflict between competing norms in these situations is essentially a matter of judicial technique, but the case law of the International Court of Justice (ICJ) suggests that where possible it prefers an integrated conception of international law to a fragmented one.[2] Apart from highlighting the formative role of international courts in determining the applicable law—a point to which we will return in the penultimate section below—this conclusion points to the danger of viewing any part of international law in isolation from the whole. Not only are the rules dynamic but so potentially is their interaction. What cannot be supposed is that environmental rules have any inherent priority over others save in the exceptional case of *ius cogens* norms. No such norms of international environmental law have yet been convincingly identified.[3] Moreover, although, as we shall see, certain environmental treaties may on their own terms have some priority over other treaties in certain contexts, it would be wrong to assume either that this is generally the case or that the opposite is true.

2 RE-INTERPRETATION AS A TOOL OF INTEGRATION?

One of the most important approaches to the integration of different bodies of law is based on techniques of interpretation, taking account of one treaty or legal norm in order to assist in the interpretation or application of another treaty or norm. The idea that treaties can in this way have a dynamic or living interpretation is an important contribution to coherence in international law. Such interpretative techniques help to avoid conflicts between agreed norms, and can save negotiated agreements from premature obsolescence or from the need for constant amendment. Changing social

---

[2] *Ibid.* at paras. 112 and 140; *Advisory Opinion on the Legality of the Use or Threat of Nuclear Weapons (UNGA)*, Advisory Opinion of 8 July 1996, [1996] I.C.J.Rep. 95 at 226 [*Nuclear Weapons*]; *Case Concerning Oil Platforms (Islamic Republic of Iran v. United States)*, Judgment of 6 November 2003, [2003] I.C.J. Rep. 90 [*Oil Platforms*]. See also *United States—Import Prohibition of Certain Shrimp and Shrimp Products*, adopted WTO Dispute Settlement Body (DSB), 6 November 1998, WTO Appellate Body Report, Doc. WT/DS58/AB/R (1998) [*Shrimp-Turtle*].

[3] In *Gabčíkovo-Nagymaros*, see note 1 above at para. 97, the court impliedly accepted Slovakia's argument that none of the norms of environmental law on which Hungary relied was *ius cogens*.

values can be reflected in the jurisprudence, a point that is particularly well observed in international human rights law,[4] but less relevant in other contexts. More importantly, changes in international law and policy can also be accommodated where appropriate.

Article 31(3)(c) of the Vienna Convention on the Law of Treaties (Vienna Convention) accordingly provides that in interpreting a treaty account shall be taken of 'any relevant rules of international law applicable in the relations between the parties.' This notably Delphic formulation conceals more than it reveals, and it is presently the subject of further study by the International Law Commission (ILC).[5] How far, if at all, might the re-interpretation of treaties by reference to environmental concerns be possible under this provision? The terms within which 'evolutionary interpretation' of a treaty is permissible under Article 31(3)(c) have been narrowly circumscribed in the jurisprudence. While accepting 'the primary necessity of interpreting an instrument in accordance with the intentions of the parties *at the time of its conclusion*,' the ICJ has also acknowledged that treaties are to be 'interpreted and applied within the framework of the entire legal system prevailing at the time of the interpretation.'[6] Its approach in cases such as the *Namibia Advisory Opinion* and *Aegean Sea Continental Shelf* is based on the view that the concepts and terms in question 'were by definition evolutionary'[7] and not on some broader conception that is applicable to all treaties. The WTO Appellate Body has given a similarly evolutionary interpretation to certain terms in the 1947 GATT Agreement. In the *Shrimp-Turtle* decision, for example, it referred, *inter alia*, to the 1992 Rio Declaration on Environment and Development, the 1982 LOSC, the 1973 Convention on International Trade in Endangered Species of Wild Fauna and Flora (CITES), the 1979 Convention on the Conservation of Migratory Species of Wild Animals, and the 1992 Convention on Biological Diversity (CBD) in order to determine the present meaning of 'exhaustible natural resources.'[8]

In all of these cases, the question at issue was not the general revision or re-interpretation of a treaty. Rather, each case was concerned with the interpretation of particular provisions or phrases, such as 'natural resources' or 'jurisdiction', which necessarily import—or at least suggest—a reference to current general international

---

[4] See, e.g., *Soering v. UK*, Series A no. 161, (1989) 11 E.H.R.R. 439 at para. 102: 'the Convention is a living instrument which . . . must be interpreted in the light of present-day conditions'; *Öcalan v. Turkey*, (2003) 37 E.H.R.R. 10 at para. 196: Taking into account the current attitude towards the death penalty in the member states of the Council of Europe, 'capital punishment in peacetime has come to be regarded as an unacceptable, if not inhuman, form of punishment which is no longer acceptable under Article 2.'

[5] For a very thorough and helpful review, see C. McLachlan, 'The Principle of Systemic Integration and Article 31(3)(c) of the Vienna Convention' (2005) 54 Int'l & Comp. L.Q. 279.

[6] *Legal Consequences for States of the Continued Presence of South Africa in Namibia (South West Africa) Notwithstanding Security Council Resolution 276 (1970) (1970–1971)*, Advisory Opinion of 21 June 1971, [1971] I.C.J. Rep. 16 at 31 [*Namibia*]; *Aegean Sea Continental Shelf Case (Greece v. Turkey)*, Judgment of 19 December 1978, [1978] I.C.J. Rep. 62 at 32–3. The ICJ's approach, combining both an evolutionary and an inter-temporal element, reflects the ILC's commentary to what became Article 31(3)(c). See 'Law of Treaties,' in A. Watts, ed., *The International Law Commission 1949–1998*, volume 2 (Oxford: Oxford University Press, 1999) Chapter 8 at 690.   [7] *Namibia*, see note 6 above at 31.

[8] *Shrimp-Turtle*, see note 2 above at paras. 130–1.

law. Ambulatory incorporation of the existing law, whatever it may be, enables treaty provisions to change and develop as the general law itself changes, without the need for any amendment. As the ICJ points out in *Oil Platforms (Islamic Republic of Iran v. United States)*, such treaty provisions are not intended to operate independently of general international law.[9] Evolutionary interpretation is thus a relatively limited task, which is consistent with the intention of the parties. It does not entitle a court or tribunal to engage in a process of constant revision or updating of treaties every time a newer one comes along. Judge Bedjaoui makes the point in *Case Concerning the Gabčíkovo-Nagymaros Project (Hungary v. Slovakia)*:

Une interprétation d'un traité qui viendrait a substituer un tout autre droit à celui qui le régissait au moment de sa conclusion constituerait une révision detournée. 'Interprétation' n'est pas 'substitution' à un texte négocié et agrée d'un texte tout autre, ni négocié, ni convenu. Sans qu'il faille rénoncer à 'l'interprétation évolutive' qui peut être utile et même nécessaire dans hypothèses très limitées, il convient de dire qu'elle ne peut pas être appliquée automatiquement à n'importe quelle affaire.[10]

According to this view, interpretation is interpretation, not revision or rewriting of treaties. The result must remain faithful to the ordinary meaning and context of the treaty 'in the light of its object and purpose.'[11] The case law not surprisingly shows that over-ambitious attempts to reinterpret or 'cross-fertilize' treaties by reference to later treaties or other rules of international law are likely to have only limited success.[12] There is no reason to think that environmental treaties are any different in this respect.

Properly employed, interpretation can nevertheless be a useful means for integrating different texts or bodies of law. The precautionary principle is a particularly good example. Adopted by consensus in Principle 15 of the 1992 Rio Declaration, the precautionary approach helps us identify whether a legally significant risk exists by addressing the role of scientific uncertainty, but it says nothing about how to control this risk or about what level of risk is socially acceptable (see Chapter 25 'Precaution'). These are policy questions, which in most societies are best answered by politicians and by society as a whole rather than by courts or scientists. Like other pre-1992 environmental agreements, the 1982 LOSC nowhere refers to any such principle or approach. Nevertheless, as the *Southern Bluefin Tuna* cases suggest, the fisheries conservation articles of the LOSC have already been given a precautionary interpretation.[13] In the same way, the definition of pollution in Article 1, the obligation to do

---

[9] *Oil Platforms*, see note 2 above at paras. 40–1. See also *Gabčíkovo-Nagymaros*, note 1 above at paras. 140–1.   [10] *Gabčíkovo-Nagymaros*, see note 1 above, separate opinion, at para. 12.

[11] 1969 Vienna Convention on the Law of Treaties, Article 31(1) [Vienna Convention]. See also *Ireland v. United Kingdom (OSPAR Arbitration)*, (2003) P.C.A. at paras. 101–5 [*OSPAR* case].

[12] See, e.g., Ireland's attempt to rewrite the LOSC in the *Ireland v. United Kingdom (MOX Plant case)* (2002) P.C.A [*MOX Plant*].

[13] See, e.g., *Southern Bluefin Tuna* cases *(New Zealand v. Japan; Australia v. Japan)*, Provisional Measures, (1999) I.T.L.O.S. nos. 3 & 4, paras. 77–9; and Judges Laing at paras. 16–19; and Treves at para. 9 [*Southern Bluefin Tuna*].

an environmental impact assessment in Article 206, the general obligation to take measures to prevent, reduce, and control pollution under Article 194, and the responsibility of states for the protection and preservation of the marine environment under Article 235 are all potentially affected by the more liberal approach to proof of environmental risk envisaged by the precautionary approach articulated in the Rio Declaration.[14]

Other contemporary concerns such as the protection of biological diversity or the sustainable use of resources can similarly penetrate older terminology in earlier treaties on the law of the sea, international watercourses, natural heritage, environmental damage, and so on. The concept of sustainable development has had a considerable evolutionary impact on existing international environmental law, and on the development of new law. Its defining role in the evolution of international law and policy on the protection of the environment secured near universal endorsement at the UN Conference on Environment and Development (UNCED). It informs not only much of the Rio Declaration but also the UN Framework Convention on Climate Change, the CBD, and Agenda 21, the programme of action adopted by UNCED. Principle 27 of the Rio Declaration calls specifically for the further development of international law 'in the field of sustainable development,' and, at the request of the Commission on Sustainable Development, the UN Environment Programme initiated a study in 1995 of 'the concept, requirements and implications of sustainable development and international law.'[15] Sustainable development also forms an important element in the elaboration of global environmental responsibility by the Rio instruments (see Chapter 26 'Sustainable Development').[16]

That changes in international law do result from such internationally endorsed principles can be observed in the decision of the ICJ in *Gabčíkovo-Nagymaros*, in which the court referred for the first time to 'this need to reconcile economic development with protection of the environment which is aptly expressed in the concept of sustainable development.'[17] The court's reliance on sustainable development has had, as a result, significant implications for the law of international watercourses and it goes far towards modernizing the older customary law along the lines indicated by the ILC and the 1997 UN Convention on the Non-Navigational Uses of International Watercourses (Watercourses Convention). The latter convention was amended in

[14] P.S. Rao, in *Report of the ILC*, Doc. GAOR A/55/10 (2000), para. 716, who concludes that the precautionary principle is already included in the principles of prevention and prior authorization and in environmental impact assessment, 'and could not be divorced therefrom.' I. Brownlie, *Principles of Public International Law*, 6th edition (Oxford: Oxford University Press, 2003) at 276, observes: 'The point which stands out is that some applications of the principle, which is based on the concept of foreseeable risk to other states, are encompassed within existing concepts of state responsibility.'

[15] *Final Report of the Expert Group Workshop on International Environmental Law Aiming at Sustainable Development*, Doc. UNEP/IEL/WS/3/2 (1996).

[16] 1992 United Nations Framework Convention on Climate Change, Article 3; and 1992 Convention on Biological Diversity, Articles 8 and 10. See also 1994 Convention to Combat Desertification in Those Countries Experiencing Serious Drought and/or Desertification, Particularly in Africa, Articles 4, 5.

[17] *Gabčíkovo-Nagymaros*, see note 1 above at para. 140.

its final drafting stages to take explicit account of the principle of sustainable utilization, which is also one of the new principles applied to high seas fisheries by the 1995 Agreement Relating to the Conservation and Management of Straddling and Highly Migratory Fish Stocks (Fish Stocks Agreement).[18] Both the 1997 Watercourses Convention and the 1995 Fish Stocks Agreement thus have the effect of redefining existing legal concepts of equitable utilization of shared natural resources and freedom of fishing, and for the first time they introduce important environmental constraints into this part of international law relating to natural resources.

What these examples show is that subtle, evolutionary, policy-driven changes in existing law may come about through the process of interpretation. In any system of law, the ability to make such changes on a systemic basis is important. For this purpose, it is neither necessary nor useful to attempt to turn either the precautionary principle or sustainable development into 'rules' of customary international law or to enshrine them in a binding treaty. Their status as general principles of law or 'interstitial norms' is more than sufficient.[19] Yet, whatever the legal form employed, we can see here that different rules and principles can and do interact in ways that tend to advance the coherence and integration of other bodies of law. Principles of this kind may be 'soft', but sustainable development and its components remain very relevant when courts or international bodies have to interpret, apply, or develop the law. Even though sustainable development cannot plausibly be represented as a legal obligation with specific normative content, it can nevertheless represent a policy goal that influences the outcome of cases, the interpretation of treaties, and the practice of states and international organizations and that leads to significant changes and developments in the existing law. In this very important sense, international law does appear to require states and international bodies to take account of the objective of sustainable development and to establish appropriate processes for doing so.

3 Inter-Relationship of Treaties in General

Interpretation can only take the systematic integration of treaties so far, and it cannot readily deal with genuine conflicts between treaties. It then becomes necessary to consider what other rules govern the inter-relationship of treaties, environmental or otherwise. How treaties of different kinds inter-relate cannot be determined in any

---

[18] 1982 Agreement Relating to the Conservation and Management of Straddling and Highly Migratory Fish Stocks, Articles 5 and 6 [Fish Stocks Agreement].

[19] The point is very cogently developed by V. Lowe, 'Sustainable Development and Unsustainable Arguments,' in A. Boyle and D. Freestone, eds., *International Law and Sustainable Development* (Oxford: Oxford University Press, 1999) 19 at 31. Article 31(3)(c) of the Vienna Convention appears to include general

a priori sense. In general international law, the relationship between successive treaties is partly governed by the intention of the parties, partly determined by the nature of the treaty, partly regulated by the relationship between special and general rules, partly determined by residual rules based on the time of conclusion of incompatible treaties, and partly dictated by the operation of law.[20] A regime of such complexity is not well suited to ensuring a coherent integration between multilateral treaties.

Given the diversity of law-making institutions and the varying participation by states in all such treaties, a measure of incoherence and uncertainty in the relationship between specific treaties may be inevitable. Moreover, the relationship between any two agreements may not be policy-driven or reflect any particular appreciation of priorities on the part of the negotiators. Two treaties that are the result of a different 'legislature'—to use Pauwelyn's description—will also be 'the reflection of a different balance of interests and one state may well have been able to push through its interests more under one treaty than under another.'[21]

The first point to appreciate is that the relationship between two treaties is first and foremost determined by the terms of those treaties. If a later treaty is 'subject to' or 'without prejudice to' an earlier agreement, then it must be interpreted and applied accordingly. The earlier treaty will then prevail in any conflict.[22] The 1997 Watercourses Convention is a good example of this approach. This agreement was intended to codify and develop the general international law relating to international watercourses—in effect, it sets out a framework for specific watercourse treaties. However, unlike the 1982 LOSC or the 1995 Fish Stocks Agreement,[23] the Watercourses Convention does not alter existing agreements, such as those governing the Nile or the Amazon, nor does it necessarily require that future watercourse agreements be consistent with its basic principles.[24] On the contrary, under Article 3, parties to later agreements may 'apply and adjust' the provisions of the convention to the characteristics and uses of specific watercourses. The Watercourses Convention is thus an optional framework code or 'guideline' whose provisions are not only subject to reservation, but may be departed from ad hoc by any of the parties.[25] Although

principles of law as an aid to treaty interpretation. Note, however, that general principles cannot override or amend the express terms of a treaty. See *EC Measures Concerning Meat and Meat Products (Hormones)*, adopted by DSB 13 February 1998, WTO Appellate Body Report, Doc. WT/DS26/AB/R (16 January 1998), at paras. 124–5 [*Meat Products*].

[20] Vienna Convention, see note 11 above at Articles 30, 41, and 53.

[21] J. Pauwelyn, *Conflict of Norms in Public International Law* (Cambridge: Cambridge University Press, 2003) at 369.   [22] Vienna Convention, see note 11 at Article 30(2).

[23] See discussion later in this chapter in section 5.

[24] 1997 Convention on the Law on the Non-Navigational Uses of International Watercourses, Article 3 [Watercourses Convention]. Parties may 'consider' harmonizing existing agreements with the convention's basic principles.

[25] *Ibid.* at Article 3(3) and agreed statements of understanding in the UN General Assembly, 51st Session, *Report of the 6th Committee Working Group*, GAOR, Doc. A/51/869 (1997), para. 8; 36 I.L.M. 719 (1997). Reservations are not prohibited.

unusual, this approach does no more than recognize the normal freedom of parties when negotiating specific bilateral or regional agreements to depart *inter se* from the general rules of international law on the subject. The point of the codification treaty is not to override this freedom, but simply to provide some certainty about the law applicable in situations where the parties have been unable to reach an *inter se* agreement. On this basis, the possibility of a conflict between the Watercourses Convention and existing or future watercourse agreements cannot arise.

The second point is that it is simplistic and fallacious to assume that in the absence of contrary wording a later treaty will necessarily prevail over an earlier one. True, Article 30(3) of the 1969 Vienna Convention provides that when not terminated under Article 59 'the earlier treaty applies only to the extent that its provisions are compatible with those of the later treaty.' However, it would be unwise to take this wording at face value. In reality, the matter is more complex for several reasons, only some of which are considered in this chapter. On its own terms, Article 30 applies only to successive treaties 'relating to the same subject matter.' What this phrase means has never been authoritatively addressed, except by scholars. It does *not* mean that Article 30 applies only between environmental treaties, for example, but not to the relationship between, say, an environmental treaty and the 1994 WTO Agreement. Rather, the prevailing view is that it is necessary to distinguish between cases of genuine conflict, to which Article 30 does apply, and the rather different relationship between treaty provisions of a general character and more specific ones, to which it does not. It is an accepted principle that a *lex specialis* takes precedence over a *lex generalis* regardless of their priority in time. Reuter thus notes that '[t]he rule of article 30 would therefore only apply to treaties with subject matters of a comparable degree of 'generality.'[26] The point can be illustrated hypothetically by contrasting an earlier treaty providing for territorial sea boundaries to be delimited by equidistance with a later treaty providing for maritime boundaries to be delimited by agreement in order to achieve an equitable result. In the absence of any contrary wording, the later treaty would not prevail despite Article 30 because its general terms simply do not conflict with the more specific rule of the earlier treaty. Here, the two provisions do not address the same issue. Article 30 never comes into play.[27]

This is an important conclusion. If correct, it means, for example, that Article 30 will not operate to give general WTO trade rules adopted in 1994 priority as treaty law over earlier, more specific trade restrictions found in CITES or in the 1989 Basel Convention on the Control of Transboundary Movements of Hazardous Wastes and Their Disposal (Basel Convention). If this had been the intention of the parties, they should have said so expressly. The issue in these examples thus remains primarily one

---

[26] P. Reuter, *Introduction to the Law of Treaties* (London: Kegan Paul International, 1995) at 132, para. 201.
[27] UN, *Official Records of the Vienna Conference on Treaties* (1969), vol. II, at 253; and Pauwelyn, see note 21 above at 364–6.

of interpretation rather than precedence.[28] As Pauwelyn points out, this approach has implicit support from the ICJ's *Advisory Opinion on the Legality of the Threat or Use of Nuclear Weapons*, where the court found that environmental treaties and customary rules of a later but more general character did not displace specific treaty rules on the use of force and international humanitarian law.[29] It did not refer to Article 30 or to rules on the precedence of later treaties.

The third point to emphasize is that Article 30 is not the only article in the Vienna Convention governing the relationship between successive treaties. Articles 41 and 58 are also important. These provisions deal respectively with *inter se* modification or suspension of multilateral treaties. Article 41 provides in part that *inter se* modification of an earlier multilateral treaty is permissible provided the modification neither affects third party rights or obligations nor 'relates to a provision derogation from which is incompatible with the effective execution of the object and purpose of the treaty as a whole.' The point is that some treaties seek to create integral regimes for the common benefit of all states, which is often reinforced by a prohibition on reservations. It would be counter-productive to allow some states parties in effect to contract out by concluding later agreements *inter se*. Many provisions of global environmental treaties potentially fall into this category. Such treaties almost always prohibit reservations and expressly or by implication frown on incompatible *inter se* modifications. A good example is the 1982 LOSC. Negotiated by consensus and as a package deal, not only are reservations prohibited,[30] but the very far-reaching terms of Article 311 give it priority over most existing treaties and some future ones. In particular, the clear implication of Article 311(3) is that the drafters sought to limit the right of parties to derogate from the convention in later agreements.

Article 311(3) is modelled on Articles 41 and 58 of the Vienna Convention, with the addition of a reference to treaties affecting the application of the 'basic principles' of the LOSC. The drafters' concern for the integrity of the LOSC thus reflects general treaty law. The assumption is that, in the event that the kind of conflict envisaged in Article 311 arises, the LOSC will prevail over a later treaty dealing with the same subject matter, notwithstanding the *lex posteriori* rule enshrined in Article 30 of the Vienna Convention. When considering such clauses, the ILC commentary concludes:

The chief legal relevance of a clause asserting the priority of a treaty over subsequent treaties which conflict with it therefore appears to be in making explicit the intention of the parties to create a single 'integral' or 'interdependent' treaty regime not open to any contracting out; in short, by expressly forbidding contracting out, the clause predicates in unambiguous terms the incompatibility with the treaty of any subsequent agreement concluded by a party which derogates from the provisions of the treaty.[31]

---

[28] I. Sinclair, *The Vienna Convention on Treaties*, 2nd edition (Manchester: Manchester University Press, 1984) at 96.   [29] *Nuclear Weapons*, see note 2 above at para. 30.

[30] 1982 United Nations Convention on the Law of the Sea, Article 309 [LOSC].

[31] Watts, see note 6 above at 678.

It has accordingly been suggested that under Article 311(3) the later inconsistent agreement may be unenforceable, even between the parties to it, not simply illegal as a breach of treaty.[32] This line of argument leads to the interesting conclusion that in the event of a true conflict between WTO law and certain multilateral environmental agreements (MEA), the latter will prevail by virtue of Article 41 of the Vienna Convention. The necessary assumption, of course, is that the MEA provisions in question are 'integral' agreements for the common benefit of all states, from which derogation *inter se* must be controlled and that WTO agreements create a network of principally bilateral relations, from which derogation *inter se* will usually be permissible.[33]

Arguments for the unenforceability *inter se* of a treaty, based on Article 41 of the Vienna Convention or Article 311(3) of the LOSC, bear some similarity to the concept of *ius cogens*. It is worth noting, however, that while a treaty will be void or become void if it contravenes a rule of *ius cogens*, this argument has proved to be of little value in international environmental law. No one has yet successfully identified any specifically environmental rules or principles with a *ius cogens* status. Of course, some human rights norms do have a *ius cogens* character, and, to this extent, the concept may affect the relationship between human rights and environmental treaties. In practice, however, human rights courts, as we shall see later in this chapter, have not tended to approach the interaction of human rights and environmental law from this perspective.

4 INTERNATIONAL ENVIRONMENTAL LAW AND WTO LAW

The principal WTO agreements, including GATT, contain no provision governing their relationship with other treaties. Article 3(2) of the WTO Understanding on Rules and Procedures Governing the Settlement of Disputes (DSU) provides only that the 'covered agreements' are to be clarified 'in accordance with customary rules of interpretation of public international law.' Subject to the proviso that rights and obligations in the covered agreements are not thereby added to or diminished,[34] this entails interpreting WTO agreements in accordance with Articles 31–3 of the Vienna Convention, and not in accordance with specific GATT canons of interpretation.[35] As we saw in the section on interpretation, this provision has enabled the Appellate

---

[32] See Pauwelyn, note 21 above at 312–13.   [33] *Ibid.* at 315–24.
[34] General Agreement on Tariffs and Trade, 1994, Annex 2 (Understanding on Rules and Procedures Governing the Settlement of Disputes), see last sentence of Article 3(2) and Article 19(2).
[35] *Shrimp-Turtle*, see note 2 above.

Body to take account, *inter alia*, of the LOSC and the environmental commitments and obligations of states and to try to apply WTO law consistently with general international law, rather than treating it as a closed or self-contained system.[36]

The LOSC remains the only environmental agreement whose inter-relationship with WTO law has been explored by an international tribunal. The WTO case law suggests that GATT need not interfere with implementation of the LOSC commitments. In *Shrimp-Turtle*, the Appellate Body held that unilateral restrictions on trade in marine living resources are more likely to be regarded as arbitrary or discriminatory under GATT if the state concerned has not first sought a cooperative solution through negotiation with other affected states.[37] Moreover, the unwillingness of the United States to negotiate a possible solution made it harder to rely convincingly on the exceptions provided for in Article XX. Together, these findings effectively reinforce rather than threaten the duty under the LOSC's Articles 116–19 to cooperate in the conservation and management of high seas marine living resources. Although the WTO ruling did not specifically require further negotiations between the parties, the United States found in practice that the easiest way to achieve its objectives was by returning to the negotiating table to conclude a regional conservation agreement for marine turtles. Unilateral trade sanctions still remained a legitimate option had the other parties refused to negotiate in good faith.

To this extent, further consideration of the relationship between the LOSC and the 1994 GATT is probably academic. If there ever is a conflict, however, it will be important to recall that, as we saw earlier, and unlike the GATT, the LOSC prevails over earlier and later treaties to the extent that there is any incompatibility according to the terms of Article 311. As an integral agreement serving the common interest of all states, the LOSC can be derogated from by the parties to the GATT only as provided for in that article. By contrast, insofar as GATT obligations are primarily a series of bilateral trade relationships applicable *inter se*, they enjoy no such priority under Article 41 of the Vienna Convention.[38] Even if the GATT is not a mere *inter se* agreement, the LOSC will still prevail insofar as it is a *lex specialis*.

Moreover, as we saw in the previous section, it has been suggested that this reasoning also applies to provisions of many other global environmental agreements, including possibly the 1973 CITES, the 1989 Basel Convention, and the 1987 Montreal Protocol on Substances That Deplete the Ozone Layer—all of which contain specific environmentally related trade restrictions. All three prohibit or strictly limit the right to make reservations. All three are arguably intended to be integral regimes for the common benefit of all states parties. According to this view, as a matter of treaty law, but only between the parties thereto, the relevant environmental provisions would prevail over incompatible WTO law, even within the WTO system of dispute

---

[36] Pauwelyn, see note 21 above.

[37] *Shrimp-Turtle*, see note 2 above at paras. 166–72. However, note the failure to reach a negotiated solution. See *United States—Shrimp, Recourse to Art 21.5 of the DSU by Malaysia*, Appellate Body Report, Doc. WT/DS58/AB/RW (22 October 2001) at 37.   [38] Pauwelyn, see note 21 above at 312–13.

settlement.[39] And if a future global environmental agreement makes specific provisions for trade sanctions that are otherwise incompatible with more general commitments under GATT, on present law and in the absence of any savings clause, it also follows that the later environmental trade rule would prevail.[40] To this extent, states are free to promote trade bans or sanctions through regional or global environmental agreements, notwithstanding GATT.

Even if these arguments about the priority of environmental treaties are wrong or insufficient, there are other possible ways to integrate WTO law and environmental law or to reconcile potential conflicts. In particular, although the exceptions envisaged in Article XX of the GATT do not mention the term 'environment', there is little difficulty interpreting 'conservation of exhaustible natural resources' or protection of 'human, animal or plant life or health' broadly enough to cover any of the existing environmentally related treaty restrictions on trade.[41] Even the precautionary principle is not incompatible with the application of WTO law, provided the evidential basis for its application exists.[42] Once again, we can see the value of interpretation. This does not mean that conflicts between WTO law and international environmental law cannot arise, but it is noteworthy that the trade and environment case law has involved unilateral action by individual states, and that the decisions have focused on issues of arbitrariness, lack of justification, or discriminatory treatment, rather than posing a straight challenge to the applicability of environmental agreements.[43] On the contrary, guided by the Appellate Body, the post-1994 WTO case law has been rather sensitive to general international law. This result may not satisfy some WTO lawyers, but, so far, it has posed no threat to the viability of international environmental law.

5 INTERACTION OF ENVIRONMENTAL TREATIES: THE LOSC AND THE CBD

The relationship between the 1982 LOSC and the 1992 CBD shows how successive treaties on rather different topics can contribute to the development of an integrated legal regime (Chapter 15 'Ocean and Freshwater Resources', and Chapter 16 'Biological

---

[39] Non-parties to these multilateral environmental agreements would however be entitled to insist on their WTO rights. See Vienna Convention, note 11 above at Article 30(4).

[40] Pauwelyn, see note 21 above at 322–4. This assumes that the earlier rule is not a *lex specialis*. For a WTO view of the issues, see the reports of the Committee on Trade and Environment.

[41] See *Shrimp-Turtle*, note 2 above. In *United States—Standards for Reformulated Gasoline*, adopted by DSB 20 May 1996, WTO Appellate Body Report, Doc. WT/DS2/AB/R (29 April 1996), the WTO Appellate Body found that clean air (and presumably also clean water) is 'an exhaustible natural resource.'   [42] *Meat Products*, see note 19 above at paras. 120–5.

[43] In addition to cases already cited, see *European Communities—Measures Affecting Asbestos and Asbestos Containing Products*, adopted by DSB 5 April 2001, WTO Appellate Body Report, Doc. WT/DS135/AB/R (12 March 2001).

Resources').[44] As we noted earlier, the 1982 convention makes no reference to biological diversity. A decade later, the 1992 Rio Conference on Environment and Development adopted the CBD, whose provisions apply both to terrestrial and marine biodiversity. Clearly, each agreement is relevant for the purpose of interpreting the other. Equally clearly, the increasingly devastating effect of unsustainable fishing practices on marine biodiversity and ecosystems is a matter that directly affects the implementation of the CBD. There is undoubtedly a possibility that implementing the latter treaty could affect rights and obligations under the LOSC.

The CBD does not prevail over the LOSC nor does it give blanket priority to the LOSC. On marine environmental matters, Article 22 specifically requires parties to implement the CBD 'consistently with the rights and obligations of States under the law of the sea.' This wording suggests that they could not, for example, ignore the rights of ships to freedom of navigation in the EEZ and high seas, whether under the LOSC or under customary law. To this extent, Article 22 of the CBD reinforces the terms of Article 311(3) of the LOSC. Within these limits, the LOSC will prevail in any conflict. On the other hand, under Article 237 of the LOSC, agreements relating to the marine environment do not have to conform to Part XII of the convention but need only be carried out in a manner consistent with the 'general principles and objectives' of the convention. This would allow CBD parties much greater latitude to depart from the terms of Part XII than from other parts of the convention, since, as a *lex specialis*, Article 237 overrides Article 311(3). Save in an extreme case, the CBD regime will therefore prevail over Part XII of the LOSC.

More importantly, however, while Article 22 also provides that existing treaty rights and obligations are not affected by the CBD, this exclusion does not apply where 'the exercise of those rights and obligations would cause serious damage or threat to biological diversity.' While in general terms the effect of Article 22 is to ensure that the LOSC will normally prevail, states parties to the CBD cannot rely on the LOSC to justify—or to tolerate—fishing that causes or threatens serious damage to biodiversity. To this extent, the CBD may have modified Parts V and VII of the LOSC. Is this permissible within the terms of Article 311(3) of the LOSC?

Here, the answer is probably yes. Since conservation of marine living resources and the protection and preservation of 'rare or fragile ecosystems' and the habitat of 'depleted, threatened or endangered species and other forms of marine life' are already envisaged by the LOSC,[45] the convention's objects and purposes can readily be interpreted to include measures aimed at protecting marine biodiversity. Thus, for example, the adoption under the CBD of protected zones intended to reduce serious damage to biodiversity on the high seas would not be incompatible with the LOSC and would be consistent with Article 22 of the CBD. However, such zones would

---

[44] *Study of the Relationship between the CBD and UNCLOS with Regard to the Deep Seabed*, Doc. UNEP/CBD/SBTTA/8/INF (2004).

[45] LOSC, see note 30 above at Articles 61, 64–7, 117–20, and 194(5).

not be opposable to non-parties to the CBD, whose LOSC rights Article 311 expressly protects. Any meaningful attempt to regulate marine biodiversity in this way would thus in practice depend principally on the parties to the LOSC rather than on the parties to the CBD.

The relationship between the LOSC and the CBD is relatively complex and operates at several different levels. It should be obvious that this relationship could not be reproduced simply on the basis of the Vienna Convention rules on the priority of treaties. It clearly had to be negotiated and carefully considered in advance. We can also see how a major law-making treaty such as the LOSC has an ongoing impact on the structuring of later law-making agreements that affect matters regulated by the LOSC. This effect is not only limited to biodiversity or fisheries but can also be observed in relation, *inter alia*, to security,[46] narcotics control,[47] trade in hazardous cargoes,[48] or the protection of cultural heritage.[49]

Moreover, this feature of the LOSC also has implications at an institutional level. The most important contribution so far made by international law to the protection of marine biodiversity is the 1995 Fish Stocks Agreement. For the first time, this agreement brings an environmental and biodiversity perspective to international fisheries regulation. To a significant extent, it gives effect to some of the general objectives of the CBD. Notice, however, that the Fish Stocks Agreement is formally an agreement implementing the LOSC, not an agreement implementing the CBD. At one level, the reason is simply that this was how the UN General Assembly chose to proceed. However, at another level, it makes sense, given the priority that the LOSC enjoys both as a matter of law and of UN policy.[50] The range of matters covered by the Fish Stocks Agreement simply could not have been addressed with the same freedom or priority as an addendum to the CBD.

A final point is that we can see from the relationship between the LOSC and the CBD that international law on the conservation of marine living resources and ecosystems is not the exclusive preserve of either treaty. A coherent and comprehensive understanding of the present environmental law of the sea may require consideration of both treaties, even for states that are not party to one or the other, or both.[51]

---

[46] 2003 Proliferation Security Initiative.

[47] 1998 UN Convention against Illicit Traffic in Narcotic Drugs and Psychotropic Substances, Articles 4 and 17.

[48] 1989 Basel Convention on the Control of Transboundary Movements of Hazardous Wastes and Their Disposal, Article 4(12).

[49] 2001 Convention on the Protection of Underwater Cultural Heritage, Article 3.

[50] Agenda 21, 13 June 1992, UN Doc. A/CONF. 151/26 (1992).

[51] See, e.g. *Shrimp-Turtle* case, see note 2 above. The United States is not a party to either agreement, yet both were relied on in the decision of the WTO Appellate Body.

6 ENVIRONMENT AND HUMAN RIGHTS

Human beings are at the centre of concerns for sustainable development. They are entitled to a healthy and productive life in harmony with nature.[52]

International environmental law is essentially anthropocentric rather than radically ecocentric in character. Occasional references to the 'intrinsic value' of the environment notwithstanding, the subject broadly seeks to serve the interests of humanity in the quality and sustainability of life on Earth. Even the protection of wilderness areas such as Antarctica or endangered species such as the great whales largely serves human-centred needs and aspirations. In principle, the protection of human rights and the protection of the environment are thus not conceptually incompatible. Indeed, it has even been suggested that human rights are themselves dependent on sustaining a natural environment of adequate quality (Chapter 28 'Environmental Rights').[53]

Nevertheless, there are inevitably circumstances where environmental objectives and the rights of particular individuals or groups may come into conflict. Establishing wildlife reserves, regulating polluting activities, or controlling resource extraction, for example, may impair the use or value of property or hamper economic development. In extreme cases, environmental regulation may amount to a taking of property or an interference with private and family life, entitling the owner to compensation.[54] Yet failing to regulate or control environmental nuisances or to protect the environment may also interfere with individual rights. Cases such as *Guerra and Others v. Italy* and *Lopez Ostra v. Spain* show how the right to private life, or the right to life or to health, can be used to compel governments to regulate environmental risks, to enforce environmental laws, or to disclose information.[55] Merely because few human rights treaties create specifically environmental rights has not impeded the 'greening' of human rights law.

Obvious questions often posed in this context are whether human rights law trumps environmental law or whether environmental rights trump the right of states to pursue economic development. As we noted earlier, such potential conflicts have not led courts to employ the concept of *ius cogens* or to give human rights automatic

---

[52] Rio Declaration on Environment and Development, Principle 1.

[53] See *Gabčíkovo-Nagymaros*, see note 1 above, separate opinion of Judge Weeramantry; R.S. Pathak, 'The Human Rights System as a Conceptual Framework for Environmental Law,' in E. Brown Weiss, ed., *Environmental Change and International Law* (Tokyo: United Nations University Press, 1992) Chapter 8.

[54] *Sporrong and Lönnroth v. Sweden*, (1983) 5 E.H.R.R. 35.

[55] *Guerra and Others v. Italy*, (1998) 26 E.H.R.R. 357; *LCB v. UK*, (1999) 27 E.H.R.R. 212; and *Lopez Ostra v. Spain*, (1994) 20 E.H.R.R. 277; *Fedeyeva v. Russia*, (2005) E.C.H.R. 376.

priority. Instead, the case law has concentrated on questions of balance, necessity, and the degree of interference. It shows very clearly that few rights are ever absolute or unqualified. As a result, it has proved relatively easy for international tribunals to accommodate human rights, environmental law, and economic development. In cases before the European Commission and European Court of Human Rights, states have been allowed a wide margin of appreciation to pursue environmental objectives, provided they maintain a fair balance between the general interests of the community and the protection of the individual's fundamental rights.[56] A similarly wide discretion has enabled states to pursue economic development, provided the right of individuals to private and family life is sufficiently balanced against economic benefits for the community as a whole. Thus, in *Hatton v. United Kingdom*, [57] additional night flights at Heathrow Airport did not violate the right to private and family life because adequate measures had been taken to soundproof homes, to regulate and limit the frequency of flights, and to assess the environmental impact. Moreover, there was no evidence of any fall in the value of the homes concerned. The state will be failing in its duty to those affected if it does not regulate or mitigate environmental nuisances or environmental risk caused by such development projects insofar as necessary to protect life, health, enjoyment of property, and family life.

The same approach has been taken under other human rights treaties. In the *Ogoniland* case, the complainants alleged that oil reserves in Ogoniland had been exploited with no regard for the health or environment of the local communities, that toxic wastes had been discharged into the environment and local waterways, and that there had been many avoidable oil spills near villages. As a result, '[t]he contamination of water, soil and air has had serious short and long-term health impacts, including skin infections, gastrointestinal and respiratory ailments, and increased risk of cancers, and neurological and reproductive problems.'[58] They alleged violations of various articles of the 1981 African Charter on Human Rights and Peoples' Rights.

The African Commission held, *inter alia*, that Article 24 of the charter imposes an obligation on the state to take reasonable measures 'to prevent pollution and ecological degradation, to promote conservation, and to secure ecologically sustainable development and use of natural resources.'[59] The commission's decision sets out specific actions required of states in fulfilment of this obligation. This is perhaps the most remarkable environmental rights case so far decided by any human rights tribunal or commission. It shows above all that uncontrolled development can violate fundamental human rights, on the basis of evidence that, unlike *Hatton*, indicated very severe harm to human rights, which could not be justified by the government.

---

[56] See, e.g., *Pine Valley Developments Ltd. v. Ireland* , Series A no 222, (1991) 14 E.H.R.R. 319; *Fredin v. Sweden*, Series A no 192, (1991) 13 E.H.R.R. 784.

[57] *Hatton v. United Kingdom*, (2002) 34 E.H.R.R. 1 (Grand Chamber).

[58] *Ogoniland* case, *Social and Economic Rights Action Centre and the Centre for Economic and Social Rights/Nigeria*, African Commission on Human and Peoples' Rights, Communication no. 155/96 (27 May 2002).   [59] *Ibid.* at paras. 52–3.

A case of such severity does not demonstrate that environmental rights will always trump development objectives, but it does have implications for the manner in which some governments allow multinationals to operate in blatant disregard of the interests of local inhabitants.

7 DISPUTE SETTLEMENT AND APPLICABLE LAW

Any attempt to consider the inter-relationship of treaties or of different bodies of international law cannot ignore the problems posed by the multiplicity of international courts and tribunals before which disputes may be brought as well as the uncertainty concerning the applicable law that may then arise. States have taken an eclectic approach to international dispute settlement, and environmental disputes are no exception. The possibilities include the ICJ,[60] the International Tribunal for the Law of the Sea (ITLOS),[61] ad hoc arbitration,[62] the WTO Dispute Settlement Body,[63] or various combinations thereof (see Chapter 45 'International Dispute Settlement').

All of these tribunals have jurisdiction to decide disputes only insofar as the parties have consented. In this context, it is open to the parties to choose the applicable law if they wish to do so and can agree among themselves. They are not constrained to choose international law, either as a whole or in part. As a consequence, disputes under certain treaties may have to be determined solely in accordance with the rules of those treaties. The 1982 LOSC is an example. Article 293(1) provides that '[a] court or tribunal . . . shall apply this Convention and other rules of international law not incompatible with this Convention.' This does *not* mean that in an LOSC environmental dispute all of international law is applicable, including customary law or other environmental treaties to which the disputing states are parties. On the contrary, tribunals deciding LOSC cases may apply general international law only insofar as it is within their jurisdiction and not inconsistent with the LOSC to do so.[64] In general terms, this means that they may apply international law where specific articles of the LOSC so provide[65] or where it becomes necessary to do so for the purpose of

---

[60] *Gabčíkovo-Nagymaros*, see note 1 above; and *Nuclear Weapons*, see note 2 above.

[61] *MOX Plant*, see note 12 above; *Southern Bluefin Tuna*, see note 13 above; *Case Concerning the Conservation and Sustainable Exploitation of Swordfish Stocks in the South-Eastern Pacific Ocean (Chile/European Community)*, I.T.L.O.S. no. 7, Order no. 2000/3 (2000) [*Swordfish*].

[62] *MOX Plant*, see note 12 above; and *Southern Bluefin Tuna*, see note 13 above.

[63] *Shrimp-Turtle*, see note 2 above; and *Swordfish*, see note 61 above.

[64] *MOX Plant*, see note 12 above at para. 19.

[65] See, e.g., under Articles 19, 21, 23, 31, 32, 34, 39, 58, 74, 83 87, 221, and 235.

interpreting or applying the LOSC.[66] For example, if the question is whether freedom of fishing on the high seas can be suspended in order to carry out nuclear tests, the legality of such tests under general international law would have to be decided in order to apply the convention's rule on the use of the high seas with 'due regard' for the rights and interests of other states.[67] However, if the question is whether an environmental impact assessment (EIA) should have been conducted under Article 206 of the LOSC, it would neither be necessary for this purpose nor permissible for the tribunal to consider whether there had also been a violation of the same obligation in customary law or under the 1992 Convention on Environmental Impact Assessment in a Transboundary Context (Espoo Convention). Article 206 can readily be applied without addressing such issues. The Espoo Convention and any customary law on EIA might of course be relevant for the purpose of interpreting Article 206, but they do not thereby become applicable law.[68]

One result of allowing the parties to limit the applicable law is that some disputes cannot be decided in accordance with all of the relevant international law potentially applicable between the parties.[69] This is particularly a phenomenon of treaty disputes arising under compulsory jurisdiction. In subscribing to regimes of dispute settlement confined to the treaty itself, the parties must be taken to have intended such a limited outcome, unless they subsequently agree otherwise. It must be admitted, however, that in such cases we are presented with a picture of law that is neither integrated nor coherent. This is an inevitable consequence of the absence of universal compulsory jurisdiction.

Uncertainty surrounding the law to be applied in certain disputes has sometimes resulted in courts encouraging, or the parties themselves seeking, an agreed solution. Three LOSC environmental cases are indicative of the difficulty. Most obviously, in *Ireland v. United Kingdom (MOX Plant Case)*, where the applicability and relationship of the LOSC, EC law, and several other environmental treaties were in issue, both the ITLOS order and the arbitral award stress the parties' duty to cooperate pending a solution in terms rather stronger than the LOSC itself would justify.[70] In *Southern Bluefin Tuna*, the ITLOS judgment also refers to the need for cooperation,[71] while the arbitral award (declining jurisdiction) left the parties with no option but to resume negotiations, based on the 1993 Convention for the Conservation of Southern Bluefin Tuna, which they did successfully. Finally, in *Case Concerning the Conservation and*

---

[66] *M. V. Saiga* Case *(Saint Vincent and the Grenadines v. Guinea)*, I.T.L.O.S. no. 2, Judgment, (1999), at para. 155.

[67] Article 87. See *Nuclear Tests Cases (Australia v. France; New Zealand v. France)*, Judgments of 20 December 1974, [1974] I.C.J. Rep. 253 and 457.

[68] *MOX Plant*, see note 12 above; and OSPAR, see note 11 at paras. 101–5.

[69] This observation is not confined to environmental disputes. See *Case Concerning Military and Paramilitary Activities in and Against Nicaragua (Nicaragua v. United States of America)*, Judgment of 26 November 1984, [1984] I.C.J. Rep. 70 at 392; and *Oil Platforms*, see note 2 above.

[70] *MOX Plant, Request for Provisional Measures* (Order), I.T.L.O.S. no. 10 (2001) at paras. 82–4 and operative para. 1; and *MOX Plant*, see note 12 above at paras. 66–7.

[71] *Southern Bluefin Tuna*, see note 13 above.

Sustainable Exploitation of Swordfish Stocks in the South-Eastern Pacific Ocean, the parties, having initiated separate proceedings before ITLOS and the WTO, rather rapidly concluded that negotiation of a provisional settlement and the resumption of cooperation were preferable to a resolution of the admittedly difficult legal questions posed by a dispute that straddled both the LOSC and WTO law.[72] Each of these cases raises important and interesting matters of LOSC law and its relationship to other treaties; however, none of them address the merits nor are they ever likely to.

8 Conclusions

Neither conflict nor fragmentation are necessary consequences of the interaction of international environmental law with other branches of international law. In practice, international tribunals have usually found various ways of applying international law as an integrated whole, except where the parties themselves have made this difficult through the balkanization of dispute settlement and the selective choice of applicable law. Rules of interpretation, priority of treaties, or a balancing of competing interests have generally provided an ample range of techniques for promoting coherence in the application of international law.

This does not mean there are no problems. On the contrary, there will always be uncertainty about how different legal regimes or different bodies of law interact. Our examination of the inter-relationship of trade, environment, and human rights law shows that difficult judgements have to be made and that there remains much for lawyers to argue over. Do they interact at all? Has the right balance between environmental regulation and individual rights been maintained? Are the terms of a treaty inherently evolutionary? Are environmental trade restrictions a *lex specialis* or a *lex generalis*, or do they form part of an integral, non-derogable regime that will prevail over subsequent agreements? What law is applicable in any dispute? The answers to such questions will rarely be obvious, and the outcomes are unlikely to be predictable, and, for this reason, they are in practice some of the most challenging questions with which any international lawyer will have to deal.

Recommended Reading

M.R. Anderson and A.E. Boyle, eds., *Human Rights Approaches to Environmental Protection* (Oxford: Clarendon Press, 1996).

P.W. Birnie and A.E. Boyle, *International Law and the Environment*, 2nd edition (Oxford: Oxford University Press, 2002).

---

[72] *Swordfish*, see note 61 above; and in the WTO, *European Community-Chile—Measures Affecting the Transit and Importation of Swordfish*, Doc. WT/DS193/1 (26 April 2000).

A.E. Boyle and D. Freestone, eds., *International Law and Sustainable Development* (Oxford: Oxford University Press, 1999).

S. Charnovitz, 'The World Trade Organisation and the Environment' (1998) 8 Y.B. Int'l Envt'l L. 98.

G. Handl, 'Environmental Security and Global Change: The Challenge to International Law' (1990) 1 Y.B. Int'l Envt'l L. 3.

C. McLachlan, 'The Principle of Systemic Integration and Article 31(3)(c) of the Vienna Convention' (2005) 54 Int'l & Comp. L.Q. 279.

J. Pauwelyn, *Conflict of Norms in Public International Law* (Cambridge: Cambridge University Press, 2003).

P. Sands, 'International Law in the Field of Sustainable Development' (1994) 65 Br. Y.B. Int'l L. 303.

R.G. Tarasofsky, 'Ensuring Compatibility between Multilateral Environmental Agreements and GATT/WTO' (1996) 7 Y.B. Int'l Envt'l L. 52.

D. Zillman, A. Lucas, G. Pring, *Human Rights in Natural Resource Development* (Oxford: Oxford University Press, 2002).

CHAPTER 8

INSTRUMENT CHOICE

RICHARD B. STEWART

THIS chapter examines the several different types of environmental regulatory instruments, including command and control requirements, economic incentive systems, and information-based instruments, and their role in international environmental regulation.[1] Research on, and both positive and normative analysis of, environmental regulatory instruments in domestic settings is relatively advanced in the United States and has more recently emerged in Europe and some other regions. In the context of international environmental regulation, there have been a number of studies of regulatory instruments in specific fields, but systematic study of the distinctive issues posed by instrument choice in the international context is still in an early stage.

Environmental regulatory instruments provide incentives for actors who cause or contribute to pollution, environmental degradation, and ecosystem stress to change their behaviour in more environmentally protective ways. These actors are producers, resource users, developers, and consumers, including government entities engaged in such activities. These instruments are designed to implement public norms of environmental protection, and redress the limitations of private law, market ordering, and criminal law in securing appropriate behavioural changes on the part of these actors. Regulatory instruments may also serve to promote changes in actors' perceptions and values, and serve expressive or symbolic functions in affirming environmental and other societal norms.

The positive study of regulatory instruments seeks to identify and explain patterns in the development, and use of different instruments to address different types of environmental problems in different institutional settings. Such patterns may be explained, for example, by the instruments' functional performance, the interests of relevant governmental and non-governmental actors, or sociological influences. From a normative perspective, regulatory instruments can be evaluated in terms of their efficacy in securing environmental protection objectives; their efficiency in achieving protection at the lowest social cost; and their ability to satisfy distributional, equity, and governance values.

The subjects of regulation can be broadly divided into three groups: the regulation of products (including their characteristics, use, and disposal); product and process methods (PPMs), including manufacturing, agriculture, and resource extraction; and other forms of natural resource use, development, or consumption. Regulatory

Thanks to Michael Livermore, Jamie Hobbs, and Jordan Fletcher for excellent research assistance and to Jonathan Wiener for extremely helpful comments.

[1] This chapter does not address the legal character of regulatory instruments, for example whether or not they are legally binding as a matter of international or domestic law. Nor does it address non-governmental regulation (see Chapter 21 'Private and Quasi-Private Standard Setting'). It also does not analyse EU environmental regulation as an international regime (see Chapter 37 'Regional Economic Integration Organizations').

programmes may be based on the protection of specific resources, such as wetlands, the atmosphere, or endangered species, against a variety of stresses. Or, they may be stressor-oriented, aimed at controlling specific types of pollution, development, or consumption activities that may affect a variety of resources.[2]

There are three basic types of regulatory instruments: command and control measures, economic incentive systems, and information-based approaches. In some regulatory programmes, these instruments may be designed as a means for achieving given environmental quality objectives, for example, the prevention of 'dangerous concentrations' of atmospheric greenhouse gases, the maintenance of sustainable wildlife populations, or the achievement of defined limits on aggregate pollution or environmental stresses (such as a phase-down of ozone-depleting substances or preventing a net loss of wetlands).[3] In other cases, including, for example, requirements for the use of best available technologies (BAT) and best environmental practices (BEP), there may be no direct linkage to a specific environmental result. Instruments also differ in the degree of flexibility they allow regulated actors, including whether they specify a given environmental result (for example, a fixed percentage reduction in emissions) while leaving the actor free to choose the means for achieving it or whether they specify the means to be used (for example, the use of designated control technologies). All of these different regulatory instruments must, in order to be effective, be backed up by requirements and arrangements for monitoring compliance and environmental performance; for record keeping, reporting, and publicity; and for enforcement and sanctions.

This chapter first describes and compares the three basic types of environmental regulatory instruments, providing brief examples from domestic and international practice. It then examines experience with their use in domestic settings before turning to the distinctive issues posed by instrument choice in the international context, and experience with the use of various different instruments in international environmental regulatory programmes. It concludes with an agenda of issues for future research.

---

[2] Regulatory instruments can also be analysed in terms of whether they employ rules or standards. See D. Bodansky, 'Rules vs. Standards in International Environmental Law' (2004) 98 Proc. Am. Soc. Int'l L. 275. Command and information-based instruments may employ either rules or standards. The most important economic instruments invariably use rules, which is a factor promoting accountability.

[3] Such objective and limitations might function as regulatory instruments if there were only one relevant actor. If they were not achieved, responsibility would be unambiguous. However, where there are multiple actors, as is commonly the case, coordinated application of instruments aimed at the conduct of the several individual actors is needed to achieve these goals. Such instruments are the focus of discussion in this chapter.

1 Basic Types of Environmental Regulatory Instruments

1.1 Command and Control Regulation

Command and control regulation specifies required or prohibited conduct for each individual regulated actor with the aim of limiting, directly or indirectly, the level of pollution, stress, or resource consumption by each. Examples include:

- Quantitative limitations on the amount of pollution, wastes, other environmental stresses, or resource use by individual actors, such as limitations on individual source emissions implementing the limitations on various air pollutants set forth in the Convention on Long-Range Transboundary Air Pollution (LRTAP Convention). The limitations imposed on various individual actors may be based on achieving an aggregate environmental quality objective (for example, the critical loads approach in the 1994 Protocol on the Further Reduction of Sulphur Emissions). Or, they may be based on the control levels achievable by particular BAT or BEP measures (the actor is not required to use such measures if it can achieve the limitation by other means). Alternatively, the levels of limitation required may be based on a balancing of costs and benefits or political compromise. Yet in all of these cases, the controls are *performance standards* that mandate the environmental result to be achieved but not the means of attaining it. Since performance standards specify only 'how much' pollution is allowed—not 'how' to achieve this limit—performance standards allow regulated actors to choose the means they deem most appropriate for achieving the required level of control and thereby promote cost savings and innovation.
- Requirements for the adoption of specified BAT control technologies, product or PPM designs, or BEP practices. These *specification standards* mandate the means that the actor must use, with the goal of preventing or limiting the amount of pollution or other stress by the regulated actor. An example is the requirement in the International Convention for the Prevention of Pollution from Ships that oil tankers have double hulls and segregated ballast tanks. In contrast to performance standards, specification standards largely eliminate flexibility by dictating 'how' to achieve control (and, in so doing, also determine 'how much'). They may be chosen when it is difficult to fix or measure environmental performance or where regulated actors lack the information to determine appropriate compliance methods.
- Prohibitions on the discharge of certain pollutants or wastes—for example, the prohibitions on the disposal of wastes at sea set forth in the Convention on the Prevention of Marine Pollution by Dumping of Wastes and Other Matter. Such prohibitions impose a quantitative limitation of zero.

- Liability for causing environmental harm under a negligence standard. Actors whose conduct falls short of the applicable standard of due care are penalized by the imposition of damages liability. In contrast to command requirements for conduct established *ex ante* by statute or by administrative regulation, which are typically more specific, the regulatory standard of due care is quite general and applied case by case in liability actions *ex post*. Non-compliance with the negligence standard is sanctioned by a monetary liability, but the same is also true for many regulatory violations.

1.2 Economic Instruments

Economic incentive systems use instruments that impose a price or opportunity cost on each unit of pollution, waste, stress, or resource consumption by regulated actors. In contrast to command measures, which require or forbid specific conduct by each actor, economic instruments enlist the price system to steer behaviour in the desired direction, while giving each actor flexibility to determine the quantity of its pollution ('how much' flexibility) as well as the appropriate control measures ('how' flexibility). Since each actor/user bears a cost for each unit of pollution, etc., it faces continuing incentives to limit and further reduce its level. The level of tax or fee or the number of allowances issued may be designed to achieve a given environmental quality result or may be based on a balancing of costs and benefits, a political compromise, and so on (see Chapter 11 'Economic Theory of International Environmental Law'). Economic instruments include:

- Environmental taxes or fees imposed on each unit of pollution, resource use, and so on. For example, many European countries have imposed taxes on the discharge of various air and water pollutants.
- Tradable pollution, stress, or resource consumption quotas, such as the emission quotas for greenhouse gases set forth in the Kyoto Protocol and in the European Union (EU) carbon dioxide emissions-trading legislation. Each quota or allowance entitles the holder to emit a given unit of pollution, take a given quantity of fish, convert a given amount of wetlands, and so on. A fixed number of quotas are issued by the government through auction or administrative allocations. Quotas can be bought and sold. The market establishes a price for quotas. All actors that pollute, use resources, and so on must hold quotas equal to their level of pollution, use, and so on. Actors bear a cost for each additional unit of pollution or resource use because they must either buy additional quotas or bear the opportunity cost of forgoing the sale of surplus quotas that they would otherwise have had. Thus, while the total quantity of pollution and so on is fixed because the aggregate number of quotas is fixed, the system operates at the level of the individual regulated actor like a tax or fee. Each regulated actor has the flexibility, etc., to set its level of discharges, resource use, and so on, but must bear a cost for each discharge unit.

- Pollution, waste, or risk 'bubbles' that allow facilities to trade off reductions of different pollutants or hazards within an overall cap, as provided for some individual industrial facilities under the US Environmental Protection Agency's (EPA) Project XL program.
- Property rights in natural resources that provide incentives for right holders to conserve them by internalizing to the right holder the costs of resource depletion or degradation—for example, the property rights that the UN Convention on the Law of the Sea (LOSC) gives to coastal states over their exclusive economic zone (EEZ) resources.
- Pure subsidies. The government purchases pollution reduction, resource preservation, and so on at a given price or by auction.[4] Pure subsidies are rarely found in domestic practice. They must be distinguished from the widespread policy of partial subsidies by government to firms through tax credits, grants, or other measures to reduce their costs of complying with command and control or other independent regulatory requirements. Some international financial transfers, such as those provided under the Multilateral Fund of the Montreal Protocol on Substances That Deplete the Ozone Layer (Montreal Protocol), which are designed to compensate developing country parties for the full incremental cost of reducing the use of ozone-depleting substances, can be regarded as true subsidies.
- Liability for causing environmental harm under a strict liability standard, as exemplified by the Superfund system of liability for hazardous waste cleanup in the United States and the EU's new environmental liability scheme. In contrast to a negligence regime, the law in this case does not establish any standard of conduct. Actors are free to choose whatever level of pollution they wish but must on cleanup, in all cases, pay a corresponding price based on the level of environmental harm caused.

1.3 Information-Based Approaches

Information-based approaches are designed to generate and provide information to various constituencies, including consumers, investors, government officials, and the public generally, about the environmental performance of actors' products or services, PPMs, or resource use and development activities and thereby provide incentives for actors to modify their behaviour.[5] These 'suasive' instruments, which

---

[4] Pure subsidies can create perverse incentives for actors to increase their levels of pollution or resource use in order to be paid more to reduce these levels. Efforts to control this problem by fixing baselines create their own problems in the context of a dynamic economy. Governments or international organizations may impose environmental regulatory requirements as a condition of financial assistance to private firms, lower-level governmental authorities, or states. These arrangements differ from subsidies because the primary purpose of the grant is not improved environmental performance but some other societal objective such as infrastructure development. The environmental regulatory instrument employed is a.function of the character of the condition.

[5] See P.H. Sand, 'Information Disclosure,' in J.B. Wiener, M.D. Rogers, P.H. Sand, and J.K. Hammit, eds., *The Reality of Precaution: Comparing Risk Regulation in the US and Europe* (forthcoming); and R.B. Stewart, 'A New Generation of Environmental Regulation?' (2001) 29 Cap. U.L. Rev. 21 at 127–51.

embody a 'reflexive law' approach to regulation, leave total flexibility to actors in choosing both the environmental result and the means for achieving it, but the level of improved environmental performance that they provide may in some cases be uncertain or weak. Information-based approaches include:

- Ecolabels and other product-based information, aimed at consumers, about the environmental characteristics of products and services or the PPMs by which they were produced. Examples include voluntary ecolabel schemes, established by non-governmental organizations (NGOs) and/or industry, for sustainably produced timber or sustainably caught fish.
- Public disclosure of pollution discharges from, and hazardous wastes and materials located at, industrial and commercial facilities, as required for example in the United States and Europe.[6]
- Programmes, such as the UN Environment Programme's Global Reporting Initiative, whereby businesses report information on their environmental performance, aimed at the general public, consumers, and investors.
- Environmental impact assessments (EIAs) on new PPM facilities, resource extraction or use activities, and development projects, which are aimed at the governmental or private bodies undertaking, authorizing, or funding such activities and the general public. An example is the Convention on Environmental Impact Assessment in a Transboundary Context (Espoo Convention), which requires states to conduct EIAs on developments with significant transboundary environmental impacts.
- Environmental goal setting, management, auditing, and reporting requirements for private firms or government bodies, generating information aimed at the organizations' management, as exemplified by the International Organization of Standardization's 14000 series standards.

These information systems can be regarded as regulatory instruments insofar as either (1) they are required by law or (2) government or other actors (such as standard-setting organizations established by business firms or NGOs) provide inducements for their adoption for the purpose of altering the conduct of environmental actors.[7] They provide incentives for improved environmental performance through a variety of mechanisms. Insofar as they are aimed at consumers or investors who value superior environmental performance, firms with superior performance will benefit economically by attracting consumers or investors. In this respect, information systems can be regarded as a form of economic instrument. Insofar as they are aimed at the general public, they may create informal, but nonetheless often effective, public and political pressures for improved performance by firms or government

---

[6] See Sand, note 5 above; B.C. Karkkainen, 'Information as Environmental Regulation: TRI and Performance Benchmarking: Precursor to a New Paradigm?' (2001) 89 Geo. L.J. 257.

[7] As an example of government incentives, the US Environmental Protection Agency offers reduced inspection burdens and enforcement leniency to firms that adopt environmental management and audit systems. Examples of non-governmental eco-information systems include the environmental management systems developed by the International Organization of Standardization and the forest product labelling and certification systems developed by industry and NGO-industry groups.

agencies. Insofar as they are aimed at the management of business firms and other organizations, they may improve environmental performance by sensitizing management to the importance of, and promoting the organizational internalization of, environmental norms (see Chapter 21 'Private and Quasi-Private Standard Setting').

1.4 Hybrid Regulatory Approaches

Hybrid regulatory measures can be created by combining elements of different instruments. An example is deposit and refund systems for post-consumer or industrial wastes, which are common in Europe and North America, under which actors must pay a fee on purchase of products or generation of wastes that they can later recover on proper disposal in accordance with command requirements. In Europe, there are also schemes to earmark revenues from such fees to finance recycling and disposal. Another example is credit-trading systems, where pollution or resource quotas are established for each actor by command systems. Those actors who reduce pollution below their quotas can sell the quota surplus to others who can use them to comply with their regulatory obligations. A third hybrid is transferable resource development rights.

A number of European countries have made substantial use of environmental agreements negotiated by government and industry, under which industry undertakes to meet defined environmental objectives on a given timetable, and the government agrees to forbear imposition of additional legally binding regulatory requirements if industry carries out its undertaking. This technique does not itself constitute a regulatory instrument for the purposes of this chapter. Such agreements could potentially use any of the regulatory instruments discussed herein in specifying the character of industry's undertaking. In practice, most agreements call for percentage reductions or limitations on the aggregate quantity of emissions or wastes—a command approach—although the targets are sometimes 'soft' and industry generally has wide flexibility in implementation.

2 CHARACTERISTICS AND PERFORMANCE OF DIFFERENT ENVIRONMENTAL REGULATORY INSTRUMENTS

Until quite recently, domestic environmental regulation relied almost exclusively on command and control instruments. In the past several decades, however, there has been growing interest in many domestic jurisdictions in alternative approaches because of the declining efficacy of command systems in achieving increasingly ambitious environmental objectives and their rapidly growing cost, complexity, and administrative and regulatory burden. In the early stages of environmental regulatory programmes, command measures could achieve significant gains at relatively low cost. However, the need to achieve progressively greater levels of reductions in residuals and stresses in order to achieve higher levels of environmental protection demanded by the public, while simultaneously maintaining economic growth, has necessitated unrelenting proliferation and intensification of highly detailed and complex command requirements. This progression has revealed some inherent shortcomings in the command approach to residuals control, including the information collection and processing demands in devising centralized controls; the piecemeal and uncoordinated character of directives; rigidity and excessive cost; and rapid obsolescence. Similar problems have surfaced in natural resource management, where ambitious centralized command approaches often proved incapable of responding to the varying and dynamic conditions and uses of different water bodies, habitats, and ecosystems.

Economic incentives, especially taxes and tradable quota schemes, have a number of important economic and environmental advantages over command regulation:

- By relying on price incentives (either through taxes or through the cost of tradable allowances), rather than on command requirements, they allow wide flexibility to regulated actors to adopt environmental protection levels and strategies best suited for their particular circumstances, and to select those measures that achieve the desired results at the lowest cost.

- These systems also impose a cost on all residuals or stresses that an actor generates, whereas under command regulation permitted levels are free. This feature of economic instruments provides strong economic incentives for sources and actors who can reduce residuals or stresses at lower cost to assume more of the reduction burden relative to higher cost sources and actors. Thus, the price system coordinates the decisions of different actors in order to promote the most cost-effective allocation of control burdens. Centralized command regulation, which tends to impose uniform BAT or other quantitative limitations on all sources within a given category, is practically incapable of achieving such an allocation. Due to significant differences in marginal control costs among different actors, this feature of economic instruments can often generate large cost savings for society. In the pollution control context, for example, some emissions trading schemes have achieved aggregate cost reductions of up to 50 per cent or more relative to command systems.

- By treating all sources of pollution and so on the same, economic instruments also tend to promote a regulatory 'level playing field'. Under command regulation, by contrast, new sources are typically subject to disproportionately stringent requirements relative to existing sources (due to pressures from existing firms and environmental advocates), discouraging investment and capital stock turnover and keeping older, more polluting facilities, cars, and so on in use longer than otherwise, with adverse environmental results.

- The imposition of a price on all residuals or stresses also provides incentives for innovation in less polluting or environmentally stressful PPMs, products, and resource activities. Those firms who succeed in such innovation will pay lower taxes or be able to sell excess quotas and, thereby, gain a competitive advantage.

• Finally, imposing a price on externalities such as pollution can help promote allocational efficiency, and reduce their extent by producing relatively higher costs and prices for more heavily polluting or environmentally damaging products, and activities, thereby reducing the extent of market demand for them.

Economic incentive systems also have potentially important governance advantages relative to command approaches. By using the price system to provide incentives, the government's task is greatly simplified. Rather than having to specify the content of detailed controls for hundreds of different types of facilities and activities, the government establishes a tax or an aggregate level of quotas that apply to all actors generating the same type of pollution or environmental stress. Detailed engineering, economic, and location decisions are made by firms in response to price incentives, based on their local circumstances. Under command regulation, information asymmetries make regulators dependent on industry for much of the information needed to devise appropriate regulations, creating risks of regulatory 'capture' by industry. In addition, regulated actors and interest groups are better able to 'game' the complex, non-transparent details of command requirements in order to extract rents and secure relative competitive advantage. These games are more difficult to carry off under tax or trading systems. Since the decisions that government must make to establish tax or trading systems—the level of tax or aggregate level of residuals or resource use—are much more limited and transparent than under a labyrinthine system of ambitious command regulation, the use of these systems promises to promote regulatory accountability to political authorities and the public.

Tax and trading systems have several potential disadvantages relative to the command system—the most important being the problem of potential environmental 'hot spots'. The very flexibility that these instruments afford can be a disadvantage if a facility or actor uses it to generate a high level of pollution or resource use in a given location, and/or if a number of facilities or activities cluster together. This risk makes their use most appropriate for pollution and other environmental problems that are regional or global in scale or in other circumstances where the primary regulatory objective is to reduce the overall level of residuals or environmental stresses. Further, the hot spot problem, to the extent that it actually exists, can be addressed by imposing constraints on the flexibility that these instruments afford, but these constraints may reduce the cost savings achieved.[8] Although strong monitoring and enforcement is essential for the efficacy of any regulatory instrument, the greater flexibility that economic instruments afford may require government to adopt or require the use by regulated actors of more elaborate monitoring, reporting, and surveillance requirements in order to ensure compliance with requirements to pay taxes on, or

[8] For discussion of emissions trading and the hotspot issue, see J.B. Wiener, 'Homesis, Hotpots, and Emissions Trading' (2004) 12 Belle Newsletter 20.

hold quotas for, all emissions.[9] The costs of these measures are generally far less than the cost savings achieved by economic instruments. Nonetheless, they pose challenges for developing and transition economy countries with weak governmental infrastructure.[10]

Although both use the price system to provide incentives for environmental protection, taxes and trading systems have somewhat different features that may affect their relative suitability for addressing different types of environmental problems. The most important is that tradable quota systems impose an aggregate limit on the total quantity of residuals or stresses, while tax systems do not. On the other hand, price systems limit the total cost of control efforts (the marginal costs of such efforts will not exceed the tax rate), while quota systems do not. Thus, the choice between the two types of instruments in particular situations may depend on the relative importance of limiting the aggregate quantity of residuals or stresses, or the aggregate costs, and the likely distribution of errors in predicting these quantities and costs. A hybrid approach is a tradable quota system with the government sale of additional quotas at a fixed price. The latter's feature would be equivalent to a tax on excess emissions, and provide a safety valve against high costs. Quota systems may have higher transaction costs than tax systems and require a sufficient number of sources or actors to establish a well-functioning trading market.

A further consideration is raised by the possibility, under a quota system, of allocating quotas gratis to existing sources rather than auctioning them. This approach has the practical political advantage of lessening resistance by existing sources to the adoption of quota-trading systems. Almost all of the tradable quota schemes that have been adopted have 'grandfathered' existing sources and actors by allocating them quotas gratis. It is not feasible to provide equivalent protection for existing sources under a tax system. This feature helps explains the US preference for tradable quota over tax systems, and the fact that the EU proposal for a carbon dioxide tax failed while a tradable quota system was adopted. Although giving out allowances helps engage participation by existing emitters, it poses equity issues because it confers gratis the value of the right to emit (scarcity rents) to emitters (command regulation also confers this valuable right without charge). In contrast, auctioning allowances would reap this value for the public (taxpayers), in a similar way to taxes. A hybrid solution is to sell some allowances and issue others as needed to engage participation or to start with a free allocation of allowances that are good for only limited periods and gradually introduce auctions.

---

[9] See D.H. Cole and P.Z. Grossman, 'When Is Command-and-Control Efficient? Institutions, Technology, and the Comparative Efficiency of Alternative Regulatory Regimes for Environmental Protection' (1999) Wis. L. Rev. 887. Questions have also been raised as to whether the assumptions about business decision-making on which economic incentive systems are based are realistic. See T.F. Malloy, 'Regulating by Incentives: Myths, Models and Micromarkets' (2002) 80 Tex. L. Rev. 531.

[10] See R.G. Bell, 'The Kyoto Placebo' (Winter 2006) Issues in Science and Technology 28. The advantages of economic instruments for such countries are presented in D. Dudek, R.B. Stewart, and J.B. Wiener, 'Environmental Policy for Eastern Europe: Technology-Based versus Market-Based Approaches' (1992) 17 Colum. J. Envt'l L. 1.

Since the efficacy of information-based instruments is often uncertain, due to the flexibility afforded to actors and the potential weakness or unpredictability of the incentives involved, and may be undermined by collective actions problems, such instruments are generally employed as a supplement to other regulatory instruments or adopted when political agreement on more direct controls is lacking.

Instrument choices in both the domestic and international contexts involve complex tradeoffs among efficacy, economic efficiency, and equity. No regulatory instrument dominates all others on these criteria in all situations. Efficacy includes consideration of administrative and organizational factors at both the levels of government regulators and of regulated actors, including information and analytical demands and the challenges of implementation, monitoring, and enforcement. Regulators may, for example, adopt prohibitions or technology-based command regulations on the ground that they are simpler to administer, comply with, and monitor than more flexible and more resource-efficient regulatory approaches. Efficacy also includes adaptability to new information and circumstances and changing societal priorities. Resource efficiency includes not only compliance outlays by regulated actors but also administrative costs; the impacts, negative and positive, of regulation on investment and innovation; and the opportunity costs of activities forgone because of regulatory requirements. Equity has several dimensions, including equity among different categories of regulated firms and individuals and distributional impacts on neighbours or citizens generally. Some critics of economic instruments claim that they are inequitable and immoral because they convey a license to pollute (a criticism also applicable to most command regulation); allow the wealthy to avoid changes in behaviour; and corrode environmental values by using prices rather than commands. In the international context, this concern has been raised by some developing countries in the context of greenhouse gas quota-trading schemes. These countries fear that such schemes will advantage the North and the multinational corporations at the expense of the South. These criticisms lack merit where economic incentive systems are properly designed and take due account of distributional equity.[11]

3 Environmental Regulatory Instrument Choice in the Domestic Context

Since analysis of instrument choice in the international context is still at an early stage, it is helpful to draw on both the much fuller domestic research and the more

[11] See R.B. Stewart, 'Economic Incentives: Opportunities and Obstacles,' in R. Revesz, P. Sands, and R. Stewart, eds., *Environmental Law, the Economy, and Sustainable Development* (New York: Cambridge University Press, 2000) 171.

limited comparative research. Domestic experience with different instruments is relevant in assessing international applications, provided that the difference in contexts is fully considered. Currently, environmental regulatory programs in industrialized societies generally use a combination of different types of command regulatory instruments as a basic foundation. For example, pollution and waste control programs generally rely primarily on a mix of BAT requirements and pollution and waste limitations based on the achievement of environmental quality standards. Some efforts have been made in Europe and elsewhere to achieve greater integration at the facility level of diverse, piecemeal pollution and waste command requirements. A similar mix of command approaches can be found in many natural resource management programs. The command and control regulatory foundation has been supplemented in many developed, and some developing, country jurisdictions by pollution or waste taxes or tradable pollution quotas; statutory systems of strict liability for clean up and, in some cases, natural resource damages; and information-based requirements for monitoring and public disclosure of pollution releases, and waste generation and storage, and for the environmental impact assessment of new facilities and development projects.[12]

There has been a growing use of tax and quota-trading instruments in both developed and developing countries over the past two decades.[13] This trend reflects the growing importance of reducing the cost of more ambitious environmental regulations—a consideration that is, for reasons developed later in this chapter, especially important in the international context. The United States has used quota- and credit-trading systems to regulate air pollution as well as water pollution and development projects that impact wetlands and wildlife habitat. For example, the highly successful quota-trading program to reduce US sulphur dioxide emissions has cost less than 50 per cent of the equivalent command regulations, saving many billions of dollars. Cost savings were the driving factor in the EU's recent adoption of a carbon dioxide emissions trading system to implement its Kyoto Protocol commitment. In general, however, Europe has favoured taxes as the economic incentive system of choice. Tax levels have typically been too low to have strong incentive effects, although a number of European countries have recently adopted taxes at rates that are high enough to have significant incentive effects. Many developing countries and countries with transition economies have adopted fees or fixed penalties based on the level of pollution in excess of regulatory standards. Often, however, the levels are too low to

[12] Environmental impact assessments especially have come to play an important role in the environmental regulatory structure of developing countries. See N. Lee and C. George, eds., *Environmental Assessment in Developing and Transitional Countries: Principles, Methods and Practice* (Chichester, NY: John Wiley and Sons, 2000); C. Wood, 'Environmental Impact Assessment in Developing Countries: An Overview,' paper given at the Conference on New Directions in Impact Assessment for Development: Methods and Practice, 24–5 November 2003.

[13] See generally, Stewart, note 11 above; J. Golub, ed., *New Instruments for Environmental Policy in the EU* (London: Routledge, 1998); and P. O'Brien and A. Vourc'h, *Encouraging Environmentally Sustainable Growth: Experience in OECD Countries*, OECD Economics Department Working Papers no. 293 (Paris: OECD Publishing, 2001) (finding recent trend in OECD countries towards market-based instruments).

have great impact or there are enforcement problems. Proceeds are often used for environmental modernization of industry and funding environmental agencies.

The widespread use of mixed or hybrid systems of environmental regulation may be explained as an effort to combine the advantages of different instruments, and to avoid the shortcomings involved in relying exclusively on a single instrument—an important lesson for international instrument choice. The precise mix of instruments chosen, however, will depend on which attributes of efficacy, efficiency, and equity are judged most important in the context of a particular regulatory problem and jurisdiction. The complexity of the tradeoffs involved is illustrated by a Resources for the Future comparative study of experience with command and economic regulatory instruments for pollution control in the United States and Europe. The study found that the performance of these different instruments depended heavily on the environmental problem being addressed, and also varied among different criteria of performance.[14] It concluded that economic instruments often achieved cost savings relative to command instruments, were superior in promoting innovation and achieving higher than expected reductions, and generally had lower information burdens and were more adaptable. Command instruments generally achieved regulatory objectives faster and with greater certainty and had lower monitoring costs. Regulated firms were more likely to oppose economic instruments because they required firms to pay taxes or obtain permits in addition to incurring compliance costs. The study found no clear evidence that command regulations in practice are better in dealing with pollution hotspots. Instrument choice in the international context will likely present similar context-specific tradeoffs.

Overall, the pattern of domestic instrument choice appears to be evolutionary in character, with near-exclusive reliance on relatively primitive command systems at the beginning; steady extension, refinement, and intensification of those systems in order to make further environmental progress and address newly discovered problems; and the addition of economic incentive and information-based instruments in response to the growing limitations of the command approach.[15] It is surprising, however, that greater use has not been made of economic instruments, especially taxes and quota-trading programs, considering the strong efficiency and innovation advantages that they have over command approaches in dealing with many types of environmental problems.

The positive political theory of instrument choice helps explain the relatively limited use to date of economic instruments.[16] Politicians have reason to favour

---

[14] W. Harrington, R.D. Morgenstern, and T. Sterner, eds., *Choosing Environmental Policy: Comparing Instruments and Outcomes in the United States and Europe* (Washington, DC: Resources for the Future, 2004).

[15] See P.O. Busch, H. Jörgens, and K. Tews, 'The Global Diffusion of Regulatory Instruments: The Making of a New International Environmental Regime' (2005) 598 Annals 146.

[16] See N.O. Koehane, R.L. Revesz, and R.N. Stavins, 'The Choice of Regulatory Instrument in Environmental Policy' (1998) 22 Harv. Envt'l L. Rev. 313; R.N. Stavins and R. Revesz, 'Environmental Law,'

spillovers? Overuse of a global commons? International trade in hazardous products? Loss of local biodiversity that is a matter of global concern? Fear that international competitiveness pressures may lead to inadequate domestic environmental
regulation? How does the structure of the problem, which is thought to require centralized or harmonized regulation, affect instrument choice?

Further, the decision rules for regulation at the international level are very different than at the purely domestic level. This difference also has significant implications
for instrument choice. Thus, as Jonathan Wiener has emphasized,[19] as a matter of
international law, states in general must voluntarily assent to any regulatory obligations that they assume (although, of course, they may be subject to various pressures
and inducements from other states to give such assent). In contrast, at the domestic
level (and in many federal systems and the EU), governments follow decisional rules
requiring far short of unanimous consent in adopting and enforcing regulatory
requirements against dissenters. As Wiener has shown, this difference, combined
with the incentive of states to 'free ride' on the efforts of others in achieving global or
regional environmental public goods, makes the ability of regulatory instruments to
enhance state participation in, and compliance with, international environmental
regulatory agreements vitally important. This consideration may, for example, call
for the use of transfer payments between states or trade sanctions in order to induce
participation. Indeed, some analysts are quite sceptical that international environmental agreements can achieve significant change in states' environmental conduct
without the use of instruments to provide such carrots and/or sticks.[20] A related,
important feature of the international setting is the free movement of investment
and trade among jurisdictions. This circumstance exacerbates collective action problems by heightening states' concerns about international competitiveness and the
leakage of investment to jurisdictions with more lax regulation, and reinforces the
importance of selecting instruments that will provide incentives for state participation and compliance.

The structure of international environmental regulation complicates the positive
political economy theory of instrument choice by creating an iterative two-level regulatory game. In purely domestic regulation, firms and other actors attempt to influence the design and implementation of regulatory programs in order to obtain
competitive advantage, extract rents, and otherwise further their interests. At the
international level, actors operate at both levels, each seeking to use the one to influence the other. Also, states are additional and very important actors. Competitiveness

---

[19] J. Wiener, 'Global Environmental Regulation: Instrument Choice in Legal Context' (1999) 108 Yale
L.J. 677 (discussing international environmental instrument choice in the context of climate regulation);
J. Wiener, 'On the Political Economy of Global Environmental Regulation' (1999) 87 Geo. L.J. 749 (dis-
cussing public choice and civic republican models of collective decision making).

[20] See S. Barrett, *Environment and Statecraft: The Strategy of Environmental Treaty-Making* (Oxford:
Oxford University Press, 2003) (discussing different environmental regulatory instruments in terms of
incentives for state participation and compliance with international agreements).

concerns are a pervasive and powerful factor. Thus, states may seek to promote adoption in international agreements of the regulatory instruments that they use domestically not only because they are familiar with them but also in order to secure competitive advantage. For example, in the negotiations leading to the 1992 UNFCCC and the Kyoto Protocol, the United States successfully advocated the adoption of emissions trading and a comprehensive approach, including all greenhouse gases and sinks, rather than a command-and-control focus on fossil carbon dioxide emissions alone, which was favoured by the EU. The United States did so in part for environmental reasons, but also because the EU approach would place the United States, with its heavy reliance on fossil fuels, at a relative competitive disadvantage and because US firms (including commodity brokers and other service professionals) had gained experience with emissions trading through US domestic programmes and were, as a result, well equipped to play in a global trading system. The EU advocated the contrary approach based on similar competitiveness considerations.[21]

As a further complication, much international regulation, including environmental regulation, does not follow the classical model of formal international agreement among states, followed by domestic implementing measures[22] (see Chapter 4 'Global Environmental Governance as Administration'). For example, many international bodies such as the Codex Alimentarius adopt international regulatory standards through decision rules that do not require unanimous consent among participating states. In many cases, such standards are adopted by expert committees or other administrative bodies. Although these standards are often not legally binding, domestic regulators often have strong practical incentives, including incentives arising from agreements by the World Trade Organization, to adopt them. In addition, extensive informal inter-governmental arrangements among domestic regulatory agencies have arisen to harmonize domestic environmental product regulation of internationally traded products, including through bilateral arrangements for mutual recognition or regulatory equivalence. Private and hybrid private-public forms of regulation are another emerging feature of international environmental regulation in such areas as environmental management and audit systems, and labelling and certification systems for forest products and coffee. Corporate environmental codes of conduct have been promoted by the UN, the Organisation for Economic Co-operation and Development (OECD), and industry and NGOs. The implications for instrument choice of these alternative forms of international environmental regulatory governance are just beginning to receive attention (see Chapter 21 'Private and Quasi-Private Standard Setting').

[21] See Wiener, *Political Economy*, note 19 above.
[22] See B. Kingsbury, N. Krisch, and R. Stewart, 'The Emergence of Global Administrative Law' (2005) 68 L. & Contemp. Prob. 15.

4.2 International Regulatory Instruments Governing Interactions among States

This subsection examines the horizontal dimensions of instrument choice in international environmental regulatory practice—the vertical dimension is discussed in the subsection that follows. Quite a number of international environmental agreements specify a distinctive set of regulatory instruments targeted specifically at various types of environmentally relevant interactions among states and their private actors, as opposed to obligations that are generic in character. Of course, these horizontal arrangements may, indeed typically will, require domestic implementing measures to control the conduct of private actors who are often involved in the relevant interactions. However, these arrangements are aimed in the first instance at transborder interactions and always specify the instruments to be used.

Trade measures designed to further environmental objectives include prohibitions by a state on the import of goods or services from another state (a command measure). Examples include the Convention on International Trade in Endangered Species of Wild Fauna and Flora; the Convention on Transboundary Movement and Management of Hazardous Wastes within Africa (Bamako Convention); and the Stockholm Convention on Persistent Organic Pollutants (Stockholm Convention). The Montreal Protocol and the Basel Convention on the Control of Transboundary Movements of Hazardous Wastes and Their Disposal (Basel Convention) prohibit trade with non-parties in ozone-depleting chemicals and hazardous wastes, respectively. Other agreements make trade conditional on prior informed consent (PIC) by the importing state, using a hybrid of command and information-based approaches. Examples include the Basel Convention (hazardous wastes where trade in them is not prohibited); the Cartagena Protocol on Biosafety (Cartagena Protocol) (genetically modified organisms); the Food and Agricultural Organization's Code of Conduct (chemical products); and the Convention on the Prior Informed Consent Procedure for Certain Hazardous Chemicals and Pesticides (PIC Convention) (chemical products). As yet, there is no example of the use in this context of price instruments such as tariffs or countervailing duties, although there has been talk in some states party to the Kyoto Protocol of using countervailing duties against US imports to offset the competitive advantages that US industry may enjoy because of the US refusal to be bound by international greenhouse gas regulatory controls.

These trade measures have various objectives, depending on the trade-environment interface of interest. They may be designed to protect the environment of the importing state by excluding commodities that will produce environmentally harmful effects in the importing state. PIC measures when combined with information disclosure requirements, may be aimed at information asymmetries. Import bans may aim to reduce the level of environmental degradation created by environmentally harmful PPMs located in the exporting state by curtailing demand for the products produced. Or they may be designed to impose economic pain on the exporting state to induce it to adopt more protective environmental measures, including participation in, and compliance with, international environmental agreements. Some agreements with trade measures, such as the Montreal Protocol, have several of these objectives.[23] The relation between objectives and instruments in this context invites further study.

Subsidy payments to states are a form of economic incentive provided in several international environmental agreements in the form of transfers from developed countries to developing countries, either directly or through a fund administered by international organizations, to induce the latter's participation and compliance with such agreements. Examples include the Montreal Protocol, the Convention on Biological Diversity (CBD), the UNFCCC, and the Stockholm Convention. In many cases, the subsidy is set equal to the incremental costs to the recipient country of complying with relevant obligations. Developed countries thereby purchase developing country contributions to environmental protection. The contractual model is further reflected in treaty conditions that make compliance by developing countries with treaty obligations dependant upon the provision of these transfers. Debt-for-nature swaps are another mechanism for transfer of pure subsidies to developing countries to promote environmental objectives.[24] While rarely found in the domestic context, pure subsidies have more often been found necessary internationally to overcome 'free rider' problems, to provide incentives for states' participation in regulatory programmes to provide global public goods, and to meet the distributional concerns of developing countries (see Chapter 41 'Technical and Financial Assistance').

State property rights in natural resources have been established by international law in order to strengthen incentives for resource conservation. One example includes the extension of national regulatory jurisdiction to resources within the EEZ that would otherwise be a global commons vulnerable to overexploitation by all states and their private actors. The objective is to provide states with the legal means and the incentive to conserve these resources. Regional fisheries agreements, such as the North East Atlantic Fisheries Commission, have followed a similar logic in allocating quotas among states.[25] The CBD recognizes state property rights over biodiversity

---

[23] Environmental regulatory trade restrictions adopted by states, which may be designed to protect domestic producers against competition, are subject to regulation under free trade regimes such as the World Trade Organization and the North America Free Trade Agreement. The legal consequences, under these regimes, of the authorization of trade measures by multilateral environmental agreements are an unresolved issue.

[24] The World Bank group, the regional development banks, UN agencies, and individual countries provide financial transfers to developing countries primarily for achieving other objectives, such as economic development, but often attach environmental conditions. As previously explained (note 4 above), these do not constitute economic instruments as defined in this chapter.

[25] The current commission was established in 1982, under the Convention on Future Multilateral Cooperation in the North East Atlantic Fisheries. Although prior to the expansion of the exclusive

within a state's borders in order to protect biological resources against unregulated exploitation by other states' private actors as well as to respond to distributional concerns of developing countries.[26]

International pollution quota-trading programmes among states are a form of economic incentive that enable states and their private actors to enjoy cost savings resulting from differences among states in the cost of limiting emissions of global pollutants or achieving other environmental objectives. They effectively create property rights in common resources, similar to the programmes discussed in the previous paragraph, but also authorize their transfer. The most prominent example are the flexibility mechanisms in the Kyoto Protocol that permit trading among states of greenhouse gas emissions allowances or credits and joint implementation arrangements. The Montreal Protocol authorizes the trading of emissions quotas by states to achieve industrial rationalization. This provision has been used infrequently because of its limited scope. Quota-trading systems can also be used, for example, in the climate regulatory context to transfer resources in the form of generous quota allocations to selected states in order to induce their participation, as exemplified by the allocations given to Russia and the Ukraine in the Kyoto Protocol, and to meet distributional concerns of developing countries.

Liability for environmental damage. International agreements increasingly provide for strict liability as a form of economic incentive to address environmental harm to other states or the global commons. Typically, liability is targeted at private actors. Examples include agreements relating to marine oil pollution, carriage at sea of hazardous and noxious substances, interstate impacts from nuclear power accidents, and transboundary shipments of hazardous wastes. Negotiations are pending to establish liability systems for transboundary shipments of genetically modified organisms (GMOs) under the Cartagena Protocol. Common characteristics include strict liability, liability channelling, liability limits, and compulsory insurance. Direct state liability is authorized in very few agreements, for example, the Convention on International Liability for Damage Caused by Space Objects, and is recognized as customary international law in some circumstances, but has been little used in part

---

economic zone to 200 miles in the 1970s, an earlier iteration of this commission played a more important role. The commission continues to allocate quotas. See, e.g., North East Atlantic Fisheries Commission, *Recommendation by Denmark (on Behalf of the Faroe Islands and Greenland), the European Community and Norway for a NEAFC Recommendation on Management Measures for Mackerel in 2005*, Report of the Twenty-Third Annual Meeting of the North-East Atlantic Fisheries Commission, 8–12 November 2004, volume II: Annexes, Annex J (2004) (establishing total allowable catch of 40,185 tonnes of mackerel and allocating quotas).

[26] Convention on Biological Diversity (CBD), Article 15 ('[T]he authority to determine access to genetic resources rests with the national governments'); L.R. Helfer, 'Regime Shifting: The TRIPs Agreement and New Dynamics of International Intellectual Property Lawmaking' (2004) 29 Yale J. Int'l L. 1 at 30–2 (describing the effect of convention's access rules as 'allow[ing] biodiversity-rich developing nations to act as gatekeepers, conditioning access by private parties . . . upon a promise to provide compensation, technology transfers, or other benefits').

because of the reluctance of states to bring claims against other states (see Chapter 44 'International Responsibility and Liability').

Information requirements for transboundary environmental impacts. International law increasingly recognizes the obligation of states to provide information on activities within their borders that may or may have generated significant environmental impacts on other states. The Espoo Convention and a number of regional agreements oblige parties to prepare EIAs on new undertakings that will likely have such impacts. EIA provisions are also found in the LOSC and the Protocol on Environmental Protection to the Antarctic Treaty (Madrid Protocol). The Cartagena Protocol requires a risk assessment in connection with international transfers of GMOs. Regional agreements and developing principles of international law require states to notify other potentially affected states of accidents or other occurrences that will have such effects.

It is significant that many of the instruments surveyed earlier in this chapter are economic instruments or otherwise have an important market-based dimension. Trade measures or transfer payments in the form of money or valuable pollution or resource quotas can provide important incentives for state participation and compliance with international environmental regulatory regimes. As Wiener also points out, trading programmes and other economic instruments can strengthen these incentives by greatly reducing the costs of achieving environmental objectives and the correlative costs of participation, and correspondingly reduce the gains from free riding. Trading programs can also provide significant profit opportunities for private actors, creating important constituencies favouring participation.

4.3 Domestic Regulatory Instruments to Implement International Environmental Agreements

The majority of international environmental agreements do not focus on interactions among states through specific rules and instruments targeted at those interactions, but rather oblige states to regulate purely domestic activities to achieve generic environmental goals. Here, a fundamental distinction is between those international agreements that specify or constrain states' choice of domestic implementing measures and, to this extent, secure a degree of uniformity in domestic regulatory strategies, and those that do not. The latter are probably the majority. Before examining the choices made in various types of agreements, this subsection will address the factors relevant to the choice between promoting uniformity and adhering to the principle of subsidiarity in domestic instrument choice (see Chapter 5 'Levels of Environmental Governance').

Several considerations favour state discretion and methodological pluralism in instrument choice. As a result of varying local circumstances and legal and institutional traditions, greater participation and more effective, efficient, and equitable regulation may be obtained by giving states flexibility to choose implementing measures than by offering them a single approach. Further, it may be desirable to allow for experimentation with alternative instruments rather than dictating a uniform approach that may turn out not to work very well. The independent value of political self-determination is another argument in favour of subsidiarity. Alternatively, agreements may fail to specify domestic implementing measures because states are unwilling for various reasons to make specific commitments or cannot agree on which measures should be chosen.

There are also various considerations favouring uniformity through international specification of the domestic instruments used to implement international regulatory programs. Experience or judgement may conclude that a specific means for achieving environmental protection is the best in particular circumstances. It may be easier to monitor and promote compliance with requirements for the use of a given instrument than with general undertakings. Harmonizing domestic product regulations can promote global trade and benefit consumers by reducing transaction costs and promoting scale economies. Requiring all states to use the same means may seem equitable, allay competitiveness concerns, and avoid the risk of excessively high costs in achieving fixed emissions or environmental quality targets. Bans and BAT requirements may be seen as serving strong moral or expressive values or ensuring a precautionary approach. On the other hand, particular instruments may be specified because they are the most familiar to the negotiators or experts in the field, based on national or other international experience.

The choice between these competing considerations is not all or nothing. International agreements may impose some constraints on domestic measures, for example, by requiring the use of command controls to limit pollution discharges by domestic sources, but allow choice among the specific types of command instruments used to achieve this limitation. Further, the choice in favour or against a degree of uniformity in particular circumstances will also be shaped by the political economy factors previously discussed, including competitiveness concerns and the interests of regulated firms, NGOs, and relevant domestic government agencies and international organizations.

4.3.1 International Agreements that Do Not Specify Domestic Implementing Instruments

The many international agreements that refrain from harmonizing domestic regulatory instruments are quite various. In many cases, states' international commitments regarding the substance of domestic measures that they are obliged to undertake are extremely vague or general.[27] Even quite generalized undertakings may be further

---

[27] See, e.g., UN Convention on the Law of the Sea (LOSC), Article 194(1), which explains that states are to take 'all measures necessary to prevent, reduce and control pollution.' UNEP regional seas agreements, cited in note 30 in this chapter; the 1968 African Convention on Conservation of Nature and

diluted by provisions that agreed measures are to be taken 'as far as possible' (or some similar qualification).[28] In some cases, such provisions may be supplemented by procedural obligations, such as monitoring and reporting;[29] by institutional arrangements, for example, requirements that states adopt systems for prior regulatory authorization for designated activities;[30] and by provisions for an integrated approach to planning and implementation.[31] However, the generality of such arrangements is often so great as to leave states virtually plenary discretion, not only in the means chosen but also in the result to be achieved. Such agreements can be viewed as largely symbolic in character, as a reflection of weakness and a lack of meaningful mutual commitment by states or, perhaps, as evidence that the problem addressed is of low priority from an international perspective. Yet, such agreements may, especially in the context of a framework convention, also provide a foundation for communication and cooperation that will later ripen into more specific commitments.

By contrast, a fair number of agreements specify quantitative targets and specific timetables for achievement by states of quantitative limitations on aggregate pollution levels or resource losses without, at the same time, specifying the measures and

Natural Resources; the 1995 Agreement for the Implementation of the Provisions of the United Nations Convention on the Law of the Sea of 10 December 1982 Relating to the Conservation and Management of Straddling Fish Stocks and Highly Migratory Fish Stocks; and the CBD.

[28] See, e.g., CBD, Article 6; and see J. DiMento, *The Global Environment and International Law* (Austin: University of Texas Press, 2003) at 44–5.

[29] See, e.g., LOSC, Articles 204–6 (states must 'keep under surveillance' and assess potential effects of activities in which they engage to determine whether they pollute the marine environment and communicate results of surveillance to other parties); CBD, Article 7; and UN Framework Convention on Climate Change, Article 12 (requiring, *inter alia*, parties to 'communicate to the [COP] . . . [a] national inventory of anthropogenic emissions by sources and removals by sinks of all greenhouse gases').

[30] See, e.g., UNEP regional seas agreements: the 1976 Convention for the Protection of the Mediterranean Sea against Pollution; the 1978 Kuwait Regional Convention for Co-operation on the Protection of the Marine Environment from Pollution; the 1981 Convention for Cooperation in the Protection and Development of the Marine and Coastal Environment of the West and Central African Region; the 1981 Convention for the Protection of the Marine Environment and Coastal Area of the South-East Pacific; the 1982 Regional Convention for the Conservation of the Red Sea and Gulf of Aden Environment; the 1985 Convention for the Protection, Management and Development of the Marine and Coastal Environment of the Eastern African Region; the 1986 Convention for the Protection of the Natural Resources and Environment of the South Pacific Region; and the 1983 Convention for the Protection and Development of the Marine Environment in the Wider Caribbean Region. Agreements may also oblige states to adopt adequate sanctions and penalties to ensure compliance by regulated actors. See, e.g., the LOSC; the 1976 Convention for the Prevention of Marine Pollution from Land-Based Sources; the 1989 Basel Convention on the Control of Transboundary Movements of Hazardous Wastes and Their Disposal; the 1991 Convention on Transboundary Movement and Management of Hazardous Wastes within Africa; the 1994 Lusaka Agreement on Cooperative Enforcement Operations Directed at Illegal Trade in Wild Fauna and Flora; and the Convention on the Protection of the Environment through Criminal Law.

[31] See, e.g., the LOSC; the 1994 Convention on Cooperation for the Protection and Sustainable Use of the Danube River, Article 2; African Convention on the Conservation of Nature and Natural Resources; the 1985 ASEAN Agreement on the Conservation of Nature and Natural Resources; and the 1987 Agreement on the Action Plan for the Environmentally Sound Management of the Common Zambezi River System.

instruments to be used in achieving these targets. These prescriptions constitute international command and control requirements, in the form of an environmental performance standard, at the level of states but not at the level of domestic actors. Examples include the Montreal Protocol, the LRTAP Convention, the Kyoto Protocol, and some international water pollution control agreements.[32] These commitments, which usually involve percentage reductions from historical baselines, involve defined, measurable objectives. A state's progress in meeting them can be monitored. In such cases, it is plausible that the failure to specify the choice of domestic instruments to achieve the aggregate limitations target reflects subsidiarity considerations rather than a lack of commitment or agreement.

The same basic structure—a performance-based command standard at the level of the state but not at the level of domestic actors—is found in international agreements where states commit to meet a well-defined environmental quality standard or natural resource management objective through appropriate domestic regulation. Such provisions, however, vary in the specificity of the environmental objectives to be obtained (including timetables); the tightness of the linkage between required action by states and the environmental objective, and the definition of states' respective responsibilities with regard to achieving environmental quality objectives for shared resources. Thus, some agreements provide environmental goals—the prevention of 'dangerous concentrations' of greenhouse gas emissions in the UNFCCC and the adoption by states of water quality objectives and criteria for shared waterbodies under the 1992 UN Economic Commission of Europe Convention on the Protection of the Marine Environment of the Baltic Sea Area (Helsinki Convention)—in quite general terms without linkages to specific mechanisms for achieving them. On the other hand, well-defined environmental quality objectives and implementing linkages are found, for example, in a number of water pollution control agreements[33] and in the Convention on the Conservation of European Wildlife and Natural Habitats.

4.3.2 *International Specification of, or Constraints on, the Choice of Domestic Instruments*

A wide range of international environmental agreements promote uniformity in instrument choice by requiring states to use specified command regulatory measures such as bans or BAT controls on relevant domestic actors, usually without linking their use to the achievement of defined environmental objectives. These measures operate as command requirements both at the level of states and of regulated actors.

---

[32] See, e.g., Annex I of the 1992 Convention for the Protection of the Marine Environment of the North-East Atlantic (requiring states to regulate point source discharges); and the 1976 Rhine Conventions of Chemicals and Chlorides.

[33] See 1976 Agreement between the United States of America and Canada on Great Lakes Water Quality (maximum concentrations, drinking water objective, and prevention of hot spots); 1976

States must use the designated regulatory technique, and the conduct of each regulated actor is subject to the prohibitions or requirements adopted through this technique. Such agreements thereby promote uniformity in domestic regulatory instruments. However, these requirements vary in specificity and, in many cases, leave states considerable flexibility to determine the precise character and extent of the constraints imposed on regulated actors' conduct.

4.3.2.1 *Command and Control Instruments*

Most environmental agreements that specify domestic instrument choice require the use of some form of command instrument. This pattern may reflect a judgement that such instruments will be more effective in achieving environmental progress than the alternatives or will be easier to monitor. Or the pattern may reflect greater familiarity with such instruments or political-economy influences such as those discussed in the domestic context.

Bans or prohibitions. Many international agreements oblige states to prohibit specified activities, including the use of driftnets for fishing, the commercial taking of whales, the incineration of hazardous substances at sea, the intentional discharge at sea of oil or oily substances or radioactive wastes, the discharge of specified pollutants by land-based sources into watercourses, the taking of migratory birds and other wild animals, the production and use of persistent organic pollutants, and mineral development in the Antarctic. Such measures may be economically inefficient because they limit or eliminate flexibility, but they may nonetheless be specified because they are judged to be more effective than alternatives, easier to monitor, or necessary for their symbolic value.

BAT and BEP requirements for PPMs. Some agreements require the use of BAT or BEP in very general terms. For example, the Bamako Convention requires the use of 'clean production methods', while the LOSC obliges states to use 'best practicable means' to prevent or control marine pollution. Other conventions, including the Convention for the Protection of the Marine Environment of the North-East Atlantic (OSPAR Convention) and the Helsinki Convention, provide for a process to specify BAT or BEP with much greater particularity. The IAEA adopts quite specific good practice guidelines for nuclear safety. In some cases, an agreement establishes a specification standard—for example, the Madrid Protocol requires the incineration of hazardous wastes. However, in many cases, it is unclear whether the requirements set forth in an agreement are specification standards, requiring the use of designated technologies or methods, or performance standards, requiring achievement of control levels achievable by such methods.

Convention on the Protection of the Rhine against Chlorides and 1991 protocols (controls must achieve drinking water quality; limit values set by Rhine Commission). See also the Convention on Long-Range Transboundary Air Pollution, including Article 1(7) of the 1988 Sophia Protocol on Nitrous Oxides; Article 1(18) of the 1991 Protocol on Volatile Organic Compounds or Their Transboundary Fluxes ('critical loads' objective). These arrangements are similar to the obligation of states under the US Clean Air Act to control source emissions to achieve national air quality standards by fixed dates.

Specification standards for product design, composition, or packaging and labelling. Examples include double hull requirements for oil tankers, limits on the sulphur content of fuels or mercury in pesticides, and labelling and information disclosure requirements for pesticides and other chemical products.

Limitation of development activities in designated protected areas for the conservation of habitat and natural resources. A number of international agreements provide for the designation of protected areas and oblige states to prohibit or restrict development activities within such areas as well as take other steps to conserve the resources in question. Examples of this approach include the Convention on Wetlands of International Importance Especially as Waterfowl Habitat, the CBD, and the Convention on the Conservation of Migratory Species of Wild Animals. The obligations provided in the first two agreements are quite general so that states have wide latitude in selecting both the means and level of protection afforded.

4.3.2.2 *Economic Instruments*

International specification of economic instruments in the purely domestic context is rare. Strict liability for environmental damage is provided in the 1993 Convention on Civil Liability for Damage Resulting from Activities Dangerous to the Environment,[34] and the pending PIC Convention. No international agreement requires domestic use of taxes or quota-trading systems, although the international greenhouse gas-trading mechanisms in the Kyoto Protocol will create strong inducements for states to adopt domestic quota, and credit-trading schemes in order to take full advantage of these flexibility mechanisms. The EU has already adopted a carbon dioxide emissions-trading scheme internally as part of its Kyoto implementation plan.

4.3.2.3 *Information-Based Approaches*

EIA and other information-based provisions for domestic activities are found in the CBD and in the UNFCCC, among others. The World Bank requires EIAs in connection with development and infrastructure project financing. There are a variety of other information-based measures emerging in international environmental law.[35]

5 Conclusion: An Agenda for Future Research

Systematic analysis of instrument choice in international environmental law is still in an early stage. The notable exception is atmospheric regulation. A vast literature has emerged regarding regulatory instruments for climate protection under the Kyoto

---

[34] See generally articles on 'Civil Liability and Accountability in International Environmental Law' (2003) 12 R.E.C.I.E.L. 225–309.   [35] See Sand, note 5 above.

Protocol and otherwise, including a discussion of the relative merits of taxes, green-house gas quota and credit trading, command and control measures, coordinated management policies, joint technology research and development, direct resource transfers to developing countries programs, and setting national emissions limitations requirements. There has also been extensive analysis of the political economy of instrument choice in the climate context.[36] The Montreal Protocol instruments and their lessons for climate and other international environmental regulatory contexts have also received considerable attention.[37] What might explain the focus on these regimes and the relative neglect of the issues of instrument choice in other areas? In the case of the global atmosphere, the environmental problems are potentially grave. The potential costs of climate regulation are staggering. In addition, the problems are novel—domestic antecedents are of limited relevance. These factors invite and justify intensive research. Yet, these reasons go only part of the way to explaining the relatively underdeveloped state of systematic analysis in other areas of international environmental law. An agenda for future research would include the issues laid out in the following sections.

5.1 Comparative Analysis of Functional Characteristics and Performance of Different Instruments

A central topic for research—for purposes both of normative evaluation and positive explanation of instrument choice—is the comparative performance of different instruments in relation to the character of the environmental problem to be addressed. A comparative analysis for command and economic instruments in Europe and the United States, such as that recently carried out by Resources for the Future, needs to be done at the international level, taking into account the several dimensions of performance—environmental effectiveness, efficiency, and equity—and the distinctive institutional features and incentive structures operating in the international context. Such analysis should address the following issues among others:

• the nature of the environmental resource at risk;
• whether the scope of the problem is global, regional, bilateral, or national;

---

[36] See, e.g., Barrett, note 20 above at 389–91 (summarizing proposals); R.W. Hahn and R.N. Stavins, 'Trading in Greenhouse Permits: A Critical Examination of Design and Implementation Issues,' in H. Lee, ed., *Shaping National Responses to Climate Change: A Post-Rio Policy Guide* (Washington, DC: Island Press, 1995) 177 and 202–4 (discussing political economy of tradable permits); S. Barrett and R. Stavins, 'Increasing Participation and Compliance in International Climate Change Agreements' (2003) 3 Int'l Envt'l Agreements: Pol. L. & Econ. 349 (discussing alternatives to the Kyoto architecture); R.B. Stewart and J.B. Wiener, *Beyond Kyoto* (Washington, DC: American Enterprise Institute Press, 2003) (evaluating alternatives and advocating quota trading system); and Wiener, *Political Economy*, see note 19 above.

[37] See, e.g., Barrett, note 20 above at 221–39.

- whether the problem relates to products, PPMs, or resource development, extraction, or use and the specific characteristics of the regulated activities in question;
- the identity of the actors whose behaviour needs to be changed in order to address the problem, including industry, agricultural actors, consumers, or government agencies;
- the sources of 'de-centralization failure' and the reasons why common or coordinated international measures are needed, such as global commons, transboundary pollution, preservation externalities, trade linkages, or competitiveness concerns such as a 'race to the bottom';
- whether the international regulatory program in question addresses interactions among states and their private actors or general domestic regulation, as discussed earlier in this chapter;
- the considerations for and against international law harmonization of domestic regulatory instruments, as discussed earlier in this chapter, and how they may vary depending on the type of environmental problem and pontential instrument in question; and
- the extent to which specification of different instruments at either the international or domestic level, can promote states' participation in, and compliance with, cooperative regulatory regimes.

Comparative study and analysis of the performance of different instruments could help improve international environmental regulatory decision-making by promoting a more systematic consideration of the armoury of available instruments to address particular environmental problems in different structural contexts and the selection of those best suited. An institutional innovation that could enhance this process would be the adoption, at the international level, of regulatory analysis and review procedures similar to those adopted in the United States and the EU, which use the tools of cost-benefit analysis to examine the relative advantages and disadvantages of different regulatory policies, including the use of different regulatory instruments, to deal with different international environmental problems.[38]

5.2 Positive Theory Regarding Instrument Choice

Another central task is to explain why different international agreement regimes do or do not specify particular instruments, both in the context of interactions among states and their private actors and in domestic implementation. Possible explanatory approaches include the following:

- Functional performance. Instruments are chosen where they are appropriate and best suited for addressing given regulatory problems, taking into account

[38] See J.B. Wiener and J.D. Graham, 'Resolving Risk Tradeoffs,' in J.D. Graham and J.B. Wiener, eds., *Risk versus Risk: Tradeoffs in Protecting Health and the Environment* (Cambridge, MA: Harvard University Press, 1995).

environmental effectiveness, efficacy, equity, and the ability to promote participation and compliance.

- Public choice. Instruments are chosen as a result of strategic interaction among
  organized interests, governmental and non-governmental, at and between the
  domestic and international levels, including interests related to international economic competitiveness.
- Sociological factors. Instruments may be chosen because they are familiar to, and
  regarded as, successful or appropriate by communities of international environmental specialists, including diplomats, policy experts, and representatives of business organizations and NGOs.[39]
- Dominant states. Powerful states may have disproportionate influence in the selection of instruments in international agreements because of their ability to use
  negotiating carrots and sticks to get their way or because of superior epistemic or
  other resources. Such states may push for or against instruments based on their
  economic or other interests or their familiarity with them.

Positive analysis would also examine the mechanisms by which international agreement or convergence on particular instruments is achieved. One mechanism is vertical borrowing or the transplant of instruments from domestic regulatory law.
International decision-makers may follow approaches that are familiar in domestic
systems, subject to the distinctive considerations, discussed earlier, in instrument
choice in the international context.[40] Another mechanism is horizontal borrowing or
transplanting from other international environmental agreements. The extent, as
well as the suitability, of such borrowing will be influenced by the extent of the
similarities and differences in the nature of the problems addressed, and the context-
specific structure of state and private actor incentives. Still another mechanism is
bottom-up harmonization or convergence though efforts to coordinate or harmonize divergent domestic regimes without a treaty, which may eventually yield a dominant instrument response that may be incorporated in international agreements.
Borrowing and transplants may be based on superior performance, consensus
among epistemic communities, other sociological factors, or the influence of dominant states or non-governmental actors. The study of these mechanisms is just beginning. For example, D.G. Victor and L.A. Coben studied international air pollution
control agreements and classified them as based predominantly on either quantity

---

[39] The classic reference is P.M. Haas, 'Introduction: Epistemic Communities and International Policy
Coordination' (1992) 46 Int'l Org. 1. For discussion of the sociological concept of acculturation as an
alternative to coercion or persuasion in the development of international regimes, see R. Goodman and
D. Jinks, 'How to Influence States: Socialization and International Human Rights Law' (2004) 54 Duke
L.J. 621. For discussion of sociological accounts of international environmental institutions, see D.J.
Frank, A. Hironka, and E. Schofer, 'Environmentalism as a Global Institution' (2000) 65 Am. Soc. Rev.
122; and D.J. Frank, A. Hironka, and E. Schofer, 'The Nation-State and the Natural Environment over the
Twentieth Century' (2000) 65 Am. Soc. Rev. 96.

[40] See J.B. Wiener, 'Responding to the Global Warming Problem: Something Borrowed for Something
Blue: Legal Transplants and the Evolution of Global Environmental Law' (2001) 27 Ecology L.Q. 1295.

instruments (establishing specific pollution limitation targets and timetables) or 'price' instruments (including not only financial instruments but BAT and other measures judged to require comparable levels of economic effort among countries). They conclude that those agreements requiring significant commitments overwhelmingly provide for quantity instruments and attribute this pattern to a 'herd mentality' among international decision-makers.[41]

Careful consideration must also be given to experience in the EU and in federal systems with a two-level structure of regulation, which may illuminate similar issues of instrument choice, including instrument harmonization, in the international context.[42] The experience most likely to be relevant is that found in systems, such as the EU, where the higher level authority mainly regulates private actors indirectly through implementing regulatory measures in member states (see Chapter 37 'Regional Economic Integration Organizations'). The first several decades of EU environment regulation involved intensifying command regulation written in Brussels, and considerable harmonization of member state regulatory techniques and results. A reaction to excessive centralization began in the 1990s, resulting in a relaxation of harmonization efforts through the adoption of framework directives implemented by member states, and increased emphasis on information-based approaches. A somewhat similar pattern can be discerned in schemes of 'cooperative federalism' between the US EPA and states. This experience may caution against ambitious instrument harmonization at the international level.

The different approaches to research summarized earlier in this chapter could be researched at two different scales. One is overall patterns or trends. For example, the foregoing review suggests that the instruments most commonly chosen to regulate transnational interactions among states and private actors—trade measures, financial transfers, and property rights systems—are those best calculated to promote states' participation and compliance in international environmental agreements. The evidence also suggests that bans, quantitative limitations with targets and timetables, and specified BAT and BEP measures are generally specified in

---

[41] See D.G. Victor and L.A. Coben, 'A Herd Mentality in the Design of International Environmental Agreements?' (2005) 5 Global Envt'l Po. 24. Another example of such research is P.-O. Busch, H. Jörgens, and K. Tews, 'The Global Diffusion of Regulatory Instruments: The Making of a New International Regime' (2005) 598 Annals 146 (studying diffusion among states of strategic environmental planning, eco-labels, energy taxes, and freedom of environmental information programs). See also P.H. Sand, *Transnational Environmental Law: Lessons in Global Change* (The Hague: Kluwer Law International, 1999). Regime effectiveness may also be an important variable in arriving at convergence of instrumental choice. Compare R. Mitchell, *International Oil Pollution at Sea: Environmental Policy and Treaty Compliance* (Cambridge, MA: MIT Press, 1994) (studying effectiveness of various environmental treaties and offering treaty drafters recommendations on provisions that can improve compliance).

[42] The relevance of this experience may, however, be limited by important differences in decision rules. Rather than the international rule of unanimous assent by lower level parties, the higher level authorities in EU and federal systems decide by some form of less than unanimous vote rule and can bind dissenters. See Wiener, 'Global Environmental Regulation,' note 19 above. In the EU, however, consent among all member states is required for new EU taxes, which doomed the proposed EU carbon dioxide tax.

relatively ambitious regimes of vertical regulation where states, by the nature of the resource and problem involved, have a strong mutual interest in making significant, verifiable environmental progress.

Alternatively, the analysis could be applied to examine, explain, and evaluate practice in specific subject areas of regulation. Why have discharges and dumping at sea generally been regulated through internationally agreed bans and specified BAT measures and civil liability systems, whereas land-based sources of marine pollution generally, with some regional exceptions, have been dealt with through much softer instruments? Why have agreements on air pollution been at the cutting edge of international environmental law? Why have environmental taxes not been used at all in international agreements, and tradable quotas only used in the Kyoto Protocol and, to a very limited extent, the Montreal Protocol, notwithstanding their growing use at the domestic level? Are these differences explained by the nature of the resource and problem in question, and the relative performance of different instruments, including information and other administrative considerations, or by the varying structure of incentives for or against international cooperation among states and private actors? Or are they explained by the predispositions of relevant international elites or the factors underlying decisions whether or not to promote uniformity among domestic instruments through international agreements? As environmental problems with the character of global public goods, including climate change, biodiversity loss, and marine resources, become more acute, will we see, as Wiener predicts, greater use of quota trading and other economic instruments because of their cost and participation efficiencies?

Thus far, international environmental law in the vertical context overwhelmingly follows a command approach, supplemented by information-based approaches. While there are examples of economic instruments, they have generally attracted less interest, and play a less important role than in a number of domestic jurisdictions. The international pattern is somewhat similar to the EU regulatory practice, which, apart from the new carbon dioxide emissions-trading system and certain subsidy programmes, has made little use of economic incentives. This parallel may suggest that economic incentives are less suited for two-level systems or that the political-economy factors at work in such systems are especially resistant to their adoption. Or, there may be other explanations altogether that would be consistent with significantly expanded future use of economic instruments in the international context (see Chapter 11 'Economic Theory of International Environmental Law'). Further, economic instruments are much more prominent in horizontal regulation.

5.3 Governance Issues

Another dimension of instrument choice that merits inclusion in the research agenda is the implication of different environmental regulatory instruments for institutional and governance issues. In the domestic context, there has been a turn to economic and information-based approaches because of the dysfunctions encountered in attempting to extend and intensify the exercise of coercive state power in the command and control mode. Although the modern regulatory state, at least in developed countries, enjoys ample power, a virtually unrelenting reliance on command regulation has made the state an increasingly maladroit and arbitrary regulator. In the international setting, on the other hand, the problem is the relative weakness of institutions. An important issue is whether economic and information-based instruments can, through their mobilization of the price and market system and non-governmental interests and incentives, better compensate for those weaknesses than command-and-control regulation. Here, a key consideration, much debated in the climate regulatory context, is the relative institutional demands, including demands for monitoring, verification, and enforcement capacities, of taxes and quota-trading programs relative to command instruments. Defenders of the command system claim that economic instruments are too complicated and difficult to police, especially for developing countries, while defenders of economic instruments argue that they are more efficient on a variety of dimensions, conserving both administrative and economic resources.[43]

The shift of authority and power from nation states to a variety of global regulatory regimes, and the governance and accountability of these regimes, is a matter of increasing concern in environmental, as in other regulatory, fields. How do different governance structures affect instrument choice and how does instrument choice in turn affect governance and accountability? In the domestic context, proponents of economic instruments assert that their use will promote public and political accountability for regulatory policy because they involve a few basic, transparent choices on the part of government. Proponents of information-based approaches argue that they will mobilize powerful private involvement and initiative in the solution of environmental problems. Such claims are often disputed by defenders of the command approach. This debate needs to be developed at the international level, where the accountability problems of governance by distant global regimes and inaccessible and inscrutable groups of experts are a mounting and legitimate concern (see Chapter 4 'Global Environmental Governance as Administration'; Chapter 32 'International Institutions'; and Chapter 30 'Legitimacy').[44]

5.4 Evolution of International Environmental Law

A final topic for research is the role and pattern of instrument choice in the past and future growth and evolution of international environmental law. Will international environmental law replicate the evolutionary trend observed in the domestic

---

[43] See Bell, note 10 above; and Dudek, Stewart, and Wiener, note 10 above. The Resources for the Future comparative study of the performance of command and economic instruments in the EU and US, see note 14 above, provides some ammunition for both sides in this debate.

[44] See Kingsbury, Krisch, and Stewart, note 22 above.

context, with a still dominant command-and-control base increasingly being supplemented, and in a few cases supplanted, by economic information-based instruments? Or will the distinctive legal and institutional characteristics of international environmental regulation produce a different pattern? As a result of its relative youth, can international environmental regulation overcome some of the political-economy constraints on regulatory innovation that operate at the domestic level and 'leapfrog' to a wider use of innovative approaches? Or will command approaches become even more entrenched at the international level? With each category of instrument, what types of command, economic, and information-based instruments are best suited for the nature of international environmental problems and institutions, and what can be done to promote their adoption?

Analysts lament the increasingly fragmented and piecemeal character of international environmental law as it expands and becomes more differentiated and more specific. Implausible grand solutions include the creation of a single international environmental organization, and integrated global planning for sustainable development. A less ambitious possibility is to replicate international initiatives taken in Europe, and elsewhere, to achieve a degree of integration in command-and-control regulations of pollution and wastes (see Chapter 37 'Regional Economic Integration Organizations'). There have been some international steps in this direction in regional agreements, such as the OSPAR Convention and the later Rhine agreements. Yet, serious fragmentation and regulatory entropy are inevitably strong tendencies in command approaches because of the need to specify separate controls for the myriad of different regulated actors and activities. As a result of the nature of the incentives that they deploy, economic and information-based instruments are potentially far better able to achieve beneficial coordination among the diverse activities of many different actors and steer them to the achievement of environmental goals.[45] Accordingly, these instruments have the potential to alleviate the piecemeal character of current international environmental law. 'Risk bubbles' that permit trading among different risks subject to an aggregate cap is one example. The Montreal Protocol limitations for a 'basket' of gases, and the adoption under the UNFCCC and the Kyoto Protocol of a comprehensive approach to setting targets and quota trading that includes most greenhouse gases and sink activities, is another.[46] Climate change and biodiversity loss are the most encompassing and urgent environmental problem that the world faces. Solutions to these two sets of related problems might be integrated by extending greenhouse gas quota-trading or tax systems to include biodiversity preservation. For example, as recently proposed, greenhouse gas emissions

---

[45] See R.B. Stewart, 'Reconstitutive Law' (1986) 46 Md. L. Rev. 86. In practice, however, the demands of simplification in a workable regulatory system limit the diversity of resource features that can be addressed within a single price-based or information-based regulatory system.

[46] See Wiener and Graham, note 38 above; and L. Guruswamy, 'The Case for Integrated Pollution Control' (1991) 54 L. & Contemp. Probs. 41.

credits could be given to developing countries that reduce deforestation, serving two major international environmental objectives through the use of a single economic instrument.

Of course, the development of a more effective international environmental regulatory system faces many problems. Greater and more systematic attention to issues of instrument choice, including both their normative and positive aspects and their relation to issues of accountability and effectiveness in international environmental governance can help us to diagnose and better address those problems and promote that development.

Recommended Reading

S. Barrett, *Environment and Statecraft: The Strategy of Environmental Treaty-Making* (Oxford: Oxford University Press, 2003).

J. Golub, ed., *New Instruments for Environmental Policy in the EU* (London: Routledge, 1998).

W. Harrington, R.D. Morgenstern, and T. Sterner, eds., *Choosing Environmental Policy: Comparing Instruments and Outcomes in the United States and Europe* (Washington, DC: Resources for the Future, 2004).

B. Kingsbury, N. Krisch, and R. Stewart, *The Emergence of Global Administrative Law* (2005) 68 L. & Contemp. Probs. 15.

N.O. Koehane, R.L. Revesz, and R.N. Stavins, 'The Choice of Regulatory Instrument in Environmental Policy' (1998) 22 Harv. Envt'l L. Rev. 313.

OECD, *Tradable Permits: Policy Evaluation, Design, and Reform* (Paris: OECD, 2004).

——, *Economic Instruments for Pollution Control and Natural Resources Management in OECD Countries: A Survey* (Paris: OECD, 1999).

——, *Handbook of Incentive Measures for Biodiversity: Design and Implementation* (Paris: OECD, 1999).

P.H. Sand, 'Information Disclosure,' in J.B. Wiener, M.D. Rogers, P.H. Sand, and J.K. Hammit, eds., *The Reality of Precaution: Comparing Risk Regulation in the US and Europe* (forthcoming).

——, *Transnational Environmental Law: Lessons in Global Change* (The Hague: Kluwer Law International, 1999).

R.B. Stewart, 'Economic Incentives: Opportunities and Obstacles,' in R. Revesz, P. Sands, and R. Stewart, eds., *Environmental Law, the Economy, and Sustainable Development* (New York: Cambridge University Press, 2000), 171.

——, 'A New Generation of Environmental Regulation?' (2001) 29 Cap. U. L. Rev. 21.

J.B. Wiener, 'Global Environmental Regulation: Instrument Choice in Legal Context' (1999) 108 Yale L.J. 677.

——, 'On the Political Economy of Global Environmental Regulation' (1999) 87 Geo. L.J. 749.

D.G. Victor and L.-A. Coben, 'A Herd Mentality in the Design of International Environmental Agreements?' (2005) 5 Global Envt'l Pol. 24.

CHAPTER 9

....

SCIENCE AND TECHNOLOGY

FROM AGENDA SETTING TO IMPLEMENTATION

....

STEINAR ANDRESEN

JON BIRGER SKJÆRSETH

1 INTRODUCTION

SOME analysts tend to see science and technology as two sides of the same coin.[1] In our opinion, the two may go together and reinforce each other, but they may also be very different animals. Science serves essentially as a vehicle for 'early warning' about environmental problems, and may provide guidance on what to do in order to alleviate or 'cure' a problem. Overall, science, therefore, usually has a 'positive' impact on the problem at hand, to the extent that it is heeded. Technology, however, can be either a blessing or a curse for the environment and resource management. On the one hand, technological change is at the root of many environmental problems linked to economic growth and unsustainable production. On the other hand, development of environment-friendly technology represents an important part of the solution to many environmental problems. The role of the chemical industry in the ozone problem is quite illustrative: stratospheric ozone depletion was caused by new technologies, but the solution was facilitated by the development of cheap substitutes to ozone-depleting substances.

In this chapter, we focus on technology as a cure for environmental problems. This focus is chosen because our point of departure is how multilateral environmental agreements (MEAs) can contribute to solve or reduce international environmental problems. More specifically, our main research question is how science and technology can contribute to enhance the *effectiveness* of international environmental policies. Even though science and technology are closely intertwined, we will conceive of them for analytical and practical purposes as serving different functions at *different levels* and in *different phases*. Science represents the search for knowledge, and this search typically takes place among knowledge producers who function within an international regime, for example, scientists operating within a scientific expert group such as the International Panel on Climate Change (IPCC). Technological innovation takes place mainly in a commercial context involving private companies, which also tend to be the target group of environmental policy. Against the backdrop of regime effectiveness, we assume that science is most important in the agenda-setting phase, providing the premises for collective policy-making. In contrast, although monitoring technology can play an important role in diagnosing problems, technological innovation is most important in the implementation phase. In international environmental cooperation, science offers advice on what to do, while technology determines the limitations and opportunities for how the problem may be tackled.

---

[1] E. Skolnikoff, *The Elusive Transformation: Science, Technology and the Evolution of International Politics* (Princeton, NJ: Princeton University Press, 1994). Skolnikoff, for example, points out how science and technology have affected world affairs, 'most easily seen through dramatic developments that have global consequences—such as the deployment of massive strategic forces (and) the nuclear accident at Chernobyl' (at 3).

We analyse science primarily in relation to research and advice within established scientific bodies associated with international regimes. Most international environmental regimes have established such bodies, composed of scientists from most or all of the member states as well as independent scientists. These bodies are usually considered both more representative as well as more legitimate compared to various domestic scientific advisory bodies. Examples and findings will be drawn primarily from the following issue areas and related international regimes: whaling, ozone, marine pollution (North Sea), air pollution (acid rain), and climate.[2]

With respect to technology, we investigate how technology can be used to enhance the effectiveness of international environmental policy. Some international environmental regimes are also linked to bodies for technological advice, and these regimes may affect technological change directly by specifying the technology to be applied. International environmental regimes also can affect technological change indirectly by banning products or activities, setting performance standards, allowing emissions trading, stimulating cooperation on technological development, stimulating the diffusion and transfer of technology to developing countries, and enhancing transparency. Technology also plays a crucial role in the implementation of regime commitments at the domestic level. The use of policy instruments as well as broader interactions between policy-makers and industry affect technological change.

This chapter will consider the following topics. First, we provide an outline of the concept of regime effectiveness and what role science and technology may have within that perspective. Thereafter, we proceed to discuss how and why science affects collective decision-making. The general role played by science within various environmental regimes is analysed before discussing what factors affect the influence and impact of science. In the fourth section, we look at the consequences of collective decision-making and the implementation of technological change. We focus on the direct and indirect links between MEAs and technological change before we zoom in on the domestic level and investigate the links between domestic policy instruments and technological change. A brief conclusion is provided in section 5.

2 EFFECTIVENESS, SCIENCE, AND TECHNOLOGY

2.1 Defining and Explaining Effectiveness

The study of effectiveness of international environmental regimes has become a fairly well-established sub-field within the broader study of such regimes since the

---

[2] See S. Andresen, T. Skodvin, A. Underdal, and J. Wettestad, *Science and Politics in International Environmental Regimes* (Manchester: Manchester University Press, 2000).

early 1990s (see Chapter 39 'Compliance Theory').[3] Over time, a consensus has evolved that it makes sense to conceive of effectiveness in terms of outputs, outcomes, and impacts. Outputs consist of the rules, regulations, and programmes flowing from the regime, and are essentially an indictor of the potential effectiveness of the regime. Outcomes are the 'positive' behavioural changes resulting from the regimes. Impacts concern the extent to which the problem in question is actually 'solved' by the regime. One indicator of problem-solving is the extent to which the goal of a regime is actually achieved. Needless to say, there are severe methodological challenges concerning causality associated with determining outcome and impact.

The question of why some regimes are more effective than others can be approached in terms of two perspectives, one focusing on the *nature of the problem*, and the other on the *problem solving capacity* of the relevant regime. With respect to the nature of the problem, the basic idea is that some problems are intellectually and politically less complicated and more 'benign' than others and, as a result, easier to solve or deal with than more 'malign' problems. The difference between the ozone and the climate problems illustrates the distinction. However, the problem-solving capacity of a regime may also make a difference in terms of effectiveness. The underlying reasoning is that some problems are more effectively dealt with because they are attacked with more political and institutional skill and energy. These two perspectives are analytical devices and, in practice, there are linkages and overlaps between them. The latter perspective, however, is more interesting for analysts as well as policy-makers as it can be more easily changed through deliberate institutional design. Problem-solving capacity can also be conceived of in terms of an *intellectual* and a *political* dimension. The intellectual challenge is to identify and diagnose the problem and to identify effective response measures. The political challenge is to mobilize relevant actors in support of collective action in pursuit of an effective solution. We now turn to how science fits into this overall analytical perspective.

2.2 Role of Science and Knowledge

At the interface between the political and intellectual dimension lies the task of transforming knowledge into decision premises. The main question we are concerned with is how scientific knowledge can be utilized in order to enhance the effectiveness of the regimes at hand. We are aware of the debate and controversy concerning the fruitfulness of separating the 'scientific' from the 'political' sphere as well as the discussions about the links between science and knowledge.[4] These are important debates with no easy answers, but we have no space, nor ambition, to entertain these

---

[3] See E. Miles et al., *Explaining Environmental Regime Effectiveness* (Cambridge, MA: MIT Press, 2002).

[4] T.S. Kuhn, *The Structure of Scientific Revolution*, 2nd edition (Chicago: Chicago University Press, 1970).

questions in this chapter. Our point of departure is simple—too simple many would claim. In line with the rationalist tradition, we assume that knowledge about the environment is a necessary but not sufficient condition for designing effective international institutions. Knowledge is necessary to diagnose problems and prescribe what to do, and science is the major supplier of 'advanced' knowledge.

As a point of departure, science represents a 'neutral' input on behalf of the resource or environment in question. Although this is a simplified assumption, reflect for a moment on the state of the art in the *absence* of science. We all know about the so-called 'tragedy of the commons' in various areas and that short-sighted economic interests tend to prevail over concerns regarding the common good. However imperfect, scientific input is needed to balance these forces. Unless we have fairly good knowledge about the environment and the natural resources in question, management tends to be based primarily on luck—not the best of steering devices. The depletion of the large whales in Antarctic waters is a stunning tale of what happens when science is weak and short-term economic interests dominate. The reason why good scientific knowledge alone is not sufficient for effective management is that a number of political factors will usually be more decisive for how management will be conducted, a point we return to in section 3.

Science plays a role in determining both the nature of the problem as well as the problem-solving capacity of a regime. Our degree of knowledge about the problem tells us how intellectually 'malign' or 'benign' the problem is. Similarly, the way we design the science-policy interface may make a difference for the ability of the regime to solve the problem. With respect to the role of science in determining the nature of the problem, our simple assumption is that, all other things being equal, the better the knowledge (and, in particular, the more consensual the knowledge), the higher the chances of increased effectiveness of the regime in question.

In regard to the role of science in relation to the problem-solving capacity of the regime, we assume that a balance between *integrity* and *involvement* is the best way to organize scientific input.[5] On the one hand, integrity is needed to ensure that the scientific input is not tilted due to influence from political and economic stakeholders. On the other hand, such stakeholders need to be involved in organizing scientific input in order to ensure that the scientists are aware of the needs of policy-makers, and present scientific results that may be utilized in practice. These assumptions proved to be somewhat simplistic when confronted with empirical reality, a topic we will return to later in this chapter. Be this as it may, science and knowledge make only a modest difference for the effectiveness of environmental regimes. Management of the environment is ultimately a political question where powerful economic actors are usually involved, and there are few, if any, examples in which science (and the environment) 'wins' when powerful counter forces are involved in the decision-making

---

[5] For a detailed account of the significance of institutional design, see Andresen, Skodvin, Underdal, and Wettestad, note 2 above.

process. In other words, the effectiveness of a regime is largely determined by the will and/or ability of states to collectively address the problems identified. Nevertheless, science is important in creating awareness about environmental problems and provides incentives that may initiate political processes.

2.3 Role of Technology in Environmental Policy

Is technology the answer to ecological challenges? This is the 'big' question. At least three arguments have been advanced against the idea that technology can protect the Earth in the long run.[6] First, technology's success is self-defeating: problem-solving creates population growth, which creates new problems, and so on. Second, the scarcity of human wisdom creates possibilities for good and bad applications of new technology—Hiroshima and Chernobyl should suffice to exemplify the latter. Third, new technology creates unanticipated consequences. Substitutes for ozone-depleting substances have, for example, proven to be powerful greenhouse gases. These arguments against technology notwithstanding, the message from history is that knowledge can grow faster than population, and technology can provide abundant green goods and services if it is wisely used.[7]

Leaving the big question aside, this chapter takes as a point of departure the common view that technology is *one* key to solving many environmental problems, particularly as environmental technology has shifted from end-of-pipe solutions to cleaner processes and products.[8] End-of-pipe technologies, such as catalytic converters, have contributed significantly to pollution abatement. Advances in renewable energy and energy-efficiency technologies have also made positive contributions. The main question, then, is not whether, but how, technological change can be stimulated to enhance the effectiveness of environmental policy.

Theories of technological change commonly identify three stages in the development cycle of technologies.[9] *Invention* is generally understood as the creation of a new technological idea; *innovation* is commonly defined as the first use of a new product, process, or system in a commercial context; and *diffusion* follows innovation as subsequent users adopt the technology pioneered elsewhere. Technological change refers to the impact arising from all three stages. Radical and incremental innovations represent different degrees of change, the latter denoting incremental and smaller improvements along a given trajectory. Radical innovation departs from the technical status quo and points to the emergence of new products and processes

---

[6] See J.H. Ausubel, 'Can Technology Spare the Earth?' (1996) 84 Am. Scientist 166.

[7] According to Ausubel, *ibid.*

[8] Organisation for Economic Cooperation and Development (OECD), *Technology Policy and the Environment* (Paris: OECD, 2002).

[9] See OECD, *Technology and Environment: Towards Policy Integration* (Paris: OECD, 1999).

that (over time) fundamentally alter the production process. In climate policy, for example, capture and sequestration of carbon dioxide represent a more radical solution than gradual improvement in energy efficiency.[10]

Like science, technology can play a role in determining the nature of an environmental problem. Advanced monitoring technology has become important to assess the state of the environment, which, in turn, is important in mobilizing political willingness to deal with environmental problems. Consider the opening statement of *Our Common Future*: 'In the middle of the 20th century, we saw our planet from space for the first time . . . From space, we see a small and fragile ball dominated not by human activity and edifice, but by a pattern of clouds, oceans, greenery and soils . . . we can see and study the Earth as an organism whose health depends on the health of all its parts.'[11] Satellite- and shuttle-based remote sensors are widely used to provide image and physical property data regarding atmospheric and ocean surface conditions. Images of the Antarctic ozone hole represent a dramatic empirical indication that something is wrong with the ozone layer, and have become important for mobilizing international and national efforts to deal with ozone depletion.

Problem-solving capacity depends heavily on technology as well. Fifteen strategies have been identified to reduce carbon emissions, each of which is based on known technology at different stages of development.[12] Technological innovation, as noted, takes place mainly within private companies in reaction to external signals. This fact has two important consequences for how we are able to analyze technological change in relation to regime effectiveness. First, we have not been able to identify any systematic literature on the impact of international environmental regimes on technological change. This does not necessarily mean that international environmental regimes do not affect technological change, but it implies that our knowledge is limited and that our approach will be exploratory.

Some international environmental regimes are linked to international bodies for technological advice, such as the Programs and Measures Committee (PRAM) to the Convention for the Protection of the Marine Environment in the North-East Atlantic (OSPAR Convention). Such committees provide an international arena for assisting the parties in identifying best available techniques/technology (BAT) for point sources, such as a power plant or industrial facility, and best environmental practice (BEP) for diffuse sources, such as agriculture. In addition to technology specifications, international regimes can affect technological change indirectly by other types of regime outputs, such as product bans, performance standards, technology transfer, emissions trading, and information disclosure. We thus assume

[10] J.B. Skjærseth and A.C. Christiansen, 'Environmental Policy Instruments and Technological Change in the Energy Sector: Findings from Comparative Empirical Research' (2006) 17(2) Energy & Env't 223.

[11] World Commission on Environment and Development, *Our Common Future* (Oxford: Oxford University Press, 1987) at 1.

[12] R. Socolow, R. Hotinski, J.B. Greenblatt, and S. Pacala, 'Solving the Climate Problem: Technologies Available to Curb CO_2 Emissions' (2004) 46 Env't 8 at 8–19.

that international environmental regimes can affect technological change *directly* and *indirectly*.

Second, there is a comparatively rich literature on public environmental policy and technological change, even though this relationship is still poorly understood. From the perspective of regime effectiveness, the link between environmental policy and technological change enters the equation when joint international commitments, or regime outputs, are *implemented*. Usually, regime outputs must be implemented at the national, and, eventually, the target group, level to induce behavioural change. Domestic policy instruments, such as regulatory and economic instruments, are particularly important in implementation processes. However, technological change is a complex process involving broader interaction between industry and policy-makers. We thus assume that the use and impact of different types of policy instruments are conditioned by the political context in which they are applied.[13] Technology has proven to be, and is increasingly regarded, as key to solving environmental problems. Technological change can be affected directly and indirectly by international environmental regimes, but it is probably mainly affected by public policy when regime commitments are implemented at the national and target group levels.

3 ROLE OF SCIENCE IN INTERNATIONAL ENVIRONMENTAL REGIMES

We begin with a brief discussion of the extent to which science is a major input to decision-makers in general. As there are strong variations regarding the extent to which science has an *impact* on decisions taken, we briefly discuss in the next subsection some factors contributing to such differences, focusing on the nature of the problem.

3.1 Why Science Matters to Policy-Makers

As noted in the introduction, most of the following observations are based on studies of five international regimes: the whaling regime, the acid rain regime, the climate regime, the ozone regime, and the North Sea regime on the prevention of marine pollution.[14] As these are long-lasting, as well as comprehensive, regimes, with several components as well as clearly distinguishable phases, we split the five regimes into

---

[13] D. Wallace, *Environmental Policy and Industrial Innovation: Strategies in Europe, the US and Japan* (London: Earthscan, 1995).   [14] See Andresen, Skodvin, Underdal, and Wettestad, note 2 above.

19 units of analysis. For example, we divide the International Whaling Commission (IWC) into three different phases, and the North Sea regime into various components as well as two phases. In the following sections, we present the main findings resulting from this project.

Scientific research is generally recognized as a major supplier of relevant knowledge. In all five regimes studied, decision-makers have turned to science for problem identification and diagnosis. In addition, in all regimes, research-based knowledge has been generally perceived as an important basis for making policy decisions, except in the last stage of the whaling regime, which we shall have more to say about later. This applies even to cases where the state of scientific knowledge was recognized to be relatively poor, for example, the North Sea regime. Scientific bodies have been established as more or less integral parts of the decision-making system in all of these regimes. Moreover, there is a tendency towards increased formalization of the links between decision-making bodies and the scientific community as regimes 'mature'. For example, while it took a few years before a scientific committee was established within the oldest of these regimes—the one surrounding the IWC—in all of the more recent regimes, scientific/technical bodies were established concomitantly with the international management bodies, and the basis for their relationship was provided in the initial treaty. Even though the pattern is not very robust, a tendency towards higher-level utilization of research-based knowledge over time can be identified. Finally, a tendency towards broadening the range of scientific inputs requested can be observed. The participation of natural scientists has expanded in scope, and economic expertise is included to an increasing extent. In the IPCC, social scientists and lawyers also have been included.

Governments rarely explicitly dispute what the scientific community considers to be 'consensual knowledge'. This statement is not to say that uncertainty and knowledge gaps are not exploited for tactical purposes in international negotiations. On the contrary, particularly in the early phases, progress is often hampered by one or more parties demanding more conclusive evidence or by competing interpretations of available information. A typical example is the position of the United Kingdom in the early phase of both the acid rain regime as well as the North Sea regime. The United Kingdom claimed that science was uncertain and, therefore, that no action was needed. In general, however, most governments are reluctant to dispute openly the factual conclusions that a clear majority of competent scientists consider 'state-of-the-art' knowledge. Moves to exploit uncertainty or favour biased interpretations are common, but open and explicit challenges seem to be rare. When President George Bush, Jr., rejected the Kyoto Protocol in 2001, he claimed that the science was uncertain and expressed doubts about the existence of a problem. However, it did not take long before he amended this position. Although the present US administration continues to reject the protocol, it acknowledges the climate change problem.

Faced with broad consensus among competent experts on the description and diagnosis of a (severe) environmental problem, governments more often do, in fact, take some kind of collective action. In other words, some substantive targets are usually set and/or regulatory measures introduced. Moreover, it seems that these steps are taken at least in part in response to scientific evidence. This is by no means to suggest that scientific evidence is a *sufficient* condition for collective action. Nor do we suggest that policy responses are typically *derived* from research-based knowledge. Only in a couple of instances, namely the later phases of the ozone negotiations and the second phase of the Convention on Long Range Transboundary Air Pollution (LRTAP Convention) regime, can the regulations adopted be seen to match the scientific advice given. Even in those cases, it would be an exaggeration to say that regulations were in any strict sense derived from scientific inputs. The typical pattern is one where new evidence about environmental damage or resource depletion leads, first, to increased attention and requests for further study, and—perhaps at a later stage— to some substantive measures designed to alleviate the problem. In other words, scientific evidence often plays a major role in *agenda setting* and often serves to precipitate *some* kind of policy response. The *substance* of this response, however, is determined essentially by politics rather than science.

Conclusive evidence is not a necessary condition for collective action. The 'normal' pattern is that broad consensus among competent experts about the nature and ramifications of a problem tend to facilitate problem solving. However, substantive measures may be agreed upon even in the absence of conclusive evidence about the amount of environmental damage. A typical case in point would be the decision of the 1987 North Sea Conference to adopt very stringent and ambitious targets to reduce pollution, even though the scientific message was very far from conclusive. The precautionary principle served to justify this shift in policy (see Chapter 25 'Precaution').[15] It also happens, although in even fewer cases, that the regulatory body moves substantially *beyond* the recommendations made by its scientific advisory body. The best-known example is probably the 1982 decision to adopt a moratorium on commercial whaling, even though the Scientific Committee of the IWC gave no such advice. Does this shift indicate that we will see more instances of proactive environmental regulation in the future? If so, it will not necessarily change the overall level of attention paid to research-based knowledge, but it may well change the *way* in which inputs from science are used and, conceivably, also the kind of inputs requested by policy-makers. However, based on available evidence, there is higher likelihood that consensual science will play a more significant role than precaution based on uncertain and disputed science.[16]

Autonomy and involvement serve different functions. Our original assumption was that a balance should be struck between involvement and autonomy. This proved to be too simplistic an assumption. Instead, autonomy and involvement seem to serve

---

[15] D. Freestone and T. IJlstra, 'The North Sea: Perspectives on Regional Environmental Cooperation,' special issue of *International Journal of Coastal and Estuarine Law* (London: Graham and Trotman, 1990).

[16] S. Andresen, L. Walløe, and G.K. Rosendal, 'The Precautionary Principle: Knowledge Counts but Power Decides,' in R. Cooney and B. Dickson, eds., *Biodiversity and the Precautionary Principle: Risk and Uncertainty in Conservation and Sustainable Use* (London: Earthscan, 2005) 39.

different functions in different stages of the science policy nexus. Autonomy is good for the *production* of science, while involvement is essential for the *transformation* of science into policy. Both the climate regime and the acid rain regime are good examples of this approach, as they have designated specific forums to deal with each of these two questions. Within the acid rain regime, there are several bodies producing basic science while the Working Group of Strategies convey the scientific findings to the policy-makers. Within the climate regime, there has been more of a sliding scale. There is a scientific core in the working groups of the IPCC, while there is a balance between science and policy in the working group plenaries. In the full IPCC Plenary, there is a political dominance.

Maybe even more important, autonomy and involvement serve different functions for different parties. This differentiation is particularly relevant between developed and developing countries in global regimes. For developed countries, particularly in Western Europe and North America, the autonomy of science is a core value that boosts its credibility. The South, however, takes a different perspective on this matter. Developing countries tend to perceive 'autonomous' science to be science done by the North—and often for the North. The more marginal their role in science, the more critical they tend to be of 'autonomous' science. For example, in the climate change regime, it has been an important challenge to increase the number of scientists from developing countries involved in climate change-related research. The important 'design' lesson, however, is that involvement and some political control over the scientific process is needed to secure the *legitimacy* of science in global regimes.[17]

The above overview indicates that science as such, as well as how the science-policy nexus is designed, do make a difference for policy-makers. Some kind of collective action usually is taken as a result of scientific findings. So far, however, we have not had much to say about the actual *impact* of science—that is, what is the 'distance' between scientific advice and collective action? It is necessary to address this question in order to determine the role of science in relation to the effectiveness of regimes. Methodologically, this is a very demanding question to answer, due to the high number of intervening variables, which make it difficult to determine causality. However, some ideas can be presented, based on assumptions about what decides the impact of science—linked to the nature of the various problems.

3.2 What Determines the Impact of Science?

A number of factors may account for the impact of scientific input on decision-makers:

- consensual knowledge versus controversial and uncertain conclusions;
- feasible cure (technology) available versus no cure available;

---

[17] For an account of the relation between effectiveness and legitimacy, see S. Andresen and E. Hey, 'The Effectiveness and Legitimacy of International Environmental Institutions' (2005) 5 Int'l Envt'l Agreements: Politics, Law and Economics 211.

- 'neutral' issues versus strong values involved;
- strong 'pushers' versus strong 'laggards';
- problems that develop rapidly and surprisingly versus those that develop slowly and as expected;
- effects visible to the public versus 'invisible' problems; and
- low political conflict versus high political conflict.[18]

Obviously, the elements listed on the left side of each of the above-listed opposites make a problem more benign, and *increase* the chance that scientific advice is followed, while the elements on the right side make a problem more malign and *decrease* the chance that scientific advice will be followed. Note that only the first factor addresses scientific knowledge. All of the other factors deal with other characteristics of a problem. According to this line of reasoning, the impact that science and knowledge are likely to have thus depends largely on non-scientific factors. The more 'benign' the other factors, the larger the impact of science is likely to be. A typical case in point is the ozone regime, which scores fairly high on all elements on the left side and which has been significantly impacted by science.[19]

As noted earlier in this chapter, institutional design did have some effect on the effectiveness of the regimes researched. However, there was one notable exception to this rule, namely the most recent phase in the whaling regime (1980 to the present). This phase of the IWC is conspicuous among the cases analysed in that it combines the *lowest* score with regard to the use of research-based knowledge with one of the *highest* scores in terms of the state of knowledge and institutional design. However, decision-makers choose not to make use of the knowledge generated. The explanation, while seemingly paradoxical, is actually straightforward. This case was the only one in our sample that was characterized by a stark conflict over *basic values*. Research can produce information on the state of a stock or an ecosystem and provide factual inputs for determining sustainable harvest levels, but there is no way it can resolve the issue of whether it is morally right or wrong to utilize a particular species for consumptive purposes. Introducing a 'rational' element represented by science, however sophisticated and accurate, has limited effect when the bargaining is over values and not numbers. Some analysts claim that the IWC is a low-effectiveness regime—not least because no attention is paid to scientific findings.[20] Others conclude that it is a highly effective regime because after years of depletion, the IWC has finally been able to protect large whales, which is one of the rare examples of a truly precautionary approach[21] (see Chapter 25 'Precaution'). This debate illustrates

---

[18] This is a modified version of A. Underdal, 'The Politics of Science in International Resource Management: A Summary,' in S. Andresen and W. Østreng, eds., *International Resource Management* (London and New York: Belhaven Press, 1989) 253.

[19] The most important lesson from the ozone regime, however, deals with the role of technology, so we will have more to say about this regime in section 4 on technology in this chapter.

[20] S. Andresen, 'The International Whaling Commission: More Failure than Success?' in E. Miles et al., see note 3 above, 379.   [21] S. Holt, 'Whale Mining, Whale Saving' (1985) 9 Marine Policy 192.

both the difficulty of evaluating regimes as well as the fact that there is no 'universal consensus' that management should be science based.

Another global regime characterized by high political conflicts is the climate regime. According to the dimensions listed earlier, it has most of the characteristics of a 'malign' problem. How has this affected the role of science in this regime? Considering that the IPCC had, in 1990, already concluded that a 60 per cent reduction in greenhouse gas emissions was required if atmospheric concentrations were to be stabilized at current levels, it seems that the crafters of the climate regime have not heeded the warnings of the IPCC. It is common knowledge that the Kyoto Protocol, for all its political and institutional merits, will have little effect on climate change. Seen from this vantage point, the effectiveness of this regime is very low, and science has not contributed much to enhance its effectiveness. Nevertheless, it should be noted that this is a long-term problem demanding long-term solutions. A 50-year time frame may be more relevant than ten to 15 years. It, therefore, may be premature to judge the effectiveness of the climate regime.

In addition, there is no doubt that science and the way it has been organized in the IPCC has played a crucial role in generating (close to) consensus about the climate change problem. In fact, the issue would never have reached the international political agenda had it not been for scientists and their work. It should be noted, however, that their role in this initial phase was made easier by close cooperation with green non-governmental organizations (NGOs) as well as by a strong demand for green policies by public opinion, particularly in the member states of the Organisation for Economic Cooperation and Development (OECD). The force of these 'benign' factors has subsequently been weakened, making it more difficult for scientists to have an influence.

4 TECHNOLOGY IN INTERNATIONAL ENVIRONMENTAL REGIMES AND NATIONAL ENVIRONMENTAL POLICY

In section 3, we analysed how and why science affects collective policy-making in the form of joint international commitments. In this section, we shall first consider how different types of international commitments affect technological change and relate to regime effectiveness. Since international commitments usually have to be implemented at the national level in order to stimulate behavioural change and problem-solving, the second part of this section analyses how public environmental policies may result in 'greener' outcomes and, eventually, problem-solving through technology.

4.1 International Environmental Regimes and Technological Change

Technology can contribute to solving many transnational environmental problems, such as ozone depletion, climate change, air pollution, marine pollution,
and releases of hazardous substances. However, this potential contribution is not
reflected in the 'design' of international environmental regimes, as very few regimes
use technology specifications as part of their rules and standards. We have previously categorized such rules and standards as direct outputs of a regime. In addition,
as mentioned earlier, international environmental regimes can affect technology
indirectly, through different types of commitments, such as bans and performance
standards (see Chapter 8 'Instrument Choice'). Note that any study of regime
impact on technological change requires demanding causal analysis of the link
between regime output and actual technological change. This implies that even
though a given regime *can* affect technology in certain ways, we do not really know
whether such effects have occurred given the lack of in-depth causal analysis.

4.1.1 *Technology Specifications in International Regimes*

Although technology specifications are rarely used in international environmental regimes, there are some important exceptions. In the late 1980s, the Paris
Commission on the Northeast-Atlantic adopted BAT standards for certain industrial
sectors within the framework of the 1974 Convention for the Prevention of Marine
Pollution from Land-Based Sources (Paris Convention). The use of BAT was then
included as a general obligation in the 1992 OSPAR Convention (Article 2), which
superseded the Paris Convention. BAT was defined as 'the latest stage of development
(state of the art) of processes, of facilities or methods of operation . . . for limiting
discharges, emissions and waste.' Since 1992, the parties to the OSPAR Convention
have adopted 12 (out of a total of 44) recommendations on BAT that provide guidance for the OSPAR Convention's strategy on hazardous substances. Likewise, the
1979 LRTAP Convention applies BAT standards where economically justified. For the
purpose of reducing and preventing air pollution, the parties shall use 'the best available technology which is economically feasible and low- and non-waste technology'
(Article 6). BAT standards also form part of the 1992 Convention on the Protection
and Use of Transboundary Watercourses and International Lakes. Finally, the concept of BAT is developed in a number of European Union (EU) directives, including
EEC Directive 76/464 on Pollution Caused by Certain Dangerous Substances
Discharged into the Aquatic Environment of the Community and the EEC 84/360 Air
Framework Directive. A more recent and comprehensive definition of BAT is laid
down in Article 2 of the EC Directive 96/61 on Integrated Pollution Prevention
Control. It provides that ' "best available techniques" (BAT) shall mean the most
effective and advanced stage in the development of activities and their methods of

operation which indicate the practical suitability of particular techniques for providing in principle the basis emission limit values designed to prevent and, where that is not practicable, generally to reduce emissions and the impact on the environment as a whole.'

In general, the use of technology specifications has two contradictory consequences with regard to technological change and effectiveness (see Chapter 8 'Instrument Choice'). First, such specifications may stifle innovation. BAT standards foreclose the possibility of an immediate innovative response since they are based on already available technology. Second, specification standards stimulate the diffusion of technology. BAT standards are typically based on the best technology in use in leading companies, and may contribute to push laggards up to the state of the art and improve the market for environmental goods and services firms.[22] The actual impact of BAT specifications depends on a wide range of factors, including their bindingness and range of application. International commitments rarely command industry to utilize a particular technology. In the case of the OSPAR Convention, for example, BAT specifications are adopted as recommendations, which are legally not binding. Technology specifications also vary as to whether or not they apply to existing installations.

International environmental regimes can also be used to underpin a 'first-mover strategy' and improve market conditions for domestic environmental technology firms. A country may force its industry to develop new technology by setting more stringent standards than in other countries. If this country is able to 'upload' these standards as BAT in international regimes, and other countries subsequently adopt similar standards, the companies in the country that first adopted the standards are likely to dominate the market. This mechanism may stimulate regulatory competition leading to more stringent standards.

4.1.2 *Commitments that Indirectly Affect Technology*

International regimes can affect technology indirectly through different types of commitments such as a *ban* on products or activities. Bans are applied mainly to chemical products, including chlorofluorocarbons (CFCs), some pesticides, and polychlorinated biphenyls (PCBs). Product bans always result in a change in technology—ranging from incremental innovation in the form of substitutes (for example, CFCs) to radical changes that restructure an industry (for example, PCB substitutes produced by new companies) (see Chapter 17 'Hazardous Substances and Activities'). Dramatic policy initiatives, such as bans, thus can induce changes in technology that benefit the environment (and, hence, increase effectiveness) over the long term.[23] Bans can also be applied to certain activities. In 1989, the Oslo Commission on the Prevention of Marine Pollution by Dumping in the Northeast-Atlantic decided to

---

[22] OECD, see note 9 above.   [23] *Ibid.*

phase out the dumping of industrial waste in the North Sea within a specific time frame. The consequences of banning this practice induced significant investments in abatement technology, no-waste technology, recycling, and even a halt in production. The titanium dioxide industry, for example, had to make major investments in order to comply with the ban.[24]

Performance commitments are widely used in international cooperation regarding the reduction of air and water pollution as well as hazardous waste management. For example, the 1990 Hague Declaration on the North Sea obliged the North Sea states to reduce emissions of 36 hazardous substances by 50 per cent (70 per cent for the most dangerous) between 1985 and 1995.[25] Such performance standards combine a clear technology-related demand—reduced emissions that can only be achieved by introducing changes to the technology in place—with flexibility in how to achieve the target—the technology to be introduced is not specified. It is reasonable to assume that the more specific and ambitious a commitment, the higher the probability that it will be effective in inducing technological change. One example is the impact of the 1991 Protocol on Volatile Organic Compounds to the LRTAP Convention on Norway. The protocol committed the parties to reduce emissions by 30 per cent between 1988 and 1999. Norway did not comply with this commitment mainly due to VOC evaporation from tankers shuttling oil on the Norwegian continental shelf. Recovery systems to be applied in shuttle tankers were in the early invention phase in the 1990s, technological innovation took longer than anticipated, and the new technology turned out to be expensive for the oil companies (estimated to cost around 2 billion Norwegian kroner). In 2001, the Ministry of Environment ordered the oil companies to take action to implement the VOC Protocol commitment after years of governmental pressure and negotiations. The same year, recovery technology was implemented on the first ships.

Commitments may also include *emissions trading*, as in the Kyoto Protocol, which has recently been implemented in the EU. Knowledge about the effects of emissions trading on technological change is limited. Experience from emissions trading in the United States, however, indicates that its effects are limited and that incremental, rather then radical, changes in technology are likely to ensue.[26] However, the value of a permit, as such, may provide an economic incentive that induces companies to identify abatement options. High permit prices also may provide an incentive for developing new technologies that can 'free up' permits at a later stage. Low permit prices, however, will probably not lead to radical changes in technology, instead, in this situation, technological change is likely to be limited to what industry would have introduced in the absence of the trading scheme.

[24] J.B. Skjærseth, 'Towards the End of Dumping in the North Sea: The Case of the Oslo Commission,' in E. Miles et al., see note 3 above, 65.

[25] J.B. Skjærseth, *North Sea Cooperation: Linking International and Domestic Pollution Control* (Manchester: Manchester University Press, 2000).   [26] OECD, see note 9 above.

Technology cooperation, diffusion, and transfer to developing countries are part of many international environmental agreements, including the Kyoto Protocol, to which we limit our discussion (see Chapter 41 'Financial and Technological Transfers'). In particular, the Kyoto Protocol's clean development mechanism is expected to induce the transfer of technology to developing countries. The Global Environmental Facility, which serves as the financial instrument of the climate regime, also finances concrete projects that assess the need for, and disseminate, information on technology and engage in technology-related capacity building. The Marrakech Accords, furthermore, established three additional funds, which deal with the transfer of technology and establish conditions for private financing. In a broad assessment of various initiatives, the OECD concludes that international technology cooperation, by sharing information, costs, and efforts, might accelerate and facilitate technical change towards more climate-friendly technologies.[27]

Information disclosure and transparency may also affect technological change. Most scholars argue that transparency increases the effectiveness of international regimes (see Chapter 29 'Public Participation').[28] Public disclosure of new environmental information may motivate companies to improve environmental performance by technological means. The 1985 Vienna Convention on the Protection of the Ozone Layer and the 1987 Montreal Protocol on Substances That Deplete the Ozone Layer are relevant examples in this regard. The ozone regime, linked to a number of international and national expert organizations, reduced the scientific uncertainty related to ozone depletion and contributed to the disclosure of information on the ozone 'hole'. Such information contributed to motivating companies to develop substitutes for ozone-depleting substances.[29]

4.2 Domestic Policy Instruments and Technological Change

Ultimately, the commitments entered into in international regimes have to be translated into national policy instruments to regulate the behaviour of target groups. Given that national governments have the authority to impose and enforce policy and regulatory instruments on target groups, such instruments can have a significant influence on technological change. Domestic environmental policy has changed the commercial conditions under which most industries operate over the past decades, and the relationship between environmental policy and technological change has

---

[27] OECD, *International Energy Technology Collaboration and Climate Change Mitigation* (Paris: OECD, 2004).

[28] R.B. Mitchell, 'Sources of Transparency: Information Systems in International Regimes' (1998) 42 Int'l Stud. Q. 109.

[29] J.B. Skjærseth, 'The "Successful" Ozone Layer Negotiations: Are There Any Lessons to be Learned?' (1992) 2 Global Envt'l Change 292.

received increased attention by scholars and practitioners alike.[30] In this section, we offer only a snapshot of this complex relationship.

Policy instruments can be defined as the means by which public authorities seek to alter the behaviour of target groups. Target groups, such as the petroleum industry, are the source of the problem in question and hold the solution to this problem, given that they 'control' the behaviour or technology that has to be modified. Governments, thus, crucially depend on their 'cooperation', be it reluctantly or willingly offered. The nature of the policy instruments chosen to address a certain problem is thus important when countries implement international environmental commitments and national policy (see Chapter 8 'Instrument Choice'). A distinction can be made between command-and-control instruments, economic instruments, voluntary agreements, and the dissemination of information.

Economic instruments, such as pollution charges, can have positive impacts over time on the development and introduction of environmentally friendly technology (see Chapter 11 'Economic Theory of International Environmental Law'). However, setting the charge at the 'right' level is extremely difficult, and, in most cases, it is deemed too low to induce radical changes. The Norwegian carbon dioxide tax, which applies mainly to the petroleum sector, is quite illustrative. The economic gains obtained from the reduced payment of carbon dioxide taxes have mainly facilitated the implementation of more energy-efficient equipment and technologies to reduce flaring in upstream petroleum operations. The tax has had some, but limited, impact in inducing more radical changes than energy efficiency such as carbon dioxide separation at the Sleipner West field.[31] Technological change in the petroleum sector is driven by many considerations that are related to specific field characteristics and other policies and instruments.

Combining regulation with economic instruments may prove most effective with regard to the development and introduction of environment-friendly technology.[32] Regulation tends to provide a strong single stimulus to introduce environmental-friendly technology, whereas economic instruments may provide continued incentives to foster innovation. The merits of portfolios of different types of policy instruments, or policy 'packages', can be illustrated by the unequal use of policy instruments and the unequal development of wind power in Norway and Denmark.[33] Denmark has invented, innovated, and diffused significantly more wind power technology than Norway. Although the reasons are extremely complex, it seems that the fact that Denmark, as opposed to Norway, has offered a wider portfolio of policy

---

[30] See, e.g., A.B. Jaffe, R.G. Newell, and R.N. Stavins, 'Environmental Policy and Technological Change' (2002) 22 Envt'l and Resource Econ. 41.

[31] A. Christer-Christiansen and J.B. Skjærseth, 'Climate Change Policies in Norway and the Netherlands: Different Instruments, Similar Outcomes?' (2005) 16 Energy & Env't 1.

[32] OECD, see note 9 above.

[33] J. Buen, *Wind Industry in Norway and Denmark: Policy Instruments and Technological Change*, FNI Report 17/2004 (Lysaker: Fridtjof Nansen Institute, 2004).

instruments (including investment subsidies, production subsidies, tax exemption for wind turbine ownership, and voluntary wind power agreements with power companies) is a significant factor in explaining the difference between the two countries.

One advantage of voluntary agreements lies in their cooperative features and potential for collective learning between and among companies, expert organizations, and authorities.[34] Voluntary agreements are considered to be 'weak' policy instruments compared to incentive-based economic instruments. In the long term, however, cooperation based on voluntary agreements may help to reduce transaction costs involved in the invention and introduction of new technology and, thereby, pave the way for radical technological change that probably would not pay off in the short term. This is partly the rationale behind the widespread use of negotiated voluntary agreements in the Netherlands.[35]

In addition to the type and combination of policy instruments applied, technological change is likely to be affected by the political context in which the instruments are adopted. Public/private partnerships for developing environmental technologies can be effective in overcoming obstacles, such as budget constraints and information gaps. Such partnerships can direct investment to critical research needs and facilitate networking among actors in the innovation process.[36] The most successful regulatory model to facilitate innovation is based on dialogue and on making environmental policy-making independent from the interests of industry.[37]

5 Concluding Comments

In this chapter, we have discussed how science and technology can contribute to enhance the effectiveness of international environmental policy. We have conceived of science and technology as separate processes, serving different functions at different levels and in different stages of the process. Let us first sum up our findings regarding the role of science. A first observation is that science represents an important decision premise for decision-makers in international environmental regimes. All of the regimes we have considered have scientific bodies as part of their institutional set up, and there is a tendency towards greater utilization of scientific research over time and a broadening of the scope of scientific input. Especially as regimes mature, governments rarely dispute scientific 'consensual knowledge' explicitly. Some

---

[34] See, e.g., P. Glasbergen, *Co-operative Environmental Governance: Public-Private Agreements as a Policy Strategy* (Dordrecht: Kluwer Academic Publishers, 1998).

[35] J.B. Skjærseth, 'Governing Technological Change by Voluntary Agreements: Climate Policy and Dutch Petroleum Production' (2005) 5 Climate Policy 419.   [36] OECD, see note 9 above.

[37] D. Wallace, *Environmental Policy and Industrial Innovation: Strategies in Europe, the US and Japan* (London: Earthscan, 1995).

kind of collective action also normally follows as a result of scientific warnings. No uniform pattern, however, can be discerned in the political responses to scientific advice. Sometimes conclusive scientific evidence is not a prerequisite for undertaking collective action. For various reasons, policy-makers may take precautionary measures. The 'normal' pattern is that science is most important in the agenda-setting phase, and that its significance declines over time as politics and governments take control of the relevant processes. To some extent, however, this can be modified by the deliberate institutional design of the science-policy nexus.

Our second main observation is that although science represents an important decision premise for decision-makers, science usually has a moderate impact on decisions taken within these regimes, unless it interacts with other 'benign' factors, including a feasible cure through the development/introduction of technology. When there are strong political conflicts, including conflicts over value judgements, the room for scientific influence is small and sometimes non-existent. That is, the substance of the response is determined essentially by politics and not by science. Regardless of these rather sobering remarks, the role of science should not be underestimated, as most of the issues discussed never would have reached the international political agenda in the absence of science.

Turning then to technology, a first observation is that much less is known about how technology can be utilized to enhance the effectiveness of international environmental policy. Our discussion of these issues, therefore, is of a more exploratory nature. However, some preliminary conclusions for further research can be drawn. First, even though technology can contribute to solving many transnational environmental problems, it is not generally reflected in the 'design' of international environmental regimes. Second, some international environmental regimes and some EU directives use technology specifications as part of their rules and standards. Third, international technology specifications may have contradictory consequences with regard to effectiveness—they may stifle innovation but facilitate the diffusion of BAT. Technology specifications in international environmental regimes may also be used to underpin a 'first mover' strategy that may stimulate regulatory competition. Fourth, international environmental regimes can affect technological change indirectly by banning products or activities, setting performance standards, allowing emissions trading, stimulating cooperation on the introduction of new technology, promoting the diffusion and transfer of technology to developing countries, and enhancing transparency.

Technology can also be utilized to enhance the effectiveness of international regimes when international commitments are implemented at the national level in the form of policy instruments. The relationship between environmental policy and technological change has received increased attention from scholars and practitioners, but even this relationship is relatively poorly understood. First, combining regulation with economic instruments may prove most effective with regard to the development and introduction of environmental-friendly technology. Second, voluntary agreements are considered 'weak' policy instruments, but they may prove effective in facilitating the development and introduction of environmental-friendly technology over the long term. Third, technological change is a complex process involving broad interaction between industry and policy-makers. The most successful interaction is based on dialogue and independence of environmental policy-making from the interests of industry.

RECOMMENDED READING

S. Agrawala, 'Structural and Process History of the IPCC' (1998) 39 Climate Change 621.

S. Andresen and W. Ostreng, *International Resource Management: The Role of Science and Politics* (London: Belhaven, 1989).

S. Boehmer-Christiansen, 'Uncertainty in the Service of Science: Between Science Politics and the Politics of Power,' in G. Fermann, ed., *International Politics of Climate Change* (Oslo: Scandinavian University Press, 1997).

A. Christer-Christiansen and J.B. Skjærseth, 'Climate Change Policies in Norway and the Netherlands: Different Instruments, Similar Outcomes?' (2005) 16 Energy & Env't 1.

P. Haas, 'Epistemic Communities and Policy Knowledge,' in N. Smelser and P. Bates, eds., *International Encyclopedia of the Social and Behavioural Sciences* (New York: Elsevier, 2001) 11578.

A.B. Jaffe, R.G. Newell, and R.N. Stavins, 'Environmental Policy and Technological Change' (2002) 22 Env't'l and Resource Econ. 41.

S. Jasanoff and M. Long Martello, 'Earthly Politics: Local and Global,' in *Environmental Governance* (Cambridge, MA: MIT Press 2005).

K. Litfin, *Ozone Discourses: Science and Politics in Global Environmental Cooperation* (New York: Columbia University Press, 1994).

OECD, *Technology and Environment: Towards Policy Integration* (Paris: OECD, 1999).

E.A. Parson, *Protecting the Ozone Layer Science and Strategy* (Oxford: Oxford University Press, 2003).

T. Skodvin, *Structure and Agent in Scientific Diplomacy on Climate Change* (Dordrecht: Kluwer Academic Publishers, 2000).

D. Wallace, *Environmental Policy and Industrial Innovation: Strategies in Europe, the US and Japan* (London: Earthscan, 1995).

PART II

ANALYTICAL TOOLS AND PERSPECTIVES

CHAPTER 10

INTERNATIONAL RELATIONS THEORY

KYLE W. DANISH

1 INTRODUCTION

SINCE the early 1990s, international rules and institutions related to international environmental law (IEL) have multiplied at an exponential rate. International environmental agreements have increased in number and rates of participation. Yet, there is little evidence that this escalation of law-making activity has had a proportional impact on the behaviour of states and other international actors. Environmental problems continue to grow more acute, and the challenge of establishing effective international responses to issues such as biodiversity and global climate change seem more difficult than ever. Environmental agreements appear to vary substantially in their rates of participation, compliance, and overall effectiveness. (see Chapter 39 'Compliance Theory'). In addition, certain environmental issues with enormous impacts, such as clean water, do not seem to make it on the law-making agenda at all.

For these reasons, in addition to analysing doctrine and practice in particular issue areas, legal scholars and practitioners now increasingly struggle to get to the bottom of broader theoretical questions about IEL, including: (1) why states and other key international actors adopt certain forms of cooperation under international law; (2) how different forms of international cooperation affect the behaviour of key actors; and (3) how international environmental laws can be made more effective in shaping actor behaviour.

To gain new perspectives and insights into these and other questions, many in the IEL community have joined other international law (IL) scholars and practitioners in turning to international relations (IR) theory. This exchange with IR theorists is one example of the broader interest among legal scholars in drawing upon the knowledge and techniques of the social sciences. This interest has spawned a set of 'law and' sub-disciplines. It also has spawned scepticism, including critiques from legal scholars who assert that something distinctive about legal norms and practices is lost when viewed through the prism of IR, economics, philosophy, or other disciplines (see Chapter 43 'Compliance Procedures').

Accordingly, the IL-IR interdisciplinary project has drawn both adherents and sceptics. For some IL scholars, the disciplines of IL and IR are complementary in that IL scholarship traditionally focuses on questions of doctrine (what is the law that governs this issue area?) and prescription (what should the law be?), while IR scholars focus on questions of explanation (why has law emerged in this area and what kind of law will work?). Seen in this light, collaboration holds the promise of designing more effective and durable international environmental laws and institutions. However, other scholars see distinct hazards in the interdisciplinary project, warning that IR theories tend to undermine the validity of international rules or even promote American hegemonic dominance.

Notwithstanding these criticisms, there is a distinct trend towards greater use of IR theory within IL scholarship generally and particularly within IEL. Conversely, among IR scholars studying environmental issues, there is rising interest in under-standing the particular forms and impacts of 'legalization' in world politics. Cross-disciplinary exchanges are increasing, and there have been a number of notable collaborations between IR and IEL scholars in recent years. This chapter reviews the major IR theories and their relevance to, and impact upon, IEL. It also identifies key emerging issues in the inter-disciplinary agenda of IR and IEL scholars and practi-tioners. Finally, it reviews sources of scepticism about this agenda.

2 REALISM AND NEO-REALISM: IR's PERIOD OF HOSTILITY TO IL

While there would seem to be a natural affinity between scholars studying inter-national law and international relations theory, there was for several decades a gulf, even a chasm, separating the two disciplines. This chasm opened up with the onset of the Cold War, when there arose an American-dominated view of international relations, which is referred to as 'Realism' and which was explicitly hostile to inter-national law. Animating this view was a deep rejection of what were perceived to be the 'legalist-moralist' views of Woodrow Wilson and proponents of the League of Nations during the inter-war years. For influential Realists such as George Kennan and Hans Morgenthau, states were not—and should not be—bound by law in the international sphere.[1]

As first formulated by Kennan and others, Realism was more a stance or diplo-matic strategy than a fully specified theory of international relations. Then, Kenneth Waltz re-conceptualized Realism as Neo-Realism (sometimes referred to as Structural Realism), thereby establishing an analytically rigorous theory of international rela-tions. Neo-Realism all but occupied the field between the early 1950s and the early 1980s and remains influential today. Neo-Realists posit that the key actors in the international system are states—not international organizations, domestic interests, non-governmental organizations (NGOs), or others. Neo-Realism further asserts that the international system is anarchic—not in the sense of being in constant violent conflict, but rather in the sense that there is no set of authoritative institutions that constrain states in the pursuit of their interests. And, in this anarchic system, each state's interests are related to material ends, specifically, the accumulation of power and wealth relative to other states.[2]

---

[1] See, e.g., G. Kennan, *American Diplomacy, 1900–1950* (Chicago: University of Chicago Press, 1951); and H.J. Morgenthau, *Politics among Nations: The Struggle for Power and Peace*, 4th edition (New York: Alfred Knopf, 1967).

[2] See, e.g., J.J. Mearsheimer, 'The False Promise of International Institutions' (1994–5) 19 Int'l Security 5; and J.M. Grieco, 'Anarchy and the Limits of Cooperation: A Realist Critique of the Newest Liberal Institutionalism' (1988) 42 Int'l Org. 485.

Under this theory, outcomes in the international system are determined by the number of states and the distribution of power among these states. Accordingly, in the Neo-Realist system, legal norms and law-based institutions do not have any independent causal effect but, rather, are epiphenomenal. States sometimes cooperate through treaties, but only at the behest of the most powerful states, and when the distribution of power changes, cooperation changes its form or ends.

So how do Realists account for the proliferation of international environmental law treaties in the past few decades? Some Neo-Realists assert that the 'low politics' of international environmental issues place these issues outside the domain of Neo-Realist analysis. In other words, because state survival ordinarily is not immediately at stake with respect to such issues, states can afford to pursue absolute gains through cooperation.[3] Alternatively, Neo-Realists argue that state activity on international environmental issues is consistent with their theory because the vast majority of international environmental treaties have not been associated with any changes in state behaviour beyond what the states would have done in the absence of the treaties, and the few regimes that have been associated with changed state behaviour have also had the active backing of a powerful ('hegemonic') state. They cite, for example, the moratorium on commercial whaling, which seems to have changed the behaviour of whaling states such as Japan, not because of the legal effect of the moratorium itself but rather because of pressure from the United States.[4]

Accordingly, with the rise of Neo-Realism to a position of prominence, several generations of IR scholars were taught that IL was a mere shadow play in the fundamentally anarchic system of state interaction, and that the study of IL was the province of idealists and utopians. During the period between the 1950s and the late 1980s, IR scholars generally were not interested in any cross-disciplinary entreaties from scholars of IL. In the 1970s, in particular, 'international law virtually disappeared from the study of international relations.'[5]

3 RISE OF NEO-LIBERAL INSTITUTIONALISM AND REGIME THEORY

3.1 Neo-Liberal Institutionalism as a Response to Realism

During the period of its ascendancy within IR, the Neo-Realist school withstood a variety of liberal attacks, including critiques that Neo-Realism could not explain the

[3] For further discussion of the view of Neo-Realist theorists regarding international environmental politics, see R.B. Mitchell, 'International Environment,' in W. Carlsnaes, T. Risse, and B. Simmons, eds., *Handbook of International Relations* (London: Sage, 2002) 500 at 504.   [4] *Ibid.*

[5] S. Krasner, 'What's Wrong with International Law Scholarship? International Law and International Relations: Together, Apart, Together?' (2000) 1 Chi. J. Int'l L. 93 at 95.

growing number of treaties, the increasing technological and economic inter-dependence of states, and the rising prominence within the international system of a wide spectrum of non-state actors in international relations. However, it took an attack from within to ease the grip of Neo-Realism on IR scholarship.

The starting point for this critique was the inability of Neo-Realism to explain the persistence, and continued influence, of certain international institutions, such as the General Agreement on Tariffs and Trade, even with the relative decline of US power. The insight of Robert Keohane and others in what has come to be known as the Neo-Liberal Institutionalist School was that states establish and maintain such cooperative arrangements out of their self-interest.[6] The Institutionalists adopted nearly all of the premises of Realism, including the notion that the international sys-tem is anarchic, that the key actors in this system are states, that more powerful states typically will dominate the international realm, and that states are rational and autonomous. Their twist was to apply a micro-economic analysis to the study of international relations, reasoning that self-interested states (even the most powerful ones) will sometimes sacrifice some of their autonomy in order to establish multi-state 'institutions' or 'regimes'—defined as 'persistent and connected sets of rules (formal and informal) that prescribe behavioural roles, constrain activity, and shape expectations'[7]—where the gains from cooperation exceed the gains from unilateral action.

In other words, regimes provide a tool that states can use to address market failures caused by barriers to collective action. In particular, regimes can offer a compelling solution to situations in which a state has 'mixed motives'. For example, states that have some interest in reducing trade in endangered species have reasons to prefer a multilateral regime—such as the Convention on International Trade in Endangered Species of Wild Fauna and Flora (CITES)—to an approach in which each state has the autonomy to regulate such trading. However, the analysis does not stop there. To the extent that CITES becomes more and more effective, the value of contraband specimens will become higher and higher, meaning that the financial rewards avail-able to a state that is willing to open its borders to trade—that is, to 'free-ride'—also increases. Given this 'mixed motives' outcome, Institutionalists argue that cooper-ation through CITES can become increasingly 'deep' only if the regime has increas-ingly powerful incentives to prevent free-riding—not only by parties to the regime but also, and perhaps even more importantly, by states that have opted to stay outside the regime.

For Institutionalists, state sovereignty implies that regimes can improve upon the unilateralist status quo only if they are self-enforcing (see Chapter 11 'Economic Theory of International Environmental Law'). And Institutionalists generally agree

    [6] See R.O. Keohane, *After Hegemony: Cooperation and Discord in the World Economy* (Princeton: Princeton University Press, 1984).

    [7] R.O. Keohane, *International Institutions and State Power* (Boulder, CO: Westview, 1989) at 3. An older definition of regimes can be found in S.D. Krasner, ed., *International Regimes* (Ithaca, NY: Cornell University Press, 1983) at 1 (defining regimes as 'principles, norms, rules and decision-making

that a regime can be self-enforcing only if it is individually rational (in the sense that no party to the regime can gain by withdrawing and no state that is outside the regime could gain by joining it) and collectively rational (in the sense that no party can gain collectively by changing the treaty).[8] Under this view, a regime can be effective only if it changes the incentive structure of the key states.

Regimes offer a number of instruments to achieve this end, thereby allowing states to exploit the clout of reciprocity at a lower transactional cost than through ad hoc cooperation or unilateral actions. Regimes allow states to pool their resources to develop information and monitor one another's performance. In addition, through conferences of the parties and other official meetings, they provide arenas for repeated iterations of negotiation and interaction. Such repeated iterations lengthen the shadow of the future—the knowledge that they will encounter each other repeatedly over time can reduce the likelihood that states will renege on their obligations.[9] Regimes thus leverage each state's concern for its reputation as a reliable bargaining partner. Regimes also provide a set of terms to clarify the scope of expected performance and, in some instances, a place for resolving disputes.

Finally, regimes provide a mechanism for organizing collective punishments or rewards. For example, parties to the ozone regime used the Montreal Protocol on Substances That Deplete the Ozone Layer (Montreal Protocol) to establish rules under which they could ban imports of ozone-depleting substances (ODS) from non-parties and non-complying parties, thereby inducing both participation and compliance. In addition, the parties worked through the regime to pool their capacity-building resources in a Multilateral Fund. Managed by the World Bank, the fund directs resources to developing country parties to offset their incremental costs of phasing out ODS.

Institutionalism has been the theory that launched a thousand research agendas, in no small part because its researchers could make use of non-cooperative game theory—a particularly potent analytical tool that has become the tool of choice of economics, which is the discipline currently in ascendancy among the social sciences.[10] Thus, Arild Underdal,[11] Michael Zürn,[12] and other IR scholars have analysed how different kinds of 'game' structures for international environmental problems lead to

procedures around which actor expectations converge in a given issue-area.'). The terms 'regime' and 'institution' are sometimes used interchangeably, but for some scholars regimes are distinguishable by their greater level of formality.

   [8] S. Barrett, *Environment and Statecraft: The Strategy of Environmental Treaty-Making* (Oxford: Oxford University Press, 2003) at xiii.

   [9] See R. Axelrod, *The Evolution of Cooperation* (New York: Basic Books, 1984) at 124.

   [10] Krasner, see note 5 above at 96.

   [11] See, e.g., A. Underdal, 'One Question, Two Answers,' in E.L. Miles, A. Underdal, S. Andresen, J. Wettestad, J.B. Skjærseth, and E. M. Carlin,, eds., *Explaining Environmental Regime Effectiveness: Confronting Theory with Evidence* (Cambridge: MIT Press, 2001) 3; and A. Underdal, ed., *The Politics of International Environmental Management* (Dordrecht: Kluwer Academic Publishers, 1998).

   [12] See, e.g., M. Zürn, 'The Rise of International Environmental Politics: A Review of Current Research' (1998) 50 World Pol. 617.

different types of regime solutions. Each of these games describes a set of circum-stances in which the players obtain certain hypothetical 'payoffs' from certain actions. Game theory captures the interdependence of international relations. In most games, a player's payoff is affected by the actions taken by other players and also by the number of times that the game will be played.

The game that provides the most difficult obstacles to cooperation is the famous 'Prisoner's Dilemma' which represents, for Institutionalists, the exemplary problem of international relations. In the context of an environmental issue, the classic Prisoner's Dilemma describes a situation in which there are two players, X and Y. Each can choose either to 'pollute' or to 'abate'. The game is played once, meaning that, without the benefit of actual experience, each player must guess how the other will play. Each player confronts the same payoff structure. The highest possible payoff occurs if both players play 'abate'. For either player, the worst possible payoff occurs if it plays 'abate' and the other player opts for 'pollute'. Without the ability to coordinate, therefore, each player's 'dominant strategy' is to play 'pollute' for it pro-vides, across the spectrum of possible plays, the highest payoff opportunities given the possible strategies employed by the other player. Thus, the Prisoner's Dilemma results in an inefficient equilibrium.

Other types of collective action problems can be represented by other types of games. For example, the 'coordination' game is more benign than the Prisoner's Dilemma. The coordination game describes a situation in which there are two coope-ration strategies that will provide the players with a high payoff. Accordingly, if the game is played sequentially—for example, if X acts first and then Y acts—the high payoff strategy can be a self-enforcing outcome. An example of a coordination game is provided by the aviation standards set by the United Nations International Civil Aviation Organization (ICAO), which include a set of standards that addresses pol-lutant emissions. Scott Barrett has explained that even though ICAO standards are voluntary, compliance is nearly universal because of the commercial incentives for manufacturers to have uniform technology requirements. Thus, once a certain num-ber of members adopt a particular technology, all members have interests in adopt-ing the same technology.[13] The ICAO provides a lesson in IEL regime strategy. Were the ICAO to attempt to set an overall emissions cap and allocate responsibility for meeting the cap, the game would be similar to a Prisoner's Dilemma, with all of its attendant compliance and enforcement difficulties. In contrast, the technology stand-ard approach, while perhaps less cost-effective, nevertheless, has the advantage of establishing a self-enforcing coordination game.

Institutionalists have used other games—including such vividly named games as 'chicken', 'stag-hunt', and 'battle of the sexes'—to represent a range of different types of collective international problems.[14] Institutionalists explain that, to improve upon

---

[13] Barrett, see note 8 above at 94.

[14] For a detailed exploration of game theory in the context of international environmental agree-ments, see Barrett, note 8 above.

unilateralism, states and other international actors have to manipulate regime design strategies to change payoffs. In these analyses, Institutionalists generally emphasize that there are almost always strong incentives for states to remain outside an agreement and 'free-ride', implying that most self-enforcing agreements are either characterized by a small number of parties or a low level of obligation or both. Indeed, Institutionalist analysis is characterized by a degree of scepticism about the potential for collective action to address the most difficult, global-scale environmental issues, such as global climate change. For Institutionalists, the greater the number of states that are needed to address a problem, and the greater the behavioural change required, the less likely that international environmental treaties can improve on the unilateral status quo.

3.2 Regime Theory and IL Scholarship

The rise of Institutionalism opened up new vistas of cross-disciplinary dialogue between scholars of international relations and scholars of international law. This is in no small part because, by the time Keohane and other international relations scholars launched Institutionalism, international legal scholars such as Louis Henkin, the adherents of the New Haven School, and others had already spent the previous three decades developing functionalist/rationalist accounts of international law. Indeed, according to IL scholar Anne-Marie Slaughter, the insight that regimes facilitate cooperation rather than mandate a utopian world government was 'an insight new only to political scientists.'[15] Like Moliere's Monsieur Jordan, these legal scholars may have been surprised to learn that they had been speaking regime theory the entire time. Even so, the Institutionalists brought to the discussion a more fully specified, more empirically rigorous analytical framework to support the functionalist explanation of treaty-based cooperation. Regime theory has provided new tools and analytical concepts for understanding why regimes develop and how they operate to change state behaviour.

And, as Slaughter, Andrew Tulumello, and Stepan Wood have observed, Institutionalists have offered another vital insight to international cooperation, namely that 'institutions that provide collective goods may be collective goods themselves, subject to the same difficulties of supply and maintenance as the underlying substantive benefits they are designed to provide.'[16] Thus, Institutionalists not only have identified a rationale for why cooperative regimes and institutions emerge, they also have identified the factors that can make such cooperation difficult to sustain.

The rich theoretical dimensions offered by Institutionalism have led to a variety of new research agendas for scholars of international environmental law. For

---

[15] A.-M. Slaughter Burley, 'International Relations Theory: A Dual Agenda' (1993) 87 A.J.I.L. 205 at 220.
[16] A.-M. Slaughter, A.S. Tulumello, and S. Wood, 'International Law and International Relations Theory: A New Generation of Interdisciplinary Scholarship' (1998) 92 A.J.I.L. 367 at 375.

example, scholars have examined the dynamic evolution of treaty regimes from framework conventions to more detailed regulatory protocols (see Chapter 20 'Treaty Making and Treaty Evolution'); the role of iteration in treaty law in overcoming Prisoner's Dilemma problems;[17] the reasons why states negotiate hard or soft norms and the comparative effectiveness of the two approaches;[18] and the factors that contribute to the effectiveness of international environmental regimes (see Chapter 39 'Compliance Theory').

4 ALTERNATIVES TO INSTITUTIONALIST REGIME THEORY: LIBERALISM AND CONSTRUCTIVISM

Even as the density of interaction between legal scholars and political scientists has increased in the past ten to 15 years, discontent with Institutionalism has emerged in both disciplines. For its critics, Institutionalism provides an incomplete account of the evolution and impact of cooperative regimes.

4.1 Liberalism

One of the central criticisms of Institutionalism has been its focus on states as the primary actors in the international system. Among Institutionalists, there is a self-awareness that treating states as the key component in international interaction is a simplification, yet they assert that it is a useful simplification. In the great majority of cases, Institutionalists argue, a model that aggregates and abstracts the varied interests and actors under the state banner is analytically powerful. They assert that it explains most of what plays out on the international stage.[19]

Yet, there is a fine line between parsimony and reductionism and, for Institutionalism's critics, the Institutionalist account omits too much, particularly in explaining a world that is increasingly interdependent and teeming with a whole variety of new actors. Slaughter, for example, has argued for a liberal theory of international law. Her liberal account disaggregates the state, arguing that interactions in the international system are determined in great measure by the type of government

---

[17] See, e.g., J. Setear, 'Ozone, Iteration, and International Law (1999) 40 Va. J. Int'l L. 193; and 'An Iterative Perspective on Treaties: A Synthesis of International Relations Theory and International Law' (1996) 37 Harv. Int'l L.J. 139.

[18] See, e.g., K. Raustiala, 'Form and Substance in International Agreements' (2005) 99 A.J.I.L. 581; D. Shelton, ed., *Commitment and Compliance: The Role of Non-Binding Norms in the International Legal System* (Oxford: Oxford University Press, 2003); and J. Goldstein et al., eds., 'Legalization and World Politics' (2000) 54 Int'l Org. (Special Issue).   [19] See, e.g., Barrett, note 8 above at 5–6.

of the interacting states—democracies act differently than other government types on the international stage.[20] A second point extensively explored by Slaughter and others is the process by which regimes lead to realignments of interests within the domestic realm of participating states, mobilizing some interests and giving them access to, and power within, new institutions. Finally, Slaughter has argued that international policies increasingly result not from state-to-state interaction but rather from interactions between international networks of sub-state actors, such as judges, law enforcement officials, and even private actors. Slaughter identifies the emergence of an increasingly active transnational society, which is neglected in classic Institutionalist accounts.

Harold Hongju Koh also has developed a transnational theory of international relations through law, but the primary focus of this theory is on the vertical, rather than the horizontal, level of interaction. Koh's 'transnational legal process' model posits that state compliance with international rules is determined not solely by the extent to which such rules provide functional benefits but also by the extent to which such rules are internalized within states through domestic legal systems.[21] In Koh's model, the key actors in this internalization process are domestic interest groups. The activities of these 'norm entrepreneurs' facilitate the interpretation and internalization of the rules within domestic law, determining in many cases whether and how states will comply with their international obligations.

With some exceptions, the implications of liberal theory for IEL have been less explored than other areas of international law. One area of potential further inquiry is whether the form of government affects rates of participation and compliance in IEL regimes. The available evidence presents a mixed picture. On the issue of participation in IEL regimes, it is not clear that a liberal democratic form of government necessarily guarantees more cosmopolitan preferences with regard to international environmental treaties.[22] For example, while President George W. Bush has come in for widespread scorn for his seemingly imperious refusal to take steps to ratify the Kyoto Protocol, President Bush's decision arguably reflects the preferences of the US polity as expressed through its representative institutions. Four years prior to the Bush announcement, the US Senate, the key domestic institution in the US treaty ratification process, unanimously passed a resolution expressing its opposition to the United States joining any treaty that did not extend greenhouse gas emission reduction obligations to developing countries.[23]

On the issue of compliance, however, at least one study suggests that liberal democracies are more likely to follow through on their IEL commitments. Edith Brown Weiss, an IEL scholar, and Harold Jacobson, an IR scholar, studied the

---

[20] A.-M. Slaughter, *A New World Order* (Princeton, NJ: Princeton University Press, 2004).

[21] H.H. Koh, 'Why Do Nations Obey International Law?' (1997) 106 Yale L.J. 2599; and H.H. Koh, 'Transnational Legal Process' (1996) 75 Neb. L. Rev. 181.

[22] J.L. Goldsmith and E.A. Posner, *The Limits of International Law* (Oxford: Oxford University Press, 2005) at 215–17.   [23] Byrd-Hagel Resolution, 1997, S. Res. 1998, 105th Cong.

compliance rates of eight states in connection with five treaties. One of their findings was that democracies performed their obligations much more faithfully than non-democracies.[24]

One way of reconciling these different findings on participation and compliance would be to conclude that, even if it is not the case that liberal states are not inherently more environmentally minded than other states, it might be that any kind of international commitment made by a liberal state—environmental or otherwise—is more deeply 'internalized' than the same kind of commitment made by another kind of state. Such deeper internalization could be the result of a more intense deliberative process and/or the incorporation of the commitment in the domestic legal system of a polity that, by its nature, is more dedicated to the rule of law.

4.2 Constructivism

Another line of criticism against Institutionalism has focused on its reliance on interest-based explanations for what causes institutions to emerge and how they operate to change behaviour. Traditional Institutionalist analyses assume that material interests (that is, security and wealth) predominate for states, that states enter regimes with their interests fully formed, and that regimes do not alter interests. Institutionalists assert that regimes change state behaviour not by changing state preferences but rather by lowering or raising the payoffs associated with acting on those preferences in particular ways. In a micro-economic sense, each state's demand for a particular collective good is given—the institution merely changes the supply.

Under the traditional form of Institutionalist theory, states encountering informal rules will make the same set of rational calculations that they make with formal rules and institutions—they will comply only if the benefits of compliance exceed the costs. Since Institutionalists do not believe that a state's preferences are readily reconstructed, they view the significance of legal norms as primarily contractual rather than constitutive. Traditional Institutionalist theory is interested in legal rules and institutions only in so far as such rules establish clear terms for what constitutes performance, and specify the circumstances under which the parties to an institution will provide rewards or mete out punishments. According to conventional Institutionalism, legal norms themselves do not shape state preferences. Thus, Institutionalism might ascribe causal significance to the phase-out schedule for ozone-depleting chemicals in so far as it precisely establishes the terms of agreement under the ozone regime, and makes clear what kind of actions will incur sanctions or incentives. On the other hand, it means little under traditional Institutionalist theory that the ozone regime reflects the 'precautionary

---

[24] E. Brown Weiss and H. Jacobson, *Engaging Countries: Strengthening Compliance with International Accords* (Cambridge, MA: MIT Press, 1998) at 511.

principle' or that compliance with the phase-out schedule is formally compelled by the norm of *pacta sunt servanda*.

For critics of Institutionalism, this account significantly discounts the role of institutions in altering state interests and, in particular, fails to capture the distinctive influence of law-based institutions and norms as distinguished from informal institutions and norms in shaping state identities. Keohane, author of some of the seminal Insitutionalist works and a keen observer of IR scholarship, has characterized the work of Institutionalism's critics as an effort to supplement Institutionalism's 'instrumentalist optic' with a 'normative optic', which explains the role of the institution in transforming state identities and preferences through a range of social processes.[25]

Constructivism is a broad label that describes a number of different theories and perspectives that share an emphasis on the social/normative aspects of state cooperation through institutions. Where Constructivists differ from Institutionalists is in their view of how states interact within the anarchic international system. Constructivists emphasize that the international system must be understood as a social structure. The international system, in their view, comprises more than just a distribution of material capabilities—it also comprises social relationships (see Chapter 3 'Paradigms and Discourses').

For example, Alexander Wendt, one of the leading Constructivists among IR scholars, describes the international system as a social structure encompassing three elements: 'shared knowledge, material resources, and practices.'[26] The first element reflects the worldview of the decision-making elites among states, including their view of which other states are their allies. This shared knowledge determines what meaning they will give to their assessment of their relative control over the second element, material resources. Thus, Wendt reasons that '500 British nuclear weapons are less threatening to the United States than 5 North Korean nuclear weapons because the British are friends of the United States and the North Koreans are not, and amity or enmity is a function of shared understandings.'[27] Finally, the third element of Wendt's Constructivism emphasizes that shared understandings emerge through state behaviour. 'Social structures exist,' Wendt explains, 'not in actors' heads nor in material capabilities, but in practices. Social structure exists only in process.'[28]

Whereas Institutionalists generally presume that states enter the international system with fully formed preferences, Constructivists emphasize that states acquire identities and interests through their participation in the international system's social structures. In other words, there is a 'mutually constitutive' relationship between states and structures in that states act on the system based on their beliefs and, through this participation, find their identities and beliefs changed—even without utilitarian calculations.

---

[25] R.O. Keohane, 'International Relations and International Law: Two Optics' (1997) 38 Harv. Int'l L.J. 487.

[26] A. Wendt, 'Constructing International Politics' (1995/1996) 20 Int'l Security 71 at 73.

[27] *Ibid.*   [28] *Ibid.*

Regimes play key roles under Constructivism, but not just as mechanisms for the diffusion of information and monitoring and for the organization of rewards and punishments. Regimes also are powerful social structures—arenas that are highly effective in generating norms and shared understandings. They both constrain actors—by creating stable patterns of behaviour—and enable them—by providing an environment for increased and focused discourse on what behaviour should be considered legitimate or illegitimate in certain issue areas.[29] Norms generated through interaction within regimes have strong effects on the behaviour and identity of actors, regardless of whether those norms are backed by coercive measures.

Threads of Constructivism can be found in much of the literature on international environmental regimes. For example, political scientists Oran Young and Marc Levy have edited a volume in which they asked researchers to analyze the impacts of different environmental regimes not only with respect to their utilitarian impacts on states (that is, regimes as 'utility modifiers' and 'enhancers of cooperation'), but also based on their social and constitutive impacts (that is, regimes as 'bestowers of authority', 'learning facilitators', and 'role definers').[30] In another book, Young has developed a typology of 'institutional tasks' performed by regimes.[31] The first three tasks—regulatory, procedural, and programmatic—are the familiar elements of any functionalist or process-related regime analysis. The last task, on the other hand, is described as 'generative' and describes the distinctively Constructivist concept of the regime as generating new social practices. Similarly, in their account of the evolution of the Nile River Basin regime, Jutta Brunnée and Stephen Toope emphasize the process by which continued interaction and discourse of the key actors around certain legal norms lead to shared understandings and a convergence of views.[32]

By emphasizing the social and discursive aspects of world politics generally and of institutions specifically, Constructivists have prompted a range of IR and IL scholars to look more closely at the impacts of non-state actors and a variety of social forces on international environmental cooperation. Thus, political scientist Peter Haas has analysed the impact of epistemic communities, groups of advocate-scientists, and other experts on international environmental cooperation (see Chapter 34 'Epistemic Communities').[33] Similarly, IR scholars Steinar Andresen[34]

---

[29] J. Brunnée and J. Toope, 'International Law and Constructivism: Elements of an Interactional Theory of International Law' (2000) 39 Colum. J. Transnat'l L. 19.

[30] O.R. Young and M.A. Levy, 'The Effectiveness of International Environmental Regimes,' in O.R. Young, ed., *The Effectiveness of International Environmental Regimes: Causal Connections and Behavioural Mechanisms* (Cambridge, MA: MIT Press, 1999) 1.

[31] O.R. Young, *Governance in World Affairs* (Ithaca, NY: Cornell University Press, 1999) at 25.

[32] Brunnée and Toope, see note 29 above.

[33] P. Haas, 'Do Regimes Matter? Epistemic Communities and Mediterranean Pollution Control' (1989) 43 Int'l Org. 377.

[34] See, e.g., S. Andresen and L. Gulbransen, 'The Role of Green NGOs in Promoting Climate Compliance,' in O. Stokke et al., eds., *Implementing the Climate Regime: International Compliance* (London: Earthscan, 2005) 169.

and Thomas Princen[35] have emphasized the roles played by NGOs in promoting the formation of, and compliance with, international environmental regimes.

A number of international legal scholars and political scientists assert that regime effectiveness rarely occurs without the emergence of a leader who can be a particular individual or a particular state(s). Weiss and Jacobson assert that '[w]hat might be termed a leader is crucial to the negotiation of environmental accords and to the promotion of compliance with them.'[36]

Constructivism and Liberalism have many overlapping interests, as do Constructivism and the thinking of the Transnational Legal Process School, which examines how state behaviour is altered when it is mediated through the particular structures of international rules and processes. All three schools assert that international cooperation is a function not merely of state preferences and bargaining but rather a range of other factors. However, Constructivists tend to cast a broader analytical net. Scholars such as Koh, who are working in the Liberal or Legal Process mode, generally confine themselves to analyzing how domestic interests or institutional/legal structures frame outcomes in the international system. Constructivists focus on these factors too, but they also probe more broadly into the sociological foundations for the internalization of legal norms. In asking why one legal norm takes root in a society while another does not, for instance, Constructivists examine such factors as the extent to which the norm corresponds to other deeply ingrained norms and the ability of 'norm entrepreneurs' to make themselves heard and begin a 'norm cascade' of internalization.[37]

Constructivist, norm-based concepts have made inroads even among the strictest Neo-Liberal Institutionalists. Though Barrett is sceptical about a variety of constructivist claims regarding international cooperation, he nevertheless agrees that to be self-enforcing an international environmental accord must not only meet criteria for rationality but also must be considered 'fair'.[38] Barrett also sees an important role for customary international law in shaping state behaviour. In many circumstances, he asserts, custom is not strictly determinative of state action, but Barrett reasons that custom often establishes a normative framework that can 'set the terms of debate' and guide negotiations in the direction of more specific rules.[39]

In the fiftieth anniversary issue of the venerable IR journal *International Organization*, IR scholars Peter Katzenstein, Keohane, and Stephen Krasner posit that the

---

[35] See, e.g., T. Princen and M. Finger, *Environmental NGOs in World Politics: Linking the Local and the Global* (New York: Routledge, 1994).

[36] *Ibid.* at 537. See also O. Young, *International Governance: Protecting the Environment in a Stateless Society* (Ithaca, NY: Cornell University Press, 1994) at 114.

[37] See, e.g., M. Finnemore and K. Sikkink, 'International Norm Dynamics and Political Change' (1998) 52 Int'l Org. 887; and R. Goodman and D. Jinks, 'How to Influence States: Socialization and International Human Rights Law' (2004) 54 Duke L.J. 621.   [38] Barrett, see note 8 above at xiii.

[39] *Ibid.* at 124 (quoting D. Bodansky, 'Customary (and Not So Customary) International Environmental Law' (1995) 3 Ind. J. Global Legal Stud. 105 at 119).

main axis of debate in the field of IR in the coming years is likely to be Rationalism/
Institutionalism versus Constructivism.[40] Indeed, Institutionalists have developed a
variety of criticisms of Constructivism. While they acknowledge that social forces
frequently play some role in state behaviour, Institutionalists nevertheless argue that
social norms usually will not trump political-economic influences on state behaviour.[41] Constructivism, they assert, presents a passable theory for interpersonal relations, but a weak explanation for most international relations. Institutionalists also
criticize Constructivism on empirical grounds. As a practical matter, it is difficult to
parse out social from material causes for behaviour. Institutionalists argue that
Constructivists sometimes offer evidence of apparent effectiveness of social forces
without taking the measure of other co-existing variables that might account for
success, such as the presence of powerful states, the number of actors involved, and
the economic incentives for action.[42] Understanding the contexts in which a norm-
based discourse has an independent effect on state identity and interests remains a
significant methodological challenge for Constructivists in both the IL and IR
communities.

5 LEGALIZATION AND IR THEORIES

In 2000, a special issue of *International Organization* brought together 13 of the leading lights of IR and IL scholarship to examine the subject of legalization and world
politics.[43] The contributors to the volume agreed on a conceptualization of legalization as a 'particular form of institutionalization characterized by three components:
obligation, precision, and delegation.'[44] As postulated by the contributors, each of
these characteristics is a matter of degree and each can vary independently. Thus, the
concept of legalization embraces a 'multidimensional continuum', ranging from
'hard' legalization (in which all three components are maximized) to 'soft' legalization (in which each is minimized) with variations in between.[45] By way of illustration, the 'hard' end of the spectrum likely would include CITES, the Montreal
Protocol, and the Kyoto Protocol to the United Framework Convention on Climate
Change. Each has well-specified obligations, fully staffed secretariats, and relatively
strong enforcement mechanisms. On the 'soft' end of the spectrum would be, for
example, the Non-Binding Statement of Forest Principles, which outlines a relatively

---

[40] P.J. Katzenstein, R.O. Keohane, and S.D. Krasner, 'International Organization and the Study of
World Politics' (1999) 52 Int'l Org. 645 at 649.
[41] See generally G.W. Downs, 'Constructing Effective International Environmental Regimes' (2000) 3
Ann. Rev. Pol. Sci. 25.   [42] *Ibid.* at 34.
[43] Goldstein et al., see note 18 above.
[44] K.W. Abbott et al., eds., 'The Concept of Legalization' (2000) Int'1 Org. 401.   [45] *Ibid.*

short set of non-binding and broadly drawn principles, and does not establish any kind of institutional mechanism for monitoring adherence to those principles. An example of a regime that might fall in the middle of this continuum is the whaling regime, which imposes a high degree of formal obligation and precise rules, but does not establish a third-party mechanism for monitoring and enforcement.[46]

This conceptualization rejects a strict dichotomy between 'legalized' and 'informal' regimes (see Chapter 6 'Formality and Informality') and, in particular, avoids the positivist presumption that only those rules enforced by a sovereign can be considered law. Having constructed this typology of legalization, the contributors use it to explore a variety of theories about why international actors opt for different forms of legalization, and the consequences of legalization in a range of settings. Kenneth Abbott and Duncan Snidal, for example, elaborate a functionalist account of legalization, reasoning that the decision as to whether to develop a legalized regime reflects a cost-benefit analysis that balances the transaction costs of negotiation and the sovereignty costs of obligation against the potential benefits of collective action.[47] Other contributors, including Ellen Lutz, Kathryn Sikkink, and Miles Kahler, examine Constructivist or cultural perspectives on legalization.[48]

For Brunnée and Toope, who have worked to extend Constructivism within IL scholarship, the bulk of the *International Organization* volume sustains outdated positivist and hierarchical notions of international law. As an alternative, they have developed an 'interactional legal theory' that aims to explain both the distinctive impact of legal norms and also how such norms can change over time.[49] Drawing on the writings of Lon Fuller, Brunnée and Toope assert that law and legal institutions emerge from the broader spectrum of social practice because law reflects both an 'internal morality' and an 'external morality'. By 'internal morality', Brunnée and Toope mean the internal processes of law-based discourse—that is, 'reasoned argument, reference to past practice and contemporary social aspirations, and the deployment of analogy.'[50] They further explain:

The conditions of internal morality ensure that rules are compatible with one another, that they ask reasonable things of the people to whom they are directed, that they are transparent and relatively predictable, and that officials treat known rules as shaping their exercise of discretion. When these conditions are met, when this particular rationality is evident, law will tend to attract its own adherence. It will be viewed as legitimate, possessing the capacity to generate moral commitment.[51]

---

[46] J.K. Setear, 'Can Legalization Last? Whaling and the Durability of National (Executive) Discretion' (2004) 44 Va. J. Int'l L. 711.

[47] K.W. Abbott and D. Snidal, 'Hard and Soft Law in International Governance' (2000) 54 Int'l Org. 421.

[48] M. Kahler, 'Legalization as Strategy: The Asia-Pacific Case' (2000) 54 Int'l Org. 549; and E.L. Lutz and K. Sikkink, 'International Human Rights Law and Practice in South America' (2000) 54 Int'l Org. 644.   [49] Brunnée and Toope, see note 29 above.

[50] *Ibid.* at 56.   [51] *Ibid.* [citations omitted].

Fuller's concept of 'external morality', as adopted by Brunnée and Toope, posits that one can expect greater adherence to, and impact from, legal norms to the extent that such norms are perceived to be fair or just.[52] It is these characteristics of legal norms, which resemble in some ways Thomas Franck's theories of legitimacy and 'compliance pull',[53] which determine the 'bindingness' of legal norms, and give them special influence on world politics. The greater the extent to which these characteristics are present, the greater the level of adherence that can be expected.

6 The Common IEL and IR Agenda

Given the significant areas of mutual interest between IR and IEL scholars, it is now becoming possible to map out a common, if not necessarily collaborative, agenda. In some ways, the agenda of IR scholars working on environmental issues is quite broad, encompassing a variety of non-legal, or perhaps pre-legal, issues. Ronald Mitchell explains that IR scholars working in this area are pursuing the following matters: (1) determining the political, economic, and social forces that cause international environmental problems; (2) determining why some of these problems make it on to the international agenda while others do not; (3) explaining why solutions are devised for some problems but not for others; (4) analysing why some mitigation policies are effective and others are not; and (5) identifying the factors determining global society's success at evaluating and improving its attempts to protect the global environment.[54]

From the international law perspective, Slaughter, Tulumello, and Wood have proposed a more general collaborative IL–IR agenda that overlaps in significant ways with the IR environmental agenda described by Mitchell. Slaughter, Tulumello, and Wood describe an agenda that: (1) identifies best practices in regime design for different types of problems; (2) identifies effective structures for negotiating new international legal instruments and institutions; (3) examines the precise processes by which actors and social structures are mutually constituted by social practices; (4) analyses the role of power and 'proof' in the discursive production of identities and shared meanings; and (5) analyses how the fundamental structures of the system of sovereign states emerged and how these structures are sustained.[55]

Rather than summarize the IEL and IR research underway in all of the areas described earlier in this chapter (many of which are explored in other chapters of this

[52] *Ibid.* at 52 [citations omitted].
[53] T. Franck, *The Power of Legitimacy among Nations* (New York: Oxford University Press, 1990).
[54] R.B. Mitchell, 'International Environment,' in Carlsnaes, Risse, and Simmons, see note 3 above, 500.
[55] A.-M. Slaughter, *A New World Order* (Princeton, NJ: Princeton University Press, 2004) at 385–94.

Handbook in greater detail), the discussion that follows focuses on regime design, which has been perhaps the most prominent area of common interest and collaboration. There has been substantial effort in this area, particularly in light of the complicated, large-scale issues that have come onto the IEL/IR agenda, including climate change and biodiversity.

Focusing on regime design research not only allows us to review an area in which much work is underway, it also allows us to hone in on some of the lines of debate between Institutionalist and Constructivist views of IEL/IR. Much IEL scholarship on regime design reflects at least an implicit orientation towards Constructivism—that is, an emphasis on the regime as a structure for discourse and norm generation. This orientation has led many IEL and IR scholars, even those who are not self-consciously Constructivists, to favour regime designs aimed at promoting more extensive discourse and norm generation to the exclusion of other types of design options. George Downs, Kyle Danish, and Peter Barsoom have described these Constructivist prescriptions as a 'Transformational' model of regime design—the prescriptions also correspond significantly with the 'framework-convention' approach widely lauded in much of the IEL literature.[56] In a number of areas, Institutionalist strategies for regime design and Transformationalist prescriptions vary strikingly, suggesting a broad agenda for further research. The discussion that follows very briefly summarizes research that has been done in three areas of regime design—(1) regime participation; (2) form of commitment; and (3) compliance—and highlights the different approaches implied by the Institutionalist and Constructivist/Transformational models.

6.1 Participation

A critical element of international environmental regime design is obtaining the optimal level of participation by states with a stake in the environmental problem or issue. Inducing key states to join the regime and deterring their withdrawal is in many ways more challenging than managing or enforcing performance by states that are parties. Non-participation or withdrawal, after all, are both legal under international law and, therefore, outside the reach of compliance norms or enforcement mechanisms. And, as Barrett observes, non-participation 'involves a deviation from cooperation at least as large as any act of non-compliance.'[57] Participation also has a dynamic aspect. From a regime design standpoint, the issue of participation involves an evaluation of whether the aim should be to launch the regime with all of the key states as parties from the beginning or to start from a base of committed states and bring in others over time.

---

[56] G.W. Downs, K.W. Danish, and P.N. Barsoom, 'The Transformational Model of International Regime Design: Triumph of Hope or Experience?' (2000) 38 Colum. J. Transnat'l L. 466.

[57] Barrett, see note 8 above at 271.

Advocates of the Transformational model of regime design favour the former approach. They recommend a strategy of lowering the price of admission in order to maximize inclusion. They argue that regimes should be broadly participatory from the outset—even if this means establishing relatively weak initial commitments—in order to expose all of the key states to the socializing influences of the regime. Highly participatory regimes, they argue, are more likely to evolve into deeper levels of cooperation.[58]

Marc Levy asserts that the experience with the Convention on Long Range Transboundary Air Pollution (LRTAP Convention) provides evidence of the effectiveness of a regime design strategy of attracting participation through the establishment of initially weak (albeit binding) commitments (see Chapter 14 'Atmosphere and Outer Space'). He argues that the LRTAP Convention's purposefully weak rules 'permitted strong consensus-building powers, whereas strong rules would have generated hostility on the part of governments.'[59] In Levy's account, weak rules lured states into the LRTAP Convention, and then scientific working groups resolved the uncertainties in favour of taking action.

Advocates of maximum inclusion offer a variety of rationales for this prescription. In some senses, it reflects high confidence of the ability of regimes to reconstruct state preferences. Thus, even states with the lowest preferences for addressing the problem should be brought within the social structure of the regime as soon as possible. Second, advocates of the Transformational model emphasize that highly participatory regimes have more powerful constitutive agents. In other words, the socialization process so central to the Constructivist view of regimes works better as the membership of the regime more closely approximates the full membership of the international community, rather than being merely a 'user's club'. Evidence for the wide-spread adherence to this prescription among IEL practitioners can be found in the 1992 Earth Summit, which attempted to enmesh nearly every state in the international system in a series of environmental accords.

Institutionalists, by contrast, argue that the record provides little evidence that highly-participatory regimes successfully improve upon a unilateralist status quo or become 'deeper' over time.[60] Moreover, constructing inclusive regimes from the beginning may mean having to accommodate the least willing actors, who can use their membership status to stymie commitment. International cooperation often follows the 'law of the least ambitious program.'[61] In addition, regimes with large numbers of members increase all of the collective action challenges of regime

---

[58] See, e.g., L.A. Kimball, 'Towards Global Environmental Management: The Institutional Setting' (1992) 3 Y.B. Int'l Envt'l L. 18 at 30.

[59] M.A. Levy, 'European Acid Rain: The Power of Tote-Board Diplomacy,' in P.M. Haas et al., eds., *Institutions for the Earth: Sources of Effective International Environmental Protection* (Cambridge, MA: MIT Press, 1993) 75.   [60] Barrett, see note 8 above at 209.

[61] A. Underdal, *The Politics of International Fisheries Management: The Case of the Northeast Atlantic* (Oslo: Universitetsforlaget, 1980) at 16 and 36.

management, including monitoring and enforcement. Because Institutionalists are sceptical about the ability of regime-based discourse to change the interests of the laggards, they see little reason to endure the significant liabilities of a design strategy of maximum inclusion. Thus, Downs, Danish, and Barsoom, for example, question the IEL emphasis on 'framework-convention' approaches, and suggest that policy-makers consider regime design strategies in which the regime would start with a small number of committed members and draw in others over time through incentives.[62] Daniel Bodansky sees merit in this strategy in the context of the international climate change regime; he has suggested that the regime might evolve in the direction of deeper cooperation if policy-makers first pursued an accord among the relatively few highest-emitting states.[63]

6.2 Form of Commitment

There is a noticeable trend in IEL, along with some other areas of IL, toward the development of 'soft law'—in the sense of legally non-binding regimes. Increasingly, commentators perceive such regimes to be something other than merely a better-than-nothing substitute for a hard law regime, but rather a form of commitment with some inherent virtues. In recent years, soft law has inspired substantial amounts of scholarship and brought together IR and IEL scholars in collaborative ventures.[64] Efforts to date have exposed significant differences in views within both disciplines, suggesting that further research is merited.

For advocates of the Transformational model of regime design, the establishment of soft law can be part of an affirmative strategy to provide more open texture for collaborative discourse and socialization. Thus, Brunnée and Toope argue that the 'pre-legal or 'contextual' regime may actually be more effective in guiding the relations of international actors.'[65] Handl similarly argues that 'abundant and well-known evidence' exists that soft law declarations such as the Stockholm Declaration and the World Charter for Nature are effective 'catalysts' leading to more ambitious commitments.[66]

In their review of international environmental regimes, David Victor and Kal Raustiala offer a more rationalist account of soft law, which they link to state concerns about compliance. Specifically, they suggest that where uncertainty about

---

[62] Downs, Danish, and Barsoom, see note 56 above; see also G.W. Downs, D.M. Rocke, P.N. Barsoom, 'Managing the Evolution of Multilateralism' (1998) 52 Int'l Org. 397.

[63] D. Bodansky, 'Bonn Voyage: Kyoto's Uncertain Revival' (2001) Nat'l Interest 45.

[64] See, e.g., Shelton, note 18 above; and E. Brown Weiss, ed., *International Compliance with Nonbinding Accords* (Washington, DC: American Society of International Law, 1997).

[65] J. Brunnée and S.J. Toope, 'Environmental Security and Freshwater Resources: Ecosystem Regime Building' (1997) 91 A.J.I.L. 28.

[66] G. Handl, 'Environmental Security and Global Change: The Challenge to International Law' (1990) 1 Y.B. Int'l Envt'l L. 3 at 8.

implementation costs is high—a condition that often holds for complex environmental regimes—states sometimes establish soft, but very precise commitments, as
an alternative to binding, but substantively weak commitments, thereby establishing
regimes that fall somewhere in the middle of Abbott and Snidal's 'legalization' spectrum. Thus, Victor and Raustiala argue that soft law can provide a mechanism that
promotes more change in state behavior than would occur if states felt compelled to
negotiate, and comply with, hard commitments.[67]

Downs, Danish, and Barsoom find little evidence to support the hypothesis that
regimes initially designed with soft law commitments foster deeper cooperation over
time than hard law regimes.[68] In addition, to the extent that some soft law regimes
appear to be effective, Institutionalists would caution that their effectiveness may be
attributable to factors other than the normative structures themselves. For example,
where the number of members of a regime is small enough, such as the shared
resource regimes analysed by Brunnée and Toope, reciprocity alone may be able to
sustain cooperation—even without the specification of precise, legal obligations.
Institutionalists also call attention to enforcement mechanisms that may be outside
the regime, and therefore not formally specified, but nevertheless very real in their
impact on the behaviour of the parties.

6.3 Compliance

Issues related to compliance with international legal obligations have been a lively
arena for interaction between IL and IR scholars (see Chapter 39 'Compliance
Theory'). Furthermore, existing scholarship on compliance throws the differences
between Transformationalist and Institutionalist analyses of regimes into particularly sharp relief.[69]

A starting point for Transformationalists is that states are predisposed to comply
with their treaty obligations, even without resort to the threat of punishment. In
their landmark work on compliance, Abram Chayes and Antonia Handler Chayes
cite a variety of reasons for this 'propensity to comply'.[70] Some of their insights map
onto Liberal and Legal Process theories. For example, Chayes and Handler Chayes
observe that states typically do not ratify a treaty until after an extensive domestic

---

[67] K. Raustiala and D.G. Victor, 'Conclusions,' in D.G. Victor, K. Raustiala, and E. Skolnikoff, eds., *The Implementation and Effectiveness of International Environmental Commitments: Theory and Practice* (Cambridge, MA: MIT Press, 1998) 659 at 684–9.

[68] Downs, Danish, and Barsoom, see note 56 above.

[69] For a more detailed analysis of the encounter of IR and IL theories regarding compliance, see K. Raustiala and A.-M. Slaughter, 'International Law, International Relations, and Compliance,' in Carlsnaes, Risse, and Simmons, note 3 above.

[70] A. Chayes and A. Handler Chayes, *The New Sovereignty: Compliance with International Regulatory Agreements* (Cambridge, MA: Harvard University Press, 1995).

vetting process, thereby ensuring that the treaty reflects the interests of a variety of domestic actors.[71]

Chayes and Handler Chayes also argue, consistent with the Constructivist theory, that states comply with their treaty obligations not merely in return for the functional benefits of the particular treaty, but also because participation in regimes now has become central to state identity and sovereignty. Chayes and Handler Chayes assert that globalization and other factors have led to increasing interdependence among states.[72] They also point to the rise of 'third wave' issues—including environmental degradation—that 'do not yield so readily to the calculus of power and interest.'[73] Under these new circumstances, Chayes and Handler Chayes argue, states are concerned about their standing in a web of regimes. They refer to this as the 'condition of the New Sovereignty', in which 'the only way most states can realize and express their sovereignty is through participation in the various regimes that regulate and order the international system.'[74] As a result of the New Sovereignty, Chayes and Handler Chayes reason that, when non-compliance does occur, it is rarely a product of wilful disobedience but instead a result of the manageable deficiencies within the treaty regime or the lack of capacity of the non-complying state.[75]

Consistent with this understanding of adherence to obligations, Chayes and Handler Chayes prescribe a 'Managerial' strategy for promoting regime compliance as opposed to a sanctions-driven 'Enforcement' strategy. Their Managerial strategy is 'verbal, interactive and consensual.'[76] A key element of this strategy is an ongoing discourse about the requirements of the regime, using the treaty as the foundational normative framework. This discourse is complemented by such 'active instruments of management' as reporting requirements, verification processes, and mechanisms that provide technical and financial assistance.

In particular, Chayes and Handler Chayes and other Transformationalists argue against hard-edge enforcement tools such as sanctions and adjudication-style dispute mechanisms. They note that sanctions and dispute settlement mechanisms are rarely used. Brunnée and Toope similarly assert that such mechanisms are usually too adversarial, backward-looking, and coercive.[77] For Transformationalists, hard-edge enforcement mechanisms present an obstacle to the kind of dialogue needed for transformation, consensus-building, and identity convergence.

Institutionalists generally acknowledge that compliance with international environmental agreements is high, even though treaties rarely incorporate enforcement mechanisms.[78] They differ with Transformationalists, however, as to whether one should therefore conclude that such mechanisms are unnecessary or harmful to cooperation. George Downs, David Rocke, and Peter Barsoom argue that compliance appears high because most international regimes require states to do little

---

[71] *Ibid.* at 5.   [72] *Ibid.* at 123.   [73] *Ibid.*   [74] *Ibid.* at 27.   [75] *Ibid.* at 10.
[76] *Ibid.* at 109.   [77] Brunnée and Toope, see note 65 above at 46.
[78] Barrett, see note 8 above at 270.

more than they would do in the absence of the regime.[79] For those few regimes that require 'deep cooperation', Downs, Rocke, and Barsoom find: (1) that non-compliance has been a problem; (2) that much of this non-compliance has been wilful rather than inadvertent; and (3) that significant efforts have been made to develop enforcement strategies.

For these reasons, Barrett 'cautions against the view that countries can solve the enforcement problem simply by appealing to a state's responsibilities, by exhortation, by naming and shaming, and by offering assistance.'[80] He further explains:

These measures may be helpful; and diplomatically, they may be necessary; but they will not suffice for remedying the hardest cooperation failures. To address these, countries must be able to make credible threats both to deter free-riding and to enforce compliance.[81]

Barrett argues that two notably successful international environmental regimes—the Interim Convention on Conservation of North Pacific Fur Seals and the Montreal Protocol—would not have been effective if their significant obligations had not been complemented by vigorous compliance mechanisms. He further cautions that international efforts to address global climate change will not be effective without careful consideration of how to address free-riding and wilful non-compliance.

7 CONCLUSIONS AND CAUTIONS

The previous sections have mapped out, in summary fashion, a potentially rich collaborative IL-IEL research agenda. Yet, this chapter ends on a cautionary note. Many IL commentators have identified a variety of hazards to embracing IR theories and the IR 'toolkit' of analytical instruments. To be sure, the long-standing resistance of IR theorists to any dialogue with IL scholars and the enduring positivism evident in many IR analyses of international rules have been sources of frustration. Another sceptical view of IR theories is that they are nothing new under the sun. To the extent that each major IR theory has an analogue in IL, one could ask whether these theories add anything other than a superfluous new layer of impenetrable social science terminology and techniques.

IR theorists themselves express scepticism about how far IR-IL collaboration can go. Political scientist Stephen Krasner, while observing that Neo-Liberal Institutionalism and Constructivism have 'created a substantive space' that can be shared by IL and IR scholars, nevertheless suggests that 'the methodological divide

---

[79] G.W. Downs, D.M. Rocke, and P.N. Barsoom, 'Is the Good News about Compliance Good News about Cooperation?' (1996) 50 Int'l Org. 379.   [80] Barrett, see note 8 above at 359.
[81] *Ibid.*

that separates political science and international law is not likely to be bridged, and that, perhaps, is not such a bad thing.'[82] He explains:

The task of political scientists is primarily to explain what is and thereby to hint at what might be. The task of lawyers is more often to elucidate not what is, but what might be. If the normative project that is central to international public law were more closely linked with the empirical project of international relations scholars, both enterprises might be enriched.[83]

The empiricism of IR, particularly in its Institutionalist forms, has been off-putting for many IL scholars. Not just the number-crunching but also the abstraction can be troubling. For example, when Barrett builds a model for analysing international environmental treaties in which states are the only actors, he is making a useful simplification in his view. Yet for many international legal scholars he is taking sides in a vigorously fought doctrinal debate about the meaning of sovereignty.[84] Abstraction also is troubling in that it threatens to omit too much of the rich context behind the evolution of law and cooperation in certain areas. Thus, when Downs, Danish, and Barsoom assign 40 different international environmental agreements scores from one to five on the basis of their 'depth of cooperation', does their analysis obscure too much of the rich complexity of individual accords?

David Bederman has suggested that the 'price that international law pays to be taken "seriously" by IR theorists is greater empiricism, positivism, and skepticism.'[85] Many IL scholars might not be willing to pay such a price. Seeing themselves as problem solvers, some IL scholars and practitioners find it difficult to embrace the scepticism at the heart of much of the IR literature and resist reducing hard-fought international rules either to a set of 'payoffs' or mere 'shared meanings'. Martti Koskenniemi strenuously warns against IL-IR collaboration. In his view, the growing currency of IR theories threatens to erode the formal underpinnings of international law, thereby making it easier for the more dominant states such as the United States to escape their obligations.[86] IR conceptualizations of the law, he asserts, encourage state actors to bypass IL's formal processes of interpretation and contestation because, to the extent that laws merely reflect interests, changed interests provide

---

[82] Krasner, see note 5 above at 98–9.   [83] *Ibid.* at 99.

[84] See, e.g., J.L. Dunoff, 'Book Review: Environment and Statecraft: Strategies of Environmental Treaty-Making, by Scott Barrett' (2004) 98 A.J.I.L. 224 (noting that Barrett's 'use of a particular understanding of "sovereignty" as a foundational *grundnorm;* the presupposition of the freedom that states have to sign, not sign, accede, or withdraw from treaties; the assumptions about the limited coercive mechanisms available to promote compliance; and even the separation of the problems of ozone and climate change (rather than a regime on "atmosphere")—all reflect theoretical assumptions as to which aspects of the international order can be taken as "given" for the analysis of international environmental diplomacy').

[85] D.J. Bederman, 'Review Essay: Constructivism, Positivism, and Empiricism in International Law: Legal Rules and International Society' (2001) 89 Geo. L.J. 469 at 471 (reviewing A. Clark Arend, *Legal Rules and International Society*).

[86] M. Koskenniemi, 'What Is International Law For?' in M. Evans, ed., *International Law* (Oxford: Oxford University Press, 2003) 89 at 102.

justification enough for deviation. Such a state of affairs distinctly favours powerful states, which have more resources to calculate and pursue their interests. '[T]he instrumentalist mindset,' he argues, 'creates a consistent bias in favor of dominant actors with many policy alternatives from which to choose and sufficient revenues to carry out their objectives.' Looking at the academic calls for IL and IR collaboration—and the proportion of IR scholars who are at US universities and think tanks—Koskenniemi concludes: 'There is no doubt: this is an American crusade.'[87]

Wood has observed that a hazard of this, or of any other interdisciplinary project, is that it can 'reinforce rather than expose or question the blind spots, silences and normative projects of the participating disciplines.'[88] He has questioned whether IR theories, by focusing solely on explaining the status quo conditions of world politics, risk reinforcing the worst tendencies of IL to legitimize and dignify existing power structures. Accordingly, Wood asserts the inter-disciplinary project is worthwhile only if it is 'counter-disciplinary' by which he means that it should be 'concerned more with destabilizing disciplinary common sense than it is with identifying common ground on which different disciplines can collaborate comfortably or multiplying the analytical tools available to be brought to bear on existing research problems.'[89]

Whatever the hazards, this is an interdisciplinary dialogue that is now fully joined. Moreover, IEL scholars and practitioners are playing a significant role in its evolution. Given that the dialogue is underway, the cautionary advice of many commentators is well taken. IEL scholars and practitioners should approach IR theory not simply to find common ground but also with a critical mind and a spirit of inquiry and invention.

Recommended Reading

S. Barrett, *Environment and Statecraft: The Strategy of Environmental Treaty-Making* (Oxford: Oxford University Press, 2003).

J. Brunnée and S. Toope, 'International Law and Constructivism: Elements of an Interactional Theory of International Law' (2002) 39 Colum. J. Transnat'l L. 19.

A. Chayes and A. Handler Chayes, *The New Sovereignty: Compliance with International Regulatory Agreements* (Cambridge, MA: Harvard University Press, 1995).

---

[87] M. Koskenniemi, 'Carl Schmitt, Hans Morgenthau, and the Image of Law in International Relations,' in M. Byers, ed., *The Role of Law in International Politics: Essays in International Relations and International Law* (Oxford: Oxford University Press, 2000) 17 at 29.

[88] S. Wood, 'Commentary: Toward a Counterdisciplinary Agenda for Research in International Law and International Relations,' in *The Measure of International Law: Effectiveness, Fairness, and Validity: Proceedings of the Canadian Council on International Law, 31st Annual Conference, 2002* (The Hague: Kluwer Law International, 2004) 260 at 260–1 [citations omitted].   [89] *Ibid.* at 264–5.

G.W. Downs, K.W. Danish, and P.N. Barsoom, 'The Transformational Model of International Regime Design: Triumph of Hope or Experience?' (2000) 38 Colum. J. Transnat'l L. 466.

J.L. Goldsmith and E.A. Posner, *The Limits of International Law* (Oxford: Oxford University Press, 2005).

J. Goldstein et al., eds., 'Legalization and World Politics' (2000) 54 Int'l Org. (Special Issue).

M. Koskenniemi, 'Carl Schmitt, Hans Morgenthau, and the Image of Law in International Relations,' in Michael Byers, ed., *The Role of Law in International Politics: Essays in International Relations and International Law* (New York: Oxford University Press, 2000) 17.

R.B. Mitchell, 'International Environment,' in W. Carlsnaes et al., eds., *Handbook of International Relations* (London: Sage, 2002) 500.

K. Raustiala and A.-M. Slaughter, 'International Law, International Relations, and Compliance,' in W. Carlsnaes et al., eds., *Handbook of International Relations* (London: Sage, 2002) 538.

A.-M. Slaughter, A.S. Tulumello, and S. Wood, 'International Law and International Relations Theory: A New Generation of Interdisciplinary Scholarship' (1998) 92 A.J.I.L. 367.

CHAPTER 11

AN ECONOMIC THEORY OF INTERNATIONAL ENVIRONMENTAL LAW

SCOTT BARRETT

1 INTRODUCTION

INTERNATIONAL law, of which international environmental law is a part, shapes and constrains state behaviour. Essentially, it tells states what they are permitted to do, what they are prohibited from doing, and what they are required to do. In this respect, international law is indistinguishable from domestic law. In other respects, however, domestic and international law could not be more different. Domestic law develops and is applied within a vertical system of governance, with a legislature that creates law, a judiciary that interprets law, and an executive that enforces law. International law, by contrast, is rooted to a horizontal system—states at once make, interpret, and enforce international law.

In a vertical system, enforcement by the state can be taken as a given. Indeed, fulfilling the need for third party enforcement is a primary responsibility of the state—a reason that states exist in the first place. In a horizontal system, outcomes must be self-enforcing. There is no world executive that is capable of enforcing international law. Externalities are common to both domestic and transnational situations, but the means for correcting externalities differ in these situations. The important economic questions in the vertical system of domestic environmental law are about such things as optimal targets (cost-benefit analysis), instrument choice (market-based instruments versus command and control, taxes versus tradable emission permits, and so on), and cost-effectiveness. In the horizontal system of international environmental law, by contrast, the most important economic questions are about *enforcement*. Optimal targets are important at the international level insofar as they provide a goal, but enforcement difficulties may mean that this ideal is unattainable. Instrument choice (see Chapter 8 'Instrument Choice') is important not only because it affects efficiency in the face of uncertainty but also because in the international context it affects enforcement. Finally, though cost-effectiveness is a desirable feature of policy at either level, in the international arena cost-effectiveness may need to be sacrificed to secure more enforcement.

The difference is perhaps best understood by comparing what may be the two greatest policy triumphs of environmental economics: in a domestic setting, Title IV of the Clean Air Act amendments of 1990; and, in the international arena, the Kyoto Protocol to the UN Framework Convention on Climate Change.

Title IV, a US law for reducing acid rain depositions in the United States and, incidentally if not deliberately, in Canada, creates a market in emission permits—an approach long advocated by environmental economists. Firms regulated under Title IV have two options. They can reduce their emissions to stay within their emission limits or they can buy or sell permits for the same purpose. This market-based approach has the advantage of limiting the costs of achieving the environmental goal of the regulation, and it has been a great success.[1]

The Kyoto Protocol, which is aimed at limiting the greenhouse gas emissions of industrialized countries, was partly styled after Title IV. Like Title IV, Kyoto creates a 'cap and trade' system. It also includes an 'offset' system, called the clean development mechanism, to allow for further cost-effective reallocations between developed and developing countries. However, Kyoto is unlike Title IV in one vital respect—Kyoto must be self-enforcing.

Participation in Title IV is not voluntary but mandated by federal law. Compliance is also enforced. Excess emissions are subject to a fine, set by Congress, of over US $2,000 per ton of sulphur. Since permit prices have been substantially below this level, firms subject to Title IV have had very strong incentives to comply. Adding to this incentive, firms that exceed their allowances must make up for the shortfall in the next year. Violators may also be sent to prison for failing to comply. Reallocations of permits may be guided as if by an invisible hand to achieve a cost-effective final allocation, but underpinning this system of trading is enforcement by the very visible hand of the state. No wonder compliance has been nearly perfect. In 2000, excess allowances amounted to just 54 tons of a total of 10 million tons available—a compliance rate of 99.999 per cent. And, remember, this is all for a law in which participation is mandatory.

The Kyoto Protocol, being a treaty, is very different. First, participation by states is voluntary—sovereignty (and international law) says that it must be. Second, compliance with Kyoto must also be self-enforcing. The market mechanisms incorporated in this agreement have a chance of working only if enforcement succeeds. If enforcement fails, the 'shadow price' on emissions—the cost of abating the last ton of emissions, which is the ton that just meets the emission cap—will be near zero. The market mechanisms incorporated in the agreement will not be used or even needed, and the environmental goals of the agreement will not be met.

As it happens, participation has been a huge problem for Kyoto. Most famously, the United States declined to participate. Other countries are participating, but many of these are not required to reduce their emissions at all, and some are actually given surplus emissions ('hot air') under the agreement. Canada and Japan were obligated to reduce their emissions substantially under the original agreement, but their participation was secured only after their original emission limits were weakened in

---

[1] See R.N. Stavins, '"What Can We Learn from the Grand Policy Experiment?" Lessons from SO$_2$ Allowance Trading' (1998) 12 J. Econ. Persp. 69.

subsequent negotiations. Once the United States declined to participate, Russia's participation was essential to bringing the agreement into force, but Russia ratified Kyoto only after being given an enhanced surplus (also agreed in subsequent negotiations) and an assurance that the European Union would support Russia's membership in the World Trade Organization (WTO). In a sense, the stance taken by the United States, which appeared a singular event at the time, is really part of a larger pattern.

The prospects for enforcement of this agreement are also uncertain. A mechanism has been designed for this purpose, but Article 18 of the Kyoto Protocol says that compliance 'procedures and mechanisms . . . entailing binding consequences' must be approved by amendment. No such amendment now exists. Compliance could in theory be helped by the trading arrangements (anything that lowers costs will presumably aid compliance). However, it is not obvious that the opportunities for trading will be fully exploited. Will voters allow their country to avoid reducing its emissions by paying another country such as Russia *not* to reduce *its* emissions? If trading is avoided, however, and compliance costs prove substantial, a different complaint may be heard: Why should a country such as Canada incur substantial costs in reducing its greenhouse gas emissions when its neighbour and main trading partner is not required to do likewise—particularly if that is likely to mean that comparative advantage in the greenhouse gas-intensive industries will shift towards the United States, thereby diluting the environmental consequences of the abatement by Canada? These kinds of questions never arose in implementing Title IV of the US Clean Air Act.

To summarize, international legal institutions must be self-enforcing, and, thus, a theory of such institutions must make enforcement endogenous (that is, part of the design of the institutions themselves). My aim in this chapter is to develop a theory of international environmental law—a positive theory that uses economic reasoning to explain key institutions such as customary law and treaties and a normative theory that uses economic reasoning to identify not only the first best outcome (an outcome that may not be sustainable by the international system) but also the second best outcome that can be sustained by the anarchic international system. Put differently, the aim of this chapter is to show how international law can restructure incentives, making it in the interest of states to change their behaviour, and so protect the environment.

2 WHY AN 'ECONOMIC' THEORY OF INTERNATIONAL ENVIRONMENTAL LAW?

The economic approach, like any, has strengths and weaknesses. Its greatest strength is that it makes sharp predictions. Put differently, it yields testable hypotheses. To obtain sharp predictions, the theory must be constructed from simplifying assumptions. To be sure, the assumptions that are used are not chosen arbitrarily, but they are limiting, which means that the interpretation of the theory must be undertaken with care. Among the key assumptions are that states are the only actors; that states are rational and motivated by self-interest; that the identities, preferences, and beliefs of states are given; and that states have preferences over their absolute gains, not those relative to other states. These assumptions are used also by other disciplines. For example, they form the foundation of the institutionalist or neo-liberal theory of international relations (see Chapter 10 'International Relations Theory').

Other assumptions could be adopted. For example, constructivist theories of international relations argue that institutions 'may be created and supported for reasons of legitimacy and normative fit rather than efficient output; they may be created not for what they do but for what they are—for what they represent symbolically and the values they embody.'[2] Both perspectives enter into debates about international institutions and organizations. Thus, the Kyoto Protocol has been criticized for failing to make a material difference to the climate and praised for making a statement about concern, purpose, and obligation. The focus of this chapter is on the former interpretation, but that is not to deny the significance of the latter.

A final comment is that the theory presented here is a theory of outcomes, not of process. For example, the theory explains what a treaty might look like. It does not explain the process of treaty negotiation or even allow process to shape treaty outcomes. This explanation is typical of the economic approach. The theory of competitive markets, for example, is a reduced-form theory, in which the process by which goods and services are traded is not modeled. The fact that process is ignored by this approach should not be taken to mean that it is unimportant.

3 WHY NOT A GENERAL THEORY OF INTERNATIONAL LAW?

A theory of international environmental law must be consistent with a broader theory of international law, but there may also exist differences. A central theme of this chapter is that, even within the environmental arena, different problems have different legal remedies. Expanding the universe to include other topics only increases such differences. As an example, international health law as it pertains to the cross-border spread of infectious diseases has, with one exception (noted later in this chapter), eschewed the use of treaties.[3] In the environmental area, by contrast, treaties are

---

[2] M.N. Barnett and M. Finnemore, 'The Politics, Power, and Pathologies of International Organizations' (1999) 53 Int'l Org. 703.

[3] See D.P. Fidler, *International Law and Infectious Diseases* (Oxford: Oxford University Press, 1999). Historically, there were a number of treaties on surveillance, reporting, and control (quarantine).

a favourite and routine legal instrument. More than 300 multilateral treaties address transnational environmental issues today.[4]

Why the difference? The main reason, I suspect, is that the control of infectious diseases would benefit less from treaties. Think, for example, of the control of measles—a highly infectious disease but one that can easily be controlled by vaccination. No treaty requires that states control measles. Yet because states can protect their own populations from imported infections by vaccinating to a critical threshold, they need not care about the levels of control adopted by other states—except insofar as they care about the well-being of persons living in these states (development).

Vaccination is essentially a defensive policy. It is akin to adding lime to lakes so as to reduce the damages from acid rain or to adapting to climate change so as to reduce the damages associated with rising concentrations of greenhouse gases, and countries have incentives to undertake these measures unilaterally. To be sure, there is a connection between defence and offence. If international cooperation in reducing emissions succeeds (fails), the need for defensive measures is reduced (increased). As well, a treaty to assist countries in reducing damages may be needed for reasons of equity. For example, an adaptation treaty may be needed as part of a larger climate treaty system, in recognition of the role played by industrialized countries in contributing to the build up of greenhouse gases in the atmosphere.[5] However, the greatest need for international environmental cooperation is in the area of offensive policy—namely, in reducing emissions, in reducing harvest rates, in protecting more habitat, and so on. The main transnational public good in the area of infectious disease control (which is analogous to the abatement of acid rain emissions or climate change mitigation) is surveillance and response, and this is the subject of the only international regulation on infectious diseases—the International Health Regulations.

Of course, in the area of international trade, treaties are common. They include a multilateral framework—the WTO—and more than 200 regional trade agreements. Yet trade is very different from environmental protection. Trade is a bilateral activity—a primary reason why the WTO dispute resolution mechanism has been so successful. Global environmental protection requires global collective action. It is thus much harder to enforce.

4 Institutions and Organizations

'Institutions,' according to Douglass North, 'are the rules of the game in a society or, more formally, are the humanly devised constraints that shape human interaction.'[6]

Following the creation of the World Health Organization, however, these regional agreements were consolidated into a single, global agreement, the International Health Regulations.

[4] S. Barrett, *Environment and Statecraft* (Oxford: Oxford University Press, 2003).   [5] *Ibid.* at 397.
[6] D.C. North, *Institutions, Institutional Change and Economic Performance* (Cambridge: Cambridge University Press, 1990) at 3.

Organizations, by contrast, are the players, 'groups of individuals bound by some common purpose to achieve objectives.'[7] North's concern is with economic perform- ance and national institutions. However, his approach can be applied also to non- economic areas and the international realm. International law can thus be seen to comprise a set of institutions that provide a framework within which states interact. States create these institutions, even as they are constrained by them. States are the primary players in this game—organizations created in turn by their citizens.

Of course, states are not the only players. Non-governmental organizations (NGOs), including firms and not-for-profit organizations, also shape the creation and evolution of international institutions. And states create international organiza- tions that play a role as well. Examples include the United Nations and its component organizations, including the United Nations Environment Programme; regional organizations such the European Union; and, of course, treaty secretariats. In this chapter, however, I take states to be the only players. This is for two reasons. First, states are the main players. State behaviour shapes customary law, and states negoti- ate, implement, and enforce treaties. Second, economic analysis of transboundary environmental protection has focused almost exclusively on the role of the state. Very few papers have considered the role played by industry—and, even in these few cases, industry's role has been indirect (see Chapter 35 'Business'). (An example is industry determining pollution levels in an underlying model of international trade, and a treaty needing to eliminate the associated 'trade leakage' by changing the incentives for states to participate.[8]) A broader theory incorporating a fuller range of NGOs does not exist. One reason for this is that the literature has focused on international agreements as an international—meaning, inter-state—negotiating problem and not as an opportunity for lobbying. This situation, in turn, is partly because eco- nomic analysis has largely ignored the need for treaty ratification. It is really in this context that domestic and international politics meet.

5 TYPOLOGY OF INTERDEPENDENCE

Why do institutions exist? Put differently, why would states *want* their behaviour to be constrained? The reason that underpins the theory developed here is that, in some situations, states benefit from mutual restraint. The most famous of all such situ- ations is the prisoner's dilemma (PD), which is shown in Figure 1. Here, there are $N \geq 2$ states, all assumed to be symmetric. Each state has a binary choice: to play Abate or Pollute. Each country's payoff increases (linearly) as a function of the num- ber of other countries that play Abate. 'Payoffs' here represent the net benefits accru- ing to a country, which may seem an abstract concept, but which can be made

---

[7] *Ibid.* at 5.   [8] See Barrett, note 4 above at 307–29.

operational. To illustrate, I shall provide estimates for a real environmental problem in the next section.

In Figure 1, the payoff to playing Pollute exceeds the payoff to playing Abate for each country, irrespective of what all of the other countries are doing. In the jargon of game theory, playing Pollute is a *dominant strategy*. In geometric terms, the two payoff curves do not cross. Self-interest thus impels every state to play Pollute. Indeed, playing Pollute is the (unique) *Nash equilibrium* of this game—that is, given the choices made by every other state, each state has no incentive to alter its own choice. In Figure 1, this equilibrium is indicated by the solid dot. Of course, what is interesting about this game is that all states would be better off if every state played Abate. This 'full cooperative' outcome is indicated by the open dot in the figure. Mutual restraint is needed to support this more efficient outcome.

The PD illustrates important economic concepts. The choice by any country to play Pollute imposes an *externality* upon all others. In other words, the outcome that any state can realize depends adversely on the decisions by other states to play Pollute—where those decisions are not made with the intention of causing harm. In the PD, this externality is also a public bad. Put differently, playing Abate is a *public good*—all states benefit from the abatement by others, and consumption of this benefit by each state does not diminish the amount available to others. The provision of public goods is often undermined by *free riding* behaviour. States benefit from the abatement undertaken by others, even if they do not abate themselves or help pay for their abatement undertaken by others. Real world examples of global public goods include climate change mitigation, ozone layer protection, and the preservation of biodiversity.

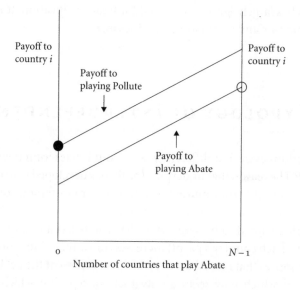

Figure 1 Prisoner's Dilemma

In domestic settings, externalities and the under-provision of public goods are referred to as market failures. In international settings, they are best called inter-state failures. Correcting market failures normally requires intervention by the state. Correcting interstate failures cannot rely upon the intervention of a world government. It must instead rely upon other approaches, including normative guidelines for behaviour or, as emphasized in this chapter, a strategic manipulation of incentives.

The PD is perhaps the most famous example of interdependence but there are many others. Figure 2 portrays a chicken game. In this case, it is in each state's inter-est to play Abate, provided the number of other states playing Abate is small. If this number is large, it is better for each state to play Pollute. In this game, there is a unique equilibrium in which some states play Abate and some play Pollute. To be precise, the equilibrium is unique with respect to the number of states that play Abate and Pollute, and is not dependant on their identities. Notice that in the game of chicken shown in Figure 2 full cooperation requires that every state play Abate. The equilib-rium is thus inefficient.

Chicken games are primarily important, as I show later in this chapter, because a treaty can *transform* an underlying PD into a chicken game. In the underlying game, states can play Abate or Pollute. In the treaty participation game, states can play Participation or Non-Participation—where it is understood that participants must play Abate (provided the treaty enters into force) whereas non-participants are free to play Pollute. In this case, the decisions by some countries to participate depend on how many other countries participate. In equilibrium, some countries participate (and therefore play Abate) and some do not (they play Pollute). The treaty improves

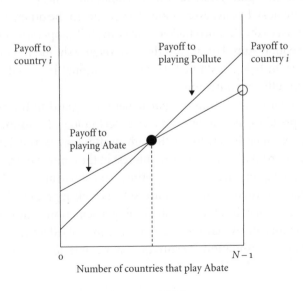

Figure 2 Chicken

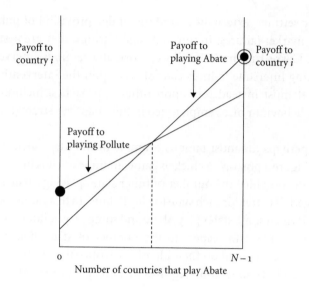

Figure 3 Coordination

welfare compared to the underlying PD (in which *all* countries play Pollute), but it is still likely to fall short of sustaining full cooperation (participation is likely to be less than full)—that is, the treaty supports a second best outcome.

Figure 3 represents a game of *coordination*. Here, each state wants to do what most of the others are doing. If most other states are playing Abate, it is better for each state to play Abate; if most others are playing Pollute, it is better for each state to play Pollute. Notice from Figure 3 that, for the coordination game, there are two equilibria (in pure strategies). In one, every state plays Abate. In the other, every state plays Pollute. In contrast to the PD and chicken games, the full cooperative outcome can be sustained as an equlibrium. This means that sovereignty should not prevent the efficient outcome from being sustained. Here, international law needs only to guide states towards the efficient outcome.

Coordination games are common, particularly in regard to the choice of technologies. The spread of the catalytic converter technology, for example, reflects in part the incentives for each state to use the same technology as its neighbours.[9] Once again, however, coordination is mainly of interest in the context of treaty design. As I show later in this chapter, a treaty can sometimes transform an underlying PD into a coordination game. Moreover, and in contrast to a chicken participation game, such a transformed game may be able to sustain full participation. Unfortunately, creating coordination incentives may require a sacrifice in cost-effectiveness—that is, the treaty that creates coordination incentives may be able to sustain only a second best outcome.

---

[9] *Ibid.* at 96–100.

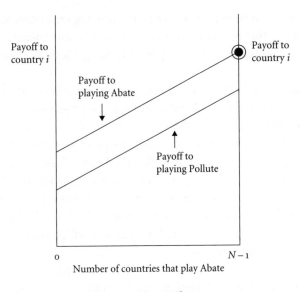

Figure 4 Non Dilemma

For completeness, there is one last situation that can be depicted using linear pay-offs. This is the non-dilemma game shown in Figure 4. In this game, states are also interdependent: each country's payoff increases in the number of others that play Abate. However, in this game every state is better off playing Abate, irrespective of what the other states do. Moreover, this equilibrium is efficient. For the non-dilemma game, there is no need for international law. Obviously, this situation is not of interest to this chapter.

6 CALCULATING PAYOFFS

How might the payoffs be calculated for a real problem? Payoffs can be taken to reflect the net benefits to a state. Just as cost-benefit analysis may underpin a domestic decision—such as whether and by how much to abate a pollutant—so may it underpin a state's decision to participate in an international agreement. The value of the theory does not depend on states developing quantitative estimates. Payoffs reflect a player's perception of its interests, and if it is true that interests determine choices then it is also true that choices reflect interests. A country may not act specifically on the basis of a cost-benefit calculation, but when a government says that climate change is a serious problem and that emissions must be reduced, and when this same government then announces a target of reducing emissions by, say, 5 per cent, then this government is essentially saying that a 5 per cent cut is better than 4 and that 6 per cent is too much. When a government sets a target of reducing emissions by 5 per cent but implements policies that reduce emissions by only 3 per cent, then its choice suggests that reducing emissions by more than 3 per cent, though desirable, was revealed to be too costly.

It happens, however, that costs and benefits are sometimes calculated quantitatively. Estimates of the costs and benefits of protecting the ozone layer, prepared by the US Environmental Protection Agency (EPA), are shown in Table 1. Three scenarios are evaluated: a situation in which nothing is done to control emissions (a 'business as usual' scenario); a situation in which the United States and other countries comply with the restrictions incorporated in the original Montreal Protocol; and a situation in which only the United States complies with these restrictions. The study first predicts ozone depletion for all three scenarios. It then calculates the costs and benefits of reducing depletion from the 'business as usual' scenario to the levels associated with the latter two scenarios.

The top rows in Table 1 show that the Montreal Protocol was predicted to have a substantial effect in reducing depletion relative to the 'no controls' scenario, especially in the long run. They also indicate that the United States on its own can reduce depletion significantly in the medium term but not in the long run. The bottom set of rows in Table 1 show the costs and benefits to the United States of undertaking the emission cuts required by the Montreal Protocol assuming either that other countries also comply with Montreal or that they do not. These estimates are for the

Table 1 Net Benefits of Ozone Protection to the United States

	Number of controls	Montreal Protocol	Unilateral implementation of Montreal Protocol by the United States
Ozone depletion (per cent)			
By 2000	1.0	0.8	0.9
By 2050	15.7	1.9	10.3
By 2100	50.0	1.2	49.0
Payoffs to the United States (billions of 1985 $US)			
Benefits	—	3,575	1,373
Costs	—	21	21
Net benefits	—	3,554	1,352
Benefit-cost ratio		170:1	65:1

Source: United States Environmental Protection Agency, Regulatory Impact Analysis: Protection of Statospheric Ozone, 1988.

United States only. Since the United States undertakes the same actions under either of the last two scenarios, the costs of taking the action are assumed to be the same. These costs are relatively low, indicating that substantial substitution possibilities exist or could be expected to exist. The benefit estimates are larger, especially for the scenario in which other countries join the United States in meeting the Montreal Protocol targets. The United States would certainly prefer that other countries join it. However, the numbers shown in the bottom right of Table 1 indicate that the United States would gain by undertaking the Montreal Protocol cuts even if other countries do not participate in the agreement.

The main benefit of reduced ozone layer depletion is avoided cancer deaths. According to an EPA study, adhering to the Montreal Protocol would avoid more than five million cancer deaths in the United States by 2165. People are willing to pay a lot to avoid the risk of premature death. Multiplying a large number of avoided deaths by a high value per death avoided results in a large benefit to protecting the ozone layer, which mainly accounts for the high benefit figures shown in Table 1.

If states really were symmetric with respect to the ozone issue—if they had the same payoff functions as those in Table 1—then ozone protection would be much like the non-dilemma game shown in Figure 4. Cooperation would not be needed. However, states are plainly asymmetric. Developing countries benefit less from ozone layer protection than industrialized countries—partly because depletion is less the nearer to the equator you are and partly because people with dark skin would be less vulnerable. The underlying game of ozone layer protection is essentially an asymmetric PD. The essential challenge for international cooperation is not to get the industrialized countries to reduce their emissions but to get these countries to compensate poor countries for reducing *their* emissions.

7 AN EXPERIMENTAL PERSPECTIVE

As already mentioned, the *Nash equilibrium* describes a situation in which no player wants to change his or her own choice, regardless of the choices made by others. The concept draws our attention to a fundamental incentive that affects behaviour in situations of interdependence. The theory presented thus far, however, is purely analytical. Its predictions spring entirely from its assumptions, and these need not reflect how real people—or states—can be expected to behave. When I develop the theory in the classroom, I always begin by playing a game and not by presenting the analytical model. I begin by distributing two cards to each student, one red and one black. I then ask the students to return one card to me, without anyone seeing which card was returned. Students are told that they will get $10 if they keep their red card and $1 for every red card handed in by any student. In a class of 25 students, if 15 hand in their red cards, these students each receive $15. The other students—those that kept their red cards—each get \$25. Plainly, handing in your red card is a prisoner's dilemma, but I do not say this until after the game is played.

I have played this game well over a hundred times, and the result qualitatively has always been the same: some students always hand in their red cards and some always keep them. The analytical model predicts that *all* students will keep their red cards. So this experiment illustrates that the theory does not predict well how real people will behave. I do not find this surprising. After all, the PD consists of *two* strong attractors. One is the outcome in which everyone keeps his or her red card. The other is the outcome in which every player hands in his or her red card. Most people feel torn when playing this game. On the one hand, participants understand that they can always do better by keeping their red cards no matter what others do. On the other hand, they also understand that if everyone behaved like this the result would be bad all around. Whenever I have played the PD in the classroom, students have been dissatisfied with the result. They have always wanted to try again—hoping they might find a way to sustain the mutually preferred outcome.

Why is the mutually preferred attractor so difficult to sustain? The reason is that the incentives favouring the inefficient outcome are strong. One powerful incentive, of course, is greed. Another, however, is fear—the fear that, should others not hand in their red cards, you could be made worse off compared with the situation in which neither you nor any other student handed in a red card. Put more colourfully, when you hand in your red card, you are vulnerable to being made a sucker. I once played a variant of this game, dividing a large class of about 50 students in half and providing additional information on a written sheet of paper distributed to the students. This sheet told the students in one group that they had a history of cooperating. The other group was told that they had a history of not cooperating. The effect was striking. Nearly all students in the former group handed in their red cards and nearly all students in the latter group did not. The greed factor was the same in both situations, but the fear factor was very different.

Before concluding the experiment, I allow the students to discuss their situation—to negotiate. Always, a number of suggestions are offered. Some students will suggest that all players show the card they are handing in—a prerequisite for 'naming and shaming'. Some students will suggest that retaliatory measures be taken against players who fail to hand in their red cards. These are sensible suggestions. However, neither can be a solution to the PD that the students were asked to play because this was a one shot game in which choices had to be made simultaneously. Still, the logic behind these reactions is instructive. As I shall explain, all good treaties do precisely what my students think is needed: they change the rules of the game. By the way, after this open discussion, I let the students choose again. The discussion usually makes little difference.[10] It seems that the students do not believe that others really will hand in their red cards, even if they pledge to do so.

---

[10] Usually the level of cooperation rises a little. However, if I then let the students choose yet again, the level of cooperation falls, mainly it seems because the students who handed in their red cards the previous time felt betrayed by those who said they would but did not.

Let me conclude by stating the obvious: these classroom experiments are unscientific. The now substantial literature on experimental game theory relies on more rigorous tests of the analytical theory, using proper controls, real money to motivate participants, and statistical analysis of the results.[11] I hope, however, that the stories I have told of my classroom games are instructive. First, even the telling of these stories helps give a 'feel' for the incentive problem. Second, the experiments reveal both the strengths and weaknesses of the analytical theory.

8 CUSTOMARY LAW

In the international setting, the law takes two main forms, treaties and custom (see Chapter 19 'Formation of Customary International Law and General Principles' and Chapter 20 'Treaty Making and Treaty Evolution'). Treaties are formal institutions, whereas customary law is an informal institution. Treaties are constructed from deliberate processes—they are negotiated and written down, plain for everyone to see. Custom, by contrast, arises spontaneously—customary law reflects how states behave, provided that they understand also that this behaviour is required of them by law. Another difference is the fact that a treaty applies only to the states that become a party to it, provided that the treaty enters into force. Customary law, by contrast, applies universally.

Most of this chapter is concerned with the treaty instrument. However, the need for treaties, and the efficacy of treaties, is shaped by custom. As well, custom changes in reaction to the treaty system. So in order to understand one instrument of the law requires understanding the other, particularly as it is the combination of the two instruments that shapes state behaviour. Finally, while the main approach used to address environmental problems is the treaty, some environmental problems can only be addressed by a change in custom.

The most dramatic development in customary law in modern times is the extension of the territorial seas and the creation of the exclusive economic zones. These developments amounted to an astonishing redrawing of international property rights arrangements over marine resources. They were a reaction to the scarcity of the ocean's resources, and they helped correct collective action problems of the kind reflected in the PD. Essentially, they nationalized a large fraction of the world's commercial fisheries, allowing unified management in many cases (of course, problems remain with fisheries that overlap different jurisdictions, with migratory species, and with the remaining high seas fisheries).

---

[11] I summarize this literature in Barrett, see note 4 above. See especially E. Ostrom, 'A Behavioural Approach to the Rational Choice Theory of Collective Action' (1998) 92 Am. Pol. Sci. Rev. 1; and E. Fehr and S. Gächter, 'Cooperation and Punishment in Public Goods Experiments' (2000) 90 Am. Econ. Rev. 980.

In other settings, custom has had less influence. For example, while custom recognizes the so-called 'no harm' principle—the principle that holds that states have a right not to be harmed by other states, including by means of pollution—custom also recognizes the rights of states 'to exploit their own resources pursuant to their own environmental policies' (as noted by Principle 21 of the Stockholm Declaration on the Human Environment) (see Chapter 22 'Transboundary Impacts'). As matters stand, neither of these conflicting rights commands supremacy. In any particular conflict, the competing claims inherent in these rights must instead be balanced, with the compromise being negotiated. Treaties ultimately resolve this kind of conflict, and they do so on a case-by-case basis. It is to this issue that I now turn.

9 THEORY OF TREATY DESIGN

As previously mentioned, there exist a huge number of treaties addressing transnational environmental problems.[12] My concern in this chapter is not so much with an evaluation of these treaties as with developing a theory that can explain the key

Table 2 Selected Post-2000 Agreements

Year adopted	Treaty
2003	Protocol on Strategic Environmental Assessment
2003	European Convention for the Protection of Animals During International Transport
2002	Convention for Cooperation in the Protection and Sustainable Development of the Marine and Coastal Environment of the Northeast Pacific
2002	ASEAN Agreement on Transboundary Haze Pollution
2001	Convention on the Conservation and Management of Fishery Resources in the South-East Atlantic Ocean
2001	Stockholm Convention on Persistent Organic Pollutants
2001	International Treaty on Plant Genetic Resources for Food and Agriculture
2001	Convention on the Protection of the Underwater Cultural Heritage

[12] For a comprehensive listing of multilateral treaties (including about 300 agreements), see Barrett, note 4 above at 165–94. Table 2 contains a partial update—a listing of selected multilateral treaties negotiated since 2000. See also R.B. Mitchell, 'International Environmental Agreements: A Survey of their Features, Formation, and Effects' (2003) 28 Ann. Rev. Env't & Resources 432.

features of environmental treaties. These key features include the minimum participation level, non-compliance penalties, trade restrictions, financial transfers, and
basic treaty obligations. I turn to these below.

9.1 Treaty Participation

Here is another game I have played with my students. As in the earlier game, every
student gets $1 for every red card handed in by anyone and $10 for keeping his or her
own red card. Unlike the earlier game, however, students this time must choose
whether or not to become a signatory to a treaty. The students are told that the treaty
has already been negotiated. The treaty says that all signatories must hand in their red
cards, *provided that the agreement enters into force* (essentially, compliance is assumed
to be enforced externally, though I relax this assumption in section 9.3 later in this
chapter). The treaty is explicit in stating that it enters into force if signed by at least
11 states. If the treaty does not enter into force, signatories can hand in their red card or
not as they please. Non-signatories may always behave as they like, whether or not the
treaty enters into force. As before, students make these choices independently, without knowing what others have decided to do.

I have played this game about ten times, and each time the number of students who
choose to ratify the agreement tends to be very close to the number of players that just
brings the treaty into force (in this game, 11). Non-signatories have always chosen to
keep their red cards, and signatories almost always choose to keep their red cards if
the agreement fails to enter into force (rarely, a signatory will choose to hand in his or
her red card even if the agreement fails to enter into force).

After playing the game once, I ask the students if they would like to revise their
choices. If the number of signatories was originally 11, students tend not to revise
their choices. If the number was initially ten or less, more students tend to ratify when
given a second chance. If the number of students ratifying the agreement was initially
greater than 11, some students may choose to play non-signatory when given a chance
to decide again. Discussion about this game reveals that the students understand that
there is a mild incentive for precisely 11 students to play signatory and for the remaining students to play non-signatory. In contrast to the PD, where students never settle
on the equilibrium, in this game students tend to converge towards the equilibrium
fairly quickly. Of course, one difference between this game and the PD is that students
cannot possibly be worse off for signing the agreement than they would be if the
agreement fails to enter into force—that is, the treaty removes the fear factor.

What kind of game is this? It is not a PD. The astute reader may recognize that it is
like a chicken game. The treaty participation game is shown in Figure 5. In this game,
you are under no obligation to hand in your red card unless you play signatory *and*
at least ten others play signatory. The treaty essentially makes the final choices of
each signatory contingent on how the other players behave. This, of course, is what

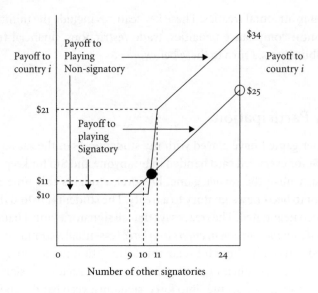

Figure 5 Treaty participation

Note: Figure not drawn to scale

the students wanted to do when they were allowed to negotiate. The difference is that the treaty allows behaviour to be contingent even when the game remains a one-shot deal.

To sum up, I have outlined how a treaty can change behaviour (assuming compliance is assured). Moreover, I have done so in a manner that is entirely consistent with international law. Under international law, countries are free to participate in treaties as they please; treaties are not binding upon non-signatories (non-parties); and signatories (parties) are expected to comply with their obligations provided the treaty enters into force. This game thus illustrates how a treaty can change behaviour by restructuring the incentives—that is, it explains why countries might negotiate treaties in the first place. There are, to be sure, weaknesses in this simple sketch. I have said nothing so far about how the entry into force number is chosen. I have also assumed (rather than shown) that signatories will comply with the treaty, provided it enters into force. These matters are taken up in the next two sections.

9.2 Minimum Participation

Where did the minimum participation level of 11 come from? It turns out not to have been chosen arbitrarily. Of course, a minimum participation of 11 is the smallest participation level capable of delivering a positive net benefit to its signatories (parties). So it is pretty obvious why the minimum participation level is not less than 11. Yet why should it not be higher? With 25 students in the classroom, it would be best if the minimum participation level were set equal to 25. This minimum participation level would maximize the aggregate payoff. So, why not set the minimum participation level equal to 25?

Suppose the minimum participation level were set equal to 25. The threat implicit in such a treaty is that, should any student fail to play signatory, the others will all choose not to hand in their red cards. If this threat were credible, of course, every student would want to participate. Yet, is this threat credible? If just one student chose to play non-signatory, would all the others allow the agreement not to enter into force? Would they all choose not to hand in their red cards? Given that one student is not participating, all the others get a payoff of $24 by handing in their red cards. They can expect to get only $10 by allowing the treaty not to enter into force. Plainly, there is a strong incentive for the remaining 24 students to rewrite their treaty and to set the minimum participation level equal to 24.

However, if a second student then refused to sign the treaty, the 23 others would also have an incentive to rewrite the treaty, this time setting the minimum participation level equal to 23. Continuing with this logic, it is easy to see that the only credible minimum participation level for this game is 11. Suppose there are ten signatories and 14 non-signatories, and the twenty-fifth state must decide whether to be a signatory or a non-signatory. If this country becomes a signatory, it gets a payoff of $11. If it becomes a non-signatory, the treaty fails to enter into force and the twenty-fifth country can expect to get a payoff of just $10. The sum of $11 is bigger and, thus, given the choices made by the other countries and given the design of this particular treaty, the twenty-fifth country will want to become a signatory. It will also want to remain a signatory. For, if this state were to withdraw, the remaining ten signatories would be no worse off for punishing this country. Their threat not to renegotiate the treaty, by changing the minimum participation level, is credible.

To sum up, the minimum participation level in a treaty cannot be chosen arbitrarily. It must take account of the incentives facing different countries. It must, in particular, be invulnerable to renegotiation. Put differently, it must be collectively rational from the perspective of the signatories to the agreement. However, this particular concept of collective rationality may be overly strong. I shall return to this concept in section 9.4 of this chapter. First, I want to return to the question of compliance.

9.3 Compliance

The treaty discussed in section 9.1 assumed that parties to a treaty had no choice but to comply. However, states *can* choose not to comply. Of course, parties are obligated to comply according to the fundamental principle of treaty law, *pacta sunt servanda*. And there is good reason for this rule—what would be the point of negotiating a treaty that parties could easily choose to violate? Why should any country comply unless it can count on the other parties to comply? (see Chapter 39 'Compliance Theory'). Abram and Antonia Handler Chayes, paraphrasing Louis Henkin, claim that 'international lawyers and others familiar with the operations of international treaties take for granted that most states comply with most of their treaty obligations most of the time.'[13] This statement may be true, though there are many instances of non-compliance.[14] However, even if all countries always complied with their treaty obligations, it may have little to do with the international norm of *pacta sunt servanda*. Instead, it may simply reflect a self-selection process. The reason is that the compliance norm applies only to countries that have ratified an agreement (provided also that the agreement has entered into force), and international law recognizes the right of any state to choose not to be a party. A country that does not want to comply could simply choose not to participate in the agreement in the first place. Put differently, the countries that choose to participate may be self-selected— they may simply be the countries with a demonstrated willingness to accept the obligation to comply.

In at least some cases, the empirical evidence seems to support this explanation of compliance. For example, upon analysing a 1985 treaty on sulphur emission cuts— the Protocol to the 1979 Convention on Long-Range Transboundary Air Pollution on the Reduction of Sulphur Emissions or Their Transboundary Fluxes (Helsinki Protocol)—E.J. Ringquist and T. Kostadinova conclude that, 'while nations ratifying the Helsinki Protocol have experienced significant emission reductions, the protocol itself has had no discernible effect on emissions.'[15] Essentially, other characteristics of these countries explain their emission reduction decisions. Empirical research by other scholars points to a similar conclusion in regard to this agreement and others like it.[16] If compliance is high with international environmental agreements, the

---

[13] A. Chayes and A. Handler Chayes, *The New Sovereignty* (Cambridge, MA: Harvard University Press, 1995) at 311.

[14] Non-compliance with fisheries agreements such as the International Commission for the Conservation of Atlantic Tunas is routine. D.P. Fidler, *International Law and Infectious Diseases* (Oxford: Oxford University Press, 1999) at 68, writes of 'the almost wholesale lack of compliance with the [International Health Regulations].' Other examples include non-compliance by North Korea with the Treaty on the Non-Proliferation of Nuclear Weapons and the recent collapse of the Growth and Stability Pact. Indeed, frequent use of the dispute settlement procedure of the World Trade Organization can also be interpreted as reflecting non-compliance.

[15] E.J. Ringquist and T. Kostadinova, 'Assessing the Effectiveness of International Environmental Agreements: The Case of the 1985 Helsinki Protocol' (2005) 49 Am. J. Pol. Sci. 86.

[16] Examples include J.C. Murdoch and T. Sandler, 'The Voluntary Provision of a Pure Public Good: The Case of Reduced CFC Emissions and the Montreal Protocol' (1996) 63 J. Pub. Econ. 33; J.C. Murdoch and T. Sandler, 'Voluntary Cutbacks and Pretreaty Behavior: The Helsinki Protocol and Sulfur Emissions' (1997) 25 Pub. Fin. Rev. 139; J.C. Murdoch, T. Sandler, and K. Sargent, 'A Tale of Two Collectives: Sulphur versus Nitrogen Emission Reduction in Europe' (1997) 64 Economica 281; and J.C. Murdoch, T. Sandler, and W.P.M. Vijverberg, 'The Participation Decision versus the Level of Participation in an Environmental Treaty: A Spatial Probit Analysis' (2003) 87 J. Pub. Econ. 337. However, see also U.J. Wagner, *The Voluntary Provision of a Pure Public Good? Another Look at CFC Emissions and the Montreal Protocol*, Department of Economics, Yale University, 2004.

reason may be that most such agreements do little more than codify how states would have behaved even in the absence of a treaty.

What about treaties that do not simply codify how states would have behaved anyway? Are treaty-specific compliance sanctions needed in these cases? Chayes and Handler Chayes argue 'no'. States, they assert, are inclined to comply and only fail to comply when they are unable, rather than unwilling, to do so. To Chayes and Handler Chayes, non-compliance is a problem to be managed—a situation more likely to be improved by the offer of assistance than by the threat of punishment. Indeed, they argue that punishment mechanisms are not only rarely incorporated in treaties and rarely used even when incorporated but also that such mechanisms are ultimately harmful to cooperation.

Political scientists George Downs, David Rocke, and Peter Barsoom offer a different view.[17] They argue that when a treaty calls for a significant change in behaviour, it requires the credible threat of punishment for non-compliance—a treaty-based compliance mechanism. Put a little crudely, Chayes and Handler Chayes commend a 'speak softly' approach to compliance. Downs and his colleagues counsel the need to 'carry a big stick'. Conceptually, however, there is an essential element missing in the approaches taken by both Chayes and Handler Chayes and Downs, Rocke, and Barsoom. Chayes and Handler Chayes consider compliance and participation as separate problems. Downs, Rocke, and Barsoom essentially conflate the two problems by failing to distinguish the punishments needed to enforce participation from the punishments needed to enforce compliance. Participation and compliance are different phenomena, but, as the problem of self-selection demonstrates, both need to be enforced if a treaty is to change behaviour.

Analysis of the joint enforcement problem reveals that deterring non-participation is the binding constraint on cooperation.[18] In other words, while a treaty must be capable of deterring both non-compliance and non-participation, the latter task is more important—if non-participation can be deterred, then non-compliance can easily be deterred. Why? The intuition is that, in order to change behaviour, a punishment must be both severe and credible. A punishment is severe if the target country is better off complying than not complying, given that the threatened punishment is carried out in the event of non-compliance. A punishment is credible if the countries called upon to impose the punishment are better off doing so than not, given that the non-compliance has occurred. Larger deviations offer greater rewards to the non-complying country and so can only be deterred by larger punishments. However, larger punishments tend also to be less credible. The largest credible deviation is for a non-complying party to behave as if it were a non-party. So if this level of non-compliance can be deterred, then all levels of non-compliance can be deterred. Deterrence of this level of non-compliance, however, is precisely the same

[17] G.W. Downs, D.M. Rocke, and P.N. Barsoom, 'Is the Good News about Compliance Good News about Cooperation?' (1996) 50 Int'l Org. 379.   [18] Barrett, see note 4 above at 269–91.

as deterrence of non-participation. Hence, if a treaty can deter non-participation, then it can easily deter non-compliance.

What this means is that the analytical theory outlined in the previous sections remains valid even when compliance is made endogenous and is not assumed. Though the theory summarized previously assumed that participating countries would comply, we now know, for the equilibrium participation level derived from this theory, that non-compliance can in fact be deterred by the threat of credible punishments. We know this because, as already demonstrated, non-participation (from the equilibrium participation level, which is 11 in the earlier example) can be deterred.

Note that mechanisms for enforcing both participation and compliance are needed. In the treaty studied previously, participation was enforced by the minimum participation clause. How would compliance be enforced? Unilateral non-compliance, short of non-participation, would typically need to be punished by reductions in the abatement by other parties—that is, by a strategy of reciprocity (as discussed in section 9.6, trade restrictions may sometimes be used to enforce both compliance and participation). Devising such a punishment can be difficult for a variety of reasons, but compliance enforcement has an additional challenge. Countries become parties to a treaty when they declare their participation. Self-reporting of compliance, however, cannot always be relied upon to be truthful. A finding of non-compliance will usually require that other countries demonstrate that a material breach has occurred.

Let me conclude this discussion with a few more observations. First, if a credible compliance mechanism is incorporated within a treaty, it would not be used in equilibrium and may not need to be used in practice. The primary role of such a mechanism is not actually to punish but to *deter* non-compliance. Put differently, the presence of the threat to punish provides an assurance to every cooperating country that the others really will comply. The credible threat to punish thus removes the fear factor noted previously. Second, such a mechanism presumes perfect verification. Self-reporting is the norm in international treaties, but independent verification is essential to any compliance enforcement. Ronald Reagan's motto for arms control treaties is appropriate here: trust but verify. Trust in these matters is not and cannot be blind. Yet trust of a different kind can be established if behaviour can be verified *and* if deviations from compliance can be punished.

9.4 Narrow and Deep versus Broad and Shallow Treaties

While credibility is important, it is not obvious that it should trump all other considerations. Suppose, for example, that participation by a certain set of countries seemed 'fair'. Could not such a participation level be accommodated by the theory? In particular, if all countries were symmetric, would fairness not require that *all* countries contribute to addressing the environmental problem? Might it not be possible to enforce such an agreement? The notion of collective rationality developed so far is too rigid to embrace such considerations. However, a weaker concept can. This weaker concept allows a trade-off between the depth and breadth of cooperation. Essentially, it can sustain an agreement comprising all countries, provided that the level of abatement undertaken by each country is lowered in comparison with the agreement studied in section 9.2.

The weaker concept of collective rationality presents countries with a simpler choice. Should any country choose not to participate in a treaty that it is generally felt it should belong to, the other countries can either ignore this country's deviation or they can allow the treaty to collapse (with the strong notion of collective rationality, these same countries would be allowed to renegotiate the treaty). Allowing a tradeoff between the depth and breadth of cooperation raises the broader question of whether countries, if given the choice, would *prefer* to negotiate a 'broad but shallow' treaty or a 'narrow but deep' one. Intuitively, if a 'narrow but deep' treaty can support participation by only a small fraction of countries, then a consensus agreement will be preferred. If, on the other hand, a 'narrow but deep' treaty supports participation by a large fraction of countries, then negotiation may favour such a treaty over the alternative of a 'broad but shallow' agreement. This theory thus helps to explain why agreements rarely include a small fraction of the countries affected by the treaty outcome. It also helps explain why treaties consisting of a large number of countries are often very weak.

This analysis assumes that the marginal costs of abatement are constant. Usually, marginal abatement costs increase in the level of abatement. It can be shown that, under such circumstances, countries will *always* prefer to negotiate a consensus agreement—that is, an agreement in which every state participates. The reason is that the total costs of sustaining a given abatement level can always be lowered by broadening participation. The Kyoto Protocol imposes emission obligations upon only a small number of countries and would thus seem to challenge this conclusion. However, having agreed to such obligations, the agreement also sought to lower the costs of realizing this overall level of abatement by a number of means, including trading in emission entitlements and the use of the 'clean development mechanism'. Both of these 'flexible' mechanisms have the effect of spreading abatement around (with increasing marginal costs, which is an essential requirement for achieving cost-effectiveness), just as in the theory demonstrated earlier. The difference really lies in the nature of the players. The theory assumed symmetric countries. Kyoto was negotiated and will be implemented by asymmetric countries. I extend the theory to consider asymmetric countries in section 9.7.

9.5 Tipping Treaties

The framework developed thus far considers interdependence only on the benefits side. Costs (technologies), however, can also be interdependent. To illustrate, imagine a situation in which countries form a network with the technology adopted by each country depending on the technology adopted by its neighbours—perhaps because costs are lower when the neighbours adopt the same technology. In this situation, the choice of a technology creates a *network externality* and there may exist multiple equilibria. For example, if there are two technologies, one 'dirty' and one 'clean', one equlibrium may involve every country using the dirty technology and another equilibrium may involve every country using the clean technology.[19] Choice of technology would then be a coordination game, resembling the game shown in Figure 3.

Although technology standards are usually disfavoured by economists because they are cost-ineffective compared with market-based regulatory instruments (see Chapter 8 'Instrument Choice'), technology standards may have a *strategic* advantage in the context of transboundary environmental protection. If network externalities are strong, the use of a technology by 'enough' countries may create incentives for the remaining countries to switch to the same technology. This situation is illustrated in Figure 6. The game on the left is the usual PD, where the payoff

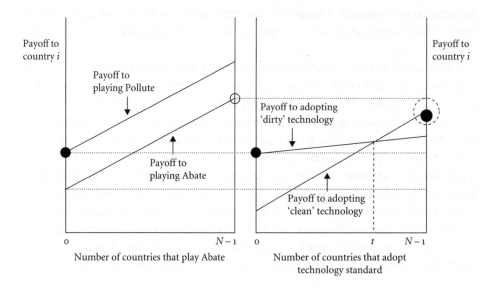

Figure 6 Tipping treaty

[19] In a spatial setting, there may also exist equilibria in which some countries use one technology and some use the other. See *ibid.* at 96–7. The equilibria realized will then depend on the extent of the network

to playing Abate assumes that abatement is achieved at minimum cost. The game on the right reflects a technology choice. Adoption of the dirty technology can be interpreted as reflecting the status quo. Adoption of the clean technology increases payoffs by supplying the public good of an improved shared environment. As a result of the network externality, as more countries adopt the technology, the incentive for others to adopt it increases. The 'tipping point' is at t. Once t other countries have adopted the clean technology, all other countries have a strong incentive to adopt it. There are thus two equilibria in this technology game. One is the equilibrium in which every country adopts the dirty technology. The other is the equilibrium in which every country adopts the clean technology.

Notice that a treaty incorporating a technology standard will typically be second best. Payoffs would be maximized if all countries played Abate, choosing the least cost means of abatement. However, as the graph on the left of Figure 6 shows, this outcome is not self-enforcing. A treaty prescribing that all parties play Abate, but without imposing a technology standard, would resemble the agreement shown in Figure 5. In some situations, the technology standard agreement shown on the right of Figure 6 will sustain a higher payoff—and so should be adopted. Choice of the technology standard carries a cost penalty but has an enforcement advantage.

Notice, finally, that the minimum participation clause in this case identifies the 'tipping point' and not the equilibrium participation level. The agreement shown on the right of Figure 6 would require parties to adopt the clean technology only when it had been ratified by at least t countries. Plainly, no country can lose by ratifying such an agreement. If the agreement fails to enter into force, the countries that ratified it would not have to change their behaviour—and so would be no worse off for having ratified it. If, however, the agreement does enter into force, then all countries will choose to ratify it, and every country will be strictly better off.

An example of such a treaty is the International Convention for the Prevention of Pollution from Ships (MARPOL Convention). This agreement requires that oil tankers incorporate segregated ballast tanks so that ballast water never mixes with the oil cargo. This treaty was not the least cost means of limiting the discharge of oil at sea, but compliance with the alternative of prescribing limits could not be enforced.[20] Compliance with the technology standard, by contrast, was easy to enforce, and, because of the network externality, choice of the technology standard also promoted participation. The value of a particular tanker increases with the number of ports to which it has access. So, as more coastal states participated in the agreement, barring other kinds of oil tankers from entering their ports, the greater became the incentive for yet other states to participate. This agreement set a minimum participation level

externality. It will also depend on history. If countries are symmetric, there can be no geography as such, and so there can exist at most two equilibria.

[20] See R.B. Mitchell, *International Oil Pollution at Sea: Environmental Policy and Treaty Compliance* (Cambridge, MA: MIT Press, 1994).

equal to 15 countries making up at least half of the world's gross tonnage. As of September 2006, however, the MARPOL Convention had been ratified by 133 states making up over 97 per cent of global tonnage—a level of participation far beyond the tipping point, which is an outcome consistent with the theory developed here.

9.6 Trade Restrictions

I have so far assumed that states are interdependent only in regard to the environment and choice of technology. However, states are interdependent in other respects too—most especially, in international trade. Indeed, trade is a problem for environmental cooperation because of the phenomenon called 'leakage'. As one set of countries cooperates by reducing pollution, comparative advantage in the pollution-intensive activity shifts towards non-cooperating countries, with the consequence that the emissions of these countries increase. This is not just a theoretical possibility. In the case of the Montreal Protocol, leakage has threatened to undermine efforts by industrialized countries to limit releases of ozone-destroying chemicals (chlorofluoro-carbons (CFCs)). As Richard Benedick, the chief US negotiator at the Montreal talks, later put it, 'India, in particular, had embarked on a policy of expanding domestic production and export markets in the South, where it anticipated outstanding commercial opportunities as the North phased out CFCs.'[21]

However, trade also opens up a possible means of facilitating enforcement. Consider an agreement that requires that parties play Abate *and* that they restrict trade with non-parties. Intuitively, such an agreement would make cooperation very unattractive if the number of parties were low. For then, cooperating countries would not only lose the opportunity of free riding; they would also lose the gains from trading with non-parties. Suppose, however, that every country but one were a party. Then the non-party would gain from free riding on the abatement efforts of the parties. Yet it would lose all the gains from trade. Provided the latter losses were large enough, the 'last' country would prefer to accede to the treaty. Intuitively, provided that 'enough' countries imposed trade restrictions, the remaining non-parties would find it in their interests to accede. Essentially, imposition of trade restrictions transforms the game into a coordination game such as the one shown in Figure 3.

Why should the trade restriction be credible? The answer is not immediately obvious because the countries that impose the restriction also lose the gains from trading with non-parties. However, recall the leakage phenomenon. As a consequence of choosing to play Pollute, non-parties increase their emissions in reaction to the cooperating countries choosing to reduce theirs. Since the leakage effect is transmitted through the trade mechanism, however, a trade restriction imposed against non-parties would wipe out the leakage effect. If the welfare consequences of leakage are

[21] R.E. Benedick, *Ozone Diplomacy* (Cambridge, MA: Harvard University Press, 1998) at 248.

large enough relative to the welfare effects of the loss in the gains from trade, the parties to the agreement would be better off imposing trade restrictions against non-parties. Trade leakage thus frustrates cooperation when trade is unrestricted but facilitates cooperation when trade is restricted. It does so by making the threat to restrict trade credible.

The main utility in trade restrictions is thus to facilitate the enforcement of an agreement to limit emissions. Again, the theory sketched here is consistent with the Montreal Protocol. As noted by Richard Benedick, the trade restrictions in this agreement were 'critical, since they constituted the only enforcement mechanism in the protocol.'[22] Note that trade restrictions are more often used for reasons other than enforcement. The Convention on Trade in Endangered Species of Wild Fauna and Flora (CITES), for example, is fundamentally a trade agreement, not an environmental agreement relying on trade restrictions for enforcement. In CITES, trade restrictions are an *end;* in the Montreal Protocol, they are a *means.*

A possible problem with the use of trade restrictions to enforce an international environmental agreement is that they may violate the multilateral trading rules. These prohibit trade restrictions imposed against parties to the WTO, arguably even when the restrictions are imposed against non-parties to an environmental treaty. However, prohibiting trade restrictions under the circumstances outlined above would plainly undermine international environmental cooperation, and there is no reason why trade liberalization should trump transnational environmental protection. Both kinds of treaty, after all, are aimed at improving welfare. In any event, it is not the imposition of trade restrictions that matters. If the restrictions were credible, they would not even be imposed in equilibrium. As it happens, the Montreal Protocol trade restrictions were not imposed. They did not need to be because the threat to impose them was credible. However, consistent with the theory outlined here, the trade restrictions did influence behaviour. According to Richard Benedick, the trade restrictions 'were indispensable to the protocol's effectiveness.'[23]

It is tempting to think that trade restrictions are an easy means of enforcing international environmental agreements. They are not. The conditions that make trade restrictions effective and credible will not apply in every case. In some cases, trade restrictions will not alter behaviour even when imposed. In other cases, trade restrictions will not be credible, even when they would alter behaviour if imposed. Both aspects of the use of trade restrictions are reflected in the recent experience of the agreement establishing the International Commission for the Conservation of Atlantic Tunas (ICCAT). Frustrated with non-participation, non-compliance, and re-flagging, ICCAT imposed trade restrictions against some countries beginning in the late 1990s. The trade restrictions probably have had some effect. They may, for example, explain why Panama acceded to the agreement in 1998. However, other countries, such as Equatorial Guinea, have not changed their behaviour, despite

---

[22] *Ibid.* at 91.   [23] *Ibid.* at 91.

being the target of trade restrictions—presumably because they can easily sell their catches to third parties. Still other countries, such as Spain, are known to have violated ICCAT but have not had to suffer trade restrictions—presumably because the threat to impose restrictions against these countries was not credible.

9.7 Asymmetric Countries

The analytical theory to this point has assumed that countries are symmetric—that is, they have different identities but the same payoff functions. This assumption is made only for reasons of convenience—it allows us, for example, to illustrate the theory by means of the simple graphs shown in Figures 1–6. However, the assumption can be justified from another perspective: symmetry matters less than one might think. If countries are just slightly different from one another, for example, all the results presented thus far will stand unaltered. If countries are *very* different from one another, however, the results will change qualitatively. Suppose, for example that, instead of there being 100 symmetric countries there were 99 symmetric countries and one very, very large country. By a 'large' country I mean a country that gains a lot from pollution abatement relative to the 99 other countries but that also is capable of polluting a great deal more than these other countries. Then it can be shown that, in the Nash equilibrium, the one 'large' country will have very strong incentives to reduce its pollution unilaterally. This is because, being large, the consequences of this country's own pollution are substantially internalized. Similarly, if there were two 'large' countries and 98 'small' symmetric countries, cooperation between the two large countries would matter the most and would not be hard to sustain. Continuing with this logic, it should be clear that the assumption of symmetry basically exposes the most serious cooperation challenge.

This reasoning relates to the perspective of enforcement. Of course, if countries are asymmetric a different challenge emerges, and this challenge involves deciding what it is that asymmetric countries should agree to do. Should they reduce their pollution by precisely the same amount? And, if so, should they reduce their pollution by the same amount in absolute or in relative (percentage) terms? Should their respective abatement obligations reflect differentiated responsibilities? There are two separate issues here. One is about cost-effectiveness, the other about equity. Cost-effectiveness will favour collective abatement achieved at minimum overall cost, which is a matter of deciding which countries will undertake the abatement and by how much. Equity is concerned with which countries *pay* for the abatement—a matter of burden sharing. As long as monetary side payments are feasible, the two concerns can be separated. And side payments *are* feasible. Moreover, they are used in practice. I discuss them in the next section.

This concern for cost-effectiveness may seem overstated. After all, some agreements, such as the Helsinki Protocol, require that states cut back their emissions by the same amount, and such an outcome is very unlikely to be cost-effective. However, and as noted previously, the Helsinki Protocol did little more than codify what states had an interest in doing unilaterally. The Kyoto Protocol is different. It requires that certain industrialized countries reduce their emissions substantially, even from the perspective of the levels that would be consistent with their national interest. Yet it is precisely for this reason that the Kyoto Protocol incorporates mechanisms meant to lower the costs of achieving the overall emission reduction—especially the provision allowing for emission trading.

Equity is important in international agreements (see Chapter 27 'Equity'), but not only, or even primarily, because countries care directly about equity. Even if countries do not care at all about equity, the agreements they negotiate may reflect considerations of equity. This is for two reasons. The first is that equitable burden sharing is a focal point for negotiations.[24] The second is that should any country believe that the arrangement put on the negotiating table is not in its interest to accept—or that it imposes an unfair burden—it can always walk away. Fairness, in the context of international negotiations, must be seen from a horizontal, not a vertical, perspective.

9.8 Compensating Payments

As previously noted, asymmetry creates the need for side payments. Indeed, it can be shown that side payments will not be used in treaty negotiations when countries are symmetric.[25] Theory, however, suggests that side payments *will* be used when countries are *strongly* asymmetric.[26] To understand this reasoning, suppose there are two types of countries. Type A countries have payoff functions that make participation in an international environmental agreement unattractive. These countries, for example, may benefit little from the provision of the global public good. Type B countries, by contrast, benefit hugely from this provision. Under these circumstances, if an agreement is negotiated to supply the global public good, and if side payments are not offered, then only (some) Type B countries will participate. However, the Type B countries will also benefit if the Type A countries can be induced to participate and help supply the public good. They, therefore, have an incentive to compensate the Type A countries for participating. Moreover, the Type A countries have an incentive to accept the offer of compensation.

The predictions of this model are once again consistent with real world experience (see Chapter 41 'Technical and Financial Assistance'). Countries are highly

---

[24] Of course, deciding what is an 'equitable' burden sharing arrangement may not be at all obvious. What I mean is not that *the* equitable arrangement will be chosen but that countries will fail to agree on arrangements that are patently inequitable.

[25] See C. Carraro and D. Siniscalco, 'Strategies for the International Protection of the Environment' (1993) 52 J. Pub. Econ. 309.   [26] For a full explanation, see Barrett, note 4 above at 335–54.

asymmetric in regard to stratospheric ozone depletion. When first negotiated, the Montreal Protocol did not offer side payments. A subsequent revision, negotiated in 1990, a year after the original agreement entered into force, offered developing countries only compensation for incremental cost—an offer that has essentially sustained full participation by developing countries. The example of the Montreal Protocol also illustrates the complementary role played by carrots and sticks. Recall that the trade restrictions in this agreement apply to all non-participating countries. They thus serve to enforce the additional obligation borne by industrialized countries—the obligation to compensate developing countries for acceding to the agreement. Additionally, the offer of compensation helps to make the application of trade restrictions against developing countries 'fair.'

10 CONCLUSION

This chapter has developed a theory of international law and, especially, of the treaty instrument, drawing from the tools of economics and game theory.[27] I began by exposing the underlying incentive problem that can only be remedied by states accepting mutual restraint. I then explained that the fundamental role of a treaty is to restructure incentives. There are a number of means by which treaties can do this, and the means that will prove most effective will depend on the circumstances specific to the problem. There is no one-size-fits-all remedy to every environmental problem. It might be asked what exactly can be gained from this approach. One thing that can be gained, I believe, is a deeper understanding of treaty effectiveness. Though many agreements have been negotiated, few seem to have made any difference. This theory explains why.

The theory can also be used for the purpose of designing better treaties. As with all good theories, this one helps to structure our imagination. It allows us to see things we may not have noticed before. In particular, it draws our attention to the enforcement challenge. This is important, because enforcement is often taken lightly. The Kyoto Protocol, for example, specifies precise emission reduction obligations and elaborate procedures for trading and offsetting emissions, but it fails (in my view at least) to create incentives for enforcement. Climate change is a colossal challenge. It is probably unreasonable to expect that the best possible treaty would be negotiated in a first round. However, the theory developed here, had it been known to the negotiators of this agreement, would at the very least have alerted them to the need to

---

[27] My approach in this chapter has been formal, though my presentation has been informal. A more careful accounting of this approach can be found in my book, *ibid.*

address enforcement head on. Enforcement will need to be addressed in future negotiations—there is no getting around this issue. The theory developed in this chapter
provides clues as to how it might be addressed.[28]

RECOMMENDED READING

S. Barrett, *Environment and Statecraft: The Strategy of Environmental Treaty-Making* (Oxford:
Oxford University Press, 2003).
——, 'The Theory of International Environmental Agreements,' in K.G. Maler and J. Vincent,
eds., *Handbook of Environmental Economics*, volume 3 (Amsterdam: North Holland, 2005)
1457–1516.
A.A. Batabyal, ed., *The Economics of International Environmental Agreements* (Aldershot:
Ashgate, 2000).
C. Carraro and D. Siniscalco, 'International Environmental Agreements: Incentives and
Political Economy' (1998) 42 Eur. Econ. Rev. 561.
M. Finus, *Game Theory and International Environmental Cooperation* (Cheltenham: Edward
Elgar, 2001).
C. Helm, *Economic Theories of International Environmental Cooperation* (Cheltenham:
Edward Elgar, 2000).
T. Sandler, *Global Collective Action* (Cambridge: Cambridge University Press, 2005).
U.J. Wagner, 'The Design of Stable International Environmental Agreements' (2001) 15(3)
J. Econ. Surveys 377.

---

[28] My own attempt is presented in Barrett, note 4 above at 393–8.

CHAPTER 12

CRITICAL APPROACHES

KARIN MICKELSON

1 INTRODUCTION: LOCATING CRITICAL APPROACHES

'CRITICAL approaches' relevant to international environmental law do not lend themselves to easy identification. A critical approach in a broad sense might be seen as any approach that challenges the fundamental assumptions of the discipline: the state-based international order, anthropocentrism and/or utilitarianism as the basis for relationships between humans and the natural world, and the standard definition of progress in terms of the current state of Northern industrial development, among others. These assumptions, of course, run through not only mainstream international law but also mainstream economics, development theory, and other disciplines.

Such an understanding, while a useful starting point, has the disadvantage of being extremely broad. As an alternative, one might take the definition of 'critical theory' as 'any social theory that is at the same time explanatory, normative, practical, and self-reflexive.'[1] In other words, such a theory attempts not only to explain and criticize current social conditions or practices but also to provide tools for those who want to improve those conditions and practices. Furthermore, it requires some degree of attentiveness to the circumstances that have made its own critical stance possible and how those circumstances might have impacted on its formulation. This definition emphasizes the fact that criticism of mainstream assumptions is a necessary, but perhaps not a sufficient, condition for an approach to be considered critical. What is also required is a fundamental rethinking of these assumptions.

International environmental law is located at the intersection of a wide range of important critical approaches in this second sense (which is at the same time narrower and potentially more far-reaching). Some emerge from other disciplines, others from non-governmental organizations (NGOs) and civil society. In the former category, there are a number of bodies of critical scholarship, such as feminist and post-colonial theories, that have gained prominence in the academy in recent decades. There are other critical approaches that have developed as specialized areas that are essentially interdisciplinary in nature, such as development studies (including post-development theory and a range of other critiques of mainstream development models). NGOs and civil society represent a rich source of critical approaches in their own right. In some instances, activism has been informed by critical scholarship; in others, notably in the case of the anti-globalization/global justice movement and the environmental justice movement, scholarship has emerged at least in part in response to the challenge posed by activists. In addition, there are some individuals

The author would like to acknowledge the invaluable research assistance of Kelly Keenan.

[1] J. Bohman, 'Critical Theory,' in R. Audi, ed., *The Cambridge Dictionary of Philosophy*, 2nd edition (Cambridge: Cambridge University Press, 1999) at 195.

who straddle the line between scholarship and activism—for example, Vandana Shiva and Martin Khor, who operate outside traditional academic circles, yet have produced a significant and influential body of writing.

The purpose of this chapter is to explore some of these approaches, and to consider how they have been deployed to analyse and critique the underlying assumptions of international environmental law and policy. The chapter is divided into five sections, covering feminist approaches, post-colonial approaches, critiques of development, the anti-globalization/global justice movement, and the environmental justice movement. It attempts not only to provide a brief overview of the relevant scholarly literature but also to describe the ways in which activism has built on (or developed) these insights.

It is important to note that critical scholarship has also had an impact on the other analytical tools and perspectives that are discussed in this part of the *Handbook*. The disciplines of international relations, economics, and environmental ethics have each undergone their own engagement with alternative perspectives that call into question some of their traditional concepts and categories. For example, there is now important feminist work in both international relations and economics that critiques the tendency in those disciplines to overlook gender and reify masculinist assumptions. In the context of environmental ethics, ecofeminism has provided an important counterpoint to both mainstream accounts of the environment that treat it as a collection of resources available for human consumption and to alternative perspectives such as deep ecology whose critiques of anthropocentrism can sometimes lose sight of the ways in which environmental degradation is linked with gender hierarchy and social injustice.

2 FEMINIST APPROACHES

Over the last several decades, the impact of feminism both in the academy and in civil society has been extraordinary. From the nature of social order to the structure of intellectual thought, almost no area of human inquiry has escaped feminist analysis and critique. None of the other critical approaches considered in this chapter have had such far-reaching effects on the ways in which we have come to conceptualize and understand a variety of previously unquestioned assumptions. Furthermore, feminist thought has influenced and intermingled with a number of the other critical approaches, giving rise in some instances to specialized sub-disciplines such as feminist post-development scholarship. The discussion here can only touch on a vast and complex field, but an attempt will be made to provide an introduction to, and overview of, feminist theory generally, feminist engagement with environment and development, feminist approaches to international law, and, finally, feminist analysis of international environmental law.

2.1 Feminist Theory: Schools of Thought

Perhaps the most striking characteristic of feminist scholarship and activism is its diversity. For this reason, many have argued that it is misleading to label 'feminism' as a monolithic entity and have instead identified a number of different schools of feminist thought. The following lists some of the most frequently discussed variants and their most salient features, though it is by no means comprehensive[2] either in breadth or depth:

- Liberal feminism is characterized by a focus on formal equality, and it critiques existing social, economic, and political structures for their failure to include women. The work of Betty Friedan, one of the cofounders and first president of the US National Organization for Women (NOW), is a well-known example of this approach.[3] Liberal feminism is frequently criticized by proponents of other feminist approaches because of its failure to engage with the ways in which existing structures are themselves gendered, and must therefore be reconceptualized in order to achieve substantive gender equality.

- Radical feminism takes as its starting point the notion that mainstream understandings of social order are deeply patriarchal, reflecting a series of embedded assumptions about appropriate gender roles and expectations. Radical feminists tend to view the incorporation of women into existing power structures as a form of window dressing that merely serves to reinforce those structures. As an alternative, they advocate fundamental change. Prominent theorists include Mary Daly, Andrea Dworkin, and Catharine MacKinnon.[4]

- Cultural feminism differs from both liberal and radical feminism in assuming that gender is based not merely on socialization, but also reflects certain inherent differences between males and females. It rejects the liberal feminist prescription for social change as simply representing the adoption of masculine values and roles, and instead celebrates feminine values as alternative, less destructive models for social interaction. Carol Gilligan's work on a female 'ethic of care' is a well-known example of this perspective.[5]

- Ecofeminism is closely connected to cultural feminism (and is sometimes characterized as a variant thereof). The connection between women and nature, which many of the other feminist approaches regard as a dangerous patriarchal construct, is central to, and celebrated by, this perspective, which regards environmental

---

[2] The focus here is on approaches that have influenced feminist thought on environment and development.

[3] See, e.g., B. Friedan, *The Feminine Mystique* (New York: Norton, 1963).

[4] See, e.g., M. Daly, *Gyn/Ecology: The Metaethics of Radical Feminism* (Boston: Beacon Press, 1978); A. Dworkin, *Pornography: Men Possessing Women* (New York: Plume, 1989); and C.A. MacKinnon, *Feminism Unmodified: Discourses in Life and Law* (Cambridge, MA: Harvard University Press, 1987).

[5] C. Gilligan, *In a Different Voice: Psychological Theory and Women's Development* (Cambridge, MA: Harvard University Press, 1982).

degradation and gender oppression as being connected both conceptually and practically. Carolyn Merchant and Vandana Shiva are among the best-known ecofeminist scholars and activists.[6]

- Post-colonial or 'Third World' feminism has criticized the tendency of 'First World' feminism to reify the experience of women in the developed world as the paradigm for female oppression. As an alternative, it has called for a more inclusive, global understanding of feminism as combining a set of common concerns with an attentiveness to local context and difference. Chandra Talpade Mohanty's work is frequently cited as a notable example of this perspective.[7]

Despite the heterogeneity of feminist scholarship, it is possible to identify a common set of concerns regarding the treatment and role of women within economic, social, and political structures. As one author puts it, '[m]any would agree that at the very least a feminist is someone who holds that women suffer discrimination because of their sex, that they have specific needs which remain negated and unsatisfied, and that the satisfaction of those needs would require a radical change (some would say a revolution even) in the social, economic and political order.'[8] Furthermore, many feminist scholars and others who utilize feminist theory and methodology in their scholarship draw on a range of approaches rather than limiting themselves to one school of thought.

2.2 Feminist Engagement with Development and Environment

The feminist engagement with development reflects a variety of approaches:

- Women in Development (WID) was the earliest form of feminist engagement with development theory and practice, and is usually dated to the work of Esther Boserup starting in the early 1970s.[9] Boserup and others highlighted the exclusion of women from many of the benefits associated with mainstream development, and pointed out the significant costs that women frequently bore because of the environmental and social effects of unsustainable and disruptive megaprojects.

---

[6] See, e.g., C. Merchant, *The Death of Nature: Women, Ecology and the Scientific Revolution* (San Francisco: Harper and Row, 1980); and V. Shiva, *Staying Alive: Women, Ecology and Development* (London: Zed Books, 1988).

[7] See, in particular, C.T. Mohanty, 'Under Western Eyes: Feminist Scholarship and Colonial Discourses,' in C.T. Mohanty, A. Russo, and L. Torres, eds., *Third World Women and the Politics of Feminism* (Bloomington: Indiana University Press, 1991) 51.

[8] R. Delmar, 'What Is Feminism?' in A.C. Herrman and A.J. Stewart, eds., *Theorizing Feminisms: Parallel Trends in the Humanities and Social Sciences*, 2nd edition (Boulder, CO: Westview Press, 2001) 5 at 5.

[9] E. Boserup, *Women's Role in Economic Development* (New York: St. Martin's Press, 1970).

- Women and Development (WAD) emerged as a radical critique of the WID perspective. Along the lines of the liberal/radical feminist distinction mentioned earlier, WAD proponents characterized WID thinking as representing a narrow focus on involving women in the modern economic sector rather than questioning the mainstream development paradigm. WAD also emphasized the extent to which this paradigm, and its linkage to global capitalism, are damaging to men as well as to women, and viewed women's oppression largely as a function of the class system and capitalist structures rather than male domination. As Lourdes Benería and Gita Sen note, '[m]odernization is not a neutral process, but one that obeys the dictates of capitalist accumulation and profit making. Contrary to Boserup's implications, the problem for women is not only the lack of participation in this process as equal partners with men; it is a system that generates and intensifies inequalities, making use of existing gender hierarchies to place women in subordinate positions at each different level of interaction between class and gender.'[10]

- Gender and Development (GAD) represents an alternative to both of the previous approaches. The GAD approach charges WAD 'with a privileging of class over gender'[11] and a failure to consider divisions within classes. According to one commentator, 'GAD addresses itself to the fundamental structures of inequity between men and women. Ideologically, GAD sees itself as centering gender and class relations rather than women *per se*.'[12] At a practical level, GAD aims at the destabilization of gender hierarchy through the development process. Caroline Moser produced an influential guide to the incorporation of gender concerns into development planning in 1993.[13]

The GAD approach has been highly influential in recent years, although commentators have noted that the WID approach continues to be dominant at the level of development practice.

Feminist development thinking has been impacted also by the increasing emphasis on environmental concerns. The early discussions of this issue (sometimes referred to as Women, Environment, and Development) focused on the impact of environmental degradation on women's lives, and the critical role that women play in environmental management at the grassroots level. Vandana Shiva is frequently mentioned as a prominent thinker in this context. As the concern for sustainability became mainstream in the late 1980s, commentators began to identify a theme known as Women, Environment, and Sustainable Development (WESD), which was

---

[10] L. Benería and G. Sen, 'Accumulation, Reproduction and Women's Role in Economic Development: Boserup Revisited,' in N. Visvanathan et al., eds., *The Women, Gender and Development Reader* (London: Zed Books, 1997) 42 at 48.

[11] K. Saunders, 'Introduction: Towards a Deconstructive Post-Development Criticism,' in K. Saunders, ed., *Feminist Post-Development Thought: Rethinking Modernity, Post-Colonialism and Representation* (London: Zed Books, 2002) 1 at 8.   [12] *Ibid.* at 10.

[13] C. Moser, *Gender Planning and Development: Theory, Practice and Training* (London: Routledge, 1993).

the focal point for discussions relating to the involvement of women in achieving sustainable development, but which also encompassed debates regarding the meaning of sustainability and the nature of development.[14]

2.3 Feminist Engagement with International Law

The feminist engagement with international law is often dated to the 1991 publication of a groundbreaking article in the *American Journal of International Law* entitled 'Feminist Approaches to International Law.'[15] In this article, Hilary Charlesworth, Christine Chinkin, and Shelley Wright argue that the international legal system has privileged men and male perspectives. At the most basic level, the institutional structures of international law exclude women from positions of power. At a deeper level, however, the fundamental assumptions of the system are at odds with the realities of women's lives. The authors draw on themes developed in feminist legal studies, such as the debate about the value of rights discourse to advance women's equality and the public/private divide, to problematize mainstream international law approaches to women's issues. Since 1991, a considerable body of feminist scholarship on international law has developed, in fields ranging from human rights to the use of force.

Despite the remarkably vibrant critiques of mainstream environmental and developmental thought on the one hand, and the emerging body of feminist international law scholarship on the other, there are few examples of scholarship applying feminist insights to international environmental law. Two examples offer an interesting contrast in approach. The first, published by Christopher Joyner and George Little in 1996,[16] drew on feminist scholarship for the purpose of overcoming mainstream assumptions about international law that might be considered problematic from an environmental perspective, notably the centrality of the sovereign state. The authors make two proposals for incorporating feminist perspectives into international environmental law. The first is the adoption of what they term a 'community security paradigm', which would involve broadening the existing understanding of security to encompass global ecological, political and economic concerns. The second is that women should be treated as an epistemic community. The notion of epistemic community, as described by Peter Haas, refers to 'a network of professionals with recognized expertise and competence in a particular domain and an authoritative claim

---

[14] For an important contribution to this theme, see R. Braidotti, E. Charkiewicz, S. Hausler, and S. Wieringa, *Women, the Environment and Sustainable Development: Towards a Theoretical Synthesis* (London: Zed Books, 1994).

[15] H. Charlesworth, Christine Chinkin, and Shelley Wright, 'Feminist Approaches to International Law' (1991) 85 A.J.I.L. 613.

[16] C.C. Joyner and G. Little, 'It's Not Nice to Fool Mother Nature! The Mystique of Feminist Approaches to International Environmental Law' (1996) 14 B.U. Int'l L.J. 223.

to policy-relevant knowledge within that domain or issue area'[17] (see Chapter 34 'Epistemic Communities'). Joyner and Little argue that '[b]y cooperating together as a unique group in society women could serve to explain and to shift attitudes on the environment in general, and on the relationship between women and nature in particular.'[18] While both of these proposals are said to represent ways of overcoming barriers to equality between the sexes, they seem to be primarily aimed at improving international environmental law. As Joyner and Little note towards the end of the article, '[n]ew legal paradigms are needed to generate new ideas for solutions to global ecological problems.'[19]

In contrast, a recent piece by Annie Rochette, entitled 'Transcending the Conquest of Nature and Women: A Feminist Perspective on International Environmental Law,'[20] takes an approach that insists on the centrality of women's concerns, while maintaining an awareness of the potential contribution of feminist approaches to environmental protection. Rochette argues that despite the increasing inclusion of references to women's concerns in international legal instruments, there are significant obstacles to the achievement of gender equality and the protection of the global environment. One is the reliance on a formal equality paradigm. Rochette draws an analogy to the WID approach: 'The assumption appears to be that the gendered impacts of environmental degradation will be addressed simply by giving women the same rights as men, and that women's role in environmental protection will be realised by giving women access to environmental and developmental decision-making.'[21] Rochette argues that this focus on formal equality and access to decision-making is problematic because, first, it fails to question the existing decision-making structures themselves; second, it fails to recognize 'intersections between gender and other systems of inequality such as race, class, culture, ability and sexuality,' which can impact on the ability of women to enjoy access to decision-making power; and, finally, because it 'leaves intact the masculinist institutions that have worked to exclude women and unsustainably exploit nature,'[22] such as Western science and technology and the capitalist global trading system.

The divergence in approach between these two attempts to apply feminist insights to international environmental law illustrates the delicate balance that must be struck between maintaining an approach that takes into account the broad range of issues that impact women's lives, and losing the focus on the concerns of women per se. This balancing act has been an important element of the feminist engagement with international environmental law and policy, and is particularly evident in

---

[17] P.M. Haas, 'Introduction: Epistemic Communities and International Policy Coordination' (1992) 46 Intl. Org. 1 at 3.   [18] Joyner and Little, see note 16 above at 264.

[19] *Ibid.* at 265.

[20] A. Rochette, 'Transcending the Conquest of Nature and Women: A Feminist Perspective on International Environmental Law,' in D. Buss and A. Manji, eds., *International Law: Modern Feminist Approaches* (Oxford: Hart Publishing, 2005) 203.   [21] *Ibid.* at 223.

[22] *Ibid.* at 223 and 224.

the work of feminist advocacy groups. These have been extremely active in the field of environment and development since the lead up to the 1992 United Nations Conference on Environment and Development (UNCED), forming coalitions across national boundaries as well as with other civil society organizations in order to promote common agendas. The Women's Environment and Development Organization (WEDO), which was founded in the United States in 1990, has been one of the most influential. WEDO describes itself as 'an international advocacy network that seeks to increase the power of women worldwide as policymakers in governance and in policymaking institutions, forums and processes, at all levels, to achieve economic and social justice, a peaceful and healthy planet and human rights for all.'

In the aftermath of the World Summit on Sustainable Development (WSSD), WEDO produced a *Gender Analysis of the WSSD Plan of Implementation*,[23] which reflects the approach that it has taken to the intersection between gender equality, environmental sustainability, and social justice. WEDO is particularly critical of the linkages drawn at the WSSD between sustainable development and existing economic structures, criticizing the failure of the Plan of Implementation to consider the negative effects of globalization, and it asserts that 'the WSSD strongly supported the existing neo-liberal economic framework.' Turning to gender concerns more specifically, WEDO recognizes a few important advances—notably on the right of women to inherit land, which was the result of intensive lobbying by the women's caucus—but concludes that the overall assessment of the WSSD from the point of view of women's interests is unpromising: 'References to gender in the Plan of Implementation provide for equal opportunity with men, but do not make gender central to sustainable development.' From WEDO's perspective, then, the Plan of Implementation's support for the existing economic system and its inadequate treatment of gender concerns are seen as being fundamentally linked. Both reflect the plan's failure to challenge problematic assumptions about the international system—a failure that may be fatal to its attempt to achieve sustainable development.

WEDO's analysis highlights a concern that underlies the feminist project more generally, namely that the mainstreaming of many feminist issues, although a sign of the success of feminist critique, is, nevertheless, a double-edged sword. On the one hand, the incorporation of gender concerns changes the terms of the debate. These concerns can no longer be treated as marginal or tangential to the 'real' business of achieving social and economic development. On the other hand, there is a tendency to see this incorporation as an end in itself rather than a means of achieving more fundamental change. Yet it is the demand for radical change that has accounted for a great deal of the energy that brought these issues onto the international agenda in the first place. This is likely to be an ongoing theme in feminist scholarship and advocacy in the future.

---

[23] *Gender Analysis of the WSSD Plan of Implementation* [copy on file with the author].

3 Post-Colonial Approaches

Since the publication of Edward Said's *Orientalism* in 1978, post-colonial theory has come to be regarded as an increasingly important body of scholarship. While associated most closely with literary criticism, it has come to influence a variety of disciplines ranging from history to law. This section will provide a brief overview of the origins of post-colonial theory and some of its major themes, before considering scholarship that draws on some of these themes in the context of international law.

3.1 Post-Colonial Theory Generally

Some authors trace the genealogy of post-colonial theory to the writings of anti-colonial authors (and activists) such as Frantz Fanon, Aimé Césaire, and Amilcar Cabral. Others have identified the work of the Subaltern Studies Group, a number of Indian historians who attempted to write post-colonial Indian history from the point of view of the oppressed (or 'subaltern' in Gramscian terms). However, post-colonial studies as a distinct area of intellectual inquiry in the North largely emerged out of literary studies. Three scholars have played a particularly prominent role in the field: the late Edward Said, Gayatri Chakravorty Spivak, and Homi Bhabha.

Said is widely regarded as the progenitor of post-colonial studies (as well as a model of the engaged post-colonial intellectual, because of his work on behalf of the Palestinian cause). In *Orientalism*, Said explored the ways in which the non-Western world was constructed in Western thought. 'Orientalism' refers to a complex set of discourses from a variety of disciplines that overlap in order to produce a body of knowledge about the non-Western 'Other'. While focusing on the analysis of discourse, Said emphasizes the ways in which this underlay justifies the exercise of Western power: 'Orientals were rarely seen or looked at: they were seen through, analysed not as citizens, or even people, but as problems to be solved or confined, or—as the colonial powers openly coveted their territory—taken over.'[24] While some have asserted that Said engages in the very kind of homogenization of the West that he criticizes in Western writings about the Orient, there is no doubt that *Orientalism* was a significant and highly influential piece of scholarship.

Spivak has been influential in feminist theory as well as in post-colonial theory. She is also associated with the Subaltern Studies Group.[25] Spivak is well known for her treatment of issues of representation and, in particular, for the notion of

---

[24] E.W. Said, *Orientalism* (New York: Vintage, 1979) at 207.
[25] See, e.g., G.C. Spivak, *The Post-Colonial Critic: Interviews, Strategies, Dialogues* (New York: Routledge, 1990).

'strategic essentialism', whereby essentialist categories ('woman', 'Third World') are used for strategic or political purposes. The work of Bhabha is the least accessible of the three, although not by any means the least influential.[26] He is particularly well known for his work on hybridity. As Ania Loomba describes this concept, it entails an insistence that 'neither coloniser nor colonised is independent of the other. Colonial identities—on both sides of the divide—are unstable, agonised, and in constant flux.'[27]

Perhaps because of its origins in literary theory, post-colonial theory has tended to focus on the analysis of literary and other texts, and has been criticized by some for its failure to engage with issues such as human rights, resource distribution, and poverty.[28] Nevertheless, as Robert Young notes, the theoretical foundation of post-colonial theory is its attempt to come to terms with systems of colonial and neo-colonial oppression. He argues:

Postcolonial critique focuses on forces of oppression and coercive domination that operate in the contemporary world; the politics of anti-colonialism and neocolonialism, race, gender, nationalisms, class and ethnicities define its terrain. Interest in oppression in the past will always be guided by the relation of that history to the present. In that sense, post-colonial theory's intellectual commitment will always be to seek to develop new forms of engaged theoretical work that contributes to the creation of dynamic ideological and social transformation.[29]

Similarly, Christine Sylvester has argued that post-colonial theory has the potential to be a source for innovative ways of thinking about development. She acknowledges its failure to engage with issues such as poverty but insists that '[p]ostcolonial studies, having neglected direct attention to such issues and their possible solutions—even in an imaginative or theoretical way—is nonetheless better placed than any Western agency to reinvent or recover postcolonial agendas of material well-being that matter on the ground.'[30] This would require a shift in focus towards practical issues but would not demand a conceptual reorientation: 'In the spirit of hybridity, postcolonial studies can read itself into the in-betweens of established and new disciplinary thinking and places—hyphenating itself and its knowledges, *on its own many terms*, with those it ostensibly despises, like neoliberalism and developmentalism.'[31]

From a different vantage point, Ania Loomba questions the validity of the accusation that post-colonial scholars fail to talk about economic exploitation, pointing out that many do deal with this subject as well as related issues, 'although their work is often not included within what is becoming institutionalised as "postcolonial

---

[26] See, e.g., H.K. Bhabha, *The Location of Culture* (New York: Routledge, 1994).

[27] A. Loomba, *Colonialism/Postcolonialism* (New York: Routledge, 1998) at 178.

[28] R. Sunder Rajan, 'The Third World Academic in Other Places; or the Postcolonial Intellectual Revisited' (1997) 23 Critical Inquiry 596 at 615–16.

[29] R.J.C. Young, *Postcolonialism: An Historical Introduction* (Oxford: Blackwell, 2001) at 11.

[30] C. Sylvester, 'Development Studies and Postcolonial Studies: Disparate Tales of the "Third World"' (1999) 20 Third World Q. 703 at 718.   [31] *Ibid.* [emphasis in original].

studies." '[32] This insight is important, given that much of the work being done in legal scholarship on issues relating to developing countries draws on elements of post-colonial theory, but it does not identify itself as 'post-colonial' *per se*, as explored in the section that follows.

3.2 Post-Colonial Theory and International Law

Despite the lack of a body of international law scholarship that could be labelled as specifically 'post-colonial', post-colonial theory is one of the strands that has informed the work of TWAIL (Third World Approaches to International Law), a network of scholars who have sought to engage with the dominant discourse of international law and its failure to take into account the perspectives and concerns of Third World peoples. TWAIL takes its inspiration from the work carried out by earlier Third World scholars, and incorporates insights from post-colonial theory and a variety of other critical approaches to international law. Among this group, the scholar who has engaged most consistently with issues relating to colonialism is Antony Anghie, who has produced an important body of scholarship on the colonial origins and history of international law. Anghie has argued that far from being a peripheral concern, colonialism has had a profound impact on international law and its principles. For example, he questions the standard genealogy of sovereignty as a product of the 1648 Treaty of Westphalia and argues that the traditional understanding of sovereignty emerged out of the colonial encounter.[33] However, Anghie is not willing to relegate colonialism to the past: '[I]t is far too simple to see colonialism as a phenomenon that is ended and may now be the subject of a valedictory judgment . . . That [the concepts of colonizer and colonized] have an enduring significance is suggested by the fact that so many vital contemporary debates are presented as debates between former colonial powers and their subjects, the developed and the developing.'[34] Furthermore, he notes, tracing the impact of colonialism is made more difficult by its complexity: 'Colonialism is not a simple phenomenon. Its forms are various and subtle. It reproduces itself through its victims and continuously creates and represses new subjects.'[35]

While Anghie's work has an obvious connection to post-colonial studies as they are generally understood, much of the work carried out by scholars associated with TWAIL has connections to the broader understanding of post-colonial critique espoused earlier by Young. In the field of international environmental law, there has

[32] Loomba, see note 27 above at xv.

[33] A. Anghie, 'Francisco de Vitoria and the Colonial Origins of International Law' (1996) 5 Soc. & Legal Stud. 321; and A. Anghie, 'Finding the Peripheries: Sovereignty and Colonialism in Nineteenth-Century International Law' (1999) 40 Harv. Int'l L.J. 1.

[34] A. Anghie, ' "The Heart of My Home": Colonialism, Environmental Damage, and the Nauru Case' (1993) 34 Harv. Int'l L.J. 445 at 505.   [35] *Ibid.* at 505–6.

been work that draws on post-colonial insights in criticizing the discipline's failure to come to terms with the perspective and concerns of the South. For example, a seemingly straightforward principle of international environmental law such as the principle of common but differentiated responsibilities can reflect fundamentally different perspectives on the roles of the South and North in responding to global environmental challenges (see Chapter 27 'Equity'). As articulated in Principle 7 of the Rio Declaration on Environment and Development, common but differentiated responsibilities are based on 'the different contributions to global environmental degradation.' Principle 7 goes on to state that developed countries 'acknowledge the responsibility that they bear in the international pursuit of sustainable development in view of the pressures their societies place on the global environment and of the technologies and financial resources they command.' From the perspective of the North, this principle can be said to reflect a pragmatic recognition of the different financial and technological capacity of the developed and developing countries, and of the current imbalance in consumption of resources as between South and North. From the perspective of the South, in contrast,

it can be said to reflect an acknowledgement of the historic, moral, and legal responsibility of the North to shoulder the burdens of environmental protection, just as it has enjoyed the benefits of economic and industrial development largely unconstrained by environmental concerns. Implicit in the latter view is a sense that the North has received a disproportionate share of the benefits of centuries of environmentally unsustainable development, and the underprivileged in the South have borne many of its costs.[36]

Thus, the principle of common but differentiated responsibilities cannot be understood without taking into account a broader historical and ethical context, in which the colonial encounter and its aftermath continue to play a critical role.

3.3 Approaches from Civil Society: The Concept of Ecological Debt

The broader sense of post-colonial critique is also apparent in some of the work carried out by civil society groups. In the early 1990s, for example, a number of Latin American activists interested in issues of environmental and social justice elaborated a concept known as 'ecological debt'. Developed as a response to the enormous external debt burden experienced not only in Latin America but also throughout the developing world, it was seen as a way of turning the concept of debt on its head. The North should be seen as a debtor rather than a creditor because the economic debt owed by the South was insignificant in comparison to the debt owed by the North

---

[36] K. Mickelson, 'South, North, International Environmental Law and International Environmental Lawyers' (2000) 11 Y.B. Int'l Envt'l L. 52 at 70.

because of the environmental damage that had been caused by its own development trajectory. This concept was discussed by Latin American NGOs during the UNCED process and was incorporated into the Debt Treaty, one of the alternative treaties produced by the NGO forum. The preamble recognizes 'the existence of a planetary ecological debt of the North' and defines it as being 'essentially constituted by economic and trade relations based on the indiscriminate exploitation of resources, and its ecological impacts . . . including global environmental deterioration, most of which is the responsibility of the North.'[37]

After several years of being discussed in NGO circles, ecological debt has become increasingly visible as a focal point for activism in recent years. In 1999, Acción Ecológica, an Ecuadorian NGO, began an ongoing campaign on ecological debt. Again, as in the work of post-colonial scholars, the emphasis is on seeing connections and continuity between past and present injustices and on demanding recognition and reparation for both. Thus, Acción Ecológica has called upon Northern NGOs to take action on a variety of fronts in relation to ecological debt. Several are based on reparation for past wrongs and damage. For example, Northern NGOs are asked to campaign for the recognition of the ecological debt in all environmental fora, for the cancellation of the payment of external debt, for compensation for damage caused by transnational corporations, and for compensation by damage due to climate change. Other proposals however, are based on the need for action in order to prevent the growth of ecological debt. For example, Northern NGOs are asked to campaign against projects and policies of the International Monetary Fund (IMF), the World Bank, the World Trade Organization (WTO), and national governments that increase ecological debt. They are asked to bring pressure to bear on national governments to reduce carbon emissions, eliminate ozone-depleting substances, and to monitor the shipment of toxic wastes and domestically prohibited products to the Third World.

4 DEVELOPMENT AND ITS CRITICS

Of all the critical approaches surveyed in this chapter, critiques of development may well be the most familiar to those working in the field of international environmental law. The notion of 'sustainable development', which was popularized in the late 1980s by the World Commission on Environment and Development (Brundtland Commission) as well as being a central theme of the 1992 UNCED and the 2002 WSSD, has come to be regarded as a central principle (and perhaps even the ultimate

---

[37] Debt Treaty, *NGO Alternative Treaties from the Global Forum at Rio de Janeiro*, 1–15 June 1992 [copy on file with the author].

aim) of international environmental law and policy (see Chapter 26 'Sustainable Development'). At the same time, however, there has been considerable debate regarding the extent to which the concept merely repackages a number of problematic assumptions about the meaning of development and the need for economic growth under a new, more benign label. This section will attempt to provide some context for this familiar debate by providing an overview of the broader critiques of development that have come out of the academy and civil society in recent years.

4.1 Development and Post-Development

The emergence of development studies as a field of scholarly inquiry is a relatively recent phenomenon. It could be characterized as an academic response to the political reality of the decolonization process of the 1950s and 1960s. While the origins of development studies lie in development economics, it quickly became apparent that an understanding of the development process required a range of disciplinary approaches. In fact, development studies might be said to be one of the first examples of a truly interdisciplinary field, combining aspects of economics, sociology, anthropology, and area studies, among others.

Development theory is a specialized sub-field of development studies that attempts to provide a conceptual framework for the development process. The earliest, and for a long time the dominant, conceptual framework of development studies was modernization theory. In this account, development was seen as a process of transformation whereby societies would gradually move ever closer to modernity, which was defined in terms of the characteristics of Western industrialized states. One of the major challenges to modernization theory came from dependency theory. Originating in Latin America in the 1960s and reaching the height of its influence in the early 1970s, dependency theory argued that the structure of the international economy was such that developing countries would never be able to achieve economic development but would instead always remain at the periphery. It is often associated with strategies such as import-substitution, which was intended to provide support for the development of domestic industry and infrastructure through the erection of trade barriers and other protectionist measures.

Despite the significant differences between modernization and dependency theories, both shared a number of common assumptions about the object and meaning of development. Frans Schuurman has argued that three characteristics were shared by dominant developmental paradigms after the Second World War:

- the essentialization of the Third World and its inhabitants as homogeneous entities;
- the unconditional belief in the concept of progress and in the makeability of society; and

• the importance of the (nation) state as an analytical frame of reference and a political and scientific confidence in the role of the state to realise progress.[38]

Schuurman notes that each of these views was increasingly under attack by the mid-1980s, with the result that development studies as a field seemed to be left without a common conceptual foundation.

Since this time, a number of alternative approaches to development have emerged that have attempted to move beyond these problematic assumptions. Post-development theory is perhaps the most visible example, although there are many others. Its premise is that orthodox understandings of development have done little to bring about prosperity in the developing world, and have instead contributed to the oppression and marginalization of large sectors of the population. In place of an essentialized Third World, post-development emphasizes an attention to context—to local cultures and conditions. Arturo Escobar, a prominent post-development scholar, has argued that the 'Third World' was in fact a product of the discourse of development, which categorized certain countries and regions as 'underdeveloped' because of their failure to conform to a particular (Western) understanding of appropriate economic and social structures.[39] This is clearly related to the rejection of the notion of progress, which was arguably the intellectual lynchpin of the entire development enterprise. Post-development scholars have criticized the failure of their predecessors to recognize the extent to which progress was defined in terms of the evolution of Western societies. This idea was in turn unquestioningly assumed to be the only valid pattern for the rest of the world. Finally, post-development scholars call into question the central role of the state as well as other alternative approaches. In its place, they emphasize grassroots empowerment and community-based decision-making.

4.2 A Post-Development Perspective on Sustainable Development

Post-development theory does not restrict its critique to traditional understandings of development. The notion of sustainable development comes under similar attack. From a post-development perspective, sustainable development does not move in any significant way beyond the existing development paradigm, and could in fact be seen as an attempt to preserve it by tinkering at the margins without changing the conceptual foundation. First, rather than requiring a re-evaluation of the human

---

[38] F.J. Schuurman, 'Paradigms Lost, Paradigms Regained? Development Studies in the Twenty-First Century' (2000) 21 Third World Q. 7 at 8.

[39] A. Escobar, *Encountering Development: The Making and Unmaking of the Third World* (Princeton, NJ: Princeton University Press, 1995).

relationship with nature, sustainable development discourse continues to see nature as a resource for human exploitation. Critics point, in particular, to the fact that the Brundtland Commission emphasized the need for economic growth. Escobar notes that 'sustainable development discourse purports to reconcile two old enemies— economic growth and the preservation of the environment—without significant adjustments to the market system.'[40] In his view, the purpose of sustainable development is to sustain not nature and culture but capital. Second, sustainable development as articulated by the Brundtland Commission could be said to 'blame the victim' by highlighting poverty as a cause of environmental degradation. As Escobar notes, '[p]opular and scholarly texts alike are filled with representations of dark and poor peasant masses destroying forests and mountainsides with axes and machetes, thus shifting visibility and blame away from the large industrial polluters in North and South, and the predatory way of life fostered by capitalism and development, to poor peasants and "backward" practices such as slash-and-burn agriculture.'[41] Finally, sustainable development discourse further reinforces the need for scientific and technological intervention in order to achieve rational utilization of the environment as a resource.

4.3 Alternatives to Development?

Post-development has itself been criticized on a variety of fronts. Perhaps the most common criticisms are that it romanticizes the 'traditional', and fails to recognize the extent to which mainstream development has been able to meet the aspirations (if not the needs) of many in the developing world. Others have accused post-development scholars of espousing a view of development for the South that could never be applicable to the North and, thus, of accepting the perpetuation of an international system that is deeply unequal. While some of this criticism may be unfair,[42] there appears to be widespread consensus that it is not enough to critique traditional development. There must be some meaningful alternative. Furthermore, those alternatives must be scrutinized to identify their own weaknesses. As a number of commentators have pointed out, it is all very well to criticize the state-centred approach to development, but, in an age of globalization, many view the state as

---

[40] A. Escobar, 'Constructing Nature: Elements for a Poststructuralist Political Ecology,' in R. Peet and M. Watts, eds., *Liberation Ecologies: Environment, Development, Social Movements* (New York: Routledge, 1996) 46 at 49.   [41] *Ibid.* at 51.

[42] For example, Wolfgang Sachs, one of the most prominent thinkers associated with post-development, has been heavily involved in proposing alternative development paths for the North. See, for example, W. Sachs, R. Loske, and M. Linz, *Greening the North: A Post-Industrial Blueprint for Ecology and Equity*, translated by T. Nevill (London: Zed Books, 1998).

potentially providing a critical buffer between the forces of global capital and local communities and regions.

This perspective is particularly important at a time when neo-liberalism seems to have stepped in where modernization theory left off, proclaiming a new age of prosperity through the unleashing of market forces and government deregulation. Frederick Cooper and Randall Packard point out that since the 1980s, two sets of critics have rejected the development framework: the 'ultramodernists', for whom 'the invisible hand of the market allocates resources optimally', and the 'postmodernists', who see development as 'one of a series of controlling discourses and controlling practices—a 'knowledge-power regime'—that has emerged since the Enlightenment, the extension of a universalizing European project into all corners of the globe.'[43] Cooper and Packard highlight this 'strange convergence of free market universalists and anti-universalist critics', noting that there are a great many questions that are left unasked. They note:

The marvelous ambiguity of the word development—eliding in a single concept notions of increased output and improved welfare—does not in itself prevent debates over its meanings, within and across national boundaries. What at one level appears like a discourse of control is at another a discourse of entitlement, a way of capturing the imagination of a cross-national public around demands for decency and equity.[44]

These demands for decency and equity are associated with a wide range of approaches to the formulation of alternatives to mainstream understandings of development. These approaches share an emphasis on the need for development that is attentive to the needs of local populations and sensitive to cultural context. One example is the subsistence perspective. Associated with the work of Maria Mies and Vandana Shiva, this perspective focuses on meeting essential human needs and has two aspects: the need for self-sufficiency (which resonates with many of the other critical approaches explored in this chapter, notably those associated with the anti-globalization/global justice movement), and the rejection of a development model based on the notion of accumulation. Shiva has emphasized the need for recovering the traditional wisdom of local communities, particularly women, as a basis for a more harmonious and sustainable relationship with nature.

Development Alternatives with Women for a New Era (DAWN) is widely regarded as an organization that has exerted considerable influence in both the alternative development and feminist communities. It is a network of women scholars and activists from the global South that has described itself as being 'committed to developing alternative frameworks and methods to attain the goals of economic and social justice, peace, and development free of all forms of oppression by gender, class, race,

---

[43] F. Cooper and R. Packard, 'Introduction,' in F. Cooper and R. Packard, eds., *International Development and the Social Sciences* (Berkeley: University of California Press, 1997) 1 at 3.
[44] *Ibid.* at 4.

and nation.'[45] DAWN advocates a 'people-centred' approach to development 'based on the values of co-operation, resistance to hierarchies, sharing, accountability and commitment to peace.'[46] It is well known for its emphasis on the need for the empowerment of women as well as their communities. In the process leading up to the WSSD, DAWN not only criticized the failure on the part of the international community to live up to its UNCED commitments, but also made a number of proposals for how the environmental and social dimensions of development could be integrated.[47] For example, DAWN called for a 'strong social framework for sustainable development,' noting that '[w]hile so far the efforts to operationalize sustainable development have focused on policies and tools to reduce environmental impacts, to internalize environmental costs and to develop preventive environmental policies and management practices, the comparable effort has to be made to internalize, share and prevent the social costs of economic growth.' It argued that 'policy measures and tools to operationalize a social framework for sustainable development should include a living wage; affordable health care; access to land, including land reform; safe drinking water and access to sanitation; clean and affordable energy for household needs; access to public education; minimum pension security guaranteed by the state and so on.'

It is unfortunate that the critiques of development and formulation of alternatives such as these have not had a broader impact on international environmental law and policy. There is widespread acknowledgment that the notion of sustainable development is problematic for a variety of reasons. For example, Günther Handl notes that ' "sustainable development," as formally characterized, invites an overly anthropocentric and instrumentalist interpretation which in the long run is apt to thwart the very pursuit of those goals that "sustainability" is said to embody.'[48] Nevertheless, few scholars in the discipline draw on the rich body of literature that has developed in the field of development studies. One exception is Alexander Gillespie, who in his book-length critique of sustainable development argues that 'the epicentre of the entire development structure and the vast underpinnings of the debate are being sidestepped or manipulated.'[49] Nevertheless, while Gillespie draws on writers such as Shiva in formulating his critique, he does not foreground their analysis.

---

[45] G. Sen and C. Grown, *Development, Crises and Alternative Visions* (New York: Monthly Review Press, 1987) at 9.

[46] Braidotti, Charkiewicz, Hausler, and Wieringa, see note 14 above at 117.

[47] Political Declaration on Sustainable Development from a Feminist Perspective, statement presented at Prepcom IV for the WSSD, Bali, Indonesia [on file with the author].

[48] G. Handl, 'Sustainable Development: General Rules versus Specific Obligations,' in W. Lang, ed., *Sustainable Development and International Law* (London: Martinus Nijhoff, 1995) 35 at 38.

[49] A. Gillespie, *The Illusion of Progress: Unsustainable Development in International Law and Policy* (London: Earthscan, 2001) at 149.

5 GLOBALIZATION AND ANTI-GLOBALIZATION

Some might argue that globalization is a phenomenon as old as recorded human history and that resistance to globalization is almost as ancient. It is only in the last 15 years, however, that the term 'globalization' has come to be a focal point for scholarly and political debate. The definition of the term is itself contested. As generally used and understood, it refers to a process of transnational or interregional integration that has a variety of aspects: economic, political, technological, and cultural. Integration is widely regarded as the key rather than mere internationalization. As David Held and Anthony McGrew note, 'the concept of globalization denotes much more than a stretching of social relations and activities across regions and frontiers. For it suggests a growing magnitude or intensity of global flows such that states and societies become increasingly enmeshed in worldwide systems and networks of interaction.'[50]

5.1 The Globalization Debate Generally

The real controversy arises with regard to the benefits and disadvantages of the globalization process. Views are frequently highly polarized. On one side, supporters of globalization view it as the means by which the international community will achieve widespread prosperity and well being. On the other, a wide array of activists and scholars argue that globalization represents a threat to cherished notions of sovereignty and self-determination, undermines the autonomy of local communities, and degrades the environment in the pursuit of endless economic growth. Needless to say, there is also considerable room in the middle occupied by those who regard the more extravagant claims on both sides of the debate with scepticism.

While few aspects of globalization have escaped critical scrutiny, economic globalization has been a focal point of concern. In particular, international economic institutions have captured much of the attention of anti-globalization activists. In recent years, the WTO has been a favourite target. Critics charge the organization with promoting the free flow of goods, capital, and services at the expense of all other values: local autonomy, environmental integrity, and fair labour practices. International financial institutions have also come under attack. Critiques of the International Bank for Reconstruction and Development (more commonly known as the World

[50] D. Held and A. McGrew, 'The Great Globalization Debate: An Introduction,' in D. Held and A. McGrew, eds., *The Global Transformations Reader* (Cambridge: Polity Press, 2000) 1 at 3.

Bank) have focused largely on its involvement in funding environmentally destructive projects such as mega-dams and export-led agriculture (frequently characterized by monocultures and an intensive reliance on chemical inputs). Critiques of the IMF have tended to focus on the destructive effect that so-called structural adjustment programmes (SAPs) have had on the capacity of developing countries to meet the needs of their populations and protect the environment. It should also be noted that while economic globalization may be the focus of criticism, the law does not escape criticism. One of the most striking features of the globalization process is its elaborate legal architecture. In the WTO context, in particular, there is an extensive treaty framework, binding dispute settlement, and an increasingly rich body of jurisprudence. Much of the critical scrutiny brought to bear on the trade regime has focused on revealing its essentially political nature, which might be obscured by the legal trappings that make it appear neutral.

5.2 Globalization and the Environment

The relationship between globalization and the environment has been a contested topic. Some view the impact of globalization on the environment as uncertain, arguing that globalization represents both a threat to environmental integrity and a potential ally in the struggle to address environmental degradation. The emphasis on economic growth that is characteristic of mainstream globalization thought and practice is thought to be antithetical to concerns for sustainability, leading to increased resource consumption and higher levels of industrial pollution. However, economic growth itself can be seen as having environmental benefits, since it can lead to the availability of more resources for environmental protection. Moreover, increasing integration can lead to enhanced cooperation on environmental issues. Similarly, international environmental regimes can themselves be seen as instruments of global integration, representing an opportunity for the elaboration of a common agenda on issues of international concern.

Others take a more clearly negative view of globalization's impact on the environment. Martin Khor, for example, has argued that there is an inherent contradiction between the paradigms represented by economic globalization, with its emphasis on trade liberalization, on the one hand, and the approach underlying UNCED, on the other. According to Khor, '[t]he UNCED approach represents one paradigm for international relations: that of consensus-seeking, incorporating the needs of all countries (big or small), partnership in which the strong would help the weak, integration of environment and development concerns, the intervention of the state and the international community on behalf of public interest to control market forces so as to attain greater social equity and bring about more sustainable patterns of production and consumption.'[51] This vision of international cooperation to achieve sustainable development is fundamentally at odds with the globalization/trade liberalization paradigm, which is described by Khor as follows:

The approach advocates a Social Darwinian philosophy of 'each man for himself, each firm for itself, each country for itself.' In this law of the social jungle, it is the right of individuals and companies to demand freedom to seek advantage and profit and to have access to the markets and resources of other countries anywhere in the globe, to implement their right to profit. The advocates of this approach want a free-market system where the strong and 'efficient' are rewarded, and the weak or inefficient may suffer losses but in any case should fend for themselves. The paradigm advocates competition, with prizes for the winners and without the supply of a cushion to compensate the losers for their loss.[52]

5.3 Alternatives to Globalization

For many activists and scholars, resistance to globalization is about embracing the local—ensuring local self-sufficiency in terms of the production of food and other essential human needs, minimizing international trade to the extent possible, and utilizing governmental intervention in order to protect local industry. A number of those espousing these views insist that changes need to go beyond the economic sphere, and should result in a fundamental shift of the nexus of the decision-making authority to the community level. (see Chapter 5 'Levels of Environmental Governance'). For example, the Living Democracy Movement, which was founded in 1999 by Vandana Shiva, is based on the idea of communities reclaiming sovereignty over natural resources and, in particular, of resisting the corporatization of critical human needs such as water and biological diversity. Shiva notes that this process calls for a reinvention of sovereignty—a theme that resonates throughout the anti-globalization movement:

The reinvention of sovereignty has to be based on the reinvention of the state so that the state is made accountable to the people. Sovereignty cannot reside only in centralized state structures, nor does it disappear when the protective functions of the state with respect to its people start to wither away. A renewed national sovereignty needs empowered communities which assign functions to the state for their protection—such is the basis of a new partnership between state and community.[53]

Others have taken a different tack, arguing in favour of globalization of a different variety. A prominent example is Richard Falk, who advocates 'globalization from

---

[51] M. Khor, 'Effects of Globalization on Sustainable Development after UNCED' (1997) 81/82 Third World Resurgence.   [52] *Ibid*.

[53] V. Shiva, 'The Living Democracy Movement: Alternatives to the Bankruptcy of Globalization,' in W.F. Fisher and T. Ponniah, eds., *Another World Is Possible: Popular Alternatives to Globalization at the World Social Forum* (London: Zed Books, 2003) 115 at 120.

below', a grassroots movement for global social and economic justice, as opposed to 'globalization from above', the traditional, elite-driven drive for economic growth to the exclusion of other values.[54] It is not globalization *per se* that is problematic, in other words, but its articulation within the current ideological climate, which is hostile to social democracy. From this perspective, some have argued against the use of the 'anti-globalization' label for the broad-based movement that resists the current model of globalization and have proposed as an alternative the term 'global justice movement', which would define it in terms of what it espouses instead of what it rejects.

On one level, there might be said to be a contradiction between a focus on local autonomy and global networks. The potential tension is apparent in the work of the World Social Forum (WSF), a forum for a discussion of globalization issues and a major actor in the global justice movement. One commentator notes that the WSF can be seen in two different ways: as an 'example of an emerging institution that may embody seeds of global democracy' or as a forum that 'provides a space for actors who may construct democratic projects in different contexts, both local and global.'[55] The WSF itself emphasizes the latter. As its name indicates, it is not intended to function as a formal organization but rather as a body to create opportunities for the discussion of common concerns and the formulation of strategies. Its Charter of Principles describes it as follows:

The World Social Forum is an open meeting place for reflective thinking, democratic debate of ideas, formulation of proposals, free exchange of experiences and inter-linking for effective action, by groups and movements of civil society that are opposed to neo-liberalism and to domination of the world by capital and any form of imperialism, and are committed to building a global society of fruitful relationships among human beings and between humans and the Earth.[56]

The WSF sees local autonomy and global solidarity as mutually supportive. Its stance reflects the fact that calls for an alternative system of global governance on the part of many global justice activists are radically different from mainstream proposals for better integration of potentially competing interests such as trade, environment, and development. As Walden Bello notes, '[t]oday's need is not for another centralized global institution but the de-concentration and decentralization of institutional power and the creation of a pluralistic system of institutions and organizations interacting with one another, guided by broad and flexible agreements and understandings.'[57]

---

[54] R. Falk, 'Resisting "Globalization-from-Above" through "Globalization-from-Below,"' in B.K. Gills, ed., *Globalization and the Politics of Resistance* (London: MacMillan, 2000) 46.

[55] T. Teivainen, 'The World Social Forum and Global Democratisation: Learning from Porto Alegre' (2002) 23 Third World Q. 621 at 624.

[56] See World Social Forum Charter of Principles, Principle 1, reproduced in Fisher and Ponniah, see note 53 above at 354.

[57] W. Bello, 'International Organizations and the Architecture of World Power,' in Fisher and Ponniah, see note 53 above at 287.

6 ENVIRONMENTAL JUSTICE

Like anti-globalization/global justice, environmental justice began as a grassroots social movement and has come to be the subject of considerable academic debate and commentary in recent years. Environmental justice has posed a fundamental challenge to mainstream environmentalism, which it has criticized for being preoccupied with the concerns of the privileged members of society and for being inattentive to issues of race, class, and gender. This section provides an overview of the origins, fundamental principles, and international dimensions of the concept of environmental justice.

6.1 Origins of Environmental Justice

The environmental justice movement originated in the United States, and grew out of a series of local struggles regarding exposure to environmental hazards in the late 1970s and 1980s. One of the most publicized examples was the battle of the residents of Love Canal, a neighbourhood in Niagara Falls, New York, which was to be relocated after significant health problems led to the discovery that the community had been built in close proximity to a toxic waste dump. Another incident highlighted the racial dimension of environmental vulnerability and was critical in galvanizing a movement for environmental justice. This event involved a mass protest against a decision to bury a large amount of PCB-contaminated soil in Warren County, North Carolina, which was a largely African-American community. Following the Warren County protests, a series of studies were carried out to research the connection between race and exposure to environmental hazards. A landmark study by the United Church for Christ Commission on Racial Justice, published in 1987,[58] indicated that race was the single most significant factor in the citing of hazardous waste facilities, and asserted that communities with significant minority populations were being targeted for such facilities. The Reverand Dr. Benjamin Chavis, co-author of the report, coined the term 'environmental racism' to refer to this phenomenon.[59]

6.2 Principles of Environmental Justice

While grassroots organizations began to organize around specific local problems, it did not take long for broader connections to be made. Robert Bullard, a leading

---

[58] United Church for Christ Commission on Racial Justice, *Toxic Waste and Race in the United States: A National Report on the Racial and Socioeconomic Characteristics of Communities with Hazardous Wastes Sites* (New York: Public Data Access, 1987).

[59] See generally R.J. Lazarus, 'Environmental Racism! That's What It Is' (2000) 1 U. Ill. L. Rev. 255.

scholar and activist in this movement,[60] has noted: 'The environmental justice framework incorporates other social movements that seek to eliminate harmful practices such as discrimination in housing, land use, industrial planning, health care and sanitation services. The impact of redlining, economic disinvestment, infrastructure decline, deteriorating housing, lead poisoning, industrial pollution, poverty and unemployment are not unrelated problems if one lives in an urban ghetto or barrio, rural hamlet, or on a reservation.'[61] Networks of activists began to form, culminating in the first National People of Color Environmental Leadership Summit, which was held in Washington, DC, in 1991. The summit adopted a statement of Principles of Environmental Justice,[62] which have come to be regarded as the 'ideological bedrock' of the environmental justice movement.[63]

The principles address a wide range of issues and seem to reflect an attempt to claim a place for environmental justice within the environmental movement while, at the same time, challenging mainstream environmentalism and demanding that it be reconceptualized. The first principle emphasizes ecological integrity: 'Environmental justice affirms the sacredness of Mother Earth, ecological unity and the interdependence of all species, and the right to be free from ecological destruction.' Immediately following, however, is a reference to the rallying cry for community organizations involved in the movement: 'Environmental justice demands that public policy be based on mutual respect and justice for all peoples, free from any form of discrimination or bias.' The principles that follow reflect the same balance. There are references to general environmental principles such as the need for 'ethical, balanced and responsible uses of land' and 'education . . . which emphasizes social and environmental issues,' along with calls for the rights of workers to safe and healthy work environments and 'the fundamental right to political, economic and environmental self-determination of all peoples.' While the scope of the principles is deliberately broad, potentially covering the entire range of environmental issues, the issues specifically mentioned are those associated with the history of the movement, particularly hazardous wastes, radioactive materials, and toxic substances. The focus is generally on the public sphere, yet the principles conclude with a reference to individual responsibility, asserting that '[e]nvironmental justice requires that we, as individuals, make personal and consumer choices to consume as little of Mother Earth's resources and to produce as little waste as possible' and going on to state that we must challenge and reprioritize our lifestyles in order to ensure the health of the natural world for present and future generations.

---

[60] See, e.g., R.D. Bullard, *Dumping in Dixie: Race, Class and Environmental Quality* (Boulder, CO: Westview Press, 1990).

[61] R.D. Bullard, 'Leveling the Playing Field through Environmental Justice' (1998–9) 23 Vt. L. Rev. 453 at 454.

[62] Reproduced in R. Hofrichter, ed., *Toxic Struggles: The Theory and Practice of Environmental Justice* (Philadelphia: New Society Publishers, 1993) at 237.

[63] J. Agyeman, R.D. Bullard, and B. Evans, 'Towards Just Sustainabilities: Perspectives and Possibilities,' in J. Agyeman, R.D. Bullard, and B. Evans, eds., *Just Sustainabilities: Development in an Unequal World* (Cambridge, MA: MIT Press, 2003) 323 at 326.

6.3 Comparative and International Dimensions of Environmental Justice: Environmentalism of the Poor

Environmental justice can be seen not only as a shift in the evolution of the US environmental movement but also as an example of what Ramachandra Guha and Juan Martinez-Alier have called the 'environmentalism of the poor'—a form of environmentalism reflected in Southern movements in which 'issues of ecology are often interlinked with questions of human rights, ethnicity and distributive justice.'[64] Parallels have been drawn between the US movement and movements in other countries, such as the rubber tappers in Brazil and the Chipko movement in India, in which struggles for environmental integrity and for social justice are seen as being fundamentally connected. In other countries, such as South Africa in the post-Apartheid era, the language of environmental justice itself has become an important theme in public discourse regarding the environment.

At the international level, attempts have been made to understand South-North environmental relations in terms of the environmental justice paradigm. Perhaps the closest analogy can be drawn in the context of the international trade in hazardous wastes, in which the development of international standards was largely driven by developing countries and NGOs. A series of well-publicized attempts to ship toxic wastes to various parts of the developing world in the 1980s heightened the concern that as environmental standards grew more stringent and disposal costs rose in the North, the South would increasingly come to be a dumping ground for Northern waste. The African nations were particularly vocal in calling for an outright ban on the export of hazardous wastes from North to South, and were the most willing to link the dumping of toxic wastes to the historical legacy of colonialism and exploitation. When the Basel Convention on the Control of Transboundary Movements of Hazardous Wastes and Their Disposal ended up regulating rather than banning such exports, a regional agreement instituting such a ban for Africa was negotiated. The Basel Action Network (BAN), an activist group working on toxics issues, specifically invokes environmental justice as a basis of its work. It describes itself as confronting 'the issues of environmental justice at a macro level, preventing disproportionate dumping of the world's toxic waste and pollution on our global village's poorest residents.'

Recently, the US movement has come to view climate change through an environmental justice lens. At the World Conference against Racism (WCAR), which was held in Durban, South Africa, in 2001, a number of representatives of US environmental organizations criticized their government for its decision to withdraw from the Kyoto Protocol to the UN Framework Convention on Climate Change, characterizing this decision as an act of environmental racism because those most

---

[64] R. Guha and J. Martinez-Alier, *Varieties of Environmentalism: Essays North and South* (London: Earthscan, 1997) at 18.

vulnerable to climate change are 'disproportionately people in the global South and poor people, people of color, and Indigenous peoples of the global North.'[65] In 2002, 28 US environmental justice, climate justice, religious, policy, and advocacy groups united to form a coalition known as the Environmental Justice and Climate Change Initiative, in order to lobby the US government to take action on climate change. In keeping with the environmental justice mandate, the initiative not only promotes alternatives that reduce greenhouse gas emissions but also emphasizes the need for governmental action targeted at assisting the communities most affected by climate change. Arguably, this is an important shift in emphasis for the environmental justice movement. While the international dimension of environmental justice was an early theme in the movement and is reflected in the Principles of Environmental Justice themselves, climate change as an issue provides a broader context in which to explore notions of the relationship between social justice and sustainability.

On this point, some commentators have expressed scepticism about the environmental justice movement's assumption that environmental sustainability and social justice are always compatible objectives, and have argued that the environmental justice movement has largely focused on the equitable distribution of environmental risks rather than the elimination of those risks.[66] Others, while acknowledging that local groups have frequently focused on opposition to the location of particular projects or facilities in their communities, point out that this is largely the result of pragmatism rather than principle. As many have argued, environmental justice is not about communities asserting 'not in my backyard'—the classic phenomenon—but about 'not in anybody's backyard'. Similarly, environmental justice advocates reject the notion that there is a tension between development and environmental integrity. Bullard has pointed out: 'Poor people and poor communities are given a false choice of "no jobs and no development" versus "risky low-paying jobs and pollution."'[67] While it may be idealistic in its demands for a fundamental restructuring of economic and social structures to reflect social justice and a harmonious relationship with nature, environmental justice emphasizes that these two objectives, while not necessarily causally linked, are morally inextricable.

7 CONCLUSION

The preceding survey highlights an interesting paradox. Although there are a number of critical approaches that are relevant to international environmental law and policy, it appears that international environmental law has generated relatively little

[65] Solidarity Statement on Environmental Justice and Climate Change, September 2001 [copy on file with author].

[66] A. Dobson, 'Social Justice and Environmental Sustainability: Ne'er the Twain Shall Meet?' in Agyeman, Bullard, and Evans, see note 63 above, at 83.   [67] Bullard, see note 61 above at 478.

critical work within its own disciplinary boundaries. This may be due to a number of factors. International environmental law itself emerged as a critique of traditional international law and of its emphasis on rigid notions of territorial sovereignty and the freedom to exploit resources without regard for long-term environmental consequences. It may be that critical energy has been channelled into this broader task. In addition, the weakness of many international environmental law norms may have immunized them from critical scrutiny, by keeping the focus on how to strengthen them. Finally, the highly technical nature of the field may make it difficult to generate critical work. Many scholars are preoccupied with analysing and explaining its technical complexities rather than deconstructing its theoretical underpinnings. Regardless of the reason, the field has remained, to a remarkable extent, as a 'critique-free zone'. Critical approaches have doubtless had some influence, but they have largely remained on the periphery of scholarly engagement.

This is a missed opportunity for a number of reasons. First, the approaches considered in this chapter can enhance our understanding of many of the changes that have already taken place within the discipline, such as the heightened concern about gender equality and South-North equity reflected in instruments such as the Rio Declaration on Environment and Development. Second, and even more importantly, these approaches offer important insights into both new and old challenges that face international environmental law at the present time: balancing environment and development, creating mechanisms to ensure that globalization does not impose an ever-increasing environmental burden, and ensuring that environmental risks and benefits are equitably distributed, among others. These are interrelated issues, as recognized by activists who draw on a variety of critical approaches to inform their work. Vandana Shiva, for example, describes the Living Democracy Movement as 'simultaneously an ecology movement, an anti-poverty movement, a recovery of the commons movement, a deepening of democracy movement, a peace movement.'[68]

Finally, while there is no lack of tools available to those interested in unpacking the presuppositions that underlie the field of international environmental law and subjecting them to critical scrutiny, it is noteworthy that these approaches do not limit themselves to critique. Instead, they provide creative and often inspiring ways of reconceptualizing our responses to environmental problems. This is not to say that there is any lack of awareness of the enormous obstacles that stand in the way. The critiques that emerge from civil society, in particular, are forced to strike a balance between envisioning alternatives and confronting the reality of entrenched power structures. However, there is little room for despair in their work. These activists may not always be optimistic about the prospects for radical change, but most seem to maintain and draw on some sense of hope for a better future. It is this sense of hope that may be the most important contribution that critical approaches can offer the discipline of international environmental law, which bears such an enormous responsibility for steering us towards a more just and sustainable international order.

[68] Shiva, see note 53 above at 120.

RECOMMENDED READING

J. Agyeman, R.D. Bullard, and B. Evans, eds., *Just Sustainabilities: Development in an Unequal World* (Cambridge, MA: MIT Press, 2003).

A. Anghie et al., eds., *The Third World and International Order: Law, Politics and Globalization* (Leiden: Martinus Nijhoff, 2003).

D. Buss and A. Manji, *International Law: Modern Feminist Approaches* (Oxford: Hart Publishing, 2005).

R. Guha and J. Martinez-Alier, *Varieties of Environmentalism: Essays North and South* (London: Earthscan, 1997).

M. Khor, *Rethinking Globalization* (London: Zed Books, 2001).

V. Shiva, *Staying Alive: Women, Ecology and Development* (London: Zed Books, 1988).

J.G. Speth, *Worlds Apart: Globalization and the Environment* (Washington: Island Press, 2003).

CHAPTER 13

ETHICS AND INTERNATIONAL ENVIRONMENTAL LAW

CHRISTOPHER D. STONE

1 ETHICS

'ETHICS' comprehends the discourse of 'right' and 'wrong', 'just' and 'unjust', 'duties' and 'rights', the morally preferable and the morally prohibited. In establishing international norms, such as those in international environmental law, one might turn to ethics for three reasons. First, as an individual (or government) engaged in the process of moral reasoning, one might be seeking guidance in identifying the morally ideal choice among the available policy alternatives: which option *ought* to be brought about?[1] Second, one might employ ethics to persuade others to endorse the same choice. Here, where ethics is employed as a discursive strategy, the arguer may find him or herself arguing from the other's principles, rather than from those the arguer would prefer. One who personally reaches vegetarianism from an animal rights perspective may seek to persuade others of this decision through utilitarian appeals, such as that rejecting meat is a means to feed more of the world's people. The third use of ethics would be to justify imposing a law or policy on others who remain unpersuaded by reason. Suppose that *we* object to *your* eating marine mammals but you (having heard us out) are not convinced. When—under what circumstances and according to what institutional arrangements—may we legitimately force our wills upon yours?[2]

Efforts to mend the global environment implicate these ethical quandaries in three ways. First, there are issues of human obligations to the non-human environment ('environmental ethics' proper). Second, there are issues of ethics among states with respect to the environment ('inter-national ethics'). Third, there are issues of ethics among generations with respect to the environment ('inter-generational ethics'). The first area can be illustrated with the question: ought we—humankind as a whole—not to kill, or cause the suffering of, whales because of something *about whales*? The second deals with questions of distribution among peoples or states: if some level of whale harvesting is justifiable, how do we allocate the allowable catch *among claimants*, for example, indigenous Arctic peoples and Japanese commercial whalers? The third deals with questions of distribution *across generations:* have we obligations to those yet to be born, and, if so, do these obligations include passing along whales to the unborn as part of their rightful legacy?

2 ENVIRONMENTAL ETHICS

As we shall use the term in this chapter, environmental ethics comes into play when we wish to evaluate environment-affecting actions on account of their impact on the

---

[1] Additionally, the actor may seek guidance on which options it ought not to perform and which lie within the zone of moral indifference.

[2] D. Bodansky, 'The Legitimacy of International Governance: A Coming Challenge for International Environmental Law' (1999) 93 A.J.I.L. 596.

environment rather than on account of their (indirect) impact on present or future humans. Thus, to contend that a forest ought not to be converted to farmland because the value of the added farmland is less than the foregone value of natural pharmaceutical inputs is not an argument of *environmental* ethics. Environmental ethics appeals to some feature of the forest (or our relation to the forest) that is not straightforwardly referenced to human use or consumption.[3] In the same way, insofar as an argument not to kill whales is based solely on the commercial value of whales as food or as amusement—measured in restaurant and whale-watching revenues—the argument is not environmental. Which elements of the 'non-human environment' deserve such an independent accounting is controversial. Among philosophers who maintain that some non-human 'things' deserve moral consideration, there is considerable disagreement as to how far 'out' from humans that concern ought to, and might coherently, run. Arguments can be found championing animals, plants, species, ecosystems, and even inanimate natural objects. Yet philosophers who would support protecting one class of objects need not, and often do not, do so for the sake of another. Those who argue for the intrinsic value of species do not always speak up for individual members and vice-versa.

To stake out a position for any of these things—to convince us that we should conserve a forest ecosystem at the sacrifice of our own well-being (less farmland)—is, of course, intellectually challenging. The environmental ethicist faces all of the obstacles that confront the proponent of conventional inter-human ethics, starting with the epistemological basis of propositions about 'rights' and 'wrongs'. How can one prove to a sceptic that it is 'wrong' to lie? The proof gets no easier when the victim is a tree.

Environmental ethics is constrained from the start because many of the epistemological 'resources' with which conventional, anthropocentric ethics have been composed are unavailable to the environmental ethicist. Some philosophers have grounded human morality in the various languages of games, cooperation, and expectations of reciprocity. Yet, if saving lions is to be justified, it cannot be on the expectation (the Androcles fable comes to mind) that any lion we may rescue will return the favour. Nor are persons and lions—let alone trees—roughly equal in power with us—a crucial condition of justice according to Hume. At the other extreme, appeals to altruism—sacrifice that carries no prospect of cooperative gain—do not provide a good grounding either. The standard philosophical moves to justify and motivate benevolence appeal to empathetic thought experiments: How would you feel if you were in Jones's shoes (and someone did that to you)? Even if we can, with some stretch, put ourselves in the hooves of a horse, there seems to be no way we can put ourselves in the banks of a river, pondering how it would feel to be dammed. Nor does it appear helpful to ask (along the lines popularized by John Rawls) what rules would we accept if, from behind a veil of ignorance, we did not know whether we would be born as a human or a bat. What would we want if we were to be born bats? And then there is a whole barrage of standard criticisms. If an

---

[3] See section 2.1 in this chapter.

x cannot take an interest in its own well-being, why should we take any interest in it? Does smallpox have moral standing? If a gazelle has rights, are we obliged to muzzle lions?

In the face of such obstacles, it is tempting to dismiss the whole exercise as futile and academic. However, to do this would be wrong. The fact is that issues of environmental ethics are already rising, inescapably, across the whole area of international environmental law. I do not mean merely that non-anthropocentric propositions have worked their way into 'soft law', for example, the 1982 World Charter for Nature's declaration that 'every form of life is unique, warranting respect regardless of its worth to man.' Consider the following contemporary controversies:

- Under the International Convention for the Regulation of Whaling, should the current moratorium on commercial whaling be extended, even for species (such as the minke) that are in no way threatened?
- Under the Agreement on Trade-Related Aspects of Intellectual Property Rights, should a World Trade Organization member be permitted to refuse recognition of patents on forms of life?
- Under the Convention on Biological Diversity (CBD) and other conservation treaties, which species (and 'mix' of life) are to be prioritized in the face of conflict?
- Under the various area and habitat set-aside conventions, which terrestrial and oceanic areas should be 'specially protected'? If we go beyond privileging the life of potential 'use'-value to humans, should we single out areas with the 'most' life, most 'higher' life, or 'rarer' life forms?
- Under the General Agreement on Tariffs and Trades, should a member be permitted to block the import of furs from animals caught in painful leg traps?
- Under the United Nations Convention on the Law of the Sea, how stringently (and at what cost) should fishing gear be restricted to protect non-commercial by-catch, such as turtles and albatrosses?

These are among the real-world questions that one might look to environmental ethicists to illuminate. What guidance can they in fact provide? In general, efforts to introduce a moral accounting for the environment have appealed to one of three foundations. The first is a variant on *homocentric* ethics. As I have remarked, in their most common expressions, appeals to human welfare ('if you do not kill whales, there will be more whales to eat in the long run') are not environmental ethics arguments, strictly speaking. But, there is one strategy that, while working within a welfarist framework, does seek to expand our accounting for the environment. While, in the final analysis it accepts our preferences (and is therefore homocentric), it does so only after modifying our preferences through environment-focused reasoning. The second is *ecocentric* ethics (environmental ethics proper), which seeks to temper our impact on non-human life and the environment on the basis of some 'good' or value that these things intrinsically (in some accounts, 'inherently') are supposed to possess—human welfare aside. The third is *human ideal*-regarding ethics, under which enjoying the environment or treating it with sensitivity is viewed as transforming us into better (as distinct from *happier*) persons.

To continue with the subject of whales as an illustration, suppose that the issue is whether to retain the moratorium on commercial whaling. An environmentalist adopting the first strategy would claim that we must weigh not only the value that people *do* place on the existence of whales (through markets and contingent valuation), but also the value that people *would* place if they thought about the matter *rightly*. The second strategy is to argue that we ought not to kill (or cause the suffering of) whales because whales have a moral right to life and to be free of unjustified pain. To adopt the third approach is to embellish the idea that, given what we know about whales, the killing of whales (not in self-defence) debases us as persons— violates, perhaps, a duty to our better selves. Let us look at these three frameworks and the issues they pose more closely.

2.1 Human Welfare-Regarding Environmental Ethics

The first foundational strategy adopts the biases of an anthropocentric framework, but assumes that what we are willing to give up for protecting non-human Nature potentially inflates (or deflates) with moral deliberations exogenous to, and prior to, the utility calculations. People asked to contingently value a whale (or its species)— 'what would you be willing to sacrifice to assure the continuing life of a/the whale?'—are apt to revise their preferences upon reflection on morally salient features: the intelligence and social relations of whales, the unique evolutionary twist they represent as terrestrial mammals that returned to the sea, and so on. In fact, much of the environmental ethics literature is dedicated to promoting just such an inflation.

There are several rubrics into which an expansive welfarist might feed these considerations. These include pointing out the market failures that leave the most uncontroversial benefits unaccounted for, such as the positive externalities of trees as carbon dioxide sequesters. In addition, the ethicist may seek to force the public to revise the value it has been placing on natural resources, emphasizing the 'existence value' (what we are prepared to pay, collectively, just for the satisfaction of knowing that x exists); the 'option value' (what we are prepared to pay for the option to have x on hand in our futures); and the 'legacy value' (what we are prepared to pay to include x as part of our legacy for future generations). The environmental ethicist may maintain that these evaluations need not be accepted as 'given', as determined by immediate polling, but that they are variables within the reach of moral argument. In this manner, human preferences are conclusive, but the burden of environmental ethics is to 'educate' humankind through enlightening discourse. I am not sure that it is possible to confine the range from which 'educative' appeals can be launched. An analysis of the *Journal of Environmental Ethics* reveals a broad orbit, from Christian spirituality to eco-feminism and the elaborations of particular mainstream philosophers.[4]

2.2 Direct Environment-Regarding Ethics

Many environmentalists believe that human-centred ethics, even an expansive welfarist vision, do not go far enough in protecting Nature, and are based on morally flawed—even arrogant—premises. These writers maintain that at least some non-humans (and perhaps the biosphere as a whole) deserve moral consideration in their own right—in the words of the 1982 World Charter for Nature, 'regardless of [their] worth to man.' If *x* is deemed worthy of moral consideration in its own right, then the question is not what humans *would* pay for *x*'s continued existence, even those whose preferences are well 'educated,' but what (if it is acceptable to employ a currency metric at all) they *ought to* pay. Efforts to frame obligations on direct respect for nature quickly encounter at least two major conceptual challenges. The first involves foundation—on what basis do we have a *prima facie* moral obligation towards non-human *things*? The second involves prioritization—assuming that we have *prima facie* obligations to both *x* and *y*, what are we to do in the case of conflict?

2.2.1 *Foundational Challenge*

Many would consider animals to present the easiest case for moral considerableness in the non-human world. If the crux of morality is to minimize the infliction of pain, then, as J. Bentham puts it, 'the question [of including animals in the moral realm] is not, Can they reason? nor Can they speak, but *Can they suffer?*'[5] Strictly speaking, Bentham's reasoning would not endow an animal with 'rights' (for the status even of human rights is uncertain under utilitarianism), but would enter its pleasures and pains along with the pleasures and pains of every other sentient creature in making the relevant utility calculations. Balancing the pain of an animal against the pleasures of people is knotty business. After all, how do we weigh the suffering of a leg-trapped animal against the pleasure of the fur wearer? Yet, even if there is no precise answer, merely in attempting to account for the suffering, we are at least rejecting the judgement (with Descartes) that animals are 'like the clock'—beyond conscious awareness, much less morally considerable.

---

[4] See C.D. Stone, 'Do Morals Matter? The Influence of Ethics on Courts and Congress in Shaping U.S. Environmental Policies' (2003) 37 U.C. Davis L. Rev. 13 at 42 (Table).

[5] J. Bentham, *Introduction to the Principles of Morals and Legislation* (1789; reprinted Oxford: Clarendon Press, 1996 (edited by J.H. Burns and H.L.A. Hart)) chapter 17 [italics in orginal]. Bentham in this passage refers to the animal's 'rights.'

However, the application of utilitarianism to non-humans remains problematical when we advance beyond the simple Benthamite pleasure-pain version to contemporary preference-satisfying modes. Granted that there are actions that we can judge to cause an animal pain, with what confidence can we say it prefers one basket of goods over another? Imagine, for example, that the issue is not harpooning whales but, by the construction of an oil-loading facility, simply dislodging them from their traditional migratory path into a more roundabout route.[6] Suppose we regard their migratory history as having endowed the whales with a prescriptive easement. Interpersonal morality and the legal system in its ordinary operations can draw on a wide range of devices, underwritten by preference-oriented utilitarianism, to identify suitable adjustments when a property right is targeted for public 'taking'. If an easement is worth $100,000 to the owner and $200,000 to the public (which needs it to operate the oil facility), the parties, if they wish to avoid a judicial determination, will presumably strike a deal at a price between those figures. However, even if there is a guardian to speak for the whales, how is he or she to know what the whale stock would regard as compensation—what amount of squid 'chummed' along the alternate route—would give the whales satisfaction equivalent to their lost easement?

Notice that the problem illustrated here is not the more common charge that assigning rights to non-humans is incoherent. The problem is that, if we do assign them rights, it is hard to preserve the utility-sensitive flexibility that survives the allocation of rights among humans—who can continuously 'correct course', mutually improving their well-being through trade. Or, if the entitlement is taken non-consensually (deliberately or accidentally), judicial awards can restore the loser to something like the *status quo ante* level of well-being. Duplicating these manoeuvres with non-humans is, however, problematical.

To say that a rights-based protection of non-humans is problematical is not to say it cannot be tried. We protect the rights of the unborn, of infants, and of senile persons, even when constructing their preferences is somewhat conjectural.[7] And those who strongly support the rights of non-human entities are not likely to be put off by the inconveniences. Moreover, to subscribe to rights for, say, animals is not a commitment to rights that are co-extensive with human rights—a position that would include some civil rights that are simply inapposite, such as the rights to worship, vote, and speak. Indeed, even those who deny animals a right to live frequently endorse a right to be free from undue pain, as evidenced by the position of the International Whaling Commission (IWC) already alluded to—killing whales is acceptable, but the pain wrought should be minimized.

---

[6] The analysis is complicated by the risk that the forced detour might extinguish the stock, but let us assume that the stock survives.

[7] e.g., *Superintendent of Belchertown State Sch. v. Saikewicz*, 370 N.E. 2d 417 (Mass. Supreme Court, 1977) (upholding the lower court's decision to withhold chemotherapy from a severely retarded patient on the conjecture that he would have suffered from uncomprehending fear if subjected to chemotherapy).

When we move away from animals in the direction of plants, neither version of utilitarianism—pleasure-pain or the preference variant—is available for guidance. Indeed, when we turn to plants, other non-utility, rights-based factors commonly called upon are also unavailable, such as the requirement that a rights-bearer 'take an interest in its life' or have 'a conscious life plan'. Nonetheless, plants share with all living things a good in the sense of having a life. Can having a life (without pain or conscious preferences) be the basis of a coherent moral claim? While a weed, lacking consciousness, does not 'take an interest' in someone not spreading Roundup on its leaves, it is certainly not incoherent to say that our doing so is against the weed's well-being. (That, after all, is why the product sells.) This has led some to argue that, just as there is a certain sort of 'speciesism' in licensing human over non-human animals, so, too it is illegitimately 'speciesist' to deny plants *prima facie* moral standing along with all of the other teleological centres of life.[8] Perhaps. However, even if we were to agree that life, *per se*, gives *prima facie* moral standing in principle, it is quite another matter to give the life of a weed substantial weight in the face of conflicting claims on the weed, such as those of the encroaching cornstalk. These conundrums may explain why, at present, with the exception of certain show-case animals, neither the lives nor the 'natural' unfoldings of individual life forms (such as an individual toad or tree) have marshalled much protection under international law.

While the movement to endow moral status on individual plants, even animals, remains peripheral on the international level, the protection of groups—species, ecosystems, portfolios of biodiversity—is well advanced, as evidenced by many treaties including the CBD, the Convention on Trade in Endangered Species of Fauna and Flora (CITES), and the Convention for the Conservation of Antarctic Living Marine Resources (CCALMR). This relative solicitude for the group over the individual raises the question on what basis do we favour species? Species lack even more transparently than individuals in the characteristics ordinarily deemed pertinent for moral considerateness, such as the capacity to feel pain, to suffer, to have a life plan, and so on. Indeed, the very concept of a species might be considered too gossamer a foundation for intrinsic ethical concern. The classification of life into species reflects human judgement—species are not, in the philosophical lingo, 'natural kinds'—and there is often controversy marking the line where one species leaves off and another begins, particularly in the face of continuing evolution.

Those who would extend moral status to species rejoin, however, by portraying the species as the logically prior entity—the individual member 'represents (re-presents) a species in each new generation.' The individual is thus portrayed as a mere token of a type, the type being considered more important than the token. While the moral considerateness of species, in their own right, is thus arguable, it is far from clear that most species-protecting conventions require it. Indeed, the

---

[8] P. Taylor, *Respect for Nature: A Theory on Environmental Ethics* (Princeton, NJ: Princeton University Press, 1986).

earliest migratory bird treaty (1868) tips off its frankly utilitarian provenance in its title: Birds Useful to Agriculture.[9] Other treaties conserve species that less transparently service human needs, but whose survival could probably be cost-justified to the 'educated' utilitarian.

Providing an ethical basis for biodiversity conservation provides a particularly ambiguous challenge. While the preamble to the CBD pays ecocentric homage to 'the intrinsic value of biodiversity,' much of the text refers to 'biological resources' defined to include 'genetic resources, organisms or parts thereof, populations, or any other biotic component of ecosystems with actual or potential use or value for humanity.' Indeed, the convention's definition of biodiversity, the variability among living organisms, is hard to pin down (what is variability and is it not always changing?), much less to characterize as something to which 'intrinsic value' can be assigned.

2.2.2 *Question of Priorities*

In the course of examining foundational questions, the ethical literature should, hopefully, sort out the ontological conundrums already alluded to, whether the unit of moral concern is to be the species of ant, the ant DNA, the ant's habitat, the anthill, the individual ant, the encompassing ecosystem—or all of them perhaps in different ways. Yet it is not enough to carve up the world into those things deemed to be morally considerable. What are we to do in the case of conflict? Do we favour the rare species of lower animal over the less rare but 'higher' one—the species that contributes most to the biomass or energy flow of the ecosystem? Surveying existing international agreements, one can infer a priority for charismatic mega fauna and intelligence creatures 'like us'. However, to defend these psychological leanings on moral grounds is another matter. For example, even if we were to accept the most extravagant claims about whales having 'higher than human intelligence',[10] it would not follow that we would thereby have more stringent duties to whales than to wallabies. Indeed, within inter-personal morality, the more demanding duties are reserved for those with the least intelligence—infants, the incompetent, and the senile. Whales, someone might argue, can fend for themselves.

Notwithstanding the apparent inevitability of ranking some life ahead of others— to acknowledge a 'great chain of being'—much of the literature goes off in the other, less helpful, direction, aiming to delegitimate prioritization. A dominant strategy among scholars is to champion a unique crucial feature—sentience, life, consciousness, or whatever—and to maintain that all things that possess that feature merit equal consideration. Thus, Peter Singer famously argues that sentience is a sufficient condition, and any effort to treat any homo sapiens differently than any other species in regard to pain infliction is 'speciesist'.[11] If there is to be no suffering for man, then

---

[9] S. Lyster, *International Wildlife Law* (Cambridge: Grotius Publications, 1985) at 63.
[10] A. D'Amato and S.K. Chopra, 'Whales: Their Emerging Right to Life' (1991) 85 A.J.I.L. 21.
[11] P. Singer, *All Animals are Equal* (Englewood Cliffs: Prentice Hall, 1989).

there should be no (human-caused) suffering for mice. To the biocentrist, for whom even privileging sentience smacks of human self-pleading, all life demands respect equally. These positions, certainly the biocentrist's, seem impossible to maintain literally—if no living thing is fair game for us, not even soy beans, then we will expire. Indeed, the principle of non-interference with life's unfolding (not merely with its existence) can lead philosophers to condemn espaliering fruit trees as immoral.

The impracticality of such biocentrism seems blatant; even the 'logic' seems strained. To grant that life and sentience are morally significant (and that all humans have them) does not entail that either is a sufficient condition for undifferentiated moral concern. Indeed, the assumption is odd, considering that conventional morality is full of differentiations among persons—duties to strangers versus duties to kin, for example. If, in the course of looking after our own security and subsistence, we find that we have to eradicate either a bee or a bear, it is hard to believe that the only legitimate method of choice is the flip of a coin.[12] Some writers have tried to backtrack from indefensible advances by speaking of *prima facie*, not absolute, obligations and burdens of proof. Thus, Paul Taylor, who maintains that humans have no greater inherent worth than any other living thing, is prepared to introduce a slew of human-favouring 'principles' that would, for example, underwrite the construction of a library at the cost of a termite colony. In other words, the escape valve principles appear loose enough to make the whole premise unhelpful. Some have taken the opposite tack, maintaining that speciesism may be 'closer to the moral truth than is species egalitarianism.'[13] Yet, if so, we need to go further in identifying the principles on which a morally acceptable speciesism is to be built. Its challenge is not only to differentiate among species but also to arbitrate the many tensions between species and individual members. To preserve a species may require actions detrimental to the individual, such as culling and imprisoning breeding stock in zoos. Why sacrifice one rather than the other?

2.3 Human Character/Ideal-Regarding Environmental Ethics

A third foundational approach is to examine and exploit, rather than reject, the specialness of humans. After all, as David Schmidtz observes, the whole premise of our having an obligation to gazelles that lions do not have is that we are unlike lions, not that we are like gazelles.[14] In this view, our duties to other creatures and to Nature are grounded on aspirations that are distinctly human. Rather than to address and revise the calculations, as per the first strategy, the ethicist seeks in this scenario to address

---

[12] The point is well elaborated in D. Schmidtz, *Are All Species Equal, in Environmental Ethics: What Really Matters, What Really Works* (New York: Oxford University Press, 2002) at 96.

[13] *Ibid.* at 99.   [14] *Ibid.* at 100.

and revise the calculator. An illustration is Immanuel Kant's declaration that '[he] who is cruel to animals becomes hard also in his dealings with men.'[15] One may feel uncomfortable with the idea that we ought not to kick a dog for our own sakes rather than for the dog's. However, particularly in cases where pain is not available as a moral guide-post, the human ideal foundation explains intuitions otherwise hard to ground. Consider why one might rue as evil the 'wanton, capricious squashing of a beetle ... [or] wild flower in the wild.'[16] Kant's take may explain the moral intuitions that Bentham cannot. The moral repugnance at traditional 'rattlesnake round-ups' in some parts of the United States, in which the torment and slaughter of snakes is accompanied by feasts and celebration, has less to do with the pain of the snakes than with the brutishness, arrogance, and ecological stupidity of the perpetrators. For a similar illustration from international environmental law, consider the Antarctic Treaty's rules against sullying the landscape with evidence of human presence.[17] We *could* attribute the motivation to straightforward utility—the cost of trash collection may be less than that which those who do not want to encounter trash would be willing to pay to have it removed. Yet I suspect that something of a human ideal is involved— a repugnance more against the sullying of humankind's character than against the sullying of the environment.

Even if we accept this reasoning, however, the challenge of prioritization cannot be dodged. An action that ill-treats something only 'sullies' our character if it is an action we ought not to do, and, for that reason, a prior determination of the moral status of the thing would appear to be critical. Why is it 'sullying' to drown sea turtles in shrimp nets but not so to eat shrimp? Certainly, in the realm of international diplomacy, an argument based on (what will inevitably be) one state's notion of 'good character' is going to be more controversial, and less effective, than arguments based on, for example, homocentric welfare claims.

3 Ethics among People with Respect to the Environment

Probably less of international environmental diplomacy is concerned with the rights *of* Nature than with the rights of people *in regard to* Nature. International ethics may even conflict with obligations to Nature. For example, poor states

---

[15] I. Kant, *Lectures on Ethics*, translated by L. Infield (London: Methuen and Company, 1930) at 240.
[16] J. Feinberg, 'Legal Moralism and Free-Floating Evils' (1980) 61 Pac. Phil. Q. 133.
[17] For example, Annex III to the Protocol to the Antarctic Treaty (Madrid) provides that '[t]he amount of wastes produced or disposed of in the Antarctic Treaty area shall be reduced as far as practicable so as to minimise impact on the Antarctic environment and to minimise interference with the

complain about trade 'sticks', such as import bans on turtle-unsafe shrimp, that are deployed to strong-arm poorer states into raising their standards.[18] Ethical disputes among states may take either corrective justice or distributive justice forms (see Chapter 27 'Equity'). In the context of climate change, it has taken both. First, there is the corrective argument that certain states, the historical emitters of greenhouse gases (the early industrializers), are obliged to bear the weight of clean-up costs because they are primarily to blame. Distributive justice emerges in arguments such as that all individuals have an equal right to the atmosphere and that, history aside, the richer states should shoulder the burden because they can better afford it (a position that may be buttressed by citing the rich states' lower marginal utility of the wealth expended in clean-up measures). However, all such arguments, justice based and otherwise, encounter objections at their very threshold: does morality even apply in the international arena—that is, can we even meaningfully discuss what distribution of whales is 'just' or 'fair'? The proponent must meet several objections.

First, there is the *strong realist* view that the actions of states are beyond moral evaluation or (what amounts to the same thing) that any 'rights' are mere dictates of 'might' and self-interest. A related view, *fiduciary realism*,[19] does not reject all ethics in the international sphere but maintains that what is ethical is for the national leader to consider exclusively duties to his own people and not duties to other people or to the global community at large. *Methodological individualism* criticizes the attribution of moral predicates to states not on moral, as much as on metaphysical, grounds—the action of states lies beyond right and wrong because there are, in reality, no 'state actions'. Only individuals act and are acted upon, have interests to advance or frustrate, and can be praised and blamed for polluting the atmosphere or depleting the ozone. Finally, *doctrinal cosmpolitanists* hold commitment to individualist accounts by virtue of their substantive moral positions. For example, for a utilitarian who is committed to evaluate actions by reference to their consequences on individual welfares, states and their boundaries are morally arbitrary. Thus, action should be guided by what conduces to the greatest happiness of persons, whichever side of a border they happen to be born on.

Assessing these positions is far beyond the scope of this chapter. Yet the underlying issues cannot be ignored. For example, if the methodological individualists are right, what are we to make of claims that contemporary Americans have a special burden to reduce carbon dioxide because 'the United States' emitted x tons of carbon dioxide in the nineteenth century? In the period of early industrialization, my

---

natural values of Antarctica, with scientific research and with other uses of Antarctica which are consistent with the Antarctic Treaty.' 1991 Antarctic Treaty, Annex III, Article 1.

[18] S. Charnovitz, 'Environmental Trade Sanctions and the GATT: An Analysis of the Pelly Amendment' (1994) 9 Am. U. J. Int'l L. & Pol'y 751.

[19] This paragraph benefits from A. Buchanan and D. Golove, 'Philosophy of International Law', in J. Coleman et al., eds., *Oxford Handbook of Jurisprudence and Philosophy of Law* (New York: Oxford University Press, 2002) 868.

forbears were living in rural Bessarabia, making the most modest demands on the atmosphere. Why should I be debited?[20]

One might question, moreover, the growing practice of multilateral environmental agreements to differentiate treaty obligations by holding rich and poor states to different standards.[21] This practice is understandable if one adopts the legal starting point of territorially defined states, some of which have more resources to put towards the chore of clean-up than others. Yet the reductionists are right to remind us that poverty and other markers of low welfare are the plight of persons, not of countries. Lightening the load on the poorest *countries* is a very rough approach to raising the incomes of the poorest *persons*. (Countries with low median incomes harbour very rich persons and vice-versa.)

Even if we put the reductionist objections aside and accept, if only for convenience, the framework of states and of just dealings among them, there remains the issue: how thick is the morality among states? How detailed and forceful are the edicts that it can offer? *Moral minimalism* holds that the obligations are relatively anaemic. In the views of some, what is right is keeping treaty obligations—*pacta sunt servanda*—and little else. Some free-standing moral imperatives may hover outside treaties, but these are limited to prescriptions with the broadest and hoariest backing in international practice, such as the demand that diplomats are not to be abused. When we turn to the controversies that actually abound in international environmental law, such as whether poor states should be allowed to destroy forests or adopt a carbon-heavy path for economic development, there is nowhere near the consensus on what is 'right' and 'fair' that one finds in genocide debates. China and India undoubtedly consider it unfair that the United States, historically the heaviest emitter of greenhouse gases, refuses to join the Kyoto Protocol; but the United States Senate considers it unfair for those countries, prospectively major polluters themselves, to refuse to put on paper *any* emission commitment to start *sometime* in the future. States with large volumes of biomass (a sink for carbon dioxide) consider it fair that they get credit, applied against the gas they produce, for the gas they withdraw. States whose emissions of greenhouse gases consist largely of methane and, therefore, which relate to the 'necessities' of agriculture, object to lumping their emissions in with the emissions that they associate with the 'luxury' uses of the developed world, such as transportation. It is not morally obtuse to wonder, as it would be with ethnic cleansing, which side is right. Many developing countries, even if they are willing to acknowledge global human rights, nonetheless reject a criticism of environmental abuses as nothing more than 'cultural imperialism' that threatens 'sovereign control over natural resources.'

---

[20] The question is not rhetorical: One might say I 'owe' by benefiting from life in an economy whose wealth was made possible by carbon-intensive activities that preceded my grandparents' immigration.

[21] See C.D. Stone, 'Common but Differentiated Responsibilities in International Law' (2004) 98 A.J.I.L. 276.

There is also an empirical aspect to the fairness controversy. It is practically an article of faith in the literature that fairness, or at least the perception of fairness, substantially influences countries to join environmental accords. However, the evidence is at best ambiguous.[22] Clearly, there are many instances of wealthy countries accepting a heavier burden than the poor. Yet these cases are consistent with the rich simply expressing their greater willingness to pay for environmental improvements in their own self-interest. Realist self-interest, not other-regarding morality, may explain the many treaties that provide for 'common but differentiated responsibility' among rich and poor signers.

4 Ethics among Generations with Respect to the Environment

A third foundation for environmental protection is based on the presumed claims of future generations. In the words of the Stockholm Declaration (from the 1972 United Nations Conference on the Human Environment), humankind is said to bear 'a solemn responsibility to protect and improve the environment for present and future generations.' The sentiment, echoed in many other documents, is undoubtedly regarded as a warrant for much of international environmental law, particularly because the concerns of international environmental law tend to be long term, and there is a conviction that future generations are un- or under-represented in politics and in market transactions and therefore need special legal protection (see Chapter 27 'Equity').

The argument that, absent special law, the unborn are 'voiceless' is a little misleading. The interests of the unborn work their way into the calculations of contemporaries in several ways. For one, if markets are working well, the future value of natural resources (their projected scarcity) manifests itself in present prices—it is false to suppose that present generations will deplete their stock with no accounting for their value to the unborn.[23] Markets aside, even in voting behaviour, the welfare of future persons is not outside any current generation's thinking. Each of us, during our own lifetimes, is presumably concerned for how our children's future will unfold after our

---

[22] For a sceptical view of the influence of ethics in international diplomacy, see D.G. Victor, 'The Regulation of Greenhouse Gases: Does Fairness Matter?' in F.L. Tóth, ed., *Fair Weather?* (Oxford: Earthscan, 1999) 193.

[23] Harold Hotelling demonstrated in 1931 that if markets for a non-renewable resource, such as coal, are efficient, then the owner will hold the coal *in situ* if and only if the anticipated growth in price equals or exceeds the social rate of interest. This should incline the owner to preserve or consume the asset at a pace that is responsive to future supply and demand, assuring some connection to the well-being of the unborn.

deaths, and concern for our children's well-being incorporates their concern for the welfare of their children, and so on. To look at it from another angle, each generation knows that to savage the environment is to erode the value of its own estates. These factors have been said to introduce an 'infinite horizon' in our thinking.

Even if the 'infinite horizon' argument for inter-generational harmony is a bit Panglossian, the tension between the present and the future is easily exaggerated. Most environmental amenities that we deem future persons to value are (not surprisingly) benefits to us. The whaling moratorium is not motivated, solely, by generosity for the unborn—that is, even if we stripped away the legacy value, the costs and benefits of whaling to us, the living, might well support the IWC's position. In point of fact, given life spans and the generational overlap, one has to labour to construct hypotheticals in which the interests of the unborn would be, by consensus, foursquare in conflict with (and not merely perhaps incongruent with) predominant contemporary self-interests. For example, one can imagine a massive public works project, such as a space vehicle that had to be launched now to intercept an asteroid not expected to collide with us for 200 years. In such a case *we* would bear all the costs and *they* would reap all the benefits. However, in the typical cases of international environmental concern, such as protecting the world from climate damage and preserving species, there is a generational overlapping of both costs and benefits.

Nonetheless, it is hard to deny the prospect of trans-generational externalities with a consequent skewing of costs and benefits. We can imagine a hypothetical argument from a yet unborn descendant that we should self-impose on ourselves some level of costs beyond the level that our own benefits (even including the satisfaction of contingent 'legacy value') would warrant. Viewed from an ethical perspective, what obligations do we have to the unborn to prevent such spillovers? The analysis of obligations to future generations may be sorted into three types of claims.

4.1 Temporally Remote Tort

First, one may argue that we have an obligation to avoid imposing a certain class of risks on the unborn—a duty to avoid temporally remote torts, such as widespread injury to remote progeny from a poorly contained nuclear waste facility. According to common standards of negligence law, an actor causing harm is liable if the expected value of the harm (the magnitude of loss, if it occurs, times the probability) exceeds the cost to the actor of avoiding the losses. To illustrate, suppose that by spending on containment $1,000 in excess of what is cost-beneficial to *us*, the living, one would avert a loss of $1,000,000 to our remote descendants. If we adopt the logic of the tort standard as our moral guide, it would seem that we are *prima facie* obliged to expend the $1,000.

I say *prima facie* because there are several avenues open for assessing and perhaps denying any obligation. The first is conceptual—that it is simply incoherent to have duties to an unidentifiable someone who does not (yet) exist. Yet to label duties to the unborn incoherent seems strained: estate planners create enforceable duties to the unborn as a matter of course. To deny it seems, moreover, morally dubious. Suppose that someone on the bank of a river were to launch a raft packed with unstable explosives. It hardly seems a defence that, because the current is slow and the nearest population lives far downriver, those put at risk are yet to be born and, therefore, the action is morally acceptable.

Some commentators, however, appeal to time discounting to justify some such future-casting risks, on the view that a positive rate of discount trivializes remote damages. Suppose the dynamite-laden raft is not expected to explode for 300 years. We can avert the risk by some preventive measure that will cost us $1,000. However, if we discount the expected $1,000,000 damage at 3 per cent, the present value of the loss is only $140. This line of reasoning alleges that the savings ($140) are not worth the investment ($1,000). We can pass on the risk in good conscience.

There is an expansive and knotty literature on whether any such discounting is applicable and, if so, what is the appropriate rate. Those who doubt the applicability of discounting point out that it was never designed for generation-skipping scenarios such as what climate change presents. Discounting applies when we wish to compare consuming $1 today with investing it and consuming $2 tomorrow—the idea was never to compare our consuming $1 today with someone else consuming, or being deprived of, $2 in their remote lifetimes. Some add that to discount (to apply anything other than a zero discount for future costs and benefits) is indefensibly to deny a future person's welfare the weight that we would give our own. Others have argued that if we weigh each present and future person equally, it is difficult to justify permitting ourselves anything beyond the most abstemious consumption, given the spectre of the unborn trillions to follow, whose aggregate welfare needs would arguably swamp our own.

Perhaps we can lift some of the weight of their otherwise oppressive welfare demands by making an adjustment for economic growth. Assume (1) a declining marginal utility of consumption, and (2) that each future generation will continue to be, as it has been, wealthier than its predecessor, even on a per capita basis. If so, then we might be warranted, after all, to apply a higher rate of discount to actions that will affect the remote future than we apply to, say, public works projects.[24] Yet, even if they will be richer and readier to handle losses, it is not clear—if domestic law is a moral guide—that the wrongdoer, the party who places the insecure dynamite on the raft, would be permitted to defend the tort on grounds of comparative utility, specifically, that the victims were richer than he and that they needed the wealth less urgently.

[24] However, see M. Weitzman, 'Just Keep Discounting, but . . . ,' in P.R. Portney and J.P. Weyant, eds., *Discounting and Intergenerational Equity* (Washington, DC: Resources for the Future, 1999) 23 (favouring a positive but low and declining rate based on the scepticism that the deep future productivity of capital is highly uncertain).

Even if our concern for future generations survive projections of robust economic growth, we might still decide to apply some sort of 'discount' for empathic distance. Our distant descendants are destined to be remote from us not only in time but also in culture, habits, kinship, and tastes. We might find them detestable, like grandchildren we relish cutting out of our wills. Perhaps at some point, the population will be scarcely 'human', dominated by cyborgs. As an empirical matter, valuation studies leave no doubt that people in fact attach less weight to the fate of the remote unborn than to nearer descendants. Yet defending such an empathic discounting as a moral principle is another matter. Is there any principle that justifies a plea by the launchers of the dynamite-laden raft that the downstream victims are far away, speak another tongue, and hold distasteful beliefs and, therefore, that the rate of discount should be especially high?

Of course, the arguments for being just to strangers remote in time does not precisely parallel those on behalf of contemporaries remote in space. If we undertake an activity that jeopardizes strangers in space—our contemporaries—we can proceed with the assurances that, should damage materialize, it is possible to make good *ex post*. The classic illustration in international environmental law is the *Trail Smelter* litigation, in which Canada was assessed damages on account of noxious fumes that wafted across the border into the United States (see Chapter 22 'Transboundary Impacts'). Providing for such *ex post* recovery serves both to internalize otherwise negative externalities and to achieve corrective justice. Pursuant to the same moral and economic considerations, we ought to be held no less accountable to strangers in time. Yet temporally remote torts present institutional complications. We will never know whether a nuclear site with a risk of leakage will in fact actually corrupt in 100 years or 200, and, if so, with what damage. The ordinary tort solution, which condones waiting and seeing and then settling up, is unavailable. We could, as an alternative, 'award' the future the mathematically expected loss. Yet the magnitude of that loss is highly conjectural. If, with good fortune, no damage does eventuate, our descendants will simply reap a windfall. Even if we are willing to buy into such a system, and escrow for our descendants the probable value of some harms, there is simply no way for us to assure delivery of the award. Suppose, for example, we decided to set aside a $1 billion investment earmarked for 'twenty-third century victims of twenty-first century avoidable fossil fuel use.' How could we prevent the fund from being ransacked in 50 years? Indeed, even if a literal lock-box were really sealed until the twenty-third century, there would be no way to assure that it would finally go to relieve the actual victims of our carbon profligacy rather than to gratify their chiefs.

Since the moral fine tuning of damage-based relief is unavailable, a concern for the unborn has to be executed through the rougher justice of self-imposed 'injunction'. In being unable to compensate with damages, *ex post*, we are left to identify certain acts that must be avoided, *ex ante*. There is, to begin with, the same problem with our uncontrollable immediate successors—they might just violate the injunction. And that aside, in deciding whether to issue an injunction in ordinary legal circumstances, the utility of the defendant's (our) conduct can be balanced against the plaintiff's (their) harm. Yet when conduct and harm are so disjointed in time, the weighing is almost unmanageably conjectural. Things can change dramatically. We cannot rule out that they (some time slice of them), with their technology and needs, will prefer us to have left our nuclear waste accessible rather than to dispose of it irretrievably. Or they may look back to conclude that the melting we are causing of the Arctic was a boon, with its opening of the Northwest Passage and the uncovering of new oil fields viewed as dominating the loss of Inuit and wildlife habitat (a judgement all the more likely if there are no Inuit remaining among them).

In the last analysis, therefore, even if future persons 'count', as of course they should, our obligation to shield them from tort-like behaviour appears to generate a less stringent and finely tuned review than that which we impose in our conduct towards contemporaries. Any sharp-edged Learned Hand test has to yield to something such as the 'Kew Gardens principle'—that is, if for a relatively modest cost we can avoid the high risk of serious, widespread bodily harm to others, then we have to bear the costs of reducing the risks to an acceptable level, no matter how remote the victims in time, kinship, or manner. What is 'relatively modest' and 'acceptable' are inevitably plastic. Perhaps we can project no greater risks on them than what we, behind a veil of ignorance as to which generation we would inhabit, would have permitted our predecessors to project onto us.

4.2 Sustainable Development

Much of the future generations literature is less concerned about quelling recklessly tortious behaviour, which typically connects specific culpable misconduct to specific victims, than about assuring the unborn that they receive 'their fair share'. This position emerges in the international environmental law literature under the rubric of 'sustainable development' (see Chapter 26 'Sustainable Development'). While artfully vague (an original intent was to gloss over the North-South tensions that erupt at international conferences—North being for conservation and South for development), sustainable development, in its application to the unborn, can usefully be divided into two distinct claims. The first is the obligation to leave future generations no less than a certain general level of welfare, and the second is the obligation to leave them certain specific assets as part of their legacy. The first position is welfarist; the second is preservationist.

4.2.1 Sustainable Development as a Welfare-Transfer Constraint

Welfarists define our obligations to the future in terms of some proxy for general welfare. Phelps's 'golden rule of capital accumulation' enjoins each generation to leave to its successor as much capital (per effective labour unit) as it would have liked to have received from its predecessor.[25] John Rawls invokes a 'just savings principle', which, while derived and calculated in a more complex manner,[26] produces much the same constraint, termed as 'a fair equivalent in real capital.' Others speak of each generation's obligation to retain and pass along equivalent 'productive capacity',[27] to live off the earth's 'earnings' without invading its 'capital', to maintain 'a standard of living at least as good as our own',[28] or to equalize opportunities. Whatever the benchmark, the point is that no constraints are imposed according to the *bases* on which welfare is to be secured, but only according to some minimum *level* to be passed along. Each generation is free to pillage natural resource capital such as coal and trees, as long as it substitutes enough capital in other forms (technology, infrastructure, social institutions, education, and so on) so that the succeeding generation can maintain the requisite floor level of well-being.[29]

Other variants include inter-generational Pareto-optimality (seeking a position from which it is impossible to advance the well-being of any person at any point in time without sacrificing the well-being of someone else in the current or some future generation);[30] inter-generational Kaldor-Hicks efficiency (no action permitted unless the benefits to the benefiting generations are robust enough that they could fund compensatory payment to the losers); and an inter-temporal wealth maximization requirement (maximizing the utility of everyone through time).[31]

4.2.2 *Sustainable Development as Preservationism*

Preservationism, by contrast, holds that among the many assets we have inherited there are some that we have a special responsibility to conserve and transmit to our descendants, and that are, therefore, non-substitutable. Leading candidates have included such widely appreciated and irreplaceable assets as the Grand Canyon, whales, and tropical forests. Various rationales are offered. Preserving some things is said to derive from duties to future generations. Or, they are said to have an existence

---

[25] See W.H. Branson, *Macroeconomic Theory and Policy*, 3rd edition (New York: Harper and Row, 1989) at 611–26.

[26] Those in the original position would seek a fair 'balancing [of] how much at each stage they would be willing to save for their immediate descendants against what they would feel entitled to claim of their immediate predecessors. J. Rawls, *A Theory of Justice* (Cambridge, MA: Harvard University Press, 1971) at 289. Rawls's larger motivation, however, is different: to allocate a 'fair share of the burden of realizing and preserving a just society' (*ibid.*) rather than to provide equal wealth opportunities of economic welfare.

[27] R. Solow, *An Almost Practical Step toward Sustainability* (Washington, DC: Resources for the Future, 1992) 19–20.   [28] *Ibid.* at 15.

[29] Put otherwise, net genuine investment must not be negative. The statement in the text is true of 'weak' but not of 'strong' sustainability which would also prohibit substitution of natural (often specifically non-renewable) resources for other forms of capital, such as man-made, without welfare comparisons. The many variants are authoritatively collected and critiqued in E. Neumayer, *Weak and Strong Sustainability*, 2nd edition (Northampton: Edward Elgar Publishing, 2004).

[30] See T. Sondler, *Economic Concepts for the Social Sciences* (Cambridge: Cambridge University Press, 2001) at 423.

[31] K. J. Arrow et al., 'Are We Consuming Too Much?' (2004) 18 J. Econ. Persp. 147.

value, and so have to be preserved for their own sake; or, because their continued existence and the appreciation of this existence fosters an ideal of human flourishing; or, because they are simply heirlooms connecting each generation to, and constructing of all of us, a true family of humankind. However persuasively these arguments can be fleshed out, their appeal presumably motivates many conventions including the Convention for the Protection of the World Cultural and Natural Heritage, CITES and the CBD.

4.2.3 *Welfarist and Preservationist Models Critiqued*

By analogy to familiar legal models, the first approach places the living in the position, roughly, of trustees managing an investment portfolio. They can, and are expected to, sell and reinvest proceeds from various holdings as conditions change and prudence dictates. Unlike the ordinary asset manager, however, the intergenerational trustees are free to distribute to themselves, as long as, at the end of their term, there is enough value left to meet their obligations to the beneficiaries. The second approach views the living as enjoying, roughly, a life estate in certain property, lacking *ius abutendi* (the right to destroy). Thus, we are 'left' with the Grand Canyon for life, then to our heirs, in perpetuity. Our obligations are to pass along—not to 'waste', alter, or even convert the favoured asset to some more beneficial use.

It is not uncommon to find in the sustainable development literature a single commentator promoting both foundations. Robert Solow, for example, while emphasizing a substitution-permitting welfare constraint (equivalent to 'productive capacity') would nonetheless insist on the preservation of 'certain unique and irreplaceable assets,' offering as illustrations Yosemite and the Lincoln Memorial.[32] The embracing of both welfarist and preservationist constraints is not surprising, given the appeal of both positions. Yet they share a common problem, and are potentially in conflict.

The common problem is that no generation can be assured that if it honours its obligation to pass along the required wealth and legacy assets, a succeeding, more profligate and dishonourable successor generation will not run through the inheritance before it reaches the third. Does that prospect remove the first generation's obligation? In general terms, the question might be put as whether a person is under a duty when his or her action is a necessary but not a sufficient condition of bringing about the morally desired result. Consider the case in which saving a drowning child requires the coordinative effort of two persons, A and B. Surely A and B are not each disobliged because the action of each, alone, cannot assure the right outcome. I am not clear why the answer should be otherwise where the required actions of A and B

---

[32] R. Solow, *An Almost Practical Step toward Sustainability* (Washington, DC: Resources for the Future, 1992) at 14. Solow indicates that these are examples of assets that would be 'preserved for their own sake,' but his choice of the Lincoln Memorial to illustrate invites questions about how he understands 'own sake'.

happen to be successive, not contemporaneous. I grant the intuition that as the chain required to bring about the good gets longer, the duty of each link may weaken. Yet, against this scenario, we must consider that after only a few duty-honouring links, *some* good has been done—perhaps the tenth generation will be cheated, but even if so, two through nine will have been (rightly) served.

A stark conflict might arise in the following way. Let us assume that we have subscribed to sustainability of the first sort—an obligation to assure our successors some prescribed minimum level of wealth or general well-being. Suppose also that the pristine Antarctic is one of the *'legacy'* assets that we are obliged to conserve. (Mineral exploitation of the continent is in fact presently under a moratorium). As long as the global economy continues fairly robust expansion we can both meet the wealth obligation and preserve the Antarctic. However, suppose that there were to be a collapse in the global economy, raising appreciable uncertainty over whether the prescribed wealth floor can be met in the *n*th generation. One way to reduce the deficit would be to mine the Antarctic of its rich troves of mineral deposits, which, although presently unreachable, will gradually become available as the technical and economic barriers to dealing with the harsh environment are overcome. Extensive mining would sully the continent and endanger its fauna and violate the 'no substitution' constraint. Thus the living would have to choose between one obligation or the other. If the likely preferences of the beneficiaries are to govern, it is hard to imagine they would not prefer their 'trustees' to waive their 'right' to the Antarctic—a right that they had no voice in formulating—and to invest the unconsumed net proceeds in general global economic growth.

The more productive wealth future generations receive in their inheritance, the greater their capacity to devise their own novel rewarding experiences. And, the greater their wealth, the better their capacity to respond to unforeseen calamities. Moreover, for all we know, our remote progeny may opt to while away their time playing video games with their robots and consider us fusty for having conserved the Antarctic or preferred a walk through an actual, rather than a 'virtual', woods.

Perhaps each generation should regard the environmental and cultural heirlooms it sets aside as individuals regard family heirlooms—not with the expectation that they will remain within the family eternally, but rather as the last things to be sold off, and then only when there is real need, and with a heavy heart.

RECOMMENDED READING

A. Buchanan and D. Golove, 'Philosophy of International Law,' in J. Coleman et al., eds., *Oxford Handbook of Jurisprudence and Philosophy of Law* (Oxford: Oxford University Press, 2002) 868.

J.P. Bruce, H. Lee, and E.F. Haites, eds., *Climate Change 1995: Economic and Social Dimensions of Climate Change*, Contribution of Working Group III to the Second Assessment Report of the Intergovernmental Panel on Climate Change (Cambridge: Cambridge University Press, 1996).

D. Schmidtz and E. Willott, eds., *Environmental Ethics: What Really Matters, What Really Works* (New York: Oxford University Press, 2002).

C.D. Stone, *Earth and Other Ethics* (New York: Harper and Row, 1987).

PART III

BASIC ISSUE AREAS

CHAPTER 14

ATMOSPHERE AND OUTER SPACE

IAN H. ROWLANDS

1 INTRODUCTION

THE purpose of this chapter is to provide an overview of key atmospheric and outer space environmental challenges that have been—and continue to be—addressed by international environmental law. To do this, the chapter is divided into seven sections. Following this brief introduction, the context is set out in the next section. In the subsequent four sections, key issue areas are investigated, namely transboundary air pollution, ozone layer depletion, global climate change, and outer space. For each of these issue areas, the particular environmental problem (or set of environmental problems) is identified and described. Key elements of the international legal response (including especially significant agreements) are then reviewed. Particularly innovative approaches taken as part of this response are then highlighted. In this way, the chapter is not meant to be exhaustive—reviewing every part of the international legal regimes to meet atmospheric and outer space environmental challenges. Instead, it is meant to be illustrative—providing the reader with a sense of the range of issues in existence and the key themes that are emerging in response. A final section summarizes the arguments developed and presents the key conclusions.

2 CONTEXT

I begin by defining terms. The title of this chapter begs the question: 'What is "atmosphere" and what is "outer space"?' The term 'atmosphere' is sometimes used interchangeably with 'air'. Moreover, it is often assumed that 'outer space' is simply the area above and beyond 'air space' (another term often used). While understandings such as these are certainly reasonable for most discussions, the effective development of international environmental law may well demand more precise definitions. To begin discussion, let me review some 'technical' definitions. The Intergovernmental Panel on Climate Change (IPCC)—an international group of climate change experts convened by the UN Environment Programme (UNEP) and the World Meteorological Organization—defines the atmosphere as the gaseous envelope surrounding the Earth. In its dry state, it contains a combination of gases made up predominantly of nitrogen and oxygen but also containing trace gases such as argon, helium, carbon dioxide, and ozone. While there is general agreement that the atmosphere begins at the Earth's surface, there is less consensus as to where it ends. The National Weather Service in the United States suggests that the atmosphere extends up to the outer limit of the exosphere (the last of the atmosphere's five distinct layers), thus reaching 10,000 kilometres above the Earth's surface. By contrast, the Karman

Line—an indicator of the edge of outer space used by the Fédération Aéronautique Internationale (FAI)—lies at a height of 100 kilometres above the Earth's surface.

Similarly concise definitions do not exist in international environmental law. While there is no piece of international environmental law with the word 'atmosphere' in its title, there is one containing the phrase 'outer space', namely the 1967 Treaty on Principles Governing the Activities of States in the Exploration and Use of Outer Space, Including the Moon and Other Celestial Bodies. Interestingly, however, the term 'outer space' is never defined in the terms of the treaty. At one point (Article 7), it is suggested that outer space is distinct from 'air space', but no further elaboration is provided. For the purpose of the discussion in this chapter, the IPCC definition of 'atmosphere' will be used. 'Outer space', meanwhile, will be the reaches beyond the atmosphere.

Of course, humankind is reliant upon the atmosphere—at its most basic level, the atmosphere's particular composition allows human beings to exist. Thus, its satisfactory condition is critical. Human activity, however, introduces substances into the atmosphere—some of which are known as 'pollutants' because their presence serves to degrade the condition of the atmosphere (at least, for human ends). Given the predominant state of the atmosphere (gaseous), most of the pollutants are also in gaseous form, arising largely from point sources on the planet's surface (for example, industrial facilities such as power stations) and, to a lesser extent, mobile sources on the planet's surface (such as different modes of transportation). The nature of the problem arising from atmospheric pollution is a function of the substance that is released, the quantity released, the location from which it is released, the prevailing meteorological conditions, and the characteristics of the location to which it is transported. Consequently, different environmental issues will be generated by, in turn, a diesel-powered local bus, a farmer who tills her field, and a factory with a 100-metre smokestack.

3 TRANSBOUNDARY AIR POLLUTION

Legislative action in the face of atmospheric pollution dates back to at least 1273. It was at this time that the first attempt to prohibit coal burning in London, England, was made and, hence, the matter was primarily 'local'. For the next six centuries, whatever efforts existed to address atmospheric pollution remained predominantly at this level. However, atmospheric pollution can have consequences that extend beyond the 'local'. Activities in one country can serve to pollute another country's lower atmosphere. Meteorological conditions do not respect national boundaries, and air currents can serve to transport pollutants from the airspace of one country into another. As a result, international disputes arising from the transboundary movement of substances by air can and do arise. Indeed, in the early part of the twentieth century, as states attempted to address increasingly severe local air pollution problems by injecting pollutants into the atmosphere at a higher level (through taller smokestacks), such efforts had the effect of dispersing the pollutants over a wider geographical range, giving rise to more transboundary problems.

In response, states have, during the last century, developed international environmental law. It is now widely accepted that states have a legal obligation to ensure that any activities that occur within their territories take into account the rights of other states regarding the protection of the environment (see Chapter 22 'Transboundary Impacts'). Often stated as being the principle that states have an obligation not to cause or allow environmental harm outside their borders, it includes the transboundary movement of pollutants through the atmosphere. The 1992 Rio Declaration on Environment and Development, for example, articulates principles that, many argue, reflect customary international law and that have direct consequences for transboundary air pollution issues. Principle 2 explicitly requires states to prevent harm to the environment of other states or of common spaces. Principles 18 and 19, meanwhile, require international notification should transboundary pollution arise from accidents or be anticipated from planned activities. In addition to these broad principles that concern transboundary impacts by any means, specific legal instruments regarding different 'kinds' of transboundary air pollution have also been developed. In this section, I review the most significant of these, considering, in particular, those that not only are most widely cited and used but also those that contain especially innovative regulatory approaches.

3.1 Transboundary Transport of Industrial Pollutants

Traditionally, the pollutants that have had the greatest environmental impact, by means of transboundary atmospheric transport, have been sulphur dioxide and nitrogen oxides. These are primarily produced by fossil fuel combustion and largely result from industrial processes, power station operation, and motor vehicle use. As a result, this issue has arisen mainly in locations where there has been intensive economic activity in close proximity to one or more international borders. The Canada–United States frontier and Europe are the two areas that have generated the most activity on this issue.

One of the first cases of international environmental law was sparked by the atmospheric transport of industrial pollutants across a border. In 1941 in the *Trail Smelter Case (United States v. Canada)*, an international arbitral tribunal (convened under the terms of an international agreement signed in 1935) responded to a complaint from the United States government (which, in turn, had been asked to intervene by residents in the state of Washington) that sulphur dioxide emissions from a smelter in Trail, British Columbia, were causing significant harm.[1] After investigation, the tribunal issued what has been called 'the most famous ruling in all of international environmental law':[2] 'no state has the right to use or permit the use of its territory in such a manner as to cause injury by fumes in or to the territory of another or the properties of persons therein, when the case is of serious consequence and the injury is established by clear and convincing evidence.' The tribunal ordered the owners of the smelter to pay US $350,000 in damages and to make changes to their operations. This ruling affirmed the customary principle of 'good neighbourliness' in such bilateral arrangements between neighbouring countries.

Moving from bilateral to multilateral settings, it is not always so straightforward to identify distinct point-sources of pollution as well as particularly affected locations. As such, it has often been the case that 'bilateral concepts of geographical contiguity and "good neighbourliness" . . . [cease] to be sufficient or adequate.'[3] Instead, a new multilateral approach involving international negotiation and treaty-making was seen to be required. This approach was forthcoming by the 1970s. Under the auspices of the United Nations Economic Commission for Europe (UNECE), a relatively complex and comprehensive regime for regulating the long-range transport of air pollutants was developed. The Convention on Long-Range Transboundary Air Pollution (LRTAP Convention) first took shape in the form of a framework agreement in 1979 (after much prompting from Scandinavian states concerned about the impact of acid rain on their territories). While not containing specific limits on emissions of industrial pollutants, it nevertheless established a structure for continued consideration of the issue. A series of eight separate protocols have been subsequently negotiated and agreed.

Although the LRTAP Convention has, as parties, states from both sides of the Atlantic Ocean, European states have played the lead in its development. Two interesting innovations in the development of the regime are particularly worth highlighting. One is the 'critical loads' approach, which was used in the 1994 Protocol on the Further Reduction of Sulphur Emissions to determine the appropriate reduction targets for different states. Rather than simply requiring all states to reduce their emissions by a particular (and identical) share, the critical loads approach attempts to differentiate national reduction targets in order to achieve environmental goals most 'effectively' (and efficiently). Using the regional acidification information and simulation model (RAINS), which was developed by the International Institute for Applied Systems Analysis in Austria, parties to the convention have estimated the vulnerability of ecosystems across Europe to pollution and then used these estimates in calculating the specific commitments of individual states.

[1] *Trail Smelter Case (United States v. Canada)*, Award, 1941, 3 U.N.R.I.A.A. 1905.
[2] V.P. Nanda and G. (Roch) Pring, *International Environmental Law for the Twenty-First Century* (Ardsley, NY: Transnational Publishers, 2003) at 226.
[3] P.H. Sand, *Transnational Environmental Law: Lessons in Global Change* (The Hague: Kluwer Law International, 1999) at 194.

The other interesting innovation arising from European activity in the LRTAP regime is the fact that with each subsequent protocol, states have broadened their focus, moving beyond the consideration of individual pollutants one by one (as in the case of the second and third protocols, which examined, respectively, sulphur dioxide and nitrogen oxides) and of only one type of effect (acid deposition). The 1999 Gothenburg Protocol to Abate Acidification, Eutrophication and Ground-Level Ozone, by contrast, targets four substances—nitrogen oxides, volatile organic compounds, sulphur dioxide, and ammonia—and three effects—acidification, tropospheric ozone formation, and eutrophication. The parties' understanding of the interplay between different chemical substances—and the consequent environmental effects—have been growing. Hence, there has been greater acceptance of the idea that not only would stronger regulatory controls on key transboundary pollutants be needed but also that the interaction among these pollutants would have to be considered as well. Though not necessarily unique to the LRTAP agreements (see Chapter 20 'Treaty Making and Treaty Evolution'), this more comprehensive approach is nevertheless deemed 'new and innovative' by many observers.[4]

In North America, although the issue of the transboundary transport of industrial pollutants began to attract more attention during the 1970s and although both the United States and Canada were parties to the LRTAP Convention, it was not until 1991 that a significant agreement—namely the US-Canada Bilateral Air Quality Agreement—was reached. The agreement governs efforts to control the two countries' sulphur dioxide and nitrogen oxide emissions. Oversight of the agreement was assigned to a bilateral Air Quality Committee, which was formed under the auspices of the International Joint Commission—a body that, though created under the 1909 Boundary Waters Treaty, had been concerned with transboundary air pollution issues for decades.

Looking ahead, there are still challenges to be met regarding transboundary air pollution on both sides of the Atlantic Ocean. New scientific information may determine that regulations need to be introduced on other substances that move across borders through the air or tightened on substances that are already being regulated. Additionally, there are other areas of the world where—with growing industrialization—transboundary air pollution has become an unfortunate reality. These areas include parts of South America, southern Africa, and southeast Asia. At present, there 'is little or no provision in any of these regions for monitoring or regulation of transboundary air pollution.'[5] Nevertheless, the LRTAP regime is continuing to serve as 'the world's most important forum for expansion of air pollution regulation and a "test tube" for new techniques, requirements, and substances.'[6]

---

[4] J. Wettestad, 'The 1999 Multi-Pollutant Protocol: A Neglected Break-Through in Solving Europe's Air Pollution Problems,' in O. Schram Stokke and Ø.B. Thommessen, eds., *Yearbook of International Co-operation on Environment and Development 2001/2002* (London: Earthscan, 2001) 35 at 35.

[5] P.W. Birnie and A.E. Boyle, *International Law and the Environment*, 2nd edition (Oxford: Oxford University Press, 2002) at 515.   [6] Nanda and Pring, see note 2 above at 237.

3.2 Major Industrial Accidents

Notwithstanding states' international legal obligation to prevent accidents that have international environmental ramifications from occurring, accidents do, in fact, occur. International law has emerged with respect to how such accidents should be dealt with. Most significant in this regard is the 1992 Convention on Transboundary Effects of Industrial Accidents, which is managed by the UNECE. The convention is designed to protect humans and the environment from the consequences of industrial accidents. It aims to do this by working both to prevent accidents and, should they occur, to reduce their severity and to mitigate their impacts. The convention was adopted in Helsinki on 17 March 1992 and entered into force on 19 April 2000.

Nuclear accidents, meanwhile, present unique challenges. Some argue that in the case of nuclear accidents there is some divergence from the widely cited notion of 'polluter pays'. While it is clear that the operator of the nuclear installation is the polluter, the potential size of a claim for damages, in light of an accident, would be such that the operator could well be bankrupted in short measure were an accident to occur. Consequently, the nuclear installation may not, on its own, be insurable. Therefore, 'in Western Europe, the uninsured risks are borne first by the state in which the installation is located and then above a certain level by a compensation fund to which participating governments contribute in proportion to their installed nuclear capacity and GNP.'[7] This regime was developed by the International Atomic Energy Agency and initially formalized in the Joint Protocol Relating to the Application of the Vienna Convention and the Paris Convention (Joint Protocol). Opened for signature in 1988, the Joint Protocol entered into force in 1992. While predominantly European in membership (20 of the 24 parties as of August 2005), it is nevertheless open to all countries and includes Cameroon, Chile, Egypt, and St. Vincent and the Grenadines among its parties. Additional agreements that were reached in 1997—the Protocol to Amend the Vienna Convention and the Convention on Supplementary Compensation for Nuclear Damage—detail the limits of the operator's liability and define the additional amounts to be provided through contributions by states.

4 OZONE LAYER DEPLETION

The Earth's stratosphere is located some 12 to 40 kilometres above the planet's surface. It is here that the so-called 'ozone layer'—that is, the part of the atmosphere with most of the planet's ozone (three atoms of oxygen bonded together)—can be found.

---

[7] Birnie and Boyle, see note 5 above at 94.

The ozone layer serves to protect life on earth from the sun's damaging ultraviolet radiation. Without the ozone layer—and with greater exposure to ultraviolet rays—people would have increased chances of skin cancer and cataracts, as well as weakened immune systems. Reduced crop yields and disruptions in marine food chains are some of the ecological consequences that would also result. Some objects—for example, building materials made with plastics and rubber—would also be prematurely weakened by ozone layer depletion.

In the early 1970s, it was theorized that chloroflourocarbons (CFCs), which are relatively stable substances that were then widely used in a variety of refrigerant, solvent, and foam-blowing applications, had the potential to catalyze the destruction of ozone in the stratosphere. Subsequent research has confirmed that a range of substances that contain the chemical elements chlorine, fluorine, bromine, carbon, and/or hydrogen eventually react with ozone in the stratosphere, thereby catalyzing ozone layer destruction.

The issue of ozone layer depletion meant that international atmospheric policy, which began by addressing bilateral issues (between contiguous countries, such as in the *Trail Smelter* case), and then developed to address regional issues (among a larger group of countries sharing a common air shed, as in the LRTAP regime), now included a global dimension as well. As a result of the long residence time of ozone-depleting substances in the atmosphere, they are transported globally and have global effects. It does not matter whether a CFC molecule has been released by means of the use of an aerosol propellant in Montreal or the disposal of a refrigerator in Melbourne as both will affect the global ozone layer in the same manner.

4.1 Building the Regime to Protect the Ozone Layer

The emerging scientific debate about potential ozone layer depletion in the early 1970s prompted international political consideration of the issue. Through the second half of the 1970s and into the 1980s, UNEP organized meetings of representatives of various governmental and non-governmental bodies to review information about the ozone layer and to develop appropriate responses. Their efforts led to the 1985 signing, by representatives from 20 states, of the Vienna Convention on the Protection of the Ozone Layer. A framework convention, it called for international cooperation on a range of issues, including scientific research and information exchange. Although it did not include legally binding obligations to reduce emissions of ozone-depleting substances, it obliged states to 'cooperate in research, observations and information exchange, and to adopt policies to control human activities that might modify the ozone layer.'[8] It also established a conference of the parties to consider subsequent protocols to fulfil the convention's obligations.

---

[8] S.O. Andersen and K. Madhava Sarma, *Protecting the Ozone Layer: The United Nations History* (London: Earthscan, 2002) at 64.

Greater public interest, ongoing scientific work, and strategic negotiating all combined to galvanize the international community's commitment to reduce the emissions of ozone-depleting substances. In 1987, representatives adopted the Montreal Protocol on Substances That Deplete the Ozone Layer. The Montreal Protocol obliges industrialized states to limit their production, and consumption, of key ozone-depleting substances by quantitatively specified amounts. It also establishes a procedure for continuing to monitor the condition of the ozone layer, and to introduce additional legal obligations upon states.

With expert assessments of the effectiveness of the ozone layer regime being 'predominantly positive',[9] there are potentially numerous elements that could be given further scrutiny. The convention/protocol approach has been called a model by some. It allows for a two-step process: first, entrenchment of the problem as one worthy of political and legal attention, coupled with continuous scientific and economic assessments of the issue, and, second, a set of concrete and specific obligations for states to take action on the problem (see Chapter 20 'Treaty Making and Treaty Evolution').

Moreover, once the protocol entered into force, the role of ongoing assessments—both scientific and economic—became critical. The architecture of the regime has allowed new information to be fed into an already-existing structure, and the challenges associated with developing new agreements have thus been avoided. Proposed adjustments, informed by the findings of the Scientific Assessment Panel, the Environmental Effects Assessment Panel, and the Technology and Economic Assessment Panel, have been discussed and, as appropriate, incorporated quickly. The effectiveness of this kind of approach encouraged one commentator to label the Montreal Protocol 'a new model for international environmental diplomacy . . . [in] that it is the world's first adaptive global environmental regime.'[10] Indeed, the flexibility arising out of the requirement to assess and review controls at least every four years has been called the protocol's 'most important innovation'[11] and 'the most impressive feature of the regime.'[12]

The Montreal Protocol originally addressed eight ozone-depleting substances (ODS): five CFCs and three halons. Ongoing scientific assessments encouraged tighter timetables as well as the inclusion of additional substances to those initially controlled. The result has been that many of the annual meetings of the parties to the Montreal Protocol have adopted amendments and adjustments to the original agreement. In 1992, for example, it was agreed that the eight original ODS—whose use by

[9] J.F.C. DiMento, *The Global Environment and International Law* (Austin, TX: University of Texas Press, 2003) at 98.

[10] E.A. Parson, 'The Montreal Protocol: The First Adaptive Global Environmental Regime?' in P.G. Le Prestre, J.D. Reid, and E.T. Morehouse, Jr., eds., *Protecting the Ozone Layer: Lessons, Models, and Prospects* (Boston, MA: Kluwer Academic Publishers, 1998) 127.

[11] D. Hunter, J. Salzman, and D. Zaelke, *International Environmental Law and Policy*, 2nd edition (New York: Foundation Press, 2002) at 545.

[12] J. Vogler, *The Global Commons: Environmental and Technological Governance*, 2nd edition (Chicester: John Wiley and Sons, 2000) at 133.

industrialized countries had been scheduled to be cut in half by 1999—would, instead, be almost completely eliminated by 1996. This same year, a range of additional substances—including hydrochlorofluorocarbons (HCFCs) and methyl bromide—were first regulated. Further restrictions on their use have since been agreed.

Turning to how these agreed commitments have been translated into action, Article 8 of the Montreal Protocol provides for a non-compliance procedure to be established—the first multilateral environmental agreement to do so (see Chapter 43 'Compliance Procedures'). In 2000, the parties set up an Implementation Committee, which was charged with considering any complaints raised by one party regarding compliance by another party. Additionally, any instances of non-compliance raised by the secretariat or by the non-complying party itself could also be considered. Intended by its drafters to be non-judicial and non-confrontational, the committee has encouraged compliance by using both sticks and carrots. For example, in its dealings with the Russian Federation during the 1990s (perhaps the most significant case of non-compliance under the terms of the Montreal Protocol), the committee often pressed for further details regarding the country's efforts to eliminate CFC production, while nevertheless accepting the arguments of some officials of international organizations that excessive penalties would jeopardize the prospects for the elimination of ODS in Russia. The strategy of the Implementation Committee has generally been successful, with compliance of the parties to the terms of the Montreal Protocol widely touted as remarkable. For Patricia Birnie and Alan Boyle, this experience shows that the Article 8 mechanisms correctly emphasize the 'importance of collective supervision and control, through multilateral negotiation and co-operation with the parties', rather than adjudication or arbitration.'[13] Thus, the regime's non-compliance process has been lauded as one that enables a 'fast and conciliatory approach to noncompliance.'[14]

The 'basket approach' to measuring the offending pollutants in the terms of the Montreal Protocol was also quite innovative. Each chemical's ozone-depleting potential was compared to that of CFC-11, which was given an ozone-depleting potential (ODP) value of 1.0. Others—such as the other chemicals in the CFC family and halons—were benchmarked against this value. This calculation provided flexibility to states to pursue reductions with respect to which substances they decided to reduce. A given state could, in theory, increase consumption of one particular kind of ozone-depleting substance if it was more than compensated for by dramatic reductions in others.

While there is not universal agreement whether the Montreal Protocol is the world's first 'precautionary treaty'[15] or simply 'one of the first to perceive the need for

[13] Birnie and Boyle, see note 5 above at 521.
[14] O. Yoshida, 'Soft Enforcement of Treaties: The Montreal Protocol's Noncompliance Procedure and the Functions of Internal International Institutions'(1999) 10 Col. J. Int'l L. and Pol'y 95, noted in J. DiMento, *The Global Environment and International Law* (Austin, TX: University of Texas Press, 2003) at 99.   [15] As noted by DiMento, see note 14 above at 100.

preventive action in advance of firm proof of actual harm,'[16] there is more wide-spread agreement that it helped to advance the use of the precautionary approach in international environmental law. Thus, it provides a precedent that diplomats can draw upon in future negotiations on global environmental problems characterized by high levels of uncertainty. While recognizing that the above represent important contributions to the development of the ozone layer regime (and to international environmental law, more generally), in the next two sections I focus attention upon two other characteristics of the regime: managing North-South issues and encouraging participation.

4.2 Managing North-South Issues

It was recognized relatively early in the development of the ozone layer regime that particular attention would have to be paid to the interests of developing countries. While developing countries were, during the 1980s, relatively small producers and consumers of ODS, their ambitions for industrialization included plans for the increased use of these substances. Developing countries argued that since the use of ODS was one of the ways in which Northern countries had catalyzed their development, why should they be denied the same opportunity? Since the production of CFCs was relatively inexpensive, involving modest levels of technologies, and the potential demand for CFCs was high in developing countries, it was thought that it was not a question of 'if' but rather of 'when'—conditions for 'take off' in terms of CFC production were in place in the developing world.

In the 1985 Vienna Convention, the provisions for ensuring the exchange of technologies to mitigate ozone layer depletion—that is, substitutes to ODS that could deliver the same services—were relatively weak. Article 4 obliged states simply to cooperate to ensure that technologies and knowledge be transferred from North to South. As such, countries could continue to follow their own laws and their own usual practices. Birnie and Boyle argue that this level of commitment was a departure from trends in international environmental law at the time, for the technology transfer provisions in the 1985 Vienna Convention were significantly weaker than the analogous provisions found in the 1982 United Nations Convention on the Law of the Sea (LOSC).[17]

It soon became clear that more had to be forthcoming in the 1987 Montreal Protocol if developing country participation was to be ensured. As it turns out, only a modest start was made at this time. More specifically, two key measures were introduced in the Montreal Protocol. First, the protocol allowed an increase in developing countries' production and consumption of ODS (up to 0.3 kilograms per person) in order to meet their basic domestic needs. And, second, developing countries had a

---

[16] Birnie and Boyle, see note 5 above at 519.   [17] *Ibid.* at 518.

ten-year grace period to implement the control obligations contained in the proto-col. Interestingly, this is one of the first tangible applications of the principle of 'com-mon but differentiated responsibilities' (see Chapter 27 'Equity'). Even still, however, this was not perceived as enough, for 'the Protocol provided only vague promises of facilitating access [to alternative substances and new technologies].'[18]

The breakthrough came in 1990 at the second Meeting of the Parties to the proto-col, when a Multilateral Fund for the Implementation of the Montreal Protocol was established. After much discussion and debate, it was agreed that the resources from this new fund would be used to finance the incremental costs of developing coun-tries' participation in the ozone layer regime. With an initial allocation of US $160 million over three years and an Executive Committee of 14 members (equally divided between representatives of the developing and the developed worlds), it secured developing country participation in the ozone layer regime—China joined soon after this meeting, and India followed suit in 1992. The arrangements for managing North-South issues in the ozone layer regime have subsequently been widely admired and cited (see Chapter 41 'Technical and Financial Assistance').

4.3 Encouraging Participation

In all environmental treaties, there is a concern that the actions of non-parties will serve to negate any benefits arising from the actions of the parties to the treaty. The ozone layer agreements were no different. In particular, concerns were voiced that states might have an incentive to stay outside of the regime in order to fill the gap with respect to the supply of ODS that would no longer be provided by those states that had ratified the agreement (see Chapter 11 'Economic Theory of International Environmental Law'). To avoid such free rider challenges, the protocol prohibited imports from, and exports to, non-parties (except those non-parties that were other-wise in full compliance with the protocol's reduction schedules). 'The evidence sug-gests that the trade provisions achieved their objectives,' giving countries such as the Republic of Korea a strong incentive to join the regime.[19]

The Montreal Protocol did not represent the first time that an international environmental agreement had employed trade measures to help meet its goals. There were already precedents for controls on trade with non-parties in the 1973 Convention on International Trade in Endangered Species of Wild Fauna and Flora (CITES), under resolutions of the parties to the 1972 Convention on the Prevention of Marine Pollution by Dumping of Wastes and Other Matter (London Convention), and in the 1946 International Convention for the Regulation of

[18] Hunter, Salzman, and Zaelke, see note 11 above at 545.
[19] D. Brack, 'The Use of Trade Measures in the Montreal Protocol,' in Le Prestre, Reid, and Morehouse, Jr., eds., see note 10 above, 99 at 101.

Whaling. Nevertheless, the ozone layer regime provides significant additional material to consider for those examining the relationship between multilateral environmental agreements and international trade agreements.

5 Global Climate Change

A range of gases in our atmosphere—most notably, water vapour, carbon dioxide, methane, and nitrous oxide—absorb infra-red radiation, making our atmosphere warmer than it otherwise would be. Without these gases—and without the surface of the planet also absorbing some of the incoming solar radiation—average global surface temperature would be minus 18 degrees Celsius instead of what it actually is, plus 15 degrees Celsius. This naturally occurring phenomenon is known as the 'greenhouse effect', and it has helped to ensure that much life has prospered on this planet.

A key environmental challenge arises, however, from the fact that a number of human activities are serving to put many of these so-called 'greenhouse gases' into the atmosphere at a faster rate than the planet can absorb them (that is, than they can be removed from the atmosphere through processes involving land-cover and/or the oceans). For the most part, it is the growing contribution of carbon dioxide from industrial activities that rely upon fossil fuel combustion that is causing the problem widely known as global climate change. There has been both an increase in the concentration of carbon dioxide since pre-industrial times (rising from 280 parts per million (ppm) in 1750 to 370 ppm in 2001) and a rise in global average temperatures (of 0.6 degrees Celsius between 1900 and 2000). Reports from the IPCC suggest that most of the observed warming at the Earth's surface over the last 50 years is likely to have been due to human activities. What is clear is that the environmental, socio-economic, and political consequences of climate change are significant.[20] And because the location of greenhouse gas emissions is relatively unimportant—at least in terms of their climate change effects—it is a truly 'global' issue.

5.1 Building the Global Climate Change Regime

While the issue of global climate change has been on a number of different scientific agendas for over a century, substantial legal attention was not directed to the issue until the mid-1980s. After a series of ad hoc gatherings, the global climate change issue became rooted in the UN system at the end of 1990. At that time, the UN General

[20] See generally Intergovernmental Panel on Climate Change, *Climate Change 2001: Impacts, Adaptation and Vulnerability* (Geneva: Intergovernmental Panel on Climate Change, 2001).

Assembly established the Intergovernmental Negotiating Committee (INC) for the UN Framework Convention on Climate Change (UNFCCC). This group was charged with negotiating a legal document in time for the 1992 United Nations Conference on Environment and Development.

Over a period of 15 months, negotiators met, debated, and eventually adopted the UNFCCC. While disappointing to some—for it did not establish quantitative commitments to limit greenhouse gas emissions—it nevertheless established a structure for international consideration of the issue. (Instead of a legally binding commitment to limit greenhouse gas emissions, there was an 'aim', on the part of industrialized countries, to return their greenhouse gas emissions, in the year 2000, to 1990 levels.) In addition to providing for annual meetings of the Conference of the Parties (COP) and establishing reporting obligations regarding national inventories and policy responses, the UNFCCC also established a number of key principles regarding the global response to climate change. These included an ambitious overall goal (namely, the 'stabilisation of greenhouse gas concentrations in the atmosphere at a level that would prevent dangerous anthropogenic interference with the climate system' (Article 2)), the idea that global climate change was a 'common concern of humankind', and that any international response should take into account the principles of equity (as described by the principle of 'common but differentiated responsibilities and respective capabilities'), sustainable development, precaution, and cost-effectiveness (see Chapter 23 'Common Areas, Common Heritage, and Common Concern' and Chapter 27 'Equity').

Entry into force of the UNFCCC in 1994 was followed, in 1997, by agreement on the Kyoto Protocol to the UNFCCC. Central to Kyoto are commitments, on the part of industrialized states, to reduce their greenhouse gas emissions by specified amounts during the commitment period of 2008 to 2012, with the overall aim of reducing their emissions by at least 5 per cent below 1990 levels. Many of the specific details regarding these commitments were left to subsequent COPs to determine. Despite the United States's declaration—in March 2001—that it did not intend to ratify the Kyoto Protocol, the agreement eventually attracted sufficient support so as to be able to enter into force on 16 February 2005.

The Kyoto Protocol—as well as the broader climate change regime—represents an important international environmental milestone. As such, there are numerous parts of it that could be identified as particularly significant and/or innovative. Birnie and Boyle, for example, argue that the process for 'supervising compliance with commitments under the convention and protocol is among the most elaborate in any environmental treaty and includes a number of significant innovations.'[21] With the sternest tests of compliance procedures yet to come, the Kyoto compliance system will continue to be monitored by those interested in innovative approaches to international environmental law.

[21] Birnie and Boyle, see note 5 above at 529.

This chapter will now focus upon two parts of the climate change regime that were agreed in Kyoto in 1997—namely the ways in which obligations and entitlements are distributed among states and the ways in which new flexibility mechanisms were integrated into the regime. Both deviated from how international environmental law had usually been carried out, and, accordingly, both have the potential to set and/or reinforce important precedents for the future.

5.2 Differentiation

While it is accepted that climate change is a 'common concern of humankind' (suggesting equality), it is also accepted that the response should be differentiated (suggesting distinctions) (see Chapter 23 'Common Areas, Common Heritage, and Common Concern'). These ideas are not particularly new. What is new, however, is the extent to which obligations were formalized as well as the extent to which they were differentiated among parties within the Kyoto Protocol. Following previous international environmental agreements (not least of all, the Montreal Protocol and the UNFCCC), developed and developing countries were treated differently under the terms of the Kyoto Protocol. Most importantly, developed countries were assigned emission limitation and reduction commitments, while developing countries were not. Unlike the Montreal Protocol, however, the process by which a party 'graduates' from one set of commitments to the other (that is, from those of developing countries to those of developed countries) is not clear. In the ozone layer regime, when a party's per capita consumption of a certain set of ODS exceeds 0.3 kilograms, that party takes on new commitments. Under the terms of the UNFCCC, however, it appears to be left to the individual party to self-declare its own 'graduation' (see Article 4(2)(g)).

Again like other international environmental regimes, there is an explicit obligation for the transfer of financial and technical assistance—from the North to the South—in order to address the environmental challenges in the climate change regime. While some kinds of assistance—for example, resources to help prepare national reports that are required by the terms of the UNFCCC—are already firmly established, others—for example, aid in adapting to the consequences of global climate change—have yet to achieve the levels that some deem necessary. As such, whether the regime is true to the principle of 'common but differentiated responsibilities' is still open to debate. Nevertheless, Birnie and Boyle argue that it is in the Kyoto Protocol that the concept of 'common but differentiated responsibility' is, for the first time, the 'explicit basis for the very different commitments of developed and developing states parties.'[22]

---

[22] *Ibid.* at 524. Similar sentiments can be found in C.D. Stone, 'Common But Differentiated Responsibilities in International Law' (2004) 98 A.J.I.L. 276 at 279.

Also within the regime, however, is the recognition that there are important differences within each of these two groups—that is, that differentiation within the countries of the South and within the countries of the North is entirely appropriate, indeed necessary. With respect to the former, those countries that would be most affected by climate change—that is, small island states, countries with low-lying coastal areas, and countries with arid and semi-arid areas, forest areas, and areas liable to forest decay (Article 4(8) of the UNFCCC)—require special consideration. Moreover, those countries that would be particularly affected by efforts to mitigate climate change—that is, reduced greenhouse gas emissions—also merit unique mention. Article 4(10) of the UNFCCC identifies fossil fuel exporting countries and users of fossil fuel for whom it is difficult to switch to other sources of energy as ones worthy of particular attention. Thus, even though the Group of 77 plus China has played a role in the development of the climate change regime, not all developing countries are considered identical—at least not in terms of the letter of the international agreements.

Turning to the North, there is even more explicit differentiation. While the developed countries' targets aim at achieving a 5 per cent emission reduction overall, individual countries have very different targets, depending upon their particular circumstances. While no specific justification for the range of commitments is given in the protocol, they vary from the most stringent (an 8 per cent reduction for many European states) to the most lenient (a 10 per cent increase for Iceland). The importance of individual positioning, in terms of the development of the Kyoto targets (for example, the efforts of the Australians to secure a relatively high target), will, no doubt, be a message taken forward into future international environmental negotiations.

5.3 Flexibility Mechanisms

The fact that states might want to meet any future emission limitation commitments 'jointly' had been envisaged in Articles 4(2)(a) and 4(5) of the UNFCCC. During the negotiations of a protocol, this possibility was explored widely, and, in the end, four so-called 'flexibility mechanisms' were included in the final agreement. Ellen Hey calls these flexibility mechanisms, from a legal and institutional perspective, 'the most noteworthy and complicating innovation introduced by the Kyoto Protocol.'[23] Philippe Sands, meanwhile, labels them 'by far the most innovative . . . aspect of the Kyoto Protocol negotiations.'[24] Here, I briefly describe each of them.

[23] E. Hey, 'The Climate Change Regime: An Enviro-Economic Problem and International Administrative Law in the Making' (2001) 1 Int'l Envt'l Agreements: Politics, Law and Economics 75 at 86.

[24] P. Sands, *Principles of International Environmental Law*, 2nd edition (Cambridge, MA: Cambridge University Press, 2003) at 372.

First, Article 4 allows two or more states listed in Annex I (the developed countries) to fulfil their emission limitation commitments together. In other words, each will be deemed to be in compliance with the terms of the Kyoto Protocol if the sum total of their combined emissions is lower than the sum total of their combined emission allowances. In theory, therefore, one state could be above its allowance, if the other is sufficiently below its allowance. While this provision was designed for the European Union (and it has been the only group of parties to take advantage of it), such a 'bubble' is available to any set of Annex I parties.

Second, Article 6 allows one developed country party to finance emission reduction activities in another developed country party and receive credit for it. The result of this transfer of emission allowances would be to increase the allowable emissions for the first country (the one paying for the emission reductions abroad), and to lower the allowable emissions of the second country (the one receiving the finance, doing the reductions, but, in turn, sending the credits abroad). It was envisioned that projects related to, for example, energy efficiency and forest conservation would result in more emission reductions than would otherwise have occurred. Identified as 'joint implementation' when initially proposed during the development of the climate change regime, it became known as 'activities implemented jointly' after 1995.

Third, an international emissions trading system is permitted by the terms of Article 17 of the Kyoto Protocol. Permits would be allocated to each party in accordance with their emission limitation obligations. Parties would then be free to trade permits among each other. Finally, a 'clean development mechanism' is proposed in Article 12 of the protocol. This flexibility mechanism is the only one to involve developing countries. In such instances, developed country parties can support the development of an emission reduction project in a developing country that serves not only to reduce greenhouse gas emissions from what they would otherwise have been, but also to advance sustainable development.

The motivation for inclusion of these flexibility mechanisms was cost-effectiveness. Since the marginal cost of emission reductions varies around the world (those countries that have highly efficient energy economies could well find it more expensive to reduce emissions than those that have taken little action), states have a motivation to meet their emission reduction commitments in other states where emissions can be reduced more cheaply. Moreover, the argument continues, because greenhouse gases are transported globally, the nature of the global climate change challenge means that an emission reduction has the same impact, irrespective of where it is achieved. Therefore, many argued that these kinds of flexibility mechanisms would not only be cost-effective (a principle recognized in Article 3 of the UNFCCC), but they would also increase the chances of widespread participation in the regime.

These flexibility mechanisms were adopted only after much debate. Many states and environmental groups had reservations. For one, there were concerns that the mechanisms would provide a means for particular developed states to 'buy their way out' of the global climate change problem, while not reflecting upon the changes that had to be made at home. A proposal to put quantitative limits on the extent to which participation in flexibility mechanisms could supplement domestic action was ultimately withdrawn, and it became widely accepted that individual states would decide their own level of involvement. Additionally, there were concerns about monitoring and verification. How could the regime ensure that the reductions traded were actually achieved? Perhaps more consequential, how could it be ensured that the baselines considered in projects arising from the clean development mechanism were genuine? There were certainly motivations to project a carbon-intensive future in the business-as-usual case, so as to generate as many emission 'reductions' (and hence credits) as possible.

It is important to recognize, however, that the flexibility mechanisms represent a noteworthy development in international environmental law (see Chapter 8 'Instrument Choice'). The introduction of market-based instruments to meet an environmental goal is significant for it represents further commodification of the international environment. Moreover, with the potential for large sums of money to be exchanged in markets, it brings in domestic players to a much greater extent. Given these results, Hey argues that the involvement of private entities in the implementation of the regime requires 'that their role be addressed at the international level or, alternatively, through establishing a close link between the relevant international and national regulations.' Rules of the game need to be clearly and unequivocally established and enforced. She goes on to argue that the pressure may require a 'paradigmatic shift in the international legal system.'[25]

6 Outer Space

Advanced technologies mean that humans have the ability to construct pieces of equipment that they can launch into outer space. In 1957, the Union of Soviet Socialist Republics (USSR) launched *Sputnik 1*—the first earth-orbiting satellite— and a year later the United States responded by launching *Explorer I*. In 1961, Yuri Gagarin—an air force pilot from the USSR—became the first human in space. Since that time, people and machines have continued to be launched into space for a range of economic, social, and political purposes. As of 2000, there were almost 9,000 human-made objects in outer space. With such activity comes the potential for environment-related challenges. Sands maintains that there are three types of environmental problems in outer space: 'orbital space debris; environmental damage caused on or to other planets as a result of human exploratory activity; and environmental damage caused on earth as a result of man-made objects falling

---

[25] Hey, see note 23 above at 90, 92.

from space.'[26] As such, there is the potential for international law to play a role in addressing these environmental challenges.

The law of outer space is based on the principles of equal access and freedom of exploitation and use by all states. The rules regulating the use of outer space that potentially have consequences for 'the environment' are embodied in a combination of international treaties and UN General Assembly resolutions. I consider the most significant of each of these.

The outer space treaty that has greatest relevance to international environmental law is the 1967 Treaty on Principles Governing the Activities of States in the Exploration and Use of Outer Space, Including the Moon and Other Celestial Bodies (Outer Space Treaty). The terms of this treaty echo many of the obligations outlined in different international environmental agreements. The treaty, for example, obliges states to ensure that they take into consideration the interests of others when conducting their activities in space. Additionally, states must inform other states of upcoming activities that have the chance to affect, negatively, the activities of those other states. Birnie and Boyle note, however, that the obligations—including the requirements to consult—are not primarily intended to 'protect the environment of Earth or outer space as such.' Instead, they are 'directed solely at protecting the interests of states in exploration and use of space.'[27] Sands agrees, noting that the approach of part of the treaty is 'directed towards the protection of human beings, rather than the protection of the environment as an end in itself.'[28]

Based on Article 7 of the Outer Space Treaty, the Convention on International Liability for Damage Caused by Space Objects (Space Objects Liability Convention) was agreed in 1972 and entered into force the same year. This treaty establishes state liability for damage caused by a space object. It was put to the test in 1978 when a Soviet nuclear-powered satellite crashed to the ground, spreading radioactive debris across an uninhabited part of the Canadian north. Canadian authorities presented a claim the following year, calling for CDN $6 million to cover the cost of restoring— to the extent possible—the territory damaged by the satellite. The matter was resolved in 1981, when the USSR paid CDN $3 million to Canada, and both sides agreed that this settled the claim. Although less than demanded, and although the rationale for the payment was not specified, many conclude that the settlement was based upon the legal arguments put forward by Canada. This remains the only claim that has been made under the terms of the Space Objects Liability Convention.

What has received less international support is the Agreement Governing the Activities of States on the Moon and Other Celestial Bodies (Moon Treaty). This treaty regulates exploitation of the moon and other celestial bodies and also declares them all to be the 'common heritage of mankind.' The Moon Treaty was opened for signature in 1979, however, it has not been signed or ratified by any state that engages in space exploration. Nevertheless, it received its necessary fifth ratification (from

---

[26] Sands, see note 24 above at 382.   [27] Birnie and Boyle, see note 5 above at 534.
[28] Sands, see note 24 above at 383.

Austria) in 1984 and thus entered into force in that year. Interestingly, it is the Outer Space Treaty, with its statement of outer space being the 'province of all mankind', that has received more widespread support. It is widely accepted that this is a 'weaker' phrase—'the province of all mankind' precludes territorial claims by individual countries but leaves open the possibility of resource use, while 'the common heritage of all mankind', by contrast, suggests that all the resources belong to all countries and that the benefits of any resource exploitation would have to be shared equitably by all states (see Chapter 23 'Common Areas, Common Heritage, and Common Concern').

Most significant of the UN General Assembly resolutions that are now accepted as part of the body of customary international law regarding outer space are the eleven Principles Relevant to the Use of Nuclear Power Sources in Outer Space. They were adopted in December 1992 and, collectively, aim to minimize the quantity of radioactive material in outer space.

Sands argues that because much of the international environmental law regarding outer space was developed 'before environmental considerations had become an important international legal issue,' it does 'not reflect some of the legal innovations which [occurred between 1992 and 2002].'[29] Similarly, Katherine Grove and Elena Kamenetskaya argue that '[t]here can be no question that the lacunae in international space law for the protection of the "space commons" must be addressed, either specifically through a new space treaty or in the general context of protecting the areas outside the jurisdiction and control of states, i.e., the "international commons" through international environmental law.'[30] John Vogler also maintains that '[t]he condition of the space environment will affect future uses and space debris poses a potentially lethal threat. Here, there is evidence of the beginnings of a regime governing orbital practices and spacecraft construction. It is evidently an area of potentially high mutual vulnerability [and] interdependence between spacecraft operators.'[31] As the private sector begins to promote private uses of space (including space tourism), they will further press for innovative approaches. Accordingly, the trail blazed by other areas of international environmental law—in both transboundary atmospheric issues and global atmospheric issues—may offer guidance.

7 SUMMARY AND KEY CONCLUSIONS

This chapter has examined the ways in which international environmental law has responded to key atmospheric and outer space environmental challenges. While the chapter has shown that the development of outer space law is still in its relative

---

[29] *Ibid.* at 382.

[30] K. Grove and E. Kamenetskaya, 'Tensions in the Development of the Law of Outer Space,' in C. Ku and P.F. Diehl, eds., *International Law: Classic and Contemporary Readings* (Boulder, CO: Lynne Rienner Publishers, 1998) 473 at 488.   [31] Vogler, see note 12 above at 118.

infancy, a series of well-established international agreements relating to the atmosphere now exist. It is upon the trends and prospects regarding the latter that this section will focus.

This chapter has revealed that the treatment of atmospheric pollution issues has evolved during the past century—moving from bilateral transboundary issues, to multilateral or regional issues, to global issues. In addition to this growth in geographical scope, the treatment of atmospheric pollution issues has also acquired greater complexity. Multiple pollutants are increasingly being considered within the same international agreement. That having been said, there is still much truth to the criticism that international policies for managing the global atmosphere 'have evolved in an ad hoc and piecemeal manner.'[32] In this respect, the 'law of the atmosphere' differs from the law of the sea, which is governed by a single comprehensive agreement, the 1982 LOSC (see Chapter 15 'Ocean and Freshwater Resources'). Despite initial proposals in the late 1980s to develop a 'comprehensive international framework that can address the interrelated problems of the global atmosphere,'[33] states ultimately decided to pursue a more piecemeal approach, perhaps reflecting their concern that a comprehensive treaty might meet the same fate as the LOSC, which at the time had still not entered into force.

However, as noted earlier, there are many links among potentially discrete parts of different efforts to manage the global atmosphere, making a wholly sectoral approach inappropriate. As John Dryzek has argued, 'for truly complex problems, those with a large number and variety of elements and interactions facing a decision system [such as the management of the global atmosphere], no intelligent disaggregation may be possible.'[34] If efforts to address atmospheric challenges proceed solely on a piecemeal basis, 'problem displacement' may well result.[35] In other words, efforts to address one atmospheric problem may simply serve to aggravate another. We have already seen evidence of this from efforts to address global atmospheric challenges: hydrofluorocarbons, a chlorine-free substance, were initially viewed as key potential replacements for ODS. However, they are also significant greenhouse gases. Therefore, while helping to address one problem, they serve to exacerbate another. As a result, linkages between these two relatively discrete regimes—that is, ozone layer and climate change—need to be, and fortunately have been, made.

Indeed, thinking about sustainability more broadly is encouraging greater cross-consideration of heretofore distinct elements. While there is certainly a price to be paid—in terms of placing additional pressures upon 'limited diplomatic resources'[36]—seemingly critical interconnections should continue to be made. Moreover, efforts to think about how different international environmental agreements could be coordinated should also be encouraged. Our atmosphere is critical

---

[32] A. Najam, 'Future Directions: The Case for a "Law of the Atmosphere"' (2000) 34 Atmospheric Env't 4047 at 4047.   [33] UN Toronto Conference on the Changing Atmosphere, Toronto, June 1988.
[34] J. Dryzek, *The Politics of the Earth* (Oxford: Oxford University Press, 1997) at 80.   [35] *Ibid.* at 81.
[36] M.S. Soroos, *The Endangered Atmosphere: Preserving a Global Commons* (Columbia, SC: University of South Carolina Press, 1997) at 281–2.

to our well-being, and management of this complex system is thus a pivotal task for humanity. The development and deployment of innovative and effective international environmental law can play a key role in ensuring that the atmosphere continues to be in a condition conducive to planetary prosperity.

RECOMMENDED READING

S.O. Andersen and K. Madhava Sarma, *Protecting the Ozone Layer: The United Nations History* (London: Earthscan, 2002).

M. Grubb with C. Vrolijk and D. Brack, *The Kyoto Protocol: A Guide and Assessment* (London: Royal Institute of International Affairs and Earthscan, 1999).

S. Oberthür and H Ott, *The Kyoto Protocol: International Climate Policy for the Twenty-First Century* (Berlin: Springer, 1999).

P. Okowa, *State Responsibility for Transboundary Air Pollution in International Law* (Oxford: Oxford University Press, 2000).

E.A. Parson, *Protecting the Ozone Layer: Science and Strategy* (Oxford: Oxford University Press, 2003).

G.H. Reynolds and R.P. Merges, *Outer Space: Problems of Law and Policy*, 2nd edition (Boulder, CO: Westview Press, 1997).

CHAPTER 15

OCEAN AND FRESHWATER RESOURCES

DAVID FREESTONE

SALMAN M.A. SALMAN

1 INTRODUCTION

In December 1970, the United Nations General Assembly (UNGA) adopted two resolutions of major significance for ocean and freshwater resources. One of them,
Resolution 2570 (C) (XXV), related to law of the sea, the seabed, and the ocean floor,
and the other, Resolution 2669 (XXV), related to international watercourses. The
resolutions set in motion two parallel, lengthy, and complex processes that resulted in
the adoption, at different later stages, of two conventions, namely the Convention on
the Law of the Sea (LOSC) in 1982 and the Convention on the Law of the Non-
Navigational Uses of International Watercourses (Watercourses Convention) in 1997.

Although it may have been simple coincidence that both issues were considered by
the UNGA in the same month, nevertheless, the legal regimes of oceans and international watercourses do have significant commonalities at a legal, as well as a practical, level. Apart from the obvious fact that most rivers flow into the oceans, both
legal regimes are based in large part on customary international law, evidenced by the
evolution of rules and principles, derived from the practice of states and patterns of
treaty practice over many centuries. As with most such customary international
law regimes, a few major issues had remained unsettled. In the law of the sea, these
unsettled issues included a lack of agreement on the maximum acceptable width of
the territorial sea around a state's coastline. In the law of international watercourses,
they included the question of how to reconcile the obligation not to cause harm with
the principle of equitable and reasonable utilization.

Both UNGA resolutions were designed to initiate a process of codification and
progressive development of the law, although each took a different path. The path of
the law of the sea was the convening of a major international conference, which took
an unprecedented nine years to complete its work. In the law of international watercourses, a more traditional approach was taken by referring the issue to the
International Law Commission (ILC) for the development of a draft convention.[1]
After nearly 25 years of work, the ILC referred its draft to the UN Sixth Committee
and the UNGA.

In the latter part of the twentieth century, both of these largely customary law
regimes have needed to respond to a range of different challenges. A greater understanding of the significance of environmental conservation and the need to maintain
the integrity of ecosystems including marine and aquatic ecosystems has resulted
in wider concerns about the increasing impact of industrial and agricultural discharges and runoff into both watercourses and oceans (see Chapter 24 'Ecosystems').

---

[1] The International Law Commission (ILC) is a UN body composed of legal experts nominated by
states, elected by the UN General Assembly (UNGA), and tasked with the codification and progressive
development of international law.

Customary international law has been slow to react to these new perspectives (see Chapter 19 'Formation of Customary International Law and General Principles'). Similarly, concern about the impacts of the increased exploitation of ocean resources—both living and non-living—has had parallels in watercourse systems where freshwater itself, as well as the living resources it carries, are becoming an increasingly scarce and highly sought after commodity.

However, there the similarities end. The law of the sea is a regime governing all aspects of ocean use under which certain areas of the ocean outside national jurisdiction—the high seas—have traditionally been viewed as being open to all—the global commons. The law of international watercourses is, by comparison, essentially sectoral, governing the use and protection of surface waters and groundwaters shared by two or more states. Nevertheless, since 1970, both regimes have proved to be complex and contentious. This chapter discusses and analyses the international environmental law aspects related to ocean resources as well as those related to freshwater resources.

2 OCEAN RESOURCES

The regulation and management of marine resources has traditionally faced fundamental issues relating to jurisdiction over the oceans. Hugo Grotius's classic work of 1609 *de Mare Liberum* envisaged an ocean unbridled by national claims, in which the mercantile nations had unrestricted rights of navigation and passage. Even in 1615, this notion was little more than a pipe dream—many nations had made traditional claims over areas of the ocean, especially over those waters fringing their coastlines, and some to much wider areas (such as Sweden's claims to sovereignty over the Baltic during the era of Gustavus Adolphus).[2] In the modern age, the challenge has been to develop legal frameworks for jurisdiction that will allow nations to exploit the many resources of the marine realm in a sustainable and orderly fashion. Voracious demands for fish as well as for fossil fuels have pressed exploration and exploitation into distant and dangerous waters. This expansion of scientific knowledge has revealed new types of resources, such as deep-sea fish species and new biological resources around deep ocean vents that function at temperatures in excess of 300 degrees Celcius. These discoveries pose unprecedented challenges to the legal regime of the oceans.

This part of the chapter will first give a flavour of the wealth of the resources in the world's oceans and the main challenges and threats facing them as well as the conservation of the marine environment. It will then look at ways that international law has

---

[2] See D.P. O'Connell, *The International Law of the Sea*, volume 1 (Oxford: Clarendon Press, 1982) at 3.

sought to address these issues through the development of general rules—culminating in the conclusion of the comprehensive 1982 LOSC, which has been called the 'constitution for the oceans'. It will then look at the development of specialized regimes addressing particular sectors, pollutants, and regions.

2.1 Marine Resources and the Conservation of the Marine Environment

2.1.1 *Marine Resources*

Marine resources are either living or non-living. In addition to fish, the living resources of the ocean include marine mammals, reptiles (such as turtles), and sea birds as well as crustacea, corals (including soft corals and deep ocean cold-water corals), and vegetation such as seaweeds and sea grasses (see Chapter 16 'Biological Resources'). The main threats that they all face come from mankind, principally from over-exploitation and the impacts of pollution. Although there are a myriad of international fisheries treaty regimes, including some bilateral ones dating back to the nineteenth century, most are creations of the post-Second World War years, and, of these, the majority were negotiated under the auspices of the UN Food and Agriculture Organization (FAO). Although these fisheries regimes are not, strictly speaking, environmental in nature, the evolution of international environmental law has introduced new concepts into their practice. Early fisheries treaties focused on the needs of human exploitation, using concepts such as maximum sustainable yield (defined in human consumption terms). The recognition by biologists—which is still not shared by many fishermen—that fishery resources are finite resources that require systematic conservation and management has been given a further boost by the growing adoption of the precautionary principle (see Chapter 25 'Precaution'), which has now been endorsed by the FAO for all capture fishery operations. Equally important has been the recognition that fish exist within a marine ecosystem and that sustainable exploitation requires an understanding of, and respect for, the parameters and constraints of this ecosystem. These concepts, which are discussed in more detail later in this chapter, are reflected in the 1995 UN Agreement Relating to the Conservation and Management of Straddling Fish Stocks and Highly Migratory Fish Stocks (Fish Stocks Agreement) and a number of other new fisheries agreements such as the 2000 Convention for the Conservation and Management of Highly Migratory Fish Stocks in the Western and Central Pacific Ocean, and the 2001 Convention on the Conservation and Management of Fishery Resources in the South East Atlantic, establishing the South-East Atlantic Fisheries Organization (SEAFO).

States may exploit the non-living resources of the ocean floor within their exclusive economic zones (up to 200 nautical miles from their coast lines) or on their continental shelf as measured in accordance with the LOSC. In some areas, such as the North Sea, states have agreed to restrict the collection of aggregates, such as gravel, from the sea bottom because of the impact that such exploitation has on fish breeding areas. Concerns are also increasingly expressed about the impact on the ecosystem of the sea floor from destructive fishing gear such as bottom and otter trawls and other dredging techniques.

The primary focus of states' exploitation of non-living resources, however, is on oil and natural gas occurring in pockets under the sea floor. The main environmental concerns have related to the emplacement of exploitation rigs on the sea floor (and their subsequent disposal) as well as leakages from platforms either through accidents or operationally from the use of oil-based muds as lubricants for the drills. Oil and gas exploitation is a lucrative industry dominated by companies from the Organisation for Economic Cooperation and Development (OECD) countries and is largely self-regulated. The industry standards are taken from best practices originating mostly from national legislation relating to North American and European waters. Although there are some regional regulatory requirements for oil and gas exploitation in the North Sea under the 1992 Convention for the Protection of the Marine Environment of the North-East Atlantic (OSPAR Convention), there is no global regime that imposes common standards.

Beyond the continental margin, the LOSC designates the deep seabed as the 'common heritage of mankind' (Article 136) and establishes an International Seabed Authority (ISA) based in Jamaica, which is the sole body authorized to develop 'rules, regulations and procedures' for the exploitation and sale of minerals found there (see Chapter 23 'Common Areas, Common Heritage, and Common Concern'). At the time the LOSC was being negotiated (1973–82), the main resources under consideration were the so-called manganese nodules (polymetallic deposits found on the deep ocean floor). Today, it appears highly unlikely that these nodules will be mined economically in the near to medium term, given the depths at which they are found. However, other resources have been discovered in the meantime, such as those associated with the deep ocean volcanic vents (so-called 'black smokers'). Not only do these vents often contain valuable minerals, but they also contain unique life forms that exist in a superheated environment. There are a myriad of possible industrial uses for these life forms, and it is clear that their exploitation needs to be regulated. However, they are not protected by the seabed regime contained within the LOSC, which only covers 'solid, liquid or gaseous mineral resources' (Article 133(a)).

A related lacuna is the inability of the LOSC regime to regulate deep sea trawl fishing over deep ocean floor habitats, which is designed to exploit deep sea species such as orange roughy and toothfish. Orange roughy (*hoplostethus atlanticus*), for example, do not reach sexual maturity until they are 30 years old, can live to 150 years, and do not breed every year. Scientists know little about them except that catches have dropped vertiginously after sustained exploitation, raising fears that they will face extinction without some form of regulatory regime.

Indeed, the full impact on the marine environment of human fishing activities is only now being properly understood. These impacts not only include direct damage to the ocean floor and marine benthic species by dredging and trawling, but also extend to depletion of threatened and endangered sea creatures such as turtles and marine mammals caught as by-catch. Scientists are now warning us of even more disturbing impacts, such as major disruptions to the marine food web by the selective culling of high-value large pelagic species such as tunas and bill fishes.[3] The FAO reports that more than 75 per cent of fish stocks are fully or over-harvested, and scientists are suggesting that fishermen are increasingly targeting smaller fish and species lower down the food chain—the trophic levels—as the higher predators becoming more difficult to find.

The 1992 UN Conference on Environment and Development in Rio de Janeiro identified a major flaw in the LOSC relating to the effective regulation of fishing for straddling and highly migratory fish stocks—species such as tunas. Chapter 17 of Agenda 21 mandated the calling of a conference on this issue and for states to take effective action to deter the reflagging of fishing vessels. The UN Conference on Straddling Fish Stocks and Highly Migratory Fish Stocks held four sessions between July 1993 and August 1995, and resulted in an innovative treaty—the 1995 Fish Stocks Agreement, which set in place new requirements for the conservation and management of these fisheries based in part on ecosystem concerns and which also imposed new obligations on states to control unregulated fishing.[4] This agreement was quickly followed by the finalization within the FAO of a non-binding Code of Conduct for Responsible Fisheries, followed by a series of international plans of action (IPOAs), including one that set out an agenda for the control of illegal, unregulated, and unreported (IUU) fishing.

2.1.2 *Marine Pollution*

The bulk carriage by sea of oil and other dangerous substances poses other threats to the marine environment. Media coverage of high profile wrecks of oil tankers such as the *Torrey Canyon* in 1967, the *Amoco Cadiz* in 1978, or, more recently, the *Exxon Valdez* in Alaska or the *Prestige* in the Bay of Biscay highlight the devastating impacts on the marine environment of huge oil spills. The international community has reacted quickly to put regimes in place to address clean-up measures and the future prevention of such accidents. However, in the wider scheme of things, marine vessel casualties are not a significant cause of environmental degradation of the oceans. Much more damaging are practices that involve the systematic disposal of contaminants into the ocean. These practices include the dumping of sewage and other waste

---

[3] D. Pauly, V. Christensen, J. Dalsgaard, R. Froese, and F. Torres, Jr., 'Fishing Down Marine Food Webs' (1998) 279 Science 860; see also D. Pauly et al., 'The Future of Fisheries' (2003) 302 Science 1359.

[4] See W. Edeson, D. Freestone, and E. Gudmundsdottir, *Legislating for Sustainable Fisheries: A Guide to Implementing the 1993 FAO Compliance Agreement and the 1995 Fish Stocks Agreement* (Washington, DC: World Bank Publications, 2001).

products at sea as well as what have been termed 'operational' discharges of contaminants through practices such as tank washing or the discharge of ballast waters from bulk carriers and from exploration and exploitation activities on the continental shelf, primarily, but not exclusively, for oil and gas. Many of these practices are controlled by specialized legal regimes.

Far more damaging still, and far more difficult to address, are the less easily identified impacts of pollution from land-based sources—either through direct discharges from factories or sewage facilities into the sea or rivers or through the indirect runoff of fertilizers, insecticides, and other chemicals, which either leach into watercourses and eventually into the oceans or enter the ocean through the atmosphere. Although the international community has begun to develop rules regulating the use of particularly harmful chemicals—such as the control of the 'dirty dozen' persistent organic pollutants (POPs) including polychlorinated biphenyls (PCBs) and dioxins by the 2001 Convention on the Prior Informed Consent Procedure for Certain Hazardous Chemicals and Pesticides—this process has really only just started (see Chapter 17 'Hazardous Substances and Activities'). Hundreds more harmful chemicals are not subject to any international regulatory regimes.

2.2 International Regulatory Responses

2.2.1 Jurisdictional Issues

Managing ocean resources presents a number of unique jurisdictional challenges. Many of the activities described earlier in this chapter take place on the open sea outside the territorial jurisdiction of coastal states. There are only a limited number of grounds recognized by international law for states to exercise criminal or civil jurisdiction so as to regulate maritime activities. The LOSC has largely codified the rules on jurisdiction, and recognizes three forms of national jurisdiction over such activities: that of the flag state, that of the coastal state, and that of a port at which a vessel calls. It is important to appreciate that these are the sole tools available for the enforcement of international rules and standards relating to the marine environment. Moreover, the rules governing the use of these are highly complex.

Vessels are subject to the primary jurisdiction of their flag state, namely the state in which they are registered and whose flag they fly. For many years, international lawyers have argued for a 'genuine link' between the vessel and its flag state—in terms of beneficial ownership or national control of the vessel. However, as regulatory requirements relating to health and safety as well as pollution control have grown in many industrialized flag states, many ship-owners have sought to escape these requirements by 'reflagging' with another state, particularly with the so-called 'open registry' states or 'flags of convenience'—states such as Panama or Liberia—which require minimal links with the vessels they register and which do not generally have the capacity to exercise effective control over these vessels. To address concerns about the jurisdictional vacuum that can arise in such situations, there has been an increased recognition of the power of port states to inspect vessels that call at their ports to ensure that these vessels are in compliance with standards established by international law—particularly those established by international treaties and conventions. This tool has been important in the policing of major treaties designed to protect safety of life at sea (1974 International Convention for the Safety of Life at Sea—as amended) as well as the oil pollution conventions. In 1995, it was recognized by the UN Fish Stocks Agreement as a legitimate basis for jurisdiction over certain types of illegal fishing.

Even the concept of coastal state jurisdiction is relatively complex. Coastal states may claim maritime zones around their shores, measured from the low-water mark or from straight baselines delineated in accordance with the provisions of the LOSC. The baseline provisions are highly technical and even include detailed provisions for drawing baselines around archipelagic states. The zones that can be claimed from these baselines include a territorial sea up to 12 nautical miles wide, in which the coastal state can exercise sovereignty; a contiguous zone out to 24 nautical miles (in which it can exercise jurisdiction over issues relating only to enforcement of customs, fiscal immigration, and sanitary laws); and an exclusive economic zone up to 200 nautical miles. The coastal state may also claim rights over the resources of the seabed and subsoil out to the edge of its continental shelf, but, in this zone and in the exclusive economic zone, it possesses sovereign rights for the purposes only of exploring, exploiting, and managing the natural resources of these zones. Moreover, the rights that coastal states may exercise in these zones are all subject to the rights of navigation of ships flying the flags of other states. While coastal states may regulate activities relating to exploitation or conservation of resources within their zones, they do not have unlimited jurisdiction over foreign vessels and must comply with the LOSC requirements (for example, the prompt release of vessels and crews arrested for breaching coastal state rules—Article 292).

In short, the LOSC has codified a complex web of rules relating to the delineation and delimitation of these zones as well as to jurisdiction within these and other zones, such as the high seas. Seabed areas beyond 200 nautical miles or beyond the edge of the continental margin constitute the deep seabed, which under the LOSC is primarily regulated by the International Seabed Authority (ISA).

2.2.2 *Regulation of Vessel-Source Pollution*

Customary international law has had problems reconciling the notion of freedom of the seas with restrictions regarding the pollution of the oceans. As a result, most environmental norms have been introduced by treaty law. These have now been codified by the LOSC requirements that all states 'have the obligation to protect and preserve the marine environment' (Article 192) and, indeed, to take proactive measures to 'prevent, reduce and control pollution of the marine environment,' including those necessary to 'protect and preserve rare or fragile ecosystems as well as the habitat of depleted, threatened or endangered species and other forms of marine life' (Article 194). Nevertheless, from a practical point of view, effective measures to implement pollution controls over vessels at sea rely primarily on flag state jurisdiction. Coastal states' rights to enforce anti-pollution measures are strictly limited as is their right to retain vessels in their ports that are in breach of national pollution control rules—unless these rules reflect international treaties. These restrictions make the process of development and enforcement of international controls on polluting activities in the ocean—such as controls on dumping or discharging from vessels—extremely complex. The majority of successful marine pollution control regimes have adopted gradualist approaches whereby ship-owners are given the space to adapt to new technologies as they build replacement vessels (for example, the approach of the 1973/78 International Convention for the Prevention of Pollution from Ships (MARPOL Convention), also discussed later in this chapter) or have used lists of prohibited or controlled substances and then, over time, have moved more substances from the controlled list onto the prohibited list. In the case of the 1972 Convention on the Prevention of Marine Pollution by Dumping of Wastes and Other Matter (London Convention, discussed later), the eventual result was a complete reversal of the burden of proof. Rather than listing substances that could not be dumped, the new approach instead lists the substances permitted to be dumped, with a ban on all others.

It is interesting that many of the new concepts now used for the management of marine living resources arose from treaty regimes established to deal with marine pollution. Both the precautionary principle and the ecosystem approach were developed in the context of regional efforts to deal with the very real impacts of multiple sources of pollution. Although there are a large number of marine environmental treaties, their development has been haphazard and essentially 'disaster driven'. The early marine pollution conventions were developed to address particular problems that came to light as a result of well-publicized pollution incidents. So, although marine pollution from oil tankers is one of the smaller causes of marine pollution, it is subject to one of the most sophisticated regulatory regimes because of the immediate scale of impacts when tankers are wrecked. For example, the 1954 International Convention for the Prevention of Pollution of the Sea by Oil broke new ground by developing a regulatory framework for the carriage of oil by sea. However, the first conventions to provide for emergency action and for compensation for oil pollution damage were developed directly in response to the world's first major oil tanker casualty—the 1967 wreck of the Liberian oil tanker *Torrey Canyon* off the coast of southwest England. The 1969 International Convention Relating to Intervention on the High Seas in Cases of Oil Pollution Casualties authorized emergency action by coastal states outside territorial waters. Two companion agreements, the 1969 International Convention on Civil Liability for Oil Pollution Damage and the 1971 International Convention on the Establishment of an International Fund for Compensation for Oil Pollution Damage, provided a basis for compensation claims against the owners and operators of oil tankers, supplemented by an international compensation fund (see Chapter 44 'International Responsibility and Liability').[5] Further, highly publicized tanker wrecks, notably the *Amoco Cadiz* off Brittany, the *Exxon Valdez* in Alaska, and most recently the *Prestige* off the coast of Spain, have led to further tightening of the regimes for the carriage of oil.[6]

However, more oil pollution is actually caused by 'operational discharges' from tanker washing and the discharge of bunkers. The main regulatory body for these issues is the International Maritime Organization (IMO), which is based in London. The IMO functions by consensus, and state delegations are often drawn from industry as well as government and non-governmental organizations. The regulatory authority for tankers—as with vessels of all kinds—is the state whose flag the vessel flies (the flag state). However, many of the states with the largest number of vessels are open registry states or flags of convenience, often without the capacity to exercise effective enforcement jurisdiction. The LOSC (Articles 218–19) does give port states authority to apprehend vessels for acts of pollution in breach of 'applicable international rules and standards' and to detain vessels that do not satisfy international construction, design, and equipment standards. Yet, generally in order for a treaty regime to apply to their vessels, the flag states must become a party to the treaty. Thus, the challenge has been to impose stricter standards on vessel owners in a way they find acceptable, so that they do not simply reflag in another state that has not agreed to the stricter standards. The IMO has done this through the gradual introduction of new technology into the construction of new tankers (for example, the use of divided hulls with so-called 'load on top' systems, which allow tankers to filter oil from ballast water, separate ballast water tanks, and even double hulls to lessen the risk of oil leaks from impacts). The 1973/78 MARPOL Convention provides the main regulatory regime for pollution from vessels of all sorts, including oil tankers, but it also extends now to the carriage of noxious liquid substances (Annex II), packaged waste (Annex III), sewage (Annex IV), garbage (Annex V), and to air pollution by a new Annex VI agreed in 1997.

This gradualist approach has been made possible by the MARPOL Convention's tacit amendment procedure (see Chapter 20 'Treaty Making and Treaty Evolution'), which allows the IMO Marine Environment Protection Committee (MEPC) to adopt technical amendments through amendment of the MARPOL annexes. These are subject to acceptance by two-thirds of the parties constituting at least 50 per cent of the tonnage of the world merchant fleet. The MARPOL requirements and also those of the London Convention, regulating dumping at sea, are incorporated by reference into the LOSC, and those provisions that are in force may now be argued to be

---

[5] Note also the significant industry voluntary compensation schemes, such as Tanker Owners Voluntary Agreement Concerning Liability for Oil Pollution (TOVALOP), dating from 1969; and Contract Regarding a Supplement to Tanker Liability for Oil Pollution (CRISTAL), which dates from 1971. See further D.W. Abecassis and R.L. Jarashow, *Oil Pollution from Ships*, 2nd edition (London: Stevens and Sons, 1985).

[6] V. Frank, 'Consequences of the *Prestige* Sinking for European and International Law' (2005) 20 Int'l. J. Marine & Coastal L. 1.

binding on all parties to the LOSC or possibly also to be part of customary law and therefore binding on all states (see Chapter 32 'International Institutions').[7] Incorporation by reference is itself an important means of introducing dynamism into the overarching framework of the LOSC so as to keep it up to date. When the LOSC text uses phrases such as 'applicable international rules and standards established by the competent international organisation,' it is recognizing that over time these organizations will develop new rules and standards that by reference will become part of the applicable regime of the LOSC.

The MARPOL Convention also recognizes that stricter regimes may be designated within 'special areas' agreed by the parties. Such regimes now apply to a number of regional seas including the northeast Atlantic, the Mediterranean, the Black Sea, and the Baltic as well as the Gulf, and the Antarctic. The IMO MEPC has also recognized that certain areas may be designated by the IMO as 'particularly sensitive sea areas' in recognition of the fact that they are particularly vulnerable to environmental threats from maritime activities. A number of sensitive areas, notably the Great Barrier Reef off the northeast coast of Australia, have been so designated, permitting a wider range of controls over shipping.[8]

2.2.3 *Regulation of Ocean Dumping*

Another high profile activity with potentially large impacts, particularly localized ones, is the dumping of waste into the oceans. The 1972 London Convention regulating dumping at sea has taken a similar gradualist approach to this issue. Again, if dumping takes place on the high seas, the only entities that can regulate this activity are the flag states and the states from whose ports the vessel sails or returns to. The 1972 Convention adopted what has now become a common approach in environmental agreements—a listing system. It initially listed substances (in its Annex I) that could not be dumped in the ocean and, (in Annex II), listed substances that could be dumped only with a permit. As public support for the elimination of dumping in the oceans has grown, the regulatory structure, which requires parties to enforce obligations against any vessels loading in their ports or their flag vessel anywhere in the world, has progressively tightened its regime. Indeed, the initial approach of listing banned substances has been entirely replaced by what is called a 'negative listing' approach. Negative listing is an important application of the precautionary principle. It reverses the presumption that any non-listed substances may be dumped. Under the negative list, only listed substances may be dumped, while the dumping of all other substances is prohibited. By the use of this approach, the parties to the 1972 London Convention have effectively ended the ocean dumping of waste.

---

[7] P. Birnie and A.E. Boyle, *International Law and the Environment*, 2nd edition (Oxford: Oxford University Press, 2002) at 353.

[8] D. Freestone and K. Gjerde, 'Particularly Sensitive Sea Areas: An Important Environmental Concept at a Turning Point' (1994) 9 Int'l J. Marine & Coastal L. (Special Issue) 431.

2.2.4 *Regulation of Pollution from Land-Based Sources*

The single largest source of marine pollution is from land-based sources, whether from direct point sources, such as factories or sewage outfalls, or from diffuse sources—such as run off from the agricultural use of pesticides and agricultural fertilizers or even from the atmosphere. These sources are more difficult to regulate by international law because the activities that give rise to the problems take place within national jurisdictions, sometimes in up-stream states and in watercourses many miles from the ocean. It is a significant example of the natural overlap with the regulation of international watercourses, which requires the watercourse states to take all measures to protect and preserve the marine environment (as discussed later in this chapter).

The search for an international instrument to regulate ocean pollution from land-based sources—a problem termed 'ubiquitous' rather than 'global'—has been elusive. In 1995, at a meeting in Washington, DC, a 'Plan of Action' was agreed, but its impacts have been disappointing as states have been slow to introduce the necessary regulatory changes. In fact, land-based pollution poses a classic 'tragedy of the commons' issue as the costs of reducing land-based sources have to be borne by coastal or riverine states, while the impacts are downstream and on the global commons—the oceans. The most successful approaches to a range of marine pollution issues have been those espoused by regional bodies, often where financing mechanisms such as the Global Environment Facility have been involved—as in the Danube/Black Sea area. Notable is the pioneering work done at the political level by the North Sea states in the context of a series of international conferences among the littoral states. The North Sea states decided not to develop a new convention, but rather to take decisions to implement existing instruments more effectively according to certain principles.

2.2.5 *Regional Approaches*

The integrated, holistic approach adopted by the North Sea states has generated a number of new approaches and principles that apply to a wider spread of pollution sources. One of those principles is the principle derived from the German *Vorsorgeprinzip*, which translates into English as the 'precautionary principle' and is now widely accepted as a general international environmental law principle (see Chapter 25 'Precaution'). This principle has spawned a number of devices under which the burden of proof is reversed in favour of conservation. A good example is the prior justification procedure pioneered by the regulatory body of the Paris Convention (the predecessor to the OSPAR Convention). Under this procedure an applicant had to prove that any proposed activity would not have deleterious environmental impacts, rather than the usual process of presuming no such impacts until they are proven. Although this approach was developed in relation to ocean dumping, the general approach is now being used more widely. Another such device is negative or reverse listing (discussed earlier in this chapter) under which only listed activities are permitted, rather than, as usual, vice versa. For land-based sources, the focus of regulation has shifted to the requirements for adoption and use of best available technology (BAT), in some situations best available technology not entailing excessive costs (BATNEEC), and best environmental practices (BEP).[9] The northeast Atlantic bodies also pioneered the integration of nature conservation into their programs, which initially focused on anti-pollution measures. These programs gave rise to the argument that a holistic approach should be taken with respect to the whole marine environment—which is the precursor to the ecosystem approach to wildlife, natural resources, and fisheries management (see Chapter 24 'Ecosystems').

At a broader regional level, the United Nations Environment Programme (UNEP) Regional Seas Programme provides a framework for the development of regional cooperation on marine environmental issues. Regional cooperation exists in some eighteen regions, of which some fourteen have concluded regional marine protection treaties. These cover the Mediterranean (1976, Barcelona), west and central Africa (1981, Abidjan), the southeast Pacific (1981, Lima), the Red Sea and Gulf of Aden (1982, Jeddah), the wider Caribbean (1983, Cartegena), East Africa (1985, Nairobi), the South Pacific (1986, Noumea), the Gulf (2001, Kuwait), northeast Pacific (2002, Antigua), and others in various stages of planning. These framework treaties are supplemented by protocols covering a wide range of issues including the regulation of land-based sources of pollution, ocean dumping, pollution from (and decommissioning of) offshore oilrigs, specially protected areas, and the protection of wildlife. Other regional regimes have been developed outside the UNEP framework including the comprehensive regime for Antarctica (1959 Antarctic Convention and 1980 Convention on the Conservation of Antarctic Marine Living Resources), the northeast Atlantic (1992, OSPAR), the Baltic (1974, Helsinki), the Black Sea (1992, Bucharest), and the Caspian (2003, Tehran).

3 FRESHWATER RESOURCES

Pursuant to the UN General Assembly (UNGA) resolution on international watercourses, the ILC started working on a draft convention on the law of the non-navigational uses of international watercourses at its twenty-third session in December 1971. After close to a quarter of a century, and a series of reports and rapporteurs, the ILC completed its work, adopted the draft convention (UN Convention on the Law of the Non-Navigational Uses of International Watercourses (Watercourses Convention)), and recommended it to the UNGA in June 1994.[10]

---

[9] E. Hey, 'International Regime for the Protection of the North Sea: From Functional Approaches to a More Integrated Approach' (2002) 17 Int'l J. Marine & Coastal L. 325 at 340–50.

[10] See (1997) 2(2) 1994 Y.B. Int'l Law Commission at 88.

It took three more years of deliberations by the UNGA's legal drafting committee, the 'Sixth Committee', acting as a working group of the whole, before the UNGA adopted the convention and opened it for signature on 21 May 1997.[11] The convention has yet to enter into force.[12]

The ILC acknowledged the valuable contribution of international organizations, both governmental and non-governmental, to the codification and progressive development of international water law. It also recalled the existing bilateral and multilateral agreements regarding the non-navigational uses of international water-courses. Indeed, the regimes addressing international rivers and lakes are among the oldest international environmental regimes, dating back to the early twentieth century. The resolutions and declarations issued by the Institute of International Law and the International Law Association (ILA) have contributed significantly to the emergence of such regimes. The Madrid Declaration, which was issued by the Institute of International Law in 1911, forbade the emptying of injurious matters, such as those from factories, into international rivers. This obligation against causing pollution was elaborated and refined by the institute in later resolutions, particularly the Salzburg Resolution of 1961 and the Athens Resolution of 1979. The ILA also addressed the issue of pollution of international watercourses in a series of resolutions and rules, particularly the Helsinki Rules of 1966.

Treaties and conventions dealing with the environmental aspects of international rivers can also be traced to the beginning of the last century. As early as 1909, the United States and Canada agreed, as part of the treaty relating to their boundary waters, that such waters and the waters flowing across their boundaries should not be polluted on either side to the injury of health or property of the other. The 1923 General Convention Relating to the Development of Hydraulic Power Affecting More Than One State (Geneva Convention) dealt with the right of any riparian state to carry out on its territory any operations for the development of hydraulic power subject to 'the limits of international law'. Such limits have been interpreted to mean the obligation of the state not to cause significant harm to other states. Thus, the work of the ILC grew out of rich historical tradition, including a considerable body of customary international law.

The Watercourses Convention aims, as stated in its preamble, at ensuring the utilization, development, conservation, management, and protection of international watercourses and promoting optimal and sustainable utilization thereof for present and future generations. The main areas that the convention addresses include the definition of the term 'watercourse'; watercourse agreements; equitable and reasonable utilization and the obligation not to cause harm; planned measures; protection,

---

[11] The convention was adopted by a vote of 103 for and three against (Burundi, China. and Turkey), with 27 abstentions.

[12] According to Article 36 of the convention, 35 instruments of ratification/accession are needed for the convention to enter into force. As of November 2006, only 14 countries have ratified or acceded to the convention.

preservation, and management; and dispute settlement. Thus, it is a framework convention that provides basic substantive and procedural principles which subsequent agreements could adopt or adjust.

This part of the chapter will discuss and analyze the environmental provisions of the Watercourses Convention, and compare them with the environmental provisions of other multilateral and bilateral watercourses agreements. It will also attempt to discern the emerging principles of international environmental law with regard to international watercourses.

3.1 Environmental Provisions of the Watercourses Convention

3.1.1 *Principle of Equitable Utilization and the No Harm Rule*

The environmental provisions of the Watercourses Convention must be seen against the backdrop of the larger debate on the relationship between the 'no harm' rule, a cornerstone principle of international environmental law (see Chapter 22 'Transboundary Impacts'), and the principle of equitable and reasonable utilization (see Chapter 27 'Equity'), which has played a central role in the law on international freshwater resources. Lower riparians tend to favour the no harm rule since it protects existing uses against impacts resulting from activities undertaken by upstream states. Conversely, upper riparians tend to favour the equitable utilization principle, precisely because it provides more scope for states to utilize their share of the watercourse for activities that may impact on downstream states.

Agreement on which rule takes priority has thus proven elusive and the issue dogged the ILC throughout its work on the watercourses topic. After the ILC completed its work, the resulting draft articles were considered by the Sixth Committee. The compromise regarding the relationship between the two principles, which is now contained in Article 5 (equitable and reasonable utilization and participation) and Article 7 (obligation not to cause significant harm) requires the state that causes significant harm to take measures to eliminate or mitigate such harm 'having due regard to' the principles of equitable and reasonable utilization. As Lucius Caflisch noted, '[t]he new formula was considered by a number of lower riparians to be sufficiently neutral not to suggest a subordination of the no-harm rule to the principle of equitable and reasonable utilization. A number of upper riparians thought just the contrary, namely that, that formula was strong enough to support the idea of such a subordination.'[13]

---

[13] See L. Caflisch, 'Regulation of the Uses of International Watercourses,' in S.M.A. Salman and L. Boisson de Chazournes, eds., *International Watercourses—Enhancing Cooperation and Managing Conflict*, World Bank Technical Paper no. 414 (Washington, DC: World Bank, 1998) 3 at 15.

However, despite the adoption of the Watercourses Convention by a large majority with this compromise language, the issue seems far from resolved for many states on both sides of the debate. It is to be noted that the three countries that voted against the convention (Burundi, China, and Turkey) and some of those that abstained, such as Bolivia, Ethiopia, Mali, and Tanzania, are upper riparian states. Still, a number of downstream states, such as Egypt, France, Pakistan, and Peru, also abstained.[14] The perception by the upstream riparians that the convention is biased in favour of downstream riparians, and vice-versa, is, no doubt, one of the main reasons for the stalling of the process of the signature and ratification of the convention. Yet, a close reading of Articles 5, 6, and 7 would lead to the conclusion that the Watercourses Convention has indeed subordinated the obligation not to cause significant harm to the principle of equitable and reasonable utilization. Some of the factors for determining equitable and reasonable utilization under Article 6 (namely existing and potential uses and the effects of the uses of the watercourse by one state on other states) relate to the causing of harm. Moreover, Article 7 on the obligation not to cause significant harm is qualified by Articles 5 and 6 and further indicates that the causing of harm may be tolerated in certain cases such as when the possibility of compensation may be considered. However, it should be pointed out that there are experts in this field who interpret the convention as having presented the two principles as equals.[15]

3.1.2 *Protection, Preservation, and Management of Watercourse Ecosystems*

The general rule laid down in Article 7 of the Watercourses Convention relating to the obligation not to cause significant harm applies both to quantity and quality of the waters of the international watercourse and is a basic principle of customary law. The causing of harm could result from a decrease in the flow of the waters as well as from adversely affecting the quality of such waters and the environment of the watercourse. The convention addresses these environmental issues in Articles 20–3 of Part IV on Protection, Preservation and Management. Article 20 requires the watercourse states individually, and, where appropriate, jointly, to protect and preserve the ecosystems of the international watercourse. The obligation is broad because it relates to the entire ecosystems of the watercourse. Such ecosystems would go beyond water and would include the fauna and flora as well as the land contiguous to the watercourse, which should be used in a manner that would not harm the watercourse. The concept of the ecosystem (see Chapter 24 'Ecosystems'), as noted by one expert, 'is and should be a broad one, its main function in ecological thought being to emphasize obligatory relationships, interdependence and causal relationships.'[16]

[14] India, which is a downstream riparian vis-à-vis Nepal and China, and upstream riparian vis-à-vis Bangladesh, also abstained.

[15] A. Tanzi and M. Arcari, *The United Nations Convention on the Law of International Watercourses* (New York: Kluwer Law International, 2001).

[16] Professor Odum, quoted in D. Hunter, J. Salzman, and D. Zaelke, *International Environmental Law and Policy* (New York: Foundation Press, 1998) at 842.

Article 21 requires watercourse states to prevent, reduce, and control pollution that may cause significant harm to other watercourse states or to their environment, including harm to human health or safety, to the use of the waters for any beneficial purposes, or to the living resources of the watercourse. The article also obliges the watercourse states to consult with each other with the view to arriving at mutually agreeable measures and methods to prevent, reduce, and control pollution. Consultation would cover matters such as setting water quality objectives and criteria, establishing techniques and practices to address pollution from point and non-point sources, and establishing lists of substances 'the introduction of which into the waters of an international watercourse is to be prohibited, limited, investigated or monitored'. Pollution is defined under Article 21 to mean any detrimental alteration in the composition or quality of the waters of an international watercourse that results directly or indirectly from human conduct.

Article 22 requires watercourse states to take all measures necessary to prevent the introduction into an international watercourse of alien or new species that may have effects detrimental to the ecosystem of the watercourse, resulting in significant harm to other watercourse states. Finally, marine environmental protection is dealt with under Article 23. It obliges watercourse states to take all measures with respect to an international watercourse that are necessary to protect and preserve the marine environment, including estuaries, taking into account generally accepted international rules and standards.

A number of observations can be made with regard to these four articles outlining the environmental obligations of the watercourse states. First, whereas the obligation to protect and preserve the ecosystems of the international watercourse under Article 20 is unqualified, the obligations with regard to pollution, introduction of alien species, and protection of the marine environment in Articles 21, 22, and 23, respectively, are qualified in different respects. Articles 21 and 22 establish significant harm as the threshold, whereas under Article 23, the watercourse states are required to take into account generally accepted international rules and standards. A statement of understanding issued by the Sixth Committee, convening as the Working Group of the Whole, clarified that the term 'significant' is not used in the convention in the sense of 'substantial' and that while the effect 'must be capable of being established by objective evidence and not be trivial in nature, it need not rise to the level of being substantial.' Another statement of understanding clarified that Articles 21, 22, and 23 'impose a due diligence standard on watercourse States.'[17] It is widely agreed that the obligation under Article 20 is also of due diligence character and thus qualified at least in this sense.[18]

---

[17] Due diligence has been defined as 'the diligence to be expected from a good government, i.e. from a government mindful of its international obligations.' See P.-M. Dupuy, 'Due Diligence in International Law of Liability,' in Organisation for Economic Co-operation and Development (OECD), *Legal Aspects of Transfrontier Pollution* (Paris: OECD, 1977) 369 at 369.

[18] See M. Fitzmaurice, 'General Principles Governing the Cooperation between States in Relation to Non-Navigational Uses of International Watercourses' (2003) 14 Y.B. Int'l Envt'l L. 3.

Second, Articles 20, 21, and 23 require action by the watercourse states individually and, only where appropriate, jointly. As such, there is no obligation for collective action. The convention does not require the establishment of joint management mechanisms. Rather, it obliges watercourse states, at the request of any of them, 'to enter into consultations concerning the management of an international watercourse, which may include the establishment of a joint management mechanism.' Third, Article 23 on protection and preservation of the marine environment extends the possibility of cooperation to other states that do not share the watercourse. This matter is important, given that acts by either group of states could adversely affect the other or the marine environment.

Although the Watercourses Convention has not yet entered into force, there is no doubt that, through the codification of basic principles, it has contributed substantially to the development of a general international legal regime for the environmental protection of shared watercourses. Moreover, the convention has exerted considerable influence on subsequent watercourses agreements, such as the Revised Protocol on Shared Watercourses in the Southern African Development Community (SADC Protocol)[19] and the Agreement on the Cooperation for the Sustainable Development of the Mekong River Basin, which are discussed later in this chapter.

The influence and relevance of the Watercourses Convention has also been underscored by the International Court of Justice (ICJ) in the *Case Concerning the Gabčíkovo-Nagymaros Project (Hungary v. Slovakia)*, which was decided by the court in September 1997, about four months after the adoption of the convention by the UNGA.[20] The case provided an opportunity for the court to address a wide range of international legal issues, including the law of treaties, state responsibility, environmental law, and the concept of sustainable development, as well as international watercourses. With regard to international watercourses, in particular, the ICJ quoted from a decision of the Permanent Court of International Justice that the 'community of interest in a navigable river becomes the basis of a common legal right, the essential features of which are the perfect equality of all riparian States in the user of the whole course of the river and the exclusion of any preferential privilege of one riparian State in relation to the others.'[21] In this connection, the court added that modern development of international law has strengthened this principle for non-navigational uses of international watercourses as well, 'as evidenced by the adoption of the Convention of 21 May 1997 on the Law of the Non-Navigational Uses

---

[19] This protocol revised and replaced the 1995 Protocol on Shared Watercourse Systems in the Southern African Development Community (SADC). The revision was specifically done to make the revised protocol consistent with the Watercourses Convention.

[20] See *Case Concerning the Gabčíkovo-Nagymaros Project (Hungary v. Slovakia)* Judgment of 25 September 1997, [1997] I.C.J. Rep. 92 [*Gabčíkovo-Nagymaros*].

[21] See *ibid.* at para. 85. See *also Territorial Jurisdiction of International Commission of the River Oder*, Judgment no. 16, [1929] P.C.I.J. 4 (10 September 1929, Series A, No. 23) at 27.

of International Watercourses by the United Nations General Assembly.'[22] Further-more, the court emphasized the concept of equitable and reasonable utilization when it directed that 'the multi-purpose programme, in the form of a co-ordinated single unit, for the use, development and protection of the watercourse is implemented in an equitable and reasonable manner.'[23]

In 2004 the ILA adopted the Berlin Rules. These rules revise all the previously adopted rules and declarations of the ILA on international water resources. Although the rules issued by the ILA have no legally binding effect, most of them are authoritative because they reflect customary international law. The Berlin Rules address in detail the protection of the aquatic environment, including the ecological integrity necessary to sustain ecosystems dependent on particular waters, ecological flows, alien species, hazard substances, pollution, and water quality standards. They also include an explicit reference to the obligation of assessing the environmental impacts of projects and programs. Although the rules go beyond the environmental provisions of the Watercourses Convention, they are based largely on these provisions, thus providing further evidence of the influence of the convention.[24]

3.2 UN Economic Commission for Europe (ECE) Convention on the Protection and Use of Transboundary Watercourses and International Lakes (UNECE Convention)

The environmental provisions of the Watercourses Convention are limited in scope when compared with the provisions of the UNECE Convention, which was adopted by the UNECE in 1992 and which entered into force in 1996.[25] Article 3 of the UNECE Convention obliges the parties to take all appropriate measures to prevent, control, and reduce any transboundary impact. It goes on to require the parties to take all appropriate measures to prevent, control, and reduce the pollution of waters causing or likely to cause transboundary impact, and to ensure that transboundary waters are used with the aim of ecologically sound and rational water management and environmental protection. It lays down three principles to guide the parties when

---

[22] See *Gabčíkovo-Nagymaros*, note 20 above at para. 85.   [23] See *ibid.* at para. 150.

[24] It should be added that the convention was endorsed by a number of international entities including the World Commission on Dams. See World Commission on Dams, *Dams and Development: A New Framework for Decision-making*, Report of the World Commission on Dams (London: Earthscan, 2000) at 253, as well as the World Commission on Water for the Twenty-First Century (see Global Water Partnership, *Towards Water Security: A Framework for Action* (Stockholm: Global Water Partnership, 2000) at 32).

[25] The United Nations Economic Commission for Europe (UNECE) encompasses Europe, Central Asia, North America, and Israel.

taking these measures. The first of these principles is the precautionary principle (see Chapter 25 'Precaution'). It requires that action to avoid the potential transboundary impact of the release of hazardous substances not be postponed on the ground that scientific research has not fully proven a causal link between those substances, on the one hand, and the potential transboundary impact, on the other hand. The second is the polluter pays principle, and the third is the sustainability principle. Under the last principle, water resources should be managed so that the needs of the present generations are met without compromising the ability of future generations to meet their own needs (see Chapter 26 'Sustainable Development'). The Watercourses Convention does not include an explicit reference to either of the first two principles. A reference to sustainability was included in the Watercourses Convention during the final drafting stages in the preamble and in Article 5 on equitable and reasonable utilization, and it has been argued that this reference implicitly recognizes the precautionary principle. Article 5 requires using and developing the international watercourse 'with a view to attaining optimal and sustainable utilization thereof.'

The UNECE Convention defines transboundary impact to mean any significant adverse effect on the environment of one state resulting from a change in the conditions of transboundary waters caused by a human activity—the physical origin of which is situated wholly or in part within an area under the jurisdiction of another party. The definition goes on to state that such effects on the environment include effects on human health and safety, flora, fauna, soil, air, water, climate, landscape and historical monuments or other physical structures, or the interaction among these factors. They also include effects on the cultural heritage or socio-economic conditions resulting from alterations to these factors. Furthermore, the convention requires the parties to develop, adopt, and implement legal measures to ensure, *inter alia*, prior licensing of waste water discharges, limits of waste water discharges based on best available technology, biological treatments for waste water, application of environmental impact assessment and other means of assessment, and minimization of accidental pollution. It also requires exchange of data and information between the parties to cover, *inter alia*, the environmental conditions of the transboundary waters, emission and monitoring data, and measures taken or planned to be taken to prevent, control, or reduce transboundary impact.[26]

Thus, the environmental provisions of the UNECE Convention are far more elaborate and comprehensive than those of the Watercourses Convention, and, accordingly, it is more protective of the environment. This should be expected given the global nature of the Watercourses Convention, which needs to take into account the regional variations and standards being used in addressing environmental issues. Moreover, the Watercourses Convention is a framework convention, which is to

---

[26] For an analysis of the UNECE Convention, see B. Bosnjakovic, 'UNECE Strategies for Protecting the Environment with Respect to International Watercourses: The Helsinki and Espoo Conventions,' in Salman and Boisson de Chazournes, note 13 above at 47.

be complemented by agreements among/between the different riparian states. Although the same could be said of the UNECE Convention, the latter provides more minimum standards and guidelines than the Watercourses Convention. It should also be noted that while the UNECE Convention pays more attention to the qualitative aspects of the shared watercourses, the Watercourses Convention is more concerned with the quantitative sharing and use of such waters. This difference in emphasis is apparent from the subordination by the Watercourses Convention of the obligation not to cause significant harm to the principle of equitable and reasonable utilization, on the one hand, and from the detailed annexes to the UNECE Convention dealing with water quality objectives and criteria, best environmental practice, and best available technology on the other hand.

Having been adopted in a regional setting, where the environmental standards of the parties are, by and large, similar and where an action by one state could easily affect the environment of other states, the UNECE Convention entered into force relatively quickly, four years after its adoption.[27] Indeed, following the success of this convention, the parties decided in 2003 to amend its provisions to allow countries outside the UNECE region to accede. This amendment, which has not yet entered into force, has particular relevance and importance to the countries that share borders with members of the UNECE and could also play a role in exporting UNECE standards to other regions.

3.3 Other Multilateral and Bilateral Agreements

As mentioned earlier, the 1909 Boundary Waters Treaty between the United States and Canada is one of the oldest treaties addressing pollution of international watercourses. The treaty also established the International Joint Commission and equipped it with considerable authority. The Boundary Waters Treaty was supplemented by the 1972 Agreement on Great Lakes Water Quality. This agreement laid down general, as well as specific, water quality objectives. The specific objectives are defined as the level of substance or physical effect that the parties agree to recognize as the maximum or minimum desired limit. These objectives were further updated and strengthened by the 1978 Water Quality Agreement. The agreement aims at restoring and maintaining the chemical, physical, and biological integrity of the waters of the Great Lakes basin ecosystem. However, the agreement states that the specific objectives represent the minimum levels of water quality, and are not intended to preclude the establishment of more stringent requirements. These agreements were followed and further strengthened by the landmark Great Lakes—St. Lawrence River Basin Sustainable Water Resources Agreement, which

---

[27] It is worth noting in this context that the non-regional members of the UNECE, the United States, Canada, and Israel, are not parties to the UNECE Convention.

was concluded in December 2005. This agreement indeed represents an interesting development because it has been concluded by the states and provinces sharing the basin,[28] whereas, all the previous agreements on the Great Lakes have been concluded by the governments of the United States and Canada themselves. The agreement bans new diversions of water from the basin, allowing only limited exceptions, and requires the states and provinces to use consistent standards to review proposed uses of the Great Lakes waters. It also requires that lasting economic development be balanced with sustainable water use to ensure that waters are managed responsibly. In this regard, the agreement requires that regional goals and objectives for water conservation and efficiency be developed and reviewed every five years by the regional body established under the agreement. The agreement also commits the parties to provide leadership for the development of a collaborative strategy to strengthen the scientific basis for sound water management. Clearly, this agreement lays down more stringent standards than the previous agreements in the region.

Similarly, the multilateral and bilateral agreements on shared watercourses in Europe that have been entered into since the conclusion of the UNECE Convention apply even more stringent environmental standards than that convention. The UNECE Convention itself states that its provisions shall not affect the rights of the parties, individually or jointly, to adopt and implement more stringent measures than those set forth in the convention. The Convention on Cooperation for the Protection and Sustainable Use of the River Danube (Danube Convention), which was concluded in 1994, two years after the UNECE Convention was adopted, is an example. Although the Danube Convention sets the sustainable development and environmental protection of the Danube as the main objectives of the convention, it goes beyond the general obligation of preventing, controlling, and reducing transboundary impacts. Article 5 of the Danube Convention requires the contracting parties to develop, adopt, and implement legal, administrative, and technical measures to ensure efficient water quality protection and sustainable water use and, thereby, also prevent, control, and reduce transboundary impact. Due regard is paid by the convention to the protection of the Black Sea and its marine environment from pollution loads from sources in the catchment area of the Danube. The Danube Convention also includes an annex containing a list of industrial sectors and industries, as well as an additional list of hazardous substances and groups of substances, the discharge of which from point and non-point sources is prevented or considerably reduced. To keep the list current with advances in science and technology, the convention entrusts the International Commission for the Protection of the Danube with the task of updating the list. Thus, the Danube Convention has adapted the environmental provisions of the UNECE Convention to a specific watercourse context and has, indeed, gone beyond the environmental requirements set forth in this convention.

[28] Those states are Illinois, Indiana, Michigan, Minnesota, New York, Ohio, Pennsylvania, and Wisconsin in the United States, and the provinces of Ontario and Quebec in Canada.

The 1999 Convention on the Protection of the River Rhine (Rhine Convention) similarly goes beyond requiring the parties to be guided by the precautionary, polluter pays, and sustainable development principles, which are also set forth in the UNECE Convention. In addition, the Rhine Convention requires that the parties be guided, *inter alia*, by the principle of preventive action, the principle of rectification, as a priority at source, and application and development of the state of the art and best environmental practice. A number of aims are spelled out in the Rhine Convention. Such aims include conserving, improving, and restoring the most natural habitats possible for wild fauna and flora in the water, on the river bed and banks, and in adjacent areas and improving living conditions for fish and restoring their free migration. They also include restoring the North Sea in conjunction with the other actions taken to protect it. It is worth noting that the first legal instrument dealing with the protection of the Rhine against pollution dates back to 1963, when the Agreement Concerning the International Commission for the Protection of the Rhine was concluded. This agreement was followed by the 1976 Convention for the Protection of the Rhine against Pollution by Chlorides, and the Additional Protocol of 1991 to the convention. These two agreements and the protocol were complemented by the Rhine Action Programme of September 1987 and later by the 1999 Rhine Convention. Thus, the Rhine can be said to be one of the first watercourses where detailed attention has been paid to the environment and, perhaps, one of the most environmentally protected watercourses in existence.

The number of multilateral and bilateral agreements dealing with the environment of international watercourses outside Europe and North America has also increased considerably in recent years. One instrument that is worth mentioning is the Agreement on the Action Plan for the Environmentally Sound Management of the Common Zambezi River System. This agreement was concluded in 1987 by Botswana, Mozambique, Tanzania, Zambia, and Zimbabwe, under the auspices of the United Nations Development Programme. It aimed at the environmentally sound water resources management of the Zambezi river system, as well as strengthening regional cooperation for sustainable development. The action plan included 19 projects covering various aspects of sustainable environmental management. Another regional instrument that has addressed environmental issues in detail is the Revised Protocol on Shared Watercourses in the Southern African Development Community (SADC), which was concluded in August 2000. Article 4(2) on Environmental Protection and Preservation consists of four parts reproducing, in more or less the same wording and order, the four articles of the Watercourses Convention dealing with the environment.[29]

Furthermore, the Agreement on the Cooperation for the Sustainable Development of the Mekong River Basin, which was concluded in April 1995, includes two

[29] For an analysis of the provisions of the SADC Protocol, see S.M.A. Salman, 'Legal Regime for Use and Protection of International Watercourses in the Southern African Development Community: Evolution and Context' (2001) 41 Natural Resources J. 981.

articles that capture some of the basic environmental provisions for shared water-courses. Article 3 states the agreement of the parties to protect the environment, nat-ural resources, aquatic life and conditions, and ecological balance of the Mekong River from pollution or other harmful effects resulting from any development plans and uses of water and related sources in the basin. Article 7 requires the parties to make every effort to avoid, minimize, and mitigate harmful effects that might occur to the environment of the river system, especially with respect to water quantity and quality, aquatic (eco-system) conditions, and ecological balance, from the develop-ment and use of the Mekong water resources or discharges of wastes and return flows.[30]

Thus, the instruments discussed in this chapter present wide-ranging approaches to the environmental protection of international watercourses. While the UNECE Convention and the other multilateral instruments in Europe and North America have gone a long way towards such protection, the Watercourses Convention and other regional watercourse instruments are not as advanced. Yet, all of these instru-ments reveal both established principles of international environmental law, such as the obligation to reduce and control pollution, as well as emerging principles, such as the obligation to protect and preserve the ecosystems of international watercourses. The over-arching obligation of states to ensure that activities within their jurisdic-tion respect the environment of other states, which is affirmed by the ICJ in the *Gabčíkovo-Nagymaros* case, will keep developing with more advances in scientific knowledge of the ecosystems of international watercourses.

4 CONCLUSION

It is interesting, but not surprising, that two discrete legal regimes exist for the two major aquatic ecosystems—oceans and watercourses. As the previous discussion has highlighted, the legal issues raised by the two systems are very different. However, there are a number of important synergies. The most significant cause of marine pol-lution is from land-based sources, and this pollution is principally carried into the sea by rivers. Many watercourse regimes—such as those of the Rhine and the Danube—are explicitly designed to restore and protect the seas into which they empty—the North Sea and the Black Sea respectively. This is surely the reason why both regimes have explicitly incorporated modern thinking on the obligations to reduce and con-trol pollution and to protect and preserve ecosystems.

---

[30] It is worth noting that only Cambodia, Lao Democratic Republic, Thailand, and Vietnam are parties to the Agreement on the Cooperation for the Sustainable Development of the Mekong River Basin. China and Myanmar, which are also riparian states of the Mekong River, are not parties to this agreement.

It is instructive to compare the virtually identical obligations in relation to both of these issues that are included in the LOSC (Articles 192 and 194) and the Watercourses Convention (Articles 20 and 21). Moreover, both regimes strike at issues that many states regard as fundamental to their sovereign rights, whether this is freedom of navigation or the use of precious freshwater resources. The need for codification was obvious in 1970, but for both regimes, the process has been arduous. After nine years of negotiation, the 1982 LOSC took a further 12 years to come into force and then only after the conclusion of a major interpretative, arguably amending, agreement in 1994. The 1997 Watercourses Convention took more than 25 years to be finalized and, nearly a decade later, has yet to command sufficient ratifications to enter into force.

RECOMMENDED READING

Ocean Resources

R. Barnes, D. Freestone, and D. Ong, eds., *The Law of the Sea: Progress and Prospects* (Oxford: Oxford University Press, 2006).

A.G. Oude Elferink, ed., *Stability and Change in the Law of the Sea: The Role of the Law of the Sea Convention* (Leiden: Martinus Nijhoff, 2005).

A.E. Boyle and D. Freestone, eds., *International Law and Sustainable Development* (Oxford: Oxford University Press, 1999).

J. Charney and L. Alexander, eds., *International Maritime Boundaries* (Dordrecht: Martinus Nijhoff, 1993).

P.H. Sand, *The Effectiveness of International Environmental Treaties* (Cambridge: Grotius Press, 1992), especially 'International Marine Environmental Treaties' at 149–254.

Freshwater Resources

L. Boisson de Chazournes and S.M.A. Salman, *Water Resources and International Law* (Leiden: Martinus Nijhoff, 2005).

C. Bourne, *International Water Law—Selected Writings of Professor Charles Bourne*, edited by P. Wouters (The Hague: Kluwer Law International, 1997).

S.C. McCaffrey, *The Law of International Watercourses—Non-Navigational Uses* (Oxford: Oxford University Press, 2001).

S.M.A. Salman and L. Boisson de Chazournes, *International Watercourses: Enhancing Cooperation and Managing Conflict*, World Bank Technical Paper no. 414 (Washington, DC: World Bank, 1998).

A. Tanzi and M. Arcari, *The United Nations Convention on the Law of International Watercourse* (The Hague: Kluwer Law International, 2001).

CHAPTER 16

BIOLOGICAL
RESOURCES

ROSEMARY RAYFUSE

1 INTRODUCTION

THE Earth's biological fecundity is staggering. While the exact number of terrestrial species is not known, it is estimated that there are between five and 30 million. Indeed, some scientists place the number as high as 50 million. Estimates of marine and, in particular, deep sea species vary widely from 500,000 to 100 million. While there is continuing debate among scientists over the extent to which global estimates of species numbers can be inferred based on limited data, it is clear that the number and diversity of both terrestrial and marine species is high.

Indicative of our very limited knowledge and understanding of the natural environment in which we humans live, only 1.9 million species have been described to date, with the conservation status of less than 3 per cent of those having been assessed. Even this modest level of assessment, however, gives cause for concern. The World Conservation Union (IUCN) expressly underestimates that among major species groups, 12 per cent of birds, 23 per cent of mammals, and 40 per cent of amphibians are threatened with extinction. In the reptile family, threat rates reach 51 per cent, particularly among turtles and tortoises, while 20 per cent of sharks and rays, 40 per cent of all freshwater fishes, and between 34 per cent and 86 per cent of plant species are under similar threat.[1] In addition, at least 20 per cent of coral reefs have been destroyed, with a further 24 per cent under imminent risk of collapse through human pressures.[2] Among the species cultivated or harvested for human consumption, the Food and Agricultural Organization (FAO) estimates that three-quarters of the genetic diversity found in agricultural crops has been lost over the last century with 1,350 of the 6,300 animal breeds used either endangered or already extinct.[3] Of the world's harvested fish stocks, the FAO has concluded that over 75 per cent are overexploited or being fished beyond their sustainable limits, with at least 10 per cent of stocks under immediate threat of extinction.[4]

The IUCN *Red List of Threatened Species* now contains 870 documented extinctions since 1500 AD, 74 of which have been in the wild, including the great auk and the Tasmanian tiger. At least another 208 species are thought to be extinct but not yet documented. From 1985 to 2006 alone, 41 extinctions in the wild occurred. In October 2004, hunters shot the last remaining female Pyrenean brown bear, consigning yet another species to extinction in the wild. The true significance of these numbers lies in the realization of the extremely small number of assessed species

---

[1] IUCN Species Survival Commission, *2006 IUCN Red List of Threatened Species:* available at <http://www.iucnredlist.org/>.

[2] C. Wilkinson et al., *Status of the Coral Reefs of the World: 2004* (Townsville, Queensland: Australian Institute of Marine Science, 2004). This report was published just days before the Indian Ocean Tsunami, which occurred on 26 December 2004 and which caused significant damage to coral reefs in the area.

[3] Food and Agriculture Organization (FAO), *Biodiversity for Food Security* (Bangkok: FAO, 2004).

[4] FAO, *The State of the World Fisheries and Aquaculture* (Rome: FAO, 2004). See also Chapter 15 'Ocean and Freshwater Resources' in this *Handbook*.

from which they are drawn. Extrapolations from these numbers conservatively indicate that current extinction rates are 50 to 1,000 times higher than extinction rates in the natural background fossil record.[5] Indeed, one estimate suggests that up to 25 per cent of all species—many of which have not yet even been described—could be extinct by 2050.[6]

Rather than being the result of naturally occurring causes, humans and human-related activities have been the main cause of extinctions since 1500 AD and represent the greatest danger to other living organisms on earth. Habitat loss and modification due to industrial, agricultural, and other activities and the introduction of invasive alien species are the most serious threats, followed closely by overexploitation due to hunting, collection, and persecution for food, medicine, the pet trade, or other purposes. Incidental mortality of non-targeted species, bio-prospecting, pollution, disease, land degradation, including desertification, deforestation, adverse climatic events such as droughts, and the introduction of transgenic or genetically modified organisms also pose threats. Beyond these, the increasing rapidity of global climate change is of major concern (see Chapter 14 'Atmosphere and Outer Space'), with fears that natural ranges for species will be unable to adapt to the unnaturally rapid changes. Climate change is already hastening the spread of invasive alien species and diseases and is likely to exacerbate human pressures on natural habitats. The consequences of this increasing habitat and species loss are both practical and ecological, threatening economic, agricultural, medical, moral, and aesthetic interests and, ultimately, the continued viability of life on earth.

It is axiomatic that as biologically renewable organisms, absent a natural mass extinctive event such as that which caused the demise of the dinosaurs or other natural extinctive processes, the continued naturally occurring viability and variability of all species within the Earth's biological chain should be assured. This assumes, however, the appropriate management of human/nature interactions. Historically, these interactions were considered a question of domestic law, reflective of states' rights to permanent sovereignty over their natural living and non-living resources. However, the potential for commercial exploitation of species, their migratory nature or transboundary dispersion, or their existence in areas beyond national jurisdiction where unlimited freedom of exploitation existed led, by the early twentieth century, to the realization that international cooperation would be necessary to protect species against human impacts (see Chapter 22 'Transboundary Impacts').

In the past century, a large number of bilateral, regional, and global agreements have been adopted relating to the protection, preservation, conservation, and management of the Earth's terrestrial and marine species and genetic resources. When viewed on paper, one might be forgiven for thinking that adequate protections have

---

[5] IUCN Species Survival Commission, see note 1 above.

[6] Millennium Ecosystem Assessment, *Ecosystems and Human Well-Being: Biodiversity Synthesis* (Washington, DC: Island Press, 2003).

been developed to ensure their continuing viability and vitality. Unfortunately, species, habitat, and genetic diversity loss is now considered to be reaching crisis proportions with potentially catastrophic consequences for humankind. This chapter examines and critically assesses the current international legal regime for the protection of the Earth's biological resources. It begins with a discussion of the meaning of the term 'biological resources,' the philosophical rationales for their protection, and the theoretical approaches thereto. It then examines the various legal regimes and regulatory measures that have been adopted. A detailed analysis of these regimes is beyond the scope of this chapter, which seeks, rather, to present a broad overview of the subject and to highlight the challenges for the future.

2 DEFINITION OF BIOLOGICAL RESOURCES

Early approaches to this topic are presented in terms of protection of 'wildlife' or 'wild flora and fauna', with an emphasis on regimes relating to the protection of predominantly terrestrial species or groups of species and terrestrial habitats. Since the 1980s, the focus has shifted, however, from ad hoc regimes for the protection of particular species of wildlife or their habitats to broader instruments intended to protect the fullness of the earth's biological diversity. This shift, which originated in the 1982 World Charter for Nature (WCN) and was made concrete in the 1992 Convention on Biological Diversity (CBD), reflects the realization of the interconnectedness of all life on Earth and the need to protect both genetic and species diversity as well as ecosystem diversity to ensure continued human existence (see Chapter 24 'Ecosystems').

As defined in the CBD, 'biological diversity' (usually shortened to 'biodiversity') means the 'variability among living organisms from all sources including, *inter alia*, terrestrial, marine and other aquatic ecosystems and the ecological complexes of which they are part; this includes diversity within species, between species and of ecosystems'. Biodiversity is thus the global resource combining the number of species, the genetic variety of species, and the variety of ecosystems on earth. Biodiversity is important not only as an economic resource but, more importantly, for providing ecosystem services and benefits to humans such as cleaning the air, disposing of wastes, recycling nutrients essential for agriculture, creating soils, and controlling disease.

In order to protect biodiversity and the 'variability among organisms', it is essential to protect the organisms themselves. These organisms are referred to in the CBD as 'biological resources', which include not just the charismatic mega-fauna and other species of flora and fauna traditionally referred to as 'wildlife' but also 'genetic resources, organisms or parts thereof, populations, or any other biotic component of ecosystems with actual or potential use or value for humanity'. In other words, the focus of the enquiry is no longer limited to 'wildlife' or 'wild flora and fauna', but includes all living organisms, including genetic material, and their naturally occurring genetic variability.

The relationship between biodiversity and biological resources is an obvious one. Biodiversity may be seen as a necessary precondition for the long-term maintenance of biological resources and, therefore, an essential environmental condition.[7] Biodiversity provides an actual or potential source of biological resources, and contributes to the richness of life on Earth as well as to the maintenance of the biosphere in a condition that supports such life. In other words, it is an 'attribute' of life. Biological resources are, however, the 'tangible biotic components of ecosystems',[8] which are equally a necessary precondition for biodiversity. Biological resources may exist in the absence of biodiversity in a species-poor or mono-culture environment. However, biodiversity cannot exist in the absence of biological resources present in their naturally occurring abundance. Thus, it is 'biological resources' and their contribution to the maintenance of the Earth's biodiversity that are the focus of this chapter.

Perhaps controversially, this chapter integrates a consideration of regimes relating to both marine and terrestrial species. With the exception of references to the 1946 International Convention for the Regulation of Whaling (Whaling Convention) and the 1982 Convention for the Conservation of Antarctic Marine Living Resources (CCAMLR), treaties relating to marine species, in particular, to fish, have generally been omitted from analyses of 'wildlife' law, primarily on the basis of their exploitative rather than conservationist objectives. Differing jurisdictional regimes have also played a part, given that terrestrial species fall wholly under national jurisdiction while marine species are often, although not invariably, located outside national jurisdiction. Yet, the fact that marine fishes are biological organisms and integral elements of the Earth's biodiversity cannot be denied. Their inclusion in a post-CBD analysis is thus *prima facie* warranted.

Moreover, marine species face precisely the same threats of over-exploitation, habitat destruction, and the introduction of alien species that terrestrial species do. In response, marine fisheries management has begun to move beyond the regulation of fisheries for the purpose of resource utilization to regulation for the purpose of conservation and long-term sustainable use on an ecosystem basis. As discussed later in this chapter, it is precisely these purposes that underlie both traditional approaches to wildlife conservation and management and the CBD regime. Additionally, the intersections between marine fisheries and other species have been amply demonstrated in problems relating to the by-catch of non-target fish species, the incidental catch of other species such as turtles, dolphins, and seabirds, and the

---

[7] P.M. Wood, 'Biodiversity as the Source of Biological Resources: A New Look at Biodiversity Values' (1997) 6 Envt'l Values 251.

[8] L. Glowka et al., *A Guide to the Convention on Biological Diversity* (Gland: IUCN, 1994) at 16–24.

effects of destructive fishing practices on corals and other benthic communities. These problems are being addressed in a range of new agreements such as the 2001 Agreement on the Conservation of Albatrosses and Petrels and the 1996 Inter-American Convention for the Protection and Conservation of Sea Turtles. Biological invasions of the marine environment are also being addressed, as evidenced by the adoption in 2004 of the International Convention for the Control and Management of Ships Ballast Water and Sediments (Ballast Water Convention). Given the similarity of threats and approaches thereto, no persuasive rationale for the exclusion of fisheries treaties remains.

3 THEORETICAL AND MANAGERIAL APPROACHES TO CONSERVING BIOLOGICAL RESOURCES

3.1 Notion of Value of Biological Resources

A number of theoretical or philosophical justifications have been articulated for conserving biological resources. As with all of international environmental law, these justifications are predominantly anthropocentric (see Chapter 3 'Paradigms and Discourses' and Chapter 13 'Ethics and International Environmental Law') and are cast in terms of the 'use' or 'value' of biological resources to humans. Value is usually categorized as being instrumental, inherent, or intrinsic. *Instrumental value* refers to the use to which an entity may be put and includes both direct-use values such as food, fibres, forest products, pharmaceuticals, chemicals, and opportunities for education and recreation, as well as indirect uses such as the services provided by biological resources and the natural ecosystems upon which we depend. Since it is individual entities or organisms that are used rather than whole species or ecosystems, the instrumentalist approach requires the conservation and protection of the whole in order to enable a continued use of the individual. *Inherent value* refers to the value of an entity prized for its own sake and includes non-use values that derive from aesthetic, spiritual, cultural, or religious considerations. These considerations may apply to individual entities or organisms but also commonly apply to particular groupings or manifestations thereof, such as forests, flocks, landscapes, mountains, rivers, or lakes. As Michael Bowman notes, both instrumental and inherent value depend on the 'existence of an external valuer or beneficiary'.[9] *Intrinsic*

---

[9] M. Bowman, 'The Nature, Development and Philosophical Foundations of the Biodiversity Concept in International Law', in M. Bowman and C. Redgwell, eds., *International Law and the Conservation of Biological Diversity* (Boston: Kluwer Law International, 1996) 5 at 15.

value, however, does not. Derived from ethical and moral considerations, intrinsic value exists independently of any economic or externally determined value and refers to the value of an entity in, of, and for itself. This approach is reflected in the deep ecology and animal rights philosophies (see Chapter 13 'Ethics and International Environmental Law').

Each of these notions of value is evident in the law relating to biological resources. The earliest and most persistent approach has been the protection of instrumental values, as reflected in attempts to conserve directly exploited species such as birds 'useful to agriculture' and whales, seals, and fish. Protection of instrumental values also lies at the heart of the 2001 International Treaty on Plant Genetic Resources for Food and Agriculture (ITPGRFA)—the objectives of which are the 'conservation and sustainable use of plant genetic resources for food and agriculture and the fair and equitable sharing of benefits arising out of their use'. Inherent values were introduced in the 1940 Convention on Nature Protection and Wildlife Preservation in the Western Hemisphere (Western Hemisphere Convention), which calls for the protection and preservation of 'scenery of extraordinary beauty . . . and natural objects of aesthetic . . . value'. Similarly, the 1968 African Convention on the Conservation of Nature and Natural Resources (African Convention) and the 1979 Convention on the Conservation of Migratory Species of Wild Animals (Bonn Convention) recognize the ever growing 'importance of natural resources' and the 'value of wild animals' from, *inter alia*, aesthetic and cultural points of view. These notions are repeated in the preambles of many conventions, although admittedly usually accompanied by more instrumental values such as economic benefit, recreation, and education. Recognition of intrinsic values is articulated in the preamble of the WCN, which recognizes that 'every form of life is unique, warranting respect regardless of its worth to man, and, to accord other organisms such recognition, man must be guided by a moral code of action'. Adopting this approach, the intrinsic value of the natural world is recognized in the 1979 Convention on the Conservation of European Wildlife and Natural Habitats (Bern Convention), the preamble of which 'recognizes that European wildlife constitutes a natural heritage possessing intrinsic, as well as other kinds of, value', while the intrinsic value of Antarctica and its ecosystem is recognized in the 1991 Environmental Protocol to the Antarctic Treaty (Madrid Protocol).

All three notions of value find expression in the CBD, the preamble of which refers to the 'intrinsic value of biological diversity and of the ecological, genetic, social, economic, educational, cultural, recreational, and aesthetic values of biological diversity and its components'. Biodiversity is recognized as being the 'common concern of humankind' and as being important 'for evolution and for maintaining life support systems of the biosphere' and 'for meeting the food, health and other needs of the growing world population'. In contrast, the definition of 'biological resources' in the CBD includes the express requirement of 'actual or potential use or value for humanity'. Arguably otiose—since all living organisms presumably have use or value, or at least potential use or value, for humanity even if yet unidentified and even if only as components of ecosystem processes necessary to human survival—the phrase was added to distinguish between 'biodiversity', which is recognized in the convention as being the 'common concern of humankind', and 'biological resources', over which states retain sovereignty and thus the ability to reap economic rewards therefrom. This essentially economic rationalist approach was adopted to ensure the participation of developing countries who sought to retain control over the financial benefits to be derived particularly from bio-prospecting and biotechnology activities utilizing genetic resources under their national jurisdiction.

The weakness of the CBD's focus on the use or value of biological resources 'for humanity' lies in our lack of knowledge of biological organisms and processes, and in inadequate domestic regimes for the ascertainment, conservation, and management of biological resources. Biological resources can be—and are being—lost before their existence, let alone their potential or actual value for humanity, has been identified. Lest the lessons of history be forgotten, it will be recalled that the 1902 Convention for the Protection of Birds Useful to Agriculture and the 1900 Convention for the Conservation of Wild Animals, Birds and Fish in Africa called for the destruction of species deemed harmful to human interests such as lions, leopards, crocodiles, eagles, hawks, herons, and pelicans. Indeed, many such species formerly excluded from protective treaty regimes are now among the most protected. In addition, relating 'use or value' purely to the economic value of biological resources is 'fraught with difficulty and uncertainty'.[10] The North Atlantic Salmon Conservation Organization (NASCO) has, for example, discovered that the economic value of wild salmon is not measured only in terms of the monetary value of catch, but also includes monetary components relating to fishers and their communities, including shipbuilders, provisioners, processing plants, and consumers as well as to communities reaping the benefit of recreational fisheries.[11] Even this broad approach to economic valuation does not begin to account for the other potential 'life support' functions of the ecological systems involved (see Chapter 11 'Economic Theory of International Environmental Law').

The strength of the CBD approach lies, however, in the potentially all-encompassing concept of 'value' reflected in its recognition of the intrinsic value of biodiversity, which allows a broad and flexible approach to the definition of biological resources beyond mere economic value. It lies also in the requirement that global *biodiversity*, as opposed to only biological resources, be protected by all states. The residual effect is that biological organisms within national jurisdiction that do not have an identified actual or potential use or value in economic terms, and biological organisms located outside the national jurisdiction of states, will still remain the common

---

[10] D. Clark and D. Downes, *What Price Biodiversity? Economic Incentives and Biodiversity Conservation in the United States* (Washington, DC: Center for International Environmental Law, 1995).

[11] See, e.g., North Atlantic Salmon Conservation Organization (NASCO), 'Report of the Technical Workshop on Development of a Framework for Assessing Social and Economic Values Related to Wild Salmon,' in *Report of the 20th Annual Meeting of the Council* (Edinburgh: NASCO, 2003) at 235–56.

concern of humankind and may therefore attract legitimate international interest in their conservation and use (see Chapter 23 'Common Areas, Common Heritage, and Common Concern').

3.2 Managerial Approaches to Biological Resources

These theoretical approaches reveal the underlying tension between the extent to which humans should exploit or preserve biological resources and are reflected in the various managerial approaches evidenced in international conventions. Early approaches to international management were purely instrumental in nature and focused primarily on the allocation of resources between different interested states, particularly in areas outside national jurisdiction. First adopted in the 1882 North Sea Overfishing Convention and the 1855 Convention for the Uniform Regulation of Fishing in the Rhine, this approach still underlies international fisheries and wildlife conventions today. Continuing over-exploitation, however, coupled with growing environmental concerns, has eventually led to a blending of allocation concerns with a realization of the need to ensure a sustainable level of exploitation. In the absence of adequate scientific knowledge and political agreement as to how to achieve this level, many species have continued to decline to the point of critical endangerment, lead- ing to calls for total bans, or moratoria, on their commercial exploitation, such as those on whaling and high-seas drift-netting.

Four essentially managerial concepts or approaches have been articulated to deal with biological resources, each of which reflects to a greater or lesser extent the philo- sophical notions of value discussed earlier in this chapter: protection, preservation, conservation, and sustainable use. Ascertaining what these terms mean and how they relate to each other is no mean feat. Suffice it to say that while the terms may overlap they are not necessarily synonymous. The terminology used will therefore qualify both the object and purpose of a treaty and the legal scope and application of its pro- visions. It is therefore important to have some understanding of the definitional dif- ferences between the concepts.

The concept of protection, which finds expression in treaties such as the 1902 International Convention for the Protection of Birds Useful to Agriculture, the 1972 Convention Concerning the Protection of World Cultural and Natural Heritage (World Heritage Convention), and the Western Hemisphere Convention, is generally considered to be the oldest, most commonly used, and most neutral, of the approaches. As a management approach, protection calls for a reaction to a threat although it does not mandate any timeframe or particular policy approach.[12]

---

[12] P. van Heijnsbergen, *International Legal Protection of Wild Fauna and Flora* (Amsterdam: IOS Press, 1997) at 43.

Preservation, on the other hand, indicates a need for a 'durable guarantee against the loss of or damage to the object to be preserved by defending it against external threats'[13] and is most often linked directly to prevention of extinction. The need for preservation was invoked to support the moratorium on commercial whaling adopted by the International Whaling Commission (IWC) in 1982. The preservationist approach is more closely associated with notions of intrinsic or existence value, although instrumentalist objectives may also be revealed. For example, while ostensibly preservationist in name, the 1911 Convention for the Preservation and Protection of Fur Seals, which prohibited pelagic sealing entirely in the international waters of the North Pacific, did so primarily to ensure the continued ability of the coastal states to exploit fur seals within areas under their jurisdiction. The contentiousness of the preservationist approach is evidenced in objections to the whaling moratorium by states who argue that the Whaling Convention reflects a conservationist rather than a preservationist approach, and that its provisions do not therefore allow a total prohibition on whaling of species of whales that could easily sustain exploitation.

The most commonly articulated approach is that of conservation, although precisely what is meant by this concept, which is not defined in the numerous treaties that invoke it, is less than clear. Two issues of particular concern are the extent to which conservation includes 'use' and its relationship with 'management'. With respect to the former, in the 1946 International Convention for the Regulation of Whaling 'conservation' does not include 'utilization'. The CBD itself does not define 'conservation of biodiversity'—the requirement of which is distinguished from the objective of 'ensuring sustainable use' of its components. On the other hand, the 1971 Convention on Wetlands of Importance Especially as Waterfowl Habitat (Ramsar Convention) refers to conservation as including 'wise use', while the 1982 CCAMLR defines conservation to include 'rational use'. More recent agreements such as the 1995 Agreement Relating to the Conservation and Management of Straddling Fish Stocks and Highly Migratory Fish Stocks (Fish Stocks Agreement)[14] and the 2000 Convention on the Conservation and Management of Highly Migratory Fish Stocks in the Western and Central Pacific Ocean (Western and Central Pacific Fisheries Convention), require both conservation and 'sustainable use'. Debate persists, therefore, as to whether conservation necessarily includes use or whether a strictly preservationist approach that precludes use and calls for absolute protection may yet inhere in the concept. The latter appears to be accepted by commentators who conclude that the concept of 'conservation' is broad enough to include both protection

---

[13] *Ibid.* at 44.

[14] 1995 Agreement for the Implementation of the Provisions of the United Nations Convention on the Law of the Sea of 10 December 1982 Relating to the Conservation and Management of Straddling Fish Stocks and Highly Migratory Fish Stocks.

and preservation as well as the maintenance, restoration, sustainable utilization, and enhancement of a natural resource or the environment.[15]

Whether or not use is an element of, or a requirement additional to, conservation, effective conservation of biological resources requires conservation on a sustainable basis of terrestrial and marine plants, animals, and micro-organisms as well as their habitat and the related living and non-living elements of the environment on which they depend, not only for their value to biodiversity but also for other values.[16] Thus, identification of appropriate management strategies and objectives to achieve conservation is still required.

The earliest management strategy, initially adopted in fisheries treaties, was that of achieving maximum sustainable yield (MSY) of a single target species. MSY is the highest quantity of biomass that can be taken from a self-regenerating stock year after year without a change in catch effort or the average size of the stock. In theory, MSY is designed to maintain productivity by ensuring that stocks are exploited at their level of 'maximum physical output and natural rate of increase, preserving highest resilience'.[17] MSY is achieved when both 'mortality and recruitment to the stock are maximised at the same time'.[18] However, MSY fails to take account of other factors such as the economic value of the catch, the cost of catching, and the natural instability of some stocks. Moreover, it fails to take into account interrelations between the targeted species and other species in the ecosystem as well as related factors such as climate change, pollution, land-use management, and the need to protect biodiversity. Thus, while MSY may be useful in establishing limits regarding consumptive use, it fails to adequately reflect non-consumptive uses. Additionally, it is highly information-intensive and may not yield reliable results if based on uncertain scientific data, inadequate interpretational scientific theories, or imprecise or politically motivated advice.

Given the shortcomings of the MSY approach, a number of alternative management strategies have been adopted in order to achieve sustainable use. The Ramsar Convention, for example, articulates an obligation of 'wise use'. The convention itself does not provide any content to this obligation, which is, in any event, qualified by the limitation that states must promote conservation and wise use only 'so far as possible'. However, over the years, the Conference of the Parties has provided substantive, albeit non-binding, articulations of the content of the duty, which equate 'wise use' to 'sustainable utilisation for the benefit of mankind in a way compatible with the maintenance of the natural properties of the ecosystem'. The 1973 Convention on International Trade in Endangered Species of Wild Flora and Fauna (CITES) adopts

---

[15] van Heijnsbergen, see note 12 above at 52; and P. Birnie and A. Boyle, *International Law and Environment* (Oxford: Oxford University Press, 2002) at 553–4. R.D. Munro and J.G. Lammers, *Environmental Protection and Sustainable Development, Experts Group on Environmental Law of the World Commission on Environment and Development* (London: Graham and Trotman/Martinus Nijhoff, 1986) at 38.   [16] Birnie and Boyle, see note 15 above at 599.
[17] FAO, 'High Seas Management: New Concepts and Techniques,' Doc. FI/HSF/TC/92/5 (1992) at para. 15.   [18] Birnie and Boyle, see note 15 above at 551.

a different strategy, which aims to promote sustainable use through regulating international trade in endangered species, thereby cutting off economic incentives to exploitation, rather than by prohibiting human use.

Derived from the concept of sustainable development (see Chapter 26 'Sustainable Development'), the more recent objective of sustainable use requires management 'in such a manner that [the resource] may yield the greatest sustainable benefit to present generations while maintaining its potential to meet the needs and aspirations of future generations'.[19] This intergenerational equity (see Chapter 27 'Equity') is to be achieved through the implementation of holistic and integrated ecosystem (see Chapter 24 'Ecosystems') and precautionary management strategies (see Chapter 25 'Precaution') that account for scientific, economic, social, and political uncertainties and that recognize the importance of both consumptive and non-consumptive uses. While admirable as an objective, the complexity, scientific uncertainty, and practical difficulty of formulating and implementing such strategies is amply demonstrated by, for example, the continuing difficulties in implementing the ecosystem approach called for in CCAMLR, and the acrimonious debates over development of a precautionary approach to fisheries within NASCO and the Northwest Atlantic Fisheries Organization (NAFO). Neither do these strategies address the underlying incompatibility of a legal regime based on state sovereignty over terrestrial living resources and marine living resources within a 200 nautical mile exclusive economic zone with the reality of transboundary, migratory, or interdependent resources and the freedom of access and exploitation in the global commons.

Achievement of the objectives of conservation and sustainable use is therefore a complex matter. It requires international cooperation in the allocation of jurisdiction over resources and their habitats as well as the establishment of obligations relating to the conduct of scientific research, the adoption of the precautionary approach, compliance, and enforcement. This action, in turn, requires the establishment of permanent international institutions to provide a forum for discussion, evaluation, coordination, and adoption of required measures and the development of dispute settlement arrangements. Moreover, it requires a consistency of approach that is quite the opposite of the fragmentary and essentially ad hoc approach taken to date, which has resulted in the adoption of a plethora of both over- and under-lapping, but discrete and often inconsistent, legal regimes. This fragmentary approach has been further exacerbated by an inconsistency of membership in the various treaty regimes. While the issue of the fragmentation of international law is beyond the scope of this chapter (see Chapter 7 'Relationship between International Environmental Law and Other Branches of International Law'),[20] it should be borne in mind when reading

---

[19] Munro and Lammers, see note 15 above at 9.

[20] See, e.g. the *Report of the International Law Commission and Its Special Rapporteur on the Topic of Fragmentation of International Law: Difficulties Arising from the Diversification and Expansion of International Law, Report of the Work of the Commission at Its Fifty-Sixth Session*, UN Doc. A/59/10 (2004).

the following sections, which examine the types of legal regimes and regulatory measures that have been adopted and their efficacy in conserving biological resources as the precondition for the maintenance of the Earth's biodiversity.

4 Types of Regimes for the Conservation of Biological Resources

International legal regimes for the conservation of biological resources—be they global, regional, or bilateral in scope[21]—generally adopt three broad approaches: regulation of harvest, protection of habitat, and regulation of trade. Regimes focusing on exotic and invasive alien species and on animal and plant genetic resources, although in some respects evidencing the development of distinct approaches, are addressed in this chapter within this broad overall framework. As will be seen, many agreements contain elements of all of these approaches. As with all international law, the efficacy of these agreements varies depending on the number and identity of the parties, the nature of the problem they are addressing, their scope of application, the specificity of their terms, their level of implementation, and their ability to adapt to changing legal and managerial concepts and realities (see Chapter 8 'Instrument Choice' and Chapter 39 'Compliance Theory').

4.1 Regulation of Harvest

4.1.1 *Harvest of Species*

Agreements regulating harvest seek to regulate and, where necessary, prohibit the taking, hunting, or killing of either a particular species or groups of species. In other words, they focus on the direct use of species through hunting, fishing, or collecting. Since states have sovereignty over the biological resources located wholly within their jurisdiction, these international agreements are aimed primarily at allocating or regulating the harvest of migratory species or those inhabiting the global commons. Two distinct but interrelated objectives underlie these agreements: the protection of endangered species and the allocation of harvest for human use of non-endangered species. Agreements relating to terrestrial species, such as the 1973 Agreement on the Conservation of Polar Bears (Polar Bear Agreement), generally reflect the former purpose or, as in the case of the various bird treaties, a combination of the two.

---

[21] For reasons of space, only global and regional treaties will be referred to in this chapter.

Agreements relating to marine species, such as the Western and Central Pacific Fisheries Convention, generally reflect the latter. Indeed, fisheries treaties are the pre-eminent example of agreements allocating harvest. These treaties generally establish regional fisheries organizations, commissions, or meetings of states parties, which are mandated to establish harvest limits and measures relating thereto in accordance with management objectives enunciated in the treaty. Outside the fisheries context, agreements such as the Whaling Convention and the Bonn Convention also establish bodies or mechanisms, such as meetings of states parties, which are either authorized to adopt regulations to control or limit harvest or to review the treaty's adoption and implementation at the national level.

A number of species-specific agreements regulate the harvest of particular species, such as vicuna, polar bears, fur seals, and southern bluefin tuna. Given the multitude of species on earth, however, effective regulation on a single species basis is impracti-cal, if not impossible. Thus, most species-related agreements apply either to a num-ber of listed species, such as whales or birds, throughout their entire range or to certain or all species within a particular geographical area. Species, the harvesting of which is to be regulated, are either named by the treaty or listed in appendices or schedules that are usually amendable in order to account for changes in the conser-vation status of listed and non-listed species. For example, the Whaling Convention lists numerous species of whales while the Bonn Convention lists dozens of species of mammals, birds, and reptiles, the harvest of which is to be prohibited by all states par-ties, including range and harvest states throughout their entire range. On the other hand, the 1966 International Convention on the Conservation of Atlantic Tunas applies to all tuna and tuna-like fishes throughout the Atlantic Ocean; the Western Hemisphere Convention applies to all flora and fauna within the Americas; and the 1980 Convention on Future Multilateral Cooperation in Northeast Atlantic Fisheries applies to all fish stocks and species within the northeast Atlantic, with the exception of those under national jurisdiction or, as in the case of tuna and anadromous stocks, otherwise regulated by another agreement. However, as the same species may be found both inside and outside the relevant convention area, regulation on the basis of geographical area does not necessarily ensure regulation throughout a species' range.

Unfortunately, a focus on regulation of harvest has proved unsuccessful in con-serving many biological resources, particularly fish, where, as noted at the outset, increasing numbers of stocks and species are being pushed to commercial and pos-sibly biological extinction. While something of a rear guard action, agreement on regulation of harvest has generally occurred only once the resource has already been depleted through over-exploitation. In other words, regulation of harvest takes place in the context of pre-existing use and is therefore fraught with difficulties. By way of example, the Polar Bear Agreement and the 1979 Convention for the Conservation and Management of the Vicuña (Lima Convention) are generally considered to be the most successful thanks to the singular and charismatic nature of the species protected and the limited number of parties involved who were agreed, at the outset, on the steps to be taken.[22] This success is in stark contrast, however, to the experience of the parties to the 1993 Convention for the Conservation of Southern Bluefin Tuna (Southern Bluefin Tuna Convention) who, although agreed on the need to conserve and restore the species, have consistently been unable to agree on the steps to be taken to do so. While polar bear and vicuña populations appear to have stabilized, the population of southern bluefin tuna has continued to decline to the extent that some parties have suggested the need to abandon the convention's objective of restoring spawning stock to 1980 levels by 2020.

As the Southern Bluefin Tuna Convention example illustrates, in the absence of a total and enforceable moratorium, the rapacious pursuit of economic gain from harvesting has, in many cases, proved impossible to counteract. Agreement on the need to regulate harvest has often been impossible to attain, as evidenced by the discussions regarding the establishment of a conservation and management regime for deep sea species in the southwest Indian Ocean. While negotiations foundered, the orange roughy fishery peaked and crashed. The South Indian Ocean Fisheries Agreement was finally adopted in 2006 in the midst of considerable uncertainty as to what fish stocks might be left to be regulated. Likewise, achieving and maintaining agreement on the precise species or stocks to be regulated has been problematic. The listing approach generally focuses only on large, visible species with obvious public appeal. Less charismatic lower life forms are therefore not regulated. Additionally, procedures for amending lists may be slow and cumbersome or wholly non-existent, and states have deliberately exploited these weaknesses to ensure species are either kept off lists or otherwise not included within the management regime of the organization. For example, while the appendices to the Bern Convention have been amended on numerous occasions, those to the Western Hemisphere Convention have not been amended since 1967. Neither is adoption of effective regulations assured. Despite mounting evidence that unregulated stocks, in particular, certain tuna and deep sea species, are threatened, a number of regional fisheries organizations have continually failed to adopt measures to regulate or restrict their harvest. The reasons for this failure are multiple but generally relate to either honest or specious and politically motivated disagreements over the science on which the calls for regulation are based (see Chapter 9 'Science and Technology').

Moreover, obligations relating to harvest—even those calling for zero harvest—are almost always qualified in some way and, thus, depending on the level of domestic legal oversight and enforcement, open to abuse. The Polar Bear Agreement allows bears to be taken in any one of five situations, including for scientific or conservation purposes or by local people using traditional methods in reliance on a traditional

---

[22] R. Churchill, 'The Contribution of Existing Agreements for the Conservation of Terrestrial Species and Habitats to the Maintenance of Biodiversity,' in M. Bowman and C. Redgwell, eds., *International Law and the Conservation of Biological Diversity* (New York: Aspen, 1996) at 71.

right. The whaling moratorium, too, is subject to exceptions for scientific and Aboriginal subsistence whaling, under the guise of which Japan has continued to conduct an essentially commercial harvest. Other agreements allow for taking of otherwise protected species where national interest or the domestic law of a state party permits, thereby providing an open invitation to do so. In the fisheries context, in particular, the problem is exacerbated by opt-out procedures that allow states to opt out entirely from the application of measures with which they do not agree. Even where states do not formally opt out, many agreements fail to provide mechanisms for monitoring implementation and compliance, and such mechanisms as do exist are not supported by enforcement techniques. This situation is being partially rectified in the fisheries context with the establishment of compliance committees within regional fisheries organizations and the provisions of the Fish Stocks Agreement, which call for third-party enforcement in certain circumstances. However, the thorny issues of compliance and enforcement both within and between states are far from resolved.

Finally, agreements regulating harvest often fail to account for three other factors: the effect of non-party range and harvesting states that are not bound by the obligations under the agreements; the relationship between targeted and non-targeted species; and other threats to species caused by a disruption of habitat from non-harvest-related activities. Each of these factors contributes to scientific uncertainty about the status of stocks or species, which in turn contributes to managerial uncertainty and the potential for over-exploitation. The first is an unavoidable consequence of the structure of the international legal system by which non-parties are not bound by treaty arrangements. Thus, for example, non-parties to the various migratory bird conventions are not bound to refrain from taking, or to preserve essential nesting, feeding, transit, or related habitats. In the fisheries context, the Fish Stocks Agreement seeks to overcome this by institutionalizing the obligation on all states to either comply with measures adopted by regional fisheries organizations or to refrain from fishing. Increasingly, regional fisheries organizations are adopting measures to promote compliance by non-contracting parties, although both their legality and their efficacy are still questionable.

The second factor is a consequence of both the harvesting methods used and the fact of harvest, which seeks to maximize the return of targeted species without reference to the effect on non-targeted species, thereby ignoring wider ecosystemic issues such as predator-prey and other biological relationships. The tuna-dolphin and shrimp-turtle controversies (see Chapter 7 'Relationship between International Environmental Law and Other Branches of International Law'), as well as assertions that whales and seals eat too many fish and are adversely affecting human-harvesting ability, are manifestations of this problem. Originally addressed in CCAMLR, which requires management measures to take into account dependant and related species, these considerations are increasingly being incorporated into measures adopted by regional fisheries organizations to control by-catch and incidental mortality.

Agreements such as the 1999 Agreement on the International Dolphin Conservation Program, the objective of which is to eliminate incidental mortality of dolphins in tuna fisheries, are also emerging.

The third factor is perhaps the least understood and represents the most difficult managerial challenge, arising as it does from the predominantly sectoral and non-holistic approach to conservation that is manifest in agreements regulating harvest, which generally fail to account for the threats posed by, for example, climate change, pollution, and disruption to breeding grounds by 'eco-tourism' activities.

4.1.2 *Harvest of Genetic Resources*

A different, but no less problematic, approach to the regulation of harvest and associated activities has been adopted with respect to genetic resources and the regulation of bio-prospecting or 'the search of biodiversity for valuable genetic and biomechanical information found in wild plants, animals and micro-organisms'.[23] Useful in the development of new drugs, crop varieties, industrial techniques, and other commodities, genetic resources were traditionally considered to be part of the 'common heritage of humankind', access to which was free to all (see Chapter 23 'Common Areas, Common Heritage, and Common Concern'). Ever the bain of any open access regime, over-harvesting was often the result. For example, *Maytenus buchananni*, a plant source of a successful anti-cancer compound was harvested to extinction by a bio-prospecting team sponsored by the US National Cancer Institute.[24] Given the potential economic significance of genetic resources, developing states, in which the bulk of the Earth's genetic resources are located, have sought to develop an international legal regime to protect their interests in genetic material found within their borders, and to ensure both the sharing of the economic benefits derived therefrom and the transfer of technology to allow for the domestic exploitation of their resources. Thus, the CBD ascribes sovereignty over genetic resources to states in whose territory they are located, and seeks to regulate access to (and, implicitly, the harvest of) genetic resources on the basis of prior informed consent of the providing state, to be given on mutually agreed terms that are to include provision by the exploiting state of a fair and equitable share of benefits derived from their use. To ensure the continued availability of these resources for humankind, providing states are, however, obliged to facilitate access and not impose restrictions contrary to the CBD's objectives. The ascription of sovereign rights is also limited to resources collected after the CBD came into force on 29 December 1993.

While the CBD applies to all genetic resources, which it defines as the genetic material of actual or potential value for humanity, access to plant genetic resources

---

[23] M. Jeffrey, 'Bioprospecting: Access to Genetic Resources and Benefit Sharing under the Convention on Biodiversity and the Bonn Guidelines' (2002) 6 Sing. J. Int'l & Comp. L. 747 at 755.

[24] C. Hunter, 'Sustainable Bioprospecting: Using Private Contracts and International Legal Principles and Policies to Conserve Raw Materials' (1997) 25 B.C. Envt'l Aff. L. Rev. 129 at 138.

specifically intended for food and agriculture is now governed by the ITPGRFA. Like the CBD, the ITPGRFA does not regulate harvest *per se*. Rather, it establishes a system of access and benefit sharing and calls for capacity building, technology transfer, and information exchange to further its objectives. As Gregory Rose notes, the primary concern of the various international instruments and institutions dealing with plant genetic resources is 'with conditions of their control, distribution and utilization, rather than with conservation'.[25] Nevertheless, the ascription of value to these resources is intended, on the one hand, to encourage providing states to conserve genetic resources in order to ensure continued financial benefit to themselves and, on the other hand, to encourage exploiting states to enter into cooperative benefit-sharing regimes to ensure the future availability of, and access to, these resources.

The ascription of value to genetic resources, which was originally intended to provide incentives for their conservation, has, however, given rise to a host of new and increasingly complex regulatory challenges. Central to the debate is the role of intellectual property rights and the relationship between the CBD and the ITPGRFA regimes and the 1994 WTO Agreement on Trade-Related Aspects of Intellectual Property Rights (TRIPS Agreement), which contains express language on genetic resources, mandating that states must grant patents for microorganisms and plant varieties. The alternative option allowed for in the TRIPS Agreement, of a *sui generis* system for plant varieties, has yet to become a reality. Quite apart from the difficulties posed by the trade-environment interface (see Chapter 7 'Relationship between International Environmental Law and Other Branches of International Law'), the relationship between the CBD and the ITPGRFA is also unclear, particularly given the former's emphasis on access and benefit sharing as opposed to the latter's emphasis on food security. Indeed, negotiation and implementation of the access and benefit-sharing regimes called for by both conventions continue to be contentious. In particular, the extent of the application of the CBD regime to genetic resources not included under the ITPGRFA regime remains unclear. Finally, neither regime regulates bio-prospecting on the high seas. This activity also falls outside the legal regime of the 1982 United Nations Convention on the Law of the Sea (LOSC). With bio-prospecting activities increasingly being conducted in ecologically sensitive high seas areas around underwater hydrothermal vents, the international community has yet to reach agreement on whether, and if so how, to regulate these potentially destructive harvesting activities and share the benefits derived therefrom (see Chapter 15 'Ocean and Freshwater Resources').[26]

---

[25] G. Rose, 'International Regimes for the Conservation and Control of Plant Genetic Resources,' in Bowman and Redgwell, eds., see note 22 above at 145.

[26] See, e.g., D. Leary, 'Bioprospecting and the Genetic Resources of Hydrothermal Vents on the High Seas: What Is the Existing Legal Position, Where Are We Heading and What Are Our Options?' (2004) 1 MacQuarie J. Int'l & Comp. L. 137; and D. Leary, 'Emerging Legal Regimes Regulating Bioprospecting for Thermophiles and Hyperthermophiles of Hydrothermal Vents' (2004) 6 Marine Biotechnology 351.

4.2 Protection of Habitat

Regulating harvest is meaningless if the destruction of a species would otherwise be brought about by the destruction of the habitat on which the species or organism depends for survival. Indeed, the traditional focus on harvesting discussed earlier in this chapter addresses a lesser threat to overall biodiversity. Rather, as noted at the outset, indirect threats to species such as habitat destruction; degradation and modification due to pollution and other industrial, agricultural, or forestry activities; habitat fragmentation due to increasing population density; and alien introductions, both intentional and accidental, are now recognized as the greatest threats to the continued survival of both terrestrial and marine species. Thus, virtually all agreements relating to terrestrial species also address the issue of habitat protection. Numerous agreements also address habitat protection in marine areas, although the protection of threatened habitats in areas beyond national jurisdiction, such as high seas sea-mounts and deep water corals, remains slow in coming.

According to the commentary to the WCN, 'habitat' means 'the place where a species lives, as well as the ecological conditions which it requires'.[27] Two definitional issues arise from this statement. The first is whether the protection of habitat is necessarily related to the protection of species or is also an independent concept. In the 1940 Western Hemisphere Convention, habitat protection was linked with the desire to protect and preserve 'representatives of all species and genera of [the contracting parties'] native flora and fauna'. The 1968 African Convention on the Conservation of Nature and Natural Resources similarly linked protection of habitat with protection of species threatened, or likely to be threatened, with extinction. A number of agreements, however, recognize that habitats are worthy of protection in their own right. The Ramsar Convention is the first such agreement concerned only with habitat, rather than both species and habitat, protection. It calls for the protection of selected wetlands on account of 'their international significance in terms of ecology, botany, zoology, limnology or hydrology'. Similarly, the World Heritage Convention applies only to habitats, albeit including habitats 'of threatened species of animals and plants of outstanding universal value from the point of view of science or conservation'. The Madrid Protocol applies to the entire 'Antarctic environment', designating the region as a 'natural reserve' dedicated to science and peace, while agreements relating to the Alps and to the marine and coastal environment of the West and Central African region are similarly aimed at protection of habitats as such. Thus, the protection of habitat, while often designed to protect the habitat of particular species that are either identified precisely or generically as threatened or endangered, may also serve other purposes.

The second definitional issue is the relationship between 'habitat' and 'ecosystem' (see Chapter 24 'Ecosystems'). The *Oxford English Dictionary* defines an 'ecosystem'

---

[27] W.E. Burhenne and W.A. Irwin, *The World Charter for Nature* (Berlin: Erich Schmidt Verlag, 1986) at 134.

as 'a unit of ecology . . . which includes the plants or animals occurring together plus that part of their environment over which they have an influence'. On this definition, as with that in the WCN, habitats are merely part of an ecosystem, which includes other essential ecological processes and life support systems. The first international agreement to specifically adopt the ecosystem approach, CCAMLR, appears to confirm this view, calling for 'prevention of changes or minimisation of the risk of changes in the marine ecosystem . . . taking into account the state of available knowledge of the direct and indirect impact of harvesting, the effect of introduction of alien species, the effects of associated activities on the marine ecosystem and the effects of environmental changes'. Although sometimes used synonymously, the terms are most often used conjunctively as in the 1981 Convention for Cooperation in the Protection and Development of the Marine and Coastal Environment of the West and Central African Region, which requires its parties to 'take all appropriate measures to protect and preserve rare or fragile ecosystems as well as the habitat of depleted, threatened or endangered species'. The 1991 Convention on the Protection of the Alps similarly requires protection and preservation of both 'functioning ecosystems' as well as flora and fauna and their habitats. This requirement includes taking measures related to air quality, soil preservation, water quality, and the management of forests. Thus, protection of ecosystems requires going beyond the protection of a mere geographical habitat location to the protection of the 'whole biological equilibrium'.[28] In this respect, and depending on how liberal an interpretation is given to the word 'habitat', many agreements for the protection of habitat may fall short of the CBD objective of ecosystem and biodiversity protection, although they necessarily contribute to it.

The most common approach taken to habitat protection is the requirement to establish protected areas, such as parks, reserves, or marine protected areas, in which activities harmful to the habitat are prohibited or strictly regulated. Perhaps the widest ranging example of this approach is found in the Antarctic Environmental Protocol, which designates all of Antarctica as a 'natural reserve'. More common, however, is the approach of the Ramsar and World Heritage Conventions, which require states parties specifically to designate significant areas of either wetlands or of cultural or natural heritage value for listing with the international secretariat established by the agreement. Having done so, parties are then required to formulate effective planning and development policies to ensure the protection of the designated areas. In some cases, these special areas are to be supplemented by buffer zones or other measures dealing with soil erosion, water and air quality, or other forms of pollution and environmental degradation that might otherwise adversely affect the protected areas.

The protected area approach, however, has its limitations. Most agreements leave a wide margin of discretion to states in selecting and designating areas for protection.

---

[28] van Heijnsbergen, see note 12 above at 162.

Indeed, the Western Hemisphere Convention requires its parties merely to explore the possibility of doing so. States may decline to designate areas, or the areas designated may not be sufficiently extensive to ensure either their viability or the viability of the species found therein. This is particularly problematic for migratory species where protected areas either do not coincide with their migration routes, are surrounded by heavily exploited areas, or are of insufficient size either to provide meaningful habitat or to ensure the essential functions of the habitat and associated ecosystems. In Australia, for example, despite their protected status, migratory birds are disappearing from the Murray-Darling River basin as a result of over-exploitation and the degradation of the riverine habitat due to existing agricultural uses. Similarly, while the nesting habitat of loggerhead turtles has been protected from tourist development in Greece, Turkey has refused to follow suit, despite both states being party to the Bern Convention. The efficacy of protected areas may also be limited by adherence to political rather than ecological boundaries or by inadequate size. Moreover, many protected areas have been imposed on local populations, giving rise to conflict.[29] Particularly when coupled with ineffective and underfunded management, such areas continue to be subject to degradation, which is often exacerbated by armed conflicts and natural disasters.

More fundamentally, vast tracts of critically important habitat areas or 'biodiversity hotspots'[30] are not subject to any international agreement, and their destruction due to pressures from increasing human population density, land clearing, and other activities continues. Hotspots are areas of high species endemism as well as high species and ecosystem diversity. The requirement of endemism is particularly important since by definition it implies that a species is found nowhere else. Thus, its survival is linked directly to the hotspot in question.[31] While numerous critical hotspots have been identified, many are located in developing tropical states and in ocean areas not subject to any relevant conservation regime. In other words, they are located in areas where states are either unwilling or unable, for any range of reasons, to protect them. The Conference of the Parties to the CBD has therefore called for the establishment, by 2010 for terrestrial areas and by 2012 for marine areas, of comprehensive, effectively managed, and ecologically representative national and regional systems of protected areas. The achievement of this goal seems unlikely, however, given the financial, capacity-building, institutional-strengthening, participatory, and other demands being raised, particularly by developing countries as well as the continued intransigence of developed countries to meet those demands. The situation with respect to high seas marine protected areas is even more precarious, with

---

[29] Churchill, see note 22 above.

[30] For a discussion of the 'hotspot' concept, see, e.g, N. Meyers, 'The Biodiversity Challenge: Expanded Hot-Spot Analysis' (1990) 10 Environmentalist 243.

[31] J.C. Kunich, 'World Heritage in Danger in the Hotspots' (2003) 78 Ind. L.J. 619 at 621.

no agreement yet being reached on the relationship between the CBD and the LOSC and the need for new legal instruments, if any. Economic interests, in particular, those of major high seas fishing states, also stand in the way of high seas marine protected area designations.

Similarly, obtaining international agreement on binding standards for the protection of forests, which are also recognized as critical habitats, has so far proven to be an insurmountable task, despite decades of attention to the issue and the general recognition of the need to curb deforestation and other threats to the world's forests. Indeed, since adoption in 1992 of the Non-Legally Binding Authoritative Statement of Principles for a Global Consensus on the Management, Conservation and Sustainable Development of All Types of Forests, the international community has not been able to agree to negotiate a legally binding agreement, let alone agree on what such an agreement would contain. The 1994 International Tropical Timber Agreement, which, in any event, applies only to tropical timber and not to all forests, is in reality little more than a commodity agreement, requiring the achievement of sustainable harvest for the purpose of promoting the industrialization of timber-producing countries. Even with this limited mandate, the parties have yet to meet their 'Year 2000 objective' of ensuring, by 2000, that all tropical timber traded by them comes from sustainably managed forests.

Somewhat more successful have been the negotiations for a convention aimed at the protection of the world's arid and semi-arid regions. Desertification caused by over-cultivation, overgrazing, deforestation, and the salinization of soil is a serious environmental and social problem, adversely affecting food production, biological resources, and biodiversity in arid and semi-arid lands. The 1994 Convention to Combat Desertification in Those Countries Experiencing Serious Drought and/or Desertification, Particularly in Africa (Desertification Convention) adopts a rather different approach to habitat protection, applying to processes and activities within states parties rather than to designated special areas. Moreover, unlike other agreements, the Desertification Convention adopts a 'bottom-up' approach,[32] treating desertification as a local resource management issue that must be addressed locally. Rather than imposing government designation and regulation from above, the Desertification Convention focuses on encouraging and creating mechanisms for local people and communities to engage in international partnerships to develop and implement national action programs that articulate long-term strategies and priorities for affected areas. This emphasis on popular participation may ameliorate the potential for conflict between competing users (see Chapter 29 'Public Participation'). Alternately, it may simply displace the conflicts downwards and outwards, rendering effective decision-making, implementation, and enforcement impossible.

---

[32] K.W. Danish, 'International Environmental Law and the 'Bottom-up' Approach: A Review of the Desertification Convention' (1995) 3 Ind. J. Global Legal Stud. 1.

4.3 Regulation of Trade

Regulation of trade can assist in the conservation of biological resources in two ways. It can be used to control the exploitation of species and genetic resources or it can be used to prevent or control the spread of alien and/or invasive species and genetically modified organisms. In particular, the international protection of genetic resources is currently achieved primarily through the regulation of transboundary trade.

4.3.1 *Control of Exploitation*

While control of the import and export of endangered or threatened species is included in a number of regional agreements, by far the most successful example of this approach is CITES, which regulates, by means of a permit system, the international trade in plant and animal species listed on its three amendable appendices. Appendix I lists species threatened with extinction, the trade in which is prohibited except in certain circumstances and with the prior approval of both the exporting and importing states. Appendix II lists potentially threatened and look-alike species, the trade in which is to be strictly regulated and permitted only upon issuance of proper documentation by the exporting state. Appendix III lists species found within the territory of one state party, where that state determines that international cooperation is necessary in controlling trade. Trade restrictions cover both species and specimens thereof and relate to the import, export, and re-export of listed species. Importantly, CITES controls only international trade and does not limit trade within a state.

CITES is often credited with being the most effective treaty regime dealing with biological resources. It is supported by an effective secretariat and an institutional network of non-governmental organizations (NGOs) that monitor international trade in wildlife and implementation by states parties to the convention. However, quite apart from any obvious shortcomings due to inadequate implementation and enforcement by states parties, CITES is now often criticized for being unwieldy and outdated. Politicization of the listing and downlisting procedures has led to major controversies, which have revealed the schism between the traditional, some say imperialistic, preservationist ethic of urban western environmentalism and the newer, post-Rio, sustainable development ethos, particularly promoted by developing countries, which sees human use of, and commercial trade in, wildlife as both desirable and necessary in order to reward local communities for, and further encourage, their conservation efforts.[33]

The continuing controversy over the CITES listing of the African elephant is instructive. Legal and illegal trade in ivory decimated populations during the 1980s.

---

[33] P. Stoett, 'Wildlife Conservation: Institutional and Normative Considerations,' in N. Schrijver and F. Weiss, eds., *International Law and Sustainable Development: Principles and Practice* (The Hague: Martinus Nijhoff, 2004) 501 at 514.

In 1989, the African elephant was listed on Appendix I, effectively banning the commercial ivory trade. Effective enforcement and conservation efforts led to an increase in elephant populations in southern African states who then sought to have the species downlisted to Appendix II in order to permit culling to control numbers and the sale of the resulting ivory to pay for ongoing conservation efforts. Opponents of the downlisting argued that this would open the door to a resurgence of illegal poaching. Nevertheless, in 1997, Botswana, Namibia, and Zimbabwe succeeded in having their populations of elephant downlisted, and, in 1999, the ivory sales were approved and went ahead. In 2000, despite attempts to have the elephants relisted on Appendix I, a further downlisting of the South African populations was agreed upon. In the meantime, as opponents of the downlisting feared, ever-increasing levels of poaching, exacerbated by poor law enforcement and excessive national culling policies, have fuelled a re-emerging and thriving illegal ivory trade. Attempts to relist the elephants on Appendix I have, perhaps not surprisingly, met with no success. Similarly, attempts to list African lions on Appendix I have likewise not succeeded, despite the significant decline in their numbers. States parties have, instead, merely been called upon to study their depletion, revenues generated from trophy hunting being considered too important for local communities to forego.

4.3.2 *Control of Alien or Invasive Introductions*

Regulating trade in endangered or threatened species is not the only aspect of trade regulation relevant to the protection of biological resources and biological diversity. Trade, itself, is one of several vectors, or pathways, for both accidental and intentional introductions of alien species into habitats in which they may become invasive and lethal to native species. Indeed, invasive alien species (IAS) are now identified as one of the most significant threats to both terrestrial and aquatic ecosystems, second only to habitat destruction (to which they often contribute) in their impact on biodiversity and nature conservation.[34] Thus, the CBD calls upon its parties to prevent the introduction of alien invasive species and to 'control or eradicate those IAS which threaten ecosystems, habitats or species'.

   A number of treaties are aimed at improving cooperation in controlling plant diseases and pests and preventing their introduction and spread across national boundaries. For example, the 1951 FAO International Plant Protection Convention and its various revisions and the 1959 Agreement Concerning Cooperation in the Quarantine of Plants and Their Protection against Pests and Diseases call for the development of national standards, restrictions on export and import, and research on phytosanitary conditions. More recently, other vectors, such as ballast water, have been identified as contributing to the spread of invasive species. The Ballast Water Convention calls upon states to prevent, minimize, and ultimately eliminate the

---

[34] A.M. Perrault and W.C. Muffett, 'Turning off the Tap: A Strategy to Address International Aspects of Invasive Alien Species' (2001) 11 R.E.C.I.E.L. 211.

transfer of harmful aquatic organisms and pathogens through the control and management of ships ballast water and sediments.

Controlling alien introductions through regulating trade is, however, fraught with uncertainty. First, the vast majority of species being transported, particularly accidentally, during trade activities has not been identified, and their potential for invasiveness has therefore not been assessed. Second, the risk of a species becoming invasive and harmful has not been subject to reliable prediction, with some species becoming invasive only many decades after their first introduction. Third, actual pathways of introduction, such as ballast water discharge, raw wood products and packaging materials, and intentional imports for the pet and ornamentals trade, have either not been adequately assessed or are subject to change. Moreover, trade regulation may fall foul of the WTO and GATT 1994 standards, in particular, the WTO's 1994 Agreement on the Application of Sanitary and Phytosanitary Measures (SPS Agreement).

Prevention of the spread of plant pests through trade regulation may also conflict with the need to protect the diversity of plant genetic resources and to ensure their international availability for research purposes. Thus, the ITPGRFA has as its objective 'the conservation and sustainable use of plant genetic resources for food and agriculture and the fair and equitable sharing of the benefits arising out of their use, in harmony with the Convention on Biological Diversity, for sustainable agriculture and food security'. Access to these resources is assured subject to the condition that provision is solely for the purpose of utilization and conservation for research, breeding, and training for food and agriculture, with pharmaceutical and industrial uses being prohibited. Benefit-sharing provisions are also included to ensure an exchange of information, access to and transfer of technology, capacity building, and the sharing of benefits arising from commercialization (see Chapter 41 'Technical and Financial Assistance'). The transboundary movement of these resources is subject to national regulation and control to ensure safety and that the objectives of the convention are met.

While the use of, and, hence, the controlled trade in, naturally occurring genetic resources is generally applauded, the use and trade in anthropogenically genetically modified organisms has been the subject of heated controversy. Throughout history, humans have sought to modify species through selective breeding techniques to improve crop and stock production and resilience. Since the 1970s, however, genetic engineering techniques have been developed whereby genes from one species may be isolated and inserted into another in ways not possible in nature to create a new, genetically modified organism. Advocates of genetic modification argue that it could result in benefits for biodiversity and the broader environment such as better agricultural efficiency and the reduced need for reliance on pesticides and other chemicals. Opponents, on the other hand, argue that the release of genetically modified organisms into the environment may pose similar types of risks to those presented by alien invasive species, with potentially wide-ranging adverse effects on biodiversity and related socio-economic impacts.

Recognizing the potential threats posed by transboundary transfers of genetically modified organisms, whether intentional or accidental, the CBD requires its parties to regulate, manage, or control risks associated with living modified organisms (LMOs) resulting from biotechnology that are likely to have impacts on the conservation and sustainable use of biodiversity, taking into account the risks to human health. The transboundary transfer of LMOs is to be conducted on the basis of an exchange of information between transferring and receiving parties on domestic regulation concerning the use and safety of LMOs as well as any other available information on the adverse effects that the introduction may have for the receiving party. Detailed procedures relating to the transboundary movement, handling, and use of LMOs are set out in the 2000 Cartagena Protocol on Biosafety to the CBD. These procedures include an advanced informed agreement procedure, whereby an exporter wishing to export certain categories of LMOs to a state for the first time must notify that state in advance and provide certain information. The importing state can then decide whether to accept or reject the import or attach conditions to it, based on a risk assessment. Unintentional transboundary transfers are also dealt with through the medium of notification and consultation requirements with respect to releases that may lead to such transfers and that are likely to have significant adverse effects. Significantly, the protocol applies only to LMOs resulting from modern biotechnology procedures. In this way, 'traditionally' engineered organisms are not covered.

5 Types of Measures Used

Given the wide range of international agreements described in this chapter, it will be apparent that a vast array of regulatory measures is needed to attain their objectives. In general, a distinction can be drawn between measures for the regulation of direct threats (harvesting and trade) and measures for the regulation of indirect threats (habitat loss and invasives), with further distinctions being drawn between *in-situ*, or on site, and *ex-situ*, or off-site, measures. As recognized in the CBD, *in-situ* conservation is a fundamental requirement of the conservation of ecosystems and habitats. *Ex-situ* measures, which refer to measures such as conservation in zoos, botanic gardens, gene banks, and scientific aquaria, also have an important role to play, particularly in the conservation of genetic resources.

Measures to be taken can either be articulated in the agreement itself or be adopted by the commission or other regulatory body, such as a meeting of the states parties, which is established by the agreement. Implementation of the measures will be carried out by state parties at the national level within their territory and in respect of their nationals, with states' compliance with their obligations usually being monitored in some manner by the regulatory body and, in an unofficial capacity, by interested NGOs. Ensuring that states comply with their obligations to adopt and enforce agreed measures remains problematic (see Chapter 39 'Compliance Theory'; Chapter 40 'National Implementation'; and Chapter 42 'Monitoring and Verification'), particularly where the measures apply in regard to biological resources located within the global commons, such as whales or fish. Securing compliance by non-state parties who seek to benefit from the free ride provided by the restraint of others also remains problematic.

5.1 Measures Regulating Direct Threats

The most direct threats to the conservation of biological resources arise from harvesting and consequential trade. Measures adopted to regulate harvest will depend on the conservation status of the species involved, with distinctions being drawn between endangered stocks or species and those less, or not, threatened. While the taking or killing of endangered species is normally prohibited, other species may also be subject to protection, particularly where their conservation status is unfavourable or where they are indigenous or endemic to a particular area. The Polar Bears Agreement, for example, places catch limits at zero. A moratorium has also been adopted on whaling. The unfavourable conservation status of albatrosses and petrels is to be improved through prohibitions on their taking, and on other interferences arising from human or human-induced activities.

Where harvest is permitted, it is often regulated through the adoption of closed seasons, during which taking is not permitted, or of closed areas. In this way, breeding, nesting, and spawning seasons and grounds and other sensitive areas, such as wildlife migration corridors, can be protected. Quantity of harvest may also be regulated through the adoption of limits on total allowable catch or take or of regulations requiring the exploitation to be based on 'reasonable', 'rational', 'optimal', or 'sustainable' use. Where overall limits are established, these may be further allocated by way of quota to either individuals or to states. Quota allocation is, however, often a fraught matter, particularly at the international level. Indeed, elucidation of criteria for the allocation of quotas is one of the most controversial issues facing regional fisheries organizations, where failure to provide equitable allocations simply encourages states to fish outside the regulatory regime.

The manner in which harvest occurs may also be regulated such that certain methods of taking will be prohibited, in order to both render taking more difficult and reduce the disruption to remaining individual specimens, other species, and the surrounding environment. The Polar Bears Agreement, for example, prohibits the use of 'aircraft and large motorized vehicles' for the taking of polar bears. The Bern Convention prohibits the use of large-scale or non-selective killing methods, including, *inter alia*, snares, gas, and poisoned baits. Measures adopted under fisheries treaties frequently restrict net mesh sizes or other fishing techniques, such as driftnetting, the use of dolphins as fish aggregating devices, and long-lining with unweighted hooks, to avoid by-catch of juvenile and non-target species including other fish, turtles, dolphins, and seabirds. These measures may be supplemented by measures articulated in separate agreements. For example, the conservation of salmon stocks was not the prime motivating factor for the moratorium on high seas driftnet fishing. Rather, broader environmental concerns over the damage driftnets cause to other marine species coalesced with coastal state claims, enshrined in the LOSC, to a preferential interest in salmon originating in their rivers. Primarily as a result of the concerted efforts of the parties to the 1992 Convention for the Conservation of Anadromous Fish Stocks in the North Pacific Ocean, the moratorium, which was adopted by a UN General Assembly resolution in 1991, is perhaps the most effectively policed and enforced international moratorium ever adopted. The unique combination of the LOSC prohibition on high seas salmon fishing and the efficacy of the United States Coast Guard in protecting US interests in 'their' salmon contribute to the moratorium's effectiveness.

As with endangered or threatened species, trade mechanisms can also be utilized to influence compliance with regulatory measures in order to ensure the continued sustainability of both the species and the harvesting activity. In the fisheries context, a number of trade-information or catch-documentation schemes have been adopted to track landings and trade flows in species such as bigeye tuna, southern bluefin tuna, and Patagonian toothfish to assist in determining where the fish were caught, by whom, and whether they were caught in accordance with the applicable regulatory measures. Information from the schemes is then used to assist in evaluating the status of the stocks and in identifying the vessels and states that are not complying with the relevant measures. Diplomatic demarches can then be made with the aim of encouraging better compliance. Where repeated non-compliance is found, it may lead to the adoption of trade-related measures, such as import restrictions, by other states against the offending state. The success of these schemes is, however, undermined by a lack of implementation and by extensive fraudulent reporting. The use of trade-related sanctions may also fall foul of GATT/WTO requirements.

Trade certification or eco-labelling schemes, which originated in the 'dolphin-friendly' tuna campaign in the United States, may also be useful in regulating harvest (see Chapter 33 'Non-Governmental Organizations and Civil Society' and Chapter 35 'Business'). Schemes adopted by both the Forest Stewardship Council and the Marine Stewardship Council are intended to promote environmentally responsible, socially beneficial, economically viable management and sustainable utilization of the world's forestry and fishery resources. The councils accredit certification organizations around the world, which then certify that harvests have come from sustainably managed forests or fisheries. Certification and labelling is then used to influence trade and individual consumer decisions (see Chapter 21 'Private and Quasi-Private Standard Setting'). Such schemes are, however, in their relative infancy, and their GATT/WTO consistency is a matter of ongoing debate.

5.2 Measures Regulating Indirect Threats

Indirect threats to biological resources arise from habitat destruction and alien introductions. In the first instance, habitat protection requires identification of areas to be protected and the adoption of national laws regulating activities, including bioprospecting, in those areas. Agreements such as the World Heritage Convention then require states to adopt policies relating to planning processes and to establish protective services. In the Western Hemisphere Convention and others, areas may be subject to varying degrees of interference ranging from strict inviolability to general public usage, while in the Antarctic access is restricted by permit. States may also be required to engage in scientific research in ecology, to adopt suitable conservation and management plans, to exchange information about habitats and their protection, to encourage the maintenance of suitable habitats for protected species, to take steps to restore degraded habitats, and to create or provide new habitat for species. This activity may include taking measures to control bush fires, limit grazing, regulate tourism, transportation, mining, and prospecting, prohibit destructive fishing practices, prevent or reduce pollution and soil, air, or water quality degradation, and limit the exploitation of plant and animal species in the protected area.

The taking of these measures may have serious financial implications for states, particularly developing countries in which much of the world's richest and most diverse habitats are found. Indeed, financial considerations underlie the ongoing debates between developed and developing countries over access to genetic resources, burden sharing, and the transfer of technology discussed in section 4 of this chapter (see Chapter 27 'Equity' and Chapter 41 'Technical and Financial Assistance'). One response is found in the World Heritage Convention, which establishes a heritage fund to assist states to meet their obligations in respect of the listed areas. A more recent approach is that found in the CBD, which requires developed states to provide 'new and additional financial resources' to enable developing countries to meet the 'agreed full incremental costs to them of implementing measures which fulfill the obligations of the Convention'. As far as developing countries are concerned, if the developed states want them to protect and conserve certain species or habitats that would otherwise be available for exploitation for the purposes of economic development, then the developed states should pay for these efforts.

Prohibitions on the introduction of alien species may be regulated through quarantine and measures relating to international transport and trade as noted in section 4.3 of this chapter. States may also be required to control domestic alien introductions to ensure the minimization of transboundary impacts. The Bern Convention not only calls for the control of such introductions, but also encourages the re-introduction of native species as a means of promoting their conservation. Aquaculture, in particular, has been identified as a threat to wild fish species leading NASCO, for example, to require its parties to adopt measures regulating salmon farming to minimize the impact of escaped farmed and transgenic salmon on wild salmon stocks. The major difficulties here are ensuring that states comply with their obligations to regulate and enforce compliance, particularly given the lack of a comprehensive and effective legal framework for evaluating damage caused by such introductions and assigning liability for the costs of rectification (see Chapter 44 'International Responsibility and Liability').

6 Biological Resources and the Twenty-First Century

As noted at the outset, given the vast amount of international law relating to the conservation of biological resources, one might be forgiven for thinking that adequate protections exist to ensure their continuing viability and vitality. Yet, this is not the case. Despite continuing regulatory and managerial efforts, the rate of loss of biological resources and biodiversity continues unabated. The world is squarely facing a total failure to meet the World Summit on Sustainable Development's goal of achieving, by 2010, a significant reduction in the rate of biodiversity loss at the global, regional, and national levels. The reasons for this continuing failure are multiple—the means of addressing them complex.

As this chapter has demonstrated, the legal regime for the conservation of biological resources, while extensive, is by no means comprehensive. Adherence to relevant treaty regimes is not universal, implementation is often patchy, and most of the treaties provide no mechanism for ensuring compliance at the national level. Additionally, the overlap between treaty regimes may give rise to uncertainty or conflict. Australia, for example, sparked a furious debate in the CCAMLR Commission when it proposed that Patagonian toothfish be listed on CITES. Other CCAMLR members refused to countenance such an overt suggestion of the failure of the CCAMLR regime. Japan's proposal that the Indian Ocean Tuna Commission should regulate the exploitation of southern bluefin tuna in the Indian Ocean similarly enraged the other members of the Commission on the Conservation of Southern Bluefin Tuna (CCSBT), who pointed out that the CCSBT regulates the exploitation of SBT globally. Disputes over the legitimacy of the International Whaling Commission's moratorium on commercial whaling led to the establishment of the North Atlantic Marine Mammal Commission. Even where the desire for cooperation between regimes is acknowledged, as between the Bonn Convention and the CBD, implementation of this cooperation is complex and time-consuming.

Moreover, many of the 'obligations' established by these treaties are hortatory rather than mandatory. Thus, compliance is both a matter of discretion and of opinion. Neither has the shift in emphasis from species and habitat conservation to conservation of biodiversity necessarily helped. Even assuming the national implementation plans required under the CBD have been adopted, their level of implementation has generally been poor. Moreover, these plans are subject to a broad range of economic and developmental considerations that are not necessarily consistent with conservation objectives. In some cases, the lack of political will to conserve biological resources and biodiversity may be obvious. In others, the political will may simply be focused more clearly on these other objectives. In this respect, the subsumption of the objective of conservation under that of sustainable development has spawned a host of new challenges, which, to date, have resulted in the diminution of the former in pursuit of the latter. Nowhere is this more evident than in the burgeoning trade versus environment debate.

Apart from the deficiencies in the legal regime, the effective conservation of biological resources is hampered, on the one hand, by a lack of scientific knowledge and, on the other, by an as yet unjustified confidence in the ability of science to save the day. With respect to the former, an inadequacy of scientific knowledge, or at least claims as to its inadequacy, have been a boon to both scientists and policymakers alike, ensuring the former are perennially occupied and allowing the latter to continue to avoid difficult conservation decisions on the basis that the science does not (or, possibly, not yet) support them. Precaution is reviled as the foe of sustainable development rather than accepted as a rational check on human destruction of the environment. Sustainable development with its insistence on the ascription of economic value, while undoubtedly a noble and useful objective, misses the point, as the old adage goes, that 'you don't know what you've got until you lose it'.

With respect to the latter, while science has succeeded in cloning sheep and breeding rainbow trout from salmon, these successes have been biologically unstable. Moreover, as recent attempts to recreate the thylocene (Tasmanian tiger) have shown, science has yet to succeed in bringing extinct species back to life. Even if it does, in the absence of adequate remaining natural habitat in which to place these species, their existence will be confined to zoos, botanical gardens, aquaria, and other man-made sideshows of what was once nature's bounty.

The issue of biodiversity protection now goes beyond the focus on biological resources themselves, to encompass threats such as global climate change. Polar bears and whales are threatened less by harvesting than they are by habitat destruction due to global warning. Climate change and associated sea temperature rise are also implicated in the failure of formerly exploited fish stocks, such as cod and pollock, to regenerate. Plant species, including important agricultural resources, are similarly challenged. The question for the twenty-first century is how to find solutions that reconcile competing economic, social, and ecological interests to ensure that biological resources are conserved and that the ecological and evolutionary potential of ecosystems is maintained. At a minimum, the usual platitudes calling for better adherence to, and implementation of, existing legal regimes, the negotiation of new ones to fill existing legal lacunae, and the provision of financial incentives and assistance to developing states to help them to meet these goals should be mentioned. However, simply doing more of that which has already shown itself to be insufficient will not suffice. At the heart of the matter lie both human rapaciousness and the vast range of 'cultural maladaptations'[35] that humans have developed, which have resulted in the undesirable biological consequences with which we are now faced. The greatest challenge is therefore to fully re-imagine our place on the planet and our role in nature—and to do so in a manner that is equitable to all.

This challenge is, in part, the objective of the CBD and the 'new generation' agreements such as the Desertification Convention and the ITPGRFA, with their emphasis on benefit sharing, information sharing, transfer of technology, financial assistance mechanisms, and, most importantly, the recognition of the importance of local control of resources. Indeed, local control and the adequate provision of financial and scientific resources to local communities to ensure effective control by those with the greatest stake in the preservation of species is arguably the most vital aspect of both cultural and species survival. However, to be fully effective, this control must be based not only on an understanding of trade and development issues, but also on a deep understanding and appreciation by all humans of the living systems of which we are but one element. The conservation of biological resources and, hence, of biodiversity in the twenty-first century will require an acceptance of the reality that our existence is dependent on theirs, not the other way round.

RECOMMENDED READING

M. Bowman and C. Redgwell, *International Law and the Conservation of Biological Diversity* (Boston: Kluwer Law International, 1996).

L. Glowka et al., *A Guide to the Convention on Biological Diversity* (Gland: World Conservation Union (IUCN), 1994).

IUCN Species Survival Commission, *2004 IUCN Red List of Threatened Species: A Global Species Assessment* (Gland: IUCN, 2004).

S. Lyster, *International Wildlife Law* (Cambridge: Cambridge University Press, 1985).

Millennium Ecosystem Assessment, *Ecosystems and Human Well-Being: Biodiversity Synthesis* (Washington, DC: World Resources Institute, 2005).

F.L. Morrison and R. Wolfrum, *International, Regional and National Environmental Law* (Boston: Kluwer Law International, 2000).

P. Sands, *Principles of International Environmental Law*, 2nd edition (Cambridge: Cambridge University Press, 2003), Chapter 11.

P. Stoett, 'Wildlife Conservation: Institutional and Normative Considerations,' in N. Schrijver and F. Weiss, eds., *International Law and Sustainable Development: Principles and Practice* (The Hague: Martinus Nijhoff, 2004) 501.

P. van Heijnsbergen, *International Legal Protection of Wild Fauna and Flora* (Amsterdam: IOS Press, 1997).

---

[35] S. Boyden, *The Biology of Civilisation: Understanding Human Culture as a Force in Nature* (Sydney: University of New South Wales, 2004).

CHAPTER 17

HAZARDOUS SUBSTANCES AND ACTIVITIES

DAVID A. WIRTH

1 INTRODUCTION

THE modern world is awash in synthetic and naturally occurring chemicals deployed with an intent to improve our quality of life. Nearly 26 million different chemicals are currently catalogued, and approximately 4,000 new substances are identified every day. While this ingenuity in manipulating the basic building blocks of matter accounts for many of the accomplishments of our industrial society, some of those chemicals may have unanticipated or undesirable consequences for human health and the environment.

1.1 Public Policies for Addressing Toxics

Toxics originate from highly diverse sources, including a wide variety of manufacturing processes that employ hazardous substances. Human beings experience

Preparation of this chapter was supported by a generous grant from the Boston College Law School Fund and draws on some of the author's previously published work.

exposure to toxics in numerous settings, and the ultimate environmental fate of hazardous substances is enormous in its scope. Toxic substances are used in consumer products, as industrial chemicals, and as pesticides. Hazardous chemicals are found in waste from manufacturing plants and households, in the workplace, and also may be transported over long distances through air and water.

Hazardous substances may have effects on human health or on the integrity of natural ecosystems or both. In addition to their intended uses, chemicals to which human beings are exposed may present risks of carcinogenicity (cancer), teratogenicity (birth defects), mutagenicity (genetic mutations), neurotoxicity (nerve damage), and a wide array of other adverse health effects. Concern for previously underappreciated health effects such as endocrine (hormone) disruption has recently increased dramatically.

Poisons such as pesticides purposely released into the environment can have unintended consequences, such as species loss through concentration at higher levels in the food chain. Pollution or chemical waste discharged into the environment as by-products of industrial manufacturing processes can disrupt terrestrial and aquatic ecosystems—some of them of considerable economic importance. Synthetic chemicals such as chlorofluorocarbons, which were once thought to be environmentally benign, can turn out to have near-catastrophic consequences of global proportions, such as the destruction of the stratospheric ozone layer.

The goals of policy interventions to combat the risks presented by toxic substances demonstrate a wide variation. Some regulatory approaches are designed to establish minimum common standards to protect health and the environment from unacceptable levels of harm. Others are intended to reduce competitive distortions that arise from divergent policy goals or approaches. Alternatively, public policies may attempt to create incentives for industry to reduce emissions of toxics or the use of hazardous substances in manufacturing processes. Finally, public policy may address toxic risks by leaving them to a system of liability, with harm from toxic exposures being addressed through general principles of compensation rather than through government regulation.

The range of options in terms of the point of policy intervention is similarly broad. Public policy may seek to reduce the use or production of toxics in favour of less hazardous substances or processes. Governmental regulation, instead or in addition, may address the removal of toxics from waste streams that pollute air, water, or soil. After harm has occurred, public policies establish criteria for determining whether compensation is appropriate and, if so, in what amount.

Further complicating the situation is the vast spectrum of policy strategies, instruments, and tools for responding to the problems created by toxics. Governments may require public authorities to evaluate and approve potentially hazardous substances as a condition for market entry. Alternatively, regulatory interventions may be required to remedy existing situations in which risks from toxic substances are present, including the removal of existing products from the market or establishing conditions of use or disposal.

1.2 International Dimensions of Regulating Toxics: Hard and Soft Law

It is increasingly apparent that the environmental and public health hazards presented by many toxic substances transcend national borders and may even be global in scope. The form of public policy interventions at the international level is significantly different from the regulatory tools typically employed by national governments. Coordinated multilateral responses often involve binding international agreements or non-binding, hortatory instruments of a kind different from the regulatory tools routinely encountered at the national level. Supranational authorities such as the European Union (EU), which exercise some but not all of the regulatory powers ordinarily associated with sovereign states, create additional analytical complexities (see Chapter 37 'Regional Economic Integration Organizations'). Last, in recent years, industry self-regulation in the form of private voluntary standards has attracted increasing attention as a public policy strategy (see Chapter 21 'Private and Quasi-Private Standard Setting').

Sovereign states have the authority to regulate private parties under their jurisdiction (see Chapter 31 'Changing Role of the State'). On occasion, states may coordinate or harmonize their policies in binding international agreements. Such an approach has considerable advantages, including enhancing the environmental efficacy of individual national responses through coordinated multilateral action; minimizing distortions in competitiveness that arise from disparate national policies; and providing a mechanism for holding other states parties to the agreement accountable through the creation of binding international obligations.

Binding treaties, however, also have drawbacks (see Chapter 20 'Treaty Making and Treaty Evolution'). Initiating a multilateral negotiation on a major new treaty or convention typically requires mustering considerable political will. Negotiations on an international agreement may take many years, and the results may represent a disappointing 'least common denominator' result, which is responsive to the needs of the least, rather than the most, ambitious positions taken in the negotiations. Even then, an international compact binds only those states that have formally accepted the obligations in it.

In response to considerations such as these, states and international institutions have often relied on less formal, non-binding instruments for situations that do not necessarily require obligations that are enforceable under international law (see Chapter 6 'Formality and Informality'). The texts of non-binding instruments, which have been widely employed in the field of international regulation of toxics, consequently are typically phrased in terms of 'shoulds' rather than the obligatory 'shalls' characteristic of binding obligations, which are more frequently found in the 'hard' law created by treaties and international agreements. One important function of this category of 'soft' instruments is consciously to establish normative expectations, which often function as standards of good practice.

In contrast to a 'hard' international agreement, a non-binding 'soft' instrument may allow states to gain experience with more ambitious, aspirational goals in a milieu that is perceived as being less risky. By contrast, under such circumstances states might commit to binding or 'hard' treaty obligations only of a modest character, if at all. Alternatively, non-binding instruments may also be appropriate for circumstances in which consensus is elusive or illusory, while, nonetheless, supporting more aggressive policy action by those states that are prepared to do so. Non-binding instruments may be attractive alternatives to a downward spiral towards a least common denominator—a result characteristic of many multilateral efforts.

A 'soft' instrument may be particularly useful for establishing normative, albeit non-binding, expectations for private parties. To accomplish this goal through a formal treaty negotiation is cumbersome at best. Since non-state actors such as private industry are not subjects of international law (see Chapter 35 'Business'), an international agreement cannot create obligations for private entities except through the intermediary of states parties to the agreement. Governmental authorities must then prescribe rules for regulated private entities within their jurisdiction. A non-binding instrument can bypass this unwieldy and time-consuming structure with exhortations addressed directly to private parties, presumably for implementation on a voluntary basis. On occasion, soft law can coalesce into binding customary law, although this is by no means necessary to ensure the efficacy of a non-binding instrument.

The concept of 'principles' is of particular importance in modern international environmental law. Although they have an analytical significance beyond any one international instrument, many of these principles are collected and codified in the Rio Declaration on Environment and Development from the UN Conference on Environment and Development. Unlike some other non-binding authorities, principles of international environmental law are not primarily intended expressly to establish normative standards. Rather, these principles are overarching aspirational precepts identified as part of a comprehensive and unifying architecture that identifies the direction in which international law should progressively evolve. Principles of international environmental law consequently are equally relevant to the development of treaties, customary law, and non-binding norms. Among the more salient principles in the field of toxics regulation are the exhortation to engage in precautionary decision-making (Principle 15 of the Rio Declaration) and the polluter pays principle (Principle 16 of the Rio Declaration).

This chapter analyses the enormous scope of international instruments addressing hazardous substances and activities by segmenting strategies for regulating toxic substances into a typology of specific junctures and regulatory theories that have been or might be employed to inform governmental interventions, whether at the national or international level. This approach offers a template for organizing and categorizing public policy responses to discrete aspects of the problem of controlling risks from toxic substances. Accordingly, this chapter begins by addressing policies designed to identify hazardous substances through testing and then progresses to treat more substantive public policy interventions designed to reduce or eliminate risks to public health and the environment from toxics.[1]

International law governing toxic substances and activities inevitably evolves in tandem with policy, legislation, and regulation at the national and (in the case of the EU) supranational level—strategies that serve as a backdrop against which multilateral efforts are negotiated and coordinated. For this reason, many multilateral instruments in the area of toxic substances and processes are designed to harmonize or extend diverse and sometimes divergent domestic regulatory approaches. Consequently, the topics below are framed by a brief discussion of domestic approaches in countries such as the United States or at the supranational level within the EU, both of which have been at the forefront of identifying public policy strategies for addressing this complex challenge. The examples, both international and domestic, have been chosen to illustrate various theories of regulation and do not aim to be comprehensive. Many national and international approaches, moreover, represent an amalgam of two or more public policy approaches and cannot necessarily be strictly compartmentalized.

2 Hazard Identification and Testing

One of the first questions inevitably encountered in crafting public policies for toxic substances, and a logical starting place for discussion, is that of identification and definition. Among the universe of elements and compounds encountered in the world, and especially those that are synthetically manufactured, some raise concern about adverse effects on human health or to the environment, while others present less cause for alarm or none at all. The level of risk that justifies a policy intervention is largely a social policy determination involving the application of judgement and values. Nonetheless, in making the distinction between 'toxic' or 'hazardous'[2] chemicals that warrant policy interventions and the remainder that do not, it is essential to have basic empirical toxicity data.

Of the tens of millions of different chemical substances known, about 100,000 are utilized in industrial processes. Of those, very few have been thoroughly tested for human toxicity or adverse environmental impacts. National legislation in the United

---

[1] Certain aspects of toxic substance regulation are addressed in other chapters, such as liability and cleanup (see Chapter 44 'International Responsibility and Liability') and private voluntary approaches (see Chapter 21 'Private and Quasi-Private Standard Setting' and Chapter 35 'Business').

[2] For the purposes of this chapter, the terms 'toxic' and 'hazardous' are used interchangeably in a non-technical sense to identify situations characterized by a heightened risk of injury, disease, or death from exposure to synthetic or extractive chemicals or substances.

States addresses the need for testing of existing chemicals and screening of new substances.[3] The Commission has formally proposed new legislation to the Council and the European Parliament consisting of a comprehensive new regulatory framework for registration, evaluation, and authorization of chemicals (REACH), which would systematize and strengthen chemical regulation by requiring the registration of existing and new chemicals.[4] As of this writing, a first reading of the proposal had been completed in both the Council and the Parliament, and formal adoption of the new system is expected by the end of 2006. The proposed registration process would require the production of basic toxicological data, including studies of ecotoxicity, if they are not already available.

2.1 Organisation for Economic Cooperation and Development (OECD) Harmonization Initiatives

Coordinating national test protocol and data requirements at the international level has significant benefits, particularly by reducing redundant or contradictory requirements from one country to another. Similarly, divergent national testing requirements can have unintended adverse consequences that can impede trade. Based on these considerations, the OECD has been actively involved for several decades in harmonizing national policies for testing chemicals.

Since 1989, a 'screening information data set' programme set out in a Decision-Recommendation on the Co-operative Investigation and Risk Reduction of Existing Chemicals has operated under the auspices of the OECD to develop basic information concerning about 600 poorly characterized international high production volume chemicals.[5] The base set of data includes the results of tests for physico-chemical properties, environmental fate, environmental effects, and health effects. As with other testing programmes, the principal goal is to assure adequate characterization of a substance to determine appropriate substantive regulatory policy for that chemical. Since the 1980s, the OECD has also had a programme to encourage the mutual recognition of test data by OECD member states—an initiative that has now extended to non-members as well.[6]

---

[3] Toxic Substances Control Act, 15 U.S.C., secs. 2601–92.

[4] See Proposal for a Regulation of the European Parliament and of the Council Concerning the Registration, Evaluation, Authorization and Restriction of Chemicals (REACH), Establishing a European Chemicals Agency and Amending EC Directive 1999/45 and Regulation (EC); and Proposal for a Directive of the European Parliament and of the Council Amending EEC Directive 67/548 in Order to Adapt It to Regulation (EC) of the European Parliament and of the Council Concerning the Registration, Evaluation, Authorization and Restriction of Chemicals, Doc. COM(2003)644 final.

[5] Organisation for Economic Co-operation and Development (OECD), Doc. C(90)163.

[6] See Decision Concerning the Mutual Acceptance of Data in the Assessment of Chemicals, OECD Doc. C(81)30, as amended by OECD Doc. C(97)186; Decision-Recommendation on Compliance with Principles of Good Laboratory Practice, OECD Doc. C(89)87, as amended by OECD Doc. C(95)8; and

The choice of forum for, and form of, multilateral cooperation for exchanging toxicity testing data is revealing. First, these efforts have taken place within the 30-member OECD, which is an international organization that is not part of the UN system, whose members are generally states with industrialized, market-oriented economies, and which is generally perceived as representing the interests of wealthier countries. Although developing countries may be invited to participate in OECD work, as in the case of certain of the OECD's efforts on the mutual acceptance of data, the OECD is not broadly representative of the interests of all countries. Second, the multilateral response has been limited to sharing those data that have been produced through existing national regulatory approaches in a largely voluntary setting, with only limited attempts to craft a harmonized system of testing at the international level. An additional reason for this relatively modest, voluntary approach may well be concerns over the confidentiality of data.[7]

2.2 Initiatives in the United Nations System

Building on a recommendation in Chapter 19 of Agenda 21, the Intergovernmental Forum on Chemical Safety (IFCS) was established in 1994. The IFCS meets approximately every three years and serves as a setting for communication among more than 150 governments, intergovernmental organizations, and non-governmental groups—including business, labour, environmental, and scientific organizations—concerned with chemicals management. The forum identifies priorities for cooperative action; recommends coordinated international strategies; facilitates the development of national regulatory infrastructure; identifies gaps in scientific knowledge related to chemicals; promotes information exchange and technical cooperation with respect to chemicals; advises governments with respect to chemical safety; and promotes cooperation between governments and non-governmental organizations (NGOs). The 2000 session of the forum (Forum III) adopted the Bahia Declaration on Chemical Safety, a statement that drew attention to the need for further action and established concrete goals for chemicals management in such areas as hazard assessments, the exchange of information, labelling, harmonized standards, infrastructure development, and the control of illegal trade.

Decision Concerning the Adherence of Non-Member Countries to the Council Acts Related to the Mutual Acceptance of Data in the Assessment of Chemicals, OECD Doc. C(97)114.

[7] The International Agency for Research on Cancer (IARC), a component of the World Health Organization located in Lyon, France, publishes a series of monographs, now covering more than 860 environmental agents, designed to relate exposure to environmental factors to the development of human cancer. The IARC ranks carcinogenic risks, and its work product may be useful to national and international authorities in evaluating risks of cancer and formulating public policies to reduce them. Unlike the OECD, the IARC is primarily a scientific research organization and not a forum for harmonizing national policies.

In 1995, also following a recommendation in Agenda 21, several intergovernmental organizations entered into a memorandum of understanding establishing an Inter-Organization Program for the Sound Management of Chemicals (IOMC). The UN World Health Organization provides secretariat services for the IOMC's activities, which include participation by the OECD, the UN Food and Agriculture Organization (FAO), the International Labour Organization (ILO), the UN Environment Programme (UNEP), the United Nations Industrial Development Organization, and the United Nations Institute for Training and Research. The United Nations Development Program and the World Bank participate as observers. Unlike the OECD's work on chemicals, the efforts of the IOMC are potentially global in reach.

The IOMC coordinates the international assessment of chemical risks; the harmonization of classification and labelling of chemicals; information exchange on chemicals and chemical risks; the establishment of risk reduction programmes; the strengthening of national capabilities and capacities for the management of chemicals; and the prevention of illegal international traffic in toxic and dangerous products. Among other things, the IOMC has facilitated the establishment of a globally harmonized system for the classification and labelling of chemicals. The IOMC implemented a voluntary prior informed consent procedure that preceded the legally binding Convention on the Prior Informed Consent Procedure for Certain Hazardous Chemicals and Pesticides (PIC Convention) (section 6.2) and has assisted countries to develop national implementation plans under the Stockholm Convention on Persistent Organic Pollutants (Stockholm Convention) (section 3.1).

Building on the IFCS Bahia Declaration and the 2002 Johannesburg Plan of Implementation at the World Summit on Sustainable Development (WSSD), the IOMC organizations and the IFCS have embarked on a strategic approach to international chemicals management (SAICM), which culminated in an International Conference on Chemicals Management held in Dubai in February 2006. The outputs from this meeting include a high-level declaration expressing a commitment to SAICM by governments, representatives of civil society, and the private sector; an overarching policy strategy describing governmental expectations from SAICM in such areas as risk reduction, knowledge and information, governance, capacity building and technical cooperation, and illegal international traffic; and a global plan of action containing a menu of 'work areas and activities', in the form of voluntary national and international actions, for implementation of the Strategic Approach. The meeting also served as a vehicle for achieving the WSSD's goal of assuring that by the year 2020 chemicals are produced and used in ways that minimize significant adverse impacts on the environment and human health. The SAICM will also address the promotion of national regulatory infrastructure, technology transfer, and improved chemicals management. An additional benefit is expected to be enhanced implementation of the major global treaties on chemicals, including the PIC and Stockholm Conventions.

3 CONDITIONS OF PRODUCTION AND USE

Public authorities may respond to the risks presented by hazardous substances, products, or processes by establishing conditions under which these substances or products may safely be used or hazardous activities conducted in a safe manner. Alternatively, if some risks are deemed to be acceptable, a governmental regulatory authority may be charged with setting out allowable conditions of use or operation. This approach may, but need not necessarily, be employed together with a requirement for governmental approval, after a governmental authority has determined that the product or substance meets a regulatory standard but nonetheless must be used or deployed under limited circumstances to meet this standard. For instance, conditions of use are contemplated by the EU's REACH proposal, as well as existing EU and US chemicals legislation (section 2). The EC Directive 96/82 on the Control of Major-Accident Hazards Involving Dangerous Substances (Seveso II Directive) (section 5) is likewise an application of this regulatory approach to hazardous activities.

3.1 Stockholm Convention

Beyond the local risks posed by their toxicity, persistent organic chemicals (POPs) such as polychlorinated biphenyls (PCBs) are a global threat because they are stable and, hence, persist in the environment for long periods; because they consequently end up widely distributed geographically, often far from the place of manufacture or release; and because they accumulate in the fatty tissue of living organisms and therefore concentrate at higher levels of the food chain. The 2001 Stockholm Convention builds on years of work by international NGOs to target a 'dirty dozen' list of pesticides and industrial chemicals.

The Stockholm Convention goes farther than prior universal agreements addressing international trade in hazardous wastes, industrial chemicals, and pesticides (section 6) by directly limiting the production and release of certain chemicals at the domestic level, whether these substances are involved in international trade or not. The Stockholm Convention consequently is an example of harmonizing national policies on conditions of use, in some cases by eliminating the use of a substance altogether, at a potentially universal, global level. The Stockholm Convention, which entered into force in 2004, targets nine chemicals and categories of chemicals for elimination: the pesticides aldrin, chlordane, dieldrin, endrin, heptachlor, mirex, and toxaphene and the chemicals hexachlorobenzene and PCBs. The agreement also strictly limits the use of DDT to control disease-carrying insects and requires governments to limit unintentional releases of PCBs, hexachlorobenzene, dioxins, and furans.

As a dynamic instrument designed to be responsive to the needs of the future as well as the present, the Stockholm Convention contains a mechanism by which the parties can apply the stringent conditions of the convention to new substances as the need arises. This mechanism expressly states that decisions to list new chemicals should be taken on the basis of a precautionary approach. Many of the original dirty dozen chemicals had already been banned in major industrialized countries under domestic law, which explains the widespread support for the treaty. More opposition is expected to the banning or restriction of new substances under the treaty, which may impinge upon profitable industries in the developed world.

The Global Environment Facility serves as the funding mechanism under the convention and has financed pilot programmes for the development of national implementation plans for the management of POPs, as required by the convention, by developing and newly industrialized countries. The convention also includes an important information-exchange component, including a clearinghouse function for sharing information provided by governments, intergovernmental organizations, and NGOs, which complements similar efforts coordinated by the IOMC.

3.2 Multilaterally Agreed Standards for Pesticides and Other Toxics

Since 1985, the voluntary FAO Code of Conduct on the Distribution and Use of Pesticides, which was newly revised in 2002, has been the internationally accepted standard for labelling, packaging, storage, and disposal, and pesticide management. Similarly, the OECD's Guidelines for Multinational Enterprises, originally adopted in 1976, were subsequently amended to include a section devoted entirely to standards addressed directly to multinational corporations in the area of the environment.[8] Both of these instruments apply not only to potentially toxic materials but also to operations involving hazardous substances or processes. Each of these efforts, consistent with its non-binding character, is addressed not only to national governments but also directly to a variety of public and private actors, including local officials, industry, workers, consumers, NGOs, and the public generally.

Alternatives to formal treaties may be particularly well suited to certain institutional settings. For example, through the process of negotiating loan agreements with sovereign states on a case-by-case basis, the World Bank is uniquely positioned to influence policies in those states, principally developing countries, which borrow from the bank. The bank's loan preparation process is governed by a series of instruments known as 'operational policies', 'bank procedures', and 'good practices' in such areas as pest management and environmental assessment (section 9.2). In principle,

---

[8] OECD, *Guidelines for Multinational Enterprises* (Paris: OECD, 2000).

the first two categories are internally binding on bank personnel and the third advisory, but the force of the instruments may vary depending on their terms.

4 Regulation of Pollutant Releases

Establishing conditions of use, as discussed in the previous section, is a public policy strategy that can be usefully employed in certain cases to reduce the risk presented by a hazardous substance or product. Such an approach may be particularly appropriate for reducing workplace risks from toxic substances or to protect those who use them, such as pesticide applicators or consumers. There may also be concern for environmental exposures to, for example, a toxic pollutant that may have adverse consequences for public health or the environment or both. While establishing conditions of use may reduce some risks resulting from exposures to toxic substances, this approach may not be sufficient to protect the public and the environment from harmful levels of exposure to pollutants released as by-products of industrial, manufacturing, or other activities.

Public policies for limiting exposures to toxic or hazardous materials may be articulated in a number of ways. One approach is to limit emissions as such—a strategy that may be expressed in a regulatory sense as an upper bound on acceptable levels of releases of the substance in question. This may be a particularly attractive option if policymakers choose to control releases based on available technology, in which case the emissions limitations may reflect the level of technology chosen, often by reference to an adjective standard such as 'best' technology or 'maximum' control. One drawback to emissions limitations phrased by reference to available technologies is that it may be difficult to correlate the regulatory standard to real-world exposures. In other words, if there are enough sources, then even stringent emissions limitations may still result in unacceptable ambient concentrations of a toxic pollutant.

Another approach is to establish limitations on environmental exposures as such, a strategy that is typically articulated as an upper limit on ambient concentrations of the substance in question. While this approach may be more directly linked to exposures, it is also not free of conceptual and practical difficulties. A regulatory authority must establish an 'acceptable' concentration or level of exposure, which may be politically controversial or scientifically difficult. Ultimately, the ambient exposure limitation must be implemented by reductions in emissions from sources, necessitating sometimes complicated extrapolations or modeling to correlate source emissions with environmental concentrations. Empirical monitoring, moreover, is necessary to assure that the regulatory targets in the form of maximum ambient concentrations have been achieved.

National and supranational regulatory approaches contain examples of each of these strategies—emissions limitations and control of ambient concentrations—with both often employed simultaneously. For example, United States law and policy for addressing air pollutants relies on an ambient approach to protecting public health and the environment from harmful concentrations of most air pollutants, including at least one toxic substance, lead.[9] Technology-based controls apply to a list of 189 other toxic chemicals pursuant to a statutorily specified schedule. The EU's air pollution legislation reflects a similar range of approaches to emissions limitations. A framework directive was adopted in 1996 with the goal of controlling ambient environmental exposures to air pollutants and monitoring their concentrations in the air.[10] By contrast, a directive adopted in 2000 addressing waste incineration requires the establishment of emissions limitations for a variety of conventional pollutants as well as toxics such as heavy metals.[11]

Likewise, United States policy with respect to water pollution includes both technology-based emissions limitations for hazardous substances as a primary approach, with limitations on ambient concentrations of toxic water pollutants as a secondary, residual strategy.[12] Similarly, under a framework directive in the field of water policy, the EU requires the attainment of basin-wide water quality objectives.[13] Pursuant to an instruction in the framework directive, the EU has established a list of 33 toxic chemicals and categories of chemicals for priority consideration, with the goal of eliminating emissions and discharges of those hazardous substances within 20 years.[14]

4.1 UN Economic Commission for Europe (UNECE) Protocols on Air Pollution

The UNECE, whose membership includes all states of both eastern and western Europe as well as Canada and the United States, has been working for several decades on questions of air pollution. A Convention on Long-Range Transboundary Air Pollution (LRTAP Convention) was concluded in 1979 under UNECE auspices (see Chapter 14 'Atmosphere and Outer Space'). The LRTAP Convention was one of the first international environmental agreements to be structured as a 'framework' convention, consciously designed to serve as a vehicle for ongoing multilateral cooperation (see Chapter 20 'Treaty Making and Treaty Evolution'). The convention

---

[9] Clean Air Act, 42 U.S.C., secs. 7401–7671q.

[10] EC Directive 96/62 on Ambient Air Quality Assessment and Management, [1996] O.J. L296/55.

[11] EC Directive 2000/76 on the Incineration of Waste, [2000] O.J. L332/91.

[12] Clean Water Act, 33 U.S.C., secs. 1251–387.

[13] EC Directive 2000/60 Establishing a Framework for Community Action in the Field of Water Policy, [2000] O.J. L327/1.

[14] EC Commission Decision 2455/2001 Establishing the List of Priority Substances in the Field of Water Policy and amending EC Directive 2000/60, [2001] O.J. L331/1. As of this writing, no specific control measures for any of these substances have yet been proposed by the Commission.

consequently articulates no more than a general commitment to 'limit and, as far as possible, gradually reduce and prevent air pollution.'

Ancillary agreements, or 'protocols,' containing substantive regulatory measures were subsequently appended to the convention. A 1998 Protocol to the LRTAP Convention on Persistent Organic Pollutants (POPs Protocol) addresses this category of toxics in the context of regional air pollution in a manner complementary to the globally applicable Stockholm Convention (section 3.1). The POPs Protocol, which governs 16 POPs—a wider coverage than the Stockholm Convention—eliminates the production and use of some substances, restricts the uses of others, establishes emissions limitations, and specifies waste management practices.

A second Protocol to the LRTAP Convention on Heavy Metals, which was adopted in 1998, addresses three toxics: cadmium, lead, and mercury. This instrument relies primarily on an emissions reduction strategy for achieving its policy goals. The agreement requires parties to it to reduce emissions of those three heavy metals by reference to a base year—an international regulatory technique frequently encountered in the regulation of toxics. The instrument also specifies numerical technology-based emissions limitations and target dates for new and existing stationary sources in 11 enumerated categories. The agreement likewise sets out technology- and process-based emissions limitations for major industrial categories, including iron and steel, non-ferrous metals, power generation, road transport, and waste incineration.

4.2 Multilateral Agreements on Land-Based Sources of Marine Pollution

Part XII of the 1982 United Nations Convention on the Law of the Sea articulates obligations for states to regulate pollutant releases on land, including toxics, that may contaminate the marine environment. In 1995, following a mandate in Chapter 17 of Agenda 21, more than 100 states participated in drafting the Washington Declaration on Protection of the Marine Environment from Land-Based Activities. The declaration launched a new initiative under UNEP auspices, the Global Program of Action for the Protection of the Marine Environment from Land-Based Activities (GPA). Among the goals of the GPA are the reduction of emissions of such toxic substances as POPs, radioactive substances, heavy metals, and hydrocarbons including oil.

Both before and after the adoption of the Washington Declaration, regional multilateral agreements addressing the environment in particular marine areas have been a principal vehicle for addressing environmental hazards from land-based sources. As of this writing, the UNEP regional seas programme, initiated in 1974 as a result of the 1972 Stockholm Conference on the Human Environment, covers 13 geographic regions. Ancillary protocols on land-based sources of marine pollution (LBS protocols) have been adopted under the auspices of many of these regional seas conventions, including those for the Mediterranean, the southeast Pacific, the Persian Gulf (ROPME Sea Area), the Black Sea, and the wider Caribbean. The post-1995 protocols, including those for the Mediterranean and the wider Caribbean—neither of which is in force as of this writing—have adopted a comprehensive basin-wide approach to sources of water pollution, including toxics, that may adversely affect the marine environment. As in the case of the UNECE LRTAP regime, to the extent that the regional LBS protocols govern substances such as POPs, these agreements are complementary to global regulatory instruments such as the Stockholm Convention (section 3.1).

In addition to requirements that parties adopt national plans and programmes, the UNEP LBS protocols contain specific regulatory requirements designed to address land-based pollution. For example, in addition to the toxics enumerated in the GPA, both the Protocol for the Protection of the Mediterranean Sea against Pollution from Land-Based Sources and Activities and the Protocol Concerning Pollution from Land-Based Sources and Activities in the Wider Caribbean Region identify organophosphorous compounds, organotin compounds, cyanides, and fluorides as substances to be addressed under the agreements. Other regional agreements addressing toxic water pollution of onshore origin that are not part of the UNEP regional seas programme include the Convention for the Protection of the Marine Environment of the North-East Atlantic (OSPAR Convention), and the Convention on the Protection of the Marine Environment of the Baltic Sea Area (Helsinki Convention).

5 HAZARDOUS PROCESSES AND INDUSTRIAL ACCIDENTS

Several major industrial accidents in the latter part of the twentieth century alerted governments and the public to the potential not only for hazardous substances but also for manufacturing processes employing them to present risks to the environment and public health. In 1976, an industrial installation in the Italian town of Seveso released a cloud of dioxin, requiring the evacuation of more than 600 people and the treatment of several times that many for dioxin poisoning. In 1984, methyl isocyanate escaped from a US-owned pesticide plant in Bhopal, India, and killed 2,000 people. In 1986, water used to combat a fire in the Sandoz Chemical Company's industrial compound near Basel, Switzerland, resulted in the release of mercury compounds, pesticides, and other agricultural chemicals into the Rhine River, which transported the pollution downstream to Germany, France, and the Netherlands, causing a massive fish die-off.

These events, as well as others less well publicized, have focused attention on manufacturing processes as a potential juncture for regulation. One obvious goal of regulatory interventions in this area is to reduce the risks of accidents such as those at Seveso and Bhopal. Addressing manufacturing processes also provides another, perhaps less apparent, opportunity to encourage shifts towards less polluting, more sustainable manufacturing practices. As illustrated by the Bhopal catastrophe, which involved foreign investment, and the Sandoz spill, a case of transboundary pollution, there is also an important international dimension to this issue.

The EEC Directive 82/501 on the Major-Accident Hazards of Certain Industrial Activities, the first and most influential instrument in the field, was adopted in 1982, amended after the Bhopal and Sandoz incidents, and overhauled and replaced by a new directive (Seveso II Directive) in 1996.[15] The Seveso II Directive addresses not only hazardous substances in industrial installations, including the storage of toxic chemicals, but also hazardous processes themselves. Under the directive, operators of industrial establishments governed by the instrument must notify the competent national authority and establish a major accident prevention policy. Operators at the most rigorous regulatory tier in addition must file a safety report, a safety management system, and an emergency plan. Unlike in the EU, no single instrument in the United States governs emergency preparedness and chemical accidents. Federal legislation nonetheless requires that public authorities, including state and local governments, must craft an emergency response plan, review it at least annually, and inform the public about chemicals in the community. Industrial installations must adopt a facility-specific risk management program and notify public authorities of emergency releases of any of 364 extremely hazardous substances.[16]

5.1 ECE Convention on the Transboundary Effects of Industrial Accidents

The Convention on the Transboundary Effects of Industrial Accidents, negotiated and adopted in 1992 under the auspices of the UNECE, is a multilateral effort along the lines of the Seveso Directives but addressed more generally to Europe and North America. Like the Seveso Directives, the convention, which entered into force in 2000, aims at protecting public health and the environment by reducing the likelihood of such events, along with measures designed to mitigate the effects of those that do occur. The convention promotes international cooperation among the parties to it before, during, and after an industrial accident.

---

[15] EC Directive 96/82 on the Control of Major-Accident Hazards, [1997] O.J. L10/13.

[16] Emergency Planning and Community Right-to-Know Act of 1986, 42 U.S.C., secs. 11001–11050; and Clean Air Act, 42 U.S.C., sec. 7412(r).

The convention obliges parties first to identify hazardous operations within their borders that could have transboundary effects in the event of an accident. After identification, parties must inform the other parties that could be affected and consult with them. The convention directs that new installations be sited in areas where the risks are minimized, and that potential transboundary effects be disclosed and analysed in advance. In the area of preparedness, hazardous operations must have both on-site and off-site contingency plans. In situations in which several parties to the convention might be affected by a hazardous operation, the convention specifies that they work together. The convention additionally articulates standards for informing and consulting with the public, including administrative and judicial remedies.

In the event of an accident, the convention requires early notification to other parties and calls on the parties to establish special notification systems for this purpose, the UNECE Industrial Accident Notification System. Additionally, parties must take action to minimize transboundary effects, in cooperation with other parties to the extent required by the situation. Each party to the convention must designate a competent authority as a focal point for communication and action with respect to the convention's obligations.[17]

5.2 Multilaterally Agreed Good Practice Standards for Industrial Accidents

As in other areas covered by this chapter, industrial accidents have been addressed through non-binding approaches and other indirect leverage points in the international system. The OECD Working Group on Chemical Accidents has adopted *Guiding Principles for Chemical Accident Prevention, Preparedness, and Response*.[18] The principles address planning, construction, management, operation, and review of the safety performance of industrial installations employing hazardous processes. The guidelines, consistent with their non-binding character, are not confined to the role of national governments but instead are addressed directly to public authorities, industry, employees, NGOs, and the public generally.

The OECD *Guidelines for Multinational Enterprises* (section 3.2) specify that private entities addressed by that instrument should maintain contingency plans to prevent and control accidents and emergencies; should report accidents immediately to public authorities; and should educate workers in the proper handling of hazardous materials so as to avoid accidents. A companion *Guidance on Safety Performance Indicators* is intended to help facilities engaged in hazardous activities,

---

[17] International Labour Organization (ILO) Convention no. 174 on the Prevention of Major Industrial Accidents adopts an analogous approach at the global level.

[18] OECD, *Guiding Principles for Chemical Accident Prevention, Preparedness, and Response* (Paris: OECD, 2003).

governmental authorities, and the local public to assess the efficacy of efforts to reduce the risk of industrial accidents and their effects should an incident nonetheless occur.[19]

Development assistance administered through the World Bank or bilateral aid agencies, and external financing of private projects through sources such as the World Bank's International Finance Corporation, are also occasions to influence public policy and private behaviour in the area of industrial accidents. The World Bank's 1998 *Pollution Prevention and Abatement Handbook* emphasizes opportunities for investment in less-polluting technologies and processes and sound management techniques in key mining and manufacturing sectors such as pesticide production and oil and gas development. Additionally, the handbook, which is intended to be applied in connection with the bank's environmental assessment policy (section 3.2), specifies the need for contingency plans to minimize accidental releases and emergency response procedures to manage accidents when they occur.

6 International Trade in Hazardous Substances, Products, and Waste

All of the regulatory strategies identified so far can be, and have been, applied within national jurisdictions and by the supranational EU to intervene in what otherwise would be unregulated markets. At the national and supranational level, those regulatory interventions typically involve imposing obligations on private parties such as businesses and industries that produce products or engage in activities that may, at least under some circumstances, pose unacceptable risks to public health or the environment.

In the international arena, analogous interventions that make use of governmental regulatory authorities or national police powers may not be possible. In a world of co-equal sovereign states whose governmental powers are generally limited by the extent of each country's territorial jurisdiction, it may be difficult or impossible for structural or legal reasons for governments to take action to abate risks that emanate from abroad. Multilateral cooperation of necessity tends to rely on consent and consensus, which may be difficult or impossible to secure so as to respond to risks from hazardous substances or activities that have a transnational dimension, leading governments and non-state actors alike to look to unilateral self-help as an alternative to concerted international action.

Internationally, the point at which something—a bulk shipment of a substance, a finished product, a service, capital, or know-how—crosses a national border consequently assumes commensurately greater importance as a potential juncture at

---

[19] OECD, *Guidance on Safety Performance Indicators* (Paris: OECD, 2005).

which regulatory requirements designed to reduce risks from toxics might be applied. Transboundary movements of hazardous substances such as industrial chemicals, pesticides, or toxic waste may also themselves present risks. For reasons such as these, the regulation of transboundary trade in hazardous substances has received considerable attention on the international level. There has also been a great deal of interest in the relationship between the agreements discussed in this section, which regulate trade in discrete categories of toxic substances through prescriptive governmental action, and the negative disciplines contained in free trade agreements such as World Trade Organization rules (see Chapter 7 'Relationship between International Environmental Law and Other Branches of International Law').

International trade in hazardous substances and products also raises significant North-South issues. After banning or severely restricting substances to protect health and the environment within their territories, industrialized countries have in some cases continued to allow those same substances to be exported. Developing countries in response have objected to a 'double standard' in which private enterprises in the industrialized world may profit at the expense of poorer countries, which may not have the technical capacity, the resources, or the governmental infrastructure to control the entry of these substances into their territory or to regulate their domestic use. Multilateral treatment of trade in hazardous substances consequently has been a vehicle for addressing the broader needs of developing countries in such areas as regulatory infrastructure, capacity building, technical cooperation, and development assistance. Negotiations on these instruments have also been permeated by delicate considerations of equity and morality.

6.1 Basel Convention on the Control of Transboundary Movements of Hazardous Wastes and Their Disposal (Basel Convention) and the Convention on the Ban of the Import into Africa and the Control of Transboundary Movement and Management of Hazardous Wastes within Africa (Bamako Convention)

The Basel Convention, which was adopted in 1989 and entered into force in 1992, was the first potentially universal, binding instrument addressing international trade in wastes, including both hazardous wastes and municipal trash. With respect to states not party to this instrument, the convention establishes a 'limited ban'. Specifically, the Basel Convention prohibits exportation from parties to non-parties and limits transboundary movements of wastes, both imports and exports, only to those states that are parties to the convention unless a party has entered into a bilateral agreement on waste shipments that satisfies Article 11 of the convention (section 8.1).

Among parties to the agreement, the core regulatory approach of the Basel Convention is the establishment of a 'prior informed consent' (PIC) regime. Accordingly, every state party to the convention may choose to ban the importation of hazardous or other wastes. With respect to other states party to the convention that have not prohibited waste imports, the government of the country of export must assure prior notification to the governments of the receiving state and any transit states in advance of a waste shipment. The shipment may not commence until the government of the proposed state of import has given its consent in writing. Based on the written consent of relevant states of import, states of export may allow exporters to use a 'general' notification procedure for up to one year for multiple shipments of the same types of wastes.

The third Conference of the Parties to the Basel Convention, which was held in Geneva in September 1995, adopted an amendment to the agreement intended to ban North-South shipments of hazardous waste intended for disposal, as defined roughly along OECD–non-OECD lines, among parties to the amendment. The amendment also phases out shipments of hazardous wastes from the same group of primarily OECD countries intended for recovery or recycling to other states outside this group. The adoption of the North-South ban amendment, which has been criticized in some quarters as paternalistic and environmentally counterproductive, is indicative of substantial continued concern about the environmental integrity of shipments from developed to developing countries.

Even before the Basel Convention was adopted, there were pressures to strengthen the rigour and intensity with which this instrument controls international trade in wastes. African states expressed concern over the Basel Convention's failure fully to ban transboundary movements of hazardous and other wastes, and no sub-Saharan African country signed the convention at the time of its adoption. Under the auspices of the Organization of African Unity (now the African Union), those countries in 1991 adopted a stronger regional agreement, the Bamako Convention. The Bamako Convention bans imports of hazardous waste into Africa and creates a PIC procedure for trade within Africa.[20]

6.2 PIC Convention

Like the Basel Convention, the PIC Convention, which was concluded in 1998 and entered into force in 2004, establishes a legally binding regime for applying PIC

---

[20] Other regional agreements include the 1996 Izmir Protocol to the Barcelona Convention for the Protection of the Mediterranean Sea against Pollution (section 4.2); the 1995 Waigani Convention to Ban the Importation into Forum Island Countries of Hazardous and Radioactive Wastes and to Control the Transboundary Movement and Management of Hazardous Wastes within the South Pacific Region; and the 1992 Central American Regional Agreement on Transboundary Movements of Hazardous Wastes.

principles to international shipments of hazardous chemicals and pesticides. The PIC Convention applies to goods in the form of chemicals in international commerce, in contrast to the Basel Convention, which applies to presumptively harmful detritus or 'bads.' As with the Basel Convention, the principal motivation for the agreement was to assist developing countries that might have limited regulatory capacity or difficulty controlling imports to implement their own domestic environmental and public health policies.

The PIC Convention addresses pesticides and industrial chemicals that have been banned or severely restricted for health or environmental reasons by parties, and which have been notified by parties for inclusion in the PIC procedure. The agreement requires that any import ban be universal and non-discriminatory. That is, a party cannot refuse to import a chemical from another party while continuing to permit domestic production or allowing imports from other parties or from non-parties. At the time it was adopted, the convention's requirements applied to 22 pesticides and five industrial chemicals. The convention also contains provisions for exchange of information concerning potentially hazardous chemicals in international trade, and channels for providing technical assistance to developing countries to improve their domestic capabilities to manage toxic chemicals and pesticides.

With respect to the covered substances, the convention requires the formal, written consent of the government of the state of import before exportation may take place. In response to a notification from the Convention secretariat, a state of import that is a party to the convention may decide to allow importation of the chemical, to prohibit importation, or to allow importation subject to specified conditions. Alternatively, the convention provides that states of import may provide an interim response. Like the Stockholm Convention (section 3.1), the PIC Convention contains a mechanism for subsequent additions to the list of covered substances.

6.3 Cartagena Protocol on Biosafety (Cartagena Protocol)

The Cartagena Protocol, an ancillary instrument to the 1992 United Nations Convention on Biological Diversity, was adopted in January 2000 and entered into force in September 2003. The protocol governs genetically modified food and crops, which strictly speaking are not toxic substances. Its public policy approach, however, is similar to those in the Basel and PIC Conventions. The Cartagena Protocol expressly articulates a public policy of precaution, and the instrument as a whole can be seen as an embodiment of this approach.

The principal regulatory vehicle in the protocol is the requirement for 'advanced informed agreement' (AIA), which is analogous to the PIC requirements established for hazardous wastes under the Basel Convention and for chemicals and pesticides in the PIC Convention. The protocol requires as a first step in the AIA process advance notice to the state of import before the first exportation of a living modified organism (LMO). The state of import then has a right to permit, deny, or impose conditions on the importation of the LMO in question and must ensure that a risk assessment has been performed. The other principal substantive aspect of the Cartagena Protocol concerns the establishment of a biosafety clearinghouse designed to facilitate the exchange of scientific, technical, environmental, and legal information on, and experience with, living modified organisms, with particular attention to the needs of developing countries.

LMOs as defined in the protocol include those intended for release into the environment, such as seeds, as well as those intended for human food or animal feed, but does not as a general matter include pharmaceuticals. LMOs intended for direct use as food or feed are not covered by the AIA procedure. As to LMOs intended for food, feed, or processing, the biosafety clearinghouse must be notified within 15 days of a decision regarding domestic use, including domestic marketing with a potential for exportation.

7 DISPOSAL OF TOXIC WASTE

The lifecycle of a hazardous substance may result in release into the environment, typically to the media of air or water, at which juncture regulatory requirements, typically in the form of emissions limitations, may apply (section 4). Alternatively, a particular toxic substance may ultimately find its way into industrial waste as a component of the detritus remaining at the conclusion of a manufacturing process. Similarly, household or consumer products consisting of or containing hazardous materials may enter the waste stream. As with releases of toxics to the environment, the treatment, storage, and disposal of hazardous waste presents risks to public health and the environment that have been addressed by regulatory policies.

In the United States, statutory requirements establish minimum technical and scientific standards for hazardous waste.[21] For instance, hazardous waste landfills must have double liners, leachate collection systems, and groundwater monitoring facilities. The principal mechanism for implementing the statute is a requirement that existing and new facilities obtain a federal operating permit. The statute also establishes the so-called 'cradle-to-grave' manifest or tracking system to ensure that waste ultimately arrives at a permitted facility. EU legislation is similar in establishing technical requirements for waste and its treatment with the goal of reducing

[21] Resource Conservation and Recovery Act of 1976, 42 U.S.C., secs. 6901–6992k.

adverse impacts on public health and the environment.[22] The legislation identifies a variety of categories of waste—municipal waste, hazardous waste, non-hazardous waste, and inert waste—and specifies requirements for landfills that may accept each category. Like the US legislation, the directive sets up a system of operating permits for landfill sites.

The binding obligations contained in the Basel Convention (sections 6.1 and 8.1) address the ultimate fate of waste governed by the agreement as part of its strategy of regulating trade in this hazardous commodity. Other international regimes target disposal more directly by attempting to harmonize national regulatory approaches.

7.1 Convention on the Prevention of Marine Pollution by Dumping of Wastes and Other Matter (London Convention)

The London Convention, for which the International Maritime Organization serves as Secretariat, is a multilateral agreement of potentially global scope designed to address one component of the disposal problem, namely dumping at sea (see Chapter 15 'Ocean and Freshwater Resources'). The London Convention, like a number of regional agreements adopted after it, adopts a listing approach. A 'black list' identifies substances, including compounds containing the toxic heavy metals mercury and cadmium, and organohalogen pesticides, whose dumping is prohibited altogether. A second 'grey list' includes substances such as wastes containing other heavy metals, which require a special permit in advance. Since its adoption in 1972, the London Convention has been amended several times, most notably to ban ocean incineration of wastes and the disposal at sea of low-level radioactive waste.

The Protocol to the Convention on the Prevention of Marine Pollution by Dumping of Wastes and other Matter, which entered into force in March 2006, supersedes the 1972 instrument for parties to both agreements. The protocol is based on a precautionary theory of regulation expressly articulated in the text and consequently is much more restrictive than the earlier instrument. To this end, the protocol, in a regulatory approach that is in direct contrast to the 1972 London Convention, prohibits ocean dumping altogether unless the activity is specifically authorized by the new agreement. Among the very restricted categories of waste for which ocean disposal is allowed are dredged material; sewage sludge; waste from fishing operations; vessels, platforms, and other man-made structures; inert, inorganic geological material; and organic material of natural origin. The protocol also prohibits ocean incineration and the exportation of wastes to other states for dumping at sea.

---

[22] EC Directive 99/31 on the Landfill of Waste, [1999] O.J. L182/1.

7.2 International Atomic Energy Agency (IAEA)
   Agreements and Standards

Nuclear safety, along with technology transfer and verification, is one of the three pillars of the IAEA's programme. After the Chernobyl accident, four binding multilateral agreements in the area of nuclear safety were adopted under IAEA auspices. One of these agreements, the Joint Convention on the Safety of Spent Fuel Management and on the Safety of Radioactive Waste Management (Joint Convention), which was adopted in 1997 and entered into force 2001, is the first binding international agreement to address the management and storage of radioactive waste and spent fuel in countries that do and do not have nuclear programmes. The Joint Convention builds on the earlier IAEA Principles of Radioactive Waste Management, which were published in 1995.

The goal of the Joint Convention is to ensure that individuals, society, and the environment are adequately protected against radiological hazards. The convention requires states parties to establish and maintain a legislative and regulatory framework to govern the safety of spent fuel and radioactive waste management through a system of licensing of facilities by a national regulatory body. The agreement sets out standards for the siting, design, construction, operation, closure, and safety assessment of spent fuel management and radioactive waste management facilities. Both existing and proposed facilities are covered by the Joint Convention, which also articulates general requirements for safe operation. Additionally, the Joint Convention sets out a regime of notification and consent for transboundary movements of radioactive waste based on the 1990 IAEA Code of Practice on the International Transboundary Movement of Radioactive Waste.

Other IAEA agreements are also designed to further the goal of nuclear safety. The Convention on Early Notification of a Nuclear Accident and the Convention on Assistance in the Case of Nuclear Accident or Radiological Emergency are intended to facilitate international preparedness for, and responses to, nuclear and radiological emergencies. The Convention on Nuclear Safety obliges states parties to operate nuclear power plants in a manner consistent with high standards of safety. The Convention on Nuclear Safety requires each party to develop and enforce safety standards, but it does not itself prescribe the standards. Consequently, there is no internationally binding instrument that sets minimum safety standards for nuclear reactors.

The IAEA has also adopted hundreds of safety standards, which are not binding on IAEA member countries, intended in part to serve as models of good practice for states in crafting their own legislation and regulations. These safety standards are further categorized as fundamental principles, mandatory requirements, and recommended guidance. Published IAEA standards in the area of radioactive waste management include those addressing the classification of radioactive waste, the predisposal management of radioactive waste, and the management of radioactive waste from medicine, industry, research, agriculture, and education.

8 INTEGRATED APPROACHES TO POLLUTION PREVENTION

As a result of the difficulty of managing hazardous substances and products once they have been produced, attention in recent years has shifted to a more comprehensive approach that focuses on minimizing the likelihood of adverse effects for the environment and public health—'pollution prevention'. In the area of hazardous substances and products, the emphasis has been on minimizing the need for toxic substances either in manufacturing processes or finished products—'toxics use reduction'.

For example, legislation adopted by Massachusetts, a subnational unit in the United States, is an effort at implementing precautionary perspectives underlying a toxics use reduction approach.[23] The statute does not regulate based on risk or 'safe' levels of exposure or emission but, instead, encourages reductions in the use of about 1,400 enumerated industrial chemicals by setting out specific, numerical reduction targets by comparison with a reference baseline. The EU's volatile organic chemicals (VOC) solvents directive adopts a similar approach by permitting Member States to adopt use reduction plans as an alternative to command-and-control end-of-pipe emissions limitations.[24]

8.1 Basel Convention

Few binding international agreements address pollution prevention as a regulatory tool, presumably because the approach is still crystallizing as a public policy option at the domestic level. One exception is the Basel Convention (section 6.1), whose overall strategy is to limit the transboundary shipments of wastes. Accordingly, the convention encourages the generation of wastes to be reduced to a minimum—a requirement that can be seen as a particularized expression of the precautionary and polluter-pays principles. In part to reduce the need for international shipments of wastes, parties to the convention are to assure the availability of facilities for sound management of wastes within their territories. Wastes may be exported only under certain conditions, including the unavailability of suitable disposal facilities in the country of generation and the need for wastes as a raw material for recycling or recovery operations in the state of import.

Other provisions of the Basel Convention indirectly encourage waste reduction. Notwithstanding the consent of the proposed state of import, the convention requires that states of export prohibit shipments of hazardous and other wastes if

---

[23] Toxic Use Reduction Act of 1989, Mass. Gen. L. ch. 21I, secs. 1–23.
[24] EC Directive 93/13 on the Limitation of Emissions of Volatile Organic Compounds Due to the Use of Organic Solvents in Certain Activities and Installations, [1993] O.J. L85/1.

there is reason to believe that the wastes will not be managed in an environmentally sound manner in the country of import. The convention also articulates an obligation for states of export to ensure that international shipments of wastes are accepted for re-import if those shipments do not conform to the terms of export. Article 11 of the Basel Convention specifies that the requirements of the convention will not apply to transboundary movements between parties and non-parties that are governed by bilateral or regional arrangements that meet certain standards. In particular, Article 11 agreements concluded after the entry into force of the Basel Convention must contain provisions that are 'not less environmentally sound' than those in the convention.

8.2 OECD Recommendation on Pollution Prevention

The OECD in 1990 adopted a non-binding Recommendation on Integrated Pollution Prevention and Control.[25] The recommendation contains an appendix entitled 'Guidance on Integrated Pollution Prevention and Control', which identifies basic principles, including the consideration of the entire lifecycle of substances and products; the anticipation of environmental effects in a variety of environmental media, including consideration of multiple pathways to exposure and movement through the environment; the minimization of waste; and the application of a precautionary decision-making approach. The recommendation also identifies the desirability of zero- or low-waste technology, recycling, and alternative manufacturing strategies designed to reduce the use of toxic substances. The form of this instrument, a non-binding recommendation adopted by wealthier industrialized countries, is perhaps indicative of the emerging nature of pollution prevention as a regulatory strategy on the international level.

9 OTHER RELATED POLICIES

Several fundamental approaches of international environmental law of a more procedural nature may also come into play in addressing public policies related to hazardous substances or processes. While not confined to situations involving toxics, these regulatory approaches have particular utility in this area.

9.1 Right to Know

One public policy approach to reducing risks from hazardous substances and activities is to inform the public of releases of potentially toxic substances, of the presence

---

[25] OECD Doc. C(90)164.

of potentially dangerous activities, or of the nature or magnitude of associated risks. Public information approaches can complement other substantive regulatory approaches, such as those related to industrial accidents (section 5). Provision of information can also comprise a complete public policy in itself, which is designed to allow consumers, workers, and members of the public to make informed choices about the risks associated with the products they purchase, the quality of the environment where they live, and potential hazards in the workplace.

As suggested by the catchphrase 'knowledge is power', information about the nature of the local environment can catalyze community activism to address appropriate responses to toxic hazards by holding local businesses and municipal governments accountable. Indeed, the anticipated release of potentially anxiety-provoking information may encourage those who have control over the situation, such as polluting industries, voluntarily to reduce risks or even to incorporate risk-reduction strategies into their ordinary business plans. Last, information disclosure is among the least intrusive forms of governmental intervention. In certain situations in which proposals for substantive prescriptive regulation may encounter political opposition, labelling and public reporting may be an effective alternative that can be expected to achieve similar or identical results.

The UNECE Convention on Access to Information, Public Participation in Decision-Making and Access to Justice in Environmental Matters (Aarhus Convention), which was adopted in 1998, articulates an express link between governmental provision of information to the public and environmental protection (see Chapter 29 'Public Participation'). To this extent, the Aarhus Convention addresses principles of democratic accountability and good government more generally. The convention, which entered into force in 2001, creates rights to information on the part of the public and obligations for public authorities regarding access to this information. An extraordinary meeting of the parties held in Kiev, Ukraine in 2003 adopted a Protocol on Pollutant Release and Transfer Registers—an approach employed at the domestic level involving the collection and dissemination of toxic emissions released into the environment.

9.2 Environmental Impact Assessment (EIA)

EIA is a component of a planning process by which environmental considerations are integrated into decision-making procedures for activities that may have adverse environmental effects. The emphasis in EIA is on the collection and analysis of information relating to the environmental consequences of a proposed action. EIA is a process-oriented analytical technique distinct from substantive environmental standards and requirements. The principal purpose of EIA is to facilitate informed decision-making through a thorough scrutiny of anticipated environmental effects.

With the assistance of this analysis, an informed decision-maker should be able to assess the advisability of proceeding with proposed actions and to modify proposals to eliminate or mitigate their adverse environmental effects.

While not confined to the field of toxics, EIA is useful for identifying and analysing potential adverse effects from hazardous substances and activities. An EIA would be expected to project the likely and potential effects of toxic substances or dangerous activities on the environment and public health. Application of the EIA methodology would likely provide an opportunity to consider less hazardous or environmentally preferable alternatives to the proposed action. The EIA would also be expected to consider mitigating measures to reduce risks from hazardous substances and activities and contingency plans in the event of a mishap.

A wide variety of international instruments encourage or mandate the application of the EIA methodology at the national level by reference to internationally harmonized criteria, to cases of actual or potential pollution of the territory of other states or of areas beyond national jurisdiction, and in development assistance projects, policies, and programmes. Any or all of these instruments could apply to a hazardous substance or process. Some agreements, such as the 1991 ECE Convention on Environmental Impact Assessment in a Transboundary Context (Espoo Convention), apply to EIA as such. Others, like the IAEA Joint Convention (section 7.2) employ EIA as a procedural tool to achieve public policy purposes related to the substantive goals of the agreement.

10 CONCLUSION

There is at present no single, overarching international institutional framework for addressing environmental and public health risks from hazardous substances and activities. Public policy has been implemented at the national, supranational, regional, and global levels, sometimes simultaneously, with considerable interaction among various settings. Like-minded countries, such as members of the OECD, may coordinate policies among themselves, or a universal strategy such as that found in the Stockholm Convention may be adopted. International instruments, as in the case of the Basel and PIC Conventions, may be consciously targeted to address North-South issues.

In almost every situation, there are also choices to be made between non-binding 'soft' instruments and binding international agreements, with advantages and drawbacks accompanying either choice of the form of instrument. And this is before even contemplating the variety of regulatory tools available to address a particular problem, ranging from modest requirements, such as access to information, to bans on particular substances or rigorous requirements for governmental approval.

While the broader picture is far from systematic or neat, this outlook is perhaps all to the good from the perspective of international policy. The difficulties in effectively reducing risks from hazardous substances and activities are varied and multifaceted at the domestic and supranational levels, and the impediments are even more imposing internationally. The wider the array of options, the greater the potential for creatively meeting new challenges. Given the scope of the problem, we can hardly afford to ignore any realistic options among this exceedingly broad array.

Recommended Reading

C. Bail, R. Falkner, and H. Marquard, eds., *Reconciling Trade in Biotechnology with Environment and Development? The Cartagena Protocol on Biosafety* (London: Royal Institute of International Affairs, 2002).

R. Brickman, S. Jasanoff, and T. Ilgen, *Controlling Chemicals: The Politics of Regulation in Europe and the United States* (Ithaca: Cornell University Press, 1985).

J. Clapp, *Toxic Exports: The Transfer of Hazardous Wastes from Rich to Poor Countries* (Ithaca: Cornell University Press, 2001).

D. Hunter, J. Salzman, and D. Zaelke, *International Environmental Law and Policy*, 2nd edition (New York: Foundation Press, 2002).

S. Jasanoff, ed., *Learning from Disaster: Risk Management after Bhopal* (Philadelphia: University of Pennsylvania Press, 1994).

K. Kummer, *International Management of Hazardous Wastes: The Basel Convention and Related Legal Rules* (Oxford: Oxford University Press, 1995).

M.A. Olsen, *Analysis of the Stockholm Convention on Persistent Organic Pollutants* (Dobbs Ferry, NY: Oceana, 2003).

M. Pallemaerts, *Toxics and Transnational Law: International and European Regulation of Toxic Substances as Legal Symbolism* (Oxford: Hart Publishing, 2003).

PART IV

NORMATIVE DEVELOPMENT

CHAPTER 18

DIFFERENT TYPES OF NORMS IN INTERNATIONAL ENVIRONMENTAL LAW
POLICIES, PRINCIPLES, AND RULES

ULRICH BEYERLIN

1 INTRODUCTION

PUBLIC international law, although mostly composed of co-equal norms, shows some elements of hierarchy. At the top of this hierarchy, norms of *ius cogens* and obligations *erga omnes* are of a higher legal quality than the mass of ordinary norms. At its bottom, in the grey area between international 'hard law' and 'soft law', are an ever-growing number of amorphous 'concepts' and 'principles', whose nature and normative quality are far from clear. This is particularly true in the field of international environmental law, which shows certain patterns of 'relative normativity' that might appear as what P. Weil calls a 'pathological phenomenon.'[1]

This chapter focuses on the various 'twilight' norms at the bottom of the normative hierarchy of modern international environmental law, such as 'precaution', 'polluter pays', 'common but differentiated responsibilities', 'equitable utilization of shared natural resources', 'intergenerational equity', 'common concern of mankind', and, last but not least, 'sustainable development'. The second section will identify these 'twilight' norms in current international environmental law and examine how legal experts and scholars assess their nature and normative quality. Given the ongoing controversy and considerable confusion concerning the status of these norms, as well as the roles they play and the effects they have, it is useful to analyse the phenomenon of 'relative normativity' in current international environmental law in more detail. R. Dworkin's legal theory, which separates 'policies' from 'legal principles' and 'legal rules',[2] may help in this respect. In the third section, this typology will be subjected to closer scrutiny in order to determine whether it proves sufficiently sound, possibly with some adaptations or modifications to provide a basis for a more reliable differentiation between the relevant norms as to their status, role, and effects. Based on this typology, the fourth section will classify the 'twilight' norms in

---

[1] P. Weil, 'Towards Relative Normativity in International Law' (1983) 77 A.J.I.L. 413 at 414. Compare also U. Fastenrath, 'Relative Normativity in International Law' (1993) 4 Eur. J. Int'l L. 305.

[2] R. Dworkin, *Taking Rights Seriously* (London: Duckworth, 1977) at 22.

question, and the final section will close this chapter by drawing some conclusions from the findings.

For a better understanding of the ensuing discussion on the problems concerning international environmental 'twilight' norms, it is useful to clarify at the outset the terminology used in this chapter. In conformity with Dworkin's terminology, 'policies' are distinguished from 'legal principles' and 'legal rules'. The term 'policies' is understood in this chapter to be a broad spectrum of non-legal concepts, including those that have the capacity to directly or indirectly steer the behaviour of their addressees. The latter subtype of 'policies' essentially corresponds to 'soft law', which encompasses a wide range of instruments that lack legally binding force but that nonetheless have normative quality in political-moral terms. This subtype of policies, as well as 'principles' and 'rules', are subsumed under the broad term of 'norms'. In this respect, the terminology used in the present contribution differs from that of Dworkin, who speaks of 'standards' instead of 'norms'.

However, the term 'standards' might give rise to misunderstandings, as it is also used in legal writings to designate those subtypes of norms that are less precise than rules.[3]

2 LEGAL DISCUSSION ON INTERNATIONAL ENVIRONMENTAL 'TWILIGHT' NORMS

2.1 Identification of 'Twilight' Norms in Current International Environmental Law

For more than three decades, international environmental law-making has been marked by two contradictory tendencies. On the one hand, states have become increasingly aware of the need to protect the global environment as a matter of 'common concern' and have put more and more joint effort into achieving this aim. On the other hand, even today, states often lack the political will to enter into international agreements entailing binding obligations. This tension is the main reason why, in cases where the issues to be regulated are politically sensitive, many international legal and non-legal environmental instruments have recourse to rather vague concepts or principles. This method of compromising in cases where states cannot agree upon more stringent rules facilitates the dynamic development of

---

[3] See, e.g., D. Bodansky, 'Rules versus Standards in International Environmental Law,' in American Society of International Law, *Proceedings of the Ninety-Eighth Annual Meeting* (Washington, DC: American Society of International Law, 2004) 275.

modern international environmental law. It allows states with heterogeneous interests and needs to enter into rudimentary agreements in which, at least initially, they commit themselves only to relatively indefinite objectives, concepts, or principles rather than to clear-cut legal obligations that might immediately infringe on their sovereignty. However, the price to be paid for making such agreements is high since vague norms tend to deprive agreements of any strength, unless an explicit agreement provides for dispute settlement, which might allow vague treaty norms to be given a more precise meaning through adjudication.

What exactly are the 'twilight' norms in today's international environmental law? Negatively answered, any norm that does not clearly set out the legal consequences that follow automatically from the presence of all stipulated facts can be seen as 'twilight'.[4] Thus, a treaty clause directing states to achieve a clearly defined result, such as the reduction of certain emissions, is a rule that entails immediately binding effects. However, what about the broad spectrum of concepts encompassed by the 1992 Rio Declaration on Environment and Development, which range from 'sustainable development' and 'inter-generational equity', to 'cooperation' and 'common but differentiated responsibilities', to 'precaution', 'polluter-pays', 'environmental impact assessment', and others?[5] Although all of these concepts are declared to be 'principles', they are hardly homogenous in nature. Some of them may vaguely point to common policy goals or may be understood as broad-ranging principles, while some others may even prove to be well-defined rules (such as requirements for environmental impact assessments).

In regard to concepts or notions such as the 'common heritage of mankind' or the 'common concern of humankind' (see Chapter 23 'Common Areas, Common Heritage, and Common Concern'), they can hardly give meaningful guidance for the conduct of states. They appear to be even more remote from norms that immediately give rise to legal effects than the just mentioned 'Rio Principles'. However, as will be shown later in this chapter, some scholars take a different view. To evaluate the quality, function, and effects of a given ambiguous concept, two questions must be answered. First, is the disputed concept structured in such a way that it may have normative quality ('normativity')—that is, the capacity to directly or indirectly steer the behaviour of its addressees? And, second, is it designed, and accordingly established, in such a way that it constitutes a legally binding norm? If both questions are answered in the affirmative, the concept in question constitutes either a legal rule or a legal principle. If only the first question is positively answered, the concept concerned is a norm that remains within the realm of 'soft law' (that is, the normative subtype of policies). If neither of the questions is answered positively, the concept is a non-normative policy.

---

[4] This definition goes along the lines of R. Dworkin's understanding of what legal rules should be. See note 2 above at 24.

[5] There may be other norms of such type, such as 'permanent sovereignty over natural resources' and 'equitable utilization of shared natural resources'.

2.2 Environmental 'Twilight' Norms as Diagnosed by Legal Experts and Scholars

In the following section, a selection of relevant writings of experts and scholars, namely an expert group of the UN Commission on Sustainable Development (CSD), another expert group from the UN Environment Programme (UNEP), and several individuals, including W. Lang, P. Sands, R. Wolfrum, A. Epiney and M. Scheyli, N. de Sadeleer as well as J. Verschuuren, will be presented in order to show that the determination of the status, role, and effects of such 'twilight' norms still needs clarification.

In 1995, a CSD expert group developed a catalogue of 'principles and concepts of international law for sustainable development.'[6] These principles and concepts are supposed to help in the development of new legal instruments by states as well as in the interpretation and application of existing treaty and non-treaty obligations. In the understanding of the expert group, the principles and concepts are norms that generate substantive and procedural obligations (for example, 'informed decision-making' and 'public participation') or constitute sources from which more detailed obligations may flow (such as the principle of 'common but differentiated responsibilities').[7] The experts stressed 'that the legal status of each of the principles . . . varies considerably; some of the principles identified are more firmly established in international law, while others are only in process of gaining relevance in international law' and stated 'that the discussion and formulation of principles . . . is without prejudice to the question of whether these are part of customary international law.'[8]

The 1996 report of a UNEP expert group compiled various 'concepts and principles in international environmental law' and declared them 'core elements' in the process of further development within this branch of law. However, it avoided any determination of the (legal) nature of these concepts and principles. Among the functions that both concepts and principles are deemed to fulfil are 'providing coherence and consistency to international environmental law; guiding governments in negotiating future international instruments; providing a framework for the interpretation and application of domestic environmental laws and policies; and assisting the integration of international environmental law with other international law fields.'[9]

---

[6] Among the total of 19 principles identified by the expert group are 'interrelationship and integration', 'right to development', 'right to a healthy environment', 'eradication of poverty', 'equity', 'sustainable use of natural resources', 'prevention of environmental harm', 'precautionary principle', 'common concern of humankind', 'common but differentiated responsibilities', 'common heritage of mankind', 'public participation', 'access to information', and 'environmental impact assessment and informed decision-making'. See *Report of the Expert Group Meeting on Identification of Principles of International Law for Sustainable Development*, Geneva, Switzerland, 26-8 September 1995, UN Doc. E/CN.17/1996/17/Add.1 (1 March 1996) at paras. 15 et seq.   [7] *Ibid.* at para. 8.

[8] *Ibid.* at para. 6.

[9] *Final Report of the Expert Group Workshop on International Environmental Law Aiming at Sustainable Development*, Washington, DC, 30 September-4 October 1996, UN Doc. UNEP/IEL/WS/3/2 (4 October 1996) Annex I at para. 29.

Lang identifies 'three different categories of principles of a decreasing legally-binding/ compulsory nature', including 'principles of existing International Environmental Law', 'principles of emerging International Environmental Law', and 'potential principles of International Environmental Law'.[10] Astonishingly, he allocates only the responsibility/liability for environmental harm, as well as the prohibition on the use of nuclear weapons and other weapons of mass destruction, to the first group of principles. Other norms, such as 'intergenerational equity', 'right to a healthy environment', 'duty not to use the environment as an instrument of warfare', and various procedural obligations, are allocated to the second category. The third group of 'potential' principles, which are characterized as 'an area of hope for many policymakers', encompasses in Lang's view the 'development and integration of environmental considerations into the development process', 'common but differentiated responsibilities', and 'precaution'.[11] Lang then asks where the boundary between policy and law is located but leaves this question open by merely saying: '[C]ustomary law is a highly difficult and complex area of law.'[12]

In contrast to Lang, Sands focuses more exclusively on the legal status of rules and principles. He discerns 'general rules and principles which have broad, if not necessarily universal, support and are frequently endorsed in practice.'[13] These include the following seven rules and principles: states' sovereignty over their natural resources and the responsibility not to cause transboundary environmental damage; preventive action; cooperation; sustainable development; precaution; polluter pays; and common but differentiated responsibility.[14] However, in his view, only the first and the third of these principles and rules 'are sufficiently well established to provide the basis for an international cause of action; that is to say, to reflect an international customary legal obligation the violation of which would give rise to a free-standing legal remedy.'[15] Sands then points to an early arbitral decision,[16] as well as to Dworkin's theory, both of which distinguish 'principles' from 'rules' and assign different legal effects to them. However, he declines to classify the environmental norms in question accordingly. He states only that '(a)ny effort to identify general principles and

---

[10] W. Lang, 'UN Principles and International Environmental Law' (1999) 3 Max Planck Y.B. UN L. 157 at 171.   [11] *Ibid.*

[12] *Ibid.* at 170.

[13] P. Sands, *Principles of International Environmental Law*, 2nd edition (Cambridge: Cambridge University Press, 2003) 231. Compare also P. Sands, 'International Law in the Field of Sustainable Development: Emerging Legal Principles,' in W. Lang, ed., *Sustainable Development and International Law* (London: Graham and Trotman, 1995) 53.   [14] Sands, *Principles*, see note 13 above.

[15] *Ibid.* at 232.

[16] *Gentini case (Italy v. Venezuela)*, M.C.C. (1903), J.H. Ralston and W.T.S. Doyle, *Venezuelan Arbitrations of 1903* (1904) at 720, 725. In this case, the following distinction was made: 'A "rule" . . . "is essentially practical and, moreover, binding . . . [T]here are rules of art as there are rules of government" while principle "expresses a general truth, which guides our action, serves as a theoretical basis for the various acts of our life, and the application of which to reality produces a given consequence"', cited in Sands, *Principles*, see note 13 above at 233.

rules of international environmental law must necessarily be based on a considered assessment of state practice, including the adoption and implementation of treaties and other international legal acts, as well as the growing number of decisions of international courts and tribunals.'[17]

In Wolfrum's view, principles are typical of international environmental law. Incorporated into policy documents, such principles are designed 'to guide the policy of States, to channel subsequent negotiations on international agreements into a particular direction, or to influence the development of international customary law.'[18] With respect to principles that have appeared in operative parts of international agreements, Wolfrum quotes Sands who states that such principles 'embody legal standards, but the standards they contain are more general than commitments and do not specify particular actions.'[19]

Epiney and Scheyli, in their treatise on international environmental law of 2000, take the view that international environmental law relies on a number of general principles that provide guidelines for relevant state action, determine the interpretation and application of existing international environmental norms, and lay the foundations for the further development of international environmental law.[20] In an earlier book, they allege that 'sustainable development' has developed into a principle of customary international law.[21] There, they even assert the existence of certain 'structural principles' ('Strukturprinzipien') in today's international environmental law that provide general orientation for the further development of international environmental law and represent touchstones for the conduct of states in this field.[22] Among these principles are said to be 'precautionary action', 'environmental impact assessment', the 'use of best available environmental practice and technology' as well as 'polluter pays'. However, the principle of 'sustainable development' is missing from Epiney and Scheyli's list,[23] which is rather surprising.

De Sadeleer deals with the status and role of the 'polluter pays', 'prevention', and 'precaution' principles, which he designates as 'the three foremost environmental principles'.[24] He sums up his analysis by stating that '[d]espite their indeterminate

---

[17] Sands, *Principles*, see note 13 above at 234.

[18] R. Wolfrum, 'International Environmental Law: Purposes, Principles and Means of Ensuring Compliance,' in F.L. Morrison and R. Wolfrum, eds., *International, Regional and National Environmental Law* (The Hague: Kluwer Law International, 2000) 3 at 6.

[19] *Ibid.* at 6. The quoted sentence of Sands, *Principles*, note 13 above at 233, is taken from D. Bodansky, 'The United Nations Framework Convention on Climate Change: A Commentary' (1993) 18 Yale J. Int'l L. 451 at 501.   [20] A. Epiney and M. Scheyli, *Umweltvölkerrecht* (Bern: Stämpfli Verlag, 2000) at 76.

[21] A. Epiney and M. Scheyli, *Strukuturprinzipien des Umweltvölkerrechts* (Baden-Baden: Nomos Verlag, 1998) at 171. See also H. Hohmann, *Precautionary Legal Duties and Principles of Modern International Environmental Law* (London: Graham and Trotman/Martinus Nijhoff, 1994) at 166 and 329.   [22] Epiney and Scheyli, see note 21 above at 15.

[23] *Ibid.* at 89, 103, and 171.

[24] N. de Sadeleer, *Environmental Principles: From Political Slogans to Legal Rules* (Oxford: Oxford University Press, 2002) at 2.

character, these directing principles have sufficient legal force to be considered normative—that is, giving rise to legal effects. For that to be the case they must fulfil two conditions: first they must be part of a binding text, and secondly they must be formulated in sufficiently prescriptive terms.'[25] Nonetheless, he admits that 'their normative character differs at several levels from that of the numerous more complete norms found in environmental law.'[26] Generally, these 'more complete norms' appear to correspond to what Dworkin calls 'legal rules'. De Sadeleer tries, however, to nuance the distinction between principles and legal rules by alleging that 'an intermediate category has arisen: that of rules of an indeterminate nature, which may be set against rules of complete and precise content.'[27] In his view, the polluter pays, prevention, and precautionary principles of environmental law illustrate the emergence of this intermediate type of rules, which 'weaken the dichotomy put forward by Dworkin.'[28] Whether this assumption persuades or not is a question that deserves further discussion.[29]

Verschuuren, in his considerations on 'principles of international law', also proceeds from Dworkin's distinction between principles and rules but stresses that no bright line can be drawn between the two. He takes the view that '[t]here is a sliding scale with a theoretical, abstract and indeterminate principle on one side and a very concrete, highly practical rule on the other. Both principles and rules can range from abstract to more concrete.'[30] Since their moral character is higher than that of rules, in Verschuuren's view, principles may, inter alia, fulfil the following functions: help define, open, or unclear statutory rules; enhance the normative power of statutory rules; increase legal certainty and enhance the legitimacy of decision-making; form the basis of new statutory rules; give guidance to self-regulation and negotiation processes between various actors in society; create flexibility in law; and, last but not least, create a necessary link between ideals and concrete legal rules.[31] Interestingly, he does not rate 'sustainable development' among the principles of international environmental law but considers it to be an 'ideal' from which principles of environmental law receive their high moral value.[32] Consequently, he stresses: 'To make the ideal of sustainable development more concrete and to implement it in concrete legal decisions, principles, such as the precautionary principle or the "polluter pays" principle, form a necessary link between the ideal, on one hand, and rules and policies, on the other'[33] (see Chapter 26 'Sustainable Development').

[25] N. de Sadeleer, *Environmental Principles: From Political Slogans to Legal Rules* (Oxford: Oxford University Press, 2002) at 368.   [26] *Ibid.*
[27] *Ibid.* at 308.   [28] *Ibid.*   [29] See the discussion in section 3.2 of this chapter.
[30] J. Verschuuren, *Principles of Environmental Law: The Ideal of Sustainable Development and the Role of Principles of International, European, and National Environmental Law* (Baden-Baden: Nomos Verlag, 2003) at 38.   [31] *Ibid.* at 38.
[32] *Ibid.* at 144.   [33] *Ibid.* at 43.

2.3 Result

What follows from our short look at the current state of the discussion on international environmental 'twilight' norms among legal experts and scholars is that it reflects utter confusion in determining the status, role, and effects of these norms. Prototypical of this muddle is the highly controversial understanding of 'sustainable development', which ranges from characterizing it as a mere political ideal (Verschuuren) to declaring it a recognized principle of customary international law (Epiney and Scheyli), with various views in between. The assessments of the other 'twilight' norms show much the same uncertainties. Actually, there does not appear to be agreement on the status, role, and effects in current international environmental relations of any of the norms in question. This fact alone gives reason for a more thorough analysis of the appearances of 'relative normativity' at the bottom of the hierarchy of norms of modern international environmental law. This analysis will be undertaken on the basis of Dworkin's theory of policies, principles, and rules.

3 DWORKIN-BASED TYPOLOGY
OF INTERNATIONAL
ENVIRONMENTAL NORMS

3.1 Dworkin's Typology and Its Reception in Doctrine

Criticizing H.L.A. Hart's legal positivism as 'a model of and for a system of rules' that neglects 'the important roles of these standards that are not rules,'[34] Dworkin counters Hart's theory of rules by differentiating three types of norms—policies, principles, and rules. Although he explains what the terms 'policy'[35] and 'principle'[36] mean, he is less concerned with their interrelationship than with differentiating between 'legal principles' and 'legal rules.' In this respect, his understanding is as follows:

The difference between legal principles and legal rules is a logical distinction. Both sets of norms point to particular decisions about legal obligations in particular circumstances, but they differ in the character of the direction they give. Rules are applicable in an all-or-nothing

---

[34] Dworkin, see note 2 above at 22.

[35] Dworkin understands 'policy' as 'that kind of standard that sets out a goal to be reached, generally an improvement in some economic, political, or social feature of the community.' *Ibid.*

[36] 'Principle' means 'a standard that is to be observed, not because it will advance or secure an economic, political, or social situation deemed desirable, but because it is a requirement of justice or fairness or some other dimension of morality.' *Ibid.*

fashion. If the facts a rule stipulates are given, then either the rule is valid, in which case the answer it supplies must be accepted, or it is not, in which case it contributes nothing to the decision.[37]

Contrary to legal rules, legal principles, according to Dworkin, 'do not set out legal consequences that follow automatically when the conditions provided are met.'[38] In his view, 'the principle is one which officials must take into account, if it is relevant, as a consideration inclining in one direction or another.' Dworkin rounds out his analysis by saying that '[p]rinciples have a dimension that rules do not—the dimension of weight or importance.'[39] Finally, he makes two seemingly contradictory observations when he states on the one hand that '[i]t is not always clear from the form of a standard whether it is a rule or a principle,'[40] while he admits on the other hand that '[s]ometimes a rule and a principle can play much the same role, and the difference between them is almost a matter of form alone.'[41]

R. Alexy does not differentiate between principles and rules but uses the contrasting pair of what is 'owed in ideal terms' ('*ideales Sollen*') and what is 'owed in real terms' ('*reales Sollen*').[42] The former must be fulfilled only as best as possible or approximately, while the latter is a type of obligation that can either be met or not.[43] While Alexy's '*reales Sollen*' appears to come very close to Dworkin's rules, Alexy's '*ideales Sollen*' apparently differs from what Dworkin means by principles. Contrary to Dworkin's principles, Alexy's '*ideales Sollen*' designates the aim that an action ideally should achieve. However, it does not circumscribe the idea(s) that should give direction to the addressee's decision-making. Whether one considers Alexy's approach to be persuasive or not, his theory cannot discredit Dworkin's distinction between legal principles and legal rules.

While Dworkin pleads for a qualitative difference between rules and principles, other theorists, such as N. MacCormick and J. Raz,[44] support the view that rules and principles show only a difference of degree since both are norms that—as A. Aarnio puts it—'have a relationship of family resemblance with one another,' and 'they have a similar or analogical role in legal discretion. Typically, principles have greater generality than rules, but otherwise there are no special characteristics to distinguish them from rules.'[45] Aarnio rejects both the 'strong demarcation thesis' and the 'weak demarcation thesis'[46] by alleging that rules and principles form a scale divided into

---

[37] *Ibid.* at 24.   [38] *Ibid.* at 25.   [39] *Ibid.* at 26.   [40] *Ibid.* at 27.   [41] *Ibid.*

[42] R. Alexy, *Recht, Vernunft, Diskurs: Studien zur Rechtsphilosophie* (Frankfurt am Main: Suhrkamp Verlag, 1995) at 177 et seq. Compare also R. Alexy, *Rechtsregeln und Rechtsprinzipien*, in Archives for Philosophy of Law and Social Philosophy, Beiheft 25 (Stuttgart: Franz Steiner Verlag, 1985) at 13 et seq.

[43] Alexy, *Recht, Vernunft, Diskurs*, see note 42 above at 204.

[44] N. MacCormick, *Legal Reasoning and Legal Theory* (Oxford: Clarendon Press, 1978; reprinted in 1995) at 152; and J. Raz, *Practical Reason and Norms* (Oxford: Oxford University Press, 1999) at 49.

[45] A. Aarnio, 'Taking Rules Seriously,' in W. Maihofer and G.Sprenger, eds., *Law and the States in Modern Times*, Proceedings of the Fourteenth IVR World Congress in Edinburgh, August 1989, Archives for Philosophy of Law and Social Philosophy (Stuttgart: Franz Steiner Verlag, 1990) 180 at 181.

[46] *Ibid.* at 180 et seq.

four parts: (1) 'rules proper' (for example, the prohibition of theft in criminal law); (2) 'rule-like principles' (for example, the principle of freedom of speech) that 'can be considered principles, but as norms they undoubtedly belong in important respects to the category of rules'); (3) 'principle-like rules' (that is, 'flexible legal rules that have a scope of application that is cognitively or evaluatively open in the same way as is the scope of value principles'); and (4) 'principles proper' (for example, the principles of equality and liberty or other value principles and goal principles).[47] Aarnio takes the view that Dworkin's 'strong demarcation thesis', which makes a qualitative distinction between rules and principles,[48] is valid if and only if one keeps an eye on the extreme ends of this scale. However, he emphasizes that 'the thesis is not valid for the area between the two extremes. In regard to applicability, there is no essential difference between open rules and principles.'[49]

There may well be the need for a typology that offers more flexibility than Dworkin's thesis of a rigid dichotomy between legal principles and legal rules. However, there are doubts whether Aarnio's alternative typology really helps in this respect. De Sadeleer offers a more flexible solution by making a distinction between 'directing principles', 'rules of an indeterminate nature', and 'rules of complete and precise content'.[50] Rather close to de Sadeleer's understanding of 'directing principles' comes V. Lowe's concept of designating sustainable development as 'a meta-principle, acting upon other legal rules and principles—a legal concept exercising a kind of interstitial normativity, pushing and pulling the boundaries of true primary norms when they threaten to overlap or conflict with each other.'[51] J. Ebbesson, pointing to normative situations that he suggests are not addressed by Dworkin's distinction between principles and rules, advocates an alternative typology that consists of three strata of norms: (1) 'balancing norms' (which allow their addressees to balance different interests against each other when carrying out a certain obligation); (2) 'goal oriented norms' (which define what to be achieved or avoided, but leave it to the addressees to decide on how to comply with the goal concerned); and (3) 'fixed norms' (which do not allow any balancing of interests, but prescribe a fixed result, such as meeting certain emission thresholds).[52]

3.2 A Plea for Upholding Dworkin's Tripartite Typology

Admittedly, Dworkin's distinction between policies, principles, and rules is vulnerable to objections in at least two respects. First, Dworkin is almost exclusively concerned with the distinction between principles and rules, while the borderline

---

[47] *Ibid.* at 184.   [48] *Ibid.* 180.   [49] *Ibid.* at 191.   [50] Sadeleer, see note 24 above at 308.

[51] V. Lowe, 'Sustainable Development and Unsustainable Arguments', in A. Boyle and D. Freestone, eds., *International Law and Sustainable Development* (Oxford: Oxford University Press, 1999) 19 at 31.

[52] J. Ebbesson, *Compatibility of International and National Environmental Law* (The Hague: Kluwer Law International, 1996) at 83.

between policies and legal principles, especially in international environmental law,[53] is crucial as well. Thus, his typology is of no help in answering the question whether, for example, sustainable development remains a mere political goal or has matured into a legal principle (see the discussion in section 4.2 later in this chapter). Second, with respect to the distinction between legal principles and legal rules, Dworkin's 'strong demarcation thesis' has been criticized for its lack of flexibility. The critics are certainly right in pointing to the fact that legal rules differ considerably from one another as to the precision of the obligations that they create. Thus, de Sadeleer's observation that the contents of legal rules can range from 'determinate' to 'indeterminate' is as correct as Ebbesson's differentiation between 'fixed' and 'goal-oriented' norms. For example, an international treaty rule, which imposes on state parties a broadly formulated obligation to embark on achieving a rather abstractly defined objective (action-oriented rule), significantly differs from a rule that contains a strictly worded obligation to achieve a clearly defined result within a fixed time limit (result-oriented rule).

However, both types of rules 'set out legal consequences that follow automatically when the conditions provided are met,' as Dworkin puts it.[54] While this undoubtedly proves true for clear-cut result-oriented rules, it is less clear in cases where action-oriented rules of indeterminate content are at stake, as is often the case in practice. Although such rules may give considerable leeway to the addressees as to how to fulfil their requirements and may raise difficulties as to their enforcement, they do not provide space for alternative actions in the way that principles do.[55] Thus, action and result-oriented rules have in common that their addressees must take action, irrespective of the determinateness or indeterminateness of the action or result that the rule prescribes. The difference between the two types of rules is gradual rather than qualitative in nature and, therefore, has no impact on the determination of the character of the norm in question. A legal rule does not transmute into a legal principle simply because of its indeterminate content. Consequently, contrary to Verschuuren's[56] and Aarnio's[57] understanding, the distinction between 'determinate' and 'indeterminate' is not a suitable criterion for separating principles from rules.

If not its indeterminateness, what else makes legal principles differ from legal rules? Do all principles have more or less the same normative quality? Negatively speaking, principles can be characterized as imperfect norms, which lack the normative force that rules have. This normative force prompts the addressee to abstain from

---

[53] Admittedly, there is also need for distinguishing policies from legal rules, especially in cases where there are doubts whether an agreement between states is governed by 'soft law' or 'hard law.' However, a state's will to be legally or non-legally bound is a criterion that usually proves sound enough to make the relevant distinction.   [54] Dworkin, see note 2 above at 25.

[55] As noted earlier, for R. Dworkin, principles are mere 'considerations inclining in one direction or another,' which only determine the addressees' decision-making process, while the result of this process is still open at that moment. See notes 36–41 in this chapter and the accompanying text.

[56] Verschuuren, see note 30 above at 38.   [57] Aarnio, see note 45 above at 181.

a prohibited undertaking or induces the addressee to take action to achieve a certain objective, irrespective of the extent to which the required action is specified in terms of contents. It is exactly this inherent effect of triggering a concrete behaviour (that is, taking or refraining from a particular action) that differentiates rules from principles—rules specify, more or less determinately, a particular action that is required, permitted, or prohibited. Principles, however, do not prescribe or proscribe such particular behaviour.

The attempt to explain in positive terms what the specific mission of principles may be raises more difficulties. Dworkin stresses that a principle only 'states a reason that argues in one direction, but does not necessitate a particular decision.'[58] Verschuuren's view is that '[p]rinciples can be seen as the link between ideals and duties, between the morality of aspiration and the morality of duty, between values and rules.'[59] Thus, principles leave the problem at hand undecided. Moreover, Verschuuren finds, as already mentioned, that principles may, *inter alia*, help define open or unclear rules, enhance the latter's normative power, and form the basis of new rules.[60] Aarnio argues that 'moral principles may be of significance in legal discretion as grounds for decision-making when choosing between different alternative meanings of a norm formulation. In so doing, moral principles "become" legally relevant.'[61]

In the author's view, principles can be understood as norms that are first and foremost designed to give guidance to their addressees for future conduct in rule-making processes as well as to shape the interpretation and application of rules already in existence. Thus, rules and principles may roughly be distinguished from each other by saying that the former are norms immediately aimed at making the addressees take action, refrain from action, or achieve a fixed result, while the latter only aim at influencing the states' decision-making, which otherwise remains open to choice, as well as their interpretation of rules.

At this point, we have at least an abstract idea of what principles are about, but we do not yet know what the features are that give principles legal nature. The answer to this question depends on whether or not the relevant principle is part of an international treaty. If incorporated into the operative part of a treaty, the principle shares the treaty's legal status.[62] Thus, it legally binds the contracting parties. However, is this also true in cases where such a principle has been put forward in a non-treaty context? A non-treaty norm can become legally binding on states only if it meets the requirements of a norm of customary international law. While it is relatively easy to judge whether norms entailing 'action-oriented' or 'result-oriented' obligations (that is, rules) have gained the status of international custom in the sense of Article 38(1)(b) of the Statute of the International Court of Justice (ICJ), principles raise more difficulties in this respect. Although they are not aimed at making states take

---

[58] Dworkin, see note 2 above at 26.   [59] Verschuuren, see note 30 above at 25.
[60] *Ibid.* at 38.   [61] Aarnio, see note 45 above at 184.
[62] It is less clear whether the same applies to a concept that is only part of the preamble of this treaty.

action to achieve a defined result, they can, at least theoretically, gain customary legal status, if the states' 'general practice' was in conformity with these principles and was accompanied by the states' *opinio iuris*. However, to provide such evidence is hard work. Proving that a state was directed by a principle when it took a decision on a particular action may be very difficult in practice because such psychological moments of decision-making are difficult to assess in terms of objective evidence. Thus, to date, only very few principles, if any at all, have cleared the hurdles in the way of becoming norms of customary international law. As will be shown in the fourth section of this chapter, most principles of international environmental law actually still belong to the sphere of morals or policies ('soft law').

Apart from these difficulties of proof, it may be asked whether the efficacy of international environmental principles really depends so much on their legal status. If one takes the view, as the author does, that 'soft law' principles are by no means inferior to legal principles but are to be seen on an equal footing with them, there are good reasons for arguing that a principle that is based on international policies or morals, in practical terms, guides states' discretion in virtually the same way as a principle that has become part of customary international law. After all, a principle, be it legal or non-legal in nature, can never automatically entail consequences in the sense that its addressees are unconditionally required to take (more or less clearly defined) action. In the words of Dworkin, a principle directs states only to take it into account 'as a consideration inclining in one direction or another' when they take their decisions.[63]

4 CLASSIFICATION OF THE 'TWILIGHT' NORMS IN DISPUTE

Based on the theoretical distinction between policies, legal principles, and legal rules made earlier in this chapter, we will now try to classify the various international environmental 'twilight' norms. With respect to each norm, two questions have to be raised. First, does the norm concerned possess the normative quality required to potentially claim the effects of either a legal rule or a legal principle? Second, has it been enshrined in a treaty or met the requirements for attaining customary legal status (see Chapter 19 'Formation of Customary International Law and General Principles')? Notwithstanding the difficulties any attempt to answer these questions unavoidably meets,[64] a closer look at some of the environmental 'twilight' norms (see

---

[63] Dworkin, see note 2 above at 26.

[64] For reasons of space constraints, the norms in question cannot be dealt with in this chapter as thoroughly as necessary, particularly as far as the second question is concerned. Thus, the answers that the author will present in the following section are at best tentative. They are mostly based on observations P. Sands has made in his 'Principles of International Environmental Law.'

the second section of this chapter) will reveal that very few of the norms alleged to be legal principles in fact deserve this label, while a number of them actually prove to be legal rules. Some of the norms that are occasionally called 'principles' will be allocated to the sphere of mere policies. However, in the future, they could develop into either legal principles or rules, provided they possess normative quality.

4.1 Principle Not to Cause Transboundary Environmental Damage

This norm is closely intertwined with what Sands calls the 'principle of preventive action'.[65] It implies the duty of a state not to allow or tolerate any activity carried out within its jurisdiction that may cause damage to the environment of other states or of areas beyond its national jurisdiction (see Chapter 22 'Transboundary Impacts'). This obligation may show a number of uncertainties, such as whether it proscribes only significant, or less serious, transboundary environmental damages. However, given the clear-cut formulation of its purpose not to cause transboundary environmental damage, the norm is result oriented. Therefore, it is a rule rather than a principle. Its addressees must take all measures needed to ensure that no (significant) transboundary harm originates from their territory—they have discretion only as to the manner in which they achieve this end. First laid down at a global level in Principle 21 of the 1972 Stockholm Declaration on the Human Environment,[66] the no harm rule has been so widely accepted in state practice that it is recognized as a rule of universal customary law.

4.2 Environmental Impact Assessment

Another norm ultimately classified as a legal rule is the duty of states to undertake an environmental impact assessment (EIA) for any proposed national activity that risks causing serious (transboundary) environmental damage. The fact that the EIA norm was included in the catalogue of the Rio Principles certainly does not justify 'downgrading' it to a principle. This argument holds all the more strongly given that the language of Principle 17 of the Rio Declaration[67] is clearly mandatory, even if rather

---

[65] See Sands, *Principles*, note 13 above at 246.

[66] Principle 21 reads as follows: 'States have . . . the responsibility to ensure that activities within their jurisdiction or control do not cause damage to the environment of other States or of areas beyond the limits of national jurisdiction.'

[67] Principle 17 states: 'Environmental impact assessment, as a national instrument, shall be undertaken for proposed activities that are likely to have a significant adverse impact on the environment and are subject to a decision of a competent national authority.'

abstract. There is no choice left to the addressees of this duty to take action or not, even though it may be difficult to determine in any particular case whether the environmental harm potentially resulting from the activity in question is sufficiently 'significant' to warrant an EIA. The obligation to undertake EIAs has been included in a considerable number of environmental treaties, most notably the Convention on Environmental Impact Assessment in a Transboundary Context, which was adopted under the auspices of the UN Economic Commission for Europe (UNECE) in 1991. However, the EIA norm not only may be binding as a matter of treaty law but also may have grown, at least in the European context, to a (regional) customary legal rule.

4.3 Precautionary Action

In contrast to the 'preventive principle', the so-called 'precautionary principle' is designed to provide the basis for early international legal action to address serious environmental threats in cases where there is ongoing scientific uncertainty with regard to the causes of these threats (see Chapter 25 'Precaution'). It was first explicitly articulated in the mid-1980s. Principle 15 of the Rio Declaration states that '[w]here there are threats of serious or irreversible damage, lack of full scientific certainty shall not be used as a reason for postponing cost-effective measures to prevent environmental degradation.' This formulation can be taken as a starting point of our inquiry as to whether the precautionary principle really deserves its designation as a 'principle'. In the author's view, this norm stipulates, albeit in negative terms, the facts that require a state precautionary action. The state concerned must face a situation that clearly indicates that the environment is going to be severely polluted or seriously disturbed unless an action averting this threat is taken, notwithstanding the lack of full scientific certainty as to causal effects. If these factors are present, taking adequate measures is not at the discretion of the state concerned. Discretion instead exists only as to the choice of measures to be taken. Although the legal consequences flowing from the state's duty to take precautionary action may be indeterminate in substance, this flaw does not affect the core of the duty that arises. There are good reasons for arguing that the precautionary principle as defined in Principle 15 of the Rio Declaration in fact meets the normative requirements of an action-oriented rule, albeit one that calls for further specification. The EIA rule discussed earlier represents one such specification. As a special emanation of the abstract precautionary rule, it has emerged as a separate self-contained rule. What remains to be determined is whether the precautionary rule has become part of customary international law. Since it has been included in a growing number of international environmental treaties, there are good reasons for arguing that it is applied in today's general practice of states accompanied by the latter's *opinio iuris*. However, as the discussion in the chapter on precaution in this *Handbook* illustrates, this conclusion remains the subject of considerable debate (see Chapter 25 'Precaution').

4.4 Polluter Pays

Principle 16 of the Rio Declaration provides that '[n]ational authorities should endeavour to promote the internalisation of environmental costs and the use of economic instruments, taking into account the approach that the polluter should, in principle, bear the costs of pollution.' Sands is right to state that 'the meaning of the principle, and its application to particular situations, remains open to interpretation, particularly in relation to the nature and extent of the costs included and the circumstances in which the principle will, perhaps exceptionally, not apply.'[68] However, neither the indeterminateness of the 'polluter pays' concept nor its 'softened' wording in Principle 16 ('should endeavour to promote') hampers its classification as a (potential legal) rule. In any case, it is not structured in such a way that it could fulfil the typical functions of a principle. It is neither designed to be taken into account in decision-making 'as a consideration inclining in one or another direction' (Dworkin) nor intended to be used merely for interpretative guidance. It directly calls for ensuring that in every case where the environment has been, or runs the risk of being, polluted, the accountable person bears the costs resulting from the pollution or from the measures taken for the purpose of preventing pollution. The possible existence of exceptions to this rule does not diminish its normative quality. Regarding the question whether 'polluter pays' has become part of customary international law, Sands rightly points to the obvious 'compromise language' adopted in Principle 16, which clearly shows that to date a number of states still have strong objections to the application of this norm at the inter-state level. Thus, 'polluter pays' is at best a recognized legal rule in the European Community, the Organisation of Economic Co-operation and Development, and the UNECE context.[69]

4.5 Common but Differentiated Responsibilities

Another concept that is often alleged to be a legal principle is states' 'common but differentiated responsibilities' to protect the environment (see Chapter 13 'Ethics and International Environmental Law' and Chapter 27 'Equity'). This concept is

---

[68] Sands, see note 13 above at 280.   [69] *Ibid.* at 280.

expressed in Principle 7 of the Rio Declaration, which states: 'States shall co-operate in a spirit of global partnership to conserve, protect and restore the health and integrity of the Earth's ecosystem. In view of the different contributions to global environmental degradation, states have common but differentiated responsibilities. The developed countries acknowledge the responsibility that they bear in the international pursuit of sustainable development in view of the pressures their societies place on the global environment and of the technologies and financial resources they command.' For the purpose of determining the normative quality of this concept, the first sentence of Principle 7 should be separated from the two that follow. It essentially contains what Sands calls the 'principle of co-operation'.[70] Notwithstanding its highly abstract wording, the character of the principle of cooperation is that of a rule, rather than a principle, because it attempts to direct conduct towards a particular goal. This is all the more definite as the first sentence of Principle 7 specifies the duty of cooperation in two respects: First, it determines what the objectives of inter-state cooperation should be, albeit abstractly. Second, by making reference to the 'spirit of global partnership', it gives some substantive, although rather abstract, guidance for assessing the performance of inter-state cooperation. However, the very essence of Principle 7 lies in the two subsequent sentences, which both use the key notion of 'responsibility', declared to be both 'common' and 'differentiated'. While the aim of the first component of responsibility is essentially the same as that of the first sentence of Principle 7, the second one, in the view of Sands, 'concerns the need to take account of differing circumstances, particularly in relation to each state's *contribution* to the creation of a particular environmental problem and its *ability* to prevent, reduce and control the threat.' Accordingly, 'it leads to environmental standards which impose differing obligations on states.'[71] It seems to follow from this understanding that 'differentiated responsibility' itself is not a rule but rather a principle functioning as a source from which subsequent rules may emerge. This conclusion is reinforced by the fact that Principle 7, certainly not by chance,[72] uses the rather ambiguous term of 'responsibility', which can hardly be interpreted as entailing an unconditional obligation to take action. The idea of 'common but differentiated responsibilities' has left several marks in the modern treaty practice of states. In particular, it is mirrored in the asymmetric obligation schemes of the Montreal Protocol on Substances That Deplete the Ozone Layer and the Kyoto Protocol to the UN Framework Convention on Climate Change. However, whether this principle has been accepted in the 'general practice' of states is uncertain as states' attitudes to this principle appear to be rather ambivalent as yet. Thus, it can hardly claim to be part of today's customary international law.

---

[70] Sands, see note 13 above at 249.   [71] *Ibid.* at 286.

[72] As is well known, the industrialized states opposed any wording of Rio Principle 7 that might be understood as an acknowledgment that due to their historic contributions to the degradation of the global environment, it is automatically first and foremost up to them to tackle this problem.

4.6 Sustainable Development

As noted earlier in section 2.3, the concept of 'sustainable development' has proven particularly vexing for the international environmental law community and thus is examined here in some detail. It has politically governed international environmental relations since at least the 1992 Rio Conference (see Chapter 26 'Sustainable Development'). Its roots go back to the early 1970s when the UN Declaration proclaimed the second UN Development Decade and the UN Stockholm Conference on the Human Environment first clearly emphasized that environmental protection and economic development must be understood as compatible and mutually reinforcing goals.[73] At first glance, the composite term 'sustainable development' describes a political value that deserves respect in today's international relations. As indicated by the term 'development', it does not set a clear target to be finally achieved but instead points to a process of interaction that should be set in motion, without saying by whom. However, some life has been given to this concept by a number of definitions. Probably the most famous one was presented by the Brundtland Commission in 1987: 'Sustainable development is development that meets the needs of the present without compromising the ability of future generations to meet their own needs.'[74] While this statement is totally silent on the impact the environment has on development and vice versa, the Rio Declaration, particularly in its Principle 4, clearly points to the interdependence between both by stating: 'In order to achieve sustainable development, environmental protection shall constitute an integral part of the development process and cannot be considered in isolation from it.'[75] Profiled in such a way, sustainable development may be understood as a normative concept that gives important impulses and political guidance for all players acting in the field of international environmental protection and development. However, there is continuing uncertainty among states in regard to the exact meaning and scope of this concept.

As indicated earlier in section 2.2, some international legal scholars have suggested that the concept of 'sustainable development' possesses normative quality and has already gained the status of a principle of customary international law. Others allocate it to the sphere of mere political ideals. Recently, sustainable development even attracted the attention of the ICJ. In its judgment in the 1997 *Case Concerning the Gabčíkovo-Nagymaros Project (Hungary v. Slovakia)*, the ICJ expressly invoked the 'concept of sustainable development' as an apt expression of the 'need to reconcile

---

[73] For the origins of this concept, see, for example, U. Beyerlin, 'Concept of Sustainable Development,' in R. Wolfrum, ed., *Enforcing Environmental Standards: Economic Mechanisms as Viable Means?* (Berlin: Springer Verlag, 1996) 95 at 96.

[74] World Commission on Environment and Development, *Our Common Future* (Oxford: Oxford University Press, 1987) at 43.

[75] Accordingly, Principle 3 of the Rio Declaration stresses that '[t]he right to development must be fulfilled so as to equitably meet developmental and environmental needs of present and future generations.'

economic development with protection of the environment.'[76] In the view of the ICJ, as a consequence of this concept, the parties 'together should look afresh at the effects on the environment of the operation of the Gabcikovo power plant.'[77] However, the court did not address the question whether this concept is of legal or non-legal quality. In this respect, Judge Weeramantry, in his separate opinion, was less reserved. He considered sustainable development to be 'a principle with normative value' rather than 'a mere concept.'[78] In his view, this principle 'is a part of modern international law by reason not only of its inescapable logical necessity, but also by reason of its wide and general acceptance by the global community.'[79] In Sands's understanding, it follows already from the ICJ's majority judgment in the *Gabčíkovo-Nagymaros* case that sustainable development 'has a legal function'. In his view, there is 'little doubt' that it 'has entered the corpus of international customary law, requiring different streams of international law to be treated in an integrated manner.'[80] Lowe qualifies these arguments as 'not sustainable'.[81] In his view, sustainable development 'is itself not a norm; it can be no more than a name for a set of norms. Indeed, it may not even be that.' He rightly points out that '[n]ormativity, by definition, must express itself in normative terms: it must be possible to phrase a norm in normative language.'[82] Later on in his study, he characterizes sustainable development as a 'meta-principle', exercising 'a kind of interstitial normativity, pushing and pulling the boundaries of true primary norms when they threaten to overlap or conflict with each other.'[83] Lowe assigns sustainable development to a category of 'modifying norms'[84] designed to establish the relationships between other primary norms. If employed by judges, a norm of such type gains normative force. According to Lowe, 'it will colour the understanding of the norms that it modifies. It is in these senses that the concept of sustainable development has real normative force.'[85]

Lowe's thesis, irrespective of its validity, reflects the extreme difficulties in determining what 'sustainable development' means in legal terms. Be it part of an international treaty or not, it is not an action-oriented rule but, rather , a principle that guides states in their decision-making. However, the borderline between legal principles and 'political ideals' (Verschuuren) is very much blurred. Taken as such, 'sustainable development' is, as shown, still highly susceptible to varied explanations. Its 'normative language' is ambiguous to such an extent that it cannot deploy any appreciable steering effect on states' environmental behaviour. For these reasons, much speaks in favour of the assumption that 'sustainable development' remains

---

[76] *Case Concerning the Gabčíkovo-Nagymaros Project (Hungary v. Slovakia)*, Judgment of 25 September 1997, [1997] I.C.J. Rep. 92 at para. 140.   [77] *Ibid.*

[78] *Ibid.* at 92.   [79] *Ibid.*

[80] Sands, *Principles*, see note 13 above at 254. Compare also P. Sands, 'International Courts and the Application of the Concept of 'Sustainable Development' (1999) 3 Max Planck Y.B. UN L. 389.

[81] Lowe, see note 51 above at 30.   [82] *Ibid.* at 26.   [83] *Ibid.* at 31.

[84] This term is tantamount to that of 'interstitial norms.' See *ibid.* at 33.   [85] *Ibid.* at 33.

below the threshold of normative quality that is an indispensable prerequisite for ascribing the quality of a (legal) principle to it. Thus, it is a political ideal rather than a legal principle. However, if Lowe's statement that sustainable development 'lacks . . . a fundamentally norm-creating character'[86] should mean that this concept can never be a source from which subsequent (legal) norms can flow, this perception is hardly persuasive. First, it somewhat contradicts Lowe's understanding that sustainable development may modify a primary norm because, if doing so, it would possibly generate a new (modified) norm. Moreover, it neglects the experience that political or moral ideals, although not possessing normativity of their own, can be catalysts in the process of further developing international law. Thus, Sands's attempt to deduce from the 'principle of sustainable development' some self-contained norms (for example, inter-generational equity; sustainable use; equitable use or intra-generational equity; and integration)[87] is entirely appropriate, irrespective of the current nature of the 'principle' itself. In the following section, two of these 'legal elements of the concept of sustainable development'[88] will be considered more closely with respect to their quality as principles, which Sands apparently assigns to them.

4.7 Sustainable Use

This concept appears to be a special emanation of 'sustainable development', which may have become a self-contained norm in international law. However, only if linked with a defined object of use may it gain normative quality. For example, the 1992 Convention on Biological Diversity (CBD) pulls sustainable use together with components of biological diversity, such as flora and fauna, and other natural resources. Furthermore, Article 2 of the CBD defines 'sustainable use' as the use of these components 'in a way and at a rate that does not lead to the long-term decline of biological diversity, thereby maintaining its potential to meet the needs and aspirations of present and future generations.' Thus, there is little doubt that 'sustainable use,' as specified by Article 10,[89] calls upon the contracting parties to take measures directed to ensure the sustainable use of natural resources. Notwithstanding its indeterminateness, it is a legal rule in this context. Due to the fact that it has been integrated in a large number of international environmental agreements,[90] it may even have gained customary legal status. However, this conclusion would require a closer examination of relevant state practice and *opinio juris*.

---

[86] *Ibid.* at 30.   [87] See Sands, *Principles*, see note 13 above at 253.   [88] *Ibid.*
[89] Article 10 of the convention specifies the rule of 'sustainable use' by determining the kind of respective actions to be taken 'as far as possible and as appropriate'.
[90] For references, see Sands, *Principles*, note 13 above at 257.

4.8 Inter-Generational Equity

The idea that as 'members of the present generation, we hold the earth in trust for future generations'[91] is, in Sands's opinion, 'well known to international law'[92] (see Chapter 27 'Equity'). Sands also presents some evidence in international practice of states being committed to this idea.[93] Even so, there may be certain doubts whether 'inter-generational equity' is of a normative quality. In contrast to 'sustainable use', it is certainly not a rule because it does not set out any 'legal consequences that follow automatically when the conditions provided are met' (Dworkin). As 'inter-generational equity' is designed to guide the discretion of states in international environmental and developmental decision-making processes, it appears to surmount the threshold of normativity and can therefore be considered a principle. If incorporated into an international environmental agreement,[94] this principle gives meaningful legal guidance for the parties to that agreement and, in this sense, is a *legal* principle.[95] It may lead parties to interpret and apply open or unclear treaty rules in such a way that the interests and needs of future generations will be met as best as possible. Whether 'inter-generational equity' has also become part of customary international law in a non-treaty context is another question that may be left open.

5 CONCLUSIONS

Current international environmental law contains at the bottom of its normative hierarchy a number of rather amorphous norms, such as 'sustainable development' and 'common but differentiated responsibilities', which are subject to ongoing doctrinal controversies as to whether they are legal norms or have to be ascribed to the sphere of 'soft law'. These norms appear to have infected the system of international environmental law with 'relative normativity', which Weil calls a 'pathological phenomenon', and to have created a high degree of legal uncertainty. For these reasons, this chapter has attempted to shed more light on these norms in order to haul them out of the sphere of twilight. It has sought to illustrate that the crucial question

---

[91] E. Brown Weiss, 'Our Rights and Obligations to Future Generations for the Environment' (1990) 84 A.J.I.L. 199.   [92] Sands, *Principles*, see note 13 above at 256.

[93] *Ibid.* at 256.

[94] For example, the 1992 UN Framework Convention on Climate Change, Article 3, paragraph 1, requires that its parties 'should protect the climate system for the benefit of present and future generations of humankind, on the basis of equity.'

[95] Lowe, see note 51 above, takes the opposite view by saying that '[i]t is hard to see what legal content inter-generational equity could have', at 27.

concerns not merely the legal status of a given norm but also the proper identification of its characteristics. This chapter has examined these questions on the basis of Dworkin's distinction between policies, legal principles, and legal rules.

The inquiry has revealed that a large number of norms that many writers call 'legal principles' actually appear to be 'legal rules'. Among them are the 'prohibition of causing transboundary environmental damage', 'environmental impact assessment', 'precautionary action', and 'polluter pays'. Although rather indeterminate in content and scope, these rules all set out determinable legal consequences: They call upon their addressees to take action in view of a certain aim, thereby preventing actors from maintaining the status quo. Obviously, a norm with the quality of a rule does not automatically gain international legal status. It remains instead in the sphere of policies ('soft law'), unless it can be shown that it either has become part of an international treaty or has been accepted in the general practice of states, accompanied by the latter's *opinio iuris*.

The task of distinguishing 'legal principles' from 'policies' has been even more complicated. Thus, the answers offered in this chapter must remain tentative in nature—the concept of 'common but differentiated responsibilities' appears to be a principle that has not yet, however, gained customary legal status. 'Sustainable development', because of its iridescent content and scope, has been assigned to the sphere of mere 'political ideals'. It is, however, an apt source from which subsequent legal norms may flow.

Since the demarcation line between legal and 'soft law' principles is seriously blurred, the distinction between them is often very difficult to make out. This causes considerable legal uncertainty. However, the detrimental effects of this uncertainty are mitigated by the fact that 'soft law' norms, especially in international environmental relations, quite often produce significant effects on the behaviour of states in political-moral terms. Indeed, as argued in section 3.2 of this chapter, whether or not a given norm is a 'principle' and, thus, a norm with the capacity to guide decisions and the interpretations or application of existing rules may be more important to its potential impact than whether it is legally binding or not.

RECOMMENDED READING

A. Aarnio, 'Taking Rules Seriously,' in W. Maihofer and G.Sprenger, eds., *Law and the States in Modern Times*, Proceedings of the Fourteenth IVR World Congress in Edinburgh, August 1989, Archives for Philosophy of Law and Social Philosophy (Stuttgart: Franz Steiner Verlag, 1990) 180.

R. Alexy, *Recht, Vernunft, Diskurs: Studien zur Rechtsphilosophie* (Frankfurt am Main: Suhrkamp Verlag, 1995).

R. Dworkin, *Taking Rights Seriously* (London: Duckworth, 1977).

U. Fastenrath, 'Relative Normativity in International Law' (1993) 4 Eur. J. Int'l L. 305.

V. Lowe, 'Sustainable Development and Unsustainable Arguments,' in A. Boyle and D. Freestone, eds., *International Law and Sustainable Development: Past Achievements and Future Challenges* (Oxford: Oxford University Press, 1999) 19.

N. MacCormick, *Legal Reasoning and Legal Theory* (Oxford: Clarendon Press, 1978; reprinted in 1995).

N. de Sadeleer, *Environmental Principles: From Political Slogans to Legal Rules* (Oxford: Oxford University Press, 2002).

P. Sands, 'International Law in the Field of Sustainable Development: Emerging Legal Principles,' in W. Lang, ed., *Sustainable Development and International Law* (London: Graham and Trotman, 1995) 53.

J. Verschuuren, *Principles of Environmental Law: The Ideal of Sustainable Development and the Role of Principles of International, European, and National Environmental Law* (Baden-Baden: Nomos, 2003).

P. Weil, 'Towards Relative Normativity in International Law' (1983) 77 A.J.I.L. 413.

FORMATION OF CUSTOMARY INTERNATIONAL LAW AND GENERAL PRINCIPLES

PIERRE-MARIE DUPUY

THERE exist a growing number of treaties dealing with many, if not all, aspects of the human environment (see Chapter 20 'Treaty Making and Treaty Evolution'). A good number of these agreements are currently in force. Over the last four decades, such instruments have combined to create a dense network of conventional obligations; nonetheless, the place and role of customary international law remains of great importance in practice for several reasons.[1] First, although they may be in force, many treaties remain for the most part unimplemented, or at best only partially implemented, regardless of what their scope and content may be. Second, not every state that is concerned, for example, by the pollution of a particular environment—be it at the regional, or even at the universal, level—is a party to the pertinent agreement. Furthermore, even if an instrument is in force between all countries concerned, it is a rare treaty that is formulated in such a fashion as to avoid all difficulties of interpretation or even of application. Thus, it is often necessary to go back to the level of general principles and customary rules.

This chapter will start with some preliminary observations on customary law-making in international environmental law, and then assess the 'banality' of the customary law-making process in the field of the international protection of the environment—that is, the fact that this process is analogous to the one in general international law. It will then review a series of theoretical and technical problems in proving the existence of customary environmental law, namely the relationship between treaties and custom; the relationship between 'soft law' and custom; and the relationship between general principles, normative concepts, and custom. This chapter will conclude with considerations regarding the problematic nature of the constantly ongoing law-making process in the absence of a legislator for the protection of the environment.

1 PRELIMINARY OBSERVATIONS ON CUSTOMARY LAW-MAKING IN INTERNATIONAL ENVIRONMENTAL LAW

It is important to note that, among the different actors concerned with issues of environmental protection at the international level (that is, states, international governmental organizations, and non-governmental organizations (NGOs)), it remains an open question as to whether a number of the basic rules that they deal with already belong to the body of well-established customary rules of international law or

---

[1] P.-M. Dupuy, 'Overview of Existing Customary Legal Regime Regarding International Pollution,' in D. Magraw, ed., *International Law and Pollution* (Philadelphia: University of Pennsylvania Press, 1991) 61–89.

whether they remain outside the realm of law, somewhere between *lex lata* and *lex ferenda*.

One of the best examples of this phenomenon is provided by the evolution of the 'precautionary principle'(see Chapter 25 'Precaution'). The manner in which this principle has been dealt with in recent times—in particular, by the World Trade Organization's (WTO) Appellate Body in *EC Measures Concerning Meat and Meat Products (Hormones)*,[2] among others[3]—is evidence not merely of the legal issues but also of the political, and, above all, the economic, issues at stake. At the same time, however, the principle's legal status remains uncertain. This example also illustrates that the question of whether a customary international rule exists is indeed very much linked with the question of how the principle in question was first launched and then actually approved. In other words, the customary law status of a rule depends on whether the principle is invoked by a majority of states, comprising both developed and developing countries, by a regional group of states (as in the case of the support expressed by the members of the European Union), or even by the international community, including international civil society. In addition, it depends on whether the principle has been referred to, or put into operation, in a treaty, in a soft law instrument, in judicial or semi-judicial decisions, or in other expressions of state practice. Therefore, the process of the *formation* of customary international law, and that of its *consolidation* as a rule of positive international law are two sides of the same coin, which is suggested by the fact that the concept of 'custom' refers to both the law-making process and to the end result of that process itself—a legally binding norm at the universal, or, more rarely, the regional, level.

If I may be allowed to rely on my experience as a lawyer having dealt with international environmental law for more than 30 years, I can say that I first confronted customary law-making in international environmental law as a scholar.[4] I encountered it again while acting as legal counsel to an international organization (the Organisation of Economic Co-operation and Development (OECD) and its Transfrontier Pollution Group), which was attempting to make sure that all of its members recognized certain principles of equal right of access to justice and non-discrimination for the victims of transboundary pollution. Principles derived from those already identified in the *Trail Smelter Arbitration (United States v. Canada)* and the *Corfu Channel Case (United Kingdom v. Albania)* (see Chapter 22 'Transboundary Impacts' and Chapter 44 'International Responsibility and Liability'). One of my

---

[2] *EC Measures Concerning Meat and Meat Products (Hormones)*, Appellate Body Report, Doc. WT/DS26/AB/R (1997), adopted 16 January 1998 [*Hormones*]; *EC Measures Concerning Meat and Meat Products (Hormones), Complaint by the United States*, Panel Report, Doc. WT/DS26/R/USA (1997), adopted 18 August 1997; and *EC Measures Concerning Meat and Meat Products (Hormones), Complaint by Canada*, Doc. WT/DS48/CAN (1997), adopted 18 August 1997.

[3] For example, see also *Southern Bluefin Tuna (Australia and New Zealand v. Japan)*, International Tribunal for the Law of the Sea, 39 I.L.M. 1359 (2000).

[4] P.-M. Dupuy, *La responsabilité internationale des Etats pour les dommages d'origine technologique et industrielle* (Paris: Editions Pedone, 1976).

most recent meetings with the 'jelly-fish'[5] of customary international law was when pleading before the International Court of Justice (ICJ) as counsel for Hungary in the *Case Concerning the Gabčíkovo-Nagymaros Project (Hungary v. Slovakia)*.[6] On each of these occasions, I felt at once convinced of my arguments, and a little embarrassed at having to demonstrate the fact that some general rules belonged to the '*corpus juris*' of customary international law. I was convinced that these principles were clearly part of customary law. However, in the absence of previous judicial decisions recognizing their status and in dealing with a relatively recent branch of international law (environmental protection), I still faced the difficulty of proving that such principles were accepted by states beyond their treaty-law formulations.

The task was relatively easy in the case of the principle of harmless use of territory (*sic utere tuo ut alienum non laedas*)—that is, the principle that a state is forbidden from using its own territory in such a manner as to harm other states. It was more difficult, at least during the eighties and early nineties, when confronted with the somewhat reformulated but very similar principle launched in 1972—Principle 21 of the Stockholm Declaration on the Human Environment. According to Principle 21, states have sovereign rights over their natural resources, and the obligation not to cause damage to the environment of other states or of areas beyond the limits of national jurisdiction. It was somewhat harder to prove before the court the customary nature of the rule requiring, as a corollary to the customary rules on good neighbourliness and Principle 21, the prior notification of all activities with the potential to cause transboundary environmental harm. While both *opinio juris* and state practice are required for custom to emerge, most scholars, without necessarily paying any real attention to state practice (which is, in any event, always problematic to assess and review), start from the assumption that such a principle belongs without any doubt to the field of customary international law. In reality, the common belief of scholars does not suffice to make the law! In this respect, it is also fair to observe that the ICJ, while formally insisting on both elements of custom, at times is rather generous in concluding that one or the other exists. As already noted earlier, it is more difficult still to demonstrate that the precautionary 'principle' is a well-defined and established customary rule in positive international law. Its formulation, implementation, impact, and implications still raise some difficult issues, whatever we may wish to be the case, not only among prudent diplomats but also within the scientific and legal communities (see Chapter 25 'Precaution'). The varying formulations of the precautionary 'principle' may imply that, in the case of scientific uncertainty, states are allowed or obliged to regulate, to prohibit, or to allow only under certain conditions activities that may cause environmental damage. The question thus remains: even if

---

[5] As Judge Jimenez de Aréchaga used to call customary international law. See E. Jiménez de Aréchaga, 'International Law in the Past Third of a Century' (1978-I) 159 Recueil des cours 9 at 9.

[6] *Case Concerning Gabčíkovo and Nagymaros Project (Hungary v. Slovakia)*, Judgment of 25 September 1997, [1997] I.C.J. Rep. 92 (25 September).

we agree that the precautionary principle has become customary international law, which of these formulations is binding upon states?

The preceding remarks do not mean that customary international law does not exist in the environmental field—quite the contrary, in fact. As I have already suggested, customary international environmental law is both omnipresent and of paramount importance. However, what the above considerations *do* illustrate is that it is often problematic to demonstrate the compulsory character of this kind of norm— in other words, to prove that the norm has been integrated into the '*corpus juris*' of general international law. This problem is exacerbated by the fact that states rarely have recourse to courts and tribunals that could state the law on this controversial point. It appears that states prefer an out-of-court solution to their environmental disputes, rather than a judicial decision by an international court or tribunal, as illustrated, for example, by the complete inactivity of the Environmental Chamber of the ICJ. In addition, even when an environmental dispute is brought before an international tribunal, it may choose not to pronounce itself on the specific legal status of the international environmental norms in question.[7] Furthermore, it also means that, when writing on international environmental law, many scholars quite innocently cite the largest possible number of opinions, treaties, and recommendations in order to convince themselves that not only must a particular rule be recognized by states as compulsory, but also that such is effectively the case in their actual practice. However, mere reiteration in different international documents may well have to be dissociated from what a state actually considers to be binding law in a specific situation. For example, a state may oppose the application of the precautionary principle with regard to the law of the sea and the sustainable utilization of fish stocks and, at the same time (through a different ministry, perhaps), invoke the principle in a dispute concerning human health in the field of international trade.

Scholarly argumentation, however, even if it can help to elucidate the existence of custom, cannot in itself furnish proof or undeniable evidence capable of convincing states of the existence of a binding obligation. Indeed, with the exception of human rights, there is probably no other field within the domain of public international law in which the distance between the academic literature and the actual practice of sovereign states is decreasing so slowly.[8]

Without necessarily over-dramatizing the issue, it seems that the technical legal (and sociological) issue of the law-making process in the field of customary international environmental law should not be arbitrarily disconnected from its ecological and political stakes. It would, of course, be ridiculous to promote the image of, on the one hand, scholars and/or NGOs as brave knights battling for the safeguarding of the environment, wielding the weapon of basic customary rules, and, on the other hand,

[7] *Hormones*, see note 2 above at para. 123.

[8] See D. Bodansky, 'Customary (and Not So Customary) International Environmental Law' (1995) 3 Ind. J. Global Leg. Stud. 105.

the image of recalcitrant sovereigns persistently seeking to escape their obligations by invoking the lack of state practice, the vagueness, or the inconsistency and, as a consequence, the non-binding effect of these same rules. Nonetheless, the issue of how, and how quickly, international legal rules and principles are recognized as binding at the universal level outside the scope of any agreement in force should not be disconnected from its political, economic, and ecological dimensions. The consideration of specific political circumstances, economic interests, or ecological characteristics linked to a particular environmental problem may lead a state to deny the binding character of a rule in a specific case, whereas the same state would be ready to accept it with reference to other environmental issues.

2 Banality of the Customary Law-Making Process in the Field of the International Protection of the Environment

In the field of the protection of the environment, as in any other, a customary rule at the universal level is defined by its legal authority over each and every state in the absence of any written legal commitment by them. Contrary to what has been suggested by some scholars who focus almost exclusively on the international law of the environment, rather than on general international law, the process of customary law-making in this branch of the law is analogous to the process in general international law. Of course, even when taking general international as a starting point, the famous theory of the 'two elements' of state practice and *opinio juris* (one 'material' and the other 'intellectual'—that is, 'psychological'), which when taken together are supposed to be necessary and sufficient for the creation of an international custom, should be considered with great care as representing an overly simplistic way of explaining a very complicated social process.[9] At the origin of a customary rule of law pertaining to the environment, as in any other branch of international law, is a complex mixture of state practice, *opinio juris*, and express or tacit expression of consent. It should be added that, while, in theory, a state's persistent objections to a certain rule of international customary law can prevent such a rule from becoming binding upon that state, in the environmental field, as in other areas of international

---

[9] The present author has systematically dealt with the general theory of international customary law and the customary international law-making process in *Droit International Public*, 7th edition (Paris: Dalloz, 2004), at 319–32; and in 'L'unité de l'ordre juridique international'(2002) 297 Cours général de droit international public Recueil des cours 157.

law, the actual practice of the 'persistent objector' is seldom sufficient to protect a dissenting state from the compulsory effect of some rules. This is especially the case when the rest of the 'international community' is largely in agreement about the binding nature of the rule in question. In those cases, a state's behaviour rarely remains coherent and comprehensive enough in the long term to achieve the desired result[10]—that is, of not being bound by the rule. An example is that of major flag states opposing the creation of the exclusive economic zone (EEZ) in the early 1980s, even though it was already recognized as part of customary international law well before the entry into force of the UN Convention on the Law of the Sea.

It has been argued by many scholars that international environmental law was unique in terms of the general norm-creation process because of its reliance on negotiations undertaken within the framework of international organizations and on an ever-increasing body of soft law instruments.[11] This phenomenon was due to the fact that the production of 'soft law' was introduced into this field sooner than it was in others. Softness here refers not only to the nature of the relevant instruments (recommendations or declarations) but also, at times, to the content itself (guidelines or standards) even if they are incorporated in binding instruments (treaties).[12] However, the emerging importance of 'soft law' in the early seventies could also be observed in the international law of economic development, including, for example, the norms dealing with permanent sovereignty over natural resources.[13] The fact that a good number of international environmental rules, such as the duty to prevent transfrontier pollution, to avoid discrimination between the victims of such pollution, or to share equitably common environmental resources, have been negotiated within the framework of international organizations does not affect the very nature (and weakness) of the law-making process. It remains very difficult, *rationae temporis*, to say exactly *from what point onwards* a particular rule may be assumed to have passed beyond the threshold of 'soft' law and crystallized into a generally binding rule. A relevant factor in this development is the process by which the norm is generated, which may be more or less rationalized through the means of institutionalized diplomacy. Another factor is the authority of the norm produced by this same process. This authority still depends—regardless of whether it is created through a harder or softer process—upon the conviction of states that the norm has become binding. This conviction in turn may depend on states' perceptions that it has become politically too costly to challenge the binding character of the norm. In other words, a state, on the basis of a cost/benefit analysis, may conclude that it is not worth continuing to challenge the existence of a rule or to persevere in denying the applicability of a rule to it.

[10] *Ibid.*, in particular, at 174 ff.
[11] G. Palmer, 'New Ways to Make International Environmental Law' (1992) 86 A.J.I.L. 259.
[12] P.-M. Dupuy, 'Soft Law and the International Law of the Environment' (1991) 12 Mich. J. Int'l L. 420.
[13] Dupuy, 'Overview of Existing Customary Legal Regime,' see note 1 above.

The fact that the customary law-making process of international environmental law is similar to that found in other areas of international law does not mean that at least some international environmental norms do not have a degree of originality. As in other areas of international law, there are a number of 'standards' of due diligence that are specific to international environmental law.[14] As far as standards for the protection of the environment are concerned, some, at least, are not defined in broad terms, referring back to the general standards of 'reasonable' behaviour of a hypothetical 'well-governed state'. Rather, they refer to scientific criteria established and periodically reviewed in the framework of international organizations, either public or private. International 'eco-standards', for example, even if not included in annexes to conventions (as they are in a large number of cases), are capable of contributing to a very precise definition of the level of diligence that legitimately may be expected from states or other actors under their control, within the overall context of good governance aimed at the sustainable management of the environment. One example is the way in which the Convention on International Trade in Endangered Species of Fauna and Flora amends the lists of species in Appendices I–III according to the changing circumstances in their conservation status. With the benefit of these general considerations, it may now be possible to synthetically review the difficulties raised by the question of whether a norm has achieved the status of customary international law.

3 THEORETICAL AND TECHNICAL PROBLEMS IN PROVING THE EXISTENCE OF CUSTOMARY ENVIRONMENTAL LAW

3.1 Relationship between Treaties and Customs

As noted earlier, the development of international law over the last three decades owes much to the increasing number of treaties of all kinds dealing, more or less systematically, with the major elements of the human environment: air, oceans, rivers, forests, the ozone layer, world climate, biodiversity, wildlife, and/or the way in which these elements are polluted by human activity (the discharge of hazardous waste, the emission of pollutants, the release of toxic gases, the over-exploitation of natural resources, and so on). A number of these conventions refer to more or less standardized forms of conduct, in terms of action, for example, against transfrontier

---

[14] P. Sands, *Principles of International Environmental Law*, 2nd edition (Cambridge: Cambridge University Press, 2003) at 155 ff.

pollution, exchange of information, prior notification, non-discrimination, the use of the best available technology, and so on.

We are, then, confronted with a classic problem. Treaties are binding only on those states that are party to them. At the same time, however, they form part of the 'state practice' contributing to the progressive crystallization of norms into customary law. As a consequence of this duality, two lines of argument confront each other. On the one hand, those who want to protect the will of the state argue that if a treaty was negotiated as a *'lex specialis'*, it is precisely because the parties to this agreement thought it necessary to explicitly set out the rule as binding upon them. The treaty itself, thus, provides evidence of the absence of any general custom or principle in the field. On the other hand, those who want to emphasize the role of treaties as evidence of state practice capable of contributing to the creation of a custom rely on international case law. The ICJ already declared in the *Case Concerning North Sea Continental Shelf (Germany v. Denmark; Germany v. Netherlands)*[15] some 35 years ago that, under certain conditions, customary international rules may emerge that are identical to treaty obligations. At issue was the question whether the method of equidistance for delimiting the continental shelf between two or more states had already passed into the corpus of international law and, as such, was binding upon every state. This rule was contained in Article 6 of the 1958 Convention on the Continental Shelf, and the court contemplated whether the rule had customary law status at the time that the treaty was negotiated or whether it had acquired that status after the treaty had entered into force.

On this occasion, the ICJ identified the conditions to be fulfilled for a treaty rule to become a rule of customary international law. The treaty provision at stake might be 'of a fundamentally norm-creating character', and benefit from 'widespread and representative participation' including that of 'states whose interests [are] specially affected.'[16] Legally speaking, the migration of an obligation from the restricted scope of a treaty, limited to a particular group of states, to that of general international law is neither theoretically nor technically impossible. This issue has been further considered by the court since 1969, for example, in the *Case Concerning Military and Paramilitary Activities in and against Nicaragua (Nicaragua v. United States)*,[17] when the ICJ reiterated that customary rules may emerge that are identical to, and coexist with, treaty law obligations.

It, nevertheless, should be accepted by scholars that the practice of citing as many treaties as possible that contain references, in analogous terms, to the same type of conduct is simply insufficient to convincingly demonstrate that a rule recognized in treaty law has also become binding in the field of custom. As a matter of fact, even the

---

[15] *Case Concerning North Sea Continental Shelf (Federal Republic of Germany v. Denmark; Federal Republic of Germany v. Netherlands)*, Judgment of 20 February 1969, [1969] I.C.J. Rep. 3 (20 February).

[16] *Ibid.* at para. 73.

[17] *Case Concerning Military and Paramilitary Activities in and against Nicaragua (Nicaragua v. United States of America)*, Judgment of 27 June 1986, [1986] I.C.J. Rep. 93 at 93–4 (27 June) [*Nicaragua*].

fulfillment of the criteria laid down by the court in 1969 is not enough to ensure that a rule has passed from a treaty into general international law. Other contextual and sociological conditions (including political ones) must be met—the balance and combination of which can hardly be given definitive formulation. To go back to an example mentioned earlier, the status of the precautionary principle very much depends on the contextual terms of reference for its application. Its meaning in the context of the protection of human health is not necessarily the same as in the context of sustainable fisheries.

3.2 Relationship between 'Soft Law' and Customs

As I have already suggested, the notion of 'soft law' has been a decisive factor in the very rapid development of new norms and principles over the past 30 years in the field of international environmental law.[18] The 1972 Stockholm Declaration[19] initiated a process of normative development that was further enlarged upon, and consolidated by, the Rio Declaration on Environment and Development, which was adopted at the first 'World Summit' in 1992;[20] even if, in this respect, the 2002 World Summit on Sustainable Development was somewhat disillusioning in not providing for further normative developments.[21] Many other declarations, however, have contributed to this process, such as, for example, the 1989 Hague Declaration on the Environment, which was adopted after the release of the Brundtland report *Our Common Future* and which called for international action for the protection of the atmosphere against global warming. Declarations of this nature have played an important role in securing formal acknowledgment by states that certain goals should be achieved in conformity with a set of general principles. In the case of the Hague Declaration, the call for an international regime on global warming and the suggested principles therein contributed to the adoption of the UN Framework Convention on Climate Change, based on the common but differentiated responsibility principle. Some resolutions and recommendations, such as the Helsinki Rules on the Uses of the Waters of International Rivers, which was adopted as early as 1966 by the International Law Association (ILA), or the 1974 OECD Recommendation 274C on Principles Concerning Transfrontier Pollution, remain central to the process that led, among other things, to the recognition of the principle of equitable use

---

[18] See, in particular, Sands, note 14 above at 35 ff.

[19] See A.Ch. Kiss and J.D. Sicault, 'La Conférence des Nations Unies sur l'Environnement' (1972) 18 Annuaire française de droit international 603.

[20] A.Ch. Kiss and S. Doumbe-Bille, 'La Conférence des Nations-Unies sur l'Environnement et le Dévelopement' (1992) 38 Annuaire française de droit international 823.

[21] See V. Barral, 'Johannesburg 2002: quoi de neuf pour le développement durable?' (2002) 2 Revue générale de droit international public 415.

of shared natural resources. This principle, in turn, was further elaborated by a UN Environment Programme (UNEP) report in 1978 on natural resources shared by two or more states[22] and then codified in the 1991 Convention on Environmental Impact Assessment in a Transboundary Context (Espoo Convention) and the 1997 UN Convention on the Law of Non-Navigational Uses of International Watercourses (Watercourses Convention).

One should, of course, systematically distinguish among this somewhat heterogeneous group of non-binding instruments—that is, between those adopted by experts acting in their personal capacity from those negotiated by state delegations with a view to setting out mere 'guidelines'. Thus, resolutions adopted by experts (such as the Helsinki Rules and the UNEP report), although they are less authoritative than those negotiated by state delegations (such as the OECD recommendations), can be extremely influential in legitimizing and shaping successive legal developments. Thus, the fact that the Espoo Convention lays down the general obligation of states to notify and consult each other on all major projects under consideration that are likely to have a significant adverse transboundary environmental impact builds upon the considerations of the OECD recommendation and the UNEP report. Along the same lines, the Watercourses Convention was largely drafted having in mind the ILA Helsinki Rules. As demonstrated by the late-night sessions in which national delegates draft non-binding instruments with extreme care, the resolutions adopted by state delegations remain closer to the expression of a potential *opinio juris*. It is fair to consider them as indications of how the law may evolve, since national delegations negotiate them while continuously weighing their normative potential. On the other hand, resolutions adopted by experts enjoy a sort of residual legitimacy since they reflect primarily the experts' contribution to the rationalization and clarification of international norms. In sum, resolutions adopted by states indicate how international law can evolve, whereas those adopted by experts indicate how international law should evolve.

Here again, the long-standing debate as to whether an accumulation of programmatic soft law instruments may help in the progressive affirmation of the emergence of a binding norm is not specific to international environmental law. The problem lies, here as elsewhere, with the discrepancy that more often than not remains between what states say and what they actually do. Expressions of *opinio juris* that are not sufficiently sustained by practice do not take us particularly far in terms of customary, and thus general, law-making. In its rich judgment in the *Nicaragua* case, the ICJ stated:

The mere fact that States declare their recognition of certain rules is not sufficient . . . to consider these as being part of customary international law, and as applicable as such to those

22 P.-M. Dupuy, 'La gestion concertée des ressources naturelles: à propos du différend entre le Brésil et l'Argentine relative au barrage d'Itaïpu' (1991) 8 Annuaire française de droit international 866–89.

States. Bound as it is by Article 38 of its Statute to apply, *inter alia*, international custom 'as evidence of a general practice accepted as law,' the Court may not disregard the essential role played by general practice. Where two States agree to incorporate a particular rule in a treaty, their agreement suffices to make that rule a legal one, binding upon them; but in the field of customary international law, the shared view of the Parties as to the content of what they regard as the rule is not enough. The Court must satisfy itself that the existence of the rule in the *opinio juris* of States is confirmed by practice.[23]

Faced, then, with diverse and inconsistent practice in terms of preventing the pollution of a shared natural resource, for example, the question is to decide whether it is nevertheless possible to ascertain the existence of a positive rule of customary international law. Scholars may think that they help in attempting to do so when they comment on the existence of customary rules in such circumstances, and they may very well have an impact in some cases. However, expressive as they are of individual opinions, their writings lack both legal force and political legitimacy. Courts (and this is no longer limited only to the ICJ but also includes the WTO Appellate Body and the International Tribunal for the Law of the Sea, which are both referred to earlier in this chapter) are, of course, in a different position since they may, at most, rationalize the picture of state practice that they perceive in a given area and assert the existence of a customary norm in cases in which there is only an apparent tendency among states not to disregard the rule in question. Once again, the ICJ case law in this respect is instructive:

The Court does not consider that, for a rule to be established as customary, the corresponding practice must be in absolutely rigorous conformity with the rule. In order to deduce the existence of customary rules, the Court deems it sufficient that the conduct of States should, in general, be consistent with such rules, and that instances of State conduct inconsistent with a given rule should generally have been treated as breaches of that rule, not as indication of the recognition of a new rule.[24]

Beyond this assessment, courts, as opposed to scholars, are restricted by the specific facts of the case and the specific formulation of the legal question by the parties to the dispute. As shown in the *Gabčíkovo-Nagymaros* dispute, the first case in which the ICJ dealt specifically with the issue of customary law-making for the protection of the environment, the ICJ's contribution remained limited because of its fear of being accused of creating the law rather than of applying it. However, the same fear has not prevented the ICJ from being more explicit in other areas of international law, such as the law regarding maritime delimitation. In this respect, a decision of an international court or tribunal depends very much on the personal beliefs, culture, and even generation of international judges, which are all factors having a bearing on the judge's sensitivity to the specificities of environmental protection, such as the possibility of transboundary and long-term effects.

---

[23] *Nicaragua*, see note 17 above at para. 184.   [24] *Ibid*. at para. 186.

3.3 Relationship between General Principles, Normative Concepts, and Customs

Another classical issue, namely that of the criteria by which to differentiate between general principles and general customary rules, does not seem to be of major interest to the discussion in this chapter (see Chapter 18 'Different Types of Norms in International Environmental Law: Policies, Principles, and Rules'). It might be argued that 'general principles' of international environmental law differ from customary norms based only on the level of generality of their formulation. Nevertheless, both kinds of norms proceed from the same progressive sedimentation of general statements, together with more or less coherent state practice and sometimes assisted by judicial consolidation. Consider, as an example, the *'sic utere tuo'* principle when it was formulated in the *Corfu Channel* case as a general principle stated authoritatively by the court in an *obiter dictum*. This decision was followed by the renewed and refurbished affirmations of the same rule in the Stockholm and Rio Declarations and then consolidated by the judicial recognition of its customary nature by the ICJ in 1996 (the *Advisory Opinion on the Legality of the Threat and Use of Nuclear Weapons*)[25] and in 1997 (the *Gabčíkovo-Nagymaros* case). The important point is that, whether referred to as 'principle' or 'custom', the rule derives its legally binding character from the same type of process.

It may, however, be significant to view some 'principles' as pertaining to a particular category that is specific to international environmental law and not to other branches of the discipline. These principles may be defined as 'normative concepts'. At their ultimate level of generalization, some key environmental concepts have been launched in the framework of the UN (and in other institutions) in the form of influential but vague concepts—the more precise content of which is to be determined on a case-by-case basis, depending on the type of action or the natural resource in question. Such concepts, due to their very broad formulation, may incorporate a whole range of potential normative developments and suggest a certain approach rather than prescribing specific conduct. The best example of such a phenomenon is provided by the 'concept' of 'sustainable development'[26] (see Chapter 26 'Sustainable Development'). As such, this concept is more of a *'Weltanschauung'*, implying a program of actions rather than a general principle in itself. Nevertheless, its legal authority depends on its recognition as a binding rule of law at the international

---

[25] *Advisory Opinion on the Legality of the Use or Threat of Nuclear Weapons (UNGA)*, Opinion of 8 July 1996, [1996] I.C.J. Rep. 95 (8 July) at para. 29. See also *Request for an Examination of the Situation in Accordance with Paragraph 63 of the Court's Judgment of 20 December 1974 in the Nuclear Test (New Zealand v. France) case*, Order of 22 December 1995, [1995] I.C.J. Rep. 347 (22 December).

[26] Y. Matsui, 'The Road to Sustainable Development: Evolution of the Concept of Development in the United Nations,' in K. Ginther, E. Denters, and P.J.I.M. de Waart, eds., *Sustainable Development and Good Governance* (Dordrecht: Kluwer Academic Publishers, 1995) 53–71.

level. Sustainable development as a concept aims, as is well known, at reconciling economic development with sound ecological management. As a 'principle', it appears frequently in treaty law, beginning with the two Rio conventions (the UN Framework Convention on Climate Change and the Convention on Biological Diversity (CBD)), and then appears subsequently in many others. However, it is formulated more precisely but in different ways in a number of soft law instruments, in particular, the 1992 Rio Declaration and the 2002 final Johannesburg Declaration on Sustainable Development. Rather than being simply understood as a 'rule' or 'principle' capable of being directly applied by states, the concept of 'sustainable development' fulfils the function of what I would call a 'normative matrix', delimitating a certain intellectual perception of what the duty to balance economic development and the protection of the environment in an equitable manner might be.

When it comes to the legal status of concepts such as 'sustainable development', the issues that arise are the same, regardless of whether they are considered to be a principle of international law or a rule of customary international law. They make us consider the extent to which, and the manner in which, their enunciation in binding and non-binding legal instruments has had a discernible impact on state practice, which might enable us to conclude that they already have been included within the scope of general international law. Nevertheless, due to their extreme generality and vagueness, such concepts, as well as when they evolve into law, always remain dependent upon complementary sources for the clarification of their veritable content—treaties, in particular. 'Sustainable development' is not a self-explanatory expression. Rather, it needs, and even implies, further normative development.

Much the same could probably be said of the 'precautionary principle'.[27] In terms of one of its possible translations, this concept implies a certain assurance that major and unconsidered risks for the environment will not be created in the absence of guarantees that such risks can be avoided. Concepts such as 'sustainable development' and the 'precautionary principle' imply the further definition of precise prescriptions and specific duties. As a consequence, they should be viewed in terms of their normative potential rather than from the formal perspective of their legal status. It remains the case, once again, that without a certain level of effective application demonstrated by the actual practice of states, the binding character of such concepts remains rather uncertain outside the scope of treaty law. Ultimately, state practice is yet again the necessary and exclusive route for acceptance into the realm of international law. And state practice is often difficult to demonstrate, in particular, for scholars, who, as noted earlier, lack the legitimacy to authoritatively determine the law, as opposed to international courts and tribunals that are endowed with this task by virtue of their statutes.

---

[27] See, among others, Ch. Leben and J. Verhoeven, eds., *Le principe de precaution, aspects de droit international et communautaire* (Paris: Editions Panthéon-Assas, 2002).

4 A CONSTANT LAW-MAKING PROCESS WITHOUT A LEGISLATOR

Whatever the sense of their public statements, most policymakers are still keen to protect the 'national' interest. Biologists and ecologists, on the other hand, have become more and more anxious as they observe the increased destruction of some of the major natural components of the human environment. Some already suggest that it may be too late to avoid catastrophic global consequences. Lawyers, somewhere in between the two, given their position as 'technicians of norms' (of their making, their implementation, their revision, and their nullification), must face up to a manifest inadequacy—the gap between, on the one hand, the uncertain political will of states to safeguard an ever more disturbed and fragile environment and, on the other, the urgent need for the implementation of integrated and comprehensive legislation at the universal, regional, and national levels, which could indeed safeguard and restore this environment.

There is, at the moment, no prospect of such comprehensive legislation, even if the progressing integration of the European Union does, in this respect, provide some hope for the future as an example of a supra-national legal system in which (environmental) integration has led to the development of a systematic body of environmental legislation[28] (see Chapter 37 'Regional Economic Integration Organizations'). At the international level, in turn, we see an ever-increasing pile of framework conventions, technical regulations, eco-standards, declarations, and recommendations dealing in one way or another with the protection of the environment. Some of them are convergent and complementary; many, however, are ill-matched. This was the case, for instance, with the international regime on plant genetic resources. The International Undertaking on Plant Genetic Resources for Food and Agriculture was based on the concept of the common heritage of mankind, while the subsequent International Treaty on Plant Genetic Resources for Food and Agriculture had to be revised to be in harmony with the CBD's approach based on national sovereignty (Articles 1 and 10). This example is, in part at least, a reflection of the absence of a coordinating legislative organ. What is perhaps most striking in this regard is the lack of an integrated UN special agency that could serve as an 'umbrella organization' for coordinating environmental policies, integrating legislation, and monitoring implementation. Within this context, general customary rules and general principles may act, in part at least, as compensation for the institutional deficiencies of the system. They may do so, for example, by promoting the coherent interpretation of many diverse rules and standards in light of the orientations and goals provided by some 'normative concepts', such as 'sustainable development' and 'precaution'. It is, in

---

[28] L. Kramer, *EC Environmental Law* (London: Sweet and Maxwell, 2003) at 348–69.

other words, precisely *because* international environmental law is based in large part on fragmented treaty law that it also needs a strong unifying basis in customary international law.

Unfortunately, the inherent weakness of customary international law—ever connected to state practice as it is—lies in the very fact that such practice is often incoherent and sparse. Ultimately, the result is that it is frequently difficult to prove convincingly that, at a given point in time, a particular pattern of conduct has acquired normative significance and thus has generated universal international law. It has been suggested by Daniel Bodansky that the debate over the legal status of any given norm may be misplaced.[29] He asserts, in particular, that although many putative norms of customary international environmental law reflect merely verbal practice (in the form of declarations and scholarly writings), rather than the actual behaviour of states, and, therefore, should not be confused with customary international law (with its traditional reliance on state practice), they may nevertheless play a significant role, particularly in setting the terms of the debate, especially in negotiations between states. This scepticism about the customary status of norms such as the precautionary principle may be understandable since state practice is sparse and often inconsistent. This position also rightly reflects the perception of a constant process of law-making that often induces states to compensate through repeated and solemn declarations for the incoherence of their own practice with regard to the actual application of these very rules. In this respect, the expression of '*opinio juris*' tends to become more normatively important than the 'material' element of the customary law-making process (that is, state practice) and even more so in the absence of frequent contributions of international courts and tribunals to the identification of what, among the declared rules, has become positive law. However, this compensatory strategy, by which declaration is substituted for action, falls short of providing the international community with a reliable legislative process, which still needs to be based on normative state practice.

Yet, there are, perhaps, some signs of hope for improvement in the situation. The first sign lies in the multiplication not only of international courts and tribunals, but also of the mechanisms for monitoring compliance. The ICJ has not, thus far, developed a particularly rich case law on international environmental law. It has also demonstrated, whenever presented with the opportunity to do so (in particular, with the *Gabčíkovo-Nagymaros* case) that it remains bound to a very traditional understanding of the concept of 'prejudice' or harm, which is quite evidently inadequate as far as environmental damage is concerned. However, the International Tribunal for the Law of the Sea, the WTO Appellate Body (albeit in a more restricted manner), and, at the regional level, the European Court of Justice, the European Court of Human Rights, and its inter-American equivalent all can be expected to have increasing opportunities to interpret the law in light of customary international law rules and the principles of public international law as applied to the protection of the

---

[29] Bodansky, see note 8 above.

human environment. Along the same lines, the recommendations and findings by compliance committees, which are nowadays established under most multilateral environmental agreements, may contribute to the development of customary law, through their non-confrontational monitoring of states' obedience to international environmental law.

A second element to be taken into consideration, in terms of the further promotion of general rules and principles, is likely to be found in the enhanced social and political pressure exercised upon the unsteady political will of states by the growing network of NGOs working at the international, regional, and local levels. They denounce unsound policies or behaviour that are potentially damaging to the environment in an increasingly effective manner. This kind of pressure has already shown that it can have a positive impact not only on the conduct of states but also, in some cases at least, on that of multinational corporations. It should be noted that both NGOs and multinational corporations traditionally are not considered bound by international customary law. The fact that active members of international civil society very spontaneously invoke general rules such as the 'precautionary principle' illustrates very clearly the role that these type of principles can play in this context. To turn back for a moment to the classical elements of the formation of customary international law, one could even venture to suggest that the *'opinio juris'* to be taken into account in the determination of customary international law is no longer simply that of sovereign states but rather that of all members of the 'international community as a whole'—including some of its non-state actors. Some of these actors, such as certain major and authentically representative NGOs, are among the most conscious components of this community and have, for a certain amount of time now, significantly contributed to the normative debate at the international level, raising the environmental awareness of states and serving as active and vocal members of the international community. Considering that the development of norms is not only a legal phenomenon but also primarily a social one (*ubi societas, ibi ius*), we can reach the conclusion that NGOs, as part of the international community, contribute to shape *opinio juris* together with states.

There is, then, not only a need but also room and hope for the development of general customary international environmental legal norms contributing to a more integrated and efficient international law in the field. Some time still remains in which this law can be developed and effectively applied—some time certainly, however, not much!

Recommended Reading

M. Akehurst, 'Custom as a Source of International Law' (1974–5) 47 Br. Y.B. Int'l L. 1.

J. Cameron and J. Abouchar, 'The Precautionary Principle: A Fundamental Principle of Law and Policy for the Protection of the Global Environment' (1991) 14 B.C. Int'l & Comp. L. Rev. 1.

J. Charney, 'The Persistent Objector Rule and the Development of Customary International Law' (1985) 56 Br. Y.B. Int'l L. 1.

M. Fitzmaurice, 'International Protection of the Environment' (2001) 293 Recueil des cours 105.

D. Freestone and E. Hey, *The Precautionary Principle and International Law* (The Hague: Kluwer Law International, 1995).

A.Ch. Kiss and J.P. Beurier, *Droit international de l'environnement*, 3rd edition (Paris: Editions Pedone, 2004).

M. Mendelson, 'The Formation of Customary International Law' (1998) 272 Recueil des cours 133.

T. Stein, 'The Approach of the Different Drummer: The Principle of the Persistent Objector in International Law' (1985) 26 Harv. Int'l L.J. 457.

P. Szasz, 'International Norm-Making,' in E. Brown Weiss, ed., *Environmental Change and International Law: New Challenges and Dimensions* (Tokyo: United Nations University Press, 1992).

CHAPTER 20

....

TREATY-MAKING
AND TREATY
EVOLUTION

....

THOMAS GEHRING

INTERNATIONAL environmental law develops predominantly through the establishment and evolution of highly dynamic environmental treaty systems. Such treaty systems are issue-specific institutional structures that are purposively established, and maintained, by their member states to govern specific areas of international environmental relations. Typically, they address collective action problems with a strong transnational, in some cases even a global, dimension. Problems of this kind cannot be addressed successfully at the domestic level, either because they have a transboundary component or because relevant countries are exploiting a common pool resource such as migratory fish, or polluting or destroying a common environmental good such as the ozone layer or a regional sea.

Environmental treaty systems are designed to facilitate and speed up the dynamic development of substantive regulations. Frequently, obligations are tightened with growing scientific and technological knowledge about a given problem and the gradual emergence of suitable abatement strategies. Dynamic treaty systems constitute hybrid structures somewhere between traditional international treaties that set forth substantive rules or standards to regulate a given area of common interest, and international organizations established for ongoing communication and decision-making purposes. In addition to substantive obligations, they include institutional components of varying design, which are, compared to multilateral agreements in other policy fields, remarkably strong. Typically, they contain arrangements for the adoption of new obligations, for decision-making on implementation issues, for internalizing scientific and technological information, for the review of implementation, and for the processing of cases of (alleged) non-compliance (see Chapter 38 'Treaty Bodies').

Important environmental treaty systems include:

- the 1971 Convention on Wetlands of International Importance, Especially as Waterfowl Habitat (Ramsar Convention);
- the 1972 Convention on the Prevention of Marine Pollution by Dumping of Wastes and Other Matter (London Convention);
- the 1972 Convention on International Trade in Endangered Species of Wild Flora and Fauna (CITES);
- the 1976 Convention on the Protection of the Mediterranean Sea against Pollution (Barcelona Convention) and its several protocols;
- the 1979 Convention on Long-Range Transboundary Air Pollution (LRTAP Convention) and its eight protocols to date;
- the 1985 Convention for the Protection of the Ozone Layer (Vienna Convention) and the 1987 Montreal Protocol on Substances That Deplete Ozone Layer (Montreal Protocol);
- the 1989 Convention on the Control of Transboundary Movement of Hazardous Wastes (Basel Convention) and the 1999 Protocol on Liability and Compensation;
- the 1992 United Nations Framework Convention on Climate Change (UNFCCC) and the 1998 Kyoto Protocol to the UNFCCC (Kyoto Protocol);

- the 1992 Convention on Biological Diversity (CBD) and the 2000 Cartagena Protocol on Biosafety (Cartagena Protocol); and
- the 1992 Convention on the Protection and Use of Transboundary Watercourses and Lakes.

This chapter examines how the establishment and operation of treaty systems such as these helps to create and develop international environmental law. Section 1 inquires into the emergence of environmental treaty systems and identifies two characteristics of the evolving law-making structure: first, the 'constitutionalization' of treaty systems through the creation of new structures for the making of international environmental law, and, second, the institutional fragmentation of international environmental governance. Section 2 examines the policy-making dimension of environmental treaty systems and identifies three areas of intra-institutional activity relevant to the law-making process: broadening and tightening commitments over time; elaborating upon, and in some cases redefining, existing obligations through an administrative process; and undertaking scientific and technical assessments to reinforce and accelerate normative development. Section 3 explores the output of the law-making process, arguing that different types of law emerge. Whereas regular treaty law is still the most important single output of environmental law-making, it is supplemented by law emerging from simplified amendment procedures and secondary decisions of competent treaty bodies.

1 Normative Development through the Establishment of New Environmental Treaty Systems

1.1 Formation of Environmental Treaty Systems

Deliberate international governance requires arrangements for collective decision-making. Tacitly emerging social norms, whether legally binding or not, can merely reflect, and subsequently stabilize, the existing behaviour of their addressees (see Chapter 19 'Formation of Customary International Law and General Principles'). If social norms are to be used to change an undesirable status quo, they must be molded *prior* to the action that they are intended to guide.[1] States intending to establish governance for an area of international relations must organize themselves, and acquire the ability to decide collectively upon social norms that indicate desired

---

[1] On the difference between spontaneous and negotiated regimes, see O.R. Young, 'Regime Dynamics. The Rise and Fall of International Regimes' (1982) 36 Int'l Org. 277 at 282–3.

behaviour. To understand how international environmental treaty law is made and developed, it is important to note that every deliberately designed international rule is inevitably related to some organizational component. It can emerge from a simple diplomatic conference or from some more complex organizational structure governing an area of international relations (see Chapter 32 'International Institutions').

Environmental treaty systems originate from inter-governmental negotiations. The traditional organizational arrangement for deliberate international governance is the temporarily established diplomatic conference. A diplomatic conference is convened when a group of actors so desires, and dissolved upon the adoption of the final act of the conference to which the treaty is attached. Alternatively, a treaty may be prepared within an existing international organization and adopted by a separately convened diplomatic conference or by a negotiating committee. Occasionally, a treaty is not only elaborated within, but also adopted by a decision of, an international organization. In all cases, the treaty is subsequently opened for signature by states and enters into force upon ratification by the number of states required by the treaty.

Decision-making in treaty-making negotiations on environmental issues, in practice, relies predominantly on the consensus principle. While frequently not even formally defined, consensus may be conceived of as the 'absence of any objection by a representative and submitted by him as constituting an obstacle to the taking of the decision in question.'[2] Conceptually, it is located somewhere between unanimity and majority voting. Like the former, it preserves the right of all parties to reject an undesired decision, but, like the latter, it does not require a positive vote by all parties. Whereas decisive actors can pursue their interests, indifference is treated as agreement. Hence, consensus decision-making requires active intervention in the negotiation process *before* the final decision is adopted.[3] What is more, decisions are not made by casting votes, but are *developed* through the gradual removal of objections against particular aspects of a draft treaty (often indicated by the bracketing of text). Settlements that are achieved are difficult to challenge later in the process because indifferent actors will tend to have accommodated themselves with the result so that support grows.

Before a negotiation process can start, pre-decisions have to be made about the relevant group of participating actors and the range of issues to be discussed. The problems of international relations are not simply 'given', but are, at least to some degree, 'socially constructed'. Accordingly, the subject of the negotiations and the emerging issue-area of the future environmental treaty system can, to some degree, be deliberately designed. Usually, the process will start with concern by interested

---

[2] Quoted from J. Sizoo and R.T. Jurjens, *CSCE-Decision-Making: The Madrid Experience* (The Hague: Martinus Nijhoff, 1984) at 57.

[3] On the implications of consensus decision-making, see B. Buzan, 'Negotiating by Consensus: Developments in Technique at the United Nations Conference at the Law of the Sea' (1981) 75 A.J.I.L. 324 at 324–47.

actors about some undesirable development, which they believe can be remedied by international cooperation. For example, during the 1980s an epistemic community of atmospheric scientists succeeded in bringing the problem of global climate change onto the international agenda (see Chapter 14 'Atmosphere and Outer Space'). In defining the problem as a subject of international negotiations, numerous questions then had to be addressed. Should the climate regime address adaptation as well as mitigation? Should it aim at binding national targets and timetables to reduce green-house gas emissions or at the development of specific policies and measures? Should it focus on all greenhouse gases or just carbon dioxide? Should it treat climate change as a task mainly for cooperation among industrialized countries or as a mat-ter of global concern? Should it be considered as just another aspect of the overall problem of protecting the global atmosphere or as a separate subject of international relations?

The delimitation of issues and actors has an immediate effect on the constellation of interests upon which substantive compromise will eventually be founded.[4] Negotiation theory demonstrates that adding or subtracting issues and parties changes opportunities for actors to pursue their interests. Since no round of inter-national negotiations, however broadly designed, can tackle all problems between all states, numerous pending issues are excluded from a negotiation. Actors may favour different delimitations of the emerging issue-area because they cannot successfully pursue interests related to excluded issues. They can expect concessions only from those actors participating in the negotiation round. Generally, an issue area must be sufficiently broad to allow for cooperation gains of all relevant parties, but it does not have to include all substantively related issues. Likewise, the group of participating actors must be sufficiently large to allow meaningful cooperation and will usually have to include the major players in the field, but it does not have to be all-inclusive. Even global problems might be successfully tackled, at least temporarily, by a comparatively small group of actors. Despite the global nature of the problem, the Montreal Protocol was adopted at a conference attended by 58 states and the European Community, and it was immediately signed by only 25 states and the European Community—including, however, most major polluters.

The initiation of a new environmental treaty system within the framework of an existing international organization, rather than through a separately established diplomatic conference, can considerably lower the organizational costs of an inter-governmental negotiation process. These costs increase dramatically with the num-ber of states involved. They include the preparation of documents in, and the translation of discussions into, usually several conference languages as well as the procedural organization of the conference process. Existing organizations provide room for the occasionally lengthy pre-negotiation of the precise terms of references

[4] J.K. Sebenius, 'Designing Negotiations toward a New Regime: The Case of Global Warming' (1991) 15 Int'l Security 110 at 110–48.

of the newly established negotiation process, and will thus legitimize an initiative if a mandate is agreed upon according to established procedures. In the absence of a suitable organizational framework, one or more interested states not only have to take the political initiative, they must also be prepared to organize and invite an intergovernmental conference and provide servicing functions.

The clearly defined memberships of established international organizations, and their specific agendas and organizational cultures, open opportunities for forum shopping and may lead to lengthy struggles over the choice of the appropriate forum. The most pertinent example of forum shopping is the decade-long struggle of the Nordic countries to put the issue of long-range transboundary air pollution on the international agenda. Originating in the 1960s as a bilateral issue between these countries and the United Kingdom, transboundary air pollution was introduced first into the Council of Europe, then into the Organisation for Economic Cooperation and Development (OECD), and finally into the Conference on Security and Cooperation in Europe and the UN Economic Commission for Europe (UNECE). Only the latter pan-European context, with its close linkage to the highly political issues of East-West relations as well as the involvement of the United States and Canada, provided the foundation for the adoption of the LRTAP Convention in 1979. In other cases, countries with diverging interests struggle over the appropriate forum. Hence, negotiations on the UNFCCC were launched by the UN General Assembly rather than by the UN Environment Programme (UNEP) because developing countries advocated a close link between the issues of environmental protection and economic development. And the regulation of trade restrictions for genetically modified organisms was disputed between the World Trade Organization (WTO), with its Agreement on Sanitary and Phytosanitary Measures, and the CBD with its Cartagena Protocol.[5]

Most global and larger regional environmental treaty systems have been established within the framework of an existing international organization or similar international structure. Most important has been UNEP, which is not a formally independent international organization, but a programme under the auspices of the UN General Assembly. UNEP has been the catalyst for such important environmental treaty systems as the Vienna Convention and its Montreal Protocol, the Basel Convention, the CBD, and several regional seas conventions protecting, *inter alia*, the Mediterranean and the Red Sea. As already mentioned, the UNFCCC negotiations were initiated by the UN General Assembly. Two important global conventions of the early 1970s, namely CITES and the London Convention, were negotiated as part of the broader process associated with the 1972 United Nations Conference on the Human Environment, which was organized by the United Nations and also led to the

---

[5] See S. Oberthür and T. Gehring, 'Institutional Interaction in Global Environmental Governance: The Case of the Cartagena Protocol and the World Trade Organization' (2006) 6 Global Envt'l Pol. 1.

creation of UNEP. Other treaty systems originated from more specialized organizations. The International Maritime Organization (IMO) provided the institutional
framework for several conventions on marine pollution from ships, including
accidental oil spills. And the UNECE assisted in the establishment of the 1979 LRTAP
Convention and the Convention on the Protection and Use of Transboundary
Watercourses and Lakes. Only a few modern environmental treaty systems were
established without the assistance of an existing institutional structure. This has been
the case especially for sub-regional cooperative projects with a limited membership,
for which no appropriate multi-purpose organization exists, such as the Convention
for the Protection of the River Rhine, the Convention for the Prevention of Marine
Pollution by Dumping from Ships and Aircraft (Oslo Convention), the Convention
for the Prevention of Marine Pollution from Land-Based Sources (Paris Convention),
and the Convention on the Protection of the Marine Environment of the Baltic Sea
Area (Baltic Sea Convention).

1.2 Two Characteristics of International Environmental Law-Making: Constutionalization of Environmental Treaty Systems and Institutional Fragmentation

1.2.1 *Constitutionalization*

An important characteristic of international environmental governance is the gradual constitutionalization of environmental treaty systems. Almost all modern environmental treaty systems create their own institutional apparatuses (see Chapter 38
'Treaty Bodies'). A few treaty systems, such as the Baltic Sea Convention and the
Oslo and Paris Conventions, establish fully independent small-scale international
organizations, while some others draw entirely upon the decision-making bodies
and secretariat of their parent organization (for example, the marine conventions
administered by the IMO). Most environmental treaty systems lie somewhere in
between, retaining a relationship to their parent organization but having their own
identity as well. Typically, a conference of the parties in which all member states are
represented constitutes the supreme decision-making body. Many environmental
treaty systems establish a secretariat that is financed by the member states and
supervised by the conference of the parties, while being hosted by the parent
organization. This arrangement can be attributed to the fact that many of the
important treaty systems of the 1970s and 1980s emerged either from loose institutional settings such as the UN Conference on the Human Environment or from
UNEP with its restricted budget. Thus, the Ramsar Convention and CITES were
facilitated until the mid-1970s by UNEP, but members were then asked to provide
their own funding. Later treaty systems such as the Vienna Convention and its

Montreal Protocol, the Basel Convention, as well as several regional seas conventions, from the beginning provided for their own administrative budgets and secretariat functions, while being attached to UNEP to avoid the creation of numerous fully independent mini-organizations.

The establishment of a permanent decision-making apparatus as a part of a modern environmental treaty system has been a consequence of negative experience with the more static arrangements of some early multilateral environmental agreements, especially in the area of the protection of nature and wildlife. It is widely seen as a major drawback that 'sleeping treaties',[6] such as the 1940 Convention on Nature Protection and Preservation in the Western Hemisphere, and the 1968 African Convention on the Conservation of Nature and Natural Resources, did not create their own institutional components, including appropriate arrangements for flexible amendment and administration. A decision-making arrangement with a mere temporary existence such as a diplomatic conference or a preparatory committee is generally not particularly well-suited for international environmental governance because substantive treaty law must then be designed so as to regulate a subject matter so comprehensively that further decisions are dispensable. In institutional economics, such an arrangement is called a 'complete contract'—in contrast to an 'incomplete contract' that deliberately leaves certain matters to subsequent decision-making.[7] Although it does not exclude amendments negotiated at further diplomatic conferences or within newly established preparatory committees (see section 3.1), the flexibility of a treaty system is thereby sharply limited.

Institutional flexibility is needed because transnational environmental problems develop dynamically, and constitute a highly unstable subject matter for regulation. They are created, and solved, by human economic activity, which depends on such factors as economic growth, technological development and changing preferences. Early attempts to regulate an environmental problem are frequently initiated under conditions of scientific uncertainty. Even highly complex substantive rules cannot be designed to account for all possible future developments within the regulated issue area. Moreover, in the absence of a permanent institutional apparatus, international treaties do not provide for arrangements for collective implementation review and conflict management. Since successful environmental governance frequently requires costly investments by states and their subjects, it regularly creates incentives for free riding and may even over-stretch the capacities of member states for action.[8]

As a consequence of their organizational arrangements, modern environmental treaty systems become themselves machineries for the making and development of international environmental law. Despite the frequent retention of links to an

---

[6] S. Lyster, *International Wildlife Law: An Analysis of International Treaties Concerned with the Conservation of Wildlife* (Cambridge: Grotius Publications, 1985) at 124.

[7] See O.E. Williamson, *The Economic Institutions of Capitalism* (New York: Free Press, 1987) at 178.

[8] A. Chayes and A. Handler Chayes, *The New Sovereignty: Compliance with International Regulatory Agreements* (Cambridge, MA: Harvard University Press, 1998).

existing international organization, many treaty systems have become virtual organizations for the management of substantive international treaties. Even if a treaty system draws upon an existing organization, this organization derives its decision-making competence from the respective treaty system. Once established, the member states may introduce specialized decision procedures that may deviate considerably from the original negotiation situation and involve scientists, experts, and non-governmental organizations. By delegating certain powers to the new entity, member states 'constitutionalize' governance within a given area of international relations.

1.2.2 *Fragmentation*

The second characteristic of international environmental governance is its institutional fragmentation. International environmental law encompasses more than 200 separately established environmental treaty systems. In contrast, the institutional landscape is much less fragmented in other problem areas such as international trade. The absence of a single international environmental organization may be attributed to the fact that most large-scale international organizations were established around the end of the Second World War, whereas international environmental affairs as a specific area of international governance developed mainly after 1970.

Although the lack of an overarching institution is frequently deplored and has led to demands for the establishment of a World Environment Organization, institutional fragmentation arguably reflects a strength, rather than a weakness, of international environmental governance. There may simply be no real need for a single comprehensive organization because many environmental problems are best tackled separately from others. It is difficult to see how lumping together several separately institutionalized treaty systems could significantly increase the opportunities for cooperation. Interests in such large issue-areas as international trade or law of the sea are often asymmetrically distributed, so that actors seek advantages on one issue while giving concessions on another. In contrast, interests regarding major environmental problems are frequently symmetrically distributed so that all actors must adopt similar measures (reduce pollution) to enjoy similar benefits from the preservation of a global or regional common (for example, the protection of the global climate, the ozone layer, or a regional sea). Linking such issues would primarily enhance the complexity of negotiations rather than create new opportunities for cooperation. Under these circumstances, the absence of a single international environmental organization allows states to design institutional arrangements tailor-made to the specific needs of a particular cooperation project.

The far-reaching institutional fragmentation of international environmental governance leads to increasing interaction between different treaty systems. Institutional interaction occurs in very different forms.[9] It may create synergy

[9] S. Oberthür and T. Gehring, eds., *Institutional Interaction in Global Environmental Governance: Synergy and Conflict among International and EU Policies* (Cambridge, MA: MIT Press, 2006).

between the institutions involved or disrupt the governance effort. On the one hand, the normative development within one institution can influence the normative development within another system. This will be true if a regional treaty system (for instance, the Oslo Convention) influences normative development in a similarly focused global system (for example, the London Convention); or if institutional innovations invented within one treaty system, such as non-compliance procedures or simplified amendment procedures, are adopted by others; or if states establish a separate institution (for example, the International North Sea Ministerial Conferences) in order to influence an existing treaty system (for instance, the Oslo Convention). On the other hand, one treaty system can influence the behaviour of states and non-state actors relevant to the implementation of another treaty system. This would be the case to the degree that incentives created under the UNFCCC and its Kyoto Protocol to plant fast-growing trees as sinks of carbon dioxide discourage the preservation and expansion of species-rich traditional forests and thereby hamper the implementation of the CBD.[10]

2 POLICY-MAKING DIMENSION OF ENVIRONMENTAL TREATY SYSTEMS

Many environmental treaty systems rely on an explicit step-by-step approach that does not aim at the comprehensive solution of a larger problem at once, but at the rapid conclusion of a set of initial instruments and the establishment of a policy-making process directed at preparing further instruments. The regulatory approach of environmental treaty systems differs significantly from that pursued in other policy fields. Instruments tend to codify realistic targets, accompanied by the expectation of sincere implementation and the opportunity to tighten obligations, if possible. With a view towards possible revision, they include provisions for the regular review of substantive obligations and for possible decisions on additional measures in light of new scientific, economic, and technological information. This approach contrasts starkly with human rights conventions, which tend to codify comprehensive catalogues of obligations and create enormous implementation deficits. And negotiations of the UN Conference on the Law of the Sea illustrated that an overall approach linking numerous separate issues to a package of overwhelming size and complexity might lead to cumbersome and time-consuming negotiations, with a significant risk of failure.

---

[10] See C.P. Pontecorvo, 'Interdependence between Global Environmental Regimes: The Kyoto Protocol on Climate Change and Forest Protection' (1999) 59 Zeitschrift für ausländisches öffentliches Recht und Völkerrecht 709 at 709–49.

The permanent law-making process not only blurs the distinction between the making and the implementation of law because later and more specific rules and decisions refine and reinterpret earlier and more general rules. It also opens the opportunity for feedback processes, through which a treaty system can adjust policy measures to the effects of its own governance activities, so as to increase its own effectiveness.[11]

2.1 Development of International Environmental Law through Political Decision-Making within Treaty Systems

The substantive obligations of almost all important treaty systems have significantly changed over time. The Montreal Protocol, which was adopted in 1987, has been amended in 1990, 1992, 1997, and 1999 in order to gradually tighten the reduction schedules for ozone-depleting substances, to extend its regulatory measures to new substances, and to introduce new supporting measures, most important of which is the introduction of a multi-million dollar multilateral fund for the financial support of developing countries. Likewise, the LRTAP Convention has adopted a whole series of protocols that have gradually expanded the scope of the regime from the control of a single pollutant, namely sulphur dioxide, to virtually all important air pollutants. The regulatory approach of the Basel Convention has been transformed from a licensing system for the international trade of hazardous wastes based upon prior informed consent into an almost total ban of exports from OECD countries to non-OECD countries. Regulation under the London Convention has been expanded to cover sources of marine pollution such as the incineration of wastes at sea and to phase out the dumping of industrial and radioactive wastes. And CITES regularly applies its trade-restricting measures to newly endangered species of flora and fauna and has also developed new regulatory approaches, such as quota systems, which are not envisaged within the treaty itself.[12]

Originally, flexibility was achieved through the split between the general obligations in the main body of a treaty and more specific rules set forth in an allegedly technical annex, which was frequently subject to a simplified amendment procedure. The 1946 International Convention for the Regulation of Whaling (Whaling Convention) was one of the first treaties to take this approach, setting forth detailed regulations in a schedule that can be amended by qualified majority vote. Similarly, CITES and the London Convention set forth their core obligations in their main

---

[11] See T. Gehring, *Dynamic International Regimes: Institutions for International Environmental Governance* (Frankfurt: Peter Lang, 1994) at 443–8.

[12] See P.H. Sand, 'Commodity or Taboo? The Regulation of Trade in Endangered Species' (1997) 6 Green Globe Y.B. 19 at 21–4.

body, while their annexes specify protected species of flora and fauna and regulated types of ocean dumping respectively. The International Convention for the Prevention of Pollution from Ships (MARPOL Convention), which was adopted in 1973/78, elaborated this model by including both mandatory and voluntary annexes.

More recently, the adoption of protocols subsidiary to existing conventions has become the most important method for the development of treaty law. The convention-protocol approach has been specifically developed to support the step-by-step approach of environmental governance. The Barcelona Convention—the first and most important project within UNEP's regional seas programme—was deliberately designed as an umbrella treaty, whose ratification was conditional upon the simultaneous acceptance of two substantive protocols, while other protocols are voluntary. So far, five protocols have entered into force and two more have been adopted. Under the 1979 LRTAP Convention, eight protocols have entered into force. These two treaty systems have developed the greatest virtuosity in employing the convention—protocol arrangement to deepen and broaden their respective regulatory approaches. The ability to agree on new sets of obligations has regularly led to the adoption of new instruments. Likewise, the Montreal Protocol, the Kyoto Protocol, and the Cartagena Protocol have supplemented the Vienna Convention, the UNFCCC, and the CBD respectively.

The convention-protocol approach increasingly reverses the original relationship between the substantive and the institutional components of a treaty system. In earlier treaties, such as the previously mentioned London Convention and CITES, the procedural machinery and auxiliary rules concerning negotiation, information, and reporting were included in conventions subsequent to agreement on substantive obligations in order to ensure that the obligations were implemented and developed. More recently, the adoption of framework conventions in the absence of substantive obligations has become a vehicle for the development of substantive obligations and their acceptance. Whereas ratification of the Barcelona Convention was still conditional upon the simultaneous acceptance of two substantive protocols, the adoption of the LRTAP Convention reflected continued disagreement among the member states about meaningful commitments to reduce the emission of key air pollutants. The parties merely agreed to establish a separate process and the necessary institutional machinery for the making of international environmental law regulating long-range transboundary air pollution as well as duties to cooperate, to report, and to provide information. Likewise, the Vienna Convention merely established the institutional machinery of the treaty system and some auxiliary obligations, because the participating states, in 1985, could not agree on hard obligations to reduce emissions of ozone-depleting substances. During negotiation of the UNFCCC in 1992, disagreement once again prevented the adoption of a clause that would have committed the parties to stabilizing their carbon dioxide emissions, so that this instrument also lacks hard substantive obligations.

By concluding a framework convention as a first step of an evolutionary regulatory process, states deliberately modify the subsequent negotiation situation in a number of ways. On the one hand, bargaining will be more institutionalized than before. The convention establishes the negotiation situation for the subsequent deliberations on substantive obligations. It defines the problem to be addressed in general terms, and it delimits the group of actors that are entitled to participate in the ensuing negotiations. Since the convention establishes the basic principles, institutions, and decision-making mechanisms, later protocols might be very concise, depending on the complexity of their regulatory approach. On the other hand, agreement on, and entry into force of, a framework convention generates permanent pressure on reluctant member states to reconsider their positions. Hence, the UNFCCC requires governments to develop greenhouse gas inventories, to formulate national strategies and measures, and to cooperate in scientific research on the problem. Due to the ongoing policy process, governments are continuously confronted with demands by other states and, increasingly, by domestic stakeholders to cooperate, and they are routinely forced to face new, or collectively evaluated, scientific insights. Such pressure appears to be more easily organized within a well-established institutional structure than, say, in the framework of a multi-purpose international organization or a separately gathered diplomatic conference.[13]

Since framework conventions, being full-fledged international treaties, require time-consuming domestic ratification, member states tend to start the permanent process of negotiating new environmental law even before the convention has formally entered into force. Such 'interim mechanisms' emphasize the importance of the process component, focusing on the development of future law, as compared to the mere implementation of the substance already agreed upon.

2.2 Development of International Environmental Law through Administrative Decision-Making within Treaty Systems

The development of international environmental law is also driven by permanent decision-making activities beyond the occasional adoption or regular amendment of treaties. Although these activities are usually considered as management or implementation of treaty provisions, they have important implications for the development of international environmental law and its effectiveness. Moreover, since such 'administrative' decision-making may be governed by more complex decision-making procedures, it can affect the process of law-making and, arguably, also the

---

[13] For criticisms of the idea that treaty systems start with non-substantive obligations and evolve over time, see G.W. Downs, K.W. Danish, and Peter N. Barsoom, 'The Transformational Model of International Regime Design: Triumph of Hope or Experience?' (2000) 38 Colum. J. Transnat'l L. 465 at 465–514; and L.E. Susskind, *Environmental Diplomacy: Negotiating More Effective Global Agreements* (New York: Oxford University Press, 1994) at 30–7 (arguing that the convention-protocol approach is 'fundamentally flawed' and attributing many general complications of treaty systems to this approach).

content of the resulting decisions. Virtually all modern environmental treaty systems provide the institutional framework for the adoption of administrative decisions of various kinds for the filling of gaps in the treaty law or for its formal or informal adjustment to changed circumstances (see Chapter 4 'Global Environmental Governance as Administration').

Regular administrative decision-making permanently renews normative expectations and bridges unexpected gaps of treaty law so as to avoid doubt about common obligations and preclude their unilateral interpretation. Such decisions reassure the members of the treaty system of the normative expectations held by the entire community of member states about their behaviour. They shape and re-shape normative agreement and reestablish the commitment entered into previously. For example, at the request of the Soviet Union, the Montreal Protocol had permitted, under certain circumstances, an increase in the production of ozone-depleting substances beyond 1986 levels. The Meeting of the Parties (MOP) 'decided' by consensus that such a production increase may not be used for export to non-parties of the protocol.[14] Similarly, the executive body of the LRTAP Convention bridged a gap in the first sulphur dioxide protocol by way of interpretation. While parties were committed to reduce their sulphur dioxide emissions by at least 30 per cent by 1993, the protocol did not address the period after 1993. Therefore, the executive body 'noted a common understanding among the Parties'[15] that an increase in such emissions after 1993 would be inconsistent with the protocol.

Administrative decision-making is also employed to relieve treaty-making negotiations from numerous tasks that could in principle also have been dealt with at the outset. It constitutes a means to accelerate the conclusion of a negotiation and to postpone the settlement of pending conflicts. The Montreal Protocol (Article 8) and its London Amendment (Article 10.1) assigned the task of adopting a non-compliance procedure and an indicative list of incremental costs to be financed by the financial mechanism to the MOP of the Montreal Protocol.[16] The Kyoto Protocol explicitly assigns a whole range of tasks to the MOP, including the elaboration of rules regarding emissions trading, the clean development mechanism, and the crediting of sink activities. These decisions were provisionally adopted in 2001 by the Conference of the Parties (COP) of the convention in the form the 'Marrakesh Accords' and were formally adopted by the first MOP of the Kyoto Protocol in 2005.

Likewise, administrative decision-making is occasionally employed to rapidly develop an environmental treaty system though the adoption of decisions that are not expressly provided for in the respective treaties. The MOP of the Montreal Protocol established in 1990 an interim multilateral fund by a simple 'decision'

---

[14] Decision I.12G, *Report of the Parties to the Montreal Protocol on the Work of Their First Meeting*, Doc. UNEP/OzL.Pro.1/5 (6 May 1989).

[15] See *Report of the Seventh Session of the Executive Body*, Doc. ECE/EB.AIR/20 (1989) at para. 22.

[16] Adopted by Decisions IV/18 and IV/5, *Report of the Fourth Meeting of the Parties to the Montreal Protocol on Substances that Deplete the Ozone Layer*, Doc. UNEP/OzL.Pro.4/15 (25 November 1992).

without a specific competence. The decision, adopted by consensus, was part of a broader agreement that paved the way for the accession of important developing countries.[17] Without a specific competence, the COP of CITES has, over time, adopted various law-making decisions, which are apparently intended to, and seem to be regarded as, formally committing the member states. The regulatory approach of the Basel Convention was first thoroughly changed by a decision of the COP of the Basel Convention that replaced the original system of prior informed consent by a ban of exports of hazardous wastes from OECD countries to non-OECD countries.[18]

Finally, administrative decision-making may create soft law instruments, if the adoption of hard law proves to be impossible. When support by the member states increases, their content may be transferred into hard law later on. Especially under the London Convention, legally binding obligations have repeatedly been preceded by recommendations. Hence, a recommendation of 1983 to prohibit the dumping of radioactive waste only became formal treaty law in 1993. Likewise, the amendments to the convention to phase out the incineration of wastes at sea and the disposal of industrial wastes at sea had been prepared by soft law instruments. Under the Montreal Protocol, the comparatively weak original control measures were first tightened by the Helsinki Resolution of 1989, before the new obligations became part of the first amendment adopted in 1990.

The increasing relevance of such administrative decision-making has changed the nature of environmental treaty systems and the process of environmental law-making. There is an implicit trade-off between the complexity of substantive regulation in the original treaty and the relevance of secondary law-making. The more detailed the substantive regulations of the treaty are, the less room exists for subsequent decision-making that might generate momentum of its own and the more traditional the legal development of the treaty system will be—and vice versa. The less elaborate the substantive treaty rules are and the more actors resort to postponing decisions to later stages of the governance process, the more important the institutional component of the arrangement will be from which such later decisions emerge and the more flexibly will the environmental law governing the issue area in question develop. Hence, the two levels of law-making become—to some degree—functional equivalents—that is, actors can increasingly choose the level at which they will deal with a given problem.

---

[17] In order to establish the fund on a permanent basis, however, the parties did not rely merely on a MOP decision, but rather did so by means of the London Amendment, which has in the meantime entered into force. See H. Ott, 'The Montreal Protocol: A Small Step for the Protection of the Ozone Layer, a Big Step for International Law and Relations' (1991) 24 Verfassung und Recht in Übersee 188. The size of the fund was US $160–240 million for a three-year period.

[18] However, the legal force of this decision was disputed by some member states. Therefore, the COP adopted at a later session an amendment to the convention, which is not yet in force. See Decision II/12, *Report of the Second Meeting of the Conference of the Parties to the Basel Convention on the Control of Transboundary Movements of Hazardous Wastes and Their Disposal*, Doc. UNEP/CHW.2/30 (25 March 1994); and Decision III/1, *Decisions Adopted by the Third Meeting of the Conference of the Parties to the Basel Convention*, Doc. UNEP/CHW.3/35 (28 November 1995).

Administrative decision-making does not necessarily have to involve all parties to a treaty system. It may also rely upon true delegation of decision-making competencies to committees or more complex decision-making arrangements. Decisions to classify endangered species of flora and fauna under CITES are guided by extensive criteria, and pass through a multi-tier procedure that assigns an important role to the Secretariat. The member states of the Montreal Protocol went a step further, and assigned decisions on funding to an Executive Board comprised of a limited number of developing and developed countries. Funds are allocated according to an indicative list of incremental costs, so that decisions are based on comparatively well-defined criteria.[19] Probably the most impressive administrative apparatus is currently established under the Kyoto Protocol for the approval, management, and control of projects under the clean development mechanism, which allows developed countries to obtain certified emission reduction credits from projects located within developing countries. This system of administrative decision-making is accountable to the MOP and operates under its general supervision and guidance.[20] However, it is designed so as to preclude immediate intervention of the political body into case-specific decision-making.

Arrangements involving true delegation are usually designed to remove certain decisions from intergovernmental bargaining and to ensure rule-based decision-making. They are well known from (semi-) independent regulatory agencies within the European Union and domestic political systems. Acceptance of resulting decisions does not rely on the consent of all parties to their precise content, but rather on the legitimacy of the procedural arrangement and the expectation that decisions can be justified by convincing arguments (see Chapter 30 'Legitimacy'). In essence, these procedures are designed to transform power-based bargaining into reason-based arguing. They rely on a division of two decision-making functions. First, general decision criteria and procedures for case-specific decision-making are elaborated. At this stage, stake-holders are at least partially hindered from acting according to their case-specific interests because any rules and procedures that they elaborate will apply to numerous different and possibly still unknown cases—thus creating a partial Rawlsian 'veil of ignorance'.[21] Under these conditions actors will tend to promote well-operating procedures and fair—that is, non-discriminating—substantive

---

[19] F. Biermann, 'Financing Environmental Politics in the South: Experiences from the Multilateral Ozone Fund' (1997) 9 Int'l Envt'l Affairs 179.

[20] See *Modalities and Procedures for a Clean Development Mechanism, as defined in Article 12 of the Kyoto Protocol*, Decision 17/CP. 7, *Report of the Conference of the Parties on Its Seventh Session, Marrakesh, 29 October-10 November 2001: Addendum: Part Two: Action Taken by the Conference of the Parties*, Volume II., Doc. FCCC/CP/2001/13/Add.2 (21 January 2002); and *Guidance to the Executive Board of the Clean Development Mechanism*, Decision 21/CP. 8, *Report of the Conference of the Parties on Its Eighth Session, New Delhi, 23 October-1 November 2002: Addendum 3. Part Two: Action Taken by the Conference of the Parties at Its Eighth Session*, Doc. FCCC/CP/2002/7/Add.3.

[21] J. Rawls, *A Theory of Justice*, 12th edition (Cambridge, MA: Harvard University Press, 1980) at 136–42.

criteria. Subsequently, the room for discretion, in which interest-based bargaining and political maneuver might ensue, will be limited so that rule-based arguments about the most appropriate option can dominate case-specific decisions.

2.3 Technical and Scientific Expertise as a Means to Accelerate and Rationalize the Development of International Environmental Law

As the development of international environmental law depends heavily on the proper scientific understanding of environmental problems, and the availability of technical solutions, all modern environmental treaty systems are designed to actively shape, in one form or another, widely accepted cognitive expectations on the scientific or technological background of political action (see Chapter 9 'Science and Technology'). In most cases, the scientific and technological assessment apparatus of environmental treaty systems do not conduct primary research. Predominantly, they evaluate available information and produce a body of knowledge that is commonly agreed within the treaty system and, thus, is more accepted than information fed into the process by any actor because it has been scrutinized by multinational teams of experts. Perhaps the most impressive example is the European Monitoring and Evaluation Programme (EMEP) of the LRTAP Convention. It was originally established to assess the import-export budgets of certain air pollutants, beginning with sulphur dioxide, for all European member states but was later employed to allocate emission targets to the member countries.[22] Similarly, under the Vienna Convention, existing information on the atmospheric chemistry of ozone depletion and the nature of ozone-depleting substances and their substitutes is regularly assessed. Likewise, the ground for the regulation of climate change was prepared by the Intergovernmental Panel on Climate Change, which continues to serve as the informal scientific and technological branch of the climate change negotiations, despite the lack of a formal relationship to the UNFCCC.

The organized assessment of the scientific and technological aspects of an environmental problem accelerates law-making because it allows the institutionalized policy-making process to start before the nature of an environmental problem, and the interests of possible contracting parties, have become clear. In general, political decision-makers will not agree on costly obligations to protect the environment, and abate pollution, until they have reliable information about the importance of a given problem. Scientific and technological assessments can help provide the prerequisites for the political acceptance of meaningful substantive obligations. Research activities

---

[22] R.R. Churchill, G. Küttig, and L.M. Warren, 'The 1994 UNECE Sulphur Protocol' (1995), 7 J. Envt'l L. 169 at 182–6.

on long-range transboundary air pollution started long before it had become clear from where the deposits of air pollutants in a given country originated, and to where the emissions were exported. Likewise, the regulation of ozone-depleting substances was preceded by the Co-ordinating Committee on the Ozone Layer, a scientific and technological structure within the framework of UNEP that assessed existing information on the atmospheric chemistry of ozone depletion, and the nature of ozone-depleting substances and their substitutes.

The assessment of environmental problems and their solutions affects the nature of international environmental law-making because it assigns an important role within the law-making process to experts, including those from non-governmental organizations and industry. 'Epistemic communities' that evolve around environmental treaty systems, frequently include both governmental and non-governmental experts (see Chapter 34 'Epistemic Communities'). Within the LRTAP Convention, EMEP was closely supervised by governmental experts, whereas the regional air pollution information and simulation model on which later regulatory approaches were based was elaborated by non-governmental scientists of the International Institute of Applied Systems Analysis in Laxenburg, Austria. During the contentious early negotiations on the Montreal Protocol, a technological assessment panel was established to bring together experts from different branches of industry, in particular, the users of ozone-depleting substances and the producers of substitutes, in order to generate common knowledge on the uses for which marketable substitutes existed. Likewise, experts from diverse nature protection NGOs are heavily involved in the assessment of endangered species within the framework of CITES.

Successful scientific and technological assessment separates two distinct functions from each other, namely the shaping of cognitive expectations on scientific and technological matters and the (subsequent) shaping of political consensus among the contracting parties. The assessment of scientific or technological knowledge is not designed to make, or replace, binding decisions, but to prepare them. If successful, such assessments produce common expectations about the relevance of the respective environmental problem and the availability of technical solutions. Whereas political decisions are founded upon interests in terms of costs and benefits, scientific and technological assessments generate reliable knowledge that helps shape preferences.

The informal power of scientific and technological assessment processes originates from the fact that convincing information is difficult for policymakers to ignore. Information that has been validated within the treaty system acquires the status of accepted evidence about the significance of an environmental problem, the particular role of a given country or the availability of certain solutions to an environmental problem. Hence, even actors intending exclusively to maximize their own utility might be inclined to change their preferences if they learn about additional implications of an environmental problem. Moreover, it becomes more difficult for a reluctant country to pursue the strategy of rejecting stringent pollution abatement measures, if a common assessment based upon an accepted methodology has proven the country to be an exporter of pollutants to neighbouring states. And a defensive strategy rejecting measures to protect the ozone layer cannot be justified by the lack of suitable substitutes for ozone-depleting substances, once the collective assessment process has revealed that such substitutes exist. In essence, the assessment of scientific and technological knowledge forces negotiators either to openly pursue parochial interests or to agree to the scientifically necessary and the technologically possible.

To the extent that scientific and technological assessment gains influence, it helps 'rationalize' the law-making process. Environmental law-making is not entirely determined by inter-governmental bargaining any more. Part of the process is withdrawn from the immediate grip of parochial state interests and submitted to expert reasoning, which tends to be based on the exchange of convincing arguments rather than bargaining power. This does not mean that ensuing substantive obligations lack political consent by the contracting parties. Rather, states are dragged into a collective learning process from which it is difficult to escape, leading state preferences to be adjusted accordingly.

3 RESULTING LEGAL STRUCTURE OF ENVIRONMENTAL TREATY SYSTEMS

The dynamic regulatory approach of environmental treaty systems has immediate implications for the evolution of international environmental law. Its development is subject to two contradictory principles. On the one hand, international treaty law cannot bind states without their consent, if only because such rules would be difficult to enforce in the absence of a well-organized enforcement power. On the other hand, this principle of state consent does not preclude states from deliberately or implicitly assigning certain decision-making competencies to international institutions to expedite collective decision-making, and the entry into force of new obligations, in order to cope with newly arising environmental problems and to exploit new political and technological opportunities for environmental protection. Accordingly, international environmental law evolves both in the traditional manner, through the adoption and revision of treaty law, and in other ways, through various forms of decisions adopted within a treaty system. As a result, the whole package of obligations entered into by states is no longer entirely reflected in treaties.

3.1 Normative Development through Traditional Forms of International Law

In spite of the required flexibility of environmental governance and the rapid evolution of substantive commitments, treaties still constitute the dominant form for the development of specific international environmental law. Soft law is relevant primarily as an intermediate step on the way to binding forms of agreement or as an additional instrument within established treaty systems, but rarely as a substitute for them. States also prefer to codify even the auxiliary and procedural obligations of important framework conventions—for example, the LRTAP Convention, the Vienna Convention, and the UNFCCC—in the form of full-fledged international treaties, although these instruments lack important substantive obligations. To add substantive obligations, they resort increasingly to the adoption of protocols, which formally constitute treaties subsidiary to the respective conventions and are open for ratification or accession only to members of these conventions.

Whereas the adaptation of the primary law of environmental treaty systems to new requirements occurs generally according to the established procedures for the amendment of international treaties, environmental treaty systems increasingly internalize the necessary institutional functions. Initially, the development of treaty law both in the form of amendments of existing treaties and the adoption of protocols was assigned to diplomatic conferences convened outside the organizational apparatus of a treaty system. This is still formally true for the Barcelona Convention and the LRTAP Convention.[23] Later treaty systems such as the Vienna Convention, Basel Convention, CBD, and UNFCCC assign the task of preparing and adopting amendments and protocols to their respective COPs.[24] Upon entry into force of an amendment in 1987, the COP of the Ramsar Convention became formally involved in treaty amendments.[25] Normally, an amendment or a new protocol must be decided upon by a certain majority of members of the treaty, frequently a two-thirds or a three-fourths majority, and they do not enter into force until ratified by a specified number of parties and only for those parties that have ratified.

Regular amendments are rarely employed to develop key substantive obligations. More frequently, treaties are amended to modify governance arrangements, such as establishing the COP of the Ramsar Convention and introducing a procedure for the amendment of the instrument, allowing the European Community to become a party to CITES,[26] and establishing the multilateral fund of the Montreal Protocol on

[23] See LRTAP Convention, Article 12; and Barcelona Convention, Articles 15 and 16.

[24] See Convention for the Protection of the Ozone Layer, Articles 8 and 9; Convention on the Control of Transboundary Movement of Hazardous Wastes (Basel Convention), Articles 15 and 17; Convention on Biological Diversity, Articles 28–9; and UN Framework Convention on Climate Change, Articles 15 and 17.

[25] M.J. Bowman, 'The Ramsar Convention Comes of Age' (1995) 42 Netherlands Int'l L. Rev. 1 at 33–8.

[26] See 1982 Bonn Amendment to Convention on International Trade in Endangered Species of Wild Flora and Fauna (CITES); 1983 Gaborone Amendment to CITES; 1982 Paris Protocol to Convention on

a permanent basis, which paved the way for the accession of a number of important developing countries.[27] The most important exception to this rule is the Montreal Protocol, which has been amended repeatedly to broaden and tighten obligations to reduce and phase out the production and consumption of ozone-depleting substances. Likewise, the regulatory approach of the Basel Convention towards the transboundary movement of hazardous wastes was transformed from a licensing system into a complete prohibition of exports from OECD countries to non-OECD countries by the amendment of 1995, after doubts as to whether a simple decision would suffice.[28]

Due to domestic ratification requirements, the development of environmental treaty systems through regular amendments and the adoption of subsidiary protocols is cumbersome and time-consuming. New obligations usually require several years to become effective. The Kyoto Protocol entered into force about seven years after its adoption in 1998, and the 1995 amendment of the Basel Convention still had not entered into force as of August 2006. To accelerate normative development, the members of the Montreal Protocol lowered the threshold for the entry into force of the London Amendments. Whereas the Vienna Convention would have required ratification by two-thirds of the Montreal Protocol parties—that is, 38 ratifications—the London Amendment provided for its entry into force upon ratification by only 20 states.

Since each amendment binds only those states that accept it, amendments create a treaty regime with different memberships for the different instruments, making it increasingly difficult to identify reciprocal commitments. For example, the amendments of the Montreal Protocol of 1990, 1992, 1997, and 1999 were, as of 22 November 2004, in force for 175, 164, 121, and 84 of the 188 members of the protocol.[29] In very rare cases, this problem may be solved by the winding up of an existing institution and the creation of a new one. For example, key members of the 1971 International Convention on the Establishment of an International Fund for Compensation for Oil Pollution Damage adopted a protocol in 1992 that created a new fund. They also withdrew their commitments from the original arrangement in order to force reluctant members to join the 1992 fund with an adapted scheme of financial compensation for environmental damage from oil spills caused by tankers.[30] Likewise, the

Wetlands of International Importance, Especially as Waterfowl Habitat (Ramsar Convention); 1987 Regina Amendment to the Ramsar Convention.

[27] See R.E. Benedick, *Ozone Diplomacy: New Directions in Safeguarding the Planet* (Cambridge, MA: Harvard University Press, 1998) at 183–8.

[28] 1995 Ban Amendment to the Basel Convention, Decision III/1, *Decisions Adopted by the Third Meeting of the Conference of the Parties to the Basel Convention*, Doc. UNEP/CHW.3/35 (28 November 1995).

[29] Decision XVI/1, *Report of the Sixteenth Meeting of the Parties to the Montreal Protocol on Substances That Deplete the Ozone Layer*, Doc. UNEP/OzL.Pro.16/17 (2004) at 42.

[30] M. Jacobbson, 'Oil Pollution Liability and Compensation: An International Regime' (1996) 1 Uniform L. Rev. 260 at 270.

Uruguay Round negotiations that established the WTO replaced the 'a la carte' approach introduced by the Tokyo Round agreements into the 1947 General Agreement on Tariffs and Trade, under which states could pick and choose which agreements to accept, with a single package of agreements that binds all WTO members.[31] It is a prerequisite for this strategy that the newly created institution generates sufficient excludable benefits that can be enjoyed only by its members. This condition is frequently not fulfilled in international environmental governance. In the case of regimes that protect a global or a regional commons, such as the ozone layer or a regional sea, replacing an existing treaty system with a new one might encourage reluctant states to refrain from joining the new institution rather than to accept its tightened obligations.

3.2 Normative Development through Simplified Amendment Procedures

Some treaty systems rely heavily on simplified procedures for the amendment of technical annexes because the regular procedure for the making and amendment of international treaty law has proven to be too slow to cope with the demand for rapid regulatory change.[32] Under such procedures, amendments are elaborated by the COPs and must be adopted by specific majorities of parties. However, in contrast to regular amendments, these amendments to annexes enter into force automatically after a specified period of time—frequently 90 days—for all member states that do not object. Aside from this simple opting-out procedure, modified procedures have developed. Under the 1992 Baltic Sea Convention, the amendment of an annex enters into force only if no member state objects. In other cases, amendments enter into force unless a certain number of member states object. For the 1979 Convention on the Conservation of European Wildlife and Natural Habitats, the quorum is one-third of the parties; for the 1992 Convention on Transboundary Effects of Industrial Accidents, it is 16 states. Under the 1946 Whaling Convention, if one member state opts out, the period of time to opt out is automatically prolonged for the other members.[33] These procedures are designed to ensure that a member state will not be committed to an amendment while other parties, possibly competitors, reject the new obligation.

Although simplified amendment procedures have been designed for the adaptation of technical details, this does not imply that these aspects are less important.

---

[31] J.H. Jackson, *The World Trading System: Law and Policy of International Economic Relations London* (Cambridge, MA: MIT Press, 1999) at 46–9.

[32] P. Contini and P.H. Sand, 'Methods to Expedite Environmental Protection: International Ecostandards' (1972) 66 A.J.I.L. 37.

[33] See 1992 Convention on the Protection of the Marine Environment of the Baltic Sea Area, Article 32; Convention on the Conservation of European Wildlife and Natural Habitats, Article 17; Convention

Occasionally, allegedly technical annexes spell out core components of a treaty system. Especially some conventions adopted in the early 1970s or before are composed of a very general main body and annexes that are subject to simplified amendment and that set forth detailed regulatory rules. For example, the Whaling Convention authorizes the International Whaling Commission to amend from time to time the annex comprising the measures for the protection of whales ('the schedule'). Likewise, the prohibition or restriction of international trade in endangered species of flora and fauna under CITES requires that species are classified as endangered or threatened. While classification decisions are subject to simplified amendment, they are occasionally highly contentious, especially if they address economically or socially important species such as certain whales or elephants and their products. Similarly, the Consultative Meeting of the London Convention could introduce, by modifying its annexes according to simplified amendment procedures, far-reaching and politically contentious new obligations to restrict and later prohibit the incineration of wastes at sea, and to phase out the dumping of industrial and radioactive wastes as an elaboration of the general obligation to prohibit the disposal of wastes at sea. Decisions of this kind are not merely of technical concern, but they are also highly political and touch upon major interests of member states.

Particularly far-reaching is the adjustment procedure of the Montreal Protocol. Under this procedure, the MOP is empowered to 'adjust', in practice to tighten, reduction targets for ozone-depleting substances that are already regulated under the protocol (Article 2.9). Adjustments enter into force for all parties six months after the decision. Parties shall make efforts for adoption by consensus, but an adjustment may also be adopted by a two-thirds majority of the parties present and voting, which must include simple majorities of both developing and developed countries. Hence, decisions become automatically legally binding even for member states that might have voted against the adjustment. Acceptance of this procedure by the member states can be attributed to particular circumstances that limit the political risk inherent in the approach. At the time it was adopted, the ozone-depleting substances in question were well known and it had been clear to negotiators that they were going to be phased out in the foreseeable future.[34] The conceptual importance of this procedure stems from the fact that it combines mandatory law-making by a MOP with majority voting. However, the procedure might have pushed the simplification of the amendment of international treaty law a step too far. Not only have all adjustment decisions so far been taken by consensus, the procedure also has not been included in any other treaty system, as far as can be seen.

on Transboundary Effects of Industrial Accidents, Article 26; and International Convention for the Regulation of Whaling, Article 5.

[34] Benedick, see note 27 above at 90.

The simplified amendment procedures of environmental treaty systems do not introduce a hierarchy of laws in which those parts subject to traditional amendment procedures, and thus under tighter control of the contracting parties, were superior to those parts subject to COP decision-making. Hierarchies of laws are well known from international organizations. Whereas the Charter of the United Nations assigns decision-making competencies to the Security Council, decisions of this body constitute secondary law that does not modify the Charter itself. It is thus remarkable that the COPs of some environmental treaty systems are entitled to change international *treaty* law, especially the annexes to environmental treaties, and, in the exceptional case of the Montreal Protocol, even possibly against the expressed will of dissenting states.

De facto, if not *de jure*, simplified amendment procedures delegate law-making functions to the COPs of environmental treaty systems, even if dissenting parties normally enjoy the right to opt out. Inaction under a simplified amendment procedure with an opt-out clause may be interpreted as implicit consent with a decision.[35] Yet, this interpretation seems to be more directed at preserving the principle of sovereign consent enshrined in international law than at accounting for the particular nature of this form of law-making. In fact, simplified amendment procedures, whether or not they contain an opt-out clause, transfer the necessary activity of law-making from individual to collective action.[36] Whereas international treaty law usually requires ratification by each individual state that agrees to be committed, under simplified amendment procedures new legal requirements emerge from the collective decision of the competent treaty body. According to both procedures, states cannot usually be bound against their will, but under simplified amendment procedures, indifferent or inactive member states become committed by decisions without individual action.

The importance of some annexes that are subject to simplified amendment procedures and the fact that these procedures create international treaty law may have led to a move away from this approach as the principal means of developing environmental treaty systems. In contrast to the conventions established in the early 1970s, such as CITES and the London Convention, later treaty systems restrict simplified amendment procedures to truly technical details lacking overwhelming general concern—with the just-mentioned limited exception of the adjustment procedure of the Montreal Protocol. As discussed earlier in this chapter (section 2.1), the convention-protocol approach replaced the convention-annex approach as the major flexibility mechanism for the making of treaty law, as exemplified in the Barcelona and LRTAP Convention systems.

---

[35] J. Brunnée, 'COPing with Consent: Law-Making under Multilateral Environmental Agreements' (2002) 15 Leiden J. Int'l L. 1 at 18–20.

[36] B. Simma, 'From Bilateralism to Community Interest' (1994-VI) 250 Recueil des cours 217 at 329–30.

3.3 Normative Development through Secondary Decision-Making

To the extent that decisions of environmental treaty systems are not directed at modifying existing, or at creating new, treaty law, they contribute to a rapidly growing body of system-specific secondary rules that are of tremendous importance in some areas of international environmental governance. In these cases, the flexibility of treaty systems is achieved through the formal or *de facto* delegation to the treaty's institutions of powers to adopt secondary decisions. Such competencies automatically establish a two-tier hierarchy of obligations. Whereas the treaty at the constitutional level remains under the tight control of the member states collectively and, with the exceptions discussed in section 3.2, also individually through national ratification, a separate body of secondary rules emerges that depends on, and is thus subsidiary to, the treaty. This body of secondary law is generated according to procedures that may, or may not, involve the COP (see Chapter 38 'Treaty Bodies'), but it derives its legitimacy and binding force from the superior treaty and from agreement among the member states.

The formal legal status of secondary decisions is ambiguous and disputed. Under the law of international treaties, secondary law-making is not specifically addressed, except insofar as the contracting parties may agree on common interpretations of a treaty and on its provisional application prior to its formal entry into force.[37] Accordingly, authoritative interpretations by the COPs of environmental treaty systems designed to close unintended gaps of treaty law may be assumed to be legally binding at least for consenting states.[38] Moreover, secondary decisions that are explicitly assigned to a decision-making body by the constituent treaties might also acquire full legal status, if treaty language suggests that legally binding force was intended by the contracting parties.[39] For example, the MOP of the Montreal Protocol was explicitly empowered to consider the feasibility of, and adopt, trade measures concerning products containing, or produced with, ozone-depleting substances (Article 8) and to elaborate the non-compliance procedure. The Kyoto Protocol explicitly assigns a whole range of tasks to the COP/MOP of the treaty system, which may have far-reaching implications and amount in fact to an exercise in legislation, rather than to the mere interpretation of treaty law. Due to their hybrid structure, environmental treaty systems might also fall under the law of international organizations, under which competent bodies can adopt legally binding *internal*

---

[37] See Vienna Convention on the Law of Treaties, Articles 31 and 25.

[38] See J. Sommer, 'Environmental Law-Making by International Organizations' (1996) 56 Zeitschrift für ausländisches öffentliches Recht und Völkerrecht 628 at 637–8.

[39] See V. Röben, 'Institutional Developments under Modern International Environmental Agreements' (2000) 4 Max Planck Y.B. UN L. 363 at 404–5.

decisions by the required majorities of parties present and voting.[40] Many important substantive decisions might be considered as internal to the legal order of the treaty system, even if they unfold certain external effects.

Remarkably, the drafters of the treaties tend to avoid express statements on the legal status of decisions. Whereas many decisions may easily be conceived of as legally binding interpretations of treaty provisions, others develop treaty systems considerably without being explicitly provided for in treaty law. The contracting parties seem to accept the ambiguous legal status of many secondary rules in exchange for the ability to employ secondary decision-making as a mechanism for the rapid development of environmental treaty systems. When an interim multilateral fund was established by the MOP of the Montreal Protocol by a simple 'decision', there was no discussion about the legal status of this instrument.[41] Likewise, upon adoption of the non-compliance procedure of the Montreal Protocol, the MOP expressly accepted the recommendation of the Legal Expert Group 'that there is no need to expedite the amendment procedure' under the Vienna Convention,[42] suggesting that, even in the absence of amendment, non-compliance decisions would have sufficient legal authority. Without a specific competence, the COP of CITES has, over time, adopted various decisions that are apparently intended to, and seem to be regarded as, legally binding. Perhaps the most important of these decisions is the introduction of quota systems for various animal products such as ivory.[43] In contrast, some parties argued that the decision of the COP of the Basel Convention to ban exports of hazardous wastes from OECD countries to non-OECD countries was not legally binding because the COP could not alter the parties' substantive obligations.[44] Whereas the decision is therefore widely considered as reflecting political, rather than formal legal, commitment, the clear wording ('the Conference . . . decides to prohibit all transboundary movements of hazardous wastes'), and the fact that it was adopted by consensus after contentious negotiations, suggest that the contracting parties nevertheless expected that it would be adhered to, and thus considered that the COP had the authority to commit the member states, even if not in legal terms.

Within a particular treaty system, decisions will generally gain *de facto* binding force, if commitment is intended by the community of member states. The precise legal status of secondary rules is of comparatively little importance for the practical

---

[40] R.R. Churchill and G. Ulfstein, 'Autonomous Institutional Arrangements in Multilateral Environmental Agreements: A Little-Noticed Phenomenon in International Law' (2000) 94 A.J.I.L. 623 at 631–58.   [41] Gehring, see note 11 above at 318.

[42] Decision IV/5 (1992), *Report of the Fourth Meeting of the Parties to the Montreal Protocol on Substances that Deplete the Ozone Layer*, Doc. UNEP/OzL.Pro.4/15 (25 November 1992).

[43] P. Sands, *Principles of International Environmental Law: Framework, Standards, and Implementation*, 2nd edition (Cambridge: Cambridge University Press, 2003) at 513–14.

[44] *Report of the Second Meeting of the Conference of the Parties to the Basel Convention on the Control of Transboundary Movements of Hazardous Wastes and Their Disposal*, Doc. UNEP/CHW.2/30 (25 March 1994) at paras. 39–50 and Decision II/12; see L. de la Fayette, 'Legal and Practical Implications of the Ban Amendment to the Basel Convention' (1995) 6 Y.B. Int'l Envt'l L. 703 at 705–8.

operation of environmental treaty systems. The contracting parties can, therefore, afford to avoid determining the issue of legal status. They tend to do so, because principled discussion in this regard might jeopardize the successful reliance on decisions as a means of governance that is more flexible than regular treaty law, and at the same time able to commit the member states more intensely than mere recommendations. Therefore, they can employ the instrument of a firmly worded decision even in cases that reach far beyond their undisputed law-making authority.

The commitment effect of decisions originates, first of all, from the consent of the contracting parties.[45] A decision that attracts the broad support of all or at least most member states reflects a promise of the supporters to honour their mutual commitment. Breaking such a promise undermines a state's reputation because offenders appear as unreliable cooperators. Therefore, the contracting parties in most environmental treaty systems seek to adopt important, if not all, secondary decisions by consensus so as to extend the consent-based binding force to all parties, even if adoption by simple or qualified majority is formally possible.

Second, such decisions may be part of larger package deals among the contracting parties and cannot be ignored without jeopardizing the whole package. In many cases, international governance depends on package deals that combine different issues, each of which is advantageous for a different group of actors. In this case, all contracting parties will be aware of the fact that *ex post* withdrawal from undesired parts of the package may prompt the withdrawal of other parties from their obligations. Accordingly, member states with an interest in a given treaty system will accept and be prepared to implement ensuing obligations irrespective of their exact legal status. Hence, whether contributions to the multi-million dollar interim multilateral fund of the Montreal Protocol were considered as legally binding or not, contributing countries could not withdraw from their commitments without risking the non-compliance of important developing countries.[46] And the ban of the transboundary movement of hazardous wastes from OECD countries to non-OECD countries was the precondition for the universal acceptance of the Basel treaty system.

Third, secondary decisions may change the situation even for actors that dislike the content of the decisions, so that unilateral rejection is not a viable option.[47] If provisions for the assessment of production and consumption figures under the Montreal Protocol, criteria for the classification of endangered species under CITES, or the rules of the clean development mechanism under the Kyoto Protocol are formulated in a particular way that has been agreed upon within the relevant COP or MOP, the treaty systems will simply operate accordingly. Alternative options are excluded by the decision, so that, unless a member state is willing to leave the system, it is forced to accept the operation of the system as it is.

---

[45] See B. Simma, 'Consent. Strains in the Treaty System,' in R. St. J. MacDonald and D.M. Johnston, eds., *The Structure and Process of International Law: Essays in Legal Philosophy, Doctrine and Theory* (The Hague: Martinus Nijhoff, 1983) at 495–7.   [46] See Benedick, see note 27 above at 188–90.
[47] Brunnée, see note 35 above at 23–31.

Fourth, environmental treaty systems replace the traditional procedures of litigation and dispute settlement under the rules of international law with internal mechanisms of norm interpretation and compliance control. The formal legal status of a decision accepted by the member states will not be relevant, unless a conflict over its content and consequences is arbitrated or litigated outside the treaty system. Whereas several environmental treaty systems explicitly envisage traditional international procedures for the settlement of conflicts, such as conciliation, third-party arbitration, or adjudication, these procedures have been used only in very few cases so far, and they are unlikely to be employed more widely in the future. Apart from being too confrontational, they do not account for the specificities of a particular treaty system. In particular, they risk involuntarily unravelling package agreements, if they dishonour informal parts of the treaty system. Instead, starting with the Montreal Protocol, several environmental treaty systems have developed their own mechanisms for implementation control and dispute settlement (see Chapter 43 'Compliance Procedures'). These quasi-judicial mechanisms reflect the desire of contracting parties to internalize the function of dealing with disputes about compliance into the overall collective decision-process of the respective treaty systems.

Finally, environmental treaty systems may develop their own internal sanctioning instruments to thwart their gradual unraveling through the 'selective exit' of contracting parties from undesired obligations. Particularly relevant are privileges granted only under the condition that obligations are fulfilled. The 'indicative list of measures' available in case of non-compliance adopted under the Montreal Protocol includes, besides assistance and the issuing of cautions, the possible 'suspension . . . of specific rights and privileges under the Protocol . . . including those concerned with industrial rationalization, production, consumption, trade, transfer of technology, financial mechanism and institutional arrangements.'[48] These measures are directed at withdrawing privileges enjoyed by the member states under the protocol, and the MOP has cautioned a number of countries in transition that it might invoke them.[49] Privileges granted under the Kyoto Protocol include, beside financial and technological assistance, the employment of the flexibility mechanisms, namely the clean development mechanism, joint implementation, and emissions trading, to reduce implementation costs. Their use currently requires that countries meet eligibility criteria, and the suspension of eligibility in cases of non-compliance might become a major sanctioning instrument of the treaty system.

The increasingly wide use of decisions by a treaty's institutions as a governance instrument that can generate commitment among the member states contributes significantly to the flexibility of modern environmental treaty systems. Whereas

---

[48] *Report of the Fourth Meeting of the Parties to the Montreal Protocol on Substances that Deplete the Ozone Layer*, Doc. UNEP/OzL.Pro.4/15 (25 November 1992), Annex V.

[49] For example, MOP Decisions X/20,21,23–28, *Report of the Tenth Meeting of the Parties to the Montreal Protocol on Substances that Deplete the Ozone Layer*, Doc. UNEP/OzL.Pro.10/9 (3 December 1998).

the making of environmental treaty law has become less flexible over time especially due to the replacement of the convention-annex approach by the more traditional convention-protocol approach, environmental treaty systems do not seem to be less flexible than before. The more traditional form of treaty-law making is complemented by the increasing use of highly flexible secondary decisions. In spite of their often unclear, and occasionally disputed, formal legal status, such decisions reflect an important part of the entire package of obligations faced by the member states of many environmental treaty systems. As long as the commitments reflected in these decisions are, within their respective treaty systems, not treated significantly different from commitments enshrined in formal treaty law, they will be honoured by the member states equally well.

4 Conclusion

The making and evolution of international environmental law are related to the establishment of numerous separately institutionalized multilateral treaty systems. Treaty systems are negotiated and adopted predominantly within the framework of existing international organizations or similar institutions. Upon their establishment, they become machineries for the making of new law and for the development of existing law in their respective areas of competence. One characteristic of the making and development of international environmental law is the fragmentation of the institutional setting from which it emerges. Environmental treaty systems govern comparatively small areas of international relations. Apparently, the contracting parties prefer the establishment of new treaty systems to the linkage of new environmental problems to existing systems. As a second characteristic, environmental treaty systems comprise, like international organizations, a permanent institutional component that enables the contracting parties to adjust obligations as necessary or appropriate to new circumstances as well as to supervise implementation and react collectively to cases of non-compliance.

In contrast to other areas of international governance, international environmental governance decidedly relies upon a step-by-step approach, and almost all important treaty systems have considerably developed over time. Through their scientific and technological apparatus for the assessment of governance-related facts, treaty systems comprise arrangements directed at creating new opportunities for cooperation among the contracting parties. Moreover, they have developed different institutional devices for the accelerated entry into force of new obligations. These arrangements include simplified amendment procedures, the adoption of secondary decisions that elaborate treaty law, the resort to soft law instruments if legally binding obligations cannot be agreed upon, and interim mechanisms to bridge the occasionally long period until a new treaty or amendment enters into force.

Environmental treaty systems partially transform intergovernmental bargaining into deliberative transnational problem-solving processes. Essentially, policy-making within environmental treaty systems remains based upon inter-governmental negotiations, and states must be assumed to pursue predominantly their parochial interests. However, assessments of scientific and technological knowledge introduce, if successfully operating, a sphere of technical deliberation into the bargaining process. Improved and collectively validated knowledge about the scope and implications of an environmental problem or about the availability of technological solutions contributes to the gradual modification of state preferences, which in turn can lead to agreement on new commitments. Moreover, the most advanced environmental treaty systems increasingly rely on the delegation of implementation decisions to specifically structured procedures that are directed at the application of general normative criteria, and avoid the mere balancing of state interests. If operating successfully, such procedures can create a process of normative deliberation.

As a result of these far-reaching internal law-making activities, the whole package of obligations entered into by the contracting parties to an environmental treaty system is no longer entirely reflected in the text of the treaty. Although the major substantive and procedural obligations remain enshrined in international treaty law, additional rules and implementation decisions add up to system-specific bodies of secondary law. Irrespective of the formal legal status of these rules, environmental treaty systems operate on the assumption that decisions that are meant to be mandatory are accepted as commitments by the parties. Moreover, the contracting parties frequently refrain from clarifying the legal status of the decisions, because this endeavour might jeopardize the use of secondary decision-making altogether. As long as they abstain from external litigation and arbitration, they remain the masters of the process, defining collectively what they are prepared to accept and which obligations they expect others to observe. As a consequence, environmental treaty systems become autonomous sectoral systems of international law, which increasingly internalize the management of conflicts about the interpretation of commitments as well as the treatment of cases of non-compliance.

RECOMMENDED READING

R.E. Benedick, *Ozone Diplomacy: New Directions in Safeguarding the Planet* (Cambridge, MA: Harvard University Press, 1995).

F. Biermann and S. Bauer, eds., *A World Environment Organization: Solution or Threat for Effective International Environmental Governance?* (Aldershot: Ashgate, 2005).

D. Bodansky, 'The Legitimacy of International Governance: A Coming Challenge for International Environmental Law?'(1999) 93 A.J.I.L. 596.

J. Brunnée, 'COPing with Consent: Law-making under Multilateral Environmental Agreements' (2002) 15 Leiden J. Int'l L. 1.

R.R. Churchill and G. Ulfstein 'Autonomous Institutional Arrangements in Multilateral Environmental Agreements: A Little-Noticed Phenomenon in International Law' (2000) 94 A.J.I.L. 623.

G.W. Downs, K.W. Danish, and P.N. Barsoom 'The Transformational Model of International Regime Design: Triumph of Hope or Experience ?' (2000) 38 Colum. J. Transnat'l L. 465.

T. Gehring, *Dynamic International Regimes: Institutions for International Environmental Governance* (Frankfurt: Peter Lang, 1994).

L.E. Susskind, *Environmental Diplomacy: Negotiating More Effective Global Agreements* (Oxford: Oxford University Press, 1994).

D.G. Victor, K. Raustiala, and E.B. Skolnikoff, eds., *The Implementation and Effectiveness of International Environmental Commitments: Theory and Practice* (Cambridge, MA: MIT Press, 1998).

W. Wijnsteckers, *The Evolution of CITES: A Reference to the Convention on International Trade in Endangered Species*, 8th edition (Geneva: CITES, 2006).

C H A P T E R   2 1

PRIVATE AND QUASI-PRIVATE STANDARD SETTING

JASON MORRISON

NAOMI ROHT-ARRIAZA

1 Introduction

MANY, if not most, standards in international environmental law (IEL) are created by states. The most common form of standard setting involves states adopting national legislation and regulations on the basis of commitments made in international or regional agreements. This article concerns a different kind of standard setting—namely that carried out by private or quasi-private entities. Private standards differ from public IEL standards in two major respects. First, the standards are aimed directly at organizations—mostly business organizations (see Chapter 35 'Business') but also in some cases non-profit or public-sector organizations—and are not aimed at states. In other words, they are market-oriented instruments that act directly on producers, and do not originate from intergovernmental agreements or instruments that apply to producers through the intermediation of national law. Second, the standards are not primarily (or at least initially) regulatory. They seek to change behaviour through a complex mix of incentives and do not rely primarily on external, deterrence-based enforcement. Organizations adopt and implement private and quasi-private standards largely as a result of market or reputational incentives, although as we will demonstrate in this chapter, both national regulation and international agreements may also push towards their adoption. These private standards may serve as gap-fillers and/or the technical basis for public law and regulation; may be precursors of subsequent public standards; or may serve for a time to show that industry can solve its own problems and that, therefore, public regulation is unnecessary. Despite these multiple functions, this chapter will illustrate that the distinction between the voluntary versus mandatory nature of private standards is increasingly blurring, as is the conceptual and practical differentiation among private, quasi-private, and public standards.

A number of factors have made private and quasi-private standards increasingly important in international environmental law. However, dissatisfaction with the limits of private standard setting has also led to increasing calls for public oversight and participation in standards-setting processes and for their transformation into mandatory, public standards. Thus, what is emerging is a complex array of standards that defy easy categorization into purely private and purely public—a trend that is likely to continue given the current emphasis on public-private partnerships and the key role of the private sector in sustainable development.

This chapter starts by examining who creates private and quasi-private standards and why. It then tackles the types of private and quasi-private standards, the implications of these standards for public policy, and the ways in which compliance with such standards is enforced. A final section discusses the advantages and disadvantages of private standard setting as compared to public, the links between public, quasi-private, and private standards, and the emergence of a hybrid standard-setting regime governing the behaviour of the private sector.

2 WHO CREATES PRIVATE STANDARDS?

2.1 Emergence of Private and Quasi-Private Standards

Private and quasi-private standards in the environmental area play a prominent role in the context of globalized business enterprises and trade. As goods move around the world, they are subject to an array of quality, safety, and environmental standards. And as national and/or regional standards have proliferated, they have given rise to efforts to create harmonized international standards that not only facilitate trade across the globe, but also help to reduce unnecessary costs associated with 'multiple registrations, inspections, certifications, labels and conflicting requirements.'[1] Some global corporations with operations in a number of different countries find it useful to standardize their internal operations, allowing them to use the same protocols throughout their organizations independently of local law, either for efficiency purposes or to help minimize environmental risks and liabilities.

In addition to those drivers internal to private actors, external drivers have also pushed towards the creation and adoption of private and quasi-private standards. Over the past two decades, consumers have increasingly linked their values with their spending and investing habits. This shift in economic paradigm now spans a wide variety of decisions, from the certified organic food people eat, to the shoes and clothes they wear, to the financial investments they make for retirement. In part as a result of this emerging change in societal expectations, companies also are beginning

---

[1] J. Cascio, 'International Environmental Management Standards: ISO 9000's Less Tractable Siblings,' *ASTM Standardization News*, April 1994 at 44.

to prefer working with suppliers and partners that have a positive track record vis-à-vis their social and environmental practices. Simultaneously serving to drive and respond to this consumer demand, non-governmental organizations (NGOs) (see Chapter 33 'Non-Governmental Organizations and Civil Society') have created multi-stakeholder alliances that have sought to expand concepts of corporate environmental and social responsibility, and have established standards as tools that underpin trade and sustainable development.

Many of these private, market-driven systems that predominate the field today stem from a general dissatisfaction with government-led 'command and control' regulatory approaches (see Chapter 8 'Instrument Choice') as well as with the failure of intergovernmental processes of the 1990s and early 2000s to result in meaningful action to advance sustainable commercial practices and protect human rights in the workplace. Consequently, stakeholders external to businesses, including investors, watchdog NGOs, social justice advocates, the general public, and even sometimes regulatory authorities themselves, have increasingly turned to incentive- and information-based approaches to supplement traditional command-and-control environmental regulation at the national level as well as to help differentiate good and bad actors in the market.

These drivers, plus others discussed later in this chapter, have led to a diversity of standard-setting processes. We focus here on three: quasi-private standard setting through the International Organization for Standardization (ISO), standard setting by industry itself and through direct industry-NGO partnerships, and the development of private standards as a result of cooperation between international governmental bodies such as the Organisation for Economic Co-operation and Development (OECD), the International Labour Organization (ILO), and the UN Environment Programme (UNEP), and the private sector, resulting in voluntary standards. These multiple pathways are now common enough that they create a burgeoning problem of proliferation of standards on the same subject matter.

2.2 ISO and Its Sister Organizations

At present, the ISO is perhaps the most recognized, and by and large well respected, international standards institution. Founded in 1946 to facilitate international trade, the ISO today is a worldwide federation of 148 national standards bodies. Membership in the ISO is voluntary and open to any country that wishes to participate. The ISO allows only one member per country. ISO members are the national standard-setting body, which may be a private entity, a government agency, or a hybrid. As a general rule, national standards bodies from industrialized countries tend to be private institutions, while in developing countries they are more often government agencies. The ISO's unique blend of government and private representation has given it a stand-alone position as perhaps the single-most recognized and accepted developer of international standards, with more than 14,000 standards published over its almost 60-year history. The scope of the ISO's work covers standards in all major fields except electrotechnical and food standards, which are the responsibilities of the International Electrotechnical Commission (IEC) and the Codex Alimentarius Commission, respectively. The ISO's stated objective is to promote the development of standardization and related global activities with a view towards facilitating the international exchange of goods and services, and towards developing cooperation in the spheres of intellectual, scientific, technological, and economic activities.

ISO standards are discussed and developed in technical committees (TCs)—some 188 are now active—which are the forums where national standards bodies and their expert delegates provide their input into the standards. National standards bodies are, in turn, composed of producers, users/consumers, government ministries, and departments and academics, among others, and their membership is supposed to ensure a reasonable balance among all interests directly or materially affected by the standard under development. Theoretically, the ISO's broad spread of interests at the national level gives it the legitimacy to enact standards with public policy implications, however, as discussed later in this chapter, it is questionable whether, in practice, the ISO or its members bodies actually achieve sufficient levels of stakeholder involvement and diversity to warrant such credibility. The international standards produced by the ISO are then further legitimized by typically being adopted by national standards bodies as 'national standards'.

The ISO's influence is exercised not only through its size and scope, but also through its status as a producer of some of the world's 'trade-legal' standards as recognized by the World Trade Organization (WTO). The WTO's Agreement on Technical Barriers to Trade, for example, requires member countries to adopt 'relevant international standards', which is an implicit reference to, among others, ISO standards, as the basis for their national standards. An adjunct Code of Good Practice specifically references the ISO, thereby lifting the ISO standards, which states may or may not adopt as their national standards, to the level of international law. This special trade-relevant status derives from the ISO's quasi-intergovernmental character and from the fact that it was established contemporaneously with other trade-facilitating organizations. Other standards developed, for example, by the NGO-led initiatives discussed later in this chapter, are not afforded the same recognition in the context of the existing international trade regime. Thus, an interesting question arises about the trade implications of ISO standards. So long as such standards are applied by private producers or through private (contractual) agreements, they would seem to be outside the purview of the WTO, but once adopted by governments as the basis for mandatory or even preferential treatment, it is conceivable that non-ISO standards that were more restrictive than the ISO ones could be subject to a WTO challenge. The case, however, has not yet arisen.

Historically, the ISO focused exclusively on the development of product specification standards, including, for example, technical measures pertaining to the height of car bumpers, film sensitivity, and screw size.[2] Its first foray into more process-oriented general standards came with the quality management series, ISO 9000, which is described in section 3.2 in this chapter. The ISO has expanded its scope over the course of the last decade to encompass environmental issues. With the creation of ISO/TC 207—dealing with environmental management in 1993, the ISO took its most notable step into the public policy arena, extending its influence beyond industry and their customers and into issues of general public interest. And the ISO is continuing (and even accelerating) its pursuit of the development of standards that directly support and advance sustainable development. In its 2003 strategic planning consultation document, *ISO Horizon 2010: Standards for a Sustainable World*, the ISO expresses its intention to continue moving into the environmental and social arenas, stating that its standards can serve 'products and services that enter into world trade and that impact on the health, safety, environment and social progress of mankind.'

As a result of the ISO's unparalleled reach, there is little doubt that any new ISO standards in the social or environmental field will continue to have a sizable (and likely growing) influence on businesses, governments, and civil society around the world. Yet, the ISO's evolution from an institution that promulgates technical engineering standards to a social and environmental standard-setting body has not been accompanied by a parallel shift in the representation of important stakeholders within the ISO. Recent evidence suggests that developing countries and numerous key stakeholder groups remain underrepresented in the ISO.[3] In addition to a lack of civil society and relevant government ministerial participation, small businesses and even some major industrial sectors tend to be underrepresented in environmental standards development, for instance, while consultants and standards bodies apparently have disproportionate influence. Part of the problem stems from the process of standards elaboration, which is done through a myriad of meetings all over the world, with no consistent funding available for NGO or developing country representatives. The language of the ISO is arcane, difficult for environmental or other civil society groups to understand and not often translated from English. Until recently, it was difficult to find environmental groups with the interest (or budget) to follow ISO proceedings consistently. Despite plans and protestations to the contrary, the ISO until the mid-2000s had taken few substantive steps towards greater inclusivity in its environmental and social standard setting.

These procedural limits also condition the rigor of ISO standards. A need for informal 'consensus' (roughly defined as the absence of sustained opposition on an

---

[2] A partial list of typical technical committees is instructive: TC1—Screw threads; TC11—Boilers and Pressure Vessels; TC35—Paints and Varnishes; TC120—Leather.

[3] See M. Morikawa and J. Morrison, 'Who Develops ISO Standards? A Survey of Participation in ISO's International Standards Development Processes,' Report by the Pacific Institute for Studies in Development, Environment, and Security, Oakland, California, October 2004.

issue of substance) to adopt a standard and the ambition to create standards applicable to large and small, developed and developing, and all types of organizations means that substance tends to be watered down to a least common denominator. As discussed in section 3 later in this chapter, these limitations have hobbled the ability of ISO environment management standards to drive sustainable development.

2.3 Non-State Environmental and Social Certification and Labelling Programmes

The perceived need for consumers to be able to distinguish sustainable from unsustainable and environmentally damaging products in the marketplace has led NGOs to create their own standards. Typically, these initiatives have consisted of normative performance and/or management standards that underpin third-party verification and certification/labelling elements. Unlike the ISO's 'systems' standards, these NGO-driven initiatives generally require performance minimums and on-the-ground outcome assessment. Organizations independently assessed as having conformed to the requirements contained in the initiative's standard(s) are entitled to include the initiative's trademark/logo on its products, promotional material, and/or facilities. Examples of such standards-based initiatives include the Forest Stewardship Council (FSC), the Marine Stewardship Council (MSC), Social Accountability 8000, and Fairtrade Labelling Organization International, among many others.

For example, the FSC certifies forests (40 million hectares in 73 countries in 2003) based on criteria that address legal issues, indigenous rights, labour rights, multiple benefits, and environmental impacts surrounding forest management. Building on this example, Unilever Corporation and the World Wildlife Fund created in 1997 the MSC to use consumer pressure to drive improved fishing practices. The MSC is now an independent organization with a Stakeholder Council composed of a balance of fisheries, processing, retail, and environmental and social interests. The MSC has to date certified a small number of fish stocks.

It remains to be seen, however, to what extent these certification programs can make inroads into mainstream markets. They assume that consumers will be willing to pay a premium for sustainability, which may only be true of some commodities or of certain luxury goods. Small producers, moreover, may find it difficult to afford the cost of third party certification (or of the implementation of the actual standards, for that matter). They also depend heavily on the credibility of the certifying/labelling organizations—any controversy may spell the end of the certification effort. Yet, it is difficult to consistently balance the many factors involved in certification in a way that satisfies competing audiences.

Over time, successful NGO-initiated standards may change into bodies that look more like formal standards institutions, albeit without the ISO's link to governments and international public law. For example, the Global Reporting Initiative, discussed later in this chapter, started as an NGO-industry collaboration based at the Coalition for Environmentally Responsible Economies (CERES), but has now created a permanent independent governing structure to develop new reporting initiatives and, eventually, to sell future standards much as the ISO does. Such initiatives may then develop a link to public law through inclusion in national legislation or public international initiatives, and may eventually carve out niches at the intersection of the public and private that are similar to (or in competition with) that of the ISO.

Of course, industry groups often create their own standards. These may range from industry- or company-specific 'codes of conduct' applicable only to their own operations to more wide-ranging standards applicable to suppliers or borrowers. The standard-setting process in this case is often quite opaque, although codes borrow heavily from each other, from the public sector standards discussed later in this chapter, and from NGO input (especially where codes are developed in response to public/NGO pressure). In certain high-profile sectors such as chemicals and banking, industry associations have played a key role in developing sector-specific codes.

2.4 Cooperation between the International Public Sector and the Private Sector

Finally, some standards straddle the line between public and private and are created by public international institutions for both public and private use. International financial institutions, for example, can set out substantive emissions and design guidelines to reduce the environmental impacts of bank-funded projects. The World Bank's Industrial Pollution Prevention and Abatement guidelines, including sector specific protocols, are then used by private financiers as well as the bank and other government agencies. Another example might be UNEP's 1994 Code of Ethics on the International Trade in Chemicals, which is aimed at private producers, references its compatibility with Responsible Care and other private standards, and yet is the product of a UNEP-convened series of consultations with industry, government, and NGO experts.

Public-private collaborations also result in more general codes of conduct aimed at industry. For example, the OECD's Guidelines for Multinational Enterprises were created as a result of a set of meetings involving OECD member governments, in consultation with industry and NGOs. The ILO's Tripartite Declaration of Principles Concerning Multinational Enterprises and Social Policy emerged from the ILO's government-worker-employer tripartite structure. Both set out a general set of obligations for private enterprises, which in the OECD guidelines includes both environment and health and safety obligations and, in the ILO case, includes principles on worker health and safety with significant environmental implications. They have more in common with other forms of public international soft law-making in terms of the access of private actors. Both are voluntary. The OECD guidelines, to the extent that they have any enforcement mechanism, use a public international process, in the form of national contact points within government ministries that are to receive complaints of violations, investigate, attempt to conciliate, and, if necessary, publish information regarding violations. The UN secretary-general's Global Compact similarly sets out a short list of broad principles, three of them concerning the protection of the environment. Private enterprises voluntarily choose to sign up to the Global Compact, which deliberately avoids enforcement machinery and relies instead on creating networks for the transmission of best practices across industry.

3 What Kinds of Private Standards Exist?

There exist a dizzying array of types of private standards and an even wider range of functions that they attempt to serve in the market today. We adopt the ISO's definition of standards as documented agreements containing technical specifications or other precise criteria to be used consistently as rules, guidelines, or definitions of characteristics, to ensure that materials, products, processes and services are fit for their purpose. Based on this broad definition, we lay out in this chapter a general (and loose) classification scheme of the types of private standards that are being developed and used today. The reader should be aware that in practice there are few clear-cut boundaries between the categories described here, with many existing standards containing elements of each of them. It is not uncommon, for example, for a single standard to include management/process requirements and performance minimums, in addition to prescriptive measurement and reporting protocols.

3.1 Technical Specifications and Performance Standards

Standard setting initially focused on product specifications, ensuring that devices such as automatic teller machine cards and kitchen appliances operate worldwide. Product specifications exist for environmentally related products such as measuring equipment, and for products and services with environmental hazards. Examples of the latter are the ISO's standards on construction and materials and engineering technologies. In the environmental arena, the vast majority of performance-oriented standards have focused on limiting an organization's adverse effects by establishing performance minimums for issues such as energy use or air or water emissions. These can apply to any stage of the product's life-cycle, for instance, production, use, and/or disposal. Standards addressing performance minimums can be qualitative (that is, minimize toxic wastes or water use) or quantitative (no more than X emissions per widget produced). Performance standards set specific goals but do not require any particular way to meet them. They may apply equally to environmental aspects covered by national regulation, by international treaty or soft law, or to unregulated aspects not covered by any government regulation.

In recent years, best-in-class standards have gained prominence in the environmental standards arena. Often, such standards have been used within the context of certification and/or labelling schemes. Best-in-class standards are typically comparative rather than absolute, in that they benchmark a producer's performance against others in the same product or service category. They can measure a single attribute (for example, energy efficiency) or they can evaluate and trade-off various attributes to obtain a measure of 'environmentally superior' products. Blue Angel in Germany or Greenseal in the United States are examples of eco-labelling schemes founded upon best-in-class performance criteria and standards for products and services. The programs grant the use of their logo to top performers that meet the minimum performance requirements.

3.2 Process and Management System Standards

The international standards developer, the ISO, was the first main player to move beyond the formulation of technical standards when it embarked on an effort to standardize quality management and assurance standards in the 1980s. Known as the ISO 9000 series, these quality management standards represented the ISO's first attempt to draft normative *systems* standards, as opposed to technical engineering specifications. The ISO 9000 standards focus on evaluating the procedures a company has in place to manage the quality of the production *process*, instead of the product itself. While not directly mandating particular 'quality levels' for products and services, the widely known and successful ISO 9000 series standards were developed to ensure that all *systems* that relate to the production of goods and services meet the same minimal quality assurance and quality control provisions.[4] To the degree that quality improvements can eliminate or minimize waste (for example, pollution), these standards have been recognized as precursors to a formal environmental management system (EMS), which more explicitly focuses on addressing organizations' environmental impacts.

Although firms have managed their environmental affairs independently for decades, over the last ten to fifteen years, standardized methods for environmental management have emerged at both the national and international levels. Voluntary

---

[4] A. Lally, 'ISO 14000 and Environmental Cost Accounting: The Gateway to the Global Market' (1998) 29(4) L. and Pol'y Int'l Bus. 501 at 504–5.

private sector standards and industry codes of conduct are examples of initiatives that have sought to harmonize environmental management practices. Developed in the late 1980s and early 1990s, examples of these voluntary environmental standards and codes include the International Chamber of Commerce Business Charter for Sustainable Development, the Chemical Manufacturers Association's (now American Chemistry Council) Responsible Care programme, and the CERES principles. While most of these codes (especially the industry-generated ones) tend to address only environmental management, some, such as the CERES principles, also focus on environmental results. Although independent of one another, these initiatives represent an evolution of voluntary standards development.[5]

3.2.1 *EMS*

The voluntary initiatives and the ISO 9000 standards discussed earlier in this chapter, along with subsequent national and regional EMS standards such as the British Standard 7750 and Europe's voluntary regulation, the Eco-Management and Audit Scheme (EMAS), served as precursors to the international EMS standard, ISO 14001. ISO 14001 and other EMS frameworks typically consist of a number of elements, such as policy setting, planning, management programs, internal auditing, and operational controls, which collectively constitute an organization's EMS. Organizations may self-declare conformance to the ISO 14001 standard but, more often, have an outside auditor certify that they meet the standard's requirements.

As with the ISO's quality management standards, prescriptive environmental performance levels are not included in ISO 14001, which instead provides a plan-do-check-act continual improvement model for organizations. Standard writers have justified the exclusion of environmental performance measures due to differences in national environmental regulations and the fear that specified levels might stifle continual improvement and innovation as well as limit market access for firms from developing countries. They also have felt that the setting of environmental performance levels, which have human health and other policy implications, falls within the remit of government, not private standard-setting bodies. Moreover, specific requirements would vary substantially among industry sectors and from large to small businesses, and the ambition of these standards was to be useful to all types and sizes of organizations.

Nonetheless, the absence of prescribed performance levels in EMSs such as ISO 14001 has diminished the credibility of the standard in the eyes of some interests external to the organizations adopting the standard. Since ISO 14001 is a systems standard, certification, even if credible, demonstrates only that a management system is in place. Any link to an actual change in the environment is indirect. External parties are primarily interested in the degree to which organizations impact the environment. And thus there has been a long-standing and unresolved

---

[5] J. Nash and J. Ehrenfeld, 'Code Green' (1996) 38 Env't 1.

debate centring on the link between certified EMSs such as ISO 14001 and improved environmental performance, especially since EMSs contain a combination of regulated and non-regulated environmental aspects and impacts. In recent years, several government-funded empirical studies in North America and Europe have failed so far to unequivocally establish that certified EMSs (ISO 14001 or EMAS) deliver environmental improvements.[6] One of the studies also found a lack of confidence in certification bodies, which were perceived as lacking sufficient technical competency and/or spending insufficient time during audits assessing companies' performance outcomes as opposed to documented policies and procedures. These studies have reinforced the reasons why EMS certifications have been met with scepticism by some government agencies, environmental organizations, and the general public in parts of the world.

3.3 Measurement and Reporting Standards

Another category of environmental standards focuses on measurement and/or disclosure of the social and environmental effects of the organization's activities. Harmonization of measurement approaches can include standards such as the air and water quality measurement standards developed by the ISO's Technical Committees 146 and 147, respectively. More recently, efforts have been made to develop greenhouse gas (GHG) accounting and reporting standards. Most notably, these include the Greenhouse Gas Protocol, which was prepared by the World Business Council on Sustainable Development and World Resources Institute (WBCSD/WRI), and the three-part ISO 14064 standard (currently under development), which provides specifications for the quantification, monitoring, reporting, and validation of GHG emissions applicable for organizations and GHG reduction projects. These protocols serve several purposes: they assist in the implementation of international treaty or national public law obligations such as the Kyoto Protocol to the UN Framework Convention on Climate Change and its associated emissions-trading schemes. They can also serve to, in effect, expand these public law schemes even to places where they do not yet apply, as in the application of the GHG protocols by US firms, either in preparation for what they see as eventual regulation or in order to participate in existing greenhouse gas emissions markets. Thus, private measurement protocols facilitate both public and private law schemes simultaneously.

A prime example of a disclosure protocol (and associated metrics) is the Global Reporting Initiative (GRI), a multi-stakeholder process and independent institution

---

[6] See 'EMS Survey Reveals Widespread Concern over Certification,' Report by Environmental Data Services, December 2003. See also 'Joint Workshop to Examine Connections between Environmental Management Systems and Permitting, Inspection and Enforcement in Regulation—Including the Formal Launch of the REMAS Project,' workshop report prepared by the Foundation for International Environmental Law and Development and the Institute for European Environmental Policy, June 2003.

whose mission is to develop and disseminate globally applicable sustainability reporting guidelines. These guidelines are for voluntary use by organizations for reporting on the company-level economic, environmental, and social dimensions of their activities, products, and services. The GRI aims to create principles on sustainability reporting that are as well accepted as financial reporting guidelines. Reports prepared using GRI guidelines are expected to follow principles of transparency, inclusiveness, auditability, completeness, relevance, accuracy, comparability, clarity, and timeliness. A GRI report is also supposed to follow specified protocols regarding data presentation, metrics, and content, although organizations have considerable flexibility in adapting the guidelines to their particular audiences and needs. Enterprises may choose to report about all the specified categories provided in the GRI guidelines or to choose less comprehensive reporting, at least during an initial period. The GRI does not attempt to dictate how an organization obtains its information, but instead to give enterprises a useful and credible template, and their multiple audiences some way of using the information to benchmark and compare results. A related facilities reporting project is developing GRI-based indicators for plant-level reporting, allowing disaggregated plant-specific data that may be more relevant to a plant's neighbours or local regulators, but less important for investors or consumers. The combination of plant- and company-level reporting allows companies to address a wide range of relevant audiences.

3.4 Proliferation of Standards Initiatives

All of these voluntary, private, and quasi-private standards have evolved in the dual context of market competition and the international legal framework. Since the inception of such schemes, government trade officials and some producers have expressed fears about growing confusion in the market place, as well as about the effects that they might have on market access and competitiveness of developing countries, particularly in cases where the programs were developed without their proper participation.[7] Regardless, the growing recognition of the positive effects of voluntary environmental and social standard-based certification and labelling systems, such as the role they play in driving market competition and innovation, as well as the potential they hold for opening new markets, has caused many original opponents to change their views and positions.

However, this competition can also have detrimental effects. The success, and even potential success, of certain NGO-led initiatives has prompted the proliferation of a

---

[7] Organisation for Economic Cooperation and Development (OECD), *Private Initiatives for Corporate Responsibility: An Analysis* (Paris: OECD, 2001); and United Nations Conference on Trade and Development, *Report of the Commission on Trade in Goods and Services and Commodities on Its Sixth Session*, Geneva, 4–8 February 2002, Doc. TD/B/EX(28)/4—TD/B/COM.1/49 (2002).

broad array of competing systems that have attempted to build on the momentum and credibility of the certification movement, while offering cheaper and less stringent alternatives. Indeed, it is precisely because NGO-led labelling and certification schemes have had significant bottom-line impacts for businesses in targeted sectors that some in the retailer/brand industries have taken a proactive role in developing competing standards and compliance systems that better suit their needs. This trend is particularly notable in the forest and coffee sectors. However, due to the poor stakeholder balance in some of these nascent industry initiatives, it is unlikely that they will result in standards and/or conformity assessment procedures that are considered meaningful by many civil society organizations. Yet, these industry groups are in the driver's seat because in many cases they represent such a large percentage of the market, and can bring their marketing and other resources to bear. And as a result, the pressing question confronting the comparatively smaller NGO-led initiatives is how to best influence the newer competing initiatives to ensure the newer initiative's credibility (and compatibility) with existing systems.

Among the industry-dominated competitors to NGO-led standards, the ISO is a case in point. In the forestry sector, for instance, some companies wanting to externally validate their environmental management practices may end up choosing to pursue ISO 14001 certification over the more rigorous (from an NGO's perspective) FSC certification. Other areas of possible competition with NGO-led initiatives may emerge when the ISO finishes drafting the GHG accounting and corporate social responsibility standards that are currently under development.

4 COMPLIANCE WITH PRIVATE AND QUASI-PRIVATE STANDARDS

Private standards are presumably 'voluntary' although they are often significantly more consequential than this label suggests. They can be considered voluntary only in that there are no legal requirements for a country to adopt them and in that there is not an entity that regulates or enforces their implementation. However, because countries often adopt private international standards such as the ISO's as national standards, and because industry norms may mandate conformity to a standard as a condition of business, they can become *de facto* requirements for competitiveness in the international market.

Participation in the standards development process itself is also not entirely 'voluntary'. Since the requirements within private standards can have significant implications for market competitiveness, various interests, particularly large multinational corporations, feel compelled to participate in the standards writing process. Requirements contained within a particular standard could have disproportionate economic consequences for a given country, industry sector, or individual company. Therefore, participation becomes virtually obligatory for potentially affected entities. Indeed, the development, diffusion, and implementation of private and quasi-private standards are driven by a swirling current of markets, risk prevention, and regulation. Each operates directly and indirectly through a number of different mechanisms, which we discuss in the next few sections.

4.1 Market Dynamics

Market mechanisms can be both positive and negative. They can take effect through requirements of financiers, investors or insurers, or through buyer specifications and government procurement. For example, after the ISO completes international standards, national standards bodies typically adopt them as national standards. Once nationalized, these standards often become market requirements (even for companies without foreign operations), for instance, as part of government or company procurement criteria, as has happened in the case of the ISO 9000 and ISO 14000 series standards.[8] Concerns within the organization about operational efficiency and environmental liabilities also play a role in the adoption of private environment-related standards. In the next sections, we discuss in more detail the various market pressures affecting all of these areas.

4.1.1 *Drivers Internal to Organizations: Eco-Efficiency, Reducing Liability*

Some organizations adopt private environmental standards, especially environmental management standards, for internal purposes, without reference to direct external pressure. They may do so for a number of reasons. In a minority of cases, corporate leadership may be convinced that a sustainable business model includes an environmental stewardship ethic. Such altruistically motivated enterprises, however, remain a small minority. A larger number of organizations, especially those engaged in manufacturing, may adopt private standards as a way to find and exploit savings opportunities and eco-efficiencies or to reduce liabilities. For example, finding ways to reduce hazardous wastes through process redesign or other pollution prevention techniques can save money on disposal costs, lower regulatory costs by obviating the need for certain permits, lower the risk of tort litigation, and reduce the quantities of raw materials used in production. There have been a host of studies over the last two decades demonstrating the economic as well as environmental benefits of such

---

[8] J. Morrison et al., *Managing a Better Environment: Opportunities and Obstacles for ISO 14001 in Public Policy and Commerce* (Oakland, CA: Pacific Institute for Studies in Development, Environment, and Security, 2000).

measures, as well as the related concepts of industrial ecology, green building, and the like. Such firms may already be implementing quality control management standards such as the ISO 9000, and it is a small step from there to EMS implementation.

Eco-efficiency and liability rationales are important to making the 'business case' for pollution prevention and other environmental protection strategies, but they are also limited. While they may drive the adoption of EMS standards, they are generally not the principal drivers of certification or reporting on environmental impacts, which can have high costs with uncertain short-term, tangible paybacks and are typically driven by external audiences. These internal motivations may lead to significant performance improvements, but it is not clear whether these improvements deal with the most urgent environmental impacts of the firm's behaviour or whether EMSs that have been adopted for internal reasons will ever lead to environmental improvements that are not deemed cost-effective, even when considering a long-term pay-back period. This uncertainty arises because a central tenet of voluntary environmental management standards is 'flexibility'—rarely, if ever, will they prescribe specific environmental improvements but rather they will allow organizations to focus on the environmental issues they themselves deem most important.

Eco-efficiency is not the only reason why firms might choose to adopt private environmental standards for their own use, even without any external drivers such as reporting or recognition. Other reasons may include improving compliance with regulatory or legal requirements, attracting or retaining qualified and forward-thinking staff, or benchmarking performance against other plants of the same company or against competitors in the same industry. These reasons merge with other, external reasons for adopting such standards, either market or regulation-based.

4.1.2 *Demands of Business Partners and Customers*

The adoption of private standards is often driven by the need to satisfy outside audiences. Voluntary environmental and social standards and their related certification, reporting, and labelling systems are increasingly becoming requirements for access to certain markets, especially in Europe and Asia. These may be either built into the contract or take the form of preferences for suppliers who meet certain requirements. Customers may require certain environmental guarantees of probity as a condition of the contract in order to minimize their own reputational exposure. Banks and insurers may be willing to lower rates if certain environmental conditions are fulfilled. In all, the adoption of certain private standards and protocols serves as a shorthand signal of environmental responsibility. For instance, as discussed earlier, while the adoption of an EMS does not guarantee superior environmental performance, it does signal to outside audiences that management is taking the issue seriously and will avoid major disasters that could tarnish the image of associated enterprises.

Government procurement is a classic example of contract-driven adoption of environmental standards. In the United States, Executive Order 13101 requires federal agencies to purchase, where possible, 'products or services that have a lesser or

reduced effect on human health and the environment when compared with competing products or services that serve the same purpose.' Europe has similar programmes,
for example, under EC Directive 2004/18 of 31 March 2004 on the Coordination of
Procedures for the Award of Public Works Contracts, Public Supply Contracts and
Public Service Contracts, governments may incorporate environmental and social
criteria into procurement. Private standards, especially third-party certification,
serve as an indicator that a product is environmentally superior, while reducing
the government's cost of obtaining the information—they are useful for both the
public and private actors. For example, the Canadian environmental agency prefers
goods and services that have been certified under Canada's EcoLogo labelling scheme
for government procurement purposes.[9]

In the private sector, industry has begun demanding the use of private standards
from their suppliers. While the ISO 14001 standard does not require that suppliers be
certified, some large corporations are requiring certification from their suppliers or
at least from suppliers of environmentally sensitive goods. For example, in 1999, both
the Ford Motor Company and General Motors announced that they were requiring
ISO 14001 certification from their suppliers. Other large corporations, such as Xerox,
IBM, Bristol-Myers Squibb, and Dole Standard Fruit Company have also required
(or strongly encouraged) their suppliers to adopt and certify to the EMS standard.
Codes of conduct and certification requirements are formalized via supplier agreements and are enforced through questionnaires and occasional on-site visits. These
practices illustrate the potential for the market to drive behavioural changes in
environmental management even for firms in countries where government regulatory authorities have been unwilling or unable to do so.

Industry associations also impose industry-specific or substance-specific standards on suppliers. For example, a number of large firms in the high-technology sector recently announced the release of the Electronics Industry Code of Conduct
(EICC), which was developed to establish and promote unified industry expectations for socially responsible practices across the electronic industry's global supply
chain. Among other things, the EICC harmonizes approaches for monitoring suppliers' performance across several areas of social responsibility, including labour
and employment practices, health and safety, ethics, and the protection of the environment. This industry-wide initiative was developed in response to repeated complaints by suppliers that the proliferation of codes has left them facing multiple,
overlapping requirements and burdensome reporting procedures.

Banks and insurers can require the implementation of management or certification programs as a condition of doing business. As of 2004, some 28 global banks,
representing more than 75 per cent of international private lending capital, had

---

[9] Environment Canada, 'Towards Greener Government Procurement: An Environment Canada Case
Study,' in T. Russel, ed., *Greener Purchasing: Opportunities and Innovations* (Sheffield: Greenleaf
Publishing, 1998).

signed on to the Equator Principles, which is a code of conduct that requires the completion of an environmental and social impact assessment and, where necessary, a management/mitigation/decommissioning plan before project finance will be available. The Equator Principles, in turn, incorporate by reference the standards of the International Finance Corporation (the commercial arm of the World Bank) and the bank itself. In the environmental area, the World Bank's *Pollution Prevention and Abatement Handbook*, along with sector-specific guidelines for some forty industries, are incorporated into an evaluation of financing for large projects.[10] Thus, standards that originate in the public international arena (which are themselves prompted by NGO and government pressures) may pass by reference into private standards, especially where the private and public functions are similar (large-project lending) and there is a felt need for consistency. Some individual banks have also developed their own principles. The Bank of America, for example, developed principles on environmental responsibility in 2004 that apply to its lending operations worldwide.

Investors also comprise a major constituency for reporting and certification initiatives. By 2003, the field of socially responsible investment (SRI) encompassed 11.3 per cent of all professionally managed investment dollars in the United States, over two trillion dollars, according to the Social Investment Forum.[11] While some SRI investments simply screen out objectionable investments such as tobacco, others engage in more complex evaluations of environmental and social records based in part on publicly reported information. Institutional investors, representing state and union pension funds, are particularly active in both seeking out environmentally sound companies, and in pushing their existing holdings to improve their ethical, environmental, and social performance. California's Public Employees' Retirement system (CalPERS), for example, has pledged to invest up to US $500 million in environmentally screened stock funds and US $200 million more in private equity to back the environmental technology sector.

Under the rubric of the Carbon Disclosure Project, a group of 155 institutional investors with US $21 trillion in assets asked large companies to provide information on carbon risk factors. In order to do so, the companies will have to use measurement and reporting protocols developed by private organizations (for example, the WBCSD/WRI Greenhouse Gas Protocol and/or the ISO 14064 standard).[12] Often, institutional investors turn to NGOs such as the Investor Responsibility Resource Center for an evaluation of a company's social responsibility profile, while these NGOs, in turn, rely on information generated from certification, labelling, and reporting systems as well as their own research. For-profit analysts have also begun to specialize in identifying environmental leaders (as evidenced by their EMS

---

[10] For a discussion of 'green banking' within the United States, see W.L. Thomas, 'The Green Nexus: Financiers and Sustainable Development' (2001) 13 Geo. Int'l. Envt'l L. Rev. 899.

[11] Social Investment Forum, *2003 Report on Socially Responsible Investing Trends in the United States* (Washington, DC: Social Investment Forum, 2003).

[12] See *Carbon Disclosure Project 2005 Report* (London: Carbon Disclosure Project, 2005).

certifications, compliance record, and performance reporting), seeing sound environmental management as a viable proxy for good management overall.[13]

4.1.3 *Demands of External Audiences: Reputational Incentives*

In addition to these contractual incentives and investor and supply chain mandates, a larger, if more diffuse, driver for the adoption of private standards is a sense that they touch on issues important to consumers. In a global economy where small shifts in market share can make all the difference, and where branding and differentiating a company's products is often key, a company's reputation as a good (or poor) environmental actor can become significant. Reputational incentives can be primarily negative—that is, an effort to avoid being tarred as an environmental predator—or positive—an effort to gain business advantages by being perceived as an environmental leader. Often companies adopt private standards as a result of both positive and negative incentives. 'Brand' industries that are vulnerable to consumer boycotts, high-profile lawsuits, or other public protests, for example, might promulgate or join codes of conduct or certification systems in an effort to avoid becoming targets. The Voluntary Principles on Security and Human Rights, a quasi-private code of conduct negotiated by the US and UK governments, major extractive industry companies, and NGOs, for instance, was largely an attempt to defuse adverse public perceptions of the security practices of oil and mining companies. Industry associations also sometimes require compliance with private standards as a condition of membership in the association. The most well-known example is the considerable revamping of the chemical industry's Responsible Care initiative, which now requires all of its members to have an industry-specific EMS in place, and to have by the end of 2007 an initial certification cycle completed by an outside auditor. At the outset, the Responsible Care initiative was largely driven by negative perceptions of the industry's environmental role. However, over time, it is possible that even though these initiatives begin for defensive reasons, as staff and management perceive that they have benefits, including real improvements in company morale or cost savings, they eventually take on a life of their own and become more substance than window-dressing.

Reputational incentives can also seek to position a company as an environmental leader, in the expectation that such a reputation will attract customers and loyal employees. Many leading companies have signed on to more than one overlapping code of conduct and/or reporting framework, although the willingness to sign on seems to vary with the stringency of the obligations required. Standards-based certification, labelling, and reporting schemes are particularly important in establishing these positive reputational incentives, as they can serve as proxies for good environmental stewardship, making it simpler for interested parties to tell leaders from

---

[13] See Innovest Strategic Value Advisors, *Corporate Environmental Governance: A Study into the Influence of Environmental Governance and Financial Performance* (New York: November 2004).

laggards. Certification and labelling require a generalized trust that the methodology of certification reflects the right issues and addresses substantive performance as well as adequate management systems and that the verifying entity has the qualifications, the independence, and the incentives to rigorously test the participant company's performance rather than soft-pedal it. These issues have been most salient in the context of self-certification or in cases where third-party certifiers have been large accounting or consulting firms with multiple connections to company management or government trade ministry officials interested in encouraging trade through certification. With the exception of organic food, certification and labelling schemes in the United States and Europe are private with some government oversight, while in the rest of the world they are more often government run. Even well regarded schemes have made controversial decisions, which in the eyes of some audiences have 'cheapened' the certification.[14]

All of these market-driven incentives share the characteristic that it is the perception, as much as the reality, that drives companies to 'voluntarily' adopt them. In other words, if producers have the impression that implementing one or more private standard could make them more attractive to business partners, consumers, investors, lenders, or procurers, they will do so even if the actual numbers of decisions that turn on the existence of such standards is limited. A dynamic will then take hold by which companies will adopt standards because their competitors have done so.

4.2 Regulatory Incentives

Regulation, or the threat of regulation, also drives the use of private standards, especially environmental management standards. Regulation may take the form of disclosure requirements, leadership initiatives that seek to reward superior environmental performance, enforcement mechanisms that require offending companies to implement private standards, or international instruments that incorporate private standards into their implementation mechanisms. Even non-existent regulation serves as a spur, by driving companies to employ private voluntary standards to avoid the imposition of more onerous mandatory ones, or as a laboratory of the viability of a policy approach.

4.2.1 Disclosure Initiatives and Private Standards

Many countries now require a public disclosure of environmental and social information through 'right-to-know' laws. In the United States, the Toxics Release Inventory requires companies to collect and make public certain toxic emissions

---

[14] Consider the opposition of Greenpeace International and other environmental groups to the certification of the Alaskan Pollack fishery by the Marine Stewardship Council, given the documented

data—some states have broader requirements that include not only emissions but also inputs and outputs of toxics in the production process. Pollutant release and transfer registers, and other mandatory corporate disclosure of environmental information, have been incorporated into the legislation of European countries and a number of developing countries, in part driven by European Union (EU) law. The Danish Ministry of Social Affairs has developed a social index for measuring the degree to which companies live up to their social responsibilities.[15] Public international law instruments, including a 2003 protocol to the Convention on Access to Information, Public Participation in Decision-Making and Access to Justice in Environmental Matters, also increasingly require the creation of pollutant release and transfer registries.

In addition, disclosure requirements are often linked to securities regulation of publicly traded firms. The UK Department of Trade and Industry, for example, mandates operating and financial review reports for quoted companies to include factors, including environmental factors, that significantly affect future operations. These requirements are similar to those of the US Securities and Exchange Commission, which require publicly traded companies to disclose risks and liabilities, including environmental liabilities and potential liabilities. French law requires companies to record in their annual reports the social and environmental consequences of their activities.[16] All of these public disclosure requirements stimulate a need for companies to find standardized, and comparable, indicators and measurements, if only to avoid a duplication of effort. Yet, because there are no uniform public standards of this kind in existence, private standards often fill the gap.

4.2.2 *Superior Performance and Public Sector Use of Private Standards as Incentives*

As new environmental challenges emerge, and some old ones resist further improvement using traditional 'command-and-control' regulation, governments have begun to explore complementary approaches to encourage companies to go 'beyond compliance'. These usually involve promising benefits such as shorter permitting times, multimedia permits, streamlined procedures, fewer inspections or positive public recognition for companies that both meet and substantially exceed compliance with environmental laws. These positive incentive-based efforts are envisioned as providing: (1) a more tailored system that will allow increased innovation by industry leaders; (2) an opportunity for tackling as-yet unregulated problems; and (3) a vehicle for efficiency gains, allowing regulators to focus scant resources on the worst problems and offenders. Opt-in is voluntary, with the existing system remaining as a baseline

---

decline of the stellar sea lion population in the fishery and the attention to the impacts on biodiversity required by the MSC certification standards. Environment News Service, 26 August 2004.

[15] See Danish Ministry of Social Affairs, *Your Tool: The Social Index* (Copenhagen: Secretariat for the Social Index, 2005).   [16] Law no. 2001–420 of 15 May 2001, J.O., 16 May 2001, at 7776, Article 46.

for companies that choose not to participate. A key theme of most of these leadership-oriented, 'beyond compliance' regulatory programmes is the fact that they are underpinned by voluntary private standards, particularly EMS and/or performance measurement and reporting standards.

For instance, in North America and Europe, the centerpiece of most such efforts is the implementation of an EMS, usually but not always modeled on ISO 14001. Most such programmes require an 'ISO 14001 plus' (or 'external value' EMS)—one that requires compliance with legal requirements, public disclosure, and stakeholder involvement. Examples of voluntary EMS-based regulatory initiatives include Europe's Eco-Management and Audit Scheme (EMAS) and the US Environmental Protection Agency's (EPA) Performance Track, as well as US state-level programs in Michigan, Wisconsin, Massachusetts, Texas, and elsewhere. The US EPA is considering providing options within existing regulatory structures for firms employing an EMS.[17]

4.2.3 *Use of Private Standards in Enforcement and Securing Compliance with Regulatory Measures*

As discussed earlier, businesses have long put private standards into place as a result of, or in order to avoid, problems with regulatory compliance. Since the mid-1990s, the US EPA's audit policy has encouraged the use of EMSs to improve compliance by serving as tools that enable early disclosure and the remediation of violations and, thereby, potentially avoiding some civil penalties. In fact, the agency has explicitly stated that criminal sanctions and civil penalties may be reduced or waived if a business can show it has implemented adequate systems for managing its environmental compliance. More recently, the EPA has gone further, requiring some firms to implement EMSs as part of settlements of environmental violation cases, often through the use of supplementary environmental projects (SEPs), in which businesses agree to pollution prevention changes or to the implementation of an EMS as part of the settlement.[18]

Even for firms that are not now in enforcement proceedings, the threat of compliance enforcement is a powerful lever for the adoption of environmental management standards. So is the potential of private litigation. Once leading industry players start adopting private standards in their operations, other players must worry that these standards will help establish what constitutes due care for purposes of tort litigation. They may adopt the standards to minimize their litigation risk. Still others may preemptively adopt private standards to dampen enthusiasm for mandatory public standards imposition. Indeed, some have suggested that the threat of mandatory

---

[17] US Environmental Protection Agency (EPA), 'Strategy for Determining the Role of EMSs in Regulatory Programs,' 12 April 2004.

[18] US EPA Office of Enforcement and Compliance Assurance, 'Guidance on the Use of EMSs in Enforcement Settlements as Injunctive Relief and SEPs,' Washington, DC, 10 June 2003.

public disclosure or corporate conduct regulatory standards motivates much of a business's enthusiasm for self-discipline and/or voluntary management practices and reporting. During the 1990s, voluntary covenants in the Netherlands and elsewhere created non-interference promises by government if industry successfully regulated itself, although enthusiasm for such bargains seems to have waned somewhat.

5 PRIVATE VERSUS PUBLIC—VOLUNTARY VERSUS MANDATORY STANDARDS

5.1 Relationship between Public and Private Standards

Neither private nor public standards exist in a vacuum. Private standards have long interacted with, and are often developed in response to, public law-making and regulatory efforts. They can serve as gap-fillers or the technical foundation for existing public laws, as portents and precursors of new public law, or as pre-emptive efforts to retard or derail public regulation. For example, in terms of a technical foundation, under Europe's 'New Approach', quasi-private standards form the underpinnings of much legislation in the EU.[19] Under this approach, which was initiated in the 1980s, the European Commission, trying to facilitate expanded regional trade, set only the 'essential requirements' for a product or service to be sold throughout the market. The technical specifics were left to voluntary standards developed by private bodies, especially the European standards body CEN (Comité Européen de Normalisation or European Committee for Standardization, known by its French acronym). This approach has been used in EU directives on the energy performance of buildings, the promotion of the use of biofuels in transport, and on waste from electrical and electronic equipment. As for gap-filling, consider measurement protocols. Treaties may specify that states are to monitor environmental impacts, but they may not specify exactly how or with what measurement approaches. Private standards are often aimed at allowing producers, and thus indirectly and ultimately governments, to employ uniform, agreed-upon measurement protocols. The GHG Protocols are a case in point. In both cases, the use of private standards reduces government costs and the time required to implement public law obligations.

Based on the recognition of these realities, government agencies have for decades actively supported the integration of voluntary consensus standards into their policies and activities. In the United States, for example, reliance upon private standards in policymaking and public standard setting goes back to the late 1970s. Voluntary

---

[19] EC Directive 98/34 Laying Down a Procedure for the Provision of Information in the Fields of Technical Standards and Regulations and of Rules on Information Services.

standards were useful, according to the Office of Management and Budget, to: (1) 'encourage federal agencies to benefit from the expertise of the private sector'; (2) 'promote federal agency participation in such bodies to ensure creation of standards that are usable by federal agencies'; and (3) 'reduce reliance on government-unique standards where an existing voluntary standard would suffice.'[20] In order to codify these policies, the US Congress in 1996 passed the National Technology Transfer and Advancement Act (NTTAA) (Public Law 104–13). The act requires federal agencies to use voluntary standards to the extent practicable, to report when they have developed agency-specific standards, and to consult with both domestic and international voluntary consensus standards bodies when developing and adopting government standards. When a voluntary standard fails to address, or is inconsistent with, the mission of a government agency, an exception clause in the NTTAA permits a governmental agency to elect or develop other technical standards.

Private voluntary standards can also presage future national or international regulation. Private standards suggest the recognition of a problem area, an approach to addressing it, and an acknowledgment that industry has both the desire and the capacity to implement controls and to do so in a manner that optimizes economic efficiency. At the international level, private standard-setting processes may be more effective and agile than multilateral negotiations, especially where highly technical protocols are at issue, since they tend to include more of the directly affected parties rather than generalist diplomats. On the other hand, industry may sometimes enter into or advocate standards-creating processes in hopes that a voluntary, private approach will forestall more onerous public regulation at either the national or international level.

An example from the regime for control of marine oil pollution may be instructive. It became clear in the wake of the 1967 *Torrey Canyon* oil spill that a regulatory regime was in the offing. Oil tanker owners negotiated a private, voluntary Tanker Owners Voluntary Agreement Concerning Liability for Oil Pollution, in part hoping to avoid stricter mandatory controls. However, the existence of a voluntary agreement did not stop the completion of a public convention, but rather showed states that the general approach was feasible and economically viable. Public international regulation of information regarding pesticides and other hazardous chemicals also followed this route from private to public.

Further evidence of this at times strained relationship between public and private standards can be found in the run-up to the 2002 World Summit on Sustainable Development (WSSD), where a coalition of groups led by Friends of the Earth International floated proposals for a multilateral treaty on corporate accountability, which would have committed states to ensuring that corporations doing business in their territory complied with certain minimum standards. While the proposal failed,

---

[20] US Office of Management and Budget (OMB), 'Federal Participation in the Development and Use of Voluntary Standards,' Circular no. A-119.

in large part due to heavy lobbying by industry, the WSSD's plan of action includes several references to corporate accountability, including the exhortation to:

[e]ncourage industry to improve social and environmental performance through voluntary initiatives, including environmental management systems, codes of conduct, certification and public reporting on environmental and social issues, taking into account such initiatives as the International Organization for Standardization (ISO) standards and Global Reporting Initiative guidelines on sustainability reporting, bearing in mind Principle 11 of the Rio Declaration on Environment and Development).[21]

The WSSD example is emblematic of the many debates surrounding both the changing nature and scope of private standards as well as their evolving role in public policy. While private standards once typically played only a technical supporting role in government policy, they are now encroaching towards becoming a centerpiece of policy instruments.

It is in this regard that the ISO's movement towards the standardization of 'management systems' (first quality, then environmental) is notable because it has marked a shift in the organization's focus from technical engineering standards to standards that have greater (and more direct) implications for society and public policy. In other words, while local communities may have little interest in the thread width of a screw used in a company's product, they are likely to be profoundly concerned about the methods by which an organization manages its environmental risks, given the potential impact on the community's welfare. In this sense, unlike all other ISO standards, which primarily affect their users (and customers), the ISO 14000 series standards directly affect a much larger set of stakeholders. These stakeholders often carry the burden of environmental 'externalities', such as the costs of resource consumption and pollution, while industry stands to enhance profits by 'externalizing' environmental impacts.

Likewise, because the ISO 14000 standards aim to tackle issues relating to the environmental performance of companies and sustainable development more generally, they enter realms that are of interest to regulatory authorities, policymakers, and the public. However, given the ISO's fifty-year history of developing technical standards almost exclusively out of an interest to industry, the institution remains heavily influenced by the private sector. Thus, as discussed earlier, while the ISO's scope of work has substantially expanded to encompass activities that may have significant societal impacts, there has not been a corresponding increase in the representation of public stakeholders. This fact has been the source of consternation to some government agencies and civil society groups who have expressed a preference for the development of public standards whenever practical and feasible.

A corollary debate has emerged regarding the appropriateness of private voluntary standards to solve pressing public policy challenges. Private voluntary standards,

---

[21] Johannesburg Plan of Implementation, 26 August-4 September 2002, UN Doc. A/CONF.199/20 (2002) at para. 18(a).

which producers must pledge to abide by and which are enforced by indirect market pressures rather than regulators, have undeniable advantages. They reduce the cost of public regulation and enforcement, shifting enforcement costs to the producers themselves, who must pay for certification or the documentation of compliance. The administration costs of private standards should be lower than for equivalent public standards. Moreover, if the leaders in an industry are conforming to private voluntary standards, regulators can use shrinking enforcement or standards development budgets to greater effect in targeting the laggards. Private standards can often be more easily arrived at and more easily revised than public agreements—contrast the less than three years it can take to develop an ISO EMS standard with the decade or more it can take for the drafting, signing, and entry into force of a treaty. In part, this contrast is due to the less than fully participatory and open nature of the private standards development process, as discussed earlier, and so it is a dubious virtue. Nonetheless, the costs of standards development are at least partially borne by the private sector, and the participation of technical personnel and those from the industries or entities to be subject to the standard may make for quicker as well as more practical and workable arrangements because the 'real parties in interest' are directly at the negotiating table.

Moreover, private standards, because they are often self-imposed, allow for more precise tailoring to the needs of a particular enterprise. An enterprise can choose to focus on certain aspects of its environmental management, for example, or choose to report on those issues of greatest concern to inside or outside constituencies. As such, it can, under ideal circumstances, create 'buy-in' throughout an organization for the environmental goals espoused rather than having these goals become routine, minimalist exercises in box checking. In theory at least, these efforts will allow for improvement beyond the threshold compliance levels specified in international or local law and will allow those enterprises with the interest and means to do so to pioneer new approaches to as yet unregulated problems.

These strengths of private standards are also their weakness. The very flexibility that businesses appreciate reduces the credibility of these standards with local community, NGO, and regulatory audiences. If enterprises can pick and choose which environmental issues to focus on, which indicators/measures to report and the like, there will be little assurance that major problems are not being swept under the rug. And if the private standards are rigorous enough in design and verification mechanisms to avoid this problem, they will also, by definition, be too rigorous to entice any but a few leading companies into choosing to implement them, despite the incentives for doing so. There is, therefore, an inherent tendency for private standards to be, overall, less stringent than public ones covering the same subject matter.

Moreover, the penalties for non-compliance with management or certification schemes, or false or misleading reporting of environmental protocols, are extremely limited. With respect to ISO standards, the ISO's Conformity Assessment Committee (CASCO) produces international standards and guides that provide information and general requirements on conformity assessment procedures—that is, deciding whether an organization has successfully implemented the standard. However, it is national accreditation bodies that set the criteria for certifiers. The International Accreditation Forum (IAF) is a world association of national conformity assessment accreditation bodies and other organizations interested in conformity assessment, mainly to ISO 9000 and ISO 14001. Its primary function is to encourage the development of a single worldwide system of mutual recognition of conformity assessment certificates, with an end goal of eliminating non-tariff barriers to trade. Both the IAF and CASCO have developed mutual recognition and other protocols. Nonetheless, harmonization of conformity assessment to private standards generally is in its infancy, as are attempts to set up worldwide standards for the qualification of certifiers, accreditation bodies, and independent standards auditors. It will take some time for these efforts to actually result in credible conformity assessment protocols that are accepted across borders, especially given the pressures on developing country certifiers and accreditation bodies to certify large numbers of companies.

Theoretically, companies can lose their ISO certification, and participants in other private schemes may be ejected from the schemes for continuing non-conformity with the standard. This happens rarely though and only after extensive negative publicity. The most common compliance assurance schemes involve private auditing and accounting firms, but several studies have shown that such audits are often incomplete and biased towards management. And with a few exceptions, such as the revamped Responsible Care programme, most industry standards do not even require external verification. A few attempts at stakeholder/labour/NGO monitoring have taken place in the labour standards context, but they have not become a widely accepted model. One complaint, therefore, is that private standards are for the most part toothless and cannot differentiate good players from bad. Related to this criticism is the more general complaint that all voluntary codes of conduct are enforced only by self-declaration and self-certification, with sporadic NGO denunciations of particularly egregious abuses being the only check.

The tension between stringency and widespread adoption has been a problem given the non-mandatory nature of private standards. With the exception of 'green' companies that stake their reputation on environmental probity, and large 'blue' companies subject to consumer scrutiny and sensitive to small changes in market share, the uptake of voluntary standards has been limited. Fewer than 25 per cent of large multinational corporations provide public information on their environmental performance, and this number has not grown significantly.[22] While most major industrial players now have some version of an EMS in place, very few provide public information derived from the EMS or pursue third party certification.

---

[22] D. Wheeler and J. Elkington, *The Recent History of Environmental and Social Reporting: Business Strategy and the Environment* (London: SustainAbility, 2001).

Environmental labelling, while growing, still covers a marginal percentage of goods sold. To truly affect environmental outcomes on a global scale, voluntary private standards are unlikely to be enough.

5.2 Revitalized Push to Create Public Standards

The combination of a lack of oversight, inadequate enforcement mechanisms, and the spotty uptake of private standards, in the midst of increasing perceptions that private enterprises play a key role in sustainable (and unsustainable) development and that states by themselves have insufficient resources to tackle emerging challenges, has led to new efforts to move standard setting for enterprise behaviour into the public realm. These efforts take several forms. First, there is the attempt to open up private/public bodies such as ISO to greater transparency and inclusiveness by providing a more prominent role for civil society organizations, small businesses, and other underrepresented sectors. Second, efforts continue to strengthen and augment existing *public* voluntary standards on corporate behaviour, including the OECD Guidelines for Multinational Enterprises, the ILO Tripartite Declaration of Principles Concerning Multinational Enterprises and Social Policy, and the UN Secretary General's Global Compact.

A third effort involves moving beyond voluntary principles, codes of conduct, and private standards towards some form of mandatory international supervision of private sector commitments. A step in this direction might involve international guidelines accompanied by a reporting and/or monitoring mechanism. One such effort includes the UN Commission on Human Rights's efforts to prepare Norms and Guidelines on the Responsibilities of Transnational Corporations and Other Business Enterprises with Regard to Human Rights. A draft version of these norms was approved by the Sub-Commission on the Promotion and Protection of Human Rights in 2003, but it has been prevented by some states and corporate interests from being more formally adopted by the UN to date. The norms include obligations on private corporations to respect national and international law on the protection of the environment, to observe the precautionary principle, and to generally conduct their activities in a manner contributing to sustainable development. The norms create a non-binding guideline recommending that business enterprises internally implement them, use them in their supply chain policies, and report on their progress. In its ongoing effort to advance the norms, the Office of the High Commissioner for Human Rights released a report linking corporate responsibilities to intergovernmental agreements in early 2005. Many of the participants in the UN process, especially NGOs, envision eventually some kind of monitoring and/or complaint system through the UN as well as through states and companies themselves, although the contours of such a system are as yet unclear. In part, the problem stems from the fact that, aside from general exhortations to respect human rights and a limited number of international crimes, such as war crimes, crimes against humanity, and genocide, international law does not impose obligations directly upon private actors.[23]

5.3 Future of Private Standards

It is evident from this analysis that private standards have played, and will continue to play, a valuable and economically efficient role in addressing pressing social and environmental problems. It is the view of the authors, however, that such private standards can (and should) only be used as a complement and supplement to public standards and that caution must be taken to ensure that they do not evolve into a complete substitute for them. It is more than likely that in coming years increased attention will focus on businesses' environmental management practices, and certification and reporting standards will almost certainly play an even more prominent role underpinning the global economic system than they do today. Public and private standards will both coexist, mutually reinforce each other, and overlap, and a variety of hybrid standard-setting processes are to be expected. It will also probably be a long-term negotiating process before states reach agreement on the appropriate nexus between public and private standards as well as the precise role private standards should play in advancing sustainable development. Meanwhile private international standards developers are moving aggressively into the sustainability field, and the differences in coverage and rigor between different kinds of private standards—especially those generated by NGO coalitions as opposed to business-led initiatives—are likely to become more salient. It is therefore urgent that those concerned with international environmental regimes consider private standards organizations and their products as an integral part of public environmental policy regimes and factor in the impact of private schemes on public regimes.

RECOMMENDED READING

C. Coglianese and J. Nash, eds., *Regulating from the Inside: Can Environmental Management Systems Achieve Policy Goals?* (Washington, DC: Resources for the Future, 2001).
C. Dankers, *The WTO and Environmental and Social Standards, Certification and Labelling in Agriculture* (Rome: Raw Materials, Tropical and Horticultural Products Service, Commodity and Trade Division, Food and Agriculture Organization, 2003).

---

[23] For an attempt to do so, see International Council for Human Rights Policy (ICHRP), *Beyond Voluntarism: Human Rights and the Developing International Legal Obligations of Companies* (Geneva: ICHRP, 2002) ; and Carlos M. Vasquez, 'Direct vs. Indirect Obligations of Corporations under International Law' (2005) 43 Colum. J. Transnat'l L. 927.

R.B. Hall and T.J. Biersteker, eds., *The Emergence of Private Authority in Global Governance* (Cambridge, UK: Cambridge University Press, 2002).

R. Krut and H. Gleckman, *ISO 14001: A Missed Opportunity for Sustainable Global Industrial Development* (London: Earthscan, 1998).

W. Moomaw and G. Unruh, 'Going around the GATT: Private Green Trade Regimes' (1997) 8 Praxis Fletcher J. Dev. Stud. 67.

M. Morikawa and J. Morrison, *Who Develops ISO Standards? A Survey of Participation in ISO's International Standards Development Processes* (Oakland, CA: Pacific Institute for Studies in Development, Environment, and Security, 2004).

J.I. Morrison, K.K. Cushing, Z. Day, and J. Speir, *Managing a Better Environment: Opportunities and Obstacles for ISO 14001 in Public Policy and Commerce* (Oakland, CA: Pacific Institute for Studies in Development, Environment, and Security, 2000).

N. Roht-Arriaza, 'Shifting the Point of Regulation: The International Organization for Standardization and Global Lawmaking on Trade and the Environment' (1995) 22 Ecology L.Q. 3.

PART V

KEY CONCEPTS

CHAPTER 22

TRANSBOUNDARY IMPACTS

GÜNTHER HANDL

1 INTRODUCTION

To date the concept of transboundary impact has served as the principal conceptual vehicle for ascertaining international rights and responsibilities regarding the environment. Other notions, such as 'intergenerational responsibility' (see Chapter 27 'Equity') or 'sustainable development' (see Chapter 26 'Sustainable Development'), while clearly gaining in importance recently, have yet to attract the international community's *imprimatur* as operational legal concepts that, in a legal system still dominated by states, could rival the function that transboundary impact plays in present-day international environmental law.

Transboundary impact highlights the crucial relevance of spatial notions, of states' territory, and the separation of cause and effect by international boundaries. As such, it does not directly speak to the mechanism through which effects might be experienced in the state of impact, or to the cause in the state of origin, but focuses instead on the effects' nature and magnitude. Although transboundary impact might be understood to include effects ranging from political and economic to ideological or intangible ones,[1] in international environmental legal discourse the notion is generally understood to involve transboundary physical effects. Transboundary impact in this former, wider sense may be subject to special treaty regimes. However, these regimes bear only indirectly on international environmental law.[2] It is the concept in the narrower sense—that is, of transboundary physical effects, by contrast—that has been the catalyst in the evolution of general international law directly applicable to the environment. The present chapter, therefore, will focus exclusively on transboundary impact in its narrower, technical sense. The focus of inquiry will be limited further to legal norms applicable to transboundary impacts on other individual states or group of states, their territory, natural resources, and people to the exclusion of transboundary effects of a global nature or affecting the global commons only. Much of international law governing transboundary impacts has an essentially bilateralist grounding. By contrast, norms applicable to the global commons more typically reflect the notion of an international communitarian interest in environmental protection. Thus, although some of the basic rules regarding transboundary state-to-state impacts may apply also to transboundary impacts of the global effects/global commons category (see Chapter 23 'Common Areas, Common Heritage, and Common Concern'), their implementation in the latter contexts can vary considerably from that involving the bilateral or plurilateral setting in which most transboundary environmental impacts tend to be located.

---

[1] For example, the transboundary impact of a state's environmental management practice in terms of a diminution of the international existence value of that state's natural resources.

[2] A prototypical illustration of such a regime guarding against intangible transboundary impacts is the 1972 Convention for the Protection of the World Cultural and Natural Heritage [World Heritage Convention].

2 TRANSBOUNDARY ENVIRONMENTAL IMPACTS IN INTERNATIONAL LAW

Rules of international law governing transboundary environmental impacts first evolved in the context of states' non-navigational uses of international water-courses. Variously viewed as grounded in the maxim of *sic utere tuo ut alienum non laedas tuo*, the concept of 'abuse of rights', or the principle of 'good neighbourli-ness' (*bon voisinage*), these rules give expression to the fact that territorial sovereign rights in general are correlative and interdependent and consequently subject to reciprocally operating limitations. While absolute territorial sovereignty was once briefly invoked in defence of transboundary injurious uses of international water-courses, today it is universally accepted that a state's freedom to engage in, or per-mit, natural resource-related activities within its territorial boundaries or subject to its control is necessarily subject to the understanding that such activities should not produce transboundary effects 'contrary to the rights of others.'[3] The specific intersection of transboundary environmental impact and prohibited state conduct has further come to be defined as the situation in which effects amount to a signifi-cantly injurious impact or, in the words of the *Trail Smelter* tribunal, are of 'serious consequence.'[4]

This view of states' interdependent environmental rights is reflected widely in treaties covering various transboundary environmental impact scenarios. It is enshrined in landmark international environmental documents such as the 1972 Stockholm Declaration on the Human Environment (Principle 21) as well as the 1992 Rio Declaration on Environment and Development (Principle 2), and has been reaf-firmed in the 2002 Johannesburg Declaration on Sustainable Development (para. 8). Further, the International Court of Justice (ICJ) in its 1996 Advisory Opinion on the *Legality of the Threat or Use of Nuclear Weapons* and, again, in its 1997 judgment in the *Case Concerning the Gabčíkovo-Nagymaros Project (Hungary v. Slovakia)*[5] expressly endorsed the prohibition of the transboundary injurious use of natural resources as

---

[3] *Corfu Channel Case (United Kingdom v. Albania)*, Judgment of 15 December 1949, [1949] I.C.J Rep. 4 at 22 (9 April): 'Every State's obligation not to allow knowingly its territory to be used contrary to the rights of others.'

[4] *Trail Smelter Case (United States v. Canada)*, Award, 1941, 3 U.N.R.I.A.A. 1905 at 1965: '[U]nder prin-ciples of international law ... no State has the right to use or permit the use of its territory in such a man-ner as to cause injury by fumes on or in the territory of another or the properties therein, if the case is of serious consequence and the injury is established by clear and convincing evidence.'

[5] 'The existence of the general obligation of States to ensure that activities within their jurisdiction and control respect the environment of other States or of areas beyond national control is now part of the corpus of international law relating to the environment.' *Legality of the Threat or Use of Nuclear Weapons*, Advisory Opinion of 8 July 1996, [1996] I.C.J. Rep. 29 at para. 226 (8 July) [*Nuclear Weapons*]. See *Case Concerning the Gabčíkovo-Nagymaros Project (Hungary v. Slovakia)*, Judgment of 25 September 1997, [1997] I.C.J. Rep. 92 at 41, para. 53 (25 September) [*Gabčíkovo-Nagymaros*].

a rule of international customary law (see Chapter 19 'Formation of Customary Law and General Principles').[6] Finally, additional evidence of broad international acceptance of the customary legal nature of the 'no significant harm rule' emerges from the International Law Commission's (ILC) recent work on international watercourses,[7] the prevention of transboundary harm from hazardous activities,[8] and shared natural resources,[9] quite apart from various pertinent resolutions of international organizations and conferences.[10]

Despite such widespread international support,[11] some commentators nevertheless maintain that relevant international practice as reflected in actual state conduct—as opposed to mere verbal reiterations of the normative position—provides insufficient support for the rule's status as international custom.[12] However, this allegation is unconvincing. Those who deny the rule's customary legal status do not base their own assertions on broad empirical evidence but rather make bald assumptions about state practice. In taking individual instances of what is pathological behaviour among states—incidents that are well-documented precisely because they are exceptional—as a guide for the general conduct of states, opponents are guilty of the same evidentiary sin of which they accuse proponents. Ultimately, the denial of the no harm rule's customary status is also irrelevant. The international legal status of the basic rule regarding significant transboundary impact is directly related to the sovereign equality of states as an axiomatic premise of the international legal order. The rule seeks to reconcile one state's sovereign right to use its territory and resources with another state's defensive invocation of the very same sovereignty-based right. Its validity, thus, does not depend on confirmation through the usual inductive process of proving customary international law, nor can it 'be invalidated by evidence pointing to manifold departures from the conduct required.'[13] True, in general, it will

---

[6] Mention might be made here also of the recent decision in the *Iron Rhine ('Ijzeren Rijn') Railway case (Belgium v. The Netherlands)*, Award of the Arbitral Tribunal of 24 May 2005, para. 59, the court of arbitration noted that 'the duty to prevent, or at least mitigate' significant harm to the environment, had now become a principle of general international law. See also *Nuclear Weapons*, note 5 above at para. 222.

[7] See Article 7 of the 1997 Convention on the Law of Non-Navigational Uses of International Watercourses [Watercourses Convention].

[8] See Article 3 of the ILC draft Articles on the Prevention of Transboundary Harm from Hazardous Activities, in *Report of the International Law Commission*, Fifty-Third Session (23 April–1 June and 2 July–10 August 2001), UN GAOR, 56th Session, Suppl. no. 10, Doc. A/56/10 (2001), 370 at 372 [Draft Articles on Prevention].

[9] See Article 7 of the draft 2004 Convention on the Law of Transboundary Aquifer Systems, in *Third Report on Shared Natural Resources: Transboundary Groundwaters*, UN Doc. A/CN.4/551 (2005) at 11.

[10] See, e.g., Commentary to Article 16 of the Berlin Rules on Water Resources, in International Law Association, *Report of the Seventy-First Conference* (Berlin, 2004) at 365.

[11] P. Birnie and A. Boyle, *International Law and the Environment*, 2nd edition (Oxford: Oxford University Press, 2002) at 109, simply note: 'It is beyond serious argument that states are required by international law to take adequate steps to control and regulate sources of serious ... transboundary harm.'

[12] See, in particular, D. Bodansky, 'Customary (and Not So Customary) International Environmental Law' (1995) 3 Global Leg. Stud. J. 105.

[13] C. Tomuschat, 'Obligations Arising for States without or against Their Will' (1993) 241 Recueil des cours 195 at 295.

neither be possible nor permissible to infer precise conduct-specific international legal rules from abstract fundamental principles, such as sovereign equality, rather than inductively from the practice of states. However, the no significant harm rule is sufficiently determinate on its own and has further been refined in state practice to provide pertinent guidance as to the basic allocation of states' corollary rights and obligations in a situation of interdependent natural resource uses.[14]

3 Prohibited Transboundary Impacts Further Defined[15]

Although in exceptional circumstances 'zero transboundary impact' might well represent the appropriate threshold,[16] it is generally agreed that states are enjoined only from causing transboundary harm that is 'serious,' 'significant,' 'substantial,' 'appreciable,' or similarly qualified. Some critics point to these qualifying words as incontrovertible evidence of the threshold's fatal lack of precision.[17] However, when viewed in context, the qualifiers' *prima facie* ambiguity turns out to be more apparent than real. First, they all convey the idea that the harm concerned must be more than *de minimis*, trivial, or simply 'detectable'. They reflect a factual judgement about 'a real detrimental effect on matters such as . . . human health, industry, property, environment or agriculture in other States.'[18] Second, states are subject to far-reaching procedural obligations—be those treaty-based or customary legal ones that facilitate clarification of whether the transboundary impacts are indeed of the kind or magnitude to cross the threshold of 'significant harm'—whatever the precise

---

[14] Even if one were to assume that as a customary legal concept the no significant harm rule might not pass muster in every judicial legal forum, it is evident that at different levels or in different settings of legal discourse the rule and its direct substantive and procedural implications do shape states' normative expectations. See Bodansky, note 13 above at 118–19 (acknowledging the influence on international environmental negotiations). By contrast, others simply deny customary international law's role as an exogenous factor affecting state behaviour. See, e.g., J. Goldsmith and E. Posner, *The Limits of International Law* (Oxford: Oxford University Press, 2005) at 42–3.

[15] Sections 3–4 of this chapter draw heavily on G. Handl, 'Trail Smelter in Contemporary International Environmental Law: Application to Nuclear Energy,' in R. Bratspies and R. Miller, eds., *Transboundary Harm in International Law: Lessons from the Trail Smelter Arbitration* (Cambridge: Cambridge University Press, 2006) 125.

[16] Thus, both in the ILC and the UN General Assembly's Sixth Committee, the view has been expressed that given the special vulnerability of groundwater, a 'zero tolerance [of harm] threshold' ought to inform a state's obligation to avoid transboundary effects. See *Report of the International Law Commission on Its Fifty-Sixth Session*, UN GAOR, 59th Session, Suppl. no. 10, Doc. A/59/10 (2004) at 130, para. 99.

[17] See, e.g., J. Knox, 'The Myth and Reality of Transboundary Environmental Impact Assessment' (2002) 96 A.J.I.L. 291 at 294.

[18] See Commentary to Article 2 of the ILC Draft Articles on Prevention, note 8 above at 388.

location in the individual circumstances of the case may be. This assessment may, moreover, be appreciably eased by international undertakings of states to publicize national pollutant release and transfer data.[19] Third, certain types of transboundary effects involving, for example, radiological, toxic, or otherwise highly dangerous substances or those otherwise affecting public health, endangering lives, or producing serious irreversible conditions, are likely to be *a priori* deemed significantly harmful.[20] Fourth, there has been a steady increase in the use of internationally agreed upon ambient environmental standards or objectives, in particular, those applicable to air and water resources, which provide a baseline against which transboundary effects can be assessed as to their permissibility under customary international law.[21] Finally, states frequently agree to use geographical markers—for example, the proximity of the causal activity to the border—as *prima facie* indicators of the 'significance' of the transboundary impact concerned.[22] In sum, in any given case of transboundary environmental interference, the task of defining 'significant harm' is, thus, clearly much less the challenge than critics make it out to be.

Assessing the legal consequences that attach to a plausible *prima facie* affirmation of the existence of such transboundary impact is, however, a different matter. The *Trail Smelter* tribunal equated the occasioning of the latter with internationally prohibited conduct.[23] However, this straightforward conceptual linkage of (factually determined) 'significance', and legal 'prohibition' of transboundary environmental harm has not been universally accepted. Rather, it has had to compete against a more complex, traditional conceptualization of threshold, which traces its origin to legal principles that evolved in relation to non-navigational uses of international watercourses.[24] According to this latter view, 'significant harm' is only one in a multiple factor-based balancing of interests of concerned states—a process that could serve as a possible corrective to the relative strictness of an obligation of avoidance simply pegged to 'significant harm'. From an environmental policy perspective, however, a persuasive case can be, and has been, made against this 'dual element' (significant

---

[19] See, e.g., the 2003 Protocol on Pollutant Release and Transfer Registers to the 1998 UNECE Convention on Access to Information, Public Participation in Decision-Making and Access to Justice in Environmental Matters [Aarhus Convention].

[20] See, e.g., Articles 25 (alien species) and 26 (hazardous substances) of the Berlin Rules on Water Resources, note 10 above at 375; or corresponding provisions of Article 21 at para. 2 (harm to human health and safety) and 23 (alien species) of the 1997 Watercourses Convention, see note 7 above.

[21] Note, e.g., the Great Lakes Water Quality Objectives established under the 1978 Agreement between Canada and the United States on Great Lakes Quality, Ottawa and its 1983 amending Protocol.

[22] Note, e.g., the 1983 Agreement between the United States and Mexico on Cooperation for the Protection and Improvement of the Environment in the Border Area, which covers activities within 100 kilometres on either side of land and maritime boundaries.

[23] Thus, the *Trail Smelter* tribunal's dictum omits any mention of 'inequitable use' as a prerequisite, additional to a finding of significant harm, to engage Canada's international responsibility.

[24] See, in particular, Article X of the Helsinki Rules on the International Law Association, *Report of the Fifty-Second Conference* (Helsinki, 1966) 497–99.

harm *plus* inequitable balance of interest) characterization of the legal threshold of prohibited transboundary environmental effects.[25]

Some instances of state practice related to transboundary air pollution as well as other evidence suggest an international acceptance of the single element—that is, a factually determined threshold of 'significant harm' as the hallmark of prohibited transboundary harm. On the other hand, it is true that in relation to the law of international watercourses the notion of 'equitable' or 'reasonable use' continues to affect the threshold of impermissible transboundary environmental effects. Thus, in its commentary to Article 7 (the obligation not to cause significant harm) of the draft Articles on the Law of the Non-Navigational Uses of International Watercourses, the ILC clearly envisaged circumstances in which 'prohibited harm' is not equated with significant transboundary harm but instead is conditioned on such harm representing an inequitable balance of interests as between the states concerned.[26] The United Nations Convention on the Law of Non-Navigational Uses of International Watercourses (Watercourses Convention) retains this approach.[27] It would certainly be possible to argue that paragraphs 1 and 2 of Article 7 of the Watercourses Convention refer to two different obligations, namely the 'prevention' of significant harm (para. 1), which is not subject to equitable use considerations, and the 'elimination' or 'mitigation' of such harm already occasioned (para. 2), which is. However, in a situation of ongoing or continuously occurring transboundary environmental effects, the obligation to eliminate or to mitigate merges with the obligation to prevent. Thus, leaving aside situations of accidental transboundary effects, it appears more appropriate to characterize the conventional threshold of prohibited harm as requiring that the conduct resulting in significant harm amounts to an inequitable use of the watercourse.

Whether or not one accepts this proposition as the appropriate test for the management of international watercourses,[28] there is substantial agreement among commentators that in relation to transboundary environmental interference generally, it would be inappropriate to condition the threshold of significant harm to considerations of equitable sharing.[29] This view has now also found expression in the work of the ILC on the prevention of transboundary damage from hazardous activities. Unlike the approach opted for in the draft Articles on the Law of the

[25] But see P. Wouters, 'The Legal Response to International Water Conflicts: The UN Watercourses Convention and Beyond' (1999) 42 German Y.B. Int'l L. 293 at 322–3.

[26] See *Report of the International Law Commission on the Work of Its Forty-Sixth Session*, UN Doc. A/49/10 (2 May to 22 July 1994) 47.

[27] See Article 7 of the 1997 Watercourses Convention, note 7 above.

[28] For a persuasive argument against, see, e.g., A. Nollkaemper, *The Legal Regime for Transboundary Water Pollution: Between Discretion and Constraint* (Dordrecht: Martinus Nijhoff, 1993) 69.

[29] See J. Lammers, 'Balancing the Equities in International Environmental Law,' in R.J. Dupuy, ed., *The Future of the International Law of the Environment* (Dordrecht: Martinus Nijhoff, 1985) 153 at 163.

Non-Navigational Uses of International Watercourses,[30] the commission's articles on prevention do not subordinate the principal obligation of prevention of significant transboundary harm to an equitable balancing of interests. Thus, the ILC's special rapporteur, in addressing the relationship between Article 3 (on prevention) and what was then Article 12 (on equitable balancing of interests among states concerned), expressly denied that the latter was meant in any way to dilute the obligation of prevention.[31]

Finally, the no significant harm obligation is one of due diligence.[32] A state is accordingly obliged only to apply restraints on transboundary injurious activities or agencies that it can reasonably be expected to adopt. This fact introduces a degree of uncertainty regarding—not the definition—but the actual operation of the threshold concept. For what is 'reasonable' under the circumstances will, of course, vary from case to case. However, the proliferation of pertinent environmental and technical standards, such as best available technology, best environmental practice, and so on,[33] which may provide *de facto*, if not *de iure*, an authoritative point of reference, provides an important counterweight. These standards can reduce—sometimes dramatically—the variability from one situation to another of what constitutes due diligence aimed at preventing or abating transboundary harmful effects. Any remaining unpredictability, it ought to be remembered, bears on the existence of a breach of the obligation, on whether the source state will actually be responsible for the transboundary harm occasioned.

4 SUBSTANTIVE LEGAL IMPLICATIONS: THE OBLIGATION TO PREVENT

Today, international law goes beyond requiring states to redress transboundary environmental impacts *ex post facto* by regulating or constraining the injury-causing

---

[30] The ILC, however, appears to follow the 1997 Watercourses Convention and to opt again for a dual element approach in defining prohibited utilization of a transboundary aquifer or aquifer systems. See proposed Articles 5 and 7 in *Third Report on Shared Natural Resources*, note 10 above at paras. 18–25.

[31] See Rao, *Third Report on International Liability for Injurious Consequences Arising Out of Acts Not Prohibited by International Law (Prevention of Transboundary Harm for Hazardous Activities)*, UN Doc. A/CN4.510 (9 June 2000) 11 at para. 21. Expressions of concern by Austria and, to a lesser extent, by the United Kingdom regarding the possibility that the relationship between the draft articles on prevention and on equitable balancing might be viewed as one of subordination of the former to the latter, prompted this clarification, a clarification that the United Kingdom found necessary but sufficient. Accordingly, the purpose of the 'equitable balancing of interests' provision 'was not to detract from the State of origin's duty of prevention . . . but rather to discuss a mutually acceptable choice of measures to give effect to that duty.' *Ibid.* at 6, note 26.

[32] See, e.g., ILC Draft Articles on Prevention, note 8 above at 391–6.

[33] See, e.g., Annexes I and II of the 1992 UNECE Convention on the Protection and Use of Transboundary Watercourses and International Lakes.

activity or agency and, instead, obliges states to take adequate measures to control and regulate in advance sources of potential significant transboundary harm.[34] Indeed, the obligation of prevention presents itself as an essential aspect of the obligation not to cause significant harm to the environment beyond national jurisdiction or control. In this sense, the obligation of prevention clearly covers situations in which transboundary harm is merely threatened, provided the risk thereof is significant in terms of a high probability of non-trivial consequences. Less self-evident, by contrast, is the answer to whether threatened transboundary harm might also be within the ambit of the obligation of prevention if the risk involved is extremely serious consequences, albeit of a low probability.

Reflecting the composite nature of the risk of harm,[35] a modified standard of proof has gradually been gaining acceptance 'with potentially greater harm calling for abstention from conduct under a proportionately lesser showing that harm will occur.'[36] In other words, even a low probability event represents a significant risk of harm and, thus, triggers the obligation of prevention, provided the probability is coupled with serious consequences. Given the fact that transboundary risks of this low probability/high consequence type are intrinsically characteristic of nuclear activities, much of the relevant international practice also concerns the nuclear activities of states. Unfortunately, the evidence that can be gleaned from both international legal instruments specifically focusing on the management of transboundary nuclear risk or diplomatic claims by risk-exposed states challenging the source state's right to create significant transboundary nuclear risks, while seemingly supportive of the modified burden of proof approach, is not free of ambiguity. A somewhat inconclusive picture also emerges from the handful of international judicial or arbitral decisions reviewing transboundary nuclear risks, primarily because these cases, as framed by the parties' arguments, do not expressly raise the issue of the type of low probability/catastrophic consequence risk.[37]

In view of these evidentiary shortcomings, the ILC's draft Articles on the Prevention of Transboundary Harm from Hazardous Activities acquire special importance. Article 1 defines the articles' scope of application as extending to activities that involve 'a risk of significant transboundary harm.' Article 2(a)—consistent with the modified burden-of-proof approach—then defines 'risk of causing significant transboundary harm' as including risks both of a 'high probability of causing significant transboundary harm and a low probability of causing disastrous transboundary

---

[34] Thus, the ILC's General Commentary on the Draft Articles on Prevention simply notes that 'the well-established principle of prevention was highlighted in the arbitral award in the *Trail Smelter* case.' See the General Commentary to ILC Draft Articles on Prevention, note 8 above at 378.

[35] That is, as the product of probability and consequence of future event.

[36] This standard was first proposed by Frederic Kirgis who asked rhetorically 'whether a disinterested decision-maker thirty years after *Trail Smelter*, in a world awakened to the existence of environmental deterioration, would find the clear and convincing standard literally applicable when there are plausible consequences magnified far beyond those considered in that case.' F. Kirgis, 'Technological Challenge to the Shared Environment: United States Practice' (1972) 66 A.J.I.L. 290 at 294.

[37] See Handl, note 15 above.

harm.' Article 3, the draft articles' key substantive provision, finally calls upon the state of origin to 'take all appropriate measures to prevent significant transboundary harm or at any rate to minimize the risk thereof.' In other words, although both of these obligations relate to future events or realizations of risk,[38] Article 3 distinguishes between situations involving 'significant transboundary harm' and those involving only a 'risk thereof', with differing associated obligations to 'prevent' and to 'minimize' respectively. This approach is, however, problematic. For the differentiation between certain harm (to be prevented) and less than certain harm (to be minimized) is a differentiation that is based on the probability of harm alone rather than on the composite of probability and consequence of the future event—the 'significance of the risk'. In this normative scheme, a 'mere' risk of significant transboundary harm thus does not attract an obligation of prevention. In its commentary, the commission acknowledges the due diligence implications of transboundary risks associated with ultra-hazardous activities. However, in describing a variety of factors bearing on the proportionately higher standard of care that is applicable, it speaks in essence of the 'measures to minimize risk'.[39] It never expressly acknowledges the possibility that logically, at the extreme end of the spectrum of consequences that could realistically be threatened, the heightened standard of due diligence might simply render inescapable the conclusion that the activity itself would be impermissible. Uncertain future harm—indeed any harm that is 'less than certain' if one follows the ILC's logic[40]—no matter how potentially catastrophic its nature and scope—does not *eo ipso* attract a legal obligation to end the risk-bearing activity.

In the final analysis, then, the ILC draft articles disappoint in that they emulate the modified burden-of proof approach only imperfectly. Yet they do confirm the fundamental persuasiveness of the approach to defining the scope of a state's international legal obligation to prevent a risk of transboundary harm. In this sense, and despite the uncertainty regarding their future formal status, they are likely to shape decisively international normative expectations.

5 PROCEDURAL IMPLICATIONS

Given that the (substantive) obligation to prevent significant transboundary harm is well established in international law, it should not be surprising that international

---

[38] Article 1 and the ILC's commentary thereto make it clear that the draft articles cover exclusively activities that involve a 'risk of causing significant harm and, as the commentary further notes, 'the element of "risk" is by definition concerned with future possibilities.' ILC Draft Articles on Prevention, see note 8 above at 385, paras. 13–14.   [39] See *ibid.* at 394.

[40] Since all situations covered by the draft articles involve 'future possibilities,' Article 3 obligations must be located on a sliding scale of probability, with the obligation to prevent harm bordering on certainty, while the obligation to minimize would arise at a somewhat lesser degree of probability whose exact location along this scale of probability remains undefined.

practice also confirms the existence of specific procedural obligations that safeguard states' basic entitlement—that is, their right to be protected against significant transboundary injurious impacts. Thus, there is extensive treaty practice—on a bilateral, regional, and global level—establishing a legal obligation for states to assess, notify, and consult prior to engaging in conduct carrying a significant risk of transboundary harm. There exists, moreover, strong evidence that these obligations are nowadays also part of general international law, either in the form of customary law or perhaps—as in the case of the obligation to assess transboundary environmental impacts—of a general principle of law.[41] Arrayed against this evidence is the fact that states often disregard these obligations—a phenomenon that is apt to raise doubt that the obligations are part of general or customary international law. Some commentators have dismissed the procedural safeguards as normatively weak[42] or as undermining the very substantive obligation of states to prevent and minimize significant transboundary impacts.[43]

However, these criticisms are too harsh, if not altogether off the mark. If the no significant harm rule is part of general international law, it stands to reason that the above procedural obligations, indispensable as they are to rendering the rule effective, must also be part of the general international legal structure within which transboundary environmental relations are being managed. Admittedly, the customary legal status of the procedural obligations concerned cannot be established by way of logical deduction. Yet there is, of course, no need for such a tenuous argument. Rather, it is a combination of characteristics that marks these obligations as general legal ones. First, there is no denying their 'substantial pedigree of international support.'[44] Apart from relevant treaties, evidence of this kind includes decisions by international tribunals and courts, diplomatic claims by states demanding compliance with these obligations as a matter of customary international law,[45] and resolutions of international organizations—both governmental and non-governmental or

---

[41] Thus, it has been suggested that 'environmental impact assessment . . . might be regarded as a general principle of law or even as [one] . . . of customary international law.' Birnie and Boyle, see note 11 above at 130.

[42] Thus, Brownlie critically refers to 'mild' procedural obligations laid down in the ILC Draft Articles on Prevention. I. Brownlie, *Principles of Public International Law*, 5th edition (Oxford: Clarendon Press; and New York: Oxford University Press, 1998) at 286.

[43] A particularly egregious example of a failure to understand the essential complementary function of procedural obligations in buttressing substantive rights and obligations of states as expressed in the no significant harm rule is the pre-UN Conference on Environment and Development's review of international environmental law by the *Harvard Law Review*. See Editors of the Harvard Law Review, 'Developments in the Law—International Environmental Law' (1991) 104 Harv. L. Rev. 1484 at 1513 ('The move towards procedural duties may in fact legitimate environmentally hazardous conduct').

[44] Birnie and Boyle, see note 11 above at 126, speaking of the obligations to notify and to consult.

[45] See, e.g., New Zealand's claim that the requirement of environmental assessment was not a treaty-based obligation but 'existed also under customary international law.' *Request for an Examination of the Situation in Accordance with Paragraph 63 of the Court's Judgment of 20 December 1974 in the Nuclear Tests (New Zealand v. France) Case*, Order of 22 September 1995, [1995] I.C.J. Rep. 288 at 299, para. 35 (22 September).

diplomatic conferences, such as those adopted at the 1992 Rio Conference on Environment and Development. Thus, Principles 17–19 of the Rio Declaration on Environment and Development give authoritative expression to the prevailing view among states that prior environmental impact assessment, notification, and consultation are part of the legal tools and methods states are required to apply to prevent or minimize the risk of adverse transboundary environmental effects. Additional supportive evidence emerges also from the recent environment-related work of the ILC[46] as well as the practice of multilateral development banks.[47] Second, the obligations represent specific manifestations of states' basic general obligation to cooperate in the prevention and minimization of transboundary environmental harm.[48] Finally, as noted, the specific procedural and substantive obligations associated with the no-significant harm rule are intrinsically interrelated—the latter, which is the obligation of prevention, becomes a realistic normative proposition only to the extent that it is being supported by the former.

It is in this vein, that the ICJ in the *Gabčíkovo-Nagymaros* case, speaking in terms of general international environmental law, refers to states' procedural obligations— namely to assess actual and potential environmental risks and negotiate in good faith—as specific consequences of their obligations to cooperate and to prevent environmental harm.[49] In the older *Lac Lanoux (Spain v. France)* case, this nexus between the obligation to cooperate for the protection of the environment, and the obligation to prevent significant transboundary harm informs similarly the tribunal's characterization of inter-state 'consultations' as being legally required.[50] By the same token, this interrelationship provides one of the key rationales for the set of procedural obligations laid down in the ILC draft articles on prevention.[51] Finally, the International Law Association's Berlin Rules on Water Resources specifically endorse procedural obligations to assess (Article 29), notify (Articles 56–7), and consult (Article 58) as part of customary international law. The commentary thereto explains this affirmation, *inter alia*, in terms of supportive state practice and the nature of the obligations as corollaries of states' general obligation to cooperate.[52]

While the case for the obligation to notify in emergency situations might arguably be strongest in terms of international support in practice, it would seem undeniable that all three transboundary impact-related procedural obligations of assessment,

---

[46] See Articles 16–17 of the draft Convention on the Law of Transboundary Aquifer Systems, note 9 above; and Articles 11–12, 17, and 28(1) of the Watercourses Convention, note 7 above.

[47] See, e.g., G. Handl, *Multilateral Development Banking: Environmental Principles and Concepts Reflecting General International Law and Public Policy* (The Hague: Kluwer Law International, 2001) at 94–7 and 123–5.

[48] See, e.g., Principle 24 of the Stockholm Declaration on the Human Environment.

[49] See *Gabčíkovo-Nagymaros*, note 5 above at paras. 112 and 139–41.

[50] *Lac Lanoux Arbitration (France v. Spain)*, Judgment of 16 November 1957, 24 I.L.R. 101 at 125–26 and 139 (1957).

[51] That is, to cooperate (Article 4), assess (Article 7), notify and inform (Article 8), and consult (Article 9). See, e.g., Commentary to Article 4, ILC Draft Articles on Prevention, note 8 above at 396.

[52] See, in particular, Commentary to Article 56, note 10 above at 399.

notification, and consultation are part of present-day customary international law. In any event, whether or not one accepts this conclusion, it is generally agreed that states disregard these obligations at their own peril. Steps in compliance therewith are important pointers in the determination of whether or not the source state has acted diligently in discharging its substantive obligation to prevent the transboundary impact concerned. At the same time, it is equally clear that the procedural obligations themselves do not imply any obligation for the source state to restrain or limit the transboundary impact-creating conduct or project.

Significant transboundary impacts or risks thereof are, moreover, subject to procedural obligations that go beyond the traditional undertakings of the source state vis-à-vis the risk-exposed state(s). These additional obligations encompass, in particular, internationally guaranteed individual rights of access to environmental information, public participation in environmental decision-making, and access to justice in environmental matters, all of which contribute to greater transparency as well as better scrutiny of human-induced environmental changes, including transboundary environmental effects. They thereby also contribute to enhancing states' ability to avoid prohibited transboundary impacts. In the environmental management context, in particular, in the wake of the Rio conference, these individual procedural entitlements have increasingly attracted international support.[53] They are, moreover, further reinforced by the principle of non-discrimination,[54] which in any given situation might provide yet another international procedural guarantee that works directly for the benefit of individuals rather than for the state actually or potentially affected by transboundary effects.[55]

Whether this measure of broad support, whose conceptual roots lie in both environmental and human rights law, permits the conclusion that public participation and access to information and to justice are generally guaranteed international individual rights related to the management of transboundary environmental impacts is, however, not as clear as some would suggest (see Chapter 29 'Public Participation').[56] However, whatever their precise legal status, it is unquestionably true that they

[53] See Principle 10 of the Rio Declaration; and Aarhus Convention, note 20 above. See further the ILC Draft Articles on Prevention, note 8 above at Article 13 ('information to the public'); ILA Berlin Rules on Water Resources, note 10 above at Article 18 (right of 'public participation and access to information'); and the Johannesburg Declaration on Sustainable Development, 4 September 2002, at para. 26.

[54] The latter is a key provision in various relevant international treaties, including the Aarhus Convention, Article 3, para. 9. It is also included in the ILC Draft Articles on Prevention, see note 8 above (Article 15), as well as in resolutions of international organizations (see, e.g., OECD Council Recommendation for the Implementation of a Regime of Equal Right of Access and Non-Discrimination in Relation to Transfrontier Pollution, Doc. C(77)28; and Article 30 of the ILA Berlin Rules on Water Resources, see note 10 above).

[55] However, there is insufficient practice to support the principle's status as one of customary law.

[56] For example, the commentary to Article 18 of the ILA Berlin Rules on Water Resources, see note 10 above at 368, simply states that '[t]here can be little room for doubt that a right of public participation has now become a general rule of international law regarding environmental management.' However, the commentary also acknowledges that 'most international environmental instruments do not contain provisions for the realization of individual rights relative to the instruments.' *Ibid.* And, somewhat

express international public policy with respect to the need to subject the risk of significant transboundary harm to a range of procedural safeguards whose activation is no longer entrusted to states alone.

6 INTERNATIONAL RESPONSIBILITY AND LIABILITY FOR TRANSBOUNDARY IMPACTS

The question of precisely what legal consequences might attach to the occurrence of significant transboundary environmental impacts (reliably ascertained) has long been a matter of contentious debate (see Chapter 44 'International Responsibility and Liability'). It has also been on the international legislative agenda for decades, without there being progress in clarifying or developing relevant rules of general international law, at least until very recently. The reasons for this situation are several. First, international environmental law naturally evolved in response to states' overriding initial concern to protect and preserve natural resources and prevent and mitigate environmental degradation. Issues of liability tended to be viewed primarily in terms of compensating transboundary environmental loss rather than of deterring it, and, thus, they also tended to be relegated to future consideration. Second, as long as the contents of states' international primary obligations regarding the environment remained relatively unsettled, the specific legal consequences said to attend breaches of these obligations—so-called 'secondary obligations' or obligations of state responsibility proper—remained themselves open to challenge primarily on account of the dearth of relevant international practice. Third, the characterization of legal consequences associated with the occurrence of significant transboundary environmental impacts is complex since both the basis and nature of the source state's obligation vary according to circumstances. Thus, significant transboundary impacts will engage this state's responsibility—that is, trigger secondary obligations to cease the injurious conduct and to repair the injury (make restitution or pay compensation) if the impact involves wrongful conduct or a lack of due diligence.[57] Arguably, even absent wrongful state conduct, a transboundary

---

inconsistently, the commentary to Article 4—the general participation of persons clause—admits that the right therein stipulated represents a 'progressive development of customary international law rather than the expression of existing law.' *Ibid.* at 349.

[57] See Articles 30, 31, and 34–7 of the ILC Draft Articles on Responsibility of States for Internationally Wrongful Acts, adopted at the Commission's Fifty-Third Session, in *Report of the International Law Commission on Its Fifty-Third Session* (23 April–1 June and 2 July–10 August 2001), UN GAOR, 56th Session, Suppl. no. 10, Doc. A/56/10 (2001) 43 at 51–3.

impact should entail the source state's obligation to ensure compensation of the harm inflicted, provided the latter is typical of a recognizably hazardous activity or conduct that 'involves a risk of causing significant harm' and, second, would otherwise remain uncompensated.[58]

However, the scarcity of international practice supportive of such a (primary) compensation obligation, as well as critics' objections to its very theoretical foundation have prevented the emergence of an international consensus acknowledging it as an essential part of a modern system of international law.[59] More than that, resistance thereto has muddied the legal waters of states' international accountability for transboundary environmental impacts generally. A final factor in the delay in the emergence of a comprehensive set of international rules on responsibility and liability is that states, in negotiating legal regimes on the redress and compensation of transboundary environmental impacts, have been reluctant to support treaty language that would unequivocally set out source state obligations to defray the costs of transboundary environmental impacts. Instead, they have preferred to promote so-called civil liability regimes, which focus on private individuals or entities—most often the principal actors concerned—as the primarily liable parties while leaving the issue of the source state's potential subsidiary or residual liability unresolved.

This traditional neglect of state responsibility and, *a fortiori*, of state liability—in itself a possible indicator of their lacking practical day-to-day operational relevance—might appear justified by the fact that international liability regimes in general have played only a marginal role in the adjustment of transboundary environmental problems. Not surprisingly, therefore, some commentators have come to question the very utility of international rules on environmental liability.[60] However, it may be too early to dismiss such rules as impractical or ineffective tools to manage transboundary environmental interference.

To begin with, there has been a re-kindling of international interest in the subject matter. Thus, in adopting the draft Principles on the Allocation of Loss from Hazardous Activities, the ILC has now finally endorsed a set of recommendations bearing on a source state's role regarding redress and compensation of transboundary environmental impacts.[61] By the same token, the International Law Institute's 1997 Resolution on Responsibility and Liability under International Law for Environmental Damage testifies to a perceived need to integrate principles of state responsibility/liability as well as of civil liability in a single overarching approach to

---

[58] See, e.g., Handl, 'International Accountability for Transboundary Environmental Harm Revisited: What Role for State Liability?' 37 Envt'l Policy and L.—2007 Nos 1/2.

[59] See, e.g., Rao, Third Report on the Legal Regime for Allocation of Loss in Case of Transboundary Harm Arising out of Hazardous Activities, UN Doc. A/CN.4/566 (2006), para. 31.

[60] See, e.g., J. Brunnée, 'Of Sense and Sensibility: Reflections on International Liability Regimes as Tools for Environmental Protection' (2002) 53 Int'l & Comp. L.Q. 351.

[61] See Draft Principles on the Allocation of Loss, note 58 above at 372. Note, however, that the draft principles are intended to provide residual rules and that their focus is on civil liability rather than state liability.

transboundary environmental harm.[62] At the same time, in some international legislative settings, states and other transnational actors continue to pursue the ideal of a comprehensive and integrated solution to the problem of liability for injurious transboundary impacts notwithstanding evident conceptual and political difficulties.[63] In short, we might well witness a gradual reassertion of the view that instead of being irrelevant, detailed and comprehensive international rules on responsibility and liability can bolster the prevention of transboundary environmental impacts, quite apart from enhancing the prospects of just and fair compensation of harm that are a result.[64]

7 INSTITUTIONALIZATION OF TRANSBOUNDARY ENVIRONMENTAL IMPACT MANAGEMENT

Whether or not this impression of reemerging support for international rules on responsibility/liability is correct, it is undeniable that normative expectations have begun to coalesce around the notion that transboundary environmental impacts ought to be managed in a formal, institutionalized manner. This trend is, of course, well-established in relation to global environmental effects or effects on areas beyond national jurisdiction or control. In either situation, for reasons of efficiency and economy or because of the obvious absence of a *prima facie* authoritative decision-maker, an international institutional structure appears indispensable to managing properly the transboundary environmental impact concerned.

However, the emergence of international management structures is observable also in relation to transboundary environmental effects—not of a global nature but, rather, of a more limited, regional nature—that is, effects upon natural resources that are shared by a limited number of states, such as common air sheds or international watercourses. This development is the result, first, of a growing international acknowledgment that environmental effects ought to be dealt with holistically—that is, in an integrated fashion that takes into account systemic ecological implications and their spatial manifestations irrespective of territorial boundaries or jurisdictional competences. Second, it is inspired by a growing realization that such patterns

---

[62] See Institut de droit international, 'Resolution on Responsibility and Liability under International Law for Environmental Damage,' 37 I.L.M. 1474 (1998).

[63] See, e.g., *Report of the Technical Group of Experts on Liability and Redress in the Context of the Cartagena Protocol on Biosafety,* UN Doc.UNEP/CBD/BS/WG-L&R/1/2-UNEP/CBD/COP-MOP/2/INF/5 (24 February 2005).

[64] See, e.g., A. Boyle, 'Globalising Environmental Liability: The Interplay of National and International Law' (2005) 17 J. Envt'l L. 3 at 25–6.

of interdependent national uses of natural resources might be best managed through joint institutional structures. In this vein, the Johannesburg Plan of Implementation emphasizes that the protection and management of the natural resource base of economic and social development may require integrated, ecosystem-oriented strategies, not just at the national level but also at the regional levels.[65]

Not surprisingly, institutional structures for the management of transboundary environmental impacts first surfaced in relation to international watercourses.[66] Today, the 'drainage basin system cum institutional structure' approach to managing transboundary impacts reflects not only international public policy on water resources, but is also a basic organizational principle of many international treaties regulating non-navigational uses of international watercourses.[67] For example, the UN Watercourses Convention adopts a basin approach emphasizing 'the protection and preservation of ecosystems,' while specifically envisaging the establishment of joint management mechanisms.[68] This trend towards addressing comprehensively the broader ecological implications of transboundary environmental degradation within a transnational management structure has, moreover, spread beyond the management of water resources to international air sheds,[69] the marine environment,[70] biodiversity,[71] endangered or threatened species, environmentally important or fragile landscapes,[72] and 'border regions' in general.[73] Notwithstanding this

---

[65] See Johannesburg Plan of Implementation, 26 August–4 September 2002, UN Doc. A/CONF.199/20 (2002) at para. 24.

[66] One of the earliest examples is the International Joint Commission established under the 1909 Treaty between the United States and Great Britain Relating to Boundary Waters, and Questions Arising between the United States and Canada. Yet, unlike more recent water agreements, including the 1978 Great Lakes Water Quality Agreement, the treaty does not adopt a drainage basin (watershed), let alone an eco-system approach, as it specifically excludes from coverage 'tributary waters' to the boundary lakes and rivers that are subject to its provisions.

[67] See, e.g., the 'Jeju Initiative,' *President's Summary of the Ministerial Segment of the Eighth Special Session of the United Nations Environmental Programme Governing Council/Global Ministerial Environment Forum*, 29–31 May 2004, at para. 17(c-d).

[68] See Watercourses Convention, note 7 above at Articles 20 and 24, respectively. Similarly, the ILC draft articles on transboundary groundwaters apply widely to 'aquifer systems' (Art. 2(c)) and encourage states to establish joint management mechanisms or commissions (Art. 8(2)). See *Third Report on Shared Natural Resources*, note 9 above.

[69] See, e.g., the 1991 Agreement between the Government of Canada and the Government of the United States on Air Quality. It is, of course, also an intrinsic feature of the UNECE-centred European-wide system of managing transboundary air pollution.

[70] See, e.g., Report on the Work of the United Nations Open-ended Informal Consultative Process on Oceans and the Law of the Sea at its seventh meeting, UN Doc. A/61/156 (2006), 2–5.

[71] See, e.g., Article 51 of Decision 391 on Common Access to Genetic Resources, 2 July 1996 (establishing an 'Andean Committee on Genetic Resources' as a joint management body for member states of the Andean Community).

[72] See, e.g., the 1971 Convention on Wetlands of International Importance Especially as Waterfowl Habitat; and the 1991 Convention on the Protection of the Alps.

[73] See, e.g., 'Border 2012: US-Mexico Environmental Program,' which is based on the 1983 Agreement between the Mexico and the United States on Cooperation for the Protection and Improvement of the Environment in the Border Area and was agreed to on 4 April 2003.

growing treaty practice, it is doubtful that, as a matter of customary law, states today are obliged to resort to international institutional mechanisms to manage transboundary impacts.

8 CONCLUSION

For the time being, the concept of 'transboundary impact' remains, at least implicitly, a cornerstone of international environmental law. The broad ecosystemic approach, although reflected in many of these agreements, is not sufficiently well-established in international practice to permit the conclusion that a new—seemingly idiosyncratic[74]—version of the obligation not to cause significant transboundary harm has emerged or is about to do so. Instead, what these normative references to ecosystem protection and preservation do signal is that states might be willing to move away from the traditional territorial sovereignty-based conceptualization of states' international environmental rights and obligations (see Chapter 25 'Ecosystems'). They suggest movement towards defining international environmental entitlement in terms of the transboundary environmental effects' consequences for the long-term stability and integrity of the ecological system that is shared by source and neighbouring states alike.

Such a reorientation of international environmental law, however, represents a radical shift. It will not occur swiftly nor will it fail to produce some backlashes. At the end of this evolutionary process, the legal relevance of 'transboundary impact' may indeed fade as a day-to-day operational legal concept. The defensive invocation of sovereignty-based environmental rights may well be replaced with rights-couched demands for protecting and preserving the 'balance' or 'integrity' of the ecological system affected or with other similar community-based arguments. Nevertheless, as long as states remain basic organizational units of civil society and unless the present anthropocentric orientation of international environmental legal thinking is abandoned, the notion that no individual political unit should be permitted to affect the shared natural system in a manner that causes, or is capable of causing, harm to other units will remain an underlying basic rationale of international environmental laws and regulations, whatever their ostensible alternative conceptual foundations.

---

[74] Thus, McCaffrey suggests that the obligation to protect and preserve ecosystems would arise 'even if failure to do so would have no readily apparent transboundary effects.' S. McCaffrey, *The Law of International Watercourses: Non-Navigational Uses* (New York: Oxford University Press, 2001) at 394.

Recommended Reading

A. Boyle, 'Globalising Environmental Liability: The Interplay of National and International Law' (2005) 17 J. Envt'l L. 3.

G. Handl, 'National Uses of Transboundary Air Resources: The International Entitlement Issue Reconsidered' (1986) 26 Nat. Res. J. 405.

——, '*Trail Smelter* in Contemporary International Environmental Law: Application to Nuclear Energy,' in R. Bratspies and R. Miller, eds., *Transboundary Harm in International Law: Lessons from the Trail Smelter Arbitration* (Cambridge: Cambridge University Press, 2006) at 125.

F. Kirgis, 'Technological Challenge to the Shared Environment: United States Practice' (1972) 66 A.J.I.L. 290.

S. McCaffrey, *The Law of International Watercourses: Non-Navigational Uses* (New York: Oxford University Press, 2001).

A. Nollkaemper, *The Legal Regime for Transboundary Pollution: Between Discretion and Constraint* (Dordrecht: Martinus Nijhoff, 1993).

P. Okowa, 'Procedural Obligations in International Environmental Law' (1996) 67 Br. Y.B. Int'l L. 275.

H. Xue, *Transboundary Damage in International Law* (Cambridge: Cambridge University Press, 2003).

CHAPTER 23

COMMON AREAS, COMMON HERITAGE, AND COMMON CONCERN

JUTTA BRUNNÉE

We have entered an era ... in which international law subserves not only the interests of individual States, but looks beyond them and their parochial concerns to the greater interests of humanity and planetary welfare ... International environmental law will need to proceed beyond weighing ... rights and obligations ... within a closed compartment of individual State self-interest, unrelated to the global concerns of humanity as a whole.[1]

1 Introduction

International law, as traditionally conceived—public international law—was designed to govern the relations of sovereign states. Even today, the structure and processes of international law remain firmly anchored in these 'Westphalian' foundations. Since there is no central law-making authority that could legislate in the collective interest, shared understandings must emerge from interstate interactions, deliberations, and negotiations. Through their involvement in the international arena, other actors—individuals, non-governmental organizations (NGOs), business entities, or international institutions (see Part VI of this *Handbook*)—may help shape these understandings. Yet they become legally binding only when there is sufficient consensus among states to generate a rule of customary international law (see Chapter 19 'Formation of Customary International Law and General Principles') or when states agree to be bound by a treaty (see Chapter 20 'Treaty Making and Treaty Evolution').

On the one hand, then, states are the makers of international law, and it is up to them to develop norms and regimes that reflect their individual values and interests, any collective values or interests they may hold, or 'the greater interest of humanity and planetary welfare.' On the other hand, states are also the enforcers of international law, if they so choose. However, this does not necessarily mean that all willing states could enforce such norms or regimes that may exist to protect collective or 'planetary' values and interests. Since public international law governs the relations of sovereign and, thus, legally speaking, equal entities, states are generally entitled to take enforcement action only when their rights are violated. Absent specific treaty-based arrangements, it is only in such cases that 'enforcement' avenues, such as calling upon the responsible state to cease the violation, seeking reparation, or taking appropriate countermeasures to induce compliance, are available at least in principle (see Chapter 44 'International Responsibility and Liability'). Of course, in practice, states only rarely invoke the responsibility of other states for breaches of international law, even when they are legally in a position to do so.

---

[1] *Case Concerning the Gabčíkovo-Nagymaros Project (Hungary v. Slovakia)*, [1997] I.C.J. Rep. 7, separate opinion of Vice-President Weeramantry, at C(c).

According to some observers, this *inter-national* law must, by definition, fail in realizing the common interests of humanity since it orders a 'world fit for governments'—an 'unsociety ruled by a collective of self-conceived sovereigns whose authority is derived neither from the totality of international society nor from the people but from the intermediating state-systems.'[2] Nothing short of a complete transformation of the global legal order is required to overcome this fatal flaw. Perhaps by professional disposition, most international lawyers are more optimistic about the potential of the existing legal order. Like Judge Weeramantry, whose separate opinion in the *Case Concerning the Gabčíkovo-Nagymaros Project (Hungary v. Slovakia)* is quoted at the beginning of this chapter, many academic commentators note the challenges inherent in the interstate structure of international law but they also find evidence that this structure is being adjusted and expanded to promote the 'greater interest of humanity.' Wolfgang Friedmann famously observed that an emerging international law of cooperation had begun to significantly modify the classical law of co-existence of states.[3] Bruno Simma traced the shifts in international law from bilateralism to community interest.[4] More recently, Ellen Hey posited the emergence of an 'international *public* law' (see Chapter 32 ' International Institutions'), through which 'common-interest normative patterns' are woven across the traditional 'inter-state normative patterns.'[5]

Writers frequently point to international environmental law for evidence of such developments and, as we will see, rightly so. However, it is important to bear in mind that contemporary international environmental law is rooted in concepts that aim to balance competing sovereign interests. Under the foundational 'no harm' principle, states' rights to use their territories and resources find their limits when serious transboundary harm is inflicted, and neighbouring states must tolerate harm that remains below this threshold (see Chapter 22 'Transboundary Impacts'). Environmental concerns have legal relevance only to the extent that they coincide with an interference with states' sovereign rights, usually related to their territorial sovereignty. Areas or environmental concerns beyond states' sovereign spheres, therefore, are difficult to capture in this framework.

This chapter examines three concepts that have emerged to respond to collective environmental concerns: 'common areas', 'common heritage', and 'common concern'. The former are areas located beyond the jurisdiction of states, like the high seas, Antarctica, or outer space. The concept of common heritage of humankind describes the status of certain resources that lie beyond the jurisdiction of states, such as the non-living resources of the seabed. The concept of common concern of humankind,

---

[2] P. Allott, *Eunomia: New Order for a New World* (Oxford: Oxford University Press, 1990) at 249.

[3] W. Friedmann, *The Changing Structure of International Law* (New York: Columbia University Press, 1964).

[4] See B. Simma, *From Bilateralism to Community Interest in International Law*, (1994-VI) 250 Recueil des cours 217.

[5] E. Hey, *Teaching International Law* (The Hague: Kluwer Law International, 2003) at 7.

finally, relates to global environmental problems, like climate change or the conservation of biological diversity, that can only be resolved if states collaborate. As will become apparent, the impact of these three concepts has been felt less in the development and application of customary law than in the development of treaty-based regimes. Today, such regimes institutionalize many collective environmental concerns and provide settings in which states' commitments can be adjusted and refined on an ongoing basis. Within these regimes, it has also been possible to develop compliance procedures that are actually invoked and that reflect the collective nature of states' interest in environmental protection.

To protect areas or resources beyond state jurisdiction, and to address common environmental concerns, international environmental law has not merely had to undergo a significant conceptual expansion, but also had to do so against the grain of the foundational structures of international law. As this chapter will illustrate, the field bears the marks of the ongoing push and pull between common-interest and interstate patterns. Yet it has also proven resilient and resourceful in its attempts to meet the attendant challenges.

2 Common Interests and the International Community

Before assessing the specific legal developments surrounding common areas, common heritage, and common concerns, it is helpful to take a broader look at what it is that makes these issues 'common', whom they are common to, and how 'commonality' is accommodated by contemporary international law. All three concepts deal with environmental challenges that call for collective action. In the case of common concerns, collective action is often quite literally required. It is impossible, for example, to combat global climate change unless states cooperate to reduce greenhouse gas concentrations in the atmosphere. Yet, the core of the concept is arguably the fact that addressing common concerns provides benefits common to all states. Such collective benefits accrue most obviously from dealing with global issues such as climate change. However, they can equally be provided by the protection of certain resources, such as biological diversity, located within the jurisdiction of individual states. A legal dimension can be added to these functional considerations: in common concern situations, states will typically find it difficult, if not impossible, to prove significant harm to their territories or to trace it back to the conduct of specific states. Therefore, a collective response is also required to avoid the legal constraints that individual states would face in attempting to tackle a common concern by invoking the responsibility of another state, assuming they were willing to do so.

Turning to common areas or resources, collaboration is required because they lie beyond the jurisdiction of individual states. *Prima facie*, all states have access to the commons, and no state is legally in a position to impose a particular approach to their use or protection. In short, it is for functional and legal reasons that areas, resources, or concerns are 'common'. From this pragmatic definition of commonality it follows, first, that it is *states* that have the requisite matters in common and, second, that it is *all* states that do so. The physical and legal attributes of the issues underlying the concepts of common area, common heritage, and common concern place them beyond the reach of individual states.

However, there is another conception of commonality, highlighted in the quote from Judge Weeramantry's separate opinion. In this conception, the three sets of issues explored in this chapter are among the 'global concerns of humanity as a whole.' States, then, are merely the facilitators of solutions and their actions will be measured not simply against their individual or collective goals but also against 'the greater interests of humanity and planetary welfare.' Further, rather than simply being a matter of necessity, the 'greater interests of humanity' might also be shaped by values that are shared around the world. This proposition might sound reasonable enough, perhaps even self-evident. But it is also complex. For example, while one may be able to deduce in pragmatic fashion that combating climate change requires collective action or that the protection of certain aspects of biodiversity provides benefits for all states, it is considerably more difficult to identify genuinely global environmental values or concerns of humanity in relation to these issues.

How do these different conceptions fit into the legal structures that were sketched in the previous section? The pragmatic account meshes most readily with classical international law. States must arrive at mutually acceptable legal solutions because the underlying concerns are beyond their individual legal capacities. However, such a thin understanding of the law of cooperation does not capture the shifts that have indeed occurred from bilateralism to collective interest or from interstate to common interest patterns. As noted earlier, the implication of the pragmatic account is that certain common issues engage *all* states. It is possible to conceive of 'all' as more than the sum of the parts and as a collective or even a community of states. Indeed, references to the interests and concerns of the 'international community' are plentiful in virtually all areas of international law. It might be objected that such references are often purely rhetorical, camouflaging thin cooperation among states as high community aspiration. It may also be said that it is not clear that merely pragmatic commonality—a functional or legal need for cooperation—can give rise to a community in any meaningful sense of the term. Or one might ask whether it is even conceptually possible for there to be a community of sovereign states. At best, some would say, there exists only an international society of states. For present purposes, it is not necessary to enter into these well-worn debates.[6] Suffice it to say

---

[6] For a comprehensive analysis, see A. Paulus, *Die Internationale Gemeinschaft im Völkerrecht* (München: Verlag C.H. Beck, 2001). See also D. Kritsiosis, 'Imagining the International Community' (2002) 13 Eur. J. Int'l L. 268.

that the interstate structures of public international law today do reflect the growing legal importance of states' collective concerns.

As will be shown in the following sections, multilateral environmental agreements (MEAs) have come to facilitate both the pragmatic coordination of individual states' efforts to address common concerns, and the cultivation and institutionalization of normative communities. However, shifts towards collective concerns are also occurring in the basic structures of general international law. There is agreement on the existence of a category of norms, referred to as *jus cogens*, from which no derogation is permissible. In deviation from the traditional voluntarist basis of international law, individual states cannot exempt themselves from these norms or make contradictory treaty arrangements. As confirmed by the 1969 Vienna Convention on the Law of Treaties, the modification of such norms, like their initial creation, is a matter for 'the international community of states as a whole' (Article 53).

Another significant 'community interest' strand in contemporary international law is the *erga omnes* effect of certain norms, in particular, norms of *jus cogens* character. As noted in the introduction to this chapter, in the traditional 'bilateral' structure of international law only a directly injured state could invoke the responsibility of another for violations. However, since the *obiter dictum* of the International Court of Justice (ICJ) in *Barcelona Traction, Light and Power Company, Ltd. (Belgium v. Spain)*, it has come to be accepted that there exist 'obligations of a State towards the international community as a whole.' These obligations, 'by their very nature ... are the concern of all States' and 'all States can be held to have a legal interest in their protection.'[7] Environmental obligations have not been explicitly identified by the ICJ as having *erga omnes* quality. However, the court did confirm in its advisory opinion in *Legality of the Threat or Use of Nuclear Weapons* that the no harm rule reaches beyond the interests of directly affected states:

[T]he environment is not an abstraction but represents a living space, the quality of life and the very health of human beings, including generations unborn. The existence of the general obligation of States to ensure that activities within their jurisdiction and control respect the environment of other States or of areas beyond national control is now part of the corpus of international law relating to the environment.[8]

Do all states have standing to hold violators to account for violations of *erga omnes* norms? For many commentators, the right of each state to invoke responsibility for violations is inherent in the very concept of obligations *erga omnes*.[9] However, the court has not pronounced itself on this point nor is there clear state practice. The International Law Commission (ILC),[10] in its Articles on State Responsibility (see Chapter 44 'International Responsibility and Liability'), chose a compromise

---

[7] *Barcelona Traction, Light and Power Company, Ltd. (Belgium v. Spain)* [1970] I.C.J. Rep. 3 at para. 33; but see also *ibid.* at para. 91 (requiring a concrete treaty mechanism to provide standing).

[8] *Legality of the Threat or Use of Nuclear Weapons, Advisory Opinion* [1996] I.C.J. Rep. 226 at para. 29.

[9] See Simma, note 4 above at 296.

[10] The International Law Commission is a UN body composed of legal experts nominated by states and tasked with the codification and progressive development of international law.

course that endorses the idea of collective interest standing but imposes limitations on remedies and countermeasures. The ILC's caution is hardly surprising. As this part of the law of state responsibility remains contentious among states, the commission's task was particularly delicate in that it involved not codification of international law, but rather charting a course for its progressive development. Under the articles, then, any state may invoke the responsibility of another for breaches of obligations owed to the international community. Similarly, obligations owed *erga omnes partes* allow all parties to a treaty to demand compliance with its terms.[11] However, if a state is not 'specially affected' by the violation, it may seek only the cessation of the violation and may not claim reparation, except in the interest of those injured (Article 48).[12] Subtle differences between 'specially affected' states and all other beneficiaries of *erga omnes* obligations also characterize the commission's approach to countermeasures. Specially affected states may resort to countermeasures, meaning that they may suspend the performance of obligations owed to the responsible state (Article 49). In other words, such states may resort to what would otherwise be violations of international law to induce the responsible state to comply with its obligations. By contrast, all other states may only take 'lawful measures' against the violating state, leaving open the precise scope of permissible responses (Article 54).

It remains to be asked whether there is any evidence in international law of the most ambitious conception of commonality and community—the idea that there exists not just a community of necessity, but also of values and that this community is comprised not merely of states but also of all humans. Through the evolution of human rights law, humanitarian law and international criminal law, individual human beings have come to be endowed with international rights and obligations. Yet if the legal conceptualization of an international community of states remains incomplete, it is even less clear what legal position 'humanity as a whole' would assume. In the environmental context, the ICJ's comments on the no harm rule in its *Nuclear Weapons* advisory opinion appear to suggest that the rule operates to protect not just the interests of states but of all human beings. The same idea, expressed in more open-ended terms, animates Judge Weeramantry's observations in the *Gabčíkovo-Nagymaros* case. However, it is not clear that the invocation of the 'greater interests' of 'humanity as a whole', in terms of positive law, reaches beyond the ground covered by *jus cogens* and obligations *erga omnes*. To the extent that there are foundational values and interests common to humanity, they may well find their way into international law. However, in terms of the making and enforcement of international law, states remain the key players.

---

[11] For a discussion of the nuances of the regime set out in the articles, see P.-M. Dupuy, 'A General Stocktaking of the Connections between the Multilateral Dimension of Obligations and Codification of the Law of Responsibility' (2002) 13 Eur. J. Int'l L. 1053 at 1069–76.

[12] States that are 'specially affected' may seek both cessation of the violation and reparation of the injury (Articles 42, 30, and 31).

3 CONCEPTUAL DEVELOPMENTS

3.1 Common Areas

Common areas are those areas that are located beyond the limits of national jurisdiction; they are not subject to appropriation by states. Not many areas remain that
fall into this category: the high seas, outer space, and, arguably, Antarctica. The central implication of the status of an area as 'common' or 'common property' is that all
states have open access to it and are entitled to exploit its resources. Thus, unless
access is regulated, the potential for a 'tragedy of the commons'—the progressive
overexploitation and, ultimately, the destruction of its resources—looms over common property regimes.[13] Aside from states' duty to cooperate or exchange information, the only generally applicable environmental obligation limiting these
freedoms is the no harm rule, which extends to the protection of areas beyond
national jurisdiction. As already noted, this dimension of the no harm rule implies
an obligation owed *erga omnes*. However, it remains unclear whether individual
states could enforce the protection of common areas on the basis of customary law.
To the extent that the no harm rule encompasses an obligation owed to the international community as a whole, the Articles on State Responsibility envisage that all
states have standing to confront responsible states. Yet since individual states will
rarely be 'specially affected' in the sense of the articles, their options would not
appear to extend far beyond demanding a stop to the harmful activity. Even these
limited options may stand on uncertain ground, as there is no state practice that
would unequivocally support their existence in customary law. New Zealand, in its
1973 application to the ICJ for interim measures to stop nuclear testing in the South
Pacific, complained, *inter alia*, about France's violation of the rights of all members
of the international community to be free from nuclear fall-out and from contamination of the high seas and atmosphere.[14] In view of France's unilateral declaration
that it would end testing, the court never decided the merits of the case brought by
New Zealand, and of Australia's parallel case. However, various separate or dissenting opinions showed the judges to be divided on the standing issue. Some judges
noted that while 'the existence of a so-called *actio popularis* in international law is a
matter of controversy,' it 'may be considered as capable of rational legal argument

---

[13] G. Hardin, 'The Tragedy of the Commons' (1968) 162 Science 1243.

[14] *Nuclear Tests case (New Zealand v. France)*, Interim Measures, [1973] I.C.J. Rep. 135 at 139.
Australia, in a parallel case, did not frame its claim explicitly in terms of the rights of all members
of the international community. It did, however, argue that the French tests would infringe the freedom of the high seas. See *Nuclear Tests case (Australia v. France)*, Interim Measures, [1973] I.C.J.
Rep. 99 at 103.

and a proper subject of litigation.'[15] For others, the applicant states had 'no legal title . . . to act as spokesman for the international community.'[16]

3.1.1 *High Seas*

With respect to the marine environment and its resources, one response to the need for regulation of use and protection has been to shrink the areas that lie completely beyond individual states' jurisdiction. The gradual expansion of states' territorial seas to 12 miles was followed by the emergence of a 200-mile zone in which states control resource exploitation and exercise regulatory jurisdiction. The 1982 UN Convention on the Law of the Sea (LOSC) consolidates these jurisdictional developments (see Chapter 15 'Ocean and Freshwater Resources'). For the remaining high seas areas, the convention's importance rests in providing a globally applicable set of provisions that expand upon the general rule against transboundary environmental harm. Indeed, the classical freedom of the high seas has been significantly modified by environmental protection requirements.

Under Part XII of the LOSC, states must 'prevent, reduce and control' marine pollution and ensure that pollution from sources under their jurisdiction or control does not harm the environment of other states or spread to the open oceans (Article 194). States must cooperate in scientific research and monitor the effects of marine pollution (Articles 200 and 204). The LOSC also calls on states to cooperate in developing appropriate regional or global standards for the protection of the marine environment (Article 197). In turn, when states regulate sources of pollution under their jurisdiction or control, they must do so in light of relevant international standards and procedures (Articles 207–12). It is perhaps with respect to the enforcement of such international standards that the LOSC most clearly reflects the *erga omnes* nature of obligations to protect the marine environment. To be sure, most enforcement powers fall to states under whose jurisdiction or control pollution occurs (Articles 213–17). Yet the convention also permits port states to institute proceedings regarding discharges into the high seas from any vessel that is voluntarily within one of its facilities (Article 218). Although only two states appear to have implemented this provision, it does represent a notable example of standing to uphold the collective interest.[17]

A large number of specialized agreements supplement the framework of marine environmental protection obligations set out in the LOSC. Regional and global agreements establish regulatory regimes for all major sources of marine pollution,

---

[15] *Nuclear Tests case (Australia v. France)*, Judgment, [1974] I.C.J. Rep. 253 at 370 (Judges Onyeama, Dillard, Jiménez de Aréchaga, and Waldock).

[16] See, e.g. Judge de Castro in *Nuclear Tests (Australia v. France)*, *ibid.* at 390.

[17] P. Birnie and A. Boyle, *International Law and the Environment*, 2nd edition (Oxford: Oxford University Press, 2002) at 376. M. Ragazzi, *The Concept of International Obligations Erga Omnes* (Oxford: Oxford University Press, 1997) at 162.

such as land-based pollution, ocean dumping, or vessel-source pollution of various kinds.[18] By contrast, liability regimes have so far focused only upon vessel source pollution. Four global agreements deal specifically with such liability: the 1992 International Convention on Civil Liability for Oil Pollution Damage, and the related 1992 International Convention on the Establishment of an International Fund for Compensation for Oil Pollution Damage, the 1996 International Convention on Liability and Compensation for Damage in Connection with the Carriage of Hazardous and Noxious Substances by Sea, and the 2001 International Convention on Civil Liability for Bunker Oil Pollution Damage.[19] All four conventions provide for ship owner liability rather than state liability, in the case of the first three supplemented by compensation funds that are financed by contributions from oil or cargo importers. None of the conventions applies to damage caused to the high seas environment. In such cases, then, recourse must be had to the general rules of state responsibility. The LOSC provides little help, containing only the observation that states 'shall be liable in accordance with international law' (Article 235).

Not surprisingly, the allocation of marine resources has been among the most contentious issues for international law (see Chapter 16 'Biological Resources'). As already suggested, one of the legal responses has been to extend the jurisdictional spheres of individual states into the oceans. The effect has been to remove the marine resources in these areas from the high seas regime and its common property implications. As most fish stocks, for example, are found within the LOSC's 200-mile exclusive economic zones, only certain high seas stocks, so-called straddling stocks, and highly migratory species remain within the common property regime. The very general provisions of the LOSC on the conservation and management of high seas living resources have since come to be supplemented by the 1995 Agreement Relating to the Conservation and Management of Straddling Fish Stocks and Highly Migratory Fish Stocks (Fish Stocks Agreement) and various regional arrangements. The Fish Stocks Agreement represents an important attempt to reinforce the *erga omnes* nature of the protection and conservation duties under the LOSC. In particular, while sub-regional and regional fisheries organizations and arrangements are the main vehicles for cooperation (Articles 8–14), even non-parties to such mechanisms are 'not discharged from the obligation to cooperate' in accordance with the LOSC and the Fish Stocks Agreement (Article 17). Further, many of the agreement's provisions are addressed to 'States' rather than 'States Parties', including obligations to cooperate in promoting compliance and enforcement (Articles 19–23). As some observers have noted, in time, the agreement might 'come to be regarded as establishing new customary rules of access to high seas fishing that are no longer based on high seas

---

[18] For an overview, see P. Sands, *Principles of International Environmental Law*, 2nd edition (Cambridge: Cambridge University Press, 2003) at chapter 9.

[19] For an overview, see R.R. Churchill, 'Facilitating (Transnational) Civil Liability Litigation for Environmental Damage by Means of Treaties: Progress, Problems, and Prospects' (2001) 12 Y.B. Int'l Envt'l L. 3.

freedoms.'[20] However, since enforcement powers, for the time being, remain predominantly with fishing vessels' flag states, illegal fishing in the high seas continues to be a problem. To date, only limited powers have been given to other states to monitor compliance with quotas and conservation requirements.[21]

3.1.2 Outer Space

Much like the high seas, outer space is treated as 'common property' that no state can appropriate and to which, legally speaking, all states have equal access (see Chapter 14 'Atmosphere and Outer Space'). These principles are enshrined, for example, in the 1967 Treaty on Principles Governing the Activities of States in the Exploration and Use of Outer Space (Articles I and II). The treaty does emphasize the interests of 'all countries' and of 'all mankind', but the focus is on 'the exploration and use of outer space for peaceful purposes' (Article I). Only brief reference is made to an obligation to conduct space exploration so as to avoid 'harmful contamination and also adverse changes in the environment of the Earth resulting from the introduction of extraterrestrial matter' (Article IX). Launch states are liable for damage caused by space objects, but environmental harm is covered only to the extent that it involves damage to another state (Article VII). Except for the extension to damage to the property of intergovernmental organizations, this limitation is maintained in the 1972 Convention on International Liability for Damage Caused by Space Objects (Article 1). Thus, as far as the protection of the commons—be it outer space, the atmosphere beyond the jurisdiction of individual states, or the high seas—is concerned, the space conventions provide only rudimentary standards. Their weakness is compounded by the lingering uncertainties as to the conditions under which the responsibility of a state for damage to the commons could be invoked. Suffice it to point to the *Nuclear Tests* cases and the earlier discussion of the law of state responsibility for illustration.

Attempts were made to complement the common property regime pertaining to outer space by a common heritage regime, notably through the 1979 Agreement Governing the Activities of States on the Moon and Other Celestial Bodies (Moon Treaty), which is discussed later in this chapter. With respect to the Earth's atmosphere, more generally speaking (see Chapter 14 'Atmosphere and Outer Space'), collective environmental protection interests have come to be expressed through the concept of common concern of humankind. Rather than on the legal status of the atmosphere, the focus here is on specific issues of concern.

3.1.3 Antarctica

Antarctica's status as a common area differs somewhat from that of the high seas or outer space. Territorial claims have been made for all but a small segment of the

---

[20] Birnie and Boyle, see note 17 above at 679.

[21] See D.R. Teece, 'Global Overfishing and the Spanish-Canadian Turbot War: Can International Law Protect the High-Seas Environment?' (1997) 8 Colo. J. Int'l Envt'l L. & Pol'y 89.

Antarctic continent, but these have been frozen since the adoption of the Antarctic Treaty in 1959 (Article IV). Any state may join this treaty, but decision-making regarding Antarctica is placed in the hands of a relatively limited number of parties that conduct 'substantial scientific activity' in Antarctica (Article IX). These 'consultative parties,' then, are effectively decision-makers on behalf of the entire international community.

For the purposes of this chapter, several features of the Antarctic Treaty are of particular interest.[22] First, Antarctica is designated exclusively for peaceful and scientific uses (Article I). Second, the Antarctic Treaty is flanked by a number of treaties that establish an extensive environmental protection regime for Antarctica. Significantly, these protective efforts apply to the entire Antarctic ecosystem—the Antarctic continent and associated marine ecosystems (see Chapter 24 'Ecosystems'). This ecosystem approach was first enshrined in the 1980 Convention on the Conservation of Antarctic Marine Living Resources (Preamble) and has been further elaborated by the 1991 Protocol on Environmental Protection to the Antarctic Treaty (Madrid Protocol) (Article 3). Third, the preambles of both of these environmental protection treaties specifically cast them as safeguarding the interests of humankind rather than merely those of the treaty parties. Fourth, the Madrid Protocol put in place a 50-year moratorium on all mineral resource activities other than scientific research (Articles 7 and 25). This arrangement effectively sidelines a 1988 Convention on the Regulation of Antarctic Mineral Resources Activities (Mineral Resources Convention) that failed to enter into force due to lack of support from key states. The moratorium is unique in the sweeping nature of the restriction that it places on the open access normally associated with common property status. Fifth, efforts have also been made to establish an innovative environmental liability regime. Indeed, the now dormant 1988 Mineral Resources Convention contained unprecedented provisions, which would have extended to the restoration or compensation of damage to ecosystems independently of damage to state interests. However, in the resumed discussion of liability issues under the Madrid Protocol, agreement has proven elusive. For the moment, therefore, reparation for damage to the Antarctic commons too could be sought only on the limited and uncertain basis of the law of state responsibility. Given the freezing of claims relating to Antarctica, particular difficulties would arise in determining which parties are entitled to invoke the law of state responsibility.

3.2 Common Heritage

As suggested in the previous section, one of the essential attributes of the commons under customary international law is the open access of all states to the resources of

---

[22] For a comprehensive review, see C. Joyner, *Governing the Frozen Commons: The Antarctic Regime and Environmental Protection* (Columbus: University of South Carolina Press, 1998).

these areas. This customary regime contains the seeds of a 'tragedy of the commons'. As we have seen, a number of treaty-based regimes have emerged to regulate use of common areas in order to safeguard the collective interest of all states in the protection of the commons and conservation of their resources. Whether or not these treaty regimes are successful in protecting the commons from 'tragedy' is open to debate. The steady decline of global fish stocks, for example, does not provide much cause for optimism. However, there is yet another dimension to the customary regime that is potentially problematic. While open access, in legal terms, means equal access of all states, in practical terms, access tends to correspond to states' technological and financial resources.

The emergence of the concept of common heritage of humankind must be seen against this backdrop. In particular, it must be understood as part of the effort by the growing number of newly independent states in the 1960s and 1970s to reshape international law to reflect developing country concerns and priorities. Thus, when Ambassador Arvid Pardo of Malta made his famous proposal that the seabed be declared the common heritage of mankind, a primary motivation was to ensure the equitable sharing of benefits from the exploitation of its resources. Little surprise, then, that industrialized countries were much less enthusiastic about the concept. A 1970 UN General Assembly resolution declaring the seabed to be common heritage had the support of 104 countries, with Western industrialized countries accounting for the 16 abstentions.[23] This pattern, of course, is not dissimilar to that of other votes on resolutions through which developing countries have sought to promote the evolution of international law on matters such as self-determination, permanent sovereignty over natural resources, or a New International Economic Order. At any rate, it foreshadowed the rocky path along which the concept of common heritage has been struggling for a foothold.

The concept did come to be the foundation for Part XI of the LOSC, which declares the 'Area'—the seabed and ocean floor beyond the limits of national jurisdiction—and its resources to be the 'common heritage of mankind' (Article 136). Part XI also sketched out what are generally recognized as the core elements of a common heritage regime. The first element is that the Area is a commons and as such not subject to appropriation by individual states (Article 137). Second, activities in the Area must be carried out 'for the benefit of mankind as a whole', and proceeds must be equitably shared among all states (Article 140). Third, the Area's non-living resources are to be managed by an international authority that regulates exploitation, ensures the equitable distribution of proceeds, and takes measures for the protection of the environment (Articles 137 and 145). Finally, the Area must be used exclusively for peaceful purposes (Article 146).

---

[23] B. Larschan and B.C. Brennan, 'The Common Heritage of Mankind Principle in International Law' (1982–3) 21 Colum. J. Transnat'l L. 305 at 318.

These elements find rough counterparts in the 1979 Moon Treaty, which declared the moon and its natural resources to be common heritage. While much less developed than the LOSC's seabed regime, the Moon Treaty too envisaged that an 'international regime' would govern any exploitation of resources, and that any benefits derived from such exploitation should be equitably shared by all states (Article 11). However, these two treaties notwithstanding, the concept of common heritage does not appear to have gained much traction. Some of the very countries most likely to undertake the exploitation of the seabed, the United States chief among them, have consistently resisted the application of the concept. Further, a 1994 Agreement on Part XI of the LOSC modified the implementation of Part XI of the LOSC to such an extent that one may ask what remains of the idea that the seabed and its resources are the common heritage of humankind, notwithstanding its reaffirmation in the agreement. The Moon Treaty has not fared much better. It too met with resistance and only a very small number of countries ratified it. In any case, the common heritage concept has not found application beyond the LOSC and the Moon Treaty.

While it has been suggested that Antarctica too constitutes common heritage of humankind,[24] the Antarctic Treaty system does not bear this out. It differs in a number of respects from the common heritage regimes described earlier. Chief among them is the fact that the Antarctic regime is not concerned with equitable allocation of proceeds from resource exploitation. Rather, exploitation plans have been put on long-term hold and the primary focus of collective concern is the preservation of the Antarctic ecosystem.

Proposals to extend the reach of the common heritage concept beyond common areas and their resources have also stalled. Both in relation to climate change and biodiversity, the concept of common concern, to be discussed in the next section, has come to be accepted as better reflecting the collective concerns relating to these issues. It was suggested at one point that plant resources were the common heritage of all (see Chapter 16 'Biological Resources'). This proposition was bound to be controversial, of course, in that it involved an application of the concept not to a commons, but to resources located within state territory, effectively purporting to convert state property into common property. Not surprisingly, it was rejected in the 1992 Convention on Biological Diversity (CBD), and again in the 2001 International Treaty on Plant Genetic Resources for Food and Agriculture. The proposal is nonetheless worth highlighting because it reveals what may be the central weakness of the common heritage concept: whether applied to common or to state property, it is motivated in large part by states' desire for access to resources rather than by genuine community interest in their protection.[25] Originally, common heritage was

---

[24] See, e.g., E.S. Tenenbaum, 'A World Park in Antarctica: The Common Heritage of Mankind' (1990) 10 Va. Envt'l L.J. 109.

[25] See I. Mgbeoji, 'Beyond Rhetoric: State Sovereignty, Common Concern, and the Inapplicability of the Common Heritage Concept to Plant Genetic Resources' (2003) 16 Leiden J. Int'l L. 821.

a conceptual device to facilitate developing country access to benefits from resources that were *de facto* largely inaccessible to them. Conversely, attempts to promote its application to biological resources within states would appear to have been designed to facilitate Northern access to resources that are *de jure* inaccessible to them. This is not to say that the concept, if actually implemented, would not be beneficial. As noted earlier, the common management and fair allocation it envisages could help address both the potential for over-exploitation and the inequities inherent in the general common area regime. And yet, it seems unlikely that the common heritage concept will deliver on that promise. Its focus on access to resources and benefits gets the concept entangled in and, it appears, sidelined by the competition that these pre-occupations entail.

3.3 Common Concern

The concepts of common area and common heritage are both inherently limited by their focus on certain geographic areas and their resources. The notion of common concern is conceptually more open ended. Indeed, it has been suggested that the 'global environment' is a common concern of humanity.[26] This idea is reflected, albeit very delicately, in Principle 7 of the Rio Declaration on Environment and Development, when it calls upon states 'to cooperate in a spirit of global partnership to conserve, protect and restore the health and integrity of the Earth's ecosystem.' However, international practice has taken a much less sweeping approach, suggesting at least some criteria for the identification of common concerns.

First, the concept is equally applicable to environmental concerns arising beyond the jurisdiction of states and within the jurisdiction of individual states. The notion of common concern has gained currency in these two contexts to the extent that the concepts of common area or common heritage were ill-suited to addressing collect-ive environmental concerns, such as those arising from climate change or loss of bio-logical diversity. However, whether the environmental concern relates to the global commons or to resources within the territories of individual states, it is the fact that all states derive common benefits from protective action that elevates it to a matter of common concern.

Second, it is not areas or resources as such that are common concerns. Rather, the concept is targeted more narrowly at specific environmental processes or protective actions. In this manner, the concept focuses upon the essence of what renders a given

---

[26] See World Conservation Union, Draft International Covenant on Environment and Development, 3rd edition (Gland: IUCN, 2004) at Article 3. See also International Law Association (ILA), New Delhi Declaration of Principles of International Law Relating to Sustainable Development, in ILA, *Report of the Seventieth Conference* (New Delhi: ILA, 2002) at para. 1.3, concluding that the 'protection, preservation and enhancement of the natural environment' are common concerns of humankind.

concern 'common', and treads gingerly around both common property regimes and the territorial sovereignty of individual states. Under the UN Framework Convention on Climate Change (UNFCCC), it is not the atmosphere or even the 'climate', as such, that is the common concern but rather the '*change* in the Earth's climate and *its adverse effects*' (preamble).[27] In turn, the CBD declares the '*conservation* of biological diversity' to be a common concern, not biological diversity as such (preamble).[28] For good measure, the preamble continues by '[r]eaffirming that States have sovereign rights over their own biological resources.'

A third element in the determination of common concerns has been their identification through treaties. In more recent treaty practice, such identification has been explicit, as in the 1992 UNFCCC and the CBD. Other treaties, which were adopted before the concept of common concern gained currency in the early 1990s, circumscribe legal consequences that closely resemble those now associated with common concern regimes. For example, although neither treaty uses the concept as such, both the 1972 Convention for the Protection of the World Cultural and Natural Heritage and the 1987 Montreal Protocol on Substances That Deplete the Ozone Layer (Montreal Protocol) amount to common concern regimes.[29]

One may ask whether common concerns must be identified by treaty to engender particular legal consequences. Indeed, must they be specifically identified at all? Or is it enough that an issue is of concern to all or a large number of states, and that its resolution requires global cooperation? Clearly, these latter features place an issue within the range of potential common concerns. However, two difficulties arise. The first relates to the need for sufficient international consensus on whether a given issue, say global forest protection,[30] is indeed of common concern. There is no reason why such consensus could not find expression in customary international law. Yet treaty negotiations may be more conducive to forging the consensus (see Chapter 20 'Treaty Making and Treaty Evolution'). When widely ratified, a treaty may also forestall further debates about this threshold issue. The second difficulty arises from the need to clarify the precise legal ramifications of common concerns. For example, even if it were agreed that global forest protection is of common concern, absent a treaty, the legal implications would be subject to debate.

Of course, over time, a growing number of treaties can also help crystallize the legal consequences that generally attach to common concerns and, thereby, contribute to the development of a customary framework. At this stage, it is possible to

---

[27] [Emphasis added].   [28] [Emphasis added].

[29] Although the preamble to the Convention for the Protection of the World Cultural and Natural Heritage declares that certain natural areas or sites should be 'preserved as part of the world heritage of mankind as a whole,' its preoccupation is arguably more in line with the concept of common concern. Notably, the preamble goes on to emphasize the duty of 'the international community as a whole to participate in the protection of . . . natural heritage of outstanding universal value.'

[30] See J. Brunnée, 'A Conceptual Framework for an International Forest Convention: Customary Law and Emerging Principles,' in Canadian Council on International Law, ed., *Global Forests and International Environmental Law* (The Hague: Kluwer Law International, 1996) 41 at 55–62.

identify a number of commonalities among common concern regimes and, thus, the contours of a potential future customary framework. The concept of common concern does not imply a specific rule for the conduct of states. Nonetheless, it signals that states' freedom of action may be subject to limits even where other states' sovereign rights are not affected in the direct transboundary sense envisaged by the no harm principle. Such limits flow precisely from the fact that the concept identifies certain types of degradation of areas or resources beyond the limits of national jurisdiction, and even of resources physically located within the territory of individual states, as of concern to all. Thus, the concept of common concern has the potential to significantly widen the range of environmental protection obligations owed *erga omnes*.[31] All states would have concomitant legal interests and could demand others to adjust their conduct accordingly. Of course, unless a treaty converts what might otherwise be an (emerging) obligation *erga omnes* into an obligation *erga omnes partes*, all the constraints of the law of state responsibility that were sketched earlier would still obtain. It may be more helpful, therefore, to conceive of the concept of common concern as entitling, perhaps even requiring, all states to cooperate internationally to address the concern.

The idea of an international responsibility to cooperate in the face of common concerns is now reflected in a number of international instruments. And, like the concept of common heritage, the concept of common concern has also come to be closely tied to South–North equity considerations (see Chapter 27 'Equity'). However, whereas common heritage regimes are concerned with equitable sharing of benefits, common concern regimes focus on equitable sharing of the burdens of cooperation and problem solving. These considerations are encapsulated in the concept of common but differentiated responsibilities, which may fairly be described as the flipside of the concept of common concern. These linkages have found expression in Principle 7 of the Rio Declaration, which reads in full:

States shall cooperate in a spirit of global partnership to conserve, protect and restore the health and integrity of the Earth's ecosystem. In view of the different contributions to global environmental degradation, States have common but differentiated responsibilities. The developed countries acknowledge the responsibility that they bear in the international pursuit of sustainable development in view of the pressures their societies place on the global environment and of the technologies and financial resources they command.

The connection is also expressed in the preamble to the UNFCCC, which acknowledges:

that the global nature of climate change calls for the widest possible cooperation by all countries and their participation in an effective and appropriate international response, in accordance with their common but differentiated responsibilities and respective capabilities and their social and economic conditions.

---

[31] See also Birnie and Boyle , note 17 above at 98–9.

Other global agreements, such as the Montreal Protocol and the CBD, reflect the underlying idea through differentiation in the obligations of developed and developing countries. As with the concept of common concern, the primary effect of the differentiation principle has been to structure treaty-based regimes. Although the principle is widely employed in treaties and frequently invoked in international negotiations, it is difficult to argue that it has acquired customary law status. Much remains controversial about the content of the principle, especially the criteria that define the basis for, and modes of, differentiation.[32] Nonetheless, taken together, existing instruments and practice suggest that states are paying attention to considerations of equity in international environmental relations and recognize that approaches to global concerns must reflect both the states' contributions to a given problem and their abilities to address it. The practical manifestations of the concept range from differentiation of commitments in terms of timelines or degree, to provision of technical and financial assistance to developing countries (see Chapter 41 'Technical and Financial Assistance'), and even to making developing country implementation of their commitments contingent upon provision of such assistance.

4 INSTITUTIONS AND PROCESSES

As the evolution of the notions of common area, common heritage, and common concern illustrates, the conceptual framework of international law has developed significantly to address collective environmental concerns. The impact of this evolution, however, has been felt not so much in the development and application of customary law as in the development of treaty-based regimes. These regimes serve to enshrine the three concepts in relation to specific areas or concerns. They also flesh out the concepts in the sense that they clarify their legal implications and outline specific commitments of states. In turn, the concepts frame the regimes and help shape their evolution and implementation.

The reference here to 'treaty regimes' highlights a central point. Today, multilateral environmental agreements usually are not one-off contracts between states but rather open-ended 'sets of implicit or explicit principles, norms, rules and decision-making procedures around which actors' expectations converge.'[33] In other words,

---

[32] For a thorough analysis, see C.D. Stone, 'Common but Differentiated Responsibilities in International Law' (2004) 98 A.J.I.L. 276. See also S. Biniaz, 'Common but Differentiated Responsibility—Remarks,' in *Proceedings of the Ninety-Sixth Annual Meeting of the American Society of International Law* (Washington, DC: American Society of International Law, 2002) 359.

[33] S. Krasner, 'Structural Causes and Consequences: Regimes as Intervening Variables' (1982) 36 Int'l Org. 185 at 186.

the adoption of an MEA is not the endpoint of the international legal process but is instead the beginning. Treaty regimes, including their institutional dimensions, are the subject of other chapters in this *Handbook* (see Chapter 20 'Treaty Making and Treaty Evolution'; Chapter 31 'International Institutions'; and Chapter 38 'Treaty Bodies'). Indeed, many of the features of treaty regimes that deal with common areas, common heritage, or common concerns, reflect wider trends in international environmental law. However, it is in the context of the legal challenges posed by the collective environmental concerns examined in this chapter that some of these features assume particular importance.

A first important dimension of treaty regimes is that they not only express, but also institutionalize, collective concerns. As the preceding discussion has illustrated, the customary law foundations of international environmental law continue to be trapped in a vicious circle of sorts. Individual states have only limited legal ability to tackle collective concerns while the legal 'community' that is said to hold the various concerns in common is not sufficiently constituted to articulate, let alone defend, its collective environmental interests. It is precisely against this backdrop that treaty-based institutionalization plays a central role. It helps constitute the collectives, or 'communities', that otherwise remain elusive but that are crucial to the legal enterprise of addressing common environmental concerns.

The institutionalization of collective concerns within treaty regimes occurs at a number of levels. Many environmental regimes establish or collaborate with forums for the exchange among scientific or technical experts (see Chapter 34 'Epistemic Communities'). For example, the UNFCCC established a permanent Subsidiary Body for Scientific and Technological Advice (Article 9). The regime also draws upon the expertise of the Intergovernmental Panel on Climate Change, which operates under the auspices of the World Meteorological Organization and the United Nations Environment Programme. Expert forums such as these are important in building consensus around the nature of collective concerns and the collective action that is required to address them. However, their role in strengthening a regime's common interest patterns, to return to Hey's terminology, is an ongoing one. Once decisions on the general thrust of collective action are made, scientific or technical expert bodies continue to make important contributions in the elaboration, refinement, or adjustment of regulatory strategies.

The legal development of the regime is usually in the hands of a plenary body, such as a Conference of the Parties (COP). The spectrum of opinions on the role of COPs is wide. Some observers see the emergence of issue-specific global legislatures.[34] Others argue that COPs increasingly resemble international organizations.[35] For yet

---

[34] See D. Anderson, 'Law-Making Processes in the UN System—Some Impressions' (1998) 2 Max Planck Y.B. UN L. 23 at 49; and G. Palmer, 'New Ways to Make International Environmental Law' (1992) 86 A.J.I.L. 259.

[35] R. Churchill and G. Ulfstein, 'Autonomous Institutional Arrangements in Multilateral Environmental Agreements: A Little-Noticed Phenomenon in International Law' (2000) 94 A.J.I.L. 623.

others, a COP is ultimately a diplomatic conference,[36] with the important difference that it facilitates continuous processes and interlocking engagements between technical experts, policy-makers, and lawyers. Whatever the case may be, COPs and their subsidiary bodies have come to be central venues for international law-making activities around collective concerns.

The phenomenon of treaty-based law-making is the second major characteristic of international law's approach to collective environmental concerns. This broader MEA phenomenon is of particular importance in the collective concern context because it significantly enhances the potential for legitimate outcomes (see Chaper 30 'Legitimacy'). Treaty-based law-making removes from debate the basic questions of who is entitled to make law for the collective and on what terms. On the one hand, collective concern treaties enshrine the background assumption that law-making is a collective enterprise. On the other hand, they settle the terms of law-making such that, while states' sovereignty is respected through consent requirements, consent processes are structured so as to maximize opportunities for collective outcomes (see Chapter 20 'Treaty Making and Treaty Evolution' and Chapter 32 'International Institutions'). Thus, the arguably most important feature of treaty-based law-making is the range of strategies that have emerged to strike a balance between the constraints of the consent requirement and the need for timely collective action.[37] To be sure, much regime development still occurs through ordinary consent-based methods. When an agreement is amended, or when an additional treaty, such as a protocol, is adopted, individual states are bound only when they consent to these instruments. And yet, the 'edges of consent' have softened considerably.[38] Under many agreements, especially when technical issues are involved, regulatory approaches can be expanded with effect for all parties except for those that explicitly opt out. Perhaps more significantly, an ever-growing array of regulatory detail is adopted through decisions of plenary bodies, without subsequent formal consent by individual states. In most cases, the resulting standards will not be legally binding, although they may well contain mandatory language.

A hybrid approach can by found in the Antarctic Treaty. Since its entry into force in 1961, no use has been made of its formal amendment procedure (Article XII). Instead, parties have relied upon the adoption of so-called 'recommended measures' (Article IX). Some of these measures are drafted in obligatory language and modify the treaty's legal framework, or even alter the rights and obligations of parties. The measures under the Antarctic Treaty become 'effective' for a party upon approval— not ratification—at the domestic level by all other parties.[39] The practice under the

[36] A.E. Boyle, 'Saving the World? Implementation and Enforcement of International Environmental Law through International Institutions' (1991) 3 J. Envt'l L. 229 at 235.

[37] See J. Brunnée, 'COPing with Consent: Lawmaking under Multilateral Environmental Agreements' (2002) 15 Leiden J. Int'l L. 1.   [38] Simma, see note 4 above at 325.

[39] See C. Joyner, 'Recommended Measures under the Antarctic Treaty: Hardening Compliance with Soft International Law' (1998) 19 Mich. J. Int'l L. 401.

Antarctic Treaty, which applies also to the Madrid Protocol, provides an early example of the technically non-binding, but nonetheless 'mandatory' rule-making that is now common under modern environmental agreements. For example, under the UNFCCC and its Kyoto Protocol, it appears that the bulk of the regulatory flesh is being put on the treaty bones through simple decisions of the plenary body. Thus, provisions on central treaty matters, ranging from inventory and monitoring requirements to the protocol's mechanisms for trading of emission units or reduction credits, are adopted in 'soft' form.[40] As the climate change regime illustrates, even soft standards are subject to tough and protracted negotiations. Nonetheless, they do facilitate agreement upon collective action and adoption of standards applicable to all parties—an important feature for efforts to address collective concerns. Equally important is that soft regulatory processes allow speedier regime development and adjustment than processes that involve subsequent ratification by individual states.

One further dimension to regime-based law-making processes is of interest. As we have seen, to the extent that international law acknowledges environmental concerns of the 'international community', the practical ramifications remain focused upon a community of states. Treaty regimes provide one arena in which non-state actors, such as international organizations, NGOs, or business entities can be directly engaged. Suffice it to point again to the climate change regime, in which non-state actors participate in myriad ways. For example, they can have observer status at COP meetings, distribute information or policy papers, meet with, or even belong to, official delegations, or report on negotiations. Although, in a formal sense, law-making remains entirely in the hands of states, non-state actors thus have considerable opportunities to provide input into law-making processes or even help shape their outcomes. In short, in the context of treaty regimes, we find at least tentative developments towards a more inclusive approach to 'global concerns of humanity as a whole.'

The third key feature of collective concern regimes is their approach to compliance and dispute settlement. As noted at various points, customary international law provides only limited options for compelling compliance with collective interest norms. In addition, states only very rarely employ even the available enforcement options provided by the law of state responsibility. Further, because collective concern issues are by definition polycentric, they do not lend themselves to traditional, bilateral dispute settlement.[41] At any rate, options for judicial dispute settlement, for example by the ICJ, are generally limited by the requirement that all parties must accept the court's jurisdiction.

---

[40] According to some observers, the Kyoto Protocol empowers the COP to adopt legally binding decisions on certain matters, such as international emissions trading. See Churchill and Ulfstein, note 35 above at 639–40.

[41] See Weeramantry, note 1 above, pointing to the additional problems that flow from the fact that the court's procedures, focused as they are upon disputes between specific state parties, are ill-suited to doing 'justice to rights and obligations of an *erga omnes* character.'

Part XV of the LOSC is unusual in this latter respect. Any party to the convention can unilaterally bring environmental disputes, including disputes relating to the high seas, before the International Tribunal for the Law of the Sea (ITLOS), the ICJ, or an arbitral tribunal (Articles 287 and 288). The relevant court or tribunal is empowered to prescribe provisional measures to forestall serious harm to the marine environment pending its final decision (Article 290). ITLOS has done so in one case concerning high seas resources—the dispute between Australia and New Zealand on the one hand and Japan on the other regarding the conservation and management of southern bluefin tuna.[42] Finally, where parties agree to jointly bring a dispute before ITLOS, 'entities other than States Parties' can join the proceedings (Article 20 of the ITLOS Statute). It would appear, then, that the ITLOS Statute recognizes in at least a limited manner that the 'community' interested in the protection of the marine environment may also include private parties, NGOs, or international organizations.[43]

However, compulsory dispute settlement is rare also in environmental agreements, partly because of states' reluctance to resort to it, and partly because it may not satisfactorily address the collective concerns underlying the agreement. Quite apart from the diffuse nature of injuries to parties' common interest in compliance with treaty commitments, addressing the regime's collective concerns requires the greatest possible degree of compliance by the widest possible range of parties. The result has been the emergence of procedures that assess parties' compliance with their treaty commitments and provide for a range of measures to facilitate or compel compliance (see Chapter 43 'Compliance Procedures').

Cooperative facilitation of compliance is the primary objective of the majority of existing compliance procedures. The procedure under the Montreal Protocol neatly encapsulates this approach, aimed, as it is, at 'securing an amicable solution . . . on the basis of respect for the provisions of the Protocol' (para. 8). This pragmatic approach recognizes the fact that non-complying parties are most likely to be states with genuine capacity limitations. By contrast, in the case of the Kyoto Protocol, only developed countries and transition countries currently have emission reduction commitments. Therefore, capacity building and financial assistance are less likely to be appropriate in promoting compliance. Moreover, the Kyoto Protocol regime has certain unique features, such as its emissions trading mechanisms, that necessitate a tougher approach to compliance. The Kyoto Protocol's compliance procedure, thus, explicitly declares its goals to 'facilitate, promote and enforce compliance' with the protocol (para. I).

All compliance procedures have in common that they can be triggered by any state party, including by a state about its own performance. Yet there is also evidence of

[42] *Southern Bluefin Tuna cases* (Provisional Measures), 38 I.L.M. 1624 (1999). Provisional measures were also indicated in the MOX plant dispute between Ireland and the United Kingdom concerning a British plant for the processing of radioactive materials. See ITLOS Order, 3 December 2001, 41 I.L.M. 405 (2001).   [43] Birnie and Boyle, see note 17 above at 223–4.

subtle movement towards a common interest pattern. For example, under the Montreal Protocol, the treaty's Secretariat can and does trigger the procedure by raising possible instances of non-compliance in its annual reports on the parties' performance and by informing the Implementation Committee (para. 3). Under the Kyoto Protocol procedure, the compliance procedure will be automatically triggered when an expert review process reveals questions about a party's implementation of its commitments (para. VI.1). While both procedures thus allow for a form of a collective-interest trigger, they do remain anchored in inter-state foundations. For example, under the Kyoto Protocol procedure, NGOs may submit 'factual and technical information' relevant to the compliance review (para. VIII.4), have access to meetings of the compliance bodies unless parties object (para. IX.2), and have access to the findings of the compliance body (para. VIII.7). Yet they cannot trigger the procedure or make formal submissions. Thus, with respect to compliance, the 'international community' in the climate change regime remains primarily one of states.

5 Conclusion

As the slow evolution of concepts such as obligations *erga omnes* and of related aspects of the law of state responsibility illustrates, international law continues to struggle with 'collective' or 'community' aspirations. Seen against this backdrop, international environmental law has made remarkable progress in its responses to both 'concerns about the commons' and 'common concerns'. Granted, the development of customary law on common areas, common heritage, and common concerns has been sluggish. Yet irrespective of their binding force, these three concepts have played significant roles in framing treaty-based efforts. In turn, treaties have fleshed out each of the concepts, and the emerging normative patterns may eventually feed back into the development of customary law. Of course, it is an open question whether effective protection of collective interests could be mounted on the basis of customary environmental law and the rules of state responsibility, especially since the latter are so rarely invoked. It is all the more important, then, that treaty regimes provide practical options for the protection of common interests. It is also safe to predict that they will remain the primary venues for 'collective concern' law-making. Often, the focus is on cooperation for functional or legal reasons. But treaty regimes have at least the potential to turn pragmatic cooperation into genuine normative communities. While by no means perfect, treaty regimes therefore offer promising settings in which to mediate between 'individual State interest' and 'the global concerns of humanity as a whole.'[44]

---

[44] Weeramantry, see note 1 above.

Recommended Reading

F. Biermann, ' "Common Concerns of Humankind" and National Sovereignty,' in *Globalism: People, Profits and Progress: Proceedings of the Thirtieth Annual Conference of the Canadian Council on International Law* (Canadian Council on International Law, 2002) 158.

J. Charney, 'Third State Remedies for Environmental Damage to the World's Common Spaces,' in F. Francioni and T. Scovazzi, eds., *International Responsibility for Environmental Harm* (Boston: Graham and Trotman, 1991) 149.

G. Hardin, 'The Tragedy of the Commons' (1968) 162 Science 1243.

D. Kritsiosis, 'Imagining the International Community' (2002) 13 Eur. J. Int'l L. 268.

A. Paulus, *Die Internationale Gemeinschaft im Völkerrecht* (München: Verlag C.H. Beck, 2001).

J. Peel, 'New State Responsibility Rules and Compliance with Multilateral Environmental Obligations: Some Case Studies of How the New Rules Might Apply in the International Environmental Context' (2001) 10 R.E.C.I.E.L. 82.

M. Ragazzi, *The Concept of International Obligations Erga Omnes* (Oxford: Oxford University Press, 1997).

B. Simma, *From Bilateralism to Community Interest in International Law*, (1994-VI) 250 Recueil des cours 217.

C.J. Tams, *Enforcing Obligations Erga Omnes in International Law* (Cambridge: Cambridge University Press, 2005).

CHAPTER 24

ECOSYSTEMS

DAN TARLOCK

1 THE POWERFUL, BUT UNCERTAIN STATUS OF ECOSYSTEMS IN INTERNATIONAL LAW

1.1 Introduction: The Powerful Appeal but Marginal Legal Status of the Ecosystem Construct

INTERNATIONAL environmental law has two overarching and related objectives: (1) the prevention of pollution and health risks from the uncontrolled application of modern technology and science that cross national borders or degrade global commons; and (2) the protection of representative natural systems or areas of 'nature' that are deemed to be of global significance from the adverse impacts of human modification. The scientific construct 'ecosystem' has profoundly influenced the development of domestic and international 'nature' protection programmes, from the reduction of greenhouse gases to biodiversity conservation. States often conserve ecosystems for their aesthetic and recreational values, but, increasingly, the primary conservation objectives are the protection of humans from the immediate and long-term health and safety risks associated with the loss of system function and services and the conservation of biodiversity for future generations. Ecosystem conservation is also a central objective of the widely accepted international norm that all countries should exploit and use their natural resources in an environmentally sustainable manner.

In 2005, the first United Nations Millennium Ecosystem Assessment evaluated 24 ecological services, found that 15 were in decline and five more stable but threatened, and linked this degradation to serious long-term effects on human well-being.[1] The assessment reflects the idea that we must now act as planetary stewards and moderate our exploitation of life support systems and natural resources. Ecosystem conservation is a central component of the stewardship project. Transnational ecosystems have been described as a manifestation of nature that form 'the psychological and spiritual backdrop of our lives.'[2] However, the primary reason that the ecosystem construct has become embedded in our consciousness is because it is assumed to be a science-based ethical imperative. A United States environmental historian has written that the 'new awareness of the environment as a living system—a 'web of life' or ecosystem—rather than just a storehouse of commodities to be extracted or a

---

[1] United Nations Environment Programme, *Living beyond Our Means: Natural Assets and Human-Well Being*, available at <http://www.unep.org/GC/GCSS-IX/DOCUMENTS/K0584573-GCSS-IX-INF8.doc> (2005).

[2] United Nations Development Programme, United Nations Environmental Programme, World Bank, and World Resources Institute, *A Guide to World Resources 2000–2001, People and Ecosystems: The Fraying Web of Life* (Washington, DC: World Resources Institute, 2000) at 4.

chemical machine to be manipulated' is the most revolutionary idea contributed by the modern environmental movement.[3]

Despite its success as an organizing principle for public policy, the ecosystem construct has not yet yielded consistent, strong legal protection norms either within states or as a matter of international environmental law. Transnational ecosystems are studied and mapped more than they are protected because there is little formal recognition of ecosystems as distinct objects of legal protection in international law. For the most part, ecosystem protection is incidental to legal regimes with other objectives. The basic reason is that it is difficult to derive universal, substantive protection norms given our current scientific understanding of ecosystems. The main protections come through procedures that require private and state actors to consider the potential impact of an activity on natural systems.

Science generally defines an ecosystem as a biological community of interdependent plants, animals, and microorganisms that occurs in a specific place associated with particular soils, temperatures, and disturbance patterns and the physical and chemical factors that make up that community's abiotic, non-living environment. This definition is purely descriptive and does not provide much guidance to those who make design about protection levels and processes. Thus, in international law the term ecosystem is very broad and has no consistent meaning. It can refer to a process of decision as well as to a substantive obligation to protect a defined resource or geographical area. In legal instruments, the term ecosystem is also often used carelessly and interchangeably with other similar terms such as environment, nature, balance of nature, ecological balance, or ecological stability.[4] These terms can imply a simple nature sensibility, a form of legal reasoning that takes into account the special features of environmental problems, such as uncertainty, or a vague, substantive protection norm.

There are overlapping, historical, conceptual, and institutional reasons for the amorphous and ultimately marginal legal status of ecosystems in international law. First, ecosystems have traditionally been seen as undifferentiated components of

---

[3] R.N.L. Andrews, *Managing the Environment, Managing Ourselves: A History of American Environmental Policy* (New Haven, CT: Yale University Press, 1999) at 202.

[4] The term 'environment' is often equated with 'ecosystem'. For example, the 1988 Convention on the Regulation of Antarctic Mineral Resources Activities defines as harm as 'any harm on the living and non-living components of that environment or those ecosystems.' *Minors Oposa v. Secretary of the Department of Environment and Natural Resources*, Supreme Court of the Philippines, 33 I.L.M. 174 at 185 (1994), which granted standing to the children of a Philippine citizen to challenge logging permits, spoke of the 'right to a balanced and healthful ecology' and to a 'sound environment'. P. Sands, *Principles of International Environmental Law I: Frameworks, Standards and Implementation* (Manchester: Manchester University Press, 1994) at 17, distinguishes environment from ecosystem because the former 'encompasses both features and products of the natural world and those of human civilization' while the latter is concerned with 'plants and animals occurring together plus that part of the environment over which they have an influence.' This distinction has considerable support, but others argue that the definition of environment should be confined to the natural environment. M.A. Fitzmaurice, 'International Protection of the Environment' (2001) 293 Recueil des cours 22 at 22–8.

other larger terrestrial or aquatic areas with a special legal status, such as national parks, protected marine areas, or nature reserves. As a matter of international law, most ecosystems are simply national territory and thus, historically, have had no distinctive legal status. Second, international environmental law remains primarily focused on the prevention of harm to one state by another (see Chapter 22 'Transboundary Impacts'). Harm can encompass ecosystem damage, but it remains legally associated with, for example, air or water pollution that causes immediate, substantial damage to human health or property. In contrast, ecosystem protection is concerned with the preservation of natural system function over time. Function impairment is harder to fit within conventional understandings of damage in international law because long-term, subtle function loss that does not pose an immediate threat to human health or life is not conventionally understood as an injury that gives rise to state responsibility (see Chapter 44 'International Responsibility and Liability'). In addition, the most serious and immediate impairment of ecosystems generally occurs within national boundaries, and, thus, the transboundary or global impacts are often difficult to measure.

The third reason for the weak legal protection of ecosystems is that ecosystem protection does not lend itself to a single national or international conservation regime. A national decision to comply with a protection mandate must be supported by a variety of public and private initiatives. The central governments of most states lack effective control of ecosystems even within their borders. In almost all countries, the control of the environment *de jure* or *de facto* is de-centralized. Multiple political jurisdictions have control over important ecosystems, and control is split between governments and private property holders, but inter-jurisdiction cooperation is essential to conservation.

The fourth reason is that the basic principles of environmental law developed before the ecosystem concept emerged as one of the central ideas of environmental protection. International environmental law still draws on the older tradition of preserving natural areas primarily for aesthetic, rather than for scientific, reasons and of conserving selected species, such as fish, birds, and fur-bearing animals, whose economic value threaten their extinction through over-exploitation. During the late nineteenth and early twentieth centuries, individual wildlife species conservation regimes were put in place, motivated largely by fears of species exhaustion. To conserve wildlife for future human benefit, regulated harvesting was substituted for unrestrained exploitation. At the same time, developed states began to wall off a few majestic, scenic areas from intensive human exploitation. While, in these efforts, nature appeared to be understood as the aggregation of the physical landscape and of all flora and fauna, early preservation decisions were made with comparatively little scientific input and before the ecosystem was understood as an appropriate focus for regulation. Finally, the fifth reason for the limited legal traction of the ecosystem concept is the evolution that the understanding of the construct has undergone since its emergence. This problem is discussed in detail in the next section.

1.2 History of the Ecosystem Concept

The ecosystem construct emerged at the end of the nineteenth century and has gone through several scientific evolutions, which have had significant implications for international protection regimes. A focus on the protection of ecosystem integrity and function replaced the earlier idea that nature was a sacred space to be protected for its natural beauty.[5] The notion that the ecosystem was the fundamental unit of nature was quickly embraced by the first generation of environmentalists because it appeared to support a categorical, science-based imperative around which a new type of legal regime could be based. However, scientific developments have undermined this assumption, and the ecosystem concept has proven to be more scientifically complex than those who embraced it assumed.

1.2.1 *Stability Hypothesis*

The most attractive policy and legal aspect of ecosystems was their presumed stability. Initially, ecologists assumed that discrete units of nature were superorganisms, which evolved through stages to become stable climax communities. By the mid-1930s, the climax theory had been replaced with the more sophisticated theory that discrete natural units should be understood as systems of individual flora and fauna that respond to various stimuli, rather than organisms that move in one direction only. In 1935, Arthur Tansley, a Cambridge ecologist, influenced by the progress of physics research at the Cavendish Laboratory, coined the word 'ecosystem'. Tansley's concept triumphed and is based on the assumptions that (1) systems rather than organisms evolve and (2) that succession, or change, is a process rather than a single end-state.[6] The American ecologist Eugene Odum built on this theory to posit a powerful stability hypothesis—namely that ecosystems tend towards stability or 'homeostasis' and that 'the limits of hemostatic mechanisms can easily be exceeded by the actions of man.'[7] Science thus supported the ethical principle 'let nature be'.[8] Yet, by highlighting the vulnerability of ecological balance to interventions by humans who, in turn, depend upon ecosystems for various 'services', such as pollution filtering, flood control, and wildlife habitat maintenance, the stability hypothesis helped tilt the debate over the reasons for ecosystem protection towards a utilitarian, anthropocentric, rather than ecocentric, outlook.

---

[5] This idea is attributed to the American ecologist Eugene Odem (1913–2002). E.P. Odum, in collaboration with H.T. Odum, *Fundamentalists of Ecology*, 2nd edition (Philadelphia: W.B. Saunders, 1959).

[6] F.B. Golley, *A History the Ecosystem Concept in Ecology* (New Haven, CT: Yale University Press, 1993).

[7] Odum, see note 5 above at 36.

[8] The American ecologist A. Leopold 'codified' this norm in his book, *A Sand County Almanac* (New York: Oxford University Press, 1949). The standard biography of Leopold is C. Meine, *Aldo Leopold: His Life and Work* (Madison: University of Wisconsin Press, 1988).

1.2.2 *Ecosystem as Dynamic Rather Than Static System*

The idea of the 'balance of nature' holds a powerful grip on human imagination,[9] but ecologists have rejected it as theology rather than science. We now realize that we know much less than we assumed about how ecosystems operate, especially as the geographic scale of the protected system increases. Most ecologists now accept the thesis that ecosystems are dynamic rather than static systems, subject to human and natural disturbances that are both predictable and random.[10] The consequences of the paradigm shift are substantial because it challenges the assumptions (1) that pure, undisturbed nature exists; (2) that it should be preserved in this state; (3) that the best way to do this is to wall it off from human actions that threaten to disturb it; and (4) that we have sufficient scientific understanding to achieve these objectives.

Some scientists go further and argue that the current concept of an ecosystem may no longer be a meaningful construct. The reason is that the new thinking on ecology undermines the crucial assumptions of the concept. Ecology has traditionally assumed that an ecosystem has definable boundaries, that it has spatial homogeneity, that we may substitute different flora and fauna and still maintain a sustainable system, that natural selection is relatively unimportant, that we can identify stability levels at different scales, and that humans are not part of ecosystems. These simplistic assumptions are now being recast as more complex, open-ended criteria that emphasize that stability is a function of the time scale of observation and the balance between '(a) rates of change in an environmental condition, and (b) rates of exchange of biota in the area.'[11] For the foreseeable future, the ecosystem concept will not be totally abandoned, but an ecosystem could be redefined as an 'ecological system' with a range of spatial scales depending on the timeframe adopted, with a wide potential, non-constant dispersal range for each species and in which species interact to maximize the system's biotic potential.

The modern dynamic conception of ecosystems has significant implications for the future of international ecosystem conservation. First, the focus of environmental protection is increasingly shifting to the restoration of previously degraded ecological systems rather than the conservation of 'natural' or undisturbed ones because there is comparatively little 'pure nature' to preserve. Second, we must integrate human activities into ecosystem protection strategies. Consistent with this understanding, modern ecology views humans not as alien, exotic species to be eliminated to the maximum extent possible but rather as important actors that interrelate with

---

[9] S. Toulmin has traced the roots of the quest for stability in Western thought from Newton to the present and argues that the pursuit of universal principles remained the norm 'up to John Dewey's time.' 'The Idea of Stability' (1999) 20 Tanner Lectures on Human Values 325 at 353.

[10] See S.R. Reice, *The Silver Lining: The Benefits of Natural Disasters* (Princeton, NJ: Princeton University Press, 2001).

[11] R.V. O'Neill, 'Is It Time to Bury the Ecosystem Concept? (With Full Military Honors, Of Course!)' (2001) 82 Ecology 3275.

ecological systems. However, many environmentalists find this idea disturbing because, in their view, it will promote ecosystem degradation. Third, as a corollary of the second point, ecosystems must be managed, not just preserved, to be effectively conserved.

1.3 Legal Challenges of Ecosystem Conservation

International environmental law's challenge is to make the ecosystem concept an operational legal norm. As the previous discussion indicates, the concept of an ecosystem is difficult to translate into legal standards. For a construct to become the basis for laws that limit human action, the scientific basis must be relatively uniformly understood, widely accepted in the scientific community, remain relatively constant, and be capable of reduction to simple principles. At the present time, it is difficult to translate our scientific understanding of ecosystems into operational legal standards. Science cannot identify the appropriate geographic scale at which protected systems should be delineated or what the management time horizon should be. At best, science can give us some guidelines for good management.

A 'healthy ecosystem' has been proposed as a normative standard, but many argue that this is just a metaphor with insufficient substantive content. Even if one overcomes the normative standard problem, there is the problem of scale. Scientists have a number of categories to describe ecosystems, which can range from a single lake to broad transnational landscapes, and, thus, the categories are often disconnected from effective conservation regimes. For example, the Canada–Mexico–United States Commission on Environmental Cooperation (CEC), which was created under a side agreement to the North American Free Trade Agreement, has identified the North American prairie ecosystem,[12] which runs from southern Canada to northern Mexico. The identification of this system as an area of international concern is an important step towards more discrete and concrete protection efforts. However, the designation of an ecosystem on the scale of the North American prairie runs the risk that there is no effective link between the designation and the system's long-term protection because no governance structure appropriate to the scale will emerge from the existing multiple state and transnational regulatory regime, and the CEC has no direct powers to compel a nation to take affirmative steps to protect the system.

In recent years, the international community has embraced the concepts of biodiversity conservation and environmentally sustainable development, but they do not yet have sufficiently clear meanings either. Thus, while both concepts communicate powerful and important ideas, they too rest on scientific (as well as ethical and economic) concepts that have yet to become operational. The construct biodiversity is

---

[12] Commission for Environmental Cooperation, *Report of the Executive Director*, Regular Session of the CEC Council, Guadalajara, 28–9 June 2001.

now replacing both nature and the ecosystem as an object of legal protection, but the addition of yet another science-based term only adds to the difficulties of formulating effective ecosystem protection standards. The broader term biodiversity, which includes everything from nature reserves to intellectual property in nature, is an invented term, which mixes ethical assertions with substantial unanswered scientific questions. The questions include queries concerning the measurement criteria. Do we measure genetic, species, evolutionary, or functional variety?[13] Thus, biodiversity remains a construct in process, and its relationship to ecosystem conservation has not been clearly defined. Ecosystems are central to biodiversity conservation because they are the unit in which species and other forms of biological diversity are conserved, but such systems are not the exclusive conservation focus.

1.4 Adaptive Management: A New Legal Paradigm for Ecosystem Conservation

The primary ecosystem conservation strategies—withdrawal of land and water from all development, one-time ad hoc development versus preservation decisions and environment impact assessment—have been undermined by the new ecology. We need dynamic regulation that incorporates a continuous process of acquiring and evaluating scientific information. These processes must produce 'regulatory science'. This is science designed to answer, to the best extent possible, causal questions about management choices and a socially desired outcome, such as the preservation of a species from extinction or the restoration of an ecosystem so that it functions more like it did prior to human intervention. For example, science-driven baselines and targets must be set so scientists can assess whether they are being maintained. The best management concept that has been developed is adaptive management.

Adaptive management was developed in the United States in the 1970s as a remedy to the static nature of environmental impact analysis. Adaptive management proceeds from the premise that a 'fixed review of an independently designed policy'[14] was inconsistent with the experience of resource managers worldwide who must make decisions against the backdrop of constantly changing conditions, significant knowledge gaps, and newly developing information. The theory asserts that rigorous but flexible procedures are necessary to manage dynamic ecosystems over time under conditions of extreme uncertainty. Thus, adaptive management complements the precautionary principle (see Chapter 25 'Precaution') because it corrects both the bias towards no action in the face of uncertainty, and the opposite bias for immediate fixes unconnected to long-term monitoring, assessment, and adjustment to changed

---

[13] See F. Bosselman, 'A Dozen Biodiversity Puzzles' (2004) 12 N.Y.U. Envt'l L.J. 364.

[14] C.S. Holling, ed., *Adaptive Environmental Assessment and Management* (New York: John Wiley and Sons, 1978) at 1.

conditions and information. Global climate change underscores the need for aggressive, precautionary, adaptive management of ecosystems. One quarter of all terrestrial species may be at risk of extinction from global change, and if we have changed our biological system to such an extent, then we do have to get worried about whether the services that are provided by natural ecosystems are going to continue.[15]

2 STATUS OF ECOSYSTEMS IN INTERNATIONAL LAW

The international law status of ecosystems can be characterized as follows: (1) no protected status; (2) direct object of protection from transboundary injuries; (3) indirect object of protection from transboundary injuries by pollution reduction regimes; (4) object of discretionary national protection influenced by international law; or (5) object of explicit international protection duties that can be legally 'hard' or 'soft' and that can be substantive or procedural.

2.1 No Protected Status: Ecosystems Are Undifferentiated Components of National Territory

International law gives states the right to control and exploit their territory. In this classical framework, a state may equally choose to conserve and manage specific ecosystems to sustain their natural functions or to consume and destroy them. More recently, this idea of discretion has also found expression in assertions of the still contested right to development.[16] Today, international law qualifies absolute claims of sovereignty through the principle that a state may not cause damage to other states or abuse shared resources, as discussed in the next section. However, to the extent that an ecosystem is confined to a single state's territory, then, according to the classical framework, states are free to do as they like. International law does not protect ecosystems as such. It considers them to be simply portions of a state's land mass or territorial sea with no distinctive legal status.

---

[15] Elizabeth Kolbett, Field Notes from a Catastrophe: Man, Nature, and Climate Change 87 (Bloomsbury USA, New York, 2006).

[16] Declaration on the Right to Development, Doc. A/RES/41/128 (December 1986), Annex; and the Right to Development, UNGA Resolution no. 55/108 (13 March 2001).

2.2 A Direct Object of Protection from Transboundary Insults

Ecosystems do have limited protection as a result of the rule against transboundary injuries (see Chapter 22 'Transboundary Impacts'). A state's activities that damage ecosystems in another state can subject it to responsibility under the transboundary harm rule, which was articulated in the *Trail Smelter Case (United States v. Canada)*,[17] and subsequently codified in Principle 21 of the Stockholm Declaration on the Human Environment and Principle 2 of the Rio Declaration on Environment and Development. For example, the continued logging of the world's tropical rainforests may contribute to the release of greenhouse gases and may disrupt regional water cycles and, thus, adversely impact a variety of ecosystems. Consistent with our increased scientific understanding of ecosystem function, the UN Environment Programme Working Group on environmental damage included the 'impairment of a viable ecological balance' among the examples of environmental damage.[18]

That said, under international environmental law, states are responsible only for demonstrable transboundary harm. Therefore, it would be difficult for a victim-state to invoke the *Trail Smelter* principle to recover ecosystem damages because we still think of transboundary injuries primarily as immediate air, water, and soil pollution rather than as ecosystem degradation. The law remains undeveloped and uncertain when it comes to the assessment of ecosystem damage, even if, for example, the 1992 amendments to the 1969 International Convention on Civil Liability for Oil Pollution Damage now allow for the recovery of 'the costs of reasonable measures of reinstatement actually undertaken or to be undertaken' (Article 1(6)). An added problem is that the no harm rule requires clear evidence not just of damage but also of the causal link between another state's activities and this damage. In many cases, ecosystem damage does not immediately manifest itself, and the evidentiary burdens may thus be difficult to meet.

The potential difficulties of establishing transboundary ecosystem damage are illustrated by an analogous argument in the International Court of Justice's (ICJ) most important environmental decision. In the *Case Concerning the Gabčíkovo-Nagymaros Project (Hungary v. Slovakia)*, Hungary attempted to invoke an environmental emergency to justify its withdrawal from a treaty involving a large dam project. However, the ICJ found that there was not a sufficient state of necessity at the time that Hungary withdrew. The court did note the emergence of new pollution and 'nature' protection norms and noted that 'vigilance and prevention are required on account of the often irreversible character of the damage to the environment and of the limitations inherent in the very mechanism of reparation of this type of

---

[17] *Trail Smelter Case (United States v. Canada)*, Award, 1941, 3 U.N.R.I.A.A. 1905.

[18] Quoted in Fitzmaurice, see note 4 above at 228.

damage.'[19] The case primarily focused on the narrow necessity excuse for treaty breach, but it also illustrates that the traditional 'no harm' rule is not well suited to the long-term protection of ecosystems.

2.3 Indirect Protection from Pollution Reduction Regimes

Ecosystems receive indirect protection under most pollution reduction regimes. Protection is indirect because the primary objective of these regimes is human health or individual species protection, but many do not and cannot differentiate between the human and non-human beneficiaries of the reduction of pollutants. For example, forests and lakes in Europe have benefited from the reductions in sulphur dioxide emissions achieved under the Convention on Long-Range Transboundary Air Pollution (LRTAP Convention), which sought to mitigate the acidification of lakes and the decline of forests (see Chapter 14 'Atmosphere and Outer Space').[20] Recently, the LRTAP regime has begun to include more explicit ecosystem protection provisions. The 1994 Oslo Protocol, which came into force in 1998, specifically establishes critical sulphur loads for Europe based on an estimate of the damage that exposure will cause to specific sensitive elements of the environment. The inclusion of ecosystem protection illustrates an important shift in the rationale for pollution prevention, from a focus on harms to humans and property towards a focus on ecosystem protection, but the shift is only partial because the focus is still on protection from specific pollutants rather than on protection from all relevant stressors.

2.4 International Law Reinforces National Protection Measures

Most countries have exercised sovereignty over their national territory by dedicating at least a portion of their territory to various forms of nature reserves or other protected areas that can sustain ecosystems. The World Conservation Union lists more than 100,000 protected sites throughout the world that cover 18.8 million square kilometres and make up 11.5 per cent of the Earth's land surface. Protected areas, such as a wetland or a temperate rainforest, often encompass an entire ecosystem or a significant part of one, but the focus remains on retaining outstanding examples of a class of ecosystem rather than on the function of the ecosystem in the larger landscape.

---

[19] *Case Concerning the Gabčíkovo-Nagymaros Project (Hungary v. Slovakia)*, Judgment of 25 September 1997, [1997] I.C.J Rep. 92 (25 September) [*Gabčíkovo-Nagymaros*].

[20] The LTRAP Convention is described in detail in Chapter 14 'Atmosphere and Outer Space' of this *Handbook*.

International instruments, such as the Convention for the Protection of the World Cultural and Natural Heritage (World Heritage Convention) and the Convention on Wetlands of International Importance Especially as Waterfowl Habitat (Ramsar Convention), have often served as an incentive for national protection as well as an additional source of national authority, in some cases augmenting incomplete central government authority. The best example of the use of international law to augment national authority is the Australian High Court's *Commonwealth v. Tasmania* decision concerning the Franklin dam. The Commonwealth of Australia petitioned the World Heritage Commission to list a large wilderness area in the island federal state of Tasmania as a world heritage site to prevent Tasmania from constructing a hydroelectric dam in the area. Commonwealth legislation was enacted to prohibit the dam. Australia's federal constitution creates a formally weak federal government, and Tasmania challenged the Commonwealth Act as being unconstitutional because there was no express grant of Commonwealth power to enact environmental laws. In *Commonwealth v. Tasmania*,[21] the High Court held that the World Heritage Convention designation allowed the Commonwealth to invoke the foreign affairs clause of the constitution, and thus gave the Commonwealth the power that it previously lacked to enact the legislation.

International environmental law is increasingly cited by domestic courts as a justification for judicial decisions that promote heritage and ecosystem conservation. This trend is especially important where no ecosystem protection duties exist in national law. For example, Nepal's Supreme Court invoked the World Heritage Convention to grant standing to a public interest plaintiff to protest the destruction of a scenic and archaeological site.[22] The Supreme Court of India has developed a strong national environmental jurisprudence that is a blend of the Western legal tradition, including international environmental law, modern 'ecological' thinking, and the country's long Dharmic tradition. The court has said that preservation of 'an ecological balance', which it has not further defined, is both a public and private duty.[23] A leading Indian scholar has described the Supreme Court's jurisprudence as one 'which proceeds closely in line with the legal ideologies which are now frequently voiced in the international fora.'[24] In a landmark decision that granted standing to the children of a Philippine national to challenge the issuance of rainforest logging permits, the Philippine Supreme Court declared that all citizens have a fundamental right to a 'balanced and healthy ecology' and a duty to protect the environment for future generations.[25]

---

[21] *Commonwealth v. Tasmania* (1983), 46 A.L.R. 625.   [22] *Harma v. Koirala*, 312 N.R.L. 1997.

[23] *Rural Litigation and Entitlement Kendra v. State of Uttar Pradesh*, A.I.R. 1987, S.C. at 364. The duty was reiterated in *Pandey v. State of West Bengal*, A.I.R. 1987, S.C. 1109; and *Virender Gaur v. State of Haryana*, (1995), 2 S.C.C. 577. It is based in Article 21 of the Indian constitution, which guarantees a right to life. *Metha v. Kamal Nath*, (2000), 6 S.C.C. 213.

[24] See C.M. Abraham, *Environmental Jurisprudence in India* (The Hague: Kluwer Law International, 1999) at 142. See also Shubhankar Dam, 'Green Laws for Better Health: The Past That Was the Future That May Be—Reflections from the Indian Experience' (2004) 16 Geo. Int'l Envt'l L. Rev. 593 at 596.

[25] *Minors Oposa*, see note 4 above at 185.

2.5 Explicit International Protection Duties

There are few explicit treaty-based ecosystem protection duties in international environmental law, likely due to the respect paid to national sovereignty. What duties that
do exist focus primarily upon global commons areas, which, with the exception of
Antarctica, do not include terrestrial ecosystems. These duties remain largely aspirational and 'soft'. Possible customary and *erga omnes* duties have yet to crystallize into
hard, if open-textured, duties. At the present time, ecosystem protection is difficult to
integrate into traditional notions of global commons, which can be subdivided into
two major subcategories: unallocated and true commons. To the extent that ecosystem impairment either affects areas beyond the jurisdiction of states or occurs within
states, international law has had difficulty in formulating protective duties, let alone
legal entitlements of other states, or 'standing', to challenge the harmful conduct. This
difficulty may explain in part why relatively greater emphasis appears to have been
placed upon procedural, rather than substantive, duties related to explicit ecosystem
protection.

2.5.1 *Ecosystems and Commons beyond State Jurisdiction*

Unallocated commons are resources that are not subject to a state's exclusive jurisdiction either because international law determines that such resources, for example,
fish in the high seas, only become a state's 'property' once they have been captured (*res
nullius*) or because international law does not recognize the possibility of territorial
claims (*res communis*), thus making the oceans, Antarctica, and outer space unallocated commons.

The idea of extra-territorial duties towards areas of global concern beyond the
jurisdiction of states has had some resonance in international environmental law. It
is reflected in Principle 21 of the Stockholm Declaration, which has been affirmed in
Principle 2 of the 1992 Rio Declaration and at the 2002 World Summit on Sustainable
Development. These declarations qualify the right to develop in accordance with the
responsibility not to 'cause damage to the environment of other states or of areas
beyond the limits of national jurisdiction.'

Aside from these general duties, more specific norms have also evolved to protect
certain commons as such, arguably with *erga omnes* effect. For example, several sections of the United Nations Convention on the Law of the Sea (LOSC), which both
reflects and extends customary international law, protect stressed marine ecosystems
from vessel- and land-based pollution and urge the adoption of fisheries conservation regimes. Article 195 requires states to 'prevent, reduce and control pollution of
the marine environment'; Article 196 requires states to take steps to control the intentional or accidental introduction of alien species; and Article 207 requires that both
coastal and land-locked states take steps to control land-based pollution. The convention has led to a number of regional sea agreements that impose more stringent
controls on land-based pollution (see Chapter 15 'Ocean and Freshwater Resources').

With varying degrees of support, the oceans, Antarctica, and outer space have all been said to have the legal status of the common heritage of humankind (see Chapter 23 'Common Areas, Common Heritage, and Common Concern'). The idea of common heritage originated in Article 136 of the LOSC, which declares that deep sea beds are 'the common heritage of mankind'. While the concept has seen less elaboration with respect to outer space, its application has arguably been extended to the Antarctic, which is the only continent that has not been divided among states. The Antarctic Treaty, which entered into force in 1961, freezes the territorial claims of the various states, and the 1991 Protocol on Environmental Protection to the Antarctic Treaty expressly imposes a number of stringent assessment and protection duties on any activity that threatens to damage the continent's ecosystems and reinforces the argument that the Antarctic is now a common area and will remain so under international law.[26] Furthermore, the Convention on the Conservation of Antarctic Marine Living Resources adopts a management regime for the exploitation and conservation of these resources.[27] Article 2 provides that any harvesting and associated activities must ensure 'the maintenance or the ecological relationships between harvested, dependent and related populations.'

2.5.2 *Ecosystems and Commons within State Jurisdiction*

Over time, ecosystem protection may also benefit from the efforts of international environmental and human rights law to modify the traditional concept of exclusive and unlimited national territorial sovereignty. For the reasons highlighted in section 1.1 earlier in this chapter, customary international law still offers only modest protection to states that suffer ecosystem damages incident to transboundary pollution. However, modern conceptions of sovereign rights could be modified by *erga omnes* duties to require more sustainable use of national territories such as tropical rainforests and wetland systems. The legal rationale is that the potential adverse global impacts of ecosystem modification may make them part of the common heritage of mankind or a matter of common concern or common interest. The international community would then have a legal interest in resources that, due to their location within states, have not traditionally been classified as global commons (see Chapter 23 'Common Areas, Common Heritage, and Common Concern').

In general, the international community still resists the extension of the common heritage principle beyond traditionally recognized common resources, especially resources located within the jurisdiction of states.[28] For example, the preamble to the

---

[26] F. Francioni, 'The Madrid Protocol on the Protection of the Antarctic Environment' (1993) 28 Texas Int'l L.J. 47.

[27] R. Tucker Scully, 'Convention on the Conservation of Antartica Marine Living Resources,' in K. Sherman, L. Alexander, and F. Gold, eds., *Large Marine Ecosystems—Stress Mitigation and Sustainability* (Washington, DC: AAA Press, 1993) 242.

[28] In 2005, the Brazilian Senate Foreign Relations and National Defense Commission held a public hearing on the threats posed by the efforts of 'the international community' to classify the Amazon

1992 Convention on Biological Diversity (CBD) states only that biological diversity is a 'common concern of human kind', which represents a rejection of stronger classifications of biodiversity that might constrain national sovereignty. Nonetheless, it is possible that some *erga omnes* protection duties could emerge from environmental treaty regimes that limit sovereign discretion to use and to consume natural resources in an unsustainable manner.[29] In any case, the idea of heritage or ecosystems of common concern continues to evolve. This evolution is manifest in the Canadian–United States Great Lakes regime. The regime is based on the 1909 Boundary Waters Treaty between the two countries, which provides that the boundary between the two countries 'shall not be polluted on either side to the injury of health or property on the other (Article 4). In elaborating this standard, Canada and the United States, through the adoption of the Agreement between the United States and Canada on Great Lakes Water Quality, have adopted an ecosystem approach to protect the water quality of the Great Lakes and to guide future pollution control strategies.[30] In addition, Canadian and United States laws, which are supported by the International Joint Commission references,[31] make it very difficult to divert substantial quantities of water from the lakes and their tributaries. Thus, they have in effect been dedicated as a bi-national, if not world, aquatic ecosystem.[32]

Some global agreements have also taken tentative steps to expand ecosystem protection beyond transboundary pollution. For example, the United Nations Convention on the Law of Non-Navigational Uses of International Watercourses (Watercourses Convention), which has not yet entered into force, applies the duty not to cause harm to ecosystems. Article 20 provides that states 'shall individually and, where appropriate, jointly protect and preserve ecosystems of international watercourses.' The term 'ecosystem' was debated and contested during the preparation of the treaty and appears to be limited to the riverbed and water-dependent land areas, but it represents an important recognition of the ecosystem idea. This

---

rainforest as 'collective public goods.' The Fleet Admiral announced that the military has prepared a strategy of resistance should the region be invaded by a 'superior power.' 'Brazil Marshall's Defences to Fight Amazon Internationalization,' Environmental New Service, 11 April 2005.

[29] The basis for such duties is that '[c]haracterization of issues such as climate change and biological diversity as the "common concern of humankind" . . . because it places them on the international agenda and declares them to be a legitimate object of international regulation and supervision, thus overriding the domain of domestic jurisdiction.' P.W. Birnie and A.E. Boyle, *International Law and the Environment* (Oxford: Oxford University Press, 2002) at 100.

[30] See National Research Council and Royal Society of Canada, *The Great Lakes Water Quality Agreement: An Evolving Instrument for Ecosystem Management* (Washington, DC: National Academy Press, 1985).

[31] International Joint Commission, *Protection of the Waters of the Great Lakes* (2000) at 35–6, described the lakes as 'a central feature of the natural and cultural heritage of the Great lakes region' and concluded that if all uses, including the maintenance of the Great Lakes ecosystem, are considered, 'there is never a "surplus" of water in the system.'

[32] A. Dan Tarlock, 'Five Views of the Great Lakes and Why They Might Matter' (2006) 16 Minn. J of Int. L., 21.

approach of the Watercourses Convention is also relevant for the evolution of customary international law. Even if an instrument has not come into force or has not been ratified by a state, it can contribute to the development of customary law. The protection duties that they adopt can be accepted as declarative of pre-existing customary law. This type of development may be underway with respect to international fresh water ecosystems.[33]

Nonetheless, treaties are still the primary source of international ecosystem protection duties regarding areas within the jurisdiction of states. There are a number of international agreements, discussed later in this chapter, that encompass direct ecosystem conservation in their objectives. However, the ecosystem construct as such is seldom used; instead, either specific ecosystems are identified or ecosystem conservation is an explicit or implicit component of broader treaty objectives.

The Ramsar Convention, which entered into force in 1975, is the most explicit international agreement addressing the protection of ecosystems, and it has served as a model for other ecosystem and biodiversity conservation instruments. The Ramsar Convention requires that members must list at least one wetland that is 'significant', based on the site's ecology, botany, zoology, limnology, or hydrology. States must include wetland conservation in national land use planning programs. The convention can promote ecosystem conservation in at least three related ways. First, a state may seek to have a site included on the list of wetlands of international importance in order to qualify for United Nations funding. Second, a state may use the endangered status as a lever to earmark additional domestic funding for the conservation of the site. For example, the Everglades National Park was placed on the endangered list in 1993, and, since that time, the United States and the state of Florida have embarked on an ambitious restoration programme. Third, the convention can support unilateral protection. In recent years, the convention's Standing Committee has played a more aggressive role in implementing the objectives of the convention. Endangered sites have been placed on an endangered list without the consent of the host state.

Another important international agreement that imposes direct ecosystem protection duties on states is the CBD. The CBD is significant because it is aimed at the conservation of internal, rather than migratory or traded, biodiversity resources. The convention requires that each country have a relatively comprehensive biodiversity conservation programme. The programme must prefer *in* to *ex situ* conservation and integrate the conservation and sustainable use of biological resources into national decision-making. Article 8's preference for *in situ* over *ex situ* conservation requires the designation of protected areas. Article 8(d) requires that these areas 'promote the protection of ecosystems, natural habitats and the maintenance of viable populations of species in natural surroundings.' Article 8(f) requires the rehabilitation and restoration of degraded ecosystems.

---

[33] M.A. Fitzmaurice, see note 4 above at 227–30; *Gabčíkovo-Nagymaros*, see note 18 above, held that the then country of Czechoslovakia violated international law by its unilateral diversion of the Danube, which caused ecological damage to Hungary's reach of the river.

Most developed and many developing countries can comply with the convention by simply designating existing parks, nature reserves, and other protected areas as the fulfillment of their Article 8 duties, regardless of how much biodiversity is conserved. However, the parties have adopted a set of 12 ecosystem management principles, which require that an explicit, forward-looking ecosystem management approach be applied to these areas. For example, Principle 7 recommends that 'the ecosystem approach should be undertaken at the appropriate and spatial scales,' and Principle 9 requires that 'management must recognize that change is inevitable.' The convention carefully balances exploitation for both commodity and knowledge production with conservation, and the principles reflect this balance. Principle 10 provides in part that states should 'protect and encourage customary use of biological resources in accordance with traditional cultural practices that are compatible with conservation or sustainable use requirements.'

The World Heritage Convention permits a state to nominate sites for inclusion on the World Heritage List that are of 'outstanding universal value'. Once a site is listed, states have a duty to protect it and other states have a duty to refrain for injuring the site. Nominations are reviewed by the convention's 21-member World Heritage Committee on the basis of various criteria, including the proposed site's natural beauty, geologic interest, and scientific value. In practice, most states designate previously delineated national parks for inclusion on the natural areas list. However, ecosystem evolution is a component of the selection criteria, although it is not the sole one. Guideline 44b.i. provides:

The sites described in 44(a)(ii) should have sufficient size and contain the necessary elements to demonstrate the key aspects of processes that are essential for the long-term conservation of the ecosystems and the biological diversity they contain; for example, an area of tropical rain forest should include a certain amount of variation in elevation above sea-level, changes in topography and soil types, patch systems and naturally regenerating patches; similarly a coral reef should include, for example, sea grass, mangrove or other adjacent ecosystems that regulate nutrient and sediment inputs into the reef.

The Convention on International Trade in Endangered Species of Wild Fauna and Flora (CITES) is not conventionally viewed as an ecosystem protection treaty. However, by focusing attention on the conservation of endangered species, it can indirectly promote national habitat conservation and thus conserve ecosystems. The convention creates a three-tiered listing system to protect species against threats due to international trade. Each party must implement CITES by designating a management and scientific authority to authorize the export and import of species in a manner consistent with the treaty. Trade is prohibited with non-parties unless they have a regulatory scheme that substantially conforms to party standards. The treaty itself makes no reference to habitat conservation, but many countries have undertaken habitat conservation efforts in an attempt to protect listed species. For example to protect its tiger populations, India created a series of tiger habitat reserves. Yet, CITES protection is weak. In China, Taiwan, and Korea, poaching that is driven by the seemingly insatiable demand for tiger bones has reversed early habitat conservation efforts in these countries.[34] The United States Endangered Species Act, which was enacted to comply with CITES, is formally focused on individual species preservation, but, in the 1990s, the act became the basis for the creation of extensive multiple species habitat conservation reserves.[35] In keeping with CITES, Canada's Species at Risk Act also contains several provisions that require or permit habitat conservation.[36]

Another example of a potentially important ecosystem-oriented treaty is the Convention on the Protection of the Alps. However, the parties have yet to take the implementation measures that are needed to flesh out the convention framework. The convention, which was ratified by the seven Alpine states and the European Union, commits the parties to 'a comprehensive policy' of cultural and environmental protection. Article 2(6) includes the protection and rehabilitation of the 'natural environment . . . so that ecosystems are able to function, animal and plant species, including their habitats, are preserved.' The convention is a work in progress, but, taken together with other European biodiversity conventions that deal with the protection of terrestrial, fresh water, and marine systems, it is an important step. The hope is that reporting requirements might ultimately produce consistent and coordinated national ecosystem protection measures and standards. Thus, the framework treaty will have evolved into a coordinated large-scale ecosystem mechanism.

2.5.3 *Procedural Duties*

The variable nature of ecosystems makes it difficult to develop substantive protection duties beyond general, undefined duties to protect and conserve the environment. It has been easier to develop general procedural duties that change the way in which decisions that threaten ecosystem stability are made. There is now a widely accepted set of procedures that should be followed for all major decisions that impact shared ecosystems such as rivers, estuaries, and other significant ecosystems. These duties include environmental impact assessment, inter-state notification and consultation, and information exchange before an activity that causes damage to a common ecosystem is undertaken. In some cases, these duties may extend to post-project monitoring and even cooperative management, as evidenced by the decision of the ICJ in the *Gabčíkovo-Nagymaros* case, referred to earlier in this chapter.

The most important procedural duty is environmental impact assessment. Domestic and international assessment duties require that all available relevant scientific and related information about the baseline conditions, the system drivers, and the likely adverse impacts of modification, which are generally ecosystem

---

[34] M.'t Sas-Rolfes, 'Assessing CITIES: Four Case Studies, Case Study 3: Tigers,' in J. Hutton and B. Dickson, eds., *Endangered Species Threatened Convention: The Past, Present and Future* (London: Earthscan, 2000).

[35] See T. Beatly, *Habitat Conservation: Endangered Species and Urban Growth* (Austin: University of Texas Press, 1994).

[36] Bill C-5, Second Session, 37th Parliament, 51 Elizabeth II (2002): Clause 41 (recovery plans must identify species habitat); Clause 57 (identification critical habitat necessary for recovery and action plans); and Clause 61 (Cabinet Orders to prohibit destruction of critical habitat).

impacts, of a project be assembled in advance. In addition, a wide range of alternatives must be investigated and mitigation programmes identified. The international duty applies primarily to activities with transboundary impacts. Important general international instruments that demand an assessment of transboundary impacts include Article 14 of the CBD and Principle 17 of the Rio Declaration. Article 206 of the LOSC requires assessment for activities that may cause 'harmful changes to the marine environment.' The UNECE Convention on Environmental Impact Assessment in a Transboundary Context, which is a regional convention that entered into force in 1997, requires that the originating state assess the transboundary impacts of a wide range of listed planned physical activities on other party states and furnish the affected state with the environmental assessment documents. The evolving expectation is that, at a minimum, assessment processes will identify mitigation measures that make a project or activity more environmentally compatible and, thus, conserve ecosystem function.

The duty to conduct an environmental impact assessment for activities that threaten either transboundary ecosystems or ecosystems of regional or global significance located entirely within one country may also be a customary international law duty. There are two rationales for this proposition. Over 100 countries, developed and developing, have impact assessment laws, so the duty is now reflected in uniform state practice. In addition, a European Economic Community directive mandates the preparation of an environmental impact statement.[37] The duty of advanced assessment can also be derived from the precautionary principle (see Chapter 25 'Precaution'). In the *Gabčíkovo-Nagymaros* case, Judge Weeramantry's separate opinion posited that all countries have a continuing duty of environmental assessment for major projects with potential adverse environmental impacts: 'EIA [environmental impact assessment], being a specific application of the larger principle of caution, embodies the obligation of continuing watchfulness and anticipation.'[38]

3 PROTECTION VISION: STEWARDSHIP SOVEREIGNTY

3.1 Sources of Stewardship Sovereignty

This chapter has sought to illustrate that the primary problem with protecting ecosystems within the framework of existing international environmental law is that the law imposes few restraints on the discretion of states to classify and manage their

---

[37] EC Directive 85/337 on the Assessment of the Effects of Certain Public and Private Projects on the Environment, 1985 O.J. L.175 at 40–4.

[38] Justice Weeramantry of Sri Lanka defined as *erga omnes* customary rules the interrelated principles of environmentally sustainable development and cautionary environmental assessment and

territory. Most ecosystems are not classified as proper objects of international environmental law because they are not transboundary resources or even global commons or unallocated resources. To better protect the planet's life support systems, the law needs to complement the *Trail Smelter* principle by requiring states to conserve ecosystems within their borders. Concepts such as the common heritage or common concern of humankind have not proven sufficient to accomplish this task. The best hope is to derive the needed complementary principle from the larger ethic of sustainable development (see Chapter 26 'Sustainable Development'). 'The maintenance of ecological conditions necessary to maintain an ecosystem supportive of human life' is a central component of any definition of sustainable development.[39] The duty to exploit and use resources sustainably, as vague and undeveloped as it is, should apply both to resources traditionally under the exclusive control of a state and those subject to international obligations. Two respected international environmental law scholars recognize the emergence of a duty of environmentally sustainable resource use that erodes traditional sovereignty, although they caution that '[o]nly where specific international regimes have been developed, as in the management of fisheries and water resources, can it be said that the concept of sustainable use has acquired some normative content or could potentially be used to judge the permissibility of natural resource exploitation.'[40]

The ethic of environmentally sustainable development can be incorporated into international environmental law by modifying the concept of exclusive territorial sovereignty to make it clear that states have primary, but not exclusive, control over resource decisions with extra-territorial impacts that extend beyond the transboundary context and, thus, owe duties to the international community. The most fitting expression of the duty of environmentally sustainable development is the idea of stewardship sovereignty. Stewardship sovereignty builds upon two jurisprudential traditions within international law—Grotian idealism and the idea of an international social contract[41]—and joins them with science-based environmental imperatives to supply a unifying perspective. Just as we have tried to impose limitations on the right of a state to make war for moral and utilitarian reasons,[42] we need to restrain the power of states to exploit ecosystems. At a minimum, we need a legal regime that requires that exploitation be done in an environmentally sustainable manner to the maximum extent possible, given a country's conservation capacity. To accomplish this, the dead-end principle of international rules based on the actual

management and posited that they have the same general applicability as the laws of human rights. *Gabčíkovo-Nagymaros*, see note 18 above at 122.

[39] C.B. Barrett and R. Grizzle, 'A Holistic Approach to Sustainability Based on Pluralism Stewardship' (1999) 21 Envt'l Ethics 23 at 25.   [40] Birnie and Boyle, see note 28 above at 89.

[41] Surveying Grotius's efforts to restrain state behaviour, H. Lauterpracht described the Groatian tradition as 'the tradition of progress and idealism,' which sought to develop international law as a 'universal moral code.' H. Lauterpacht, 'The Grotian Tradition in International Law,' in E. Lauterpacht, ed., *International Law: Being the Collected Papers of Hersch Lauterpacht*, volume 2 (Cambridge: Cambridge University Press, 1975) 307 at 359 and 363.

[42] T. Meron, 'International Law in the Age of Human Rights' (2003) 301 Recueil de cours 24.

consent of all states must be replaced with one based on what Fernando Tesòn, following Rawls, has called 'rational hypothetical consent'.[43]

The idea is not as radical as it seems. The idea of limited, rather than absolute, sovereignty has some acceptance among both development and developing nations. The case *Commonwealth v. Tasmania*, in which the Australian High Court accepted the World Heritage Convention as a restraint on its internal resource use, as well as a confirmation of the constitutional protection of rainforests in the 1988 Brazilian constitution, is a promising example of the acceptance of stewardship obligations by individual countries. Thus, stewardship sovereignty simply applies a basic and increasingly widely accepted principle of modern environmental ethics to international law. There is a lively debate about the source and scope of environmental ethics (see Chapter 13 'Ethics and International Environmental Law'), but there is an emerging global consensus that we must replace the Greco-Judeo-Christian tradition that considers humans to be despots over nature[44] with the principle that we are stewards of the earth[45] and must at least approach all exploitation decisions with much more caution and humility than we have in the past.

3.2 Core Principles

Stewardship is an evolving concept, but it contains three core consensus-building principles. The first is the principle of inter-generational equity articulated by Edith Brown Weiss.[46] This standard permits resource exploitation subject to the constraint that we leave the resource in no worse shape than when we started. As a leading environmental philosopher has noted, 'environmentalists will achieve more by appealing to the relatively non-controversial and intuitive idea that the use of natural resources implies an obligation to protect them for future users—a sustainability theory based on intergenerational equity—rather than exotic appeals to hereto unnoticed inherent values in nature.'[47] The second principle is that environmentally sustainable,

---

[43] F.R. Tesòn, 'International Obligation and the Theory of Hypothetical Consent' (1990) 15 Yale J. Int'l L. 84 at 109. Tesòn argues we that '[i]f actual consent cannot lay the foundation for international obligation, perhaps we should give special foundational status not to *any* consent, but only to *rational* consent.' Tesòn has elaborated his critique of traditional international law, which divorces the issue of state legitimacy from normative principles, in F.R. Tesòn, 'The Kantian Theory of International Law' (1992) 92 Colum. L. Rev. 53.

[44] J. Passmore, *Man's Responsibility for Nature* (London: Duckworth, 1974), remains the leading exponent of this position.

[45] See R. Attfield, *The Ethics of Environmental Concern*, 2nd edition (Athens, GA: University of Georgia Press, 1991), for a forceful exposition of this provocative thesis.

[46] E. Brown Weiss, *In Fairness to Future Generation: International Law, Common Patrimony, and Intergenerational Equity* (Dobbs Ferry, NY: Transnational Publishers, 1989).

[47] B.G. Norton, 'Why I Am Not a Nonanthropecentrist: Callicott and the Failure of Monistic Inherentism' (1995) 17 Envt'l Ethics 341 at 356.

rather than unrestrained, development must be the norm of the future and follow from inter-generational equity. The final core idea is the precautionary principle, which reinforces the first two because it posits that all development decisions, especially those involving resources of extra-territorial significance, must be made with an eye to the preservation of options for future generations (see Chapter 25 'Precaution').

Adaptive management, which is discussed earlier in this chapter, can implement stewardship sovereignty, by incorporating the modern vision of a dynamic ecosystem into effective ecosystem management regimes. Adaptive management has increasingly been adopted, at least in principle, as the central management strategy for ecosystem restoration and management.[48] We now recognize that all ecosystem conservation is an ongoing experiment, which requires a continuous process of acquiring and evaluating new scientific information, and adapting it to the ecosystem management experiment that is being undertaken. Adaptive processes cannot eliminate all risk of ecosystem function loss. The hope is that scientific information may be able to limit the risk and convince all interested parties, especially with entitlements to consume and exploit a resource, that the minimization of the risk of function loss can be managed and accommodated in a fair and effective manner.

4 CONCLUSION

Many of the treaties, customary rules, and soft law instruments that make up international environmental law either directly or indirectly protect ecosystems. However, ecosystems as such remain under-protected. They are generally not recognized as discrete objects of protection by international regimes. Rather, they are, by and large, classified as national territory subject to the exclusive control of nation states. To carry forward the project of protecting our planetary life support systems, a wide range of ecosystems—internal and cross-border—must be recognized as distinct objects of international conservation duties. International protection norms must be complemented by national laws and policies that ensure that ecosystem conversation becomes an integral component of environmentally sustainable development for all areas of the planet.

---

[48] For example, EC Directive 2000/60 Establishing a Framework for Community Action in the Field of Water Policy requires that all member states develop river basin plans for both international and national rivers. The protection of aquatic and related terrestrial ecosystems is an important component of the directive, and it is widely understood that adaptive management strategies must be developed and implemented to comply with the directive.

Recommended Reading

D. Botkin, *Discordant Harmonies: A New Ecology for the Twenty-First Century* (New York: Oxford University Press, 1990).

S. Bundiansky, *Nature Keepers: The New Science of Nature Management* (New York: Free Press, 1995).

P. Coates, *Nature: Western Attitude Since Ancient Times* (Berkeley: University of California Press, 1998).

G.C. Daily, ed., *Nature Services: Societal Dependence on Natural Ecosystem* (Covelo, CA: Island Press, 1997).

F. Golley, *A History of the Ecosystem Concept in Ecology* (New Haven, CT: Yale University Press, 1993).

J.B. Hagen, *An Entangled Bank: The Origins of Ecosystem Ecology* (New Brunswick: Rutgers University Press, 1992).

Simon A. Levin, ed., *Encyclopedia of Biodiversity* (San Diego: Academic Press, 2001).

E. Mayr, *Evolution and the Diversity of Life* (Cambridge, MA: Belknap Press of Harvard University, 1976).

E.O. Wilson, *The Diversity of Life* (Cambridge, MA: Harvard University Press, 1992).

CHAPTER 25

PRECAUTION

JONATHAN B. WIENER

1 INTRODUCTION

PRECAUTION is a strategy for addressing risk. Risk of future harm is always uncertain. At its essence, precaution entails thinking ahead and taking anticipatory action to avoid uncertain future risks. Doing so necessitates the capacities to identify hazards and opportunities, to forecast scenarios and their associated outcomes, and to take anticipatory measures to manage causes before adverse outcomes occur. This idea is not new—success at risk assessment and management, including the astute exercise of precaution, has been central to the survival of the human species over millennia as well as to its continuing health and prosperity.[1] Early hominids had to forecast and avoid risks such as predators, poisons, and adverse weather. Modern humans use risk analysis to invest, insure, and protect, including precaution against uncertain future risks.

Precaution finds expression in timeless commonsense adages such as 'better safe than sorry'. Yet precaution is far easier said than done. On one hand, advances over time in scientific methods of risk identification and prediction have uncovered more subtly related causes and effects that unfold over longer latency periods, thereby calling for ever-earlier actions to anticipate uncertain future effects and to manage the suspected present causes. On the other hand, recognition that in the real world we confront multiple interconnected risks means that simple adages are insufficient or incoherent. Of course, one prefers 'safe' to 'sorry', but the real questions are 'better safe against this or against that?' and 'what are the consequences of seeking safety?' The serious issue is safe versus safe, not safe versus sorry. And because every human institution is imperfect—including both markets and government, both private and public—precautionary regulations of technological risks can also create new 'countervailing' risks.[2] 'Better safe than sorry' may be an old adage, but 'the cure is worse than the disease' has at least as old a pedigree. Advocates of precaution advise innovators of new technologies to 'look before you leap' and invoke Hippocrates's adage 'first, do no harm', but innovators say the same to government regulators.

At a deeper level than simplistic maxims, applying precaution as a legal concept involves several more complex issues, including the optimal balance between benefits and costs, safety and innovation, and risk-aversion and risk-taking; assumptions (often unstated) about vulnerability or thresholds and resilience or assimilative capacity (and the evidentiary requirements for demonstrating each); the tradeoff between false negative errors (neglecting a significant risk) and false positive errors

---

[1] For a popular account, see P.L. Bernstein, *Against the Gods: The Remarkable Story of Risk* (New York: John Wiley and Sons, 1996).

[2] See J.D. Graham and J.B. Wiener, eds., *Risk vs. Risk: Tradeoffs in Protecting Health and the Environment* (Cambridge, MA: Harvard University Press, 1995); and J.B. Wiener, 'Precaution in a Multi-Risk World,' in D. Paustenbach, ed., *Human and Ecological Risk Assessment: Theory and Practice* (New York: John Wiley and Sons, 2002) 1509.

(overreacting to an insignificant risk); the optimal response to uncertainty and irreversibility; the plural consequences of precaution in an interconnected multi-risk world, including effects on target risks, countervailing risks, and ancillary benefits; the role of law in constraining or empowering government; and the societal selection of which risks to regulate. These complex considerations mean that the astute exercise of precaution requires far more than an earnest commitment to protecting health, safety, and the environment. Intelligent precaution requires careful consideration of facts, values, consequences, and tradeoffs.

2 PRECAUTIONARY PRINCIPLE (PP)

The PP is an attempt to codify the concept of precaution in law. The PP is the most prominent—and perhaps the most controversial—development in international environmental law in the last two decades. Fifteen years ago, advocates forecast that the PP 'could become *the* fundamental principle of environmental protection policy and law.'[3] Even then, '[t]he speed with which the precautionary principle has been brought on to the international agenda, and the range and variety of international forums which have explicitly accepted it within the recent past, are quite staggering.'[4] Today, the forecast is partly confirmed: 'If international environmental law were to develop Ten Commandments, the precautionary principle would be near the top of the list.'[5] Yet the controversy continues: 'The precautionary principle may well be the most innovative, pervasive, and significant new concept in environmental policy over the past quarter century. It may also be the most reckless, arbitrary, and ill-advised.'[6]

States have adopted versions of the PP in their domestic law since at least the 1970s. The concept of '*Vorsorgeprinzip*' in German law dates at least to the early 1970s, which is about the same time that similar doctrines were introduced in Swedish law and Swiss law. In the 1992 Maastricht Treaty, the European Union (EU) expressly provided that EU policy on the environment 'shall be based on the precautionary principle' (Article 130R, now renumbered Article 174). In February 2000, the European Commission elaborated its interpretation of the PP in an important statement.[7] In

[3] J. Cameron and J. Abouchar, 'The Precautionary Principle: A Fundamental Principle of Law and Policy for the Protection of the Global Environment' (1991) 14 B.C. Int'l & Comp. L. Rev. 1 at 2.

[4] D. Freestone, 'The Precautionary Principle,' in R. Churchill and D. Freestone, eds., *International Law and Global Climate Change* (London: Graham and Trotman, 1991) 21 at 36.

[5] D. Bodansky, 'Deconstructing the Precautionary Principle,' in D.D. Caron and H.N. Scheiber, eds., *Bringing New Law to Ocean Waters* (Leiden: Koninklijke Brill NV, 2004) 381.

[6] G.E. Marchant and K.L. Mossman, *Arbitrary and Capricious: The Precautionary Principle in the EU Courts* (Washington, DC: AEI Press, 2004) at 1.

[7] Communication from the Commission on the Precautionary Principle, Brussels, Doc. COM(2000)1 (2 February 2000).

1999, Canada incorporated the precautionary principle in its revised Canadian Environmental Protection Act. In February 2005, France adopted the PP as part of its environmental charter and constitution.[8]

In the United States, precautionary pre-market safety review of new drugs under the US Federal Food, Drug and Cosmetic Act began before World War Two, and the precautionary prohibition of carcinogens in food dates to the Delaney Clause in 1958, although neither of these laws used the term 'precaution.' Landmark court decisions in *Ethyl Corp v. EPA* and *TVA v. Hill* expressly endorsed the notion of 'precautionary' regulation under the Clean Air Act and the Endangered Species Act, respectively.[9] However, the ruling in *Industrial Union Department, AFL-CIO v. American Petroleum Institute et al.* (the *Benzene* case),[10] which required a risk assessment prior to regulating workplace hazards, and the 1983 guidebook on risk assessment from the National Academy of Sciences, cast doubt on whether anticipatory precaution is required or even allowed in US federal regulation, at least if precaution means adopting regulatory policies before conducting a scientific risk assessment. Still, precaution is often invoked; for example, the US Food and Drug Administration adopted 'precautionary measures' to shield the blood supply from mad cow disease (BSE and vCJD) in 1999, and the city of San Francisco adopted a modest version of the PP in 2003. Thus, precaution has been adopted in numerous specific US laws, but the United States has not officially adopted the PP as a general basis for regulation.[11]

Given this history, one view is that the United States was more precautionary than Europe in the 1970s, but that since 1990 the positions have reversed so that now Europe endorses the PP and seeks proactively to regulate risks, while the United States opposes the PP and waits more circumspectly for evidence of actual harm before regulating.[12] Others argue that the pattern is more complex, with precaution adopted (or not) by different states for different risks, depending more on the specific context and societal processes of risk selection than on a uniform approach to regulation—a pattern of precautionary particularity, not principle.[13] For example, viewed very generally, Europe appears to have been more precautionary than the United States regarding such risks as marine pollution, genetically modified foods, climate change, toxic substances, phthalates, and antibiotics in animal feed, whereas the United States appears to have been more precautionary than Europe regarding such risks as chlorofluorocarbons (CFCs) and stratospheric ozone protection,

---

[8] Environment Charter of 2004, Article 5, adopted as part of the French Constitution (attached to the Preamble) on 28 February 2005.

[9] *Ethyl Corp. v. EPA*, 541 F.2d 1 (D.C. Cir. 1976); and *TVA v. Hill*, 437 U.S. 153 (1978).

[10] *Industrial Union Department, AFL-CIO v. American Petroleum Institute et al.*, 448 U.S. 607 (1980).

[11] J.S. Applegate, 'The Precautionary Preference: An American Perspective on the Precautionary Principle' (2000) 6 Human & Ecological Risk Assessment 413.

[12] See D. Vogel, 'The Hare and the Tortoise Revisited: The New Politics of Consumer and Environmental Regulation in Europe' (2003) 33 Br. J. Pol. Sci. 557.

[13] See J.B. Wiener, 'Whose Precaution after All ? A Comment on the Comparison and Evolution of Risk Regulatory Systems' (2003) 13 Duke J. Comp. Int'l L. 207.

nuclear power, mad cow disease (especially in blood donations), fine particulate matter air pollution, cigarette smoking, youth violence, and terrorism and weapons of mass destruction (see section 5 below). Yet there is also variation within the United States and Europe. And, in any case, these are selective examples. A quantitative analysis of a much larger sample of almost 3,000 risks over the last three decades found no significant pattern of shifting relative transatlantic precaution.[14]

In international environmental law, versions of the PP have been adopted in over 50 multilateral instruments, including several treaties on marine pollution adopted in the 1980s, the Montreal Protocol on Substances That Deplete the Ozone Layer (1987), the Rio Declaration on Environment and Development (1992, paragraph 15), the UN Framework Convention on Climate Change (UNFCCC) (1992), the Convention on Biological Diversity (1992), the Cartagena Protocol on Biosafety (2000), and the Stockholm Convention on Persistent Organic Pollutants (2002).[15] Some scholars point to even earlier international environmental treaties that employed the logic, if not the terminology, of precaution, such as the Convention on the Prevention of Marine Pollution by Dumping of Wastes and Other Matter (London Convention) (1972), the Convention on International Trade in Endangered Species of Wild Fauna and Flora (CITES) (1973), and the Organisation for Economic Co-operation and Development Declaration of Anticipatory Environmental Policies (1979).

Yet not all states have consented to the PP in international law. For example, although the United States has ratified most of the treaties just mentioned, it has repeatedly urged use of the term 'precautionary approach' rather than 'principle', and it has stayed out of the 1997 Kyoto Protocol to the UNFCCC and the 2000 Cartagena Protocol. And disputes in the World Trade Organization (WTO) over precautionary restrictions on beef hormones, asbestos, and genetically modified foods have raised the question whether international trade law, particularly the Agreement on the Application of Sanitary and Phytosanitary (SPS) Measures, precludes the precautionary principle by requiring regulation to be based on risk assessment. In response, some have asserted that the PP may now be so widely adopted that it is ripening into an enforceable norm of customary international law,[16] potentially binding states even if they have not consented to it explicitly (see Chapter 19 'Formation of Customary International Law and General Principles'). Others have argued that state practice on precaution is so diverse and inconsistent, and the formulations of the PP so varied (see next section), that no clear and binding norm can be discerned.[17]

---

[14] J.K. Hammitt, J.B. Wiener, B. Swedlow, D. Kall, and Z. Zhou, 'Precautionary Regulation in Europe and the United States: A Quantitative Comparison' (2005) 25 Risk Analysis 1215.

[15] A. Trouwborst, *Evolution and Status of the Precautionary Principle in International Law* (The Hague: Kluwer Law International, 2002) at 63.

[16] See J. Cameron and J. Abouchar, 'The Status of the Precautionary Principle in International Law,' in D. Freestone and E. Hey, eds., *The Precautionary Principle and International Law* (The Hague: Kluwer Law International, 1996) 29; and O. McIntyre and T. Mosedale, 'The Precautionary Principle as a Norm of Customary International Law' (1997) 9 J. Envt'l L. 221.

[17] See J.B. Wiener and M.D. Rogers, 'Comparing Precaution in the US and Europe' (2002) 5 J. of Risk Res. 317 at 343 (observing that divergent state practice regarding the PP undermines its claimed status as

3 VERSIONS OF THE PRECAUTIONARY PRINCIPLE

In the face of risks, government has two basic strategies: *ex ante* precautions, *ex post* remedies, or a combination. *Ex post* remedies include cleanup projects and tort litigation in the courts. *Ex ante* precautions include scientific research and regulation administered by agencies. Some regulations are more *ex ante* than others, intervening earlier to anticipate the time path over which the risk is forecast to become manifest. On these sliding scale dimensions, regulation can be said to be 'more precautionary' when it intervenes earlier and/or more stringently to prevent uncertain future adverse consequences.

Despite widespread endorsement of precaution as a *strategy* in many (but not all) cases, there is no single agreed statement or understanding of the PP as a *principle*.[18] Nor is it clear whether the PP is meant to be an aspirational principle or a binding rule. If it is an aspirational principle, then it can more easily be vague and ambiguous but will be of little help in making difficult policy choices. If it is a binding regulatory rule, then it must be more concrete but will more often be arbitrary. Two experts sympathetic to the PP observe: 'Paradoxically, we conclude that the application of precaution will remain politically potent so long as it continues to be tantalizingly ill-defined and imperfectly translatable into codes of conduct, while capturing the emotions of misgiving and guilt ... [I]t is neither a well-defined nor a stable concept. Rather, it is has become the repository for a jumble of adventurous beliefs that challenge the status quo of political power, ideology, and environmental rights.'[19]

Versions of the PP diverge on several key issues. These include:

- Is the PP part of the mainstream process of risk assessment and risk management or is it an alternative? The view that the PP is inconsistent with, and an alternative to, the traditional risk assessment/risk management framework is held by

customary international law). US courts have so far rejected claims that the PP or related environmental norms constitute enforceable customary international law. See *Beanal v. Freeport-McMoran, Inc.*, 197 F.3d 161, 167 (5th Cir. 1999); and *Flores v. Southern Peru Copper Co.*, 343 F.3d 140, 158–61 (2d Cir. 2003).

[18] See P. Sandin, 'Dimensions of the Precautionary Principle' (1999) 5 Human & Ecological Risk Assessment 889 (finding 19 versions, with significant differences regarding threat, uncertainty, action, and command); D. VanderZwaag, 'The Precautionary Principle in Environmental Law and Policy: Elusive Rhetoric and First Embraces' (1999) 8 J. Envt'l L. & Practice 355 (identifying 14 formulations); C.D. Stone, 'Is There a Precautionary Principle?' (2001) 31 Envtl. L. Rep. 10790 at 10799 (finding no coherent statement, 'disarray'); and Bodansky, see note 5 above at 383–6 and 391 (finding key differences on multiple dimensions, including legal instruction (reason not to postpone action, licence to act, duty to act), trigger of application, and what action should be taken, hence the PP has 'not moved ... towards consensus' and 'the only point of overlap is a truism').

[19] A. Jordan and T. O'Riordan, 'The Precautionary Principle in Contemporary Environmental Policy and Politics,' in C. Raffensperger and J. Tickner, eds., *Protecting Public Health and the Environment: Implementing the Precautionary Principle* (Washington, DC: Island Press, 1999) 15.

both advocates (who dislike the risk-based approach and see the PP as a desirable alternative) and critics (who favour the risk-based approach and see the PP as undesirable). In contrast, the European Commission takes the view that the PP is part of risk management.[20] Similarly, the San Francisco version of the PP calls for an analysis of alternatives and their consequences. And many see the PP already at work in traditional risk assessment through the adoption of conservative default assumptions and methods for calculating risks.

- Does the PP apply only to the environment or more broadly to all health and environmental risks? The Rio Declaration (paragraph 15) and the Maastricht Treaty (Article 130r, now Article 174) address the environment, but the European Commission, the Court of Justice of the European Communities, the WTO, and other bodies have considered the PP to be equally relevant to health, food, and consumer safety risks.

- What degree of risk triggers the PP? Some versions refer to uncertain, serious, or irreversible risks (for example, the Rio Declaration), but some versions omit these trigger criteria.

- What action should be taken under the PP? Most versions give no real guidance, simply stating that uncertainty is no excuse for inaction, or warrants action, without saying what that action should be. Other versions call for a ban on the proposed product or activity until uncertainty is reduced to some degree, usually by shifting the burden of proof onto the proponent of the product or activity. Some versions call for adoption of best available control technology, but others do not.

- May costs be considered? Some versions exclude cost and many analysts pose the PP in opposition to cost-benefit analysis. But the Rio Declaration (paragraph 15) refers to 'cost-effective' measures, and the European Commission maintains that precautionary regulation must be based on an analysis of costs and benefits.

- Does the PP require zero risk? Most versions do not, and the European Commission explicitly states that the PP 'must not aim at zero risk', but some versions lean toward banning activities posing any uncertain risk. For example, 'where potential adverse effects are not fully understood, the activities should not proceed'.[21] Risks are never 'fully understood', so this version would amount to a ban.

- Is there a difference between 'precaution' and 'prevention'? Early versions used the terms interchangeably. For example, the Bergen Declaration (1990, paragraph 7) provided that the PP requires states to 'anticipate, prevent and attack' risks. By contrast, the European Environment Agency has argued that precaution applies to 'uncertain' risks whereas prevention applies to 'known' risks.[22] It is not clear, however, what is meant by a 'known' risk. Either there is no such thing (because all risks are uncertain), in which case prevention is an empty set and the PP applies to all

[20] See Communication from the Commission, note 7 above.

[21] United Nations General Assembly, *World Charter for Nature*, UNGA Resolution 37/7 (1982).

[22] European Environment Agency (EEA), *Late Lessons from Early Warnings: The Precautionary Principle 1896–2000*, Environmental Issue Report no. 22 (Luxembourg: Office for Official Publications of the European Communities, 2001 and Copenhagen: Earthscan, 2001).

risks, or there are many 'known' risks (in the sense of well-understood cause and effect relationships), in which case the PP is only about risks for which there is fundamental ('true' or 'deep') uncertainty about the cause-and-effect or hazard-and-harm relationship, and the PP applies only to those few rare and temporary cases of utter mystery that later become understood as scientific advances.

From all of these variations, it is useful to consider three archetypal versions of the PP.

3.1 Version 1: 'Uncertainty Does Not Justify Inaction'

In its most basic form, the PP permits precautionary regulation in the absence of complete evidence about the particular risk scenario. A common phrasing is: 'Where there are threats of serious or irreversible damage, lack of full scientific certainty shall not be used as a reason for postponing measures to prevent environmental degradation' (Bergen Declaration (1990) and the Rio Declaration (1992), paragraph 15, which adds 'cost-effective' before 'measures'). In short, uncertainty does not justify inaction: 'The precautionary principle is formulated in many ways, and differences between them may be significant. However, all formulations have an essential element in common: rational decisions may and should be taken on the basis of uncertain science, despite a "lack of full scientific certainty" or of "conclusive evidence to prove a causal relation between inputs and their effects." '[23]

   This version of the PP does not go very far. Its salient merit is that it rebuts the frequently heard claim that 'uncertainty warrants inaction' (or, stated another way, that regulation should not occur unless regulatory authorities 'prove' that a risk is 'real') or, similarly, that regulation is unwarranted because the 'assimilative capacity' of the environment can be assumed to absorb residuals without adverse effect until the contrary is shown. If these claims were valid, *ex ante* regulation would never be warranted. Only *ex post* tort liability could constrain risks. If we are ever to act before harms occur, then we must act in the face of uncertainty. Responding to these claims that uncertainty warrants waiting, as just noted, and to the particular challenge of finding a basis for anticipatory action to assess and prevent transboundary harms under international law (which until the 1970s had emphasized *ex post* state liability for transboundary harm, as under *Trail Smelter Arbitration (United States v. Canada)*),[24] this version of the PP states that we may act in advance of actual harm. But it does not say what we should do. It only permits action, rather than compelling it. It responds only to the situation of 'lack of full scientific certainty', but there is *never* 'full scientific certainty' or 'conclusive evidence'. We always face uncertainty, and we

---

[23] C. Henry, 'The Essence of the Precautionary Principle,' in K. von Moltke and C. Weill, eds., *European Precautionary Practice*, Les actes de l'IDDRI no. 1, Proceedings of the International Workshop, Paris, 3–4 December 2002 (Paris: Institut du Développement Durable et Relations Internationales, 2004) 29.   [24] *Trail Smelter Case (United States v. Canada)*, Award, 1941, 3 U.N.R.I.A.A. 1905.

must *always* make decisions under uncertainty. This version of the PP does not answer the real question, which is *what* action to take in the face of (inevitable) uncertainty.

3.2 Version 2: 'Uncertainty Justifies Action'

A second version of the PP is somewhat more aggressive. It says that uncertain risk justifies action. For example, the 1998 Wingspread Conference concluded: 'When an activity raises threats of harm to human health or the environment, precautionary measures should be taken even if some cause and effect relationships are not fully established.'[25] Similarly, the German Federal Interior Ministry wrote: 'The principle of precaution commands that the damages done to the natural world (which surrounds us all) should be avoided *in advance* and in accordance with opportunity and possibility . . . it also means acting when conclusively ascertained understanding by science is not yet available.'[26] Or, '[a]ccording to the precautionary principle, the more uncertain the risk, the more justified is some form of regulatory intervention.'[27] Article 5 of the 2004 French Environment Charter provides: 'When the environment is at risk from serious and irreversible harm, even if this cannot be scientifically proven, public authorities must, through the application of the precautionary principle and according to their competences, implement procedures to assess the risks and adopt temporary and appropriate measures to prevent the damage occurring.'

Like the first version of the PP, this version is based on a truism. Since cause and effect relationships are never 'proven' or 'fully' or 'conclusively' established (even in retrospect), we are always dealing with uncertain and probabilistic relationships. This version, while calling for proactive precautionary measures, still does not address the real question of *what* measures should be taken. Still, version 2 is more precautionary than version 1, insofar as version 2 affirmatively impels regulatory intervention rather than just permitting it. Yet if precaution itself would have adverse consequences, this affirmative principle would be too strong (hence, the French qualification to adopt 'temporary and appropriate' measures). And if greater uncertainty itself warranted more regulatory action, it would perversely skew social investments away from more certain risks.

[25] Quoted in Raffensperger and Tickner, see note 19 above at 343.

[26] S. Boehmer-Christiansen, 'The Precautionary Principle in Germany—Enabling Government,' in T. O'Riordan and J. Cameron, eds., *Interpreting the Precautionary Principle* (London: Cameron May, 1994) 31 at 37.

[27] W.E. Wagner, 'The Precautionary Principle and Chemical Regulation in the U.S.' (2000) 6 Human and Ecological Risk Assessment 459 at 461.

3.3 Version 3: Shifting the Burden of Proof

A third version of the PP requires forbidding the potentially risky activity until the proponent of the activity demonstrates that it poses no (or acceptable) risk: 'As described in the Wingspread Statement on the Precautionary Principle, the applicant or proponent of an activity or process or chemical needs to demonstrate to the satisfaction of the public and the regulatory community that the environment and public health will be safe. The proof must shift to the party or entity that will benefit from the activity and that is most likely to have the information.'[28] This version of the PP is more precautionary than the first or second version. Unlike the first two versions, version 3 specifies a particular action to take in the face of uncertain risk: forbid the activity unless the standard of proof is met by the proponent. Version 3 has two key components: shifting the *burden* of proof to the proponent of the activity or product and setting a *standard* of proof (what must be demonstrated—no risk, *de minimus* risk, 'safety', acceptable risk, or something else).

Depending on the standard of proof, version 3 could invite overregulation. What counts as 'safe' is unclear. Some interpretations of version 3—for example, the World Charter for Nature quoted earlier—would impose a standard of proof of no risk. Such a measure would often yield overregulation where the risk of the substance or activity is small relative to its benefits. For example, many medicines are toxic at some dose, as are vitamins and oxygen, and no drug company could offer proof that they were not toxic or posed no risk of harm at all doses. More generally, because, as Paracelsus taught, 'the dose makes the poison,' potentially every substance would have to be banned if proof of no toxicity or no harm were the universal principle. As a result, real world applications of version 3 tend to employ a more balanced standard of proof. In the *Benzene* case (cited above), the US Supreme Court held that 'safe' does not mean 'no risk' but rather means 'no significant risk', and then left it up to the federal Occupational Safety and Health Administration (OSHA) to determine which workplace health risks are 'significant'. Laws requiring pre-market approval of new products typically require that product proponents demonstrate 'acceptable risk' or 'no unreasonable risk' or 'net benefits'.

Meanwhile, version 3 does contain the useful idea of putting the *burden* of proof on the party best able to generate the information needed to make the decision. This idea is analogous to the notion of putting the burden of accident avoidance on the 'least cost avoider'.[29] California's Proposition 65 and the 1996 protocol to the London Convention take this approach: substances initially listed may be removed from the list if producers demonstrate that the substance falls below a threshold of risk.

The stringency of version 3 can also be seen by analogy to criminal law. Violence is a problem of public risk and public health. Version 3 would shift the burden of proof

---

[28] P.L. deFur, 'The Precautionary Principle: Application to Policies Regarding Endocrine-Disrupting Chemicals,' in Raffensperger and Tickner, see note 19 above at 345–6.

[29] G. Calabresi, *The Costs of Accidents* (New Haven, CT: Yale University Press, 1970).

from 'innocent until proven guilty' to 'guilty until proven innocent'. Yet such a shift in criminal law would be opposed by many who favour version 3 for environmental risks. Talbot Page argued that version 3 should apply to environmental law but not to criminal law on the ground that, although both protect public health, the cost of mistaken precaution in criminal law is foregone liberty, but in environmental law it is only money.[30] Page's analysis, however, neglects the possibility that environmental precaution could create countervailing risks that harm health and impair liberty.

4 Normative Analysis of the Precautionary Principle

As noted at the outset, despite the common sense of precaution as a strategy in many (but not all) cases, the PP as a legal principle remains controversial. The crux of the controversy is precisely the fact that, judged on its consequences, precaution is desirable in some but not all cases, whereas the PP seems to insist on precaution in all cases of uncertain risk. Efforts to connect the PP to consequentialist decision-making, such as the European Commission's 2000 communication, are efforts to enable precaution where warranted based on the expected consequences, but to avoid mandating precaution in all cases.[31] This section examines the variables relevant to such a consequentialist normative framework for precaution.

As noted earlier, uncertainty is the primary focus of the PP. Health and environmental problems are regularly characterized by uncertainty about probability, severity, timing, and cause-effect relationship. Moreover, latency between cause and effect means that waiting for better evidence may mean missing the opportunity to address the cause. Thus, if uncertainty is cited as a reason not to act, the result may be incurring the harm. Hence, version 1 of the PP offers a sensible rebuttal to the generic claim that uncertainty justifies inaction or that the environment can assimilate all residuals absent proof to the contrary.

Uncertainty, however, can also be handled in standard decision analyses, without invocation of the PP. Uncertainty can be quantified in calculations of expected value. Risk premia for uncertainty can be added to expected benefits and costs. Moreover, uncertainty does not justify inaction, but neither does uncertainty itself justify action. The choice depends on the relative expected consequences of each action compared to alternatives. Uncertainty affects all risks, including the countervailing

---

[30] T. Page, 'A Generic View of Toxic Chemicals and Similar Risks' (1978) 7 Ecology L.Q. 207.

[31] For approaches to melding the PP with consequentialist decision analysis, see, for example, the symposium in volume 4 of the *Journal of Risk Research* (2001); R.B. Stewart, 'Environmental Regulatory Decisionmaking under Uncertainty' (2002) 20 Res. L. & Econ. 71; and C. Gollier and N. Treich, 'Decision Making under Uncertainty: The Economics of the Precautionary Principle' (2003) 27 J. Risk & Uncertainty 77.

risks induced by precaution. We never decide under certainty—the hard question is not whether uncertainty justifies action or waiting, but rather what action to take given the degree of uncertainty.

A distinct basis for precaution is irreversibility. As noted earlier, many versions of the PP cite the threat of irreversible damage. It has long been observed that irreversible impacts warrant precautions as a way to preserve the option value of greater flexibility—that is, to defer the irreversibility while more can be learned.[32] However, irreversibility cannot simply mean impossible to reverse, because in a world with a one-way flow of time, all choices are irreversible in that sense, even trivial ones. Risks neglected may prove irreversible, but, likewise, the costs and countervailing risks of precautionary regulation are also irreversible opportunities foregone. To evaluate precaution, one must compare the seriousness of 'irreversible' impacts, including the options lost and the cost and time needed to reverse or heal the results.[33]

A third factor favouring precaution is the possibility of catastrophe. Worst-case or catastrophic scenarios may warrant special efforts to avoid them even if they are very unlikely because their harms would be so great, and because people tend to put more value on preventing a single devastating incident than they do on preventing an equal number of deaths spread out over multiple smaller incidents.[34] As with uncertainty, the problem of catastrophic risk can also be handled with standard decision analysis. A very low probability multiplied by a very large harm can yield a significant expected value, and risk premia can be added for the greater value of avoiding devastating incidents. Advocates of precaution argue that the PP is needed to counter the heuristic error that people may make in neglecting or ignoring very low-probability risks,[35] but critics counter that people also sometimes exaggerate the risk of low-probability catastrophic and dreaded events, and, indeed, invocation of the PP may be selectively spurred by such errors of exaggeration.[36] Meanwhile, some suggest that the probabilities of risks may follow a 'power law' distribution such that worst-case scenarios are not so unlikely.[37]

All of these factors, however, also characterize the risks that precaution may *induce*. In a world of multiple contending risks, the factors just noted (uncertainty, irreversibility, catastrophe, and skewed probability distributions) can attach to *both*

[32] See K.J. Arrow and A.C. Fisher, 'Environmental Preservation, Uncertainty, and Irreversibility' (1974) 88 Q. J. Econ. 312; and C. Henry, 'Investment Decisions under Uncertainty: The "Irreversibility Effect" ' (1974) 64 Am. Econ. Rev. 1006.

[33] See C.R. Sunstein, 'Irreversible and Catastrophic' (2006) 91 Cornell L. Rev., 841.

[34] See R.A. Posner, *Catastrophe: Risk and Response* (New York: Oxford University Press, 2004).

[35] D. Dana, 'A Behavioral Economic Defense of the Precautionary Principle' (2003) 97 Nw. U. L. Rev. 1315.

[36] See P. Slovic and E.U. Weber, *Perception of Risk Posed by Extreme Events* (Columbia University Center for Hazards and Risk Research, 2003).

[37] See D.A. Farber, 'Probabilities Behaving Badly: Complexity Theory and Environmental Uncertainty' (2003) 37 U.C. Davis L. Rev. 145.

the target risk being reduced by precaution *and* the countervailing risks that are created by precautionary actions. Measures to reduce one uncertain irreversible catastrophic risk might induce another.[38] For example, banning nuclear power might induce global warming, while preventing global warming by shifting to a new energy technology such as nuclear fusion or space-based solar power might introduce uncertain new risks of irreversible catastrophic impacts. Or banning genetically modified foods might perpetuate hunger in poor countries and hasten the irreversible conversion of tropical forests to farmland. Banning a product might induce the risks of substitute products. Historically, introducing the seemingly benign CFCs in order to replace highly toxic refrigerants turned out to yield a new and unintended countervailing risk of stratospheric ozone depletion.

Thus understood, the PP should not call for precautionary regulation of uncertain irreversible risks if such regulation would itself yield the very dangers the PP seeks to avoid. At the extreme, the PP could swallow itself, prohibiting both the risky activity and the risky regulation of this activity. Of course, the countervailing risks might be small or worth running in some cases, and there might also be ancillary benefits of regulation. The central point is that invoking the PP cannot escape the need to weigh the full portfolio of consequences.

Greater precaution reduces the risk of false negatives (inattention to significant risks) but increases the risk of false positives (attention to insignificant risks—false alarms). Avoiding false negatives is often cited as the primary benefit of the PP.[39] Yet overreaction to false positives (or even to true positives) also entails harms: opportunities foregone, innovations rejected (including those that would improve human and environmental health), public cynicism about future warnings (the 'crying wolf' syndrome), and new countervailing risks. As noted earlier, Talbot Page argued in 1978 that false positives are worth tolerating in the environmental context because their cost is only money, but this argument assumes that money is lexically less important than environmental protection regardless of its magnitude, and, more importantly, it neglects the countervailing adverse health and environmental impacts of precautionary measures.

The real world does not come one risk at a time. It is an interconnected web of multiple interdependent risks. In a multi-risk world, prudent precaution requires analysis of the full portfolio of expected consequences. Such analysis is needed for both new technologies and new public policies. The portfolio of consequences includes reduction of the target risk, costs, ancillary benefits such as other risks reduced, and countervailing risks increased.

[38] See, e.g., Graham and Wiener, note 2 above; F.B. Cross, 'Paradoxical Perils of the Precautionary Principle' (1996) 53 Wash. & Lee L. Rev. 851; and C.R. Sunstein, *The Laws of Fear: Beyond the Precautionary Principle* (Cambridge: Cambridge University Press, 2004).

[39] European Environment Agency, *Late Lessons from Early Warnings: The Precautionary Principle. 1896–2000*, note 22 above.

In addition, a dynamic approach recognizes that knowledge improves over time. Both 'wait and learn' and 'act and learn' are plausible strategies—the choice between them depending on the relative expected consequences. Precaution is 'act and learn', to preserve the option value of avoiding irreversibility. As such, precaution must be accompanied by further research and adaptive management towards the updating of the initial policy over time. Thus, the French version of the PP calls precaution 'temporary', and the European Commission requires precaution to be 'provisional' as new science is gathered. The challenge is to design institutions and incentives to generate this new science and to apply it to update policies. The concern is that once policies are adopted, institutions become reluctant to review and revise them.

In sum, version 1 of the PP is helpful to decision-makers as a rebuttal to the mistaken claim that uncertainty warrants inaction. Latent risks mean that inaction under uncertainty may invite future harms. Irreversibility and catastrophe offer additional warrants for precaution. Version 1 of the PP, however, like any permissive principle of law, authorizes the exercise of government power while leaving unaddressed the serious question, namely, what action government should take in the face of such risks. On the other hand, versions 2 and 3 of the PP could be counterproductive. They incur the costs of false positives and neglect the countervailing risks of regulation. In the real world of multiple risks and imperfect government, precaution itself may be a risky activity. Amidst multiple risks, we need to exercise precaution against excessive precaution. Or, to put it differently, given the reality of multiple interrelated risks, we need a principle of optimal precaution rather than of maximum precaution. Precautionary regulation should be based on full portfolio impacts analysis and followed by continuing research to foster learning and adaptive revisions. Ultimately, we need to seek 'risk-superior' options that reduce multiple risks in concert.

5 FUTURE OF THE PRECAUTIONARY PRINCIPLE

The reality of precautionary regulation has been more moderate than the extreme versions of the PP sometimes advocated. When the EU and domestic legal systems have adopted precaution, they have included qualifications and exceptions to account for costs, countervailing risks, and provisionality. Extreme forms of the PP are unlikely to be implemented (though examples such as the Delaney Clause do arise). Rather, the trend in Europe appears to be towards a reconciliation of the PP with the principle of proportionality and with methods of regulatory impact analysis (RIA) under the Better Regulation initiative. The new Barroso Commission (stimulated by the Lisbon Agenda for economic growth and by UK Prime Minister

Tony Blair's emphasis on regulatory reform) has issued new RIA guidelines[40] and may construct a centralized process of regulatory review.[41]

Moderation may also be inspired to address the concerns of developing countries. Poorer countries face pressing needs to develop, eradicate poverty, and attract investment. For them, the costs of highly precautionary policies may loom much larger than do those costs in wealthier countries. Further, poorer countries may sensibly choose different tradeoffs among risks, such as favouring reduction of large near-term risks even if this requires tolerating some small long-term risks that the PP would address. For example, developing countries may resist the application of the PP by Europe or other trading partners as a means to impose restrictions on developing countries' use of genetically modified foods to combat hunger and of pesticides such as DDT to combat malaria. As the conversation about precaution broadens to become less a transatlantic dispute and more a global dialogue, the greater variety of interests may foster a more moderate approach to the PP than some of the articulations to date.

Meanwhile, the US government, while criticizing the PP in the environmental sphere, has adopted the logic and language of the PP as the centerpiece of its new National Security Strategy, pledging to anticipate and prevent terrorist attacks despite uncertainty.[42] In essence, the US approach is the converse of the EU's, which endorses the PP in the environmental arena and criticizes it in the national security arena (at least insofar as it authorizes *unilateral* precautionary use of force), although some European states, such as the United Kingdom, appear to favour the PP in both arenas. This turn of events may invite further diplomatic friction, but it also offers a fresh opportunity for governments to reassess the advantages and disadvantages of precaution in each context.[43]

The future thus offers two contrasting paths. On the one hand, there could be a continuation of precautionary particularity: the selective use of precaution by different states against different risks, often driven by heuristic reactions to recently visible or dreaded risks. On this path, no shared understanding on optimal precaution would emerge. Precautionary particularity would serve domestic interests and would

---

[40] European Commission, *Impact Assessment Guidelines*, Doc. SEC(2005) 791 (15 June 2005), with 15 March 2006 update.

[41] See, J.B. Wiener, 'Better Regulation in Europe' forthcoming in (2006) 59, Current Legal Problems .

[42] The National Security Strategy of the United States of America, 17 September 2002, Introduction and Part V ('We cannot let our enemies strike first . . . [but must take] anticipatory action to defend ourselves, even if uncertainty remains as to the time and place of the enemy's attack. To forestall or prevent such hostile acts by our adversaries, the United States, will, if necessary, act preemptively . . . America will act against such emerging threats before they are fully formed . . . The greater the threat, the greater is the risk of inaction and the more compelling the case for taking anticipatory action to defend ourselves, even if uncertainty remains as to the time and place of the enemy's attack'). On the similar UK position, see D. Runciman, 'The Precautionary Principle' (April 2004) 26(7) London Review of Books.

[43] See J. Stern and J.B. Wiener, 'Precaution against Terrorism,' (2006) 9 J. Risk Research 393.

offer some avenues for hybridization (legal borrowing) across states, but it would also give rise to repeated disputes among states over mismatches in the selection of specific risks and precautionary measures, especially in cases of international trade in products regulated differently in different countries.

Alternatively, if these developments stimulate mutual understanding of both the merits and demerits of the PP and a forthright conversation about a sensible middle ground, they could lead to a new transatlantic and even global consensus on the criteria for optimal precaution based on analyses of consequences. This consensus could be embodied in international accords on environment, development, and security. It could also play a role in the emergence of a new body of global administrative law (see Chapter 4 'Global Environmental Governance as Administration'), including shared rules and norms for international regulatory policy. This consensus could support the creation of a network of national and international institutions to conduct full portfolio impact analyses of national and international precautionary measures in diverse domains (including health, safety, environment, and security), both restraining unwarranted precaution and prompting desirable precaution.

RECOMMENDED READING

D. Bodansky, 'Scientific Uncertainty and the Precautionary Principle' (September 1991) 33 Env't 4.

J. Cameron and T. O'Riordan, eds., *Interpreting the Precautionary Principle* (London: Cameron May, 1994).

D. Freestone and E. Hey, eds., *The Precautionary Principle and International Law* (The Hague: Kluwer Law International, 1996).

J.D. Graham and J.B. Wiener, eds., *Risk vs. Risk: Tradeoffs in Protecting Health and the Environment* (Cambridge, MA: Harvard University Press, 1995).

J. Morris, ed., *Rethinking Risk and the Precautionary Principle* (Woburn, MA: Butterworth-Heinemann, 2000).

C. Raffensperger and J. Tickner, eds., *Protecting Public Health and the Environment: Implementing the Precautionary Principle* (Washington, DC: Island Press, 1999).

P.H. Sand, 'The Precautionary Principle: A European Perspective' (2000) 6 Human and Ecological Risk Assessment 445.

A. Trouwborst, *Evolution and Status of the Precautionary Principle in International Law* (The Hague: Kluwer Law International, 2002).

J.B. Wiener, 'Precaution in a Multi-Risk World,' in D. Paustenbach, ed., *Human and Ecological Risk Assessment: Theory and Practice* (New York: John Wiley and Sons, 2002) 1509.

——, 'Whose Precaution after All ? A Comment on the Comparison and Evolution of Risk Regulatory Systems' (2003) 13 Duke J. Int'l & Comp. L. 207.

CHAPTER 26

SUSTAINABLE DEVELOPMENT

DANIEL BARSTOW MAGRAW
LISA D. HAWKE

1 INTRODUCTION

THE paradigm of sustainable development evolved over many years through attempts to take account of concerns regarding economic development, environmental protection (including human health), and social development (including human rights). Its adoption and core content evidence a profound change in the way society views the relationship between economic activity and the natural environment. Nevertheless, although sustainable development is now viewed by the international community as the overarching framework for improving quality of life throughout the world (and by many as the best approach to maintaining a healthy planet), important disagreements exist about its precise meaning and implications, and resistance to it still surfaces from time to time. This chapter examines the evolution and content of the concept of 'sustainable development', its legal status and function, and its implications for principles and tools of international environmental law.

2 ORIGIN AND EVOLUTION

In 1971, as a precursor to the Stockholm Conference on the Human Environment, a group of persons experienced in development and environment produced *Development and Environment: The Founex Report*, which addressed the efforts, especially by developed countries, to protect the environment and developing countries' struggle to achieve economic development. The report was one of the earliest documents to identify the specific environmental issues that developed and developing countries face with respect to matters such as agriculture, transport, and human settlements. The purpose of the report was to draw attention to the relationship between economic growth, poverty, and environmental protection and to conceptualize environmental policy with these linkages in mind with an eye to the Stockholm Conference.[1]

The main purpose of the Stockholm Conference was to be a practical means and source of encouragement for governments to work towards protecting and improving the human environment.[2] The Stockholm Declaration on the Human

---

[1] Preparatory Committee for the United Nations Conference on the Human Environment, *Development and Environment: The Founex Report* (Founex, Switzerland, 4–12 June 1971) at para. 5.1. Five regional meetings on development and environment were also held as well as a meeting of scientists from developing countries (see, for example, International Council of Scientific Unions Special Committee on Problems of the Environment, Environmental Problems in Developing Countries Report, Canberra, Australia (24 August–3 September 1971)).

[2] G.A. Res. 2581(XXIV), UN Doc. A/RES/2581(XXIV) (8 January 1970).

Environment, which emerged from this conference and was endorsed by the United Nations General Assembly (UNGA) in 1972, deals with the integration of economic, environmental, and social justice issues. For example, the preamble mentions human rights, economic development, and developing countries' priorities; Principle 1 relates to human rights; Principle 8 relates to economic and social development; Principle 11 relates to the effects of environmental policies on development and international economies; Principle 21 includes the economic activity of exploiting natural resources; and Principle 23 relates specifically to developing countries. Thus, without using the phrase 'sustainable development', the Stockholm Declaration foreshadowed the holistic approach embodied in this concept and helped give rise to it.

The first publicly visible use of the term 'sustainable development' was most probably in 1980 when it appeared in the World Conservation Strategy (WCS), a document prepared by the International Union for Conservation of Nature and Natural Resources (IUCN). The WCS defined sustainable development as 'the integration of conservation and development to ensure that modifications to the planet do indeed secure the survival and well-being of all people.' [3] The WCS examined the contribution of living resource conservation to human survival and sustainable development, identified the priority conservation issues and the main requirements for dealing with them, and proposed ways for effectively achieving the strategy's aim.

The term 'sustainable development' was given international prominence and refined in 1987 by the World Commission on Environment and Development (WCED or the Brundtland Commission), an independent body created by the UNGA. Its report, *Our Common Future*,[4] brought the term 'sustainable development' to the forefront of international discourse and policy-making. The Brundtland Commission's discussion of sustainable development emphasized that technology and social organization are affecting the natural environment, and its provision of what are now referred to as 'environmental services', in ways that limit societies' ability to meet current and future needs and, thus, that the environment must be protected. Soon thereafter, the 1990 Dublin Declaration by the European Council on the Environmental Imperative identified sustainable development as one of the objectives of the European Community.[5]

The 1992 UN Conference on Environment and Development (UNCED) in Rio de Janeiro, Brazil, was the first time that the world's governments officially adopted sustainable development as the development paradigm. Sustainable development is the underlying theme of the five instruments adopted by the 172 countries

---

[3] International Union for Conservation of Nature and Natural Resources (currently World Conservation Union) (IUCN), *World Conservation Strategy: Living Resource Conservation for Sustainable Development* (Gland, Switzerland: IUCN, 1980).

[4] World Commission on Environment and Development, *Our Common Future* (Oxford: Oxford University Press, 1987) at 43–6.

[5] Declaration by the European Council on the Environmental Imperative, Bull. Eur. Comm. No. 6 (1990) at 17.

represented by heads of state or other national leaders at UNCED. For example, the Rio Declaration on Environment and Development, which contains 27 key principles to guide the integration of environment and development policies, focuses on sustainable development in Principle 1 ('[h]uman beings are at the centre of concerns for sustainable development. They are entitled to a healthy and productive life in harmony with nature.'). Agenda 21, a comprehensive global plan of action for the implementation of sustainable development, was designed to create a 'global partnership for sustainable development.' The United Nations Framework Convention on Climate Change (UNFCCC), a legally binding international agreement intended to stabilize greenhouse gases in the atmosphere at a level preventing dangerous anthropogenic interference with the climate system, provides, in Article 3, on principles that '[t]he Parties have a right to, and should, promote sustainable development.' The Convention on Biological Diversity (CBD), a legally binding agreement that strives to conserve the world's genetic, species, and ecosystem diversity emphasizes 'sustainable use'. Finally, the Statement of Principles on Forests expressed the global consensus on the management, conservation, and 'sustainable development' of the world's forests.

In 1994, sustainable development was recognized as an objective of the World Trade Organization (WTO) in the first paragraph of the preamble to the Marrakech Agreement Establishing the World Trade Organization (WTO Agreement).[6] The role of sustainable development as the overarching paradigm was also being challenged, however. In 1994, during negotiations related to the International Conference on Population and Development (ICPD), a battle to recognize 'sustained economic growth' as a paradigm ensued. Some developing country delegations expressed the view that 'sustained economic growth' was more important than sustainable development, and that sustainable development was a guise for keeping developing countries in a subservient position. Other countries resisted these arguments, expressing their view that environmental and health protection and social justice cannot be ignored in order to achieve a healthy economy and society over the long term. The final ICPD Programme of Action reaffirmed the primacy of sustainable development while also recognizing the importance of economic growth, through the use of the phrase 'sustained economic growth in the context of sustainable development.'

The debate continued in connection with the 1995 World Summit for Social Development. Developing country negotiators insisted on language stating that 'sustained economic growth and sustainable development are equally important.' Norway and the United States, later joined by the European Union, argued that sustainable development remained the appropriate paradigm. This issue was the final one decided on the brink of the head-of-state summit. The process of negotiating this issue revealed that high-level politicians from developing countries readily acknowledged the need to integrate social, economic, and environmental considerations.

[6] Marrakech Agreement Establishing the World Trade Organization, 15 April 1994, 33 I.L.M. 15 (1994).

The result was a clear reaffirmation of sustainable development as the paradigm, and, for the first time in a United Nations instrument, an explicit linkage was made between economic development, social development, and environmental protection. Paragraph 6 of the Copenhagen Declaration on Social Development makes this clear: 'We are deeply convinced that economic development, social development and environmental protection are interdependent and mutually reinforcing components of sustainable development, which is the framework for our efforts to achieve a higher quality of life for all people.'[7]

The years following the Social Summit showed that developing countries remained suspicious that demands for environmental protection would interfere with their economic development. Many difficult negotiations ensued, including about who will pay the costs that are required to achieve sustainable development. Nevertheless, international discussions continued to utilize sustainable development as the fundamental organizing concept.

In 2000, the UNGA adopted the United Nations Millennium Declaration, which reaffirmed the UNGA's support for principles of sustainable development agreed upon at UNCED. The declaration identified six fundamental values to be essential to international relations, including freedom, equality, solidarity, tolerance, respect for nature, and shared responsibility.[8] The UNGA stated that '[p]rudence must be shown in the management of all living species and natural resources, in accordance with the precepts of sustainable development . . . The current unsustainable patterns of production and consumption must be changed in the interest of our future welfare and that of our descendants.'[9] The Millennium Declaration also identified eight goals, known as the millennium development goals (MDGs), which all 191 United Nations member states have agreed to try to achieve by the year 2015. MDG-7 focuses on environmental sustainability, and the first of three targets under MDG-7 is to '[i]ntegrate the principles of sustainable development into country policies and programmes; reverse loss of environmental resources.'

At the World Summit on Sustainable Development (WSSD) in Johannesburg, South Africa, in 2002, representatives from around the world again reaffirmed their commitment to sustainable development. The WSSD Plan of Implementation recognizes poverty eradication, changing unsustainable consumption and production patterns, and protecting and managing the natural resource base for economic and social development as 'overarching objectives of, and essential requirements for, sustainable development.'[10]

---

[7] Copenhagen Declaration on Social Development, UN Doc. A/CONF.166/9 (19 April 1995) at para. 6.

[8] United Nations Millennium Declaration, G.A. Res. 55/2, UN Doc. A/RES/55/2 (8 September 2000) at I, para. 6.   [9] Ibid.

[10] Johannesburg Plan of Implementation, in *Report of the World Summit on Sustainable Development*, Johannesburg, South Africa, 26 August-4 September 2002, UN Doc. A/CONF.199/20 (2002) at para. 11. Adopted at the seventeenth plenary meeting of the World Summit on Sustainable Development on 4 September 2002.

In May 2005, the United Nations released the *Millennium Development Goals Report*, which detailed the progress, if any, made towards achieving the MDGs. The report states that most countries have committed to the principles of sustainable development by incorporating them into national policies as well as agreeing to relevant international instruments. However, it also states that these good intentions have not resulted in sufficient progress to reverse the loss of environmental resources.[11]

Also in 2005, the UNGA adopted the 2005 World Summit Outcome, as a follow-up to the 2000 Millennium Summit.[12] The World Summit Outcome, which frequently uses the term 'development' as an apparent shorthand for 'sustainable development', reaffirms the Millennium Declaration (para. 3) and recognizes sustainable development as a key element of United Nations activities (para. 10). The environment *per se* is mentioned relatively infrequently (see, for example, para. 10), and uncertainty may have been reintroduced regarding the relationship between sustainable development and sustained economic growth (para. 19, for example, lists both of these concepts as 'commitments'). Taking the 2005 World Summit Outcome as a whole, together with the other instruments mentioned earlier and the fact that day-to-day discourse at the United Nations and elsewhere routinely use the term 'sustainable development', sustainable development as described in this chapter remains the overarching paradigm for both development and environmental protection.

3 MEANING

The most often quoted definition of 'sustainable development' is the one contained in the Brundtland Commission's report, *Our Common Future*:

Sustainable development is development that meets the needs of the present without compromising the ability of future generations to meet their own needs.
  It contains within it two key concepts:

- the concept of 'needs,' in particular the essential needs of the world's poor, to which overriding priority should be given; and
- the idea of limitations imposed by the state of technology and social organization on the environment's ability to meet present and future needs.[13]

While the international community has not agreed to this definition in any legally binding instrument, the definition is so frequently cited that it has acquired a quasi-official status. Considering the Brundtland Commission's definition together with

---

[11] *Millennium Development Goals Report* (New York: United Nations, 2005) 30, Goal 7: Ensure Environmental Sustainability.

[12] See 2005 World Summit Outcome, G.A. Res. 60/1, UN Doc. A/RES/60/1 (24 October 2005).

[13] World Commission on Environment and Development, see note 5 above at 43.

official intergovernmental statements such as the Copenhagen Declaration on Social Development, the Millennium Declaration, the World Summit on Sustainable Development, and the 2005 World Summit Outcome, referred to earlier, sustainable development may be considered to consist of the following core elements:

- the needs of present and future generations must be taken into account (inter-generational equity);
- the needs of the world's poor must receive priority, and abject poverty must be eliminated (intra-generational equity);
- the environment needs to be preserved at least to a significant degree; and
- economic, social, and environmental policies must be integrated.

The first of these elements, inter-generational equity, is stated very clearly in the Brundtland Commission's definition (see Chapter 27 'Equity'). It finds further support in many other international instruments, for example, in Principle 3 of the Rio Declaration, which states that '[t]he right of development must be fulfilled so as to equitably meet the developmental and environmental needs of present and future generations.' It is also recognized in national jurisprudence, as demonstrated, for example, in the well-known case of *Oposa v. Factoran*.[14] In this case, the petitioners sought to 'prevent the misappropriation or impairment' of Philippine rainforests by deforestation, and asserted that they represented their generation as well as future generations in addressing the present and future harms. The Supreme Court of the Republic of the Philippines allowed the petitioners to sue for cancellation of timber license agreements, and granted them standing to represent their generation and generations yet unborn, based on the constitutional right to a balanced and healthful ecology and the 'twin concepts of "inter-generational responsibility" and "inter-generational justice." ' The court stated that this right belongs to a different category of rights, since it is concerned with the self-preservation and self-perpetuation of humanity, therefore, the right to a balanced and healthful ecology need not even have been written in the Constitution as it was assumed to exist from the inception of humankind.[15]

The role of intra-generational equity in achieving sustainable development is indicated by the Brundtland Commission's statement that overriding priority should be given to the needs of the world's poor. Similarly, Principle 5 of the Rio Declaration provides that '[a]ll states and people shall cooperate in the essential task of eradicating poverty as an indispensable requirement for sustainable development, in order to decrease the disparities in standards of living and better meet the needs of the majority of the people of the world.' Intra-generational equity finds further support in many other international instruments, such as the second sentence of paragraph 6 of the Copenhagen Declaration: 'Equitable social development that recognizes empowering the poor to utilize environmental resources sustainably

---

[14] *Oposa v. Factoran*, G.R. No. 101083 (30 July 1993) (Supreme Court, Republic of the Philippines).

[15] *Ibid.* at 7. See also Constitution of the Republic of the Philippines, Article II at para. 16.

is a necessary foundation for sustainable development.' This concept of intra-generational equity is also found in MDG-1 ('[e]radicate extreme poverty and hunger') as well as in the Millennium Declaration (paras. 6, 11, and 21) and the 2005 World Summit Outcome (paras. 11 and 19).

That the environment must be preserved is clear from the Brundtland Commission's conclusion that human and technological capital are not infinitely substitutable for natural capital, therefore, natural capital itself needs to be pre-served. This idea can be traced back to pre-Stockholm UNGA Resolution 2849 (XXVI), which states that 'the rational management of the environment is of funda-mental importance for the future of mankind.'[16] The crucial importance of protect-ing the environment is also clear from a myriad of other international instruments. For example, the first target of MDG-7 includes 'revers[ing] loss of environmental resources'; and the International Law Association's 2002 New Delhi Declaration on Principles of International Law Relating to Sustainable Development (ILA Sustainable Development Principles), states that '[t]he protection, preservation and enhancement of the natural environment, particularly the proper management of climate system, biological diversity and fauna and flora of the Earth, are the common concern of mankind' and that states are under a duty to manage natural resources in a rational, sustainable way.[17] Indeed, the increasing recognition of the critical import-ance of environmental services and of the fact that nature is the true infrastructure of society implies clearly that the environment must be preserved, at least to some significant extent.

The need to integrate economic, social, and environmental policies is a logical out-growth of the foregoing three aspects of sustainable development and is explicit in the first sentence of paragraph 6 of the Copenhagen Declaration, quoted earlier, and in the numerous subsequent repetitions of this language in international instru-ments. It finds further support in paragraph 5 of the 2002 Johannesburg Declaration on Sustainable Development, which states that 'we assume a collective responsibility to advance and strengthen the interdependent and mutually reinforcing pillars of sustainable development—economic development, social development, and envir-onmental protection—at the local, national, regional, and global levels.'[18] Moreover, paragraph 10 of the 2005 World Summit Outcome, referred to earlier, reinforces this responsibility by emphasizing that sustainable development is to be a key element of United Nations activity.

Identification of these core elements, however, does not eliminate significant disagreements about what they imply or require. One important question is what the need to achieve equity—or simply the practical necessities of achieving progress

---

[16] G.A. Res. 2849 (XXVI), UN Doc. A/RES/2848(XXVI) (20 December 1971).

[17] New Delhi Declaration of Principles of International Law Relating to Sustainable Development, 70th Conference of the International Law Association Resolution 3/2002 (2–6 April 2002).

[18] Johannesburg Declaration on Sustainable Development, 4 September 2002, UN Doc. A/CONF. 199/L.6/Rev.2 (2002).

towards sustainable development—requires developed countries to do in terms of assisting developing countries by providing funding, technology, and capacity building. It is well recognized that developing countries, generally speaking, lack the financial and other resources (for example, scientific, technical, regulatory, legal, and institutional resources) needed to make the desired progress towards sustainable development (see Chapter 41 'Technical and Financial Assistance'). This topic arises in virtually every serious international discussion of sustainable development, including in the context of negotiating or implementing multilateral environmental agreements, and is a source of significant North-South tension.

Another critical question involves how to view inter-generational sustainability. Is this a question of 'utility' (in the neo-classical economic sense) or should one instead view this question in terms of the ongoing ability of nature to provide essential environmental services (biological and physical), such as providing sufficient raw material inputs and sufficient capacity to absorb wastes (an approach that some economists refer to as addressing 'throughputs')? The former approach leads to the goal of enabling each future generation to be at least as well off as the present generation with respect to the future generation's utility or happiness as experienced by that generation. The latter approach leads to the goal of enabling future generations to be at least as well off as the present generation with respect to their access to environmental services. How one approaches the question of inter-generational sustainability thus has profound implications. For example, should developed countries restrict themselves to achieving a level and type of resource use that both ensures a good life for their populations and also is within the carrying capacity of the biosphere if generalized to the whole world? And is the current drive for quantitative economic growth through trade and investment liberalization good policy?[19] Our sense is that many economists are intellectually addicted to growth and that economic theory needs to take into account the crucial roles that environmental services perform and the effects that economic growth can have on the biosphere's ability to continue to provide these services.

The generality of the concept of sustainable development raises yet another issue. One could ask whether the concept is so vague as to be meaningless and not of any practical use. The generality of the concept, however, is both inevitable and appropriate because the concept must provide guidance and inspiration to policy-makers while simultaneously being capable of application in a wide variety of contexts, involving different economic realities, ecological conditions, population characteristics, legal systems, cultures, values, and preferences. Indeed, in practice, sustainable development must be tied closely to local conditions. Because of the simultaneous needs for global generality and local specificity, the tools and approaches used by countries and sub-national units in their efforts to achieve sustainable development

[19] See H.E. Daly, *Beyond Growth, The Economics of Sustainable Development* (Boston, MA: Beacon Press, 1998) at 1–3; see also H.E. Daly, *Sustainable Development: Definitions, Principles, Policies*, invited address (Washington, DC: World Bank, 2002).

are of particular importance. The implications of sustainable development for such tools are addressed in section 6 of this chapter, following a discussion of sustainable development's legal status and function (section 4) and its implications for important principles of international environmental law (section 5).

4 LEGAL STATUS AND FUNCTION

Countries, commentators, and courts have taken a variety of positions with respect to the normative status of sustainable development (see Chapter 18 'Different Types of Norms in International Environmental Law: Policies, Principles, and Rules'). Issues relating to the legal status and function of sustainable development can be best assessed by examining its possible status under the three major sources of international law—international agreements, customary international law, and general principles of law (see Chapter 19 'Formation of Customary International Law and General Principles' and Chapter 20 'Treaty Making and Treaty Evolution')—and also by considering its use at the domestic level in municipal law. This chapter addresses each of these in turn.

4.1 International Agreements

When the term 'sustainable development' appears in a binding international agreement, its legal implications depend both on where it appears in the instrument and on the precise text in which it is used. Use of 'sustainable development' in the preamble of an instrument is primarily important for determining the object(s) and purpose(s) of the treaty and in interpreting the treaty. It may carry less normative weight than if identical words were to appear in the operative text of the same instrument. An example of preambular use is the first paragraph of the preamble of the WTO Agreement, which recognizes sustainable development as an objective of the agreement. The WTO Appellate Body used this preambular language as a guide to the interpretation of Article XX(g) of the General Agreement on Tariffs and Trade (GATT), in the 1998 *United States—Import Prohibition of Certain Shrimp and Shrimp Products*.[20] Sustainable development plays a similar role in the preamble of the North American Free Trade Agreement (NAFTA), in which the parties resolve to '[p]romote sustainable development.'[21]

[20] *United States—Import Prohibition of Certain Shrimp and Shrimp Products*, adopted WTO Dispute Settlement Body, 6 November 1998, WTO Appellate Body Report, Doc. WT/DS58/AB/R (1998); and General Agreement on Tariffs and Trade, 30 October 1947, 55 U.N.T.S. 194.
[21] North American Free Trade Agreement, 1 January 1994, 32 I.L.M. 612 (1993).

Sustainable development—or 'sustainability'—is sometimes expressly identified as an 'objective' in the operative text of an international agreement. For example, Article 2 of the UNFCCC states that the objective of the agreement is to stabilize greenhouse gas concentrations in a timeframe allowing 'economic development to proceed in a sustainable manner'; and Article 1 of the CBD states that '[t]he objectives of this Convention . . . are . . . the conservation of biological diversity [and] the sustainable use of its components.' In these instances, the term does not directly create obligations but is of use in identifying the object(s) and purpose(s) of the agreement, in interpreting it, and thus in assessing the consistency of parties' and signatories' actions with respect to it. The effect of using the term 'sustainable development' in this context is thus similar to using it in a preamble. However, in this case, it would be beyond cavil that sustainable development indeed is among the objects and purposes of the agreement, and should be given significant weight in interpreting and applying the provisions of the agreement.

When 'sustainable development' is included as a 'principle' in a binding international agreement, the text may create rights or obligations on the part of the parties, depending on the wording of the text. The fourth principle in Article 3 of the UNFCCC, for example, states that '[t]he Parties have a right to, and should, promote sustainable development.' The use of the word 'right' indicates that parties have a legal right to promote sustainable development. In contrast, the use of 'should' is hortatory and, thus, does not, by itself, impose a legal obligation on parties to promote sustainable development. By definition, the term 'principle' implies a higher normative content than 'objective'. Beyond that, any practical difference between including sustainable development as an 'objective' and including it as a 'principle' may depend primarily on the wording of the provision rather than on its title.

4.2 Customary International Law

The possible status of sustainable development as customary international law is the subject of considerable disagreement (see Chapter 19 'Formation of Customary International Law and General Principles'). This disagreement is related to the fact that numerous international instruments of varying normative status mention sustainable development, often many times in the same instrument and typically (as described earlier) in an important role. Some of these instruments are legally binding, such as the CBD. Others are non-legally binding international declarations, which have been adopted by large numbers of states and sometimes the UNGA. Examples of non-legally binding instruments include the Copenhagen Declaration on Social Development, the Johannesburg Declaration on Sustainable Development, the ILA Sustainable Development Principles, and the 2005 World Summit Outcome, referred to earlier in this chapter. Unless such an instrument purports to be codifying an existing norm of international law, its legal implications can best be understood by considering its relevance to determining whether sustainable development has become, or is in the process of becoming, a norm of customary international law.

In any event, at one end of the spectrum, sustainable development has been identified as nothing more than a global policy, with no normative value. Somewhat further along the spectrum towards sustainable development being a binding legal norm is the view that sustainable development is 'soft law'—that is, a normative statement supported by a political or other commitment and, thus, something more than policy even though it is not legally binding (though it may become binding in the future). An apparently related position—but one that does not use the term 'soft law'—is that sustainable development is more than just a policy goal and that neither the category of non-normative policy statement nor the category of customary international law accurately characterizes sustainable development.[22]

It is not entirely clear where the International Court of Justice (ICJ) stands in this respect. In its decision in the *Case Concerning the Gabčíkovo-Nagymaros Project (Hungary v. Slovakia)*, the ICJ, after referring to new 'norms and standards' that have been developed to deal with the relationship between economic activities and environmental protection, stated that the concept of sustainable development expresses 'the need to reconcile environmental protection and economic development.'[23] Although recognizing sustainable development only as a 'concept', the majority indicated that the concept has substantial relevance. However, they failed to develop the analysis further. This analysis seems to fall short of stating that sustainable development is one of those new norms or standards to which the majority referred.

In the same case, however, Judge Christopher Weeramantry authored a separate opinion in which he stated: 'I consider [sustainable development] to be more than a mere concept, but as a principle with normative value which is crucial to the determination of this case.'[24] Weeramantry also stated that 'the law necessarily contains within itself the principle of reconciliation. That principle is the principle of sustainable development.' He further stated that he considers sustainable development to be 'a part of modern international law by reason not only of its inescapable logical necessity, but also by reason of its wide and general acceptance by the global

[22] See M.-C. Cordonier Segger and A. Khalfan, *Sustainable Development Law Principles, Practices, and Prospects* (Oxford: Oxford University Press, 2004) at 45–6.

[23] *Ibid.* See also *Case Concerning the Gabčíkovo-Nagymaros Project (Hungary v. Slovakia)*, Judgment of 25 September 1997, [1997] I.C.J. Rep. 92 (25 September) at para. 140 [*Gabčíkovo-Nagymaros*]. The court stated: 'Throughout the ages, mankind has, for economic and other reasons, constantly interfered with nature. In the past this was often done without consideration of the effects upon the environment. Owing to new scientific insights and to a growing awareness of the risks for mankind—for present and future generations—of pursuit of such interventions at an unconsidered and unabated pace, new norms and standards have been developed, [and] set forth in a great number of instruments during the last two decades. Such new norms have to be taken into consideration, and such new standards given proper weight, not only when States contemplate new activities, but also when continuing with activities begun in the past. This need to reconcile economic development with protection of the environment is aptly expressed in the concept of sustainable development.' *Ibid.*

[24] *Gabčíkovo-Nagymaros*, see note 23 above, separate opinion of Vice-President, Judge Weeramantry.

community.'[25] Weeramantry appears to consider sustainable development a legal principle of customary international law with an *erga omnes* character and, thus, is at the other end of the spectrum from those who consider sustainable development to be only a policy, with no normative content.[26]

Vaughn Lowe has stated that sustainable development law describes a group of congruent norms, which can be analysed as a 'metaprinciple, acting upon other legal rules and principles—a legal concept exercising a kind of interstitial normativity, pushing and pulling the boundaries of true primary norms when they threaten to overlap or conflict with each other.'[27] The precise role of this 'metaprinciple' is unclear (as is how it came into existence); but in terms of its function, it may be similar to the customary international law norm to act in good faith, which is relevant in several different contexts (for example, cooperation, negotiation, and dispute settlement) and which is highly fact-dependent in its application.

Although Lowe's reference to 'true primary norms' suggests that the sustainable development metaprinciple is somehow different than other customary international law norms, he does not say that clearly. Thus, unless Lowe is positing an entirely new type of international law (which he does not claim to do), the sustainable development metaprinciple seems to be best understood as a norm of customary international law.

The role of the metaprinciple might be somewhat similar to that of a preamble to an agreement (described earlier). Like preambular language, a metaprinciple helps in clarifying appropriate objectives and in interpreting norms, particularly when they threaten to overlap or conflict with one another. The reference to 'overlap or conflict' also brings to mind the principle of integration, discussed later in this chapter, because the principle of sustainable development surely favours reconciliation over conflict, as in the idea that trade and environmental protection can (and should) be mutually supportive. It does seem clear that Lowe's use of 'interstitial' does not refer simply to filling gaps in the legal structure because of the reference to (gap-less) situations in which existing norms threaten to overlap or conflict. It is possible that Lowe's and Weeramantry's views are quite similar. Weeramantry refers to reconciliation, which could apply in a situation of possible overlap or conflict, and of the desirability of avoiding 'normative anarchy,' which is reminiscent of Lowe's goal of avoiding conflict.

[25] *Ibid.*

[26] Judge Christopher G. Weeramantry, vice-president of the International Court of Justice, *Sustainable Development: An Ancient Concept Recently Revived*, invited address at the United Nations Environment Programme's Global Judges Symposium on Sustainable Development and the Role of Law, Johannesburg, South Africa, 19 August 2002.

[27] Vaughn Lowe, 'Sustainable Development and Unsustainable Arguments,' in A. Boyle and D. Freestone, eds., *International Law and Sustainable Development: Past Achievements and Future Challenges* (Oxford: Oxford University Press, 1999) 19 at 30–1.

4.3 General Principles of Law Recognized by Major Legal Systems

General principles of law, as this category is most commonly understood by international lawyers, are principles that are widely shared among states representing major legal systems around the globe (see Article 38 of the ICJ Statute). The key question, therefore, is whether and how the concept of sustainable development has been embraced by states' domestic laws.

Sustainable development has been incorporated into municipal (domestic) law of some states, such as Australia and Canada (see section 4.4 later in this chapter). The number and range of states that incorporate sustainable development in their domestic legislation, however, is not yet sufficient for this concept as such to have reached the level of a general principle of law under Article 38 of the ICJ Statute. It is possible, however, that some of the principles related to sustainable development may have such wide recognition that they have become general principles of law. For example, as discussed in section 5, precaution is an inevitable and essential element of all domestic regulatory regimes aimed at protecting health, safety, and the environment. Although details may vary from country to country as to, for example, the burden of proof, the standard of proof and the technical methodology in assessing new chemicals or foods, it most probably is the case that it is a general principle of law, within the meaning of Article 38 of the ICJ Statute, that a country may regulate in the face of scientific uncertainty where the risk to the environment (or health or safety) is serious.

There is yet no definitive judicial or arbitral ruling on this question or on the status of precaution as customary international law, however. For example, in *EC Measures Concerning Meat and Meat Products (Hormones)*, the Appellate Body declined to take a position: 'The status of the precautionary principle in international law continues to be the subject of debate among academics, law practitioners, regulators and judges . . . We consider . . . that it is unnecessary, and probably imprudent for the Appellate Body in this appeal to take a position on this important, but abstract question.'[28] Alternatively, in *Southern Bluefin Tuna (New Zealand v. Japan; Australia v. Japan)* (Order), the International Tribunal for the Law of the Sea (ITLOS) seems to have based its ruling on the precautionary principle. The tribunal, in light of scientific uncertainty, ruled that the parties 'should act with prudence and caution to ensure that effective conservation measures are taken to prevent serious harm to the stock of southern bluefin tuna (see Chapter 25 'Precaution').[29]

---

[28] *EC Measures Concerning Meat and Meat Products (Hormones)*, Apellate Body Report, WTO Doc. 98-0099, WTO Doc. WT/DS26/AB/R, and WTO Doc. WT/DS48/AB/R (AB-1997–4). See also *EC Biotechnology (GMOs)*, Interim Panel Report, para. 7.87 (2006).

[29] *Southern Bluefin Tuna cases* (Provisional Measures), 38 I.L.M. 1624 (1999) at para. 77.

4.4 Sustainable Development in Municipal (Domestic) Law

On the national level, the concept of sustainable development as the integration of environmental concerns with all other policy areas is usually formulated as a procedural rule to be applied by legislative and administrative bodies. This approach, for example, has been adopted in those states that utilize the tools identified in section 6 of this chapter, such as environmental impact assessments (for example, the United States's practice of conducting environmental assessments of prospective free trade agreements) and natural resource accounts.

Some countries have also expressly included sustainable development as a substantive requirement in their domestic law. In Australia, for example, the term 'sustainable development' has been written into domestic statutory law. The National Environment Protection Council Act states that 'the concept of ecologically sustainable development should be used by all levels of Government in the assessment of natural resources, land use decisions and approval processes.'[30] In addition, Australia's Environment Protection and Biodiversity Conservation Act states that wildlife conservation plans must minimize 'any significant adverse social and economic impacts, consistently with the principles of ecologically sustainable development.'[31] The Canadian Environmental Protection Act also includes sustainable development in several sections. For example, the preamble states: '[T]he Government of Canada seeks to achieve sustainable development that is based on an ecologically efficient use of natural, social and economic resources and acknowledges the need to integrate environmental, economic and social factors in the making of all decisions by government and private entities.'[32]

Sustainable development may also influence domestic law even when it is not explicitly mentioned in a statute. For example, the United States National Environmental Policy Act recognizes 'the critical importance of restoring and maintaining environmental quality to the overall welfare and development of man, [and] declares . . . to use all practicable means and measures, including financial and technical assistance, in a manner calculated to foster and promote the general welfare, to create and maintain conditions under which man and nature can exist in productive harmony, and fulfill the social, economic, and other requirements of present and future generations of Americans.'[33] While this statute, which antedated UNCED by

[30] National Environment Protection Council Act, 1994 (Australia).

[31] Environment Protection and Biodiversity Conservation Act, 1999 (Australia).

[32] Canadian Environmental Protection Act, 1999, ch. 33 (Canada). The statute reads: 'An Act respecting pollution prevention and the protection of the environment and human health in order to contribute to sustainable development.' The declaration also states: 'It is hereby declared that the protection of the environment is essential to the well-being of Canadians and that the primary purpose of this Act is to contribute to sustainable development through pollution prevention' (*ibid*).

[33] National Environmental Policy Act, § 101, 42 U.S.C. § 4331 (1969).

two decades, does not include the term 'sustainable development', it embodies the concepts of inter-generational equity and of integrating social and economic development with protection of the environment.

5 IMPLICATIONS FOR PRINCIPLES OF INTERNATIONAL ENVIRONMENTAL LAW

The concept of sustainable development has implications for key concepts in international environmental law, including integration, equity and the duty to cooperate, precaution, good governance, and prior informed consent for local communities. These concepts are considered in the following section.

5.1 Integration

Perhaps the most important implication of the concept of sustainable development is its focus on a holistic approach to policies that may affect development and environment. Sustainable development is based, to some degree, on the interdependence of the biosphere (that is, the connective layers of earth, water, and air on which life depends), of human endeavours *inter se*, and of human activities and nature. Taking account of these interdependencies requires integrating a wide variety of factors. Indeed, as described in section 3 earlier in this chapter, integration of economic, social, and environmental policies is one of the core elements of sustainable development. The principle of integration thus highlights the need for policy-makers to take into account the interdependencies and importance of nature, to be inclusive and comprehensive in their analyses, and to consider the impacts and implications of proposed policies. Principle 4 of the Rio Declaration expresses this concern as follows: 'In order to achieve sustainable development, environmental protection shall constitute an integral part of the development process and cannot be considered in isolation from it.' The principle of integration thus emanates from sustainable development.

The principles of good governance and of prior informed consent by communities, described immediately below, are examples of developments that reflect the principle of integration.

Sustainable development requires governance free of official corruption. Corruption often interferes with efforts to achieve all core aspects of sustainable development (both intra- and inter-generational equity, environmental protection, and sound policy integration). For example, public resources may go to a few relatively well-off officials or their families instead of being used for the public good; projects may be selected for their potential to generate bribes rather than for their potential to further the public good; less-efficient contractors may be chosen resulting in waste and inefficiency; and environmental regulations may not be enacted or enforced. Attention to sustainable development and the need to integrate relevant policies were most probably factors leading to the recent flood of anti-corruption treaties (for example, the Inter-American Convention against Corruption, the Convention on the Fight against Corruption Involving Officials of the European Communities or Officials of Member States of the European Union, the Council of Europe Criminal Law Convention on Corruption and the Council of Europe Civil Law Convention on Corruption, the OECD Convention on Combating Bribery of Foreign Public Officials in International Business Transactions, and the United Nations Convention against Corruption) and corresponding municipal legislation (often building on the 1978 US Foreign Corrupt Practices Act). As a result of this spate of activities, the principle of good governance may be an emerging norm of customary international law.

Achieving sustainable development requires that natural resources be used in an equitable and sustainable manner. International human rights norms require that those affected by decisions have a right to express their views during the decision-making process. Consistent with the principle of integration, these have been integrated into a requirement that local communities (including, but not limited to, indigenous communities) have both the right to participate in any decisions that will affect them, including decisions affecting the resources on which they depend, and substantive rights (referred to as community-based property rights) to such resources, the content of which depends both on international human rights norms and local law and custom. Even apart from the issue of equity, the role that these communities play is critically important to achieving sustainable development, *inter alia*, because of the frequent need to involve them in protecting natural resources, and because of the knowledge they possess from traditional practices. This has become a particularly important issue in the context of creating protected areas, the CBD (Article 8(j), regarding access to genetic resources), the World Intellectual Property Organization (regarding genetic resources, traditional knowledge, and folklore), and the International Bank for Reconstruction and Development (World Bank, under the rubric 'broad community support'), and it may be relevant to other activities and institutions as well, including the clean development mechanism under the Kyoto Protocol to the UNFCCC (which requires project proponents and the approval body to invite and consider the comments of stakeholders, including individuals, groups, or communities affected, or likely to be affected, by the proposed project activity). There may be an emerging international norm of prior informed consent (sometimes also referred to as free, prior informed consent) in this context, and, in any event, its effective implementation will be critical to achieving sustainable development in many situations.

5.2 Equity and the Duty to Cooperate

The principles of inter-generational and intra-generational equity are core elements of sustainable development and, in fact, have emanated in part from—or in tandem with—this concept (see Chapter 27 'Equity'). Many international instruments refer to inter-generational and intra-generational equity, such as the UNFCCC and the CBD as well as the widely accepted definition of sustainable development in the Brundtland Commission report, quoted earlier. Inter-generational equity, even if its generality makes it difficult to apply in concrete situations, at least requires that some good faith effort be made to consider the interests of future generations. Intra-generational equity likewise requires that the possible impact of policies and decisions on the poor be taken into consideration. Inter- and intra-generational equity thus have implications with respect to the assessment of environmental and other impacts, as discussed in section 6.

A particularly thorny equity issue has to do with equity between developed and developing countries. This issue is not a core element of sustainable development, which is concerned with equity between generations and between individuals, rather than between countries. Nevertheless, the North-South context played an important part in the negotiations leading up to the 1992 Earth Summit and the multilateral environmental treaties (MEAs) adopted at the summit and thereafter. The North-South context, moreover, has important practical implications for sustainable development. Whether sufficient effective assistance is forthcoming from developed countries and whether developing countries make appropriate use of assistance will be very important in determining progress towards sustainable development (see Chapter 41 'Technical and Financial Assistance').

The North-South context has, in particular, given rise to the principle of common but differentiated responsibilities (CBDR), which is now reflected in virtually all multilateral environmental agreements (MEAs). The principle of CBRD can be regarded as a further specification of the duty to cooperate as contained in, among other instruments, the Rio Declaration. Principle 7 of the Rio Declaration states: 'States shall cooperate in a spirit of global partnership to conserve, protect and restore the health and integrity of the Earth's ecosystem. In view of the different contributions to global environmental degradation, States have common but differentiated responsibilities.' This principle—which is directly related to equity between countries and, practically, though not necessarily theoretically, related to intra-generational equity—takes into account each state's contribution to the creation of environmental problems in connection with its ability to prevent, control, and reduce them. The first aspect—the duty to cooperate—is well established in international law (see, for example, Articles 55 and 56 of the Charter of the United Nations), and applies at the global, regional, and bilateral levels. The second aspect—CBDR—as mentioned, is included in most MEAs to achieve equity and encourage universal participation. CBDR takes various forms, including different standards or commitments for developed countries and for developing and economy-in-transition countries, delayed compliance for developing and economy-in-transition countries, and commitments to transfer financial and other resources from developed to developing and economy-in-transition countries (see Chapter 41 'Technical and Financial Assistance').

The implementation of CBDR, thus, is not only crucial to the attainment of sustainable development but also has affected the nature of the obligation to cooperate in international environmental law. For developing countries, sustainable development, through CBDR, has conditioned the duty to cooperate upon the receipt of financial and technological assistance, and, for developed states, it has broadened the duty to cooperate to include the commitment to transfer financial and technological assistance. An example of the former is a provision contained in many MEAs that stipulates: '[T]he extent to which developing country Parties will effectively implement their commitments under the Convention will depend on the effective implementation by developed country Parties of their commitments under the Convention related to financial resources and technology.'[34]

5.3 Precaution

All states have the duty to protect the environment and thus prevent harm to the environment, a principle contained in Principle 21 of the Stockholm Declaration and Principle 2 of the Rio Declaration and recognized by the ICJ in its advisory opinion in *Legality of the Use of Nuclear Weapons*.[35] Prevention remains the point of departure in international environmental law. However, in case of scientific uncertainty, states may be faced with the duty to adopt precautionary policies or measures (see Chapter 26 'Precaution'). While the nature of what might be appropriate measures in such a context often is contentious, sustainable development, based on equitable considerations as discussed in the previous section, also has affected what such measures might legitimately entail in a developing or an economy-in-transition state.

Given the prevalence of scientific uncertainty, precaution, which is often also referred to as the 'precautionary principle' or the 'precautionary approach', now is one of the most commonly encountered concepts in international environmental

---

[34] See UN Framework Convention on Climate Change, Article 4.
[35] *Legality of the Threat or Use of Nuclear Weapons*, Advisory Opinion, 8 July 1996, [1996] I.C.J. Rep. 226.

law. Some countries oppose referring to precaution as a 'principle', however, because of a concern that it could easily disguise trade protectionism. Precaution is thus one of the most controversial concepts of sustainable development. Precaution also is an essential part of all municipal (domestic) systems for protecting health, safety, and the environment. This is because regulators seldom, if ever, possess all the scientific and other information they need and want, but they nevertheless have to make decisions one way or another—they must make decisions in the face of uncertainty. The exercise of precaution is thus critical to protecting the environment in the face of competing demands and is one of the core elements of sustainable development.

The concept of precaution is articulated in many international instruments, including binding international agreements such as the CBD and the Cartagena Protocol on Biosafety, as well as the UNFCCC. The most commonly used definition is found in Principle 15 of the Rio Declaration: '[i]n order to protect the environment, the precautionary approach shall be widely applied by States according to their capabilities. Where there are threats of serious or irreversible damage, lack of full scientific certainty shall not be used as a reason for postponing cost-effective measures to prevent environmental degradation.' By virtue of the term 'according to their capabilities,' Principle 15 links precaution to CBDR and thus, more directly, to sustainable development. If capabilities are limited in terms of scientific knowledge or technical or financial capabilities, which is likely to be the case in developing and economy-in-transition countries, thresholds for precautionary action may be lower. As a result of the need for developed countries to transfer financial and technological resources to developing and economy-in-transition countries, the latter countries are to some extent dependent on the former countries in how they implement precaution. Moreover, if capabilities are strong, as is likely to be the case in developed countries, the definition of precaution implies that stronger measures should be taken. The concept of sustainable development thus implies that implementing precaution may entail different consequences in dissimilar contexts, and it may thus have profound implications for what may be considered appropriate precautionary policies and measures in a given context. The manner in which precaution is defined and applied in these different contexts in the future will be significant both in determining success in achieving sustainable development and in elaborating its substantive content.

6 IMPLICATIONS FOR TOOLS OF INTERNATIONAL ENVIRONMENTAL LAW

Various tools and approaches have been used to pursue sustainable development. Generally speaking, these tools help gather needed information, set priorities, understand inter-relationships, build credibility and support, and improve implementation and monitoring of sustainable development policies and laws. As a result, all tools used to pursue the protection of the environment, such as, for example, corporate responsibility mechanisms (see Chapter 21 'Private and Quasi-Private Standard Setting'), transparency, public participation and access to justice (see discussion later in this chapter), impact assessment tools, education, and monitoring and verification (see Chapter 42 'Monitoring and Verification'), can support the attainment of sustainable development. Sustainable development, however, has had significant consequences for how and where these tools are utilized and has made their proper use a matter of international concern.

Education offers a pertinent example. Its importance to attaining sustainable development was emphasized by the Decade of Education for Sustainable Development, which was proposed at the WSSD in 2002 and proclaimed by the UNGA to comprise the period between 2005 and 2014.[36] Education is a primary instrument of change towards sustainable development because it is essential to individual and societal capacity building. Public education, in particular, fosters values, actions, and lifestyles that are required to achieve a sustainable future, which often involves changes in the behaviour of individuals, business, non-governmental organizations (NGOs), intergovernmental institutions, and governments. The UN Educational, Scientific, and Cultural Organization has emphasized that the 'education and full and equal engagement of women and girls is crucial to ensuring balanced and relevant Education of Sustainable Development messages and to providing the best chance for changed behaviors for sustainable development in the next generation.'[37] In the remainder of this section of the chapter, we discuss by way of example two sets of tools (transparency, public participation, and access to justice and impact assessment and accounting techniques) to illustrate how sustainable development has affected the tools associated with environmental law.

6.1 Transparency, Public Participation, and Access to Justice

Transparency, public participation, and access to justice have been and will remain crucial instruments at the national level of decision-making for attaining sustainable development. They allow for the active engagement of individuals and civil society organizations in providing information and other input with respect to all aspects of sustainable development. They are particularly critical tools because of the importance of integrating local aspects into decisions regarding sustainable development.

---

[36] G.A. Res. 57/254, UN Doc. A/RES/57/254 (21 February 2003) at paras. 1–2.
[37] See generally United Nations Educational, Scientific and Cultural Organization (UNESCO), Education for Sustainable Development (United Nations Decade 2005–14), *Gender Equality* (Paris: UNESCO, 2006).

Moreover, as Principle 10 of the Rio Declaration, the Convention on Access to Information, Public Participation in Decision-making and Access to Justice in Environmental Matters (Aarhus Convention), and the 1994 Draft Declaration of Principles on Human Rights and the Environment (see Chapter 28 'Environmental Rights') illustrate, their use at the national level has become a matter of concern at the international level of decision-making (see Chapter 29 'Public Participation').

Sustainable development, however, also has resulted in the enhanced importance of these tools at the international level of decision-making, *per se*. This development is particularly evident in those situations where international institutions, such as development banks, make decisions regarding projects to be executed in developing and economy-in-transition countries (see Chapter 32 'International Institutions'). Since such projects may have considerable impacts on individuals and groups in society, their participation in decision-making regarding relevant projects becomes important both at the national level and at the international level of decision-making. This point can be illustrated with reference to the World Bank, which has adopted Operational Policy/Bank Procedure (OP/BP) 4.01 on Environmental Impact Assessment. OP/BP 4.01 determines, among other things, that project-affected groups and local NGOs are to be involved in the environmental impact assessments that are to be conducted for projects carried out with the assistance of the World Bank. While these assessments are carried out within the state concerned, their outcome directly affects decision-making at the international level—in this case, project-related decisions of the World Bank. Moreover, NGOs and representatives of civil society participate in international meetings as observers and in consultations regarding individual projects (see Chapter 33 'Non-Governmental Organizations and Civil Society').

In addition, the establishment of the World Bank Inspection Panel illustrates a similar development with respect to access to justice, albeit a procedure that involves a quasi-judicial process. In this case, communities or groups of at least two individuals may submit a complaint against the World Bank, alleging that they have suffered or are likely to suffer harm as a result of the World Bank not abiding by its own internal rules, such as OP/BP 4.01.

Sustainable development, due to its focus on integration and the links that it establishes between individuals, states, and international institutions, through, for example, the need for poverty alleviation, good governance, and environment and development, thus has changed the nature of transparency, public participation, and access to justice. The use of these instruments, while originally conceived as of concern to individual states, has become a matter of international concern. Moreover, such tools are now also being employed at the international level of decision-making—that is, to decisions taken by international institutions. The Almaty Guidelines in Promoting the Application of the Principles of the Aarhus Convention in International Forums, which were adopted by the parties to the Aarhus Convention, also illustrate this point[38]—access to information and public participation are a matter of concern at the international level, *per se*.

6.2 Impact Assessment and Accounting Techniques

The concept of sustainable development also has crucially affected the nature of impact assessments and the accounting techniques used in such assessments and other valuations. Principle 17 of the Rio Declaration refers to the need to conduct environmental impact assessments (EIA) in the following terms: EIAs 'shall be undertaken for proposed activities that are likely to have a significant adverse impact on the environment and are subject to a decision of a competent national authority.' Principle 17 as well as the Convention on Environmental Impact Assessment in a Transboundary Context illustrate that EIAs and the manner in which they are conducted are a matter of concern to the international community, as are transparency, public participation, and access to justice. As already discussed in the previous section, EIAs are also conducted in those cases where international institutions, such as the World Bank, are involved in decision-making and are thus relevant at the international level of decision-making, *per se*.

The scope of EIAs, however, also has been influenced profoundly by sustainable development, extending their scope to global impacts and international agreements. In the United States, for example, Executive Order 13141 and its Guidelines for Implementation require assessment and consideration of the environmental impacts—including the global impacts in some circumstances—of trade agreements.[39]

Sustainable development also has had far-reaching consequences for the nature of the assessments to be conducted and the methods of accounting to be used in conducting impact assessments and other valuations. In essence, these consequences amount to both a broadening of the issues to be considered in the assessment, to issues other than environmental consequences, and to the introduction of new accounting techniques. A relevant example of the former is the process of sustainability assessment; a relevant example of the latter is natural resources accounting.

Sustainability assessment is a process designed to enable policy-makers to engage in integrated decision-making on projects, plans, policies, and programmes. Sustainability assessments differ from EIAs because they address social and economic as well as environmental outcomes. Ideally, sustainability assessments are

---

[38] Almaty Guidelines in Promoting the Application of the Principles of the Aarhus Convention in International Forums, Annex to Decision II/4, *Report of the Second Meeting of the Parties*, Doc. ECE/MP.PP/2005/2/Add.5 (20 June 2005).

[39] See Executive Order No. 13141, 64 Fed. Reg. 63, 169 (18 November 1999).

characterized by an integrative approach to improving social, economic, and environmental outcomes and increased information resulting from the identification of relevant social issues. Efforts are currently underway to identify sustainable development criteria, and conduct pilot projects because sustainability assessments remain primarily aspirational due to difficulties in integrating environmental, social, and economic aspects. An interesting example of a framework for conducting sustainability assessments are the CBD's *Akwé: Kon Guidelines*, which outline best practices for conducting environmental, cultural, and social impact assessments.[40]

Sustainable development also has given rise to the recognition that the accounting techniques used, in order to be accurate, need to reflect the use of natural assets in addition to produced capital consumption.[41] Conventional accounting procedures such as gross domestic product, however, focus solely on the measurement of economic performance and growth as reflected in market activity and disregard essential factors such as the depletion of natural resources, thus failing to provide policy-makers and the public with the complete picture.[42] Natural resource accounting does include such factors (often in non-monetized form), and thus provides a more comprehensive assessment of the sustainability of growth and development by displaying both positive and negative changes in the environment over the period in question, including the full impact resulting from the depletion and degradation of natural capital (for example, changes in the extent of forest cover).

Natural resource accounting also avoids some of the problems associated with cost-benefit analysis (also referred to as benefit-cost analysis), a widely used, and sometimes legally mandated, methodology for evaluating the economic feasibility of a proposed policy, programme, or project (hereinafter referred to jointly as a project). In a cost-benefit analysis, the projected benefits and costs of a project over time are calculated and compared. In theory, this comparison indicates whether the project will reap more benefits than it will cost, and which projects among several alternatives will reap the largest gains as well as the relative importance of, and relationship between, relevant variables. In practice, however, cost-benefit analysis encounters serious problems. For example, it is very difficult, if not impossible, to accurately assign economic values to the social and environmental impacts of a project. Many of these impacts are, by their nature, non-monetary or non-quantifiable, at least not in any reasonably accurate way—for example, how much is a human life, an ecosystem, a species, a view of a mountain range, or a national park worth in monetary terms, both now and in the future? Similarly, how should the myriad of environmental services (for example, air and water purification, provision of food, pollination of plants, prevention of erosion, provision of shade and windbreaks, provision of fuel, and

---

[40] See *Akwé: Kon Guidelines* (Montreal: Secretariat of the Convention on Biological Diversity, 2004).

[41] United Nations Department of Economics and Social Affairs Statistics Division and United Nations Environment Programme Economics and Trade Unit Division of Technology, Industry and Economics, *Integrated Environmental and Economic Accounting: An Operational Manual*, UN Doc. ST/ESA/STAT/SER.F/78 (2000).   [42] *Ibid.*

recreation) be valued? Other difficult questions include how should externalities be taken into account; how should distributional issues be calculated and considered; what discount rate should be used to convert future costs and benefits into present value; and how should the values that future generations will place on specific items or services be calculated. It is expected that sustainability assessment processes and natural resource accounting methodology will address some of these problems.

7 CONCLUSIONS

Sustainable development, which was adopted by the international community in 1992 as the paradigm, but not a legal norm, for improving the quality of life for people around the world, has had profound effects on international environmental law. While significant differences and uncertainties remain regarding its precise meaning and legal status, its four core elements are clear: inter-generational equity; intra-generational equity; the need to protect the environment; and the need to integrate economic, social, and environmental policies. It is also clear that the concept of sustainable development has not only expressly appeared in many international environmental instruments (both legally binding and non-legally binding) but has also affected both international environmental law principles and the tools used to implement these principles.

With respect to principles, sustainable development has significantly altered the content of the duty to cooperate, for both developing and developed states, through the principle of CBDR. Similarly, sustainable development has affected the duty to protect the environment in the face of scientific uncertainty and thus precaution. In the case of developing countries, for example, the content of precaution is dependent both on their capabilities and on the extent to which developed states transfer financial and technical assistance to developing states in order to enhance those capabilities. Sustainable development thus has further contextualized both the duty to cooperate and the notion of precaution.

At the level of tools, sustainable development has resulted in such tools and their use at the national level now being of concern to the international community *per se* as well as fostered the use of these instruments at the international level. The concept of sustainable development also has had profound effects on the nature of the impact assessments and accounting processes. In particular, it has resulted in broadening their scope both geographically and with respect to the elements assessed, to include social and economic considerations as well as environmental ones, and thus facilitate a more holistic assessment of the projects or activities concerned. How sustainable development has had these effects—whether as a non-normative policy, as soft law, as a reconciling norm of customary international law (as submitted by Judge

Christopher Weeramantry), as a 'metaprinciple' to avoid conflict (as submitted by Vaughn Lowe), or simply through the normative power of the actual—will probably remain the subject of debate among lawyers for many years.

Recommended Reading

A. Boyle and D. Freestone, eds., *International Law and Sustainable Development: Past Achievements and Future Challenges* (Oxford: Oxford University Press, 1999).

M.-C. Cordonier Segger and A. Khalfan, *Sustainable Development Law: Principles, Practices, and Prospects* (Oxford: Oxford University Press, 2004).

D. Magraw, 'Legal Treatment of Developing Countries: Differential, Contextual and Absolute Norms' (1990) 1 Colo. J. Int'l L. & Pol'y 69.

Millennium Ecosystem Assessment, *Ecosystems and Human Well-Being: Synthesis* (Washington, DC: Island Press, 2005).

H.E. Daly, *Beyond Growth: The Economics of Sustainable Development* (Boston, MA: Beacon Press, 1998).

CHAPTER 27

EQUITY

DINAH SHELTON

1 INTRODUCTION

In 1997, the United States Senate voted ninety-seven to zero in favour of a resolution stating that the United States should not join any agreement on climate change that would require the industrialized countries to reduce their greenhouse gas emissions, unless the agreement imposed similar obligations on developing country parties. In March 2001, President George W. Bush rejected the Kyoto Protocol, which did indeed establish targets and timetables for developed countries but not for developing ones. Whatever the impact of the Senate resolution on the US rejection of the Kyoto Protocol, the resolution implicitly suggested to the administration and the public that a climate change agreement that failed to treat states parties in an equal manner was discriminatory and thus unfair. If such perceptions of fairness or equity do indeed impact the level of participation and positive action among heterogeneous states, then they are likely to factor in the long-term success of an environmental regime or agreement. To assess the potential impact of equity on international environmental law, this chapter examines the various meanings attributed to the term equity in international law generally and in international environmental law in particular; the roles equity has played in multilateral environmental agreements; and how different equitable principles are, or may be, implemented in practice.

2 DIFFERENT MEANINGS OF EQUITY

Equity has many different meanings, and the precise nature of the concept is obscure. In international law equity is often used as a synonym for fairness or justice. Thomas Franck, for example, considers equity as subsumed in the concept of fairness, which in his view has both procedural and substantive dimensions.[1] The procedural aspect is concerned with reaching decisions by the 'right process', while the substantive dimension aims at distributive justice.[2]

The procedural and substantive dimensions of equity are often perceived as interrelated, based on the assumption that fairer proceedings lead to fairer outcomes.[3] The concept of environmental justice, for example, seeks to ensure procedural equity through decision-making based on relevant criteria, and with the participation of those affected in order to produce outcomes that treat all affected groups fairly. The

---

[1] T. Franck, *Fairness in International Law and Institutions* (Oxford: Clarendon Press, 1995) at 7–9.

[2] *Ibid.* at 7.

[3] Franck, *ibid*, who argues that the two dimensions are more likely to be in tension because procedural fairness favours stability and order while distributive justice strives for change to achieve a fair outcome.

environmental justice movement has emerged as a result of correlations found, within some countries, of race and poverty with the allocation of environmental burdens, in particular when and where minority communities have been systematically excluded from decision-making processes to determine the distribution of environmental risks. For example, in 1983, the US General Accounting Office investigated the demographics of communities around hazardous waste landfills and found that three out of four waste sites were located in minority communities predominately composed of poor persons.[4] Another seminal study by Robert Bullard concluded that, within the United States, race is the factor of highest correlation between environmental burdens and groups.[5] Overcoming traditional exclusion or under-representation of affected groups in the decision-making process (procedural fairness) is expected to produce greater equity in the allocation of benefits and harm (distributive justice).

At the international level, some developing countries argue that they too are bearing a disproportionate environmental burden due to the export of pollution from wealthier countries, while they are unable to share in the benefits derived from the activities producing the pollution. While developing states have the legal right to exercise their sovereignty to exclude hazardous enterprises, waste, and products, in practice they often lack clean substitutes or the material and human resources necessary to enforce their environmental laws or to reject foreign investment activities that are harmful to the environment. In addition, some of these countries assert that they may be injured by future climate change to which they have largely not contributed, and which is due to industrial and other processes from which they have not benefited. In their view, it is equitable for the cost of cleanup or reduction of pollution to be borne by those who were responsible for creating the problems.

In addition to concerns about the equity of general rules (including whether they comport with notions of distributive and retributive justice), equity also relates to law in the sense of providing individualized justice. In this perspective, the relationship between equity and law is rooted in an Aristotelian understanding of the limits of positive law. Law is intended to be stable, coherent, and transparent, allowing those bound by it to foresee the legal consequences of their actions. Law is also intended to apply to all of its subjects without discrimination, which implies treating like cases alike and dissimilar situations in ways that take account of relevant differences. However, law-makers can never anticipate all future circumstances, and must enact the law in general terms. Law-makers also may disagree over what constitutes relevant differences when formulating laws. Subsequent unforeseen events may show gaps in the law, or enforcement may produce a decision contrary to the original

---

[4] See US General Accounting Office, *Siting of Hazardous Waste Landfills and Their Correlation with Racial and Economic Status of Surrounding Communities*, Doc. GAO/RCED-83–168 (1983); see also G. Torres, 'Environmental Justice: The Legal Meaning of a Social Movement' (1998) 15 J. L. & Com. 597.

[5] R.D. Bullard, *Dumping in Dixie: Race, Class and Environmental Quality* (Boulder, CO: Westview Press, 1990).

purpose of the law. Equity thus allows for exceptional adjustments or correctives to fulfil the underlying and overarching purpose for which the law was adopted by affording individualized justice (equity *contra legem*). Equity in this understanding also may provide a basis for decision in the absence of law or when it is necessary to fill in gaps in existing norms, such as when new issues emerge that give rise to disputes (equity *praeter legem*). Finally, the law itself may choose equity as the rule of decision (for example, delimitation of some maritime boundaries), especially when different circumstances among subjects of the law necessitate differential treatment (equity *infra legem*).[6]

In international law, an additional issue arises. Do considerations of equity arise at the inter-state level, involve individuals, or are they relevant with respect to both states and individuals? In international law and the law regarding sustainable development, in particular, two principles have been developed that seek to infuse a greater degree of fairness among individuals and states, both present and future. These are the principles of intra-generational equity and inter-generational equity.

2.1 Intra-Generational Equity

Intra-generational equity aims to assure justice among human beings that are alive today. International human rights law sets the minimum standards of treatment in the civil, political, economic, social, and cultural realms, but it also recognizes that the exercise of rights cannot be absolute because each person's rights will collide with the rights of others (see Chapter 28 'Environmental Rights'). Article 29 of the Universal Declaration of Human Rights incorporates the equitable principle of abuse of rights in foreseeing that one's exercise of rights may be limited to secure the rights and freedoms of others. In the field of environmental protection, states and the international community must fairly allocate and regulate scarce resources to ensure that the benefits of environmental resources, the costs associated with protecting them, and any degradation that occurs (that is, all the benefits and burdens) are equitably shared by all members of society. In this regard, equity is an application of the principle of distributive justice, which is discussed below, as it seeks to reconcile competing social and economic policies in order to obtain the fair sharing of resources.

The term 'sustainable development' can also be seen as encompassing an international understanding of intra-generational (as well as inter-generational) equity in its effort to strike a fair balance between the often conflicting goals of economic development and environmental protection (see Chapter 26 'Sustainable

---

[6] M. Akehurst, 'Equity and General Principles of Law' (1976) 25 Int'l & Comp. L.Q. 801.

Development'). Indeed, many of the principles in the Rio Declaration on Environment and Development reflect this balance as well as other aspects of intra-generational equity, such as a concern for the least well-off in society. Principle 6, for example, mandates particular priority for the special situation and needs of developing countries, particularly the least developed and those most environmentally vulnerable.

2.2 Inter-Generational Equity

Inter-generational equity is based on the recognition of two key facts: (1) that human life emerged from, and is dependent upon, the Earth's natural resource base, including its ecological processes, and is thus inseparable from environmental conditions; and (2) that human beings have a unique capacity to alter the environment upon which life depends. From these facts emerges the notion that humans that are alive today have a special obligation as custodians or trustees of the planet to maintain its integrity to ensure the survival of the human species. Those living have received a heritage from their forbearers in which they have beneficial rights of use that are limited by the interests and needs of future generations. This limitation requires each generation to maintain the corpus of the trust and pass it on in no worse condition than it was received. Another way to consider the issue is to view current environmental goods, wealth, and technology as owing to the progress of prior generations. This debt cannot be discharged backward so it is projected forward and discharged in the present on behalf of the future.

The concept of trust involves understanding the relationships between the trust corpus, the trustees and beneficiaries, and the obligations imposed on the latter. Generally, these obligations require conserving and maintaining the trust resources, thus placing constraints on the present generation of beneficiaries. Meeting the obligation does not mean that no change is possible, but it does call for minimizing or avoiding long-term and irreversible damage to the environment. The implications of the principle of inter-generational equity are three: first, that each generation is required to conserve the diversity of the natural and cultural resource base so that it does not unduly restrict the options available to future generations to satisfy their own values and needs. Second, the quality of ecological processes passed on should be comparable to that enjoyed by the present generation. Third, the past and present cultural and natural heritage should be conserved so that future generations will have access to it. These rights and obligations derive from a notion of human society that extends beyond the totality of the current planetary population, giving it a temporal dimension. In fact, the idea of cultural rights is one that has long carried with it a concept of community over time. What is new is the application of this idea to natural resources.

In the international environmental law context, the 1972 Stockholm Declaration on the Human Environment enunciated the principle of 'a solemn responsibility to protect and improve the environment for present and future generations' (Principle 1). The principle has also been incorporated in many environmental agreements since that time. The 1997 International Atomic Energy Agency's Joint Convention on the Safety of Spent Fuel Management and on the Safety of Radioactive Waste Management provides an example. Article 4 of this convention obliges states parties to take steps to avoid actions that impose reasonably predictable impacts on future generations greater than those permitted for the current generation and to generally avoid imposing undue burdens on those to come.

It may be objected that there are no rights-holders present to correspond to the obligations imposed. Without identifiable individuals can there be rights and duties? Edith Brown Weiss posits that the rights-holders are not individuals, who remain in the future, but generations, some of which are here and some of which are in the future. Generations hold these rights as groups in relation to other generations. Since the future individuals are indeterminate, a guardian or a representative of the group may enforce these rights.[7] For example, in *Minors Oposa v. Secretary of the Department of Environment and Natural Resources*, the Philippine Supreme Court found that present generations have standing to represent future generations in large part because 'every generation has a responsibility to the next to preserve that rhythm and harmony for the full enjoyment of a balanced and healthful ecology.'[8]

Finally, several subsidiary rules in domestic trust law could be important in fleshing out the application of the principle of inter-generational equity, such as those that require the trustee to monitor and report on the status of the trust corpus. For each society, these rules could be transposed into legal obligations for the government to monitor the state of the environment and provide information periodically to the public. Monitoring and reporting requirements are already common in national and international environmental law,[9] and, in a few instances, the gathering and dissemination of information is implicitly or explicitly linked to inter-generational equity. The International Convention for the Regulation of Whaling, for example, establishes a commission that collects and analyses statistical information on the current condition and trend of whale stocks, and the effects of whaling activities on the 'great natural resource' of whales, which the preamble says should be safeguarded

---

[7] E. Brown Weiss, *In Fairness to Future Generations: International Law, Common Patrimony and Intergenerational Equity'* (Dobbs Ferry, NY: Transnational Publishers, 1989) at 95–7.

[8] *Minors Oposa v. Secretary of the Department of Environment and Natural Resources*, Philippine Supreme Court, 33 I.L.M. 168 (1994).

[9] Monitoring and reporting are required of states parties to most major environmental agreements, including the Convention on International Trade in Endangered Species of Wild Fauna and Flora, Article VII; the Convention on Biological Diversity, Article 26; the UN Framework Convention on Climate Change, Article 12; and the Montreal Protocol on Substances That Deplete the Ozone Layer, Article 7.

for future generations.[10] Article 4 of the UNESCO Convention for the Protection of the World Cultural and Natural Heritage requires each state party to ensure the identification, protection, conservation, presentation, and transmission to future generations of the cultural and natural heritage situated in its territory. Each state party is asked to submit to the World Heritage Committee an inventory of property forming part of the cultural and natural heritage. The committee keeps the list up to date and also periodically prepares a list of world heritage in danger.

3 EQUITY AND INTERNATIONAL LAW

Concepts of equity have emerged in different contexts in international law, reflecting the different meanings discussed before, in the second part of this chapter. Equity thus has been invoked *contra legem*, in opposition to the basic rule of sovereign equality between states, to fill in gaps when new issues emerge (*praeter legem*) and as a principle to govern the interpretation of legal norms (*infra legem*). This section looks at the relationship between international law and equity in the light of these three meanings.

3.1 Sovereign Equality and Equity

For most of its history, international law regulated bilateral and reciprocal relations, and allocated rights and responsibilities on the basis of sovereignty and legal equality among states. Strictly legal, that is, formal equality demands rules of identical treatment, to ensure full respect for the sovereignty of each state regardless of size or wealth. Where such equal treatment is perceived as unjust, equitable norms may be adopted and applied to treat states unequally. For example, the norm of equitable utilization of transboundary waters by riparian states, discussed in section 3.1.1 later in this chapter, ensures the possibility of adjusting the otherwise required equal allocation of a shared resource between riparian states to ensure a 'fair' distribution.

Sovereign equality as a basic constitutional principle of the international legal system also requires non-intervention or non-interference with decisions taken by each government concerning matters within the state's territory or jurisdiction. Particularly relevant for international environmental law is the translation of this notion into the principle of (permanent) sovereignty over natural resources and, thus, non-interference with the manner in which a state uses its natural resources. Principle 21 of the Stockholm Declaration begins by invoking this principle as it

[10] 1946 International Convention for the Regulation of Whaling, at pmbl. para. 1 ('recognizing the interest of the nations of the world in safeguarding for future generations the great natural resources represented by the whale stocks') and Article 4.

proclaims that 'States have, in accordance with the Charter of the United Nations and the principles of international law, the sovereign right to exploit their own resources pursuant to their own environmental policies.' However, the sovereignty of each state also implies that its resources are not harmed by the conduct of other states (see Chapter 22 'Transboundary Impacts'). Hence, Principle 21 continues by balancing the principle of permanent sovereignty with the 'responsibility to ensure that activities within their jurisdiction or control do not cause damage to the environment of other States or of areas beyond the limits of national jurisdiction.' This balance can be seen as an application of equitable principles of abuse of right or good neighbourliness among equal subjects of the international legal system.

In dispute settlement, Article 38(2) of the Statute of the International Court of Justice (ICJ) provides for equity to be applied as individualized justice (*contra legem*) if the parties so agree, but this option has never been utilized because states are apparently unwilling to confer such broad discretion on the court. Nor is equity applied as an independent source of law. Instead, the ICJ has applied equity primarily within rules that call for its application or to interpret or fill in gaps in existing law (*praeter legem*). Most of these cases concern resource allocation, where it is clear that the international community has determined that elements of distributive justice should play a role.

In the *Case Concerning the Continental Shelf (Tunisia/Libya)*, the ICJ called equity a legal concept that is a direct emanation of the idea of justice, which it is bound to apply as a general principle of law in achieving an equitable or just solution to a case.[11] In fact, the court has variously referred to equitable principles, procedures, methods, and results or solutions without always providing clarity about these four aspects of equity or how they interrelate with legal norms. In delimiting maritime boundaries, however, the ICJ has indicated that tribunals 'will always have regard to equity infra legem, that is, that form of equity which constitutes a method of interpretation of the law in force, and is one of its attributes.'[12]

The ICJ aims to avoid purely subjective views of justice between the parties when it makes use of equitable principles in a case. The ICJ decided the *North Sea Continental Shelf* case, 'in accordance with equitable principles' as a matter of customary international law.[13] Subsequently, it described 'the justice of which equity is an emanation' as '... justice according to the rule of law: which is to say that its application should display consistency and a degree of predictability; even though it looks with particularity to the more peculiar circumstances in an instant case, it also looks

[11] *Case Concerning the Continental Shelf (Tunisia/Libya)*, Judgment of 24 February 1982, [1982] I.C.J. Rep. 18.

[12] *Case Concerning the Frontier Dispute (Burkina Faso/Republic of Mali)*, Judgment of 22 December 1986, [1986] I.C.J. Rep. 554 at 567. For the use of equity in maritime boundary cases, see also *North Sea Continental Shelf Cases (FRG/Den./Neth.)*, Judgment of 20 February 1969, [1969] I.C.J. Rep. 3; *Case Concerning Delimitation of the Maritime Boundary in the Gulf of Maine (Canada/United States of America)*, Judgment of 12 October 1984, [1984] I.C.J. Rep. 246; and *Case Concerning the Continental Shelf (Libya/Malta)*, Judgment of 3 June 1985, [1985] I.C.J. Rep. 13.

[13] *North Sea Continental Shelf Cases*, see note 12 above at 3 and 53.

beyond it to principles of more general application.'[14] This passage suggests that the court seeks a degree of legal certainty in its choice and application of norms, but it must take into account the facts, the situations, and the specific interests or claims of the parties. Equitable norms themselves provide no guidance in selecting among the various facts or factors that could weigh in the decision. Thus, an element of subjectivity is probably present in all efforts to achieve an equitable result.

3.2 Distributive Justice in International Law

Imposing equal obligations on subjects of law that are unequal in relevant ways may be perceived as unjust if they exacerbate inequalities or impose unfair burdens on those least able to bear them. Legal systems, including the international legal system, often seek therefore to base the distribution of goods and the burdens of society according to the principle of distributive justice, seeking substantive equality by treating like alike and unlike differently according to various criteria such as prior entitlement, just desserts, or need.

International law has allocated both shared resources and environmental burdens through the equitable principle of distributive justice. The principle of distributive justice implies that relevant dissimilarities warrant adjustment or special treatment. Such an equitable approach may call for accommodating pervasive inequalities of economic development or lack of capacity to tackle a given problem, by imposing differential obligations or providing preferential treatment. These unequal relationships seek to foster true equality, largely through favouring the least developed or most affected states.

3.2.1 *Distributive Justice in Allocating Resources: Equitable Utilization*

Equitable utilization of shared natural resources is a widely accepted principle applied in apportioning watercourses, fish stocks, and the continental shelf. It is based on the notion of 'fair sharing' among those utilizing the resource, as a matter of intra-generational equity. It finds expression in Article 2 of the 1997 UN Convention on the Law of Non-Navigational Uses of International Watercourses (Watercourses Convention), which calls on the parties to take all appropriate measures to ensure that international watercourses are used in a reasonable and equitable way (see Chapter 15 'Ocean and Freshwater Resources').

The status of equitable utilization as a fundamental norm in the field of shared natural resources was affirmed by the ICJ in the *Case Concerning the Gabčíkovo-Nagymaros Project (Hungary v. Slovakia)*.[15] In the *Fisheries Jurisdiction Cases (UK v.*

---

[14] *Case Concerning the Continental Shelf (Libya/Malta)*, see note 12 above at para. 45.

[15] *Case Concerning the Gabčíkovo-Nagymaros Project (Hungary v. Slovakia)*, Judgment of 25 September 1997, [1997] I.C.J. Rep. 92 (25 September).

Iceland; FRG v. Iceland), the ICJ stressed the obligation of reasonable use and good faith negotiations aimed at an equitable result, taking into account the needs of conservation and the interests of all exploiters of the resource.[16] Thus, the notion of equitable utilization is one of distributive justice, attempting to make a 'reasonable' allocation or reach a fair result in distribution of a scarce resource, based on what are deemed to be relevant factors, such as need, prior use or entitlement, and other interests.

As developed in practice and in the Watercourses Convention, equitable utilization involves the substantive allocation of rights and procedural equity, including the duties of notification and consultation. On a substantive level, each party is held to have an equal right to use the resource, but since one party's use can impact the beneficial uses of others and not all uses can be satisfied, some limitations are necessary. The Watercourses Convention states that equitable and reasonable uses are to be 'consistent with adequate protection of the watercourse' (Article 5). The phrase suggests that uses that would substantially harm the watercourse could be inherently inequitable and indicates how positive rules may restrict the scope and application of equitable principles.

Notions of entitlement stemming from prior uses, strict equality, proportional use based on population, and priority accorded to certain uses all have been asserted at one time or another as a basis for determining what is an equitable allocation. In some instances, the parties agree in advance on certain divisions or priorities. The 1909 Boundary Waters Treaty between the United States and Canada relies upon equality of use for the generation of power (each country being entitled to use half of the waters along the boundary) and equitable sharing of water for irrigation. In contrast, the 1959 Nile Agreement between the Sudan and Egypt for Full Utilization of Nile Waters confirmed the 'established rights' of each party, without identifying them, while additional amounts were allocated on other equitable bases. While the latter agreement seems to view established rights as guaranteed by law, most other instruments take the better view and include prior entitlements as one factor in determining equitable allocation.

The idea of equitable utilization in the past had as a corollary that no use had inherent priority over any other. Instead, determining what uses were equitable involved balancing a number of factors in each individual case. Today, there appears to be a move towards recognizing that some resource uses do have priority over others. In the use of freshwaters, for example, emphasis is being placed on the satisfaction of basic human needs—that is, the provision of safe drinking water and sanitation. The Watercourses Convention provides that in the event of a conflict between the uses of an international watercourse, special regard is to be given to the requirements of vital human needs (Article 10), while the UN Committee on Economic,

---

[16] *Fisheries Jurisdiction Cases (United Kingdom v. Iceland; Federal Republic of Germany v. Iceland)*, Judgments of 25 July 1974, [1974] I.C.J. Rep. 3; and [1974] I.C.J. Rep. 175.

Social and Cultural Rights, in its General Comment 12 on the Right to Water, insists that priority be given to safe drinking water and sanitation, with a guaranteed minimum amount to be provided to every person. Thus, a strictly legal approach grounded in human rights may alter the weighing of factors by designating one use as inherently more important than all others.

Equity as distributive justice in the allocation of limited resources also plays a role in the rules governing the common heritage of mankind (see Chapter 23 'Common Areas, Common Heritage, and Common Concern'). Once resources have been identified as part of the patrimony of all humanity, it becomes essential to articulate principles for sharing the management and benefits from such resources and the rules to govern their use. Such rules may promote exploitation, as with deep seabed mineral resources, or may reject extractive operations in favour of conservation, as in Antarctica. The issue of fairness in the allocation of benefits has been a major issue in debates regarding the resources of the deep seabed, while much of the discussion about Antarctica has concerned procedural fairness and participation in decision-making. It may also be considered that the deep seabed regime is focused on intra-generational equity, while the Antarctic designation as a nature reserve in Article 3 of the Madrid Protocol on Environmental Protection to the Antarctic Treaty gives priority to inter-generational equity.

3.2.2 *Distributive Justice in Allocating Burdens: Financial and Other Arrangements*

Wealth disparity among nations and its consequences in affecting levels of technology, training, and human living conditions bring the question of the distribution of burdens onto the international agenda. In the environmental field, past contributions to global environmental problems have also played a role in notions of distributive justice. Within states, taxes and spending programmes address the needs of the poor, and liability or licensing regimes among other techniques may make the polluter pay. At the international level, the acceptance of a need for distributive justice in sharing the burdens of international society has been slow in coming despite the evident needs and claims of the least developed countries.

The limits of the traditional approach of reciprocal rights and duties among formally equal states became evident after the emergence of large numbers of new and fragile states following decolonization. Newly independent countries quickly realized that political independence was insufficient to guarantee economic independence and control over their natural resources. This recognition led many of them, especially in the 1970s, to make a concerted effort to gain preferential treatment in what was to become the New International Economic Order. The 1974 Charter of Economic Rights and Duties of States, which was one of the major instruments of this period, refers to equity throughout the text, in connection with, *inter alia*, equitable sharing, equitable prices, and equitable terms of trade. The effort was essentially to apply the principle of distributive justice to construct new legal and political arrangements to allow developing countries to overcome the inheritance of the colonial past. Developing countries see this form of equity as a potential means to overcome the inequality and poverty they experience despite the formal or legal equality of states. Preferential treatment for developing countries within the World Trade Organization and the General Agreement on Tariffs and Trade reflects one application of this notion as it is designed to help developing countries increase their economic position in accordance with equitable principles. Differential treatment in trade agreements has allowed these countries to derogate from some of the obligations imposed on developed states.

Efforts to elaborate a new international economic order that would impose a fundamentally altered set of principles of international law on developed states, based on distributive justice, permanent sovereignty over natural resources, and the transfer of technology, ultimately failed as a set of unilateral demands. Nevertheless, the aim of realizing economic self-determination was not lost. It instead resurfaced in an altered form with the emergence of international environmental issues. Developing countries were able to press the issue of equitable burden-sharing for several reasons. First, they hold the major part of the Earth's biological resources and need or want to use them for economic development. At the same time, developed states have an interest in the conservation and sustainable utilization of these resources, many of which are the source of desired products as well as ecological processes (for example, tropical forests as carbon sinks). Second, developing countries could focus on fairness in pointing out the predominant responsibility of wealthier states for pollution. Third, developing states could legitimately plead their inability to participate in or comply with environmental protection agreements due to poverty and the need to develop.

In general, concern about the equitable distribution of the burdens of environmental protection has increased for these reasons and has led to the creation of a series of financial mechanisms, exemptions, provisions for the transfer of technology, and flexibility in the time required for compliance with international obligations. Capacity building through the provision of financial resources and the transfer of technology is widely included in global multilateral environmental agreements and often becomes a condition for compliance by developing countries, as in the Montreal Protocol on Substances That Deplete the Ozone Layer (Montreal Protocol) (Article 5(5)) (see Chapter 41 'Technical and Financial Assistance'). Explicitly stating that economic and social development and poverty eradication are the first and overriding priorities of developing country parties, the Convention on Biological Diversity (CBD) and the UN Framework Convention on Climate Change (UNFCCC) make the provision of financial resources and the transfer of technology from developed country parties a condition for the implementation of treaty obligations by developing country parties. Other conventions, such as the Convention to Combat Desertification in Those Countries Experiencing Serious Drought and/or Desertification, Particularly in Africa, express a concern for the special needs and circumstances of developing countries, particularly the least developed, in combating environmental degradation.

It may be argued that equity plays a more important role in international environmental law than in any other area of international law. At least since the 1972 Stockholm Conference on the Human Environment, international environmental law has sought to fairly allocate the benefits and burdens involved in natural resources and their protection, based on historic responsibility, capacity, and need. At Stockholm, poorer states asserted the greater responsibility of industrialized countries to remedy the environmental problems that the latter states were accused of creating. The Stockholm Declaration recognized that environmental protection is a major issue that affects the well-being of people and economic development throughout the world, acknowledging that environmental problems in developing countries are caused by a lack of development. Principle 5 calls for sharing among all mankind the benefits from the use of non-renewable resources, while Principle 9 calls for the transfer of 'substantial quantities' of financial and technological assistance to supplement the domestic effort of developing countries to remedy environmental deficiencies. Several other principles call for particular attention to the needs of developing countries in meeting the costs of environmental safeguards.

Twenty years later, the Rio Declaration on Environment and Development echoed many of these principles and developed others in its effort to balance the two elements in its title. Principle 3 of this declaration refers to the 'right to development', which is to be fulfilled so as to equitably meet the developmental and environmental needs of present and future generations. Principle 6 calls for giving special priority to the situation and needs of developing countries, particularly the least developed and those most environmentally vulnerable. While these principles focus on elements of need as a basis for distributive justice, Principle 7 shifts to take into account responsibility and capacity: 'In view of the different contributions to global environmental degradation, States have common but differentiated responsibilities. The developed countries acknowledge the responsibility that they bear in the international pursuit of sustainable development in view of the pressures their societies place on the global environment and of the technologies and financial resources they command.' Thus, the declaration identifies at least three factors that could be taken into account in the equitable allocation of benefits and burdens: need, responsibility, and capacity.

Several equitable principles have become common in international environmental agreements. Indeed, almost all multilateral environmental agreements dealing with shared or common natural resources contain equitable principles. Equitable benefit sharing is one of the objectives of the CBD, and equitable utilization is a fundamental principle applicable to the allocation of non-navigational uses of international watercourses. The first principle governing the UNFCCC is that the parties should protect the climate system for the benefit of present and future generations of humankind 'on the basis of equity and in accordance with their common but differentiated responsibilities and respective capacities' (Article 3). This principle not only calls for equity generally but identifies several factors to be taken into account in deciding what is equitable. The second principle adds the factor of need as a further element.

4 WHY HAS EQUITY BECOME PROMINENT IN INTERNATIONAL ENVIRONMENTAL LAW?

Issues of equity have become prominent in international environmental law for two main reasons. First, international environmental law involves limits on the use of resources—that is, how to conserve and allocate increasingly scarce or threatened shared natural resources and public goods, such as commercial fish stocks or international rivers and lakes. It is in conditions of scarcity within a community (and this assumes that states sharing resources form a community)—where it is agreed that all are entitled to a share of the resource and none is entitled to all of it—that questions of equity as distributive justice arise. Note that while all may agree that there should be a fair distribution, it is far more difficult, as discussed below, to attain agreement on what constitutes the fair method of allocation.

The second reason for the prominence of equity is that environmental law imposes burdens and costs as it seeks to reduce pollution as the major cause of environmental degradation. It must allocate the burden among countries whose emission levels and capacities to reduce them differ greatly. Vast wealth disparities around the globe have resulted in great variation in the nature of environmental problems, the role of each state in contributing to global environmental deterioration, and each state's ability to prevent and remedy harm to the environment. At the beginning of the twenty-first century, the industrialized world, with 20 per cent of the global population, generated more than 80 per cent of the world's pollution and used about 80 per cent of global energy and mineral resources, but the environmental impacts that resulted from this production and consumption, particularly with respect to anthropogenic climate change, affected disproportionately the development of poorer countries. Developed countries also accounted for 83 per cent of the world's gross domestic product (GDP), with the gap between developed and developing countries in per capita GDP increasing during the last 30 years of the twentieth century, making developing countries relatively poorer than before. Poverty itself has come to be seen as a major source of environmental degradation. At the same time, developing countries hold most of the Earth's biological resources, partly because of lack of industrialization and partly for reasons of climate. These countries assert a right to share in the benefits resulting from the use of such resources by others and an equitable sharing of the burdens of pollution. As a result, international environmental law has moved considerably away from formal equality towards grouping states to allocate burdens and benefits based on responsibility for harm and financial or technological capacity to respond (see Chapter 26 'Sustainable Development' and Chapter 41 'Technical and Financial Assistance').

These questions of allocation of shared resources, responsibility for conserving a state's own natural resources and controlling pollution, and the distribution of costs arising from pollution prevention and environmental degradation have brought the issue of equity to the fore. In particular, an understanding that unilateral, bilateral, or even regional solutions are likely to be ineffective in resolving global issues such as climate change have led to a recognition of the need to encourage full participation by states in environmental regimes through acknowledging different capacities and responsibilities. Distributive justice has been a particular focus in balancing competing but equally valued rights or interests. Equity can be seen in this context as a counterpoint to the classical insistence on the formal equality of states and as providing a compromise between permanent sovereignty over natural resources and a common concern such as the conservation of biological diversity. In this sense, negotiators must rely upon equity to resolve conflicts in applying the two parts of the Stockholm Principle 21: the right to use resources and the duty not to cause transboundary environmental harm.

5 Principles for Determining Equitable Allocation

In most legal systems, equity has traditionally played a major part in determining the distribution of rights and responsibilities in conditions of scarcity and inequality. However, the assertion that like cases must be treated alike and those that are different handled otherwise requires determining which similarities and differences are relevant in which situation. To take an example from within national legal systems, income differences are generally accepted as a proper basis for allocating tax burdens but not for voting in national elections. Thus, while the general value of equity or fairness is largely accepted in the context of scarcity and inequality, debate centres on the appropriate principle on which to determine equitable allocation—whether decisions should be based on need, capacity, prior entitlement, 'just deserts', the greatest good for the greatest number, or strict equality of treatment. The various factors may point towards allocation in one direction or in many different directions. In addition, a single factor, such as need, may be asserted by more than one actor or group of actors. These latter problems have complicated international negotiations, for example, over access to, and equitable benefit sharing of, the use of genetic resources. The principle of common but differentiated responsibilities, which seeks to balance the different principles for achieving equitable allocation, at present provides the basis for achieving equitable allocation in international environmental law. Prior to focusing on the principle of common but differentiated responsibilities, this chapter first discusses the different bases for achieving equitable allocation.

5.1 Different Principles for Attaining Equitable Allocation

Formal equality (for example, per capita distribution) is one method of allocating resources and burdens. As noted earlier, rules are generally deemed just if they apply to all without discrimination. Yet equal treatment may yield extreme outcomes when pre-existing economic or other inequalities exist in society. At the international level, when allocations are based on formal equality, moreover, the issue of whether the appropriate apportioning unit is the state or the individual may arise, as in determining permissible emission levels. Requiring all states to implement environmental agreements in identical fashion would make many developing countries, or groups in those countries, worse off, at least in the short term. From the perspective of equity towards the most vulnerable or least well off, environmental protection should not result in further deterioration of their well-being. In order to address this problem, non-equal or differential obligations can and are being imposed as equitable means to foster substantive equality in the long term. The acceptance at Rio and henceforth of the principle of common but differentiated responsibilities seems to suggest a contraction of the use of formal equality as a means of allocation in environmental law.

Notions of *entitlement* uphold the existing distribution of goods if they were justly acquired according to the rules in force at the time of acquisition. Entitlement protection is contained in some environmental laws and agreements that 'grandfather' existing activities by exempting them from retrofitting to meet more exacting and newly enacted standards or allowing emissions to continue at pre-existing levels. For example, some international environmental agreements, such as the 1987 Sulphur Protocol to the Convention on Long-Range Transboundary Air Pollution, require equal reductions in pollution from historic baseline levels. The rewards that this system grants to those who have the goods may be too high to result in what is considered to be a fair distribution. An entitlement approach also may serve to deny essential goods to others.

Traditional international law largely reflects ideas that protect entitlement. The dominant principle is that all states, including those newly created, have equality of opportunity as sovereigns, but pre-existing natural endowment and activities make older states substantially stronger in wealth and power and developing states substantially stronger in natural (biological) resources. Since traditional international law entitles all states to an equal right to obtain or use common resources, from fish in the high seas to the geostationary orbit, technologically advanced states have the ability to, and may choose to, acquire the greatest part of the resources from the common area. Equality of rights, however, does not necessarily bring about equality of outcomes and the least favoured may find themselves in a continually declining position.

Different *capacities* (from each according to his or her ability) may be the decisive factor chosen to achieve distributive justice, as expressed in environmental agreements that require the member states of the Organisation for Economic Cooperation and Development (OECD) or other groupings of countries to finance poorer countries or transfer technology because they have the ability to do so. One problem that can arise is making the relevant determinations of ability to pay. States may argue that various factors make if fair for them to be grouped with the poorer countries. The Kyoto Protocol classifies Saudi Arabia and Singapore as 'developing', while Bulgaria is classified as developed, even though its economy remains one in transition. Without objective criteria to determine the groupings, along with the flexibility to move states from one group to another, the problem will largely be a political one. Some treaties avoid this problem by incorporating notions of capacity generally, requiring each state party to take measures 'in accordance with its particular conditions and capabilities' or 'as far as possible and as appropriate.'[17]

Inequalities in the ability to access the benefits of natural resources and address environmental impacts are evident. While the reality of environmental interdependence imposes a need for inter-state cooperation, states are impacted differently by specific environmental conditions, have greater or lesser interest in or impact on a particular problem, and may lack the human or financial capacity to take actions deemed prudent or necessary by the international community. It is clear that the expenditures necessary to prevent or abate environmental hazards can be high in the short term. This factor often provokes in developing countries rational fears that participation in international environmental treaties may decelerate or limit industrial development. As a result of these types of considerations, the Food and Agricultural Organization's Code of Conduct for Responsible Fisheries recognizes that the capacity of developing countries to implement the recommendations of the code have to be taken into account because existing inequality with regard to resources and capacities influences the ability of such states to take action on specific environmental problems.

Different *needs* (to each according to his or her need) as a basis for equitable allocation are recognized in the Rio Declaration and reappear, for example, in the UNFCCC. In implementing the convention, the parties are to be guided by 'the specific needs and special circumstances of developing country Parties, especially those that are particularly vulnerable to the adverse effects of climate change, and of those Parties, especially developing country Parties, that would have to bear a disproportionate or abnormal burden under the convention.'[18] The question of what would

---

[17] Convention on Biological Diversity, Articles 6–11.
[18] UN Framework Convention on Climate Change, Article 3.2.

be 'disproportionate' is left open. Article 4(8) adds that all parties are to consider what actions, including funding, insurance, and transfer of technology, may be necessary to meet the specific needs of specially affected states. Determining need, like determining capacity, may require the development of objective criteria and the assessment of the situation over time of each state party.

Different *historical responsibility* or 'just deserts'—that is, past and present contribution to environmental harm, is deemed by developing countries to be one of the most relevant factors in allocating burdens. The 1991 Beijing Declaration on Environment and Development stated the view of the developing world that 'the developed countries bear responsibility for the degradation of the global environment. Ever since the Industrial Revolution, the developed countries have over-exploited the world's natural resources through unsustainable patterns of production and consumption, causing damage to the global environment, to the detriment of the developing countries.' Fairness and a morally coherent response suggest that these states, which attained their current developed status through imposing non-internalized costs on the environment, take the major abatement actions, rather than demanding that everyone equally mitigate the externalities, including those not responsible for initially creating the problem. Equity, in this sense, is justified as a means of corrective justice, requiring remedial conduct to correct past wrongs.

The polluter pays principle, which requires that the entity causing environmental harm should bear responsibility for the costs ensuing from that harm, is an economic principle requiring the internalization of externalities. However, it is also compatible with corrective justice since it serves a reparative function by making those states that caused most environmental harm pay for the remediation or losses suffered by others. Similarly, compensatory or reparative justice for historical wrongs and takings may be a basis for equitable (preferential) treatment for developing countries, especially where colonizing states built their industrial development on the exploitation of natural resources of their colonies.

5.2 Common but Differentiated Responsibilities

The principle of *common but differentiated responsibilities* may incorporate some or all of the different factors relevant to equity. It is a multifaceted concept, with most formulations referring to different historical responsibilities as well as to different capacities and needs. Given this, states may plead for recognition of acquired rights or prior uses. In response, other states could stress the polluter pays principle, the principle of good neighbourliness, or the needs of its population as a basis for limiting activities, even when there are acquired rights. Where such conflicts arise in negotiations, states may agree upon priorities or select one or more of the factors to be the basis of decision. Failure to agree may lead to long-term disputes over determining a fair allocation of resources or burdens.

All of the texts adopted at Rio include some formulation of the principle of common but differentiated responsibilities. Principles 6 and 7 of the Rio Declaration are particularly important in affording priority to the needs of the least developed and most environmentally vulnerable states while expressing the general principle of common but differentiated responsibilities. The latter was especially controversial, with neither developed nor developing countries satisfied with the result.[19] The United States issued an interpretive statement indicating its view that the principle does not 'imply a recognition . . . of any international obligations.'[20] The legal status of common but differentiated responsibilities is, in fact, not entirely clear. It is referred to explicitly and applied in several multilateral environmental agreements, but whether it is a fundamental principle of international environmental law, a bundle of some or all of the above factors that lead to equitable decision-making, or itself a rule of equity remains debated. Its formulation could encompass, and in some formulations has encompassed, the notion of the historic responsibility of the North for the environmental degradation it produced in achieving its wealth. In this sense, the principle of common but differentiated responsibilities appears as a legal concept involving redistribution of wealth because the North took a disproportionate amount of the Earth's environmental goods. Principle 7 of the Rio Declaration, however, speaks not of historical responsibility but rather of the responsibility of developed countries for the *present and future* pursuit of sustainable development in view of the pressures their societies are placing on the global environment and on the resources they command.

In the context of the Montreal Protocol, negotiator Richard Benedick observed at least three possible interpretations of the principle: (1) a justifiable effort to achieve equity (distributive justice) between richer and poorer states in general; (2) a formula for balancing the performance of developing countries according to the technological and financial assistance given to them; and (3) an opportunity for developing countries to extract the maximum possible transfer of wealth as a precondition for accepting responsibility for protecting the environment (because of historical responsibility?).[21] Given the many meanings and factors involved in determining

---

[19] The Group of 77 had proposed a stronger formulation: 'The major cause of the continuing deterioration of the global environment is the unsustainable patterns of production and consumption, p articularly in developed countries . . . In view of their main historical and current responsibility for global environmental degradation and their capability to address the common concern, developed countries shall provide adequate , new, and additional financial resources and environmentally sound technologies on preferential and concessional terms to developing countries to enable them to achieve sustainable development.' Rio Conference on Environment and Development, UN Doc. /CONF.151/PC/WG.III/L.20/REV. 1 (1992).

[20] Rio Conference on Environment and Development, UN Doc. A/CONF.151/26 (Vol. IV) (1992) 20.

[21] R. Benedick, *Ozone Diplomacy: New Directions in Safeguarding the Planet* (Cambridge, MA: Harvard University Press, 1998) at 24.

equity, it is not surprising that when developing countries look at past actions of the developed states, they see historical responsibility for the harm done, while developed countries see prior entitlement (this debate could be considered to fall within the scope of inter-generational equity). Looking forward, developing countries assert their present and future needs, while developed countries point to the wealth of biological resources predominately found in the developing world. The ambiguities involved in the principle of common but differentiated responsibilities make it essential to observe how it and other equitable principles can be implemented in practice to reduce disagreements in these perspectives of the North and the South.

6 DIFFERENT WAYS OF IMPLEMENTING PRINCIPLES OF EQUITY

The implementation of environmental equity calls for appropriate or fair benefit and burden sharing among all those who have an interest in a shared resource, which implies distributive justice and participatory processes to manage the shared resources. Equity thus has both substantive and procedural aspects.

6.1 Substantive Rules of Equity

In practice, some multilateral environmental agreements set forth a general objective or objectives and a set of obligations applicable to all states parties but then differentiate the specific duties by category of states. Article 4(1) of the UNFCCC, for example, sets out the obligations of all parties; Article 4(2) specifies the obligations of developed country parties (listed in Annex I), while paragraphs 4(3)–4(5) set forth obligations for OECD countries (listed in Annex II). This type of distinction often reflects the respective contributions of developed and developing countries to emissions, while seeking to avoid future contributions by developing countries—an application of equity that seeks to enhance the status of the poorest and most disfavoured communities. In other agreements, developed countries promise to provide material aid to developing countries in exchange for which the developing states mitigate environmental harm from industrialization, such as by avoiding or reducing the use of ozone-depleting substances. This compensatory inequality or preferential treatment centres on capacity building through the allocation of resources and technology. Examples of redistribution include aid mechanisms and technology transfer (see Chapter 41 'Technical and Financial Assistance').

Determining the factors that are relevant for differentiating obligations is difficult, and substantive measures of equity may be applied in one of several ways. The principle of equitable burden sharing between legally equal parties can involve allocating costs on the basis of ability to pay or the party's contributions to the problem rather per unit or per capita. Emissions can be allocated on the basis of past or current emission levels, promoting stability in the international economic order by maintaining current practices, and limiting the entry of new polluters. This approach, however, constitutes an entitlement approach that benefits neither the environment nor the most disadvantaged countries, rewarding those who have done the least to curb emissions. In the climate change regime, differentiated responsibilities to attain emission reductions reflect a variety of factors, including different starting points, economic structures and resources, past and present contributions to atmospheric pollution, and capacity to perform.

Since differential treatment is concerned with the realization of substantive equality over time, in order to enhance the social and economic development of those worst off in the world, it seeks to provide remedial measures to achieve what drafters agree would be a more just society. Temporary exceptions may be created therefore to allow actors to enjoy the rights established by the rules in force. The Montreal Protocol, for example, exempted from its targets and timetables for ten years those developing states whose consumption of chlorofluorocarbons was less than 0.3 kilograms per capita—a criterion that all developing states satisfied initially.

Agreements concerning natural resources, biodiversity, or the global genetic pool not only denominate those resources that are a common concern of humankind but also reaffirm state sovereignty. The objectives of the CBD set forth in Article 1 reflect the effort to balance equitably the many relevant concerns. Listed in this article are conservation, sustainable use, and the equitable sharing of the benefits arising out of the utilization of genetic resources, along with appropriate access, appropriate transfer of relevant technologies, and appropriate funding. This complex list of factors reflects the competing equitable claims involved in the biodiversity regime. Traditional practice has involved an open regime of capture for biological resources, including those species located within areas where states exercise sovereignty or jurisdiction. Some states, which tend to be those states that have the technological capacity to make use of the resources, appear to believe they have an 'acquired right' of traditional free access. The issue of need is divided because the economic value of many of the resources lies in food supply and medicine (some 80 per cent of all medicines are derived from biological resources)—products that are needed in all parts of the world. The countries where these resources are predominately located, however, are few (17), and 15 of them are developing countries, which need the income derived from the use of these resources. Despite the potential life-saving value of new medicines, developing countries feel it is fair to demand compensation for access and use of their biological resources. The parties negotiating the CBD attempted to determine fair allocation of the resources, taking all of these elements into account.

On the one hand, authority to determine access to genetic resources rests with national governments and is subject to national legislation (Article 15.1). On the other hand, each state party must endeavour to create conditions to facilitate access to genetic resources for environmentally sound uses by other parties, and should not impose restrictions that run counter to the convention's objectives. The parties must mutually agree on terms based on prior informed consent by the party providing the genetic resource. Contractual agreements on access are likely to become the primary method by which public and private entities gain access and negotiate a share of the benefits upon a payment of collection fees, royalties, or other form of benefit sharing. The CBD also requires that developed country parties provide new and additional financial resources to developing countries, and develop a financial mechanism to provide resources to developing country parties (see Chapter 41 'Technical and Financial Assistance').

6.2 Procedural Rules

Procedural fairness involves notification, access to information, and cooperation, including participation in decision-making, because equitable solutions based on balancing the interests of those affected can occur only if the interests are represented and properly articulated (see Chapter 29 'Public Participation'). In consequence, all parties potentially affected should have the right to participate equally in decision-making. The Global Environment Facility (GEF) is an example. It provides new and additional grant and concessional funding to meet the agreed incremental costs of measures to achieve agreed global environmental benefits. Most of the funds come from developed countries, but the Council has a plurality of members from developing countries (16 from developing countries, 14 from developed countries, and two from economies in transition states). If a vote is necessary, the decision must be adopted by 60 per cent of both the total number of participants and 60 per cent of total contributions. As a consequence, agreement will have to be reached across the groups before action is taken.

The element of procedural fairness is also found in the CBD. The CBD, like other recent agreements, includes the technique of prior informed consent to ensure that parties are informed of the risks and benefits of any decision they may make. This transparency is intended to provide legitimacy and fairness to transactions. The conferences of the parties have devoted considerable attention to the procedural aspects of equitable access. Thus, the Bonn Guidelines, which were adopted at the sixth Conference of the Parties in 2002, emphasize the prior informed consent of the source state (which is also required by Article 15 of the CBD), and recommend that consent be obtained from indigenous or local communities on whose traditional lands the resources are located (see Chapter 36 'Indigenous Peoples').

The traditional principle of equitable utilization of shared resources also requires sharing of information about uses in order to ensure that the initiating state has all of the data necessary to evaluate whether or not its proposed use is equitable. The principle of prior notification concerning new uses that may affect other states now appears settled in treaty and practice, and will serve to lead to correlative obligations of consultation and negotiation as part of an ongoing process to ensure that shared resources are used by all parties in an equitable and reasonable manner. These duties are detailed in international watercourse agreements, including the Convention on the Law of Non-Navigational Uses of International Watercourses, where these considerations are found in Articles 8–9 and in Part III.

7 Conclusions: Equity Matters in a Just Society and Instrumentally

There is growing recognition of the interdependence of states and of problems that are insoluble through unilateral action, leading to acceptance of the moral principle of solidarity or partnership. Interdependence underscores the search for a just global society, which is a quest as old as human civilization. To many, a just society involves ensuring that the natural components of the environment continue to sustain life in all of its diversity, and that the natural benefits that humans enjoy are fairly shared among all those present and to come. The moral dimension of equity is such that it is often deemed synonymous with justice and is an end in itself.

The recognition that global resources are shared or of common concern or heritage has given rise to a duty to assist those states unable to participate in the utilization of the resources. Equity in international environmental law thus means a rational sharing of the burdens and costs of environmental protection, discharged through the procedural and substantive adjustment of rights and duties. Equity in the sense of fairness also means warning states of imminent peril and cooperating to resolve problems that will impact the ecological processes or resources on which future well-being depends.

Equity is important and, with its emphasis on fairness, is more attractive to many than economic efficiency or open conflict as a means of deciding how to allocate and sustain limited commons resources. Without a cooperative and equitable solution to the issue of allocation, competitive utilization of the resource may continue until the resource is depleted. Equitable or differentiated obligations may induce participation in action among the competing states as well as among states that may not have any direct interest in a specific environmental issue. Developing countries have noted that ozone depletion, which is of greater concern to developed countries, has been addressed more rapidly and seriously than desertification or other issues of greater interest to the South. Such observations may be a disincentive to cooperation, notably, the 2002 GEF decision to fund desertification projects, which seems at least in part a response to criticisms heard before, and during, the World Summit on Sustainable Development that the limited mandate of the fund was unfair.

Equity also may be justified on the basis of self-interest. Developed countries gain from secure access to primary resources situated largely in developing countries. More generally, environmental protection is in everyone's interest, and the adjustment of legal obligations to achieve better protection is self-interested. An allocation of burdens that takes into account the more vulnerable position of developing states may benefit all through inducing their cooperation to improve global environmental conditions. Moreover, Scott Barrett's work has indicated that agreements perceived to be fair are not only likely to induce greater participation, but are more likely to be self-enforcing and thus successful over the long term.[22]

In sum, equitable approaches are not only based in morality and a sense of justice, but may also foster more effective action on issues of common concern and more effective implementation of norms. Equity, as reflecting notions of fairness and legitimacy, may produce more or better compliance with environmental agreements. In practice, therefore, equitable differentiation probably has become the price to be paid to ensure universal participation in environmental agreements concerned with global problems. Yet, it should not be forgotten, as Thomas Franck has noted, that '[t]he law promotes distributive justice not merely to secure greater compliance, but primarily because most people think it is *right* to act justly.'[23]

Recommended Reading

M. Akehurst, 'Equity and General Principles of Law' (1976) 25 Int'l & Comp. L.Q. 801.

E. Brown Weiss, *In Fairness to Future Generations: International Law, Common Patrimony and Intergenerational Equity'* (Dobbs Ferry, NY: Transnational Publishers, 1989).

P. Cullet, *Differential Treatment in International Environmental Law* (Burlington, VT: Ashgate Publishing, 2003).

A. Dobson, *Justice and the Environment* (Oxford: Oxford University Press, 1998).

T. Franck, *Fairness in International Law and Institutions* (Oxford: Clarendon Press, 1995).

L. Gündling, 'Our Responsibility to Future Generations' (1990) 84 A.J.I.L. 207.

M. Janis, 'Equity in International Law' in R. Bernhardt, ed., (1984) 2 Encyclopedia Pub. Int'l L. 109.

D. McGraw, 'Legal Treatment of Developing Countries: Differential, Contextual and Absolute Norms' (1990) 1 Colo. J. Int'l Envt'l L. & Pol'y 69.

C. Redgwell, *Intergenerational Trusts and Environmental Protection* (Manchester: Juris Publishing, Manchester University Press, 1999).

F. Toth, ed., *Fair Weather? Equity Concerns in Climate Change* (London: Earthscan, 1999).

---

[22] S. Barrett, *Environment and Statecraft: The Strategy of Environmental Treaty-Making* (Oxford: Oxford University Press, 2003).   [23] Franck, see note 1 above at 8.

CHAPTER 28

ENVIRONMENTAL RIGHTS

JOHN G. MERRILLS

1 INTRODUCTION

INTERNATIONAL environmental law and the law of human rights embody distinct but related concerns of the modern world. On the one hand, since the future of humanity depends on maintaining a habitable planet, effective measures to protect the environment are crucial to any project for advancing human rights. In this sense, then, human rights rely ultimately on achieving a secure environment. On the other hand, because human rights law already protects interests such as those concerned with life and the home, claims at the international level relating to a variety of environmental matters are now possible by those affected. Accordingly, the exercise of established human rights is already contributing something to environmental protection.

The relation between the environment and human rights has led, as might be expected, to considerable interest in the subject of 'environmental rights'—meaning by that the possibility of formulating claims relating to the environment in terms of human rights.[1] As well as the case law concerned with specific human rights mentioned earlier, we therefore find environmental treaties with provisions on freedom of information and similar guarantees and, at the most general level, a discussion of the advantages of adding a broad 'right to environment' to the list of traditional human rights. Indeed, in a regional context, this latter step has already been taken in the 1988 Protocol of San Salvador (San Salvador Protocol), which provides in Article 11(1) that '[e]veryone shall have the right to live in a healthy environment and to have access to public services,' and in the 1981 African Charter on Human and Peoples' Rights (African Charter), which lays down in Article 24 that '[a]ll peoples shall have the right to a generally satisfactory environment favourable to their development.'

Now to say that, as part of their basic human rights, individuals have the right to live in a healthy environment, or to speak, as the African Charter does, of the right to 'a generally satisfactory environment' as a collective right, is, like other invocations of environmental rights, to use the language of human rights to promote or consolidate certain social values. In this respect, debates about 'environmental rights' are no different from those over abortion, self-determination, euthanasia, the right to development, and many other issues in which rights are asserted, challenged, and argued about from different points of view. As these examples show, rights talk is both pervasive and exciting. However, it is plainly also often confused and inconclusive, partly, no doubt, on account of genuine disagreements, but sometimes because theoretical considerations that should underpin the discussion of legal and moral

---

[1] See, for example, A. Boyle and M. Anderson, eds., *Human Rights Approaches to Environmental Protection* (Oxford: Clarendon Press, 1996); and D. Shelton, 'Environmental Rights,' in P. Alston, ed., *Peoples' Rights* (Oxford: Oxford University Press, 2001) 185.

questions are ignored or taken for granted. This chapter reviews some of these considerations as they relate to the issue of human rights in general and environmental rights in particular.

2 VALUE OF RIGHTS

Moral, legal, and social issues of current concern are now so often discussed in terms of human rights that it may seem odd to begin by asking whether the concept is really needed or whether what may seem to be gained by framing questions in terms of rights could not be achieved just as effectively in other ways. However, this is the right place to start because the answer can help to avoid some common misunderstandings about what it means to have a right and, more fundamentally, because without a grasp of the justification for rights—that is, an appreciation of what they are for—it is scarcely possible to have a sensible discussion about the case for new human rights, such as environmental rights, in a moral or legal context.

The first mistake that reviewing the need for rights can help to avoid is assuming that rights are no more than a way of expressing preferences or interests. Preferences are commonly dressed up as 'rights' for rhetorical purposes, but the two are far from synonymous and appreciating the distinction between them is crucial for thinking clearly about either. Whereas rights concern entitlements—that is, things to which morality or valid rules of law give us a claim—preferences are just that, things we may want, but that we have no warrant for other than personal desire. Thus, I may want the last jam tart (or a healthy environment for my children), but whether I can claim these things as my human rights is an entirely separate question.

A second mistake is to think that human rights are co-extensive with morality. In other words, it is to assume first that the language of rights is essential to bring any moral considerations into play, and then that dealing with a matter in terms of rights exhausts moral argument. Of course, discussion of human rights involves morality, but the reverse is not true, and it is perfectly possible to examine the morality of a course of action without bringing rights into the picture at all. For example, it may be clear that my desire for the last jam tart (or for a clean environment) is nothing more than a preference (that is, that I have no right to these things), but it might nevertheless be morally right for me to have them. As Loren Lomasky puts it, 'if P enjoys chocolate cake and I do not, it is right for me to give my piece to him although he has no right to it.'[2] Similarly, because there is a difference between asking whether I have a moral right to something and asking whether it is morally right for me to have it,

---

[2] See L.E. Lomasky, *Persons, Rights and the Moral Community* (New York: Oxford University Press, 1987) at 8.

finding that a right exists may only be the first step in the process of moral reasoning. Thus, assuming that I could establish that I have a right to that last jam tart or to a clean environment, it would remain to be determined whether exercising my right was morally the right thing to do in the particular circumstances. So in Lomasky's example, the morally right thing for me to do with my piece of chocolate cake is obviously not to eat it myself (thereby exercising my right) but to give it to P instead.

Why, then, is there a need for rights and what would be lost if they did not exist? Rights and preferences tend to be confused—sometimes it must be said deliberately—because when there are conflicting demands, whether in relation to jam tarts or the environment, having the desired objective recognized as a right is a crucial means of establishing priorities. When preference confronts preference the result in moral terms is a stand-off. When right confronts preference, on the other hand, the holder of the right has a trump card with which to pre-empt preferences and other non-moral considerations. What is true here of moral rights is true *a fortiori* when such rights are translated into law. Thus, the incorporation of environmental rights into national constitutions or their adoption into international treaties does not guarantee that the holder of such rights will always be successful when they come into conflict with other rights, but it certainly means that environmental rights must always be taken into account and also that good reasons will be needed for denying them effect.

If rights are a good way of ensuring that something is taken seriously, designating an entitlement a *human* right is even better, on account of the status of this class of rights in legal and moral discourse. However, what are human rights for? The most convincing justification, it is submitted, is that human rights are intended to ensure the basic conditions needed for rights-holders to pursue their various goals.[3] Originally developed as a way of recognizing the unique value of every individual, human rights have now been extended to collectivities where they fulfil a similar function in promoting and protecting the autonomy of ethnic and religious minorities, indigenous peoples, and other groups.[4] A comparable development has been the extension of rights to cover economic, social, and cultural matters, as well as the civil and political sphere. These broadenings of the field of human rights are not without their own conceptual problems, which are further considered later in this chapter, and even in the original sphere, the individual's rights have, of course, provided endless scope for debate among philosophers and lawyers. For present purposes, however, the significant point is that a persuasive rationale for human rights is that they enable us to address the realization of individual and group autonomy, which would be difficult, if not impossible, to achieve in other ways, thereby giving them a special place in legal and moral argument.

[3] This theme is developed in Lomasky, see note 2 above at chapters 2 to 4.
[4] For excellent surveys of this issue, see J. Crawford, ed., *The Rights of Peoples* (Oxford: Clarendon Press, 1988); and Alston, see note 1 above.

3 What Rights Do We Have?

Having established that the concept of human rights can be grounded in the idea of autonomy and self-realization, it is now possible to consider whether, or to what extent, this provides a basis for treating environmental concerns as involving rights. Whether it is correct to say that environmental rights exist in a moral sense raises wider issues than can be considered in this chapter (see Chapter 13 'Ethics and International Environmental Law'), so the present inquiry is not concerned with this question, but with the preliminary question of whether recognizing environmental rights is consistent with the rationale of human rights. The legal status of environmental rights is clearly also a separate question, although one to which the current inquiry is relevant because if the conclusion were to be that the idea of environmental rights as moral entitlements made no sense, it would be difficult to argue the case for their recognition as legal rights, given the close relation between law and morals in this area.

If we take first the proposition that individuals may be said to enjoy certain moral rights with regard to environmental matters, it is not difficult to see how conceptually such things as a right to compensation for harm, a right to be consulted and to make representations on issues of concern, and a right of access to environmental information can all be accommodated within the idea that rights exist in order to promote self-realization and individual development. The same can plainly be said of the broader 'right to live in a healthy environment,' or the equivalent, when expressed as an individual right. Whether or not there are legal rights to give these entitlements effective expression, as in the San Salvador Protocol, it is not unreasonable to see the rights of the individual as in issue when what is at stake is bound up with life, property, and control of one's affairs as the above matters unquestionably are. Although therefore the notion of environmental rights would probably have seemed strange to the pioneers of human rights, there is nothing in this concept or its rationale that looks to be incompatible with their thinking.

What about the proposal that the right to a clean, healthy, or 'satisfactory' environment should be regarded as a collective right? In this case, the proposition is that groups or communities, defined in some way, should be the beneficiaries of a right on the ground that it is vital to their existence or survival. The right would be an economic, social, or cultural right and, as such, constitute a claim on the resources of a wider community, which is also to be defined, rather than simply a protection from interference, but this distinction, already well recognized in human rights law, is not in itself problematic. Likewise, there would appear to be no obvious reason why groups as well as individuals should not enjoy rights of this kind. It is easy to imagine situations in which environmental conditions may be so bound up with the life of communities as to justify placing groups in a position analogous to that of individuals.[5] Indeed, it could be argued that by formulating the right to a satisfactory environment as a collective, rather than an individual, right, the African Charter more accurately captures its essence. Group rights, as will be seen, do present conceptual problems, but if the question is whether as a matter of principle there is a justification for treating a 'right to environment' as a collective right, the answer must be yes.

It is tempting to leave the discussion of the possible justification for environmental rights at this point and move on to other matters. Before doing so, however, a word should be said about why in terms of legal policy there may be a case for not recognizing such rights and the alternatives to doing so. From the earlier discussion of the difference between preferences and rights, it will be recalled that if a preference can be turned into a right, the position of the new rights-holder is much strengthened, especially in comparison with rivals whose preferences have not been so transformed. There may also be other effects, however. Suppose that instead of being confronted with a mere preference, our rights-holder is confronted with another rights-holder. We are now back to the same position of preference being confronted with preference, with the important difference that, as Lomasky has explained,[6] since both parties are armed with rights, accommodation through compromise may now be much less appealing.

The tendency for disputes to become more acrimonious when rights are at stake can also be seen elsewhere. A rights-holder confronted by a rival with a mere preference will expect to get his way, and, although the purpose of rights is to ordain such priorities, the natural tendency to 'stand on our rights' cannot be said to do much to promote social harmony or, in some cases, social welfare. When there are only competing preferences, we can try to maximize social welfare by utilizing a cost-benefit analysis. However, once a preference is converted into a right, trade-offs can no longer be considered in the same way. Moreover, a proliferation of rights and rights-holders not only multiplies the opportunities for rights-holders to come into conflict with each other, but also generates a tension between rights as a basis for actions and other moral considerations. Thus, a society that over-emphasizes legal and moral rights may find it difficult to maintain community values such as cooperation, generosity, and civic duty, which are not identified with the concept of rights.

Does it follow from these gloomy prognostications that there is never a good case for recognizing new rights? Certainly not. As consideration about the importance of different aspects of life evolves and the world itself changes, so new rights are bound to emerge and must be acknowledged if the concept of human rights is to fulfil its purpose. What the above warning is intended to induce is a certain caution. Not everything that could be recognized as a new human right needs to be so treated and evaluation should take account of the disadvantages as well as the benefits of doing so.

---

[5] For examples of such situations, see W. Shutkin, 'International Human Rights Law and the Earth: The Protection of Indigenous Peoples and the Environment' (1990–1) 31 Va. J. Int'l L. 479.

[6] See Lomasky, note 2 above at 5.

This leads to a more specific point. In deciding whether new rights are needed, it is important to take account of what is already in place. There is no need to create new rights to deal with matters that are already covered by existing rights. Indeed, to do so may be counter-productive. An example of such a case is the proposal that the 'right to sleep' should be recognized as a human right.[7] Would this really serve any useful purpose? There is already a prohibition of torture and inhuman or degrading treatment, which would cover many situations. Working conditions are regulated by many conventions of the International Labour Organization, while domestic noise may raise an issue under the right to respect for the home, and so on. Consideration of the kinds of cases to which environmental rights might be relevant suggests that their position may be very similar. It is not that the interests guarded by environmental rights are unworthy of protection; it is rather that in many instances they are adequately protected already. For example, the violation of the collective right to a 'general satisfactory environment' found by the African Commission on Human and Peoples' Rights in *The Social and Economic Rights Action Centre and the Centre for Economic and Social Rights v. Nigeria*[8] was accompanied by violations of so many other individual and collective rights as to add relatively little to the decision.

When a new right is suggested, it is therefore always worth asking both how what is proposed is to be defined and whether the putative right is sufficiently distinct from established rights for it to be sensible or useful to create another conceptual boundary. Thus, to take again the proposed right to sleep, it may be better to address the very different situations in which harmful sleep deprivation can occur via established principles concerned with torture, labour standards, and so on, which can put these issues in their appropriate context, than to invent a new somewhat amorphous right. Similarly, with regard to environmental rights, someone's right to know about environmental projects may not really be so different from the right to know about other matters as to justify the creation of a new right. Accordingly, deciding what rights to recognize is more than a matter of deciding what might be justified in theory, but it also requires attention to how rights affect social behaviour and to what rights may already exist.

4 WHO CAN HAVE RIGHTS?

Rights cannot exist as free-floating abstractions but need rights-holders, for the function of rights, as has been seen, is to protect potential growth areas for the benefit of someone or something, and, hence, the idea of a right without a rights-holder

---

[7] For discussion of this and other 'new' human rights, see P. Alston, 'Conjuring Up New Human Rights: a Proposal for Quality Control' (1984) 78 A.J.I.L. 607.

[8] See *The Social and Economic Rights Action Centre and the Centre for Economic and Social Rights v. Nigeria* (2001), text reprinted in (2003) 10 I.H.R.R. 282 [*Ogoni*]; see also D. Shelton, 'Case-Note' (2002) 96

is a contradiction in terms. The identity of the rights-holder is clearly crucial to the content of the right concerned. Thus, the contrasting formulations in the San Salvador Protocol and the African Charter of, respectively, an individual and a collective environmental right necessarily give the right concerned different meanings on account of their very different rights-holders. A more fundamental point is that, in any system in which rights are important, an entity has to fulfil certain criteria in order to qualify as a rights-holder at all, and what those criteria are (that is, how rights-holders are defined), moulds the contours of the legal or moral system concerned. What then is needed to be a rights-holder?

Considering first the question of group rights, it is clear that identifying the proper rights-holders presents extremely controversial issues.[9] With the possible exception of 'inter-generational rights', which are discussed later in this chapter, the problems of identification appear to be similar for all types of collective rights and are not peculiar to environmental rights. However, it is also worth noting that deciding who holds a particular collective right depends very much on the nature of the right concerned. Therefore, it should not be assumed that establishing who is entitled to self-determination, for example, will also establish who is entitled to claim any collective environmental rights that may be recognized or vice-versa.[10] In this respect, there is an obvious difference between individuals as rights-holders and groups. Whereas the former normally stand on a footing of equality, the latter, lacking as they do an intrinsic identity, must be constructed conceptually for particular purposes, which plainly complicates the problem of identification.

When the relevant rights-holder has been identified, further questions arise concerning membership of the group and the authority to act on its behalf. In regard to membership, allowing the group to decide eligibility, leaving it for individuals to decide for themselves, or adopting external criteria such as race, religion, or culture all have advantages and limitations. With respect to the authority to act, groups, however composed, cannot function like individuals and so need suitable arrangements for authorizing action. At the legal level, such arrangements are usually quite precise. In less formal settings, however, the position will often be more obscure, and it may be unclear who has the right to speak for the group and to assert (or waive) its claims.[11] A great deal must depend on the organization and cohesiveness of the group. Consequently, one test of whether a particular group right can be recognized should perhaps be whether there is a constituency to which the new right belongs

A.J.I.L. 937; and F. Coomans, 'The *Ogoni* Case before the African Commission on Human and Peoples' Rights' (2003) 52 Int'l & Comp. L.Q. 749.

    [9] See, for example, J. Crawford, 'The Rights of Peoples: "Peoples" or "Governments"?' in Crawford, see note 4 above, at 55.

    [10] See J. Crawford, 'Some Conclusions', in Crawford, see note 4 above, at 159 and 169–70.

    [11] See D. Makinson, 'Rights of Peoples: Point of View of a Logician', in Crawford, see note 4 above, 69 at 77–8.

such that we are not only able to identify the collective rights-holder, but also to determine who is entitled to act on its behalf.

Identifying rights-holders in the case of individual rights is an altogether more straightforward matter. Since we are now concerned with the rights of individual human beings rather than groups, the problem of identifying the standard claimant, which causes so much difficulty with collective rights, simply does not arise. Accordingly, if environmental rights are recognized as human rights, it can be on the same basis as other rights, which means treating them as legal or moral entitlements of all humans. There is, of course, a need to consider the position of children, the insane, people in comas, and the like, whose capacity to possess the full range of rights, or to exercise them, may be questionable or, in some cases, may call for additional rights. Yet these are familiar problems and do not require further discussion in this chapter.[12] There are, however, other cases of particular interest in the context of environmental rights about which something should be said.

One such case concerns the position of future generations and whether we should think of those not yet born as possible holders of environmental rights.[13] This is different from the controversial question whether foetuses should be treated as having rights, since the present issue concerns not the rights of a person (or something) that in the normal course of events will emerge as an individual but, rather, with the 'rights' of everyone born in the future in relation to our management of the environment today. This might therefore be thought of as a special type of collective right rather than as an indefinite number of individual rights and, as such, poses the conceptual problem of defining the rights-holder, which has already been discussed. It also raises other difficulties, however.

First, there is the question of who is to be regarded as competent to assert and exercise the rights concerned. Although the idea of one person being authorized to act on behalf of another is familiar in other contexts, the type of delegation involved in inter-generational rights would plainly have to derive not from designation by the principal (as in most cases of agency), but on authorization from the present community (as in guardianship, for example). Although there would probably be no shortage of volunteers for the role of 'guardian of the rights of future generations,' the problems of deciding who should exercise this role and securing legitimacy for the appointee's decisions are plain. And this consideration leads to a second issue, namely the standard by which the activities of such guardians could be judged.

The content of any notional inter-generational rights could obviously not depend on the guardians' discretion. For rights of this kind to perform their function, there would need to be a standard to allow an assessment of whether a posited claim was for

---

[12] For a suggested approach to such problems, see Lomasky, note 2 above at 152–228.

[13] The issue was raised but not resolved in the case of *EHP v. Canada*, Comm no. 67/1980, which was decided by the Human Rights Committee, reprinted in *Selected Decisions of the Human Rights Committee*, volume 2 (October 1982–April 1988) 20.

too much or too little. Such a standard could be formulated only by reference to a current assessment of what future generations might need in order to pursue their goals. As the expectations here relate to the whole of future human history, it is only necessary to ponder the question to appreciate the impossibility of providing a sensible answer. No one can know what life will be like in future centuries or how future generations will view our present concerns. Consequently, there can be no useful debate about rights in this context. Instead of treating future generations as shadowy rights-holders, we would therefore be better occupied reviewing the claims to rights of those currently alive, along with their various responsibilities.

A similar conclusion follows if we consider the claims of another supposed class of rights-holders, namely animals. By definition, 'animal rights' cannot be human rights, but animals are sensate creatures, are affected by our treatment of the environment, and, unlike future generations, are part of the here and now. All of these factors might lead one to think that, if there are to be human environmental rights, there ought to be animal environmental rights too. However, on closer analysis, the case for such rights turns out to be unconvincing. If, as suggested earlier, the moral case for rights rests on the concept of autonomy and self-realization, then animals fail to qualify for membership of the moral community on the ground that they are not generators of personal value.[14] This does not mean that how we treat animals, including their fate as part of the natural environment, is a matter of moral indifference. However, acknowledging that there is a moral dimension to the treatment of animals is quite different from thinking of them as having rights.

The proposal that various inanimate objects such as mountains, rivers, trees, or Earth itself should be held to have rights is even less convincing.[15] As in the case of animals, the argument for creating new classes of rights-holders is that these are all elements of the biosphere and, as such, are affected by human activity. Assigning rights in this wholesale manner certainly avoids anthropocentrism, which can be a drawback of a human rights approach to environmental protection. As with animals, however, presenting the issue as one of rights not only runs counter to the theoretical basis of rights but is also quite unnecessary. We have no difficulty in accepting that it is morally wrong to destroy a masterpiece by Rembrandt, yet do not regard this as any kind of argument for giving rights to paintings. In the same way, how we treat mountains and other parts of the natural world, including animals, raises significant moral issues irrespective of their supposed rights. This is also true of how our treatment of the environment may affect future generations. Since rights are not the whole of morality, the idea that only by creating new rights and new classes of rights-holders can we encourage a responsible attitude towards the environment is one to be rejected.

---

[14] See Lomasky, note 2 above at 223.
[15] See P.S. Elder, 'Legal Rights for Nature: The Wrong Answer to the Right(s) Question' (1984) 22 Osgoode Hall L.J. 285.

5 ISSUES OF DETERMINACY
AND CONSISTENCY

When investigating rights, it is not enough to find that there may be justification for holding that a particular right exists and to establish who can hold it. It is also necessary to consider who has an obligation by virtue of the right, what the scope of that obligation is, and how the right relates to other rights. Although in the nature of things it is not always possible to deal with these matters with absolute precision, it is important to move as far as possible in that direction, as indeterminacy on such questions in the moral sphere tends to weaken the case for having such rights at all, while, in law, it burdens judges and other decision-makers with a legislative responsibility that may be beyond their capacity or inappropriate constitutionally. The issue of environmental rights illustrates these points rather clearly.

5.1 Who Bears the Corresponding Obligations?

Dealing first with the question of the bearers of the obligation, it is evident that, in relation to the individual, the primary obligation in regard to whatever environmental rights exist must be owed by the state. Under domestic constitutions and international human rights law, obligations are owed to individuals by the state, and the function of rights is to provide a means for such obligations to be enforced. At the moral level, things are more complicated, for while it is obvious that a case can be made for imposing such obligations on the state, moral responsibility does not stop there but extends also to individuals, corporations, and others whose activities can affect us adversely. Naturally, such wider moral responsibilities can be translated into legal duties in suitable cases, since there is no reason to treat the state as exclusively responsible where activities affecting the environment are concerned.

In regard to collective rights, the issue of who has the corresponding obligation is just as important but more difficult to resolve. A good deal depends on the prior question of who is regarded as the rights-holder. To take the example of an assumed 'right to a clean environment', if the rights-holder is regarded as the state, which is a possible approach, then the corresponding obligation must rest on other states. In contrast, if we follow the African Commission on Human and Peoples' Rights and consider the rights-holders to be groups within the state,[16] then it will be the state itself that has the primary obligation. As with individual rights, it is again worth noting that the primary obligation need not be the exclusive obligation. Thus, it has been pointed out that so-called peoples' rights in international law,

[16] See the *Ogoni* case, note 8 above.

such as the environmental right in Article 24 of the African Charter, might well involve obligations for non-state entities as well, although the issue is far from clear.[17]

5.2 Content of Rights

Turning now to the content of rights, we encounter a different type of indeterminacy. In this case, the problem is to establish the extent of a given right—that is to say, what may properly be claimed—so that whoever owes the obligation can know when it has been discharged. Knowing what the justification for rights is helps by indicating what we should be looking for and ruling certain things out, which makes agreement or disagreement on the question of justification very significant. So, for example, basing rights on autonomy and self-realization can provide a broad indicator of their scope and implications. At the same time, establishing an agreed basis for rights can only go so far, and an operational concept of rights calls for close attention to the scope of rights individually. Human rights guarantees are normally drafted in quite general terms and so typically feature a good deal of indeterminacy, and, at the moral level, where we lack an authoritative procedure for resolving such problems, indeterminacy is even more pronounced. In other words, there is all the more reason for not rushing to embrace new rights without considering their implications.

Individual environmental rights relating to compensation, information, and so on appear sufficiently focused for their scope as moral rights to be reasonably clear, and, although they must be sharpened if they are also to function as legal rights, they do not seem to present any unusual definitional problems. However, the same can hardly be said of the right of peoples to 'a generally satisfactory environment favourable to their development,' as set out in Article 24 of the African Charter or the individual's right 'to live in a healthy environment,' proclaimed in Article 11(1) of the San Salvador Protocol. The problem of deciding what these, or similar formulations of economic, social, and cultural, rights actually mean has been noted by Alan Boyle[18] and need not be reiterated. It may, however, be worth making a couple of points about this form of indeterminacy in relation to the concept of rights in general.

One point is that there is nothing in the above or similar provisions that is inconsistent with the concept of a right *per se*. In other words, there is no basis for saying that rights exist only if their content can be precisely defined. Thus, rights 'to all you can eat' or 'to stay with Aunt Doris whenever you like' are perfectly intelligible as rights although both are somewhat indeterminate in content. The difficulty with such rights, and this is the other point, is not a conceptual one but a practical one,

---

[17] See Makinson, note 11 above at 80.

[18] See A. Boyle, 'The Role of International Human Rights Law in the Protection of the Environment,' in Boyle and Anderson, eds., see note 1 above at 43.

stemming from the vague and apparently open-ended nature of the commitment.[19] This can obviously lead to disagreement about what it means to have such a right[20] and, at an earlier stage, produce an understandable reluctance to enter into imprecise commitments of this type. Both consequences may be seen at the international level where certain recognized rights such as the right to self-determination have spawned endless argument, and a general resistance to the idea of 'peoples' rights' reflects a wariness of their implications. If the aim therefore is to improve protection of the environment, the effort put into promoting general environmental rights might be better directed to more specific aims.

5.3 Relationship between Different Rights

Advocates of new human rights or those seeking to extend existing rights sometimes argue their case in terms that appear to ignore the existence of other rights or the need to relate the right under consideration to them. This is understandable, given that proponents of particular issues often come to these matters from a background of special expertise or interest. Nevertheless, the tendency for rights to be discussed, as it were, in separate compartments, which is encouraged by the practice already noted of formulating certain rights in rather vague terms, is to be deplored. A coherent concept of rights calls for a given right, whether actual or proposed, to be considered alongside other rights, for only in this way is it possible to appreciate what any current right really means or to understand the possible significance of a new right for a legal or moral system.[21]

The need to avoid extravagant thinking, which is a real risk if rights are treated in isolation, may be seen by considering the way in which nearly all rights have to be qualified to take account of other legitimate interests. Thus, the International Covenant on Economic, Social and Cultural Rights speaks in Article 2 of each party's obligation 'to take steps . . . *to the maximum of its available resources* with a view to achieving *progressively* the full realisation of the rights recognised in the present Covenant,' while Article 4 of the International Covenant on Civil and Political Rights allows derogation from most of its provisions 'in times of public emergency.' Although not framed in terms of other rights, these are, in effect, different ways of recognizing that the guarantees of the respective covenants are qualified by such considerations. Plainly, any 'environmental human rights' already in existence, or which may be created in the future, are likely to be subject to similar limitations.

---

[19] See Makinson, note 11 above at 80–1.

[20] For instance, a report in the British press described a dispute between the proprietor of a seafood restaurant and a client, which occurred when the latter, having accepted an offer to consume 'all he could eat' for a fixed price, ordered his fourth plate of oysters. How the dispute was resolved is not recorded.

[21] For exploration of this point with reference to the issues of self-determination, development, and cultural identity, see Makinson, note 11 above at 83–92.

Provisions such as those just quoted, which have their counterpart in moral argument about rights, cannot take care of all possible conflicts between rights or conflicts between rights and other interests such as public order or social welfare. Although priorities can sometimes be established by means of other explicit arrangements, there are many situations in which resolution of such matters must emerge from practice. This is, of course, not a reason for refusing to think about such issues in advance, and it is important when introducing new rights to try to do so. It must be recognized, however, that only so much can be achieved—a reasonable aim being to deal with obvious cases of potential inconsistency.[22] It is not possible to review these exhaustively in this chapter, but it may be useful to briefly indicate the kinds of issues that supporters of environmental rights may need to address in order to deal with the question of consistency.

The types of conflicts that may arise can for convenience be divided into three broad groups. First, there are conflicts between individual rights. Does a right to environmental information, for example, include the right to information that is commercially sensitive or that relates to a person's private life? Then there are possible conflicts between collective rights. Does group A's right to a clean environment entitle it to prevent group B from carrying out an ecologically damaging practice that may be part of its indigenous culture?[23] Finally, there are the possibilities for conflict between individual rights and collective rights. Does group A's right to a clean environment entitle it to interfere with X's property rights? Conversely, should the individual's right of access to decision-making processes entitle a person to participate in, say, the deliberations of an ethnic minority of which he is not a member?[24] It is not necessary to work out how these and other conflicts might be resolved to appreciate that new rights should not be created without considering their relation to existing concepts.

6 LEGAL RIGHTS AND MORAL RIGHTS

Much of the discussion so far has concerned moral rights, although a substantial proportion of it is no less relevant in the legal sphere. It is now time to say something about legal rights and, more specifically, about the conceptual issues that arise when legal rights are closely linked to moral rights, as is the case with human rights law in general and environmental rights in particular. For the lawyer, the starting point

---

[22] For one approach to resolving such problems, see T. Meron, 'On a Hierarchy of International Human Rights' (1986) 80 A.J.I.L. 1.

[23] See the example of the Dogrib Indians, cited by Brownlie, in Crawford, see note 4 above at 7.

[24] Conflicts of this type are discussed in G. Triggs, 'The Rights of Peoples and Individual Rights: Conflict or Harmony?' in Crawford, see note 4 above at 141.

must be that whatever the procedure for identifying moral rights, law has its own processes and criteria, which must be utilized in legal contexts, frustrating though this can sometimes be for activists. Another way of putting the point is to say that legal rights and rules, and their moral counterparts, make up distinct normative systems, each with their own logic and criteria of identification. Although a natural rights theorist might disagree, it is therefore an error to maintain that a certain moral right (the right to a clean environment, say) must automatically be considered a right in international law, just as it would be to make the same argument about the rules of chess or any other normative system.

To avoid misunderstanding, it should be appreciated that the point being made in this case is concerned only with how we identify legal rights, not with what may be termed their pedigree. It goes without saying that the inspiration for legal rights has often come from morality, just as we might see the game of chess as a stylized representation of a medieval battlefield. However, we do not identify the rules of chess by studying medieval battles, and we should likewise identify legal rules by legal, not moral, criteria. In a similar way, to insist on the distinction between legal rights and moral rights is not to deny that morality exercises an important influence on how legal rules develop and are applied. Thus, an increasing interest in environmental issues generally has led in recent years to greater attention to these considerations in judicial decision-making, but whether this consequence means we can yet speak of 'environmental rights' is an entirely different question.

Since international law is grounded in treaties and state practice, there is a temptation to use the proliferation of environmental treaties and the development of rules of customary international law concerned with states' rights and duties with regard to the environment as a basis for deriving rights for individuals and groups. It is, of course, true that an increasing number of treaties now deal with environmental matters, that principles of customary law have developed, and that there is an abundance of 'soft' law in this area. However these, like the International Court of Justice's creation of an environmental chamber, show recognition of the environment's significance as a legal and political issue, but are no more evidence of individual or collective environmental rights than Article 2(4) of the Charter of the United Nations proves the existence of a 'right to peace'.[25] Naturally what begins as a matter for states may inspire developments in human rights, as has happened at the regional level in the African Charter and in the San Salvador Protocol. Yet, such a result is different from being able to show that it has happened generally.

More plausible perhaps is the attempt to derive environmental rights from references to the environment in human rights case law.[26] This has the merit of utilizing legal material that is genuinely concerned with human rights, but the evidence

---

[25] See Brownlie, note 23 above at 14.

[26] See, for example, M. Thorne, 'Establishing Environment as a Human Right' (1991) 19 Denver J. Int'l L. & Pol. 301.

should not be made to take more weight than it can bear. As already mentioned, environmental considerations can be, and in practice are, recognized as relevant in human rights cases under treaties such as the European Convention on Human Rights that make no mention of the environment specifically. Examples are cases concerning planning issues in relation to property rights, aircraft noise in relation to the right to respect for private life and the home, and the dumping of nuclear waste in relation to the right to life.[27] It is useful to gather such cases together for illustrative purposes or to support an argument that in some form environmental rights ought to be recognized in international law. However, using such cases to show that these rights are already part of the law is more questionable (although they are, of course, a reminder that human rights practice today must regularly address environmental issues).

To suggest that there are improper ways of identifying environmental rights is not the same as saying that such rights cannot be created. It is worth noting, however, that the potential for confusion is not confined to the situation in which the question is whether the declaration of a new right would be premature. Even if the evidence is compelling, there is also the problem, mentioned earlier, of determining the precise significance of what has been found, specifically the relation between environmental (or other) emergent human rights and the rest of the legal system. International law provides a good illustration of this kind of problem, although a similar issue can arise in domestic legal systems, especially with regard to constitutional rights.

One pitfall stems from what may be characterized as the fragmentation of complex systems of law into distinct specialities (see Chapter 7 'Relationship between International Environmental Law and Other Branches of International Law').[28] The danger is that having identified legal rights of unquestionable authenticity on a given subject, the specialist in this field may lose sight of the fact that 'human rights law', 'environmental law', 'the law of the sea', 'international criminal law', or whatever are not separate disciplines in the sense that law is distinct from moral philosophy, but are simply convenient divisions for teaching, research, and other purposes. Claims that this or that speciality needs its own rules on, say, sources, treaties, or state responsibility should therefore be treated rather sceptically, if international law is to retain coherence. Assuming, then, that, in some form, environmental rights are to form part of international law now or in the future, it will be just that—a part of international law—and not a component of a discrete subject whether styled 'international environmental law' or 'human rights'.

Another pitfall is that when new rights are recognized, not only are conceptual walls erected around them but other parts of the system, when they cannot be ignored, are treated as subordinate to the new arrival. In the human rights field, this can be done by insisting (1) that the chosen right or set of rights are so important that

---

[27] See R. Desgagne, 'Integrating Environmental Values into the European Convention on Human Rights' (1995) 89 A.J.I.L. 263.   [28] See Brownlie, note 23 above at 15.

they should take precedence over all other human rights, and (2) that they have the status of *ius cogens* and so should prevail over all other norms of international law as well.[29] The motives behind such moves are obvious enough. If securing recognition for environmental rights—first as moral, and then as legal, rights—dramatically increases the force of environmental arguments, as it does, then it is logical to try to go one step further and attempt to climb to the top, using the foothold that one has established on the legal ladder. As with the question of whether such rights exist, however, these moves are allowable only if they satisfy the system's established criteria of legitimacy. The scope of rights and their relation to other rights are not matters for mere assertion, but questions to be settled by reference to the specific content of norms and the evidence of practice. Likewise, although there will always be room for argument about the content of *ius cogens* at a given time, international law has criteria for determining the status of its norms, including human rights norms, which are no less relevant for 'environmental rights' than for other elements in the system.

7 CONCLUSION

Rights play a key role in the debate about law and morals, but they raise conceptual issues that need clarification. In this chapter, I have tried to make this clarification by examining the idea of environmental rights and bringing out its implications. We have seen that the concept of rights plays a vital role by marking out growth areas for individuals or for groups. This can provide a theoretical basis for environmental rights of various kinds, although whether it is necessarily appropriate to address environmental issues through the concept of human rights is another matter. Three specific questions were then examined: (1) the need to establish who can be a rights-holder; (2) the need to identify who is under corresponding obligations; and (3) the need to consider the scope of a given right and its relation to other rights. Finally, to take account of some specific features of law and legal argumentation, this chapter has briefly reflected on the evidence needed to establish rules of international law and to determine their relative status within the system.

As far as possible, I have sought to relate the points made to environmental law in particular, although I have refrained from detailed consideration of certain matters, such as environmental ethics and equity, which are discussed in other chapters (see Chapter 13 'Ethics and International Environmental Law' and Chapter 27 'Equity'). I am conscious that in this rapid survey of the conceptual issues surrounding rights, I have dealt rather briefly with several matters that could be examined in greater

---

[29] For an example of such reasoning, see Thorne, note 26 above at 332.

depth. Questions such as the basis of human rights or the relation between legal and moral rights will no doubt continue to exercise lawyers and philosophers as long as their disciplines exist. The value of a rights-based approach to the legal and policy challenges posed by the environment is, of course, also a subject for continuing debate. If this chapter has done nothing else, I hope that it has at least demonstrated that environmental rights generate conceptual problems that are complex, interesting, and central to this issue.

RECOMMENDED READING

P. Alston, 'Conjuring Up New Human Rights: A Proposal for Quality Control' (1984) 78 A.J.I.L. 607.

A. Boyle and M. Anderson, eds., *Human Rights Approaches to Environmental Protection* (Oxford: Clarendon Press, 1996).

J. Crawford, ed., *The Rights of Peoples* (Oxford: Clarendon Press, 1988).

P.S. Elder, 'Legal Rights for Nature: The Wrong Answer to the Right(s) Question' (1984) 22 Osgoode Hall L.J. 285.

L.E. Lomasky, *Persons, Rights and the Moral Community* (Oxford: Oxford University Press, 1987).

W. Shutkin, 'International Human Rights Law and the Earth: the Protection of Indigenous Peoples and the Environment' (1990–1) 31 Va. J. Int'l L. 479.

D. Shelton, 'Environmental Rights,' in P. Alston, ed., *Peoples' Rights* (Oxford: Oxford University Press, 2001) 185.

M. Thorne, 'Establishing Environment As a Human Right' (1991) 19 Denver J. Int'l L. & Pol. 301.

UN Commission on Human Rights, Sub-Commission on Prevention of Discrimination and Protection of Minorities, *Human Rights and the Environment*, Final Report of the Special Rapporteur, UN Doc E/CN. 4/Sub. 2/1994/9 (6 July 1994).

CHAPTER 29

PUBLIC PARTICIPATION

JONAS EBBESSON

1 Introduction

Two intimately related developments regarding public participation in environmental decision-making can be discerned in international law. First, there are increasing efforts at the international level to adopt standards designed to govern public participation in national-level decision-making. Second, a growing number of procedures govern public participation in international decision-making, within the framework of international environmental agreements and international institutions. While the two types of procedures are to be distinguished, both are driven by similar motivations and pursue common goals. Moreover, the relevant norms in these two contexts interact and influence each other, giving rise to an international body of law concerning public participation in environmental matters. This chapter considers that body of law and how it has been applied to decision-making in both international and national contexts.

The chapter first discusses the contexts in which international law on public participation in environmental matters has developed and is to be understood, both politically and conceptually. It then explores the rationales for public participation. Subsequently, it analyses existing international norms regarding participation, related to international and national levels of decision-making respectively, and addresses how they have given rise to emerging normative patterns.

2 Contexts and Concepts

2.1 Political Context: Increased Involvement of Non-State Actors

The development of international norms concerning public participation in environmental decision-making reflects the general move in international governance, as well as in numerous states, towards expanding the involvement of non-state actors in decision-making procedures. Governments have lost the exclusive mandate, if they ever had it, to represent the public and to speak and act on behalf of public interests.

International law and policies on public participation in decision-making concerning environmental matters address participation in international *as well as* national contexts, institutions, and proceedings. However, the norms pertaining to these two contexts have not developed in tandem, and they differ considerably in regard to their content, geographical scope, and structure. Moreover, the roles and functions of public participation in international and national contexts differ. In spite of this situation, the norms concerned increasingly interact with and influence each other, resulting in some degree of normative integration between the international and national contexts. Regardless of whether the given laws and policies concern public participation at the national or international level, they address activities and procedures related to the environment, whereby individuals and groups can

- increase their general awareness;
- express their views;
- influence and engage themselves in law- and policy-making;
- affect decision-making concerning specific activities, plans, and programmes;
- trigger reviews of administrative decisions; and/or
- have existing laws enforced.

The massive presence and intense engagement of non-state actors in *international* environmental decision-making has a long history. There were a few cases of non-governmental organization (NGO) activism in the second half of the nineteenth century, when NGOs pushed for the adoption of a convention on bird protection. In the early twentieth century, environmental NGOs were also involved in international meetings on the regulation of fishing activities, and in promoting the development of international law for the protection of certain marine mammals. Yet, the difference is striking between these early cases and the activism shown at the UN conferences devoted to environmental issues in Stockholm in 1972 (UN Conference on the Human Environment (UNCHE)), in Rio de Janeiro in 1992 (UN Conference on Environment and Development (UNCED)), and in Johannesburg in 2002 (World Summit on Sustainable Development (WSSD)). It is estimated that in Rio about 2,400 NGO representatives participated in the conference (and 17,000 persons attended the parallel NGO forum). In Johannesburg, some 8,000 people represented NGOs, business, and other civil society groups at the conference (and many more participated in the hundreds of side events). Although these figures are outstanding, today such participation has grown even more pervasive, with NGOs attending almost every intergovernmental conference and meeting held within the framework of environmental agreements or intergovernmental organizations.

Despite the long history of NGO engagement in international environmental matters, the rules and regulations on the participation of non-state actors are of a more recent origin, dating back to the 1970s. Most international environmental regimes, whether of regional or global scope, now have accreditation processes and regulations concerning the participation of non-state actors. However, there are only a few intergovernmental institutions—*international development banks* being an exception (see Chapter 32 'International Institutions')—where the engagement of non-state actors extends beyond participation in decision-making to include the means and procedures by which the acts and decisions of the institution may be challenged.

The development of international norms and policies regarding public participation in *domestic* environmental decision-making can be traced back to before 1992.

Principle 10 of the Rio Declaration on Environment and Development, which was adopted at UNCED, has nevertheless been particularly influential for this development by suggesting a level of international consensus of policy formation. It provides that

[e]nvironmental issues are best handled with the participation of all concerned citizens, at the relevant level. At the national level, each individual shall have appropriate *access to information* concerning the environment that is held by public authorities, including information on hazardous materials and activities in their communities, and the opportunity to *participate in decision-making processes*. States shall facilitate and encourage public awareness and participation by making information widely available. Effective *access to judicial and administrative proceedings*, including *redress* and *remedy*, shall be provided [emphasis added].

While the motives for international rules on the participation of non-state actors in international forums are obvious, it may seem less apparent why international norms should address public participation in domestic decision-making proceedings. As Principle 10 indicates, public participation in this context embraces access to information, participation in decision-making, and access to judicial and administrative proceedings. These matters, and, in particular, judicial and administrative proceedings, belong to what traditionally was considered to be within state sovereignty. As such—with the exception of international human rights law—they have remained outside the scope of international law. This is no longer the case. Many states have expanded the participatory rights for individuals and NGOs of their own accord. Increasingly, however, international law is also imposing a duty on states to develop participatory processes at the national level, although, in most cases, it does not determine the precise manner in which states are to organize such participation. As indicated, there are also some signs that the norms and procedures applicable to participation in, respectively, the international and national contexts of decision-making are being integrated. This development is in line with the general observation that the divide between the 'international' and the 'national' is being relaxed.

The amplified voice of NGOs in international contexts implies a radical shift in the manner in which decisions are being made at the international level. Giving non-state actors a more influential role in law-making and the implementation of existing laws challenges the state-centred nature of international law. This does not mean that states have surrendered their decision-making and law-making powers. Rather, the increased involvement of non-state actors, at least in part, serves to legitimize the policies and laws adopted by states and, thereby, supports the regulatory activities of states. Non-state actors have also obtained formal recognition as partners in the implementation of international policies. This means that states are neither exclusively representing public concerns in environmental decision-making nor solely responsible for implementing international agreements and commitments. This development is reflected in, for example, the multiple stakeholder 'partnership' concept, which was key to the manner in which environmental problems were addressed at the 2002 WSSD.[1] Whatever its impact on public involvement in environmental decision-making, the partnership concept reflects the perception that international environmental policies and laws in general, if they are to be effective, require the participation of a diversity of actors.

2.2 Conceptual Context: Legal Fragments and Normative Patterns

In legal discourse as well as in law- and policy-making, 'the public' is often defined negatively as encompassing almost all actors *outside* the public—governmental—administration. Thus, it includes individuals, groups, NGOs, social movements, indigenous peoples, and local communities, which are not affiliated with the government or public administration. In most cases, however, the private corporate sector, when acting commercially, but not necessarily when organized in lobby groups, is excluded from the concept of 'the public' and is recognized as a separate category of stakeholders (which is not addressed in this chapter) (see Chapter 33 'Non-Governmental Organizations and Civil Society' and Chapter 35 'Business'). Despite this broad notion of 'the public', it will be evident that in international contexts and institutions, NGOs are privileged compared with other, less institutionalized non-governmental and non-corporate actors.

While UNCED[2] as well as at the WSSD[3] repeatedly referred to good governance and public participation, neither conference spurred the development of a comprehensive global treaty on public participation in decision-making regarding the environment. Part of the reason is found in the recent origin of this field of international law, the political facet of public participation, and the intimate relationship between public participation in decision-making and issues of governance and state sovereignty. These are all factors that complicate the achievement of sufficient consensus on a global scale for the development of legally binding norms. Thus, so far, the existing international rules and principles on public participation rarely go beyond regional application. Principle 10 of the Rio Declaration does not reflect a general principle of international law, but, by suggesting a level of consensus regarding the desirable direction of policy formation, it has framed legal discourse and induced legal development, in particular at the regional level. The 1998 UN Economic

---

[1] E.g., Johannesburg Plan of Implementation, in *Report of the World Summit on Sustainable Development*, Johannesburg, South Africa, 26 August–4 September 2002, UN Doc. A/CONF.199/20 (2002) at paras. 49, 106, 146, and 167.

[2] United Nations Conference on Environment and Development (UNCED), Agenda 21, 13 June 1992, UN Doc. A/CONF. 151/26 (1992) at paras. 1.3, 3.2, 8.3, 8.16, 8.25, 10.10, 15.5, 16.33, 18.9, 18.22, 18.59, 28.1, 33.8, 33.16, 36.3, 36.10, 39.1. and 39.3.

[3] Johannesburg Plan of Implementation, at paras. 2, 45, 62, 71, 138, 139, 141, 163, and 164.

Commission for Europe (UNECE) Convention on Access to Information, Public Participation in Decision-Making and Access to Justice in Environmental Matters (Aarhus Convention) is at the forefront of these developments. Since the geographical scope of the UNECE is not limited only to the European Continent, the Aarhus Convention and other agreements adopted under its auspices may include also the United States and Canada (although the Aarhus Convention has not been ratified by either of these states) as well as a number of states in Asia (previously parts of the Soviet Union). In addition, more modest developments can be noticed in other regions. Finally, some limited steps have been taken at the global level to flesh out the legal implications of Principle 10 of the Rio Declaration, for example, by rather vague provisions in treaties of global scope and, more convincingly, by the work of the International Law Commission (ILC).

Apart from regional treaties and the abstract clauses in global environmental treaties, the normative development regarding public participation in decision-making has taken place mainly by way of intergovernmental policy documents, declarations, decisions, recommendations, guidelines, and action plans. The legal relevance of these documents differs, with none of them by itself establishing legal obligations for states. The bits and pieces contained in these documents generally are not the result of coordinated decision-making processes. Nevertheless, they provide fragments of a normative pattern, which can be fully depicted only if these documents are studied together with relevant regional arrangements as well as with draft documents of global relevance. In addition, one needs to consider these developments in international environmental law in light of the already established norms of international human rights law, such as the right to political participation and to a fair trial. They provide a conceptual link to participatory rights, access to information, and access to justice, as contained in, for example, the Rio Declaration and the Aarhus Convention. All of these elements are crucial in order to avoid mere *pro forma* participation in decision-making processes—that is, access to information is a prerequisite for meaningful participation, and access to justice is a means to having decisions and decision-making processes reviewed.

3 WHY PUBLIC PARTICIPATION?

Why, then, have governments come to endorse public participation in environmental decision-making even in policy documents of global relevance?[4] In answering this question, one can identify different rationales that foster legal development as well as

---

[4] See, e.g., Agenda 21, paras. 23.2, 8.18, 27.9, 27.10, and 27.13; 2000 Malmö Ministerial Declaration, adopted by the Global Ministerial Environment Forum, Sixth Special Session of the Governing Council

different roles that members of the public play when participating in decision-making regarding the environment. In terms of governance, the increased confidence in—and need for—public participation reflects an expansive notion of democracy where the involvement of citizens and NGOs is conceived not only as furthering selfish interests, but also as contributing to promoting public environmental interests. This understanding diverges from the 'standard liberal' approach, according to which public interests should be enforced, or even invoked, only by governmental and administrative institutions. Whatever its merits, the latter approach accords badly with various welfare rights such as the protection of the environment, which require integration of public and private interests, often of a diffuse, collective, and fragmented character, in the decision-making process.

Pressure from influential NGOs and the awareness of governments themselves that participatory elements are needed to enhance the legitimacy of decision-making have also spurred the development of international and national regimes for public participation (see Chapter 30 'Legitimacy'). Public involvement serves to legitimize environmental decisions, partly because of environmental arguments. However, factors relating to democratic decision-making are just as important. The trust in public authorities and the acceptance of decisions are enhanced if members of the public have a say—not only by voting—in the development, application, implementation, and enforcement of legal norms and policies, as well as in decision-making concerning specific projects. Such participation is particularly relevant in domestic contexts. Yet, given the increased impact of international decision-making (see Chapter 32 'International Institutions'), such decisions also require pluralistic participatory structures in order to induce legitimacy.

Another set of arguments that promote participatory rights relates to international human rights law. As mentioned, the international rules on public participation in environmental decision-making—including access to information and access to justice—draw on, adapt, and develop concepts already recognized in international human rights law. For instance, the right of members of the public to participate in environmental decision-making furthers and specifies the generally acknowledged right to political participation.[5] Likewise, the right to access to effective judicial proceedings and remedies in environmental matters draws on the right to a fair trial, set out in most human rights documents,[6] while also adapting it to the specific features of environmental problems.

---

of the United Nations Environment Programme, 31 May 2000; and 2002 Johannesburg Plan of Implementation, at para. 119.

[5] E.g., 1948 Universal Declaration of Human Rights (UDHR), Article 19; 1966 International Covenant on Civil and Political Rights (ICCPR), Article 25; 1969 American Convention on Human Rights (ACHR), Article 23; and 1981 African Charter on Human and People's Rights, Article 13.

[6] E.g., UDHR, Article 10; ICCPR, Article 14; European Convention on Human Rights (ECHR), Article 6; and ACHR, Article 8.

Of course, there are also straightforward environmental motives for promoting public participation in decision-making. Governments and public authorities sometimes fail to consider essential environmental concerns when seeking to realize different, often conflicting interests. Moreover, environmental authorities are not able to act in all cases where environmental laws are not complied with, either because they are understaffed or blocked, for political reasons, from enforcing existing environmental laws. In these cases, allowing members of the public to initiate proceedings and invoke acknowledged environmental concerns, which are otherwise at risk of being ignored, may lead to better decisions and more effective application and enforcement of existing—international and national—environmental law. Participation may also provide an opportunity to determine (and question) what constitutes a health or environmental problem in the first place. Such problems and concerns cannot be reduced to objective criteria only, defined, for example, in decibels, concentrations, or the number of specimen. They also involve subjective perceptions of whether the effects on humans and the environment is a 'problem' or not. Finally, participatory procedures provide for communication, for exchanging 'second thoughts' and reflections among those involved, and for thinking in terms of alternatives, which are all essential elements in any sustainable development policy.

In terms of diplomacy and negotiation techniques, there are moments and circumstances in which privacy and secrecy may be necessary to achieve certain results, but this does not challenge the general presumptions in favour of transparent and participatory decision-making structures. An argument sometimes made *against* public participation is that it is time-consuming, obstructing, and costly. To be sure, democratic elements and institutions are seldom without costs, but, to the extent that participatory elements enhance legitimacy, the quality of decisions, and even the democratic quality of society, this economic argument becomes less convincing. Most certainly there are cases when participatory entitlements are misused, but there is no persuasive evidence that this is common practice. Moreover, the expanding participation of non-state actors does not mean that states have lost their power. It is not a zero-sum game, and, as already pointed out, public participation even helps to make governmental decisions more effective by enhancing the legitimacy and, thus, the acceptance level of decisions taken. Generally, more relevant criticisms against NGOs' participation are concerns about their accountability and transparency and about the geographical regions and societal classes whose interests they represent. For instance, who funds the NGOs and to what extent can the overwhelming number of NGOs from Western countries claim to represent public interests of other countries or the wider international community?

4 International Contexts, Institutions, and Decision-Making

4.1 NGOs as Representatives of the Public

A common feature of the public participation arrangements in international environmental regimes is that NGOs—whether international, national, technical, scientific, or policy-oriented—are given an almost exclusive mandate to represent civil society. Other less institutionalized segments of society, such as individual actors, networks, and social movements, are generally disregarded. Except for review procedures within the framework of a few regional environmental arrangements and some international development banks, NGOs are thus given a privileged position to attend meetings and voice their concerns and agendas. While this may simplify the practical arrangements of international meetings, it has the effect of precluding views and concerns of less organized groups and communities from being heard at international meetings.

The point is not that NGOs are generally more representative of public interests than their governments when participating at international meetings and in decision-making. Rather, they may influence international decision-making by invoking recognized public interests in parallel to governments themselves, and bring attention to issues and arguments that would otherwise be ignored. Even when their formal role is limited to that of an 'observer', NGOs may influence the development and implementation of environmental laws and policies by pushing the agenda, providing expertise, lobbying, monitoring, and even enforcing environmental duties. In performing these functions, NGOs also act as 'whistle-blowers' by demanding attention for urgent concerns and as 'watch-dogs' by, for example, pressuring governments to implement international commitments. In yet other cases, NGOs may challenge decisions in review procedures, either in their own name or as full-powered representatives of persons affected by the decisions.

4.2 Public Participation in Decision-Making and Access to Information

Several UN bodies, such as the UN Environment Programme (UNEP), the Commission on Sustainable Development (CSD), the International Labour Organization, the International Maritime Organization, the UN Educational,

Scientific, and Cultural Organization, the Food and Agricultural Organization, and the World Health Organization (WHO), as well as secretariats of multilateral environmental agreements (MEAs) (see Chapter 38 'Treaty Bodies'), have adopted accreditation programmes that apply to NGOs. Other international organizations, with differing degrees of engagement in environmental and health matters, such as the Organisation for Economic Co-operation and Development (OECD), the European Union (EU), and the Organization of American States (OAS), have also adopted processes and schemes for NGO accreditation (the World Trade Organization (WTO) still maintains a rather rigid approach to NGO involvement). Most MEAs adopted after the mid-1980s follow the standard formula for NGO participation at Meetings of the Parties, and in subsidiary bodies, that was first adopted in 1973 in the framework of the Convention on International Trade in Endangered Species of Wild Fauna and Flora (CITES). Accordingly, with some differences, the following treaties as well as numerous regional agreements, all set out that any body or agency, whether national or international, governmental or non-governmental, which is qualified as competent in the subject matter covered by the respective agreement, and which has informed the secretariat of its wish to be represented at a Meeting of the Parties, may be admitted unless a minority of the parties present—at least one-third—objects:

- 1992 UN Framework Convention on Climate Change (UNFCCC) and the 1997 Kyoto Protocol;
- 1992 Convention on Biological Diversity (CBD);
- 1987 Montreal Protocol on Substances That Deplete the Ozone Layer;
- 2001 Stockholm Convention on Persistent Organic Pollutants (Stockholm Convention);
- 1998 Convention on the Prior Informed Consent Procedure for Certain Hazardous Chemicals and Pesticides in International Trade;
- 1989 Basel Convention on the Control of Transboundary Movements of Hazardous Wastes and Their Disposal;
- 1979 Convention on the Conservation of Migratory Species of Wild Animals; and
- 1994 Convention to Combat Desertification in Those Countries Experiencing Serious Drought and/or Desertification, Particularly in Africa (Desertification Convention).

Even where an MEA or the constitutive document of an international organization does not provide for admitting NGOs as observers, the relevant forums rarely bar the parties from adopting participatory arrangements. In such cases, the legal basis for NGO participation is usually found in decisions by the forum in question, such as a conference of state parties or a governing body of an international organization (for example, the Convention on Wetlands of International Importance Especially as Waterfowl Habitat (Ramsar Convention), the International Whaling Commission, and the WHO).

Once accredited, NGOs may attend meetings and lobby state representatives, but they may not take part in the formal decision-making—that is, they may neither vote on nor veto decisions. Accreditation does not necessarily imply a right for NGOs to attend all sessions (some may be closed and some may be informal, which usually depends on the rules of procedure or decisions taken by the chairperson), but, in general, it entails the right to observe meetings and to submit documents, proposals, and petitions for consideration by the parties. In most environmental regimes, NGOs are given the right to address the meeting. Some regimes also entitle NGOs to participate in the meetings of committees or expert groups (for example, the Ramsar Convention), either as full members or observers, or to nominate candidates to certain committees (for example, the Aarhus Convention, where NGOs are entitled to nominate members of the compliance committee). Finally, some environmental regimes permit NGOs (and individuals) to make formal complaints and trigger enforcement and review procedures, for example, through compliance committees (see section 3.3). So while the observer status provides for differing degrees of participation in different regimes, it usually entails more opportunities than mere passive observation.

As pointed out, the rudimentary right of NGOs to be represented at Meetings of the Parties to environmental agreements is usually dependent on a minority of the state parties not blocking their participation. As far as the legal basis for NGO participation is concerned, the treaty parties may of course review and change their policies and, if the legal basis is not set out in the treaty, change their decisions providing for NGO participation. Moreover, there are generally no means for the NGOs themselves to have the accreditation regulation enforced or a decision concerning their presence appealed. Despite these considerations, and the formulation in most relevant treaties that NGOs 'may' be represented at meetings, a group of states representing less than one-third of the membership cannot formally (but maybe politically) block their participation. Therefore, it is too simple to argue that these provisions do not provide a participatory *right* at all. Rather, the participatory right of NGOs is a narrowly defined, qualified, and conditioned right, but it may be sustained even against the will of some state parties.[7] Likewise, it is too simple to dismiss decisions and regulations for NGO participation adopted at Meetings of the Parties as purely political, 'non-legal', or 'non-binding'. Although decisions and regulations can be altered, they do bind the treaty parties or the international organization in question until duly changed in accordance with the rules of procedure.[8]

An interesting and innovative (and possibly controversial) initiative was the set of guidelines adopted in 2005 by the Aarhus Convention parties in order to generally

[7] I leave aside that some regimes have certain rules for national non-governmental organizations (NGOs), which allow the home state to veto the NGO's presence.

[8] In this respect, decisions by Meeting of the Parties concerning procedural or organizational issues differ from most decisions relating to the parties' performances in general.

promote access to information and public participation in international forums.[9] Yet, it is difficult to observe a general trend in the operative policies, regulations, and/or guidelines for public participation of international organizations (such as the UN, the OECD, the OAS, and the EU), except that they have expanded rather than reduced the scope for non-state participation. Within the UN system, the legal basis for public participation is found in the mandate given to the Economic and Social Council (ECOSOC) to provide for 'consultative arrangements' with NGOs.[10] NGOs fulfilling the ECOSOC criteria (time of existence, non-profit structure, and a democratic decision-making structure) may attain different consultative status, depending on the purpose and scope of the organization[11] and thus contribute to the UN work programmes. The more than 2,500 NGOs with such status serve as technical experts and advisers, take part in the implementation of programmes, and provide interventions, statements, and proposals for new initiatives. These organizations are generally invited to attend international conferences organized by the United Nations (1972 UNCHE, 1992 UNCED, and 2002 WSSD), but other NGOs may also be admitted by the respective conference secretariat, in accordance with guidelines agreed to by states and preparatory committees.

In addition to providing for NGO participation through accreditation, some treaty secretariats and international institutions have established various forms of communication centres, discussion forums, dialogue routines or procedures for commenting in order to enhance public involvement (for example, the CBD, the CSD, the Commission for Environmental Cooperation under the North American Agreement on Environmental Cooperation (NAAEC), the UNECE, and UNEP). These arrangements differ considerably from one regime to the other, but they may allow for members of the public to submit comments and views about a convention and its implementation. Even more important for access to information has been the establishment of useful and informative websites in the second half of the 1990s, by most intergovernmental organizations and treaty secretariats within and outside the UN system. This development has made the relevant information far more available than before. In some regimes, the task of providing relevant information is set out in the treaty, but, more often, it is based on decisions by the parties or on the general mandate given to the Secretariat. Generally speaking, however, neither such communication policies or dialogue routines nor the practices for placing information on the web amount to rights for members of the public to participate in decision-making or to access information.[12]

---

[9] Almaty Guidelines in Promoting the Application of the Principles of the Aarhus Convention in International Forums, Annex to Decision II/4, *Report of the Second Meeting of the Parties*, Doc. ECE/MP.PP/2005/2/Add.5 (20 June 2005).

[10] Compare Charter of the United Nations, Article 71, according to which the Economic and Social Council (ECOSOC) 'may make suitable arrangements for consultations with non-governmental organizations concerned with matters within its competence.'

[11] ECOSOC Resolution 1996/31.

[12] In this respect, the EU is a special case, where members of the public can indeed claim and enforce a right to access to documents held by the organization's institutions, although subject to secrecy restrictions.

4.3 Access to Justice

Essentially, most international review or dispute settlement proceedings against *states*—such as the International Court of Justice, the International Tribunal for the Law of the Sea, and the WTO Dispute Settlement Body—can be initiated only by the states themselves. Although the practice of the WTO Dispute Settlement Body shows that it may be possible for NGOs to act as *amicus curiae* under the discretion of the institution resolving the dispute,[13] this possibility does not amount to a right for NGOs to participate in or trigger such procedures nor to submit briefs. More readily available for non-state actors are the international human rights tribunals and institutions with global or regional jurisdiction. These procedures, by focusing on the application of international norms within the national legal system of a state, can be used by members of the public to challenge states for violations of international law concerning the protection of health and the environment (see Chapter 28 'Environmental Rights').[14] At least in theory, the Permanent Court of International Arbitration and other arbitral tribunals may consider cases in which non-state actors bring a claim for compensation for damage against a state or corporation. However, since such cases can be brought before these tribunals only with the consent of the state or corporation concerned, they are quite unlikely to arise in practice.

Hence, apart from the human rights courts, there is still no international court readily available for recourse by individuals or NGOs when states violate international norms on the protection of health and the environment.[15] Nor do any of the global environmental agreements provide a review system that can be triggered by members of the public. The few regional review mechanisms and procedures established for this purpose in Europe and North America—the Standing Committee of the 1979 Convention on the Conservation of European Wildlife and Natural Habitats (Bern Convention), the Council of the Commission for Environmental Cooperation (CEC), which was established by the 1993 NAAEC, and the 1998 Aarhus Convention Compliance Committee (applicable to Europe and parts of Asia)—are based on different logics and have different objectives and varying degrees of independence.

The review procedures of the Bern Convention and the Aarhus Convention are established for the purpose of promoting compliance with the international law standards set out by the conventions themselves (on, respectively, nature protection

See EC Regulation 1049/2001 Regarding Public Access to European Parliament, Council and Commission Documents, [2001] O.J. L145/43.

[13] *United States—Import Prohibition of Certain Shrimps and Shrimp Products*, Appellate Body Report, adopted 6 November 1998, Doc. WT/DS58/AB/R (12 October 1998).

[14] This aspect was relevant in *Fadeyeva v. Russia*, 55723/00 Eur. Ct. H.R. (9 June 2005), where the European Court of Human Rights (ECrtHR) held that Russia violated Article 8 of the ECHR, because of the health deterioration of the plaintiff (applicant) from industrial emissions. See also Daniel García San José, *Environmental Protection and the European Convention on Human Rights*, Human Rights Files no. 21 (Strasbourg: Council of Europe Publishing, 2005).

[15] Again, the EU is a special case, where the European judicature in certain situations can be available for members of the public to challenge the implementation of EU law in the member states.

measures and procedural arrangements related to public participation). The NAAEC procedure, however, is primarily intended to ensure enforcement of national environmental protection standards. The common feature of these regimes is that they all allow for triggering by individuals and NGOs, and also permit these individuals and groups to submit *amicus curiae* briefs in the fact-finding phase. Still, the three review bodies differ considerably in terms of their structure, degree of independence, and judicial properties. Whereas NGOs take active part in the standing committee meetings of the Bern Convention, the Council of the CEC consists of only cabinet-level (or equivalent) representatives of the parties. The Aarhus Convention Compliance Committee is an independent, although non-judicial, body where the committee members are nominated by the parties, signatories, and accredited NGOs, and they act in their personal capacity. The regimes also differ in terms of the remedies available. In no case is the international review body competent to take decisions that are legally binding on the parties. However, in the two European regimes, the committees can adopt independent findings of non-compliance and may in some cases recommend measures to be taken by the non-compliant states that would bring that state back into compliance. Given certain circumstances—for instance, in cases of serious or consistent non-compliance—these review bodies may also recommend that the other parties to the convention adopt measures against the non-compliant state. The Council of the CEC may make publicly available only a factual record of the case in point. While none of the review bodies is judicial in a strict sense, the NAAEC provides a far more politicized structure than the other two bodies and cannot really be said to grant access to justice against the failing NAAEC party.

Legal scholars and NGOs have criticized these review systems, not least the NAAEC, for lacking teeth. While this criticism is well founded, the Aarhus Convention, as well as the Bern Convention (and even the NAAEC) go well beyond other international environmental arrangements in providing access to a review procedure for members of the public. The effectiveness and relevance of these mechanisms much depend on the legal basis and rules of procedure but also on the self-perception of the review bodies—their engagement, integrity, and the use they make of discretionary powers in interpreting and applying the rules concerned. Given that none of the regimes discussed makes it possible for non-state actors to enforce a decision against a failing party, the impact of the decisions and findings resides in the authoritative interpretation of the treaty and in the authority of the review body itself. Such decisions and findings exert political pressure on the failing state to comply with applicable rules and standards, and may induce other treaty parties to initiate international dispute settlement procedures against it. Findings and recommendations by the international review body may also be used by non-state actors as evidence of a legal or factual nature in domestic procedures against the government of the failing state.

One of the few instances where non-state actors may challenge decisions by *international institutions* is provided by international development banks (another example being the EU). These procedures were adopted in response to several developments, including the call in Agenda 21 that development banks should consult with NGOs and provide accurate and timely information about their programmes,[16] and the criticism from NGOs about World Bank projects. In a sense, these procedures—the World Bank Inspection Panel, the Inter-American Development Bank investigation mechanism, and the Asian Development Bank accountability mechanism—resemble the review systems established within the regional environmental regimes discussed earlier. Like the regional review mechanisms, these procedures provide some degree of independent evaluation of the banks' activities and result in findings that are not legally binding for the banks and/or the borrowing state involved.

The issue at stake in the review procedure established by development banks is not whether financial support can be justified for a specific project—say, a dam—considering the harm caused to the peoples and the environment affected. Rather, as in the case of the World Bank, it concerns whether the process leading to a possible contract follows the bank's operational policies for environmental assessments and consultations with project-affected groups. A finding of a violation of these policies does not as such suspend or cancel the lending agreement between the bank and the borrowing state. Instead, it may lead to a reconsideration of the manner in which a project is being implemented. Moreover, in cases of non-compliance with contractual conditions on the part of the borrower, the bank—and not the Inspection Panel—has some discretion to decide on such measures.[17]

The essential participatory element in the World Bank review procedure is that affected groups of persons may submit complaints to the Inspection Panel for failures of the bank—not the borrower—to comply with its policies and procedures concerning a project financed by the bank.[18] The Inspection Panel is intended to carry out investigations independently (for example, by interviews, consultations, on-site inspections, and *amicus curiae* briefs from NGOs). Still, it acts under the authority of the bank's Executive Board; a politically sensitive body, which also takes the final decision in case of a violation of bank policies. So despite the relative independence and effectiveness of the Inspection Panel and its availability for non-state actors, the World Bank review procedure remains essentially an in-house review system. While its judicial analogy is therefore even weaker than that of the Aarhus Convention (but not weaker than that of the NAAEC), it is difficult to compare the effectiveness of the review systems since they operate in such different contexts. Broadly speaking, however, the effectiveness of the review procedures in the World

---

[16] Agenda 21, paras 27(9), 33(14), and 38(7).

[17] Compare International Bank for Reconstruction and Development (IBRD), *General Conditions: Conditions for Loans*, 1 July 2005, Article VII; and International Development Association (IDA), *General Conditions for Credits and Grants*, 1 July 2005, Article VI.

[18] IBRD Resolution no. 93-10 and IBRD Resolution no. IDA 93-6.

Bank and other development banks depend on the self-perception and integrity of the panels—that is, on the same factors that matter for the review procedures within the regional environmental agreements discussed earlier.

5 NATIONAL CONTEXTS, INSTITUTIONS, AND DECISION-MAKING

5.1 Non-Discrimination or Minimum Standards?

The possible forms for environmental decision-making in national contexts and institutions are numerous and include the issuing of permits; environmental impacts assessments; requests by supervisory authorities; hearings, appeals, and reviews proceedings; private litigation; citizen suits; and class actions. Environmental decision-making ranges from decisions concerning specific activities, installations, and substances to decisions concerning plans, programs, policies, and even the adoption of laws and executive regulations. Thus, to be relevant, international norms concerning public participation in domestic decision-making should be both flexible enough to be adaptable to the different decision-making structures, and sufficiently clear to ensure some minimum standards for public participation and access to information. Access to information matters not only because it facilitates meaningful participation in the various forms of environmental decision-making, but also because it enables members of the public to continuously assess matters that affect their living environment.

One approach to meet the needs for flexibility in a transboundary context, without harmonizing the standards for access to information, public participation, or access to justice in domestic contexts, is to prohibit discrimination on the basis of nationality and residence. The logic of non-discrimination is to ignore state borders and provide for equal participation regardless of such borders when decisions are made that affect health and the environment. In other words, if an activity may cause transboundary effects, the state that decides on the permit must ensure equal access to its decision-making procedures to those affected in other states, by applying its national criteria for standing and participation. In some regimes (for example, the Aarhus Convention and the 2003 Protocol on Strategic Environmental Assessment to the Convention on Environmental Impact Assessment in a Transboundary Context), the non-discrimination principle also applies to planning decisions and/or access to information.

Equal access to remedies for injured parties was incorporated already into the 1909 US-Canada Boundary Water Treaty. Much later, in 1974, the non-discrimination principle was given a far wider scope of application—to almost any decision-making concerning the permissibility of environmentally hazardous activities—by the Convention on the Protection of the Environment, concluded between the Nordic states. This endeavour, in turn, inspired the OECD to adopt recommendations with broader geographical reach on equal access in procedures concerning transboundary pollution.[19] Since then, non-discrimination has been further acknowledged as a principle of environmental law in national and international settings. It is applied by numerous states, formulated in international policy statements, and laid down in various regional treaties. In the global context, the ILC has actively promoted the codification of the principle: first, by drafting what was to become the 1997 UN Convention on the Law of Non-Navigational Uses of International Watercourses (Watercourses Convention) and, second, by its draft articles on International Liability for Injurious Consequences Arising out of Acts not Prohibited by International Law (Prevention of Transboundary Harm from Hazardous Activities) (Draft Articles on Prevention), which were submitted to the UN General Assembly in 2001.[20] The UN Watercourses Convention has not yet entered into force, the OECD recommendations are not legally binding, and the ILC Draft Articles on Prevention have not been formally endorsed by states as yet. Even so, these and other international treaties (for example, the Aarhus Convention and the 2003 African Convention on the Conservation of Nature and Natural Resources), policy documents and drafts, as well as national laws support the claim that, in environmental matters, the procedural dimension of the non-discrimination principle has achieved global recognition as a legal principle.

The merit of non-discrimination in environmental contexts is the implied indifference to state borders in decision-making. This being said, unless other international rules are also applicable, the transboundary rights implied by the non-discrimination principle fully depend on the law of the state where the activity is to take place. If generous participatory rights are granted to locals, then equally generous rights must be given to equally affected persons on the other side of the border. If, on the other hand, a state applies restrictive rules on standing and access to remedies, it only has to ensure equally limited rights across the border. Thus, ignoring state borders in decision-making does not as such ensure participatory rights.

A more ambitious approach, therefore, is to define internationally the minimum requirements for public participation in decision-making, access to information, and access to justice, to be implemented in national systems. Contrary to the notion of non-discrimination, however, minimum international legal standards for public participation are few and far between. For the time being, such standards are being

---

[19] OECD Recommendation on the Implementation of a Regime of Equal Right of Access and Non-Discrimination in Relation to Transfrontier Pollution, Doc. C(77) 28(Final), 16 I.L.M. 977 (1977).

[20] International Liability for Injurious Consequences Arising out of Acts not Prohibited by International Law (Prevention of Transboundary Harm from Hazardous Activities), see International Law Commission (ILC), *Report on the Work of Its Fifty-Third Session*, UN Doc. A/56/10/suppl.10 (2001) 366–436 [Draft Articles on Prevention].

developed regionally, particularly in Europe and parts of Asia and in North America, whereas the references to public participation in existing global environmental agreements are modest, despite the strong endorsement of public participation in environmental decision-making at the 1992 UNCED.

5.2 Public Participation in Decision-Making and Access to Information

The regional regimes for Europe and parts of Asia—the Aarhus Convention, in particular—are by far the most advanced international legal instruments providing for public participation in decision-making and access to information in environmental matters. The Aarhus Convention establishes minimum rights for public participation in decision-making procedures concerning specific activities and installations, plans, programmes, policies, executive regulations, and generally applicable rules. Thus, it provides a bottom floor for harmonization and goes further than merely prohibiting discrimination. In addition to promoting generous rules as to who may participate, it sets out that environmental NGOs are deemed to have a sufficient interest to take part in decision-making and submit complaints to legal review. Obviously, participatory rights do not imply a veto for members of the public, but the decision-making procedures must be transparent and provide for participation—including opportunities to submit comments and opinions—at an early stage in the process, and due account shall be taken of the outcome of the participatory procedures. Members of the public are also granted a right to access to any environmental information held by public authorities, without having to show a particular interest in the case. The presumption is that all environmental information should be publicly available, unless refusal to disclose information is justified by any of the listed grounds. To make this right more useful, the Aarhus Convention also obliges the parties to keep and update 'an adequate flow' of environmental information. While these provisions are rather vague, they will be strengthened by the Protocol on Pollutant Release and Transfer Registers, which was adopted in 2003, and which prescribes that publicly available pollutant release and transfer registers be established.

The Aarhus Convention applies to most states in the UNECE region (with the exception of, for example, Canada, the United States, and Russia, which are not parties). It is also open to accession by states outside the UNECE region, so, theoretically, it could expand into a treaty with global application, although this is quite unlikely (and at the time of writing, no state outside the UNECE has yet acceded to it). In order to understand the full significance of the Aarhus Convention, its normative context in Europe needs to be taken into consideration. First, it applies in parallel with other UNECE environmental conventions, which set out more narrowly defined provisions on access to information and participatory structures in decision-making with respect to environmental impact assessments, water issues, and industrial accidents.[21] These conventions provide substantive content, which is relevant in claims of non-compliance and domestic cases, with respect to the type of information to be provided, the nature of participation to be afforded, and the standards to be implemented by the parties.

Second, apart from the environmental regimes, the European Court of Human Rights (ECtHR) has taken a wide and principled approach to access to environmental information. According to its jurisprudence, a state violates the fundamental right to respect for privacy and family life if it fails to provide essential information about hazardous activities that enables members of the public to assess the risks they and their families might run.[22] This finding shows the close linkage between environmental law and human rights law by construing an environmental 'right-to-know' with far-reaching implications for the right to access to environmental information in Europe.

By comparison, the legal arrangements and minimum standards for public participation in decision-making and access to information in other regions are less ambitious. This is also the case with the North American counterpart, the NAAEC, which is more concerned with access to enforcement remedies and sanctions than with participatory structures. While the NAAEC also intends to promote transparency in law-making and access to environmental information held by public authorities, it falls far short of a right-based structure, such as that of the Aarhus Convention and the jurisprudence of the ECtHR. The regional nature conservation agreements for, respectively, southeast Asia and Africa are even more removed from such a structure and level of ambition in providing for public participation in decision-making and access to information.[23] Nevertheless, in the global context, the relevance of these initiatives is not to be found in the drafting details, but rather in the fact that they show that issues of public participation in environmental matters are the subject of international negotiations and legal development also outside Europe and North America.

For the time being, there is no counterpart to the Aarhus Convention at the global level, despite the link to the right to political participation in different human rights instruments. The MEAs that endorse public participation in decision-making and the dissemination of information (for example, in the UNFCCC, the Desertification

[21] 1991 Espoo Convention on Environmental Impact Assessment in a Transboundary Context (Espoo Convention), Articles 3 and 6; 1992 Convention on the Transboundary Effects of Industrial Accidents, Article 9; and 1999 Protocol on Water and Health to the 1992 Convention on the Protection and Use of Transboundary Watercourses and International Lakes, Articles 5, 9, and 10.

[22] Compare ECHR, Article 8. *Guerra and Others v. Italy*, 14967/89 Eur. Ct. H.R. 7 (1998) (19 February 1998).

[23] 1985 ASEAN Agreement on the Conservation of Nature and Natural Resources, Article 16; 2003 African Convention on the Conservation of Nature and Natural Resources (Maputo, Mozambique, 11 July 2003), Article XVI. At the time of writing, neither the 1985 ASEAN agreement nor the 2003 African convention was in force.

Convention, the Stockholm Convention, the CBD, the Cartagena Protocol on Biosafety, the Montreal Protocol, and the Ramsar Convention), basically aim to improve public awareness about, and engagement in environmental problems, without granting the public a right to take part in environmental decision-making or to obtain environmental information. Even though these agreements should be interpreted in light of the Rio Declaration and other policy documents, and may become the starting points for more progressive norms on public participation and access to information in the future, they currently are far from reflecting the right-based approach of the Aarhus Convention or even Principle 10 of the Rio Declaration.

Given this lack of more substantial treaty law concerning public participation in decision-making and access to information in environmental matters, the ILC Draft Articles on Prevention provide one of the few legally relevant references to public participation in a global legal context: 'States concerned shall, by such means as are appropriate, provide the public likely to be affected by an activity within the scope of the present articles with relevant information relating to the activity, the risks involved and the harm which might result and ascertain their views.'[24] The provision correctly conceives of access to information as closely related to public participation. In addition to the duty of states to make relevant information on hazardous activities and related risks available to members of the public, it provides—clearly inspired by the post-Rio developments in environmental and human rights law—that states shall 'ascertain their views'. Hence, members of the public shall at least be ensured some opportunity to comment on proposed activities, and these views should be taken into due account. How else can the views be ascertained? If incorporated into a multilateral agreement, the thrust of the ILC Draft Articles on Prevention would remain far from the Aarhus Convention approach, and the parties would retain considerable leeway in designing the participatory arrangements. Nevertheless, it would push beyond the references to public participation in existing global environmental agreements. The ILC Draft Articles on Prevention imply a more rights-based approach to participation—although the term 'right' is avoided—and have a broader scope of application than the mentioned MEAs of global application, since the draft articles would apply generally to hazardous activities.[25] They also make decision-making a two-way street and not just a matter of governments providing information to members of the public.

5.3 Access to Justice

In contrast to public participation in decision-making, most human rights conventions do set out a right to fair trial, which may also provide access to justice in cases about human health and/or the environment. As far as international environmental agreements are concerned, the right to access to justice in environmental matters is

[24] ILC Draft Articles on Prevention, see note 20 above, Article 13.

[25] *Ibid.* at Article 13; and see ILC, *Report on the Work of Its Fifty-Third Session*, note 20 above at 422–5.

again made most explicit in the Aarhus Convention and the NAAEC. Both agreements construe access to justice as an essential element of public participation in decision-making—that is, as a means to enforce environmental laws, correct erroneous administrative decisions, and push competent authorities to do their job. International law thus becomes a vehicle to improve the effectiveness of national as well as international environmental laws.

The Aarhus Convention links access to justice to the participatory and informational elements. The parties to the convention must ensure that members of the public have access to a court or another independent and impartial body established by law in order to be able to challenge: (1) refusals by public authorities to grant requests for environmental information; (2) the legality of decisions concerning specific activities; and (3) other violations of national environmental law by private and public bodies. Parties are also obliged to fulfil minimum standards concerning remedies and due process. In defining criteria for standing, the Aarhus Convention reflects the complexity of the interests to be considered and balanced against each other in environmental decision-making. It, thus, deviates from international human rights law by relaxing the distinction between private and public matters. It also promotes wider access to justice to members of the public, for example, by providing for judicial review of decisions in cases where this would not necessarily follow from the human rights regimes. Another element that distinguishes the Aarhus Convention from human rights regimes is that it grants environmental associations, subject to relevant requirements under national laws, access to justice in environmental matters and a right to act on behalf of public environmental interests.

In a sense, the approach to access to justice in the NAAEC is even broader in scope than that of the Aarhus Convention, as it obliges the state parties to generally ensure judicial and administrative enforcement proceedings, whereby violations of domestic environmental laws can be sanctioned and remedied. The NAAEC also requires that the parties provide adequate remedies to sue private actors, request governmental action, and seek injunctions as well as ensuring due process in existing forms of environmental proceedings.

Outside Europe, parts of Asia, and North America, the institutional arrangements and the standards set out are far less ambitious, notwithstanding a reference to access to justice in the 2003 African Convention on the Conservation of Nature and Natural Resources. While the existing global environmental agreements are silent on the issue, access to justice does have a firm basis in international human rights law, through the established right to a fair trial. Therefore, and because human rights law has increasingly come to include environmental considerations, the most likely avenue for developing a regime on access to justice in environmental matters on a global level would be through the mutual integration of international human rights law and environmental law.[26]

---

[26] Compare Joint UN Environment Programme–Office of the UN High Commissioner for Human Rights (OHCHR) Expert Seminar on Human Rights and the Environment, *Human Rights and the Environment: Conclusions of a Meeting of Experts*, OHCHR Doc. HR/PUB/02/2 (14–16 January 2002).

6 Conclusions

Despite the patchy development of international rules for public participation in environmental decision-making and despite the rather fragmented normative pattern established so far, this process has changed the image of international environmental law. International environmental law is no longer limited to defining emission standards, technical requirements, or other measures to reduce pollution levels or protect nature. It is also concerned with governance and democratic structures in international and national contexts and institutions. Moreover, the development of norms regarding public participation in decision-making indicates that a strict divide between international and national law risks concealing the mutual—formal and informal—influences of such norms and procedures in the making, as well as in the application, of environmental law.

Even though the references in globally applicable MEAs remain vague when it comes to defining public participation, they nevertheless show some consensus regarding the desired policy direction. They endorse, rather than preclude, the ongoing normative development that expands participatory elements in decision-making. They in fact provide an important element in the structure of international environmental law. The described regional regimes with more substantial provisions both link into and complement these global agreements.

Notwithstanding the dominance of European and North American arrangements for public participation in domestic environmental decision-making, and the lack of similar international arrangements for other parts of the world, access to justice and public participation in decision-making are not merely 'Western' preoccupations. The southeast Asian and African agreements show that, even outside Europe and North America, public participation in environmental decision-making is not perceived as a national concern only. There are also other signs for increasing interest in participatory structures of environmental decision-making outside Europe and North America. In Africa, Latin America, and the Asia-Pacific region, NGO activism is increasing, domestic measures are being developed on public participation, and intergovernmental meetings have been held in these regions to discuss the issue and to promote public engagement. Despite these signs that the door is not closed for a global dialogue on public participation, the lack of attention devoted to public participation at the 2002 WSSD, in spite of the focus on 'partnership', may suggest that legal development will continue primarily through regional regimes rather than a global environmental agreement.

Irrespective of the level at which norms on public participation are developed, one essential concern is how to ensure that these arrangements do not result merely in *pro forma* participation. Access to information, participation in decision-making, and access to justice in national contexts represent fundamental values related to democracy. However, since they also serve to legitimize governmental decisions, there is always the risk that governments may abuse them, without providing members of the public with meaningful ways to voice their concerns and have those concerns taken into account. At the national level, transparency in public administration as well as the division of governmental power between the executive and the judiciary go a long way towards providing a safeguard against such abuse. The international participatory and review procedures that have been adopted within the framework of environmental agreements and international development banks face the same risk. This is particularly the case with respect to the review mechanisms that allow for complaints to be submitted against states or international organizations, but where the government or international organization in question retains a significant amount of control over the review body. In these cases, much depends on the extent to which the review body is able to assert its discretionary powers and thus establish a degree of independence. This independence is crucial to avoiding *pro forma* participation, and thus will play a key role in determining whether or not the participatory structures prescribed by international law can enhance the effectiveness of environmental law, induce legitimacy, and improve the protection of health and the environment.

RECOMMENDED READING

S. Charnovitz, 'Two Centuries of Participation: NGOs and International Governance' (1996–7) 18 Mich. J. Int'l L. 184.

J. Ebbesson, 'The Notion of Public Participation in International Environmental Law' (1997) 8 Y.B. Int'l Envt'l L. 51.

A. Gowlland Gualtieri, 'The Environmental Accountability of the World Bank to Non-State Actors: Insights from the Inspection Panel' (2001) 72 Br. Y.B. Int'l L. 216.

V. Koester, 'Review of Compliance under the Aarhus Convention: A Rather Unique Compliance Mechanism' (2005) 2 J. Eur. Envt'l & Planning L. 31.

L.A. Malone and X. Pasternack, *Defending the Environment: Civil Society Strategies to Enforce International Environmental Law* (Ardsley, NY: Transnational Publishers, 2004).

R. Mushkat, 'Public Participation in Environmental Law Making: A Comment on the International Framework and the Asia-Pacific Perspective' (2002) 1 Chinese J. Int'l L. 185.

K. Raustiala, 'The "Participatory Revolution" in International Environmental Law' (1997) 21 Harv. Envt'l L. Rev. 537.

UN Economic Commission for Europe, *Access to Information, Public Participation and Access to Justice in International Forums and Addendum: Survey of Selected Access to Information, Public Participation, and Access to Justice Rules and Practices in International Forums*, UN Doc. ECE MP.PP/2002/18, CEP/2002/13 and ECE MP.PP/2002/18/Add.1, CEP/2002/13/Add.1 (12 September 2002).

F. Yamin, 'NGOs and International Environmental Law: A Critical Evaluation of their Roles and Responsibilities' (2001) 10 R.E.C.I.E.L. 149.

D. Zillman, A. Lucas, and G. Pring, eds., *Human Rights in Natural Resource Development—Public Participation in the Sustainable Development of Mining and Energy Resources* (Oxford: Oxford University Press, 2002).

CHAPTER 30

LEGITIMACY

DANIEL BODANSKY

1 INTRODUCTION

CAN the International Whaling Commission (IWC) ban commercial whaling under the auspices of a treaty whose declared purpose is the 'orderly development of the whaling industry'? Should a majority of the parties to the Montreal Protocol on Substances That Deplete the Ozone Layer (Montreal Protocol) be able to compel dissenting states to reduce their production and consumption of ozone-depleting substances? Do decisions by the Antarctic Treaty consultative parties constrain the activities of non-member states? Should World Trade Organization (WTO) dispute settlement panels be the mechanism for deciding the legality of trade measures contained in multilateral environmental agreements? These questions all raise, in different forms, the issue of legitimacy. The terms 'legitimacy' and 'illegitimacy' are often used as general labels of approval and disapproval. Yet legitimacy has a more precise meaning in political theory and sociology, focusing on the justification and acceptance of political authority—the authority of the IWC to ban commercial whaling, for example, or of the WTO to review measures adopted pursuant to environmental agreements. A legitimate institution is one that has a right to govern—for example, based on tradition, expertise, legality, or public accountability—rather than one relying on the mere exercise of power.

The problem of legitimacy is one of the oldest in political theory. What gives some people the right to govern others? Conversely, apart from fear of punishment, why should those subject to authority obey? These questions have been central preoccupations of philosophers since the time of Plato, and have become even more pressing in modern times, due to the rise of liberal theory, which views individuals as naturally free and rational, not subject to the authority of others. To paraphrase Rousseau, '[i]f men are born free, what can justify their chains?'[1]

Traditionally, the weakness of international institutions has made legitimacy a less pressing issue in international law than in domestic law. To the extent that international law consists merely of specific treaty commitments, which states are free to accept or reject, the problem of political authority does not arise. However, as international institutions develop with the power to bind non-consenting states, this has begun to prompt concern about the problem of legitimacy (see Chapter 32 'International Institutions'). Perhaps the most dramatic illustration is the 'democratic deficit' debate within the European Union (EU), resulting from the growing authority of unelected EU institutions.[2] The revitalization of the UN Security

This chapter is adapted, in part, from D. Bodansky, 'The Legitimacy of International Governance: A Coming Challenge for International Environmental Law?' (1999) 93 A.J.I.L. 596.

[1] J.-J. Rousseau, *The Social Contract*, bk. I, ch. 1, translated by M. Cranston (London: Penguin Books, 1968) ('Man was born free, and he is everywhere in chains. How did this transformation come about? ... How can it be made legitimate?').

[2] See, e.g., F. Scharpf, *Governing in Europe: Effective and Democratic?* (Oxford: Oxford University Press, 1999); and J.H.H. Weiler, *The Constitution of Europe: 'Do the New Clothes Have an Emperor' and*

Council in the early 1990s and the strengthening of the trade regime's dispute settlement system under the WTO Uruguay Round Agreements have raised similar concerns.[3] Indeed, one critique of globalization is that it involves a transfer of decision-making authority away from the nation-state towards a variety of unelected and unaccountable international or transnational bodies. As Susan Marks observes, '[w]hile state powers remain pivotal... so too is the impact of political initiative, decision-making, and action in other fora.'[4]

In recent years, legitimacy has begun to emerge as an issue not only in international law generally but also in international environmental law more specifically. The growing severity and complexity of international environmental problems has increased the need for institutions with greater legislative, administrative, and adjudicatory authority, which can respond flexibly to new problems and information through the development, implementation, and enforcement of international norms. Whether the international community is successful in developing such institutions will depend in part on whether they are accepted as legitimate. The issue of legitimacy is thus emerging as a significant factor in the development of international environmental law.

2 CONCEPT OF LEGITIMACY

The concept of legitimacy relates to the grounds or justifications of political authority. Legitimacy and illegitimacy are properties of decision-makers and decision-making processes—institutions (and, by extension, their commands), as well as the more informal networks and rule structures that exercise authority over others.

Legitimacy is most easily understood by contrasting it with two other bases of governance: rational persuasion and power. Consider the question of why someone might follow another's directive—a regulatory requirement adopted by an international environmental institution, for example, or a decision by a compliance body (see Chapter 39 'Compliance Theory'). One possibility is that the addressee of the decision—an individual, for example, or a company or state—is rationally persuaded that the decision is correct, based on whatever standard of correctness it chooses to apply—self-interest, societal interest, justice, legality, and so forth. The

Other Essays on European Integration (Cambridge: Cambridge University Press, 1999) at chapters 8 and 10.

[3] D.D. Caron, 'The Legitimacy of the Collective Authority of the Security Council' (1993) 87 A.J.I.L. 552; R.B. Porter et al., *Efficiency, Equity and Legitimacy: The Multilateral Trading System at the Millennium* (Washington, DC: Brookings Institution Press, 2001); and D. Esty, 'The World Trade Organization's Legitimacy Crisis' (2002) 1 World Trade Rev. 7.

[4] S. Marks, 'Democracy and International Governance,' in J.-M. Coicaud and V. Heiskanen, eds., *The Legitimacy of International Organizations* (Tokyo: United Nations University Press, 2001) 49.

losing side in a WTO dispute, for example, might accept the WTO panel's decision because it finds the panel's reasoning persuasive about what, legally, the GATT requires. Or a state might accept a more stringent requirement to phase out ozone-depleting substances because it agrees that the decision is justified on environmental grounds and is, therefore, in its long-term self-interest. Or a Western European state might accept a commitment to reduce its emissions of greenhouse gases because it acknowledges that such a commitment is fair, given its historical contribution to the global warming problem and its capacity to act. In cases such as these, obedience is unproblematic because the actor, at some level, agrees with the content of the decision, if not *ex ante*, then at least as a result of the decision-maker's arguments.

At the other end of the spectrum, an individual or state might comply with a directive due, not to agreement, but rather to outside pressure. The losing party in a domestic lawsuit might believe that the court was mistaken, but comply with the court's decision for fear of being imprisoned or fined. Or a state might find a WTO panel decision unpersuasive but nonetheless implement the decision in order to avoid the imposition of retaliatory trade measures by the winning side. Pressure can take many forms—military, economic, or political. At the extreme, when it leaves an actor no real alternative, we refer to it as compulsion or coercion. Although examples of coercion are rare in international environmental law, lesser forms of pressure are not uncommon. In the 1980s, for example, the United States used the threat of trade and fishing sanctions to induce whaling states to accept the IWC's moratorium on commercial whaling. Similarly, at the multilateral level, the Montreal Protocol includes provisions that seek to pressure states to join by imposing restrictions on trade with non-parties.

Legitimacy represents a third possible basis for compliance. Even if a state does not agree with, say, a WTO panel decision—even if it believes the panel incorrectly interpreted the GATT—it might still accept the decision because it recognizes the WTO dispute resolution process as legitimate. Legitimacy lies somewhere between rational persuasion and compulsion as a basis for action. In contrast to rational persuasion, legitimacy involves the notion of deference (or in the stronger case, obedience)—that is, performing an act not because one is convinced, on the merits, that the act is right but simply because another has directed it. As the legal philosopher, Scott Shapiro, explains, in discussing the idea of a command:

Commands differ from arguments. Arguments are meant to persuade. They attempt to convince the person that they ought to act in certain ways and they do this by presenting to the interlocutor the reasons that make the recommendations worthy. Commands, on the other hand, are not designed to convince their addressees of the wisdom of their contents. Subjects who obey them do so not because they believe that the actions commanded are worthy of obedience, but rather in virtue of the fact that they were so commanded.[5]

---

[5] S. Shapiro, 'Authority,' in J. Coleman and S. Shapiro, eds., *Oxford Handbook of Jurisprudence and Philosophy of Law* (Oxford: Oxford University Press, 2002) 386 (discussing the distinction between power and authority made by Robert Paul Wolff in his classic work, *In Defense of Anarchism* (1970)).

In contrast to compulsion, however, which also involves the notion of obedience, legitimacy has a normative quality. When an institution has legitimate authority, it has a right to rule, and its subjects have a corresponding obligation to obey. In contrast, a gunman, to use the familiar example, has power but not legitimate authority. He may compel compliance through the threat or use of force, but, as Shapiro notes, 'he is unable to impose the moral obligation to comply.'[6]

Legitimacy, thus, differs from both coercion and rational persuasion. Unlike coercion, the command of a legitimate authority serves not only as a reason for action, but also as a justification, and deviations from the command are subject to criticism. However, unlike rational persuasion, the justification for action provided by legitimacy has a content-neutral quality. It relates to the qualities of the decision-maker or the decision-making process—its legal authority, for example, expertise, democratic accountability, or reliance on the right kinds of reasons—rather than the content of the decisions themselves. In this respect, legitimacy differs from the concept of justice, which in most formulations has a substantive component (see Chapter 13 'Ethics and International Environmental Law'). This is why there is no contradiction in saying that a particular law or decision is misguided, inequitable, or even unjust, but still legitimate, for example, because it was duly enacted by a democratically elected legislature or handed down by a court with proper jurisdiction.

The concepts of rational persuasion, compulsion, and legitimacy are, of course, ideal types. In practice, an international institution may rely on all three. For example, WTO dispute resolution panels claim a right to decide disputes, pursuant to the Dispute Settlement Understanding agreed to by WTO member states. They claim, that is, to have legitimate authority. Yet WTO panels also present reasons for their decisions, aimed at persuading states and non-governmental entities that their decisions are correct. And if neither legitimacy nor rational persuasion proves sufficient, WTO panels can authorize the imposition of trade measures against the losing state in order to compel compliance. Indeed, the WTO example illustrates that the three concepts are not merely complementary but also, at a deeper level, interlinked. Even when the losing side does not accept a panel's legitimacy and must be compelled to obey, it is still critical that other states view the dispute settlement system as legitimate since this is what justifies the imposition of trade measures by the winning party—this is what distinguishes the WTO enforcement system from unilateral compulsion. And one of the potential reasons why states may accept the dispute settlement system as legitimate is the requirement that panels give reasons for their decisions, bringing us full circle back to the notion of rational persuasion.

Many writers contrast legitimacy, not with rational persuasion, but rather with self-interest. However, self-interest, as a basis of action, cross-cuts the distinction I am making between legitimacy, power, and persuasion. It can serve as a persuasive argument to follow a command. For example, a state may be persuaded to reduce its

---

[6] *Ibid.* at 385.

use of ozone-depleting substances by the argument that this is in its long-term self-interest. But self-interest might also serve as a basis of legitimacy—a state might accept a WTO panel decision with which it substantively disagrees, and which it believes is contrary to its immediate interests, because it believes that it has a long-term self-interest in the maintenance of the WTO dispute resolution system. Finally, coercion—although often contrasted with self-interest—itself relies on self-interest (except in cases of pure compulsion, when the actor loses its power of agency). Through the threat of force or sanctions, coercion seeks to raise the costs of non-compliance so that the actor has an interest in complying.

Legitimacy has two dimensions, one empirical and the other normative. On the one hand, we can ask whether, as a factual matter, an institution's authority is accepted by those whom it purports to govern (for example, individuals or states)—whether it has de facto or 'popular' legitimacy. This is a question of sociology and political science. On the other hand, we can ask whether the institution's authority is normatively justified; that is, whether there are good reasons why it should have the right to make the decisions it does. This is a question of political philosophy.

The distinction between popular and normative legitimacy is fundamental. If legitimacy did not have a normative as well as a sociological dimension, we could only describe what states think, not criticize their views or persuade them to change their minds. Criticism and persuasion require a normative vantage point—they require the ability not only to describe but to evaluate. Indeed, although many writers focus on popular legitimacy, normative legitimacy is conceptually prior. What people accept as legitimate reflects their view about what they believe is normatively justified. So popular legitimacy logically presupposes normative legitimacy. Yet the fact that an institution has popular legitimacy—based, say, on tradition or charisma—does not mean that its claim to authority is well founded. For example, nobody would conclude that Nazi Germany, which commanded considerable public acceptance, was normatively legitimate.

The question of legitimacy is not merely of theoretical interest; it also has significant practical implications. Legitimacy represents a potential basis of compliance with international environmental law, apart from self-interest or power. But its importance does not stop there. As Max Weber argued, a regime's legitimacy has wider ramifications, influencing its development and stability.[7] The willingness of states to accept an institution such as the Kyoto Protocol's Compliance Committee and give it greater decision-making authority depends, in part, on whether they trust it to make good decisions. All other things being equal, institutions regarded as legitimate, such as the European Court of Human Rights, tend to get more business, while those regarded as illegitimate get less.

---

[7] M. Weber, Economy and Society, edited by G. Ross and C. Wittich (Berkeley, CA: University of California Press, 1978).

In determining a regime's popular legitimacy, whose views count: those of states or of civil society? Traditionally, the answer has been states. An international institution's popular legitimacy was a function of whether states accept its decisions as authoritative. Yet, as non-governmental actors become more influential in the international legal process, and as international environmental law has growing implications for private actors, the attitudes of individuals, non-governmental organizations (NGOs), and business towards international environmental institutions are likely to move to centre stage.[8]

3 A TYPOLOGY OF LEGITIMACY THEORIES

Thus far, we have been considering the general concept of legitimacy. We now turn to particular conceptions or bases of legitimacy, such as public accountability, legality, and expertise.[9] These conceptions of legitimacy can be grouped into three broad categories: source-based, procedural, and substantive.

Source-Based Theories—Historically, authority has usually been legitimated by its origin or source. Often, religion has served to legitimate authority—leaders have claimed to rule by divine right or to have a mandate from heaven. In medieval times, custom played a significant role. Today, source-based approaches to legitimacy remain important, but the consent of 'the people'—or, in the case of international law, the consent of states—has replaced God as the principal source of legitimate authority. Indeed, according to the voluntarist theory of international law, all international rules rest on the consent of states, expressed either explicitly in treaties or implicitly in state practice.

Process-Based Theories—Authority can also be legitimated in procedural terms. Judicial legitimacy, for example, depends on due process rights such as the right to be heard, the right to confront witnesses, the right to an impartial judge, and the requirement that judges provide reasons for their decisions,[10] while administrative law typically includes requirements intended to promote public accountability, for example, by requiring governmental agencies to provide the public with notice of proposed rules and an opportunity to comment (see Chapter 4 'Global Environmental Governance as Administration'). Efforts to

[8] Already, the EU's democratic deficit debate and the controversies surrounding the WTO, the World Bank and other globalizing institutions largely reflect the concerns of civil society rather than of states. Jutta Brunnée refers to the former as 'vertical legitimacy' and the latter as 'horizontal legitimacy.' J. Brunnée, 'COPing with Consent: Law-Making under Multilateral Environmental Agreements' (2002) 15 Leiden J. Int'l L. 1 at 13–14.

[9] See R. Dworkin, *Taking Rights Seriously* (Cambridge: Cambridge University Press, 1977) at 134 (distinction between concepts and conceptions).

[10] T. Tyler, *Why People Obey the Law* (New Haven, CT: Yale University Press, 1990).

promote greater transparency in international environmental negotiations and in institutions such as the World Bank and the WTO reflect a procedural orientation.

Outcome-Based Theories—In contrast to these 'input-based' approaches to legitimacy, the old adage 'nothing succeeds like success' suggests that an institution's outputs can also help to legitimate it.[11] If an institution is seen as doing a good job governing—for example, by producing economic growth, public order, or social justice—people will be more inclined to accept its authority in the future. An institution's effectiveness, thus, can help earn it a measure of deference and trust. This has been one of the principal explanations for the acceptance, during the post-Second World War period, of the international trade regime.[12]

These three bases of legitimacy are not mutually exclusive. Different types of institutions, exercising different types of authority, may rely on different theories of legitimacy. In Western states, for example, the legitimacy of legislative authority rests primarily on popular consent, expressed through periodic elections. In contrast, judicial and administrative authority—with a weaker basis in popular consent—have been legitimized primarily in procedural or substantive terms.

Often, an institution may be evaluated according to multiple conceptions of legitimacy, which reinforce or undermine one another. A democratically elected regime, for example, derives significant legitimacy from its source. But if—like Weimar Germany—it fails to maintain public order or economic stability, it may eventually lose legitimacy. Conversely, the WTO and the EU have been very successful in promoting economic growth, but their lack of democratic accountability has, nevertheless, led to legitimacy concerns.

Some believe that conflicts such as these between different bases of legitimacy are not isolated or accidental phenomena, but reflect the fact that different bases of legitimacy in some respects work at cross-purposes, making tensions between them inevitable.[13] Although democracy is widely regarded as the touchstone of legitimacy in the modern world, it appears, at times, to be incapable of addressing problems effectively—hence, the increasing efforts to move politically sensitive issues out of the political arena, through the use of non-partisan commissions, independent central banks, and so forth, which rely for their legitimacy on expertise and effectiveness. In the international environmental arena, the same tension is apparent. Greater transparency and public participation in negotiations, for example, may make states more reluctant to make difficult compromises in order to reach a successful outcome. Similarly, the global character of the UN climate change regime, although often seen

---

[11] For discussions of input- versus output-based theories of legitimacy, see Scharpf, note 2 above; R. Keohane and J.S. Nye, Jr., 'The Club Model of Multilateral Cooperation and Problems of Democratic Legitimacy,' in Porter, see note 3 above at 264.

[12] Keohane and Nye, see note 11 above.

[13] See, e.g., R.A. Dahl, 'A Democratic Dilemma: System Effectiveness versus Citizen Participation' (1994) 109 Pol. Sci. Q. 23.

as crucial to the regime's procedural legitimacy, may raise transaction costs and make it harder for the regime to achieve results.

Finally, conceptions of legitimacy are not necessarily universal. Developed and developing countries, for example, often focus on very different aspects of a regime in assessing its legitimacy. Developed countries, for example, tend to focus more on the efficiency of substantive outputs while developing countries focus more on equity; developed countries focus more on transparency and developing countries more on universality and sovereign equality. The extent to which different countries share a common conception of legitimacy is an empirical question, which cannot be answered *a priori*.

4 Why Is Legitimacy a Growing Issue in International Environmental Law?

Traditionally, international environmental law—like international law more generally—has relied on two bases of legitimacy: state consent and legality. Consent has played the primary role. Much if not most international environmental law has developed through a consensual process. States recognize that they cannot solve some transnational or global environmental problem through individual action, so they agree to collective action by means of a reciprocal exchange of promises— they agree, for example, to limit their use of ozone-depleting substances or to restrict the import and export of endangered species. Since consent is generally regarded as a legitimate basis of obligation, these commitments persist through time and continue to bind states, whether or not they still agree with what the commitments provide.

In addition, to the extent that states can legitimately bind themselves not simply to rules but also to the authority of institutions, then legality also plays an important legitimating role. The term 'legitimacy' derives from the same Latin root as 'law', and the *Oxford English Dictionary* continues to define 'legitimacy' as 'the condition of being in accordance with law or principle.' Legal legitimacy is what connects an institution's continuing authority to its original basis in state consent. The authority of the Security Council, for example, derives from the Charter of the United Nations, to which UN member states have consented, and its continuing legitimacy depends on acting in accordance with the Charter. The connection between law and legitimacy is fundamental to the idea of the rule of law, which makes political authority subject to the restraint of general, open, and relatively stable rules. Legality is especially central to the legitimacy of adjudicatory bodies, such as the International Court of Justice or the WTO's Appellate Body, which have authority only to apply the law, not to make it, and are, hence, particularly vulnerable to claims that their decisions lack legal legitimacy.[14]

Generally, concerns about the legitimacy of international environmental issues have related to one or both of these bases of legitimacy. The challenge in the 1980s by Malaysia and other developing countries to the legitimacy of the Antarctic Treaty system (ATS), for example, had to do with the issue of consent. In essence, the developing states questioned the right of the ATS to govern the Antarctic, an area widely viewed as part of the global commons (see Chapter 23 'Common Areas, Common Heritage, and Common Concern'), when most states had not consented to the ATS. They proposed instead that Antarctica be placed under the auspices of an institution with global membership, namely the UN General Assembly.

Critics of the IWC's moratorium on commercial whaling, in contrast, have focused on the issue of legal legitimacy. They claim that the IWC, in adopting the moratorium, acted contrary to the International Convention for the Regulation of Whaling (Whaling Convention) for two reasons. First, the moratorium is inconsistent with the convention's stated purpose, namely, 'to make possible the orderly development of the whaling industry,' and, second, the decision lacked a scientific basis, as required by the convention. As one Norwegian critic of the IWC put it, whaling states signed on to play cricket, but now find themselves pressured to play a game of chess instead.[15]

Two factors are likely to further undermine consent and legality as bases of legitimacy for international environmental law. First, the coming generation of environmental problems will be likely to require the development of more expeditious and flexible law-making techniques, which do not depend on consensus among states. Consensus decision-making is time-consuming and difficult, and tends to result in least-common-denominator results. This is why the UN Charter requires consensus only among the five permanent members of the Security Council and, otherwise, allows the Security Council to make decisions by a qualified majority vote. Yet voting rules such as these, by departing from consensus decision-making, raise legitimacy concerns, which have grown more pronounced as the Security Council's mandate has expanded and it has begun to exercise quasi-legislative authority. Among multilateral environmental agreements, the Montreal Protocol is still the only one to include a non-consensual decision-making mechanism, namely its adjustment procedure (thus far, never used), which allows a qualified majority of parties to tighten the stringency of its control measures on ozone-depleting substances. But calls are periodically made to move further in this direction—for example, through the establishment of a new supranational organization with broad legislative and enforcement powers.[16]

---

[14] See, e.g., C.E. Barfield, 'Free Trade, Sovereignty, Democracy: The Future of the World Trade Organization' (2001) 2 Chi. J. Int'l L. 403.

[15] A. Pollack, 'Commission to Save Whales Endangered Too,' New York Times (18 May 1993) at C4.

[16] See G. Palmer, 'New Ways to Make International Environmental Law' (1992) 86 A.J.I.L. 259. In 1989, 24 countries (including Germany, France, and India) adopted the Declaration of The Hague, which

Of course, to the extent that international decision-making processes such as the UN Security Council and the Montreal Protocol adjustment procedure are created by treaties, they ultimately rest on state consent—consent not to specific obligations or decisions but rather to an ongoing system of governance. However, the persisting questions about the legitimacy of the EU and the Security Council illustrate that general consent, even in combination with the principle of legal legitimacy, may not be sufficient to insulate an ongoing governance system from criticism on legitimacy grounds. General consent to broad decision-making mechanisms involves a much more significant surrender of autonomy than consent to specific obligations—and, therefore, raises more serious concerns about legitimacy—since, in giving its consent, a state does not know what particular constraints may be imposed on it in the future. General consent may be enough to legitimate a relatively limited decision-making mechanism such as the Montreal Protocol adjustment procedure, where the range of possible decisions is narrowly circumscribed. Yet when an institution must respond to changing problems in changing ways, 'any concept of consent is unlikely to have any significant application . . . unless we conceive it as a process, as a relationship . . . that must be constantly renewed and maintained.'[17]

Moreover, even if treaties provide international institutions with a sufficient grounding in state consent, the transfer of decision-making authority away from the nation state has, to a significant extent, not been to international organizations, but rather to informal networks of government officials and private entities, which lack a clear consensual basis. According to Anne-Marie Slaughter, these transnational networks constitute the 'real new world order.'[18]

A second factor that has diminished the legitimating force of state consent is the fact that international environmental law increasingly governs the conduct of non-state actors—ship builders and operators who must conform to the requirements of the International Convention for the Prevention of Pollution from Ships (MARPOL Convention); producers and consumers of ozone-depleting substances, whose activities are limited by the Montreal Protocol; and so forth. It has become almost commonplace that international environmental law now addresses subjects that, in the past, were addressed by national law. The corollary is that, the more international environmental law resembles domestic law, the more it should be subject to the same standards of legitimacy. Particularly when state consent is given by the executive branch, with little or no control by the legislature, then it may not be enough to legitimate the regulation of private conduct.

called for the development of 'new institutional authority' with non-unanimous decision-making powers.

[17] P.H. Partridge, *Consent and Consensus* (London: Pall Mall, 1971) at 29–30.
[18] See A.-M. Slaughter, *A New World Order* (Princeton, NJ: Princeton University Press, 2004).

5 ALTERNATIVE BASES OF LEGITIMACY

If state consent and legality no longer suffice to legitimate international environmental regimes, what are the possible alternatives? Democracy, public participation, and expertise are among the leading candidates. In terms of the typology elaborated earlier, democracy is principally a source-based approach, public participation a procedural approach, and expertise a substantive approach.

5.1 Democracy

In the modern world, democracy has become the touchstone of legitimacy, both because it rests on the will of the people (a source-based rationale) and, to a lesser extent, because it is seen as promoting their common welfare (a substantive rationale). Yet 'democracy' can mean many different things—popular democracy, representative democracy, pluralist democracy, or deliberative democracy, to name a few.[19] What might it mean in the context of international environmental law? Democracy among states or among peoples? A system of majority decision-making or simply greater participation and accountability?[20]

At the international level, many developing countries use the term 'democracy' to refer to 'one-state–one-vote', as compared to voting rules that give some states more influence than others—for example, by weighting their votes (the approach used by international financial institutions such as the World Bank) or by giving them veto power. Yet this usage is, at best, questionable, since one-state–one-vote gives disproportionate influence to smaller states. There is nothing obviously democratic about a system that gives 10,000 inhabitants of a small-island state the same weight as one billion inhabitants of China or India.

In the domestic arena, democracy typically is considered to mean a system of popularly elected representative bodies, majority decision-making, and protection of minority rights. At the international level, the only institution that remotely fits this description is the European Parliament, which is popularly elected and makes

[19] D. Held, *Models of Democracy*, 2nd edition (Stanford, CA: Stanford University Press, 1996). George Orwell included 'democracy' in his category of 'meaningless words.' See Marks, note 4 above at 47.

[20] See D. Bienen, V. Rittberger, and W. Wagner, 'Democracy in the United Nations System: Cosmopolitan and Communitarian Principles,' in D. Archibugi, D. Held, and M. Köhler, eds., *Re-Imagining Political Community: Studies in Cosmopolitan Democracy* (Cambridge: Polity Press, 1998) 287.

decisions by majority vote. One approach to bolstering the legitimacy of international environmental law would be to establish new environmental institutions governed by popularly elected representatives or to modify existing institutions along these lines.[21]

However, this approach not only is politically unrealistic, but also would suffer from a legitimacy deficit of its own. Democratic rule depends on the existence of a *demos*—a shared sense of peoplehood or community—which is absent at the international level. A *demos* is more than a random collection of individuals or even a group bound together by common interests. It requires a 'foundation not only of shared values, but also of shared experience, so that people identify with the political system to which they belong, and can trust its procedures and their outcomes.'[22] As Fritz Scharpf has noted, within stable democratic states, the sense of collective identity necessary for democracy is 'more or less taken for granted.'[23] The acceptance of the majority's right to govern, even by those in the minority, reflects this sense of common identity or *demos*.

Prior to the eighteenth century, most political theorists believed that a democratic community could exist only in a small city-state. The establishment of the United States demonstrated that democracy is also possible in a large nation-state. The question now in Europe is whether there is a European *demos*—whether Europe constitutes the kind of community that can be governed democratically.[24] However, regardless of the answer to this question, the international community more generally still seems very far from developing a shared sense of community. Theoretically, a global *demos* could develop in the future. Yet, as a practical matter, the diversity of cultures, religions, social and economic conditions, and histories makes the prospects for a global *demos* very dim. Why would Americans, Spaniards, Japanese, Saudis, Brazilians, or Indians feel bound by the decisions of a foreign majority concerning permissible levels of carbon dioxide emissions or measures to protect biological diversity? Why would they view a majority decision-making procedure as legitimate? And, from a normative perspective, why should they?

Of course, democracy has a vital role to play at the domestic level. Making foreign policy-making more democratic would help ameliorate the concerns about state consent and give international environmental law greater legitimacy vis-à-vis individuals. And democracy might play a significant role at the regional level, where people from different states may share the same language or religion or have common histories, traditions, and sensibilities. Yet, at the global level, democracy does not appear to offer a viable alternative to state consent.

---

[21] See, e.g., H. French, 'Strengthening International Governance' (1995) 3 Env't & Dev. 65 (proposing the establishment of a new institution composed of representatives of national parliaments); and R. Falk and A. Strauss, 'Toward Global Parliament' (Jan/Feb 2001) 80 Foreign Affairs 212.

[22] A. Arblaster, *Democracy* (Minneapolis, MN: Open University Press, 1994) at 76.

[23] Scharpf, see note 2 above at 8.

[24] J. Weiler, 'European Democracy and Its Critique' (1995) 18 W. Eur. Pol. 4.

5.2 Participation and Transparency

Like democracy, public participation and transparency aim to make government more accountable to those affected by its decisions (see Chapter 29 'Public Participation'). They seek to enable stakeholders to have an input into the decision-making process, to give them a sense of ownership in that process, and to subject institutions to public scrutiny. However, in contrast to democratic governance, where the public wields power through the ballot box, participation and transparency do not, in themselves, give the public any real decision-making authority. Instead, their influence is more partial and diffuse. Consequently, they confer a relatively weak form of legitimacy.

Indeed, the significance of public participation may result less from its legitimating role than from the de-legitimating effect of a lack of participation. Restricted participation tends to provoke dissatisfaction on the part of those excluded. Even if public participation, by itself, is not sufficient to legitimate an institution, it may be necessary to avoid concerns about illegitimacy.

Traditionally, the issue of participation related primarily to participation by states. The challenge by developing states to the legitimacy of the Antarctic Treaty System, for example, focused on the requirement that states undertake substantial activities in Antarctica in order to become full participants in the regime—a requirement that effectively raised the price of membership and prevented most developing countries from joining. Similarly, the lack of effective participation, initially, by developing countries in the Intergovernmental Panel on Climate Change raised legitimacy concerns, and led to the establishment of an ad hoc working group to encourage greater developing country involvement. Indeed, in the climate change regime, the demand for universal participation had the somewhat curious result that all of the parties to the UN Framework Convention on Climate Change (UNFCCC) were allowed to participate (and potentially obstruct) the Kyoto Protocol negotiations, even though from the outset, states agreed that the protocol would impose obligations on only a small subset of states, namely industrialized countries.

Today, participation by the public, not just by states, has emerged as a major issue. In the EU, limited public participation has been an important element of the democratic deficit critique. The arcane and often opaque quality of EU governance makes public participation difficult, both on the legislative side, where Council deliberations have traditionally been confidential, as well as on the implementation and enforcement side, where the use of committees to elaborate and apply standards is notoriously obscure. The public's limited access to WTO dispute resolution processes has provoked similar criticisms.

In the international environmental sphere, significant progress has been made in opening up negotiations and decision-making procedures to non-governmental groups. The 1998 Convention on Access to Information, Public Participation in Decision-making and Access to Justice in Environmental Matters seeks to consolidate and extend these gains, by requiring parties to promote transparency and participation in 'international environmental decision-making processes and within the framework of international organizations in matters relating to the environment.'[25] However, counterbalancing this trend, international standards are being elaborated, increasingly, not through inter-governmental negotiations but by quasi-private bodies such as the Codex Alimentarius Commission and the International Organization for Standardization, in which business representatives and government experts predominate, with only limited opportunities for public access and input (see Chapter 21 'Private and Quasi-Private Standard Setting').

Although public participation and transparency can serve as important sources of legitimacy, two caveats are in order. First, there is the question of who exactly is participating. Even if international meetings were opened up and NGOs given unrestricted access, relatively few members of the public would, in practice, be able to participate. The phrase 'public participation' is thus a bit of a euphemism. It refers to participation, not by the 'public'—whatever that might mean—but by non-governmental groups such as Greenpeace or the International Chamber of Commerce. Whether these self-selected groups represent the 'public interest' or only their own private interests is debatable (see Chapter 33 'Non-Governmental Organizations and Civil Society' and Chapter 35 'Business').

Second, although public participation and transparency are important, they are not the only values at stake. International environmental law also seeks to achieve effective results. Sometimes, this may require confidential negotiations, in which states feel free to express their views and make difficult compromises.[26] When states are on public view, they typically feel they must reiterate and defend their official positions. Breakthroughs almost always occur only at the eleventh hour, when participation and transparency are put aside and a relatively small group of negotiators meet behind closed doors to hammer out the final agreement. Thus, the goals of public participation and transparency may sometimes conflict with the goal of effectiveness.

5.3 Expertise and Effectiveness

In part, we judge an institution by its fruits. Until recently, the international trade regime's success in promoting economic growth helped to legitimate it. Similarly, the EU's success in promoting peace and prosperity in Europe served as the

[25] 1998 Convention on Access to Information, Public Participation in Decision-Making and Access to Justice in Environmental Matters (Aarhus Convention), Article 3(7). In 2005, the parties to the Aarhus Convention adopted the Almaty Guidelines, which provide more detailed guidance on public participation in international forums. UN Doc. ECE/MP.PP/2005/2/Add.5 (20 June 2005).

[26] For example, historians of the US Constitutional Convention generally agree that, if the convention's deliberations had been subject to the sharp glare of publicity, the delegates would not have been able to negotiate as ambitious an instrument.

foundation of its popular legitimacy. In the international environmental arena, the Antarctic Treaty System is an example of a regime claiming substantive legitimacy. Its proponents typically defend it by pointing to the regime's 40-year record of success in preserving Antarctica as a zone of peace and science.

The substantive success of a regime might be judged in different ways and have various origins. Some writers, for example, have justified democracy not only on source-based grounds but also on substantive grounds, as the form of government most conducive to political stability, economic growth, and social welfare.[27] An alternative tradition dating back to Plato focuses on expertise as a basis of decision-making. Expert authority reflects the view that certain types of issues are technical in nature—that, as such, they have right and wrong (or at least better and worse) answers and that certain people possess special expertise about what those answers are. The authority of doctors rests on these foundations, as does the authority of lawyers and judges. We choose as judges, for example, people with specialized training in law, who are therefore presumably experts, rather than lay people.

At least some environmental questions seem appropriate for expert decisions. What levels of whaling, for example, are sustainable? Which ozone-depleting substances have substitutes available? What loadings of acid deposition can an ecosystem tolerate? These are technical questions, which should be answered by those with the relevant expertise (see Chapter 9 'Science and Technology'). Although expertise is valued for substantive rather than procedural reasons—it is valued, in other words, because it produces desirable outcomes, not because experts have any intrinsic right to decide—following the decision of an expert does not require agreeing with the decision's content. It simply requires accepting that the expert has special knowledge, which entitles her decisions to deference. The doctor-patient relationship provides a good illustration. A patient follows a doctor's orders not because he or she is rationally convinced that the treatment is correct—in most cases, the patient will have no basis to judge—but rather because of the doctor's perceived expertise. In this sense, expertise, like all conceptions of legitimacy, has a content-neutral quality.

As bases of legitimacy, technocracy and democracy stand in sharp contrast with one another. The fact that both conceptions of legitimacy remain important reflects the fact that we want government institutions to be both effective in solving problems and subject to public control. As Charles Lindblom notes:

On the one hand, people want policy to be informed and well-analyzed. On the other hand, they want policymaking to be democratic. In slightly different words, on the one hand they want policymaking to be more scientific; on the other, they want it to remain in the world of politics.[28]

---

[27] See, e.g., A. Sen, 'Democracy as a Universal Value' (1999) 10 J. of Democracy 3.

[28] C.E. Lindblom, *The Policy Making Process*, 2nd edition (Englewood Cliffs, NJ: Prentice Hall, 1980) at 12. Thus, in Anglo-American legal systems, the expertise of the judge is complemented by the participation of the lay jury.

Expertise plays a particularly important role in legitimating administrative agencies, which are seen as primarily technocratic. Many international environmental regimes make the need for scientific expertise explicit, including the Whaling Convention and the WTO's Agreement on the Application of Sanitary and Phytosanitary Measures. In *EC Measures Concerning Meat and Meat Products (Hormones)*,[29] the WTO Appellate Body, while recognizing that science does not dictate any particular level of protection, nonetheless struck down the EU's beef hormone ban because it was not rationally supported by any specific scientific studies.

However, the relationship between expertise and decision-making is complex. On the one hand, disregarding science may help to de-legitimate a decision-making process, as the controversy over the IWC moratorium on commercial whaling illustrates. Yet technical expertise is rarely a sufficient basis for environmental decision-making. Most problems involve issues not simply of fact but also of policy and value.[30] Consider, for example, the problem of global warming. Like most environmental problems, global warming has many potential solutions: energy efficiency standards, taxes, tradable emission allowances, and so forth. Science can provide us with useful information about the feasibility and effectiveness of these options. Yet, ultimately, the choice between them is a policy question, not a scientific one.

Science also cannot tell us what level of risk is acceptable. The UNFCCC defines as its ultimate objective the stabilization of greenhouse gas concentrations at levels that would prevent 'dangerous' anthropogenic interference with the climate system. Yet deciding what is 'dangerous' involves questions of value as well as fact, and, for this reason, the Intergovernmental Panel on Climate Change—the principal source of expert opinion on climate change—has expressly refrained from attempting to resolve the issue. Like any issue of risk management, assessing risks is a scientific task, but deciding how to respond requires value judgements about what levels of risk are acceptable.[31]

Even with respect to purely technical questions, which have right and wrong answers, expert decision-making poses difficult issues. First, it may not be certain what those right answers are. Most international environmental problems involve significant uncertainties. So deciding what to do depends not only on science but also on a non-scientific judgement about how to act in the face of uncertainty. Second, identifying who qualifies as an expert can prove to be a stumbling block, particularly when it is possible to find 'experts' on different sides of virtually any question. Moreover, without public accountability and oversight, expert decision-making

---

[29] *EC Measures Concerning Meat and Meat Products (Hormones)*, WTO Doc. WT/DS26/R/USA (18 August 1997).

[30] Perhaps in part because issues of science and values are typically intermixed, 'epistemic communities' typically share not only scientific beliefs about social or physical causation, but also normative beliefs and values (see Chapter 34 'Epistemic Communities').

[31] See R.H. Moss, 'Avoiding "Dangerous" Interference in the Climate System: The Role of Values, Science and Policy' (1995) 5 Global Envt'l Change 3.

poses the danger of regulatory capture: experts may make decisions on the basis, not of their expertise but, rather, of their relationships with the regulated industry. This is a particular problem whenever industry experts are given a special role in the decision-making process.

The absence of any simple relation between technical expertise and decision-making, however, does not negate the importance of scientific expertise in legitimating international environmental regimes. Even the precautionary principle relies on science to identify the risks that might warrant a precautionary approach (see Chapter 25 'Precaution'). Otherwise, there would be no rational basis for determining when precautionary action is warranted. Although science cannot answer questions of value, expertise can provide a legitimate basis of decision-making when there is no significant disagreement over values—when people have shared goals and the principal issue is how to achieve those goals. Expert legitimacy thus depends only on what Fritz Scharpf has called 'thin identity' rather than 'thick identity'—that is, perceptions of shared interests as opposed to the commonalities of history, language, and culture that democratic legitimacy presupposes.[32] Since thin identity is more widely shared than thick identity, expertise may represent a more achievable basis of legitimacy for global environmental regimes than democracy.

6 CONCLUSION: BUILDING LEGITIMACY OVER TIME: HOW TO DEVELOP TRUST IN INTERNATIONAL ENVIRONMENTAL INSTITUTIONS?

International environmental law faces a dilemma. On the one hand, effectively addressing problems such as climate change will require more authoritative systems of international governance, which do not depend on consensus among states. Yet, without a firmer basis of legitimacy, states may be unwilling to entrust international environmental institutions with the necessary decision-making authority. Building the legitimacy of international environmental institutions poses a formidable challenge. Legitimacy involves trust—trust that an institution will make decisions appropriately. Yet trust is easier among neighbours than strangers. So, as the scale of governance increases, trust becomes more difficult to achieve. This is a problem even within nation-states or at the regional level. In the United States, the federal government in Washington is seen by some as remote and unresponsive to local concerns, and, in the EU, critics question why seemingly distant institutions in

---

[32] Scharpf, see note 2 above.

Brussels can override the democratically adopted choices of member states. Needless to say, the problems of remoteness and unfamiliarity are even more intense at the global level.

Under the best of circumstances, building legitimacy typically takes time. It is a long-term project. An institution like the US Supreme Court today has enormous legitimacy—it can decide the outcome of a presidential race or the status of wartime detainees, without any real question that its decisions will be followed. Yet this legitimacy did not exist from the outset. When the court was established, it was not a foregone conclusion that the political branches would respect its opinions. Instead, the court's legitimacy developed over time. The same is true internationally. The European Court of Human Rights considered literally no cases during its first decade. Today, it issues more than 700 judgments per year. What changed? The obvious answer is that the European court gained legitimacy. Over time, states and potential litigants became familiar with it and developed confidence in its decisions.[33]

However, legitimacy—like trust more generally—is a fragile phenomenon. It is easier to destroy than to build up. We may not know precisely what would make an institution legitimate. Yet we have a pretty good idea what would cause it to lose legitimacy: bias, illegality, failure to consider scientific evidence, secrecy, exclusion of the public, and inequity. These are the things to be avoided, if an institution is to fend off charges of illegitimacy and have time to gain the confidence of states and other international actors.

RECOMMENDED READING

S. Bernstein, 'Legitimacy in Global Environmental Governance' (2005) 1 J. Int'l L. & Int'l Relations 139.

D. Bodansky, 'The Legitimacy of International Governance: A Coming Challenge for International Environmental Law?' (1999) 93 A.J.I.L. 596.

I. Clark, *Legitimacy in International Society* (Oxford: Oxford University Press, 2005).

J.-M. Coicaud and V. Heiskanen, eds., *The Legitimacy of International Organizations* (Tokyo: United Nations University Press, 2001).

T.M. Franck, *The Power of Legitimacy among Nations* (Oxford: Oxford University Press, 1990).

I. Hurd, 'Legitimacy and Authority in International Politics' (1999) 53 Int'l Org. 379.

---

[33] As the European Court of Human Rights illustrates, however, the process of legitimation is complex, and an institution can to some degree become a victim of its own success. The court's increased workload has led to a huge backlog of cases (65,000 as of the end of 2003), which undercuts the court's effectiveness and, hence, its output-based legitimacy. Yet the proposed solution—a new process to filter out unmeritorious cases, including decisions on admissibility by individual judges—could undercut the court's procedural legitimacy.

R. Keohane and J.S. Nye, Jr., 'The Club Model of Multilateral Cooperation and Problems of Democratic Legitimacy,' in R.B. Porter et al., *Efficiency, Equity and Legitimacy: The Multilateral Trading System at the Millennium* (Washington, DC: Brookings Institution Press, 2001) 264.

M. Kumm, 'The Legitimacy of International Law: A Constitutionalist Framework of Analysis' (2004) 15 Eur. J. Int'l L. 90.

S. Shapiro, 'Authority,' in J. Coleman and S. Shapiro, eds., *Oxford Handbook of Jurisprudence and Philosophy of Law* (Oxford: Oxford University Press, 2002) 382.

PART VI

ACTORS AND INSTITUTIONS

CHAPTER 31

CHANGING ROLE
OF THE STATE

THILO MARAUHN

SINCE the early days of modern public international law, the state has been the most important subject thereof. However, today, the state neither is the sole, nor necessarily the primary, actor in international (environmental) relations. In recent years, the role of the state and, notably, the ability of the state to address environmental risks and threats have increasingly come to be scrutinized. While states' standard setting remains important, commentators have argued that the ability and willingness of states to implement and enforce such standards have major weaknesses. This so-called implementation deficit[1] has been discussed since the early 1980s, both at the national and at the international levels. As a consequence, the traditional reliance on national implementation has been questioned[2]—stimulating more fundamental debates on the state as an actor in international environmental relations.

Apart from doubts prompted by the observable limitations of national implementation, the role of the state is increasingly questioned from the perspective of legal and political theory.[3] A growing literature claims the demise of the state.[4] However, doubts regarding the role of the state should not be overdrawn. On the one hand, as a descriptive matter, the state is much less in decline than is often claimed. On the other hand, from a normative perspective, it must be asked whether an early demise of the state would not destabilize the international legal order and entail more problems than benefits. In the environmental and in other contexts when states have indeed 'failed' they have not been replaced by meaningful and effective local, regional, or supranational actors. The point is most graphically illustrated by the many instances where the United Nations has met the limits of its capacity to provide alternative governance, such as in the context of trusteeship administrations in Kosovo or East Timor. Simply put, if a state's administrative capacity breaks down, there is nothing to replace it properly, even in the less dramatic situations of day-to-day environmental governance failures. It is against this background that initiatives such as the New Partnership for Africa's Development (NEPAD) have actually called for strengthening and reconstructing statehood.[5] In other words, the state remains a truly important actor in international relations. It forms part of international governance, which has become multilevel governance. It is, thus, the changing role of the state rather than its demise that deserves to be addressed in this chapter.

---

[1] M. Bothe, 'Vollzugsdefizit im Völkerrecht-Überlegungen zu 30 Jahren Umweltrecht,' in H.J. Cremer, T. Giegerich, and D. Richter, eds., *Tradition und Weltoffenheit des Rechts* (Heidelberg: Springer, 2002) 83.

[2] D.H. Cole and P.Z. Grossman, 'When Is Command-and-Control Efficient? Institutions, Technology, and the Comparative Efficiency of Alternative Regulatory Regimes for Environmental Protection' (1999) Wis. L. Rev. 887 at 887–938. Yet see R.I. Steinzor, 'Reinventing Environmental Regulation: The Dangerous Journey from Command to Self-Control' (1998) 22 Harv. Envt'l L. Rev. 103 at 103–202.

[3] M. Reisman, 'Designing and Managing the Future of the State' (1997) 8 Eur. J. Int'l L. 409.

[4] R.A. Falk, *Law in an Emerging Global Village* (Ardsley, NY: Transnational Publishers, 1998).

[5] See generally C.R. Ezetah, 'Legitimate Governance and Statehood in Africa: Beyond the Failed State and Colonial Self-Determination,' in E. Kofi, ed., *Legitimate Governance in Africa* (The Hague: Kluwer Law International, 1999) 419.

Historically, states did not easily accept environmental responsibility. Having done so, however, it took them a while to move from standard setting towards implementation, which became a matter of attention only after much interdisciplinary and public debate. Today, states have to find their place within a complex environmental governance structure, which is based on a multitude of international environmental agreements, integrates a broad variety of actors, and extends across multiple and differing layers of governance, depending on the environmental problem at hand. Due to the perceived inadequacy of pure command and control strategies, questions of instrument choice and, notably, a growing focus on incentive-based techniques of environmental governance (see Chapter 8 'Instrument Choice') have also changed the role of the state. While negative incentives come close to command-and-control strategies, the whole spectrum of positive incentives ('carrots') offers a much broader perspective on steering the behaviour of individuals, groups, and even states. Thus, perhaps counter-intuitively, the increased reliance on 'carrots' rather than 'sticks' has not weakened the role of the state but rather strengthened it. Allowing a choice of action, carrots are considered more acceptable by the addressees of environmental legislation than sticks, enabling the state to expand the scope of environmental governance while, at the same time, relying upon a broader variety of means. These shifts are crucial given the need for states to position themselves between the conflicting trends of privatization and internationalization of environmental policies.[6]

1 WESTPHALIAN MYTH OF UNIMPAIRED FREEDOM OF ACTION

The starting point of this chapter is what was long considered a state's more or less unimpaired freedom of action and inaction, which is often said to be grounded in the so-called Westphalian system. This historical explanation, however, is questionable since territoriality and sovereignty can be traced further back in history than the political system established on the basis of the Westphalian peace.[7] In addition, the concept of territorial sovereignty as such remains elusive. In their environmental relations, states never really enjoyed absolute territorial integrity nor absolute territorial sovereignty. Rather, co-existence and cooperation have always been elements of

---

[6] On these developments, compare K.E. Maskus and J.H. Reichman, 'The Globalization of Private Knowledge Goods and the Privatization of Global Public Goods'(2004) 7 J. Int'l Econ. L. 279; and M. Zürn, *Regieren jenseits des Nationalstaats* (Frankfurt am Main: Suhrkamp, 1998).

[7] For a balanced assessment of Westphalia's relevance, see H. Steiger, 'Der Westfälische Frieden—Grundgesetz für Europa?' in H. Duchhardt, ed., *Der Westfälische Friede* (München: Oldenbourg, 1998) 33.

environmental sovereignty, illustrating that the idea of the Westphalian system tends to be misinterpreted and over-estimated, *de facto* and *de iure*.[8]

Taking a closer look at the traditional characteristics of statehood and sovereignty as they have emerged over time, with particular reference to environmental sovereignty, it has to be conceded that since the age of enlightenment and the establishment of territorial systems of governance, territory has always been essential to statehood. As one of the conceptual and definitional elements of statehood even today, territory is invariably taken into account in inter-state relations. However, notwithstanding the legal characteristics of territorial sovereignty in principle, states early on had to cope with the fact that the environment as such, and natural resources in particular, do not necessarily conform to the territorial boundaries agreed upon between sovereign states (see Chapter 22 'Transboundary Impacts'). In the past, transboundary issues primarily focused on rivers and lakes. Today, concerns relating to resources such as air, the global climate, and groundwater have made it abundantly clear that it is impossible to construct a 'hermetically sealed' sphere of sovereignty. Sovereignty over such resources can only be a claim, never a fact.

Nevertheless, the claim has remained important both to international law in general as well as to international environmental law in particular. In order to become operational, sovereignty must be split up into freedom of action, which is mostly characterized as territorial sovereignty, and the protection of territory against outside interference, which is mainly considered in terms of territorial integrity. These concepts are still relevant today although, in light of the numerous rules that have been developed and agreed upon in international environmental law, they are less central than in the early days of international environmental law.[9]

While it is true that international environmental agreements have come to the fore only after the Second World War, especially after the 1972 Stockholm Conference on the Human Environment,[10] states began to cooperate much earlier on where they had to co-exist alongside the same natural resource. In fact, treaties dealing with the shared utilization of natural resources have been concluded from the second half of the nineteenth century onwards. Most of the early treaties were bilateral, addressing surface water, fisheries, and even the protection of birds. Some of the agreements that were concluded during the first half of the twentieth century may already be considered to pursue genuinely ecological, as opposed to merely resource conservation or sharing, objectives.

These agreements illustrate that states deployed the concept of sovereignty as a claim, but actually adopted pragmatic approaches in light of shared natural

---

[8] A. Osiander, 'Sovereignty, International Relations, and the Westphalian Myth' (2001) 55 Int'l Org. 251.

[9] D.A. French, 'A Reappraisal of Sovereignty in the Light of Global Environmental Concerns' (2001) 21 Legal Stud. 376.

[10] *Report of the Conference on the Human Environment and Action Plan*, UN Doc. A/CONF.48/14/Rev. 1 (1972).

resources. While this pragmatism did not prevent conflicts, it demonstrates that—perhaps in distinction to other fields of international law—the environmental context has always led states to seek cooperation with each other. It may be argued that the physical fact of a resource transcending political boundaries stimulated legal cooperation. In short, the so-called Westphalian system of absolute sovereignty and integrity could never be operational to the full with respect to transboundary natural resources.

The over-estimation of Westphalian concepts of sovereignty can further be illustrated by reference to early arbitral awards in international environmental relations, including the *Behring Sea Fur Seals Arbitration (Great Britain v. U.S.)*,[11] the *Trail Smelter Arbitration (U.S. v. Canada)*,[12] and the *Lac Lanoux Arbitration (Spain v. France)*[13]—the very cases that tend to be cited to show the Westphalian roots of international environmental law. It was the decline in seals because of over-exploitation on the high seas that led to the 1893 *Bering Sea Fur-Seals* case. The arbitral tribunal rejected the position of the United States, which sought to rely upon its territorial jurisdiction to protect seals against being taken on the high seas, but recognized the need for conservation to prevent over-exploitation and the decline of a hunted species. The dispute leading to the *Trail Smelter* case arose out of the activity of a smelter situated in Canada whose emissions of sulphur dioxide caused damage in the United States. The United States was awarded damages on the basis 'that under the principles of international law . . . no State has the right to use or permit the use of its territory in such a manner as to cause injury by fumes in or to the territory of another of the properties or persons therein, when the case is of serious consequences and the injury is established by clear and convincing evidence.'[14] The arbitral tribunal in the *Lac Lanoux* case, which involved a water diversion dispute between France and Spain, concluded that prior consultation and negotiation were required not only by treaty stipulation but more generally by a principle of customary law.[15]

All three cases illustrate that states sought to balance their mutual interests rather than the interests of the ecosystem as such. However, states were seeking compromise and cooperation, which can best be illustrated by the fact that the nine-point plan for conservation adopted by the arbitral tribunal in the *Bering Sea Fur-Seals* case still serves as a model for fisheries commissions today.[16] Thus, it may be argued that

---

[11] *Bering Sea Fur Seals Arbitration (Great Britain v. U.S.)*, 1898, 1 Moore's International Arbitration Awards 755, reprinted in 1 I.E.L. Rep. 43 at 67 (1999).

[12] *Trail Smelter Case (United States v. Canada)*, Award, 1941, 3 U.N.R.I.A.A. 1905 [*Trail Smelter*].

[13] *Lac Lanoux Arbitration (Spain v. France)*, 24 I.L.R. 101 (1957).

[14] See *Trail Smelter*, note 12 above.

[15] See D. Rauschning, 'Lac Lanoux Arbitration,' in R. Bernhardt, ed., *Encyclopedia of Public International Law* (Amsterdam: North Holland, 1997) 111.

[16] F. Orrego Vicuña, 'From the Bering Sea Fur-Seals Case to the 1999 Southern Bluefin Tuna Cases: A Century of Efforts at Conservation of the Living Resources of the High Seas' (1999) 10 Y.B. Int'l Envt'l L. 40 at 40–7.

Westphalian sovereignty has been, and is of, limited relevance for international environmental law and that its significance tends to be over-estimated even today.[17]

2 CONTEMPORARY STATEHOOD

The basic criteria of statehood as reflected in state practice, doctrine, and pertinent legal documents alike have remained more or less unchanged—people, territory, and government—with the need for an effective government becoming increasingly important. In general international law, this latter factor has been much discussed in light of the phenomenon of state failure. From the perspective of inter national environmental law, effective government is an indispensable factor for the implementation of international environmental agreements (see Chapter 40 'National Implementation').

International environmental obligations—while formally addressed to the state—are, in substance, often primarily concerned with the behaviour of non-state actors, in particular, private entities, including individuals, corporations, and similar types of actors. International environmental law, however, rarely addresses such private individuals and entities directly. Usually, it requires states to adopt implementing legislation, which then will address the behaviour of private actors. In this respect, the state is indispensable as a legislator and enforcement agency for international environmental law. It may thus be argued that sovereignty in the context of international environmental law has become very much operational. It is not an end in itself but rather a tool for the development and implementation of international environmental law.

The perspective taken here thus focuses on statehood as an element of a global system of environmental governance. This perspective is not simply about replacing one notion with another. Rather, it involves replacing a status-oriented approach with an action-oriented model. Governance refers to processes and systems that make an organization or a society work. Global governance consequently may be described as 'a continuing process through which conflicting or diverse interests may be accommodated and co-operative action may be taken. It includes formal institutions and regimes empowered to enforce compliance, as well as informal arrangements.'[18] This conception, in turn, leads to a notion of international environmental governance that includes the development of common interests of states and related

[17] O. Elias, 'Regionalism in International Law-making and the Westphalian Legacy,' in C. Harding, ed., *Renegotiating Westphalia* (The Hague: Martinus Nijhoff, 1999) 25.
[18] Commission on Global Governance, *Our Global Neighbourhood* (New York: Oxford University Press, 1995) at 2–3. See also M. Koskenniemi, 'Global Governance and Public International Law' (2004) 37 Kritische Justiz 241.

institutions.[19] The effective steering capacity of international environmental law very much depends on the proper combination of various levels and techniques of governance. It requires international, regional, national, and also sub-national or local governance (see Chapter 5 'Levels of Environmental Governance'). While international governance structures have been established—including international organizations with secretariats, compliance committees, and numerous other organs—the actual functioning of the system depends on the activities performed at the national level. Only if states participate in these systems and if they adopt national implementing legislation and enforce such legislation (see Chapter 40 'National Implementation') will the international level be able to succeed in its governance activities. Contemporary statehood and its relevance for international environmental law can best be illuminated by focusing on the roles assumed by states in this context, namely as authors, addressees, and guardians of the law.

2.1 States as Authors of International Environmental Law

Within the de-centralized system of international law, states are still the primary authors thereof. This assessment also applies to international environmental law: treaties are normally adopted and ratified by states; customary international environmental law is based on state practice and *opinio juris* as derived from official statements; and even general principles of international environmental law are developed on the basis of principles of national environmental law—that is, they are ultimately state-authored provisions.[20] The role of states as authors of the law, however, has changed over time. While the final decision within law-making processes still rests with states, they have lost relative importance in the process of law-making. Many multilateral environmental agreements have been drafted under the auspices of international organizations.[21] Furthermore, the participation of non-governmental organizations (NGOs) in international environmental conferences has had an impact on the substance of the law. In addition, the resolutions of international organizations and the declarations adopted by global conferences have changed the law-making process (see Chapter 20 'Treaty Making and Treaty Evolution' and Chapter 32 'International Institutions'). While none of these types of documents are

---

[19] U. Beyerlin, 'State Community Interests and Institution-Building in International Environmental Law' (1996) 56 Zeitschrift für ausländisches öffentliches Recht und Völkerrecht 602.

[20] For a discussion of the continued relevance of state consent in law-making, see D.B. Hollis, 'Why State Consent Still Matters: Non-State Actors, Treaties, and the Changing Sources of International Law' (2005) 23 Berkeley J. Int'l L. 137.

[21] See J. Sommer, 'Environmental Law-Making by International Organisations' (1996) Zeitschrift für ausländisches öffentliches Recht und Völkerrecht 628–67.

binding *per se*, they have contributed to the development of international environmental law. Thus, resolutions adopted by the statutory bodies of UNEP, the FAO, the IMO, IAEA, and others have invited states to act on the basis of the principles embodied therein, thus developing a significant law-making effect without, however, depriving states of their final say in the law-making process. The continued relevance of states as authors of international environmental law is not second-best but remains legitimate for at least two reasons.[22] First, states enjoy a comprehensive legitimacy as actors in public international law (see Chapter 30 'Legitimacy'). Second, states still bear primary responsibility as addressees of those rules and—in so far as the behaviour of non-governmental actors and private individuals is concerned— they remain the primary implementing agents of such rules. In a de-centralized legal system, making the law without paying tribute to those most affected by the law will deprive the law of its very effectiveness. If international environmental law is designed to have an effect 'on the ground', then it must accommodate the interests of states. This is best done at the stage of law-making. Thus, states legitimately are and remain the primary authors of international environmental law.

2.2 States as Addressees of International Environmental Law

States are not only authors but also addressees of international environmental law. Even though international environmental governance must eventually have an impact on private actors, these actors are hardly ever directly addressed by international law. Consequently, states are faced with at least three different types of obligations: obligations to refrain, obligations to prevent, and obligations to preserve. While obligations to refrain from certain conduct that is harmful to the environment are a typical feature of municipal environmental law, addressed to private entities, similar obligations are included in international agreements, although they are directed towards states. International environmental law includes obligations to refrain from transboundary environmental harm, from polluting transboundary watercourses, from dumping hazardous waste on land or at sea, from releasing particular substances into the atmosphere, from destroying ecosystems or biodiversity, and so forth, even though these obligations must be implemented domestically to have an impact on the behaviour of non-state actors. In light of this fact, the most important type of obligations addressed towards states includes obligations to prevent the environmentally harmful conduct of non-state actors. Such obligations include the adoption of legislation, the establishment of an administrative infrastructure (such as licensing systems and supervisory bodies), and sometimes even the enforcement of criminal law, which always necessitates governmental activities.

---

[22] D.M. Bodansky, 'The Legitimacy of International Governance: A Coming Challenge for International Environmental Law?' (1999) 93 A.J.I.L. 596.

As a third category of obligations addressed towards states, the obligation to preserve may require more than the mere prevention of the further degradation of the environment either by the state's own conduct or by activities of non-state actors under its jurisdiction. For example, the obligation to preserve parts of an ecosystem may require improvements with regard to a particular environmental resource. Thus, the preservation of the marine environment may necessitate improvements of water quality in coastal areas, or the protection of the Earth's climate may require measures of reforestation under the clean development mechanism of the climate change regime (see Chapter 14 'Atmosphere and Outer Space').

2.3 States as Guardians of International Environmental Law

Finally, states act as guardians of international environmental law, traditionally, in the context of law enforcement, with an initiating role in connection with compliance control procedures. The traditional international law-enforcement perspective still focuses on state responsibility for breaches of international law, and the secondary obligations (normally an obligation to make reparations) resulting therefrom. There seems to be widespread agreement, however, on the limited effectiveness of the state responsibility regime in environmental matters.[23] As the examples of the Chernobyl accident, the Sandoz chemical spill, and the salination of the Rhine illustrate, even when the facts and causal links are clear, there may be no recourse to the law of state responsibility. Retorsions and reprisals are not really an option in the case of common goods and, thus, largely fail to meet the needs of international environmental law. It may thus be argued that the role of states has changed to the most significant extent where they act as guardians of the law. In light of the ineffectiveness of traditional international law-enforcement mechanisms, new compliance control mechanisms have been developed with a less dominant role for individual states (see Chapter 43 'Compliance Procedures'). Since collective, rather than unilateral, enforcement; cooperation rather than confrontation; prevention rather than repression; and compliance assistance rather than sanctions have become the characteristics of the 'enforcement' of international environmental law, the contribution of states to this system has become largely, though not exclusively, procedural. They may initiate the procedure, provide relevant data for the assessment of their own or another party's compliance, and participate in decision-making with regard to reactions in the event of non-compliance.[24]

---

[23] M. Bothe, 'The Evaluation of Enforcement Mechanisms in International Environmental Law: An Overview,' in R. Wolfrum, ed., *Enforcing Environmental Standards Economic Mechanisms as Viable Means?* (Berlin: Springer, 1996) 13 at 27–9.

[24] T. Marauhn, 'Towards a Procedural Law of Compliance Control in International Environmental Relations' (1996) 56 Zeitschrift für ausländisches öffentliches Recht und Völkerrecht 696.

Contemporary statehood thus can best be understood as part of a global system of (environmental) governance with states assuming particular roles within this system. The specifics of these roles change over time as the international legal system is also undergoing processes of transformation.

3 TRANSFORMATION OF THE INTERNATIONAL LEGAL SYSTEM

States played the decisive role in the early development of international environmental law. This centrality corresponds to the general characteristics of international law more or less until the end of the Cold War. However, changes that the international legal system in general underwent in the second half of the twentieth century also prompted changes in the role of the state in international environmental law. Additionally, such systemic changes unleashed the potential for change inherent in international environmental law rooted, in particular, in an increasing readiness of non-state actors within international environmental regimes to develop their own ideas on changes and improvements. The transformation of the international legal system occurred over a period of years with a broad variety of inputs. Since it is not possible in this chapter to focus on all relevant changes, this section picks up two developments that can be illustrated quite well in referring to developments in international environmental law: the growing plurality of actors and the growing plurality of regimes. As a consequence, state-to-state networks have partially been replaced by inter-linked networks of states and other actors.

3.1 A Growing Plurality of Actors

Until the early 1970s, states could be considered not only the primary, but nearly the only, actors in international environmental law. They were the authors, addressees, and enforcers of the limited rules of international environmental law that existed at that time. However, some international environmental regimes had already been established, which over time led to a progressive institutionalization of international environmental law and thus to the gradual rise in importance of a new type of international actor. First attempts at institutionalizing international environmental protection had been made during the nineteenth century. In the twentieth century, the International Whaling Commission (IWC) was set up under the International Convention for the Regulation of Whaling, which was signed in 1946. Later, the International Commission for the Protection of the Rhine was established. However, the major impetus for developments in this field arose from the United Nations

Conference on the Human Environment, which was held in Stockholm in 1972. It led to the establishment of the United Nations Environment Programme (UNEP), and a multitude of other international environmental institutions. Today, we may even speak of a proliferation of international environmental regimes and institutions such that it is difficult to identify a coherent system of international environmental organizations (see Chapter 32 'International Institutions'). While there have been attempts to cluster such regimes and institutions around either UNEP or the Commission on Sustainable Development (CSD), no such effort has so far been successful.[25] Indeed, as in international law in general,[26] there are tendencies towards a fragmentation of international environmental law.

It is not only international organizations that have contributed to the broadening of the spectrum of actors in international environmental law. NGOs have also played an increasingly prominent role (see Chapter 33 'Non-Governmental Organizations and Civil Society'). Indeed, international environmental law has not only taken note of NGOs but has granted them varying degrees of legal status, in contrast to general international law, more generally, where the status of NGOs is more doubtful. Moreover, in light of their considerable—positive and negative—impacts on environmental protection, commercial actors, including national and, in particular, transnational corporations, must also be borne in mind (see Chapter 35 'Business').

Finally, we have to consider more closely the role of the individual in international environmental law. It is true that there still is a lot of scepticism vis-à-vis a human right to a healthy environment,[27] notwithstanding the tremendous amount of literature that has been published in this regard (see Chapter 28 'Environmental Rights'). Whether such a right exists or not need not be resolved in this chapter because international human rights institutions have drawn upon other well-established human rights to address environmental considerations. For example, the European Court of Human Rights has built upon the protection of one's home and privacy in order to establish a human rights basis for protection against at least certain activities detrimental for the human environment.[28]

The complexity of international environmental relations arising out of the plurality of actors is thus of a dual nature, which can be described by reference to the notions of internationalization and privatization. Internationalization, as understood for present purposes, refers to the increasing number of government-based actors beyond the state, such as regional and universal (inter-governmental) organizations, while privatization refers to the increasing number of non-governmental

[25] See U. Beyerlin and T. Marauhn, *Law-Making and Law-Enforcement in International Environmental Law after the 1992 Rio Conference* (Berlin: Umweltbundesamt, 1997) at 46–50 and 62–3.

[26] M. Craven, 'Unity, Diversity and the Fragmentation of International Law' (2003) 14 Finnish Y.B. Int'l L. 3.

[27] Cf. A.E. Boyle and M. Anderson, eds., *Human Rights Approaches to Environmental Protection* (Oxford: Clarendon Press, 1996).

[28] H. Post, 'Hatton and Others: Further Clarification of the "Indirect" Individual Right to a Healthy Environment' (2002) 2 Non-State Actors and Int'l L. 259.

actors at the local, national, regional, and international levels, reflecting, to a certain extent, the environmental concerns not only of civil society but also of the business community. Both categories of new actors are non-state actors. They differ, however, in that inter-governmental organizations can be more easily considered to be instrumental for state or public interests, whereas non-governmental organizations focus on private interests, notwithstanding the fact that they often claim to be representing public interests.

3.2 A Growing Plurality of Regimes

Apart from an increasing diversity of actors in international environmental relations and law, an important development since 1972 has been the increasing number of international regimes. States have not only moved from bilateralism in environmental law to multilateralism, but they have negotiated a broad variety and large number of international environmental agreements. While the sheer number of such agreements is impressive, it has also given rise to various problems that have repercussions for the role of the state. First, many regimes are sectoral, which means that they address a particular environmental problem, a particular source of pollution, or a particular part of the environment. This approach is often mirrored at the national level by implementation measures within the branch of government that is most concerned with a given sector. Different branches of government may then have to address conflicts arising out of different environmental regimes. Some of the more recent international instruments have moved towards integrated pollution control and integrated environmental protection to alleviate the resulting problems.[29] Second, the proliferation of environmental regimes has also increased the administrative burden resting upon states. Aside from the national implementation of agreements, an increasing burden results from reporting obligations (see Chapter 42 'Monitoring and Verification') and compliance procedures (see Chapter 43 'Compliance Procedures'). Third, the growing number of regimes has given rise to the development of a sprawling international and quasi-international bureaucracy. This phenomenon also places a burden upon traditional statehood and governance. In certain respects, one may consider the displacement of national bureaucracies by an international bureaucracy to be a positive step towards better protection of the global environment. That said, whether environmental problems can be better solved at the international than at the national level, or whether 'subsidiarity'[30] (see Chapter 5

---

[29] Cf., among others, K. Wieriks and A. Schulte-Wülwer-Leidig, 'Integrated Water Management for the Rhine River Basin, from Pollution Prevention to Ecosystem Improvement' (1997) 21 Natural Resources Forum 147 at 147–56; and O. MacIntyre, 'The Emergence of an "Ecosystem Approach" to the Protection of International Watercourses under International Law' (2004) 13 R.E.C.I.E.L. 1.

[30] For a discussion of subsidiarity in European environmental law, compare S. Mahmoudi, 'Subsidiarity and the Environment' (1995) 6 Finnish Y.B. Int'l L. 505.

'Levels of Environmental Governance') should play an important role in international environmental law, is a question that cannot be finally answered in this chapter.

What can be said is that political agreement and environmental governance at the global level have not yet been achieved—they are not even in sight. The development of international environmental law largely follows the traditional patterns of consent-based treaty-making. There is very limited secondary 'legislation' by international environmental institutions and there is no global environmental agency to coordinate or oversee treaty implementation. The powers of UNEP and the CSD are limited. While both were once considered potential nuclei for full-fledged international organizations, they have not been able to realize such ambitions. To illustrate the obstacles that stand in the way of the development of a more centralized coordinating agency, suffice it to point to the difficulties encountered in establishing merely closer cooperation between the various secretariats of multilateral environmental agreements.

International environmental law has attempted to address at least some of the concerns related to the inter-relationship and interdependence of resources and actors by developing concepts that reflect the global nature of certain environmental problems. Relevant concepts include those of the global commons, common interest, common concern, and—arguably the only one generally accepted as a matter of law—common heritage (see Chapter 23 'Common Areas, Common Heritage, and Common Concern'). While these concepts highlight the global character of an environmental issue, it is doubtful that they truly develop new legal coordinates or point towards a new level of law-making and law-enforcement.

3.3 From State-to-State Networks towards Inter-Linked Networks

Before developing perspectives on optimizing international environmental governance, it is useful to take a closer look at the types of relationship that have emerged between states and the other (new) actors referred to earlier in this chapter. Basically, it is possible to distinguish between inter-state relations, relations between states and international organizations, and relations between non-state actors and states. While inter-state relations remain central to international environmental law, the overall trend appears to be towards replacing state-to-state networks with inter-linked networks.

3.3.1 *Inter-Linking the State with New Actors*

International law has primarily developed on the basis of inter-state relations. The same is true for international environmental law, which largely follows the accepted patterns of legal development, in form and, to an extent, also in substance. As far as form is concerned, international environmental law primarily is based on treaties and customary international law, both typical modes of inter-state legal regulation. Newer approaches to treaty-making, such as the framework convention and protocol approach, have made law-making in international environmental relations somewhat quicker and more responsive (see Chapter 20 'Treaty Making and Treaty Evolution') but have not led to major changes in legal form or a major shift towards secondary law-making by international bodies (see Chapter 32 'International Institutions'). The situation is different when it comes to the substance of the rules of international environmental law, where the conceptual framework of inter-state relations plays an increasingly limited role. Similarly, the law of state responsibility as one of the tools to enforce standards in international law is based on the elements of an internationally wrongful act committed by a subject of international law—the state. However, notwithstanding a large body of literature on state responsibility in the environmental context and many international efforts to develop responsibility and liability regimes in this area (see Chapter 44 'International Responsibility and Liability'), virtually no environmental disputes have actually been resolved on the basis of the law of state responsibility. One of the difficulties may be that, in many situations, what is at issue is state responsibility for the behaviour of private persons. Perhaps the most prominent discussion of recent years was the debate about environmental responsibility after the Chernobyl disaster.[31] In the end, state responsibility was not successfully applied to this situation, nor did states substantially improve environmental standards as a consequence of those discussions.[32]

Quite apart from these questions concerning the role of the law of state responsibility, new issue areas have emerged where the substance of international environmental law can no longer be read exclusively on the basis of inter-state relations in the first place. For example, climate change is an issue that goes far beyond inter-state conflicts of interest since the resource in question and the effects of environmentally harmful activities are not limited to a particular state. In addition, it is difficult to establish a clear causal nexus between specific polluters and atmospheric degradation. The so-called greenhouse effect is both complex and truly global. In contrast, traditional inter-state relations do pattern other recent agreements, as in the context of biodiversity where the concepts of access to genetic resources and benefit sharing have led to rights and obligations of a reciprocal nature.[33]

While the United Nations did not originally encompass organs or agencies that focused upon environmental concerns, today, there does exist a range of relevant

---

[31] F. Zehetner, 'Tschernobyl: Zur völkerrechtlichen Wiedergutmachungsproblematik' (1986) Umwelt-und Planungsrecht 326.

[32] Additional agreements were reached under the auspices of the International Atomic Energy Agency (IAEA). See among others M.T. Kamminga, 'The IAEA Convention on Nuclear Safety' (1995) 44 Int'l & Comp. L.Q. 872.

[33] See T. Marauhn, 'Die Erhaltung der Biologischen Vielfalt und die nachhaltige Nutzung ihrer Bestandteile,' in K. Lange, ed., Nachhaltigkeit im Recht (Baden-Baden: Nomos Verlag, 2003) 87.

specialized UN agencies, such as the Food and Agriculture Organization (FAO), the UN Educational, Scientific, and Cultural Organization UNESCO, the World Health Organization (WHO), the World Meteorological Organization (WMO), the International Maritime Organization (IMO), and the International Atomic Energy Agency (IAEA). The United Nations has also established specialized organs to address environmental problems. These include UNEP, which was established on the basis of the 1972 Stockholm summit outcomes, and the CSD, which was established on the basis of a decision of the 1992 Rio summit. While there is still no general organization that is tasked with the protection of the international environment, a growing number of secretariats have been created to administer the international implementation of environmental treaties. Environmental treaties have also established an extensive network of supervisory bodies, conferences of the parties, commissions, and working groups (see Chapter 38 'Treaty Bodies'). The result is that a vast diversity of institutions is involved in some aspect of global environmental governance, giving rise to growing problems of coordination and consistency within the system (see Chapter 32 'International Institutions').

States have not made use of international institutions by transferring sovereign powers to these organizations but, rather, by relying upon them as forums for lawmaking, whereby decisions taken under their auspices normally remain subject to the approval by states parties. Some transfers of responsibilities have occurred in the context of technical monitoring[34] and, to a limited extent, in the context of supervisory bodies, such as treaty-based compliance or implementation committees. These latter bodies are authorized to receive and evaluate reports submitted by state parties, and they may even propose certain consequences in case of non-compliance (see Chapter 43 'Compliance Procedures'). However, the final determinations of non-compliance and decisions on response measures generally remain political decisions taken by states, which confirms the broader point that there has been only a very limited transfer of responsibility to international environmental institutions. Instead, states have made use of international institutions as providers of legal and technical expertise. Notably, developing states have turned to international (environmental) institutions for assistance with capacity building and training.[35] However, facilitation of such assistance is a task that has now largely moved to the UN Development Programme, the World Bank, and regional development banks (see Chapter 41 'Technical and Financial Assistance').

The relationship between states and NGOs is ambivalent. NGOs are normally established according to municipal law and are thus at least partially dependant upon acceptance by states. While they often claim to act in the common interest of

---

[34] For example, in the case of the European Evaluation and Monitoring Network (EMEP) under the LRTAP Convention. See J. Wettestad, 'Acid Lessons? LRTAP Implementation and Effectiveness' (1997) 7 Global Envt'l Change 235.

[35] D. Navid, 'Compliance Assistance in International Environmental Law: Capacity-Building, Transfer of Finance and Technology' (1996) 56 Zeitschrift für ausländisches öffentliches Recht und Völkerrecht 810.

societies, they do not normally represent the general public but provide a voice to particular groups within society. Indeed, even certain industry pressure groups have organized themselves as NGOs so as to participate in the international environmental arena, where a prerequisite for observer status, for example, is usually that the group be non-profit. Many intergovernmental organizations grant NGOs some status in their fields of activity, allowing them to observe international law-making processes, make submissions, or even participate in non-compliance procedures.[36] NGOs can certainly complement or contribute to governmental activities with regard to the environment. The relationship between states and NGOs thus deserves further reflection, in particular, when states are trying to identify areas of common concern and common interests.

Apart from industry pressure groups participating in international negotiations, transnational corporations are another actor with particular relevance in international environmental relations (see Chapter 35 'Business'). While transnational corporations (TNCs) are in part subject to the laws of their home country and their host country, their economic power tends to have a major impact on several states. Through the emergence of *lex mercatoria*[37] and the use of commercial arbitration, transnational corporations have contributed to the development of law not totally outside the reach of governmental control but with a certain life of its own. This phenomenon has given rise to concerns with regard to labour standards and other regulatory issues.[38] In the 1980s, the UN General Assembly sought to influence the behaviour of TNCs by adopting a (non-binding) code of conduct.[39] Some 20 years later, the UN launched the so-called 'Global Compact' as a voluntary corporate responsibility initiative, and, in 2003, the UN Sub-Commission on the Promotion and Protection of Human Rights approved a set of norms on the Responsibilities of Transnational Corporations and Other Business Enterprises with Regard to Human Rights. High profile events, such as the Bhopal disaster in India[40] and *The Social and Economic Rights Action Centre and the Centre for Economic and Social Rights v. Nigeria* case in Nigeria,[41] continue to press the question how to control the activities of transnational corporations if the host state is not capable and the home state not

---

[36] F. Yamin, 'NGOs and International Environmental Law' (2001) 10 R.E.C.I.E.L. 149.

[37] P. Zumbansen, 'Lex mercatoria: Zum Geltungsanspruch transnationalen Rechts' (2003) 67 Rabels Zeitschrift für ausländisches und internationales Privatrecht 637 at 637–82.

[38] J.M. Diller, 'Social Conduct in Transnational Enterprise Operations: The Role of the International Labour Organization,' in R. Blanpain, ed., *Multinational Enterprises and the Social Challenges of the Twenty-First Century* (London: Kluwer Law International, 2000) 17.

[39] Centre on Transnational Corporations, *The United Nations Code of Conduct on Transnational Corporations* (New York: United Nations, 1986).

[40] K.F. McCallion, 'Institutional and Procedural Aspects of Mass Claims Litigation and Settlement: The Exxon Valdez and Bhopal Gas Disaster Cases,' in International Bureau of the Permanent Court of Arbitration, ed., *Institutional and Procedural Aspects of Mass Claims Settlement Systems* (The Hague: Kluwer Law International, 2000) 43.

[41] *The Social and Economic Rights Action Centre and the Centre for Economic and Social Rights v. Nigeria* (2001), text reprinted in (2003) 10 I.H.R.R. 282. See J.P. Eaton, 'The Nigerian Tragedy,

willing to act. It is important to develop legal mechanisms to deal with these situations. One option is to rely on municipal liability regimes, making use of policies adopted by those corporations. Another option is the further elaboration of international standards, binding or non-binding, to govern TNC conduct. Under principles 7, 8, and 9 of the Global Compact, business is requested to support a pre-cautionary approach to environmental challenges, to undertake initiatives to promote greater environmental responsibility, and to encourage the development and diffusion of environmentally friendly technologies. However, in many cases, it is the economic power of TNCs that acts as a constraint on governmental policies, be it at the national or international level. Whatever the source (domestic or international) and legal force (binding or non-binding) of efforts to shape the corporate practices of TNCs, the adoption of environmentally friendly corporate policies very often is a result of either NGO pressures, or finds its origin in the interest of such corporations to protect their reputation for marketing purposes.[42] Overall, while the rise of TNCs may not affect the formal powers of states, it certainly does impact their factual ability to make international environmental law applicable to these corporations and to enforce it within the municipal system.

While the individual remains primarily a subject of domestic law, he or she, nevertheless, has gained a greater role in international environmental law. This is particularly the case in the context of environment-related human rights law. Of course, individuals also play a role as members of NGOs that are active at the international or national levels in pressing for the development or implementation of international environmental law, and as claimants under municipal environmental law helping to enforce its implementation. Other new opportunities to push for the implementation of environmental standards have been provided by the World Bank Inspection Panel,[43] which gives individuals and groups of individuals some voice with regard—among others—to environmental consequences of development projects. However, these developments are of limited impact and do not fundamentally change the role of the state in international law.

3.3.2 *Cross-Cutting Relationships and 'New' Networks*

Having thus identified various links between the state and other actors in international environmental relations, it is important to note that, on top of these links, cross-cutting relationships and 'new' networks have developed that do have implications for states. Thus, the activities of new actors and their inter-relationships will

---

Environmental Regulation of Transnational Corporations, and the Human Right to a Healthy Environment' (1997) 15 Boston U. Int'l L.J. 261.

   [42] M. Anderson, 'Transnational Corporations and Environmental Damage: Is Tort Law the Answer?' (2002) 41 Washburn L.J. 399.

   [43] A. Gowlland Gualtieri, 'The Environmental Accountability of the World Bank to Non-State Actors: Insights from the Inspection Panel' (2001) 72 Br. Y.B. Int'l L. 213.

have an impact on the role of the state. In addition, the state as such is not a homogenous actor. It needs organs to act and organs are ultimately made up of human individuals. While such individuals are bound by governmental policies, they nevertheless establish networks among themselves. For example, epistemic communities emerge that as such have an impact on governmental activities (see Chapter 34 'Epistemic Communities'). Cross-cutting relationships thus have to be scrutinized carefully. While a detailed analysis cannot be provided in this chapter, some aspects can be highlighted.

From a lawyer's perspective, it is difficult to assess the effect on international environmental law of interactions between various individuals acting in their capacity as organs of states or as non-state actors. While it is possible to identify the status as well as the rights and obligations of actors endowed with legal personality, it is much more difficult to get a precise idea of the inter-personal mechanisms and their impact on the law. A useful tool is social network analysis.[44] Such analysis has emerged as a key technique in modern organizational studies. It focuses on the social structure between actors, both individuals and organizations, and highlights the ways in which they are interconnected. Law-related social network analysis can demonstrate that such networks operate on many levels, within corporations as well as NGOs, among both categories of non-state actors, within governments, among government departments, within international organizations, and between all of these different levels. In practical terms, social network analysis may play a decisive role in clarifying how problems are solved, how organizations run, and to what degree particular actors manage to achieve their goals. This type of information is particularly important in the context of international environmental relations because of the variety of actors and individuals involved. Above all, however, knowledge about environment-related international networks is important in order to develop international environmental regimes that are effective in a dual sense. They effectively address a particular environmental problem, and their implementation and compliance instruments are adequate to meet the objectives of the regime.[45]

One of the interesting phenomena in international environmental relations is the fact that highly specialized governmental officials and their counterparts within international organizations as well as other types of non-state actors tend to share similar approaches to the issues with which they deal. This commonality often serves as an incentive to maintain contact with each other across the boundaries of their respective political frameworks. Such sharing of approaches creates valuable channels for information flow, the possibility of discussing new perspectives, and an informal basis for the development of common ideas and positions. Epistemic communities that have developed over time may agree on how to address particular

---

[44] J. Scott, *Social Network Analysis: A Handbook* (Newbury Park: Sage Publications, 2000).

[45] For a European perspective, see K.H. Ladeur, *The New European Agencies: The European Enviroment Agency and Prospects for a European Network of Environmental Administrations*, European University Institute working paper (1996).

environmental problems, even though governmental and other actors have difficulty reaching agreement. It is against this background that epistemic communities have contributed to the development of international environmental law.[46] For example, in the 1970s, the World Conservation Union (IUCN) co-sponsored environmental treaties (including the Convention on Wetlands of International Importance Especially as Waterfowl Habitat, the Convention on International Trade in Endangered Species of Wild Fauna and Flora, and the Convention on the Conservation of Migratory Species of Wild Animals). Epistemic communities can both weaken and strengthen the role of the state in international environmental law.

From the perspective of states, overlapping networks can be useful in a number of respects. They provide sources of information that would otherwise not be available to states, and they facilitate communication between various types of actors. In addition, overlapping networks have the potential to provide synergies when implementing international environmental regimes. At the same time, there are some potential downsides. For example, overlapping networks may blur the lines of accountability and responsibility precisely because they cut across traditional categories of actors. Also, they contribute to the development of communities, the legitimacy of which is limited to the expertise of participating individuals. These ambivalent tendencies have to be borne in mind when turning to a closer view on contemporary statehood, and the roles assumed by states in contemporary international environmental law.[47]

The role of states must be contrasted with the comparative advantages of non-state actors. International organizations bundle national interests, balance them, and contribute to the development of common interests and concerns. Even if certain states are dominant in one or another international organization, NGOs have gained access to such international organizations contributing at least to increased transparency. Specialized international organizations have the potential to absorb the knowledge and input of epistemic communities, providing stronger input in favour of environmental concerns than is possible at the national level. Also, international institutions can coordinate and supervise the implementation of international environmental agreements and, in particular, can contribute to compliance control and compliance assistance at the international level.

Private non-state actors play a more ambivalent role than international organizations. Nevertheless, they also enjoy certain comparative advantages within a multilevel system of international environmental governance. While NGOs, in principle, represent only their constituencies, they nevertheless have managed to put environmental issues of common concern on the international agenda. The record of business entities is less positive in this regard. They have at times, for example, sought to keep issues off the international agenda.

---

[46] P. Haas, 'Introduction: Epistemic Communities and International Policy Coordination' (1992) 46 Int'l Org. 1.

[47] B.H. Desai, 'Mapping the Future of International Environmental Governance' (2002) 13 Y.B. Int'l Envt'l L. 43.

4 PERSPECTIVES: OPTIMIZING INTERNATIONAL ENVIRONMENTAL GOVERNANCE

From an international environmental law perspective, statehood must be evaluated as an element of a larger system of international environmental governance. Although the role of states as authors and guardians of the law has changed in a number of respects, states have remained of essential importance for international environmental law. Neither have they become obsolete nor has an effective international bureaucracy been established that is able to perform governmental functions to a sufficient degree. While international environmental governance does not necessarily depend on statehood, states do contribute in significant ways to effective environmental governance. Since international organizations lack the authority and capacity to implement international norms directly, national implementation is essential, and it may be argued that states are a necessary intermediate level for the implementation of international environmental standards. Only states have sufficient legislative means at hand, and only states can provide the indispensable administrative infrastructure. In other words, states continue to play a crucial role as addressees of international environmental law. States, however, do not act in isolation. They are networked with other states and, increasingly, act under the supervision of international compliance control procedures. In addition, cross-cutting networks of epistemic communities, of NGOs, and of other actors have an impact on state behaviour.

States enjoy certain comparative advantages in international environmental governance. They are well-established actors, equipped with the necessary tools to participate both in international environmental law-making and in its implementation. States have the capacity to participate in cooperative law enforcement vis-à-vis each other as well as to implement and enforce standards vis-à-vis their own citizens and entities subject to their jurisdiction and control. The participation of states in international environmental governance, thus, is an asset that cannot be easily left aside. However, states also suffer from certain deficiencies. Their activities are often guided by national interests rather than common interests or concerns. To make matters more complex, such national interests are subject not only to pressure from inside but also from outside. For example, sometimes states are less powerful than they perceive themselves to be, such as in relation to TNCs.[48]

---

[48] On the complex interrelationship between states and transnational corporations in international environmental law, see D.M. Ong, 'The Impact of Environmental Law on Corporate Governance—International and Comparative Perspectives' (2001) 12 Eur. J. Int'l L. 685.

As all different categories of actors in international environmental law enjoy certain comparative advantages, an important question is how to optimize[49] international environmental governance. It is neither easy to define nor to achieve such an optimum. However, it is possible to state that in most cases there is a more, rather than a less, important role for the state to play within the increasingly overlapping networks of states, international organizations, and non-governmental actors. Roles are not only pre-defined but can also be attributed to actors on the basis of incentives agreed upon in multilateral treaties.[50] This is a matter that should be observed more closely in the future. Given the strength of states as actors in international environmental relations, incentives should be developed and included in multilateral agreements to make use of their potential within multilevel international environmental governance. For example, the interest of states in an economic use of natural resources will stimulate their contribution to preserve such resources as a basis for development. Providing a utilitarian justification for the preservation of the environment may thus help to optimize environmental governance.

In the final analysis, the state still has a strong role to play in international environmental law—perhaps a stronger role than during the period of 'coexistence.' This growing role is due to the fact that new forms of governance have given the state much broader thematic scope to intervene and many more instruments to influence the behaviour of other actors. While it is true that some traditional mechanisms have been weakened, the overall assessment of the role of the state in international environmental law is positive. The law is not confronted with a paradigm shift but is experiencing a transformation of the role of the state that may—if properly used—be much to the benefit of international environmental law as a whole.

[49] D.C. Esty, 'Toward Optimal Environmental Governance' (1999) 74 N.Y.U. L. Rev. 1495.

[50] Thus, the Convention on Biological Diversity provides a utilitarian justification for the preservation of diversity, building on the direct and indirect usefulness of biological resources to humanity. The interests of host states in their biological resources and their economic use are deployed to provide for conservation. See R. Wolfrum, 'The Convention on Biological Diversity: Using State Jurisdiction as a Means of Ensuring Compliance,' in R. Wolfrum, ed., *Enforcing Environmental Standards: Economic Mechanisms as Viable Means?* (Berlin: Springer, 1996) 373. See also F.X. Perrez, 'The Relationship between "Permanent Sovereignty" and the Obligation Not to Cause Transboundary Environmental Damage' (1996) 26 Envt'l L. 1187.

Recommended Reading

K.W. Abbott and D. Snidal, 'Hard and Soft Law in International Governance' (2000) 54 Int'l Org. 421.

G. Loibl, 'The Role of International Organisations in International Law-Making International Environmental Negotiations' (2001) 1 Non-State Actors and International Law 41.

W.R. Moomaaw, 'International Environmental Policy and the Softening of Sovereignty' (1997) 21 Fletcher Forum of World Affairs 7.

N. Schrijver, 'The Changing Nature of State Sovereignty' (2000) 70 Br. Y.B. Int'l L. 65.

R. Wolfrum, 'Means of Ensuring Compliance with and Enforcement of International Environmental Law' (1999) 272 Recueil des cours 9.

CHAPTER 32

INTERNATIONAL INSTITUTIONS

ELLEN HEY

1 INTRODUCTION

MUCH of international environmental law addresses common interest problems—that is, problems that are of concern to the international community as a whole (see Chapter 23 'Common Areas, Common Heritage, and Common Concern'). Addressing such problems requires cooperative action, common rules and standards, and continuous decision-making among relevant actors. In the course of engaging in these activities, a framework of global environmental governance has emerged in which international institutions play important roles. Moreover, within this framework, under the influence of the concept of sustainable development (see Chapter 26 'Sustainable Development'), issues are addressed that go to the heart of the South-North relationship and the inequalities that prevail in this context. The South-North context, in fact, largely accounts for the complex institutional structure of the framework of global environmental governance. In this framework, many of the rules and standards, or norms, are adopted within multilateral environmental agreements (MEAs), but other international institutions, such as the Global Environment Facility (GEF), administer part of their implementation in the South. These institutions themselves also adopt rules and standards, which they apply together with MEA-based norms to projects conducted in the South. International institutions provide the platform where these two inter-related governance issues (common interest and South-North context) are addressed through cooperation among a variety of actors, including states (see Chapter 31 'Changing Role of the State') and non-state actors such as the corporate sector (see Chapter 35 'Business') and non-governmental organizations (NGOs) (see Chapter 33 'Non-Governmental Organizations and Civil Society').

The international institutions involved in global environmental governance are a heterogeneous set of actors. Their legal status, competences, and tasks vary considerably. They are linked to each other through cooperative arrangements, which concern a multitude of different topics ranging from reciprocal observer status at each other's meetings to the establishment of new international institutions. In engaging in global environmental governance, through normative development as well as through decision-making in individual situations, international institutions have moved beyond the interstate paradigm, which is central to the traditional doctrine of international law. In so doing, a body of law has emerged that, as a system, has traits of what in national law is considered to be public law in general and administrative law in particular (see Chapter 4 'Global Environmental Governance as Administration'),[1] rather than private (contract) law, which is a body of law with which traditional

---

[1] The term 'public law' is used in the broad sense as used in Dutch (*publiekrecht*) and German (*öffentliches Recht*) law, where it refers to constitutional and administrative law—two bodies of law that in Dutch and German law are conceptualized as intimately interrelated. For a broad conceptualization of 'public law,' see M. Loughlin, *The Idea of Public Law* (Oxford: Oxford University Press, 2003; paperback,

interstate law shares many traits.[2] As a result, contemporary international law can be characterized as a legal system that is undergoing systemic change and in which two normative patterns operate and interact with each other—what I have elsewhere referred to as the interstate normative pattern and the common interest normative pattern.[3]

This chapter addresses the roles of international institutions in global environmental governance and presents international institutions as exercising public powers within this framework. Conceptualizing international institutions in this manner carries with it the normative postulation that international institutions are exercising delegated powers that should be subject to limitations and to the requirement of accountability.[4] First, an overview of, and the linkages between, different international institutions will be provided. Thereafter, two distinct roles of international institutions will be discussed: their roles in normative development and in decision-making in individual situations, with the latter focusing on decisions taken in the selection of projects for funding and in compliance procedures. Finally, I will return to the public law character of international environmental law and the characterization of the framework of global environmental governance.

2 INSTITUTIONAL FRAMEWORK OF GLOBAL ENVIRONMENTAL GOVERNANCE

As mentioned earlier, the international institutions that participate in global environmental governance are a heterogeneous set of actors, which are linked to each

2004). See also B. Kingsbury, N. Krisch, and R. Stewart, 'The Emergence of Global Administrative Law' (2005) 68 L. & Contemp. Probs. 15.

[2] See H. Lauterpacht, *Private Law Sources and Analogies of International Law (with special reference to arbitration)* (London: Longmans, Green and Company, 1927). See also Separate Opinion by Judge ad hoc E. Lauterpacht in Order of the International Court of Justice (ICJ) of 17 December 1997 in the *Case Concerning the Application of the Convention on the Crime of Genocide (Bosnia Herzegovina v. Yugoslavia), Counter Claims,* [1997] I.C.J. Rep. 243. Lauterpacht in paragraph 23 of his opinion makes the point that 'an international tribunal of essentially civil . . . jurisdiction' is ill equipped to deal with issues that arise in the context of the settlement of a dispute under Article IX of the Convention on the Prevention and Punishment of the Crime of Genocide, which are of a criminal law nature. He refers to these difficulties as 'systemic.' Similar problems may arise in relationship to international environmental law as pointed out by Judge Weeramantry in his separate opinion in the *Case Concerning the Gabčíkovo-Nagymaros Project (Hungary/Slovakia),* 25 September 1997, [1997] I.C.J. Rep. 92 (25 September). In paragraph C(c) of the opinion, Weeramantry points to the *inter partes* nature of the procedure at the ICJ, in which it is difficult to do justice to rules of an *erga omnes* character, if they were to arise in a case.

[3] E. Hey, *Teaching International Law: State-Consent as Consent to a Process of Normative Development and Ensuing Problems,* inaugural lecture (The Hague: Kluwer Law International, 2003).

[4] See also P. Allott, *Eunomia: A New Order for a New World* (Oxford: Oxford University Press, 1990) at 167–77.

other through a variety of cooperative arrangements. When screening these institutions from the point of view of their origin, the following stand out.

- Treaty-based institutions, such as the conferences or meetings of the parties (COPs or MOPs) and secretariats to MEAs and their protocols as well as subsidiary bodies such as those on scientific and technical cooperation and on compliance (see Chapter 38 'Treaty Bodies').
- UN specialized agencies, which are international organizations that are established by treaty but have a special relationship with the United Nations based on the agreements that they conclude with the Economic and Social Council (ECOSOC) pursuant to Article 57 *juncto* Article 63 of the Charter of the United Nations (UN Charter). Examples of specialized agencies are the International Bank for Reconstruction and Development (IBRD or World Bank), the International Maritime Organization (IMO), the Food and Agriculture Organization (FAO), the UN Industrial Development Organization (UNIDO), and the International Fund for Agricultural Development (IFAD). Linked to specialized agencies are other institutions that play important roles in global environmental governance. In the case of the World Bank, the World Bank Inspection Panel and the Prototype Carbon Fund (PCF) are relevant examples.
- UN General Assembly (UNGA) bodies, which have been established pursuant to Article 22 of the UN Charter. Relevant examples are the UN Development Programme (UNDP), the UN Environment Programme (UNEP), and the UN Institute for Training and Research (UNITAR).
- Institutions based on cooperative arrangements between other international institutions, which include the GEF, the Inter-Organization Programme for the Sound Management of Chemicals (IOMC), and the Intergovernmental Panel on Climate Change (IPCC).

In addition, mention should be made of the UNGA, ECOSOC, and the Commission on Sustainable Development (CSD), all of which perform coordinating functions, as well as courts and tribunals that engage in dispute settlement functions (see Chapter 45 'International Dispute Settlement').

This listing illustrates that various different types of institutions participate in global environmental governance. The institutions based on cooperative arrangements, moreover, are illustrative of one type of link that exists between international institutions. However, the three institutions listed as examples fulfil very different functions: the GEF is a financial mechanism (see Chapter 41 'Technical and Financial Assistance'), the IOMC develops rules and standards for harmonizing the classification and labelling of chemicals and has established risk reduction programmes, and the IPCC is a scientific advisory body (see Chapter 9 'Science and Technology'). In functional terms, the three institutions might, if compared to the other institutions listed, be characterized as follows. The GEF, as a financial mechanism, more closely resembles the PCF and IFAD than it does the IOMC or the IPCC. The IOMC resembles COPs, when they engage in normative development for the purposes of further developing an MEA-based regime. The IPCC performs a task similar to that of the Joint Group of Experts on the Scientific Aspects of Marine Pollution (GESAMP), which is also based on a cooperative arrangement among other institutions. While the above characterization serves to illustrate that very different types of institutions participate in global environmental governance and that these institutions cooperate in setting up new institutions, the institutional dynamics of global environmental governance are more complex.

MEAs in many cases were developed through the United Nations, its specialized agencies, or programmes of the UNGA.[5] Moreover, the secretariats of most MEA-based regimes are either linked to the United Nations[6] or administrated by its agencies or programmes,[7] although some have an independent status.[8] Beyond the MEAs and their protocols, most of the substantive standards and rules are developed by way of MEA-based institutions or through cooperative arrangements entered into by various MEAs (see Chapter 20 'Treaty Making and Treaty Evolution'). Other institutions, specialized agencies, or programmes of the UNGA also may be involved in such cooperative arrangement, of which the IOMC is a pertinent example.[9] In addition, both specialized agencies and UNEP also participate in the development of rules and standards. Examples in this case are the FAO, under whose auspices the Code of Conduct for Plant

[5] For example, the United Nations Framework Convention on Climate Change (UNFCCC) was developed under the auspices of the United Nations, the Convention on Biological Diversity (CBD) under the auspices of UNEP, while conventions related to vessel-source pollution, such as the Convention on the Prevention of Marine Pollution by Dumping of Wastes and Other Matter (London Convention) and the Convention for the Control and Management of Ships' Ballast Water and Sediments (BWM Convention) were developed under the auspices of the International Maritime Organization (IMO) and the International Treaty on Plant Genetic Resources for Food and Agriculture (ITPGRFA) under the auspices of the FAO. Moreover, the FAO and UNEP together participated in the development of the Convention on the Prior Informed Consent Procedure for Certain Hazardous Chemicals and Pesticides (PIC Convention).

[6] For example, the UNFCCC and the Convention to Combat Desertification in Those Countries Experiencing Serious Drought and/or Desertification, Particularly in Africa (Desertification Convention), established their own, essentially independent secretariats, which are linked to the United Nations.

[7] For example, the secretariats of the CBD, the Vienna Convention on the Protection of the Ozone Layer (Vienna Convention), the Basel Convention on the Control of Transboundary Movements of Hazardous Wastes and Their Disposal (Basel Convention), and the Convention on Trade in Endangered Species of Wild Fauna and Flora (CITES) are administered by UNEP. The secretariat of the PIC Convention is administered jointly by UNEP and the FAO. The IMO provides the secretariat for MEAs related to vessel source marine pollution. Relevant examples are the London Convention, the International Convention for the Prevention of Pollution form Ships (MARPOL Convention) and the BWM Convention. Likewise, the FAO provides the Secretariat for the Agreement to Promote Compliance with International Conservation and Management Measures by Fishing Vessels on the High Seas (Compliance Agreement) and the ITPGRFA.

[8] The Secretariat of the International Convention for the Regulation of Whaling provides an example.

[9] The IOMC was established in 1995 by way of a memorandum of understanding concluded between four UN specialized agencies (the FAO, the International Labour Organization (ILO), UNIDO, and the World Health Organization (WHO)), UNEP, and the Organisation for Economic Co-operation and Development (OECD). In 1997, UNITAR joined the IOMC. The World Bank and UNDP, furthermore, are observers in the IOMC. The WHO administers the secretariat of the IOMC.

Germplasm Collecting and Transfer (PGCT Code of Conduct) was developed, and UNEP's role in the development of the Global Programme of Action for the Protection of the Marine Environment from Land-based Activities (GPA). A further point to note is that some of the instruments developed within these agencies or programmes serve to implement more than one MEA. The PGCT Code of Conduct and the IOMC provide relevant examples. The former assists in the implementation of both the Convention on Biological Diversity (CBD) and the International Treaty on Plant Genetic Resources for Food and Agriculture, while the IOMC serves to implement the Convention on the Prior Informed Consent Procedure for Certain Hazardous Chemicals and Pesticides in International Trade (PIC Convention) and the Stockholm Convention on Persistent Organic Pollutants (Stockholm Convention). The content of an MEA-based regime, in fact, can only be grasped if the decisions taken within the regime in question,[10] as well as those that originate in other institutions linked to the regime, are considered together with the MEA and its protocols.

The World Bank plays a pivotal role in the framework of global environmental governance. It cooperates in the implementation of MEA-based commitments in developing and economy-in-transition states through a variety of funds, such as the GEF and the PCF. In addition, it finances projects that may serve to implement MEAs in these countries outside these funds. The GEF, as the financial mechanism for various MEAs, performs an important role in implementing the MEA-based commitments of developed states to transfer finances and technology to developing states (see Chapter 41 'Technical and Financial Assistance'). The World Bank both administers the GEF Fund and functions as one of the implementing agencies of the GEF. The other implementing agencies of the GEF are UNEP and UNDP. Since 1999, four regional development banks (the African Development Bank, the Asian Development Bank, the European Bank for Reconstruction and Development, and the Inter-American Development Bank), IFAD, the FAO, and UNIDO have joined the GEF as executing agencies. Other UN specialized agencies operate as executing agencies of GEF projects on an ad hoc basis.[11] The GEF operates on the basis of guidance from relevant COPs, internal World Bank policies, and its own rules, such as those related to portfolio and project criteria.

The network depicted in this section of the chapter provides the institutional setting in which global environmental governance unfolds through normative development and decision-making in individual situations. The resulting rules, standards,

---

[10] The *CITES Handbook* (Nairobi/Stevenage: UNEP/Earthprint, 2005), for example, is crucial to understanding the impact of CITES as the *Handbook for the International Treaties for the Protection of the Ozone Layer*, 6th edition (Nairobi/Stevenage: UNEP/Earthprint, 2003) is for understanding the Vienna Convention and its Montreal Protocol on the Protection of the Ozone Layer (Montreal Protocol). Likewise, the impact of the Kyoto Protocol can only be grasped if account is taken of the decisions adopted at the first COP/MOP of the protocol.

[11] An example is provided by the Global Ballast Water Program, executed by the IMO, with UNEP acting as the implementing agency.

and decisions together, as suggested earlier, harbour traits of public law and reveal an evolving common interest normative pattern in international law.[12]

3 INTERNATIONAL INSTITUTIONS AND NORMATIVE DEVELOPMENT

Except in the formation of customary international law (see Chapter 19 'Formation of Customary International Law and General Principles'), normative development in the traditional international legal system depends on a highly formalized notion of state consent, which serves both to transform relevant rules and standards into binding law and to legitimize those same rules and standards (see Chapter 30 'Legitimacy'). This notion of state consent leads to the assumption that a rule or standard, or a set of rules and standards in the form of a treaty, legally bind a state only if that state explicitly has consented to the rule, standard, or treaty in question. Furthermore, it implies that, unless explicitly agreed in the relevant constitutive document, an international institution cannot adopt rules and standards that legally bind its member states.

While there are examples of international institutions that have been endowed with the competence to adopt general rules that legally bind their member states, they are few and far between. The European Community (EC) is probably the best-known example (see Chapter 37 'Regional Economic Integration Organizations'), while the UN Security Council also has developed such a competence.[13] In addition, a large number of MEA-based institutions have been given the express competence to amend technical annexes subject to a so-called opting-out procedure. In these cases, the COP of an MEA or the MOP of a protocol has the competence to adopt amendments to such annexes either by consensus or a majority vote, with the amendments binding all states parties, except those states that object to the amendment.[14] These procedures thus provide individual states, if they so wish, with the option of relying on formal state consent even if expressed in a negative manner. The Montreal Protocol on Substances That Deplete the Ozone Layer (Montreal Protocol) and the PIC Convention have dispensed with the requirement of formal state consent

---

[12] Other areas of international law where this pattern can be discerned are, for example, international criminal law and international human rights law.

[13] The resolutions adopted by the Security Council regarding terrorism provide an example. See, in particular, UN Security Council Resolution 1373(2001), which in paragraphs 1 and 2 provides general rules that legally bind states in combating terrorism.

[14] See, e.g., Article 30, *juncto* Article 29, of the CBD, which apply to amendments of annexes to the CBD or to its protocols such as the Cartagena Protocol on Biosafety. Similarly, see Article 16, *juncto* Article 15, of the UNFCCC and Article 21, *juncto* Article 20, of the Kyoto Protocol.

in a more fundamental way where the entry into force of certain amendments to their annexes is concerned. Under the Montreal Protocol, the MOP has the competence by consensus, and, if consensus is not available, by a two-thirds majority vote of both developed and developing states, to adjust the stringency of control measures for substances already controlled under the protocol, with legally binding effect for all states parties.[15] In practice, however, such adjustments have been adopted by consensus. Under the PIC Convention, the COP is competent to add or remove chemicals or groups of chemicals from Annex III (substances subject to the prior informed consent procedure) by consensus, with such amendments legally binding all parties once they have been adopted.[16]

The Montreal Protocol and the PIC Convention significantly depart from the procedure applicable to the amendment of annexes found in most MEAs (that is, formal ratification or opting-out), even if the text of the Montreal Protocol promises a greater possible departure from this procedure than witnessed in practice. Decision-making by consensus, even if it assumes that no state parties disagree with the proposed amendment, does not entail the formality traditionally associated with state consent, which assumes that state consent must be expressly given[17] or that states at least must have the option of expressly communicating their dissent (opting-out). Such a formal moment at which states express consent or have the opportunity of expressing dissent is lacking where COPs or MOPs take decisions by consensus with binding effect or where states do not have the option of reassessing the decisions adopted.

A further departure from the traditional requirement of formal state consent, however, also is common practice in global environmental governance. This departure involves international institutions developing rules and standards that are not legally binding, but that do apply generally to the states parties to an MEA-based regime (see Chapter 20 'Treaty Making and Treaty Evolution'). Two types of rules and standards can be distinguished: those that apply to all or specified groups of states parties, such as Annex I states under the Kyoto Protocol, in their activities to implement the regime, and those that apply to international institutions when they take decisions about projects that serve to implement MEAs in developing and economy-in-transition states. An example of the former are the decisions of the COP/MOP of the Kyoto Protocol, which provide the means by which the protocol will be implemented, including, for example, the conditions under which parties to the protocol may engage in emissions trading or participate in the clean development mechanism.[18] An example of the latter are the decisions that COPs regularly adopt and that provide

---

[15] Article 9(2), of the Montreal Protocol.

[16] See Articles 7 and 9, *juncto* Article 22(5), of the PIC Convention.

[17] See Articles 11–16 and 39 of the Vienna Convention on the Law of Treaties.

[18] See, e.g., Decision 2/CMP.1 on the Principles, Nature, and Scope of the Mechanisms Pursuant to Articles 6, 12, and 17 of the Kyoto Protocol, which was adopted at COP/MOP.1(2005) of the Kyoto Protocol.

guidelines that the GEF is to apply in developing and selecting projects that serve to implement MEAs in developing and economy-in-transition states.[19] What the two types of decisions have in common is that both affect the commitments and entitlements of parties to the MEA in question. In the case of the climate change regime, for example, the first type of decision provides the conditions that Annex I parties must meet to be entitled to participate in the flexible mechanisms and the second type of decision determines whether a developing or economy-in-transition state, in fact, is able to profit from the commitments regarding the transfer of financial and technical means contained in MEAs (see Chapter 41 'Technical and Financial Assitance'). The relevant COPs or MOPs normally adopt such decisions on the basis of consensus. However, if no consensus is available they may be adopted by a two-third majority vote.

In addition to MEA-based institutions, other international institutions, such as UN specialized agencies and UNEP, also engage in normative development. Relevant examples are the World Bank's Operational Policy/Bank Procedures (OP/BP) 4.01 on environmental assessment policy as well as OP/BP 4.10 on indigenous peoples, which internally bind the bank's personnel; the FAO's PGCT Code of Conduct, which is voluntary and addresses states, collectors, and others involved in the collection and use of plant germplasm; and the Guidelines on Waste Water Management, which were developed within the framework of the GPA with the assistance of UNEP. Again a distinction can be made between rules relating to the execution of projects in developing and economy-in-transition states (OP/BP 4.01) and guidelines and codes of conduct that address the activities of states and non-state actors (FAO Code of Conduct and Guidelines on Waste Water Management). Similar guidelines and codes of conduct are also adopted through cooperative endeavours that are engaged in by international institutions. A relevant example in this respect is the aforementioned IOMC, whose Strategic Approach to International Chemicals Management (SAICM) provides, among other things, rules and standards for the harmonization of classification and labelling of chemicals.

What these instruments have in common is that they establish rules and standards that are meant to affect the behaviour of states and non-state actors, and may have significant consequences for such actors. It is in this respect that they give rise to normative development. World Bank OP/BP 4.01, for example, determines that proposed consultation with project-affected groups and local NGOs be registered in the project concept document—a requirement that is likely to affect the status of NGOs in environmental assessment procedures. More generally, OP/BP 4.01 is likely to co-determine, if not determine, the standards for conducting environmental impact assessments in developing and economy-in-transition states. The

---

[19] See, e.g., UNFCCC, Decision/CP 11 on Additional Guidance to an Operating Entity of the Financial Mechanism, which was adopted at COP-11(2005) of the UNFCCC; and Decision VII/20 on Further Guidance to the Financial Mechanism, which was adopted at COP-7(2004) of the CBD.

legal consequences of such decisions also may be illustrated with reference to a decision of the European Court of Justice (ECJ). In *Mondiet*, the ECJ found that an EC Council regulation prohibiting driftnets was valid, based on, among other things, a non-legally binding UNGA resolution banning the use of driftnets.[20] Rules and standards developed within the framework of the IOMC may have similar consequences. Also relevant in this context is the WTO Appellate Body (AB) ruling in *United States—Import Prohibitions of Certain Shrimp and Shrimp Products* in which the AB suggested that it might be more open to considering internationally agreed rules, as opposed to unilateral rules, as a basis for instituting an import ban, without specifying whether such decisions would have to be legally binding or not.[21]

The instruments referred to also share another trait, which is that they are not based on formal state consent, even if states participate in their negotiation and adoption—the latter often by consensus. Formal state consent, however, is not absent from the framework of global environmental governance. It can be traced to the MEAs and their protocols to which states formally consented as well as to the constitutive treaties establishing relevant international institutions. For UNEP, this is the UN Charter, which endowed the UNGA with the competence to establish subsidiary organs. For the GEF, the relevant treaty is the Articles of Agreement of the IBRD, which gave the World Bank the competence to establish new institutions—a competence that was not attributed to UNEP or UNDP,[22] which are the other two institutions that *de facto* established the GEF. Formal state consent in these situations can be conceptualized as states consenting to a process of normative development, the outcome of which is unknown when consent is given. It is in this context that issues of legitimacy arise (see Chapter 30 'Legitimacy') and that decision-making processes and procedures deserve attention. While it might be argued that states formally consented to those processes and procedures when they became parties to the treaties in question and that, therefore, no problems ensue, I suggest that problems of legitimacy do arise, and that they are related to the assumption prevalent in public law that public powers are delegated powers that are to be subject to limitations and to the requirement of accountability.[23] Three considerations inform this assertion. First, the approach adopted in environmental decision-making introduces a large degree of informality in decision-making, while formality in law tends to protect the weaker party. Second, in many situations, such as for UNEP and the GEF, formal state consent is very far removed in time from the moment when the rules and standards materialize. Third, in practice the mandates of some of the institutions involved in

---

[20] Case C-405/92, *Mondiet* [1993] E.C.R. I-6133. The relevant UN General Assembly Resolution is UNGA Resolution 44/225 on Large-scale Pelagic Driftnet Fishing and Its Impact on the Living Marine Resources of the World's Oceans and Seas (22 December 1989).

[21] *United States—Import Prohibitions of Certain Shrimp and Shrimp Products*, WTO Doc. WT/DS58/AB/R (98–000) (12 October 1998).

[22] See Article 5, sec. 2(b)(v), of the Articles of Agreements of the IBRD, and paragraph 5 of UNGA Resolution 29/3351 (18 December 1974).   [23] See text at note 4 above.

global environmental governance have changed significantly over time. An example of the latter is the World Bank, which when it was established was not envisaged as a major player in global environmental governance.

Is the answer, then, to return to the formal exigencies of the traditional notion of state consent? Given the governance issues at stake, I suggest that this approach would be impractical, if not impossible. I also suggest that answers will not be found in dwelling on whether, due to a lack of formal state consent, certain rules and standards of international environmental law are binding or not so binding. Such queries tend to overlook the extent to which non-legally binding rules and standards may affect the MEA-based commitments and entitlements of states as well as the interests of private actors. Instead, based on the role that relevant rules and standards play, we should ask ourselves how their legitimacy can be secured. This question, I suggest, requires a focus on the decision-making processes and procedures employed and the introduction of a degree of formalism in these procedures. It is only through the introduction of a degree of formalism in these processes and procedures that their transparency and openness to meaningful participation by all states concerned, including balanced representation of Southern and Northern states, can be attained and that the attribution and delegation of norm-making powers to international institutions can be regulated. In the case of the GEF, the latter—the *locus* of decision-making competence (MEAs or the GEF)—seems to be a continuous bone of contention between the various MEAs and the GEF. Evidence of this situation is provided by the repeated admonitions contained in COP and other MEA-based documents that the GEF adopt more transparent, country-driven, and participatory approaches in its working methods and provide greater feed-back to relevant COPs on its work.[24]

A further point that the earlier analysis raises is that the distinction between rules that are external and those that are internal to the institution, which is often made in the literature on the law of international institutions,[25] has become blurred in the framework of global environmental governance. The blurring of this distinction is apparent from, in particular, the guidelines that MEAs adopt to guide the work of the GEF. While these guidelines apply generally to projects that are to be implemented in developing and economy-in-transition states, they are addressed to the GEF. Such guidelines, although usually of a more general nature, are similar to the rules that the GEF itself adopts and to those adopted by the World Bank in that they all have the function of setting the standards that the GEF is to apply in determining the eligibility of projects for

---

[24] See, e.g., UN Doc. UNFCCC/SBSTA/2004.INF.9 (15 June 2004), which contains the report of the fifth meeting of the Joint Liaison Group. The Joint Liaison Group facilitates synergy between the UNFCCC, the CBD, and the Desertification Convention and is attended by members of the secretariats and the chairpersons of the scientific subsidiary bodies of the three MEAs. See also CBD Decision VII/20, note 19 above.

[25] See H.G. Schermers and N.M. Blokker, *International Institutional Law*, 4th revised edition (Leiden: Martinus Nijhoff, 2003) at paragraphs 1196 and following.

funding. In other words, these rules and standards are intended to guide the operational policies of the institution in question. Such rules and standards, however, may also foster normative development, for example, in determining the applicable rules and standards on environmental impact assessment (World Bank OP/BP 4.01).

4 INTERNATIONAL INSTITUTIONS AND DECISION-MAKING

International institutions also play a role in global environmental governance as decision-makers in individual situations. Such decisions most prominently are taken in the selection of projects that serve to implement MEAs in developing and economy-in-transition states, and within compliance-related procedures. The selection of MEA-related projects in developing and economy-in-transition states typically takes place within funds linked to MEAs. In these situations, the bodies in question interpret and apply the rules and standards discussed in the previous section. Compliance procedures have been established within most MEAs, and in these procedures the substantive rules and standards adopted with the framework of an MEA and related protocols are interpreted and applied to individual states.

In traditional international legal doctrine, the assumption again is that international institutions have the competence to adopt decisions in individual situations with binding legal effect for a state, only if that state has formally consented thereto. Not many international institutions have been endowed with this competence. The EC again is the example *par excellence* (see Chapter 37 'Regional Economic Integration Organizations'). In addition, the competence of the Security Council to take decisions in situations where it determines that there is a threat to the peace, breach of the peace, or act of aggression on the basis of Chapter VII of the UN Charter falls within this category.

In global environmental governance, however, decisions that are not of a binding legal character but that have potential consequences for states and non-state actors are routinely taken by financial mechanisms and by compliance committees. In the case of decisions on the eligibility of individual MEA-related projects that are financed by the GEF, the competence to take such decision is found in MEAs (where they refer to the establishment of a financial mechanism), the agreements concluded between the COPs of MEAs and the GEF,[26] and the instruments establishing the

---

[26] See, e.g., the Memorandum of Understanding between the Conference of the Parties to the Convention on Biological Diversity and the Council of the Global Environment Facility, annexed to Decision III/8 (1996) of the COP to the CBD.

GEF.[27] For those funds administered directly by the World Bank or decisions on projects taken by the bank, this competence is found in the internal rules adopted by the bank.[28] In the case of compliance procedures, the competence to take decisions in individual situations finds its basis in MEAs, and the subsequent decisions of COPs or MOPs by which they establish compliance commissions. With the exception of decisions taken by the enforcement branch of the Kyoto Protocol compliance regime, the ensuing decisions, in the case both of compliance regimes and of individual projects, are non-legally binding. Both types of decision-making will be reviewed later in this chapter. A comprehensive overview of the different financial mechanisms or compliance procedures will not be undertaken in this chapter, as these are presented elsewhere in the *Handbook* (see Chapter 41 'Technical and Financial Assistance' and Chapter 43 'Compliance Procedures').

4.1 Decision-Making in the Selection of Projects

Decision-making in global environmental governance as related to the selection of projects is intimately related to the concept of sustainable development (see Chapter 26 'Sustainable Development') as translated into the principle of common but differentiated responsibilities. This principle is the basis for, among other commitments, the commitment of developed states to transfer financial and technological assistance to developing states, which to a large extent is implemented by way of funds, many of which are administrated by the World Bank. As a result, the COPs of MEAs, the funds themselves, and the World Bank adopt rules and standards that guide the financial mechanisms in the selection and design of projects in developing and economy-in-transition states. These guidelines also may influence normative development, as discussed earlier with reference to World Bank Operational Policies and Bank Procedures, such as OP/BP 4.01 on environmental impact assessment. Moreover, such rules and standards impact not only states but also individuals and groups in society.

While exercising similar functions, the legal characteristics of the funding mechanisms vary considerably. The IFAD, for example, is a UN specialized agency, which was established in 1977 as an outcome of the 1974 World Food Conference.[29] IFAD

---

[27] Originally, the GEF was established by World Bank Resolution 91–5. The GEF was reformed in 1994 on the basis of the IBRD, Executive Directors' Resolution no. 94–2, 24 May 1994; IBRD Resolution 487, 7 July 1994; UNEP, Governing Council, Resolution SS.IV.1, 18 June 1994; and a decision of UNDP's Executive Board (excerpt from the report of the UNDP Executive Board Meeting, Doc. DP/1994/9, 13 May 1994) *juncto* Instrument for the Establishment of the Restructured Global Environment Facility.

[28] For the Prototype Carbon Fund, this is IBRD Resolution no. 99–0, as amended by IBRD Resolutions no. 2000–1 and 2003–3.

[29] Agreement Establishing the International Fund for Agricultural Development (13 June 1976).

cooperates with other international institutions on the interface between poverty, food security, and environmental concerns related thereto, such as desertification and land degradation. The Multilateral Fund for the Implementation of the Montreal Protocol (Montreal Protocol Fund), on the other hand, operates under the terms of reference set out by the parties to the Montreal Protocol.[30] The World Bank, UNDP, UNIDO, and UNEP act as implementing agencies for the Montreal Protocol Fund, while UNEP also acts as the fund's treasurer. In addition, the World Bank administers several funds, including the GEF and the PCF. The GEF serves as the funding mechanism for a number of MEAs, including the UN Framework Convention on Climate Change, the CBD, and the Convention to Combat Desertification in Those Countries Experiencing Serious Drought and/or Desertification, Particularly in Africa, and operates under the guidance of the COPs or MOPs of the MEAs.[31] The PCF, when established in 1999, was unique in that it includes among its investors both states and other public entities as well as private actors.[32] More recently, other similar funds such as the Community Development Carbon Fund and the Bio-Carbon Fund have been established within the bank. Moreover, the World Bank administers donor country specific funds, such as the Netherlands Clean Development Facility and the Italian Carbon Fund.

Funding mechanisms typically adopt portfolio and project criteria to guide them in their work. These criteria serve to determine what type of projects and which particular projects are eligible for funding from the institutions concerned. In the case of the Montreal Protocol Fund, such criteria are developed in close cooperation between the MOP of the Montreal Protocol and the Executive Committee of the fund, which ultimately decides on such criteria by consensus and, if consensus is not available, by a double three-fourths majority vote among the five members representing donors and the five members representing recipients. In the case of the GEF, the council decides on such criteria by consensus and, if consensus is not available, by a double majority vote consisting of 60 per cent of the members present and 60 per cent of the votes representing donors. The GEF Council consists of 32 members, with 14 representing donor states, 16 representing developing states, and two representing economy-in-transition states. Individual projects require the approval of the GEF senior executive officer, and a minimum of four council members may request that a project be subjected to review by the council. While the GEF ultimately operates under the guidance of the relevant COPs or MOPs, the relationship has continued to be somewhat problematic as evidenced by the report of the fifth meeting of the Joint Liaison Group and the regularly adopted COP decisions regarding the financial mechanism.[33] Common themes in these documents are the need to enhance transparency, to focus more on country-driven initiatives, and to enhance capacity

---

[30] For the terms of reference of the multilateral fund, see the *Handbook for the International Treaties for the Protection of the Ozone Layer*, note 10 above at 298.

[31] See text at notes 26 and 27 above.   [32] See note 28 above.   [33] See note 24 above.

building. In addition, these documents refer to the need to reconsider the incremental costs approach in view of, in particular, climate change adaptation projects, especially in regard to the additional climate change funds, such as the Least Developed Country Fund, that are administered by the GEF but that are not part of the GEF Fund.[34]

Within the PCF, the Participants Meeting is the main organ and decides on portfolio and project criteria. It is composed of the public and private entities that have invested in the fund and whose voting rights depend on the size of their investment in the fund. The Participants Meeting, while taking most decisions on the basis of a simple majority, adopts portfolio and project criteria developed by the World Bank, which is the trustee of the PCF, on the basis of a two-thirds majority vote. In developing such criteria, the Host Country Committee, consisting of recipients of PCF funding, advises the trustee. The trustee selects the individual projects to be financed by the PCF with the advice of the Host Country Committee and the Participants Committee. The latter consists of seven members with alternatively three or four members representing respectively private or public donors to the fund. In the Participants Committee, each member has one vote and most of its decisions are taken by a simple majority of the members present and voting. Project concept notes, which are prepared by the Fund Management Unit, that propose projects for inclusion in the fund's portfolio, however, can be objected to by the Participant Committee if at least two of its members object to inclusion of the project in the portfolio within 30 days of the presentation of the note by the trustee.

What is noteworthy regarding these funding mechanisms is, first, that they do not operate under the one-state–one-vote system that applies in the MEAs that they seek to implement and that provide their *raison d'être*. Reasons of efficiency seem to dictate this choice, in the sense that it is impractical for one hundred plus states to decide on individual projects. Second, within the GEF and even more so within the PCF, the equal positions of donors and recipients in decision-making has been abandoned, with an international institution—that is, the World Bank and the fund secretariats administered by the Bank—performing crucial decision-making functions. Developed states, as it were, seem to have outsourced the implementation of their MEA-based commitment to transfer funds to developing states to the World Bank and funds administered by the bank, and, in the course of doing so, the balanced representation of developing and developed states prevalent in MEAs has been abandoned to a lesser or greater extent. This is all the more relevant given that, in the World Bank itself, developed states hold a majority of the votes, due to the weighted voting system applied in the bank. The fact that developing and economy-in-transition states approve the project documents once the project has been selected for implementation in their country adds formal state consent, but does not necessarily legitimize the projects in question. After all, such states have a limited role in determining the rules of the game—the portfolio and project criteria—at least with

---

[34] See report of the Joint Liaison Group, note 24 above.

respect to those funds administered by the World Bank. The recipients of funding thus seem to be in a position where they may choose to play the game according to the rules set predominantly by others or not at all, with the latter not being a realistic option, given their dependent position.

Decisions on the eligibility of projects may have significant effects for states and other actors, with formal state consent playing only a marginal role in the process. In this situation, lawyers typically raise the question whether the relevant decisions are legally binding. And, if they are not, as is true of most of the decisions taken by international institutions that operate in the framework of global environmental governance, then the situation is regarded as not being legally relevant and, thus, beyond legal discourse. I suggest that this approach is incomplete because it does not take into account the role that such decisions play, and places the discourse regarding their legitimacy in the realm of politics only. The public law analogy introduced in this chapter suggests that this approach is incomplete, if not incorrect.

In the case of decision-making in individual situations, as in normative development, formal state consent is too far removed in time from the moment when a decision on the eligibility of a project is taken to afford that decision legitimacy (see Chapter 30 'Legitimacy'). Alternatively, where a developing state or economy-in-transition state formally consents to a project, the context in which the decision is made takes away from the legitimizing role that formal state consent plays in traditional international law. Thus, we might again pose the question whether a return to the formal doctrine of state consent is the answer. Again, I suggest that this approach would be impractical, if not impossible. Instead, as in the case of normative development, I suggest that the formalization of the decision-making processes and procedures is required if decisions are to be regarded as legitimate. Such processes and procedures, in the case of decisions taken in individual situations, should be open to participation, transparent, and result in reasoned decisions. Especially where individual projects are concerned, the participation not only of states but also of individuals and groups in the society concerned would seem to be important, given the implications that such projects may have for them—for example, where the displacement of population is concerned. Moreover, under certain circumstances, those individuals and groups should have the possibility to appeal decisions taken if they suffer detrimental effects or their interests have not been accounted for. The World Bank Inspection Panel offers such a procedure.[35] Its jurisdiction, however, extends

---

[35] The World Bank Inspection Panel's decision in *China/Western Poverty Reduction Project Investigation Report*, Request Number RQ99/3 (4 April 2004) at paragraphs 34–45 and 180–6, in particular, is illustrative with respect to, among other policies, OP/BP 4.01. In this decision, the panel interpreted OP/BP 4.01 and found that the World Bank had classified incorrectly the project as a category B, instead of a category A, project. As a result, the environmental impact assessment conducted was found to be too narrow—category A projects require a more intensive environmental impact assessment than category B projects.

only to projects executed by the IBRD and the International Development Agency, and does not extend to all projects financed through the GEF or other funds managed by the World Bank.

4.2 Decision-Making in Compliance Procedures

Treating compliance procedures in a section that deals with decision-making in individual situations implies a departure from the approach generally found in academic writing, in which compliance procedures have been regarded mostly as alternatives to dispute settlement procedures. This analysis has merit, given that these procedures arise because of a possible breach of one or more international rules or standards that are part of an MEA-based regime. However, the manner in which these procedures have unfolded might also merit another characterization—the introduction of decision-making in individual situations with the object of introducing feedback loops that will facilitate the overall implementation of the MEA in question and thus further what is in the common interest.[36]

Compliance committees generally adopt non-legally binding decisions, which are subject to endorsement by a non-legally binding COP decision. The Kyoto Protocol compliance regime, as adopted by the COP/MOP, is an exception to this general practice. In this case, the so-called enforcement branch is competent to adopt what are generally considered to be legally binding decisions, even if the regime itself was adopted on the basis of a non-legally binding COP/MOP decision.[37] Whether legally binding or not, findings of non-compliance have normative effect for individual states. A state's privileges under the MEA in question may be suspended and, in some cases, even a state's MEA-based entitlements may be effected.[38] Moreover, the state in

---

[36] The compliance regime under the Convention on Access to Information, Public Participation in Decision-making and Access to Justice in Environmental Matters (Aarhus Convention), however, is an exception to this development, to the extent that it entitles natural and legal persons to submit complaints of non-compliance (see Decision I/7, Doc. ECE/MP.PP/2/Add. 8 (1 April 2004) (see Chapter 29 'Public Participation')). In this case, the natural or legal persons' individual rights are the primary object of concern, even if upholding these may be in the common interest. This aspect of the Aarhus Convention compliance procedure makes it comparable to the individual complaint procedures available under international human rights treaties, such as Protocol I to the International Covenant on Civil and Political Rights.

[37] See Annex to Decision 27/CMP.1 on Procedures and Mechanisms relating to Compliance under the Kyoto Protocol, which was adopted at COP/MOP 1(2005) of the Kyoto Protocol (Annex to Decision 27/CMP.1). In view of the nature of the decisions of the enforcement branch and Article 18 of the Kyoto Protocol, requiring amendment of the protocol if binding consequences ensue from the non-compliance procedure, the COP/MOP decided to consider further the question of whether the protocol should be amended (see paragraph 2 of Decision 27/COMP.1).

[38] See the indicative list of measures that might be taken by the MOP to the Montreal Protocol attached to the non-compliance procedure of the Montreal Protocol (*Handbook for the International*

question will be required to increase its overall efforts and investments, with or without the assistance of a financial mechanism, in order to attain implementation of the MEA. Findings of non-compliance thus have consequences for the state involved. Moreover, such findings can have consequences for non-state actors.

Under the non-compliance procedure of the Montreal Protocol, the implementation committee, for example, in addition to assistance, may recommend that a state that is found to be in non-compliance restrict its exports[39] or request that other state parties cease exports to the state in question, so as to help the latter return to compliance.[40] While such recommendations and requests are rare—the implementation committee and the ensuing MOP decision usually limit themselves to cautioning states and foreshadowing other measures, if the state does not meet the applicable rules and standards in the future—if adopted, they affect not only the state in question but also traders in both the state in question and other states.

A further illustration of how findings of non-compliance may affect both states and non-state actors is provided by the manner in which similar findings, adopted within Convention on International Trade in Endangered Species of Wild Fauna and Flora (CITES), have resounded in EC case law. The CITES Standing Committee, a body of limited representation, may adopt a notification containing a recommendation to suspend trade with a certain member state that is not in compliance with CITES. Such decisions are based on, among other things, reports submitted by the CITES secretariat, administered by UNEP, and have been taken because a member state is found not to be properly implementing CITES within its territory[41] or because a member state has failed to meet its reporting requirements under the convention.[42] While not legally binding, these notifications may affect the rights of relevant states under CITES as well as the opportunities for traders in both the state concerned and other states. These consequences may ensue because other parties to CITES, based on such recommendations, may take measures prohibiting fauna and flora originating in the notified state from entering their territory. Significantly, the ECJ in *Commission v. France* found that it was illegal to import certain species of wild cats from Bolivia into the European Union (EU) based on Community legislation in conjunction with a CITES notification.[43] The case in fact turned on the CITES notification. Decisions taken by other compliance committees may have a similar effect.

Treaties for the Protection of the Ozone Layer, see note 10 above at 297) as well as paragraphs XIV and XV of the Annex to Decision 27/CMP.1.

[39] MOP Decision VII/18 on compliance with the Montreal Protocol by the Russian Federation, in *Handbook for the International Treaties for the Protection of the Ozone Layer*, see note 10 above at 214.

[40] MOP Decision XVII/26 on Non-compliance with the Montreal Protocol by Azerbaijan, in Doc. UNEP/OzL.Conv.7/7 – UNEP/OzL.Pro.17/11 (25 January 2006) at 57.

[41] See, e.g., CITES Notification 2005/038, concerning Nigeria.

[42] See, e.g., CITES Notification 2004/023, concerning Algeria, Central African Republic, and Guinea-Bissau; withdrawn with respect to Algeria, Notification 2005/19.

[43] Case C182/89, *Commission v. France*, [1990] E.C.R. I-4337. The relevant notification was contained in a legally non-binding resolution adopted by the COP to CITES, Conference Resolution 5.2 (30 April

Decisions of the Kyoto compliance committee, for example, might result in the traders being barred from trading in emission units from states that have been found not to be in compliance with the protocol.

Formalization of compliance procedures again, I suggest, is a factor that will contribute to securing the legitimacy of ensuing decisions. Given the interests at stake in compliance procedures, such procedures should be transparent, result in reasoned decisions that are proportional, and be subject to scrutiny through, for example, an appeals procedure. Compliance procedures, however, have not attained this degree of formalization. Decisions are published but only in a summary fashion, and appeals procedures are not available. The Kyoto Protocol procedure again provides an exception. Both in the case of the facilitative and enforcement branch, reasoned decisions are expressly required,[44] and, in the case of the enforcement branch, an appeal procedure is provided for if the party in question 'believes it has been denied due process.'[45] The latter consists of an appeal to the COP/MOP, which, if it agrees by a three-fourths majority, may override a decision of the enforcement branch, in which case it is to refer the matter of the appeal back to the enforcement branch.[46] These important conditions, which are unique to the Kyoto Protocol compliance procedure, may well in the future serve to legitimize its decisions.

5 GLOBAL ENVIRONMENTAL GOVERNANCE: ADMINISTRATIVE LAW IN THE MAKING

Within the framework of global environmental governance, international institutions have taken on a variety of roles, some of which have been highlighted in this chapter. In particular, their roles in normative development and decision-making in individual situations have been discussed. In addition, the inter-linkages between the various institutions were pointed out. Most significantly, the chapter highlights that within global environmental governance formal state consent, which is pivotal to the traditional doctrine of international law, plays only a limited role. It serves at most to legitimize processes of normative development. This, in turn, implies that formal state consent no longer suffices to legitimize the rules and standards developed or the decisions taken in individual situations. Other sources of legitimacy are required, and this chapter suggests that one potential source of legitimacy is to be found in the formalization of the processes and procedures employed, both in normative development and in decision-making.

1985). This resolution was adopted before the institutional restructuring that was introduced in CITES in 2002, it was at that time that the Standing Committee was established.

[44] Paragraphs VII(7) and IX(9) of the Annex to Decision 27/CMP.1.
[45] Paragraph XI, Annex to Decision 27/CMP.1.   [46] *Ibid.*

This depiction of global environmental governance suggests that both normative development and decision-making that unfold in this context do not fit the patterns associated with the interstate pattern of international law. Instead, they provide an illustration of an emergent common interest pattern in international law and harbour traits of public and, in particular, administrative law (see Chapter 4 'Global Environmental Governance as Administration'). While such conceptualizations of law are particular to national law and lead to different connotations in different national legal systems, most legal systems have conceptualized the requirement that power exercised by public institutions is to be controlled by way of law.[47] Such conceptualizations in national legal systems find expression in notions such as government subject to law (*rechtstatelijkheid*), rules on the attribution and delegation of power, transparency, the right of interested parties to participate in decision-making, the requirements that decisions be proportional and reasoned, and review mechanisms through which interested parties may appeal decisions taken in individual situations. Such notions, however, cannot be transferred to the international level of governance without further thought for the simple reason that democracy has not materialized, and is highly unlikely to materialize, at the international level anywhere in the near future (see Chapter 30 'Legitimacy'). By implication, participation in normative development has to be conceived of in terms different from law-making processes through parliament. Decision-making by consensus, as in MEAs, might in this case be an alternative, provided that measures are taken to ensure the meaningful participation of less powerful states—in particular, developing states. Such meaningful participation, however, is equally relevant in bodies of limited composition engaged in decision-making in individual situations where the relevant rules and norms are interpreted and applied. It is important to note in this respect that developing states and economy-in-transition states, in particular, are the object of decision-making in these contexts. The overwhelming majority of individual non-compliance situations and all decisions on the allocation of projects concern these states.

Returning to the opening section of this chapter where reference was made to two inter-related governance issues—the common interest and the South-North context—I suggest the following. Addressing common interest problems as such necessitates a relaxation of the formal notion of state consent, and requires a focus on decision-making processes and procedures because we cannot hope to protect the global environment by means of a system of law that is akin to national contract law. The South-North context, however, even more strongly demands a focus on these processes and procedures and on legitimacy in this context. Legitimacy cannot be achieved if developed states and international institutions in which developed states have an overwhelming influence have an unbalanced say in decision-making. Not achieving legitimacy in the South-North context, furthermore, runs the risk of

---

[47] See T. Koopmans, *Courts and Political Institutions* (Cambridge: Cambridge University Press, 2003).

alienating developing states from the framework of global environmental governance, which would endanger the protection of the common interest. It is for these
reasons that the role of international institutions in normative development and,
in decision-making in individual situations, requires our scrutiny. The lens provided
by national public law and, in particular, administrative law, offers helpful tools in
this respect.

RECOMMENDED READING

J. Brunnée, 'COPing with Consent Law-Making under Multilateral Environmental Agreements' (2002) 15 Leiden J. Int'l L. 1.

D. Bodansky, 'The Legitimacy of International Governance: A Coming Challenge to International Environmental Law?' (1999) 39 A.J.I.L. 596.

B.S. Chimni, 'International Institutions Today: An Imperial Global State in the Making'
(2004) 15 Eur. J. Int'l L. 1.

J.M. Coicaud and V. Heiskanen, eds., *The Legitimacy of International Organizations* (Tokyo:
United Nations University Press, 2001).

E. Hey, 'Sustainable Development, Normative Development and the Legitimacy of Decision
Making' (2003) 24 Netherlands Y.B. Int'l L. 3.

B. Kingsbury, N. Kirsch, R.B. Stewart, and J.B. Wiener, eds., *The Emergence of Global
Administrative Law* (2005) 68 L. & Contemp. Probs. 1.

S. Marks, *The Riddle of All Constitutions: International Law, Democracy and the Critique of
Ideology* (Oxford: Oxford University Press, 2000).

K. Michelson, 'South, North, International Environmental Law and International
Environmental Lawyers' (2000) 11 Y.B. Int'l Envt'l L. 53.

D. Shelton, ed., *Commitment and Compliance: The Role of Non-Binding Norms in the International Legal System* (Oxford: Oxford University Press, 2000).

R. Wolfrum and V. Röben, eds., *Developments of International Law in Treaty-Making* (Berlin:
Springer, 2005).

CHAPTER 33

NON-GOVERNMENTAL ORGANIZATIONS AND CIVIL SOCIETY

PETER J. SPIRO

1 INTRODUCTION

NON-GOVERNMENTAL organizations (NGOs) have enjoyed a meteoric rise on the world stage over the past decade. The Cold War and the Westphalian system at its zenith marginalized NGOs insofar as they merited any form of attention through a state-centred lens. Globalization, by contrast, has centred them as key international actors, and the emergence of NGOs comprises a central feature of the new structure of international decision-making. In a mere 15 years, NGOs have moved from being an actor not widely recognized among academics, policymakers, or the public, to one understood as being consequential among both elite and popular audiences.

Beyond recognition, the accelerated rate at which NGOs have made their debut into world politics poses a first-order analytical challenge. To some extent, this challenge reflects the continuing institutional instability that characterizes decision-making in the wake of globalization—it is difficult to isolate the nature of NGO participation in a dynamic that remains otherwise fluid. Yet the difficulties in situating NGOs on the global landscape also result from the affront they pose to the old order. Among the features of emerging decision-making structures, NGO participation may be the least amenable to traditional models of world politics. For political leaders and scholars alike, their place and legitimacy as independent global actors remains contested.

International environmental law-making has presented a useful vehicle for the study of NGOs and civil society in this new global context. Along with human rights, international environmental law stands at the forefront of international law-making. A relatively new area of intensive international regulation, its institutional features are thus only now being mapped out, and can reflect the evolving role of NGOs in a way that more entrenched regimes cannot. International environmental law sheds light on the crystallizing NGO role insofar as it now accounts (again, along with counterparts in the human rights arena) for a significant band of the NGO spectrum.[1] Some of the most globally prominent NGO activity concerns international environmental law. The area should thus present a leading indicator on the place of NGOs in the future institutional structure of international law.

This chapter attempts to distil major theoretical approaches to NGO participation in international law both generally and with specific application to international environmental law. The chapter extracts three models from the major academic work on the question: liberal, stakeholder, and post-national (see Chapter 10 'International Relations Theory'). The liberal model continues to centre the state as the primary locus of decision-making authority, while allowing the indirect influence of NGOs

---

[1] See M. Keck and K. Sikkink, *Activists across Borders: Advocacy Networks in Traditional Politics* (Ithaca, NY: Cornell University Press, 1998) at 11 (documenting increase in proportion of international NGOs focused on environmental issues from 14 per cent in 1953 to 26 per cent in 1993).

on the shape of international decisions. Domestic, transnational, and institutionalist variants of the liberal model frame the relevant terrains of NGO activity differently, as bounded or not bounded by national borders, but always with states as the key target actors and ultimate repositories of power. Stakeholder and post-national models, by contrast, recognize independent NGO power inside public international institutions under the former approach and outside public institutions altogether under the latter.

All three models accurately describe a segment of NGO participation in international environmental law-making. Insofar as the Liberal model hews to a state-ordered worldview, it may lose traction as an explanatory framework for considering the place of NGOs. Liberal models are at least implicitly offered as universal theories of global political ordering, to serve as the exclusive tool for understanding international politics. But Liberal theory is ill-equipped to explain evolving new pathways of NGO participation. It is only as good as far as it goes—that is, in explaining how NGOs work through states to advance their agendas. Otherwise, it is an approach in denial. Stakeholder and post-national models fill the resulting gap by confronting, explaining, and justifying novel forms of NGO participation, at the same time that they accept the fact of state-channelled influence. As those forms of participation ramify and entrench, the scholarly challenge will migrate correspondingly as these new approaches are refined. The continued application of both the post-national and stakeholder models may be necessary, if they both reflect developments on the ground. It is possible, however, that the private ordering of post-national regimes will find its way back to public institutional settings, which would mark the ascendancy of the stakeholder analysis.

Some parameters for the discussion should be noted up front. First, this chapter considers NGOs as being representative of some element of civil society. The definition of NGO remains elusive. Standard categorizations limit NGOs to non-profit entities, as will this chapter, although the theoretical models described earlier can also be deployed to describe corporate participation at some level of generality (see Chapter 35 'Business'). Although it is not yet in popular usage, John Gerard Ruggie's 'civil society organizations' would perhaps better characterize the entities under discussion here.[2] This chapter will also bracket the role of non-representative NGOs, variously described as 'expert', 'advisory', or 'scientific', and the related phenomenon of epistemic communities (see Chapter 34 'Epistemic Communities'). Expert NGO participation cannot be explained in terms of governance values, insofar as expert NGOs do not purport to serve as political agents.[3] In practice, of course,

[2] See J.G. Ruggie, 'Reconstituting the Global Public Domain—Issues, Actors, and Practices' (2004) 10 Eur. J. Int'l Rel. 499 at 501.

[3] As T. Princen and M. Finger observe, scientific NGOs by themselves cannot 'promote regime change', because only activist NGOs can 'politicize the biophysical.' See T. Princen and M. Finger, *Environmental NGOs in World Politics* (London: Routledge, 1994) at 221. Keck and Sikkink distinguish NGOs from epistemic communities insofar as the latter seek to persuade rather than to politicize. Keck and Sikkink, see note 1 above at 161.

many representative NGOs engage as experts (and some expert NGOs represent constituencies, if only of experts). But the theories of participation will differ. The NGOs addressed in this chapter have sometimes been described as 'activist' NGOs, although that label should properly equate activism with political activity of any description, without the implication of aggressivity.

This chapter will also not attempt a proof of NGO impact on international environmental law. Although difficult to establish empirically, there appears to be some agreement that NGOs have been influential in the making, evolution, and implementation of various international environmental regimes. Even those who oppose NGO participation at least implicitly acknowledge their impact. By assuming the fact of NGO influence, the chapter focuses on channels of causality and justification. In the process, it ignores the Realist model of international relations theory, which would deny the consequentiality of NGOs and of international law more generally. As this denial increasingly conflicts with developments on the ground, realism adds nothing to the analytical toolbox.

Finally, the chapter means in no way necessarily to valorize NGOs or their agendas or to accept descriptions of NGOs along the lines of the 'conscience of the world' or 'guardians of the environment.' NGOs are no more angelic than are the individuals of which they are composed. As with other political and corporate (in the sense of collective) entities, institutional incentives may lead to conduct that is not necessarily in the general public interest. Accountability concerns are appropriately levelled at any group of entities wielding power, although accountability-based arguments against NGO participation in world politics have been exaggerated. As with other representative entities, the legitimacy of NGO participation in international law-making can be framed in process and democratic terms (see Chapter 30 'Legitimacy'). The North/South divide among states is also projected onto the universe of NGOs—disparate interests and disproportionate influence along a North/South axis may raise additional legitimacy concerns. However, just as states themselves continue to be imperfectly accountable (and, in some cases, may be grossly so), NGOs cannot be dismissed along political, analytical, or normative valences, insofar as they represent discrete constituencies, simply because they are subject to distinctive accountability mechanisms. Although these mechanisms themselves may be fair game for further study and refinement, they do not take NGOs off the table.

2 ESTABLISHING APPROPRIATE VARIABLES

Much of the growing literature on NGOs in international environmental decision-making disaggregates NGO participation in terms of their roles and functions at various junctures in the decision-making process. This approach is linear, considering the sequence of decision-making phases and how NGOs are participating in each. While this approach facilitates a descriptive account of NGO participation, it may fail to address foundational questions. A more useful typology can be constructed from agency relationships and causal chains. Mapping out the features of NGO activity across the decision-making cycle isolates the ways in which NGO participation is (or is not) novel in the realm of world politics.

The linear analysis typically breaks down the decision-making sequence into three or more phases in the establishment of environmental regimes—in effect, amounting to a before, during, and after. The 'before' consists of agenda setting and events that bring a particular issue into the policymaking orbit; the 'during' includes the negotiations themselves; and the 'after' comprises implementation and enforcement. As David Tolbert notes, NGO 'roles generally correspond chronologically to the international community's response to an issue of environmental protection.'[4] Kal Raustiala disaggregates NGO participation in the negotiations phase to include the monitoring of national delegations for domestic publics, reporting on negotiations, and facilitating domestic political compromises both during negotiations and for the purposes of domestic ratification. Margaret Keck and Kathryn Sikkink evaluate the success of non-state networks by isolating 'stages' in issue politics to include 'defining an issue area, convinc[ing] policymakers and publics that the problems thus defined are soluble, prescrib[ing] solutions, and monitor[ing] their implementation.'[5] A number of case studies of NGO participation in international environmental decision-making implicitly take the same sort of approach by organizing analysis on a chronological basis, considering NGO inputs along the road to establishing an international environmental law regime.

This approach has utility in establishing the fact of NGO influence. Decisions (especially in the context of treaty development) are undertaken on a linear basis. Even if actor influence is difficult to measure precisely, describing the totality of NGO participation in the context of any particular process is likely at least to demonstrate the proposition that NGOs are consequential to the process. The effect is both to demonstrate cumulative influence (established by the possibility of influence at any number of decision-making points) as well as to highlight particular junctures at which such influence is probable (the monitoring of agreements as an example, with respect to which NGOs develop data that would otherwise go undelivered). To the extent that this has been the basis point for assessing the place of NGOs in international decision-making—do they make a difference?—it may explain the tendency to highlight decision-making phases as a controlling variable.

---

[4] D. Tolbert, 'Global Climate Change and the Role of International Non-Governmental Organizations,' in R. Churchill and D. Freestone, eds., *International Law and Global Climate Change* (London: Graham and Trotman, 1991) 95 at 98.   [5] Keck and Sikkink, see note 1 above at 201.

The approach fails to isolate essential and causal qualities of NGO participation, however. One could after all undertake a similar analysis of state influence without necessarily shedding any more light on the nature of state power, other than that it exists. Accounts that break out decision-making phases are prone to describe different mechanisms of influence under cover of different kinds of decisions. Unless common elements are extracted, this may result in something less than a full understanding of NGO participation—this kind of influence for that component of the process, another kind for another component. Such analysis fails to isolate the sources of NGO power and the essential qualities of NGO participation.

Some analyses, including representative work in the models described later in this chapter, are less vulnerable to this critique insofar as they maintain relational variables. Post-national approaches, for instance, look beyond state decision-making to focus on interactions between NGOs and other non-state actors. Liberal theory, by contrast, situates NGO activity as it bears on state decision-making. But the virtue of these models is also their limitation. By situating NGO activity relative to another set of actors, these analyses miss the rest of the spectrum. Restrictive relational premises often go unexamined. It is simply assumed that situating NGOs relative to other types of actors will best illuminate their new place. By surveying the full range of relational possibilities, this chapter assesses the strengths of the three dominant models.

3 NGOs in Liberal Theory: Acting through the State

Liberal theory continues to represent a central tradition in much of the international relations literature, and it continues to centre the state as the primary actor in world politics. One can isolate three distinctive strands of the Liberal model as it confronts the role of NGOs in international environmental law-making: domestic/two-level, transnational/Constructivist, and supranational/Institutionalist. Each situates NGO activity relative to state behaviour.

3.1 Domestic/Two-Level Approaches

State-bounded Liberal approaches to NGO participation work from Robert Putnam's model of world politics as a two-level game, with domestic political preferences as a variable in interstate relations.[6] This account extends the politics of 'public interest'

---

6 R. Putnam, 'Diplomacy and Domestic Politics: The Logic of Two Level Games' (1988) 42 Int'l Org. 427.

or 'pressure' groups to matters of international concern. Domestic NGOs mobilize on global issues in the same way that they mobilize on domestic ones, deploying the same political assets to the end of influencing a state's external policies. To the extent that NGOs are able to marshal domestic political power to promote international ends, they are able to indirectly affect matters of world politics.

This dynamic clearly—and now uncontroversially—explains part of NGO influence on international environmental law-making. Insofar as states remain dominant in the establishment of formal international regimes, it strategically behoves NGOs to work domestic political channels where, through votes and other forms of political leverage and bureaucratic influence, they may influence state policy, which, in turn, may influence international outcomes.

For some commentators, this remains the primary channel of NGO influence. As Abram Chayes and Antonio Handler Chayes conclude, NGOs 'exert their major influence through the domestic political process.'[7] In considering the role of NGOs in climate change agenda-setting, Peter Newell focuses almost exclusively on the impact of NGOs within the boundaries of domestic politics, highlighting their ability (or inability) to enlist domestic media and public opinion behind the climate change agenda and isolating domestic relationships with governmental decision-makers as a key variable to success, both in a pressure group model.[8] The state-bounded approach may also explain the increasingly common practice of including NGO representatives on state delegations to international conferences, an innovation of the earlier twentieth century that entered the mainstream with the Rio process. Although the opportunity for influencing state positions is then magnified by proximity in negotiating rooms, NGO influence in this context remains indirect and, in principle, subject to state control. In all cases, NGOs work within the boxes of their respective states by way of influencing state behaviour at the international level.

Although this traditional Liberal lens on the role of NGOs clearly accounts for a substantial channel of NGO influence in international environmental decision-making, state-bounded approaches fail to explain the full reality of NGO participation in international environmental law-making. The premise that NGOs restrict themselves to influencing 'home' states is no longer sustainable. Many NGOs are now multinational in composition and identity, so that only in a nominal sense can they be identified as having a 'home state' in the first place. Even where environmental NGOs have such a national identity, they increasingly operate across national borders to work in other domestic and intergovernmental spaces to influence international policies.

---

[7] A. Chayes and A. Handler Chayes, *The New Sovereignty: Compliance with International Regulatory Agreements* (Cambridge, MA: Harvard University Press, 1995) at 252.

[8] P. Newell, *Climate for Change: Non-State Actors and the Global Politics of the Greenhouse* (Cambridge: Cambridge University Press, 2000) at 128–36.

3.2 Transnational Approaches

The transnational approach to NGOs abandons the premise of boundary-restricted activity. Transnationalism highlights how national or subnational NGOs work to advance their national, even local, agendas by enlisting foreign and international agents. Key to much of this inquiry into NGO activity—comprising an important strain of Constructivist international relations theory—is the development of transnational advocacy networks comprised primarily of NGOs. Advocates facing 'blockages' in their domestic political contexts develop transnational networks that then apply leverage on other states and international institutions, which will in turn pressure the home state in which the blockage is suffered. This 'boomerang effect' supplies a model for transnational advocacy efforts. The basic innovation is to recognize transnational NGO activism both below and beyond the state.

Although transnational approaches first gained considerable traction with respect to the study of international human rights developments, they have also been deployed to assess the participation of NGOs in international environmental protection efforts. Keck and Sikkink hold out Brazilian rain forest deforestation as a case study. Unable to influence policymaking in Brazil, local activists turned to US and European NGOs, who in turn pressured the multilateral banks (both directly and through their own governments), who in turn pressured Brazil to attend to deforestation. In the mid-1980s, prominent US NGOs, including the Environmental Defense Fund and Natural Resources Defense Fund, worked with Brazilians to enact US legislation calling on the World Bank to pay closer heed to environmental aspects of its financing activities. The bank, in turn, forced subnational authorities to accept the institutional participation of local NGOs in forest-related policymaking. When this deal soured, Brazilian NGOs, together with the Friends of the Earth and Oxfam, filed a complaint with the World Bank Inspection Panel, established in 1993 as a channel for direct NGO input into bank oversight. Although this complaint was ultimately rejected, the episode forced the World Bank to recognize the environmental implications of its projects. The case study presents an example of activists ' "shop[ping]" the entire global scene for the best venues to present their issues [to] seek points of leverage at which to apply pressure.'[9]

So framed, the transnational model accurately describes the relatively new phenomenon of transnational organizing to advance domestic ends. Yet therein lies its limitation. Much transnational scholarship remains focused on the state as the ultimate target of activism. In this sense, it is ill-equipped to explain the emergence of an NGO role in such global regimes as climate change that relate to transnational environmental phenomena. Where activists enlist foreign NGOs to pressure foreign states to pressure the target state, the model remains two level, with the added interplay of

---

[9] Keck and Sikkink, see note 1 above at 200.

cross-border pressure group activity.[10] Where activists work through international institutions, an additional level is added, but under the transnational approach it is categorically indistinguishable, simply another pressure point. This may explain why transnational approaches tend to be Constructivist, emphasizing the consequentiality of ideas. Acting as transnational norm entrepreneurs, the argument runs, advocacy networks act to transform an issue discourse, as a result of which states, by way of their identity as such, adjust their behaviour to conform with the new norm. Without this premise, it would be necessary to unpack the features of NGO-target relationships that might affect NGO leverage (and to consider why an NGO based in one country would have any leverage with decision-makers in other countries or in international institutions in the first place). Elevating the place of ideas allows transnationalists to under-specify what else might stand behind the impact of NGO activity through networks in foreign states and international institutions, and how domestic and international contexts might present different explanatory and normative variables. Transnationalist scholarship, like Constructivism more generally, appears incapable of predicting when an idea will gain purchase and why it will gain purchase before some actors and not others. Insofar as it is grounded in established political theory, it self-consciously transfers models of domestic political pluralism to the international level.

3.3 Supranational/Institutionalist

Where much transnationalist literature ultimately plays to the local, Institutionalism focuses on the global. This third variant on the Liberal theme seeks to explain the function of NGOs in international institutions. As with transnationalism, however, it remains state-centric in the sense that it seeks to situate NGOs relative to states. As Institutionalist theory more broadly explains international regimes as serving state interests, so too does it find NGO participation in those regimes to serve state interests. Far from depleting state power, the argument runs, NGO participation actually strengthens the regulatory powers of states and the state system.

[10] M. Finnemore and K. Sikkink themselves make the connection, suggesting a 'two-level norm game.' See M. Finnemore and K. Sikkink, 'International Norm Dynamics and Political Change' (1998) 52 Int'l Org. 887 at 893. Much Constructivist international relations theory, in other words, works from the premise of segmented domestic and international political spaces. This tendency is not necessary to Constructivist theory, and there are important Constructivist scholars, such as John Gerard Ruggie, who have turned their sights on non-state power structures. Perhaps the fact that Constructivism is largely reactive to previous, state-centric international relations work explains the continued focus on state actors in Constructivist scholarship. As leading Constructivist scholar Alexander Wendt notes, on the one hand, Constructivism is 'substantively open-ended and applicable to any social form.' On the other, in the context of world politics, 'it may be that non-state actors are becoming more important as initiators of change, but system change ultimately happens *through* states.' See A. Wendt, *Social Theory of International Politics* (Cambridge: Cambridge University Press, 1999) at 9 and 193.

Raustiala, for example, describes various functions served by NGOs that facilitate the effectiveness of international environmental institutions and the place of states within them. Given that NGOs are politically powerful and sometimes possess superior information, states have various incentives to integrate NGOs into the structure of international decision-making. On the information side, the resulting benefits of NGO participation include supplying 'off budget' policy research and development to states; providing states with information about the compliance of other parties with multilateral regimes; policing national delegations in the context of international negotiations, tipping off home governments as necessary to the possibilities of bureaucratic misbehaviour; and undertaking onsite reporting for delegates of often-complex negotiations as they unfold (as undertaken in many multilateral environmental agreement settings by the *Earth Negotiations Bulletin*). On the political side, because NGOs are powerful domestic political players, their inclusion on negotiating delegations can smooth domestic acceptance of international regimes and enhance the probability of co-opting political actors that might otherwise oppose government preferences, both during negotiations and in the post-negotiations context of domestic ratification efforts. They also undertake capacity-building programmes in national settings to advance treaty compliance. In the end, however, states retain control of the decision-making process.

If Constructivism pits NGOs against states, as Anne Marie Slaughter sums up, then the Institutionalist approach puts NGOs in their service.[11] Where transnationalism seeks to explain how transnational NGO activity impacts policymaking at the national level, Institutionalism considers the NGO role in cementing intergovernmental regimes. But in both cases, the state remains the relational constant. As Raustiala asserts, 'in order to work, international environmental cooperation must rely on the legitimate coercion over private actors which only states, and their organizations, wield.'[12]

The supranational/Institutionalist model accounts for some portion of NGO participation in international environmental law-making. Such participation facilitates the establishment and implementation of international environmental regimes. But the model falls short on several fronts. It does not appear to recognize NGO interests or identities distinct from those of states (as with the core traditional Liberal model, it presumes that NGOs are subject to being characterized as 'domestic').[13] If NGO functions serve state interests, why do states not undertake such functions on their own? Inside international institutions, the model implicitly denies NGO influence, except (perhaps) through participation on state delegations, and has difficulty accounting for mechanisms of independent NGO participation (other than to

---

[11] A.M. Slaughter, 'International Law and International Relations' (2000) 285 Recueil des cours 11 at 101.

[12] K. Raustiala, 'States, NGOs, and International Environmental Institutions' (1997) 41 Int'l Stud. Q. 719 at 736.

[13] See *ibid.* at 724 ('states are inextricably linked to the societies within which NGOs flourish').

emphasize that such participation is at the mercy of states). Outside such institutions, the model denies that power can be exercised without state participation. This leaves a swath of activity comprising consumer action, codes of conduct, labelling campaigns, and private standard-setting regimes theoretically orphaned, presumably of no consequence in the scheme of international environmental protection. This Liberal model, as with the other two, leaves too much activity unexplained.

4 NGOs as Stakeholders: Acting through International Institutions

In contrast to Liberal perspectives on NGO participation in world environmental politics, stakeholder models independently situate NGOs in the context of public international institutions. This approach highlights the direct participation of non-state actors in international decision-making, as a matter of both practice and aspiration. The stakeholder model explains and justifies the growing, unmediated role of NGOs in international organizations. In this construct, the state may remain the primary target of regulatory activity, but it is displaced by international institutions as the key decision-making platform. In this context, NGO participation is not dependent on state power.

The stakeholder model can be summed up with the notion of giving NGOs 'a place at the table.' As Richard Shell suggests in the context of world trade—which of course implicates international environmental protection values—the model 'emphasizes direct participation . . . not only by states and businesses, but also by groups that are broadly representative of diverse citizen interests[;] the priorities for global society are open-ended and subject to deliberation by those whose lives will be affected.'[14] Also addressing the organs of world trade (in which the formal monopoly of state power has been better defended), Daniel Esty argues that '[p]ermitting NGOs to participate would thus allow the organization to hear important voices which would otherwise be unrepresented or under-represented.' He elaborates:

A citizen who cares very deeply about ending whaling, for instance, almost certainly will find his or her views better represented in international fora by the World Wide Fund for Nature than by his or her own government, which has many goals it must simultaneously pursue. At the very least, listening to NGOs offers a cut across the grain of territorial representation . . . The participation of NGOs in WTO debates also can help to compensate for deficient representativeness at the national level.[15]

[14] G.R.Shell, 'Trade Legalism and International Relations Theory: An Analysis of the World Trade Organization' (1995) 44 Duke L.J. 829 at 910–11.
[15] D.C. Esty, 'Non-Governmental Organizations at the World Trade Organization: Cooperation, Competition, or Exclusion' (1998) 1 J. Int'l Econ. L. 123 at 131–2.

The stakeholder model thus frames NGOs as representative entities at the international level. As early as 1989, Philippe Sands noted that NGOs 'represent interests of people with particular concerns' in calling for NGO standing in international institutions.[16]

In modern practice, the stakeholder model perhaps best explains the parallel conference phenomenon, in which NGOs have convened shadow gatherings to coincide with major intergovernmental issue summits. If the 1972 Stockholm Conference on the Human Environment witnessed the innovation of the parallel conference, the 1992 UN Rio Conference on Environment and Development saw its flowering, with 22,000 NGO representatives descending on Rio for the meeting. The NGO conferences evidenced a push from the ground-up for non-state representation in norms-setting processes. In this context, NGOs have emerged as a sort of third estate, representing environmentalist constituencies outside and inside the tent. This role has sometimes been explicitly recognized, as with Agenda 21's characterization of NGOs as 'partners for sustainable development.'

The stakeholder model best comprehends the formal mechanisms of NGO participation. Other examples from the international environmental law context include the formal NGO observer status that is now enabled in all major environmental treaty regimes. This status typically affords NGOs rights of intervention in public treaty negotiating sessions as well as in ongoing treaty proceedings, including annual conferences of the parties in such regimes as climate change and ozone protection. The Council of the Global Environment Facility provides for the participation of up to five NGO representatives in Council meetings. The UN Environment Programme (UNEP), through its 'Major Groups and Stakeholders Branch', has adopted procedures allowing for NGOs to comment on UNEP working documents in the same time frame as governmental representatives. The World Bank has established an advisory committee composed of NGO representatives, with an aim to bring human rights and environmental values into bank decision-making. As noted earlier, NGOs have standing to initiate formal complaints before the Bank Inspection Panel. Although it remains exceptional among the major multilateral environmental agreements, NGOs are central players in monitoring state-party compliance with the Convention on International Trade in Endangered Species of Wild Fauna and Flora (CITES). The European Regional Convention on Access to Information, Public Participation in Decision-making and Access to Justice in Environmental Matters allows NGOs to nominate members of its compliance committee.

Liberal Institutionalist theorists discount these mechanisms of participation in the context of otherwise centring international regimes. Observer rights are only that—in some cases, regime procedures expressly deny negotiating rights to NGOs— as states 'have clearly restricted and determined' the scope of NGO activities short of

---

[16] P.J. Sands, 'The Environment, Community and International Law' (1989) 30 Harv. J. Int'l L. 393 at 401.

full participation in negotiation and other components of the law-making process.[17] As Raustiala notes, in late-stage negotiations, states retreat into so-called informal-informals from which NGOs will be excluded. As for monitoring functions, Institutionalism plays it as another example of service provision, with NGOs assuming a task to the benefit of state power.

This perspective would seem to underestimate the actual scope of NGO power in international environmental law-making. Formal participation mechanisms now appear to be consequential. Such participation enhances the legitimacy of international environmental institutions. By way of proving the point, one need only posit the counterfactual of states moving to formally rescind NGO rights of participation. Any such effort would likely fail, and, were it to succeed, it would only be to the ultimate detriment of the institution involved. The growth of formal participation rights has been unidirectional, establishing a trajectory in which NGO participation is entrenched and enhanced. It is difficult to put together a scenario in which the evolution of NGO practice over the last 30 years or so is reversed. Likewise, the crucial NGO role in advancing treaty compliance—sometimes enshrined in formal undertakings between treaty secretariats and NGOs, as is the case in the CITES regime[18]—seems to go beyond the Liberal Institutionalist vision of NGO participation. NGOs are using treaty-based institutions to advance their own agendas in a way that would otherwise not necessarily serve the collective interest of states as such (although state and non-state interests may of course often coincide), especially in those contexts where transborder harms are not at issue. That states would otherwise under-enforce, for instance, a regime against trade in endangered species seems likely. Even where transborder harms are at issue, as in the ozone and climate change contexts, NGOs have been able to work directly with secretariats and compliance bodies by way of using treaty obligations as a tool to overcome state preferences that would otherwise result in non-compliance. Insofar as these NGO compliance-oriented activities within international institutions are not undertaken through state agents, they are difficult to explain in Liberal terms.

The trajectory is also being entrenched by the growing influence of NGOs in standard setting through informal channels within international institutions. Such groups as Greenpeace, the World Wide Fund for Nature (WWF), and the World

[17] Raustiala, see note 12 above at 734.

[18] Article XII of the Convention on International Trade in Endangered Species of Wild Fauna and Flora (CITES) authorizes the Secretariat to be 'assisted' by 'suitable' NGOs that are 'technically qualified in protection, conservation, and management of wild fauna and flora.' The Secretariat has a formalized arrangement with Trade Records Analysis of Flora and Fauna in Commerce (TRAFFIC) to provide capacity-building activities, and TRAFFIC has been an important monitoring agent of CITES compliance. Although TRAFFIC is constituted as a technical scientific expert body, it is a joint venture of the World Conservation Union and the World Wide Fund for Nature, the latter of which qualifies as an advocacy membership NGO of the sort addressed in this chapter. NGO activity in enforcing CITES trade-management requirements have in at least one instance been described as 'paramilitary' in nature, with US-based NGO WildAid undertaking enforcement in Thailand with little governmental supervision. See *Report of the CITES Tiger Mission Technical Team*, COP-12 Doc. 33 (2002), Annex at 17.

Conservation Union (IUCN) are major political players in international environmental law-making. Greenpeace, in particular, in effect launders its influence through formal channels. For example, Greenpeace and other groups have paid membership dues for smaller states that would not otherwise have joined the International Whaling Commission, in order to stack state votes in favour of a whaling moratorium. Greenpeace itself was reported to have prepared required member submissions and then to have assigned Greenpeace members to sit as delegates for these 'states of convenience'.[19] The London-based Centre for International Environmental Law (CIEL) (now the Foundation for International Environmental Law and Development) was instrumental in establishing the Alliance of Small Island States (AOSIS) in 1989. CIEL, together with Greenpeace, coordinated the positions of 37 state members of AOSIS for purposes of climate change policy. AOSIS has been in turn a prominent force in the climate change negotiations. Insofar as NGOs were nominally representing state parties, the practice does not directly challenge traditional paradigms of state primacy, and it would be accurate to say that the power of the states involved (as a Liberal Institutionalist would argue) was greatly enhanced by the NGO effort. Yet the groups involved, especially the member-based Greenpeace, are surely also representing the interests of constituencies beyond the states behind whose nameplates they sit. Given the disparity in resources—in this case, weighing heavily in favour of the NGOs, in contrast to the examples of environmentalist NGOs sitting in large, developed-state delegations—it would be surprising if there were not some, and perhaps many, cases in which the NGOs have been formulating the policy, both goals and specifics, in a sort of tail-wagging-the-dog dynamic. This brand of delegation capture might be described as a sort of stakeholder model *sub rosa* or as proof that some form of stakeholder participation will emerge even if states persist in maintaining a monopoly on formal power in international institutions. Indeed, delegation capture and other channels of informal NGO influence raise transparency concerns, insofar as it no longer remains clear who at the negotiating table is speaking for whom.

These developments may point to the eventual consummation of the stakeholder approach in the form of a tripartite global environmental organization. Modelled on the International Labour Organization, such a centralized decision-making institution would be comprised of representatives of governments, corporations, and NGOs. The proposal recognizes NGOs as representing constituencies on a level of parity with and independent of states. Such an arrangement could be accounted for only through a stakeholder lens, as state-centric approaches would have difficulty processing direct NGO participation. Although a global environmental organization remains far over the horizon, the idea has enjoyed high-profile support.[20] In the meantime, the United Nations Global Compact presents a sort of halfway house

---

[19] See Chayes and Handler Chayes, note 7 above at 265.

[20] See, e.g., G. Palmer, 'New Ways to Make International Environmental Law' (1992) 86 A.J.I.L. 259 and D.C. Esty, 'The Value of Creating a Global Environmental Organization' (June 2000) Env't Matters: Annual Review 13.

for realizing such stakeholder visions, relating broadly to social practices including the environment. The Global Compact is styled as a 'forum' rather than a decision-making institution, and its structure is rudimentary. But the membership combines corporations and NGOs in a direct relationship with the United Nations. Global Compact principles hold that subscribing corporations should 'support a precautionary approach to environmental challenges', 'undertake initiatives to promote greater environmental responsibility', and 'encourage the development and diffusion of environmentally friendly technologies.' The compact has more than 1,500 corporate signers as well as major NGO affiliates (including the WWF and IUCN). The Global Compact may or may not evolve into a major entity, but its design does reflect a move towards stakeholder approaches and enhanced, direct participation on the part of non-state actors in relations with international institutions. Even if such visions of centralized stakeholder governance through a global environmental organization or the Global Compact fail to coalesce, they highlight the utility of enhanced NGO status in international environmental law-making.

The stakeholder model does appear well equipped to the task of explaining and justifying the emerging terms of NGO participation in international environmental law or at least better equipped than Liberal approaches. The model's leap is to accept the possibility of NGO power beyond the state and to rationalize such power on the basis of NGO representativeness. It implicitly assumes, however, that the consequentiality of NGOs (and of other actors) is located in public institutional settings alone. This assumption leaves extra-institutional activity outside the model.

5 NGOs as Freelancers: Acting through the Marketplace

This slack is taken up by post-national models of non-state action. Post-nationalism highlights the exercise of power outside of state and intergovernmental structures. In both the Liberal and stakeholder models, NGOs influence states and/or international institutions to the end of constraining the behaviour of states and of the private actors for which states may be held accountable. Post-nationalism, by contrast, posits a capacity on the part of NGOs directly to act against entities whose behaviour is sought to be constrained—be they states, other governmental entities, or non-state actors. The international environmental arena has proven particularly fertile ground for the development of the post-national model, insofar as (in contrast to the context of international human rights) the ultimate targets of normative regimes and NGO mobilization are typically private corporate actors (see Chapter 35 'Business'). There is a vast potential for international environmental standard setting to play out without any participation on the part of the state, much less state primacy.

The political space of the market is key to post-national conceptions of international environmental decision-making. NGOs have exploited the global competitiveness of global markets to discipline corporate actors. Insofar as markets offer expanded choice, NGOs harness the possibility of choice to advance their agendas and to reflect and build sympathetic constituencies. Paul Wapner pitches NGOs as disseminating an 'ecological sensibility' under which '[t]hey persuade vast numbers of people to care about and take actions to protect the earth's ecosystems.'[21] As part of a spectrum of resulting behaviours, consumers begin to take environmental practices into account in their marketplace decisions, initiated or coordinated by NGO leaderships. Once this muscle is demonstrated, it need not be deployed in particular cases; the capacity suffices to establish leverage and the possibility of influence. To the extent that NGOs can credibly threaten to divert buyers—in effect, to distort the market in favour of political ends—they can influence corporate decision-making with respect to environmental and other policies. As John Ruggie observes, 'civil society organizations have managed to implant elements of public accountability into the private transactional spaces of transnational firms.'[22] As this power shows itself to be persistent, NGOs can move away from ad hoc initiatives towards broader, sustained efforts to constrain corporate and state power in lieu of formal public regulation.

The arc here is from 'naming and shaming' campaigns to negotiated codes of conduct. Greenpeace and other international environmental NGOs innovated the consumer boycott as an extra-institutional policy tool. Companies have often relented when faced with such campaigns. Indeed, often the mere threat of a boycott will cause a target actor to back down. In the context of climate change, for example, while a recalcitrant ExxonMobil finds itself facing a sustained boycott campaign in the form of 'stop Esso', other major energy concerns have undertaken to voluntarily reduce greenhouse gas emissions—at least in part to mitigate consumer opprobrium on the issue. In one notable case, Royal Dutch Shell desisted from scuttling oil rigs in the North Sea in the face of a Greenpeace protest, even though it was later acknowledged to have been the more environmentally friendly decommissioning option, and even though Greenpeace had refrained from working the issue through available international institutional channels (the 1971 London Convention on the Prevention of Marine Pollution by Dumping of Wastes and Other Matter and the 1992 OSPAR Convention for the Protection of the Marine Environment of the North-East Atlantic). States, too, have been the target of successful boycotts, through the vehicle of home corporations and products, as when France halted nuclear testing in the wake of a Greenpeace campaign that cut into its market for wine exports. Selective investment stands as a riff on the boycott strategy, with socially conscious investors either shunning share ownership in corporations deemed unfriendly to the environment or working from within, in the form of shareholder resolutions, to exert

[21] P. Wapner, *Environmental Activism and World Civic Politics* (Albany, NY: State University of New York Press, 1996) at 42.   [22] See Ruggie, note 2 above at 514.

pressure towards better environmental corporate policy. Short of boycotts, the mere reporting of information by NGOs can pull corporations towards better environmental practices.

Because boycott campaigns, from the NGOs' standpoint, are costly, risky, and enjoy no guarantee of success, NGOs have also developed less confrontational means to persuade corporate and state actors. Multinational corporations have come to understand NGO capacities and have internalized and anticipated NGO views in corporate decision-making (Chapter 35 'Business'). This understanding is not necessarily a matter of guesswork and prediction but increasingly involves behind-the-scenes dialogue between corporations and NGOs on sensitive issues of environmental and other policies. This communication reflects the fact of NGO power. Corporations understand that they ignore NGOs at their peril.

This dynamic is now moving away from ad hoc accommodations to the emergence of broader regimes developed and pressed by NGOs on corporations in the form of codes of conduct and certification schemes (see Chapter 21 'Private and Quasi-Private Standard Setting'). Developed in 1989 in the wake of the notorious *Exxon Valdez* oil spill, the Valdez Principles comprised an early attempt to formulate principles of good environmental corporate citizenship. Now known as the CERES Principles, after its sponsoring entity, the Coalition for Environmentally Responsible Economies, signatory companies agree to monitor and improve their environmental impacts; work towards improved waste disposal and energy conservation; inform the public of dangerous conditions or incidents; and undertake self-evaluation of environmental practices through generally accepted environmental audit procedures. Although the CERES Principles have been a mixed success (only about 60 corporations have agreed to the principles, although among them are such large concerns as Ford, General Motors, and the Bank of America), they illustrate the possibility of an NGO-originated regime with broad implications for corporate environmental practices, and for international environmental protection generally. Beyond formal adherents, the principles may explain corporate moves towards incorporating environmental matters into accounting practices as well as a general trend towards acknowledging green values in corporate public relations. (Royal Dutch Shell now combines financial and social reports into one, for example.) Such reporting, as undertaken even in the absence of some formal commitment, may demonstrate the possibility of corporations being 'stung', in Wapner's formulation, by the environmental sensibilities pressed through NGOs.

Sector-specific certification schemes comprise more narrowly drawn, but more deeply elaborated, voluntary codes relating to environmental practices. The forest certification program developed by the Forest Stewardship Council (FSC) (founded by environmental and human rights NGOs and timber industry representatives in 1993) presents an example of an increasingly refined, specified set of articulated practices relating to the sustainable management of international forest resources. This code and its associated certification scheme have captured a substantial slice of developed world lumber markets, most prominently undertakings by prominent American-based home improvement retailers to stock only such wood as carries the certification seal. As Benjamin Cashore notes, the strength of this and similar initiatives 'derive their policy-making authority not from the state, but from the manipulation of global markets and attention to customer preferences.'[23] The FSC's governance structure applies a tripartite stakeholder approach, with chambers for corporations, environmental NGOs, and other non-state actors including indigenous peoples and interested individuals. Other such certification schemes with environmental implications are found in the context of various foodstuffs, from coffee to chocolate. The Marine Stewardship Council has been established (through a 1997 joint initiative on the part of Unilever, the world's largest buyer of seafood, and the WWF) on the FSC model, to advance sustainable fisheries practices, to which a number of large buyers and processors have signed on. Similar approaches are found in the human rights context, most successfully with respect to textile manufactures and the diamond trade. Other efforts look to developing softer norms on a partnership basis, without ambitions to establish standing institutions. Constituted on a tripartite basis with representatives of civil society, the corporate sector, and governmental leaders, the World Commission on Dams (WCD) undertook a study examining criteria for the planning, financing, construction, and operation of dams and then disbanded. Notwithstanding its expiration, the WCD is generally considered to have been a significant force in sketching basic norms in this area.

These NGO-driven schemes are often politely dismissed because they are voluntary, and thus cannot even purport to set mandatory standards for corporate environmental practices in the way of command-and-control governmental regulation. This objection is, of course, true as a formal matter. No corporation is legally compelled to subscribe to any of these various codes. As a practical matter, however, there may be (depending on market conditions) tremendous pressures for corporations to sign on. As in boycott situations, where persisting with the offending practice will result in measurable losses to the bottom line, refusal to comply with codes of conduct may also emerge as ill-advised policy even from traditional, non-socially responsible business metrics. In theory, at least, such privately generated regimes can result in something that starts to look like law in both its refinement and its real-world pull towards compliance. The codes, too, can 'sting' corporate actors into proactive environmental practices. When the major US materials retailer Home Depot found that it could not satisfy demand through FSC-certified wood products, it began itself to lobby foreign producers and governments to adopt sustainable forestry practices, to great effect in Canada and Chile.

Perhaps the more subtle challenge to such regimes is the counter posing of private standard setting by corporate-dominated institutions (see Chapter 21 'Private and

---

[23] See B. Cashore, 'Legitimacy and the Privatization of Environmental Governance: How Non-State Market Driven Governance Systems Gain Rule-Making Authority' (2002) 15 Governance 503 at 513.

Quasi-Private Standard Setting'). In this case, the International Organization for Standardization (ISO) looms as a corporate-dominated alternative to NGO-sponsored codes. Long a forum for harmonizing technical standards, during the 1990s, the ISO expanded its reach to include environmental auditing and management standards, denominated as the ISO 14000 series. As with the NGO-driven regimes, the standards are voluntary. They largely speak to how corporations should address environmental issues as a matter of internal management procedures and how environmental issues plug into the corporate chain of command. They do not dictate conformity with substantive parameters. They are nonetheless perceived to be increasingly consequential and 'fast becoming a requirement for doing business in world markets.'[24] The ISO has been nominally constituted on a stakeholder basis, providing for NGO participation in the formulation of ISO standards. However, observers have questioned the efficacy of non-corporate voices in ISO decision-making. By controlling the institutional levers of a non-state regime, corporate interests may pre-empt more protective mechanisms that would be formulated by NGO-driven processes or by public regulation.

The prospect is of 'greenwash'—not so much with the ISO, in particular, but with nimble corporate responses to environmental activism generally. For all the green evident in annual reports and smokestacks emblazoned with ISO 14000, the question remains as to whether the changed public relations amounts to better environmental practices. While it is true that codes of conduct are not only voluntary, but also unenforceable in the way of public regulatory schemes, this again ignores non-formal enforcement mechanisms available to NGOs in the form of mobilizing sympathetic consumer constituencies. Through the information-forcing and monitoring activities of the codes and their NGO sponsors, corporations can be made to pay for non-conformity with code schemes to which they have (or have not) subscribed. Even if this form of discipline is inexact (as, of course, are public regulatory schemes as well), it would seem substantial enough to be processed into corporate decision-making. In short, 'greenwashing' is probably undertaken at a company's peril.

It is also in elaborating the post-national model that the putative lack of accountability among NGOs should be most seriously considered. In other models, NGO activity is mediated either through the state or through international institutions, in which case NGO unaccountability is backstopped by other institutional actors. In the post-national model, NGOs exercise power directly against target entities, in which case resulting arrangements may be more infected by the unaccountable actor. Or so the argument would run. Of course, with some notable exceptions (the Sierra Club among environmental NGOs), NGOs are not formally democratic in the sense that they are subject to one member–one vote governance. Yet they are subject to other effective accountability mechanisms. NGOs may be internally accountable insofar as

---

[24] V. Haufler, *A Public Role for the Private Sector: Industry Self-Regulation in a Global Economy* (Washington, DC: Carnegie Endowment for International Peace, 2001) at 37.

members exercise some loose oversight of their executive directorates. NGOs compete among themselves for members and leadership positions—a misstep by one can be exploited by another. As for external accountability—that is, to other actors—as repeat players in institutional contexts, public or private, NGOs becomes responsible to processes, which constrain their capacities to opt out of institutional bargains.[25]

As a descriptive matter, the post-national model would now seem essential to understanding the place of NGOs in the international environmental process. Only from formalist premises can one deny the consequentiality of NGO activity outside of state or public international institutional settings. At the same time, the post-national orientation does not reject the continuing significance of the public regulatory arena. In this respect, the post-national analytic takes off where the other models stop, by way of expanding the horizon of standard-setting activity. Where Liberal models defend the primacy of states and stakeholder approaches assume the primacy of public institutions, post-nationalism explores beyond the public/private divide.

6 NGOs AND THE FUTURE OF INTERNATIONAL ENVIRONMENTAL LAW-MAKING: RELEGALIZING NORMS?

Which model will best describe NGO participation in international environmental law going forward will depend in some measure on the balance between public and private institutional decisional settings. Only post-nationalism will be able to account for such developments as unfold outside of public entities—that is, outside of the scope of governmental or intergovernmental sponsorship. In the short term, post-national responses to international environmental issues are likely to increase, at least where public law prospects are limited. In the long run, however, there may be a migration back and up to public institutions at the supranational level, in which case the stakeholder model would likely prove the dominant explanatory perspective on the NGO role.

There is nothing inevitable about perfecting the public institutional management of international environmental law issues. Non-state-sponsored codes of conduct—the endpoint of the post-national dynamic—can in theory operate as effectively as legal regimes. They may, however, be systematically more unstable than public forms of global regulation. To the extent that codes are unable to establish and maintain monopoly positions, for example, target actors will face the prospect of shifting

---

[25] For an elaboration, see P.J. Spiro, 'Accounting for NGOs' (2002) 3 Chi. J. Int'l L. 161.

regimes—what represents 'the law' today may be displaced by another regime to-morrow. Moreover, insofar as post-national schemes allow the unmediated exercise of NGO power, they may be subject to greater deviations from the initial expectations of acceding parties. The upshot is greater uncertainty where regimes remain the crea-ture of private institutional or extra-institutional mechanisms.

Corporations abhor uncertainty. Once major corporations are implicated in codes of conduct and similar regimes, they then have an incentive to press for their adop-tion as law. Even if public law regimes are more costly over the short run, their prom-ise of greater stability over the long run may draw corporate support. To the extent that codes of conduct are pressed more effectively on large, multinational manufac-turers than on others, a lack of universality in the private scheme gives rise to com-petitive disadvantages. The result may be corporate pressure for legalization. But the upshot will not be a return to government as usual. Not only will the resulting regimes be international, they will ever more likely be born of processes in which NGOs and other non-state actors are extended increasingly formal participation roles. This will demand the continued reordering not only of international envir-onmental institutions but of the theory that may explain it.

RECOMMENDED READING

B. Arts, *The Political Influence of Global NGOs: Case Studies on the Climate and Biodiversity Conventions* (Utrecht: International Books, 1998).

M. Keck and K. Sikkink, *Activists beyond Borders: Advocacy Networks in International Politics* (Ithaca, NY: Cornell University Press, 1998).

E.E. Meidinger, 'Forest Certification as Environmental Law Making by Global Civil Society,' in Errol Meidinger et al., eds., *Social and Political Dimensions of Forest Certification* (Remagen-Oberwinter: Forstbuch, 2003).

P. Newell, *Climate for Change: Non-State Actors and the Global Politics of the Greenhouse* (Cambridge: Cambridge University Press, 2000).

T. Princen and M. Finger, *Environmental NGOs in World Politics: Linking the Local and the Global* (New York: Routledge, 1994).

K. Raustiala, 'States, NGOs, and International Environmental Institutions' (1997) 41 Int'l Stud. Q. 719.

P. Wapner, *Environmental Activism and World Civic Politics* (Albany, NY: State University of New York Press, 1996).

F. Yamin, 'NGOs and International Environmental Law: A Critical Evaluation of Their Roles and Responsibilities' (2001) 10 R.E.C.I.E.L. 149.

CHAPTER 34

EPISTEMIC COMMUNITIES

PETER HAAS

1 INTRODUCTION

As the world becomes more globalized, decision-makers grow uncertain about what their interests are and how best to achieve them, and ideas become increasingly important as maps or frames for decision-makers in an unfamiliar setting. With the end of the Cold War, decision-makers cannot rely on geopolitical doctrines as a guide for various areas of foreign policy and international practice.

The environment provides a telling issue area in which to address the role of ideas in an increasingly uncertain global policy context. This chapter looks at the concept of 'epistemic communities', the role of epistemic communities in institutionalizing ideas in international relations, and, in particular, the role played by ecological ideas in the development of international environmental law and the role played by sympathetic international environmental lawyers in converting such rules of nature to rules of man.

2 EPISTEMIC COMMUNITIES

2.1 Concept of Epistemic Communities

The concept of epistemic communities was developed by 'soft' Constructivist scholars of international relations concerned with agency. Soft Constructivists, in general, focus on the role of various types of norms, principled beliefs, causal beliefs, and discourses in establishing roles and rules in international relations—that is, determining the identities, interests, and practices that shape the identification of actors in international relations (see Chapter 10 'International Relations Theory').

The concept helps international relations (IR) scholars to describe the actors associated with the formulation of causal beliefs and the circumstances, resources, and mechanisms by which new ideas or policy doctrines get developed and influence the political process as well as to understand and explain the broader process by which their ideas shape politics. Epistemic communities are important actors that are responsible for developing and circulating causal ideas and associated normative beliefs and, thus, help to identify state interests and preferences as well as to identify legitimate participants in the policy process, and influence the form and content of negotiated outcomes by shaping how conflicts of interest will be resolved. Attention to epistemic communities provides a way to understand agency in politics and policy formation. Under conditions of complexity, decision-makers are uncertain of their

A number of international lawyers have educated me about their craft. I thank Cesare Romano, Peter Sand, Edith Brown Weiss, Kal Raustiala, Dan Esty, Laurence Boisson de Chazournes, Alexandre Kiss, and Naomi Roht-Arriaza.

goals or how to achieve them. Ideas may play important roles in framing the policy debate and in predisposing outcomes highlighted by each perspective.

Epistemic communities are networks—often transnational—of knowledge-based experts with an authoritative claim to policy relevant knowledge within their domain of expertise. Their members share knowledge about the causation of social or physical phenomena in an area for which they have a reputation for competence, and a common set of normative beliefs about what actions will benefit human welfare in such a domain. Members are experts with professional training who enjoy social authority based on their reputation for impartial expertise. In the environmental realm, they are primarily scientists and engineers, and, in economic matters, they are economists. Such individuals may hold positions in multiple locations over their careers: academia, think tanks, governments, and even within firms. Few are drawn to non-governmental organizations (NGOs) because most NGOs value principled beliefs over causal beliefs in formulating and justifying their policy discourses. Their beliefs are at an analytic level below those of John Dryzek's 'discourses', although their political involvement can contribute in a causal way to the institutionalization of such broader discourses (see Chapter 3 'Paradigms and Discourses'). In particular, they are a group of professionals, often from a number of different disciplines, who share all of the following characteristics:

- shared consummatory values or principled beliefs, which provide a value-based rationale for social action by the members of the community;
- shared causal beliefs or professional judgement, which provide analytic reasons and explanations of behaviour, offering causal explanations for the multiple linkages between possible policy actions and desired outcomes. While they need not agree on every element—in fact they are likely to disagree vehemently about some elements—they do agree both about the core assumptions and causal forces from which their models of the world derive as well as about the means by which such disagreements can potentially be reconciled;
- common notions of validity, including inter-subjective, internally defined criteria for validating knowledge; and
- a common policy enterprise, including a set of practices associated with a central set of problems that have to be tackled, presumably out of a conviction that human welfare will be enhanced as a consequence.

This combination of factors—especially the socialized truth tests and common causal beliefs—distinguish epistemic communities from other types of policy networks and groups active in politics and policy-making. Unlike other organized interest groups active in politics and policy-making, epistemic communities are bound by the truth tests to which they were socialized. Thus, they are more likely to provide information that is politically untainted and, therefore, more likely to 'work', in the political sense that it will be embraced and followed by political authorities concerned about the need for appearing impartial. Their advice is also more likely to be technically effective, in the sense of obtaining the desired goals, than would be policies derived by political compromise. Politically, their reputation for expertise and impartiality provides a social provenance, in the sense of the pedigree imparted, for example, by antique appraisers that confer confidence in their advice by potential consumers.

2.2 Intellectual History of Scholarship about Epistemic Communities

Constructivism has achieved an intellectual status as one of the dominant approaches in IR (see Chapter 10 'International Relations Theory'). The ideational focus was absorbed into the broader constructivist programme developed in international relations and comparative politics that looked at the role of beliefs and ideas in shaping state interests and practices, with epistemic communities providing a mechanism by which new ideas are developed and circulated and providing a means for focusing on agency when studying international cooperation and governance. Consequently, the role of causal ideas and epistemic communities in explaining international cooperation has received increased attention. Causal ideas and epistemic communities are now generally regarded as significant sources of state interests under conditions of complexity and uncertainty, as a main source in the origins and forms of multilateral regimes, and as important actors in the broader processes of social learning, reflexive governance, and identity formation. In other words, Constructivists have demonstrated that globalization makes actors uncertain about their interests and policies, and that various forms of social constructs (ideas) play a significant role in helping actors plot their course in uncertain conditions.

The focus on causal ideas and their transmission mechanisms has been largely eclipsed since the late 1990s by more attention to the role of norms and principled beliefs. A variety of critiques have been offered of the epistemic communities' research programme.[1] Some of these challenges include the following:

- epistemic communities' knowledge base is itself socially constructed and represents the potential systematic bias of those responsible for articulating research agendas;
- it is difficult to isolate the influence of the causal beliefs of epistemic communities from the institutional influence of the formal institutions with which they are associated;
- epistemic communities' scholarship has lacked a compelling theory of the state and has not paid sufficient attention to the domestic politics of the countries in which epistemic communities exercise a potential influence; and
- better appreciation is needed for those ideas that are likely to prove attractive to decision-makers in response to uncertainty.

[1] For an overview of these critiques and some trenchant rejoinders, see C. Dunlop, 'Epistemic Communities: A Reply to Toke' (2000) 20 Politics 137–44.

These critiques have led to increased analytic clarification, and to stronger theoretical foundations and refinements for the constructivist epistemic communities' research programme. While states are key juridical actors and act wilfully, they vary in their administrative and political ability to formulate environmental (and other) policy, to absorb ideas domestically and from abroad, and to enforce policies at home. States are functionally differentiated, and vary widely according to their state/society relations and their technical capacity to formulate and enforce public policies in technical domains. State capacity in this sense is issue specific—that is, regulatory potential varies by issue because the nature of the state's institutions, their resources, and policy networks vary by issue. Consequently, governance varies depending on the issue area.

Epistemic communities are most likely to emerge initially under circumstances affected both by issue and state characteristics. They are likely to be found working on substantive issues where scientific disciplines have been applied to policy oriented work such as environmental protection, economic development, and energy policy. Thus, epistemic communities arise in disciplines associated with natural science, engineering, ecology, and even economics. They usually emerge around specific topics whose research support is relatively inexpensive and not directly related to the explicit mission of the sponsoring research body. Consequently, the research and policy guidance of the epistemic community will be relatively independent of the explicit agenda of the research sponsor. Epistemic communities thus will enjoy broader political influence on issues such as the environment and ecology, rather than in areas such as nuclear energy, because their findings are seen as being impartial or independent of explicit political influence. Environmental research is relatively inexpensive, compared to that of nuclear energy, and is conducted through networks of researchers who are not directly associated with the government or government laboratories. Epistemic communities are also most likely to emerge in countries with well-established research capacity and where scientists enjoy some autonomy from the state. In such social settings, the knowledge base will be relatively untainted and, as a result, will enjoy a stronger political authority and legitimacy. States will also look for new ideas after highly publicized crises. Such crises, potential or actual environmental disasters, or economic crises will prompt decision-makers to take action to ameliorate pressure from domestic constituencies and from abroad.

The empirical experience with the global reception of environmental ideas does not directly engage the question of which ideas will matter at such points, other than saying that new ideas must have some affinity with existing beliefs or discourses and that there is a strong path-dependent element to the dynamics of causal ideas once they are institutionalized. In the early 1970s, when international institutions were founded to address global environmental threats under the influence of the United Nations Conference on the Human Environment (UNCHE), there were few contending epistemic communities. In fact, there were only three major intellectual approaches to international environmental management. Traditional resource managerial approaches were widely discredited by the Limits to Growth study and the 1973 oil crisis. Market-based approaches to environmental management were weakly advanced by economists, the World Bank, and the General Agreement on Tariffs and Trade at the UNCHE, but they and their institutional backers generally paid little heed to the conference. Market-based approaches did receive more attention in the 1990s, particularly in the drafting of the Kyoto Protocol. Access to information—a form of economic instrument that confers information and improves the prospects for informed consent and contracting—also became more prominent, especially in the 1998 Convention on Access to Information, Public Participation in Decision-Making and Access to Justice in Environmental Matters and the 1998 Convention on the Prior Informed Consent Procedure for Certain Hazardous Chemicals and Pesticides in International Trade. What is striking analytically, however, is the relative infrequency with which the negotiated outcomes that correspond to the dominant expertise paradigm—economics—have been adopted. Even in the climate change regime, for example, market mechanisms are instrumentally applied to achieve the substantive goals, identified by scientists, of ensuring that anthropogenic greenhouse gas emissions do not exceed the carrying capacity of the atmosphere. Market mechanisms as such, however, are primarily concerned with means rather than ends. They seek to provide mechanisms that improve environmental quality, but they are agnostic about the desirable level of environmental quality to be pursued. Conversely, epistemic communities specify the desirable environmental target, and work backwards to develop the policy instruments that meet the desired ends. Even with the popularity of market-based discourses in the 1990s, negotiated outcomes that are in force —including the 2001 Stockholm Convention on Persistent Organic Pollutants—continue to reflect the command and control approach of the ecological epistemic community, which derived environmental standards from the causal beliefs of the community. The ecological epistemic community's ideas persist.

Capturing the ideational high ground after the UNCHE left the nascent ecological epistemic community as the only game in town to assert a technical claim to expertise for addressing the new agenda of issues. Subsequently, this approach has retained its dominance as the presumptive approach to environmental management. Still, the ecological beliefs of the epistemic community at least corresponded loosely to the overarching policy paradigm, and political imperatives, of the time by continuing to assert the role of the state in promoting environmental protection, even while specifying the legitimate domain to which the state should exercise sovereignty.

More generally, some hypotheses were offered about which ideas are likely to be favoured in response to uncertainty and crises. Thus, some analysts suggested that it is not the accuracy of objective truth that matters but, rather, the political function that potential ideas serve. In either case, truth alone is insufficient since politicians must believe that these ideas serve some political utility in order to apply them (see Chapter 9 'Science and Technology'). Judith Goldstein has suggested that ideas that have been regarded as successful in the past are likely to enjoy favour,[2] such as trade liberalization, while John Odell has suggested that simple ideas will enjoy an edge over more complicated ones.[3] Moreover, Jeffrey Garrett and Barry Weingast suggest that ideas that are favourable to cementing political coalitions, either internationally or domestically, will prevail.[4] In general, if there is only one candidate, it is likely to prevail. The political factors associated with selection are only salient if there exist a large number of competing ideas. In practice, the universe of available causal policy ideas is not very large and there may not be a vast opportunity for political competition at moments of selection that follow crises.

More attention also has been paid to the broader dynamics by which ideas are transferred internationally. While they may initially be developed and consolidated in advanced democracies, they will be emulated and borrowed in other countries with sufficient domestic scientific capacities. International institutions are also likely to play an influential role in the broader transmission pattern. Major formal international organizations (IOs) that can play a role are those that enjoy strong organizational resources, and some autonomy from their member governments, through a combination of secretariat skills, porous organizational boundaries, and executive leadership. Such institutions are most likely to be immediately responsive to recognizing changes in the policy environment, and to absorbing new ideas about their underlying missions. In the environmental realm, these institutions included the UN Environment Programme (UNEP), the World Bank, the UN Economic Commission for Europe (UNECE), and the UNCHE. Subsequently, organizations may transmit the new ideas to member states through training programs and the demonstration effect, as well as to other international organizations through joint activities.

This makes it possible to analytically disentangle the causal effects of ideas from the institutions associated with them. It is possible to control the influence of the institution by looking at the same institution's behaviour over time, subject to the ideas that enjoy popularity within it. For instance, the World Bank encouraged much stronger environmental policies after the 1987 reforms that had the effect of lodging more ecological ideas within the bank. Thus, epistemic communities and causal ideas have played a determinative role in influencing the ends to which institutional resources will be deployed in practice.

More generally, studies have separated two distinct mechanisms by which ideas disseminate internationally. One is through active social learning, through which individual decision-makers are persuaded of the virtue of new ideas through direct exposure to epistemic community members or international institutions acting on their behalf. Such social learning is most likely to lead to robust changes in national

---

[2] J. Goldstein, *Ideas, Interests and American Trade Policy* (Ithaca, NY: Cornell University Press, 1993).

[3] J.S. Odell, 'Understanding International Trade Policies' (1990) 43 World Politics 139.

[4] G. Garrett and B. Weingast, 'Ideas, Interests and Institutions,' in J. Goldstein and R.O. Keohane, eds., *Ideas and Foreign Policy* (Ithaca, NY: Cornell University Press, 1993) 173.

practices as a consequence of profound long-term shifts in the appreciation of the national interest and how countries' prospects for material welfare are influenced by ecological stability. An example of this pattern is the European acid rain regime (Long-Range Transboundary Air Pollution Convention (LRTAP)), in which the concept of critical loads was developed by the UNECE and the Institute for Applied Systems Analysis and disseminated through key countries to inform international treaties on sulphur and nitrogen oxide emissions, as well as national policies and legislation adopted to implement treaty obligations.

A second pattern of dissemination lacks the social element of direct contact that social learning entails. This second pattern is one of policy borrowing—of emulation of patterns of behaviour and policies from salient countries and organizations. While policy borrowing is a major pattern by which ideas diffuse internationally and lead to policy harmonization, it would not be possible without the causal operation of social learning that institutionalizes ideas in the major countries and institutions from which others borrow. Instances of this process have to do with adoptions of economic incentives for environmental protection in Europe, and the widespread application of toxic chemical standards developed by the United States or the World Health Organization.

Social learning is better understood now as a path-dependent process of collective social change. New ideas are solicited by uncertain policy-makers in the aftermath of well-publicized disasters or shocks, which encourage decision-makers to seek guidance for responding to new and uncertain issues. Such conditions are more frequent under conditions of globalization and complexity. Through the steps described earlier in this chapter, new ideas imparted to decision-makers by epistemic community members lead to changes in state understandings of the policy environment and of their own national interests, and eventually to changes in state practices as well. These beliefs become institutionalized through the redeployment of state resources and through the consolidation of administrative practices and laws.

2.3 Ecological Epistemic Community and Multilateral Environmental Governance

A new environmental management doctrine based on ecological principles emerged in the 1960s. Since 1972, the ecological epistemic community has increasingly institutionalized this new management doctrine in state policies and practices, in the programmatic activities of international institutions, and in international regimes. As a consequence of the international institutionalization of ideas held by the ecological epistemic community, states have undertaken more comprehensive styles of environmental management for transboundary and global environmental threats, leading to selective improvements in environmental quality. Members of the ecological epistemic community subscribed to holistic ecological beliefs about the need for policy coordination subject to eco-systemic laws (see Chapter 24 'Ecosystems'). Their ideas about ecological management were based on a systems perspective of environmental and social systems. Ecological management proposals favour setting comprehensive environmental standards based on conservative estimates of the ability of ecosystems to sustain stress, which are subject to the epistemic community's technical understanding of the behaviour of particular ecosystems. They promoted international environmental regimes that are grounded on policies that offered coherent plans for the management of entire ecosystems, sensitive to interactions between environmental media (such as air and water), sources of pollution, and contending uses of common property resources. Rather than limiting themselves to more traditional policies for managing discrete activities or physical resources spaces within fairly short-term time horizons, they proposed treaties, in which bans and emissions limits were set for multiple contaminants, with environmental standards for each contaminant set according to the scientific understanding about its environmental impact and its interactive effects with other contaminants.

Over time, the ecological epistemic community added a broader social component regarding the need for widespread stakeholder participation in research and negotiations, out of the belief that such non-state actors, and particularly indigenous peoples, would have access to vital ecological knowledge outside the traditional domain of ecological sciences (see Chapter 36 'Indigenous Peoples'). Moreover, such non-state actors, it was felt, would prove powerful political forces for compliance once management efforts were designed.

The ecological epistemic community has been associated with distinctive patterns of environmental cooperation. Treaties concluded with its input reflect causal beliefs about environmental management. These treaties are based on environmental standards that reflect the epistemic community's technical understanding of the ability of specific environments to sustain stress. An example is the 'critical loads' approach of the 1994 Sulphur Protocol to the LRTAP Convention, which differs from more common patterns of institutional bargaining where negotiated outcomes are solely based on compromise. Patterns of institutional bargaining embrace universal standards that are based on political compromise, but have no clear relationship to environmental quality, such as the arbitrary, across-the-board cuts in pollution contained in early European air pollution agreements or North Sea emission controls. In the absence of technical consensus on the behaviour of the North Sea and the impact of individual pollutants on the overall health of the ecosystem, North Sea diplomats adopted 30 per cent and 50 per cent reductions in the emissions of a wide array of chemicals. Such standards, while politically attractive, lack any clear connection to overall environmental quality and, thus, may impose economic costs without any offsetting environmental benefit.

In contrast, when regimes are negotiated with the involvement of members of the ecological epistemic community and strong international institutions, they develop through a process of 'social learning'. Negotiations occur with a scientific discourse, in which political debate and compromise reflect expert consensus on the behaviour of ecosystems and their ability to sustain stress. The substance of regimes reflects scientific consensus about the most important environmental threats, and negotiated standards reflect consensus about the degree of environmental stress the target environment can sustain. Social learning generates treaties with differentiated national obligations and substantive commitments, based on expert consensus on causes and environmental effects. Agenda setting is responsive to scientific advice and publicized crises. States' interests may be altered as a consequence of being exposed to new ideas, and negotiated treaties will reflect an increased willingness to sacrifice short-term economic gains for longer-term collective environmental protection.

Since the 1970s, an increasing number of regimes have been developed through the process of social learning. Only regimes negotiated in the shadows of the ecological epistemic community, and strong international institutions, have yielded patterns of comprehensive environmental management through a process of social learning. Ecological epistemic community members, often working with UNEP, have helped draft comprehensive international environmental regimes governing marine pollution, acid rain, stratospheric ozone protection, wetlands protection, protecting migratory species, polar bears protection, and the preservation of Antarctica. An increasing proportion of all environmental regimes are now based on the comprehensive ecological approach promoted by the ecological epistemic community as it has increased in vigour and influence, and countries have institutionalized their ideas. In 1973, three out of 11 major international environmental regimes (or clusters of MEAs) were based on ecological management styles; in 1985, seven out of 22; and, in 1995, 11 out of 25 or 12 out of 25, if the climate change regime's commitment to stabilizing atmospheric concentrations at safe levels is interpreted as an ecological management frame. The application of ecological management ideas to environmental regimes spanning a number of geographic areas and functional activities means that most states have accepted ecological obligations for governing a wide variety of human activities.

Conversely, treaties and regimes concluded without input from the ecological epistemic community yielded political compromises that were based on across-the-board reductions or least-common-denominator-type negotiated outcomes. Instances of the non-social learning regimes include fisheries management, whaling, marine dumping, and the Baltic and North Seas. Table 1 provides examples of some of the variety of negotiated environmental outcomes that characterize the environmental regimes that were established since the UNCHE. Social learning has yielded comprehensive ecological efforts with the combination of epistemic community involvement and strong international institutions. Such comprehensive efforts entail differentiated national obligations and substantive commitments, based on the experts' consensus on the causes of environmental degradation.

Table 1: Major Multilateral Environmental Agreements (in force) and
Their Negotiated Form (as of 2005)

	Strong Institutions	Weak Institutions
Ecological epistemic community	*Social learning* ozone European acid rain Persian Gulf (pre 1980) South Pacific southeast Pacific Antarctica migratory species polar bears wetlands toxics	

No ecological epistemic community	*Institutional bargaining*
	Red Sea
	Black Sea
	Baltic
	North Sea (1987–)
	marine dumping
	   (London Convention)
	operational oil pollution
	   (International
	   Convention for the
	   Prevention of Pollution
	   from Ships)
		Least common denominator
		Caribbean
		West Africa
		East Africa
		North Sea (1972–87)
		fisheries management
		   Persian Gulf (1980–)

Institutional bargaining results from strong institutions that encourage states to compromise in the absence of epistemic consensus. Such treaties and regimes tend to involve disjointed treaties with uniform national regulatory obligations chosen for their political and emotional appeal. Finally, least-common-denominator results of weak collective obligations result from negotiations undertaken in the absence of strong institutions or strong scientific consensus, such as with most fisheries agreements, where the institutional context for treaty negotiation and national enforcement is extremely weak, and where fisheries biologists, although able to demonstrate that over-fishing is occurring, cannot convincingly identify sustainable fishery yields.

The climate change and biodiversity regimes shed light on the nature of the consensual knowledge shared by the ecological epistemic community. They, however, have not been included in the table because, while in each case there exists a cohort of like-minded environmental specialists who believe that action is necessary in order to prevent calamitous climate change or loss of biodiversity, the knowledge base is insufficiently mature (or 'useable') in each instance to provide meaningful targets and deadlines for decision-makers to apply (see Chapter 9 'Science and Technology').

3 Epistemic Communities and International Environmental Lawyers

International environmental lawyers do not themselves constitute an epistemic community. However, they have played a key role in institutionalizing the ideas and actual participation of the ecological epistemic community in the formation of international environmental law and regimes.

3.1 International Environmental Lawyers Are Not an Epistemic Community

While there is now an active community of international environmental lawyers involved in the development and interpretation of international environmental law, they remain a policy community and not an epistemic community. Their shared beliefs take a different form from that of the ecological epistemic community discussed earlier, and they lack the social authority enjoyed by the ecological epistemic community.

International law as a field lacks the social authority or legitimacy of the technical authority commanded by epistemic communities. Legitimacy in the ecological epistemic community rests on the internally consistent substantive nature of the ideas put forth for policy-makers by experts, and on the transparent way in which such ideas are developed and gain consensus. International environmental law and international law more generally is philosophically and epistemologically different from the social domain of ecological science. Whereas ecology and the technical domains in which epistemic communities operate are the realms of hybrid and brute facts, where claims about physical phenomena may be evaluated by recourse to mechanisms independent of the subject of study, law is a different activity. Law operates in the domain of social facts. The substantive domain of law is not subject to the type of shared tangible understandings that characterize the political domain in which ecological facts are identified for public policy. While international environmental law as a corpus may provide a presumptive backdrop against which negotiations and treaty drafting occurs,[5] international lawyers lack the authority in environmental policy circles that scientists and engineers enjoy directly.

International environmental law also lacks epistemic status for sociological reasons. International lawyers lack the public respect for impartial views about the world to which their advice is deployed, for the reasons mentioned earlier in this chapter. In addition, the professional knowledge base of international environmental law is insufficiently institutionalized to generate common truth tests and a tight sociological network. Law school curricula tend to offer only one elective course on international environmental law, and there are few professional career path opportunities for international environmental lawyers in the absence of litigation opportunities in the realm of international environmental law. The array of professional niches for international environmental lawyers remains fairly narrow and is limited to policy analysts and law school professors.

International environmental law texts now exist, but they are largely collections of treaties rather than volumes based on a deductive set of propositions from which conclusions about institutional design and appropriate behaviour may derive. Thus, international environmental law lacks the core causal beliefs and truth tests that define an epistemic community.

3.2 International Environmental Lawyers and the Translation of the Ecological Epistemic Community's Ideas into International Environmental Law

International environmental lawyers have played an active role in the development of international environmental law and in the conversion of causal ideas of the ecological epistemic community into treaties for the management of environmental threats by institutionalizing scientists' involvement in collective decision-making and in drafting treaties based on the scientists' insights. Since the UNCHE, a core network of individuals has been involved in the formulation of much of the corpus of international environmental law. A small clique of lawyers initially worked for the Stockholm secretariat, and cut their teeth drafting the 1972 Convention on the Prevention of Marine Pollution by Dumping of Wastes and Other Matter. Subsequently, their rules of thumb were reproduced, and they acquired the status of precedent among the broader community of international lawyers. The cadre of sympathetic lawyers grew, with their foundations and institutional memories residing in UNEP's legal office (now called the Environmental Policy Development and Law unit), in the World Bank's legal office, and in some government offices. Some figures

---

[5] I. Johnstone, 'The Power of Interpretive Communities,' in M. Barnett and R. Duvall, eds., *Power in Global Governance* (Cambridge: Cambridge University Press, 2005) 185.

include Patrick Szell (United Kingdom), Johann Lammers (Netherlands), Winfried Lang (Austria), and Peter Sand (Food and Agriculture Organization, UNEP, the UNECE, and the World Bank).

These lawyers have developed a kernel of procedural techniques by which ecological principles of environmental management would be applied to environmental law. These techniques include the following:

- the umbrella convention-protocol sequence—this technique was developed in the 1972 Convention on the Prevention of Marine Pollution by Dumping of Wastes and Other Matter (London Convention) and the Protocols on Marine Dumping and Emergency Co-operation. Initially, in the regional seas treaties, this technique required states to commit not only to broad amorphous principles but also to more specific binding commitments as well, since states in most cases had to ratify at least one protocol. However, this no longer seems to be true for current multilateral environmental agreements (MEAs), which allow a state to become a party to the main treaty only, without ratifying the subsequently adopted protocol. The climate change and the biodiversity regimes are both relevant examples (see Chapter 20 'Treaty Making and Treaty Evolution');
- conference of the parties (COPs) and treaty amendments—COPs, through their decisions, develop the MEA-based regimes, thereby circumventing the problem of having to amend the treaty. In addition, by provisions such as those developed under the auspices of the Montreal Protocol on Substances That Deplete the Ozone Layer, diplomats, based on expert advice, can approve environmental standards by amending an annex to the protocol without having to go through time-consuming domestic ratification processes (see Chapter 32 'International Institutions' and Chapter 38 'Treaty Bodies');
- lists of banned or regulated substances—the 1972 London Convention differentiates between banned substances (black list) and regulated substances (grey list). As of March 2006, for those states that are parties to the 1996 protocol, this system will be replaced by a ban on all dumping of wastes at sea, except for those substances listed (the so-called reverse listing approach). Both systems require the identification of substances and the setting of appropriate standards and, thus, the involvement of environmental specialists;
- standing expert committees and panels—most international environmental regimes have been designed to have standing scientific panels associated with them for the provision of timely environmental monitoring and policy information. Such arrangements provide the regularized mechanism by which individual scientists and epistemic community members may be recruited and involved in international environmental treaty making; and
- the establishment of dedicated voluntary trust funds so that regimes may be self-supporting—these funds have the effect of making the conventions financially self-supporting as well as creating more resources for programmatic activities.

More broadly, international environmental lawyers have come to appreciate international environmental negotiations as an exercise in communication and learning, where individual parties develop new ways of understanding the world, others, and themselves as a consequence of being exposed to the causal ideas articulated by the ecological epistemic community. Such a reflexive approach also provides the means by which international law development can accelerate past a snail's pace dictated by the least enthusiastic party.

4 CONCLUSION

Over the last 30 years, the environment has become firmly established on the international diplomatic agenda, and, through regime formation, binding rules have been developed for most human activities affecting environmental quality. Substantively, the focus on international environmental regimes has shifted from discrete environmental standards to ecosystem protection. Procedurally, it has come to rely much more heavily on the expert advice of the ecological epistemic community.

The ecological epistemic community is one of the principal vehicles by which new ideas of ecological sustainability and governance have evolved. International environmental lawyers have helped provide the institutional mechanisms by which these ideas have reached and been disseminated to states and other actors. Constructivist theories of IR help to provide the explanatory parameters by which these processes occur as well as shedding light on their effects.

RECOMMENDED READING

E. Adler, 'Constructivism and International Relations,' in W. Carlsnaes, T. Riss, T. Risse, and B. Simmons, eds., *Handbook of International Relations* (Beverly Hills, CA: Sage, 2002) 95.

S. Andresen et al., *Science and Politics in International Environmental Regimes* (Manchester: Manchester University Press, 2000).

P. Contini and P.H. Sand, 'Methods to Expedite Environmental Protection: International Ecostandards' (1972) 66 A.J.I.L. 37.

E.B. Haas, *When Knowledge is Power* (Berkeley, CA: University of California Press, 1990).

P.M. Haas, 'Environment: Pollution,' in P.J. Simmons and Chantal de Jonge Oudraat, eds., *Managing Global Issues* (Washington, DC: Carnegie Endowment for International Peace, 2001) 310.

——, ed., 'Knowledge, Power and International Policy Coordination' special issue (1992) 46 Int'l Org.; reprinted as P.M. Haas, ed., *Knowledge, Power and International Policy Coordination* (Columbia, SC: University of South Carolina Press, 1997).

P.M. Haas, and E.B. Haas, 'Learning to Learn' (1995) 1 Global Governance 255.

E.L. Miles, A. Underdal, S. Andresen, J. Wettestad, J.B. Skjaerseth, and E.M. Carlin, *Environmental Regime Effectiveness* (Cambridge, MA: MIT Press, 2002).

J.G. Ruggie, 'What Makes the World Hang Together?' (1998) 52 Int'l Org. 557.

J. Searle, *The Construction of Social Reality* (New York: Free Press, 1995).

CHAPTER 35

BUSINESS

STEVEN R. RATNER

BUSINESS is a central actor in international environmental law. Industry, far more than states, engages directly in environmental degradation as well as the prevention and remediation of its harms. Two conclusions follow, which are both obvious to even a casual observer of environmental policy. First, business will aggressively seek to influence the content and application of environmental law and, second, environmental law will be effective only to the extent that it controls the behaviour of business. Yet the state-centric paradigm of traditional international law continues to skew the analysis of international environmental regimes away from this reality. Both treaties and treatises regard private economic actors as secondary players, and see states as the overwhelmingly dominant targets and prescribers of environmental law. The result is a paradox. Proponents of international environmental law see it as a cutting-edge subject of international law—one that shows the law responding to dynamic collective action problems—yet the field is trapped as much as, if not more than, other areas of international law in a doctrinal straitjacket that gives lopsided attention to states.

This chapter seeks to expose some of the divergences between doctrine and reality, and to suggest ways of understanding the field that take proper account of business. It does so first by examining the roles and goals of business entities with respect to international environmental law. It then examines how international law has accommodated the place of business in environmental policy with respect to two key issues: (1) corporations as the target of legal obligations; and (2) corporations as participants in the process of international environmental law, particularly with respect to law-making and implementation. I conclude with some thoughts regarding a reconceptualization of the doctrine.

Before beginning, it is necessary to clarify that the scope of actors under the term 'business', as used in this chapter, is large. In particular, it is not confined to large, transnational corporations (TNCs) but, instead, includes small and large businesses operating in one state alone. Moreover, it extends to business-initiated non-governmental organizations (BINGOs), both those composed of, or representing, businesses within one state as well as those with a more international profile.

1 BUSINESS AND ENVIRONMENTAL REGULATION

1.1 Two Visions of International Business

The relationship between business and international environmental law can be seen from two distinct perspectives. First, domestic and international businesses create a need for international environmental protection through their capacity to disturb the ecosystem without regard to interstate borders. Pollutants emitted as part of business activity can harm common spaces or move across state boundaries, as with the case of oil released from tankers or ozone-depleting substances. Products produced by business may be inherently hazardous and create extraterritorial harm, as with radioactive materials, pesticides, or persistent organic pollutants (POPs).[1] And business activity can disturb, without actually polluting, disparate geographical areas or common spaces, as with fishing, logging, or bio-prospecting.

However, the transboundary environmental impact of companies is not sufficient in explaining the need for international regulation, for, in principle, many of these manifestations could be handled through strong domestic laws. Yet, the control of business through domestic law faces systemic obstacles. On the one hand, the home government (that is, the state of incorporation or residence) of a TNC that causes pollution elsewhere may have little interest in regulating harmful activity that takes place beyond its borders. On the other hand, if the state hosting the TNC's operations is in the developing world, it may lack the technical expertise and human resources required for effective regulation. Equally significant, it may also lack the desire to do so in the face of economic pressure to welcome foreign business with as few restrictions as possible. (Domestic regulation of purely local companies in the developing world faces these two obstacles for the same reasons.) And, in the case of transboundary pollution, the country in which the damage occurs may lack effective jurisdiction over a company operating in another country.

This vision of the corporation as a threat to the environment, which requires international regulation, competes with a second vision, one initiated by business itself, that sees the corporation as an instrument of environmental improvement. According to this view, corporations can pay attention to the environmental impact of their products and processes. Indeed, businesses can enhance the ecosystem through involvement in remediation. It also emphasizes that governments cannot act alone. Thus, large TNCs can ratchet up a developing state's environmental performance by establishing environmentally sensitive operations where the local law does not require them. Or they can serve as a source of knowledge and training for their affiliates (and governmental officials) in developing countries that exceeds the training that governments offer through official development assistance. Chapter 30 of Agenda 21 represents the first major UN recognition of this role for business.

These two views of the corporation are also part of a larger debate between North and South about foreign investment. For many years, governments of less developed capital-importing countries saw corporations through the first lens, and proposed international norms allowing states to control the conduct and profits of foreign entities. Defending their economic interests, corporations, supported by Western governments, fought fierce ideological, political, and legal battles from the 1960s

---

[1] See R.J. Fowler, 'International Environmental Standards for Transnational Corporations' (1995) 25 Envt'l L. 1 at 8–10.

through the 1980s over, for instance, the ability of host states to expropriate without full compensation. By the 1990s, the beginnings of an accommodation could be seen, as developing countries desperate for foreign investment created legal regimes that were favourable to capital inflows, and some TNCs saw the advantages of accepting various codes (often non-binding) on their conduct abroad.

Yet, as noted, the very need of developing countries for investment has also limited their incentives to regulate foreign-based TNCs operating in their territory. Seeing themselves as lacking the leverage, expertise, and bureaucracy to control corporate environmental conduct, poor host states have sought to transfer some of the regulatory onus to richer home states. Prominent examples of this burden-shifting are the conventions on the transboundary movement of potentially hazardous items, including the 1989 Basel Convention on the Control of Transboundary Movements of Hazardous Wastes and Their Disposal, the 1998 Convention on the Prior Informed Consent Procedure for Certain Hazardous Chemicals and Pesticides in International Trade (PIC Convention) (regarding pesticides), the 2000 Cartagena Protocol on Biosafety (Cartagena Protocol) (on genetically modified organisms), and the 2001 Stockholm Convention on Persistent Organic Pollutants (Stockholm Convention). The result is a more effective constraint on TNC activity than developing states can muster.

1.2 A Diversity of Corporate Attitudes

John Drahos and Peter Braithwaite identify two basic approaches of business to international environmental regulation. Many businesses are still dominated by the economic dynamic of the race to the bottom. In this case, the corporation seeks to lower costs and bolster profits by operating in the least restrictive legal environment. States seeking to attract companies for their economic benefits will lower their standards to accommodate them. Home states, seeking maximum tax revenue, will be reluctant to regulate companies' extraterritorial conduct. A second perspective sees no contradiction between economics and environmentalism. Businesses adopting this view emphasize how corporations profit by following or developing the 'best available technology' or the 'world's best practice'. Consumers will respond to environmentally friendly companies, and those in the lead—practising 'eco-efficiency'—will gain a competitive advantage over others.[2]

Yet business attitudes cannot be grouped simply into anti-regulation and pro-regulation. For one thing, nearly all businesses, large and small, domestic and international, seek certainty in legal regimes above all, whether with regard to the environment, taxation, or employment. A new, but permanent, regulation will prove

[2] J. Braithwaite and P. Drahos, *Global Business Regulation* (Cambridge: Cambridge University Press, 2000) at 267–70 and 279.

much more attractive than uncertainty, even if the new rule imposes additional costs. Moreover, corporations divide up along many other lines, with much debate about whether these differences correspond to attitudes about regulation. Will companies that cause only domestic impacts approach regulation differently from TNCs? The former may oppose international regulation if they are unable to influence it (because they are small economic actors) or fear the higher standards resulting from it; they may favour it if it results in overall lower standards; or they may be agnostic if it does not have an effect on their operations at all. What about regional differences? While European companies have lately shown greater interest than US companies in the best available technology model, and tend to be leaders in the various BINGOs promoting the broad notion of corporate social responsibility (CSR), they were laggards in the 1980s with respect to the development of the ozone regime. What about large companies versus small ones? Small companies will usually have to bow to the wishes of major players in a particular industry, but this does not translate into either an anti-regulatory attitude or a preference for a particular form of regulation. This difficulty in mapping corporate attitudes has made cross-sectoral analysis of international environmental regimes difficult, and, as a result, most academic treatments have dealt with each industry or pollution problem independently.

2 Business as the Target of International Environmental Law Duties

2.1 The Limits of Orthodoxy

International law doctrine has resisted the concept that companies themselves have legal duties. That doctrine views corporations as fundamentally different from states, with only states enjoying the full range of legal rights and duties and the capacity to make claims for violations of rights. This characterization repeatedly appears in the deliberations of the International Law Commission (ILC) and the Institut de Droit International and academic treatments (including other chapters in this *Handbook*). This posture remains even though the law has long accepted rights for non-state actors, for example, in treaties letting individuals sue states in regional courts or letting foreign investors sue states in the International Centre for the Settlement of Investment Disputes, or imposed duties upon them, as in the corpus of international criminal law.[3] Yet the penumbra of legal personality casts a shadow over attempts to

---

[3] 1965 Convention on the Settlement of Investment Disputes between States and Nationals of Other States.

evaluate the normative role for non-state actors. As stated in a major treatise, private persons cannot, in general, be liable under international law because the state is a 'screen' between them and international law.[4]

The pull of the orthodoxy is seen in a terminological splitting of hairs between 'responsibility' and 'liability' (see Chapter 44 'International Responsibility and Liability'). Thus, scholars have argued a variety of propositions: (1) only states can be 'responsible' for violations of international law because of their unique personality, and corporations can only be 'liable' under domestic law ('civilly liable' under private domestic law, though the possibility remains for criminal liability);[5] and (2) only states can be responsible for violations for the same reasons, but corporations can be liable under international (and not merely domestic) law.[6] Some scholars focus on the acts triggering liability or responsibility rather than the state/corporate distinction. Thus, (3) 'liability' arises only for acts not prohibited by international law, so that a state (or conceivably a corporation) may be liable for certain harmful consequences of its acts even if the state is not legally responsible because those acts— typically, some kind of pollution—are not prohibited under international law;[7] and (4) a state is responsible for breaches of international law but liable for (and only for) the consequences of those breaches.[8] For non-lawyers, the use of the term 'responsibility' clouds matters even more, since legal responsibility, whatever it is, is certainly narrower than the responsibility envisaged in the concept of CSR.

The doctrine also at times distinguishes between international law that directly regulates corporate activity, and that which allocates jurisdictional competence of states to regulate corporate activity.[9] Under the former approach, international law sets uniform standards for the behaviour of corporations, while, under the latter (an 'allocation regime'), it decides which state will regulate the activities of corporations under its domestic law.[10] A pure allocation regime enables governments to apply diverse national standards without having to agree on an international standard.

---

[4] See, e.g., Nguyen Quoc Dinh, *Droit International Public*, edited by P. Daillier and A Pellet, 7th edition (Paris: LGDJ, 2002) at 649.

[5] See, e.g., P. Sands, *Principles of International Environmental Law*, 2nd edition (Cambridge: Cambridge University Press, 2003) at 869–70 and 873.

[6] See Resolution of the Institut de Droit International, *Responsibility and Liability under International Law for Environmental Damage*, 1997, Strasbourg, Article 1.

[7] See International Law Commission, Draft Articles on Prevention of Transboundary Harm from Hazardous Activities, UN Doc. A/56/10 (2001) 370, Article 1.

[8] See A. Boyle, 'State Responsibility and International Liability for Injurious Consequences of Acts Not Prohibited by International Law: A Necessary Distinction?' (1990) 39 Int'l & Comp. L.Q. 1.

[9] See Fowler, note 1 above at 19.

[10] A similar distinction has been adopted in international criminal law between treaties establishing international crimes (such as genocide) and those giving some or all states jurisdiction to prosecute offences (such as torture). See B. Simma and A.L. Paulus, 'The Responsibility of Individuals for Human Rights Abuses in Internal Conflicts: A Positivist View,' in S.R. Ratner and A.M. Slaughter, eds., *The Methods of International Law* (Washington, DC: American Society of International Law, 2004) 23 at 32.

The problem with these two sets of distinctions—between responsibility and liability and between direct regulation and the allocation of jurisdiction—is that the practice of actors in the international environmental process is so pragmatic, and catholic, as to render them without much utility as a way of understanding the field.

2.2 Treaties

2.2.1 *Civil Liability Conventions*

The strongest examples of international duties that apply directly to corporations are found in the civil liability conventions. These treaties implement the polluter pays principle, which reflects a policy preference among many states that corporations are legally responsible for their pollution and its consequences. Consider three such treaties:

- The 1960 Paris Convention on Third Party Liability in the Field of Nuclear Energy states directly that the 'operator of a nuclear installation shall be liable' for damage to or loss of life or property (Article 3) and that the liability is strict liability, with exceptions only for armed conflict and grave and exceptional natural disasters (Article 9). It goes on to specify the maximum amount of damages. Moreover, it contains a jurisdictional allocation clause providing that jurisdiction over suits against operators normally rests with the territorial state, with judgments enforceable in other states parties.

- The International Convention on Civil Liability for Oil Pollution Damage (1969, amended in 1984 and 1992) makes the 'the owner of a ship at the time of an incident . . . liable for any pollution damage caused by the ship as a result of the incident,' with liability again strict and subject to some (indeed a longer list of) exceptions (Article III). It also contains a cap on damages, though it does not allocate jurisdiction to one state alone, allowing suits in any state where pollution or preventive measures take place; and, again, judgments are enforceable in any other state party.

- The 1989 Basel Convention on the Control of Transboundary Movements of Hazardous Substances (Basel Convention) (along with its 1999 protocol) engages in a two-pronged approach. The original convention declares that '[i]llegal traffic in hazardous wastes or other wastes is criminal' and requires all parties to punish exports inconsistent with the convention, though it does not contain a jurisdictional allocation structure in the event that more than one state chooses to prosecute. The 1999 protocol provides a civil liability regime in case of incidents involving the transboundary movement of such substances, whether legal or illegal. The generator or exporter assumes liability—which is strict and subject to some exceptions—until the disposer takes control of them. The 1999 protocol also allocates jurisdiction, giving a right of action in the state where the damage or incident occurred or the defendant has his or her principal place of residence or business (Article 17), again providing for mutual recognition of judgments.

In essence, these treaties combine substantive duties on companies with jurisdictional allocation provisions. It is frankly difficult to see what is left of either the distinction between responsibility and liability or between direct regulation and jurisdictional allocation. Plainly stated, the treaties place duties on businesses not to cause pollution. What varies is simply the scope of the duty (due diligence, strict liability), the penalties (civil fines versus criminal penalties), and the enforcement architecture (shared versus unique jurisdiction to hear private claims).

2.2.2 *Other Conventions*

Beyond the relatively small arena of liability conventions lies the rest of the universe of international environmental treaties, which formally place obligations only on states. Yet, even these accords clearly set specific rules, of which corporations must at a minimum be aware and, depending on the ratification patterns, with which they must comply. The 2001 Stockholm Convention prohibits or severely limits the production, use, import, and export of POPs. Like other treaties, it sets international standards for industry conduct and prescribes conduct for—or allocates various responsibilities to—different states (for example, producers, exporters, and importers) to enforce the standards. Similarly, the International Convention for the Prevention of Pollution from Ships (MARPOL Convention) sets forth very specific standards for the construction, design, and equipment of oil tankers, which builders, owners, and operators of oil tankers must take account of, even though the standards apply to tankers only through the intermediation of national law. These more typical environmental law treaties do not use the language of direct corporate liability, and, thus, a distinction could be made between the two types of treaties. For the liability conventions, the treaty (once it enters into force) creates the corporate duty, but victims of the prohibited activity will be able to make corporations accountable for a failure to carry out the duty only by suing in the courts of the relevant state party, whereas for the typical environmental treaty, the treaty itself does not speak of a corporate obligation, and corporations need only follow its strictures when they engage in the prohibited activity vis-à-vis a state party that has mandated compliance under domestic law.

I admit that there is a distinction between the liability conventions and the other treaties. Indeed, I have put special emphasis on liability regimes to show that the law creates duties on companies that even an orthodox international lawyer should accept. However, in the end, the practical convergence of the two sets of treaties from the perspective of business entities seems far more important than the lawyer's distinctions between them. In both cases, (1) the treaty sets international standards for the activity; (2) business needs to be aware of these standards; (3) business faces its greatest exposure for failure to comply with these standards when they carry out activities within the jurisdiction of states parties, because the treaty requires states parties to take certain enforcement actions; and (4) less-than-universal ratification of the treaty creates gaps in the effectiveness of the regime and opportunities for business to exploit these gaps.[11]

Of course, treaties that include some allocation of jurisdiction will vary in terms of which states have jurisdiction to regulate, and certain regimes will be easier than others for corporations to evade. It is far simpler for a company, faced with a treaty giving flag states jurisdiction to enforce an international standard, to reflag its vessel to that of a non-party than it is for a company, faced with a treaty giving exporting states jurisdiction to enforce an international standard, to change the location of its exports to a non-party. This allocation mechanism is the key to the success of the Basel Convention and other regimes. However, in both situations, states have effectively created standards on corporations, and these corporations will consider the possibilities of adjusting their business depending on their willingness to comply with them.

2.3 Soft Regulation

Soft international instruments have already recognized the critical role of business entities in environmental degradation and protection. Numerous non-binding regulatory instruments emanating from international organizations are targeted at—and phrase their commitments as directed towards—business. For example, the Food and Agriculture Organization's (FAO) International Code of Conduct on the Distribution and Use of Pesticides is divided roughly equally between commitments for governments and commitments for industry. The Bonn Guidelines on Access to Genetic Resources provide not only standards for governments to regulate bio-prospecting, but responsibilities for commercial users of bio-resources and recommendations for private agreements between users and providers of these resources. The hesitancy of governments to use the language of direct obligations on corporations in treaties is clearly less manifest with respect to soft law instruments (though the non-binding documents from the World Summit on Sustainable Development (WSSD) were deliberately worded to avoid such expressions).[12] Yet, if one believes that soft law is really a form of international law, these

---

[11] States could create pure allocation regimes without any international standards, in which case one cannot speak of an international duty on a company. Examples include the 1974 OECD Principles of Transfrontier Pollution, which call for non-discrimination in application of domestic law but announce no international standards, and the UN Convention on the Law of the Sea's grant to flag states of jurisdiction over environmental aspects of shipping that are not regulated by international standards. But these do not typify environmental treaties.

[12] E. Morgera, 'From Stockholm to Johannesburg: From Corporate Responsibility to Corporate Accountability for the Global Protection of the Environment?' (2004) 13 R.E.C.I.E.L. 214.

commitments are further proof of the anachronistic nature of the view that only states can be the subject of duties.

3 CORPORATIONS AS PRESCRIBERS OF NORMS

The stakes for corporations in the content of international environmental law are so great that business is actively involved in its prescription. The standards/allocation distinction, while not particularly useful from a legal point, does highlight different policy preferences of business. In some cases, industry will push for uniform international standards. Mitchell has suggested that corporations will generally prefer these to be low, and will seek to eliminate competitive disadvantages for companies governed by stricter regulations.[13] Moreover, large TNCs would find global standards easier to administer. Global standards nonetheless can improve environmental protection by placing more stringent controls on corporations than domestic standards, in particular, in developing countries. In other situations, companies will seek allocation regimes (without any international standards) to take advantage of situations of lower standards in some states.[14] Yet even pure allocation regimes could improve environmental quality if the state with the higher standards, rather than the one with the lower standards (typically the place of incorporation over the place of operation), had mandatory jurisdiction to regulate the company. The same company may take a different position on different issues.

Corporations participate in the prescription of international environmental norms in three distinct ways: interaction with individual governments; independent participation in international law-making fora; and the prescription of industry codes of behaviour.

3.1 Interaction with Governments

The corporation's most obvious target of influence is government. Business entities are continually lobbying governments to incorporate their views in official positions. At one extreme, a business may seek influence, only to find itself shut out of discussions. At the other, the company may be so powerful that it captures the government, which then becomes its advocate in interstate negotiations. In the middle lie a range of possibilities, as business and government discuss the latter's positions to be taken

---

[13] R.B. Mitchell, *Intentional Oil Pollution at Sea: Environmental Policy and Treaty Compliance* (Cambridge, MA: MIT Press, 1994) at 110.   [14] Braithwaite and Drahos, see note 2 above at 285.

at international venues, with government mediating among business, consumer, environmental, labour, and other interests.

Numerous case studies have documented this process. In the case of acid rain, automobile manufacturers in Europe heavily influenced their governments' positions, with British, French, and Italian opposition to decreases in nitrogen oxide emissions determined by the positions of their car makers, and Germany's position in favour determined by the ability of German car makers to incorporate catalytic converters more easily.[15] Food and drug companies based in the United States, Canada, Australia, Argentina, Chile, and Uruguay that export genetically modified organisms (GMOs) (and their BINGO, the Global Industry Coalition) influenced the position of these states on trade in GMOs in the negotiations over the 2000 Cartagena Protocol and succeeded in limiting the protocol's scope.[16] Much, but not all, US industry has lobbied the US administration and Congress—quite successfully—against binding standards on greenhouse gases.

As part of, or in addition to, lobbying, industry can provide critical (and often one-sided) information to governments, especially those too poor to conduct scientific studies. In some cases, industry representatives serve on governmental delegations as members or advisers. The line between advising and lobbying is often thin. Japan's government-chosen commissioner on the International Whaling Commission has traditionally been the head of Japan's domestic whaling BINGO. Veterans of, or those sympathetic to, the shipping industry long controlled most of the committee work of the International Maritime Consultative Organization (IMCO, which is now the IMO).[17] Indeed, such participation effectively crosses the line to the second category of corporate involvement.

3.2 Independent Participation in International Venues

Corporate involvement through governmental delegations represents no challenge to a state-centric view of international law. Indeed, it reinforces it by suggesting that corporations can be successful only if they can first convince states to endorse their positions. Yet direct involvement by corporations in international organizations, conferences of states parties to treaties, and other intergovernmental meetings suggests a weakening of the paradigm (see Chapter 29 'Public Participation'). For many

[15] M.A. Levy, 'European Acid Rain: The Power of Tote-Board Diplomacy,' in P.M. Haas et al., eds., *Institutions for the Earth: Sources of Effective International Environmental Protection* (Cambridge, MA: MIT Press, 1993) 75 at 95.

[16] A. Gupta, 'Advanced Informed Agreement: A Shared Basis for Governing Trade in Genetically Modified Organisms?' (2001) 9 Indiana J. Global Leg. Stud. 265; see also State Department Fact Sheet on Cartagena Protocol on Biosafety, 8 March 2004.

[17] R.M. M'Gonigle and M.W. Zacher, *Pollution, Politics and International Law: Tankers at Sea* (Berkeley, CA: University of California Press, 1979) at 277.

years, intergovernmental institutions have allowed individual businesses or BINGOs to participate in their norm-setting agenda. Business is more than happy to oblige. Business might have a consultative status that merely allows it to attend meetings, but it must lobby governments to achieve its goals so that the basic model discussed earlier in this chapter is preserved, but in a setting more efficient for influencing multiple governments. Consultative status may allow BINGOs or individual business to table papers at intergovernmental meetings. Some 700 companies sent representatives to the 2002 Johannesburg Summit, and the International Chamber of Commerce and the World Business Council on Sustainable Development (WBCSD) jointly set up a new BINGO—the Business Action for Sustainable Development—to represent business interests. One result of their work was the watering down of the Johannesburg Plan of Implementation's references to corporate responsibility as well as the lack of any efforts to draft a convention on business duties.[18]

Business participation can be still more direct. Representatives of the pesticide and chemical industries have served on groups of experts of the FAO and the UN Environment Programme (UNEP) that determined the substances subject to the prior informed consent (PIC) regime in soft law instruments and treaties. European and US BINGOs provided technical expertise and lobbied to protect their interests. The Montreal Protocol on Substances That Deplete the Ozone Layer has a Technology and Economic Assessment Panel (TEAP) to provide technical advice to the parties on implementing their obligations; TEAP and its working groups consist of both governmental and industry representatives.[19] More recently, the Conference of the Parties to the Convention on Biological Diversity created a panel of experts and an ad hoc open-ended working group to address access to, and the benefit sharing of, genetic resources—both contain representatives of industry who have been nominated by governments. The two groups worked closely with the Swiss government on a proposal that it had prepared with Swiss companies, resulting in the 2002 Bonn Guidelines, which were a key step to a regime on bio-prospecting. The conference that prepared the Stockholm Convention appointed an expert group that included representatives of various chemical industry BINGOs.

International law has, at this stage, no norms governing participation by non-state actors in international organizations, and each international organization or conference has developed its own procedures. As a theoretical matter, vast participatory rights are possible, including voting, membership in decision-making organs, and budgetary contributions, similar to the structure of the International Labour

---

[18] See World Summit on Sustainable Development, Johannesburg Plan of Implementation, in *Report of the World Summit on Sustainable Development*, Johannesburg, South Africa, 26 August–4 September 2002, UN Doc. A/CONF.199/20 (2002) at para. 49.

[19] J.H. Knox, 'A New Approach to Compliance with International Environmental Law: The Submissions Procedure of the NAFTA Environmental Commission' (2001) 28 Ecology L.Q. 1 at 49–50. The involvement of business in the PIC and ozone regimes can also be seen as an example of corporate roles in implementing international environmental law, discussed further in section 4 below.

Organization (see the discussion of the World Bank's prototype carbon fund later in this chapter).

3.3 Prescription through Private Codes

As discussed further in other chapters in this *Handbook*, industry has developed its own codes in numerous areas of the environment—in some cases, accompanied by enforcement mechanisms (see Chapter 21 'Private and Quasi-Private Standard Setting'). Some are merely pledges by individual companies to conduct operations according to vague principles—a sort of politically correct window-dressing for their public persona. Others are industry-wide standards monitored by impartial third parties with sanctions for non-compliance. In some situations, businesses are trying to take the initiative away from the mandatory regulation by states or international organizations by addressing an issue on its own terms. In others, they may be trying to influence the content of an expected mandatory regime. For example, with respect to oil pollution, during the negotiations on compensation for oil pollution damage, the major tank owners created the Tanker Owners Voluntary Agreement on Liability for Oil Pollution. Eventually, joined by nearly all privately owned tanker owners, the agreement required members to take out insurance sufficient to compensate states for preventive and cleanup costs associated with crude oil spills. The agreement filled an important gap in remediation law until the 1992 expansion of the compensation regime under the International Oil Pollution Prevention Fund.[20] Similarly, the 1994 Code of Ethics on International Trade in Chemicals was drafted by UNEP in consultation with industry and eventually endorsed by a broad range of chemical companies and BINGOs. It represented a heightened set of expectations for business, beyond those in previous soft law instruments prepared by the FAO and UNEP, and formed a critical stepping stone to the PIC Convention.[21]

Today, the coverage of private codes is enormous. The International Organization of Standardization (ISO) is perhaps at the apex of sophistication with its series 14000 standards. Other codes are industry-specific, such as those of Responsible Care in the chemical industry, which contains a set of general principles and encourages national associations to adopt detailed codes of conduct to carry out the principles.

The use of the term 'codes' or 'private codes' rather than 'norms' or 'law' reflects the orthodoxy's insistence that only states can make international environmental law— even soft law. Yet international standards represent yet another challenge to the orthodoxy, for many of them have the key hallmarks of law: (1) prescription by

---

[20] S. Bloodworth, 'Death on the High Seas: The Demise of TOVALOP and CRISTAL' (1998) 13 J. Land Use & Envt'l L. 443.

[21] W.B. Chambers, 'WSSD and an International Regime on Access and Benefit Sharing: Is a Protocol the Appropriate Legal Instrument?' (2003) 12 R.E.C.I.E.L. 310 at 317.

authoritative bodies, namely broadly representative industry groups with detailed expertise in environmental issues as well as in the technical areas of a certain sector; (2) actual compliance by critical actors; and (3) effective mechanisms for inducing compliance, such as auditing with the public exposure of results, and the use by other private actors (for example, purchasers and insurance companies) of linkages to the benefits they provide. Indeed, industry leaders and some scholars have suggested that these codes are far more important to the environmental conduct of industry than anything promulgated by governments.[22]

If codes can exhibit these core indicia of law, is there, then, any added value in the appraisal of the international environmental law landscape to distinguishing between law (treaty, custom, and soft) and private code? I would suggest that the law/private code distinction remains a useful analytic construct because the former offers two potential advantages compared to the latter. First, although corporate codes may be authoritative among corporations, instruments resulting from the pre-scriptive process of states have a greater potential for legitimacy among all interested actors in the international environmental process. State-prescribed norms probably have a better chance of reflecting non-business interests—such as those of environmental NGOs, labour unions, human rights, and individuals—than do business codes. The output of state-dominated processes may not, in fact, be any more pro-tective of the environment—in that states have numerous other interests beyond such protection—but, at least, it comes closer to incorporating the views of a multi-tude of relevant viewpoints (in UN jargon, 'stakeholders'). Even joint business-NGO initiatives can suffer a legitimacy deficit on this account, as each is prone to capture by the other.

Second, although corporate codes may be effectively enforced through private mechanisms, norms issued by states have a greater likelihood of enforcement through the coercive power of the state, including its courts and regulatory bodies. These public bodies will be more receptive to norms that governments have endorsed than to those from business alone. Governments will be reluctant or even legally unable to enforce business-initiated codes, however salutary they may be, until those norms have been re-issued through governmental channels. If an international con-vention endorses a certain standard on emissions and industry endorses a higher standard, only the former will be enforced by governments. At the same time, in the absence of norms created by treaty or of decisions of an international organization, governments may enforce non-binding codes (as some base their procurement deci-sions on a product's compliance with ISO standards). The World Trade Organization (WTO) Agreement on the Application of Sanitary and Phytosanitary Measures, while giving special status to codes developed by three international organizations, allows governments to rely upon private codes as a scientific basis for controlling the importation of products (if the organizations producing them are open to all WTO

---

[22] See, e.g., Braithwaite and Drahos, note 2 above at 615–16.

members). Moreover, even binding codes risk under-enforcement in states whose regulatory structures are weak.

4 BUSINESS ROLES IN THE IMPLEMENTATION OF INTERNATIONAL ENVIRONMENTAL LAW

Environmental law demonstrates the possibilities, as well as the hazards, of extensive business involvement in the implementation and enforcement of international law. Business has begun to engage in the sort of roles previously seen as the province of governments.

4.1 Cooperative Projects

Many business entities, in particular, large TNCs or BINGOs, have access to significant resources to promote compliance with international environmental law. One option is simple technical training. For example, the WBCSD produces guides for companies to operate in more environmentally sensitive ways. Business can also assist governments, particularly by funding conferences and other programmes in developing countries. The world's leading pesticide BINGO has sponsored educational programmes, training, and the transfer of equipment to some developing countries to improve pesticide management.[23]

Beyond training, companies participate actively in projects, particularly in the developing world, with the stated goal of meeting various hard or soft environmental commitments. At the Johannesburg Summit, governments gave their formal stamp of approval to a prominent role for business in carrying out the (non-treaty) commitments of Agenda 21, Rio + 5, and the Johannesburg Plan of Implementation itself. They endorsed and announced the formation of 200 so-called Type II partnerships of governments, business, NGOs, and local communities to supplement governmental undertakings. The WSSD Prepcom, the UN General Assembly (in Resolution 56/76 of 2002), and the UN Commission on Sustainable Development (CSD) produced guidelines on these partnerships that emphasize transparency,

---

[23] D.G. Victor, ' "Learning by Doing" in the Nonbinding International Regime to Manage Trade in Hazardous Chemicals and Pesticides,' in D.G. Victor, K. Raustiala, and E.B. Skolnikoff, eds., *The Implementation and Effectiveness of International Environmental Commitments: Theory and Practice* (Cambridge, MA: MIT Press, 1998) 221 at 254–5.

accountability, and close involvement with governments in implementing projects. Of the 319 partnerships registered with the CSD as of early 2006, 43 per cent had business and industry partners.[24] Yet many scholars and NGOs have criticized the Type II partnerships as more of a publicity stunt than a coherent part of the WSSD process. Beyond concerns that the partnerships will become an excuse for governments to ignore their own commitments, they note that the various UN guidelines are too vague and give the CSD no authority to ensure that the partnerships will actually advance the specific priorities in the Johannesburg Plan of Implementation or include the relevant stakeholders. Reporting by corporations is voluntary, and the commission's role is merely to foster dialogue on the success of these programs.[25]

Outside the WSSD process, the World Bank has created a prototype carbon fund (PCF), which is funded by six governments and 17 companies, including BP/Amoco, Deutsche Bank, Mitsubishi, and Statoil. The PCF funds projects in developing countries that reduce or contain carbon emissions, allowing the participating governments to purchase emission reduction units that lower their cost of compliance with the Kyoto Protocol to the UN Framework Convention on Climate Change. And business has undertaken a particularly innovative role regarding bio-prospecting. While governments and industry have worked to produce guidelines on the environmental and intellectual property issues associated with the process (with the goal of a legally binding regime), a number of businesses, principally in the pharmaceutical area, have concluded agreements directly with developing world governments or NGOs. In these contracts, the company is allowed to harvest certain plants, insects, or other specimens for research in exchange for certain benefits to the local actors. The first, a 1991 contract between US-based Merck and a Costa Rican scientific NGO, gave the latter funding, equipment, and a share in the future earnings from any drugs marketed using the specimens. Another biotechnology company, Diversa, has concluded agreements with institutions in Kenya, Ghana, and elsewhere that similarly combine royalties with scientific training and support for research. Other companies are partnering with academic institutions under the auspices of several US government agencies to engage in bio-prospecting in ten states in Asia, Latin America, and Africa.

4.2 Monitoring and Enforcement of Business Behaviour

Businesses also monitor company compliance with rules or standards. The resulting audits may be consumed internally or seized upon by outside actors, such as

[24] UN Economic and Social Council, *Partnerships for Sustainable Development—Report of the Secretary General*, prepared for fourteenth session of the Commission on Sustainable Development, UN Doc. E/CN.17/2006/6 (11–22 April 2005).

[25] See, e.g., C. Bruch and J. Pendergrass, 'The Road from Johannesburg: Type II Partnerships, International Law, and the Commons' (2003) 15 Geo. Int'l Envt'l L. Rev. 855.

consumer, labour, and environmental NGOs, to mobilize shame against companies. Among the most successful and best regarded monitors is the Swiss company SGS. The executive board of the clean development mechanism (CDM) under the Kyoto Protocol has accredited SGS and 15 other companies to validate proposed CDM projects, monitor their emissions, and certify their emission reductions. At the same time, global accounting firms have faced accusations from NGOs of inadequate monitoring and capture by their clients.

Industry is also capable of inducing compliance through more significant carrots and sticks. The major studies of oil pollution by Michael M'Gonigle, Mark Zacher, and Ronald Mitchell give a picture of the range of inducements and sanctions.[26] After the adoption by IMCO in 1969 of amendments to the MARPOL Convention, which required ships to use the load-on-top system (LOT) and to limit intentional discharges of oil residues in empty tankers, most large oil companies agreed to compensate independent tank owners for the additional costs associated with LOT, thereby encouraging its use. When amendments in 1973 and 1978 required more effective oil pollution prevention measures, such as the installation of segregated ballast tanks, classification societies—that is, large corporations that measure numerous characteristics of a ship and classify them—withheld certification from ships that did not meet the MARPOL Convention rules. Insurance companies provided insurance only if the standards were met. In the years before the Stockholm Convention, the world's leading pesticide BINGO required its members to comply with the FAO's non-binding Code of Conduct on the Distribution and Use of Pesticides as a condition for membership.[27]

Business efforts at enforcement have potential advantages compared to state or interstate enforcement. States might not agree upon certain standards at all on a certain issue, in which case industry's efforts to enforce its own standards may represent the only form of environmental protection. States may also agree upon standards but not upon an enforcement strategy, which industry might develop for self-interested reasons. In addition, states might agree upon a strategy, but some might be economically unable to carry out their enforcement obligations or simply not be parties to the relevant treaties. The cooperative attitude by many large companies towards elements of the export control regimes in the PIC Convention, the Stockholm Convention, and the Cartagena Protocol—for example, making the necessary notifications even if their home state is not a party—helps overcome structural shortcomings in the developing world. In this sense, private enforcement fills gaps in the public enforcement regime.

Second, from an economic perspective, industry may impose greater costs upon non-complying companies than can government. The denial of certification to a product, the public revelation of an audit revealing unsound practices, or the denial

---

[26] See Mitchell, note 13 above; and M'Gonigle and Zacher, note 17 above.
[27] Victor, see note 23 above at 255.

of membership in a leading BINGO could prove more devastating to a firm's reputation than any fine. Third, and also from an economic perspective, industry enforcement may be cheaper and more efficient than enforcement through regulation or liability regimes. Enforcement entities may be cheaper to run and less corrupt, and the targets might more easily internalize compliance costs when those imposing the costs are business partners working alongside them during their operations.

Finally, enforcement by industry, whether of its own standards or of those developed by governments, can take place in a club-like atmosphere of repeat players with a stake in maintaining their reputation within an industry. And when businesses work together with NGOs, international organizations, or other groups in the enforcement process—as occurs in the case of the Fair Labor Association with respect to worker rights—the advantages of the club can be combined with the advantages of outside perspectives. Nonetheless, most such partnerships—for example, the Global Reporting Initiative or the WBCSD—limit their role principally to encouraging businesses to adopt favourable policies rather than the more assertive forms of enforcement.

On the negative side, businesses face incentives to downplay or ignore violations. At the most basic level, if the major players, or enough minor players, in an industry see environmental regulation as limiting profits, then the prospects for enforcement by individual businesses or BINGOs are constrained. Industry codes can have free riders; the club-like atmosphere within an industry can just as easily translate into modest costs for violators; all parties may have an incentive to keep violations hidden from the public; and auditors are typically paid by those they are auditing. As much as business portrays itself as progressive environmentally, the enforcement role of governments, international organizations, non-business NGOs, and individual victims of pollution (through civil liability) remains critical.[28] Most empirical studies offer a decidedly mixed picture of company monitoring, emphasizing the need for both public and private enforcement.

4.3 Litigation

Litigation in international and domestic venues represents a more adversarial mode of business participation, one oriented towards resisting the implementation of environmental controls. In the WTO, businesses have prodded and litigated alongside states in order to perpetuate environmentally sensitive or damaging activities by asserting that another state's environmental policies were inconsistent with the

---

[28] See, e.g., N. Gunningham and D. Sinclair, *Voluntary Approaches to Environmental Protection: Lessons from the Mining and Forestry Sectors*, paper for OECD Global Forum on International Investment, Conference on Foreign Direct Investment and the Environment, 7–8 February 2002.

General Agreement on Tariffs and Trade. Mexico, on behalf of its tuna fleet, challenged the United States in the early 1990s, and four Asian states acted to protect their fishing fleets against US legislation in the *United States—Prohibition of Shrimps and Certain Shrimp Products* proceedings in the mid-1990s.[29] Indeed, if the United States did impose the measures to protect its domestic fishing fleets, as the claimants alleged, then corporations were shadow players on the respondent's side too.

The European Court of Justice (ECJ) has also heard cases involving business interests in cases referred from national courts. In the 1982 case of *Syndicat National des Fabricants Raffineurs d'Huile de Graissage and Others v. Groupement d'Intérêt Economique 'Inter-Huiles' and Others,* [30] the plaintiff, which had been granted sole authority to collect waste oils under a French law implementing an European Community (EC) directive, sued a competitor for unapproved collections and exportations to other EC states. The court upheld the competitor's claim that France's prohibition on exportation by unauthorized collectors was inconsistent with the free movement of goods. It held that environmental protection could be assured as long as the oils were exported to an authorized disposal entity in another state. In *Etablissements Armand Mondiet v. Armement Islais* (1992),[31] the plaintiff manufacturer of driftnets sued the defendant tuna fisher after the latter cancelled its contract for nets following a new EC regulation banning the use of certain nets. When the French courts found the cancellation justified based on *force majeure*, assuming the regulation was valid, the ECJ upheld the regulation as within the EC's competence. *Mondiet* and subsequent cases have explicitly incorporated principles of international environmental law in construing Community law.

In arbitrations under the North American Free Trade Agreement (NAFTA), US companies have challenged Mexican and Canadian environmental measures under the treaty's investment protection provisions. Tribunals have upheld domestic regulatory actions on the environment against most claims, although in *Metalclad v. Mexico*, a NAFTA panel found that a Mexican state's efforts to regulate a toxic waste dump constituted an expropriation,[32] and in *S.D. Myers v. Canada*, a panel found that Canada's ban on polychlorinated biphenyl (PCB) exports violated NAFTA's minimum standard of treatment.[33] As with the WTO and ECJ proceedings, the claimants in these cases, in part, alleged that the respondent's actions were motivated by a protectionist desire on behalf of its domestic companies.

Corporations have also been involved in domestic litigation. In a few cases, domestic courts have entertained suits by states against businesses under the civil liability

---

[29] *United States—Import Prohibition of Certain Shrimp and Shrimp Products*, adopted WTO Dispute Settlement Body, 6 November 1998, WTO Appellate Body Report, Doc. WT/DS58/AB/R (1998).

[30] *Syndicat National des Fabricants Raffineurs d'Huile de Graissage and Others v. Groupement d'Intérêt Economique 'Inter-Huiles' and Others*, Case 172/82, [1983] E.C.R. 555.

[31] *Etablissements Armand Mondiet v. Armement Islais*, Case C-405/92, [1993] E.C.R.I-6133.

[32] *Metalclad Corporation v. United Mexican States*, ICSID Case no. Arb(AF)/97/1; 40 I.L.M. 35 (2001).

[33] *S.D. Myers v. Government of Canada*, 40 I.L.M. 1408 (2001).

terms of environmental conventions. Domestic courts have found that certain damage was covered by the insurance scheme created under the treaty (in particular, the International Convention on Civil Liability for Oil Pollution Damage).[34] Cases by alleged victims of environmental harm against companies under the US Alien Tort Claims Act, which seek to rely on international environmental norms, have not resulted in any successes for plaintiffs. In other cases, domestic courts have decided cases against corporations for environmental damage based on the forum state's environmental law that is itself based on the polluter pays principle or its general tort law. On the other hand, cases dealing with overseas environmental damage brought in the United States, Canada, the Netherlands, Australia, and the United Kingdom (for example, the claim against Union Carbide in the United States for the Bhopal disaster) have often been dismissed on the basis of *forum non conveniens*. Yet in *Thor Chemicals* and *Cape PLC*, concerning operations by UK subsidiaries in South Africa that created hazards for workers and residents, the British courts rejected defenses of *forum non conveniens*, causing both companies to settle for fairly large amounts.[35]

5 EXITING THE DOCTRINAL THICKET

From a reading of treaties, inter-state arbitrations such as *Trail Smelter*, and treatises, one would get the impression that the onus for both prevention of pollution and reparation for harm is on states and their governments, when states are neither the principal polluters nor the principal remediators. The participation of corporations as critical targets, prescribers, and enforcers of norms stands as an almost parallel universe to the doctrine that places states in a unique position. International relations scholars have tended not to fall prey to this blindness. They examine the behaviour of states at international negotiations but have few illusions about why states adopt the positions they do, who else is participating in these negotiations, and what happens in terms of compliance mechanisms and patterns. They perceive states as unique actors in some sense—the ability to enter into treaties—but ultimately as one of many in the international environmental law process—in Drahos and Braithwaite's words, as just another 'loci of legitimacy and power waiting to be captured, networked and used as vehicles for the regulatory models of individual model mongers.'[36]

Rather than incorrectly describing reality to fit the doctrine, it is time for doctrine to modernize itself. One solution is to return to first principles of jurisprudence—

---

[34] See the discussion in Sands, note 5 above at 918–22.

[35] These are discussed in H. Ward, 'Towards a New Convention on Corporate Accountability? Some Lessons from the Thor Chemicals and Cape PLC Cases' (2001) 12 Y.B. Int'l Envt'l L. 105.

[36] Braithwaite and Drahos, see note 2 above at 275.

rights and duties—and to ask, directly and without preconceived doctrinal cat-egories—who has them under international environmental law? One might start with rights (of states and non-state actors alike) and construct duties from these rights. As Joseph Raz has stated, 'there is no closed list of duties which correspond to the right . . . A change of circumstances may lead to the creation of new duties based on the old right.'[37] The field of international human rights is obviously organized around the latter paradigm—rights first, though scholarly treatments now consider more carefully who bears the corresponding duties.[38] International environmental law has been more nuanced—for example, in the tension between the two parts of the transboundary harm principle (the right to exploit resources and the duty not to cause damage to other states). Although the idea of a human right to a clean environ-ment is gaining acceptance among states, this notion, as well as the rest of inter-national environmental law, still focuses on the corresponding duties of states and ignores Raz's admonition about the range of dutyholders. Alternatively, one may construct a legal system as Kant did, based on duties, and ask which duties each inter-national actor possesses regarding environmental protection.

Reconceptualizing international environmental law in terms of duties means ask-ing these fundamental questions: Who bears the duties? What are their scope? How normatively grounded are they in terms of our views of appropriate prescriptive processes? How are they enforced—by whom and in what venues? Where does the system need new duties and new dutyholders? From this perspective, the companies fit in alongside states, international organizations, and non-state entities such as NGOs. Treaties, state practice, and case law will be reappraised for the extent to which they create duties. Corporate standards and strategies must not be relegated to a sep-arate narrative but integrated into the discussion of every environmental law issue. States will not drop out of the picture. To the extent that they control access to venues and membership in intergovernmental organizations, they will always occupy a spe-cial place in our consideration of duties—but this place will be less dominant than suggested by the International Law Commission, the Institut de Droit International, or keepers of the orthodoxy. I suspect most practising international environmental lawyers are already asking these sorts of questions. It is time for doctrine to catch up with them.

[37] J. Raz, *The Morality of Freedom* (Oxford: Oxford University Press, 1986) at 171.
[38] See, e.g., S.R. Ratner, 'Corporations and Human Rights: A Theory of Legal Responsibility' (2001) 111 Yale L.J. 443.

Recommended Reading

P. Barrios, 'The Rotterdam Convention on Hazardous Chemicals: A Meaningful Step Toward Environmental Protection?' (2004) 16 Geo. Int'l Envt'l L. Rev. 679.

J. Braithwaite and P. Drahos, *Global Business Regulation* (Cambridge: Cambridge University Press, 2000).

A. Daniel, 'Civil Liability Regimes as a Complement to Multilateral Environmental Agreements: Sound International Policy or False Comfort?' (2003) 12 R.E.C.I.E.L. 225.

R.J. Fowler, 'International Environmental Standards for Transnational Corporations' (1995) 25 Envt'l L. 1.

A. Gupta, 'Advanced Informed Agreement: A Shared Basis for Governing Trade in Genetically Modified Organisms?' (2001) 9 Indiana J. Global Leg. Stud. 265.

R.B. Mitchell, *Intentional Oil Pollution at Sea: Environmental Policy and Treaty Compliance* (Cambridge, MA: MIT Press, 1994).

Organisation for Economic Cooperation and Development, *Corporate Responsibility: Private Initiatives and Public Goals* (Paris: OECD, 2001).

S.R. Ratner, 'Corporations and Human Rights: A Theory of Legal Responsibility' (2001) 111 Yale L.J. 443.

S. Tully, 'The Bonn Guidelines on Access to Genetic Resources and Benefit Sharing' (2003) 12 R.E.C.I.E.L. 84.

D.G. Victor, ' "Learning by Doing" in the Nonbinding International Regime to Manage Trade in Hazardous Chemicals and Pesticides,' in D.G. Victor, K. Raustiala, and E.B. Skolnikoff, eds., *The Implementation and Effectiveness of International Environmental Commitments: Theory and Practice* (Cambridge, MA: MIT Press, 1998) 221.

CHAPTER 36

INDIGENOUS PEOPLES

RUSSEL LAWRENCE BARSH

> Indigenous peoples and their communities and other local communities have a vital role in environmental management and development because of their knowledge and traditional practices. States should recognize and duly support their identity, culture and interests and enable their effective participation in the achievement of sustainable development.
>
> Principle 22, Rio Declaration on Environment and Development

1 INTRODUCTION

INDIGENOUS peoples have sought to protect their way of life by asserting the indivisibility between indigenous culture and the land on which indigenous communities live, in national as well as international forums. Gradually, the international community has recognized distinctive rights for indigenous peoples. This chapter first treats the emergence of indigenous peoples' rights in international law in its historic context. Subsequently, it addresses conceptual issues related to the position of indigenous peoples in international law. These conceptual issues concern critical distinctions and assumptions related to the definition of what constitutes an 'indigenous people' and, especially, the distinction between minority and indigenous peoples' rights and the collective representation of indigenous peoples. The chapter then moves on to address the role of indigenous peoples in international environmental law with a focus on distinctively indigenous rights and responsibilities.

While this chapter addresses indigenous rights as they relate to international environmental law, a broader perspective is also developed. The latter relates to the content of indigenous peoples' rights as intimately related to their land and, thus, to the environment. More succinctly put, indigenous rights, and especially substantive rights, relate to the environment, regardless of whether they are pursued in the context of the International Labour Organization (ILO) or the Commission on Sustainable Development (CSD).

2 DEVELOPMENT OF THE CONCEPT OF INDIGENOUS PEOPLES IN INTERNATIONAL LAW

The legal concept of indigenous peoples emerged in the League of Nations period and continues to evolve in theory and application. It generally applies to groups that base their claims on the distinctive territoriality of their cultures, and would be regarded as the inhabitants of non-self-governing territories, but for their geographic location within an existing state and their small size. Indeed, indigenous peoples have long maintained that the failure of international institutions to recognize their right to self-determination constitutes discrimination on racial or cultural lines. While indigenous peoples' representatives at inter-governmental meetings continue to press this argument, governments have increasingly responded by making concessions with respect to 'internal' self-determination—that is to say, the right of indigenous peoples to govern themselves within their own traditional territories, subject to the 'external' self-determination and territorial integrity of the states within which indigenous peoples live.

The terms 'colonies', 'native inhabitants', 'indigenous population', and 'peoples not yet able to stand by themselves' appear interchangeably in Articles 22 and 23 of the 1919 League of Nations Covenant, which promises them 'just treatment' at the hands of administering powers. While the League of Nations Covenant identifies 'peoples' as the objects of protection, existing colonial boundaries were respected in practice and little attention was paid to the diversity of cultures found within these territorial units. Former European colonies that had achieved their independence prior to 1919 were omitted altogether from the concept of 'peoples' contained in the covenant. Consequently, no consideration was given to the possibility that some of these states, for example, in the Americas, could be composed of indigenous societies dominated by small numbers of European settlers.

Although the Charter of the United Nations expressly recognizes the equal right of all 'peoples' to self-determination, it describes the object of international protection only as 'non-self-governing territories,' without referring to 'indigenous peoples' (as the League of Nations Covenant does) or to historically and culturally distinct groups. The Charter thereby appears to ratify the League of Nation's practice of respecting colonial boundaries regardless of their relationship to ethnographic realities. The UN General Assembly (UNGA) strengthened this impression in 1960 with Resolution 1514, which defines non-self-governing territories as lands administered by a geographically separate and culturally distinct state. This definition excluded encircled groups, such as tribal peoples in the interior rainforests of Brazil, even if they had experienced military subjection, economic exploitation, and continued social marginalization.

UNGA Resolution 2025 in 1970, entitled the Declaration on Friendly Relations among States, reopened the issue of 'internal colonization' by conditioning the territorial integrity of existing states on the extent to which their governments 'effectively represent the whole of their population.' A state that persists in exploiting or excluding indigenous peoples may therefore be legally obligated either to bring them voluntarily into power-sharing arrangements at the national level or, if that fails, to accept an internationally supervised exercise of self-determination—such as a referendum of indigenous peoples on their future relationship with the state.[1] This

---

[1] Best argued by E.-I.A. Daes in her capacity at that time as chairperson of the Working Group on Indigenous Populations, in *Explanatory Note Concerning the Draft Declaration on the Rights of Indigenous Peoples*, UN Doc. E/CN.4/Sub.2/1993/26/Add.1 (1993) at 4–6.

viewpoint is consistent with the views of the International Court of Justice in the *Case Concerning East Timor (Portugal v. Australia)*[2] and in the *Legal Consequences for States of the Continued Presence of South Africa in Nambia (South-West Africa) Notwithstanding Security Council Resolution 276*,[3] on the implications of *carence de souveraineté* or gross failure of the duties of the state with respect to human rights and self-determination. A distinction between 'indigenous' and colonized peoples continues to be made in practice, however, due to the reluctance of the international community to intervene in cases of internal colonization.

The particular situation of 'indigenous' peoples emerged in the 1950s, while the UNGA was preoccupied with dismantling empires in Africa and Asia. Latin American states asked the ILO to investigate the increase of unemployment and poverty in that region's rapidly expanding cities. In a 1957 report, the ILO concluded that the region's urban problem was actually a land problem. Industrialization and the exploitation of natural resources were displacing indigenous peoples ('Indians'), and landless indigenous peoples were migrating to cities where they remained marginalized and exploited as unskilled workers. The ILO study led to the adoption of the 1959 Convention on Indigenous and Tribal Populations (No. 107), which was the first international instrument to address the situation of 'indigenous' peoples as a separate category from non-self-governing territories or minorities. It applies only to economically and culturally distinct groups living within the borders of independent states, in particular, 'indigenous populations' that pre-existed the state and its dominant population (the typical case in the Americas) and 'tribal' groups that have existed on the margins of dominant societies for millennia (more typical of Asia and Africa). A few European, African, and Asian states ratified the convention, but 15 of its 27 ratifications were in Latin America. The ILO eventually responded to indigenous criticism by adopting a stronger instrument, the 1989 Convention on Indigenous and Tribal Peoples (No. 169), which has been ratified by 17 states (all but three of them in Latin America). Both instruments are currently in force.

The situation of indigenous peoples had meanwhile attracted the attention of the UN Commission on Human Rights. An encyclopaedic study of conditions of indigenous peoples by José R. Martínez Cobo, which was undertaken from 1971 to 1983,[4] was accompanied by a global mobilization of indigenous peoples led by the formation of the World Council of Indigenous Peoples and its successful bid for non-governmental organization (NGO) status with the UN Economic and Social Council (ECOSOC). Human rights NGOs organized global conferences on indigenous peoples in Geneva in 1977 and 1981, leading to the establishment of

---

[2] *Case Concerning East Timor (Portugal v. Australia)*, Judgment of 30 June 1995, [1995] I.C.J. Rep. 90.

[3] *Legal Consequences for States of the Continued Presence of South Africa in Nambia (South-West Africa) Notwithstanding Security Council Resolution 276*, Advisory Opinion of 21 June 1971, [1971] I.C.J. Rep. 3 at 28–34.

[4] For an overview, see *Study of the Problem of Discrimination against Indigenous Populations; Volume V: Conclusions, Proposals and Recommendations*, UN Doc. E/CN.4/Sub.2/1986/7/Add.4 (1986).

a Working Group on Indigenous Populations within the Sub-Commission on Prevention of Discrimination and Protection of Minorities in 1982; the proclamation of 1993 as the International Year of Indigenous People and 1994–2003 as the International Decade for Indigenous People; the establishment in 2002 of the Permanent Forum on Indigenous Issues as an expert advisory body to ECOSOC, with governmental and indigenous experts appointed by the secretary-general; and the adoption of a draft United Nations Declaration on the Rights of Indigenous Peoples (UNDRIP)[5] by the Human Rights Council, with the recommendation that it be adopted by the UN General Assembly, which could take place as early as December 2006.

3 CONCEPTUAL ISSUES RELATED TO THE POSITION OF INDIGENOUS PEOPLES IN INTERNATIONAL LAW

3.1 Critical Assumptions and Distinctions

The international legal concept of 'minority' arose in the same era and political environment that shaped the League of Nations' use of the term 'indigenous', and although the two concepts share certain traits, they should be carefully distinguished. Contemporary law on the protection of minorities arose from the 1919 Treaty of Versailles, which led to a realignment of national borders throughout Europe and to the adoption of 23 multilateral treaties on the protection of 'minorities' in central and eastern Europe and the Middle East. Article 27 of the International Covenant on Civil and Political Rights (ICCPR) extended the principles contained in the League of Nation's minority treaties to all countries 'in which ethic, religious, or linguistic minorities exist.' Although states have not been able to agree on a single definition of 'minorities', there is general agreement on the relevance of numerical inferiority, collective solidarity, and the desire to perpetuate their distinctive identities, including, in particular, their language and nationality.[6]

Indigenous people in many countries have enjoyed some degree of recognition, 'protection' or supervision as minorities. In North America, Brazil, and some Australian federal states, for example, indigenous communities were concentrated

---

[5] Draft Report to the General Assembly on the First Session of the Human Rights Council, UN Doc. A/HRC/1/L.10, at 58–70 (30 June 2006).

[6] See J. Deschênes, *Proposal Concerning a Definition of the Term 'Minority,'* UN Doc. E/CN.4/ Sub.2/1985/31 (1985).

on 'reserves' supervised by state authorities.[7] Indigenous organizations, however, have objected vigorously to any association of their situation with the concept of 'minorities'. The concept of minority rights focuses on entrenching the legal equality of minorities with other citizens, as well as limited albeit non-territorial autonomy with respect to language, culture, and religion. As the Permanent Court explained in *Minority Schools in Albania*,[8] the purpose of the minority treaty regime was to ensure the right of the protected groups to perpetuate their linguistic, religious, and cultural identities. Although Article 27 of the ICCPR entitles persons to enjoy minority rights 'in community with other members of their group,' minority rights are individual in nature. The aim is to protect the right of individuals to choose freely the degree to which they remain ethnically separate or integrate into national society. In contrast, indigenous rights are group rights. Indigenous peoples have sought, not equality, but rather some degree of collective territorial autonomy, arguing that *territorial* sovereignty is indispensable for the enjoyment of their distinctive ways of life.

Indigenous peoples have justified their distinctive claims on the basis that the uniqueness of their cultures and the gravity of their situation require a different approach. First, indigenous peoples argue that, in contrast to minorities, they are defined by a special relationship with the land. 'The relationship with the land and all living things is at the core of indigenous societies.'[9] The claim that indigenous peoples are the best and most legitimate custodians of their traditional lands has enjoyed growing popularity. It gained political legitimacy when the UN Conference on Environment and Development (UNCED), in Chapter 26 of Agenda 21, recognized that '[i]ndigenous peoples and their communities have an historical relationship with their lands' as well as a distinct role in achieving sustainable development. This argument also implies limitations on the rights of indigenous peoples, however. If indigenous peoples' rights flow from their relationship to traditional lands, it would seem to follow that unsustainable use is incompatible with the collective ownership of those lands. Furthermore, displacement, relocation, or urbanization would appear to diminish a group's identity and rights as an indigenous people.

Second, indigenous peoples contend that they differ from minorities in that they have been, and continue to be, consistently made targets of genocide and ethnocide—that is, state actions that aim at, or result in, the physical destruction of a group or its cultural distinctiveness. This broad claim is difficult to dispute or to assess. The 1948 Convention on the Prevention and Punishment of the Crime of Genocide was not adopted with particular reference to indigenous peoples nor do other existing international norms regarding genocide address the reconstitution of the victims' territorial sovereignty, which is the principal aim of indigenous peoples. The UN

---

[7] However, the indigenous leaders contended that the state administration of reserves was in reality a form of colonial oppression with the aim of eventually coercing indigenous peoples to assimilate into national society.   [8] *Minority Schools in Albania*, [1935] P.C.I.J. (ser. A/B) No. 64.

[9] *Indigenous Peoples and Their Relationship to Land; Final Working Paper Prepared by the Special Rapporteur, Mrs. Erica-Irene a. Daes*, UN Doc. E/CN.4/Sub.2/2001/21 (2001) para. 13 at 7.

Commission on Human Rights long resisted any expansion of the definition of genocide to include ethnocide, moreover. However, UNDRIP expressly prohibits acts of ethnocide such as displacement, forced assimilation, and the removal of children from indigenous communities (Article 8).

As a result of vigorous objections by indigenous groups to any association of their situation with the concept of 'minorities', the UN Commission on Human Rights maintained separate working groups for the elaboration of declarations on minorities and indigenous peoples from 1982 to 1993. As adopted, the Declaration on Minorities reiterates the long-standing principles of equality and limited autonomy, adding that states should also promote and, within their means, contribute financial resources towards minorities' perpetuation of their distinctive characteristics.[10] By comparison, UNDRIP reflects their demand that they enjoy as much collective territorial power as they choose.

The term 'indigenous peoples' has never been authoritatively defined. As a result, there continue to be instances where the indigenousness of a particular individual or group is ambiguous and contested by the state.[11] In the exercise of its authority to hear individual communications (complaints) arising under the ICCPR, the Human Rights Committee has examined several disputes of this nature. As a general rule, the committee reasoned in a case from Canada, 'persons who are born and brought up on a reserve [that is, within a state-designated indigenous community], who have kept ties with their community and wish to maintain those ties must normally be considered as belonging to that minority' [sic].[12] Likewise, an individual's way of life is an appropriate criterion for ethnic membership.[13] However, the committee has held that a group of mixed European and African ancestry is not an indigenous people, while acknowledging that they 'developed their own society, culture, language and economy, with which they largely sustained their own institutions, such as schools and community centers.'[14] It is difficult to dispel the impression that an outdated notion of 'race' has played some role in this decision.

A more precise and satisfactory definition of 'indigenous' may gradually evolve in practice, if UN organs and treaty bodies take a purposive approach in which a group's entitlement to classification as 'indigenous' is a function of the nature of its claims and aspirations. Historically and geographically, distinct groups seeking greater control over traditionally used lands and living resources in order to protect

---

[10] Declaration on the Rights of Persons Belonging to National or Ethnic, Religious and Linguistic Minorities, UNGA Resolution 135 (1992).

[11] *Report of the Special Rapporteur on the Situation of Human Rights and Fundamental Freedoms of Indigenous People, Mr. Rodolfo Stavenhagen*, UN Doc. E/CN.4/2002/97 (2002) para. 107 at 30.

[12] *Lovelace v. Canada*, Communication no. 24/1977 (1980), reprinted in *Selected Decisions under the Optional Protocol*, UN Doc. CCPR/C/OP/1 (1985) 83–7, para. 14 at 86 [*Lovelace*].

[13] *Kitok v. Sweden*, Communication no. 1987/195, reprinted in UN Doc. CCPR/C/33/D/197/1985 (1988), paras. 9.1, 9.5, 9.6, and 9.7 [*Kitok*].

[14] *Diergaardt v. Namibia*, Communication no. 760/1997, reprinted in UN Doc. CCPR/C/69/D/760/1997 (2000) para. 2.1 at 2.

or achieve good human-ecological relationships (rather than mere cultural distinct-iveness) stand to benefit most from claiming indigenousness. Other historically disenfranchised and culturally distinct groups may find it easier to claim rights as minorities (if they are dispersed inside an existing state) or as non-self-governing territories (if they are geographically separate from the state or regionally concen-trated within it, possibly as a majority, and lack power in governing the state).

3.2 Collective Representation of Indigenous Peoples

Whether or not indigenous peoples are 'peoples' in the sense of Article 1 of the Charter of the United Nations (that is, entitled to the exercise of collective self-determination), there is little doubt that indigenous peoples hold and exercise rights as groups. In particular, they claim, and to a growing degree enjoy, rights to lands traditionally occupied or used by them, including a measure of collective regulatory control over the allocation and permissible uses of these lands and resources. This control raises the questions: Who speaks on behalf of indigenous groups? Who are their legitimate representatives? Given the existence of state-recognized organizations and groups of indigenous people, as well as international indigenous NGOs, traditional polities, and grassroots movements, it is necessary to determine which entities are eligible to exercise internationally recognized col-lective rights, such as land rights.

This question does not arise in human rights law more generally since multilateral human rights mechanisms are individualistic, and respond to claims made by indi-viduals claiming group membership or leadership.[15] Nor does it ordinarily arise in the case of NGOs, the most numerous non-state participants in UN activities, because they are recognized solely for the purpose of 'consultation' and not to assert their own claims against individual states. The ILO is an exception. National trade union associations have the right to vote, and the ILO accordingly has long-standing procedures for determining whether particular trade unions are genuinely represen-tative. With respect to indigenous groups, the UN, thus far, has largely avoided the problem of determining whether putative leaders or their organizations are legit-imate and representative.[16]

At the national level, many states have administrative procedures for confer-ring political recognition on particular organizations as the legal representatives of indigenous peoples. In Canada, for example, the federal Minister of Indian and

---

[15] For example, *Lovelace*, see note 12 above, and *Kitok*, see note 13 above.

[16] However, see *Mikmaq People v. Canada*, Communication no. 205/1986, reprinted in UN Doc. A/47/40 (1992), Annex IX, 214, in which the state party challenged the representative legitimacy of a trad-itional leader; and *Mahuika v. New Zealand*, Communication no. 547/1993, reprinted in UN Doc. CCPR/C/70/D/547/1993 (2000), in which members of several 'tribes' challenged the authority of national indigenous leaders to settle a fishing rights dispute.

Northern Affairs has legislative authority to determine which geographical communities constitute 'Indian Bands' or First Nations for the purposes of holding and governing reserved lands, while the Canadian prime minister is entrusted by the constitution with discretion to determine which national organizations of indigenous people may participate in intergovernmental conferences and negotiations.[17] Australia accepts as 'Aboriginal' any person that asserts an indigenous identity, and is recognized as being indigenous by an indigenous community. However, it negotiates land matters only with judicially determined 'traditional custodians' and distributes national social spending through an elected national indigenous council created and governed by federal legislation. Most Latin American states confer legitimacy on particular regional and national indigenous organizations by dealing with them. The identification of specific indigenous nations, tribes, or peoples is generally ad hoc.

Since the 1970s, intergovernmental bodies such as ECOSOC, the ILO Governing Body, and secretariats of other specialized agencies have privileged particular indigenous organizations by conferring consultative NGO status upon them, as well as selecting them as partners in the delivery of financial and technical assistance. There is a growing risk of competition between organizations legitimized by community roots, and organizations made credible by international recognition and support. Some indigenous people fear the emergence of a global indigenous elite that is significantly more removed from accountability to grassroots communities than state-sponsored, national-level indigenous organizations. A meeting of intergovernmental agencies and indigenous organizations in 1992 concluded that there is 'a responsibility on agency officials that deal with indigenous issues to be sensitive to this matter and to ascertain the legitimacy and representativity of persons purporting to speak and act on behalf of indigenous peoples.'[18]

Traditional leaders and customary institutions of community self-government may be more democratically representative and accountable than institutions that are officially recognized by the state and that depend on the state for legitimacy or financial support. Traditional polities operating under local customary laws have often survived, and continue to evolve from, pre-colonial forms of organization of indigenous peoples themselves, and, in many instances, they enjoy broad grassroots support in the absence of elections or other forms of legitimization promoted by the international community. However, it cannot simply be assumed that traditional leaders are just, accountable, or broadly representative. The most authoritative voice of a particular indigenous people is a question of fact no less relevant than the indigenousness of the group or the identification of its individual members.

[17] *Twinn v. Canada* [1987] 2 F.C. 450 (F.C.T.D.); and *The Queen v. Native Women's Association of Canada* [1994] 3 S.C.R. 627.

[18] *Note by the Secretariat: Report of a Consultation between Representatives of Indigenous Peoples and International Development, Human Rights and Other Agencies*, UN Doc. E/CN.4/1993/AC.4/TM.3/1 (1993) para. 19 at 5.

4 ROLE OF INDIGENOUS PEOPLES IN INTERNATIONAL ENVIRONMENTAL LAW

When indigenous peoples' organizations began actively asserting themselves in the United Nations system in the 1970s, they generally regarded themselves as colonized peoples or non-self-governing territories. However, it quickly became clear to them that member states were unwilling to address indigenous peoples' concerns through the decolonization machinery of the United Nations, whereas the doors to human rights bodies such as the Commission on Human Rights were open. At first, indigenous people were reluctant to associate their claims with the individualistic framework of human rights law, which treats only states and individuals as bearing international rights and responsibilities. Yet over the course of the 1980s, indigenous people began to participate in UN human rights bodies and succeeded in persuading them to recognize: (1) collective or community rights; (2) the important role of property rights, including land tenure and intellectual property, to human rights as well as environmental sustainability; and (3) the importance of involving grassroots organizations directly in the multilateral policy-making process. Once legitimized in the context of human rights, these principles were advanced successfully in the preparatory process for the UN Conference on Environment and Development (UNCED), where indigenous peoples became part of a broader platform shared by grassroots organizations of farmers, peasants, fishers, women, and youth, especially from developing countries. The principles were also incorporated into the final acts of UNCED and the Cairo Conference on Population and Development; in the text of the Convention on Biological Diversity (CBD); in the policies and practices of the UN CSD; in the 2002 Johannesburg Plan of Implementation[19] of the World Summit on Sustainable Development (WSSD); and in UNDRIP.

4.1 Community Rights and Partnerships

At international NGO conferences in 1977 and 1981 and at early meetings of the Working Group on Indigenous Populations in 1982–5, indigenous organizations argued the need for recognition of collective human rights as well as for individual responsibilities to the community. Many governments expressed concern that this approach undermined the post-1945 human rights paradigm of individual rights and state duties, and compared indigenous proposals with arguments made by the Soviet Union to justify the suppression of individual dissent and political opposition on the

---

[19] Johannesburg Plan of Implementation, in *Report of the World Summit on Sustainable Development*, Johannesburg, South Africa, 26 August–4 September 2002, UN Doc. A/CONF.199/20 (2002).

basis of community interests. On the other hand, the indigenous perspective won the sympathy of many African states as well as of NGOs from developing countries, especially in the context of their efforts to shift international development activities from large-scale industrial projects to small-scale community-based activities.

By the time of the UNCED preparatory negotiations in 1989–92, states as well as a broad spectrum of grassroots NGOs echoed indigenous leaders' focus on land and other forms of tangible and intangible property as collective human rights, interwoven with the right to self-determination. Indigenous peoples' insistence on recognition of community ownership and control of land evolved into a more general principle: 'local communities' have a major 'role' to play in achieving sustainability as partners in decision-making and implementation on the ground. It follows that governments should respect the distinctive interests and perspectives of local communities, and pursue development through a more decentralized system of 'partnerships' with communities. 'Partnership' implies genuine reciprocity: mutual respect, informed consent, and shared benefits. Privileging grassroots communities in this way ensures that people who live closest to forests, estuaries, oceans, and other critical ecosystems continue to have a significant stake in conservation as well as a direct voice in state measures for ecosystem protection.

4.2 Land and Ecological Knowledge

The protection of indigenous peoples' land rights differs from the general right to property as protected in, for example, Article 5(d)(v) of the UN Convention on the Elimination of Racial Discrimination (CERD). The latter secures the right of everyone 'to own property alone as well as in association with others' without discrimination. Narrowly construed, this norm leaves states considerable latitude to restrict the ownership of property, provided they apply the same restrictions to all sectors of society. Indigenous peoples have argued that they have been persistent victims of discrimination with respect to the right to own land and, in particular, that they have been denied the right to hold, use, and conserve their lands and living resources collectively as self-defined communities. In support of these claims, indigenous leaders have maintained that collective ownership of land is more compatible with sustainable use than individualized tenure systems, and that indigenous cultures foster sharing, moderation, and conservation. Their arguments go beyond the right to equal treatment by the state, implying that states must recognize some form of collective land ownership based on the traditions or customary laws of indigenous peoples.

While some states and NGOs seized upon this argument as support for greater public (state) control of land, others generalized the indigenous position to other landless, dispossessed, or displaced communities of peasants, fishing peoples, forest dwelling hunters, nomadic herders, and the *favelas* surrounding the world's expanding cities. Indigenous demands for land helped energize a broader argument for security of land tenure in cities as well as the countryside, which was justified as a means of promoting development, human rights, and more moderate population growth. Security of tenure was expressly endorsed by states in these terms at the International Conference on Population and Development in 1994 and has subsequently been invoked routinely by the Committee on Economic, Social and Cultural Rights and the Committee on the Elimination of Racial Discrimination.[20]

Land tenure has been recognized as a right solely in the context of individuals and communities, not corporations. As such, it is conceptually grounded in the contention that security of tenure creates an incentive for good stewardship. Importantly, it is also based on the assertion that indigenous peoples and other 'local communities' have accumulated valuable knowledge of the dynamics of the ecosystems from which they have traditionally drawn a livelihood, and have devised ways of managing living resources to ensure their long-term survival. To this extent, the security of land tenure recognized by international conferences in the 1990s is not an end in itself, but rather is being linked to a presumed capacity of local communities to contribute to sustainability as well as a responsibility on their part to do so.

Indigenous peoples also successfully linked the diversity of their cultures, values, and interests with the protection of biodiversity.[21] In his address to the General Assembly celebrating the launch of the International Year of the World's Indigenous People (1993), the UN Secretary-General equated cultural and biological diversity, agreeing with indigenous leaders that the loss of indigenous cultures continues to deprive humanity of the practical knowledge and experience necessary for its survival.[22] Like land tenure, cultural diversity is arguably a functional right in the sense that it can be abused by using it destructively or selfishly in ways that are incompatible with environmental sustainability. While cultural diversity has long been recognized in general terms by the UN Educational, Scientific, and Cultural Organization—in particular, in its 1966 Declaration of the Principles on International Cultural Cooperation[23]—and the freedom of different groups to enjoy their cultures was recognized by CERD when it was adopted the same year, the CBD was the first binding instrument to recognize the rights of indigenous people and other 'local communities' to intangible elements of their cultures such as medicinal knowledge.

---

[20] 'Programme of Action,' in *Report of the International Conference on Population and Development*, UN Doc. A/CONF.171/13 (18 October 1994) Annex, para. 6.27 at 41: 'Governments should respect the cultures of indigenous people and enable them to have tenure and manage their lands, protect and restore the natural resources and ecosystems on which indigenous communities depend for their survival and well-being.'

[21] For a review of these linkages, see L. Maffi, ed., *On Biocultural Diversity: Linking Language, Knowledge, and the Environment* (Washington, DC: Smithsonian Institution Press, 2001).

[22] *Opening of International Year of Indigenous Peoples Is Marked at General Assembly Ceremony*, UN Press Release no. GA/8447 (10 December 1992) at 1.

[23] Adopted by the UNESCO General Conference, 14th Session, 4 November 1966. Article 1 refers to the 'rich variety and diversity' of cultures, proclaims them all to be of equal 'dignity and value,' and calls upon every people 'to develop its culture.'

States in Africa, Asia, and Latin America have relied on the CBD to claim national ownership and control of the diverse ecological knowledge systems that exist within their frontiers, together with the genetic and species diversity found within their territories. To this extent, state claims may conflict with the interests and rights of local communities as established by the CBD. Indigenous peoples not only succeeded in achieving recognition of collective property in communities, but also in juxtaposing community rights with the rights of states—a dynamic tension governed by competing claims to good stewardship.

5 DISTINCTIVELY INDIGENOUS RIGHTS AND THE ENVIRONMENT

Indigenous peoples have gradually achieved a large measure of legal personality as distinct societies with distinctive collective rights as well as a distinct role in national and international decision-making. Their public international legal status is an intermediary between non-self-governing territories and minorities—an immediate right to internal self-determination and the possibility of achieving external self-determination in particular circumstances, under international supervision. As the UN Secretary-General explained at the launch of the International Year of the World's Indigenous People, the rights of indigenous peoples involve a balancing of individual and collective dimensions within the framework of protecting 'cultural authenticity'.

The rights specific to indigenous peoples, as distinguished from rights that they may share with minorities and other culturally, ethnically, or religiously distinct groups within states, are the focus of the two ILO conventions referred to earlier in this chapter. Similar norms have evolved in the practice of intergovernmental committees entrusted with the implementation of UN human rights conventions and from the text and implementation of the CBD. Although conventions are binding only on state parties, many of the same norms received universal approval in Agenda 21, which is the final act of UNCED, including the recognition of land rights, protection from environmental degradation, and the right of indigenous peoples to participate in decisions that affect them. There have also been parallel developments in state practice, often in response to international criticism, such as *sui generis* arrangements for local autonomy or self-government.[24] These standards may appropriately be regarded as having achieved the status of customary international law.

---

[24] See, e.g., H. Hannum, *Autonomy, Sovereignty and Self-Determination: The Accommodation of Conflicting Rights*, revised edition (Philadelphia, PA: University of Pennsylvania Press, 1996).

5.1 Distinctive Political Rights: Self-Definition and Participation

Contemporary public international law recognizes the right of indigenous peoples to collective participation in decisions that may directly affect them (see Chapter 29 'Public Participation') as well as the right to determine their own identity as 'indigenous' (self-definition). The determination of particular groups' eligibility to exercise indigenous rights, and their individual membership, is a crucial threshold issue with both substantive and procedural elements. ILO Convention 107 attempted a broad sociological definition of 'indigenous populations'. As early as 1984, however, a study by the Sub-Commission on Prevention of Discrimination and Protection of Minorities proposed 'self-definition' as a complementary or alternative approach,[25] and self-definition was added to ILO Convention 169 five years later as a 'fundamental criterion' of indigenous status. Hence, if a state party contested a group's self-definition, the reasonableness of the state's views would be subject to ILO review, with the burden of persuasion resting *on the state*. CERD has adopted a similar approach: self-identification of an individual as a member of an indigenous group should be sufficient 'if no justification exists to the contrary.'[26] Self-definition by indigenous peoples is also the standard advanced by Article 33 of UNDRIP.

In accordance with Articles 4(2) and 6 of ILO Convention 169, state actions aimed specifically at indigenous peoples must not be 'contrary to the freely expressed wishes of the peoples concerned.' Any measures affecting indigenous peoples must be preceded by 'good faith' consultations 'with the objective of achieving [their] agreement or consent.' These consultations include development activities within the territories occupied or used by indigenous peoples (Article 7(1)), according indigenous communities a certain degree of control over resources such as minerals that may be owned by the state. States are moreover obliged to respect the institutions of indigenous peoples, provide support for the 'full development' of those institutions, and deal with indigenous people through 'their [own] representative institutions' (Articles 5(b), 6(1), and 8(2)). States must implement the convention with the participation and the 'cooperation' of indigenous peoples (Articles 2(1) and 33(2)). Taken together, these principles support internal self-government or, in the terms used by some commentators, internal self-determination. UNCED echoed these norms in calling upon states to ensure the 'active participation' of indigenous peoples in national legislation and development planning that may affect them, including 'greater control over their lands, self-management of their resources' and the right to preserve their 'customary and administrative systems and practices.'[27]

[25] *Study of the Problem of Discrimination, Volume V: Conclusions, Proposals and Recommendations,* UN Doc. E/CN.4/Sub.2/1986/7/Add.4 (1986).

[26] General Recommendation VIII(38), *Report of the Committee on the Elimination of Racial Discrimination,* UN Doc. A/45/18 (1990) at 79.   [27] Agenda 21, paras. 26.3(a)(ii), 26.3(b), and 26.4.

ILO Convention 169 requires that states make good faith efforts to reach agreement with indigenous peoples' own 'representative institutions'—that is, institutions chosen by indigenous peoples rather than by the state—before taking actions that affect these peoples. The political rights of indigenous peoples, therefore, extend beyond the general human right to participate in the political life of the state guaranteed in Article 25 of the ICCPR, which refers specifically to voting and candidacy for public office, and the rights of minorities to 'participate effectively in decisions' that affect them, as set out in Article 2(3) of the UN Declaration on the Rights of Persons Belonging to National or Ethnic, Religious and Linguistic Minorities (Declaration on Minorities). In a dispute challenging the Canadian government's decision to negotiate the text of a constitutional amendment with four selected indigenous organizations, the Human Rights Committee took the view that Article 25 does not guarantee all indigenous groups a voice in national affairs.[28] However, Canada's exclusion of some indigenous nations from the amending process is inconsistent with the ILO convention, which, while not ratified by Canada, has increasingly been cited as a general source of law by intergovernmental human rights bodies, such as CERD and the Inter-American Commission on Human Rights. It is now also inconsistent with UNDRIP.

There has also been recognition, at least in practice, of indigenous peoples' right to collective participation in international decision-making, for example, in the 'partnership' theme of the International Year and International Decade of the World's Indigenous People.[29] The *sui generis* standing of indigenous peoples in the international community is exemplified by the establishment of the Permanent Forum on Indigenous Issues by ECOSOC.[30] Half of the independent experts on this advisory body to ECOSOC are nominated by member states, and half are nominated by indigenous peoples' organizations, which for this purpose have organized themselves into regional caucuses. The forum has a mandate to develop policy and 'raise awareness and promote the integration and coordination of activities relating to indigenous issues' throughout the UN system, including operational programmes and specialized agencies.

Indigenous peoples' organizations were among the first grassroots organizations to seek a direct role in international decision-making in the 1970s and 1980s. For the previous 100 years, only a small number of international NGOs enjoyed access to international institutions. Most NGOs were devoted to peace and humanitarian aid, and many of them were linked with women's organizations. However, the 1919 Constitution of the ILO conferred standing on organizations of 'workers'. Originally aimed at empowering trade unions, regardless of whether they had been sanctioned by the state, this provision gradually acquired a broader interpretation. In the 1980s, it was applied to groups that shared a means of subsistence, including craftspeople,

---

[28] *Mikmaq People v. Canada*, Communication no. 205/1986, reprinted in UN Doc. A/47/40 (1992) Annex IX, 214, para. 5.5 at 216.   [29] See, e.g,. UNGA Resolution 163 (1993).

[30] ECOSOC Resolution 2000/22 (28 July 2000).

peasant farmers, home workers, and hunting or fishing communities as well as indigenous and tribal peoples.

Indigenous leaders meanwhile demanded a greater voice in the UN Commission on Human Rights and its subsidiary bodies. Existing ECOSOC rules favoured NGOs with topical interests and broad international membership rather than communities or cultural groups. Indigenous organizations such as the World Council of Indigenous Peoples, the International Indian Treaty Council, and the Four Directions Council successfully argued that they represented coalitions of nations and peoples and should be recognized even if they operated in only one or two states. With the conferral of consultative status on the Grand Council of the Crees of Québec, ECOSOC opened the door to NGO status for individual indigenous nations. By the time the Preparatory Committee for UNCED began meeting, a dozen indigenous peoples' organizations enjoyed ECOSOC consultative status, and more than a hundred other indigenous groups were participating in the annual sessions of the Working Group on Indigenous Populations without the need for ECOSOC accreditation. These precedents paved the way for a more inclusive form of NGO status that welcomed grassroots movements and community-based organizations into the UNCED process and, ultimately, into the post-UNCED work of the CSD, the CBD Conference of the Parties, and the World Bank (see Chapter 33 'Non-Governmental Organizations and Civil Society').

International financial and trade institutions have also begun to accord *sui generis* standing to indigenous peoples. In updating its policy on projects affecting indigenous or tribal peoples, the World Bank directed its staff to ensure the 'informed participation' of indigenous peoples in project planning, with 'full respect for their dignity, human rights, and cultural uniqueness,' and with 'full consideration' being given to their own preferences, with the aim of protecting them from adverse impacts and securing for them 'culturally compatible social and economic benefits.'[31] More recently, a WTO panel accepted the standing as *amicus curiae* of two Canadian indigenous nations to submit arguments on land rights and the implications of unsettled land claims on the pricing of forest products.[32] WTO panels have previously accepted factual briefs from environmental NGOs that had no direct interest in the outcome of the dispute. In *United States—Provisional Anti-Dumping Measure on Imports of Certain Softwood Lumber from Canada*, however, indigenous communities argued that the Canadian pricing scheme at issue had direct adverse effects on their land rights, and US authorities supported this argument. In fact, if not in name, then, indigenous communities were parties to the trade dispute and stood to benefit from the WTO decision.

---

[31] World Bank, 'Indigenous Peoples,' World Bank Operational Directive 4.20 (1991).

[32] *United States—Provisional Anti-Dumping Measure on Imports of Certain Softwood Lumber from Canada* (Case DS247), Brief of Natural Resources Defense Council, Defenders of Wildlife, Northwest Ecosystem Alliance, Grand Council of the Cree (Eeyou Istchee), and Interior Alliance (10 May 2001).

In paragraph 3 of its Johannesburg Plan of Implementation, the WSSD recognized that partnerships with 'major groups' such as indigenous peoples 'are key to pursuing sustainable development in a globalizing world.' It may reasonably be argued that consistent international practice has ripened into a norm that inter-governmental bodies cannot act legitimately without the broad and effective participation of indigenous peoples' organizations. This argument gains strength from Article 41 of UNDRIP, which implies a direct operational relationship between indigenous peoples and UN agencies.

5.2 Distinctive Substantive Rights

Article 27 of the ICCPR guarantees to 'minorities' the substantive rights to practice and perpetuate their distinctive languages, cultures, and religions.[33] For indigenous peoples, there is a functional relationship between distinctiveness and the collective rights to land, territory, and self-determination. This point was recognized by the Human Rights Committee in *Ominiyak v. Canada*, when it held that state-sponsored encroachments on the lands traditionally used by indigenous peoples for hunting, fishing, herding, or other means of earning their livelihood may violate the ICCPR. The committee, in particular, found that '[t]he rights protected by Article 27 include the right of persons, in community with others, to engage in economic and social activities which are part of the culture of the community to which they belong.'[34] Consistent with the views of indigenous peoples, international law recognizes that the perpetuation of indigenous cultures depends upon the heightened protection of land rights, environmental quality, and local knowledge systems.

5.2.1 *Rights to Land and the Environment*

ILO Convention 107 recognizes the right of indigenous peoples to 'ownership, collective or individual . . . over the lands which [they] traditionally occupy,' including respect for customary laws and procedures governing the use and transmission of rights to land (Articles 11, 12, and 13(1)). The convention specifies that indigenous people may not be removed from their traditional lands without their 'free consent' except for reasons of national security, public health, or 'development' and, even then, only after restitution in the form of lands of equal value.

The exceptions in favour of national security and development were nevertheless unacceptable to indigenous peoples, leading to the adoption of higher standards in 1989. ILO Convention 169 recognizes the right of indigenous peoples to the 'ownership and possession' of the 'total environment' that they occupy or use, as well as the

---

[33] *Report of the Human Rights Committee*, UN Doc. A/49/40 (1990) Annex V, at 107.

[34] *Ominiyak v. Canada*, Communication no. 167/1984, UN Doc. A/49/40 (1990) Annex IX(A), 1–30, para. 32.2 at 27.

rights to be protected from environmental degradation, involuntary removal, and unwanted intrusions by non-members of their groups (Articles 7(4), 13(2), 14(1), 16(1), and 18). This formulation extends the rights of indigenous peoples to living resources such as wildlife and fish, and to water, whether located on lands they permanently 'occupy' or lands that they traverse seasonally to 'use'. ILO Convention 169 also broadly recognizes the 'institutions' of indigenous peoples, which implies that indigenous peoples exercise some degree of local control of land use, inheritance, the use of water, and the harvesting of plants, fish, and wildlife. In cases where indigenous peoples have historically been displaced or otherwise deprived of lands they have traditionally occupied or used, states must establish appropriate procedures for the settlement of land claims.

Minerals are *not* included in the scope of indigenous land rights in ILO Convention 169, and, consistent with the non-discrimination provisions of CERD, they may be retained by the state if the state retains the right to minerals located beneath other privately owned lands as well. The state must negotiate with indigenous peoples for access to state-owned minerals, however, whether or not state law imposes this requirement on state dealings with other surface owners.

The substantive right to land guaranteed in ILO conventions has been applied in quasi-judicial procedures. The ILO Committee on the Application of Conventions and Recommendations has pressed India to provide adequate restitution in kind to tribal people displaced by the construction of hydroelectric dams, and has advised state parties such as Brazil and Peru that they have a duty to demarcate indigenous territories and to take effective action against invasions by settlers.[35] The Inter-American Commission on Human Rights has drawn on the ILO conventions for guidance in cases such as *Mayagna (Sumo) Indian Community of Awas Tingni v. Nicaragua*.[36]

Three years after the adoption of ILO Convention 169, UNCED called upon all states, 'in full partnership with indigenous people and their communities,' to settle land claims; recognize the value of traditional knowledge and resource management practices; and protect indigenous peoples from 'activities that are environmentally unsound or that the indigenous people concerned consider to be socially and culturally inappropriate.'[37] UNCED also recognized indigenous peoples' 'right to subsistence' from living marine resources, as well as their right to a share of forest resources.[38] The Committee on the Elimination of Racial Discrimination

[35] For example, *Report of the Committee of Experts on the Application of Conventions and Recommendations* (International Labour Conference, 1996), 83rd Session, Report III (Part IVA) at 269 (India); *Report of the Committee of Experts on the Application of Conventions and Recommendations* (International Labour Conference, 1991), 78th Session, Report III (Part IVA) at 354 (Brazil) 359 (Peru); and *Report of the Committee of Experts on the Application of Conventions and Recommendations* (International Labour Conference, 1993), 80th Session, Report III (Part IVA) at 310 (Brazil).

[36] *Mayagna (Sumo) Indian Community of Awas Tingni v. Nicaragua*, [2001] I.A.C.H.R. 9 (31 August 2001).   [37] Agenda 21, paras. 26.3(a)(ii), 26.3(b), and 26.4.

[38] Statement of Principles on Forests, in Agenda 21, at para. 17.83 at principle 5(a).

subsequently construed CERD as requiring states 'to recognize and protect the rights of indigenous peoples to own, develop, control and use their communal lands, territories and resources and, where they have been deprived of their lands and territories traditional owned or otherwise inhabited or used without their free and informed consent, to take steps to return those lands and territories,' or to provide compensation or restitution in kind.[39] The universality of ratification of CERD, together with the breadth of consensus achieved at UNCED, suggest that the land rights of indigenous peoples have attained the status of customary international law. At a bare minimum, indigenous peoples are entitled to prompt and effective demarcation of their lands, the just resolution of their land claims, and some form of international oversight or good offices to promote fair play by states.[40]

The Johannesburg Plan of Implementation recognizes that 'traditional and direct dependence of renewable resources and ecosystems . . . continues to be essential' to indigenous peoples. Building on the conclusions of the International Conference on Population and Development, the plan also calls on governments to 'promote, as appropriate, land tenure arrangements that recognize and protect indigenous and common property resource management systems' (paragraph 6(h); also see paragraphs 38(d) and 43(h)).

With the adoption of UNDRIP, the land-rights provisions of ILO Convention 169 will become universal standards with one important improvement. Article 26 of UNDRIP recognizes the right of indigenous peoples to lands and resources 'which they have traditionally owned, occupied or otherwise used or acquired'; the past tense suggests a stronger right to restitution than the ILO Convention.

5.2.2 Intellectual and Cultural Property Rights

Principle 22 of the Rio Declaration, which was quoted at the beginning of this chapter, recognizes the importance of indigenous knowledge, cultures, and 'traditional practices', whereas Agenda 21 calls on states to 'respect, record, protect and promote the wider application' of indigenous knowledge 'with a view to the fair and equitable sharing of the benefits.'[41] These principles reappear in the legally binding provisions of the CBD. State parties are obligated to 'respect, preserve and maintain [the] knowledge, innovations and practices' of indigenous communities, insofar as they embody 'traditional lifestyles relevant for the conservation and sustainable use of biological diversity' and to promote the wider use of indigenous knowledge and practices 'with the approval and involvement of the holders of such knowledge' (Article 8(j)). In addition, state parties agree to 'protect and encourage customary use of biological resources in accordance with traditional cultural practices that are compatible with conservation or sustainable use requirements' (Article 10(c)). These principles were

[39] In its General Comment XXIII(51), UN Doc. CERD/C/SR.1235 (18 August 1997).

[40] *Indigenous Peoples and Their Relationship to Land; Final Working Paper Prepared by the Special Rapporteur, Mrs. Erica-Irene A. Daes*, UN Doc. E/CN.4/Sub.2/2001/218, paras. 152–8 at 41–3.

[41] Agenda 21, para. 15.5(e).

reiterated in paragraph 42(j) of the Johannesburg Plan of Implementation, which requires governments to share the benefits of traditional or local knowledge with indigenous peoples on 'mutually agreed terms', and in paragraph 41(b), which emphasizes the applicability of this norm to traditional medicine.

Read together, the provisions of the CBD secure the rights of indigenous peoples to continue to use living resources in accordance with traditional, sustainable practices; to own, control, and perpetuate their traditional ecological knowledge systems and practical know-how with the assistance of the state; and to market their ecological knowledge and know-how if they choose. With respect to land rights, then, the CBD is more restrictive than the ILO conventions or CERD because it conditions continued access to land on the nature of land use—customary, traditional, and sustainable. However, the CBD is the only convention that protects the intellectual property of indigenous peoples explicitly, albeit 'subject to national legislation,' which allows states some leeway to adopt divergent national standards. If a state has ratified multiple instruments, the highest standard of protection for indigenous peoples will presumably be applied. This will be strengthened by the adoption of UNDRIP, which recognizes the rights of indigenous peoples broadly to 'maintain, control, protect and develop their cultural heritage, traditional knowledge and traditional cultural expressions,...including human and genetic resources [and] knowledge of the properties of fauna and flora'.

The CBD addresses land rights within a human-ecological framework—that is to say, it aims to protect cultural systems of land use and conservation. In its comments on the identity and rights of indigenous peoples, the Human Rights Committee has also emphasized a connection between cultural distinctiveness, distinctive ways of earning a livelihood, and rights to land and living resources. This emphasis implies that indigenous peoples' claims to territory and territorial authority are strongest where they can demonstrate significant, albeit sustainable, human utilization of the environment.

5.3 Right to External Self-Determination

The UN system has to a large extent recognized the right of indigenous peoples to some form of autonomy, self-government, or 'internal' self-determination. However, international indigenous organizations continue to demand UN recognition of their right to 'external' self-determination as a justiciable human right rather than merely as a political programme of the UNGA. This remains the main point of contention in the drafting of UNDRIP, helping delay its transmission to the UNGA for 13 years. The final text of UNDRIP affirms indigenous peoples' 'right to self-determination' (Article 3), but focuses on the exercise of this right by means of 'autonomy or self-government in matters relating to their internal and local affairs' (Article 4), and the right to 'maintain and strengthen their distinct political, legal, economic, social and cultural institutions' with state financial assistance (Article 5),[42] borrowing the language of ILO Convention 169. This implies an incremental approach—negotiating the terms of the political relationship between indigenous peoples and states under some form of international oversight. By its silence, UNDRIP also leaves open the possibility of exercising external self-determination without drawing attention to it; for example, in a situation where a state gives indigenous peoples little choice but to seek statehood of their own for their self-preservation. Significantly, UNDRIP expressly recognizes the right of indigenous peoples divided by states' borders to 'maintain and develop contacts, relations and cooperation' across these borders, which if not exactly a right to reunification is, at a minimum, recognition of a unique quasi-international status.

Indigenous organizations also demand recognition of the treaties many indigenous peoples previously concluded with states, as international instruments that can be enforced by the International Court of Justice (ICJ). Indigenous peoples' quest for full international personality finds some support in the opinions of the ICJ on the legitimacy of territorial acquisition,[43] and in the status of treaties made by European powers with non-European societies.[44] Their argument receives some support form Article 37 of UNDRIP, which affirms that such treaties are legally binding on states, but stops short of opening the ICJ to disputes over treaties between indigenous peoples and states, as indigenous leaders have long demanded. The Human Rights Committee has thus far declined to consider such arguments,[45] but has nonetheless asked states to strengthen the autonomy and territorial integrity of indigenous communities as a means of perpetuating their cultures.[46]

It may be argued that the question of indigenous peoples' right to the full measure of 'external' self-determination has become more symbolic than substantive as states and international institutions increasingly recognize the 'internal' self-determination, self-government, and territorial rights of indigenous peoples. As small societies, indigenous peoples stand to benefit most from continuing political and economic relationships with the states within whose borders they now live. The physical security, freedom, and well-being of indigenous peoples are desperate in many countries, to be sure. However, the implementation of existing

---

[42] See also Articles 18–20, 32 and 35, which also paraphrase ILO Convention 169; Article 14 contemplates separate schools.

[43] *Western Sahara, Advisory Opinion*, Opinion of 16 October 1975, [1975] ICJ Rep. 12. Compare the disregard of indigenous occupation of *Eastern Greenland (Denmark v. Norway)*, [1933] P.C.I.J. (ser. A/B) No. 53.

[44] *Case Concerning Right of Passage over Indian Territory (Merits) (Portugal-India)*, Judgment of 12 April 1960, [1960] I.C.J. Rep. 6.

[45] For example, *Mikmaq People v. Canada*, Communication no. 205/1986, reprinted in UN Doc. A/47/40 (1992) Annex IX, at 214.

[46] For example, *Concluding Observations on the Third Periodic Report of Canada*, UN Doc. CCPR/C/79/Add.105 (7 April 1999) at para. 8.

norms by states that respect international law can improve the conditions of indigenous peoples in those states in the near term, while the most abusive states are unlikely to be moved by arguments of self-determination any more than they have thus far been persuaded to recognize the lesser standards of autonomy or 'internal' self-determination.

6 INDIGENOUS RESPONSIBILITIES

Although the legal status of indigenous peoples continues to evolve, they already enjoy a privileged position as quasi-state actors, and not merely as part of the wider trend towards NGO participation in policy discussions and program implementation. To this extent, it may be argued that the organizations and authorities of indigenous peoples bear the same responsibility to respect internationally recognized human rights as the states in which they reside.[47] Indigenous leaders have divided on this issue at international conferences, with many insisting that self-determination must include the right to deviate from international instruments such as the ICCPR. Like some UN member states, some indigenous peoples maintain that cultural differences render UN instruments less than universal in authority. Others contend that their cultures have always valued individual freedom and individual diversity; hence, they have nothing to fear from human rights norms. The Human Rights Committee has implicitly upheld the 'reasonableness' of decisions taken by indigenous authorities to exclude certain individuals from sharing community economic resources,[48] but it may someday rule in favour of an individual grievance. In the meantime, UNDRIP provides that indigenous peoples must exercise their rights 'in accordance with international human rights standards' (Article 34), without discrimination on the basis of gender (Article 44), and with due regard for the values of 'democracy', 'fairness', and 'good governance' (Article 46).

More particularly, indigenous peoples' reliance on arguments derived from their 'special relationship with the land' implies an obligation to continue to use the biosphere sustainably. This does not necessarily bar cultural change or improvements in material standards of living, provided that change is achieved without sacrificing the biological diversity or productivity of traditional territories. It does strongly suggest that indigenous peoples, as subjects of international law, not only enjoy collective rights to be recognized and protected by the international community, but specific obligations to the international community with respect to the objects of international environmental law. A state may be unwise to allege an indigenous

---

[47] See, e.g., the admonition given the Navajo Nation in a land dispute with another indigenous people, the Hopi. Sub-Commission on Prevention of Discrimination and Protection of Minorities, Resolution 1989/37 (1989).

[48] *Kitok v. Sweden*, Communication no. 1987/195, reprinted in UN Doc. CCPR/C/33/D/197/1985 (1988) 12.

people's waste of its territory as justification for dispossession. However, a case can be made for holding indigenous peoples accountable for the stewardship of their territories in international bodies such as the Conference of the Parties of the CBD, in much the same way as if they were state parties. To do so would naturally raise the question of whether indigenous peoples are adequately represented in the governance structure of the CBD treaty system through their current consultative status as non-governmental observers without votes.

Respect for international legal norms can be viewed as a negative burden—that is, a limitation on sovereignty or self-determination. As they emerge from the shadows of colonialism into a growing role as non-state actors on the multilateral stage, indigenous peoples may also owe the international community positive duties such as contributing expertise and resources to worldwide challenges such as climate change, AIDS, poverty, and the destruction of life in the oceans—in other words, a duty of international cooperation. As the president of the Métis National Council of Canada argued at the first annual session of the Permanent Forum, indigenous peoples that are relatively wealthy, like wealthy states, have obligations to the less fortunate.

7 CONCLUSIONS

The international legal status of indigenous peoples continues to be a work in progress, with relatively little in the way of explicit rules in widely accepted conventions. Indigenous peoples continue to press their positions on self-determination, autonomy, and territorial integrity through a wide range of international forums, in particular, the Permanent Forum on Indigenous Issues, the UN Commission on Human Rights, the Conference of the Parties of the CBD, and the supervisory machinery of CERD and the ILO, as well as the Inter-American Commission of Human Rights. At this stage, their gains in standing and participation exceed their achievements in the field of substantive law, and their rights enjoy greater weight in practice than may appear from a survey of the provisions of UN conventions. Likewise, indigenous peoples continue to exert their greatest influence on international decision-making through human rights bodies, although the primary objects of their attention, ultimately, are land and the environment.

Recommended Reading

P. Alston, ed., *Peoples' Rights* (New York: Oxford University Press, 2001).

S. James Anaya, *Indigenous Peoples in International Law* (New York: Oxford University Press, 1996).

R.H. Barnes, A. Gray, and B. Kingsbury, eds., *Indigenous Peoples of Asia* (Ann Arbor, MI: Association for Asian Studies, 1995).

R.L. Barsh, 'The Challenge of Indigenous Self-Determination' (1993) 26 U. Mich. J.L. Reform 277.

——, 'Is the Expropriation of Indigenous Peoples' Land GATT-able?' (2001) 10 R.E.C.I.E.L. 13.

——, 'Who Is "Indigenous"? A Survey of State Practice,' in J.E. Magnet and D.A. Dorey, eds., *Aboriginal Rights Litigation* (Markham: Lexis Nexis Butterworths, 2003) 93.

M. Battiste and J. (Sákéj) Henderson, *Protecting Indigenous Knowledge and Heritage: A Global Challenge* (Saskatchewan: Punch Publishing, 2000).

L. Maffi, ed., *On Biocultural Diversity: Linking Language, Knowledge, and the Environment* (Washington, DC: Smithsonian Institution Press, 2001).

S. Pritchard, ed., *Indigenous Peoples, the United Nations and Human Rights* (London: Zed Books, 1998).

M. Riley, ed., *Indigenous Intellectual Property Rights; Legal Obstacles and Innovative Solutions* (Walnut Creek: AltaMira Press, 2004).

REGIONAL ECONOMIC INTEGRATION ORGANIZATIONS

THE EUROPEAN UNION AS AN EXAMPLE

LUDWIG KRÄMER

1 INTRODUCTION

ALTHOUGH there are a number of regional economic integration organizations such as Mercosur in Latin America, ASEAN in Asia, NAFTA in North America, that also have environmental issues on their agenda, this chapter will focus on the European Union (EU). There are several justifications for this decision, the most relevant is that the EU, through the European Community (EC), is the only regional organization that has the declared policy to pursue both the objectives of economic growth and environmental protection, because it accepts that, in the long term, it cannot reach one objective without the other. Environmental protection thus occupies a central place in overall EU policy. Furthermore, the EU has adopted numerous environmental instruments that legally bind its member states.

At the international level, the EC has the competence to negotiate and conclude treaties with states that are not members of the EU. For environmental matters, this competence is not exclusive but shared with member states, which, therefore, also participate in the negotiation and conclusion of international environmental agreements. As the EU increasingly tries to speak at the international level with one voice in environmental matters, it has the potential of progressively growing into a role of an important negotiator, initiator, and actor that influences the evolution of international law. Whether the EU actually takes on that role remains to be seen, given its own internal structure.

2 EU's INSTITUTIONS AND PROCEDURES

Before progressing with the analysis that will be conducted in this chapter, a short remark needs to be made about the two related but distinct entities: the EU and the EC. The EU was established by the 1992 Treaty on European Union (EU Treaty), which entered into force in 1993 and was subsequently amended. It encompasses the so-called European Communities: the EC and Euratom, which are distinct legal entities but which have the same member states.[1] The precursor of the EC was the European Economic Community, originally established in 1958 with the entry into force of the Treaty of Rome. Even though the EU and EC are distinct entities they share the same institutions to various degrees. The term European Union is used to refer to the general cooperative framework among the member states and encompasses the EC. The term European Community refers to the supra-national entity engaged in developing policies, including an environmental policy, that are common to the member states. While the EC has the competence to enter into international treaties with non-member states (known as third states) and adopt legislation that is binding on the member states, the EU does not have such competences.

The EU at present has 25 member states,[2] which are, in classical public international law terms, 'sovereign'. Some member states, such as France, Great Britain, Spain, or Germany, are influential players in international policy-making in general. The accession of Bulgaria and Romania is planned for 2007—accession negotiations with Turkey and Croatia have commenced, and the countries of the southern Balkan might be members by 2020. The EC and, respectively, Norway, Switzerland, Iceland, and Liechtenstein have entered into close cooperation agreements that also cover environmental matters. While the primary aim of the EU is to reach an ever-closer union of the peoples of Europe, the final form and content of this union have not yet been determined. The EU Treaty provides for cooperation on, and the development of, common policies on both internal matters (among the member states) and external matters (with third states), although the most intense form of cooperation is in the area of economic affairs and conducted through the EC.

Although the EU Treaty does not mention environmental protection, the EC Treaty contains detailed provisions on the environment. According to its Article 2, the EC has the task to 'promote throughout the Community a harmonious, balanced and sustainable development of economic activities, a high level of employment and of social protection . . . a high level of protection and improvement of the quality of the environment, the raising of the standard of living and quality of life, and economic and social cohesion and solidarity among member States.' To achieve this task, the EC has to pursue, next to other policies, 'a policy in the sphere of the environment' (Article 3(1) of the EC Treaty). The objectives, principles, and decision-making procedures of the environmental policy are laid down in Articles 174–6 of the EC Treaty. These provisions allow the EC to adopt measures that have binding

---

[1] The EC and Euratom were originally based on separate treaties, respectively the EC Treaty (Treaty of Rome, as amended); the Treaty Establishing the European Atomic Energy Community (Euratom Treaty); and Treaty on the European Union (Maastrict Treaty), which have been incorporated into the EU Treaty.

[2] Member states are: Belgium, Germany, France, Italy, Luxemburg, Netherlands (founding members); Great Britain, Denmark, Ireland (accession 1973); Greece (accession 1982); Spain, Portugal (accession 1986); Austria, Finland, Sweden (accession 1995); Estonia, Latvia, Lithuania, Poland, Czeck Republic, Hungary, Slovakia, Slovenia, Cyprus, Malta (accession 2005).

effect on the EC member states and/or on private persons. With regard to states that are not members of the EU, Article 174(4) expressly provides that both the member states and the EC shall cooperate, within their respective spheres of competence, with other countries and international organizations and may conclude agreements with them. Such treaties, when concluded by the EC, are binding upon the EC itself and all of its member states (Article 300(7) of the EC Treaty).

The EC institutions that are relevant for the elaboration and implementation of EC environmental policy are as follows:

- the European Parliament, whose 732 members are elected by general free elections in which the citizens in the EC member states participate;
- the Council, which is composed of the governments of the member states and within which each member state's votes are weighed according to the size of its population (Article 205 of the EC Treaty);
- the Commission, which is independent from the Council and the European Parliament and acts in the general interest of the EC (Article 213 of the EC Treaty). Its members function in their individual capacity and are appointed by the Council for a period of five years; and
- the Court of Justice, which has as its task to ensure that 'in the interpretation and application of this Treaty the law is observed' (Article 220 of the EC Treaty).

In environmental policy as well as in all other policy areas, apart from political declarations and resolutions, the institutions mainly act by adopting legally binding regulations, directives, and decisions (Article 249 of the EC Treaty). Regulations are directly binding for each citizen within the EU. Directives address the member states and oblige them to transpose the directive's requirements into national law and reach the objectives fixed in the directive, leaving them some discretion as to the means that they employ to reach these ends. Decisions concern particular situations and are directly binding for the addressee, which may be a member state as well as a private person or entity. These three instruments—regulations, directives, and decisions—have in common that, once adopted according to the prescribed procedures, they need not be 'ratified' or otherwise approved by member states. Rather, the adoption of such an instrument at the EC level obliges the addressees, be they member states or private actors, to conform to the instrument's content.

The Commission has a monopoly on the right of initiative when it comes to making proposals for the adoption of a regulation, directive, or decision related to the environment. Council and Parliament may not adopt any instrument without a formal proposal having been submitted by the Commission. A Commission proposal is subject to consideration by the European Parliament and the Council, with the Economic and Social Committee, representing private stakeholders, and the Committee of the Regions, where regional and local authorities are represented, submitting advisory opinions. In order for a regulation, directive, or decision to be adopted, a qualified majority is required in the Council as well as a majority in the European Parliament. This is the so-called co-decision procedure set out in

Article 251 of the EC Treaty. Where the Parliament amends a Commission's proposal, unanimity is required in the Council, unless the Commission agrees to the amendment. In some particularly sensitive policy areas—ecological taxes, town and country planning, quantitative management of water resources, soil protection, and measures that significantly affect a member state's choice of energy sources or the structure of its energy supply—the Council, upon proposal of the Commission and having heard the other forums mentioned earlier, decides alone and by unanimity.

The EC has adopted legislation in practically all areas of environmental policy. These EC-wide provisions—the so-called 'positive integration' measures—stand next to measures that ensure the free circulation of goods and together they seek to balance economic and environmental concerns. Normally, this makes it unnecessary for member states to adopt supplementary environmental measures and, at the same time, avoids the need for the Court of Justice to weigh environmental and economic considerations in the interpretation of the more general provisions of the EC Treaty itself.

In comparison to public international law, in particular, the following specificities mark EC (environmental) law. First, environmental legislation is adopted almost entirely on the basis of majority decisions, with the agreement of about 70 per cent of member states being sufficient for the adoption of a legally binding instrument. In practice, this process prevents one or two member states from vetoing the adoption of legislation until their specific requirements are satisfied. Second, the Commission's right of initiative also allows the initiating of legislative action in cases where member state's governments would be reluctant to see new initiatives taken. The Commission's proposal, at a minimum, starts an extensive discussion within the other EC institutions on the merits of the proposal, even if the Council and the European Parliament were to decide not to adopt it. Third, the Commission has the task of ensuring that the law is applied. It therefore has to ensure not only that EC environmental law is incorporated into the national law of member states but also that it is actually applied and enforced. Fourth and related to the previous point, the Court of Justice contributes to the effective enforcement of EC law. By the end of 2004, the court had delivered more than 400 judgments in environmental matters—about 80 per cent of these judgments were pronounced as a result of the Commission taking the initiative to bring a case against a member state for not properly incorporating, applying, or enforcing EC environmental law. It is important to note that the very large majority of these cases did not concern transboundary matters, but rather the implementation of EC environmental law within a member state. Fifth, EC law also affects citizens who may be granted rights or have obligations imposed on them directly by EC environmental law. Moreover, where citizens are directly and individually concerned by a measure, they have access to the Court of Justice. Finally, EC law distinguishes itself from public international law by the fact that, based on EC law, in the case of a conflict between national and EC law, EC law prevails (see Chapter 40 'National Implementation').

3 Development of EC Environmental Law

The EC Treaty, which became effective in 1958, originally pursued purely economic objectives. It did not contain any provision on environmental policy or law. By the end of the 1960s, the Commission, however, became convinced that environmental measures were necessary at the European level and gradually managed to persuade the Council—that is, the member states—that this was indeed the case (see Chapter 5 'Levels of Environmental Governance'). In the absence of an explicit provision in the EC Treaty authorizing the adoption of an environmental policy and related law, the best way forward was considered to be the adoption of European environmental action programs, which, for a period of several years, determined the objectives, principles, and priorities of European measures. This joint European policy programming was so successful that it was maintained even after the insertion of a specific environmental chapter into the EC Treaty in 1987. In 1993, the European Parliament was given the power to co-decide in the adoption of environmental action programmes, which, at the same time, attained the status of an official instrument in the common environmental policy.

The first European environmental action programme, adopted in 1973, launched comprehensive research programmes. This development eventually barred the practice of adopting European legislative measures, mainly as a reaction to pollution incidents or to plans by a member state to adopt national legislation. In the latter case, the purpose of EC legislation was to avoid disparate national standards that might create technical barriers to trade within the EU or, more generally, go against the overall objective of integrating member states, economies, and citizens into an ever-closer union. These efforts to develop a European environmental policy were facilitated by the fact that, from the outset, the protection of the environment found considerable public support. The basic decision of the EC Treaty to create a trading area, in which state borders did not constitute economic borders, enabled the Commission to successfully resist all attempts by member states to limit EU environmental actions to transboundary issues. The Commission was assisted in this endeavour by the fact that the EC Treaty, prior to 1987, did not contain explicit provisions on environmental policy. Thus, environmental measures had to be based mostly on trade provisions, which meant the establishment of harmonized standards.

The Commission thus successfully argued that environmental measures were necessary for the establishment and the functioning of the EC-wide internal market. Its member states accepted this reasoning, as they acknowledged the fact that many environmental problems required the taking of legislative measures throughout the territory of the EC. It was mainly for this reason that legislation on the quality of bathing water or of drinking water, on the environmental impact assessment of projects, on the protection of habitats including provisions on hunting, and on urban waste waters or municipal waste were adopted by the EC, even though such measures had no transboundary dimension. While it has been argued that, under the subsidiarity principle, such matters might best be left to member states, this argument did not bar the EC from adopting environmental measures that lacked a transboundary dimension.[3]

With regard to capacity building, the Commission's legislative and programming proposals obliged the Council to regularly meet as an 'environment council'. At present, there are six such meetings per year. While in the early 1970s, only a few member states had an autonomous environmental ministry or department, this situation gradually changed. Today, all 25 member states have a central environmental ministry—about one-third of them also have a regional environmental infrastructure in place with legislative and administrative responsibilities.

At the EC level, the Commission's environmental department grew from half a dozen staff members in the 1970s to some 600 in 2005. Other Commission departments, including energy, transport, trade, regional policy, consumer protection, and industry, are also under continuous pressure to consider the environmental aspects of their respective policies. An autonomous agency, the European Environment Agency, is charged with providing reliable data and information on the state of the environment. The system, in addition, is assisted by scientific bodies that are charged with the development of a common European scientific opinion on the environment, health, safety, and other matters.

Progressively and with the accession of new member states, EC legislation has become not only more systematic and comprehensive, but also of a more general and framework character, leaving the details either to subsequent EC legislation or to the member states themselves. European environmental law-making has also been exposed to two, sometimes, opposite pressures. On the one hand, member states and their regions have pushed to maintain their power to freely adopt—or not adopt—environmental provisions. On the other hand, vested interest groups have identified the EU as a new power centre, one where they should concentrate their lobbying efforts. The Commission's right of initiative, which has often been supported by pro-environmental member states, has counterbalanced this trend, supported by public opinion favouring pro-environmental initiatives.

This slow, but progressive, change in the legislative trend since the early 1990s is marked by the fact that more general or framework directives are being adopted at the EC level. It is then left to member states, under the provision of Article 176 of the EC Treaty, to legislate on details and to maintain or introduce more stringent and more detailed environmental provisions at the national level. Examples of this trend

---

[3] On the subsidiarity principle and EU environmental law, see K. Lenaerts, 'The Principle of Subsidiarity and the Environment in the European Union: Keeping the Balance of Federalism' (1993–4) 17 Fordham Int'l L.J. 846–95.

are found in the water, air, waste, and noise sectors.[4] This trend does not manifest itself in product-related legislation, which is normally based on Article 95 of the EC Treaty, because uniform standards—the 'level playing field'—are of primary importance to producers and traders.

The EU had adopted, by the end of 2005, some 250 pieces of environmental legislation. These texts cover all essential areas of environmental concern, in particular, fresh water and marine water quality and management; air pollution; noise; environmental characteristics of products; waste management; biodiversity and nature protection; climate change; industrial installations as well as cross-cutting issues such as environmental impact assessments of plans and projects, access to environmental information, the prevention of industrial accidents, and the remediation of environmental damage. This EC legislation is regularly reviewed, updated, and adapted to changing situations.

EC legislation establishes a comprehensive set of provisions to protect the environment and humans. No significant sector appears to have been left out. It is mainly for this reason that national environmental legislation in a number of EU member states practically mirrors EC law and details it, but does not significantly go beyond the EC measures. At present, it is generally estimated that between 70 and 80 per cent of national environmental legislation in EU member states finds its origin in EC legislation. For some member states in southern or eastern Europe, this figure is close to 100 per cent. Even in European states that are not EU members, EU environmental legislation plays a very significant role. This is due to the fact that such states either are adopting EU environmental legislation in view of their possible future membership in the EU or because of their close cooperation with the EU.

4 CHARACTERISTICS OF EU ENVIRONMENTAL LAW AND POLICY

4.1 Choice of the Legal Basis

The original objective of the 1958 EC Treaty, which was to integrate the economies of the member states into an internal market, as well as the absence of explicit provisions on the protection of the environment resulted in the fact that EC-wide trade-related measures were already largely in existence when EC environmental legislation appeared on the scene. The introduction in 1987 of a specific legal provision into the EC Treaty to allow for the adoption of EC environmental legislation ensured that

---

[4] See, e.g., the EC Directive 2000/60 Establishing a Framework for Community Action in the Field of Water Policy, [2001] O.J. L327/1.

environmental measures could be adopted either on the basis of this new provision (Article 175 of the EC Treaty) or, where the environmental measures impacted on trade, on the trade provisions of the EC Treaty. In the case of the latter, relevant articles of the EC Treaty are Article 95, regarding trade-related environmental measures that may affect trade within the EC,[5] and Article 133, concerning environmental measures that may affect international trade.[6]

The choice of the correct legal basis is relevant for two reasons. First, the procedure with respect to the elaboration of the legislative instrument varies under the different provisions of the EC Treaty. For example, the European Parliament has a much smaller role in the area of international trade (Article 133 of the EC Treaty) than in the area of environmental policy. Second, the residual powers of member states to maintain or introduce national environmental legislation after the adoption of an EC measure vary considerably. For measures adopted on the basis of Article 175, member states may maintain or introduce more stringent national environmental protection measures provided that these provisions are compatible with the general requirements of free trade within the EC (Article 176 of the EC Treaty). In contrast, under Article 95, member states can deviate from EC legislation only under very restrictive conditions—laid down in Article 95—and after the approval of the Commission. Moreover, member states have no residual rights when an EC measure is adopted on the basis of Article 133.

In practice, the Council and the European Parliament have adopted practically all product-related environmental legislation, including those that ban or restrict the use of products, on the basis of Article 95 of the EC Treaty, thus ensuring the largest possible free circulation of products within the EC. In contrast, EC legislation on trade in endangered species, on trade in hazardous waste, and on trade in ozone-depleting substances as well as the decision to ratify the Cartagena Protocol on Biosafety, where the Commission proposed both Article 133 and Article 175 as an appropriate legal basis, were based on Article 175 of the EC Treaty. In these areas, it was considered that the environmental elements of the subject matter prevailed over the trade aspects. This differentiation met with the approval of the Court of Justice.[7]

---

[5] Measures concerning the harmonization of environmental production standards as well as environmental measures that address the freedom of competition within the EU typically are adopted on the basis of Article 95. Relevant examples are EEC Directive 90/220 on the Deliberate Release into the Environment of Genetically Modified Organisms, [1990] O.J. L117/15; and EC Directive 93/12 Relating to the Reduction in Sulphur Content of Certain Liquid Fuels, [1993] O.J. L74/81.

[6] Measures concerning the import and export of products typically are adopted on the basis of Article 133. Relevant examples are EEC Regulation 2455/92 Concerning the Export and Import of Certain Dangerous Chemicals, [1992] O.J. L251/13; and EEC Regulation 3254/91 Prohibiting the Use of Leghold Traps in the Community and the Introduction into the Community of Pelts and Manufactured Goods of Certain Wild Animal Species Originating in Countries Which Catch Them by Means of Leghold Traps or Trapping Methods Which Do Not Meet International Humane Trapping Standards, [1991] O.J. L308/1.

[7] See, e.g., Court of Justice of the European Community (CJ), Opinion 2/00, 6 December 2001, [2001] E.C.R. I-9713 (concerning the proper legal basis for ratification of the Cartagena Protocol on Biosafety).

In practice, member states only rather exceptionally have exercised their residual legislative powers pursuant to Articles 95 or 176 once an EC legislative measure has been adopted. Several reasons may account for this outcome. In some cases, member states may fear disadvantaging national economic operators by adopting more stringent environmental measures. In addition, EC environmental legislation is, with respect to its substance and for numerous member states, innovative and progressive. Finally, national public opinion normally does not ask for more stringent measures. The derogating possibilities thus seem to have more psychological than practical relevance.

4.2 Legislative Instruments

Legislative instruments—regulations and directives—remain the principal instrument of EU environmental policy. They create the necessary legal security for member states, economic operators, and citizens. In the past, member states, for reasons of subsidiarity and a fear of losing too many responsibilities to the EU, preferred directives to regulations and general legal provisions to precisely drafted obligations. In contrast, the Commission, the European Parliament, and public opinion in the member states normally favoured more precise and detailed provisions, as environmental protection continued to be perceived as important and as a relatively popular policy by citizens. As mentioned earlier, the EC has adopted more recently so-called framework directives.

Initially, legislative instruments contained a considerable number of procedural requirements—such as standards for issuing permits and requirements for impact assessments, planning, consultation, and reporting—because for many environmental sectors and in numerous member states the necessary legal infrastructure had yet to be established. Information and participation rights for citizens progressively gained importance, due to greater transparency, better governance, and a general move towards a system of open society in Europe.

The EC rarely recurred to recommendations or other non-binding instruments such as voluntary agreements since experience in the member states, at the European level and by other regional European organizations, showed that such instruments, not being enforceable, were not effective. Where recommendations were adopted, this was mainly due to pressure from member states who played the subsidiarity card or from vested interest groups that wished to avoid binding legislation. Neither did the EC give member states the option of allowing the private sector to develop its own voluntary instruments in order to regulate certain issues. It was felt that such an approach would lead to too great a differentiation in the application of EC law and thus work against, rather than in favour, of political, social, economic, and environmental integration within the EU. The Court of Justice also has consistently held that

EC environmental legislation had to be incorporated into national law by way of binding legislation in order to enable economic operators and private persons to know their precise rights and obligations.

4.3 Regulatory Tools and Approaches

4.3.1 *Command and Control*

Early EC environmental legislation concentrated on command and control provisions (see Chapter 8 'Instrument Choice'), in conformity with the prevailing convictions in continental Europe at the time. With the enlarged EU and the growing influence of Anglo-Saxon thinking, legislation became more flexible and general, setting a framework for action but leaving more discretion to national/local authorities. EC law itself also developed a tendency of laying down principles in framework directives and then elaborating the further details in more technically oriented 'daughter' directives.

Over time, there also has been a clear trend away from precise emission standards and towards concentration (quality) standards, even though it is recognized that the latter are hardly enforceable. Furthermore, without much public discussion, the EU has decided, as a matter of principle, not to harmonize standards for industrial installations, although free trade requirements continue to press for uniform production standards. All of these trends, though, have not yet seriously put into question the general conviction that command and control measures remain the core approach to the effective protection of the environment in Europe.

4.3.2 *Economic Instruments*

The use of economic instruments at the European level, such as tax relief, financial incentives, subsidies, or charges (see Chapter 8 'Instrument Choice'), has traditionally been negligible. This situation can be explained by the fact that the EU has practically no income of its own but depends, for the fulfilment of its tasks, on financial transfers from its member states. Furthermore, the adoption of ecological taxes requires a unanimous Council decision. Such a decision cannot be reached at present as several member states, for reasons of principle, are opposed to the adoption of EC tax provisions.

For these reasons, attempts to introduce an eco-tax on energy failed in the 1990s, and no further attempts were made to introduce taxes or charges at the EC level. The adoption of the Kyoto Protocol in 1997 introduced an international trading scheme for greenhouse gas allowances, and prompted the EU to rethink the role of economic instruments in environmental policy. As a result, and as the EU took on a global leadership role on climate change issues, the EU adopted in 2003 a directive on emission trading in greenhouse gas allowances in order to gain experience in this new type of instrument and in the hope of sharing its experience with other countries. The climate change sector might see the adoption of additional economic instruments in the future.

Eco-taxes and other economic instruments increasingly are used by EU member states, with countries in northern and central Europe recurring to such instruments more frequently than countries in southern and eastern Europe. An even more extended use of such instruments at the member state level, however, is inhibited by apprehensions of creating competitive disadvantages for the national economic operators with respect to competitors from other EU member states.

4.3.3 *Private Standard Setting at the EC Level*

Two European standardization bodies, the European Committee for Standardization (CEN) and the European Committee for Electrotechnical Standardization (CENELEC), have a membership that goes beyond the geographical area of the EU. Both bodies have detailed working arrangements with the International Organization of Standardization and national standardization organizations. They are financially supported by the EU but elaborate their standards in complete autonomy, almost without any participation of public interest groups or representatives of the public interest. Mechanisms are provided to enable the EU to incorporate such standards into EU legislation. Environmental standards, however, rarely emanate from these bodies. The absence of officials from the EU or from member states as well as from environmental groups in the CEN/CENELEC working groups rather feeds reservations against the results of the standardization process, and neither the CEN nor the CENELEC are particularly interested in promoting environmentally friendly industrial standards.

Private standard-setting instruments such as corporate codes, self-commitments, and other initiatives from the business community (see Chapter 21 'Private and Quasi-Private Standard Setting'), as mentioned earlier, do not play a significant role in European environmental policy. Very few voluntary environmental agreements with economic associations have been concluded—their success does not appear evident. Recent attempts to promote environmental protection through measures of corporate social responsibility have not yet shown any visible effect. In general, it may be assumed that even economic operators prefer legislation to privately agreed standards, as legislation establishes legal certainty and creates a level playing field for all competitors, including importers.

4.3.4 *Integration*

Article 6 of the EC Treaty states that '[e]nvironmental protection requirements must be integrated into the definition and implementation of Community policies and activities . . . in particular with a view to promoting sustainable development'

(see Chapter 26 'Sustainable Development'). Efforts have been ongoing to implement this provision in the EC's general activity with limited success in most policy
areas. This is not really surprising since comprehensive institutional structures, legislation, and networks have been built-up over the years to organize the respective
sectors, such as energy, transport, trade, competition, agricultural, fisheries and
industry policy sectors. Moreover, those sectors involved do not necessarily welcome new challenges from the environmental sector. The integration of environmental requirements into other policies must therefore be understood as a process
that requires continuous efforts—the establishment of administrations and the
political determination to breath life into Article 6—in order to enable it to become
more than a reflection of wishful thinking. More recently, economic and political
crises in the agricultural and fisheries sector have contributed to promoting the
integration of environmental requirements into the policies for these sectors.
However, in these as in other sectors, the integration of environmental considerations is far from satisfactory.

4.3.5 *Planning*

Early on in the development of EU environmental policy, it was clear that the environment in the EU could not be protected without the active involvement of local,
regional, and national administrations and of its citizens. Accordingly, planning
instruments became an important policy tool in the form of clean-up plans or management plans to be elaborated by the responsible authorities in member states. EC
legislation required the elaboration of such plans and their regular updating, in areas
such as air pollution, discharges to water, waste management, and ambient noise.

In the early 1990s, EC legislation introduced the requirement that planning be
of a trans-national character. The above-mentioned EU environmental action programs were the most obvious example of transboundary planning. At the same time,
under the influence of Anglo-Saxon thinking, the effectiveness of European legislation, and environmental legislation in particular, began to be assessed in economic
terms. Cost-benefit assessments, life-cycle analyses, economic impact assessments, and
other economic tools were used to pre-vet environmental legislation at the EU level
(see Chapter 11 'An Economic Theory of International Environmental Law'). These
procedures were used despite the fact that no recognized method enabled the full
assessment of the social and economic value of environmental degradation or of the
short-term and, in particular, long-term effects of environmental impairment. In spite
of this, the protection of the environment increasingly was perceived as a cost element,
and these different economic tools were sometimes used to prevent new environmental legislation from being advanced, paving the way for a *de facto* deregulatory policy.

With regard to environmental planning by member states, in the area of freshwater management and nature protection, strong signals were given to national
administrations to plan beyond their national frontiers. Moreover, in the area of

climate change, the introduction of emission trading in 2003 cannot be implemented without transboundary administrative cooperation. In contrast, transboundary planning was, until recently, largely rejected in the areas of waste management and air pollution.

5 CONCEPTS AND PRINCIPLES IN EU ENVIRONMENTAL LAW

The EC Treaty refers to several environmental concepts and principles. However, overall EC environmental law can be characterized as rather pragmatic and down to earth in its approach. This point is probably best illustrated by the procedural, instead of substantive, attitude taken to environmental rights and by the fact that the European legislature has not sought to provide legal content to the notion of inter-generational equity.

5.1 Sustainable Development

The EC Treaty provides that sustainable development is one of the aims of EC policy, without defining this notion. With some reluctance, the EU accepted that 'sustainable development' also included, besides an economic and social dimension, an environmental aspect. In practice, the term is increasingly used to promote economic growth under the slogan of 'competitivity of the European economy', and to cut back on environmental standards. It thus remains to be seen whether the increased economic pressure on politicians and the legislature will lead, in the future, to EC environmental measures being adopted only if, and to the extent that, they are economically sound—whatever that means.

5.2 Principles

The EC Treaty also formulates a number of specific environmental principles: the principles of precaution and prevention; the polluter-pays principle; the principle that environmental damage should be rectified at the source; and the above-mentioned principle that environmental requirements should be integrated into the definition and implementation of other EC policies. There is a divergence of opinion, whether these principles can be enforced in court or whether they instead constitute guidelines for political action.

In practice, these principles may be, and are being, used by the EC institutions to justify and explain specific legislative or administrative measures. However, only in extreme cases are they likely to constitute an obstacle to the adoption of EC legislation. Nor have member states or private persons ever contested an EC legislative measure or administrative decision before the Court of Justice based on the argument that it contradicted one of the EC environmental principles. With regard to member states' laws, the Court of Justice in several rulings has confirmed that their compatibility with EC law could be justified on the basis of the environmental principles contained in the EC Treaty. It, however, has never annulled a national measure based on the argument that it contradicted EC environmental principles.

The precautionary principle (see Chapter 25 'Precaution'), in particular, has on several occasions been used to justify the adoption of EC health- and/or environmental-related decisions or measures. The argument used has been that in the absence of scientific certainty EC institutions are allowed to take measures in order to protect human health or the environment. The Court of Justice approved of this practice and also applied the precautionary principle in the agricultural and pharmaceutical sector, using the integration principle contained in Article 6 of the EC Treaty to ensure the general application of the precautionary principle in EC law.

5.3 Environmental Rights

Another consequence of the pragmatic character of EC environmental law is that EC law does not provide for an individual right to a clean or healthy environment as a human right (see Chapter 28 'Environmental Rights'). Rather, the discussion in Europe over the last 30 years has come to the conclusion that such a right could not be formulated in a meaningful way that would make it enforceable in courts. Several recently adopted member state constitutions, however, do provide a right to a clean environment.

Efforts within the EU have concentrated on giving citizens procedural rights against public administrations, in particular, the right of access to information, the right to participate in decision-making, and the right of access to the court in environmental matters (see Chapter 29 'Public Participation'). Directives on the first two of these rights and on access to justice, where these rights have been impaired, have been amended or adopted in light of the entry into force of the Convention on Access to Information, Public Participation in Decision-making and Access to Justice in Environmental Matters (Aarhus Convention), as was legislation to apply these rights with regard to the EU institutions. General legislation on access to justice in environmental matters is considered by member states to be within their competence rather than an EC competence.

6 IMPLEMENTATION AND ENFORCEMENT

Monitoring of the implementation and application of EC environmental legislation is probably the area where EC environmental law differs most from public international environmental law (see Chapter 42 'Monitoring and Verification'; Chapter 43 'Compliance Procedures'; and Chapter 45 'International Dispute Settlement'). The basic provisions in this regard are laid down in the EC Treaty: member states must do everything to comply with their obligations under the EC Treaty and under the regulations, directives, or decisions adopted by the EC institutions (Article 10). The Commission, acting in the general interest of the EU, must ensure that EC legislation is applied by the member states (Article 211), and the Court of Justice has to ensure that the law is applied (Article 220).

Where the Commission is of the opinion that a specific member state has infringed its obligations under EC environmental law, it may take legal action against this member state. This procedure is divided into a pre-judicial procedure between the Commission and the member state in question, and a judicial procedure before the Court of Justice (Article 226 of the EC Treaty). The Court of Justice may find that a member state has not complied with its obligation under EC law by not transposing a specific EC environmental instrument into its national law, by not transposing it correctly or with regard to its entire territory, or by not complying with EC law in a specific individual case. Following such a judgment, the member state in question is obliged to take the necessary measures in order to comply with the court's judgment (Article 228(1) of the EC Treaty). If the member state does not do so, the Commission may submit a second case to the court, this time requesting the court to impose a monetary penalty on the member state (Article 228(3) of the EC Treaty). The court may then decide on the amount of the penalty, taking into account the seriousness, duration, and economic capacity of the member state in question.

This procedure has proven to be very successful in environmental matters since the Commission takes its function as watchdog quite seriously. At present, at any given time some 1,300 infringement cases are pending against member states. While about 90 per cent of all cases are solved during the pre-judicial phase and thus not brought before the Court of Justice, the court, by mid-2005, had delivered more than 400 judgments against member states in environmental matters. Member states completely and unreservedly accept the judgements of the court, even if in a particular procedure a judge of their own nationality may not be sitting on the bench. The judgments themselves have not really raised concerns with regard to national sovereignty, subsidiarity, or other legal constructs. The threat of having to pay a monetary penalty, moreover, has proven to be a very efficient means to ensure compliance with EC law, even though the pre-judicial and judicial procedures take some time. By mid-2005, the court had actually imposed such a monetary penalty in three cases.

These cases involved Greece for the ongoing operation of an unauthorized landfill, also elsewhere in this chapter (€20,000 per day);[8] Spain for ongoing pollution of inland bathing waters (€647,000 per year and per polluted bathing water);[9] and France for the prolonged breach of an EC measure for the conservation of marine resources (€20 million plus €57.6 million for every six months of continued non-compliance).[10] The negative effect of procedural delays is compensated by the publicity that is given to the Commission's pre-judicial or judicial action, which often leads to extensive public discussions and to pressure on the national or regional governments to adapt their legislation or practice and align to EC law—which member states co-adopt through their role in the Council.

In the past, the implementation by member states of international conventions to which the EC is a party but which had not been transposed into EC law was not monitored by the Commission, even though Article 300(7) of the EC Treaty explicitly specifies that international conventions that are concluded by the EC are binding on EC institutions *and* on the member states. In autumn 2004, the Court of Justice finally clarified that the Commission also has the responsibility to monitor the implementation by member states of the provisions of international conventions that have been concluded by the EC, and that member states are in breach of their obligations under EC law when they do not comply with the provisions of such international conventions, even where no transposition into EC legislation has taken place.[11]

The Commission explicitly encourages individuals, environmental groups, and other persons to file complaints regarding potential breaches of EC (environmental) law and has publicly committed itself to systematically pursue any such complaint. At present, some 600 environmental complaints are filed with the Commission every year. As a result, the Commission is able to gain rather detailed knowledge of the practical application of EC environmental law by national, regional, or local authorities. This complaint procedure, which is actively supported by the European Parliament, has resulted in giving the impaired environment somewhat of a voice and has had the effect that environmental issues are constantly discussed in the European context.

Generally, the procedure to monitor the legislative and practical application of EC environmental law by the EC institutions is more intense than in most EC member states. The monitoring of EC environmental law is a very powerful cornerstone of EC environmental policy, as the environment has neither a voice nor (national) frontiers and is thus bound to rely on public support for its protection. The system ignores questions of state sovereignty and considers environmental protection as

---

[8] Case C-387/97, *Commission v. Greece* [2000] E.C.R. I-5047.

[9] Case C-278/01, *Commission v. Spain* [2003] E.C.R. I-14141.

[10] Case C-304/02, *Commission v. France*, 12 July 2005 (not yet published in E.C.R. I).

[11] Case C-239/03, *Commission v. France*, 7 October 2004 (not yet published in E.C.R. I).

such, independently of the reports and information submitted by governments of member states, which all too often are silent on actual or potential cases of deficient application of EC environmental law. The Commission's commitment to the general European, rather than to any state's, interest contributes to the monitoring system's success, even though the risk remains of seeing the implementation policy influenced through pressure on its staff, selective staff appointments, political interventions, or other means. Data on complaints, infringement procedures, judgments, and other details are regularly published, although not always with the transparency that one would wish to see. Indeed, a truly European public opinion is still in an embryonic stage and might, as the principle of an 'open society', take a long time before it is fully established everywhere.

7 EU AS AN INTERNATIONAL ACTOR

The international ambition of the EU is at present purely rhetorical. EU foreign policy with regard to environmental protection does not constitute an exception to this statement. The EU's institutions, infrastructure, and decision-making procedures were conceived, constructed, and further developed in order to integrate sovereign states into an ever closer union. Efforts were thus concentrated on forming this European union rather than on having the EU play an international role. As EU member states, in particular, France, Great Britain, and Germany as well as Italy, Spain, and Poland, have more or less strong foreign policy ambitions, the EU appeared on the international scene as a body where, *de facto*, the individual EU member states, and not the EU as such, play the dominant role. When confronted with international problems, the EU has tried to reach a common position through internal coordination, but it was only very exceptionally able to develop pro-active proposals for the solution of international conflicts or controversies.

Environmental policy fitted and fits well into this pattern. The EU's environmental administration is organized to act within the regional European context rather than to take global initiatives and to assume global responsibility. Therefore, the administration is strongly concentrated on EU-internal environmental problems. Since the mid-1970s, the EU participated in international global or regional discussions on environmental issues, and often reached common positions with respect to international conventions or policies by intensely coordinating and harmonizing the different national attitudes of its member states in reaction to proposals or suggestions made by others. However, EU member states have hardly ever given the EU, represented by the Commission, a general negotiating mandate that would have allowed the introduction of 'autonomous' European proposals into international environmental negotiations. This attitude was facilitated by a provision in the EC Treaty, according to which a mandate for the EU to negotiate international conventions required an explicit—*de facto* unanimous—decision by the Council—that is, by the EC member states. Member states in designing Commission mandates made sure that such mandates were narrow, linked to internal coordination and approval procedures, and not too progressive. Furthermore, the EC rule that EC member states are not allowed to take international initiatives themselves if these deviate from existing EC environmental law resulted in the fact that member states, neither separately nor via the EC institutions, suggest progressive measures in international environmental negotiations.

This constitutional situation has resulted in the EC taking a re-active, rather than a pro-active, role in global environmental discussions. Its generally positive approach to a high level of environmental protection has led the EC to be generally in favour of more and more stringent international environmental provisions, and to positively accept many suggestions from other states or international bodies that have gone in this direction. Such a positive reaction was facilitated by the fact that in these international environmental discussions, the Commission as well as the member states were normally represented by officials from environmental, instead of trade or foreign policy, departments. However, the internal structure and decision-making procedures have ensured that the EC itself was generally unable to take the initiative for new global measures or innovative new proposals. In those cases where other states submitted a new proposal that was already covered by EC environmental law, internal coordination was necessary to examine whether the proposal went beyond the existing provisions, and whether it was necessary to agree on a common EC position. Where the subject matter of the proposal was not yet covered by EC law, the EC, as such, in the absence of negotiating instructions, could normally not take a position but had to leave the reaction to the individual member states.

Other elements added to this restraining situation. For example, EC development policy was, and is to a considerable degree, marked by the colonial past of several of the EC member states. It has not developed into an integrated multilateral European policy but is strongly influenced by member states' efforts to maintain a development policy on the basis of bilateral contacts with developing countries. This situation has made it more difficult for the EC as a whole to develop, and put into operation, an environmental strategy in multilateral environmental negotiations on waste, tropical forests, or water as well as on capacity building, the transfer of technology, and environmental cooperation. The conclusion of the Lomé Convention and the Cotonou Agreement with a large number of developing countries did not change this deficiency in the environmental dimension of EC development policy.

The EC's role in the climate change negotiations, especially for the Kyoto Protocol to the UN Framework Convention on Climate Change, despite the leadership role assumed by the EC at the international level, illustrate the earlier-made remarks. Within the EC, practically no government, and almost no members of the public, contest the necessity to reduce the emission of greenhouse gases in order to fight climate change. Furthermore, due to general and historical considerations, all EU member states accept that industrialized countries have to take the lead in combating climate change. It was with this attitude that the EC went to the Kyoto negotiations, with the internally agreed objective to obtain a 15 per cent reduction of greenhouse gas emissions by developed countries as compared to 1990. Not only was this object-ive not reached—the outcome was a 5.2 per cent reduction—but the EC also accepted the inclusion of several new greenhouse gases as well as new implementa-tion instruments—emission trading, a clean development mechanism, and joint implementation—which were, at that time, almost entirely unknown and untested in Europe. The reason for these far-reaching compromises was the endeavour to reach a worldwide consensus, though the EC knew that it was not yet equipped to make effective use of all of these instruments.

When the United States later proved unwilling to join Kyoto, the EC took respon-sibility for ensuring the entry into force of the Kyoto Protocol, as it was of the opin-ion that all efforts for a global joint venture to combat climate change would be lost if this first serious effort failed. Not having many economic or political assets with which it could bargain—military assistance and support, financial aid, trade facil-ities, and investments were all in the hands of the EC member states—the EC largely depended on the will of other countries (Canada and China) to follow common sense and, in the case of Russia, economic self-interest and accept the Kyoto Protocol as the way ahead.

Also at the regional level, the EC concentrated itself on internal political, eco-nomic, and ecological integration rather than on trying to establish a coherent sys-tem of European environmental standards beyond the EC boundaries. After a failed attempt to establish an EC agency to clean up the river Rhine in the early 1970s, the EC accepted that pollution of regional oceans and rivers would be left to the secretariats of regional conventions rather than regulate such matters via EC legislation. The EC thus became a party to relevant regional conventions and supported initiatives within their framework as well as relying on intergovernmental cooperation. The EC took a similar stance in areas such as atmospheric pollution and nature protection as well as with respect to agreements that covered more horizontal environmental aspects such as transboundary environment impact assessments or access to infor-mation, participation in decision-making, and access to justice in environmental matters. In all of these areas of regional environmental cooperation in Europe, the EC did not generally play a very active role. It left initiatives for the elaboration of agree-ments or subsequent protocols either to contracting parties—which might be EC member states—or to the secretariats of the regional organizations or conventions. Furthermore, this generally more passive approach also explains at least partly the different degree of success in regional environmental cooperation in different parts and sectors in the European region. Indeed, the EC did not seek to ensure compliance by its own member states with the provisions of these regional conventions, even when it was a party to them. It remains to be seen, whether the earlier-mentioned judgment of the Court of Justice, in Case C-239/03, will change this situation.

In view of the present lack of US leadership in global environmental issues, which is likely to last for the foreseeable future, it might well be that, in the future, the EC will be required to be a more active player on the international scene. Its internal constitutional and political structures, however, make it unlikely that the EC will be able to fully accept and act on such a role. It is rather more likely that the EC will continue to leave initiatives at the international level, be they on policy or on legal questions, to third states and member states or to other international bodies, limiting itself to cooperate, to try to find long-term solutions to environmental problems, and to generally act as a constructive and loyal partner—one that is willing to share its own 'internal' environmental experience with the international community. The EC might act differently, where it has already developed EC legislation on a specific subject and thus has already been capable of adopting a joint position. This is because the 'export' of such a joint position might not raise internal tensions and, indeed, might be in the EU's competitive interest by making its standards the common international standard. An example is the international discussion on a protocol with regard to liability for damage caused by genetically modified organisms or products. Here, the EC has come to the internal agreement that the development of specific provisions on liability for damage caused by such products is not desirable. It, therefore, is likely to also actively promote this approach at the international level.

8 LESSONS TO LEARN FROM THE EU ENVIRONMENTAL EXPERIENCE

Over the past 30 years, the EC has developed a comprehensive and dense legal network for its internal environmental protection policy, which has evolved from a marginal role to becoming a core policy of the EC. Having established the link between EC environmental policy and sustainable development, the former is likely to remain at the core of EU policy, even if economic considerations might figure more prominently. EC internal environmental law and policy, despite some of the difficulties discussed, is an uncontested success story. It is much more successful than any juxtaposition of national environmental policies and laws could have been. The environmental provisions that were adopted allow any member state that has the political will to do so, to develop a coherent and efficient environmental policy. No significant sector of environmental policy can be identified where a state's environmental efforts could not have been realized because of the state's member-ship in the EC. In contrast, numerous examples can be given where state environ-mental legislation would not exist without prior EC legislation on this matter.

The EC's contribution to the development of international law lies in a number of major achievements that are perhaps not all innovative but that are easily forgotten. The first lesson to learn from the EC is that protection of the environment will be inadequate as long as the principle of national sovereignty remains sacrosanct in environmental matters. The environment knows no frontiers, and, more and more, standard setting in water and air, waste management, nature conservation, climate change, and biodiversity protection will have to be undertaken in a context that exceeds national geographic and legal frontiers. And as the protection of the envir-onment is largely in the hands of states and public authorities, measures that can be enforced against states are a necessity in environmental matters.

The second lesson is that while states and public authorities have the task to pro-tect the environment, all too often public authorities at the local, regional, or national level will tolerate, accept, or favour environmental impairment, through their action, inertia, or passivity. More than any other sector of law, environmental law needs robust, credible, and strong enforcement procedures in order to remain credible. The length of judicial procedures requires an efficient, speedy, and smooth dispute settle-ment procedure that is independent of parties and acts prior to the intervention of courts.

The third lesson to learn from the EC's experience is that citizens' active involve-ment in the monitoring of the environment is indispensable. Public authorities hold the power to protect or not to protect the environment. Sharing this power with its citizens is indispensable if the general interest in environmental protection, which is confronted with numerous vested interests, is to be kept on the agenda—an open society is crucial for the protection of the environment.

The fourth lesson is that environmental principles and provisions alone are not sufficient to adequately protect the environment. Agriculture, energy, transport, trade, and fisheries law—the different sectors of economic and administrative law—progressively need to be influenced by environmental considerations and 'greened'. Environmental law must not be considered as just one more sector of law, besides many others. Rather, it needs to be integrated into laws applicable to other policy areas. This process is not self-sustaining but requires active steering.

Fifth, the making of (environmental) law is not exclusively an issue of putting provisions on papers and taking them through the regulatory machinery. It is neces-sary to bring decision-makers together regularly, to ensure confidence building, and to generate synergistic effects among them. Achieving this process requires much more frequent meetings than once every five or ten years. Moreover, it is doubtful whether global meetings on environmental issues, even if held frequently, can achieve this result. Regular regional UN meetings with fewer participants, fewer topics, and less red carpet might well help in addressing important regional environmental problems and exploring solutions that cannot be realized at the global level.

Sixth and finally, it should be remembered that environmental law is not an end in itself—it is a tool to protect the environment. Environmental standards need to be prepared, drawn up, adopted, and put into daily practice. Regional environment action programs drawn up under UN guidance could contribute to ensure better regional cooperation, more consideration for the making of environmental law, and more reflection on the ways and means to develop environmental law principles, such as those of the 1992 Rio Declaration, and to make environmental law a reality, not only an intellectual game with glass beads.

From the perspective of public international law, the EC could be seen as an actor that demonstrates how much progress can be achieved in environmental law and policy as long as the solutions are not looked for at the global level but instead where attention is more focused on the regional aspect. In particular, the combined impacts of the policy postures of the United States and of developing states, with the former systematically subordinating environmental concerns to trade consider-ations at the international level, and the latter perceiving environmental protection as an impediment to economic growth, makes it unlikely that adequate global solu-tions to urgent environmental problems—climate change, loss of biodiversity, omnipresence of chemicals, water of insufficient quality and quantity, urbanization, erosion, and desertification—can be found. There is one planet but, for the fore-seeable time ahead, not one governance system for this planet. Seen from this per-spective, the EC efforts to protect the regional environment could be considered as an alternative option to global environmental solutions, embedded in international principles and overall objectives. European environmental policy and law, with all of its imperfections, can try to make environmental protection a daily reality, an applied system of law, and a part of the United States' and of European policy. The EC, thus, is more of an actor on the regional than on the international scene. However, its results in effectively protecting, preserving, and improving the European environment are impressive.

The EC's future is more uncertain than the future of states. The recent and pro-jected enlargements undoubtedly constitute a risk to further internal EC integration, and thus also to the consolidation and intensification of environmental protection measures. The difficulties of adapting to globalization might lead EC member states, and the EC itself, to choose between economic competitiveness and environmental protection, though empirical data show that European states with a strong environ-mental policy are generally economically more competitive than states with a weak environmental policy. Should the attempts to adopt a constitution for the EU fail, the cutting back of the EU to some form of free trade area is an option that might be attractive to some. European environmental law is bound to be negatively affected by such an evolution, and, under such circumstances, it would probably suffer signifi-cant regress.

RECOMMENDED READING

N. Haigh et al., *Manual of Environmental Policy: The EC and Britain* (London: Cartermill (loose-leaf)).

J. Jans, *European Environmental Law*, 2nd edition (Groningen: Europa Law Publishing, 2002).

L. Krämer, *Casebook on EU Environmental Law* (Oxford: Hart Publishing, 2002).

——, *EC Environmental Law* (London: Sweet and Maxwell, 2003).

M. Lee, *EU Environmental Law: Challenges, Change and Decision-Making* (Oxford: Hart Publishing, 2005).

R. Macrory, ed., *Principles of European Environmental Law* (Groningen: Europa Law Publishing, 2004).

M. Pallemaerts, *Toxics and Transnational Law* (Oxford: Hart Publishing, 2003).

H.W. Rengeling, ed., *Handbuch zum europäischen und deutschen Umweltrecht*, 2 volumes, 2nd edition (Köln: Heymann, 2002).

R. Romi, *L'Europe et la protection juridique de l'environnement*, 3rd edition (Paris: Editions Victoires, 2004).

N.J. Vig and M.G. Faure, eds., *Green Giants? Environmental Policies of the United States and the European Union* (Cambridge, MA: MIT Press, 2004).

CHAPTER 38

TREATY BODIES

GEIR ULFSTEIN

1 INTRODUCTION

THE 'treaty bodies' established by many multilateral environmental agreements (MEAs) represent a new form of international cooperation. These bodies, and, in particular, their 'conferences of the parties' (COPs), are not merely intergovernmental conferences since they are established by treaties as permanent organs and have subsidiary bodies and a secretariat, while they also differ from traditional inter-governmental organizations (IGOs). These new institutional arrangements grew out of the 1972 UN Conference on the Human Environment in Stockholm. The first environmental treaty to use the term conference of the parties was the 1973 Convention on Trade in Endangered Species of Wild Fauna and Flora (CITES). Although a few MEAs have used an existing IGO,[1] or have established a new IGO,[2] more recently, COPs have become the preferred institutional machinery for cooperation under MEAs. They have been established, for example, by global treaties addressing climate change, ozone depletion, and biodiversity as well as by regional agreements addressing acid rain in Europe and hazardous wastes in Africa.

Treaties parties may have several reasons for choosing the COP model rather than traditional IGOs. First, using an existing IGO may have the disadvantage of including states that are not parties to the relevant MEA. Second, the establishment of a new IGO may be perceived as more costly and bureaucratic. Third, COPs offer greater flexibility since they do not have a permanent seat but may instead convene meetings in different countries and in different parts of the world.

The next section briefly describes COPs, their subsidiary bodies, and their secretariats. Sections 3 to 5 then discuss, respectively, the decision-making powers of COPs with respect to internal matters, their substantive decision-making powers, and their capacity to act at the external level. A cross-cutting issue in these three sections is the question of the international legal personality of COPs and their implied powers. Finally, section 6 reflects on the applicability of treaty law and international institutional law to the activities of the COPs, the extent to which the treaty bodies in the form of COPs are unique features in international law, and whether the COPs serve their intended functions.

---

[1] For example, several agreements dealing with marine pollution rely upon the International Maritime Organization (IMO).   [2] For example, international fisheries commissions.

2 STRUCTURE AND FUNCTIONS
OF TREATY BODIES

The COP, as the supreme organ under MEAs that are applying the COP model, is composed of all treaty parties.[3] COPs meet regularly, usually annually or every second year. A bureau elected by the COP may act on its behalf between its regular meetings and serves as a facilitating organ during the COP's sessions. The functions of COPs are spelled out in their constitutive MEAs, although COPs may have implied powers as well. Typical functions with respect to matters internal to the MEA include establishing subsidiary bodies, adopting rules of procedure, and giving guidance to subsidiary bodies and the secretariat (see section 3). In addition, COPs are instrumental in developing parties' substantive cooperation under the MEA by adopting new binding or non-binding commitments by the parties (see section 4). Finally, COPs may act at the external level by entering into arrangements with states, IGOs, or the organs of other MEAs (see section 5).

Protocols to MEAs, insofar as they are formally separate agreements, may have their own institutional structure (see section 4 later in this chapter). The substantive linkage between the parent convention and the protocol—and full or partial overlap in membership between the two—may, however, militate in favour of joint institutions or meetings. The Montreal Protocol on Substances That Deplete the Ozone Layer (Montreal Protocol) to the Vienna Convention for the Protection of the Ozone Layer (Vienna Convention) is an example of a protocol that establishes a separate Meeting of the Parties (MOP), which meets in conjunction with the COP of the convention. In contrast, the plenary body of the regional Convention on Long-Range Transboundary Air Pollution (LRTAP Convention) also serves as the governing body of its relevant protocols. The Kyoto Protocol to the UN Framework Convention on Climate Change (UNFCCC) provides that the COP of the convention shall serve as the MOP of the protocol, but parties to the convention that are not parties to the protocol may participate only as observers when the COP acts in this capacity.

Subsidiary bodies may be established through provisions in a MEA itself or, as already mentioned, by decision of the COP. They may have different functions, including financial assistance (as in the case of the Montreal Protocol's Executive Body), technology transfer, compliance (as in the case of the Montreal Protocol's Implementation Committee), or scientific advice. Subsidiary organs may have the same membership as the COP, but they may also be established with a limited membership. Although most subsidiary organs are composed of state representatives,

---

[3] This plenary organ may have different denominations, such as Meeting of the Parties (MOP) or Executive Body.

some compliance bodies, such as the Kyoto Protocol's compliance committee, are composed of persons acting in their individual capacity.

A permanent secretariat may be designated in the MEA itself, or the MEA may establish an interim secretariat and leave the final decision to the COP. While the COP and subsidiary bodies are independent organs, many MEAs locate their secretariats with existing IGOs, such as the United Nations, the UN Environment Programme (UNEP), the UN Economic Commission for Europe (UNECE) or the International Maritime Organization (IMO), although some establish more autonomous secretariats. For example, the UNFCCC is 'institutionally linked' to the United Nations but without being fully integrated into any of its departments or programmes. The Convention on Wetlands of International Importance Especially as Waterfowl Habitat (Ramsar Convention) is unusual in that it uses a non-governmental organization (NGO)—the World Conservation Union (IUCN)—as its secretariat. When an MEA uses an existing IGO to perform secretariat functions, the location of the MEA secretariat may be different from that of the host organization. For example, the secretariat of the Convention on Biological Diversity (CBD) is based in Montreal, whereas the 'host', UNEP, is based in Nairobi.

The functions of the secretariat are generally spelled out in the MEA. Typical functions include conducting studies, preparing draft decisions for the COP and subsidiary bodies, providing technical assistance to the parties, and receiving and circulating reports on the implementation of commitments. The secretariat may also serve as the conduit for cooperation with other MEAs and relevant international organizations and bodies, including financial institutions.

3 COMPETENCE AT THE INTERNAL LEVEL

The powers of the COP at the internal level—that is, in matters relating to the operation of the MEA—may be set out explicitly in the MEA. Typical powers include adopting rules of procedure, adopting financial regulations and the budget, establishing new subsidiary bodies, and providing guidance to these bodies and the secretariat. More general powers may also be provided, authorizing the COP, for example, to exercise other functions required for the achievement of the objective of the MEA. Through such specific and general powers, the COP is provided with authority at the internal level corresponding to that which is provided in the constitutive instruments of the IGOs.

In addition to the powers explicitly granted by the MEA establishing a COP, COPs may have implied powers. The doctrine of 'implied powers' has been developed for international organizations, where it found its authoritative expression in the Advisory Opinion of the International Court of Justice in *Reparation for Injuries*

Suffered in the Service of the United Nations (*Reparations* case).[4] By emphasizing the object and purpose of the IGO, this doctrine has provided the legal basis for decision-making that is not expressly set out in the convention establishing the international organization, including decisions at the internal level.[5] The institutional set-up of COPs, with their subsidiary bodies and secretariats, is so similar to those of traditional IGOs that this doctrine arguably also applies to the decision-making powers of COPs.[6] In the absence of express authority for powers at the internal level, resort may thus be had to the 'implied powers' of the COP (for example, to establish subsidiary organs).

The institutional structure of MEAs is hierarchic, with the COP being the supreme body. This formation means that the subsidiary bodies and the secretariat must respect the decisions and instructions adopted by the COP. The organization hosting the secretariat has no power to instruct either the COP or its subsidiary bodies. There may, however, arise some questions concerning the allocation of competence between the COP and the host organization to instruct the secretariat. The point of departure should be that, whereas the officials of the secretariat are employed by the host organization and, as such, are under its instruction, any failure to execute decisions of the COP would amount to a breach of the cooperation arrangement between the COP and the host organization.

The rules of procedure for COPs generally provide for decision-making in internal matters by simple majority. As with IGOs, internal decisions, such as guidance by the COP to subsidiary bodies and the secretariat, should be considered binding unless the MEA or the relevant decision itself specifically indicates that a certain type of decision was intended to be non-binding.

4 SUBSTANTIVE DECISION-MAKING

COPs, together with their subsidiary bodies and secretariat, have important roles in developing the substantive commitments of MEA parties. The parties will usually meet in the subsidiary organs as well as in the COP, hammering out decisions

[4] *Reparation for Injuries Suffered in the Service of the United Nations*, Advisory Opinion of 11 April 1949, [1949] I.C.J. Rep. 174. The case concerned the capacity of the United Nations to bring a legal claim. The court considered that 'the Organization must be deemed to have those powers which, though not expressly provided . . . are conferred upon it by necessary implication as being essential to the performance of its duties.'

[5] See *Effects of Awards of Compensation Made by the U.N. Administrative Tribunal*, Advisory Opinion of 13 July 1954, [1954] I.C.J. Rep. 47 at 53.

[6] R.R. Churchill and G. Ulfstein, 'Autonomous Institutional Arrangements in Multilateral Environmental Agreements: A Little-Noticed Phenomenon in International Law' (2000) 94 A.J.I.L. 623 at 632–3.

through negotiations in these permanent forums. This process is far more effective than convening ad hoc diplomatic conferences for defined purposes (see Chapter 32 'International Institutions').

The governing MEA will set out the decision-making powers of the COP in relation to the adoption of new substantive commitments. Virtually all COPs may adopt amendments to their governing MEA that contain new legal obligations. Such amendments will, however, require subsequent ratification by states parties to the MEA in order to create binding obligations for individual parties. Generally, a minimum number of ratifications are required in order for an amendment to enter into force. This type of amendment process is well known from other multilateral treaties, including treaties establishing IGOs.

Several MEAs reflect the framework treaty-protocol approach, whereby the COP is allocated powers to adopt protocols to the MEA that contain new commitments. Examples include the Vienna Convention and its Montreal Protocol, and the UNFCCC with its Kyoto Protocol. In these cases, the normal treaty-making approach has been applied, but use has been made of the institutional machinery established by the MEA to further develop the regime by way of protocols. However, since they are treaties in their own rights, these protocols also require subsequent ratification to bind individual states, and a minimum number of ratifications to enter into force.

Several MEAs provide for their COPs to adopt or amend annexes to the MEA or its protocols, subject to the non-acceptance of these decisions by individual parties. Annexes are often of a 'technical' nature, but they may also involve controversial political issues, such as lists of prohibited substances or of protected animals or plants. Relevant examples can be found under the Montreal Protocol, CITES, and the Convention on the Conservation of Migratory Species of Wild Animals (CMS). Although the parties retain the formal right to make a notification of non-acceptance, there may be considerable political pressure not to make such a notification. By requiring action by states in order for them not to become committed rather than to become committed—opting-out, instead of opting-in—the efficiency of law-making is greatly enhanced.

The most advanced form of delegated powers to the COP is found in treaties that authorize it to adopt binding decisions. This approach has the advantage of allowing for a more speedy process and of preventing states from staying outside new commitments, since otherwise they could do so by non-ratification or non-acceptance of amendments or protocols. In such cases of binding COP decision-making, we may truly speak of international legislation. However, it seems that the only MEA-based example of such explicit powers is Article 2.9 of the Montreal Protocol, which allows the adoption of certain new obligations—with binding effect for all parties—by a 'double majority' of developing and developed states. Although Article 2.9 has never been used, one cannot exclude the possibility that the mere existence of this option can help achieve solutions based on consensus.

A controversial issue is whether COPs can have law-making powers without the explicit authority to make binding decisions being given in the text of the MEA (see Chapter 20 'Treaty Making and Treaty Evolution' and Chapter 32 'International Institutions'). Generally, such powers would encroach on the sovereignty of states and should not easily be presumed. However, Article 17 of the Kyoto Protocol, for example, enables the COP to adopt 'rules' relating to the operation of the system for trading in emissions of greenhouse gases. The use of the word 'rules' suggests that such measures are intended to be legally binding. This idea is supported by the fact that this article refers to 'relevant principles, modalities, rules and guidelines,' indicating that 'rules' are different from, for example, non-binding 'principles' or 'guidelines'. Such an interpretation is also supported by substantive considerations. For instance, a party that makes use of the 'rules' on emissions trading by buying emission quotas cannot, arguably, be accused of non-compliance with the protocol when it wants to add these quotas to the emission limits of the protocol.[7]

It may be added that the question of the binding character of decisions by MEA bodies has also arisen in relation to decisions establishing non-compliance procedures as well as to decisions adopted by compliance bodies operating under such procedures (see Chapter 43 'Compliance Procedures'). In the climate change regime, for example, the COP decision on compliance, which was adopted as part of the so-called Marrakesh Accords,[8] left it up to the COP/MOP[9] 'to decide on the legal form of the procedures and mechanisms on compliance.' Article 18 of the Kyoto Protocol specifically provides that any 'procedures and mechanisms' entailing 'binding consequences' shall be adopted by amendment, so unless the COP/MOP adopts an amendment relating to compliance, the Kyoto compliance procedure cannot entail 'binding consequences'. This provision leaves uncertain the legal status of measures adopted by the Enforcement Branch of the Compliance Committee in response to non-compliance. For example, it may be argued that deduction of emission quotas at a penalty rate as a response to non-compliance with a party's assigned amount of emissions, which is one of the most significant consequences envisaged, is a 'binding consequence' requiring the amendment procedure.[10] Absent such an amendment, it remains unclear whether, and with what legal effect, this consequence could be imposed.[11]

---

[7] *Ibid.* at 639. More sceptical about the binding character is J. Brunnée in 'COPing with Consent: Law-Making under Multilateral Environmental Agreements' (2002) 15 Leiden J. Int'l L. 1 at 24–6.

[8] The Marrakesh Accords were adopted by the COP of the UN Framework Convention on Climate Change (UNFCCC) in 2001 (Decision 24/CP. 7).

[9] The COP/MOP is the Conference of the Parties to the UNFCCC serving as the Meeting of the Parties to the Kyoto Protocol, but with voting rights only for representatives from the parties to the protocol (see the Kyoto Protocol, Article 13).

[10] See G. Ulfstein and J. Werksman, 'The Kyoto Compliance System: Towards Hard Enforcement,' in O.S. Stokke, J. Hovi, and G. Ulfstein, *Implementing the Climate Regime: International Compliance* (London: Earthscan, 2005) 39 at 58.

[11] The sensitive nature of this issue is illustrated by the fact that, at its first meeting in December 2005, the COP/MOP was unable to reach final agreement on it. It adopted the compliance procedures and mechanisms by simple decision but provided for consideration of an amendment with a view to making a decision by its third meeting in 2007.

COPs may also engage in interpretation of the provisions of their governing MEA or protocol. To the extent that such interpretation is expressly authorized by the governing MEA or protocol, it appears intended to be of a legally binding character. An example would be Article 10(1) of the Montreal Protocol, which establishes that contributions from developed countries to the protocol's financial mechanism shall 'meet all agreed incremental costs' incurred by developing countries in complying with commitments under the protocol. The MOP was to decide on an 'indicative list' of incremental costs, which it did in 1992.[12] The fact that there was express authorization of this decision in the Montreal Protocol means that it should be considered to be of a binding nature.

However, interpretation of MEAs may also be undertaken in the absence of such explicit authorization. For example, the Consultative MOP to the Convention on the Prevention of Marine Pollution by Dumping of Wastes and Other Matter has decided that 'dumping' under the convention covers the disposal of waste into or under the seabed from the sea but not from land by tunnelling.[13] In such cases, the interpretation could be considered subsequent practice by the parties to a treaty, which, according to Article 31(3)(b) of the Vienna Convention on the Law of Treaties, is an element that may be taken into account in interpreting the treaty. On the other hand, if international institutional law applies, the COP, like an IGO organ, would be regarded as the author of the practice, and not the states parties. In either case, provided the interpretation adopted by the COP is uncontested and not modified by further practice, it should carry considerable weight in interpreting the relevant terms of the MEA. Of course, certain interpretative acts may be so far-reaching that they may better be understood as an attempt to amend the MEA between all parties or to modify the MEA between the parties voting in favour of the decision (Articles 39 and 41 of the Vienna Convention on the Law of Treaties, respectively). Since the MEA will usually contain an amendment procedure requiring subsequent ratification by states parties, such a form of simplified amendment or modification should not easily be presumed.

Finally, the COPs may adopt decisions that concern substantive commitments but are not meant to be of a binding character—'soft law' measures. The parties may apply such measures in order to develop their commitments without being ready to undertake new legal obligations. Soft law measures may be effective in themselves, but they may also be the first step in adopting binding regulations. For example, the ban on the export of hazardous waste from Organisation for Economic Co-operation and Development (OECD) countries to non-OECD countries was first adopted by a COP decision under the Basel Convention on the Control of

---

[12] 'Indicative List of Categories of Incremental Costs,' Doc. UNEP/Ozl.Pro.4/15, reprinted in (1992) 3 Y.B. Int'l Envt'l L. 822.

[13] London Consultative Meeting of the Parties, Resolution LDC.41 (13) (1990), reprinted in (1990) 6 Int'l Org. & the Law of the Sea: Documentary Yearbook 332. See Churchill and Ulfstein, note 6 above at 641.

Transboundary Movements of Hazardous Wastes and Their Disposal and subsequently adopted as an amendment to the convention.[14] Non-binding decisions may also contribute to developing new customary international law, for example, as expressions of *opinio juris* in relation to concepts such as 'sustainable development' (see Chapter 26 'Sustainable Development') or the 'precautionary principle' (see Chapter 25 'Precaution').

The voting procedures for adopting new substantive commitments—be they of a binding or non-binding character—will follow from provisions in the relevant MEA or protocol or from the COP's rules of procedure. Most MEAs provide that the parties shall try to reach a consensus decision, but, if this proves impossible, they will allow decisions to be taken by a qualified majority. However, some MEAs establish special procedures, such as the requirement of a 'double majority' of developed and developing countries in the Montreal Protocol, when exercising the 'legislative' functions mentioned earlier. Similar voting arrangements may also be found in subsidiary organs, such as the Enforcement Branch of the Compliance Committee under the Kyoto Protocol, which requires a three-quarters majority and a majority both among developed and developing states for making decisions.

5 COMPETENCE AT THE EXTERNAL LEVEL

Most of the attention devoted to the powers and functions of MEAs has focused on standard setting, and the implementation of these standards within the scope of the agreement. MEAs, however, may also need to have a 'foreign policy'—for instance, the relationship to the IGO hosting the secretariat must be arranged; there may be a need for agreement with the state hosting the secretariat and meetings of the parties; implementation of commitments may require financial assistance and capacity building and, hence, arrangements with international financial institutions; and, finally, because some environmental problems are inter-connected, it may be necessary to require cooperation between different MEAs and IGOs involved in the environmental field (see Chapter 32 'International Institutions').

Several questions of international law are relevant when assessing the capacity of the COPs to enter into arrangements at the external level. First, to what extent does the COP have the necessary 'international legal personality' to enter into binding agreements under international law? Second, would the subsidiary bodies and the secretariat be bound by these agreements? Third, would these agreements be directly binding, and would they be so for the states parties to the MEA? And, finally, would

---

[14] Decision II/12, *Report of the Second COP*, Doc. UNEP/CHW.2/30 b (1994) and Decision III/1, *Report of the Third COP*, Doc. UNEP/CHW.3/35 (1995).

MEA organs other than the COP have the competence to enter into such agreements? It may be asked whether these questions are merely legal niceties. However, similar questions arise for IGOs, and, to the extent that the organs of MEAs serve comparable functions, these issues must also be addressed with respect to cooperation under MEAs.

MEAs do not contain explicit provisions setting out their treaty-making capacity. This absence of explicit provisions is, however, also common to most IGOs, without preventing them from enjoying such legal capacity. Furthermore, several provisions of MEAs may be taken to provide treaty-making capacity, such as the catch-all phrase in Article 7(2) of the UNFCCC, which states that the COP 'shall make, within its mandate, the decisions necessary to promote the effective implementation of the Convention'; Article 7(1) authorizing the COP to '[s]eek and utilize, where appropriate, the services and cooperation of, and information provided by, competent international organizations and intergovernmental and non-governmental bodies'; and the powers of the secretariat under Article 8(2)(f) to 'enter, under the overall guidance of the Conference of the Parties, into such administrative and contractual arrangements as may be required for the effective discharge of its functions.'

The main basis for accepting the international legal capacity of IGOs at the external level has, however, been the doctrine of 'implied powers' referred to earlier in this chapter on the competence of the MEA organs at the internal level. The reason for establishing COPs, subsidiary bodies, and secretariats rather than formal IGOs was 'institutional economy' and not a desire to have less effective institutions. Furthermore, there is a need for MEA organs to act at the external level. Hence, 'implied powers' should be equally acceptable as a basis for the treaty-making capacity of MEAs as for that of IGOs.[15]

It should also be assumed that it is the COP, as the supreme body of the MEA, just as it is the IGO, that has the competence to enter into binding agreements, unless a corresponding competence for the subsidiary bodies or the secretariat follows directly from the MEA or from decisions by the COP. Agreements entered into would be binding for all the MEA bodies, but not for the states parties as such. The states parties must, however, respect such agreements when they act as members of the COP or of other MEA bodies. Similarly, the agreements will not be binding for the organization hosting the secretariat, but the secretariat must respect the agreements as part of their secretarial responsibilities.

If we take a look at the arrangements actually entered into by COPs, we find, first, that the relationship with the organization hosting the secretariat is not based on a

---

[15] The UN Office of Legal Affairs stated in an opinion of 4 November 1993 that the UNFCCC established 'an international entity/organization with its own separate legal personality, statement of principles, organs and a supportive structure in the form of a Secretariat' (Articles 3, 7–10). United Nations Office of Legal Affairs, *Arrangements for the Implementation of the Provisions of Article 11 of the UN Framework Convention on Climate Change Concerning the Financial Mechanism* (4 November 1993) para. 4.

binding or non-binding agreement, but rather on parallel decisions of the COP and of the organs of the host organization on their mutual relationship. Thus, the COP of the UNFCCC decided at its first meeting in 1995 (Decision 14/CP.1) that 'the Convention secretariat shall be institutionally linked to the United Nations, while not being fully integrated in the work programme and management structure of any particular department or programme.' The UN General Assembly responded by adopting Resolution 50/115 of 20 December 1995, which '[e]ndorse[d] the institutional linkage between the Convention secretariat and the United Nations, as advised by the Secretary-General and adopted by the Conference of the Parties.'

In regard to the arrangements made between the MEA organs and the state hosting the secretariat or meetings of such organs, we find agreements, such as on privileges and immunities, which should be considered to be of a legally binding nature. Examples are the 1996 Agreement between the United Nations, the Federal Republic of Germany, and the Secretariat of the UNFCCC and the 1998 Agreement between the Multilateral Fund for the Implementation of the Montreal Protocol and Canada. These agreements were accepted by the COPs, respectively, of the UNFCCC and of the Montreal Protocol.

Separate financial institutions may be set up under MEAs, such as the Multilateral Fund of the Montreal Protocol, or use may be made of existing financial arrangements, such as the Global Environment Facility (GEF). The UNFCCC establishes that a mechanism for the provision of financial resources, including the transfer of technology, is 'defined' and that arrangements shall be agreed upon between the COP and the 'entity or entities' entrusted with the operation of this mechanism (Article 11(1) and (3)), which is the GEF. The COP of the UNFCCC entered in 1996 into a memorandum of understanding (MOU) with the Council of the GEF. MOUs are generally meant to signify non-binding, rather than binding, arrangements. The non-binding character of the MOU between the COP of the UNFCCC and the GEF is also supported by its wording. On the other hand, nowhere is it suggested that the non-binding status of the arrangement was chosen because the COP lacked competence to enter into binding agreements (see Chapter 41 'Technical and Financial Assistance').

There is an obvious need for arrangements formalizing cooperation between different MEAs in order to facilitate a more comprehensive approach to international environmental problems. The CBD provides that the COP shall contact the executive bodies of other relevant conventions so as to enter into 'appropriate forms of cooperation' with them (Article 23(4)(h)). This provision has formed the basis for memoranda of cooperation with the secretariats of relevant MEAs, such as the Ramsar Convention, the CMS Convention, and CITES. The memorandum of cooperation with the Ramsar Convention's Secretariat is called an 'agreement', and requires a year's written notice for termination, which could indicate its binding character. On the other hand, the term 'memorandum of cooperation' and its wording lead to the conclusion that it is a non-binding arrangement. This conclusion also seems to hold true for the other memoranda of cooperation entered into by the secretariat of the CBD. It should not necessarily be taken to indicate a lack of international legal personality, but rather that internationally binding agreements are not necessary or desirable for such coordination between secretariats.

6 Conclusions

The establishment of treaty bodies by MEAs may be regarded as part of a more general trend in international law towards the institutionalization of cooperation between states to solve common problems. MEAs are treaties and, as such, the tenets of treaty law are applicable. International institutional law should, however, supplement treaty law when assessing the powers of the treaty bodies.

Although we find some similarities in the institutional set-up of treaties outside the field of international environmental law, it is difficult to find other examples of treaties establishing COPs with a comparable role in standard setting and with subsidiary organs and a permanent secretariat. True enough, human rights treaties and some arms-control treaties provide for their parties to meet from time to time but, typically, only for considering amendments to the treaty and/or electing members of supervisory organs. Supervisory organs of human rights treaties may have some resemblance to those set up under non-compliance procedures in MEAs, but the human rights organs are composed of independent experts and not of representatives from the states parties. The composition of the Compliance Committee of the Kyoto Protocol is, however, comparable in this respect to that of human rights supervisory organs.[16]

As in most forms of international institutions, there have been disagreements over the powers of COPs, both in substantive decision-making and in relation to compliance control. A more policy-oriented question is how the cooperation between different MEAs should be facilitated and, indeed, to what extent there is a need for a more comprehensive approach to international environmental problems. Possible avenues are more formalized cooperation between relevant MEAs, a strengthened role for UNEP, or even the establishment of a World Environment Organization.[17]

---

[16] Another example is the Compliance Committee under the Convention on Access to Information, Public Participation in Decision-Making and Access to Justice in Environmental Matters (see Chapter 29 'Public Participation').

[17] See B.H. Desai, 'Mapping the Future of International Environmental Governance' (2000) 13 Y.B. Int'l Envt'l L. 21; B. Desai, *Institutionalizing International Environmental Law* (Ardsley, NY: Transnational Publishers, 2004); and S. Charnovitz, 'A World Environment Organization' (2002) Colum. J. Envt'l L. 323.

On the other hand, concern has also been raised, particularly by the United States, about the increasing powers of MEA organs.[18] Finally, to the extent that it is acknowledged that more effective international cooperation is needed in order to address urgent environmental challenges, more attention may be directed towards the legitimacy of decision-making under MEAs (see Chapter 30 'Legitimacy'), such as the roles of public participation, the scientific basis for decisions, and state consent.[19] All of these questions must be carefully considered. Yet, in the meantime, it is fair to say that MEAs with their COPs, subsidiary bodies, and secretariats have generally been successful in providing a non-bureaucratic and dynamic framework for environmental cooperation.

RECOMMENDED READING

D. Bodansky, 'The Legitimacy of International Governance: A Coming Challenge for International Environmental Law?' (1999) 93 A.J.I.L. 596.

J. Brunnée, 'COPing with Consent: Law-Making under Multilateral Environmental Agreements' (2002) 15 Leiden J. Int'l L. 1.

S. Charnovitz, 'A World Environment Organization' (2002) 27 Colum. J. Envt'l L. 323.

R. Churchill and G. Ulfstein, 'Autonomous Institutional Arrangements in Multilateral Environmental Agreements: A Little-Noticed Phenomenon in International Law' (2000) 94 A.J.I.L. 623.

B. Desai, *Institutionalizing International Environmental Law* (Ardsley, NY: Transnational Publishers, 2004).

E. Hey, 'Sustainable Development, Normative Development and the Legitimacy of Decision-Making' (2003) 34 Netherlands Y.B. Int'l L. 3.

R. Lefeber, 'Creative Legal Engineering' (2000) 13 Leiden J. Int'l L. 1.

F.X. Perrez, *Cooperative Sovereignty: From Independence to Interdependence in the Structure of International Environmental Law* (The Hague: Kluwer Law International, 2000).

V. Röben, 'Institutional Developments under Modern International Environmental Agreements,' in J.A. Frowein, R. Wolfrum, and C.E. Philipp, eds., *Max Planck Yearbook of United Nations Law*, 3rd edition (Dordrecht: Martinus Nijhoff, 1999) 363.

G. Ulfstein and J. Werksman, 'The Kyoto Compliance System: Towards Hard Enforcement,' in O.S. Stokke, J. Hovi, and G. Ulfstein, *Implementing the Climate Regime: International Compliance* (London: Earthscan, 2005) 39.

[18] J. Brunnée, 'The United States and International Environmental Law: Living with an Elephant' (2004) 15(4) Env. J. Int'l L. 617 at 636–8.

[19] D. Bodansky, 'The Legitimacy of International Governance: A Coming Challenge for International Environmental Law?' (1999) 93(3) A.J.I.L. 596 at 624. See also E. Hey, 'Sustainable Development, Normative Development and the Legitimacy of Decision-Making' (2003) 34 Netherlands Y.B. Int'l L. 3.

PART VII

IMPLEMENTATION AND ENFORCEMENT

CHAPTER 39

COMPLIANCE THEORY

COMPLIANCE, EFFECTIVENESS, AND BEHAVIOUR CHANGE IN INTERNATIONAL ENVIRONMENTAL LAW

RONALD B. MITCHELL

1 INTRODUCTION

STATES have spent considerable time and resources negotiating over 1,500 bilateral and over 700 multilateral environmental agreements, and have been signing such agreements at rates averaging about 20 multilaterals and 30 bilaterals per year.[1] Yet, after states negotiate such agreements, a central question becomes: 'so what?' Which of these international environmental laws have made a difference and how much of a difference and what type of difference have they made?

2 COMPLIANCE, EFFECTIVENESS, AND THE EFFECTS OF INTERNATIONAL ENVIRONMENTAL LAW

International lawyers and legal scholars often assess the effects of international environmental agreements (IEAs) in terms of the extent to which states comply with their commitments. International relations scholars tend to examine IEA effects through a broader set of questions (see Chapter 10 'International Relations Theory'). They are concerned with any behavioural or environmental changes that can be attributed to an IEA—whether these changes involve compliance or not and regardless of whether

The material in this chapter is based upon work supported by the National Science Foundation under Grant no. 0318374 entitled 'Analysis of the Effects of Environmental Treaties' September 2003–August 2006. Any opinions, findings, and conclusions or recommendations expressed in this material are those of the author and do not necessarily reflect the views of the National Science Foundation. This chapter has benefited from helpful comments from the editors of this volume.

[1] R.B. Mitchell, 'International Environmental Agreements: A Survey of Their Features, Formation, and Effects' (2003) 28 Ann. Rev. Env't & Resources 429 at 438–9.

these changes were desired, unintended, or even perverse. International relations scholars also focus on the reasons why states change their behaviour and what aspects, if any, of an IEA explain those changes.

To see the difference between these approaches, consider four categories of behaviour: treaty-induced compliance, coincidental compliance, good faith non-compliance, and intentional non-compliance. This typology highlights that the compliance/non-compliance distinction does not always correspond well to the IEA influence/non-influence distinction. A strict focus on compliance creates two analytic problems. First, it overstates an agreement's influence by conflating coincidental compliance and treaty-induced compliance. States may comply with IEAs for a variety of reasons unrelated to their influence. For example, states join agreements to prescribe or proscribe actions that they plan to take or to refrain from taking in any event. Economic changes (for example, a recession or a major increase in oil prices) may also produce reductions in production that lead parties to an agreement to reduce their emissions of a regulated pollutant, bringing them into compliance with an agreement for reasons unrelated to agreement influence. Thus, equating compliance with IEA influence is analytically misleading if the compliant behaviours would have occurred even without the IEA.

Second, assuming non-compliance implies an IEA's lack of influence also misleads. States may make real efforts to foster an agreement's goals, but fall short of the agreement's legal standards in what can be called good-faith non-compliance. Thus, an agreement that establishes challenging behavioural rules might lead parties to undertake a range of environmentally beneficial behaviours that fall short of compliance, but nevertheless constitute more behavioural change than would have occurred had the rules been less aggressive. Although IEA comparisons do not yet allow empirically well-supported claims in this regard, it seems plausible that, for example, the moratorium on commercial whaling has led to fewer whales being killed than would have been killed had negotiators agreed to a low, but non-zero, commercial whaling quota.

Thus, evaluating compliance and non-compliance with an IEA is sometimes less useful than considering (1) whether actors have behaved differently than they would have absent the agreement and (2) why they have behaved as they have. Framed in this way, identifying the effects of IEAs raises several subsidiary questions. In what follows, I delineate these issues to highlight how the questions that legal and international relations scholars ask about the influence of IEAs—and the different ways in which they answer them—reflect different analytic goals and often explain what appear to be contradictory assessments of any particular IEA. Rather than prompting unproductive disagreements, this diversity of approaches to, and evaluations of, IEAs offers a deeper and richer understanding of when, how, and why some IEAs perform well and others perform poorly. I review the theoretical terrain and illustrate that nominally 'competing' perspectives have different insights to offer those seeking to improve the practice of international environmental law.

2.1 Identifying an Indicator of IEA Influence

First, we must ask: what should be evaluated? Where should we look for an IEA's effects?[2] We need an indicator of influence—that is, some phenomenon that we would expect to be influenced by an IEA. Three potential indicators are implied by the public policy trichotomy of outputs, outcomes, and impacts. Outputs can be thought of as the laws, policies, and regulations that states adopt to implement an IEA and transform it from international to national law (see Chapter 40 'National Implementation'). The advantage of using national laws and regulation as evidence of IEA influence is that their adoption is usually easy to identify (since they are almost always public documents), and is a necessary precondition for behavioural changes in most countries. In addition, an IEA's influence is often clearly evident in legislative or regulatory language that references, or uses language from, the IEA. And, we would be rightly sceptical of attributing drastic reductions in emissions to an IEA in states whose governments have never adopted laws or policies aimed at encouraging such reductions. Yet new laws and policies seem incomplete indicators of IEA influence. Although necessary, they are certainly not sufficient to induce the behavioural changes that might produce environmental improvement.

We can also look for an IEA's influence in outcomes—that is, in changes in how governments or sub-state actors behave. Behavioural change is useful as an indicator since IEAs almost always identify behavioural changes that must occur to achieve agreement goals. Behavioural changes are necessary links in the causal chain from IEAs to environmental improvement—however, once again, we would be sceptical of crediting an IEA with any environmental improvement without evidence of change in some relevant human behaviour. The difficulties of using behaviour as an indicator of IEA influence are that (1) many behaviours are not readily observable, especially when those individuals engaging in them have incentives to keep them secret; (2) behaviours change in response to numerous non-IEA influences; and (3) demonstrating convincingly an IEA's influence on a particular behaviour is usually more difficult than on legislation or regulation. Behaviour is also somewhat unsatisfactory as an indicator of IEA effectiveness, since even significant changes in behaviour are often insufficient to resolve an environmental problem.

We can also look for IEA influence in impacts—that is, in changes in environmental quality. Using environmental improvement as evidence of IEA influence has the advantage of focusing on the ultimate object of concern as well as the motivation, at least avowed, for negotiating IEAs. Equally important, the absence of environmental improvement provides a valuable source of feedback to IEAs: if environmental quality is not improving, it suggests that further—or at least different—actions are necessary. The disadvantages of using environmental quality as an indicator are that so

---

[2] A. Underdal, 'One Question, Two Answers,' in E.L. Miles et al., eds., *Environmental Regime Effectiveness: Confronting Theory with Evidence* (Cambridge, MA: MIT Press, 2002) 1.

many factors other than IEAs—and even other than human behaviour—influence environmental quality, and often these factors include natural variation, making the isolation of IEA influence from other factors challenging at best.

Beyond the choice of laws and regulations, behaviour, or environmental quality, one must also choose whether to look at the indicators defined by the negotiators as being important or at other indicators. The Convention on International Trade in Endangered Species of Wild Fauna and Flora (CITES) can be evaluated in terms of trade in endangered species, the hunting and harvest of these species, or efforts to protect these species. The International Convention for the Regulation of Whaling (ICRW) can be evaluated in terms of its effect on the whaling industry, the population of whales, or the legal standing of whales. And pollution agreements can be assessed through ambient pollution levels, reduced cancer rates, or reduced resource use.

2.2 Identifying a 'Comparator' of IEA Influence

Having chosen an indicator of IEA influence, one also needs a 'comparator' or a point of reference against which observed outputs, outcomes, or impacts can be compared. Three types of comparators are possible: the legal standard established in the IEA, the 'counterfactual' of what would have happened without the IEA, or some desired goal, either as defined by the IEA or by the analyst.

2.2.1 *Assessing IEA Compliance*

Using the legal standards established in an IEA as the comparator corresponds to assessing compliance. If an IEA establishes clear standards regarding the passage of certain implementing legislation; the banning, limiting, or requiring of certain behaviours; or the meeting of certain environmental quality targets, then we can compare actual legislation, behaviours, or environmental quality to those standards and identify those actors who are or are not in compliance with particular provisions of an agreement. Such assessments provide the foundation to allow various responses to these actors, in ways that may increase the effects of an existing treaty on those actors' behaviours. Thus, such assessments may contribute to improving the performance of existing agreements. After an agreement comes into force, the relevant questions for many people are 'which actors complied with, and which violated, their legal obligations', and 'what actions can be taken to increase the likelihood that all actors comply more in the future.' Such assessments are regular elements in meetings of the parties or other institutional aspects of IEAs, but are also frequently undertaken by non-governmental organizations (NGOs). A major advantage of adopting legal standards as the comparator is that, at least in many cases, they can be easily identified simply by reading the IEA. A major disadvantage, however, is that high and even perfect levels of compliance may tell us little about IEA influence.

2.2.2 *Assessing IEA Goal Achievement*

Using a goal as a comparator—whether the goal is specified by the IEA's negotiators or some other goal separately identified by the analyst—corresponds to assessing treaty success. Comparing outputs, outcomes, and impacts to specified goals can help identify how existing agreements, even if well-complied with, fall short of their goals and can identify the need for new agreements with new, more aggressive, goals. Such assessments foster the negotiation of new IEAs and the renegotiation of existing IEAs. Those seeking to foster international environmental progress often undertake such assessments to investigate whether problems are being resolved and, if progress has been made, to identify ways in which to 'move the bar' so that environmental progress can continue.

2.2.3 *Assessing IEA Effects Using Behavioural Change and Counterfactuals*

Yet, those focused on assessing compliance or goal achievement often fail to carefully assess whether, or how much of, what occurs was caused by the IEA. Both compliance and goal achievement can be simply 'happy coincidences' that occurred for reasons completely separate from the IEA's influence. If we desire to attribute compliance or goal achievement to an IEA—that is, to identify them as effects—our analysis must also incorporate counterfactuals. A counterfactual is an analytically established baseline of 'what would have happened otherwise.' A counterfactual approach focuses on whether the legislation or regulations put in place, the behaviours engaged in, or the environmental quality experienced would have been any different had the IEA not existed. Such an assessment helps identify which actions would not have been taken otherwise. Comparing observed outputs, outcomes, and impacts to what would have happened otherwise—rather than to an IEA's legal standards—allows identification of a broader range of IEA effects than is possible with a narrow focus on compliance. Such an approach can highlight cases where actors are altering their behaviours in response to an IEA, but in ways that may fall short of, exceed, or produce results quite different from those intended by the IEA's negotiators. Using counterfactuals can inform the renegotiation of existing, or the negotiation of new, agreements by identifying which elements of an IEA or which external factors have led to particular effects, be they better than expected, worse than expected, or simply different than expected. Such assessments can also identify factors that inhibit IEA influence by examining cases in which we would expect significant IEA influence, but have seen little or no influence to date. A major advantage of a counterfactual or 'effects-oriented' assessment is that it can be applied in many cases in which the other approaches are difficult or impossible. Thus, an effects-oriented approach allows us to derive important insights from the many IEAs that lack clearly defined legal standards or clearly identified goals. Of course, the obvious challenge lies in establishing a convincing counterfactual of what laws, behaviours, and environmental qualities would have existed otherwise that would provide the basis for comparison and for inferences about the IEA's influence.

Whether a compliance, goal achievement, or effects orientation is most appropriate depends on the goals of the analyst. Identifying compliers and violators even if we cannot determine whether their actions are due to an IEA or not can be useful in knowing how to induce greater compliance, whether with sanctions, rewards, or some alternative response. Identifying goals that have been achieved and goals that have fallen short provides motivation for further efforts and insight into where to place such efforts. Distinguishing states and sub-state actors who have been influenced by an IEA from those who have not, or IEAs that have had significant influence from those that have not, sheds valuable light on how to design IEAs, even when the actions of those being influenced fall far short of either compliance or goal achievement.

2.3 Selecting the Level of Analysis

Assessing an IEA's influence also requires identifying the level at which to assess the IEA. In some instances, we want to determine either the average or aggregate influence of an IEA across a range of countries in order to compare the performance of different agreements. In other instances, we want to assess the influence of a particular IEA on a particular country. In yet other instances, we want to compare the effects of several different rules within a single agreement in order to determine which rule is most effective.

The goals of evaluating an IEA also shape the type of questions and obstacles faced by this evaluation. Consider an effort to assess the influence on a particular developed country of an IEA that requires developed countries (1) to reduce their emissions of a certain pollutant by 20 per cent; (2) to contribute to a pollution reduction fund; (3) to collaborate with other countries in scientific research; and (4) to provide annual reports on emissions. How do we assess the IEA if the country reduces its emissions by 12 per cent, does not contribute to the pollution reduction fund, does extensive collaborative research, and provides detailed annual reports on emissions? We might decide to disaggregate the analysis, looking at each of the four requirements. Yet how do we compare the influence of the IEA on this country with its influence on another country that performed 'better' on two of the requirements but 'worse' on the others? How do we compare this agreement's influence to that of another pollution agreement that required a 5 per cent reduction in a pollutant that was much harder to control or that involved only developing country parties? And how, if at all, do we compare the effects of any pollution-regulating IEA to a wildlife-preserving IEA? These questions demonstrate that claims made about IEAs that appear plausible and reasonable often require analytic assumptions and judgements that involve choices about aggregation and comparison that are, upon examination, neither obvious nor straightforward.

2.4 IEA Influence and Endogeneity

Assessing IEA influence also requires addressing endogeneity. Endogeneity problems arise when the factors responsible for a problem also influence the policies adopted to resolve it. In the domestic sphere, endogeneity is less of an analytic obstacle since the actors adopting regulations are rarely the targets of regulation. However, most international treaties require collective efforts by actors who are simultaneously regulators and targets of regulation. As a result, the forces that determine environmental behaviours also determine the design of the agreement as well as which states become parties. This creates two additional challenges to accurately assessing IEA influence. First, it reminds us that agreements are often acceded to only when states—and by those states that—are ready to limit environmental harm. Therefore, the most common comparisons used as evidence of IEA influence—that is, how the behaviours of parties differ from their behaviour prior to membership and from the behaviour of non-parties—may not confirm IEA influence. Rather, these comparisons may simply indicate that when states' interests become more environmental, they negotiate and become parties to agreements that require them to take actions that they would have taken anyway, and states whose interests have not changed end up remaining non-parties. Second, the possibility of endogeneity clarifies that comparing the influence of different IEA strategies requires surmounting the major methodological hurdle that those strategies most likely were not 'randomly assigned' to different IEAs. For example, we cannot assess the value of sanctions relative to rewards by simply comparing the average performance of sanction-based IEAs to reward-based IEAs—the types of problems for which states are willing to agree to include sanctions in an agreement differ systematically from those in which they are willing to agree to include rewards.[3] And those systematic differences also influence how much or how little states change their behaviour in response to the IEA. These methodological problems can be surmounted—for example, only comparing IEAs that are independently identified as addressing the same problem type—but ignoring them is a recipe for drawing inaccurate conclusions about what makes IEAs work well.

[3] R.B. Mitchell and P. Keilbach, 'Reciprocity, Coercion, or Exchange: Symmetry, Asymmetry and Power in Institutional Design' (2001) 55 Int'l Org. 891.

3 Understanding the Influence of IEAs: How and Why Do They Make the Differences They Make?

Any analysis of IEA influence requires that we ensure that the IEA really is responsible for any changes in outputs, outcomes, or impacts that we observe, and that we can identify how and why those IEAs have had the influence they have had. Most IEAs have not been analysed in this way. Agreements on stratospheric ozone depletion, dumping of wastes in the North Sea, and dumping of radioactive wastes globally are some that have been judged as being influential. Those addressing trade in endangered species, the world's natural and cultural heritage, tropical timber, and many fisheries regimes have been judged as being less effective.[4] Yet such judgements depend considerably on whether one is most concerned with compliance, goal achievement, or behavioural change and counterfactuals.

3.1 Two Models of Actor Behaviour

International relations scholars view environmental agreements as having the potential to influence the behaviour of actors—whether individuals, corporations, or states—through two different behavioural logics: a logic of consequences or a logic of appropriateness.[5] These logics, corresponding relatively closely to 'rational actor' and 'normative' models respectively,[6] establish rather different understandings of why actors comply with or violate international environmental law (IEL).

The dominant understanding of why actors behave as they do corresponds to a rationalist logic of consequences. Within this logic, actors behave as they do as a result of explicit and instrumental calculations of how the consequences of the behaviours they have available will influence their interests. In this logic, actors come to behavioural decisions with clear and well-established goals and interests. They compare the consequences of engaging in their available alternatives using such information as they have about their alternatives, the potential consequences of those alternatives, and the likely actions of other actors. Within this decision context,

---

[4] Miles et al., see note 2 above; E. Brown Weiss and H.K. Jacobson, eds., *Engaging Countries: Strengthening Compliance with International Environmental Accords* (Cambridge, MA: MIT Press, 1998); and M.J. Peterson, 'International Fisheries Management,' in P. Haas et al., eds., *Institutions for the Earth: Sources of Effective International Environmental Protection* (Cambridge, MA: MIT Press, 1993) 249.

[5] J. March and J. Olsen, 'The Institutional Dynamics of International Political Orders' (1998) 52 Int'l Org. 943.

[6] O.A. Hathaway, 'Do Human Rights Treaties Make a Difference?' (2002) 111 Yale L.J. 1935.

they choose behaviours based on 'what is best for me'. This logic adopts a 'rational actor model' of behaviour in which actors are strongly invested in determining what actions are in their interests, and carefully gather information about available alternatives and consequences in order to calculate, quite consciously, the relative costs and benefits of their alternatives to determine which maximizes their utility. Within this logic, IEAs influence decisions by altering the consequences of engaging in certain behaviours—or the ability to engage in those behaviours—in ways that alter the actors' calculations of what is in their interests. Actors' goals are assumed to be determined by factors such as a state's position in the world relative to other states; the material, economic, political, and social resources as well as the constraints it is operating under; the preferences and dispositions of its citizenry; and other factors, all of which are assumed to be impervious to the influence of international law.

An alternative approach, which many lawyers take as a starting point and which recent theoretical work in international relations now recognizes, understands behaviour as a response to an interplay of norms and identity (involving elements of both socialization and internalization) in a process characterized as 'a logic of appropriateness.'[7] Rather than calculating how available choices help or harm their interests, actors choose among behaviours based on an assessment of 'what is the "right" thing to do in this situation for someone like me.' In this view, IEAs establish or codify norms regarding what is 'right' and 'wrong' behaviour in particular situations for particular actors. Within this logic, agreements influence decisions by signalling that certain behaviours are 'appropriate' and others are 'inappropriate' or by signalling that actors' behavioural choices will lead other actors to consider them as being a particular type of actor. Indeed, most legal proscriptions and prescriptions transform what was, prior to successful negotiations, a relatively undifferentiated spectrum of behaviours into the dichotomous categories of compliance and violation. Even if, as is often the case in IEL, consequences for compliance or violation are not defined in the agreement and do not seem likely in practice, the simple placement of behaviours into those social categories may have significant influence over some actors.

In this view, actors respond to IEAs based on the social identities that they have or seek to have. Rather than asking themselves 'what is in my interests', actors ask 'how do I want to see myself' and/or 'how do I want other actors to see me?' Thus, IEAs help define what a state must do to be considered 'environmental' or 'green'. Equally important, they also define what a state must do to be considered a 'law abiding' state. The aspects of international environmental law that 'do the work' in this model are not the threats of sanctions for violation or promises of reward for compliance but, rather, the desire of actors to do what is right, what is legally required, or what others expect of them. Indeed, norms may operate through different mechanisms. Strongly socialized actors may accept either the broad legal meta-norm of *pacta sunt servanda*—that is, that legal agreements are to be observed—or the more IEA-specific norm that states should take certain actions to 'protect the environment.'

---

[7] Compare, e.g., March and Olsen, see note 5 above, and Hathaway, see note 6 above.

For those states or sub-state actors that internalize such norms, law takes on a 'taken for granted' character in which behaviours are engaged in with little if any calculation. Such actors identify what behaviours are legal and give little thought to engaging in those that are not. Such actors are driven by an internal commitment to seeing themselves as having particular identities. Consider a set of states or corporations generally committed to either environmental protection or law conformance but that are engaged in behaviours that a new IEA bans. If those actors promptly bring themselves in line with the agreement, especially if doing so is costly or if they do not seriously consider the costs, we can assume that these actors are operating according to a logic of appropriateness. For example, judges and lawyers, especially those in states with a strong rule-of-law tradition, may 'import' IEL into domestic legal decisions and structures with little consideration of the economic impacts of such rulings.[8]

Less strongly socialized actors engage in a calculus about their behavioural choices, but it is a calculus in which the perceptions of others, rather than their material responses, are central. A government may choose to violate an environmental agreement, but it cannot choose to do so and still have other states or even their own domestic audiences perceive them as 'green' and 'law-abiding'. Thus, the desire to be viewed by domestic and international audiences as a good environmental citizen may lead some governments to give little if any thought to violating an agreement. Interestingly, this logic helps explain why states that object to an agreement's rules or, in some cases, that have withdrawn from an agreement, may nonetheless behave in line with some aspects of those rules. Thus, Norway, Japan, and Iceland all opposed the ICRW's moratorium on commercial whaling (see Chapter 16 'Biological Resources'). However, rather than simply ignore the moratorium, each country has sought to whale in ways that allow it to remain in compliance with the ICRW's provisions: Iceland has withdrawn from the agreement so that it would no longer be bound; Norway has remained a member but has followed the ICRW's 'opt out' procedures so the moratorium would not be binding on its whaling; and Japan has issued scientific permits for the whales that it kills annually. And, all three countries have kept their whaling well below pre-moratorium levels, and have selected levels and hunting techniques based on scientific principles delineated in the agreement. Thus, even cases that demonstrate the inability of IEL to achieve certain goals may demonstrate the power of norms to produce outcomes that we might not expect otherwise.

The intellectual distinctions between these models are valuable in assessing both whether and how IEL influences the behaviour of states. However, the value of the intellectual distinction should not be confused with a notion that IEL always, or even in particular cases, operates only through one or the other logic. Indeed, the distinction's value may lie precisely in its ability to generate competing observable implications from each of the models, which would allow us to identify IEAs that work

---

[8] E.g., H. Koh, 'Why Do Nations Obey International Law?' (1997) 106 Yale L.J. 2598; and K. Raustiala and A. Slaughter, 'International Law, International Relations and Compliance,' in W. Carlsnaes et al., eds., *Handbook of International Relations* (London: Sage Publications, 2002) 538.

mainly through one logic, those that work mainly through the other, those in which the two logics are mutually reinforcing, and those in which the operation of each logic appears to undercut the other.

3.2 Explaining Compliance and Other Behaviour Changes

This distinction between models of state and sub-state actor behaviour provides a foundation for understanding not only when we should expect states to comply or violate IEAs, but also when we should expect to see evidence of IEA influence in the form of treaty-induced behavioural change. This chapter's initial distinction between treaty-induced and coincidental compliance sheds light on factors that explain, and conditions that foster, behavioural change. Consider first the reasons for coincidental compliance—that is, reasons why states behave in accord with a particular IEA even when that IEA lacks any causal influence. How impressed should we be by Louis Henkin's oft-quoted claim that 'almost all nations observe almost all principles of international law and almost all of their obligations almost all of the time?'[9] High compliance levels owe much to the fact that international law reflects negotiation among the actors that will be subject to it. States often negotiate treaties precisely 'for the promotion of their national interests, and to evade legal obligations that might be harmful to them.'[10] To the extent that states negotiate because they see that reaching agreement on some issue is in their interests, we should interpret subsequent behaviour that conforms to this agreement as most likely a reflection of those interests rather than as the influence of international law that codified those interests. The lack of mining in Antarctica has more to do with the availability of cheaper alternatives than with any IEA rules banning such mining, which themselves were possible only because the pressures to mine in Antarctica were not extreme. Economic and political conflicts have often led fisheries agreements to set catch limits that are at or above the levels that the parties can reasonably catch. When agreements require little or no change in behaviour or require behavioural changes the parties planned to make anyway, we should expect high compliance, but we should not interpret this compliance as evidence of agreement influence.

When agreements reflect lowest common denominator negotiations, most states and companies will find themselves already in compliance. Indeed, many states are parties to agreements that regulate behaviours that they are not, or are only minimally, engaged in, as evident in the many non-whaling members of the ICRW and the many countries that are parties to, but not significantly engaged in the behaviours

---

[9] L. Henkin, *How Nations Behave: Law and Foreign Policy* (New York: Columbia University Press, 1979) at 47.

[10] H.J. Morgenthau, *Politics among Nations: The Struggle for Power and Peace* (New York: McGraw-Hill, 1993) at 259.

regulated by, the International Tropical Timber Agreement or the Montreal Protocol on Substances That Deplete the Ozone Layer (Montreal Protocol). When leader states convince laggard states to contribute to solving an environmental problem, the 'leader' states are likely to have already established and implemented legislation that exceeds the requirements. A 1985 protocol to the Convention on Long-Range Trans-boundary Air Pollution (LRTAP Convention) required a reduction of sulphur dioxide emissions by 30 per cent from 1980 levels by 1993—a standard that many parties had already met before the agreement was signed. Even improvements in 'laggard' state behaviour must be examined carefully since they may reflect pressures by leaders on laggards to clean up their pollution that would have occurred even without an agreement—for example, because industries in leader states pressured their governments to 're-level the playing field' by demanding that foreign governments make their competition meet the same environmental standards. In other cases, the reaching of an agreement is itself evidence that the interests of the states involved have changed (otherwise the agreement would have been reached earlier). Often, these changes in interests could be expected to prompt corresponding changes in behaviour even without an agreement. Even agreements that require behaviours that appear costly at the time of negotiation may become either cheaper or even economically advantageous to conform to if favourable, but independent economic or technological conditions prevail. In short, a reasonable starting assumption when we observe compliance is that the behaviour in question reflects the short-term and self-interested behaviour of the parties, defined narrowly and independently of the actions of other states, and that such behaviour would have occurred anyway.

To urge that we start with such an assumption is not, however, to imply that we should end with it. Agreements can influence behaviour in several ways, with agreement influence evident either as treaty-induced compliance or good faith non-compliance. Start by considering how agreements may influence states when they operate within a logic of consequences. The process of international negotiation may lead states that are involved, while remaining self-interested, to re-define their interests in broader and longer-term ways even while not leading them to see their interests as interdependent on the actions of other states. Environmental negotiations require states to consider the environmental impacts of economic activities—impacts that are often sufficiently long term, unclear, ambiguous, or indirect that they would not be considered in a state's decision-making. Agreements that promote scientific research may show that particular behaviours harm the states engaged in them, independent of any impacts they may have on other states. Thus, reductions of acid precipitants under the LRTAP Convention appear to have been due, at least in part, to scientific efforts under that convention that clarified the local (rather than the foreign) effects of acid rain on forests, lakes, and fisheries (see Chapter 14 'Atmosphere and Outer Space'). By making the environmental costs of otherwise beneficial economic activities clearer and more salient, negotiations lead states to change their policies and behaviours, not because they adopt a logic of appropriateness but because they have new content in the consequences they consider. Thus, joining an agreement may alter how states calculate costs and benefits by raising the costs of certain behaviours and the benefits of others, both through quite material retaliation as well as through more social retaliatory effects. These dynamics as well as other related ones can lead states to take actions that are clearly in their interests but that they would not have taken otherwise.

IEAs may also provide opportunities for states to eschew independent action in favour of interdependent decision-making. The environmental realm, in particular, may appear to states as a realm in which they can reject the 'relative gains' model common to security and economic affairs, feeling free to improve their state's well-being in absolute terms without concerns that others will take advantage of them. Since environmental degradation is usually a by-product, rather than an intended outcome, of economic decisions, states can more readily assume that other states are not selecting levels of environmental degradation as part of a strategic game among states. States need not make worst case assumptions about other states and can use past experience and other factors to more accurately predict how other states will behave. For states who view the benefits of reducing a pollutant as contingent on how many other states also do so, the ability to reliably predict the reductions by other states may provide enough reassurance to take action that might otherwise seem too risky. And over time, initially reluctant states may gain information and confidence based on the changed behaviours of others and alter their behaviours accordingly.

Experience with an agreement also may bring behaviours more in line with agreement goals and rules due to habit, institutional inertia, or domestic legal implementation and internalization. These processes are consistent with states operating within a logic of consequences, but one that recognizes that states do not constantly recalculate decisions. Governments, corporations, and individuals may engage in a careful rational calculation about behaviours when a new treaty rule is adopted or enters into force, but standard-operating procedures, group think, and bounded rationality may make this choice, once it has been made, hard to revisit. Once agreement-consistent behaviour begins, bureaucratic and corporate supporters of such behaviour gain power and resources, while their opponents lose power and resources. Thus, pollution treaties may foster the development of corporations and corresponding corporate interests that supply pollution-reduction technologies while hindering the development of corporations that produce polluting technologies. Material capabilities may atrophy so that violation becomes more difficult or expensive. Mothballing whaling or fur-sealing ships or retooling factories that produced chlorofluorocarbons may involve processes that are as, or more, costly to undo as to do. In short, international rules allow actors to simplify or reduce the number of decisions they must make in a complex decision environment.

Now, consider how agreements may influence states when they operate within a logic of appropriateness. When an IEA simply codifies existing environmental norms, of course, any norm-driven behaviour cannot be attributed to the IEA's influence. However, IEAs can strengthen existing norms or generate new ones. In these cases, it may be difficult to analytically separate what aspects or 'how much' behaviour has been prompted by norm-strengthening or norm-generating dynamics and how much by other, more instrumental, paths of influence. This analytic obstacle should not, however, be taken as evidence that norms are not a potentially powerful path of IEA influence. Governments often publicly discuss whether to join or comply with a particular IEA's provisions. They may refuse to join an agreement or, if they join, they may take reservations, request extensions of or opt out of particular provisions, use escape clauses, or withdraw altogether. However, the social context within which these discussions occur changes as the norms strengthen. When an agreement's norms are weak or non-existent—as when an IEA has just been signed or has few parties—government officials can legitimately ask 'are these commitments in our country's interest?' As norms strengthen, however, it becomes increasingly difficult to maintain an interest-based, rather than a norm-based, framing of this question. Thus, discussions in the United States of whether to test nuclear weapons in the atmosphere would have a significantly different, and more normatively driven, tone today than they did in 1960 before the Limited Test Ban Treaty was adopted. And the discussion in France and China to stop atmospheric testing presumably had a more normative tone because of the US and Soviet ban than they would have had without that ban.

Norms may operate at this general level—influencing all states relatively equally—but norms may also operate at the more specific level implied by the focus on identity of the logic of appropriateness. Certain types of states may be more susceptible to the general norm of *pacta sunt servanda*. Thus, we might expect democratic states to comply more often with international agreements because of the normative commitments of a state's government.[11] A democratic state will tend to value an identity as a country that is subject to the 'rule of law'—behaving in conformance with international commitments represents one social 'marker' of such an identity. Some states (for example, the Scandinavian states) may, at least for periods of time, want to maintain self-perceptions and international reputations as environmental leaders—perceptions undercut by failures to meet international environmental commitments. When doing so has large domestic costs, these pressures may not be determinative, as evident in Norway's ongoing commitment to commercial whaling; but, in less demanding cases, these pressures may tip the balance in favour of fulfilling IEA commitments. Equally important, international law influences, and is relied on by, judges, bureaucrats, and other actors within states. The aggregate effect of large numbers of such actors responding to international law in particular ways can alter the

---

[11] E. Neumayer, 'Do Democracies Exhibit Stronger International Environmental Commitment?' (2002) 39 J. Peace Res. 139.

internal dynamics of a state's legal system in ways that dispose the state to meet its environmental commitments. In short, state behaviour may reflect both a logic of consequences and a logic of appropriateness.

There is a normative dimension as well when states that are not yet complying ask 'should we comply' or when states are complying and ask 'should we violate'. A country that has behaved in line with an IEA's provisions for years may find it rhetorically difficult to argue that doing so is no longer in its interests. Its previous conformity with the agreement will have strengthened the general norm surrounding the IEA as well as specific normative expectations about that country by its own citizens and other states. Governments have an easier time using instrumental and interest-based arguments to reject a norm initially, but need stronger arguments to reject a norm that they have previously supported and urged others to support.

These normative forces may be even stronger at the corporate level. Businesses promulgate and train personnel in corporate procedures that reflect domestic and international laws, even when violations are likely to go undetected. Corporations cannot flout domestic laws the way states may flout international law. They cannot, at least publicly, discuss whether to comply or violate certain rules—whether international or not—based on whether doing so is in their interests or not. Indeed, certain multinational corporations adopt international rules even when these rules are not, or have not yet been, implemented through their home government's domestic laws since doing so is in line with a norm, and corporate culture, among many corporations that see themselves as abiding by all legal rules. In some cases, corporations will adopt particular behaviours simply because they reflect some IEA provision, without considering whether a violation is likely to be caught and sanctioned. And companies sometimes have little say in the matter. For instance, companies that transport oil and other cargo internationally are quite dependent on companies that build, insure, and classify large tanker and container ships, and these latter companies have a strong norm of requiring all those they do business with to meet international marine pollution standards regardless of where those ships are flagged.[12] Companies often do not ask 'is complying with these laws in our interests' but instead simply ask 'what is the law?'

3.3 Explaining Non-Compliance, Violation, and the Failure to Change Behaviour

When states or sub-state actors fail to adopt behaviours in line with an IEA, the reasons may simply be the converse of those just delineated. Commitments may go unfulfilled because, in line with a logic of consequences, actors calculate costs and

---

[12] R.B. Mitchell, *Intentional Oil Pollution at Sea: Environmental Policy and Treaty Compliance* (Cambridge, MA: MIT Press, 1994).

benefits and find the former to exceed the latter. Likewise, agreements that have not yet generated strong normative expectations are likely to have less influence than those that have. However, there are three additional factors to consider. The foremost of these is incapacity. States and sub-state actors may fail to fulfil their IEA commitments because they lack the resources to do so. Financial, administrative, or technological incapacities can all inhibit behavioural change. The failure of developing countries to meet their environmental commitments often reflects more pressing concerns, and the lack of adequate resources, more than a conscious decision that compliance is not in their interests. Indeed, the shift to a facilitative rather than an enforcement model of compliance in many environmental agreements—including compliance-financing mechanisms under the Montreal Protocol and the UN Framework Convention on Climate Change—reflects the increasing recognition of the role of incapacities in non-compliance (see Chapter 43 'Compliance Procedures').

Precisely because many, and perhaps most, IEAs require that governments alter the behaviour of a myriad of sub-national actors, governments that lack relevant administrative capacities may fail to alter the behaviours of those actors. Governments may lack requisite informational or regulatory infrastructures. Thus, efforts in developing countries to induce peasant farmers to restrict tree clearing or wetland draining may fail for lack of the knowledge regarding who is engaged in those activities or the ability to readily communicate new rules to them. Effective regulatory infrastructures may be lacking: tankers registered in Liberia and Panama rarely enter these countries' ports, making flag state inspections under international marine pollution agreements difficult. Incapacities may sometimes be less country-specific. Negotiators may establish standards that exceed the capacities of current technologies—the hope that regulatory necessity will prompt technological innovation may prove unfounded, leaving companies with no, or only prohibitively expensive, ways to comply. Cultural, social, and historical contexts also may make compliance significantly more difficult to elicit from the companies and citizens of one country than another. The economic trajectories of some states' economies make them harder to alter than others. Similarly, the policy styles of different governments may all but preclude adoption of policy instruments that would facilitate achievement of particular policy goals within that state's available resources.

States may also fail to achieve as much behavioural change as intended due to inadvertence. Consider environmental rules establishing aggregate national targets for pollution reduction by specified deadlines. An unexpected economic boom may lead a tax established in good faith at a level deemed sufficient to achieve a 7 per cent reduction in carbon dioxide emissions by a specified date to induce only a 3 per cent reduction by that deadline. The inherent uncertainty regarding ultimate environmental affects that is characteristic of many policy strategies, particularly those giving targeted actors flexibility, means that even developed states' efforts to alter their citizens' and companies' behaviours may fail to achieve their intended results. Programmes adopted because they performed well in one country may, for a variety of reasons, perform less well in others. Innovative policies based on sound theoretical predictions about their environmental effects may, in the messy real world of implementation, face obstacles that reduce or even eliminate any significant influence on behaviour.

Finally, normative and ideological factors need not always support an IEA. When an IEA's dictates fail to reflect the concerns of particular states, those states may well reject the IEA completely. Norms of fair treatment or norms regarding the right to develop may trump norms of environmental protection. Some developing countries, most notably Malaysia, vigorously objected to negotiating a forestry agreement at the 1992 United Nations Conference on Environment and Development in Rio unless it included temperate and boreal, as well as tropical, forests.[13] Likewise, many developing countries joined the Montreal Protocol only after their economic situations were properly reflected in the agreement's terms. Indeed, the ongoing conflict between environmental protection and trade may reflect a normative divide between states' attempts to square their identity as environmental states with their identities as economically 'liberal' states.

4 Systems and Strategies for Inducing Behavioural Change

The foregoing sections have delineated reasons why states and sub-state actors fulfil, or fail to fulfil, IEA commitments and have discussed the processes by which IEAs may wield influence. They have not, however, explored the various ways IEAs attempt to promote compliance, behavioural change, and environmental improvement nor shed light on which IEAs perform better and how to improve IEA designs so that they achieve these goals. Central to questions of IEA influence are questions about how we explain the variation in performance of IEAs. Numerous case studies conducted in recent years have demonstrated clearly that, for any given IEA, certain countries are more likely to be influenced by the agreement than others.[14] More recently, however, various scholars have sought to look at a larger set of cases to identify the sources of variation across IEAs rather than sources of variation across countries.[15] This work

---

[13] E.A. Parson et al., 'A Summary of Major Documents Signed at the Earth Summit and the Global Forum' (1992) 34 Env't 12.

[14] E.g., Brown Weiss and Jacobson , see note 4 above; D.G. Victor et al., eds., *The Implementation and Effectiveness of International Environmental Commitments* (Cambridge, MA: MIT Press, 1998); and O.R. Young, ed., *Effectiveness of International Environmental Regimes: Causal Connections and Behavioural Mechanisms* (Cambridge, MA: MIT Press, 1999).

[15] C. Helm and D. Sprinz, 'Measuring the Effectiveness of International Environmental Regimes' (2000) 44 J. of Conflict Resolution 630; Miles et al., see note 2 above; R.B. Mitchell, 'A Quantitative Approach to Evaluating International Environmental Regimes' (2002) 2 Global Envt'l Pol. 58.

sheds valuable light on the ways in which IEAs can be designed and re-designed to increase their ability to influence the behaviour of member states.

For over a decade, this rich empirical work has often been discussed in terms of whether IEAs, and international law more generally, achieve better results with an 'enforcement' or a 'managerial' approach. Those committed to an enforcement view see states as operating according to a logic of consequences, but a logic of consequences in which sanctions are far more influential than any alternative ways of altering consequences. They contend that inducing significant behavioural change requires international agreements with 'teeth' in the form of potent sanctions.[16] Most international agreements are 'shallow' and require parties only to engage in behaviours they would have engaged in anyway. To the extent that they require 'deep' cooperation involving significant behavioural change, they will lack influence unless the IEA can threaten sanctions that make behavioural changes, however costly, cheaper than not making them. By contrast, those committed to the managerial view contend that states have many mechanisms other than sanctions with which to induce actors to behave in ways consistent with an agreement.[17] They view state behaviour as being dependent on both a logic of consequences and a logic of appropriateness, and see state failures to meet their commitments as generally reflective of incapacity, inadvertence, or normative differences. Sanctions, while sometimes useful and effective, are more often inappropriate or ineffective, and altering behaviour requires procedures that encourage and facilitate compliance rather than punishing non-compliance. This either/or model of management versus enforcement captures important analytic distinctions but, in the process, obscures or ignores a large variety of ways by which IEAs influence state behaviour. In many cases, IEAs have components of both models and, in others, their components do not readily fit into these overly simplified categories.

A basic distinction exists in whether IEAs are regulatory (identifying proscriptions or prescriptions for parties); procedural (establishing regular collective decision-making processes); programmatic (fostering the pooling of parties' resources for joint projects); or generative (fostering development of new social practices).[18] The Montreal Protocol and a variety of other pollution-related agreements establish, in their agreement texts, regulatory limits on certain behaviours. By contrast, many fisheries agreements establish procedural institutions to generate scientific advice for use by the parties to set annual quotas that are often advisory rather than regulatory in nature. The Global Environment Facility operates under a programmatic instrument designed to finance projects and programmes in developing countries. Requirements in the Convention on Wetlands of International Importance Especially as

---

[16] G.W. Downs et al., 'Is the Good News about Compliance Good News about Cooperation?' (1996) 50 Int'l Org. 379.

[17] A. Chayes and A. Handler Chayes, *The New Sovereignty: Compliance with International Regulatory Agreements* (Cambridge, MA: Harvard University Press, 1995).

[18] O.R. Young, *Governance in World Affairs* (Ithaca: Cornell University Press, 1999) at 24ff.

Waterfowl Habitat (Ramsar Convention) that countries make 'wise use' of their wetlands may best be characterized as generative. These distinctions between four major types of IEAs have implications in terms of which might be expected to have the largest behavioural effects. Yet, at present, we have little systematic empirical information regarding which types of legal norms are most or least effective in altering behaviour. More generally, the social and political process of defining 'the problem', and how it should be addressed, condition any agreement's effects since they determine the costs, obstacles, and resistance to achieving it. Aggressive goals may motivate significant efforts or may be ignored as unachievable; more realistic goals may achieve prompt results but provide little motivation for further effort. The means chosen also surely matters, but even simple questions, such as whether binding agreements induce more change than non-binding resolutions remain open.[19] It is generally difficult in any but regulatory regimes to assess compliance since the standards for doing so are either quite vague or difficult to identify. However, this need not mean that non-regulatory agreements do not significantly influence behaviour.

4.1 Systems of Regulation

Regulatory IEAs have, for analytic purposes, three distinct systems that contribute to their ability to induce behaviour change.[20] Effective agreements attempt to match these systems to the problem being addressed. The first system is a primary rule system that includes an IEA's overarching goals as well as its more specific proscriptions and prescriptions. Primary rule systems can vary, *inter alia*, in whether they involve aggressive or limited goals; are specific or vague; proscribe, prescribe, or permit certain actions; ban or only limit behaviours; target relatively few or many actors; or regulate acts of omission or acts of commission. Deciding which activity to regulate and who will regulate it will dictate which actors with what interests and capacities must change their behaviour, how large and costly those changes will be, and whether other factors will reinforce or undercut compliance incentives. Designing more specific rules clarifies what is expected for those predisposed to comply, and removes the opportunity to claim inadvertence or misinterpretation for those predisposed to violate.[21]

Regulatory regimes also have information systems that generate information regarding the indicators of outputs, outcomes, and impacts that are central to determining (1) how actors have behaved—as a basis for responding to them in ways that enhance agreement performance and (2) what progress has been made towards the

---

[19] E. Brown Weiss, ed., *International Compliance with Nonbinding Accords* (Washington, DC: American Society of International Law, 1997).

[20] R.B. Mitchell, 'Compliance Theory: An Overview,' in J. Cameron et al., eds., *Improving Compliance with International Environmental Law* (London: Earthscan, 1996) 3.

[21] Chayes and Handler Chayes , see note 17 above.

agreement's goals—as a basis for revising the agreement. Regulating highly transparent activities or those that involve transactions between actors can reassure actors regarding the actions of others, and allow them to protect their interests if necessary. How information is generated and processed varies considerably, including the self-reporting that is common to most IEAs, through systems of implementation review and sunshine methods to independent verification systems such as TRAFFIC's database for monitoring trade in endangered species under CITES.[22] Systems that supply incentives for, and build the capacity to, report perform better than others that sanction non-reporting or that fail to address practical obstacles to reporting. Many IEAs rely, whether explicitly or implicitly, on NGOs that often have both the incentives and capacity to monitor the agreement-related behaviours of governments and corporations. As environmental threats and concerns increase, intrusive monitoring and verification provisions may be added to some IEAs.

A regulatory regime's third system is its response system, which consists of its strategy for altering the behavioural decisions that actors make. Although direct 'tit-for-tat' reciprocity is thought to be central to effective trade and arms control agreements,[23] it is less likely in environmental realms. In the latter, agreement supporters are usually unwilling to degrade their environment to retaliate for such behaviour by others and, even if they did, such actions would have little influence on those unconcerned about the environment. In response, various scholars have stressed enforcement strategies involving the linkage of economic sanctions to careful monitoring and verification; 'management' using diplomacy, norms, and rewards; and a range of other strategies including eco-certification, prior informed consent, and the simple promotion of norms.[24]

4.2 Strategies of Regulation

In devising regulations, IEAs select from six ideal types of response systems: punitive, remunerative, preclusive, generative, cognitive, or normative. IEAs can rely primarily on one of these approaches or combine aspects of several. The first two strategy types attempt to alter behaviour by altering the consequences of engaging in the behaviours available to the targeted actors. These strategies assume that actor behaviour stems from decision-making based in a logic of consequences and seek to alter that logic either through negative 'punitive' strategies or positive 'remunerative' ones.

---

[22] On systems of implementation review and sunshine methods, see Victor et al., note 14 above; Brown Weiss and Jacobson , see note 4 above.

[23] R. Axelrod, *The Evolution of Cooperation* (New York: Basic Books, 1984).

[24] J. Wettestad, 'Science, Politics and Institutional Design: Some Initial Notes on the Long-Range Transboundary Air Pollution Regime' (1995) 4 J. Env't & Dev. 165; Downs et al., see note 16 above; Chayes and Handler Chayes , see note 17 above; Victor et al. , see note 14 above; and Brown Weiss and Jacobson, see note 4 above.

Punitive strategies seek to convince targeted actors that not fulfilling their IEA commitments will be noticed and that other states, NGOs, or their own citizens will impose economic, political, or social penalties such that—even if there is some chance the violation will go unnoticed—fulfilling those commitments becomes the more attractive alternative. As discussed in much of the literature on deterrence, the success of a strategy depends on the threat's credibility and potency—that is, on whether other actors are likely to detect such failures, are likely to respond to such failures when detected, and are likely and able to respond in ways that are costly relative to the pre-existing benefits of violation over compliance. A strategy of remuneration or rewards seeks to convince states that fulfilling their IEA commitments will be to their benefit not only due to the environmental benefits of cooperative action with other states, but also due to additional, direct, and specific benefits provided by other actors. These most often involve financial rewards for compliance, either involving making loans or grants available or offering improved trade relations.

Both these strategies require the coupling of after-the-fact monitoring with contingent responses. They operate by providing signals to targeted actors about how particular behaviours will be responded to after they occur in hopes of influencing choices before they occur. They depend on the IEA's information system being able to identify what actors did, and on its response system being able to mobilize the threatened or promised responses. The informational requirements of punitive strategies tend to be particularly demanding. The threat of sanctions tends to drive information out of the system—targeted actors have incentives to find clandestine ways to continue existing behaviour. By contrast, the promise of rewards can be made contingent on targeted actors performing requisite behaviours, and also providing convincing evidence of having done so.

Both strategies also face problems due to the incentives other actors have not to respond. Sanctions themselves pose a collective action problem among potential sanctioners because they involve diffuse benefits even if the sanctions succeed, but with concentrated costs that depend only on their being imposed. It also may be difficult to 'target' sanctions on an offending state and avoid spill-over effects on others. Punitive strategies also frequently face a 'sanctioning problem' because the costs to the 'senders' imposing the sanctions exceed the benefits that would accrue to the sender if the offending state changed its behaviour in the desired manner.[25] And, even when a given state's benefits from sanctioning exceed its costs, there may be domestic political objections to sanctioning both from those sectors that will bear the costs of sanctioning, and from others demanding that all states that would benefit from the effective sanctions contribute to them. Remunerative strategies face similar obstacles: states that would benefit if the target is responsive have incentives not to contribute to their provision, and the incentives to actually provide the promised reward decline, and may vanish, once the targeted state has fulfilled its commitments.

[25] R. Axelrod and R.O. Keohane, 'Achieving Cooperation under Anarchy: Strategies and Institutions,' in K. Oye, ed., *Cooperation under Anarchy* (Princeton, NJ: Princeton University Press, 1986) 226.

Two strategies that receive less attention are not contingent on knowing how actors behave, relying on altering the opportunities actors have to engage in particular behaviours rather than the consequences of doing so. 'Preclusive' strategies seek to remove opportunities for actors to engage in proscribed behaviours. Unlike punitive strategies, preclusive strategies increase the difficulty or costs of engaging in specific behaviours, rather than the costs of having engaged in those behaviours. Thus, the Montreal Protocol bans parties from exporting specified chemicals to non-parties— to the extent that parties fulfil this commitment they actually prevent non-parties that lack the domestic ability to produce these chemicals from increasing their emissions of the ozone-depleting substances the agreement sought to reduce. Preclusive strategies, such as the eligibility requirements for emissions trading under the Kyoto Protocol or the CITES ban on trade with countries lacking adequate regulatory frameworks, nicely illustrate a form of IEA influence that a focus on compliance would miss—although the behaviour of non-parties cannot be considered non-compliant, such strategies may influence the behaviour of non-parties. Similarly, much of the influence of the International Convention for the Prevention of Pollution from Ships has been attributed to the response of shipbuilders who, although not required to do so by the agreement, incorporated the convention's environmental standards in their shipbuilding practices, effectively precluding any company—whether within a party state or not—from purchasing a ship that was not built to these standards.[26]

Generative strategies, by contrast, attempt to create new opportunities and enhance capacities for actors to meet their IEA commitments. In this case, the goal is to provide opportunities that are preferred by those who would otherwise choose to ignore or violate their IEA commitments. Unlike remunerative strategies, generative strategies do not require monitoring and the contingent provision of rewards. Rather than rewarding actors for having engaged in some behaviour, the strategy seeks to make it easier or less costly to engage in that behaviour in the first place. For example, port state control agreements make ship inspections far more effective at detecting violations of marine pollution agreements. These agreements require member maritime authorities to enter daily inspection reports in a central database; such up-to-date inspection information helps each maritime authority target their limited inspection resources on ships that other countries' maritime authorities have either not inspected recently or found in violation of international standards.[27] The agreements have created a new resource, a database that maritime authorities find it in their interest to use—there is no need to reward those who use it, it simply needs to be made available.

Neither preclusive nor generative strategies require well-developed information systems. Neither strategy involves contingent responses to the behaviours of targeted

---

[26] Mitchell, see note 12 above.

[27] G.C. Kasoulides, *Port State Control and Jurisdiction: Evolution of the Port State Regime* (London: Martinus Nijhoff, 1993).

actors, and so they need not monitor behaviour to distinguish actors based on how they behave. The nature of these strategies allows them to influence actors independent of knowing how the actors behaved with respect to the agreement's proscriptions or prescriptions. Just as banks place locks on their vaults and trash cans in their lobbies to make it harder for people to rob the bank but easier for people not to litter, so too environmental agreements can be structured to make violating their provisions more difficult and fulfilling their provisions easier. That said, effective versions of these strategies are often not available. Preclusive strategies work only if the parties that are supportive of an IEA control resources that other parties need to violate that IEA's provisions. Thus, IEAs that prohibit the export of banned substances to non-parties will have little influence on countries that have indigenous capabilities to produce those substances. Likewise, generative strategies require that alternatives are available that most actors will see as more attractive than the existing behaviours that run counter to IEA goals—a situation that is often not the case.

Finally, IEAs can adopt one of two strategies that involve altering the perceptions of targeted actors, by changing either the information or the value structure of the targeted actors. Cognitive strategies, or 'labels', involve efforts to provide states with information about the choices they face and the consequences of those choices for them and for others, with the expectation that improved information alone will alter their calculation of what choices best promote their interests. This strategy assumes that actors operate in a logic of consequences mode and engage in the behaviours that the IEA seeks to restrict—or refrain from behaviours that the IEA seeks to promote—only because they lack full and accurate knowledge of the consequences of their choices. IEAs regulating pesticides and hazardous waste seek to promote prior informed consent about these substances in the belief that simply ensuring the provision of better information will lead to either fewer or safer imports.

Normative strategies attempt to induce a much deeper change in the actors they target. They seek to alter actors' underlying values and norms and the goals they pursue. Rather than alter the means by which actors pursue pre-existing ends, such strategies seek to change the ends actors pursue or their beliefs about whether particular means are ever appropriate for pursuing their ends. Such strategies seek to induce actors using a logic of consequences to adopt a logic of appropriateness. By altering how an issue is framed and the terms of debate and by engaging actors in dialogue about an issue, such strategies can, over time, convince actors to alter what they view as appropriate goals to pursue and the appropriate means by which to pursue them. The incorporation of concepts such as 'the common heritage of mankind' (see Chapter 21 'Private and Quasi-Private Standard Setting'), 'sustainable development' (see Chapter 26 'Sustainable Development'), or the 'precautionary principle' (see Chapter 25 'Precaution') involve efforts to shift how particular problems are perceived and discussed, and thereby influence how states behave with respect to issues involving resources with open access, economic development, or adoption of technologies, respectively. Embedding these concepts in international law raises the rhetorical standard against which governments are judged when defending—to others or to their own polities—the extraction of deep sea-bed resources, the exploitation of their own country's natural resources, or the release of genetically modified organisms. Re-framing a debate so that certain actions are deemed illegitimate does not preclude those actions but may create pressures that, at the margin and over time, make actors who would previously have engaged in such actions see doing so as inappropriate.

Cognitive and normative strategies also have virtues and flaws. Both strategies, when successful, can lead to long-term, internalized shifts in actors. Subsequent monitoring or manipulation of incentives is unnecessary to maintain the desired behaviour. If actors become convinced that the consequences of their behaviour harm their own interests, whether other states manipulate these consequences or not, they will alter their behaviour without further pressure. Likewise, if actors become convinced that certain behaviours are simply inappropriate, they are likely to adopt and maintain corresponding behaviours. The fundamental weakness of cognitive strategies lies in the fact that, in many cases, more accurate information will only reinforce an actor's sense that their current behaviour is in their interests, even if not in the interests of others. Likewise, normative strategies depend on long-term efforts to shift the terms of debate and the perceptions of targeted actors. Such strategies may take longer to induce change than the environment can withstand. More important, it is simply quite hard to convince a state to adopt a logic of appropriateness that would lead them to reject a behaviour that the calculations of a logic of consequences suggest has considerable material benefits.

Finally, an important strategic element of international environmental regulation involves deciding whether rules should involve binding or non-binding commitments. This chapter focuses on binding international environmental law. Yet countries have established a variety of forms of non-binding international environmental cooperation, from declarations such as those that came out of the Stockholm, Rio, and Johannesburg conferences to ongoing programmes of bilateral aid involving environmental contingencies to joint policy statements made by heads of state. Although some research has been conducted on the effects of non-binding environmental commitments,[28] systematic efforts will need to compare the influence of binding and non-binding instruments under comparable conditions before any credible claims can be made about which of these approaches is more effective and under what conditions.

5 OTHER CONSIDERATIONS

Much literature on IEA effects has focused on 'how do regimes influence the environmental behaviours of states?' but is more usefully guided by framing the question

---

[28] Brown Weiss, ed., see note 19 above.

as 'what explains variation in the environmental behaviour of states?' The latter question directs our attention to the many non-legal drivers of environmental behaviours that either hinder or facilitate IEA efforts. Accounting for the influence of economic, technological, political, and other factors on environmental behaviours not only improves the accuracy of claims of IEA influence by discounting alternative explanations, but also clarifies whether an IEA's influence depends on—and is 'large' or 'small' relative to—these other influences. Beyond the influence of IEA design discussed earlier, the numerous other factors that drive environmental degradation can be categorized as involving characteristics of the environmental problem, of the country, and of the international context.[29]

Characteristics of the environmental problem explain not only the likely effects of an agreement on a given behaviour, but also the variation in these behaviours (over time, across actors, and across problems) that have nothing to do with the agreements. Obviously, problems that pose large, immediate, and visible environmental threats but require relatively cheap changes to avert them benefit from these factors, regardless of the type of agreement reached. Problems that require restraint in current behaviour are likely to do better than those whose resolution demands new behaviours or technologies, since the latter face obstacles due to incapacity as well as incentives. Actors have stronger incentives to continue the behaviours that cause some environmental problems than others—contrast the resistance to regulation of carbon dioxide with that of the regulation of chlorofluorocarbons. Market structures can reinforce or undercut regulatory efforts—the effectiveness of a 1911 fur seal agreement owed much to the fact that a single market for seal skins in London made monitoring easy.[30] Marine pollution agreements benefit from the incentives that shipbuilders and ship insurers have to monitor and enforce them while, by contrast, endangered species agreements create shortages and price increases that encourage smuggling.[31] The influence of an IEA depends on other factors beyond the negotiators' control, including how many states contribute to the problem, the scientific uncertainty about the problem and its resolution, the positions of corporate interests, and the level of concentration of the regulated activity.[32] These factors can change, and thereby influence behaviours, independent of any IEA. New science can mobilize action if an activity is shown to involve large and immediate costs for those engaged in it or on others who have clout with those who engage in it. Polluting behaviours often decline if environmentally friendly technologies become economically attractive whereas extractive behaviours (for example, fishing or whaling) tend to be less responsive to technological developments because environmental damage is more inherent to those behaviours.

[29] Brown Weiss and Jacobson , see note 4 above.

[30] K. Dorsey, *The Dawn of Conservation Diplomacy: U.S.-Canadian Wildlife Protection Treaties in the Progressive Era* (Washington, DC: University of Washington Press, 1998).

[31] Mitchell, see note 12 above; and H.K. Jacobson and E. Brown Weiss, 'Assessing the Record and Designing Strategies to Engage Countries,' in Brown Weiss and Jacobson, see note 4 above at 521.

[32] *Ibid*. at 536, Figure 15.2.

Country characteristics explain why countries vary in their environmental degradation and in their responsiveness to agreements. Economic factors, political forces, policy styles, and demographic and social characteristics all help explain why some countries adjust and others do not. Likewise, IEA influence varies across countries due to stable forces such as history and social and cultural commitments, geographic size and heterogeneity, and resource endowments; factors that vary more over time such as level of development, type of government, the role of NGOs and environmental parties, and attitudes and values; and immediate drivers such as administrative and financial capacity, leadership changes, and the activities of civil society groups.[33] In some cases, IEAs increase their influence by taking such factors into account. Thus, marine pollution agreements had little influence on ships when flag states were the only ones with enforcement rights. They became more effective when they extended enforcement rights to port states that were both more concerned and more able to enforce them.[34]

Characteristics of the international context also influence environmental practices.[35] Large-scale shifts—the end of the Cold War, the start of the war on terrorism, global economic booms or busts, democratization, globalization, the development of new technologies—can alter how, and how many, countries protect the environment. The ebb and flow of global environmental concern helps explain when individuals, corporations, and countries adopt environmental behaviours and design clean technologies or do not. Global concern is promoted by international conferences such as the 1972 UN Conference on the Human Environment, the 1992 UN Conference on Environment and Development, and the 2002 World Summit on Sustainable Development and by major scientific reports on problems such as climate change, biodiversity, or ozone loss.[36] NGOs such as the Worldwide Fund for Nature and Greenpeace and intergovernmental organizations such as the UN Environment Programme and the World Bank have led countries to focus on environmental problems and have provided financial and informational resources to address them. These forces overlap and interact with agreement features to promote behavioural change. One potentially important element of IEA success in the future may be the interplay among IEAs and other international institutions, as illustrated both by the efforts to coordinate among the Convention on Biological Diversity, the Ramsar Convention, and CITES and by the possibility of incompatibilities between IEA commitments and World Trade Organization (WTO) law (see Chapter 37 'Regional Economic Integration Organizations' and Chapter 38 'Treaty Bodies'). The dynamics of such interactions among IEAs, and between IEAs and non-environmental institutions, has prompted a lively debate about whether the increasing density of environmental agreements fosters or inhibits the ability of each to achieve its objectives, and

---

[33] *Ibid.* at 535.   [34] Mitchell, see note 12 above.

[35] Jacobson and Brown Weiss, see note 31 above at 528.

[36] R. B. Mitchell et al., eds., *Global Environmental Assessments: Information and Influence* (Cambridge, MA: MIT Press, 2006).

about whether integrating all environmental agreements into a global environmental organization would facilitate or impede environmental progress.

In examining the influence of IEAs, two final caveats are in order relating to the influence of IEAs relative to that of other international organizations, national governments, and non-state actors. The first caveat is that IEAs have little if any persuasive power of their own. Their ability to influence behaviour depends on supportive governments, corporations, NGOs, and individuals taking the steps necessary to 'breathe life into' IEA provisions by monitoring the behaviour of relevant actors, responding to those behaviours in ways that foster behavioural change, shedding light on the environmental and economic consequences of particular behaviours, and engaging various actors in normative dialogue. Where a strong network of supportive actors exists, IEAs will tend to be influential regardless of their precise terms and even regardless of whether they are binding or not. Where such a network is absent, IEAs will be less likely to be influential. The second caveat is that, in evaluating the influence of IEAs, it is too often forgotten that we should compare them to the many alternatives ways we might mitigate environmental degradation and improve environmental quality. We should not only compare performance across IEAs but also compare, on some basis, whether the same amount of social, political, and economic resources would produce more impressive results if applied to the tasks of incorporating environmental considerations into fundamentally non-environmental international law such as WTO law, inducing corporations to adopt environmental standards as is being done under the non-governmental International Organization for Standardization or having NGOs operate alone or with multinational corporations and governments to improve environmental protection through policies such as debt-for-nature swaps or the Johannesburg Summit 'type two' partnerships.

6 CONCLUSION

The scholarship and practice of international environmental law can be improved if those analysing the effects of IEAs couple two questions traditionally posed by international lawyers—'are states complying with their IEA commitments?' and 'are IEA goals being achieved?'—with a crucial third question regarding the extent to which IEAs are responsible for the policies, behaviours, and environmental quality that we observe after an agreement is signed. Compliance often may not be a meaningful indicator of IEA impact, arising from economic, political, or social circumstances that foster those outcomes rather than from the relevant IEA's influence. Nor is non-compliance always evidence that an IEA lacks influence—IEAs may deserve credit for significant progress that falls short of compliance for a variety of reasons.

The behaviours of non-parties—and of corporations in non-party states—may be influenced by IEAs, even though these behaviours cannot be categorized as being compliant or not. State and sub-state actor behaviours are driven by two logics, one of consequences and one of appropriateness. IEAs influence behaviour through six strategies that either alter the evaluations of costs and benefits among alternatives that characterizes the former or alter the sense of what is right and wrong that characterizes the latter. Using insights from international relations scholarship to more carefully identify whether, when, and how IEAs alter policies and behaviours and improve environmental quality provides opportunities to help make international environmental law more effective in the future than it has been in the past.

Recommended Reading

E. Brown Weiss and H.K. Jacobson, eds., *Engaging Countries: Strengthening Compliance with International Environmental Accords* (Cambridge, MA: MIT Press, 1998).

A. Guzman, 'International Law: A Compliance Based Theory' (2002) 90 Cal. L. Rev. 1823.

C. Helm and D. Sprinz, 'Measuring the Effectiveness of International Environmental Regimes' (2002) 44 J. Conflict Resolution 630.

H. Koh, 'Why Do Nations Obey International Law?' (1997) 106 Yale L.J. 2598.

E.L. Miles et al., eds., *Environmental Regime Effectiveness: Confronting Theory with Evidence* (Cambridge, MA: MIT Press, 2002).

R.B. Mitchell, 'A Quantitative Approach to Evaluating International Environmental Regimes' (2002) 2 Global Envt'l Pol. 58.

—— and T. Bernauer, 'Empirical Research on International Environmental Policy: Designing Qualitative Case Studies' (1998) 7 J. Env't & Dev. 4.

K. Raustiala and A. Slaughter, 'International Law, International Relations and Compliance,' in W. Carlsnaes et al., eds., *Handbook of International Relations* (London: Sage Publications, 2002) 538.

D.G. Victor et al., eds., *The Implementation and Effectiveness of International Environmental Commitments* (Cambridge, MA: MIT Press, 1998).

O.R. Young, ed., *Effectiveness of International Environmental Regimes: Causal Connections and Behavioural Mechanisms* (Cambridge, MA: MIT Press, 1999).

CHAPTER 40

NATIONAL
IMPLEMENTATION

CATHERINE REDGWELL

1 INTRODUCTION

NATIONAL implementation constitutes a key element in ensuring compliance with international environmental law.[1] It plays a dominant role in ensuring non-state actors' compliance with international environmental norms, particularly where international environmental law has been translated, directly or indirectly, into national law. It may also afford opportunities for non-state actors successfully to challenge national implementation of international environmental law through judicial review, national rules on standing and remedies permitting (see Chapter 29 'Public Participation'). Although international environmental law is less developed than human rights law in terms of individual enforcement of rights through national courts, there is significant case law upon which to draw where courts have invoked, directly or indirectly, international environmental norms. An exhaustive survey of such invocation is beyond the scope of this chapter; however, it will consider the trends in domestic judicial enforcement, and the role that national courts play in both developing and enforcing international environmental law. It will also consider the nature of the international norms in question, and the impact that this factor exerts on national implementation (both legislative and judicial), drawing upon the extensive literature on implementation and compliance with international environmental law (see Chapter 39 'Compliance Theory'). In so doing, this chapter will not focus on any particular treaty or set of obligations, though the extent of reliance upon national measures of implementation under different treaties will be touched upon.[2] The impact on instrument choice at the national level will also be observed (see Chapter 8 'Instrument Choice').

Notwithstanding its importance for the effectiveness of international environmental law, national implementation is not generally addressed in any detail in the leading international environmental texts. For example, Patricia Birnie and Alan

---

[1] Although this chapter will focus primarily on legislative implementation and judicial enforcement of international environment law at the state level, examples will also be drawn from the regional, especially the EU, level (see Chapter 37 'Regional Economic Integration Organizations'). Also acknowledged, though beyond the scope of this chapter, is the role of international institutions in the implementation of international environmental law, both at the level of institutional/treaty cooperation (e.g., the role of Interpol and the Memorandum of Understanding between the Convention for the Protection of the World Cultural and Natural Heritage (World Heritage Convention), International Council on Monuments and Sites, and the United Nations Educational, Scientific, and Cultural Organization as well as Interpol and the Convention on International Trade in Endangered Species of Wild Fauna and Flora) and in the relations between international financial institutions and borrower countries (for example, World Bank Operational Directive 4.01 on Environmental Assessment and 4.04 on Natural Habitats).

[2] Nor will this chapter explore in any depth the link between implementation and enforcement of international environmental law in national law and other areas of international law such as trade and human rights (see Chapter 7 'Relationship between International Environmental Law and Other Branches of International Law').

Boyle observe that '[t]he extent to which public international law and treaties can be invoked or enforced by national courts varies across jurisdictions . . . and is beyond the scope of this book.'[3] Conversely, national treatments tend to isolate the discussion of international environmental law from the discussion of substantive national legal developments, with national implementation thus only obliquely touched upon.[4] There are some exceptions to this general difficulty in ascertaining the nature and extent of national implementation of international environmental law, and these include: (1) in-depth analyses of the implementation of particular treaty instruments[5]; (2) in-depth analyses of implementation of international environmental law in a single or multiple jurisdictions[6]; (3) reports on national implementation prepared by individual treaty secretariats; and (4) comparative studies of the role of international environmental law before national courts.[7] Evidence of environmental state practice may also be found in traditional sources of state practice such as international law yearbooks including, of particular relevance, the *Yearbook of International Environmental Law* (country and region reports).

1.1 What Is Implementation?

A natural threshold question in a chapter addressing national implementation is 'what is implementation'? An expansive definition might include policies, strategies, implementation, enforcement, and strengthening endogenous capacity in terms of finance, scientific, and technological expertise. Recent UN Environment Programme (UNEP) guidelines on compliance with, and enforcement of, multilateral environmental agreements (MEAs) exclude the activities of non-state actors from the definition of 'implementation,' which encompasses, '*inter alia*, all relevant laws, regulations, policies, and other measures and initiatives, that contracting parties adopt

---

[3] P. Birnie and A. Boyle, *International Law and the Environment*, 2nd edition (Oxford: Oxford University Press, 2002) at 265. P. Sands, *Principles of International Environmental Law*, 2nd edition (Cambridge: Cambridge University Press, 2003), addresses general issues of national implementation, compliance, and reporting in about eight pages (at 174–82).

[4] See, e.g., J. Glazewski, *Environmental Law in South Africa* (Durban, South Africa: Butterworth, 2002); S. Bell and D. McGillivray, *Ball and Bell on Environmental Law*, 6th edition (London: Blackstone, 2005); S. Elworthy and J. Holder, *Environmental Protection Text and Materials*, 2nd edition (Cambridge: Cambridge University Press, 2005); S. Divan and A. Rosencranz, *Environmental Law and Policy in India*, 2nd edition (Delhi: Oxford University Press, 2001); A. Lucas et al., eds., *Environmental Law and Policy in Canada*, 3rd edition (Toronto: Emond Montgomery, 2003); and W.H. Rodgers, *Rogers' Hornbook on Environmental Law*, 2nd edition (St. Paul, MN: Thomson-West, 1994).

[5] For example, R. Reeve, *Policing Trade in Endangered Species: The CITES Treaty and Compliance* (London: Royal Institute of International Affairs/Earthscan, 2002).

[6] For example, J.V. DeMarco and M.L. Campbell, 'The Supreme Court of Canada's Progressive Use of International Environmental Law and Policy in Interpreting Domestic Legislation' (2004) 13 R.E.C.I.E.L. 320.

[7] For example, M. Anderson and P. Galizzi, eds., *International Environmental Law in National Courts* (London: British Institute of International and Comparative Law, 2002).

and/or take to meet their obligations under a multilateral environmental agreement and its amendments, if any.'[8] This chapter will adopt a shorthand definition of national implementation as 'measures parties take to make international agreements operative in their domestic law,'[9] although attention will also be paid to non-governmental organization (NGO) involvement with implementation at the national and supranational levels.

The chapter is divided into several sections. Following this introduction, section 2 addresses national implementation of international environmental law, embracing legislative, administrative, and judicial methods of implementation. Enforcement is principally the focus of this last method—be it direct or indirect enforcement of international environmental law through the courts. Direct enforcement includes the exercise of police powers by the state in prosecuting environmental offences. Indirect judicial implementation and enforcement of international environmental law may occur in a myriad of ways, including through the invocation of international environmental law principles in private litigation or as a defence invoked by the state in judicial review of a decision to revoke a licence or permit. Section 2 addresses both, before concluding with reference to procedural issues of jurisdiction, standing, and remedies.

To some extent, all three types of implementation mechanism addressed in section 2—legislative, administrative, and judicial—might be termed 'hard' or 'legal' enforcement, which engages the public institutions of the state (legislature, bureaucracy, and courts) in the implementation and enforcement of international environmental law. Increasingly, however, there are 'softer' mechanisms of implementation and compliance control, which are actively encouraged under international environmental law treaties. This development draws on the role of major groups in the implementation of international environmental law addressed in Chapters 23–32 of Agenda 21, and may be seen in the context of the development of public participation in environmental decision-making more generally. Stakeholder involvement in national implementation has been actively encouraged under a number of international environmental law treaties, including the 1971 Convention on Wetlands of International Importance Especially as Wildfowl Habitat (Ramsar Convention) and the 1972 Convention for the Protection of World Cultural and Natural Heritage (World Heritage Convention). Such encouragement extends not only to ensuring public participation in decision-making by public authorities, but also to less formal methods of communication with all affected shareholders and to processes of consultation between private parties, for example, natural resources companies and stakeholders (see Chapter 29 'Public Participation').

---

[8] UNEP Governing Council Decision SS.VII/4, 'Compliance with and Enforcement of Multilateral Environmental Agreements,' Doc. UNEP(DEPI)/MEAs/WBG.1/3 (February 2002) Annex II.

[9] Reeve, see note 5 above at 16 (citing the definition contained in the draft report of the Nordic Research Project on the Effectiveness of International Environmental Agreements, Finnish Ministry of the Environment, 1995).

Following on from this consideration of national implementation of international environmental law, section 3 shifts the focus to the role accorded national implementation *in* international environmental law. Specific national implementation techniques mandated or encouraged by specific environmental treaty texts, and in soft law instruments, are identified. Since monitoring and reporting obligations are now common in international environmental treaty arrangements, section 4 addresses international oversight of national implementation. Obstacles to effective national implementation, and the international response thereto, are examined in section 5 before turning in the final section to offer some conclusions.

1.2 Impact of Domestic Constitutional Legal Orders on Implementation

A further threshold issue is the extent to which the domestic constitutional legal order impacts upon the implementation of international environmental law. The challenge of effective national implementation through legislative, administrative, and judicial measures is one faced by all states, regardless of their constitutional system. Even for constitutional systems that recognize the possibility of the direct effect of international law through constitutional provision or a doctrine such as self-executing treaty obligations, there are few international environmental obligations that are capable of such execution. Yet differences will clearly arise in consequence of the different constitutional accommodations of international law within the domestic legal order, be it direct effect or judicial receptivity to international law arguments. Nonetheless, such studies as have taken place on judicial enforcement of international environmental law have not found appreciable differences between common and civil law jurisdictions in this regard.

One key difference that does arise is legislative competence with respect to environmental matters—an issue particularly important for federal states. There are examples of constitutional challenge to federal legislative competence that have arisen explicitly in the environmental field. For example, the well-known 1983 *Commonwealth of Australia v. State of Tasmania* (*Tasmanian Dam*) case in the High Court of Australia involved a legal challenge to a proposed dam development affecting a site in Tasmania that had been designated under the World Heritage Convention.[10] Tasmania wished to go ahead with a project that impacted on a federally designated wilderness park and that federal legislation had rendered illegal. The case arose from a constitutional challenge to the federal legislation. The Australian High

---

[10] *Commonwealth of Australia v. State of Tasmania* (*Tasmanian Dam* case), (1983) C.L.R. 1; reprinted in A. Palmer and C. Robb, eds., *International Environmental Reports*, Volume 4: *International Environmental Law in National Courts* (Cambridge: Cambridge University Press, 2004) 13.

Court was willing to find that acceptance of an international obligation was sufficient to confer upon the Commonwealth of Australia the power to make laws implementing such obligations. In a close decision (four to three), the court also held that there was a legal duty under the World Heritage Convention to protect designated world heritage sites. However, the courts in other federal states have been more reluctant to conflate external treaty-making powers and internal subject-matter competence to legislate. Thus, in a challenge to the federal Ocean Dumping Control Act involving federal competence to implement the 1972 Convention on the Prevention of Marine Pollution by Dumping of Wastes and Other Matter (London Convention), the Supreme Court of Canada found the statute to fall within federal competence, but did so on the basis of the 'national' importance of reducing and eliminating marine pollution, and it expressly rejected a general principle of federal jurisdiction to implement international agreements.[11] In contrast, in the United States, a case concerning federal legislation giving effect to a migratory birds treaty with Canada established that the federal government has authority to adopt legislation to implement treaties—although some have recently questioned this result.[12] One of the controversial features of the case is that the treaty was concluded only after federal legislation was held unconstitutional on the basis that the US Constitution does not provide an expressly enumerated federal power to regulate the hunting of migratory birds.

These cases highlight one of the difficulties of national implementation for federal states, where the competence to conclude international agreements is not necessarily matched by competence to legislate. Such constitutional impediments may not be relied upon where breach of an international obligation assumed by the state is concerned,[13] even in the case of a radically decentralized state such as Belgium. In reality, however, the practice of federal states including provincial/state representatives in their negotiating teams and (where extant) the constitutional requirement of a role for the national legislative body in the ratification process mitigates many of the worst effects of these constitutional obstacles.[14] Exceptionally, the matter may be one that is raised for inclusion in the text of the environmental instrument itself.

---

[11] *R. v. Crown Zellerbach*, [1988] 1 S.C.R. 401, reprinted in Palmer and Robb, see note 10 above at 67 (applying the 'national concern' test of the residual peace, order, and good government clause in the constitution).

[12] *Missouri v. Holland*, 252 U.S. 416 (1920), reprinted in Palmer and Robb, see note 10 above at 492.

[13] See Article 27 of the 1969 Vienna Convention on the Law of Treaties (Vienna Convention); but see Article 46 on the manifest violation of internal law.

[14] States may also attach a federalism clause to their instrument of ratification. See, e.g., the United States' federalism understanding attached to its 1992 ratification of the 1966 International Covenant on Civil and Political Rights. However, experience under the 1991 Convention on Environmental Impact Assessment in a Transboundary Context suggests that other states may be unwilling to accept either a federalism clause embedded in the treaty text (rejected during negotiation of the convention) or a federalism understanding made on ratification. Canada made a reservation on ratification of the convention which stated: 'Inasmuch as under the Canadian constitutional system legislative jurisdiction in respect of environmental assessment is divided between the provinces and the federal government, the

Article 34 of the World Heritage Convention is one such 'federalism clause', which was addressed to states parties that 'have a federal or non-unitary constitutional system' and require federal governments to discharge their obligations and to ensure that their constituent units do so where implementation of the World Heritage Convention comes under their jurisdiction. However, Ben Boer's 1992 analysis of the Australian experience under the World Heritage Convention suggests a lack of cooperation between the federal, state, and territorial governments—and a 'lack of political maturity in relations between the elements of the Australian federation in environmental management' which 'seems to be contrary to the spirit of Article 34.'[15]

These constitutional issues of the relationship between legislative competence and the exercise of external relations powers are likewise confronted in the European Union (EU) (see Chapter 37 'Regional Economic Integration Organizations'). There are few areas of exclusive EU competence of relevance to international environmental law. Much more frequently encountered is shared or mixed competence, which is reflected in the participation clauses of recent international treaties such as the 1992 UN Framework Convention on Climate Change (UNFCCC), which provides for the participation of both the EU and the member states. Some treaties do not, of course, provide for the direct treaty participation of non-state entities—the original text of the 1973 Convention on International Trade in Endangered Species of Wild Fauna and Flora (CITES), for example, (and a 1983 amendment so providing has yet to enter into force)—but this omission has not prevented the EU from giving effect to CITES by regulation directly binding on the member states and subject to the full enforcement powers of EU law.[16] Moreover, a rare instance of the direct effect of an environmental treaty provision is found in the European Court of Justice's (ECJ) 2004 judgment on a preliminary ruling reference from the Cour de Cassation in France. In this case, the ECJ held that Article 6(3) of the 1980 Athens Protocol for the Protection of the Mediterranean Sea against Pollution from Land-Based Sources (now Article 6(1) of the 1996 amended protocol) has direct effect 'so that any interested party is entitled to rely on those provisions before national courts.'[17] Such regional reinforcement is a potent additional tool in the implementation of international environmental law.

Government of Canada in ratifying this Convention, makes a reservation in respect of proposed activities (as defined in this Convention) that fall outside of federal legislative jurisdiction exercised in respect of environmental assessment.' Objections were made to this reservation (but not to treaty relations arising with Canada) by Finland, France, Ireland, Italy, Luxembourg, Norway, Spain, and Sweden, all questioning the compatibility of the reservation with the object and purpose of the convention. Canada responded by affirming its reservation as non-severable.

[15] B. Boer, 'World Heritage Disputes in Australia' (1992) 7 Envt'l L. and Litig. 247 at 256; for more recent analysis see B.W.Boer and G.Wiffen, *Heritage Law in Australia*, (Oxford University Press, 2006).

[16] EC Council Regulation 338/97, [1997] O.J. L61/1, replacing an earlier 1982 regulation.

[17] Case C-213/03, *Syndicat professionnel coordination des pêcheurs de l'Etang de Berre et de la region v. Electricité de France*, 15 July 2004, C228/25 (Second Chamber) at para. 47.

2 NATIONAL IMPLEMENTATION OF INTERNATIONAL ENVIRONMENTAL LAW

As indicated earlier, national implementation may be divided into three separate, yet clearly related and overlapping, parts: legislative, administrative, and judicial implementation. National laws and regulations implementing substantive treaty obligations have the advantage over administrative and judicial implementation of greater transparency and, generally, clarity in the application of the legal principles, whether as a guide to conduct or in the application of the law by the courts in the event of violation. Legislative implementation of a state's international obligations performs a 'delegated normativity' function, conditioning not only state but also non-state actors' behaviour. It can also demonstrate a preventative, even precautionary, approach to the implementation of environmental measures. Of course, to the extent that interlocutory and other proceedings are available in judicial enforcement, as well as mandamus (requiring public action), cessation (the administrative authorities requiring a party to desist in conduct that is potentially environmentally harmful), or other orders in administrative law, it is possible to see a weak reflection of this preventative approach in the other areas of national implementation.

2.1 Legislative Implementation

There is increasing sophistication in international environmental treaties regarding the methods of implementation. The question 'is legislation necessary?' is familiar in the EU context, especially with respect to the implementation of directives, and it resonates in international environmental law as well. There are two aspects to this question. The first aspect is to consider the extent to which domestic law already fulfils the obligations assumed. If no legislative implementation takes place, there is the risk that overarching treaty objectives will not be achieved. This is particularly problematic with the 1992 Convention on Biological Diversity (CBD), with its soft obligations, including (1) no listing mechanism (unlike the Ramsar Convention and the World Heritage Convention); (2) the fact that its substantive provisions are peppered with qualifying language 'as far as possible' and 'as appropriate'; and (3) it performs a framework role in bringing together other, more specifically worded, biodiversity-related treaties (Ramsar Convention, the Convention on the Conservation of Migratory Species of Wild Animals (Bonn Convention), the Convention on the Conservation of European Wildlife and Natural Habitats (Bern Convention), and CITES). Yet Article 6 requires states to 'develop . . . or adapt for this purpose' existing national strategies plans or programmes, suggesting that at least a degree of legislative implementation will be required to fulfil these CBD obligations. Moreover, it is difficult to see how the in situ conservation obligations of Article 8, such as the requirement to establish a system of protected areas, can be accomplished without legislative implementation (or the adaptation of existing legislative measures).

The second aspect of the question is whether the treaty permits non-legislative (soft) implementation, for example, by circular or other method. Under a number of treaties, such as the 1973 International Convention for the Prevention of Pollution from Ships and its 1978 protocol (MARPOL Convention) and the 1996 Protocol to the London Convention, there are a range of measures indicated, including administrative. However, in carrying out the obligation to implement in good faith, it may prove necessary to legislate effectively to regulate the activities of territorial sub-units (the Australian example with Tasmania and the World Heritage Convention), and effectively to control the activities of non-state actors within and beyond the state (for example, on the high seas). Legislation is most likely to be necessary when implementation obligations require the state to exert due diligence in respect of the activities of non-state actors—inspection powers of the flag state, for example—and where adequate deterrent sanctions are to be imposed. It is difficult to imagine how, for example, the 1989 Basel Convention on the Transboundary Movement of Hazardous Wastes and Their Disposal (Basel Convention) could properly be implemented without, *inter alia*, a legislative framework for the issuance of permits and the sanctioning of breach of permit conditions. Liability regimes, as yet not extensively developed under international environmental law, perhaps most clearly underscore the necessity for a legislative response.

In addition, national constitutional and/or legislative provisions may directly mandate the implementation of international environmental treaty obligations. We find something along these lines in South Africa's National Environmental Management Act,[18] which empowers the minister to pass domestic legislation or regulations to give effect to any international instrument to which South Africa is a party. It also requires the minister to report on 'the international environmental instruments for which he or she is responsible' and to submit 'an Annual Performance Report on Sustainable Development' as part of South Africa's commitment to implementing Agenda 21 (section 26).

2.2 Administrative Implementation

In a World Resources Institute publication in 1990, which he later updated, Peter Sand identified a new phenomenon in international (environmental) law—transnational administrative implementation and enforcement (see Chapter 4 'Global Environmental Governance as Administration'). In essence, Sand noted the development

---

[18] National Environmental Management Act 107 of 1998.

of national focal points and implementation authorities and enhanced cooperation between them. Examples include cooperation between customs authorities under CITES (for example, the 'mutual recognition' of permits), and the exchange of information and notification obligations between hazardous waste authorities under the regional and global waste regimes or between port authorities under the MARPOL Convention[19] (cooperating in, *inter alia*, 'alert diffusion'). Thus, while it may be the foreign ministries that are most actively engaged in the negotiation of the treaty text, it is the administrative authorities of the state upon which fall many of the practical issues of implementation and enforcement. This suggests the development of a functional horizontal cooperation at the sub-state level.

2.3 Judicial Enforcement

The role of the judiciary in the implementation and enforcement of international environmental law was recognized in UNEP's Montevideo Programme III, which was adopted in 2001, and which identifies the judiciary as one of the key target groups for capacity building. A UNEP Global Judges Symposium was held on the eve of the Johannesburg World Summit on Sustainable Development (WSSD) in 2002, and it adopted the Johannesburg Principles on the Role of Law and Sustainable Development. These principles affirm, *inter alia*, 'that an independent judiciary and judicial process is vital for the implementation, development and enforcement of international environmental law.'[20] There have been a number of studies of judicial implementation of international environmental law, including a three-volume compendium of summaries of environment-related cases by UNEP. While this would appear ample testament to the potential of the judicial role to implement key international environmental principles such as the precautionary principle and the principle of intergenerational equity, only seven of the 69 cases discussed therein overtly address international environmental law.[21]

Of course, many national cases that are concerned with implementation and enforcement of domestic planning and environmental laws will serve to implement

---

[19] Bolstered by the port state enforcement provisions of the 1982 United Nations Convention on the Law of the Sea (LOSC) and by memoranda of understanding between maritime authorities in various geographic regions, the first one between 14 such authorities in Europe (the 1982 Paris Memorandum).

[20] For discussion of these principles, and subsequent developments, see Lord Justice Carnwath, 'Judicial Protection of the Environment: At Home and Abroad' (2004) 16 J. Envt'l L. 315.

[21] Volume 1 examines issues of standing, environmental impact assessment, choice of forum, public trust doctrine, the precautionary principle, polluter pays principle, and riparian right to water; Volume 2 summarizes cases on planning control, police power and compulsory acquisition in environmental management, and the place of culture in environmental management (mainly New Zealand and Australian cases); and Volume 3 addresses forum and jurisdiction, physical planning, pollution control, enforcement, rights of local community to use local natural resources, and animal protection. As indicated, some 69 cases are included in the three volumes, only about seven of which overtly address

key treaty and customary obligations. The difficulty lies in tracing the connection in these cases to implementation of international obligations, in the absence of an express link (such as explicit reference to the treaty obligation sought to be implemented/enforced). Excluded from consideration in this chapter is judicial enforcement of national laws designed to implement international law, where the court has not referred to the international obligation(s) in question as an aid to interpretation. As indicated earlier, a significant number of the cases reported in the UNEP compendium fall within this category. The justification for such exclusion is that such cases, while telling us much about domestic implementation of domestic environmental law, tell us little about domestic implementation of international environmental law.

As Daniel Bodansky and Jutta Brunnée observe, there is a further methodological difficulty in examining case law that appears to rely on international environmental law. Based on the 12 jurisdictions represented in their analysis, they note that in a 'surprisingly large number of cases, courts refer to norms of international environmental law without explaining whether they regard them as rules of decision, as an interpretative aid, or as principles that, despite currency at the international level, are simply drawn from national sources.'[22] Alice Palmer and Cairo Robb, in their collection of approximately 50 cases from 26 jurisdictions, identify two categories of cases: (1) those that demonstrate direct reliance on international environmental instruments and principles; and (2) cases that elaborate domestic approaches to environmental issues 'influenced' by international environmental law or contributing to international developments. Yet they acknowledge their broad brush approach, embracing a consideration of international obligations, broader international debates, comparative law elements, and domestic factors (such as issues of constitutional and procedural law), 'all of which are necessary constituents of principled environmental decision-making.'[23]

In examining the judicial implementation and enforcement of international environmental law, it should also be recognized that the courts play a role supplemental to the state's political organs, with whom the principal implementation obligation resides. The success of this supplemental role will depend on a variety of factors, not the least of which is the desirability of judicial law-making and the competence/expertise of the judiciary in the environmental sphere. Only a few states have taken the step of establishing specially designated environmental courts, such as

international environmental law, principally in cases relating to land use (World Heritage Convention, the Ramsar Convention, and the CBD) or involving principles such as the precautionary principle or the polluter pays principle.

[22] D. Bodansky and J. Brunnée, 'Introduction: The Role of National Courts in the Field of International Environmental Law,' in Anderson and Galizzi, see note 7 above.

[23] Palmer and Robb, see note 10 above at xiii. Palmer and Robb acknowledge that this volume of the international environmental law reports is 'less rigorously focused on the international dimension' than the three previous volumes on early decisions, trade and environment, and human rights and environment.

New Zealand's Environment Court and the Australian state of New South Wales' Land and Environment Court. According to one recent survey of 12 jurisdictions, 'the role of national courts in implementing international environmental law has been rather limited to date [2002].'[24] If one obstacle to more active involvement of national courts is, indeed, judicial *horror iuris non domestici* in some instances,[25] then UNEP's judicial capacity building, promoting judicial networking, and the sharing of information should produce dividends—but these are for the long term.

It is important also to acknowledge that, unlike in the human rights and trade law fields, for example, there is no central dispute settlement mechanism for international environmental law nor any specialized regional or international court competent to apply and enforce international environmental law along the lines of the European, African, or Inter-American Courts of Human Rights, with access for non-state actors (see Chapter 45 'International Dispute Settlement'). Thus, unlike human rights plaintiffs, environmental plaintiffs face domestic legal obstacles to enforcement of environmental rights/interests that cannot generally be surmounted by recourse to a supranational body. Even at the interstate level, proposals for an international environmental court have not prospered, and the Environmental Chamber of the International Court of Justice (ICJ), which was first designated in 1992, has yet to be pressed into service by states. In consequence, plaintiffs' only recourse may be national judicial implementation and enforcement measures.

As already indicated earlier, direct enforcement by domestic courts of international environmental law is rare. In dualist states, there is no possibility for the direct enforcement of treaty obligations (save for EU law) without domestic legislative implementation. Environmental treaty obligations are rarely of sufficient precision to give rise to direct effect even in monist states. Direct application and enforcement of customary international law is possible in both systems, but, again, specific instances are relatively rare. One such instance is the Indian Supreme Court's adventurous decision in *Vellore Citizens' Welfare Forum v. Union of India* (1996), where it found the concept of sustainable development, the precautionary principle, and the polluter pays principle to be part of customary international law and, hence, applicable as part of Indian domestic law.[26] A decision of the 'Green Bench' of the court,[27] the judgment reviewed a plethora of both hard (UNFCCC and the CBD) and soft law (Stockholm Declaration on the Human Environment, Rio Declaration

---

[24] Bodansky and Brunnée, see note 22 above at 9.   [25] *Ibid.* at 21.

[26] *Vellore Citizens' Welfare Forum v. Union of India*, (1996) 5 S.C.C. 647, discussed by M. Anderson, 'International Environmental Law in Indian Courts,' in Anderson and Galizzi, see note 7 above at 156 and reprinted in Palmer and Robb, see note 10 above at 270.

[27] The Indian Supreme Court persuaded High Courts in several states—the Bombay, Calcutta, Madras, and Gujarat High Courts, e.g.—to devote greater judicial resources to environmental cases through the designation of a 'green bench.' See S. Divan and A. Rosencranz, *Environmental Law and Policy in India*, 2nd edition (Dehli: Oxford University Press, 2001) at 4. For critical case studies of the Court's jurisprudence, see L.Rajamani, 'Public Interest Environmental Litigation in India' (2007) Journal of Environmental Law (forthcoming).

on Environment and Development, Brundtland report,[28] and Agenda 21) instruments in determining that sustainable development is part of customary international law and, thus, part of domestic law (and also found no conflict with statutory law and consistency with the Indian Constitution). This bold decision has been followed in a number of subsequent cases in India. It is unusual in its reliance on customary international (environmental) law, since many other courts that invoke environmental principles choose to avoid a discussion of their legal status—most notably with respect to the polluter pays principle, the precautionary principle, sustainable development, and intergenerational equity. Thus, for example, in the celebrated case of *In Re Minors Oposa* (1993)[29] before the Philippines Supreme Court, which involved a legal challenge to the grant of timber licences in remaining rainforest brought by the legal representatives of minors, the court held that the plaintiffs had standing to challenge the award of the licences, since the resulting deforestation would cause harm to both present and future generations. Intergenerational equity was relied upon, yet it is far from clear that the court applied intergenerational equity as a rule of *international* law. Similar conclusions may be drawn regarding the concept of intergenerational equity before the Canadian courts.[30] Another excellent example of judicial 'dodging' of the international legal status of an environmental principle is the application of the precautionary principle by the Land and Environmental Court of New South Wales as a 'statement of common sense.'[31]

More frequently encountered in domestic judicial decisions is the application of international environmental law in the interpretation and application of domestic law. This indirect application typically arises in the use of international environmental law as an aid to interpretation, especially where recourse to the treaty or other instrument assists the interpretation of the implementing domestic legislation. Thus, for example, in the Dutch case of *GJP Ziers*,[32] an administrative decision to approve hotel construction with adverse impact on badger habitat was adjudged 'unreasonable' because of incompatibility with the requirements of the 1979 Bern Convention. In seeking standing for judicial review of the United Kingdom secretary of state's decision to offer offshore blocks for petroleum licensing in the northeast Atlantic region, Greenpeace relied successfully upon the EEC Directive 92/43 on the Conservation of Natural Habitats and of Wild Fauna and Flora as influenced by, *inter*

---

[28] G. Brundtland, *Our Common Future: the World Commission on Environment and Development* (Oxford: Oxford University Press, 1987).

[29] *In Re Minors Oposa*, 33 I.L.M. 173 (1994); reprinted in Palmer and Robb, see note 10 above at 382.

[30] J.V. DeMarco, 'Case Note: *Imperial Oil Ltd v. Quebec (Minister of the Environment)*' (2004) 13 R.E.C.I.E.L. 108. For a broader discussion, see J.V. DeMarco. and M.L. Campbell, 'The Supreme Court of Canada's Progressive Use of International Environmental Law and Policy in Interpreting Domestic Legislation' (2004) 13 R.E.C.I.E.L. 320–32.

[31] *Leatch v. National Parks and Wildlife Service and Shoalhaven City Council*, [1993] N.S.W. L.E.C. 191, reprinted in Palmer and Robb, see note 10 above at 57.

[32] *GJP Ziers*, Afd G RvS, 30 December 1993, A.B. 1995, no. 24, discussed in A. Nollkaemper, 'International Environmental Law in the Courts of the Netherlands,' in Anderson and Galizzi, see note 22, 183 at 187, and reprinted in Palmer and Robb, see note 10 at 359.

alia, the CBD, in arguing that the secretary of state had failed to take account of the impact of petroleum activities upon coral and cetaceans in the area.[33] There is nothing unique in the use of international environmental law in these techniques; rather, they are a reflection of the general relationship between domestic and international law. As such, other doctrines may come into play, including the widely applied presumption that legislators do not intend to legislate inconsistently with the international obligations of the state. The opportunities for such application are, however, few and far between when contrasted with the human rights field. This distinction is, in part, a reflection of the many difficult procedural issues arising for environmental plaintiffs (see section 2.3.1 below).

The Dutch and UK cases cited above are both examples of successful individual/ NGO judicial challenges to state action using international environmental law instruments and principles. There are further examples where the state invokes the provisions of international environmental law to resist challenges by individuals to regulatory or other measures adopted by the state to implement its international environmental obligations. Most common are challenges to planning consent refusals or planning enforcement measures that affect individuals' ability commercially or otherwise to develop land. Thus, for example, the World Heritage Convention was successfully relied upon by the United Kingdom in a challenge to a refusal of planning consent for coal mining activities in Northumberland[34] and by Egypt in a challenge to the revocation of hotel building permits near the Great Pyramids.[35]

Apart from direct challenges to state action, in a few cases, private parties have invoked international environmental law in litigation against other private parties. This approach runs the risk that the obligation relied upon will be held to apply only to states. Such was the fate of the *sic utere tuo* rule in the Dutch *Reinwater Foundation* case, where Dutch horticulturalists sued a French potash mining company for harm caused by the dumping of saline waste in the Rhine. The plaintiff sought to argue that the rule applied to relations between individuals. The Rotterdam District Court in 1979 was convinced, but the Hague Appeal Court in 1986 was not.[36] In 1997, a US court likewise rejected the application of the polluter pays principle, the precautionary principle, and the proximity principle in a case between private parties (non-state corporations), in *Beanal v. Freeport-McMoran*.[37] In general, courts have been

---

[33] *R. v. Secretary of State for Trade and Industry, ex parte Greenpeace Ltd.* [2000] 2 C.M.L.R. 94 (Q.B. Div.), also reprinted in Palmer and Robb, see note 10 above at 462.

[34] *Coal Contractors Limited v. Secretary of State for the Environment and Northumberland County Council* [1993] E.G.C.S. 218.

[35] In an International Centre for the Settlement of Investment Disputes arbitration, see *Southern Pacific Properties (Middle East) Ltd v. Egypt*, 1993, 32 I.L.M. 933 (1993).

[36] The case was reported in (1980) 11 N.Y.I.L. 326 (District Court) and (1988) 19 N.Y.I.L. 496 (Appeal Court). See further discussion in A. Nollkaemper, 'International Environmental Law in the Courts of the Netherlands,' in Anderson and Galizzi, see note 32 above, 183; for extracts of the cases, see Palmer and Robb , see note 10 above at 340.

[37] *Beanal v. Freeport-McMoran*, 969 F. Supp. 362 (D. La. 1997); see also *Amlon Metals v. FMC*, 775 F. Supp. 668 (S.D.N.Y., 1991).

reluctant to give horizontal direct effect to international environmental law principles in the absence of legislative implementation. In consequence, the state continues to play an important intermediary role in the application of such principles within domestic law, highlighting once again both the importance especially of legislative implementation and the need to make provision for the 'effective enforcement of environmental rights,' as required by Article 19 of the Economic Commission for Europe's 1998 Convention on Access to Information, Public Participation in Decision-Making and Access to Justice in Environmental Matters (Aarhus Convention) (see Chapter 29 'Public Participation').

2.3.1 Procedural Issues

Among the reasons frequently cited for the relative paucity of domestic case law on international environmental issues is the procedural obstacles to litigation. These are familiar arguments both in domestic law, which has seen significant legal developments in terms of access to information, justice, and decision-making, and on the international plane. Judicial resolution of environmental disputes may encounter three particular difficulties: (1) jurisdiction; (2) standing; and (3) remedies. It is rare for these issues to be directly addressed by international law, thus leaving them largely for domestic courts to resolve.

2.3.1.1 Jurisdiction

Where the defendant is an international corporation and/or the damage alleged is transboundary in nature, conflict of laws issues may well arise. Domestic courts may decline jurisdiction on the basis that courts in another state are better placed to adjudicate the matter (*forum non conveniens*). Such was the fate of Ecuadorian indigenous groups challenging Texaco's oil development activities in Ecuador before US courts pursuant to, *inter alia*, the Alien Tort Claims Act.[38] Indeed, a number of individuals and groups have sought unsuccessfully to launch Alien Tort Claims Act proceedings in the United States against US multinationals arising from natural resource activities abroad alleged to infringe international human rights and environmental standards. Jurisdiction may also be declined on the basis that the plaintiff is suing the 'wrong' defendant, as discussed earlier.

2.3.1.2 Standing

There is no level—domestic, regional, or international—where the issue of standing does not loom large for environmental litigants. Even the progressive 1998 Aarhus Convention fails to harmonize this thorny issue, with its access to justice provisions (Article 9) requiring the demonstration of a 'sufficient interest' (or impairment of a right if such is required for standing under domestic administrative law), yet relying

---

[38] *Aguinda v. Texaco*, 142 F. Supp. 2d 534 (S.D.N.Y., 2001), upheld by the US Court of Appeals (Second Circuit), 16 August 2002. Court proceedings have since been launched against Texaco in Ecuador.

to a significant extent upon national legislation. More innovative is Article 9(2), which recognizes that NGOs may constitute 'the public concerned' with a sufficient interest for standing (and, where the administrative procedural law of a state party to the convention requires this as a precondition for standing, deems such organizations to have rights capable of being impaired).

It is certainly the case that restrictive rules on standing are frequently identified as the most significant barrier to domestic implementation of international environmental law through the courts, preventing suitable cases from reaching the judicial domain. As indicated earlier, the principle of intergenerational equity was famously relied upon by the Philippines Supreme Court to confer standing on minors wishing to oppose the grant of timber licences in one of the last remaining areas of untouched forest in the Philippines. *In Re Minors Oposa* finds an echo in progressive decisions of the Indian Supreme Court,[39] yet these cases remain on the whole exceptional. Nor is it the case that domestic jurisdictions readily acknowledge the standing of plaintiffs to claim on behalf of the environment, a domestic echo of the international judicial reluctance to develop *actio popularis*.[40] Nonetheless, there have been some progressive developments, including the recognition of the standing of NGOs such as the Sierra Club and Greenpeace to challenge private and public action detrimental to the environment at the national and regional levels. Moreover, where permitted, public interest intervention in cases before domestic courts can be an effective method for introducing international environmental law and policy arguments. A recent survey of six major environmental cases before the Supreme Court of Canada concludes that in four of these cases such issues were considered only because of the arguments of the public interest interveners.[41]

2.3.1.3 *Remedies*

Linked to the problems of standing are remedies, especially where plaintiffs seek to bring an *actio popularis*. The Indian case of *Vellore* is unusual not only in the award of compensation to individuals directly suffering harm from the pollution of the watercourse, but also as it directed that an environmental trust fund be established, by the polluter, to finance general ecological clean-up. Generally speaking, there is no harmonization of remedies under international environmental law, save for the few examples of liability and compensation regimes established principally in connection with hazardous activities (for example, nuclear, hazardous waste, and maritime

---

[39] See further M. Anderson, 'International Environmental Law in Indian Courts,' in Anderson and Galizzi, see note 7 above, 183.

[40] The *locus classicus* on standing for the national environment is C. Stone, 'Should Trees Have Standing?' published in the course of proceedings in *Sierra Club v. Morton* (1972) 45 S. Cal. L. Rev. 450. Other judicial techniques include recourse to public trust and related doctrines. This may be contrasted with the human rights context where *actio popularis* has been recognized by Article 24 of the 1981 African Charter on Human and Peoples' Rights, and Article 11 of the 1988 San Salvador Protocol to the 1969 American Convention on Human Rights, for example.

[41] DeMarco and Campbell, see note 30 above.

transport of petroleum) (see Chapter 17 'Hazardous Substances and Activities' and Chapter 44 'International Responsibility and Liability'). The function of these regimes is to channel and to limit liability, with a maximum ceiling set for compensation (thus ensuring an insurable risk for the operator). Those plaintiffs seeking to escape such restrictions—the plaintiffs in the *Amoco Cadiz* oil spill off the coast of northern France in 1978, for example—must seek recourse through domestic courts (in this case, the courts of the United States, the state of incorporation of the ship owner, a vertically integrated petroleum company).

3 REQUIREMENTS IMPOSED BY INTERNATIONAL ENVIRONMENTAL LAW WITH RESPECT TO NATIONAL IMPLEMENTATION

Turning now to consider the extent to which international environmental law addresses the issue of national implementation, this third section examines specific implementation obligations contained in soft law and binding treaty instruments. The strong linkage between implementation and reporting obligations is highlighted in section 4, before section 5 turns to examine the obstacles to national implementation and some international responses.

3.1 Soft Law Instruments

The importance of national implementation of international environmental law is recognized in key soft law instruments. The 1972 Stockholm Declaration, in keeping with the environment and planning linkage present in many developed municipal legal systems of the time, places significant emphasis upon domestic policy and planning (Principles 11–17). The 1982 UN General Assembly Resolution 37/7 on a World Charter for Nature reaffirms in its preamble 'the need for appropriate measures, at the national and international, individual and collective, and private and public levels, to protect nature and to promote international co-operation in the field.' Such measures include implementation of the applicable international legal provisions for the conservation of nature and the protection of the environment (para. 21(c)). Here again, the importance of national policies and strategies is emphasized, but, unlike the Stockholm Declaration, implementation is not made the sole purview of states. The World Charter for Nature embraces wider participation by other public authorities, international organizations, individuals, groups, and corporations, to the extent that they are able. This theme is continued in the 1992 Rio Declaration, especially in the accompanying Agenda 21, though Principle 11 of the

Rio Declaration places squarely on states the obligation to enact 'effective' environmental legislation.

Annual national reporting on the implementation of Agenda 21 has occurred through the Commission on Sustainable Development (CSD), which was established as a result of Rio. Annual national reports are supplemented by a five-year cycle of country profiles, thus far Rio+5 (1997) and Rio+10 (2002), the latter marked by the WSSD in Johannesburg. The purpose of these periodic country profiles is to help countries monitor their own implementation progress, while facilitating information sharing and exchange, and to 'serve as institutional memory to track and record national actions undertaken to implement Agenda 21.'[42] The WSSD saw the further production of 'national assessment reports,' a form of self-appraisal of ten years' implementation of Agenda 21 and of the further issues developed by the CSD (for example, energy).

3.2 Treaty Implementation Requirements

Despite the growing importance of soft law, the focus of this chapter is upon national implementation of 'hard' obligations, in particular, treaty obligations. This focus reflects the reality that the vast majority of binding international environmental obligations are grounded in treaty instruments. It is axiomatic that treaty obligations are binding and must be implemented in good faith, expressed in the maxim *pacta sunt servanda*. The strength of this obligation was underscored by the ICJ in the 1997 *Case Concerning the Gabčíkovo-Nagymaros Project (Hungary v. Slovakia)*,[43] and, as already noted above, the High Court in Australia drew upon it in elaborating the Commonwealth of Australia's obligations under the World Heritage Convention.

Requirements of national/regional[44] implementation are frequently spelled out in treaty texts, with varying degrees of specificity. Implementation obligations may include the following.

- The development of policies and strategies for implementation. For example, Article 6 of the CBD requires each contracting party to develop national strategies, plans, or programmes for the conservation and sustainable use of biological diversity or to adapt existing strategies and so on for this purpose.

---

[42] According to the Division for Sustainable Development in the UN Department of Economic and Social Affairs. The World Summit on Sustainable Development in 2002 produced a plan of implementation and kick-started further partnership arrangements with the private sector, which are also being monitored by the Commission on Sustainable Development.

[43] *Case Concerning the Gabčíkovo-Nagymaros Project (Hungary v. Slovakia)*, 25 September 1997, [1997] I.C.J. Rep. 92.

[44] Multilateral agreements may encourage the conclusion of bilateral and regional agreements to buttress implementation. For example, Article 14 of the 2000 Cartagena Protocol on Biosafety to the CBD directly encourages such agreements consistent with its objectives, as does Article 197 of the 1982 LOSC.

- The requirement to adopt laws, regulations, and other measures that take into account internationally agreed rules and standards and recommended practices and procedures or that are no less effective than such global rules and standards. An example of the former, a type of indirect standard setting, is found in Article 60(3) of the 1982 Convention on the Law of the Sea (LOSC), which requires that states, when abandoning offshore installations, 'take into account' any generally accepted international standards established by the competent international organization, namely, the 1989 IMO Guidelines and Standards for the Removal of Offshore Installations and Structures on the Continental Shelf and in the Exclusive Economic Zone. An example of the latter—an obligation of result—is found in Article 210 of the LOSC, which requires that '[n]ational laws, regulations and measures shall be no less effective in preventing, reducing and controlling . . . pollution [from dumping] than the global rules and standards.'
- The requirement to designate an appropriate authority to issue permits, maintain records, and monitor compliance/environmental conditions. Such obligations are commonly found in pollution treaties, such as Article VI of the 1972 London Convention.
- The requirement that states take 'appropriate measures' to prevent and punish contraventions of the treaty. An example is found in Article VII.2 of the London Convention. 'Appropriate measures' may be more precisely spelled out, as in the MARPOL Convention requirements that states shall prohibit violations and shall establish sanctions in respect thereof (Article 4).
- The requirement that states undertake monitoring, control, and surveillance, including through observer schemes. Many examples may be found, especially with respect to treaties regulating living resources, such as the 1995 Agreement for the Implementation of the Provisions Relating to the Conservation and Management of Straddling Fish Stocks and Highly Migratory Fish Stocks, the 1946 International Convention for the Regulation of Whaling, the 1980 Convention on the Conservation of Antarctic Marine Living Resources, and the 1978 Convention on Future Multilateral Co-operation in the North-West Atlantic Fisheries.
- The possibility of upward derogation. This is generally permissible and, indeed, frequently exhorted. An example of such exhortation is found in Article 3(3) of the 1996 Protocol to the London Convention. Upward derogation takes the state beyond implementation of treaty obligations *per se*, although it is grounded upon them.
- Setting a time limit for completing implementation of certain provisions of the agreement, which is an approach found in some regional seas agreements.[45]

Certain implementation techniques contain elements of substantive obligation, such as requirements to conduct a prior environmental impact assessment[46] or to utilize

---

[45] See, e.g., Article 4(4)(a) of the Convention for the Protection of the Mediterranean Sea against Pollution (Barcelona Convention) and Article 2(3)(a) of the Convention for the Protection of the Marine Environment of the North-East Atlantic.

[46] See Article 4(3)(c) of the Barcelona Convention and Article 8 of the CBD.

best available techniques (BAT) and best environmental practices (BEP). Both types of requirements are found in the 1995 revised Convention for the Protection of the Mediterranean Sea against Pollution (Barcelona Convention), for example. The regional 1992 Convention for the Protection of the Marine Environment of the North-East Atlantic (OSPAR Convention), likewise utilizes BAT and BEP (Article 2(3)) as well as making provision for access to information (Article 9). Another example is the obligation not to transfer damage from one part of the environment to another nor to transform one type of pollution into another, found in Article 3 of the 1996 Protocol to the 1972 London Convention.[47]

A common technique in pollution control and eradication treaties is to set forth specific prohibitions, which states are required to implement through the application of specific 'measures', but to leave the method and means to the state. Such prohibitions are essentially obligations of result. This regulatory approach is both a reflection of the essentially horizontal and decentralized character of international law-making, and of the specific bargains and compromises embedded in specific environmental treaty-making. In consequence, regulatory or non-regulatory techniques may be employed, including soft implementation through codes of conduct and industry voluntary agreements and the like (see Chapter 21 'Private and Quasi-Private Standard Setting'). The latter are of particular import in 'regulating' non-state actor behaviour.

Since Rio, some environmental implementation obligations are also conditioned by the principle of common but differentiated responsibility (see Chapter 27 'Equity' and Chapter 26 'Sustainable Development'). This principle is enunciated in Principle 7 of the Rio Declaration and is reflected in Article 3 of the 1992 UNFCCC. Article 6 of the CBD also conditions implementation by providing that each party shall implement measures for conservation and sustainable use 'in accordance with its particular conditions and capabilities.' Such language leads to different standards in national laws, and parties undertake common obligations but have differential obligations with respect to the implementation of such obligations. Implementation standards are thus conditioned by context, taking into account the particular capabilities and circumstances of developing state parties.

4 IMPLEMENTATION REVIEW

The first generation of international environmental treaties rarely provided for any degree of monitoring or oversight of national implementation. Increasingly, however, modern environmental treaties provide for a comprehensive feedback loop, from implementation, to monitoring, to reporting, to international review, and to

---

[47] See also Article 195 of the 1982 LOSC.

non-compliance mechanisms (see Chapter 42 'Monitoring and Verification' and Chapter 43 'Compliance Procedures'). The latter are now sometimes referred to as 'review institutions.' For example, Kal Raustiala, in his 2001 study for UNEP on reporting and reviewing institutions in ten MEAs, defines review institutions broadly to embrace 'specific institutions, formal or informal, that gather, assess, and take decisions based on information relevant to the implementation of, compliance with, adjustment of, and effectiveness of obligations contained in MEAs, as well as in subsidiary agreements and authoritative decisions of the parties.'[48] This underscores the evolutionary nature of many international environmental treaty instruments, and the dynamic effect of decision-making by the conference of the parties, as well as the impact of the work of treaty subsidiary bodies and secretariats (see Chapter 38 'Treaty Bodies'). Perhaps the most striking example of monitoring and reporting obligations giving rise to new prescriptions is the evolution of the 1979 Convention on Long-Range Transboundary Air Pollution. Its further development started with a protocol containing modest monitoring and information-gathering functions, but the treaty has since grown into a major framework agreement with a number of protocols addressed to specific air pollutants, several of which are already 'second generation' (for example, the 1994 Oslo Protocol on Further Reduction of Sulphur Emissions, supplementing the 'first generation' 1985 Sulphur Protocol).

Under many recent international environmental agreements, states parties not only have the obligation to implement, but also have an express obligation to report upon such implementation. Through reporting, it is possible to obtain a snapshot of overall implementation and enforcement patterns. Such reporting obligations might include:

- supplying the text of implementing laws and measures—for example, the MARPOL Convention requires submission of 'the text of laws, orders, regulations and other instruments which have been promulgated on the various matters within the scope of the present Convention' (Article 11(1)(a)), while the 1996 Protocol to the London Convention requires all 'administrative and legal measures taken to implement the provisions of this protocol, including a summary of enforcement measures' to be supplied (Article 9(4(2)). In the latter example, description is to be supplemented by an assessment of the effectiveness of implementation and enforcement measures, and by the identification of problems encountered in their application (Article 9(4)(3));
- transmission of specimens of the documentation employed when implementing the permitting or certification systems required by a number of international environmental treaties, such as the oil pollution certificates required under the MARPOL Convention (Article 11(1)(c));

---

[48] K. Raustiala, *Reporting and Review Institutions in Ten Multilateral Environmental Agreements* (Nairobi: UNEP/Division of Early Warning and Assessment, 2001).

- supplying records of the nature, quantity, time method, and location of disposed waste or other pollutants as well as the results of monitoring environmental conditions (for example, Article 9(4)(1) of the 1996 Protocol to the London Convention); and
- publication of records kept, and of the results of monitoring, as well as the compilation of official reports, or summaries thereof, reflecting the application and enforcement of the treaty (for example, Article 11(1)(e) and (f) of the MARPOL Convention).

The link between reporting, implementation, and compliance has also given rise to a relatively new phenomenon in the context of national implementation of international environmental obligations, namely compliance review (see Chapter 43 'Compliance Procedures'). This type of review occurs through the scrutiny of individual states' implementation performance by an Implementation Committee (for example, the 1987 Montreal Protocol on Substances That Deplete the Ozone Layer to the 1985 Vienna Convention for the Protection of the Ozone Layer (Vienna Convention) and the 1997 Kyoto Protocol to the 1992 UNFCCC) or by another body and/or by the Conference of the Parties (for example, CITES). Many recent instruments make some provision for the future establishment of an implementation review procedure, such as the compliance mechanism envisaged under the 2000 Cartagena Protocol on Biosafety (Cartagena Protocol) to the 1992 CBD or the vaguer provision in the 1996 Protocol to the London Convention, which empowers the COP to 'establish subsidiary bodies, as required, to consider any matter with a view to facilitating the effective implementation of this Protocol' (Article 18(1)(2)). Reports submitted by the contracting parties are to be reviewed by 'an appropriate subsidiary body' (Article 9(5)). Typically, compliance procedures are designed to ensure a return to compliance through a range of techniques, including the possibility of facilitative and/or coercive measures (for example, access to facilitative financing or the suspension of trading privileges).

5 IMPLEMENTATION FACILITATION

A number of obstacles to effective national implementation may arise and come to be highlighted under treaty-based non-compliance or other procedures. Under the Vienna Convention, for example, a number of non-compliance cases have arisen from an inability of states to carry out their reporting obligations effectively. For developing country parties, this is often a consequence of a lack of financial resources and technical expertise. Implementation of the CBD, especially for developing country parties, is hampered by inadequate scientific knowledge of the full extent of biodiversity contained within their borders since much of the taxonomic research is carried out by developed countries. In situ conservation under the CBD may require the designation of protected areas, with the need to enforce such designation. CITES is dependent on the issuance of certificates and the careful monitoring of points of entry for illegally traded flora and fauna, as are, indeed, the 1989 Basel Convention and the 2000 Cartagena Protocol to the CBD, which regulate the transboundary movement of waste and of living modified organisms, respectively. In general, there are six types of obstacles to national implementation, which may operate individually or collectively: (1) financial; (2) technical; (3) scientific; (4) legal and administrative; (5) political; and (6) textual (that is, the treaty text itself may be insufficiently clear and precise to give rise to precise obligations for national implementation).

In recognition of these barriers to implementation, implementation facilitation is now a key feature of contemporary environmental treaty arrangements. It is part of an emphasis upon capacity building, and developing countries claim it is an expression of common but differentiated responsibilities, as noted earlier. For example, under the 1966 Protocol to the London Convention, the duties of the Secretariat include 'providing advice on request on the implementation of this Protocol and on guidance and procedures developed thereunder' (Article 19(2)(2)). Under the revised 1995 Barcelona Convention, the Secretariat may, at a party's request, assist a party 'in the drafting of environmental legislation in compliance with the Convention and the Protocols' (Article 14(2)). Such facilitation is also evident under a number of other treaty instruments, which include trust fund arrangements to facilitate implementation and compliance. The Ramsar Convention, Vienna Convention, and World Heritage Convention funds are cases in point. There is a clear link, therefore, between implementation and compliance, with such funds available to assist national implementation where, essentially, the state is in non-compliance with its obligations under the convention owing to a lack of capacity and/or of resources. There is also an obvious link to international financial institutions, bearing in mind the role of the World Bank as the trustee of the Global Environmental Facility, which is administered jointly with the UN Development Programme and UNEP—the purpose of which is to provide facilitative financing for the additional incremental costs incurred by developing states in meeting their environmental obligations under, *inter alia*, the CBD and the UNFCCC (see Chapter 41 'Technical and Financial Assistance'). Implementation facilitation also occurs through the ordinary loan arrangements of the World Bank, which have 'mainstreamed' the environment and which peg project compliance measures to international environmental standards. Other international institutions have a role to play in capacity building, such as the Commonwealth Secretariat and its involvement in financing legal expertise in the drafting of maritime legislation for the implementation of the 1982 LOSC in Africa and the Caribbean region, in particular.

International environmental law has also responded to the problem of a lack of scientific knowledge and expertise impeding national action. Where a lack of scientific certainty arises from the nature of the environmental problem itself, such as climate change or the precise impacts of marine pollutants, the precautionary principle has evolved (see Chapter 25 'Precaution'). Lack of scientific knowledge may also relate to a lack of indigenous expertise linked to finance and capacity. The Global Taxonomic Initiative under the CBD aims at closing the developing country knowledge gap with respect to biological diversity through species identification. In addition, the clearing house mechanisms established under a number of recent environmental agreements, including the CBD, are a web-based system to facilitate the exchange of knowledge and expertise through the parties themselves, including examples of implementing legislation.

Ultimately, the question is one of the allocation of scarce national resources in the face of competing national demands. The political will to ensure effective implementation of existing and future environmental obligations is a crucial factor. It may be influenced by external pressures, such as regular meetings of the Conference of the Parties and compliance review, and by internal pressures generated by civil society and the role of major groups in the sustainable development process, which was acknowledged at Rio in Agenda 21.

6 Conclusion

Notwithstanding very significant evolution in international environmental law during the past 30 years, in particular, we still do not have a complete picture of the extent to which it is implemented by legislative/executive action at the domestic level. A recent trend in international environmental law doctrine is to emphasize the need for effective implementation and enforcement of the existing rules rather than the promulgation of further substantive norms. This emphasis upon national implementation is evident in the influence of the Rio Conference—'Think Globally, Act Locally.' Yet the techniques available for assessing the extent—not to mention the effectiveness—of such implementation are still rudimentary and incomplete. In consequence, it is difficult to examine, say, the relative paucity of international environmental case law and to draw from it conclusions regarding the effectiveness of national implementation. Is national legislation so well designed and implemented that few cases arise in practice? Or is this relative paucity a result of judicial restraint/ aversion to international environmental law? Or is there a record of poor implementation that is coupled with very restrictive standing requirements, cost rules, or the like, deterring potential litigants? Or is it that there are cases we simply do not know about—a general problem of the dissemination of state practice in the environmental context? What is clear is that, as a relatively new area of international law, international environmental law will be increasingly invoked in horizontal and vertical proceedings before national courts, and legislative implementation and enforcement will continue to be scrutinized by supranational bodies via national reporting and monitoring obligations as well as (in some cases) via non-compliance procedures. It is unlikely that international environmental law will achieve as high a profile as international human rights law before national courts. Yet there is some cause for optimism in the extent to which international environmental law is permeating national policy discourse, legal instruments, and, slowly but inexorably, judicial decision-making.

RECOMMENDED READING

M. Anderson and P. Galizzi, eds., *International Environmental Law in National Courts* (London: British Institute of International and Comparative Law, 2002).

J.V. DeMarco and M.L. Campbell, 'The Supreme Court of Canada's Progressive Use of International Environmental Law and Policy in Interpreting Domestic Legislation' (2004) 13 R.E.C.I.E.L. 320.

J. Ebbesson, *Compatibility of International and National Environmental Law* (The Hague: Kluwer Law International, 1996).

F.L. Morrison and R. Wolfrum, eds., *International, Regional and National Environmental Law* (The Hague: Kluwer Law International, 2000).

A. Palmer and C. Robb, eds., *International Environmental Reports*, Volume 4: *International Environmental Law in National Courts* (Cambridge: Cambridge University Press, 2004).

R. Reeve, *Policing Trade in Endangered Species: The CITES Treaty and Compliance* (London: Royal Institute of International Affairs/Earthscan, 2002).

P. Sand, *Lessons Learned in Global Environmental Governance* (Washington, DC: World Resources Institute, 1990).

——, 'Lessons Learned in Environmental Governance' (1991) 18 B.C. Envt'l Aff. L. Rev. 213.

UNEP, *Compendium of National Decisions on Matters Related to Environment*, Volume 1 (Nairobi: UNEP, 1998); Volumes 2–3 (Nairobi: UNEP, 2001).

CHAPTER 41

TECHNICAL AND
FINANCIAL
ASSISTANCE

LAURENCE BOISSON DE CHAZOURNES

1 INTRODUCTION

TECHNICAL and financial assistance plays an important role in the furtherance of environmental protection. Since the end of the 1980s, important changes have modified its contours, aims, and legal structure. The emergence of new principles, such as the principle of sustainable development (see Chapter 26 'Sustainable Development') and the principle of common but differentiated responsibilities (see Chapter 27 'Equity'), have introduced new facets to this notion, and the implementation of these principles has resulted in a complex mosaic of financial mechanisms and funding sources, which are linked to global conventions, multilateral institutions, bilateral aid, and private sector investment.

The principle of sustainable development plays a catalyzing role in the integration of environmental concerns into development assistance. International institutions, such as the United Nations Development Programme (UNDP), and multilateral and regional development banks, such as the World Bank and the European Bank for Reconstruction and Development (EBRD), have incorporated environmental objectives into their development aid schemes. At the same time, the principle of common but differentiated responsibilities furnishes a specific rationale for the provision of technical and financial assistance within multilateral environmental agreements (MEAs). To a large extent, this principle also determines the institutional structure associated with MEAs. Donor states may provide assistance for various reasons, including altruism and self-interest. However, the principle of common but differentiated responsibilities arguably entails legal consequences, linked to the requirement to take into account the needs and differentiated capabilities of developed and developing countries in the protection of the global environment. Pursuant to the principle, all states share common responsibilities for the protection of the environment for the benefit of present and future generations, although developed countries have specific responsibilities, one of them being the provision of technical and financial assistance to developing countries.

Through their contributions to financial mechanisms, such as the Multilateral Fund for the Implementation of the Montreal Protocol on Substances That Deplete the Ozone Layer (MFMP)[1] and the Global Environment Facility (GEF),[2] developed

---

The author would like to thank Mara Tignino, researcher in the Faculty of Law at the University of Geneva, for her invaluable help in the preparation of this chapter.

[1] The London Amendment, which was adopted in 1990 at the second Meeting of the Parties to the Montreal Protocol on Substances That Deplete the Ozone Layer (Montreal Protocol), established the Multilateral Fund for the Implementation of the Montreal Protocol (MFMP) on Substances That Deplete the Ozone Layer (Article 10 of the Montreal Protocol). See *Report of the Second Meeting of the Parties to the Montreal Protocol on Substances That Deplete the Ozone Layer*, Doc. UNEP/OzL.Pro.2/3 (1990) at Annex II, 'Amendment to the Montreal Protocol on Substances that Deplete the Ozone Layer.'

[2] Established in 1991 as a pilot project under the auspices of the World Bank, with the participation of the UN Environment Programme (UNEP) and the UN Development Programme (UNDP), the Global

countries contribute to the production of global public goods. In fact, financing projects in issue areas such as ozone depletion, climate change, or biodiversity benefits the international community as a whole. This notion is reflected in the concept of incremental costs, which is closely connected to the provision of technical and financial assistance. It relates to the extra costs that developing countries may incur in providing environmental benefit to the international community. Such costs may involve the introduction of new technologies or alternative methods of production and also training programmes. Through the provision of technical and financial assistance, developed countries contribute to covering such costs in order to provide developing countries with adequate means for implementing MEAs.

Other functions of technical and financial assistance include, *inter alia*, capacity building, disaster relief, financing of pollution control equipment, and compliance assistance. Among these various targets, capacity building has received the most political emphasis. As specified in Agenda 21, 'capacity-building encompasses the country's human, scientific, technological, organizational, institutional and resource capabilities.'[3] Effective environmental management by governments requires scientific and technical expertise, adequate infrastructure for environmental monitoring, and management and complex decision-making processes, which in many countries are not available. These factors explain why the transfer of technology and the provision of financial aid, including loans, credits or grants, are all part of the broader issue of capacity building. The provision of technical and financial assistance involves different types of actors, including public, private, multilateral, and bilateral entities. One of main public sources of financing for developing countries is official development assistance (ODA), yet this source of funding has declined since the 1990s. International financial institutions (IFIs), such as the World Bank, as well as private actors increasingly play a role in funding environmentally friendly projects. Financial mechanisms have been established to serve as vehicles for assistance to developing countries. Good examples of this practice are the MFMP and the GEF. Private sector involvement in funding activities related to the protection of the environment has been endorsed, among others, at the 2002 World Summit on Sustainable Development (WSSD). It is exemplified by the Prototype Carbon Fund (PCF), which was established under the auspices of the World Bank.

This chapter will first provide a picture of the different types and sources of technical and financial assistance, such as ODA, international institutions, and public/private partnerships. In so doing, the chapter will also address the relationship between technology transfer and intellectual property rights (IPRs), especially in light of agreements such as the Convention on Biological Diversity (CBD). The aim

---

Environment Facility (GEF) was restructured in 1994 and amended in 2003. See Instrument for the Establishment of the Restructured Global Environmental Facility, as amended by the Beijing Declaration of the Second Global Environmental Facility Assembly (16–18 October 2002), 44 I.L.M. 1002 (2005) at 7–21.

[3] United Nations Conference on Environment and Development, Agenda 21, 13 June 1992, UN Doc. A/CONF. 151/26 (1992) at para. 37.1.

and nature of technical and financial assistance will then be assessed. The objectives of technical and financial assistance vary significantly depending on the agreement concerned, and they have been progressively enlarged. Finally, the legal structure of financial mechanisms will be analysed, in particular, its relationship with the principle of common but differentiated responsibilities.

2 Different Types and Sources of Technical and Financial Assistance

The polymorphous character of financial and technical assistance is reflected in the multiple channels through which it may be provided. ODA, which is aimed at alleviating poverty, is provided through bilateral, regional, and international channels, and it is one of the sources of public funds for developing countries. Specific environmental mechanisms, such as those based on MEAs, constitute another channel through which assistance reaches developing countries. These mechanisms are intended to provide new and additional resources—that is, resources over and above ODA. While specific environmental mechanisms and ODA may have different objectives and features, it is important to bear in mind that they may both play a role within the activities of an institution. For example, the World Bank and the UNDP are providers of technical and financial assistance emanating both from ODA channels and from environmental mechanisms.

2.1 Levels of ODA and the Proposed International Finance Facility

Although there has been a decline in the provision of ODA, this form of assistance remains an essential means for financing development and for realizing objectives agreed upon by the international community, such as the millennium development goals (MDGs).[4] The role played by ODA in providing financial resources to developing countries has been at the centre of debates at international conferences held during the early 2000s. The Conference on Financing for Development, which was held

---

[4] The millennium development goals (MDGs), relying on the United Nations Millennium Declaration set out time-bound and quantified targets in order to address the fight against poverty. The eight MDGs deal with poverty in a multi-dimensional perspective, ranging from halting income poverty, hunger, disease, while, at the same time, promoting gender equality, education, and environmental sustainability. United Nations Millennium Declaration, UN Doc. A/RES/55/28 (September 2000).

in Monterrey in 2002, and the WSSD, held in the same year, reaffirmed the commitment of developed countries to the provision of ODA.[5] In particular, the Monterrey conference adopted an ambitious resolution—known as the Monterrey Consensus—which reaffirms the target of dedicating 0.7 per cent of the gross domestic product (GDP) of developed countries to ODA.[6] Furthermore, many states announced increased contributions or pledged to meet fixed dates for reaching the target. The European Union (EU) set a target for member states of 0.39 per cent by 2006. This increase will permit the EU to reach the target of dedicating 0.7 per cent of their GDP to ODA by 2015.[7]

In order to achieve the MDGs by 2015, there are calls for developing new strategies. The commitment of G-8 members to provide an additional US $50 billion a year by 2010, compared with 2004, is a step in this direction.[8] Increases in donor aid should also be accompanied by the establishment of innovative financing mechanisms. The proposal to create an International Finance Facility (IFF), formulated in 2003 by the United Kingdom's Treasury and Department for International Development, provides an example.[9] According to a document released by the UK government in September 2005, the IFF would leverage additional money from the international capital markets by issuing bonds, based on legally binding long-term donor commitments.[10] The document envisages that long-term commitments would increase the effectiveness of aid as well as its predictability and stability. Moreover, legally binding pledges by donors would be subject to recipient countries meeting one or more financing conditions such as adherence to good governance.

The 2005 draft document outlining the outcome of the WSSD recalls in rather soft terms the need to achieve 'the target of 0.7 per cent per cent of gross national product for official development assistance by 2015 and to reach at least 0.5 per cent of gross national product for official development assistance by 2010.' While this draft document underlines the urgent need for additional ODA commitments and encourages

---

[5] *Monterrey Consensus of the International Conference on Financing for Development*, Report of the International Conference on Financing for Development, Monterrey, Mexico, UN Doc.A/CONF.198/11 (18–22 March 2002) at 9, para.42. See also Johannesburg Plan of Implementation, in *Report of the World Summit on Sustainable Development*, Johannesburg, South Africa, 26 August–4 September 2002, UN Doc. A/CONF.199/20 (2002) at 56, para. 85(a).

[6] However, at the occasion of the same conference, the United States took a different position announcing the creation of a 'compact for global development' and the establishment of a 'millennium challenge account.' See Remarks by the President of the United States at United Nations Financing for Development Conference, Cintermex Convention Center, Monterrey, Mexico, US Department of State, 22 March 2002.

[7] See Presidency Conclusions, Barcelona European Council, Doc. SN 100/1/02 REV 1 (15–16 March 2002). In June 2005, the Council of the European Union, reaffirming the 2002 Barcelona commitments, set the target of 0.56 per cent by 2010.

[8] G-8 Summit, *Gleneagles Document on Africa*, 8 July 2005, at para. 28.

[9] UK Department for International Development, *International Finance Facility* (London: HM Treasury, January 2003).   [10] *Ibid*. at 4.

broad participation in the IFF,[11] the UN WSSD limits itself to recognizing 'the value of developing innovative sources of financing' and notes that some countries will implement the IFF without using committing language.[12]

2.2 Greening of Development Aid within International Institutions

While ODA does not generally aim at specific environmental objectives, increased concerns about the environment have led IFIs and other organizations to enlarge their 'green' activities. Poverty reduction strategies have become significant tools through which funds are channelled to alleviate poverty. As strategic documents reflecting national development priorities over a period of three to five years, poverty reduction strategies have become one of the principal means by which multilateral funding is being allocated. Although environmental concerns are often integrated in these documents, there is still a considerable variation across countries in the degree to which such concerns have been mainstreamed. In this context, it is important to develop an understanding of the links between environment and poverty and to promote better integration of environmental and natural resource concerns in poverty reduction strategies.[13]

Multilateral development banks such as the World Bank and organizations such as the OECD and the EU have developed other strategies and tools for integrating environmental objectives into development aid.[14] Since the late 1980s, the World Bank has adopted a number of operational directives (now operational policies) related to the environment.[15] Additionally, the World Bank has developed new programmatic lending instruments, which support policy and institutional reforms that address links between poverty reduction and the environment. In particular, since

---

[11] See the *Revised Draft Outcome Document of the High-level Plenary Meeting of the General Assembly of September 2005*, submitted by the president of the General Assembly, Doc. A/59/HLPM/CRP.1/Rev.2 (5 August 2005) at para. 22.

[12] United Nations General Assembly, *2005 World Summit Outcome*, Doc. A/RES/60/1 (16 September 2005) at para. 23(d).

[13] In this regard, see J. Bojö and J.B. Rama, *Poverty Reduction Strategies and Environment: A Review of Forty Interim and Full Poverty Reduction Strategy Papers* (Washington, DC: World Bank, 2002).

[14] For example, see Organisation of Economic Cooperation and Development (OECD), *Development Assistance Committee: Guidelines on Environment and Aid: No. 1, Good Practices for Environmental Impact Assessment of Development Projects* (Paris: OECD, 1992); and OECD, *Recommendation on Common Approaches on Environment and Officially Supported Export Credits* (Paris: OECD, 2003). See also the conclusion of the Partnership Agreement between the Members of the African, Caribbean and Pacific Group of States and the European Community and its Member States, Cotonou, 2000, Articles 1 and 20(e).

[15] These include Operational Policies on Environmental Assessment (OP 4.01); on Natural Habitats (OP 4.04); on Forests (OP 4.36); on the Safety of Dams (OP 4.37); and on Projects on International

2001, it has developed an environment strategy aimed at creating a portfolio of investments devoted to environmental issues and has started to 'mainstream' environmental issues into sectoral lending programs. The World Bank also has adopted a stronger role in dealing with threats to global environmental goods, such as climate change and loss of biodiversity. This is largely the result of its position as the implementing agency of the GEF, as will be explained later in this chapter.

2.3 Involvement of the Private Sector and the Non-Governmental Sector

Over the past several decades, with the decline of the relative importance of ODA, non-state entities have emerged as significant actors in development aid. For example, in the 1970s, 70 per cent of the resource flow from the United States to the developing world was ODA-based and 30 per cent originated from the private sector. Today, the numbers are reversed: 85 per cent of the resource flow from the United States to the developing world originates from the private sector and 15 per cent from the public sector.[16] The 1992 UN Conference on Environment and Development (UNCED) and, more strongly, the Monterrey conference and the WSSD have paved the way for the 'privatization' of assistance.[17] The WSSD, in particular, led to the establishment of a range of new 'partnership' arrangements between governments, the private sector, and civil society groups. The private sector and other actors, thus, have become increasingly involved in providing the necessary funds. In fact, private investment flows have become pivotal to the realization of sustainable development.

A relevant example of the increasing involvement of private actors in funding environmentally friendly projects is the PCF, which was established within the World Bank and the Clean Development Mechanism (CDM) created under the Kyoto Protocol. This mechanism, in addition to others, involves private actors, through the use of private resources as well as public resources, in the development of what was hitherto considered to be a public financing system. As mechanisms intended to channel private sector investment towards climate friendly projects, the PCF and the CDM aim to support the development of a new set of international arrangements for public/private partnership, which will be discussed later in this chapter. Another conduit for the involvement of the private sector is the International Finance

Waterways (OP 7.50). See L. Boisson de Chazournes, 'Policy Guidance and Compliance Issues: The World Bank Operational Standards,' in D. Shelton, ed., *Commitment and Compliance: The Role of Non-Binding Norms in the International Legal System* (Oxford: Oxford University Press, 2000) 281.

[16] Global Development Alliance, *Expanding the Impact of Foreign Assistance through Public–Private Alliances* (Washington, DC: US Agency for International Development, 2003) at 3.

[17] See Agenda 21, at para. 33.16; and Johannesburg Plan of Implementation, at para. 80(d) and (e), 81, and 82.

Corporation (IFC). In order to be eligible for IFC funding, a project must meet a number of IFC criteria. It must be technically, environmentally, and socially sound with good prospects of being profitable for the local economy and must satisfy IFC environmental and social standards.[18]

The Global Development Alliance, which was developed by USAID and launched in 2001,[19] also responds to the changed environment, and is a means by which the private sector acts as a financier of development aid. This alliance combines resources and capabilities of various actors and emphasizes public/private sector partnerships. Alliances among government, civil society, and the private sector complement and multiply the impact of ODA. Hence, donors use ODA to catalyze the involvement of the private sector, both domestic and foreign, in development assistance.

The instruments establishing the UN Global Compact[20] and the Equator Principles, which were endorsed by almost 40 private banking institutions,[21] both refer to human rights and environmental principles and, thereby, underscore the need to focus on the environmental and social responsibility of private actors (see Chapter 21 'Private and Quasi-Private Standard Setting' and Chapter 28 'Environmental Rights'). Although these instruments are not legally binding, their endorsement by companies illustrates the will of the private sector to support the implementation of environmental standards in their activities. The development of these instruments fits in with the increased role of civil society, of which the private sector is considered to be a part. There is, in other words, a call for the private sector to be accountable—to accept obligations in return for the voice and, indeed, the influence it is being accorded at the international level (see Chapter 35 'Business').

The increasing involvement of non-state actors in the provision of financial and technical assistance has been criticized as an off-loading of development issues onto the private sector, and there are concerns dealing with potential conflicts of interest and impartiality in the decision-making process. Moreover, it is important to appreciate that, while large developing countries, such as China or India, may count on private investments, for the poorest and smallest developing countries, ODA continues to be one of the most significant means for implementing development goals because of the difficulties they face in attracting private investment flows.[22]

---

[18] For example, see International Finance Corporation (IFC) Operational Policies: on Environmental Assessment (OP 4.01, October 1998); on Natural Habitats (OP 4.04, November 1998); on Pest Management (OP 4.09, November 1998); on Forestry' (OP 4.36, November 1998); and on International Waterways (OP 7.50, November 1998). See also the World Bank, *Pollution Prevention and Abatement Handbook* (Washington, DC: World Bank Group, 1998); and IFC, *Environmental and Social Guidelines for Occupational Health and Safety* (Washington, DC: IFC: 2003).

[19] Global Development Alliance, see note 16 above.

[20] The ten principles of the UN Global Compact, 1999.   [21] Equator Principles, 2003.

[22] C. Toulmin and T. Bigg, *Financing for Environment and Development* (Paris: Institut du développement durable et des relations internationales, 2004) at 6.

2.4 Intellectual Property Rights and Technology Transfer

Technology transfer provisions have special legal features, due to their thorny relationships with intellectual property rights (IPRs). These features distinguish technology transfer obligations from other forms of technical and financial assistance. The complex links between the transfer of technology and IPRs are best illustrated by the provisions of two treaties, namely the CBD and the 2001 International Treaty on Plant Genetic Resources for Food and Agriculture (ITPGRFA). Since the 1970s, developing countries have called for improved access to technology, and have emphasized the need to enhance their technological capabilities.[23] Specific provisions on the transfer of technology have been incorporated into various international instruments. In such instruments, two broad and overlapping categories of technology-related provisions can be distinguished. The first category focuses on the development of national measures for the protection of IPRs. This type of provision is contained in specific instruments related to the protection of property rights over industrial property or artistic works.[24] In addition, the World Trade Organization (WTO) Agreement on Trade-Related Aspects of Intellectual Property Rights (TRIPS Agreement) refers to criteria and objectives regarding the protection and enforcement of IPRs. The second category of provisions focuses on measures for the transfer of technology to, and capacity building in, developing countries. These instruments deal with the transfer of specific technologies for the protection of human health and the environment, including biodiversity, climate change, and ocean resources.[25]

While the protection of genetic resources had become an issue of international concern during the 1980s,[26] the technological developments that have taken place

---

[23] United Nations, Declaration on the Establishment of a New International Economic Order, Doc. A/RES 3201 (1974); and United Nations, Programme of Action on the Establishment of a New Economic Order, Doc. A/RES 3281 (1974).

[24] See 1883 Paris Convention for the Protection of Industrial Property, as amended in 1979; and the 1886 Bern Convention for the Protection of Literary and Artistic Works, as amended in 1979.

[25] See, e.g., Montreal Protocol, Article 10A; 1992 Convention on Biological Diversity (CBD), Article 18; 1994 United Nations Framework Convention on Climate Change (UNFCCC), Articles 4.1(c), 4.3, 4.5, 4.7-4-10, 9.2 (c), 11, and 11.1; 1997 Kyoto Protocol to the UNFCCC (Kyoto Protocol), Articles 10 and 11; 1994 Convention to Combat Desertification in Those Countries Experiencing Serious Drought and/or Desertification, Particularly in Africa (Desertification Convention), Articles 6(e) and 16–18; and 1992 United Nations Convention on the Law of the Sea (UNCLOS), Articles 62, 143–4 and 266–77, and Annex III, Basic Conditions of Prospecting, Exploration and Exploitation, Article 5. For a complete list on provisions on technology transfer, see UN Conference on Trade and Development, *Compendium of International Arrangements on Transfer of Technology: Selected Instruments*, Doc. UNCTAD/ITE/IPC/Misc.5 (2001).

[26] FAO Conference, International Undertaking on Plant Genetic Resources for Food and Agriculture, Resolution 8/83 (23 November 1983).

since, particularly in biotechnology engineering, have enhanced the importance of regulating access to, and the benefit sharing of, genetic resources, especially because of the economic benefits involved. The technology-related provisions in both the CBD and the ITPGRFA reflect the particularly problematic nature of the relationship between IPRs and technology transfer obligations in the context of regulating the conservation and sustainable use of genetic resources.[27] On the one hand, the social, economic, ecological, and cultural importance of biological diversity, genetic resources, and their derivatives as well as their uses for biotechnology applications have received increased recognition. On the other hand, this recognition has prompted sovereignty and property concerns and has raised a range of new conceptual and practical policy and legal questions. While developed countries claim access to genetic resources and their uses for biotechnology applications as well as for the strengthening of IPRs, developing countries assert their sovereign rights over the genetic resources situated in their territories and the right to the transfer of technologies that are relevant to the conservation and sustainable use of biological diversity.

The CBD and the ITPGRFA reflect attempts to balance these concerns. Article 16(2) of the CBD is particularly relevant in the sense that contracting parties recognize that 'in the case of technology subject to patents and other intellectual property rights, such access and transfer shall be provided on terms which recognize and are consistent with the adequate and effective protection of intellectual property rights.' In its fifth paragraph, Article 16 recognizes that IPRs may influence the implementation of the convention and stipulates that states 'shall cooperate in this regard subject to national legislation and international law in order to ensure that such rights are supportive of and do not run counter to its objectives.'

The ITPGRFA delineates a regime for benefit sharing that provides direct and indirect links to IPR instruments. In this sense, it provides a legal framework that is more developed than the one provided for by the CBD. The main institutional innovation of the ITPGRFA is found in the establishment of a multilateral system of access and benefit sharing for plant genetic resources for food and agriculture (PGRFA). Some key features of this multilateral system are the exchange of information, technology transfer, capacity building, and sharing of monetary and other benefits of commercialization.[28] With respect to technology transfer, the ITPGRFA, in Article 13, establishes only a general obligation to facilitate access to technologies for the conservation, characterization, evaluation, and use of PGRFA. Specific mention is made of the fact that even technologies protected by IPRs should be transferred under 'fair and most favourable terms,' in particular, in the case of 'technologies for use in conservation as well as technologies for the benefit of farmers in developing countries.' The ITPGRFA seeks to ensure access to, and transfer of technology to,

---

[27] See CBD, Articles 15, 16, and 19; and International Treaty on Plant Genetic Resources for Food and Agriculture (ITPGRFA), Articles 12 and 13.   [28] ITPGRFA, Article 13.2(a), (b), (c), and (d).

developed countries also through the establishment and maintenance of all types of partnerships, including those involving the private sector in research and human resources development.[29]

3   NATURE AND AIM OF FINANCIAL AND TECHNICAL ASSISTANCE

Technical and financial assistance provided through ODA, IFIs, and public/private partnerships increasingly deals with activities related to environmental issues. The aim of technical and financial assistance, however, has evolved over time. It may involve both the more traditional aim of development aid, namely that of assisting developing countries in overcoming technical difficulties through providing emergency relief or setting-up training programmes, as well as new types of projects such as the financing of investment projects that aim to benefit the global environment.

3.1 Traditional Nature and Aim of Technical and Financial Assistance

At the universal and regional levels, several conventions commit parties to respond to requests for technical assistance from states likely to be affected by pollution incidents and emergencies at sea. Article 198 of the 1982 UN Convention on the Law of the Sea, for example, requires states to cooperate, in accordance with their capabilities in eliminating the effects of pollution caused by pollution incidents. This requirement is also reiterated in most regional seas agreements.[30] Under the 1990 International Maritime Organization's (IMO) International Convention on Oil Pollution Preparedness, Response and Cooperation, the assistance provided by parties may consist of training as well as ensuring the availability of relevant technology, equipment, and facilities to prepare for and respond to oil pollution incidents and joint research and development programmes. International organizations, such as the IMO, and regional organizations, such as, for example, the Regional Marine Pollution Emergency Response Centre for the Mediterranean Sea, also may have a role in coordinating the provision of technical assistance and advice for states faced

[29] *Ibid.*, Article 13.2(b)(ii).
[30] For example, see 1992 Helsinki Convention on the Protection of the Marine Environment of the Baltic Sea, Annex VII, Regulation 8.

with major oil pollution incidents at sea. Similar provisions are also contained in the 1986 Convention on Assistance in Cases of Nuclear Accident or Radiological Emergency.

Technical and financial assistance also serves as a significant tool to help developing countries in training national experts as well as in providing at least part of the supporting capital for putting into place pollution control equipment or operational activities. For example, the general trust fund established by the 1984 Protocol on Long-Term Financing of the Cooperative Programme for Monitoring and Evaluation of the Long-Range Transmission of Air Pollutants in Europe (EMEP) to the 1979 Convention on Long-Range Transboundary Air Pollution provides technical and financial assistance for the gathering of data and monitoring of air pollution by providing pollution control equipment and training on how to use the equipment. Helping countries put this equipment into place contributes to the implementation of, and compliance with, environmental agreements.

Technical and financial assistance can also contribute to the development and implementation of national legislation. For instance, under the trust fund for the 1973 Convention on International Trade in Endangered Species of Wild Fauna and Flora (CITES), which is administered by UNEP, the Secretariat provides technical assistance for supporting the development of CITES-related legislation and for conducting national wildlife trade policy reviews.[31] Other functions may include the strengthening of national capacities to submit reports providing data on the implementation of, and compliance with, the agreements concerned.

Financial mechanisms established under environmental agreements may also help countries that are seeking to accede to a convention. For example, countries that are seeking to become parties to the Convention on Wetlands of International Importance Especially as Waterfowl Habitat may ask for a grant to support activities necessary for the identification, delineation, and mapping of a site to be included on the List of Wetlands of International Importance.[32]

In its traditional form, technical and financial assistance mostly address issues from a sectoral or specific viewpoint, and their main aim is to help countries overcome technical obstacles to the protection of the environment. More recently, however, different types of projects have emerged. These projects promote multi-sectoral approaches and proper environmental governance, and their aim is to achieve global benefits. Financial and technical assistance, relying on the principle of common but differentiated responsibilities, has become a means to address common concerns shared by developed and developing countries, moving from the concept of donors and recipients to one of partnership to solve global problems.

---

[31] Conference of the Parties, 'National Wildlife Trade Policy Reviews,' Decision 13.75 (2004).

[32] Ramsar Small Grants Fund for Wetland Conservation Wise Use (SGF), Operational Guidelines for the Triennium 2006–2009, as amended by Standing Committee Decisions SC29-13, SC30-13, and SC34-17 at para. 14.

3.2 Provision of Global Public Goods and the Changing Nature and Aim of Technical and Financial Assistance

Financial mechanisms such as the MFMP and the GEF are means for promoting global benefits. The global environment is the perfect example of a global public good. The degradation of the atmosphere, the oceans, and the ozone layer threatens people's lives everywhere, and their protection benefits both present and future generations. Their conservation thus provides an opportunity for dealing with issues of common interest (see Chapter 23 'Common Areas, Common Heritage, and Common Concern'). Management and conservation of global public goods requires integrated rather than fragmented solutions among states, especially between developed and developing countries. Under the Montreal Protocol, the projects financed include institutional strengthening and technical assistance to meet the incremental costs incurred by developing countries when changing from ozone-depleting technologies to more ozone-friendly technologies, and when phasing out the consumption of ozone-depleting substances. Within the GEF, the projects financed include five focal areas: ozone depletion, loss of biodiversity, climate change, land degradation, international waters, and persistent organic pollutants. The GEF mechanism has allowed for synergies among its focal areas and contributed to raising more resources than individual funds created for specific purposes would have been capable of. Projects in each of these areas address issues of environmental governance, thus assisting countries to integrate global concerns into their sustainable development policies. In so doing, they rely on the principle of public participation and on impact assessment techniques and promote the establishment of accountability mechanisms at the national level.

The broad scope of the GEF activities requires a constant effort by donor countries to increase the level of their contributions. Donor countries commit money every four years through a process called the GEF Replenishment. Over the years, donor countries have increased their commitments. In 1994, 34 countries pledged US $2 billion to fund the first GEF Replenishment; at the second GEF Replenishment in 1998, 36 states committed US $2.75 billion; and in 2002, 32 donor countries pledged US $3 billion to the third GEF Replenishment.[33] The replenishment phases have contributed to the strengthened recognition and position of the GEF as a crucial financial mechanism for the management of common interests.

---

[33] See Resolution no. 2002-0005 of the IBRD Executive Directors approving the third GEF Replenishment of the GEF trust fund (19 December 2002). The text of the resolution is available in *Instrument for the Establishment of the Restructured Global Environment Facility* (Washington, DC: Global Environment Facility, 2004) at 59–68. The fourth GEF Replenishment is still under negotiation, and it should be concluded by 2006. See Meeting on the Fourth Replenishment of the GEF Trust Fund, *Draft Negotiating Text: Still under Discussion: Policy Recommendations for the Fourth Replenishment of the GEF Trust Fund*, Doc. GEF/R.4/30 (19–20 December 2005).

The natural and cultural heritage protected by the 1972 Convention for the Protection of the World Cultural and Natural Heritage (World Heritage Convention) provides another example whereby financial mechanisms are used to achieve global benefits. The World Heritage Fund aims to compensate heritage 'host' countries for their special conservation efforts on behalf of the world community. The World Heritage Fund provides about US $3 million annually to support activities by states parties in need of international assistance for protecting the natural and cultural sites that are part of the World Heritage List.[34]

The MFMP and the GEF, as providers of global benefits, also play a role in inducing and restoring compliance with environmental agreements (see Chapter 43 'Compliance Procedures'). For instance, the Montreal Protocol's non-compliance procedure has been invoked on several occasions by parties that are encountering difficulties in implementing the protocol, including Russia, Belarus, Ukraine, and a number of other states from Eastern Europe and the former Soviet Union. Various measures have been recommended by the Meeting of the Parties to the Montreal Protocol to deal with these problems of non-compliance, including the provision of technical and financial assistance, notably through the GEF. In these situations, GEF financing has been used as an incentive for compliance and has contributed to the resolution of the issues through the Montreal Protocol's non-compliance procedure. The non-compliance procedures adopted by the the parties to the Kyoto Protocol[35] and to the 1998 Convention on Access to Information, Public Participation in Decision-Making and Access to Justice in Environmental Matters[36] provide additional examples where technical and financial assistance play an important role in both avoiding non-compliance and restoring compliance with treaty obligations.

Non-compliance procedures established under various MEAs thus offer an additional framework for providing financial and technical assistance. As institutional vehicles, they further the conditionalities that are attached to the provision of such assistance. In so doing, they are contributing to the promotion of sustainable development policies and actions at the domestic level. Through the performance of oversight functions, the Montreal Protocol and Kyoto Protocol compliance bodies thus contribute to the building up of environmental regimes by developing criteria for national environmental governance as conditions for the provision of technical

---

[34] For the budget 2006–7, see *Presentation of the World Heritage Fund and Budget 2006–2007*, Decision 29 COM 16; and *Decisions adopted at the Twenty-Ninth Session of the World Heritage Committee*, Doc. WHC-05/29.COM/22 (2005) at 161.

[35] Under the purview of the facilitative branch, the Kyoto non-compliance mechanism may provide technical and financial assistance to facilitate the implementation of the protocol. See Decision 27/CMP.1, *Procedures and Mechanisms Relating to Compliance under the Kyoto Protocol*, Doc. FCCC/KP/CMP/2005/8/Add.3 (November 2005) at 92–103.

[36] See Decision I/7, *Review of Compliance*, Doc.ECE/MP.PP/2/Add.8 (2 April 2004) (see Chapter 29 'Public Participation').

and financial assistance. Non-compliance procedures also provide a means for institutionalizing technical and financial assistance, promoting the accountability of global for a, and addressing issues of common interest.[37]

4 FINANCIAL MECHANISMS

Since the UN Conference on the Human Environment in Stockholm in 1972, creating trust funds has become one of the most important techniques for transferring financial and technical resources aimed at the protection of the environment. Three main types of trust funds have evolved over time. First generation trust funds mostly have focused on sectoral and technical approaches. Such trust funds have been established at the initiative of states, international organizations, or non-governmental organizations (NGOs). In this case, the contributions made by developed countries were not conceived as aiming to benefit the international community as a whole. Instead, they were perceived as a means of offering technical assistance to developing countries and of facilitating the operations of the international institutions involved.

Due to the global nature and complexity of the problems to be tackled (that is, climate change, biological diversity, and the ozone layer), international cooperation regarding technical and financial assistance needed to be strengthened, which has led to the establishment of a different type of trust fund, often referred to as second-generation trust funds. In particular, these financial mechanisms exhibit the following characteristics: they are an essential means for implementing MEAs; the types of projects and activities financed through these mechanisms have been expanded; and the number of institutional partners involved in the running of these mechanisms has increased. They contribute to shaping the legal commitments in the area of technical and financial assistance and in fostering global public goods. More recently, *sui generis* mechanisms are also emerging as a new means for achieving environmental aims. Established in the context of public/private partnerships, they exemplify the emphasis placed on the need for synergy between the public and the private sectors.

The establishment of new financial mechanisms during the last two decades has also strengthened international law on financial and technical assistance.

---

[37] These bodies and procedures may be considered as part of the so-called field of 'global administrative law.' It is defined as 'the mechanisms, principles, practices, and supporting social understandings that promote or otherwise affect the accountability of global administrative bodies, in particular by ensuring they meet adequate standards of transparency, participation, reasoned decision, and legality, and by providing effective review of the rules and decisions they make.' B. Kingsbury, N. Krisch, and R.B. Stewart, 'The Emergence of Global Administrative Law' (2005) 68 L. & Contemp. Probs. 17.

Developing countries require financial and technical resources from developed countries for implementing issues of common interest—this is not only an issue of fact but also of law.

4.1 Financial Mechanisms of the First Generation

Trust funds established on the basis of specific environmental agreements, such as the 1989 Basel Convention on the Control on Transboundary Movements of Hazardous Wastes and Their Disposal (Basel Convention), primarily aim to provide financial resources for supporting the costs of the activities of the secretariats charged with the administration of the conventions. Technical cooperation trust funds also may be used to enable representatives from developing countries to attend the meetings that take place within the framework of MEAs. Yet, some of these funds also promote technical cooperation activities in order to implement the agreements, notably through the financing of programs for state capacity building. For instance, the CITES trust fund provides financial support for capacity building and conducting scientific research,[38] and the Basel Convention technical cooperation trust fund covers a broad range of activities, including technical assistance in the implementation of the convention as well as assistance in case of accidents and liability issues caused by transboundary movements of hazardous wastes.[39]

Trust funds may also be used to support general functions such as the direction and coordination of environmental activities engaged in by an international institution. The UNEP Environment Fund is a prime example.[40] It is an important source of financing for the implementation of UNEP activities. Apart from a contribution from the UN's regular budget, UNEP depends entirely on voluntary contributions to the Environment Fund. In 2005, contributions to the Environment Fund reached US $59.2 million.[41]

Although the first generation of financial mechanisms deal with a wide array of activities, the provision of technical and financial assistance from developed to developing countries is perceived as a relation between donor and recipient countries, and is not considered to benefit the international community as a whole. Furthermore, the legal structure of the commitments relating to the provision of technical and financial assistance is also different. Not relying on the principle of common but differentiated responsibilities, the contributions to first generation financial mechanisms often have a voluntary nature. These funds do not cover investment or risk

---

[38] See Decision 13.1, *Strategic Vision and Action Plan*, CoP13 Decisions (2003) Annex I, at 129–47.

[39] Decision V/32, *Enlargement of the Scope of the Technical Cooperation Trust Fund*, Doc. UNEP/CHW.5/29 (1999).   [40] General Assembly Resolution 2997 (XXVII) (15 December 1972).

[41] UNEP, *Annual Report* (Hertfordshire: Earthprint, 2005) at 76–7.

management projects, which play a significant role in the context of the second generation financial mechanisms. Moreover, the amount of contributions made to first generation funds is significantly lower than the financial resources administered by the financial mechanisms created in the wake of UNCED.[42]

4.2 Financial Mechanisms of the Second Generation

One of the prominent characteristics of the second-generation funds is the fact that through their contributions, developed countries are providers of global public goods. The financing of the incremental costs incurred by developing countries, under financial mechanisms such the MFMP and the GEF, as mentioned earlier, benefits the international community and furthers the common interests of all states. These mechanisms are characterized by the involvement of several institutional partners. The GEF is managed by three institutions as implementing agencies, namely the World Bank, the UNDP, and UNEP.[43] While these organizations share some common responsibilities, they also have distinct roles. The World Bank, as the trustee of the GEF, is responsible for investment projects and the mobilization of private sector resources, while the UNDP has the primary role of ensuring the development and management of capacity-building programmes and technical assistance projects. For its part, UNEP is responsible for overseeing the development of scientific and technical analysis as well as for promoting environmental management consistent with the purpose of the GEF. In addition, in 1999, the GEF Council established formal links with seven international organizations, including four regional development banks.[44]

The GEF Secretariat has also made efforts to enhance the involvement of the private sector in the GEF. The private sector is involved in the GEF via the implementing agencies, including the World Bank and UNDP. The World Bank, for its part, draws

---

[42] For a comparison on the financial resources, for example, see *Contributions and Pledges to UNEP's Environment Fund*, in UNEP, *Annual Report*, see note 41 above; Resolution no. 2002-0005 of the IBRD Executive Directors Approving the third Replenishment of the GEF Trust Fund, see note 33 above; and Decision XIV/39, *2003–2005 Replenishment of the Multilateral Fund*, Doc. UNEP/OzL.Pro.14/9 (2002).

[43] The MFMP has four implementing agencies: the World Bank, UNEP, the UNDP, and the UN Industrial Development Organization (UNIDO). The implementing agencies assist recipient enterprises to prepare projects that are reviewed by the Secretariat and then considered by the Executive Committee. The World Bank, in its capacity as one of the implementing agencies, created its own fund, the Ozone Projects Trust Fund, with funding provided by the MFMP.

[44] These organizations are known as GEF 'executing agencies' and they are: the African Development Bank, the Asian Development Bank (ADB), the European Bank for Reconstruction and Development, the Inter-American Development Bank (IDB), the International Fund for Agricultural Development, the UN Food and Agricultural Organization, and UNIDO. In particular, the IDB and the ADB have been both granted direct access to GEF resources for the implementation of GEF projects. See GEF, *Joint Summary of the Chairs*, GEF Council Meeting, Doc.GEF/C.20 (14–15 October 2002) at 5.

upon the investment expertise of the IFC. This allows for the IFC'S projects generating global environmental benefits to obtain GEF funds. An open issue remains the fact that, regardless of the potential profitability of most private investments, the GEF provides concessional funding in the form of grants and subsidies to recipients. Nonetheless, this type of funding can be seen as seed money or risk grants for initiating a project. It is in line with the concept of public/private partnerships that was promoted at the WSSD in Johannesburg in September 2002.[45]

The institutional framework in which second generation financial mechanisms operate is also innovative, notably in the context of their relations with the bodies established by MEAs. In fact, the activities of these financial mechanisms are carried out in conjunction with guidelines and criteria forged by the Conference of the Parties (COPs) of the various MEAs. The COPs determine the eligibility criteria for the allocation of grants and concessional funding and decide on the policy and program priorities. The executive bodies of the financial mechanisms such as the GEF Council and the Executive Committee of the MFMP act in conformity with the priorities established by the relevant COP.

The relationship of the GEF and the MFMP to MEAs is a crucial component of their mandate and *raison d'être*—it pertains to their political legitimacy. The assistance provided by these funds is critical to advancing the aims of the conventions in developing countries and for promoting issues of environmental governance. They assist these countries in integrating global environmental concerns into their sustainable development strategies, policies, and actions. Moreover, by placing the financial and technical activities to be undertaken within conventional legal frameworks, the MEAs provide a framework within which to assess the legitimacy of the actions undertaken by these financial mechanisms.[46]

In 2005, the GEF Council decided to introduce allocation criteria based on an index of a country's potential to generate global environmental benefits and on an index of performance in the biodiversity and climate change focal areas.[47] Some states members of the GEF Council, however, expressed doubts in relation to this

[45] In June 2006, the GEF Council asked the GEF Secretariat, with the help of the IFC and the implementing and executing agencies, to develop a project proposal for the establishment of a public/private sector partnership fund for Council consideration. *GEF Strategy to Enhance Engagement with the Private Sector*, GEF Council Meeting, Doc. GEF/C.28/14 (6–9 June 2006).

[46] Memorandums of understanding have been concluded to this effect between the GEF and the Conference of the Parties (COPs). See Decision 12/COP.2, *Memorandum of Understanding between the Conference of the Parties of the UNFCCC and the Council of the GEF*, Doc. FCCC/CP/1996/15/Add.1 (29 October 1996); Decision 8/COP.3, *Memorandum of Understanding between the Conference of the Parties of the CBD and the Council of the GEF*, Doc. UNEP/CBD/COP/3/38 (11 February 1997); Decision 6/COP.7; *Memorandum of Understanding between the Conference of the Parties of the UNCCD and the Council of the GEF*, Doc. ICCD/COP(7)/16/Add.1 (25 November 2005); and Decision 19/COP.1, *Memorandum of Understanding between the Conference of the Parties of the Stockholm Convention on Persistent Organic Pollutants and the Council of the GEF*, Doc. UNEP/POPS/COP.1/19 (31 January 2005).

[47] GEF, *Joint Summary of the Chairs*, Special Meeting of the Council, Doc.GEF/C.26 (August 31–1 September 2005), at Annex I, Decision on the Resource Allocation Framework.

decision.[48] The new approach may transform the dynamics of the GEF from an area-focused mechanism governed by environmental and operational criteria to a country 'performance-based framework' for the allocation of GEF resources involving the application of criteria of a political nature. This distinction raises concerns as to the legitimacy and the institutional position of the GEF, which is to operate on the basis of the guidance provided by the COPs that have designated the GEF as the financial mechanism for MEAs.

The decision-making process in the second generation financial mechanisms is also relevant. It indicates states' willingness to ensure that these funds are administered collectively, representing the interests of donor and recipient countries. The governing principle in the decision-making process is that of consensus within the MFMP and within the GEF. If 'no consensus appears attainable,' other procedures are provided for. In the MFMP's Executive Committee, a two-thirds majority of the parties representing a majority of developed and developing countries is required.[49] In the GEF, the voting procedure provided for is characterized by the principle of a double-weighted majority, which requires a 60 per cent majority of the total number of participating states as well as a 60 per cent majority of the total amount of contributions made to the trust fund of the GEF.[50]

Eligibility criteria in financial mechanisms mostly focus on state-driven projects. However, there is an emerging trend favouring the provision of such assistance to actors other than states. In this context, an interesting model is the GEF's Small Grants Program, which is administered by UNDP. It provides grants of up to US $50,000 to finance activities of NGOs and community-based organizations. With its grassroots approach, this program has helped to develop innovative ways for promoting sustainable development and increasing the visibility of the GEF at the local level. Also relevant is the GEF medium-sized grant program (MSP), which is open to NGOs (albeit not exclusively) for grants below US $1 million.[51] Expedited procedures were established to allow MSP grants to be processed in a simpler and quicker way than larger grants. In practice, MSP grants do not yet fully benefit from expedited procedures—an issue that is the subject of complaints from NGOs.[52]

Since these financial mechanisms are based on agreements that seek to address issues of common concern, and implement the idea that global benefits can only be achieved through cooperative action, the legal regime established by these agreements has to be perceived from a global perspective. The interdependence of the

---

[48] *Ibid.* at Annex IV, Statements by Council Member representing Argentina, Bolivia, Chile, Paraguay, Peru, and Uruguay.

[49] *Report of the Second Meeting of the Parties to the Montreal Protocol on Substances that Deplete the Ozone Layer*, Doc. UNEP/OzL.Pro.2/3 (1990) Appendix II, Terms of Reference of the Executive Committee.

[50] Instrument for the Establishment of the Restructured Global Environmental Facility, see note 2 above at Article 25(c).

[51] See UNDP and GEF, *Strategic Framework, Including Addendum*, March 2002, at 4.

[52] See GEF Council Meetings, *Compilation of NGO Interventions*, 13 May 2003, at 3.

actions to be put in place by developed and developing countries as well as the role of the principle of common but differentiated responsibilities constitute the main pillars of these agreements. The provision of technical and financial assistance by developed countries to developing countries through these financial mechanisms is one way in which the latter principle is being implemented.

4.3 *Sui Generis* Financial Mechanisms

As mentioned earlier, new partnership arrangements between governments, the private sector, and other civil society-actors, such as indigenous and local communities and NGOs are presently regarded as important instruments for furthering sustainable development.[53] Some of the financial mechanisms that have been concluded in this context will be discussed in this section. New vehicles for technical and financial assistance include *sui generis* mechanisms such as the PCF and the Rain Forest Trust Fund. Both mechanisms were established within the World Bank and draw upon the experience of this institution in administering such mechanisms. The PCF is a rather elaborate institutional structure based on public-private partnership. It uses private and public financial resources in support of climate-friendly projects, and it involves the private sector in the development of a comprehensive and coherent financing system for the reduction of global concentrations of greenhouse gas emissions. The objective of the PCF is the funding of projects in developing countries and countries with economies in transition that aim to reduce global concentrations of greenhouse gases, thereby contributing to compliance with the commitments under the Kyoto Protocol.[54]

The resolution establishing the PCF opens this mechanism both to public and private sector participants, whose participation in the PCF must be approved by the trustee—that is, the World Bank.[55] It provides that 'each Public Sector Participant

---

[53] The Monterrey Consensus and the Johannesburg Plan of Implementation have flagged the significance of such types of partnerships. *Report of the International Conference on Financing for Development*, see note 5 above at 5–7, paras. 20–5; and *Report of the World Summit on Sustainable Development*, see note 5 above at paras. 80(d) and (e), 81, and 82.

[54] IBRD Instrument Establishing the Prototype Carbon Fund, IBRD Resolution no. 99-1 Authorizing Establishment of the Prototype Carbon Fund, approved by the Executive Directors of the IBRD on 20 July 1999 (as amended by Resolution no. 2000-1 on Changing the Terms of a Second Closing and on Certain Other Amendments to the Instrument Establishing the Prototype Carbon Fund, approved by the Executive Directors of the IBRD on 15 May 2000, and by Resolution no. 2001-3 on Changing the Composition of the Participants Committee, and on certain other amendments to the Instrument Establishing the Prototype Carbon Fund, adopted by the Executive Directors of the IBRD on 22 March 2001).

[55] The resolution distinguishes between 'eligible private sector participant,' meaning 'any person, other than an Eligible Public Sector Participant, organized in a country Party to the UNFCCC and whose participation in the Fund has been approved by the Trustee,' and 'eligible public sector participant,'

will be required to contribute U.S. $10 million to the Fund and each Private Sector Participant will be required to contribute U.S.$5 million to the Fund.'[56] These payments can be made at any time during the life of the fund.[57] Both public and private investors in the fund participate in decision-making based on the size of their contribution to the fund. The World Bank ensures that the projects financed comply with the project selection criteria. Projects have to comply with guidelines, modalities, and procedures adopted by the parties to the UN Framework Convention on Climate Change (UNFCCC) and the Kyoto Protocol. Moreover, the World Bank is also responsible for ensuring complementarity between GEF-financed projects and the projects financed by the PCF.[58]

Projects financed under this mechanism help to reduce the concentration of greenhouse gases in the atmosphere, and leverage additional financial resources through the involvement of the private sector. The PCF attracts these resources by supporting the creation of 'carbon assets'—that is, verified and certified emission reductions—which are produced by PCF-funded projects.[59] The fund aims to put into practice the innovative market mechanisms introduced by the Kyoto Protocol, and it illustrates that these mechanisms may be used to the advantage of the World Bank's borrowing countries in furtherance of their sustainable development. In particular, the fund aims to develop projects related to renewable energy technology such as geothermal, wind, solar, and small hydro energy.[60] Through the creation of this fund, the World Bank provides an important example on how to channel private and public resources in order to create new financial resources addressing global concerns such as climate change.

The Rain Forest Trust Fund has served as another laboratory for experimenting with innovative strategies aimed at the protection and sustainable use of natural resources in the Amazon and Atlantic rainforest located in Brazil.[61] It provides funds for a pilot programme to conserve the Brazilian rainforest. Financial resources for the

meaning 'any government, agency, ministry or other official entity of a country Party to the UNFCCC and whose participation in the Fund has been approved by the Trustee.' IBRD Instrument Establishing the Prototype Carbon Fund, see note 54 above, Article I, paras. 16 and 17.

[56] *Ibid.*, Article IV.

[57] Six governments and 17 companies have contributed US $180 million to the Prototype Carbon Fund (PCF), which currently has 28 projects under preparation. See *Carbon Finance Annual Report* (2005) at 4.   [58] *Ibid.*

[59] Since the establishment of the PCF, the World Bank has agreed to administer other carbon funds. They include the Netherlands Clean Development Mechanism (CDM) Facility (established in 2002), the Community Development Carbon Fund (established in 2003), the Italian Carbon Fund (established in 2004), and the BioCarbon Fund (established in 2004). In addition, in 2002 and 2003, carbon funds have been established within a number of other institutions, including the IFC and the European Bank for Reconstruction and Development.

[60] *Project Selection Criteria and Project Portfolio Criteria*, Schedule I to the Instrument Establishing the Prototype Carbon Fund, see note 54 above.

[61] Resolution no. 92-45 of the Board of Executive Directors of the World Bank, *Establishment of the Rain Forest Trust Fund*, (24 March 1992) (including its background note).

fund are provided by the G-7 group of countries (Canada, France, Germany, Italy, Japan, the United Kingdom, and the United States), the Netherlands, the EU, and Brazil and total about US $345 million.

From its inception in 1992, the pilot programme has sought to involve a wide range of stakeholders at different levels of decision-making. Projects are identified and prepared by the Brazilian government and its national agencies in consultation with other stakeholders such as the World Bank and the donor countries. The World Bank coordinates the preparation of projects between the government of Brazil and the donors. It also administers the Rain Forest Trust Fund and oversees ongoing projects, using the same standards, rules, and procedures that apply to projects financed by World Bank loans.[62] The pilot programme also emphasizes the participation of civil society organizations, from project preparation and monitoring to the evaluation of the impact of the pilot program as a whole.[63] NGOs also have access to small grants administered by the UNDP for activities consistent with the objectives of the program.[64] The programme therefore has begun to create a singular model of international and national cooperation, showing that global and local needs related to tropical rainforests can gradually be integrated.

The involvement of the private sector, both in Brazil and abroad, should also be strengthened. In particular, the role of the private sector as a partner for the programme could be much larger than at present, stimulating investments in projects that will lead to the sustainable use of forest resources. Private business involvement is important for promoting the implementation of sustainable forest management practices, the production of certified timber, the provision of fund research, and the financing of investments. Since its 2000 institutional review, the pilot programme has been trying to identify and address the means to open the way to greater private sector involvement.[65]

Finally, some remarks should be made about the CDM. Although not a funding mechanism as such, the CDM illustrates the increased role of market mechanisms and the private sector in channelling funds to climate-friendly projects. Moreover, it provides a means of joint implementation of the Kyoto Protocol between developed and developing countries. The CDM is designed to allow countries with emission reduction obligations under the Kyoto Protocol to achieve emission reductions credits from projects in developing countries. Like the PCF, the CDM aims to reduce

[62] See the background note, *ibid.* at paras. 37 and 38.   [63] *Ibid.* at para. 39.

[64] *Ibid.* at para. 12. For instance, the Amazon Working Group, which is a coalition of more than 320 non-governmental organizations (NGOs) in the Amazon, and the Atlantic Forest Network, linking NGOs in the Atlantic rainforest to the pilot program, are receiving financial support to strengthen their capacities in the context of the pilot program. See R. Abers, *Civil Society Participation in the Pilot Program to Conserve the Brazilian Rain Forest*, Rain Forest Trust Fund Study, working paper (Brasilia: Pilot Program to Conserve the Brazilian Rain Forest and Department of Environmentally and Socially Sustainable Development, Latin American and Caribbean Region Strategic Compact, 2001).

[65] See Indufor Oy and STCP Engenharia de Projetos Ltda, *Mid-Term Review of the Pilot Program to Conserve the Brazilian Rain Forest, Final Report of the Evaluatory Phase*, 31 October 2000.

the cost of compliance of developed countries with the Kyoto Protocol commitments, while providing developing countries with additional funds and advanced technologies. The CDM thus captures some innovative aspects of the emerging climate change regime, by creating a platform for a coordinated approach between developed and developing countries as well as between public and private entities to implement the Kyoto Protocol.

Under the CDM, a project participant is either an Annex I state party to the Kyoto Protocol or a private and/or public entity authorized by such a party to participate in CDM project activities.[66] The Meeting of the Parties of the Kyoto Protocol exercises the main authority over the mechanism. An 'executive body' supervises the works of the CDM as carried out by the designated operational entities (DOEs), which are charged with the task of validating proposed CDM project activities, and of verifying and certifying reductions in the emissions of greenhouse gases of CDM projects.[67] Private actors are integrated in the institutional framework of the CDM, and they play an active role in developing, executing, financing, and supervising CDM project activities.

The success of the CDM will depend, on the one hand, on the amount of investment it is able to stimulate in greenhouse gas mitigation activities and, on the other hand, on the long-term benefits of such activities. Although, the spread of project activities and host countries is relatively wide, proposed CDM project activities are concentrated in a few countries such as India, Brazil, China, and Indonesia. These countries are recipients of a significant proportion of the flow of direct investments, and many of the poorest nations do not appear to be attracting significant interest in investment in CDM projects. Such outcomes can undermine the rationale of the CDM and weaken support for the Kyoto Protocol commitments.

4.4 Financial Mechanisms as Part of the Legal Structure of Financial and Technical Assistance

In general, states may be reticent to consider their commitments to financial mechanisms as being mandatory. It has been noted that non-binding commitments, especially within a treaty framework, may create shared expectations among stakeholders and, thus, may have the same *de facto* weight as legal obligations.[68] Under the MEAs

---

[66] See Decision 3/CMP.1, *Modalities and Procedures for a Clean Development Mechanism as Defined in Article 12 of the Kyoto Protocol*, Doc. FCCC/KP/CMP/2005/8/Add.1 (December 2005) at 6–29, paras. 28–34.

[67] In accordance with the modalities and procedures of the CDM, the Executive Board accredits operational entities that meet the CDM accreditation requirements and recommends the designation of such entities to the COP. See Decision 3/CMP.1, *ibid*. at 11, paras. 20(a) and (b).

[68] See M. Bothe, 'Legal and Non-Legal Norms: A Meaningful Distinction in International Relations?' (1980) 11 Netherlands Y.B. Int'l L. 65 at 85.

adopted in the wake of the 1992 UNCED, the whole legal regime is in fact built on shared responsibilities between groups of countries. The overall objectives of MEAs cannot be achieved without state parties acting collectively and in the common interest. The establishment of financial mechanisms and the way in which they operate are part of this collective endeavour. These financial mechanisms, whether within or outside the MEAs in question, constitute a powerful incentive to carry out all elements of these MEAs, whether fully binding or not.

The evolution in the nature and aim of technical and financial assistance as one means of protecting global public goods has given rise to new features in the legal structure for the provision of technical and financial assistance. This legal structure relies on the principle of common but differentiated responsibilities, which, in turn, relies on technical and financial assistance as an implementing tool[69] in order to achieve global benefits and protect global public goods. The effectiveness of agreements such as the Montreal Protocol, the UNFCCC, and the CBD is dependent upon both developed and developing countries implementing their differentiated substantive commitments undertaken on the basis of these conventions.

Both developed and developing countries need to take steps to protect global public goods. Developing states, however, in many cases lack both the financial and technical resources to effectively implement these agreements. Moreover, they may also have good reason, given the historical contribution of developed states to environmental degradation and the greater capacity of developed states, not to make the protection of global public goods their first policy priority. As a result of these considerations, developing states' implementation of MEAs is to a large extent dependent on the transfer of funds and technology from developed states. This is no longer only a question of fact, but also of law by virtue of the provisions in MEAs that explicitly make implementation by developing states dependent on developed states providing financial and technical assistance. Developed states thus are to provide assistance to developing states in order for the latter to be able to meet the incremental costs of environmental projects, which produce global public goods.

The Montreal Protocol, for example, provides that the capacity of developing countries to fulfil the obligations set out in the protocol 'will depend upon the effective implementation of the financial co-operation as provided by Article 10 and the transfer of technology as provided by Article 10A.' Such an explicit provision, adopted on the basis of the principle of common but differentiated responsibilities, set a legal precedent that has been incorporated in MEAs such as the CBD, the UNFCCC, and the Stockholm Convention on Persistent Organic Pollutants.[70]

---

[69] See UNFCCC, Article 3.1; CBD, Article 18.2 and 19.2; Desertification Convention, Article 5.a and 6.b; Kyoto Protocol, Article 10; and 2001 Stockholm Convention on Persistent Organic Pollutants (Stockholm Convention), Article 12.

[70] See Montreal Protocol, Article 5.7, CBD, Article 20.4; UNFCCC, Article 4.7; and Stockholm Convention, Article 13.4.

Linking developing states' compliance with MEAs to the provision of financial and technical assistance by developed countries is a clear manifestation of the principle of common but differentiated responsibilities. This principle thus not only provides the basis for sharing common responsibilities and acknowledging differentiated responsibilities with respect to the protection of the global environment, but it also functions as a defence in case developing countries are unable to comply with the treaty in question. In the event that developed countries do not provide technical and financial assistance through the agreed channels, developing countries may invoke this situation in defence of their non-compliance with the commitments under the relevant agreements. By implication, action will not be taken against developing states until they have been provided with financial or technical assistance. Compliance by developing states in this context, thus, is assessed from the angle of developed countries' behaviour—developing states having been given the power to pressure developed states to ensure that they have the necessary means to meet their commitments.[71]

In contrast to other MEAs, the Convention to Combat Desertification in Those Countries Experiencing Serious Drought and/or Desertification, Particularly in Africa contains provisions that weaken the concept of shared responsibilities between developed and developing countries in the implementation of the convention. In particular, the convention, in Article 20(7), states that implementation by developing countries 'will be greatly assisted by the fulfilment of . . . obligations . . . in particular those regarding financial resources and transfer of technologies.' This approach probably is due to the fact that combating desertification was not regarded as beneficial to the overall international community and thus as not involving a global public good. However, the recent inclusion of land degradation as one of the focal areas of the GEF has changed this perception. Supporting the incremental costs of projects related to the prevention and control of land degradation is now directly linked to the provision of global environmental benefits. It has now been recognized that land degradation, manifested in destroyed forests and degraded water resources, has repercussions on biodiversity and on the hydrological cycle and induces climate change.[72]

---

[71] Under the Montreal Protocol, it is provided that when the provision of technical and financial assistance does not work adequately, developing states may notify the Secretariat. The latter will transmit a copy of the notification to the Meeting of the Parties, which must decide on appropriate action. During the period between notification and the Meeting of the Parties at which the appropriate action is to be decided, the non-compliance procedures cannot be invoked against the notifying party. Montreal Protocol, Articles 5(5)-(7). Although the Montreal Protocol in its Article 5 confers this power to developing and economy-in-transition states, these countries have not yet invoked this defence. See G.M. Bankobeza, *Ozone Protection. The International Legal Regime* (Utrecht: Elven International Publishing, 2005) at 118 and 270.

[72] Between 2002 and 2004, the GEF has funded more than US $72 million worth of projects focused primarily on combating deforestation and desertification having global benefits.

5 CONCLUSIONS

Since the early development of international environmental law in the 1970s, financial and technical assistance has been conceived as an important instrument in enhancing the protection of the environment. However, over time, the contours, functions, and legal structure of financial and technical assistance have changed, making it a complex institution. The sources and channels though which it may be provided are many, and the aim of financial and technical assistance has gradually evolved to include the promotion of global benefits.

Assistance aimed at compensating developing countries for the extra costs incurred in the implementation of MEAs, based on the notion of global benefits and global public goods, in fact, has been a crucial development. Financial and technical assistance has also become a tool for promoting environmental governance through the adoption by states of policies and actions aiming at participation, impact assessment, and accountability mechanisms. Another important development is the establishment of new types of legal and institutional mechanisms through which financial and technical assistance is provided. The principles of sustainable development and common but differentiated responsibilities confer new legal meaning on these mechanisms and procedures. The establishment of financial mechanisms, moreover, has encouraged new ways of cooperation among a wide array of actors.

Through the financing of environmental projects, the private sector increasingly plays a role in the furtherance of common interest issues. Yet, this trend towards the 'privatization' of assistance requires that the lines of allocation of responsibilities be clearly set so as to avoid bias and conflicts of interests. In this context, financial mechanisms such as the GEF or other trusted-based institutions are a particularly appropriate means of avoiding both bias and indeed, allegations of bias. The recently established financial mechanisms reveal the new legal features of financial and technical assistance. These mechanisms can be powerful incentives in promoting compliance with treaty commitments. Their establishment is part of the collective endeavour pursued by states in order to address issues of common interest.

RECOMMENDED READING

M.A. Bekhechi, 'Some Observations Regarding Environmental Covenants and Conditionalities in World Bank Lending Activities' (1999) 1 Max Planck Y.B. UN L. 289.

L. Boisson de Chazournes, 'The Global Environment Facility Galaxy: On Linkages among Institutions' (1999) 3 Max Planck Y.B. UN L. 243.

——, *The Global Environment Facility as a Pioneering Institution: Lessons Learned and Looking Ahead*, GEF Working Paper 19 (Washington, DC: GEF, November 2003).

E. Hey, 'Exercising Delegated Public Powers. Multilateral Environmental Agreements and Multilateral Funds,' in R. Wolfrum and V. Röben, eds., *Developments of International Law in Treaty Making* (Heidelberg: Springer, 2005) 437.

N. Matz, 'Environmental Financing: Function and Coherence of Financial Mechanisms in International Environmental Agreements' (2003) 6 Max Planck Y.B. UN L. 473.

——, 'Financial Institutions between Effectiveness and Legitimacy—A Legal Analysis of the World Bank, Global Environment Facility and Prototype Carbon Fund' (2005) 5 Int'l Envt'l Agreements 265.

M. Netto and K.U. Barani Schmidt, 'CDM Project Cycle and the Role of the UNFCCC Secretariat,' in D. Freestone and C. Streck, eds., *Legal Aspects of Implementing the Kyoto Protocol Mehcnaisms* (Oxford: Oxford University Press, 2005) 180.

P.H. Sand, 'Institution-Building to Assist Compliance with International Environmental Law: Perspectives' (1996) 56 Zeitschrift für ausländisches öffentliches Recht und Völkerrecht 780.

C. Toulmin and T. Bigg, *Financing for Environment and Development* (Paris: Institut du développement durable et des relations internationales, 2004).

R. Wolfrum, 'Means of Ensuring Compliance with and Enforcement of International Environmental Law' (1998) 272 Recueil des cours 9.

CHAPTER 42

MONITORING AND VERIFICATION

JØRGEN WETTESTAD

1 INTRODUCTION

GOOD monitoring and verification of practices in international institutions are important in building trust between and among cooperating parties, and in strengthening wider societal confidence. In the international context, monitoring has to do with the ascertainment and reporting of states' behaviour. Verification refers to procedures and systems for quality and reliability checks of the reported data. Finally, compliance has to do with the relationship between state actions and international commitments—and responses to possible mismatches.[1] Within the field of environment, monitoring and verification systems have been developed since the mid-1970s, mainly to underpin and facilitate assessments of the follow-up of not very sophisticated or finely tuned international commitments. A classic example is the 1985 Helsinki Protocol within the Convention on Long-Range Transboundary Air Pollution (LRTAP Convention), which calls for a flat-rate 30 per cent cut in sulphur dioxide emissions. Monitoring of such agreements was mainly based on national reports with little or no verification of the data. International commitments have differentiated and grown in sophistication since this time. For instance, the 1994 Oslo Protocol (which succeeded the 1985 Helsinki Protocol) to the LRTAP Convention established moderately differentiated emission ceilings among the parties. Monitoring and verification systems have also developed but not dramatically.

Recent years have witnessed an increasing interest in flexible international policy instruments, chief among them being emissions trading. A well-respected research institute has characterized this development as representing a 'fundamental systems change in environmental governance.'[2] This observation refers to the complex multi-level character of international emissions trading, involving actors at the sub-national, national, and international levels in an unprecedented way in international environmental politics. What does this complex 'systems change' mean with regard to monitoring and verification? As far back as 1995, Abram Chayes and Antonia Handler Chayes believed that the adoption of tradable emission permits as a regulatory instrument would probably require closer performance monitoring.[3] Are flexibility mechanisms a new challenge, and do they require new procedures and solutions with regard to monitoring and verification? This is a significant question and one that is addressed in this chapter.

The chapter first reviews in section 2 the development of monitoring and verification procedures and practice in international environmental institutions over time.

---

[1] E.g., O.S. Stokke, J. Hovi, and G. Ulfstein, eds., *Implementing the Climate Regime: International Compliance* (London: Earthscan, 2005).

[2] Centre for European Policy Studies (CEPS), *Greenhouse Gas Emissions Trading in Europe: Conditions for Environmental Credibility and Economic Efficiency* (Brussels: CEPS, 2002) at 6.

[3] A. Chayes and A. Handler Chayes, *The New Sovereignty: Compliance with International Regulatory Agreements* (Cambridge, MA: Harvard University Press, 1995) at 189.

Main components of such procedures are the character of the reporting systems (that is, who, what, and when?) and the character of verification (for example, independent tracking of emissions and space for environmental non-governmental organizations (NGOs) and other third parties?). Monitoring and verification procedures have developed in three stages. First, there was a relatively lax initial reporting phase with little independent input or access for third parties. Second, the picture changed in the 1990s, with better reporting and increased independent input and access. And, finally, new or adjusted monitoring and verification mechanisms emerged in response to the growing sophistication and flexibility of policy instruments.

The bulk of the empirical material in this chapter will be drawn from 'atmospheric' regimes (see Chapter 14 'Atmosphere and Outer Space') such as the LRTAP Convention, the ozone layer regime (comprising the Vienna Convention for the Protection of the Ozone Layer (Vienna Convention) and the Montreal Protocol on Substances That Deplete the Ozone Layer (Montreal Protocol)), and the climate change regime (including the United Nations Framework Convention on Climate Change (UNFCCC) and the Kyoto Protocol). Examples from other regimes such as the Convention on International Trade in Endangered Species of Wild Fauna and Flora (CITES) (see Chapter 16 'Biological Resources'), and the North Sea cooperation will also be utilized. In the field of international environmental politics, there are good reasons to look closely at the European Union (EU) (see Chapter 37 'Regional Economic Integration Organizations'). First, it is an important region in the global economy and what the EU does with environmental policies and procedures matters. Second, compared to the international environment and resource regimes mentioned earlier, the EU is a complex and, in many ways, advanced institution in terms of verification and compliance procedures. The chapter, therefore, examines global and regional regimes and institutions as well as pollution and resource management regimes. Although this should go some way towards establishing some of the trends in international environmental politics, the empirical coverage is clearly limited.

Section 3 investigates more fully the increasing use of flexibility mechanisms and related challenges to monitoring and verification. There is a clear movement towards the use of flexible mechanisms, particularly emissions trading, as central environmental policy instruments, both at the domestic and international levels. Indeed, as a central element of the 1997 Kyoto Protocol, emissions trading will start in 2008. However, inadequate monitoring can undermine the efficiency of trading programs.[4] To what extent and how does this development create changing needs and challenges for the international community with regard to monitoring and verification? What are the main lessons of previous trading systems with regard to effective design? Since there is almost no international track record to learn from in the field of the environment, we look first at to two interesting domestic systems: the US

---

[4] See, e.g., J. Kruger and W.A. Pizer, *The EU Emissions Trading Directive: Opportunities and Potential Pitfalls* (Washington, DC: Resources for the Future, 2004) at 24.

sulphur dioxide and nitrogen oxides trading system and the UK carbon dioxide trading system. At the international level, the EU has adopted an important forerunner emissions trading programme, so we shall take a detour there before addressing global challenges to emissions trading and flexibility mechanisms. Section 4 winds up the chapter with a summary and some concluding reflections.

2 Overview of the Development of Monitoring and Verification Approaches and Central Drivers for Change

2.1 Introduction

As indicated, this section will review and seek to explain changes in monitoring and verification approaches over time in successive stages. This review will include a discussion of questions such as:

- What are the main features and functions of reporting requirements? How far are reporting requirements complied with? Are reports used for the assessment of national compliance? Are they used for the assessment of changes in national behaviour/policy reform and/or the assessment of overall progress of the regime/institution?
- How reliable are national reports? For instance, within the whaling regime, Chayes and Handler Chayes have pointed out the occurrence of wilful Russian misreporting.[5]
- What other sources of information are there? And do interested third parties (environmental NGOs for instance) have access to them?
- What are the main existing verification mechanisms? Here, one can distinguish between discussions at conferences of the parties and international inspections.

In order to shed some explanatory light on the evolution in monitoring and verification mechanisms, we then follow other studies of international environmental politics[6] by comparing fundamental problem characteristics with problem-solving capacity (with institutional characteristics as a central element).[7]

---

[5] Chayes and Handler Chayes, see note 3 above at 155.

[6] E.g., E.L. Miles et al., *Environmental Regime Effectiveness: Confronting Theory with Evidence* (Cambridge, MA: MIT Press, 2002).

[7] In practice and over time, these factors often interact. Hence, institutional progress may lead to reduced scientific uncertainty and controversy and an overall more benign collaborative problem.

Factors influencing monitoring and verification include:

- problem characteristics (for example, high uncertainty as well as many and diverse emission sources complicate good reporting);
- trust (the general atmosphere and level of trust between the regime parties will probably matter). A relaxed atmosphere and high levels of trust would doubtless foster an open and critical discussion of national reports and, hence, make verification easier;
- design of commitments (for example, precise and quantified commitments probably lead to better national reports than diffuse and qualitative commitments);
- administrative capacity (as the administrative capacity to deal with reporting has been weaker in developing countries than in developed countries, the establishment of specific funds or other arrangements to assist developing countries in enhancing their administrative capacity could help improve reporting); and
- general institutional 'maturity,' which has to do with the fine-tuning and improvement of national and international reporting and monitoring arrangements.

2.2 Baseline: Lax National Reporting and Limited Independent Input and Access for Third Parties

In the formative years of international environmental cooperation, the primary, and, in most cases, only, basis for assessing parties' compliance with international policies was national reports. The ozone regime, for instance, which is the international regime set up to protect the ozone layer, was primarily based on the 1985 Vienna Convention and the 1987 Montreal Protocol. The Vienna Convention contained only a generally worded paragraph on the transmission of information: '[I]n such form and at such intervals as the meetings of the parties to the relevant instruments may determine' (Article 6). In conjunction with much more detailed and precise obligations in the 1987 Montreal Protocol, a more elaborate monitoring, verification, and compliance regime began to take form. This monitoring and verification system has two main pillars.[8] First, pursuant to Article 7, the parties are required to provide annual data on the production, imports, and exports of all controlled substances, both with regard to 1986 baseline data and annual data thereafter. Second, the Secretariat receives these reports, processes and analyses them, and produces summary compliance reports (which are made public) for the Implementation Committee (see discussion later in this chapter) as well as for the Meetings of the Parties.

---

[8] S. Oberthür, *Production and Consumption of Ozone Depleting Substances 1986–1999: The Data Reporting System under the Montreal Protocol* (Berlin: Deutsche Gesellschaft für Technische Zusammenarbeit, 2001).

The importance of industrial and technological substance substitution as well as the trade component raised concerns about industrial secrecy and competitiveness. Hence, there was a confidentiality dimension surrounding the national reports, adding to the national-based, de-centralized character of the system. Nearly all data involved were confidential, and only the total national production and consumption of regulated substances were reported publicly. Due to commercial considerations, only broad groups of chemicals were reported, and exports and imports were not reported as separate categories. An additional issue in this context was the refusal of the member states of the EU to provide national consumption data, which made it impossible to assess the compliance of individual European states. Member states of the EU reported only to the EU Commission, and these reports were confidential (see Chapter 37 'Regional Economic Integration Organizations').

Although the specific data requirements differed slightly in other comparable international regimes, the basic picture was similar. Take, for instance, the 1979 LRTAP Convention. The convention text called for nothing more elaborate than a general form of information exchange, expressed in Article 4 of the convention. It was followed, however, by increasingly specific commitments on emissions reporting in subsequent protocols. For instance, the 1985 Sulphur Dioxide Protocol stated that 'each Party shall provide annually to the Executive Body its level of national annual sulphur emissions, and the basis upon which they have been calculated' (Article 4). Article 6 called for information on national programmes, policies, and strategies. So the principal initial element in the monitoring of state performance was the parties' annual reports to the Secretariat on emissions, and on procedures and measures adopted for the abatement of emissions and the measurement of acid precipitation.

An additional source of data *potentially* relevant for verification purposes was provided by the European Cooperative Monitoring and Evaluation Programme (EMEP), which itself was based on a protocol to the LRTAP Convention, adopted in 1984. The EMEP has three main elements: emissions data, measurements of air and precipitation quality, and atmospheric dispersion models.[9] Under the LRTAP Convention, periodic public reviews of national reports and data collected through the EMEP were conducted. However, this information source was not actively utilized for verifying compliance within the regime, probably due in part to the initial East-West confidence-building and non-intrusive character of the regime.

In order to find an independent verification mechanism with some bite, we have to go to the CITES. On the one hand, CITES's monitoring relied (and relies) on conventional national reporting, including annual reports on all trade in species of

[9] The European Cooperative Monitoring and Evaluation Programme (EMEP) sampling network consists of some 100 stations in 33 countries, and the work has been coordinated by three international centres: two in Oslo and one in Moscow. A specific EMEP financing protocol was established in 1984. For more discussion about EMEP and the role of EMEP within the LRTAP Covention, see J. Di Primio, *Monitoring and Verification in the European Air Pollution Regime* (Laxenburg, Austria: IIASA, 1996) at WP-96-47.

relevant flora and fauna and biennial reports on legislative, regulatory, and administrative measures taken. On the other hand, by providing for independent verification, CITES represents something of a departure from other early international regimes. Starting in the mid-1970s, a practice was developed under CITES of independent reviews of national reports about trading. This independent system was started by the World Conservation Union (IUCN) and the World Wildlife Fund and developed into the Trade Records Analysis of Flora and Fauna in Commerce (TRAFFIC) monitoring network. This network now spans 22 offices in eight regional programmes around the world. TRAFFIC informs the Secretariat directly of non-compliance but also works through its regional offices with national CITES authorities. Some argue that cooperation with the TRAFFIC network has given CITES one of the best operational information sources of any international environmental regime.[10]

With regard to general compliance with reporting requirements in the regimes discussed earlier, one must conclude that compliance was initially relatively lax, although it was better in developed states than in the economy-in-transition states and developing states. This result is not surprising, as administrative capacity in environmental matters was better developed in developed states. Looking again at the ozone regime as an example, only 57 (42 per cent), of the 136 parties due to report for 1994, had reported by October 1995.[11] Moreover, many reports were 'consistently incomplete'—of the 126 parties due to report for 1993, only 69 (54 per cent) had reported complete data by October 1995.[12] In addition, baseline data were missing for a number of countries.

NGOs and other civil society representatives enjoyed some measure of access to relevant reports about international processes at the domestic level, although access varied and, in some cases, was clearly very restricted (for example, in the then Communist countries). Despite these limitations, it was possible to gain some understanding of national processes related to international regimes, including implementation efforts. When it came to international bodies and related overviews of reporting practices, practice was generally even more restrictive. Take the North Sea cooperation as an example, which was initially based on the 1972 Convention for the Prevention of Marine Pollution by Dumping from Ships and Aircraft (Oslo Convention) and the 1974 Convention for the Prevention of Marine Pollution from Land-based Sources (Paris Convention). The initial Oslo and Paris Convention texts referred only to 'Contracting Parties' as relevant actors, and, throughout the 1980s, NGO participation was limited to occasional brief presentations to Commission delegates before the annual meetings.

---

[10] R. Reeve, *Policing International Trade in Endangered Species—The CITES Treaty and Compliance* (London: Royal Institute of International Affairs/Earthscan, 2002) at 68.

[11] H.O. Bergesen and G. Parmann, eds., *Green Globe Yearbook* (Oxford: Oxford University Press, 1996) at 107.   [12] *Ibid.*

How did things shape up in the EU? The EU uses directives as the main instrument in its environmental policy-making. As with the international regimes mentioned earlier, oversight was facilitated mainly through national reporting. Here too, reporting practice was initially lax and uneven.[13] It should be noted that the EU institutionalized access to information by the public. For instance, the 1990 directive on freedom of information on the environment made most of the government-held data on environmental issues available to the public and included information on emissions, policies, and legislation.[14]

What explains this initial monitoring and verification picture? With regard to fundamental problem characteristics, most transboundary monitoring and verification processes suffered from considerable scientific uncertainty on issues such as national emission levels and effects. This uncertainty complicated the process of putting together comprehensive and detailed national reports. The Cold War and East-West confrontation also influenced reporting within some environmental regimes. In the case of the LRTAP Convention, Eastern European country reports with exactly the same emission figures year after year did little to enhance confidence and trust.

In terms of institutional capacity growth, the 1970s and 1980s represented an institutional warm-up period, nationally and internationally. Many countries struggled to build the necessary domestic institutional emissions reporting capacity consistent with international reporting and verification requirements. International policies were either not very sophisticated or very ambitious. Take, for instance, the aforementioned 1985 Helsinki Protocol, which was agreed to under the LRTAP Convention. This protocol required a flat-rate 30 per cent reduction of sulphur dioxide emissions by 1993 (with a 1980 baseline). Many countries knew already at the signing of the protocol that they had achieved, or were close to achieving, this target.[15] Within the issue area of international marine pollution control and the North Sea cooperation, the regulations and recommendations contained vague and imprecise formulations, with very few verifiable targets and timetables.[16] Few and vague targets meant a lack of points to focus on in national reporting and substantial discretion in the design and content of such reports.

---

[13] According to K. Collins and D. Earnshaw, 'The Implementation and Enforcement of European Community Environment Legislation,' in D. Judge, ed., *A Green Dimension for the European Community: Political Issues and Processes* (London: Frank Cass, 1993) 219, 'non-notification' and, hence, inadequate reporting of measures put into place domestically to implement EU directives was a considerable problem.

[14] EC Directive 90/313 ([1990] O.J. L 41/56), which was further strengthened in 2003 by the adoption of EC Directive 2003/4 on Public Access to Environmental Information ([2003] O.J. L 41/26). This directive establishes the 'right' to access rather than the 'freedom' of access.

[15] T. Laugen, *Compliance with International Environmental Agreements: Norway and the Acid Rain Convention*, Report 3 (Lysaker, Norway: Fridtjof Nansen Institute, 1995).

[16] J.B. Skjærseth, *North Sea Cooperation: Linking International and Domestic Pollution Control* (Manchester: Manchester University Press, 2000).

2.3 A Changing Picture in the 1990s: Better Reporting and Maturing Institutions

In the early 1990s, things started to change both in terms of reporting practices and procedures. With respect to reporting practices, the ozone regime is again an interesting example. On the one hand, there were clear improvements in reporting, mostly with regard to the major ozone-depleting substances (ODS)—that is, chlorofluorocarbons and halons. On the other hand, significant problems still remained. According to Sebastian Oberthür, data quality was 'moderate at best'. Discrepancies between global production and consumption data and between production data available from industry and production reported to the ozone regime Secretariat showed serious and continuing problems.[17] Reporting also improved within the LRTAP Convention. However, according to experienced participants in the regime, by the late 1990s, the weakest point in the scientific political complex was still the emission data.[18] As pointed out by Juan di Primio,[19] 'some data can be questioned because time-series are overtly incomplete, and/or show constant rounded figures for long periods, and/or consider as provisory emissions for previous emissions for previous years.' The CITES case is more ambiguous. Although the quality of reporting improved, non-reporting and late reports were being increasingly noted towards the end of the 1990s.[20]

Moving on to procedural changes, the 1992 UNFCCC was a forerunner in terms of designing a verification process with a significant independent review element. At the first Conference of the Parties, states decided that national reports should be subject to in-depth reviews carried out by expert review teams. These teams are staffed by experts nominated by the parties and chosen by the UNFCCC Secretariat, ensuring that membership reflects both a balance between Annex I and non-Annex I parties and a diversity in expertise.

Implementation committees were established within several regimes. The ozone regime's Implementation Committee was the first to be established in 1990. The committee is composed of ten members, two from each of the five main geographical regions of the world, elected for a two-year period.[21] The parties to the LRTAP Convention decided as part of the 1994 second Sulphur Protocol to establish an Implementation Committee comprising eight legal experts. It came into being in

---

[17] Oberthür, see note 8 above.

[18] Interview with Lars Lindau, Swedish Environmental Protection Agency, 21 October 1999. Lindau has been chairman of LRTAP Convention's Working Group on Abatement Techniques.

[19] Di Primio, see note 9 above at WP-96-47, p. 43.   [20] Reeve, see note 10 above at 62–8.

[21] The committee's main formal functions are to consider and report on any complaint from, or reference by, a party; to consider and report on the annual report of the Secretariat; to request, where necessary, further information on cases before it; to undertake, 'upon the invitation of the Party concerned,' data compilation inside the territory of that party; and to exchange information with the financial mechanism of the Montreal Protocol.

1997, at which point the mandate was broadened to cover the review of compliance with all of the LRTAP protocols. Most recently, within the framework of the 1997 Kyoto Protocol, the parties established a Compliance Committee composed of a Facilitative Branch and an Enforcement Branch, each with ten members (see Chapter 38 'Treaty Bodies' and Chapter 43 'Compliance Procedures').

Do these committees perform a verification function? With the exception of the Enforcement Branch of the Kyoto Protocol's Compliance Committee, this function is performed only to a limited extent, it seems. The LRTAP Implementation Committee, for example, initially concentrated efforts on reviewing reporting procedures and practices, including the publishing of overview tables of reporting 'scores'. However, investigations seem to have been geared more towards procedural matters than data-related matters. Nevertheless, in the case of the LRTAP Convention, some claim that this work has had positive effects on reporting. According to the convention's twenty-fifth anniversary book,[22] 'the completeness of emission data reporting has improved significantly since the Implementation Committee began to review it as a matter of course each year. For example, the level of emission data reported for the 1985 Sulphur Protocol was 99 per cent in 2003, while it had been 86 per cent in 1998'.

In addition to the establishment of implementation and compliance committees, regime bodies—such as the secretariats and the conferences of the parties—became more active in the field of reporting, verification, and compliance. As indicated earlier in this chapter, this was certainly the case in the ozone regime, but a similar development also took place within the LRTAP Convention.[23] The case of CITES is particularly interesting in this regard, as the role of the secretariat as a data verifier has been very prominent all along. As noted by Rosalind Reeve: 'The [Secretariat] wields considerable power, since not only does it review and verify information, but it also makes recommendations to the COP and the standing Committee, which on occasion are far reaching and often acted upon.'[24] In several regimes, COP meetings, during the 1990s, started tentatively to utilize other evidence than national reports. In the ozone regime, for example, evidence produced by the Global Ozone Observing System was used to verify reports of emission cuts by a group of parties.

With regard to the possibilities for wider societal insight and independent verification by NGOs, certain changes in access procedures and practices can be noted. For instance, within the North Sea regime, the 1992 OSPAR Convention increased NGO access to information and meetings within the regime, inspired by the more inclusive

[22] *Clearing the Air—Twenty-Five Years of the Convention on Long-Range Transboundary Air Pollution* (Geneva: UN LRTAP Convention, 2004) at 120.

[23] J. Wettestad, 'Enhancing Climate Compliance: What Are the Lessons to Learn from Environmental Regimes and the EU?' in Stokke, Hovi, and Ulfstein, see note 1 above at 209.

[24] R. Reeve, 'Verification Mechanisms in CITES,' in T. Findlaw and O. Meier, eds., *Verification Yearbook 2001* (London: Vertic, 2001) 137 at 151.

approach adopted by the North Sea conferences.[25] Within the climate change regime, the 1992 UNFCCC adopted a fairly inclusive approach in terms of access for NGOs, providing them with observer status.[26] On verification and compliance, in particular, access was offered with some success in the negotiations on the Kyoto Protocol's compliance regime, which was finalized in the 2001 Marrakesh Accords. Again, however, CITES seems to be the exception. In this case, a somewhat different dynamic may have taken place. Considered to be one of the most liberal regimes in terms of NGO inclusion, in the late 1980s, as government participation expanded and a related formalization of the general mode of operation of the regime took place, NGO involvement grew increasingly difficult.

Shedding some light on the overall dominant trend of sharpened procedures and practices, improvements can be explained by an interplay of changing problem characteristics and institutional maturation. With regard to changing problem characteristics, a general and diffuse development was the increasing knowledge of the parties about their emissions and ways to deal with them. This increase in knowledge facilitated better reporting. A much more specific and certainly spectacular change happened in the Eastern Europe, with democratization and increased openness developing from the early 1990s. For instance, within the LRTAP Convention, these changes undoubtedly contributed greatly to an increased transparency in Eastern European states, and more reliable reporting of emissions data. This transparency, in turn, increased basic trust among the parties. In addition, one can also note a more general drive towards increased openness in international environmental policy processes throughout the 1990s. This openness was apparent in the 1992 Rio Declaration[27] and was taken a significant step further with the adoption of the 1998 Convention on Access to Information, Public Participation in Decision-Making and Access to Justice in Environmental Matters (see Chapter 29 'Public Participation').

Environmental regimes also matured institutionally, together with the general sense of trust. Within the ozone regime, a significant factor was the fine job done by the Secretariat in elaborating data forms and accompanying instructions for filling them out.[28] As regimes began to review compliance, this put an even greater

---

[25] The 1992 Convention for the Protection of the Marine Environment of the North-East Atlantic replaced the 1972 Oslo and 1974 Paris Conventions, referred to earlier in this chapter and is generally referred to as the OSPAR Convention.

[26] S. Oberthur et al., *Participation of Non-Governmental Organisations in International Environmental Governance: Legal Basis and Practical Experience* (Berlin: Ecologic, 2002); and L.H. Gulbrandsen and S. Andresen, 'NGO Influence in the Implementation of the Kyoto Protocol: Compliance, Flexibility Mechanisms, and Sinks' (2004) 4 Global Envt'l Pol. 4 at 54–76.

[27] Particularly Articles 4, 5, and 6–8. See J. Jendroska, 'Public Participation and Information in the Emissions Trading Directive' (2004) 1 Envt'l L. Network Int'l Rev. 8.

[28] As noted by Reeve, see note 10 above at 278, another important factor was the threat of losing 'Article 5' status and, hence, access to funds in the case of continuing inadequate reporting.

premium on accurate, reliable reporting and verification.[29] As stated in the LRTAP Convention's twenty-fifth anniversary book, '[i]n the Convention's early years there was no call or need for a compliance regime. In time the need for introducing a compliance system grew stronger and in 1997 the Executive Body established the Implementation Committee.'[30]

Institutional maturation also included the establishment of financial mechanisms to provide assistance for, among other things, monitoring and reporting (see Chapter 41 'Technical and Financial Assistance'). The most striking example is probably the establishment in 1990 of the multilateral fund within the ozone regime. As pointed out by Beth DeSombre and Joanne Kauffman, '[t]he process helped Article 5 countries discover the extent of their ODS use and what would need to be done to meet their obligations under the Protocol.'[31] Article 5 countries received funding for the establishment of ozone 'focal points,' and the fund arranged for experts to advise the focal points on data reporting. Finally, growing institutional maturity also meant increased learning and interaction between regimes, also with regard to monitoring and compliance arrangements. Both the LRTAP Convention and the climate change regime were influenced by the ozone regime in this regard.

2.4 Recent Trends: More Advanced and Flexible Policies

In recent years, more weight has been given to differentiated, flexible, and generally more sophisticated policies. A good example is the 1999 Gothenburg Protocol to Abate Acidification, Eutrophication and Ground-Level Ozone (Gothenburg Protocol) within the LRTAP regime. In contrast to earlier LRTAP protocols, which targeted a single pollutant (for example, sulphur dioxide) and one main environmental effect (for example, acidification) at a time, the 1999 Gothenburg Protocol targets the four substances of nitrogen oxides, volatile organic compounds (VOCs), and ammonia and the three effects of acidification, tropospheric ozone formation, and eutrophication.[32]

The Gothenburg Protocol took the differentiation of national emission ceilings that had started in the 1994 Oslo Protocol a significant step further. This myriad of national commitments represents a considerable monitoring and verification oversight challenge, but, according to the LRTAP Convention sources, it also enhances

---

[29] Within the realm of research, this was reflected in increasing attention given to the implementation of international environmental commitments (see Chapter 39 'Compliance Theory' and Chapter 40 'National Implementation').   [30] *Clearing the Air*, see note 22 above at 165.

[31] E. DeSombre and J. Kaufman, 'The Montreal Protocol Multilateral Fund: Partial Success,' in R. Keohane and M. Levy, eds., *Institutions for Environmental Aid: Pitfalls and Promise* (Cambridge, MA: MIT Press, 1996) 89 at 120.

[32] J. Wettestad, *Clearing the Air: European Advances in Tackling Acid Rain and Atmospheric Pollution* (Aldershot, UK: Ashgate, 2002).

the general prospects for ratification and compliance. The general impression from the convention's 25-year anniversary book is one of institutional maturation within the regime in the last decade, including the functioning of the Implementation Committee. However, the book also notes that 'there is still . . . a long way to go before the Convention's implementation and compliance regime is as effective as it could, or should, be.'[33] An option that is mentioned in order to enhance the effectiveness of the implementation and compliance regime is the introduction of a system of performance auditing similar to that of the Kyoto Protocol.

2.5 Winding Up: The Development of Monitoring and Verification Mechanisms

Let us return to the issues mentioned in section 2.1. We note a clear improvement in reporting standards (less clear, perhaps, in the CITES regime, in part because the reporting standards were high to begin with). Understandable differences between North and South remain. Reports are mainly used by treaty bodies such as the conferences of the parties for the assessment of national compliance. These assessments were initially mild in tone and short on criticism but acquired more 'teeth' over time. Assessments of changes in national behaviour and policy reforms are included to some extent, for instance, in the LRTAP Convention's periodic review reports. Standards of national reporting have improved and generally are considered accurate.

With respect to sources that are additional to the national reports, their use continues to vary. Within the LRTAP regime, the EMEP has provided an independent corrective of sorts, but the EMEP data have never been actively used for verification purposes. The same goes for the Global Ozone Observing System within the ozone regime. Information is more easily available for interested third parties, such as environmental NGOs, than it was before. However, the role played by such information in monitoring and verification has been limited. Having said that, the CITES TRAFFIC network has become an important independent source of information. This fact may have something to do with what is being monitored. Transboundary trade, which CITES oversees, may after all be less complex for NGOs to monitor than the complex transboundary movements and atmospheric chemistry addressed by the 'atmospheric' regimes. The same factors may account for the role of organizations such as Greenpeace in providing information on whaling in the context of the International Whaling Commission.

Existing verification mechanisms figure mainly as discussions at conferences of the parties. As noted earlier, these discussions have generally had a mild and not very

---

[33] *Clearing the Air*, see note 22 above at 165.

critical character, but they have developed into more critical exercises over time. Although international inspections are rare, they are envisaged in the complex and important climate change regime (that is, the expert review teams) and are being considered within the LRTAP regime.

3 Zooming in: The Increasing Use of Flexibility Mechanisms and the Related Challenges of Monitoring and Verification

3.1 Introduction

As noted, there is a clear trend towards an increasing use of various flexible mechanisms, and particularly emission trading, as central environmental policy instruments, both at the domestic and international levels (see Chapter 8 'Instrument Choice'). The inclusion of such instruments was no doubt integral to getting the Kyoto Protocol on climate change adopted in 1997. In Europe, domestic greenhouse gas emissions trading systems (ETS) in Denmark and the United Kingdom have been followed by the development of an ETS at the EU level. As indicated, this development has been characterized as a systemic change in environmental governance.

However, without good monitoring and effective verification, instruments such as emissions trading can easily become 'book keeping device(s) which substitute paper transactions for real world reductions.'[34] Moreover, as emphasized by economists, in order to be a cost-effective policy instrument, emissions trading needs to replace other existing environmental policy instruments. Hence, such trading should be just as verifiable as the policy instruments they replace. Important questions include: What are the main lessons regarding monitoring and verification in connection with relevant domestic ETS schemes so far? Has adequate monitoring and verification taken place, including reasonable access for other societal actors? What is the main institutional set-up for handling these matters within the emerging EU ETS; does it point towards a successful monitoring and verification system; and, finally, what are the implications for monitoring and verification of global trading under the Kyoto Protocol?

As there is virtually no international track record to learn from when addressing these questions, it is necessary first to sum up important experiences obtained at the

---

[34] International Energy Agency (IEA), *International Emission Trading—From Concept to Reality* (Paris: IEA, 2001) at 13.

national level in recent years. Within the field of air pollution and climate change, there are several domestic experiences in the United States and United Kingdom from which lessons may be learned.

3.2 Domestic Experiences: Good Transparency, but High Monitoring and Verification Costs?

The United States started a sulphur dioxide trading programme in the mid-1990s and a regional nitrogen oxide trading programme in the late 1990s. As summarized by Joe Kruger and William Pizer,[35] the sulphur dioxide programme started in 1995 and targets emissions from large electric power units (over 20 megawatts per hour) in the continental 48 states. In the second phase, which runs from 2000 on, approximately 3,000 units at more than 700 power plants have been included. The nitrogen oxide trading programme is a multi-jurisdictional partnership between federal and state governments that is probably more analogous to the EU ETS than the sulphur dioxide programme. The nitrogen oxide trading programme has evolved in geographic scope over time—first, encompassing nine north-eastern states in the late 1990s before it was expanded in 2004 to include 19 states and the district of Columbia.[36] With regard to coverage, the programme includes large industrial boilers (such as petroleum refineries, pulp and paper plants, and steel plants) as well as electric generating units.

With regard to monitoring and verification, the sulphur dioxide and nitrogen dioxide programmes are implemented largely at the federal level by the US Environmental Protection Agency (EPA), which also runs electronic allowance and emissions registries and is responsible for the verification of emissions data. There are detailed and continuous emissions monitors (CEMS) for both programmes. All power units have had to install CEMS. Emissions are reported electronically to the EPA, there are extensive electronic auditing procedures, and there are even occasional on-site audits of facilities. A facilitating element is that the emissions sources to be monitored do not vary much. The sulphur dioxide programme consists entirely of electric power plants, and, although the nitrogen dioxide programme also includes some other industrial sources, they can be monitored in a manner similar to power plants. Verification is carried out centrally at the EPA. The system relies heavily upon electronic reporting and auditing of data. This has made it possible to process and analyze emissions data and to make data available to the public on the Internet. There are no confidentiality requirements involved. Over time, the registry systems have developed considerably. There is an Emissions and Allowance Tracking System (EATS), which tracks both emissions and allowances, and includes the ability of

[35] Kruger and Pizer, see note 4 above.
[36] Two additional states will be added in 2007. See *ibid.* at 9.

using the system for multiple pollutants, of communicating with other registry systems, and of providing electronic reports on data to the government or the public. Overall, the US sulphur dioxide case has been characterized as a success, not least in terms of cost-effectiveness.[37] However, what about monitoring and verification? The impression is rather positive. An 'unprecedented level' of transparency has been noted, primarily due to the EATS.[38] Yet authors have also pointed out considerable monitoring and reporting costs.[39]

Turning to the UK greenhouse gas ETS, this system was initiated in 2000 but did not actually start operating until March 2002. The system covers all six main greenhouses gases and a range of industries. The initial scheme was voluntary, and the government provided £215 million of funding to support it over a five-year period in order to encourage participation. Thirty-one organizations ('direct participants') took on targets to reduce their emissions compared to 1998–2000 levels, aiming to deliver close to 12 million tonnes of additional carbon dioxide-equivalent emission reductions over the period 2002–6. The scheme is also open to 6,000 companies with climate change agreements (CCA). According to the Department for Food, Environment and Rural Affairs, the direct participants achieved 4.6 million tonnes of carbon dioxide-equivalent emission reductions in the first year of the scheme, and nearly 5.2 million tonnes in the second year. In the first year, 866 of the CCA actors entered into the UK ETS.

Regarding monitoring and verification, a central element is an Internet-based registry that records and tracks the ownership and transfer of emission allowances. All market participants must have an account with the registry. There is also a verification system, with verifiers accredited by the UK Accredation Service. With respect to the verification costs in the UK system, these have ranged from €5,000 to €7,500 for a simple site to €10,000 to €20,000 for more complex sites.[40]

The first major review of the scheme was conducted by the National Audit Office (NAO) in the spring of 2004.[41] The overall assessment was that the scheme was a 'pioneering initiative with significant achievements.'[42] However, the journal *ENDS Report* was critical, pointing out that 'the UK's fledgling carbon market is now awash with allowances, thanks to a combination of "hot air" allocations, weak targets and on-going investment in abatement.'[43] Nevertheless, both the NAO and the *ENDS*

---

[37] See, e.g., IEA, note 34 above at 30–1.

[38] Concerted Action on Tradeable Emissions Permits (CATEP), *Institutional Requirements, Emissions Trading Policy Briefs 4, Concerted Action on Tradeable Emissions Permits* (CATEP, 2003) at 7.

[39] E.g., R.N. Stavins, 'Lessons from the American Experiment with Market-based Environmental Policies,' in J. Donahue and J. Nye, eds., *Harnessing the Hurricane: The Challenge of Market-Based Governance* (Washington, DC: Brookings Institute Press, 2002) 6; and Concerted Action on Tradeable Emissions Permits, see note 38 above at 6.   [40] Kruger and Pizer, see note 4 above at 19.

[41] National Audit Office, *The UK Emissions Trading Scheme—A New Way to Combat Climate Change*, report by the Comptroller and Auditor General, Doc. HC 517, session 2003–4 (21 April 2004); and 'Watchdog Fails to Bite on UK Emissions Trading Scheme' (April 2004) 351 ENDS Report 27 at 27–30.

[42] 'Watchdog Fails to Bite on UK Emissions Trading Scheme,' see note 41 above.   [43] *Ibid.* at 29.

Report agreed that the creation of the allowance registry was an important 'but often over-looked' institutional success.[44] In the NAO review, a clear majority of participants emphasized how their participation in the system had improved their collection of data on energy use and the measurement of emissions.[45] Furthermore, the NAO also 'verified the verification procedure' and expressed general satisfaction with this part of the scheme.[46] However, substantial costs were again pointed out.

3.3 EU System: Much More Complex Challenges than in the Domestic Systems?

There are several institutional differences between the US and UK domestic contexts and the EU multinational context. Compared to the United States, the main difference is, of course, that the EU member states are sovereign states and that the EU is, overall, much more heterogeneous and multi-jurisdictional in character, leading to the fact that competences are shared between the member states and the European Community (see Chapter 37 'Regional Economic Integration Organizations').[47] Moreover, while the US emissions trading system focuses on emissions that are directly measured, the greenhouse gas emissions at the heart of the EU system (and the global climate change regime) will mainly be calculated indirectly on the basis of energy usage. Compared to the UK emissions trading system, the EU system is a much more complex system.[48] In addition, the UK trading system is a financial incentive-based system, which is quite different from that of the EU. These elements imply that caution is required when inferring lessons from the US and UK systems for the EU.

The main elements of the EU system are as follows. From 1 January 2005, companies with activities covered by the EU ETS are to keep track of their emissions and produce a report on annual emissions that must be verified by a third party (similar to the verification of the financial accounts of a company). At the same time, they must make sure that they are in possession of a sufficient number of emission allowances to cover their emissions. Member states decide upon, and issue, allowances by the end of February each year, operate national registries, collect verified emissions data, and make sure that a sufficient number of allowances are surrendered by each company each year to cover their annual emissions. Each member state must also produce a regular annual report to the EC Commission. The commission will operate an

---

[44] *Ibid.* at 30.   [45] National Audit Office, see note 41 above.

[46] The National Audit Office specifically reviewed the application of the verification procedure for two randomly selected companies and concluded that '[we] were satisfied that they had been applied appropriately' (*ibid.* at 15).   [47] Compare Kruger and Pizer, see note 4 above at 38.

[48] J. Wettestad, 'The Making of the 2003 EU Emissions Trading Directive: Ultra-Quick Process Due to Entrepreneurial Proficiency?' (2005) 5 Global Envt'l Pol. 1.

electronic European registry system and prepare an annual report on the basis of member states' reports.

The requirement for independent verification was established in Article 15 of the 2003 EC Directive 2003/87 Establishing a Scheme for Greenhouse Gas Emission Allowance Trading within the Community and amending EU Directive 96/61 (ETS Directive). Independent auditors/verifiers are appointed by the competent national authority, and emissions from all activities are subject to verification. Moreover, 'where appropriate', verification shall be carried out on the site of the installation (Annex V, sections 6, 7). However, serious concern has been expressed about differing monitoring, reporting, and verification requirements across the EU. For instance, as of mid-2005, according to the CEPS research institute, there were more than fifty different systems in operation.[49] It is also unclear whether verifiers will be able to operate across borders.[50] Hence, there is a considerable harmonization challenge involved.

The decade-long operation of emission reporting systems and registries in the climate change context, beginning with the 1992 UNFCCC, could easily lead one to expect a good emissions data foundation for the operation of the EU ETS. A specific EU monitoring mechanism for carbon dioxide and other greenhouse gases has also been in operation since 1993.[51] The data situation is nevertheless still not satisfactory. According to consultants Enviros,[52] 'contrary to the impression put out by some analysts, there is no single source of accurate base year data for the sectors affected by the EU ETS across the EU and in particular the accession states.' Compared to the quite narrow scope of the US system (that is, utilities and industrial boilers), the EU system has more regulated sources and more industrial sectors, and some of these sectors have quite varied sources of emissions (such as iron and steel). This multiplicity and variety of sources increases the challenges in terms of data.

Regarding the possibilities for wider societal access and verification, the EU ETS Directive, like the US system, requires member states to make emissions and allowance data available to the public. The registry system has two tiers. First, there is a national component (national registries), which also includes a community registry. Second, there is a 'Community Independent Transaction Log' connected to all national registries in order to enable and check exchanges between them. All in all, several important building blocks of a good monitoring and verification system have been put into place. Yet incomplete data and limited harmonization across member

[49] CEPS, *Reviewing the EU Emissions Trading Scheme: Priorities for Short-Term Implementation of the Second Round Allocation*, Part I, CEPS Task Force Report (Brussels: Centre for European Policy Studies, 2005) at 10.

[50] 'New Rules for Verification under EU Emissions Trading Scheme' (May 2005) 364 ENDS Report 40.

[51] J. Wettestad, 'The Ambiguous Prospects for EU Climate Policy: A Summary of Options' (2001) 12 Energy & Env't 139.

[52] Enviros, *European Emissions Trading Scheme: Executive Briefing Two* (London: Enviros Consulting, 2004) at 1.

states indicate that there is still a considerable way to go before a well-functioning system is in place. Calls have been heard for moving towards a single system, which would bring down transaction costs and improve mutual trust.[53]

3.4 Monitoring and Verification of Global Trading within the Kyoto Protocol

As of 2008, all of the flexibility mechanisms established in the Kyoto Protocol will be in operation—that is, global emissions trading—with assigned amount units (AAUs) as the main 'currency'; joint implementation (JI) with emission reduction units (ERUs) as the 'currency'; and the Clean Development Mechanism (CDM) producing certified reduction units (CERs) or removal units (RMUs) from sink projects. However, as decided in the EC Directive 2004/101 Establishing a Scheme for Greenhouse Gas Emission Allowance Trading within the Community, in Respect of the Kyoto Protocol's Project Mechanisms,[54] CERs generated by CDM projects will be useable in the EU ETS from its beginning in 2005.

With respect to global emissions trading, Annex I parties may acquire AAUs from other Annex I parties that find it easier to meet their emission targets. Hence, it is important to keep in mind that trading within the Kyoto framework is geared much more towards the national level and the responsibilities of the parties than is the case in the EU scheme. The monitoring and verification challenges are nevertheless of the same nature as those discussed in connection with the EU scheme—that is, getting good baseline data, establishing the necessary registries, achieving harmonized procedures and practices, and so on. CDM and JI projects will be particularly challenging since the data situation is generally (even) less satisfying in economy-in-transition states and developing countries involved as host countries in such projects. Three main registries will be established: first, a national registry maintained by each Annex I party (containing accounts for holding of ERUs, CERs, AAUs, and RMUs by the parties); second, a CDM registry maintained by the Executive Board of the CDM, containing CER accounts for non-Annex I parties participating in the CDM; and, third, an international transactions log (ITL) maintained by the UNFCCC Secretariat. The ITL is not expected to be online until 2008. Given the complexity of managing such a system, the EU pilot scheme is likely to provide valuable experience and a knowledge base from which to start trading under the Kyoto Protocol.

With regard to JI, an important challenge is related to the data and baseline situation in non-EU Eastern European countries, such as Russia and Ukraine. With

---

[53] See CEPS, note 49 above at 4.

[54] EC Directive 2004/101 Establishing a Scheme for Greenhouse Gas Emission Allowance Trading within the Community, in Respect of the Kyoto Protocol's Project Mechanisms, [2004] O.J. L 30/15.

regard to CDM, a hotly debated issue has been the use of 'sinks' (that is, afforestation and reforestation projects). The room for such projects has been strictly limited under the Kyoto Protocol, and they are in fact excluded entirely from the EU pilot scheme.[55] The extent to which such projects represent additional efforts is unknown—in other words, measures that would not have come about without the climate change policy impetus. Moreover, sinks are not permanent. In general, it has been maintained that assessing the additionality and, hence, the real emission reductions of JI projects will be easier than those of CDM: 'In most cases, JI projects can reasonably be expected to lead to an actual reduction of emissions by the replacement of old plants with more modern and efficient operations. This is intrinsically easier to assess—and contain—than an investment that is claimed to displace some other projected new construction, which may be more common under the CDM.'[56] In the same vein, Einar Telnes from the Norwegian verification company Veritas has noted that 'we're verifying something that's not there, namely the greenhouse gases that would have been emitted in the absence of these projects.'[57] These problems have led to the establishment of elaborate certification and verification procedures, which also mean potentially high transaction costs related to such projects.

4 CONCLUDING COMMENTS

The main question asked in this chapter was to what extent do flexibility mechanisms represent totally new challenges, and require new procedures and solutions regarding monitoring and verification? In order to answer this question, the first section of the chapter summed up some important elements and lessons from the monitoring and verification of international environmental commitments. A main finding is that, for a long time, international environmental commitments were only monitored, with very little verification. However, verification has increased over time, through the use of review teams and the establishment and operation of compliance committees. Hence, although the increasing use of flexibility instruments can benefit from established monitoring procedures and some relevant baseline data, the foundation is not 'rock solid' in regard to data, verification instruments, and practice, in particular.

[55] Annex I parties are only allowed to use RMUs from sink projects to account for up to 1 per cent of the party's emissions in its base year. M. Buckens and H. Belin, *The European Emission Trading Scheme: Mechanisms and Issues*, European Union Policies Series (Brussels: EIS, 2004) 27.

[56] M. Grubb, C. Vrolijk, and D. Brack, *The Kyoto Protocol—A Guide and Assessment* (London: Royal Institute of International Affairs/Earthscan, 1999) at 199.

[57] A. Doyle, 'Brazil Garbage Dump Could Be Climate Trailblazer,' Reuters News Service/Planet Ark (2 December 2004).

The increasing use of international emissions trading and other flexibility mechanisms undoubtedly means more complex multi-level governance systems and, hence, increasing challenges. Yet institutional capacity is also increasing, not least on the verification side. Formal access to data by the public will probably increase as well, partly due to electronic registries at various levels. Hence, no dramatic change in terms of the balance between challenges and capacities should be expected. If a change in this balance occurs, the change will probably be more towards an improving situation.

However, there are a number of more specific challenges involved. As indicated, the emissions baseline data are shaky, particularly in the economy-in-transition states and developing countries. Moreover despite the fact that formal access to data and relevant information may increase, the complex and multi-level character of the flexible instruments may mean that access in practice for NGOs and the public at large will remain unchanged or even possibly decrease. Finally experience from the US and UK trading systems indicates potentially high verification costs. High costs may decrease the attractiveness of flexibility instruments in a long-term perspective.

RECOMMENDED READING

E. Brown Weiss and H. Jacobson, eds., *Engaging Countries: Strengthening Compliance with International Accords* (Cambridge, MA: MIT Press, 1998).

A. Chayes and A. Handler Chayes, *The New Sovereignty: Compliance with International Regulatory Agreements* (Cambridge, MA: Harvard University Press, 1995).

E.L. Miles, A. Underdal, S. Andresen, J. Wettestad, J.B. Skjærseth, and E.M. Carlin, *Environmental Regime Effectiveness: Confronting Theory with Evidence* (Cambridge, MA: MIT Press, 2002).

R. Reeve, *Policing International Trade in Endangered Species: The CITES Treaty and Compliance* (London: Earthscan, 2002).

O.S. Stokke, J. Hovi, and G. Ulfstein, eds., *Implementing the Climate Regime: International Compliance* (London: Earthscan, 2005).

D.G. Victor, K. Raustiala, and E.B. Skolnikoff, eds., *The Implementation and Effectiveness of International Environmental Commitments* (Cambridge, MA: MIT Press, 1998).

J. Wettestad, *Designing Effective Environmental Regimes: The Key Conditions* (Cheltenham, UK: Edward Elgar Publishing, 1999).

F. Yamin, ed., *Climate Change and Carbon Markets: A Handbook of Emissions Reduction Mechanisms* (London: Earthscan, 2005).

Yearbook of International Co-operation on Environment and Development 2003/2004 (London: Earthscan, 2004).

COMPLIANCE PROCEDURES

JAN KLABBERS

In the year 2525, the future historian working on a history of the ozone layer (by then long depleted, no doubt) may get a somewhat strange, and arguably distorted, picture of his or her topic when relying all too heavily on the reports of the Implementation Committee under the non-compliance procedure for the Montreal Protocol. Take, for example, the report of the thirty-second meeting of the Implementation Committee, a meeting held in Geneva in July 2004.[1] Two things catch the eye. One is that only the poorer nations seem to have compliance problems—the report refers to Pakistan, Lesotho, and Bosnia and Herzegovina; China, Cameroon, and Egypt; Libya, Somalia, and the Marshall Islands, plus a host of other not very well-to-do states. The only exception (if that is what it is) is Israel, but then again, so our future historian will realize, in international politics Israel was often, in the late twentieth and early twenty-first centuries, in the dock for reasons not necessarily related to its behaviour. Either way, all this suggests that non-compliance, at least under the Montreal Protocol, is most of all a poor nation's problem,[2] which, in turn, suggests, somewhat maliciously perhaps, that those poor states are the main culprits for the depletion of the ozone layer, while the richer states are doing their best to provide technical assistance in cleaning up the environment, either individually or through international organizations such as the World Bank, the UN Environment Programme, and the UN Development Programme (see Chapter 41 'Technical and Financial Assistance').

The second impression that our future historian will get is that, somehow, compliance seems to be intensely negotiable. Many of the states accused of non-compliance claim, in response, that the yardstick against which their behaviour is being tested is itself incorrect.[3] And at least one member of the Implementation Committee has proven to be highly sympathetic, noting that 'the quality of data reporting inevitably improve[s] over time,'[4] which, in effect, would suggest that indeed the low baselines have not been set realistically. While the committee, as such, has not automatically accepted such a line of reasoning, it has not rejected it out of hand either. Instead, the matter has been moved forward to the committee's thirty-third meeting.[5] Either way, flexibility is the name of the game—flexible norms, flexible baseline values, flexible

Thanks to Katja Keinänen and Tuomas Kuokkanen for intelligent discussion.

[1] Implementation Committee, Doc. UNEP/OzL.Pro/ImpCom/32/6 (11 August 2004).

[2] And in a sense, it is, as compliance or non-compliance procedures (the terms will be used interchangeably) place great emphasis on helping states that lack the capacity to comply. As Jutta Brunnée puts it, 'non-complying parties are most likely to be states with genuine capacity limitations.' See J. Brunnée, 'Enforcement Mechanisms in International Law and International Environmental Law' (2005) Envt'l L. Network Int'l Rev. 3 at 11.

[3] Typically, baseline values for the consumption of risky substances are identified; states are then supposed to reduce their consumption percentage-wise. As a result, it becomes attractive for states to revise their baseline upwards, and, indeed, this would seem to be the standard line of defence: the baseline was set unrealistically low. See Implementation Committee, note 1 above at paras. 42–51 (concerning the Philippines, Lebanon, and Thailand) and paras. 59–61 (concerning Saint Vincent and the Grenadines).

[4] *Ibid.* at para. 956.   [5] *Ibid.* at paras. 100–2.

implementation, and flexible assistance. The result may be that the protection of the ozone layer will become subordinated to the process,[6] and concentration on procedures may provide a cover that will hide a fundamental lack of agreement among the relevant actors.

1 CHARACTERISTICS OF NON-COMPLIANCE PROCEDURES

The Montreal Protocol on Substances That Deplete the Ozone Layer was among the first international agreements in which a specific non-compliance procedure was envisaged, and it is generally held to be the most developed example to date. Article 8 of the protocol instructs the parties to 'consider and approve procedures and institutional mechanisms for determining non-compliance with the provisions of this Protocol and for treatment of Parties found to be in non-compliance.' In its current version, the procedure was accepted at the tenth Meeting of the Parties (MOP) in Cairo in 1998.[7] Under the Montreal Protocol, the procedure can be initiated by either a complaint from another contracting party, on the basis of self-criticism by the party concerned, or on the initiative of the Secretariat administering the protocol. The party concerned may express worries about its capacity to meet the requirements set in the protocol (and its various adjustments), and ask for lenience or assistance. An especially established Implementation Committee will hear the case and make recommendations to the MOP, which usually adopts them through a decision. A typical decision may then identify the issue, note a lack of compliance, observe attempts on the part of the state concerned to remedy the situation, and recommend assistance while also recommending that the party concerned not be stigmatized but 'continue to be treated in the same manner as a Party in good standing.' Nonetheless, if only to make sure that the party concerned takes things seriously, the threat of sanctions is not excluded. Should it fail to meet the commitments indicated by the MOP, the parties may consider measures, including export restrictions.[8]

The procedure under the Montreal Protocol has been quite actively used. In 1998, nine decisions were taken, all of them relating to eastern European states. Five years later, the tally had risen to 20 decisions, all involving states from Eastern Europe, Asia,

---

[6] Then again, it has been noted that the overall consumption of some of the substances depleting the ozone layer (chlorofluorocarbons (CFCs)) has been brought down from 1.1 million tonnes in 1986 to 90,000 tonnes in 2002, and if it can be demonstrated that the consumption of CFCs has not been replaced by the consumption of other harmful substances, then surely this qualifies as a success. See K. M. Sarma, 'Compliance with the Ozone Treaties' (unpublished paper, 2004) at 7.

[7] See Doc. UNEP/OzL.Pro.10/9 (3 December 1998), Annex II.

[8] The language is taken from a random example. Decision X/25 concerning Lithuania, as reproduced in *ibid.* at 37–9.

Latin America, and Africa. Moreover, in addition to decisions on non-compliance, it is now also common to take decisions on 'potential non-compliance', which typically are the result of a failure to provide satisfactory explanations for consumption data and are 'potential' in the sense that much depends on whether satisfactory explanations are forthcoming. No particular sanctions, however, have yet been decided upon.

Non-compliance procedures have become rather prevalent in international environmental law, allowing one commentator to observe that 'it appears that establishing such a compliance mechanism has become standard practice in the environmental context.'[9] In addition to the Montreal Protocol, non-compliance procedures have been set up under the Convention on Long-Range Transboundary Air Pollution (LRTAP Convention) (to address compliance with its various protocols), the Convention on Environmental Impact Assessment in a Transboundary Context, the Kyoto Protocol to the UN Framework Convention on Climate Change, the Basel Convention on the Control of Transboundary Movements of Hazardous Wastes and Their Disposal (Basel Convention), the Convention on Access to Information, Public Participation in Decision-Making and Access to Justice in Environmental Matters (Aarhus Convention), the Cartagena Protocol on Biosafety, and the Convention on the Protection of the Alps.[10] Moreover, such procedures are being negotiated for other agreements, including the Convention on the Prior Informed Consent Procedure for Certain Hazardous Chemicals and Pesticides, the Stockholm Convention on Persistent Organic Pollutants, and the International Treaty on Plant Genetic Resources for Food and Agriculture (ITPGRFA), while the possible establishment of compliance procedures under the London Protocol to the Convention on the Prevention of Marine Pollution by Dumping of Wastes and Other Matter, and the Water and Health Protocol to the Convention on the Protection and Use of Transboundary Watercourses and International Lakes is under discussion.

Allowing for variations across regimes, most mechanisms have at least one compliance committee, usually composed of representatives of a limited number of parties (eight to fifteen) to the underlying multilateral environmental agreement and reporting back to the plenary body set up by that agreement (often dubbed the Conference of the Parties (COP) or MOP). As in the case of the Montreal Protocol, final decision-making then rests with the COP or MOP. Usually, the individuals sit as representatives of states, highlighting the diplomatic nature of non-compliance procedures. Sometimes the compliance procedure is envisaged in the original treaty or in a protocol thereto and sometimes it is based on a decision by the MOP or COP.

---

[9] See T. Kuokkanen, 'Putting Gentle Pressure on Parties: Recent Trends in the Practice of the Implementation Committee under the Convention on Long-Range Transboundary Air Pollution,' in J. Petman and J. Klabbers, eds., *Nordic Cosmopolitanism: Essays in International Law for Martti Koskenniemi(Leiden: Martinus Nijhoff/Brill Academic Publishers*, 2003) 315 at 316.

[10] In addition, the North American Free Trade Agreement (NAFTA) has a similar procedure, but as NAFTA is not an environmental agreement alone, the dynamics are bound to be different.

Typically, compliance procedures involve standing committees—creating ad hoc committees whenever a complaint or request is submitted would be too time-consuming and impractical.

Submissions regarding non-compliance can usually be brought either by other contracting parties (but this is rarely done) or by the non-complying parties themselves, or action can be initiated by the secretariat established by the agreement in question. The Aarhus Convention (see Chapter 29 'Public Participation'), moreover, allows for actions to be initiated by members of the public, including non-governmental organizations and private citizens.

While there is some uncertainty about the binding nature of compliance procedures, the spirit behind them would suggest that final outcomes would be recommendatory in nature (see Chapter 38 'Treaty Bodies'). After all, the point of compliance procedures usually is to facilitate compliance, and, to this end, the compliance committee may provide advice or assistance (for example, with respect to technology transfer or capacity building), invite further reporting, or request a compliance action plan. By contrast, the procedure itself is best seen as being compulsory in nature—once a state is faced with a submission made against it, it is expected to cooperate. The most elaborate procedure devised to date is without a doubt the procedure developed under the Kyoto Protocol.[11] Remarkably, the procedure looks, in part, like a judicial procedure, complete with conditions relating to the admissibility of complaints (Article VII), procedural guarantees (Article VIII), the possibility of appeal (Article XI), and possible consequences attached to a finding of non-compliance (Article XV).

Another innovation involves dividing the tasks of the Kyoto Protocol's Compliance Committee into two branches: a facilitative branch, which works to nip compliance problems in the bud, and an enforcement branch, which deals with non-compliance after the fact. In addition, the committee consists of a plenary (all 20 of its members, which is to be co-chaired by the chairs of the two branches) and a bureau and is assisted by the Secretariat set up under the Kyoto Protocol. All in all, the result is an elaborate, complex structure, which gives the impression of a judicial organ dressed in political (or bureaucratic) garb.[12]

An almost judicial element is also envisaged in Article 21 of the ITPGRFA. This article is the basis upon which a non-compliance procedure will be set up, and it provides for 'legal advice or legal assistance' to states involved in a non-compliance procedure. Again, this process would suggest a gradual formalization or judicialization

---

[11] For the text, see Decision 24/CP.7 plus annex, which was adopted at the eighth plenary meeting of the Conference of the Parties to the UN Framework Convention on Climate Change and reproduced in Doc. FCCC/CP/2001/13/Add.3 (21 January 2002), at 64–77.

[12] The procedure being established under the Cartagena Protocol on Biosafety, while less elaborate and detailed than the one under the Kyoto Protocol, also has a judicial feel to it. It includes rules on the admissibility of submissions, on admissible information, and on what sort of measures can be taken. The text is annexed to Doc. UNEP/CBD/BS/COP-MOP/1/15 (14 April 2004) at 98–101.

of the non-compliance procedure. The degree to which non-compliance procedures are actually used varies from regime to regime. While the procedure under the Montreal Protocol is actively used, as is the procedure overseeing compliance with the various protocols negotiated under the LRTAP Convention,[13] the committee that was set up in 2002 under the Basel Convention reported in 2004 that it had not yet received any submissions.[14]

2 WHY NON-COMPLIANCE PROCEDURES?

Compliance with agreed upon norms is usually, but not always, considered to be a virtue. Not only does compliance denote trustworthiness, but it also maintains the balance of rights and obligations (or of advantages and disadvantages; gives and takes) that usually form the basis of the agreement. Given the general dearth of studies in international law on compliance, the topic's current popularity seems curious. Since roughly the late 1980s and early 1990s, when Thomas Franck published his groundbreaking work on the legitimacy of international law, and argued that much of the force of legal rules depended on their 'compliance pull',[15] and Abram Chayes and Antonia Handler Chayes pioneered the managerial approach to compliance,[16] compliance issues have moved from a distant background—as something most often dependent on the 'political will' of actors—into a prominent position. The end of the Cold War may have suggested a diminished role of 'political will' and so may partly be responsible for the focus on compliance, as may the rise of environmental issues, which has suggested that, in the nature of things, a bit of progress is better than no progress at all.

Still, perhaps the most curious thing about special non-compliance procedures is that they exist at all as alternatives to traditional dispute settlement procedures (see Chapter 45 'International Dispute Settlement'). Their soft nature, divorced from traditional enforcement considerations and justifications, suggests, after all, a disappointment with the law. It suggests that the traditional approach to law, which

---

[13] T. Kuokkanen reports eight substantial cases by the end of the year 2002. See Kuokkanen, note 9 above at 321.

[14] See *Report of the Second Session of the Basel Convention Implementation and Compliance Committee*, Geneva, Doc. UNEP/CHW/CC/2/3 (29 April 2004) at para. IV.

[15] See T.M. Franck, 'Legitimacy in the International System' (1988) 82 A.J.I.L. 705; and T.M. Franck, *The Power of Legitimacy among Nations* (Oxford: Oxford University Press, 1990).

[16] See A. Chayes and A. Handler Chayes, *The New Sovereignty: Compliance with International Regulatory Agreements* (Cambridge, MA: Harvard University Press, 1995).

labels behaviour as either legal or illegal, is incapable of dealing with present-day circumstances. And it suggests, most worryingly perhaps, that compliance has become subject to negotiations.

Compliance (or non-compliance) procedures are usually said to exist, and be necessary, in international environmental protection because the environment cannot, for a number of reasons, be entrusted to the workings of traditional international law. In particular, so the argument often goes, the regular system of state responsibility is not particularly suitable for environmental protection (see Chapter 44 'International Responsibility and Liability'). There is, for example, often no real wrongfulness at issue—causality between behaviour and environmental degradation is frequently difficult to establish with the degree of precision that the law would insist on; traditional remedies are often inaccessible due to inflexible rules on standing; responsibility comes after the breach and generally cannot restore the *status quo ante*; the standards of environmental protection (due diligence, significant harm, and so on) are often regarded as too indeterminate to be enforceable by traditional means; and non-compliance can have numerous causes that a focus on formal breach of treaty cannot easily accommodate.

There is a lot of truth in this perspective. International law, and, in particular, its enforcement-related notions and doctrines, is very much a system for and between states. The jurisdiction of international tribunals is based on the voluntary acceptance thereof by the parties and is, thus, it is often thought, of little help when parties are unwilling to go to court or to submit their disputes to arbitration or other binding dispute settlement procedures.

The general rules on what to do in case a state violates an international legal norm (the 'internationally wrongful act') also come with problems in the environmental context. It is not usually the case, for instance, that states themselves pollute, but, more often, environmental damage is caused by entities within states. However, it is built into the traditional notions of international law that the law cannot claim direct authority over entities within states but can only do so indirectly, by claiming authority over states in the hope that states will, through legislation or by allowing international provisions to be self-executing, 'pass the buck'. In a sense, then, the state is only a fringe player—it may be guilty of failing to legislate, but it will not, in the typical scenario, be itself guilty of polluting the environment.

Another problem is that few rules of international law are so clear and precise that departures from the norm can be characterized without debate as being internationally wrongful acts, and this applies both to customary rules and to treaty provisions. Often, what may appear at first sight as an internationally wrongful act can be recast as being merely a difference in interpretation of the norm at hand. As a result, it becomes awkward to apply the law on state responsibility to what might well be a *bona fide* misinterpretation or, maybe, not even a misinterpretation but rather a competing interpretation. This line of thought holds all the more true, arguably, in matters that are highly technical, such as the protection of the Earth's environment, where typically neither the norms to be respected nor the yardsticks with which to measure respect for these norms are very clear.

Also rather useless are the rules on material breach of treaty that were laid down in the Vienna Convention on the Law of Treaties. Article 60 of the convention defines a material breach as 'a violation of a provision essential to the accomplishment of the object or purpose of the treaty' and thus focuses on the importance of the provision breached rather than on the gravity of the breach itself. By so doing, Article 60 greatly misses its target. The distinction between a material breach and a 'regular' breach, which is so vital to the drafters of the Vienna Convention on the Law of Treaties, has—understandably—all but disappeared in practice,[17] with the result that since breaches typically trigger the law of state responsibility rather than the law of treaties, the consequences of breach are, arguably, less clear cut than they would have been under the codified law of treaties.

Finally, the remedies that general international law has to offer are also not always considered very useful. Many remedies presuppose an identifiably injured or affected party, which is something difficult to establish in regimes based on what political scientist Robert Keohane once described as 'diffuse reciprocity'.[18] Surely, depleting the ozone layer cannot be seen to merely affect a single identifiable state but rather to affect the planet at large. To some extent, Article 60 of the Vienna Convention on the Law of Treaties aims to provide solace by rendering it possible for individual parties to a treaty regime, other than those directly injured, to take steps, but this possibility comes with two drawbacks. Not only is it politically awkward to take measures against another state without being directly injured (nor will there be much incentive to do so), it is also the case that the main remedy at the disposal of non-directly injured states is a suspension of the treaty's regime. The cure in this case is considerably worse than the disease.

In short, those who argue that general international law is not very well equipped to address environmental concerns do have a point—and it is a point that many states seem to share since they hardly ever resort to traditional dispute settlement procedures to settle environmental disputes. Perhaps surprisingly though, the establishment of a non-compliance procedure does not really seem to answer most of the problems that general international law faces or, if it does, it merely disguises the existing political problems. For instance, a non-compliance procedure does not render indeterminate norms more specific without turning into law-making or without sacrificing the same political flexibility that is so often heralded as one of the virtues

---

[17] Fine examples are the *Rainbow Warrior (New Zealand and Greenpeace v. France)*, 30 April 1990, reprinted in 82 I.L.R. Rep. 499 (1990); and the *Case Concerning the Gabčíkovo-Nagymaros Project (Hungary/Slovakia)*, Judgment of 25 September 1997, [1997] I.C.J. Rep. 92 (25 September).

[18] See R.O. Keohane, 'Reciprocity in International Relations,' in R.O. Keohane, ed., *International Institutions and State Power: Essays in International Relations Theory* (Boulder, CO: Westview Press, 1989) 132.

of non-compliance procedures.[19] Non-compliance procedures also have their own problems as far as procedural niceties such as standing are concerned, as is recognized in the various academic papers analyzing the connections between non-compliance procedures and general international law.[20] Causality does not become clearer under a non-compliance procedure, and standards of wrongfulness do not become more exact (or exacting) either.

It would seem then that the most important role for non-compliance procedures relates to two possibilities. First, they may enable a more pro-active stand, identifying compliance problems before non-compliance actually occurs, and thus help forestall degradation rather than focus on patching things up after the fact. Second, they might help parties concentrate on the non-intentional causes of non-compliance. In particular, non-compliance procedures might be of assistance in identifying a lack of resources or capacity as a key to non-performance. In both cases, flexibility would seem to be a clear asset: a flexible, non-adversarial, non-accusatory procedure might just help convince states to turn to compliance mechanisms both with respect to themselves and with respect to others. Yet, in both cases, a serious commitment to fighting environmental degradation on the part of those states is presupposed as well as a serious commitment to fighting environmental degradation along the lines agreed in the treaty or protocol at hand.

3 THEORETICAL CONSIDERATIONS

Whether non-compliance procedures actually are successful is a complicated matter, dividing political scientists and lawyers alike. Proponents of the use of non-compliance procedures suggest that the sources of wrongful acts are, most often, such things as a lack of capacity or a lack of resources, or genuine differences of interpretation, rather than a case of bad faith. If so, the argument continues, it makes little sense to punish states for what is, in effect, a good faith effort to comply.[21] Instead of using sticks, it might be better to lure states into compliance with carrots, including such things as technical assistance and financial assistance.

---

[19] J. Werksman makes a virtue out of a possible vice: 'Through the exploration of an individual case, parties come to a better understanding of the scope of their obligations.' See J. Werksman, 'Compliance and the Kyoto Protocol: Building a Backbone into a "Flexible" Regime' (1998) 9 Y.B. Int'l Envt'l L. 48 at 53.

[20] See, e.g., M. Fitzmaurice and C. Redgwell, 'Environmental Non-Compliance Procedures and International Law' (2000) 31 Netherlands Y.B. Int'l L. 35.

[21] The inevitable counterargument will be, of course, that states should not sign up to commitments they cannot keep. Moreover, if there is uncertainty about key notions, then usually the uncertainty results from fundamental disagreement rather than from insecure or sloppy drafting.

At the heart of the theory behind compliance procedures is not just the consideration that general international law does not really work but also a diagnosis as to why general international law cannot even be expected to function properly. International law generally presupposes, so it seems, a binary way of thinking, yet, in real life, compliance can come in varying degrees. Compliance, as Chayes and Handler Chayes write, 'is not an on-off phenomenon.' The systemic problem for regime-builders is not so much to ensure literal compliance (as traditional legal thought insists) but rather 'to contain deviance within acceptable levels.'[22]

Others firmly disagree. Writers coming from the realist or political economy tradition suggest that, at the very least, much compliance would take place simply for the reason that states, when constructing regimes, tend to construct them so as to coincide with their interests: '[S]tates will rarely spend a great deal of time and effort negotiating agreements that will continually be violated.'[23] In such a setting, non-compliance makes fairly little sense, and the existence of non-compliance procedures will hardly contribute to compliance with the agreed upon norms. Those same authors contend, moreover, that when analyzed up close, many successful regimes owe their success to the possibility of sanctions, and they point out that increased depth of cooperation is often accompanied by increased sanctions possibilities, with the sanctions regimes of the European Union and the World Trade Organization being among the favourite examples. Given the relative absence of sanctions in international law, this does not amount to a plea for an increased use of traditional, 'hard' dispute settlement mechanisms. Yet it does not unequivocally support an increased use of non-compliance procedures either.

Empirical evidence is inconclusive, partly for the classic reason that it is difficult to establish causality in the social sciences (see Chapter 39 'Compliance Theory'). Some work suggests that non-compliance procedures can be highly effective. Others suggest, using the same materials, that effectiveness ultimately results from the availability of hard sanctions. And as some sanctions are usually available, if only in the form of withholding benefits, no firm conclusions can be drawn either way. As Kal Raustiala concludes with respect to the Montreal Protocol's non-compliance procedure, it 'can be interpreted as supporting either the norm-driven approach of managerialism or the rationalist, enforcement-focused views of its critics.'[24]

Hence, the jury is still out on whether non-compliance procedures are capable of influencing state behaviour in ways that other mechanisms cannot or in ways that are more effective or persuasive. And it is more than likely, as Benedict Kingsbury has written, that our views on compliance cannot be seen in isolation from our theories

[22] See Chayes and Handler Chayes, note 16 above at 17.

[23] See G.W. Downs, D.M. Rocke, and P.N. Barsoom, 'Is the Good News about Compliance Good News about Cooperation?' (1996) 50 Int'l Org. 279 at 283.

[24] See K. Raustiala, 'Compliance and Effectiveness in International Regulatory Cooperation' (2000) 32 Case W. Res. J. Int'l L. 387 at 420.

about international law and international relations in general (see Chapter 10 'International Relations Theory').[25] The realist is bound to insist on the availability of sanctions, however defined, and the liberal institutionalist is bound to insist that sanctions are not the only thing that might work—and never the twain shall meet.

Perhaps the problem then resides in asking the wrong (because unanswerable) question: whether the analysis ought to concentrate on what effectiveness is actually pursued? Lawyers grow up in the expectation that law ought to be instrumental and that it ought to function in the service of some desired result. It may be the case, however, that this is an overstatement and that law is used not just (or not always) as a rational means to some rational end but also as a symbolic exercise, giving the impression that something is being done about some problem without actually doing much about it. The rationality of the instrument may be a 'political rationality,' to borrow Martti Koskenniemi's term, rather than an instrumental rationality.[26] This applies to soft instruments no less than to harder regimes.

4 LEGAL ISSUES

The emergence of non-compliance procedures raises a few intricate legal problems. Perhaps two ought to be singled out. One is the question of the voluntary nature of the procedures or their outcomes—what if a state refuses to cooperate, gives every impression of not taking the procedure very seriously, or ignores the recommendations resulting from the non-compliance procedure? The second, related question is how the non-compliance procedure relates to international law's general enforcement mechanisms. It is convenient to start with this latter issue.

Non-compliance procedures typically leave existing enforcement mechanisms intact. Typically, the non-compliance procedure is an addition to the existing framework, and the existing framework may simply be general international law or, less often, a specifically designed adversarial procedure. The standard formula is that the non-compliance procedure is 'without prejudice' to existing mechanisms. Yet, it is not very clear what this means in terms of law. The most obvious literal reading would suggest that in a case where a state faces submissions under both procedures simultaneously, the general procedure would take precedence. This conclusion follows from the more substantive argument that under a general procedure, the

---

[25] See B. Kingsbury, 'The Concept of Compliance as a Function of Competing Conceptions of International Law' (1998) 19 Mich. J. Int'l L. 345.

[26] See M. Koskenniemi, 'Comment on the Paper by A. Handler Chayes, A. Chayes, and R.B. Mitchell,' in W. Lang, ed., *Sustainable Development and International Law* (London: Graham and Trotman, 1995) 91 at 93.

concrete rights of an individual party will inevitably be at stake. Dismissing this right in favour of the more elusive common interest might be difficult to sell to the disgruntled party and might, more generally, be difficult to reconcile with liberal rights thinking. Surely, under any version of liberalism, a concrete right cannot be trumped by reference to a common interest, and a concrete right to be compensated cannot be trumped by saying that the guilty party promises to make a good faith effort to do better in the future.

On the other hand, the non-compliance procedure finds its *raison d'être* precisely in the attempts to defuse the adversarial or confrontational nature of dispute settlement, so why should it not be allowed to prevail? Would that not imply that the procedure is, at best, a poor man's alternative rather than a full-fledged compliance procedure in its own right? And, would not the accused state have a right, if such a procedure exists, to see it utilized rather than the more adversarial and unfriendly procedure before a court or arbitration tribunal?

A number of related issues also surface. For instance, if a state has developed a plan to improve its environmental compliance following a non-compliance procedure, does this intention immunize it against more formal action? If an aggrieved state has participated in a non-compliance procedure, will it be estopped from claiming individual compensation under a formal procedure? And what does 'participated' mean in this case? Does it matter whether it was represented in the Implementation Committee or whether it did not block a consensus within the COP or MOP? Can a victim state (or any other party, for that matter) ask for interim measures of protection?

To some extent (but not exclusively perhaps), these are hypothetical situations, which are not expected to materialize any time soon. Yet, the very circumstance that these questions can be asked to begin with suggests that there is still something rather undeveloped about non-compliance procedures. And this is the paradox since such a procedure must remain undeveloped in order to retain the desirable degree of flexibility. Any attempt to answer ancillary questions; any attempt to formalize the procedure and spell out the rights and legal positions of the parties to a dispute brings the non-compliance procedure closer to the judicial procedure (as, indeed, the enforcement branch of the procedure under the Kyoto Protocol suggests) and thus misses the mark.

By the same token, the procedure may work best if (and as long as) its results are seen as voluntary. If they come to be seen as binding, the accused party may be better off with the procedural guarantees offered by regular dispute settlement. Such guarantees include the possibilities of appointing an ad hoc judge or helping to select an arbitration panel or court chamber; the possibilities of winning time that judicial procedure typically offers; and the substantive possibility, in all but the most blatant cases, that the state will be found not responsible, either due to the ambiguity of the norm concerned or the uncertain connection between a private company's behaviour and the state concerned.

There is, as yet, little experience with states unwilling to participate or to comply. The most cited case here is that of Russia under the Montreal Protocol, which was finally resolved by Russia agreeing to a deal involving financial assistance in order to help it comply.[27] Other incidents are unknown or unreported,[28] which might spell a great success rate but may also be due to self-selection—procedures will probably not start if there is an indication that the state in non-compliance is unwilling to abide, as the diplomatic costs would be considerable.

5 COSTS AND BENEFITS

Prosper Weil, in a classic piece, warned against the relativization of international law's normativity by such developments as the emergence of *jus cogens* norms, *erga omnes* obligations, international crimes of states, and soft law, not because he would be unsympathetic to attempts to introduce normative gradations *per se* but rather because he felt that legal thought would not be able to accommodate such subtlety. Whereas politics and morality come in infinite shades of grey, law, by contrast, must insist on retaining its 'simplifying rigor'. In order to have any use at all, law would need to be able to translate moral and political nuances into simple dichotomies of binding versus non-binding, legal versus illegal, responsible versus non-responsible. Otherwise, law would lose its distinctiveness and, therewith, its specific social function.[29]

The creation of non-compliance procedures may eventually, as protagonists claim, be beneficial to the environment. It is not inconceivable that non-compliance procedures contribute to the more effective management and containment of environmental problems and that the environment would be worse off without them. Yet, if Weil is right, this success comes at a systemic cost—the cost of giving up the rule of law in favour of a specific set of goals. This may sound overly dramatic, but it is nonetheless a concern to be taken seriously. As the above-mentioned example of sympathy towards rethinking baseline values suggests, anything seems negotiable under a non-compliance procedure, including compliance. From there it is but a

---

[27] For a useful discussion, see J. Werksman, 'Compliance and Transition: Russia's Non-Compliance Tests the Ozone Regime' (1996) 56 Zeitschrift für ausländisches öffentliches Recht und Völkerrecht 750.

[28] Although on occasion, the laconic language or lack of cooperation suggest that states do not take a procedure too seriously. The Implementation Committee operating under the various protocols to the Convention on Long-Range Transboundary Air Pollution once was compelled to note that 'Ireland stated that it was not in a position to describe the progress that it had made towards compliance.' It also noted that attempts to get Spain to comply had remained ineffective: 'Despite repeated attempts, the secretariat has been unable to establish contact with the relevant authorities in Madr [sic].' See UN Doc. ECOSOC EB/AIR/2004//6 (15 September 2004) at paras. 25 and 29.

[29] See P. Weil, 'Towards Relative Normativity in International Law?' (1983) 77 A.J.I.L. 413.

small step to suggest that the binding force of law is negotiable since law is about as binding as states want it to be. This conclusion, in turn, can only come to mean that law will lose whatever force it may have and will becomes indistinguishable from politics and morality—someone's politics, at any rate, and someone's morality, usually those of the stronger parties.

There is, in other words, a clear connection between attempts to formulate soft law instruments and non-compliance procedures. Both may be effective in the short run. Yet, a soft law instrument can only be violated softly, giving rise to a soft form of responsibility, established by a soft tribunal. And the archetypical soft tribunal is, indeed, the non-compliance procedure, which aims to avoid such fierce terms as responsibility, compensation, damages, and even breach. (It is no coincidence surely that we do not speak of breach procedures but, instead, use the far softer euphemism of non-compliance, as if a breach is not really a breach.) By the same token, we also speak of commitments and consequences rather than obligations and sanctions.

On the other hand, a systemic argument usually fails to persuade when pitted against a strong substantive argument. If non-compliance procedures do help clean up the environment, then why should it matter that they may do so by diluting the traditional concept of law? The very idea of law itself is, one could argue, only an instrument, a tool to realize society's goals, and it may well need to be replaced as soon as better tools come along. There are at least some examples of domestic institutions that have developed softly, in managerial rather than in a judicial mode, yet still have managed to grow into their proper role without incurring systemic costs. A case in point is the Constitutional Council (Conseil constitutionnel) in France. Initially composed of elderly statesmen rather than lawyers, it turned 'into a true constitutional court because of its decisions.'[30]

6 Concluding Remarks

In the end, non-compliance procedures, from the instrumental perspective, may have quite a lot to offer. They may, as some empirical evidence suggests, contribute to compliance with treaty commitments and, if those treaty commitments indeed help clean up the environment, then so much the better. Still, there is a price to pay and that is the price of dilution. By creating a highly political, diplomatic way of inducing compliance, the law may end up rendering itself superfluous, and if the law is no longer a viable option then neither is the rule of law, giving those who wield political power eventually a blank check to do as they see fit.

[30] See T. Koopmans, *Courts and Political Institutions: A Comparative View* (Cambridge: Cambridge University Press, 2003) at 72.

It is no great surprise, therefore, that the paradox involving non-compliance procedures has already become visible and that some have identified a trend towards greater involvement of national courts in ensuring compliance with international environmental standards.[31] The flexibility of a non-compliance procedure approach should, ideally, be surrounded by procedural guarantees and clear and lucid standards, which, in turn, would render the procedures indistinguishable from standard judicial procedures. Yet the more the non-compliance procedure comes to resemble the judicial procedure, the less flexible, and therefore the less useful, it will become.

Recommended Reading

A. Chayes and A. Handler Chayes, *The New Sovereignty: Compliance with International Regulatory Agreements* (Cambridge, MA: Harvard University Press, 1995).

G.W. Downs, D.M. Rocke, and P.N. Barsoom, 'Is the Good News about Compliance Good News about Cooperation?' (1996) 50 Int'l Org. 279.

T.M. Franck, *The Power of Legitimacy among Nations* (New York: Oxford University Press, 1990).

G. Handl, 'Compliance Control Mechanisms and International Environmental Obligations' (1997) 5 Tulane J. Int'l & Comp. L. 29.

B. Kingsbury, 'The Concept of Compliance as a Function of Competing Conceptions of International Law' (1998) 19 Mich. J. Int'l L. 345.

M. Koskenniemi, 'Breach of Treaty or Non-Compliance? Reflections on the Enforcement of the Montreal Protocol' (1992) 3 Y.B. Int'l Envt'l L. 123.

R. Lefeber, 'From the Hague to Bonn to Marrakesh and Beyond: A Negotiating History of the Compliance Regime under the Montreal Protocol' (2001) 14 Hague Y.B. Int'l L. 25.

R. Mitchell, 'Regime Design Matters: Intentional Oil Pollution and Treaty Compliance' (1994) 48 Int'l Org. 425.

K. Raustiala, 'Compliance and Effectiveness in International Regulatory Cooperation' (2000) 32 Case W. Res. J. Int'l L. 387.

R. Wolfrum, 'Means of Ensuring Compliance and Enforcement of International Environmental Law' (1998) 272 Recueil des cours 9.

---

[31] See A. Nollkaemper, 'Compliance Control in International Environmental Law: Traversing the Limits of the National Legal Order' (2002) 13 Y.B. Int'l Envt'l L. 165.

CHAPTER 44

INTERNATIONAL RESPONSIBILITY AND LIABILITY

MALGOSIA FITZMAURICE

1 Introduction: Scope of the Chapter

THIS chapter addresses the consequences of the causation of transboundary environmental harm within several international legal regimes: state responsibility for breach of general environmental obligations; international civil liability regimes for harmful consequences of high risk activities (such as nuclear and oil-related activities); liability regimes in multilateral environmental agreements (MEAs); and the emerging general system of liability for harmful consequences of lawful activities involving high risk. The chapter will offer an overview of these international legal regimes and will assess their strengths and weaknesses, their usefulness as tools of environmental protection, and their effectiveness as systems of compensation.

After more than 50 years of work, the International Law Commission (ILC) codified the general (customary) regime for state responsibility in the Articles on Responsibility of States for Internationally Wrongful Acts (ILC Responsibility Articles),[1] which were adopted in 2001. The law of state responsibility is based on the distinction between two types of rules: 'primary rules', which are those that establish the obligations of states, and 'secondary rules', which are concerned with the breach of primary rules and with the consequences of such breach. The term 'state responsibility' is now widely used to denote secondary rules, following the decision of the ILC to limit its articles on state responsibility to these. As will be shown in this chapter, state responsibility for environmental damage has played a relatively limited role in environmental law, due in part to the fact that it does not cover the liability of private actors, who are those largely responsible for pollution. Furthermore, the state responsibility regime leaves unclear the extent to which states are responsible in relation to the environment towards the community of states generally (*erga omnes*) or towards group of states based on multilateral treaty regimes (*erga omens partes*).

---

[1] Draft Articles on Responsibility of States for Internationally Wrongful Acts, *Report of the International Law Commission on Its Work of Its Fifty-Third Session*, 56 U.N. GAOR Supp. (No. 10) at 43, UN Doc. A/56/10 (2001) [*ILC Report on Fifty-Third Session*]. See J. Crawford, *The International Law Commission's Articles on State Responsibility, Introduction: Text and Commentaries* (Cambridge: Cambridge University Press, 2002).

In the 1970s, the ILC also started work on a system covering the harmful consequences of lawful but high-risk activities. In 1997, facing insurmountable conceptual
difficulties, the ILC decided to divide the liability topic into two projects. The first
project involved work on primary obligations relating to the prevention of transboundary harm from hazardous activities, and, in 2001, it resulted in the adoption of
a draft convention. The second project involved work on liability for injurious consequences of acts not prohibited by international law. After years of conceptual
struggle and 'misplaced emphasis',[2] the ILC is currently in the process of deciding
what direction this project should take. It has switched its focus to the practical aspect
of the allocation of loss and seems to be abandoning the concept of state liability in
favour of civil liability.

The development of civil 'high risk' liability regimes marked a change of emphasis,
channelling liability away from the state towards the operators. A further change of
emphasis is reflected in a fundamental shift away from the compensatory approach
of responsibility or liability regimes towards more pro-active systems set up in MEAs,
aimed at encouraging and assisting states to fulfil their obligations in relation to the
protection of the environment (see Chapter 43 'Compliance Procedures'). In a yet
further development, states have begun to complement the compliance-oriented
aspect of MEAs through the introduction of liability regimes within the MEAs themselves. On the one hand, important benefits derive from this incorporation of liability regimes into MEAs, such as their espousal of the polluter pays principle, the
provision of compensation for victims, and their deterrent effect on potential polluters. However, on the other hand, their inclusion substantially increases the complexity and costs of negotiating MEAs, to an extent that may not really be justified by
the benefits.

2 PRIMARY RULES OF INTERNATIONAL
ENVIRONMENTAL LAW

States' obligations arising under primary rules derive both from treaty and from general customary international law. In the environmental field, it is in fact treaties that
have come to play by far the greater part in regulating state conduct. To appreciate the
challenges that arise in applying the law of state responsibility in the environmental
context, it is nonetheless important to consider the evolution of the field against the
backdrop of its customary law foundations.

---

[2] P.S. Rao, *First Report on the Legal Regime for Allocation of Loss in Case of Transboundary Harm Arising
Out of Hazardous Activities*, UN Doc. A/CN.4/531 (21 May 2003) at para. 16.

2.1 Evolution of Primary Rules

The traditional foundation of the regulation of the international behaviour of states in the environmental field is the customary law rule prohibiting the causation of transboundary damage—a rule that has its roots in the principle of state sovereignty (see Chapter 19 'Formation of Customary International Law and General Principles' and Chapter 22 'Transboundary Impacts'). This classical approach to state responsibility developed on the basis of the award in the *Trail Smelter Arbitration (United States v. Canada)*, in which the tribunal relied on 'the principle of general international law' prohibiting a 'State . . . to use or permit the use of its territory in such a manner as to cause injury by fumes in or to the territory of another or the properties or persons therein, when the case is of serious consequences and the injury is established by clear and convincing evidence.' The same basic premise underlay the decision of the International Court of Justice (ICJ) in the *Corfu Channel* case, in which the court referred to 'every State's obligation not to allow knowingly its territory to be used so as to cause harm to the citizens or property of other States.'

The *Trail Smelter* rule was taken up in Principle 21 of the Stockholm Declaration on the Human Environment and Principle 2 of the Rio Declaration on Environment and Development, which extend the duty to prevent transboundary harm to areas outside states' jurisdiction or control. The rule, which has become one of the few uncontested norms of customary international environmental law in the environmental field, was confirmed by the ICJ in the 1996 Advisory Opinion on the *Legality of the Threat or Use of Nuclear Weapons*.

The rule against significant transboundary environmental harm appears to include as well the duty to adopt preventive measures to protect the environment. Already in the *Trail Smelter Arbitration*, Canada was ordered to adopt measures to prevent further injury, and such a duty is now at the core of numerous contemporary environmental treaties.[3] The same approach was adopted by the International Law Commission in Article 3 of the 2000 draft Convention on the Prevention of Transboundary Harm.[4]

Beyond the realm of the rule prohibiting transboundary harm, it remains difficult to identify uncontested principles of international environmental law. The paucity of judicial practice on principles such as precaution (see Chapter 25 'Precaution') or sustainable development (see Chapter 26 'Sustainable Development'), and the divergence of views on their legal status among states and academic observers alike, complicate the task. Therefore, answering the central background questions of the law of state responsibility, pertaining to the status or content of the primary rule that was breached, is particularly taxing within international environmental law.

---

[3] P. Birnie and A. Boyle, *International Law and Environment* (Oxford: Oxford University Press, 2002) at 111–12.

[4] It requires all parties to adopt 'all appropriate measures to prevent or minimise risk of significant transboundary harm.'

2.2 Due Diligence and the Strict/Absolute Liability Standard

The concept of due diligence derives from general international law. It is a relative concept, depending on the circumstances and issue at hand and taking into account the diverse conditions of particular states. There is almost unanimous agreement that the prevention of harm is an obligation of due diligence. This conclusion is reflected in the ILC's draft Convention on the Prevention of Transboundary Harm (Articles 3–7). From a practical point of view, however, the due diligence concept poses a host of evidentiary difficulties—causality being one of them. The paucity of international law practice, judicial or otherwise, concerning the definition of the standard of care required by states makes it very difficult to develop the law of state responsibility into a satisfactory framework for environmental protection.

One alternative way forward, which has been suggested by some writers, is the adoption of strict liability as a general standard for environmental damage.[5] However, the standards of strict or absolute liability are themselves not free from difficulties, due to the difference between the concepts of strict liability and liability for risk. Moreover, some writers have distinguished between strict and absolute liability, in that strict liability offers greater range of exculpatory factors precluding responsibility than absolute liability.[6] Furthermore, there is no prevailing state or treaty practice or case law that supports a general strict or absolute liability standard. The only relevant claim was based on the 1972 Convention on International Liability for Damage Caused by Space Objects, a convention that does establish an absolute liability standard, but this case was settled by an *ex gratia* payment and is, therefore, of no value as a precedent. In any case, other environmental treaties, such as the 1997 United Nations Convention on the Law of Non-Navigational Uses of International Watercourses, are based on the due diligence standard. Clarity on the prevailing standard cannot be sought in national laws, which also differ greatly in their support for strict or absolute liability.

2.3 Question of Harm

The question of harm (damage)[7] too has caused many differences of views, misunderstandings, and misinterpretations. Like the question of fault, the issue of harm is

---

[5] See, e.g., L.F.E. Goldie, 'Liability for Damage and the Progressive Development of International Law' (1965) 14 Int'l & Comp. L.Q. 1189; G. Handl, 'Balancing of Interests and International Liability for the Pollution of International Watercourses' (1975) 13 Canadian Y.B. Int'l L. 156 at 167–70; and A.L. Springer, *The International Law of Pollution* (Westport: Quorum Books, 1983) at 133–4.

[6] L.E.F. Goldie, 'Concepts of Strict and Absolute Liability and Ranking of Liability in Terms of Relative Exposure to Risk' (1985) 16 Netherlands Y.B. Int'l L. 174at 175.

[7] In this chapter, the words 'harm' and 'damage' are used interchangeably.

not covered by the ILC Responsibility Articles, since it was seen to belong to the realm of primary, rather than secondary, rules.[8] In *Trail Smelter*, the Arbitral Tribunal recognized only economic harm. Yet the contemporary concept of harm arguably encompasses not only injury to persons and property, but also to the intrinsic value of the environment, including individual components and whole ecosystems.[9] However, defining and evaluating purely ecological harm is complex and has remained controversial, as is evidenced by the problems that have arisen in this respect in national laws. Moreover, an additional problem arises in international law as it is unclear which entity, if any, would be entitled to claim for harm to common spaces—that is, areas beyond national jurisdiction. A further issue concerns the threshold of harm—that is, the level at which transboundary harm becomes impermissible or, in the terminology of the law of state responsibility, 'wrongful'. This question is not settled. While the *Trail Smelter* case set the threshold of harm at a 'serious' level, Principles 21 and 2 of the Stockholm and Rio Declarations do not include any references to a threshold of harm. In turn, the treaty-based formulations that do exist differ from each other in this regard. For example, the 1997 United Nations Convention on the Law of Non-Navigational Uses of International Watercourses and the ILC draft Convention on the Prevention of Transboundary Harm appear to lower the threshold of harm to 'significant', which is defined by commentaries to these instruments as 'not necessarily substantial but more than trivial.' In short, the ambiguities in the threshold of harm contribute to the general confusion regarding the workings of the law of state responsibility in relation to the environment.

3 STATE RESPONSIBILITY (OBLIGATIONS OF STATES UNDER SECONDARY RULES)

3.1 General Framework of the Law of State Responsibility— *Chorzów Factory* Case

The general principles of state responsibility are applicable in the context of the breach of environmental law norms. These general principles can be traced back to

---

[8] J. Crawford, *International Law Commission, First Report on State Responsibility*, UN Doc. A/CN.4/490/Add.4 (1998) at para.117.

[9] See Birnie and Boyle, note 3 above at 12–4; and A. Boyle, 'Reparation for Environmental Damage in International Law: Some Preliminary Problems,' in M. Bowman and A. Boyle, eds., *Environmental Damage in International and Comparative Law* (Oxford: Oxford University Press, 2002) 17. See generally on the legacy of *Trail Smelter* Arbitration, R. Bratspies and R. Miller, eds., *Transboundary Harm in International Law, Lessons from Trail Smelter Arbitration* (Cambridge: Cambridge University Press, 2006).

the judgment in the *Chorzów Factory* case, according to which an illegal act (or omission) requires reparation.[10] This requirement is further developed in the following statement of the court:

'The essential principle contained in the actual notion of an illegal act is that reparation must, as far as possible, wipe out all the consequences of the illegal act and re-establish the situation which would in all probability have existed if that act had not been committed. Restitution in kind, or if that is not possible, payment of a sum corresponding to the value which restitution in kind would bear; the award if need be of damages for loss sustained which would not be covered by restitution in kind or payment in place of it—such are the principles which serve to determine the amount of compensation for an act contrary to international law.'

3.2 Introduction to the Work of the ILC on State Responsibility

'State responsibility' was one of the original topics that the ILC was charged to codify when it was set up in 1948. Work on this topic started in 1956 and, originally, was limited to the narrow topic of diplomatic protection (though within this limited topic, the ILC's initial work addressed both primary and secondary rules). However, it was soon decided that the work on state responsibility should cover a much wider range of international obligations. At this stage, it became apparent that it would in fact be impossible to codify rules relating to the content of international obligations generally ('primary rules'), due to their infinitely varying nature. It was therefore decided to limit the work to secondary rules, and this work started in 1963 and led, in 2001, to the adoption of 59 ILC Articles on Responsibility of States for Internationally Wrongful Acts (ILC Responsibility Articles). These articles concentrate on the 'framework or matrix of rules of state responsibility identifying whether there has been a breach by a State and what were its consequences'[11]—that is, on secondary rules.

The ILC Responsibility Articles on state responsibility are 'rigorously general in . . . character.'[12] As one commentary has noted, they apply to 'all types of international obligations regardless of their source, subject matter, or importance to the international community. They apply to both acts and omissions, to treaty obligations and customary norms, to breaches of bilateral as well as multilateral obligations, and the whole gamut of particular subject areas—human rights law, environmental law, humanitarian law, economic law, the law of the sea, and so forth.'[13] As a result of their generality, the secondary rules of state responsibility can be articulated independently of the primary rules of obligation.

---

[10] *Case Concerning Factory at Chorzów (Claim for Indemnity)*, 1928 P.C.I.J. (ser. A) No. 17.
[11] Crawford, see note 1 above at 2.   [12] *Ibid.* at 12.
[13] D. Bodansky and J.R. Crook 'The ILC's State Responsibility Articles' (2002) 96 A.J.I.L. 773 at 779–80.

3.3 Main Elements of the ILC's Approach to State Responsibility

In the codification of these secondary rules, the ILC adopted the following broad approach. In Part 1 of the articles, it envisaged, as the necessary basis to trigger state responsibility, the commission of an internationally wrongful act by a state—an act or omission that is attributable to a state under international law and that constitutes a breach of an international obligation (Article 2). Such an internationally wrongful act entails the international responsibility of a state (Article 1). Chapter 5 of Part 1 identifies circumstances that preclude a finding of wrongfulness. These circumstances include *force majeure*, distress, necessity, compliance with peremptory norms, self-defence, consent of the state against which an otherwise wrongful act has been committed, and the fact that the wrongful act constituted a countermeasure in response to a prior breach of international law (Articles 20–7).

Part 2 of the Articles deals with what is referred to as the 'content of the international responsibility of a State,' which, broadly speaking, refers to the issue of remedies. These remedies are defined in general terms as reparation for injury, which can be accomplished in a number of ways, including restitution, compensation, and satisfaction. The final Part 3 of the Articles deals with the implementation of the international responsibility of a state. This part includes, first, rules on the 'invocation' of responsibility. As will be discussed in more detail later in this chapter, while an 'injured State' (Article 42) may always invoke the responsibility of another for a breach of international law, the articles also outline certain circumstances under which other states may invoke that responsibility (Article 48). Further, this part fleshes out the concept of countermeasures, by which is meant actions taken by an injured state against the state that is responsible for an internationally wrongful act in order to induce that state to comply with its obligations under Part 2 (Article 49).

Unfortunately, at this stage in the development of international environmental law, once one looks beyond stating the general principle that breaches of international law incur state responsibility, one encounters numerous problems. First of all, environmental treaties, to the extent that they address the issue, employ very different definitions of 'environment'. Moreover, the content of many of the fundamental primary environmental rules remains vague and subject to significant disagreement between states (such as, for example, in the cases of the precautionary principle, sustainable development, and intergenerational equity) (see Chapter 25 'Precaution'; Chapter 26 'Sustainable Development'; and Chapter 27 'Equity'). Case law, which might help address the difficulties concerning the primary norms in the field, is scant. There are also further questions, specific to environmental law, that put in doubt the usefulness of the application of the general law of state responsibility. One such problem, to be discussed further in section 3.5 in this chapter, is the standing of states to invoke responsibility of other states in the case of breach of obligations owed *erga omnes* (to the whole community of states) and *erga omnes partes* (owed to the parties of a multilateral treaty).

3.4 Reparation

The ILC draft Article 31 articulates a single system of reparation, which applies to all of international law, including environmental law: '1. the responsible State is under an obligation to make full reparation for the injury caused by the internationally wrongful act. 2. Injury includes any damage, whether material or moral, caused by the internationally wrongful act of a State.' The forms of reparation envisaged by the law of state responsibility are restitution, compensation, and satisfaction, 'either singly or in combination' (Article 34). Article 35 on restitution describes it as the re-establishment of the situation that existed before the wrongful act was committed, unless restitution is materially impossible or involves a burden out of all proportion to the benefit deriving from restitution instead of compensation. Article 36 on compensation describes the obligation to compensate for the damage, 'insofar as such damage is not made good by restitution.' Compensation will cover any financially assessable damage, including loss of profits, insofar as it is established. Satisfaction is the form of reparation that is employed when restitution or compensation cannot be used. It may take the form of an acknowledgment of the breach, an expression of regret, or a formal apology (Article 37).

In practice, a number of hurdles stand in the way of reparation for environmental harm. The first and fundamental problem is, again, the question of the content of the primary rule. Aside from the previously mentioned concerns, to the extent that the scope of international environmental protection requirements remains uncertain, some environmental harm may simply fall outside the realm of what states can be held legally responsible for.[14] For example, beyond the prohibition of transboundary damage, what is the scope of obligations to protect global commons or to protect ecosystems? In addition, cases involving environmental harm often raise particularly complicated causation questions. The general standard provided by the ILC Responsibility Articles may not prove too helpful in this context. The ILC commentary to the articles simply describes the link that must exist between the wrongful act and the injury in order for state responsibility to arise as a sufficient causal link, which is not too remote.[15]

The main forms of reparation—restitution and compensation—raise specific kinds of difficulties in the environmental context. Article 35 on restitution focuses on the restoration of the *status quo ante*.[16] In principle, the utility of restitution to remedy environmental harm should be obvious. It may also avoid some controversies, as it relates to restoration of a pre-existing factual situation, which does not involve the

---

[14] See note 9 above at 21–2.   [15] Crawford, see note 1 above at 295.   [16] *Ibid.* at 213.

complex valuation questions associated with compensation. However, in some cases, environmental harms are irreversible, and, hence, restitution will be impossible. In other cases, restitution may be possible but will entail unreasonable burdens. As a result, restitution may not always be an option or may have to be complemented by compensation to ensure full reparation.

It is generally agreed that compensation is due only for established 'financially assessable damage', including environmental harm. Indeed, the UN Compensation Commission assessed Iraq's liability for environmental damage and the depletion of natural resources. The ILC certainly considered environmental harm to fall into this category, as the commentary to the ILC Responsibility Articles suggests by singling out pollution as one of the areas in which states may seek compensation for harm suffered. As the ILC also observed in its commentary to the articles, generally in the practice of states, when compensation has been awarded, payments have been made to reimburse the injured state for expenses reasonably incurred in preventing or remedying pollution or compensating for the diminished value of polluted property. Therefore, as the law stands at present, compensation will include clean-up costs and property devaluation. The ILC acknowledged, however, that actual damage would often extend to such environmental values as biodiversity, amenity, so-called 'non-use' values, which are, 'as a matter of principle, no less real and compensable than damage to a property, though [they] may be difficult to quantify.'[17] Similarly, it is unclear whether notional or non-market based value to depleted resources would be covered under the formulation of 'financially assessable damage.'[18]

Finally, there are also other forms of non-quantifiable, non-individual harm to the environment, which cannot be remedied based on available methods of reparation. The ILC Rapporteur singled out as such the release of chlorofluorocarbons (CFCs) or other ozone-depleting substances causing environmental harm. Arguably, these kinds of diffuse wide-spread releases can only be addressed by special treaty regimes, which not only allocate risk but also introduce standards of conduct for the parties.[19]

The above considerations indicate that the general legal framework of the law of state responsibility is relevant to the reparation for environmental harm that can be evaluated on a traditional basis. International practice confirms that compensation for environmental harm encompasses restoration, clean-up costs, and harm to persons and private property. However, other elements that one may see as encompassed in the notion of environmental harm, such as the loss of biological diversity, wild fauna and flora, or ecosystems, escape the classical structure of reparation under the law of state responsibility. Therefore, when neither restitution nor compensation can be resorted to, satisfaction is the only remaining means of reparation for the injured state to rely on.

---

[17] *Ibid.* at 223.   [18] Birnie and Boyle, see note 3 above at 24.
[19] Crawford, see note 1 above at para. 118.

In sum, the value of the law of state responsibility in cases of transboundary harm currently is limited. There is no certainty as to the applicable standard of fault. And even if claims for compensation are limited to 'financially assessable damage', the interpretation of this phrase has yet to take full account of the particular demands of environmental valuation. This suggests not that we abandon the goal of compensating for environmental loss but, instead, that we focus on methods of valuation and on overcoming the objection that something that is not necessarily 'property' and that has no 'market value' has no 'financial or economic worth'.[20]

3.5 State Responsibility and the Multilateralism of Environmental Obligations

One of the problems of the law on state responsibility has been how to overcome the classical bilateralism of the duty/right paradigm[21] and how to reflect the features of the many environmental obligations that have as a goal the protection of the common interest. Concerns regarding certain common areas or systems, such as the ozone layer, the climate system, or the high seas are good examples of common interests that should be protected. However, there may not be an obvious injured state when environmental harm is caused in these cases. The classical bilateral approach to international obligations flows from a particular concept of 'injury', which is rooted in a legal interest.[22] It may be relevant to observe that both climate change (although with respect to climate change, there are likely to be at least some injured states, such as small island states) and biological diversity have been defined as having the character of 'common concern', and deep-seabed mining together with outer space as having the character of the common heritage of humankind. Such concepts presuppose a 'legitimate interest' of the international community as a whole (see Chapter 23 'Common Areas, Common Heritage, and Common Concern'). The concept of obligations *erga omnes* may help address these types of issues. It relates to concerns in the protection of which all states have a legal interest.[23] However, many aspects of the legal character of *erga omnes* obligations are still arguable, and the concept 'is frequently invoked for more that it can bear.'[24] In 1974, the ICJ did not address the

---

[20] Boyle, see note 9 above at 25–6.

[21] J. Crawford, *Third Report on State Responsibility*, UN Doc. A/CN.4 (507) (2000) at 43, para. 96.

[22] *South West Africa Cases (Ethiopia/South Africa; Liberia/South Africa)*, Judgment of 18 July 1966, [1966] I.C.J. Rep. 20 at 20–3.

[23] *Barcelona Traction, Light and Power Company, Limited (Belgium/Spain)*, (Second Phase), Judgement of 5 February 1970, [1970] I.C.J. Rep. 32 at para. 33 [*Barcelona Traction*]; see also *Advisory Opinion* on *Legal Consequences of the Construction of a Wall in the Occupied Palestinian Territory*, Judgment of 9 July 2004, [2004] I.C.J. Rep. 9 at paras. 154–9 and dispositif subpara. 3(d).

[24] *Barcelona Traction*, see note 23 above, Judge Higgins's separate opinion, para. 37; see also paras. 38–9.

legal possibility of an *actio popularis* by any state to enforce common environmental interests.[25]

Important changes were introduced by Articles 42 and 48 of the ILC Responsibility Articles, which manage in many respects to capture the expanding multilateralism of contemporary legal obligations. Even considering that Article 48 probably represents, at least in part, progressive development rather than existing customary law, it constitutes an important development.[26] It has been met, however, with a certain degree of scepticism by states.

Article 42, which stipulates when a state can invoke the responsibility of another, rests on the concept of directly injured states. Article 42 applies not only to bilateral obligations, but also to collective obligations owed to the international community (*erga omnes*) or to a group of treaty parties (*erga omnes partes*). However, only when it is directly affected can a state invoke the responsibilities of another for violations of such obligations. Article 48 does suggest a way forward for third states wishing to redress breaches of obligations of public interest, irrespective of direct injury to them. It encompasses *erga omnes* obligations flowing from custom and obligations deriving from the multilateral environmental regimes that have been set up, for example, by the treaties on climate change and biodiversity, in the implementation and maintenance of which all parties have a common legal interest (obligations *erga omnes partes*).[27] In fact, given the current state of customary law, collective obligations are almost entirely found in treaties. However, even when third states have standing under Article 48, they have only a very limited right to seek reparations and to adopt countermeasures in the event of the breach of community obligations. It appears that third states only have the right to seek cessation and assurances and guarantees of non-repetition of any breach of an obligation owed to the international community (Article 48). The law of countermeasures is also very limited. The adoption of countermeasures is only allowed on behalf of an injured state, and, in the case of 'victimless' breach, their use is altogether banned (Article 54).[28]

The unclear character of obligations *erga omnes* and, to a certain extent, *erga omnes partes*, coupled with the problems relating to reparations and countermeasures in cases of a breach of the obligations owed to the community of states, suggest the need for other more effective systems of ensuring compliance with such obligations. It appears that, at least in cases of obligations *erga omnes partes*, such a solution may be provided by treaty-based compliance mechanisms. Despite the promise of Article 48 of the ILC Responsibility Articles, the articles' basic framework has not overcome the classical bilateralism of the redress of harm between states. The institutions of reparation and countermeasures traditionally rely on the bilateral relations of states.

---

[25] *Nuclear Tests Cases (Australia v. France, New Zealand v. France)*, Judgment of 20 December 1974, [1974] I.C.J. Rep. 253 at 387.

[26] J. Peel, 'New State Responsibility and Compliance with Multilateral Obligations: Some Case Studies of How New Rules Might Apply in the International Context' (2001) 10 R.E.C.I.E.L. 82.

[27] Crawford, see note 1 above at para. 106(a).   [28] Peel, see note 26 above.

Additionally, the general procedural requirements that standing before international courts requires consent and a well-defined legal interest preclude the submission of a claim of state responsibility in cases of 'victimless' harms to the global commons.

4 Development of Primary Rules of State Liability—Liability for Injurious Consequences of Acts Not Prohibited by International Law

It was thought that the customary law standard of due diligence, without a clear normative content and requiring a complicated burden of proof, was not adequate to cover ultra-hazardous activities, such as those emanating from a nuclear power plant. These considerations prompted the International Law Commission to begin work in 1978 on the Articles on Liability for Injurious Consequences of Acts Not Prohibited by International Law.[29] This regime was to be based on a standard of strict liability for activities involving risk of significant transboundary harm, which either is unforeseeable or, if foreseeable, is unpreventable even if a state takes due care.

The conceptual premise of this regime was the lack of wrongfulness on the part of the state conducting the activity or under the jurisdiction of which the relevant activities occurred. Therefore, the ILC sought to propound liability rules that would apply without a previous finding of responsibility for a wrongful act or omission. The conceptual basis is that certain activities are justified from a cost-benefit standpoint and should not be prohibited. However, if they cause injury, both the polluter pays principle and the notion of compensatory justice suggests the need for compensation by the state causing the injury to the state suffering the harm.[30] This approach resulted in the separation of the liability topic from that of state responsibility—an approach that was seen by many to be 'fundamentally misconceived'.[31] The key complaint of the critics was that in the law of state responsibility, the issue is not whether the relevant activity as such is unlawful but whether the home state fulfils its due diligence duty to avoid causing transboundary harm.[32]

---

[29] J. Brunnée, 'On Sense and Sensibility: Reflections on International Liability Regime' (2004) 53 Int'l & Comp. L.Q. 351.

[30] This notion is included in legal principles and recommendation adopted by the Brundtland Commission Experts Group on Environmental Law of the World Commission on Environment and Development, Summary of Principles in Annex 1 to *Our Common Future* (Oxford: Oxford University Press, 1987).

[31] See, e.g., A. Boyle, 'State Responsibility and Liability for Injurious Consequences of Acts Not Prohibited by International Law: A Necessary Distinction?' (1990) 39 Int'l & Comp. L.Q. 1.   [32] *Ibid.*

Finally, following sustained criticism of several drafts, the ILC decided to further divide the liability topic into a part on the prevention of transboundary harm from hazardous activities and a part on liability for injurious consequences. The liability part is focused on the legal regime for allocation of loss from transboundary harm arising out of hazardous activities, on which two reports have been thus far submitted. It has now been reoriented to focus on civil, rather than state, liability. The first (prevention) part was completed in 2001 with the adoption of the draft convention on the primary obligation of states concerning harm prevention. The draft convention outlines primary rules of conduct aimed at preventing or minimizing the risk of significant transboundary harm (Articles 1 and 3). In other words, the fundamental premise underlying the draft convention is the need for management of risk and cooperation and consultation between states. Harm is defined broadly as losses to persons, property, and the environment, although there is no definition of what encompasses the environment. The commentary to the draft convention explains that risk of causing significant harm refers to a combined effect of the probability of occurrence of an accident and the magnitude of its injurious impact.[33]

In keeping with what the ILC considered to be the basic standard of international environmental law, the level of care incorporated in the duty of prevention is that of due diligence. It encompasses the adoption of all appropriate measures for the prevention of significant transboundary harm by the state of origin (Article 3).[34] The draft convention affirms a number of important procedural obligations between states, which have to contribute to the avoidance of significant transboundary harm: cooperation (Article 4); notification and information (Article 8); consultation on preventive measures (Article 9); and exchange of information (Article 12).

The draft convention is animated by a principle of the equitable balancing of interests, which emphasizes consultations between states to find the best possible solution regarding measures to be adopted in order to prevent significant transboundary harm or minimize the risk thereof (Article 9(2)). Article 10 provides a non-exhaustive list of factors to be taken into account in order to achieve an equitable solution. It is worth noting that the principle of equitable balancing of interests has long played a pivotal role in the context of the transboundary management of certain types of resources, notably freshwater resources. In the draft convention, the principle relates to the adoption of equitable measures for harm prevention, which places the balancing of interests in a totally different context. The interests of all involved states have to be considered, therefore departing from traditional bilateralism of international environmental law.

Another important feature of the draft convention is that it builds on existing international customary law, notably the no harm rule derived from the *Trail Smelter Arbitration*. By contrast, the previous liability drafts of the ILC had been attempts to promote progressive development of international law. The draft convention

---

[33] *ILC Report on Fifty-Third Session*, see note 1 above at 387.   [34] *Ibid.* at 392.

clarifies the content of environmental procedural rules and, most importantly, confirms the duty of due diligence as the standard underlying international environmental obligations.

5 CIVIL LIABILITY REGIMES

5.1 Introduction

Given the difficulties inherent in establishing the direct liability of states in relation to environmental damage under the state responsibility or liability regimes, an alternative system has been developed based on civil liability regimes. These regimes recognize the competence of national courts, either in the state where the damage was caused or in the state of nationality of the polluter, to decide cases regarding the liability of the actual parties causing damage outside the state in which they are based. Such decisions thereby become enforceable in other states parties to the agreement. This system has been used to address a number of objectives, largely aimed at remedying shortcomings in the system of state responsibility or liability. Thus, first, the system has been perceived as embodying the polluter pays principle, although as will be seen later in this chapter, it does not do so in a completely pure form. Second, the system has been used to establish a principle of absolute liability with respect to ultrahazardous activities. Third, it has been used, particularly through recent protocols to existing civil liability regimes, to clarify the inclusion of environmental damage as a head of claim. Fourth, the system is used to establish liability for economically beneficial activities that involve certain risks even when performed with due care, such as the maritime transportation of oil and other hazardous cargo and nuclear activities.[35]

Civil liability regimes arose, initially, in relation to particular forms of ultrahazardous activity, notably in regimes relating to nuclear activities and to oil pollution by ships. In fact, these two regimes (both of which are described in more detail later in this chapter) remain the most significant examples of civil liability regimes. However, the concept has been introduced on a wider basis in the meantime. Thus, states started to include civil liability regimes as a part of more general regimes set up under MEAs—for instance, the 1999 Basel Protocol on Liability and Compensation for Damage Resulting from Transboundary Movements of Hazardous Wastes and Their Disposal (Basel Liability Protocol) to the 1989 Basel Convention on the Control of Transboundary Movements of Hazardous Wastes and Their Disposal (Basel Convention). The recent International Maritime

---

[35] T. Gehring and M. Jachtenfuchs, 'Liability for Transboundary Environmental Damage: Towards a General Liability Regime?' (1993) 4 Eur. J. Int'l L. 92 at 93 and 94; L. A. de la Fayette, 'New Approaches for Addressing Damage to the Marine Environment,' (2005) 2 J.M.C.L. 167.

Organization (IMO) conventions—namely, the 1996 International Convention on Liability and Compensation of Hazardous and Noxious Substances by Sea (HNS Convention) and the 2001 International Convention on Civil Liability for Bunker Oil Pollution Damage—evidence the trend of the expanding number of (at least sectoral) civil liability regimes, which, however, as observed below are fraught with difficulties. As noted earlier, the ILC is still working on the Liability for Injurious Consequences of Acts Not Prohibited by International Law project, in which the focus has been switched from state to civil liability.

There are a number of common features of the nuclear and oil pollution civil liability regimes that may now be said to be typical of civil liability regimes, as they are largely reproduced in MEA-based civil liability regimes. These features include the strict liability of the operator; the limitation of this liability at a certain ceiling; and mandatory insurance or other form of financial security to cover the liability of the operator. Further, given that these liability ceilings may not be sufficient to cover the damage suffered by injured parties, the regimes have introduced (usually by supplementary convention) additional tiers of compensation. In relation to nuclear liability, this additional tier is funded by the states themselves and, in the case of oil pollution, by the oil industry. Another common feature is that the nuclear and oil pollution regimes recognize harm to the environment, primarily in the guise of costs of reinstatement of the affected environment.

There are also several inherent problems with civil liability regimes, which render them unsuitable for certain types of environmental damage. Problems arise, in particular, when there are difficulties in establishing a causal link between the damage, the activity, and the defendant, as in global climate change, ozone depletion, transboundary air pollution, and marine pollution, in relation to diffuse sources of harm from land-based pollution.[36]

5.2 Nuclear Liability

The civil liability regimes in relation to damage resulting from the peaceful use of nuclear energy are structurally very similar to those that deal with oil pollution damage. Some of the difficulties with these regimes stem from the fact that, since the early 1960s, two separate major regimes have co-existed. The first one came into existence under the auspices of the International Atomic Energy Agency (IAEA) (the 1963 Vienna Convention on Civil Liability for Nuclear Damage), and the second under the Organisation for Economic Co-operation and Development (OECD), and was set up by the 1960 Convention on Third Party Liability in the Field of Nuclear Energy (Paris Convention) and the 1963 Brussels Supplementary Convention. The new

---

[36] R. Churchill, 'Facilitating (Transnational) Civil Liability Litigation for Environmental Damage by Means of Treaties: Progress, Problems, and Problems' (2001) 12 Y.B. Int'l Envt'l L. 3 at 41.

regime set under the Vienna Convention was directed at worldwide participation. The parties to the Paris and Brussels Conventions are basically OECD members.Both these conventions were amended by the 1964 Additional Protocol and 1982 Protocol.

In 1988, a Joint Protocol Relating to the Application of the Vienna Convention and the Paris Convention (Joint Protocol) was adopted. The Joint Protocol established a link between the conventions, combining them in effect into one expanded liability regime. Parties to the Joint Protocol are treated as though they are parties to both conventions and a choice of law rule is provided to determine which of the two conventions should apply to the exclusion of the other in respect of the same incident. In 1997, the Protocol to Amend the Vienna Convention (in force in 2002) and the Convention on Supplementary Compensation for Nuclear Damage were adopted (not in force). In 2004, the parties to the OECD Paris and Brussels Conventions signed the Amending Protocol (not in force), which brought the Paris Convention more in line with the IAEA 1997 conventions. The amendments are aimed at the provision of compensation for more people for a broader scope of nuclear damage to include environmental damage and economic costs. They also shifted more of the burden of insurance onto industry and extended the definition of nuclear damage to include environmental damage and economic costs. The scope of application is also broadened. The definition of nuclear damage also contains the costs of measures to reinstate a sigificantly impaired environment, and the cost of preventive measures. Additionally, the geographical scope of the Paris Convention has been expanded.

The Paris Convention set a maximum liability of 15 million Special Drawing Rights—SDR (about €18 million), but this was increased under the Brussels Supplementary Convention up to a total of 300 million SDR (about €360 million), including contributions by the installation State up to 175 million SDR (€210 million) and other parties to the convention collectively on the basis of their installed nuclear capacity for the balance. The most important features of the revised Paris Convention, as amended by the 2004 Protocol include an increase in the nuclear operator's liability amount to a new minimum of €700 million. In addition, the minimum liability amount applicable to low-risk installations and transport activities will climb to €70 million and €80 million respectively.

The most important feature of the revised Brussels Supplementary Convention is a substantial increase in the three tiers of compensation under the convention. The first tier, corresponding to the minimum liability requirement under the Paris Convention, jumps to €700 million and continues to be provided by the operator's financial security, failing which it must be provided by the installation state from public funds.

The second tier climbs to a new high of €500 million and continues to be provided from public funds made available by the installation state. The third tier (international) rises to €300 million and continue to come from public funds provided by all contracting parties. Total compensation available under the revised Paris-Brussels regime is now €1.5 billion, compared to the previous amount of €300 million IMF Special Drawing Rights (approximately €350 million).

Amended by the 1997 Protocol, the 1963 Vienna Convention sets the possible limit of the operator's liability at not less than 300 million SDR (about €360 million). The Convention on Supplementary Compensation for Nuclear Damage defines additional amounts to be provided through contributions by states parties collectively on the basis of installed nuclear capacity and a UN rate of assessment, basically at 300 SDRs per MW thermal (that is, about €360 million total).

The liability regimes were motivated by the recognition that, while the nuclear industry required encouragement for development, nuclear activity involves risks of serious accidents. Against this background, the core foundations of the conventions are the same: liability is absolute—no proof of fault or negligence is necessary (only a few exceptions are allowed); liability is channelled exclusively to the operator— either a state or a private party of the nuclear installation or a ship (in certain cases, a carrier or a handler of nuclear material may be treated as an operator); limitations may be placed on total duration or amount of liability; and payment up to the set limit of liability is supported by compulsory insurance or security held by the operator and guaranteed by the state of installation or registry. Under the Vienna Convention, the upper ceiling is not fixed, but it may be limited by the legislation of each state.

Recognizing that the amount for which the operator can be liable may not be sufficient to cover the damage suffered by injured parties, the Paris and Vienna Conventions provide for additional funds under supplementary conventions. This provision for payment of damages over and above the limited liability of the operator can be seen as compromising the polluter pays principle, notably because the additional payments are funded by the state.

The practical significance of the nuclear liability regime, however, may be questioned because major nuclear powers remain non-parties, such as the United States, Canada, South Korea, and Japan. Furthermore, some non-nuclear states did not ratify these conventions because they considered that victims might be able to obtain higher compensation under national laws than that provided by the conventions.[37] States with a majority of the world's 440 nuclear power reactors are not parties to any nuclear liability conventions. Moreover, and probably related to these facts, neither convention has ever been the basis for a claim.[38]

5.3 Liability for Oil Pollution

Oil pollution damage is covered by an extensive number of conventions, adopted under the auspices of the IMO: the 1969 International Convention on Civil Liability for Oil Pollution Damage, as amended by the 1992 protocol (CLC Convention), which was a result of the *Torrey Canyon* catastrophe. Final amendments were

[37] *Ibid.* at 10. The Russian Federation ratified the 1963 Vienna Convention in 2005.
[38] *Ibid.* at 9 and 10.

adopted in 2000 (amendments in force), including to the 1971 International Convention on the Establishment of an International Fund for Compensation for Oil Pollution Damage, as amended in 1992 (Oil Fund Convention) and again in 2000. The 2000 amendment raised the maximum amount of compensation payable by the fund for a single incident, including the limit established under the 2000 CLC Convention amendments, to 203 million special drawing rights (SDR) (US $260 million), up from 135 million SDR (US $173 million).[39]

The amended conventions are widely used, and compensation of many hundred of millions of US dollars has been paid under them. The 1992 CLC Convention is based on the strict liability of the ship owner. However, ship owners can exonerate themselves if they prove that the loss resulted from war, hostilities, insurrection, civil war, natural phenomena, such as hurricanes that are of an exceptional character or persistence, or was wholly caused intentionally by a third party or by the negligence of those responsible for navigational aids (Article 3).

The oil pollution liability regime was originally based on a two-tier system in which the owner of the tanker that caused the spill is strictly liable for the payment of compensation under the first tier, up to a maximum amount. The tanker owner is required to hold requisite insurance coverage, in which the source of money is provided by the Protection and Indemnity Clubs (P&I Clubs). The second tier, which covers liability above the ceiling on the liability of the owner under the first tier, is paid out of a supplementary fund set up by the Oil Fund Convention. The fund is made up of contributions from persons who receive oil by sea in contracting states. The concerns regarding the impact of liability limits and two-tiered compensation systems on the implementation of the polluter pays principle in the nuclear liability context do not apply with quite the same force in the oil pollution context. Since the additional payments are funded by the oil industry, it is possible to view the approach as providing 'a very wide definition of the polluter in the case of an accident to an individual ship,'[40] by extending the definition of a polluter from the actual individual operator to the industry as a whole.

In May 2003, a new protocol establishing a Supplementary Fund for Oil Pollution Damage was adopted (in force 2005), which introduced a third tier of compensation for oil pollution damage—the aim of which is to supplement the compensation available under the 1992 CLC and Oil Fund Conventions with an additional third tier of compensation. The protocol is optional and participation is open to all states parties to the 1992 Oil Fund Convention. Annual contributions to the fund will be made in respect of each contracting state by any person who, in any calendar year, has received total quantities of oil exceeding 150,000 tons.

---

[39] However, only if three states contributing to the fund receive more than 600 million tonnes of oil per annum. The maximum amount is still raised to 300.740 million special drawing rights (SDR) (US $386 million), up from 200 million SDR (US $256 million). It entered into force in 2003.

[40] Churchill, see note 36 above at 40.

The Supplementary Fund has available an amount of about £436 million (US$ 845 million), in addition to the amount of around £162 million (US$ 314 million) which is available in the present 1992 Fund after the increase which took effect on 1 November 2003. As a result, the total amount available for compensation for each incident in the states which are members of the Supplementary Fund is approximately £597 million (US$ 1, 159 million). The Supplementary Fund only covers incidents which occur after the entry into force of the protocol. One of the effects of the protocol will be the possibility of the payment of the compensation at 100 per cent of the amount of the damage agreed between the Fund and the victim in almost all cases. It will also avoid the need to fix the level of payment below 100 per cent of the amount of the damage suffered during the early stages of most major incidents as has been the case in respect of several recent incidents.

The conventions cover oil pollution damage that occurs in the territory, territorial waters, and the exclusive economic zone of a state party. An important factor of a successful claim is a uniform interpretation of the definitions and common understanding of what constitutes an admissible claim. The governments of the member states of the 1992 Oil Fund Convention have established policies and guidelines with a certain degree of flexibility.[41] Claims in respect of pollution damage can fall under the following broad categories: preventive measures (including clean-up); damage to property; economic losses; and reinstatement/restoration of impaired environment. Of these, claims for preventive measures are the most complicated. The problem is the interpretation of 'reasonableness' of measures adopted by a government or a public body. What constitutes reasonable measures must be decided in each case, and the reasonableness of a measure is difficult to determine in the absence of any clear-cut interpretation. Thus, compensation for clean-up operations always constitutes a problem.

Spills may cause economic loss, such as an impairment of fishing activity or a reduction in tourism, and such loss may be consequential (that is, the direct result of physical damage to a claimant's property) or purely economic (that is, where the claimant did not suffer any damage to his own property but cannot conduct normal economic activities). The validity of the second type of claim is unclear, and it would seem that the only admissible type of claim is one involving loss or damage caused by oil contamination. Therefore, the starting point is the pollution not the incident itself. Thus in order to qualify for compensation, there must be a reasonable degree of geographic and economic proximity between contamination and the loss or damage sustained by a claimant.

Reasonable reinstatement measures are aimed at enhancing the speed of natural recovery of an environment impaired by an oil spill. There are a number of criteria to

---

[41] *Oil Spill Compensation, A Guide to the International Conventions on Liability* (London: International Petroleum Industry Environmental Conservation Association and International Tanker Owners Pollution Federation Limited, 2004).

be fulfilled for such costs to be admissible. These criteria are aimed at demonstrating that the measures were technically justified, and were likely to enhance significantly the natural process of recovery, and that the costs were reasonable and not out of proportion to the extent or duration of the damage and the benefits likely to be achieved. Compensation is payable only for reasonable measures that are actually adopted or to be adopted and only when a claimant has sustained an economic loss that can be quantified in monetary terms. Claims based on abstract quantification calculated according to theoretical models or claims of a punitive nature designed to punish a polluter are inadmissible.[42]

Although, the oil civil liability regimes have proved to be a useful tool in obtaining compensation in a large number of cases, it may be said that there are a number of problems that may arise in relation to them, such as the lack of certainty as to the precise, fixed, and objective definition of damage, which is re-defined by the court in each case, depending on the particular circumstances of a case; the difficulties relating to the interpretation of 'reasonableness'; the only partial implementation of the polluter pays principle (encompassing, at present, operators as well as persons who receive oil and, in the case of nuclear liability, the state); the high burden of proof; and often lengthy litigation.

5.4 General MEAs Setting Up Civil Liability Regimes

Attempts to set up general civil liability regimes under MEAs were seen as one way to overcome the problems inherent in the paradigm of state responsibility for transboundary environmental harm. While there are now several such regimes adopted or under development, the focus in this chapter will be on the 1999 Liability Protocol to the Basel Convention, which (though it is not yet in force) typifies such regimes and allows us to highlight the challenges involved in their establishment.

The drafting of the Basel Liability Protocol was completed after six years of protracted negotiations. Its aim is to set up 'a compensation regime for liability and for adequate and prompt compensation for damage' deriving from the transboundary movement and disposal of hazardous wastes (Article 1). Article 6 imposes a duty to notify other states concerned of the proposed transboundary movement of hazardous wastes. The whole process of exporting such wastes is very complicated, therefore, there may be many different parties liable. However, the protocol identifies as the party usually liable the actual exporter, who is strictly liable, albeit only up to a certain limit (Article 12 and Annex B). The protocol also imposes time limits on making claims of ten years from the date of the incident, and of five years from the date when the claimant knew, or ought reasonably to have known, of the damage (Article 13).

---

[42] *Ibid.* at 10–12.

Damage is defined as including loss of life or personal injury; loss or damage to property; loss of income deriving from an economic interest in use of the impaired environment; and costs of certain measures taken to prevent, minimize, or mitigate damage or to effect environmental clean up (Article 2). One of the contentious issues during negotiations was the problem of supplementary payments in the event of damage to the environment exceeding the liability limits set by the protocol. Article 15(1) provides that in such an event any supplementary measures must be covered by existing mechanisms. It is understood that such a mechanism is provided by the Technical Co-operation Trust Fund, established under the Basel Convention and supplied by voluntary contributions. Developing countries, however, were in favour of a separate fund. The Basel Liability Protocol provides for the possibility of liability based on fault in cases of damage caused by non-compliance with the requirements of the Basel Convention or through intentional or negligent conduct (Article 5).

The Basel Liability Protocol demonstrates the complexity of designing viable civil liability regimes and of the issues and interests to be reconciled. The protocol had to take into account the economic interests of industry, including insurance concerns, relating to waste transfer and concerns of transit and recipient countries as to the risk involved in movements of such materials and securing proper compensation. It also had to be acceptable to both developed and developing countries.

5.5 Conclusions on Sectoral and MEA-Based Civil Liability Regimes

If holding states liable for environmental harm is fraught with difficulty, it would appear that civil liability regimes are also not always an adequate or suitable tool for ensuring compensation. Another drawback is that civil liability treaties do not 'provide compensation in the case of damage to non-economic components of the environment (such as fauna or flora not exploited by man) where it is not possible to take measures to restore the environment.'[43] Thus, they do not address the problem of compensating for damage to the environment as such. Practice demonstrates as well that states are very reluctant to ratify liability regimes, and that there is no single system that provides a general pattern that could be applied across the board. In fact, such a solution is impossible, as liability regimes should fit structurally the activity in question. Thus, the one successful liability regime, namely that which is available for oil pollution damage, would not necessarily be a model for other areas. Even this regime is not free from shortcomings, as noted earlier in this chapter, since compensation under this regime is based on reasonableness—a concept that lends itself to many different interpretations. Some states that are parties to the oil liability

---

[43] Churchill, see note 36 above at 34.

regime—for example, France in case of the *Amoco Cadiz* spill—have in the past decided to initiate claims outside the treaty regime in US courts because possible compensation is higher.

In sum, the apparent trend towards the negotiation of liability regimes must be carefully considered in order to avoid wasting precious negotiating resources on regimes that will not prove effective in preventing or compensating environmental damages. Each issue area must be closely scrutinized to determine whether a civil liability regime would be beneficial for redressing environmental damage, as it clearly appears that several environmental fields are not suitable for such regimes.

5.6 Development of a General Regime on Civil Liability— Work of the ILC on a Liability Regime

In 2003, Special Rapporteur Rao submitted the first report on the liability regime. Although the project retains the old title on liability for injurious consequences, it is in fact now becoming a legal regime for the allocation of loss in case of transboundary harm arising out of hazardous activities and focuses only on the issue of civil liability. The main premise of the commission's work will be to develop a model that would be both general and residual in character.[44] The Rapporteur drew several very important conclusions for his future work from the criticism of the previous work of the ILC, which was characterized by a very piecemeal and unfocused approach. In his first report, the Rapporteur presented the main principles on which civil liability and compensation would rest, namely that liability is to be attributed to the person most in control of the activity—that is, the operator who has to take out insurance to cover his liability; that the casual link between the person and the activity should be reasonably traced; and that the limited liability of the operator should be supplemented by additional funding mechanisms. The state should also ensure that means are available within the legal system, in accordance with international standards, for the equitable and expeditious compensation and relief of victims of transboundary harm, since harm to persons and property is compensable. Where actual restoration of the environment or natural resources is impossible, costs incurred to introduce equivalent elements could be reimbursed.[45] It may be noted that the basic points covered in the draft largely follow the format established in the nuclear and oil pollution conventions.

In his second report, Rao presented the views of states on the allocation of loss.[46] Support was given for assigning liability first to the operator, as the main beneficiary

---

[44] Rao, see note 2 above at para. 152.   [45] *Ibid.* at para. 153.

[46] P.S. Rao, *Second Report on the Legal Regime for Allocation of Loss in Case of Transboundary Harm Arising Out of Hazardous Activities*, UN Doc. A/CN.4/540 (21 May 2003).

of the activity and the creator of the risk. An important feature of such a scheme is that it is in line with the polluter pays principle. However, the issue concerning the types of harm eligible for compensation is one of the matters not solved and one that remains in dispute. Both states and the ILC were of the view that harm to persons, property, including the elements of state natural heritage and state patrimony, as well harm to the environment and natural resources within the jurisdiction or control of a state should be covered. Harm to global commons remains a contentious issue. Some of the members of the ILC felt that global commons are sufficiently protected through several conventions, such as the 1982 UN Convention on the Law of the Sea (however, these conventions do not contain rules on liability). Some were of the view that a more integrated approach to the regulation of the global commons should be centred on obligations *erga omnes*. Numerous obstacles were mentioned preventing inclusion of redress of harm to the environment *per se*, such as problems in establishing a causal connection, the standing of parties to sue, and the quantification of harm.[47] In 2004, the the ILC adopted the complete set of draft principles, which differed in certain fundamental aspects from the set proposed by the special rapporteur in his second report. In particular, it changes the principles from hard law to soft law by replacing the imperative 'shall' to the persuasive 'should' in the operative provisions of the draft. Principle 1 as adopted by the ILC confirms that the principles apply to 'damage caused by activities not prohibited by international law which involve a risk of causing significant transboundary harm through their physical consequences.' Thus liability is not absolute as that would be on liability for 'unforseeable damage'.[48]

The difficulties of setting up an efficient and general liability regime are illustrated by the failure to enter into force of the 1993 Council of Europe Convention on Civil Liability for Damage Resulting from Activities Dangerous to the Environment (Lugano Convention), which harmonizes laws on environmental damage but which due to several factors, such as its incorporation of unlimited liability and the existence of a number of sectoral liability treaties, will probably never become binding.

In conclusion, the work of the ILC on civil liability for environmental harm, although conceptually different from the earlier drafts, may still encounter difficulties, which may be summarized as follows: (1) civil liability regimes are not uniform and therefore may make it problematic to set up a general system, such as the 1993 Lugano Convention; (2) the scope and the extent of the role of the state in redress of

---

[47] *Ibid.* at para. 36.

[48] International Law Commission, *Report on the Work of the 56th Session of the ILC 2004*, Supplememnt no. 10, Doc. A/59/10; see, in depth, A. Boyle, 'Globalising Environmental Liability: The Interplay of National and International Law' (2005) 17 J. Envt'l L. 3. On 26 May 2006, the Drafting Committee completed the second reading of the set of draft principles, having taken into account the comments and observations of governments, suggestions by the Special Rapporteur, and the debate in plenary. The draft principles have retained the same title and structure as adopted on first reading (A/CN.4/L.686).

victims is unclear; (3) the scope of compensation for harm is ill-defined and the compensability of the intrinsic value of the environment is questionable, as is the compensability of harm to the global commons; and (4) for environmental harm to be eligible for compensation, there usually must be an anthropocentric element.

6 CONCLUSIONS

The lack of effectiveness of state responsibility as a means of addressing environmental harms results, in part, from the vague and ill-defined nature of the many primary rules of international environmental law. The due diligence requirement that is inherent in many of these primary rules is also not well suited to allowing for compensation of transboundary environmental harm. However, other reasons for the ineffectiveness of state responsibility flow from the outlook and structure of its secondary rules. For example, the goals of state responsibility are not focused directly on promoting compliance with environmental norms. Rather, state responsibility is reactive and aimed at setting up a system of dealing with the consequences of breaches of the norms of international law. It is triggered only by the commission of a wrongful act by a state. In addition, state responsibility may shape the behaviour of states to a certain extent through deterrence. However, by definition, state responsibility has very limited indirect influence, mediated through a state, on the private actors who are primarily responsible for causing pollution.

Efforts have been made to fill at least the latter gaps through the development of various civil liability regimes. It would appear that these regimes were intended as a means both for encouraging environmental protection and for enhancing the chances of pollution victims being compensated. As for the first of these roles, three potential benefits are generally mentioned. First, they can help with the implementation of the polluter pays principle. Second, they play a potential role as an economic instrument, providing incentive for compliance with environmental standards and, thereby, preventing the occurrence of environmental harm. Finally, they are supposed to provide a 'back up' system, which can be activated in the event of the occurrence of environmental harm, notwithstanding the legal framework of the underlying protection regime. Close scrutiny reveals, however, that there is as yet little supporting evidence for these arguments. There is a marked absence internationally and domestically of evidence indicating the effectiveness of either the preventive or incentive functions of strict liability regimes.[49] Sadly, there are no clear indications that they shape the behaviour of the polluter.

---

[49] Brunnée, see note 29 above at 365.

These weaknesses in the responsibility and liability approaches to environmental protection highlight the need for a 'new way'. Given the importance of preventing environmental harm, this new way may lie in the development of compliance regimes that help keep harms from occurring in the first place.

Recommended Reading

B. Baker Röben, 'Civil Liability as a Control Mechanism for Environmental Protection at the International Level,' in F. Morrison and R. Wolfrum, eds., *International, Regional and National Law* (The Hague: Kluwer Law International, 2000) 821.

T. Berwick, 'Responsibility and Liability for Environmental Damage: A Roadmap for International Environmental Regimes' (1998) Georgetown Int'l Envt'l L. Rev. 257.

D. Bodansky and J. Crook, 'Symposium: The ILC's State Responsibility Articles: Introduction and Overview' (2002) 96 A.J.I.L. 773.

M. Bowman and A. Boyle, eds., *Environmental Damage in International Environmental and Comparative Law* (Oxford: Oxford University Press, 2002).

E.H.P. Brans, *Liability for Damage to Public Natural Resources, Standing Damage and Assessment* (The Hague: Kluwer Law International, 2001).

J. Brunnée, 'Of Sense and Sensibility: Reflections on International Liability Regimes as Tools for Environmental Protection' (2004) 53 Int'l & Comp. L.Q. 351.

R. Churchill, 'Facilitating Transnational Civil Liability Litigation for Environmental Damage by Means of Treaties; Progress, Problems, and Prospects' (2001) 13 Y.B. Int'l Envt'l L. 3.

J. Crawford, *The International Law Commission's Articles on State Responsibility: Introduction, Text and Commentaries* (Cambridge: Cambridge University Press, 2002).

T. Gerhing and M. Jachtenfuchs, 'Liability for Transboundary Environmental Damage: Towards the General Liability Regime?' (1993) 4 Eur. J. Int'l L. 92.

P. Okowa, *State Responsibility for Transboundary Air Pollution in International Law* (Oxford: Oxford University Press, 2000).

T. Scovazzi, 'State Responsibility for Environmental Harm' (2001) 13 Y.B. Int'l Envt'l L. 43.

CHAPTER 45

INTERNATIONAL DISPUTE SETTLEMENT

CESARE P.R. ROMANO

1 INTRODUCTION

TYPICALLY, in all international agreements, as well as in all manuals of international law, the section on dispute settlement comes last. This *Handbook* is no exception. The reason for this seemingly universal rule is quite obvious. Dispute settlement is to international law what pathology is to medicine. It is about the worst-case scenario, when the consensus that made it possible for rules to be created does not exist anymore, and parties argue as to what these rules actually mean and if, by whom, to what extent, and with which consequences, they have been violated. It is a place where parties hope they will never have to go.

Of course, in international treaties, dispute settlement clauses follow the description of the agreed rules. As a result of this eventual and ancillary function, the law and procedure of international dispute settlement has long been the Cinderella of international law. After lengthy negotiations on the substance of an environmental agreement, diplomats tend to cut and paste dispute settlement procedures from previous treaties without much thought about what would happen if these procedures actually needed to be used.

In the past two decades, a series of considerations has modified this casual attitude towards international dispute settlement, particularly in the environmental sphere. Environmental factors have been increasingly acknowledged to be a relevant source of international tension and disputes and even of actual threats to international peace and security.[1] Four considerations seem to justify heightened attention to the prevention and settlement of environmental disputes. First, there is the growing demand and need for access to natural resources, coupled with a limited or at least shrinking resource base. Second, the nature and extent of international environmental obligations has enormously increased as states assume broader and deeper commitments. The thickening web of agreements and norms increases the likelihood that disputes might arise about how to interpret the scope of these obligations. Third, as these increasing international environmental obligations affect national interests, and impose on states large administrative, economic, and political burdens, states that do not comply with environmental obligations are perceived to gain an unfair competitive advantage (see Chapter 39 'Compliance Theory'). Fourth, as national economies are increasingly globalizing, states are more likely than ever to be dragged into international disputes caused by environmentally degrading activities of their nationals or in defence of nationals affected by activities elsewhere.

---

[1] The Inventory of Conflict and the Environment, a project of the School of International Service of the American University, lists more than 120 examples of international disputes or outright conflicts caused directly or indirectly by environmental problems during the nineteenth century. While the criteria used for inclusion in the database are rather large, and, at the same time, the database does not claim to be comprehensive, it can still provide some useful insight on the range, scope, and complexity of the field. The Inventory of Conflict and the Environment, information available at <http://gurukul.ucc. american.edu/ted/ice/ice.htm> (14 January 2006).

The canonical way of treating international dispute settlement begins by recalling the obligation that states have under the UN Charter to settle international disputes peacefully and by means of their own choice. Then, traditional exposés analyze one by one the whole gamut of typical dispute settlement means available, ranging from the so-called 'diplomatic means', such as negotiation, enquiry, mediation, or conciliation, to those whose outcome is legally binding (also known as adjudicative means), such as arbitration and settlement by way of standing international judicial bodies.

While this tried and tested approach has some merits, it is by and large a vestige of an old world where adjudication was ultimately regarded as a sort of 'continuation of diplomacy by judicial means,' to paraphrase the famous quote from Carl von Clausewitz. The traditional approach puts too much stress on the *settlement* of disputes, while environmental policy usually focuses on the *management* of environmental problems leading to disputes. Whether a dispute caused by an environmental problem is settled depends, first and foremost, on whether the environmental problem that caused the dispute is resolved. The legal case eventually litigated can address only a specific aspect, typically a specific *legal* aspect, of a complex environmental problem. Closure of this particular aspect, diplomatically or judicially sanctioned, can exhaust a case but, *per se*, does not necessarily mean that the whole dispute is extinguished. This depends on how the environmental problem is managed, which is largely why there is a trend towards equipping modern international environmental regimes with two salient characteristics. First, there is the internalization of dispute settlement procedures. Complex environmental regimes contain within themselves the institutions, procedures, and rules to tackle disputes arising out of the implementation of the regime's norms (see Chapter 38 'Treaty Bodies'). In these regimes, law-making and law-enforcement functions are part of the same continuum. Second, the development of so-called non-compliance procedures (see Chapter 43 'Compliance Procedures') has very often blurred the classical distinction between diplomatic means and adjudication, and warped the classical categories of international law such as state responsibility and liability (see Chapter 44 'International Responsibility and Liability'), counter-measures, and, of course, dispute settlement.

The settlement of environmental disputes can be explored along many other different themes and variables. One could explore permanent bodies and procedures and compare them to ad hoc solutions. Or one could look first at cases where, for a certain body or procedure to be activated, the consent of both parties needs to be obtained and compare this to cases where the will of just one of the parties suffices to start compulsory dispute settlement. Procedures and bodies whose pronouncements have a binding effect could be compared to those that do not have binding powers. Bodies and procedures where only states have standing could be contrasted with procedures that are open to non-state entities. Dedicated dispute settlement bodies and procedure could be contrasted to non-specialized ones. Each of these themes would likely yield valuable insight.

This chapter examines international dispute settlement in the field of the environment by contrasting dispute settlement by way of procedures contained in international environmental agreements (endogenous) to dispute settlement by way of procedures either of non-environmental agreements or of environmental agreements other than the one under which the dispute arose (exogenous). While the frequency of endogenous procedures is on the rise, their relevance has been historically minimal, and has been further undermined by the emergence of non-compliance procedures. However, resort to exogenous procedures is on the rise and has yielded a substantial record.

The reason why this peculiar approach has been chosen, out of all possible ones, is that it highlights some emerging problems affecting international dispute settlement well beyond the specifically environmental realm: the problem of disharmonic dispute settlement clauses; the phenomenon of fragmentation of a single dispute into several distinct cases; the fact that international environmental disputes, being polymorphous, very often can be looked at from the point of view of different and uncoordinated legal regimes or specific sets of international law; and, lastly, the ongoing multiplication of fora, actors, and levels of jurisdiction. Interestingly enough, these issues first emerged in the context of certain environmental disputes that will be discussed later in this chapter.

2 Dispute Settlement within International Environmental Agreements

Many of the earliest international environmental agreements, concluded between the nineteenth century and the 1970s, did not provide for any dispute settlement procedure at all. Yet, gradually things have changed. In 1972, a study on the frequency of dispute settlement clauses in international treaties, in all areas of law, not only in environmental treaties, determined that only a quarter contained express provisions for the settlement of disputes.[2] However, the same study also found that the frequency of dispute settlement clauses had constantly increased over time both in absolute and relative terms. Another study carried out at the beginning of the 1980s, this time focused only on multilateral environmental agreements (MEAs), concluded that one-third of existing agreements contained some dispute settlement

[2] C. Reithel, *Dispute Settlement in Treaties: A Quantitative Analysis* (Ph.D. dissertation, University of Washington, 1972).

provisions.[3] During the mid-2000s, more than 20 years and hundreds of treaties later, more than half of all MEAs contain some dispute settlement provisions.[4]

While it is evident that dispute settlement provisions in international environmental agreements are becoming increasingly frequent, one must wonder whether they are bringing anything new to the field. *Prima facie*, the answer is no. After all, the classical categories of judicial and diplomatic means have been crystallized by a century-long practice, and it is hard to imagine any new procedure for the settlement of disputes that could not be traced back to them. Despite the large number of agreements containing settlement clauses, cutting and pasting reduces diversity. Most of the environmental agreements containing dispute settlement provisions offer the same two-stage scheme, with marginal variations. First, there is a general obligation to peacefully settle disputes by having recourse to any diplomatic means to which the parties can agree. Such means generally track Article 33 of the UN Charter verbatim. Then, should the dispute fail to be settled, there are two options: either the agreement leaves it at that, not providing for any further method or forum, or it provides for a specific further stage of dispute settlement. Typically, this further stage consists of either conciliation, resolution by international adjudication (either by an arbitral tribunal whose procedure might be spelled out in an annex or by a standing international body, such as the International Court of Justice (ICJ)), or reference to some organs of the treaty in question whose decision will be binding. This second level can be activated either unilaterally—that is, at the request of either party to the dispute, with built-in mechanisms and timetables to prevent stalling by the other party—or it needs the consent of both parties to be activated.

Nonetheless, closer scrutiny reveals some distinctive features. First, while in the early years, the designation of standing institutions or procedures for dispute settlement, such as the ICJ or the Permanent Court of Arbitration, was relatively rare and states relied on special or ad hoc arrangements, this trend has been recently reversed. Second, it is undeniable that procedures contained in environmental agreements have taken advantage of the increased level of sophistication of modern dispute settlement mechanisms. The most recent agreements provide parties with a spectrum of options rather than a single procedure. Several include no less than three or four mechanisms, some of which may be invoked simultaneously, providing for an ideal, though not desirable, escalation of the dispute, from informal, non-contentious, and non-adversarial procedures such as consultation and negotiation, to more formal, contentious, and adversarial procedures such as adjudication. This process indicates the existence of a trend to move away from the treatment of dispute settlement clauses as a sort of afterthought, opting instead to include articulated, carefully drafted, and broad provisions. This tendency reached its apex with the 1982 United

---

[3] A.C. Kiss, 'Le reglement des différends dans les conventions multilaterals relatives à la protection de l'environnement,' in R.J. Dupuy, ed., *The Settlement of Disputes on the New Natural Resources* (The Hague: Martinus Nijhoff, 1983) 120.

[4] C. Romano, *The Peaceful Settlement of International Environmental Disputes: A Pragmatic Approach* (London: Kluwer Law International, 2000) at 39.

Nations Convention on the Law of the Sea (LOSC), which contains what is probably the most detailed, comprehensive, and complex dispute settlement clause ever. Dispute settlement options are tailored to particular categories of disputes, by providing, for instance, the establishment of special chambers within the International Tribunal for the Law of the Sea (ITLOS) or the exclusion of certain categories of disputes from the otherwise mandatory and binding procedures.

Be that as it may, although dispute settlement procedures in environmental agreements are becoming increasingly common and elaborated, in reality they are very rarely used. Traditional dispute settlement can be crudely summarized as a procedure that can be used only as a result of a breach of international law, and is bilateral and confrontational in nature, where a judicial or quasi-judicial body external to the agreement makes a decision, allocating blame for past action without providing a positive remedy.

Traditional international dispute settlement can work if it can be resorted to without causing great prejudice to the political relations between the parties. Disputes can occur without ever being made public and leaving a trace. Disagreements between states might remain merely at the level of cocktail party anecdotes without ever becoming suitable for public examination. Diplomats and dispute management processes might be able to dispose of them swiftly without letting them reach a critical level. Indeed, even when a dispute is brewing, diplomats usually tend to avoid dangerous labelling. Funnelling a dispute through a formal procedure (even when the procedure is nothing more than a generic call for negotiations) obliges the parties to the dispute to recognize being in disagreement. Such recognition might be undesirable, however obvious it might be, simply because it might affect other areas of the parties' relations.

Adjudication will be resorted to only if the law is fairly, but not too, clear or if the parties agree to give the dispute settlement body a large leeway or even to engage in creative law-making. Yet, states are unlikely to take action that will result in a precedent being set by which they themselves might later be judged. Few states have an environmental record so clean as to be able to throw the first stone. In addition, increasingly specific legal regimes or organizations are endowed with dispute settlement bodies or procedures that provide an alternative to 'external' bodies and procedures. The emergence of the so-called non-compliance procedures (see Chapter 43 'Compliance Procedures') has not only dramatically changed the way in which international environmental regimes work but it has also further undermined classical dispute settlement procedures. In contemporary international environmental law, there is a strong tendency towards the institutionalization and internalization of decision-making and dispute management processes within individual treaty regimes. Several multilateral environmental agreements and, in particular, those concluded since the beginning of the 1970s, establish permanent institutions (for example, a conference of the parties, a secretariat, several technical and scientific bodies, a fund) to pursue the agreements' goals, manage the resources that have been entrusted to them, and monitor compliance and address issues as they arise.

Yet, most importantly, traditional international dispute settlement works mostly in cases where an environmental dispute is essentially localized, in contrast to being widespread or global. Environmental problems that concern a large number of states and actors at once, where the issues at stake are of a common or even global nature, are ill-suited to traditional dispute resolution, unless two clearly divided groups can be identified, which is very rarely the case. Indeed, traditional dispute settlement is essentially a bilateral exercise, where the claims of one party are rebutted by another part and the opposing legal claims are scrutinized by a standing body through the crucible of the presentation of submissions and responses.

It should not be surprising therefore that there are very few examples of international environmental disputes arising out of environmental agreements that have been addressed through the formal dispute settlement procedures (diplomatic or adjudicative) contained in the same agreements. Among the most recent examples, one can cite the *MOX Plant Case (Ireland v. United Kingdom)*, which was tackled through the dispute settlement clauses of two different environmental agreements and which will be discussed (and cited) later in this chapter.

3 DISPUTE SETTLEMENT OUTSIDE INTERNATIONAL ENVIRONMENTAL AGREEMENTS OR THROUGH PROCEDURES CONTAINED IN ENVIRONMENTAL AGREEMENTS OTHER THAN THE ONE AT ISSUE

International environmental agreements and their dispute settlement clauses do not exist in a void. They are part and parcel of a much wider canvas. It is a principle of international law that, although states have an obligation to settle their disputes peacefully, they are free to use whatever means they can agree on to do so. At any time, the parties to a dispute, by agreement, can decide to resort to other dispute settlement procedures and institutions outside the confines of the given treaty. To illustrate with some examples in the environmental field, the 1996 Protocol to the 1972 Convention on the Prevention of Marine Pollution by Dumping of Wastes and Other Matter provides that, should the parties not be able to settle a dispute by diplomatic means, the dispute shall be settled by arbitration 'unless the parties . . . agree to use one of the procedures listed in . . . the 1982 United Nations Convention on the Law of the Sea [LOSC]' (Article 16.2). Incidentally, under the 1996 Protocol, arbitration can be restored to regardless of whether the parties to the dispute are also parties to the LOSC.

More broadly, the 1997 Joint Convention on the Safety of Spent Fuel Management and the Safety of Radioactive Waste Management provides that, should the parties not be able to settle a dispute by diplomatic means, 'recourse can be made to the mediation, conciliation and arbitration mechanisms provided for in international law' (Article 38).

The agreement to resort to dispute settlement procedures and institutions outside the scope of the given agreement can also be reached *a priori*. For instance, Article 33(1) of the 1997 Convention on the Law of the Non-Navigational Uses of International Watercourses reads: 'In the event of a dispute between two or more parties concerning the interpretation or application of the present Convention, the parties concerned shall, in the absence of an applicable agreement between them, seek a settlement of the dispute by peaceful means'. Hence, should such an agreement exist, it would normally take precedence over the dispute settlement clauses of the convention itself, but as we will see, this seemingly straightforward issue is not devoid of considerable difficulties.

Obviously, environmental agreements are only a specific facet of the larger world of international law. The disputants might be parties to other non-environmental treaties that might provide for different dispute settlement procedures. For instance, it is common practice among states to conclude so-called bilateral Treaties of Friendship, Commerce and Navigation, which provide that in case of a dispute between the parties, one, or both by agreement, may refer it to a permanent or ad hoc body or procedure. There are also a number of multilateral treaties that provide for specific procedures or fora. For instance, the 1928 General Act of Arbitration for the Pacific Settlement of International Disputes provides that '[a]ll disputes with regard to which the parties are in conflict as to their respective rights shall . . . be submitted for decision to the Permanent Court of International Justice [now the International Court of Justice], unless the parties agree . . . to have resort to an arbitral tribunal' (Article 17).

In addition, a number of international organizations are endowed with their own very sophisticated judicial bodies and dispute settlement regimes. For instance, all members of the World Trade Organization (WTO) are subject to the dispute settlement system of that organization. To become members of the Council of Europe, ratification of the 1950 European Convention on Human Rights and its protocols is required. It follows that acceptance of the jurisdiction of the European Court of Human Rights is necessary to become members of that organization. The acceptance of the jurisdiction of the European Court of Justice is implicit in the ratification of the EC Treaty. Interestingly, the jurisdiction of these bodies is compulsory—albeit not necessarily exclusive—thus providing an exception to the general principle of freedom of choice of dispute settlement means.

Since it is quite common for a particular dispute to touch upon more than one treaty (and environmental disputes, being multifaceted, are particularly prone to do so), and because a given act of a state may violate obligations under more than one treaty, these exogenous dispute settlement clauses and institutions provide for a much larger array of means to which states, perhaps unsurprisingly, increasingly resort. Yet that is not all. As much as states might have disputes over the implementation of particular treaty provisions, disputes might also arise about the interpretation and compliance with obligations arising out of customary international law and general principles of law in the field of the environment, such as the obligation not to use one's territory as to cause damage to others or the so-called 'precautioary principle'.

Many of the early landmark international environmental disputes settled by way of international adjudication arose out of the violation of customary international law and were settled outside the framework of any particular international environmental treaty. For instance, the *Trail Smelter Arbitration (United States v. Canada)* between the 1920s and 1940s, which is one of the *loci classici* of international environmental law, did not concern the violation of any particular international treaty between the two countries.[5] Nor did the *Bering Sea Fur Seals* dispute, between Great Britain and the United States, or the *Nuclear Tests* dispute, between Australia and New Zealand on the one hand and France on the other, during the 1970s and again during the early 1990s.[6] In other cases, the treaties whose breach was invoked were not, *per se*, environmental treaties, but the dispute involved environmental matters and the judgments dealt with the existence or lack thereof of customary norms of international environmental law. For example, the *Lac Lanoux* dispute between France and Spain, litigated in the 1950s before an arbitral tribunal, dealt with the 1866 Third Treaty of Bayonne, fixing the boundary between the two countries. The *Case Concerning the Gabčíkovo-Nagymaros Project (Hungary v. Slovakia)* revolved around the 1977 treaty concluded between the two countries providing for the building of hydroelectric works. More recently, in the *Case Concerning Pulp Mills on the River Uruguay*, Argentina claimed the violation by Uruguay of the 1975 Statute of the River Uruguay, which established a common framework and institutions for the management of the river.[7]

Be that as it may, while in the early days of international environmental law international adjudicative bodies did contribute, sometimes decisively, to its development, nowadays codification and law-making by states and international organizations has greatly reduced the room that international courts and tribunals have to compose international norms and principles in the environmental field.

---

[5] *Trail Smelter Case (United States v. Canada)*, Award, 1941, 3 U.N.R.I.A.A. 1905.

[6] *Bering Sea Fur Seals Arbitration (Great Britain v. U.S.)*, 1898, 1 Moore's International Arbitration Awards 755, reprinted in 1 I.E.L. Rep. 43 at 67 (1999); *Nuclear Tests (Australia v. France)*, [1973] I.C.J. Rep. 99 (Interim Protection Order of 22 June); and *Nuclear Tests (New Zealand v. France)*, [1973] I.C.J. Rep. 135 (Interim Protection Order of 22 June).

[7] *Lac Lanoux Arbitration (Spain v. France)*, 24 I.L.R. 101 (1957); *Case Concerning the Gabčíkovo-Nagymaros Project (Hungary v. Slovakia)*, [1997] I.C.J. Rep. 92 (25 September), and *Case Concerning Pulp Mills on the River Uruguay (Argentina v. Uruguay)*, Provisional measures, 13 July 2006, <http://www.icj-cij.org/icjwww/idocket/iauframe.htm>.

4 Some Problems with Contemporary International Environmental Dispute Settlement

As the preceding discussion has illustrated, international environmental disputes can arise both from the interpretation and implementation of treaties, and of customary international law and general principles of law. They can be tackled either through bodies and procedures endogenous to the given treaties or through those that are exogenous. To this complex matrix, one should add the existence of an extensive, and constantly expanding, array of procedures and fora for dispute settlement, which is increasingly accessible not only to states but also to a number of diverse actors, including international organizations, corporations, and individuals. This situation is both a challenge and an opportunity. On the one hand, it multiplies opportunities for disputes to be addressed in a structured and law-based institutional and legal setting before they escalate. On the other hand, it raises the question of the possible or actual conflict between different legal regimes and dispute settlement procedures. The following sections will illustrate four practical problems. Although the disputes used to illustrate them are all generated by environmental problems or concerns, these problems are also very much representative of the larger challenges international law and international dispute settlement face in the contemporary world.

4.1 Disharmonic Dispute Settlement Clauses

First, there is the problem of synchronizing dispute settlement clauses in environmental agreements with those of other treaties, environmental or otherwise. Ideally, treaties should contain provisions to this end, spelling out which dispute settlement procedure or forum takes precedence. When there is none, general principles of law, such as the *lex specialis* and the *lex anterior* principles, or rules contained in the 1969 Vienna Convention on the Law of the Treaties, could help to resolve the riddle.[8] Yet, because of the abstract and general nature of these principles and rules, their application to concrete cases might be far from automatic, and parties to the dispute might disagree on them. This disagreement creates a sort of 'Catch 22' situation, where

---

[8] In 2000, the issue of the fragmentation of international law and the difficulties arising from the diversification and expansion of international law was placed on the long-term work agenda of the International Law Commission (ILC). So far, the focus of the ILC work has been international law norms that can counteract fragmentation, in particular, those on the interpretation of treaties, more than international institutional considerations and dispute settlement procedures.

a third party is needed to make a binding decision about which dispute settlement procedure will be used to settle the dispute.

The *Southern Bluefin Tuna (New Zealand v. Japan; Australia v. Japan)* dispute can be used to illustrate the point.[9] In a nutshell, the dispute pitted Japan against Australia and New Zealand over the conservation and management of southern bluefin tuna stocks in the south Pacific. In 1993, the three states had concluded an agreement to this end. The agreement contains a typical dispute settlement clause that is found in many environmental agreements. Article 16 of the Convention for the Conservation of Southern Bluefin Tuna (SBT Convention) provides:

1. If any dispute arises between two or more of the Parties concerning the interpretation or implementation of this Convention, those Parties shall consult among themselves with a view to having the dispute resolved by negotiation, inquiry, mediation, conciliation, arbitration, judicial settlement or other peaceful means of their own choice.
2. Any dispute of this character not so resolved shall, with the consent in each case of all parties to the dispute, be referred for settlement to the International Court of Justice or to arbitration; but failure to reach agreement on reference to the International Court of Justice or to arbitration shall not absolve parties to the dispute from the responsibility of continuing to seek to resolve it by any of the various peaceful means referred to in paragraph 1 above.

As often happens, the parties could not agree to have the dispute referred to the ICJ or an ad hoc arbitration. However, all three states were parties to the LOSC. Like the 1993 SBT Convention, the LOSC provides that states have a general duty to peacefully settle disputes. To do so, they are free at any time to agree on any means they choose, ranging from negotiations to judicial settlement. However, if settlement is not reached by means of the procedure chosen by the parties, and the parties have explicitly excluded no other procedure, then either party is entitled to trigger the compulsory dispute settlement procedure of the LOSC. Under the LOSC regime, in certain cases and for certain categories of disputes, parties can unilaterally refer the matter to adjudication. They also have a choice between two kinds of ad hoc arbitration (so-called Annex VII and VIII), ITLOS and the ICJ, with Annex VII ad hoc arbitration being the default procedure.

Two bodies considered the question of which dispute settlement procedure was to be applied: the LOSC procedure providing for unilateral activation or the procedure in the SBT Convention providing for consensual activation? First, ITLOS considered the matter in the course of deciding whether it could order provisional measures to suspend Japanese fishing, as requested by Australia and New Zealand. Under Article 290(5) of the LOSC, '[p]ending the constitution of an arbitral tribunal to which a dispute is being submitted . . . any court or tribunal agreed upon by the parties or, failing such agreement within two weeks from the date of the request for provisional measures, the International Tribunal for the Law of the Sea . . . may prescribe, modify or revoke provisional measures . . . if it considers that *prima facie* the tribunal

---

[9] *Southern Bluefin Tuna cases* (Provisional Measures), 38 I.L.M. 1624 (1999).

which is to be constituted would have jurisdiction and that the urgency of the situation so requires.'

ITLOS found that the fact that the SBT Convention applied to the parties did not preclude them from recourse to the dispute settlement procedures of the LOSC. Only in the event that Australia, New Zealand, and Japan could agree to submit the dispute to arbitration under Article 16 of the SBT Convention would the LOSC dispute settlement procedure be overridden. Since they could not come to such an agreement, the tribunal concluded that Australia and New Zealand were not precluded from unilaterally resorting to the Annex VII arbitral tribunal.

The Annex VII arbitral tribunal found differently. It concluded that it lacked jurisdiction. While ITLOS read Article 16 of the SBT Convention not as an agreement to exclude compulsory dispute settlement procedures but rather as an agreement on the need to agree, the arbitral tribunal held that 'the absence of an express exclusion of any procedure . . . is not decisive.' The fact that Article 16 made referrals to binding settlement conditional upon agreement between the parties clearly indicated the intent of the parties to the SBT Convention to remove proceedings from the reach of compulsory procedures of any kind, including the compulsory procedures of the LOSC.

True, ITLOS reached its conclusion while seized by a request for provisional measures, where it needed only *prima facie* jurisdiction to proceed, while the arbitral tribunal had to rule on whether it actually had jurisdiction. The difference between a finding of *prima facie* jurisdiction and a determination of jurisdiction by an arbitral tribunal is profound. In order to have a finding of *prima facie* jurisdiction, it is simply necessary that a lack of jurisdiction not be manifest. The threshold of *prima facie* jurisdiction is thus much lower than the one that had to be cleared in the merits phase before the arbitral tribunal. Still, the different results are remarkable. The example illustrates how quite common and seemingly straightforward dispute settlement clauses can engender significant disagreement *per se*.

4.2 Fragmentation and Cluster Litigation

The second problem is the phenomenon of fragmentation of a single *dispute* into several distinct *cases*—that is to say, a single environmental problem (pollution by A in the territory of B) giving rise to several distinct legal cases dealing with discrete legal aspects of the same dispute. Again, another actual case helps to illustrate the point. Throughout the 1990s, Ireland and the United Kingdom were entangled in a dispute over a so-called 'MOX plant'. The plant in question, operated by British Nuclear Fuels (BNFL), a government-owned company, is located in Sellafield, in northwest England on the coast of the Irish Sea. It reprocesses fissile plutonium and uranium from spent nuclear fuel consigned by foreign utility companies to manufacture mixed oxide fuel (MOX). The Irish were concerned about routine radioactive discharges from the MOX plant as well as the frequent transports of nuclear materials from and to the plant via the Irish Sea. In short, it was a typical environmental dispute. On the one hand, there was a state, which wanted to use its territory to carry out a legitimate, but potentially polluting, economic activity, and, on the other hand, there was a neighbouring state that questioned the risk-assessment and the cost-benefit analysis made by the first state and tried to have the activity blocked.

BNFL decided to build the plant in 1992 and got the go ahead from the UK government the year after. Alarmed by the likely intensification of MOX-related activities at Sellafield, Ireland urged the United Kingdom to prepare an environmental impact assessment, and sought to obtain environmental and safety information on MOX production at the plant and associated nuclear transports. In particular, Ireland asked the United Kingdom to supply information including: (1) details of secured and forecast sales volumes; (2) details of required annual production capacity; (3) figures for the sales volumes and sales prices assumed for MOX fuel; (4) details of plant capacity and commissioning start dates for plutonium commissioning; and (5) the number of annual voyages relating to the MOX plant operation. Without this information, which did not directly pertain to the marine environment, Ireland claimed it could not verify whether the building of the plant was economically justified as required under certain European Community directives. The information, Ireland argued, would also help it assess the pattern and intensity of the MOX plant operation, which would likely affect the environmental quality of the Irish Sea. However, the United Kingdom rejected Ireland's request, on the grounds that the information was commercially sensitive, as competitors of BNFL could take advantage of it.

After years of unsuccessful diplomatic efforts to obtain the information in question, and with the commissioning of the plant looming, Ireland started two separate dispute settlement procedures under two different conventions. First, in June 2001, it started dispute settlement proceedings under the 1992 Convention for the Protection of the Marine Environment of the North-East Atlantic (OSPAR Convention), requesting an ad hoc arbitral tribunal.[10] Article 9(2) of the OSPAR Convention provides for access to information 'on the state of the maritime area, on activities or measures adversely affecting or likely to affect it and on activities or measures introduced in accordance with the Convention.' Article 9(1) requires the parties to the convention to make such information available 'to any natural or legal person, in response to any reasonable request . . . as soon as possible and at the latest within two months.' This requirement is subject to the exceptions recognized under Article 9(3) including 'commercial and industrial confidentiality.' Second, as the British government did not yield, Ireland instituted in October 2001 arbitral proceedings against the United Kingdom under the LOSC, alleging that the United Kingdom violated basic obligations of the convention with regard to the protection of the marine environment, including the obligation to carry out an assessment of environmental

---

[10] *Dispute Concerning Access to Information under Article 9 of the OSPAR Convention (Ireland v. United Kingdom)*, Final Award, 2 July 2003, 42 I.L.M. 1118 (2003).

impacts.[11] Pending the constitution of an arbitral panel, on 15 November 2001, a month before the MOX plant was scheduled to open, Ireland requested provisional measures from ITLOS to prevent the operation of the new MOX plant and to freeze the transport of radioactive materials to and from it.[12]

Despite this legal barrage, Ireland did not succeed in stopping the commissioning and operations at Sellafield. In the case under the OSPAR Convention, the arbitral tribunal denied Ireland's information requests because Ireland failed to establish that each category of the redacted commercial information pertained to an activity or measure involving 'an adverse effect' on the maritime area presently or prospectively. In the LOSC case, while Ireland had asked ITLOS essentially to order the United Kingdom to immediately suspend the commissioning of the MOX plant and to stop movements of radioactive materials through the Irish Sea, all the tribunal did was to require that the United Kingdom and Ireland cooperate in the exchange of information, monitoring, and the prevention of pollution from the MOX plant.

In short, as a result of Ireland's desperate attempts, three different international adjudicative bodies (arbitral tribunals under the OSPAR Convention, the LOSC (further discussed later in this chapter), and ITLOS) have dealt with different legal aspects of essentially the same dispute, concerning the adequacy of transboundary environmental impact assessments regarding the proposed MOX project. The example perfectly illustrates how submitting disputes to dispute settlement procedures does not necessarily lead to their settlement.

However, this is not the whole, nor the end, of the story. Besides being parties to the LOSC and the OSPAR Convention, the United Kingdom and Ireland are also members of the European Community. As such, they are both party to the Treaty Establishing the European Atomic Energy Community (EURATOM) and the Treaty Establishing the European Community (EC). They are also subject to the jurisdiction of the European Court of Justice (ECJ) in actions brought by the European Commission or by the infringement of those treaties. The European Commission tracked the dispute with a certain concern and, eventually, stepped in, reclaiming the centrality and supremacy of European institutions and legal order.

First, the Commission initiated infringement proceedings against Ireland before the European Court of Justice, claiming that, by submitting the dispute to a tribunal outside the Community legal order, Ireland had violated the exclusive jurisdiction of the ECJ about issues concerning the interpretation or application of EC law. Since, upon ratifying the LOSC, the EC had deposited a formal declaration to assert its exclusive competence over pollution prevention provisions under the LOSC to the extent that such provisions affect the Community's common rules,[13] the Annex VII arbitral tribunal decided to stay the proceedings pending a decision on the matter by the ECJ.

---

[11] *MOX Plant Case (Ireland v. United Kingdom)*, 24 June 2003, 42 I.L.M. 1187 (2003).

[12] *MOX Plant Case (Ireland v. United Kingdom)*, 41 I.L.M. 405 (2002).

[13] Declaration made pursuant to Article 5(1) of Annex IX to the Convention on the Law of the Sea (LOSC) and to Article 4(4) of the agreement relating to the implementation of Part XI of the LOSC.

On 30 May 2006, the ECJ ruled against Ireland, finding that it had failed to respect the ECJ's exclusive jurisdiction on the interpretation and application of Community law, and that, by not consulting with the Commission before initiating arbitral proceedings, it had hindered the achievement of the Community's tasks and jeopardized the attainment of the objectives of the Community treaties.[14]

Finally, it should be noted that one year later, on 3 September 2004, the European Commission threatened to start infringement proceedings against the United Kingdom before the ECJ for failure to provide appropriate information about nuclear material stored at Sellafield, and to grant EURATOM safety inspectors sufficient access to the site. Although the EC Commission's step against the United Kingdom cannot be directly linked to the Irish actions, it is surely notable that the 'guardian of the treaties and custodian of the common European interest' felt compelled to take action in the face of the UK's obstructionism over the extent and nature of operations at Sellafield after three different, and non-EC, international adjudicative bodies had been seized of the matter.

4.3 Competing and Parallel Legal Regimes

The third problem, which is a variant of the problem just illustrated, arises when the same issue can be looked at from the point of view of different and uncoordinated legal regimes (see Chapter 7 'Relationship between International Environmental Law and Other Branches of International Law'). This is often the case in the trade and environment context, for instance. Since 1991, when Chile began preventing Spanish fishing vessels that were carrying swordfish destined for the United States from docking in Chilean ports, Chile and the EC have been at loggerheads. The Chilean unilateral regulation in question is Article 165 of the Chilean Fisheries Law, which prevents any vessel from trans-shipping or landing vessels in Chilean ports when its catches do not comply with Chilean law.

On the one hand, the EC took issue with Article 165 in that it arguably treads on notions of open trade and the freedom of the transit of goods. Safeguard measures enacted by Chile not only make exportation to Chile impossible, but they would make re-exportation to American markets impossible as well. The EC additionally took issue with the jurisdictional implications of the regulation because it applied to fish caught outside Chile's 200-mile exclusive economic zone (EEZ). On the other hand, Chile has continually maintained that Article 165 is a necessary and equitable environmental measure aimed at remedying a widely accepted and acknowledged fisheries depletion problem. Chile's goal is to pressure other nations' boats fishing beyond the 200-mile limit to pursue the activity in a responsible, transparent, and regulated manner. To this end, in 2000, Chile, Colombia, Ecuador, and Peru signed the Framework Agreement for the Conservation of Living Marine Resources on the

---

[14] *Commission of the European Communities v. Ireland*, Case C-459/03, Grand Chamber Judgment, 30 May 2006, 2 OJ C 165 (2006).

High Seas of the Southeast Pacific, which is also known as the Galapagos Accord. With this accord, these three countries committed to the same regulatory measures adopted by Chile a decade before.

Is this an environmental dispute or a trade dispute? Well, both. Trade *and* environmental disputes are nothing new. In the 1990s, the WTO dispute settlement system dealt with some of them (for example, *United States—Restrictions on Imports of Tuna (Tuna Dolphin I* and *II*), and *United States—Prohibition of Shrimps and Certain Shrimp Products (Shrimp-Turtle*)).[15] However, the dispute over swordfish stocks is new because it is the first case where the same dispute was submitted to two different adjudicative bodies that, to decide the case, would arguably use rather different sets of international law: trade law and the law of the sea.

First, in November 2000, the EC requested and obtained the establishment of a WTO dispute settlement panel to determine whether Chile's action restricting access to Chilean ports had violated, *inter alia*, the Articles V and XI of the General Agreement on Tariffs and Trade. When Chile, in response, threatened to refer the matter to ITLOS, alleging a violation of the provisions in the LOSC, relating to the protection of the marine environment and high seas fishing, the EC, unable to prevent the unilateral activation of the LOSC dispute settlement procedure, agreed to play along and have the case submitted to a five-judge special chamber of ITLOS. The ITLOS chamber was to decide, among other things, not only whether the EC was in breach of its obligations to ensure the conservation of swordfish under the LOSC, but also whether Chile had violated the LOSC by extending its own conservation measures to fishing on the high seas.

To summarize, the same dispute had been transformed into two completely different and arguably antithetical cases. Each party selected the forum that would apply what it perceived to be the most favourable body of law to particular aspects of the dispute. For the EC, Chile's banning of access to ports for its vessels was trade related and should be decided in light of international trade law.[16] Chile, in contrast, considered the dispute to be environmental, pertaining to the protection of an endangered marine species, which should be decided in light of the law of the sea.[17]

It is plausible to imagine that the two dispute settlement bodies seized of the matter (the ITLOS special chamber and the WTO dispute settlement system) could reach antithetically different conclusions—each correct based on the body of law the dispute settlement body applied. The ITLOS special chamber might find in favour of Chile, relying on the relatively pro-environment LOSC provisions, while the WTO, espousing the doctrine of 'free trade' and based solely on a trade-promoting treaty, might decide in favour of the EC. The LOSC system seems to provide more leeway in

---

[15] *United States—Restrictions on Imports of Tuna*, 39 GATT B.I.S.D. 155 (1993), reprinted in 30 I.L.M. 1594 (1991); and *United States—Prohibition of Shrimps and Certain Shrimp Products*, WTO Doc. WT/DS58/AB/R (98–000) (12 October 1998).

[16] *Chile—Measures Affecting the Transit and Importation of Swordfish*, Request for Consultations by the European Communities, Doc. WT/DS193/1 (26 April 2000).

[17] *Case Concerning the Conservation and Sustainable Exploitation of Swordfish Stocks in the South-Eastern Pacific Ocean (Chile v. European Community)*, Judgment of 20 December 2000, 40 I.L.M. 475 (2001).

assessing unilateral measures and in treating negotiations as a paramount, but separate, issue. The WTO clings to the notion that such measures can be adopted only after proper negotiations and must, in any event, be compatible with the agreements. Each conclusion would be legally correct because they would be reached within the confines of separate and self-contained legal regimes.

Would such decisions help settle the dispute? Surprisingly, the answer is 'possibly, despite all'. One might argue that it is exactly the far-flung implications of this embarrassing situation that led the EC and Chile to reach a negotiated deal in January 2001. Chile restored access for EC fishing vessels to Chilean ports, while the EC agreed to bilateral and multilateral scientific and technical cooperation on the conservation of swordfish stocks. Accordingly, and pending the ratification of the agreement, the EC requested a suspension of panel proceedings in the WTO, and Chile and the EC asked ITLOS to do the same.[18]

In the absence of formal rules of coordination among the various, and increasingly numerous, international judicial bodies and procedures, which could address issues of *litis pendens* and forum shopping in an organic way and, more significantly, in the presence of the worrisome phenomenon of segmenting international law into specialized, self-contained, and ultimately conflicting regimes, issues such as those raised by the *Swordfish* case will appear again. Environmental concerns, which ultimately can be found at the core of most disputes, are particularly fertile ground. Whether the result will be a clash of judgments or a remarkable convergence of minds of the tribunals asked to adjudicate these cases, within the confines of their respective bodies of law, remains to be seen.

4.4 Multiplication of Actors and Levels

All of these problems would be complex enough in a world where only states (that is, governments) have access to international fora. In this simple world, there are two parties in any dispute, which, despite disagreeing on the specific instance, have much in common and which tend to reason and act along familiar lines. Moreover, the interactions between them can be explained by relatively unsophisticated game-theory and bi-dimensional models. However, one of the hallmarks of the current age of globalization is the transformation from an international system comprised of a limited number of governmental actors to a new, and still fluid, system where a host of entities other than states are the bearers of rights and duties as a matter of international law, and act not only on the international scene but also domestically to

---

[18] *Case Concerning the Conservation and Sustainable Exploitation of Swordfish Stocks in the South-Eastern Pacific Ocean (Chile v. European Community)*, Order 2001/1, International Tribunal for the Law of the Sea (15 March 2001); and Order 2003/2 (16 December 2003). *Chile—Measures Affecting the Transit and Importation of Swordfish, Arrangement between the European Communities and Chile*, Communication by the European Communities, Doc.WT/DS193/3, adopted 6 April 2001 and Add. 1, adopted 9 April 2001 and Add. 2, adopted 17 November 2003.

protect those rights and enforce the rights of governments (see Chapter 29 'Public Participation').

For instance, when France resumed nuclear testing in the South Pacific in 1995, a veritable barrage of actual and potential legal actions and dispute settlement procedures arose. On the classical inter-state level, diplomatic means were employed between France, Australia, and New Zealand. Then, as France did not relent, New Zealand tried to have the ICJ consider the matter,[19] and other states of the region considered invoking the activation of the conciliation mechanism contained in Article 27(4) and Annex II, Part 2, of the 1992 Convention on Biological Diversity. Individuals and non-governmental organizations instituted proceedings before the European Commission of Human Rights,[20] the UN Human Rights Committee,[21] and the ECJ,[22] as well as national courts.[23] Interestingly, all of these cases were eventually dismissed.

This example illustrates, on the one hand, that there is a growing supply of forums where certain legal aspects of complex international disputes can be litigated by a large and increasingly diversified host of players. On the other hand, there is an increasing demand for redress and access to justice by non-state entities that largely stems from the shortcomings of national legal systems. Think, for example, of the difficulties encountered in holding corporations accountable for environmental damage in countries other than their state of nationality (for example, Union Carbide in India for the Bhopal catastrophe, or Chevron Texaco in Ecuador for environmental damage). Yet, as the earlier example of the nuclear tests underscores, demand for judicial redress, and the offer of such redress, rarely meet. This tells much about the inherent limitations of judicial and quasi-judicial remedies at the international level as well as about the still spotty and widely diverse role that international law plays in domestic legal systems. It also explains why, despite the remarkable list of fora—national, international, and transnational—where any given dispute, or aspects of it, could be litigated, calls for more dispute settlement mechanisms are as strong as ever, at all levels and for and by all kinds of actors. Experimentation and exploration are still very much the order of the day.

[19] *Request for an Examination of the Situation in Accordance with paragraph 63 of the Court's Judgment of 20 December 1974 in the Nuclear Tests Case (New Zealand v. France)*, Order of 22 September 1995, [1995] I.C.J. Rep. 288.

[20] The inhabitants of Tahiti and Mangareva claimed violation by France of Articles 2, 3, 8, 13, and 14 of the European Convention on Human Rights, and of Article 1 of the Additional Protocol (right to property). *Noel Narvii Tauira and Eighteen Others v. France*, Application 28204/95, (1995) 83 D.R. 112.

[21] The plaintiffs claimed violation of Articles 6 and 17 of the Covenant on Civil and Political Rights. *Vaihere Bordes and John Temeharo v. France*, Decision of 30 July 1996, Communication no. 645/1995, UN Doc. CCPR/C/57/D/645/1995.

[22] Inhabitants of Tahiti challenged, before the European Court of Justice, the decision by the European Commission not to use the powers it possess under the EURATOM Treaty in relation to the French tests. *Danielsson and Others v. Commission*, Order of the President of the Court of First Instance, 22 December 1995, Case T-219/95 R [1995] E.C.R. II-3051.

[23] *Association Greenpeace France*, Conseil d'Etat, 29 September 1995, Actualité juridique-Droit administrative, 10 October 1995, at 749.

One can mention, for instance, the creation, in 1993, by the ICJ of a Chamber for Environmental Matters, or the adoption in 2001 and 2002 by the Permanent Court of Arbitration of the optional rules for arbitration and conciliation of disputes relating to natural resources and the environment.[24] Another notable development is the creation of panels at the World Bank (1994), the Inter-American Development Bank (1995), and the Asian Development Bank (1995), which allow individuals or groups to challenge projects financed by these international organizations in violation of their own policies, such as those requiring environmental impact assessments. Under the North American Agreement on Environmental Cooperation individuals can file complaints that one of the states party to the agreements is failing to effectively enforce its environmental laws (Article 14.1).

Finally, the UN Compensation Commission (UNCC), which is the body created by the UN Security Council to decide on claims of reparations against Iraq for damage caused during the 199091 Kuwait war, should be noted. The UNCC received approximately 170 environmental claims from governments and international organizations seeking a total of about US $80 billion dollars in compensation for environmental damage and the depletion of natural resources in the Persian Gulf region and for costs incurred by governments outside of the region in providing assistance to countries that were affected by the environmental damage.

In addition to the intergovernmental level, there are also procedures at the grass-roots and transnational levels that one could mention, including the International Court for Environmental Conciliation and Arbitration, which, despite its name, is not an international organization but rather a private association constituted under Mexican law and composed of legal scholars and environmental activists, or the Latin-American Water Tribunal (Tribunal Latinoamericano del Agua). Finally, throughout much of the 1990s, there have been discussions about the creation of an International Environmental Court that could hear international and transnational environmental cases, but to date, it still remains only a proposal.[25]

5 Conclusions

There are no international judicial or quasi-judicial bodies solely dedicated to environmental disputes, the partial exception being the Chamber for Environmental Matters of the ICJ. However, the polymorphic nature of environmental disputes

---

[24] Permanent Court of Arbitration, Optional Rules for Arbitration of Disputes Relating to Natural Resources and/or the Environment, 40 I.L.M. 202 (2002); *Optional Rules for Conciliation of Disputes Relating to Natural Resources and/or the Environment* (The Hague: Permanent Court of Arbitration, 2002).

[25] A. Rest, 'Need for an International Court for the Environment? Undeveloped Legal Protection of the Individual in Transnational Litigation' (1994) 24 Envt'l Pol. & L. 173; and E. Hey, *Reflections on an International Environmental Court* (The Hague: Kluwer Law International, 2000).

makes a wide variety of fora potentially usable, which are almost impossible to list. Cases involving environmental issues have been brought before the ICJ, ITLOS, the WTO dispute settlement system, the European Court of Human Rights, the Inter-American Court of Human Rights, judicial bodies of regional economic integration organizations (such as the ECJ), inspection panels, international and transnational arbitral tribunals, and compensation and reparations bodies. This also explains why, besides dispute management and settlement procedures endogenous to international environmental regimes, there are no international judicial or quasi-judicial bodies solely dedicated to deal with environmental disputes.

The fragmentation of law in specialized and self-contained regimes; the institutionalization of international decision-making and enforcement processes; the proliferation of international judicial bodies; the erosion of the divide between the domestic and international legal spheres; and the multiplication of subjects of international law beyond the state-centric classical models, are all characteristics of contemporary international law. Many of these changes to the international law fabric originally took place in the environmental field. Between the 1970s and early 1990s, international environmental law was the *avant-garde* of international law, and the drive is not over yet. Several of the most interesting cases, heralding many of the features and problems in the field of international dispute settlement in the twenty-first century, stem from environmental disputes. While it is clear that there is no shortage of fora and procedures to address them, we are still rather far from an international judicial system (that is, a structured and organized institutional order), as the cases presented illustrate. This unsatisfactory state of affairs makes it difficult to appease the increasing demands on international dispute settlement bodies and procedures, and creates all sorts of incentives for parties (all actors, not only states) to exploit jurisdictional competition by engaging in abusive forum shopping, starting cluster litigation in multiple forums, and challenging judgments that should be final if they are ever to be able to bring about the settlement of a dispute. The road ahead is unclear, but, as much as environmental disputes have provided many of the cases that heralded these problems, it is likely that they will also provide the occasions to start addressing them.

RECOMMENDED READING

A. Adede, *The System for Settlement of Disputes under the United Nations Convention on the Law of the Sea: A Drafting History and Commentary* (Dordrecht: Martinus Nijhoff, 1987).

R. Bilder, 'The Settlement of Disputes in the Field of International Law of the Environment' (1975) Recueil des cours 139.

J.G. Merrills, *International Dispute Settlement*, 3rd edition (Cambridge: Cambridge University Press, 1998).

K. Oellers-Frahmand and A. Zimmermann, eds., *Dispute Settlement in Public International Law*, 2nd edition (Berlin: Springer, 2001).

C. Robb, ed., *International Environmental Law Reports*, 3 volumes (Cambridge: Cambridge University Press, 1999).

C. Romano, *The Peaceful Settlement of International Environmental Disputes: A Pragmatic Approach* (London: Kluwer Law International, 2000).

Y. Shany, *The Competing Jurisdictions of International Courts and Tribunals* (Oxford: Oxford University Press, 2003).

Y. Shany, 'The First MOX Plant Award: The Need to Harmonize Competing Environmental Regimes and Dispute Settlement Procedures' (2004) 17 Leiden J. Int'l L. 815.

R. Wolfrum and N. Matz, *Conflicts in International Environmental Law* (Berlin: Springer, 2003).

INDEX

....